ADVANCED Java PROGRAMMING

Uttam K. Roy

Assistant Professor

Department of Information Technology

Jadavpur University, Kolkata

OXFORD

UNIVERSITY PRESS

Oxford University Press is a department of the University of Oxford. It furthers the University's objective of excellence in research, scholarship, and education by publishing worldwide. Oxford is a registered trade mark of Oxford University Press in the UK and in certain other countries.

Published in India by
Oxford University Press
YMCA Library Building, 1 Jai Singh Road, New Delhi 110001, India

First published in 2015

ISBN-13: 978-0-19-945550-8
ISBN-10: 0-19-945550-3

Typeset in Times New Roman
by Mukesh Technologies Pvt. Ltd, Puducherry 605005
Printed in India by Magic International (P) Ltd, Greater Noida

Dedicated to
my beloved wife *Banhishikha*
and
my sweet baby *Rimisha*

FEATURES OF

Comprehensive Coverage

Extensive coverage of topics such as JSP, JNDI, JMS, Java and CORBA, J2EE, and JSF in separate chapters provides detailed insight into Advanced Java Programming.

SOCKET PROGRAMMING

REMOTE METHOD INVOCATION

JAVA SERVER PAGES

JAVA MESSAGE SERVICE

JAVA DATABASE CONNECTIVITY (JDBC)

19.4.3 An Example

In this section, we shall develop a simple but elegant client–server socket application using SSL. In this application, the client sends a string to the server. The server prints the string and sends it back to the client. The client finally prints it. Although this application is very simple, it demonstrates basic steps required to develop almost all SSL-based secure applications.

19.4.3.1 Writing the Server

In a traditional (non-SSL) socket application, the server program first creates a `java.net.ServerSocket` object. In an SSL-enabled socket application, the equivalent object is `javax.net.ssl.SSLServerSocket` object and is created in a slightly different way. All constructors of `SSLServerSocket` class are protected. Consequently, those constructors cannot be used to instantiate `SSLServerSocket` objects. The instances are created using `SSLServerSocketFactory` class. An instance of this factory is usually created as follows:

```
SSLServerSocketFactory factory = (SSLServerSocketFactory)
SSLServerSocketFactory.getDefault();
```

The `SSLServerSocket` object is then created using `createServerSocket()` method on this factory:

```
SSLServerSocket sss = (SSLServerSocket) factory.createServerSocket(6789);
```

19.4.3.2 Writing the Client

The client first creates a `SSLSocketFactory` as follows:

```
SSLSocketFactory factory = (SSLSocketFactory) SSLSocketFactory.getDefault();
```

The counterpart of `Socket` in SSL is `SSLSocket` which is created as follows:

```
SSLSocket ss = (SSLSocket) factory.createSocket(args[0], 6789);
```

The complete source code (`SSLClient.java`) is given below:

```
import javax.net.ssl.*;
import java.io.*;
public class SSLClient {
  public static void main(String[] args) {
```

After recompilation, we can then run the server and client directly whose output is shown in Figure 19.5:

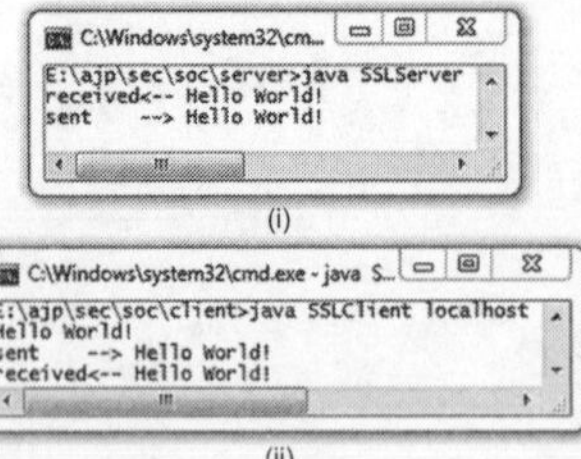

(i)

```
C:\Windows\system32\cmd.exe - java S...
E:\ajp\sec\soc\client>java SSLClient localhost
Hello World!
sent     --> Hello World!
received<-- Hello World!
```

(ii)

Application-based Examples

The book tries to give the practical applications of the concepts of Advanced Java Programming by providing ample application-based examples, with step-by-step explanations.

THE BOOK

Codes and Screenshots

Readers can thoroughly understand each topic with the help of program codes and screenshots.

The following is a complete source code (`CalculatorPublisher.java`) of the web service publisher:

```
import calc.ws.*;
import javax.xml.ws.Endpoint;
public class CalculatorPublisher {
  public static void main(String[] args) {
```

If everything goes well, the browser's screen looks as shown in Figure. 18.2:

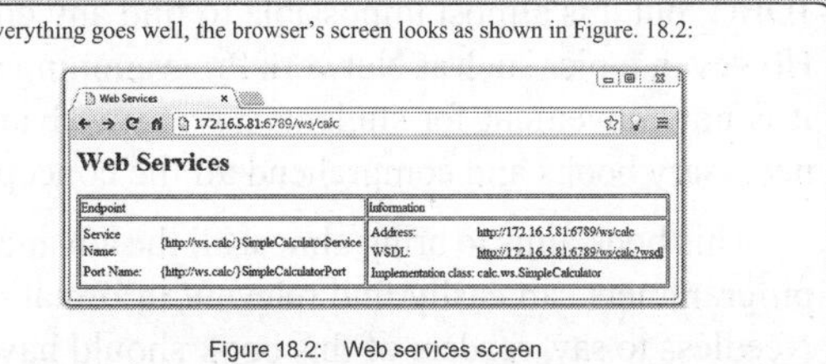

Figure 18.2: Web services screen

20.9.1 Installing Apache Tomcat web server

To install these servlets, we need a web server. Any web server that supports servlets may be used. A list of web servers supporting servlets may be found in Table 20.1 and Table 20.2. Note that the procedure for installing servlets varies from web server to web server. Please refer

23.2 INSTALLING HIBERNATE

We assume that the latest version of Java is already installed on your computer. Download .zip (for windows) or .tgz (for Unix) from `http://hibernate.org/orm/downloads`. We downloaded the file `hibernate-release-4.3.1.Final.zip` and when unzipped, a set of files was generated. A sample screen shot is shown in Figure 23.1:

Name	Date modified	Type	Size
documentation	1/22/2014 12:07 PM	File folder	
lib	1/22/2014 12:07 PM	File folder	
project	1/22/2014 12:07 PM	File folder	
changelog.txt	1/22/2014 11:59 AM	Text Document	332 KB

Software Information

The book lists steps for installation and configuration of relevant software (wherever necessary), which is required for executing the examples explained therein.

Chapter-end Pedagogy

It comprises keywords, objective-type questions (with answers), and subjective-type questions for students to test their understanding of the concepts.

KEYWORDS

catch block—Contains code to handle exceptions

Checked Exception—A set of exceptions that must be caught or declared to be thrown

Custom Exception classes—User-defined exception classes that represent meaningful exceptional situations

Nested try-catch— A `try`, `catch` or a `finally` block containing another set of try-catch-finally blocks

Runtime exception—A set of exceptions that need not be caught or declared to be thrown explicitly

throw—A keyword used to throw an exception

EXERCISES

Objective-type Questions

1. What is the full form of JNDI?
   (a) Java Network and Directory Interface
   (b) Java Naming and Directory Implementation
   (c) Java Network and Directory Implementation
   (d) Java Naming and Directory Interface

6. Which of the following are JNDI properties?
   (a) java.naming.factory.initial
   (b) java.naming.provider.url
   (c) Both a) and b)
   (d) None of the above

Subjective-type Questions

1. What is the difference between a SignedObject and SealedObject?
2. Show how objects can be transferred over the network keeping object's confidentiality and intrigrity.

10. What is a message digest?
11. What properties does a message digest satisfy?
12. What do you mean by signing a JAR file multiple times? What is its usefulness?

PREFACE

The power of Java is unquestionable and is well-known to everyone in the software community. Numerous books are available on core Java. However, the real power of Java primarily lies in Java's advanced concepts. Although there are many books available on these topics, most of them focus on a specific technology. For example, it is not impossible to find dozens of books on Socket programming, RMI, JNI, Servlets, JSP, and JDBC, but it is almost impossible to find any engineering/science curriculum, which has subjects like these. However, topics such as Network Programming and Advanced Java are very common. In these circumstances, it is not convenient for students having "Advanced Java" as a subject in his/her course to purchase all the necessary books and comprehend all the concepts included therein.

This book aims to bring almost all the advanced concepts of Java under a common roof so that experienced programmers can easily find relevant information whenever necessary and can become experts in this field. Needless to say, readers of this book should have good working knowledge of core Java.

ABOUT THE BOOK

This book covers, in depth and with extensive examples and references, the primary technical issues that every Java expert should understand, such as JNI, Socket programming, RMI, JavaMail, Java XML-RPC, Soap, Security, Servlet, JSP, JDBC, Hibernate, JNDI, JMS, CORBA, and many others. Each chapter provides detailed working examples illustrating the functioning of these technologies and how they can be used to build robust Java-based applications. This book provides real-world examples supported with ample screenshots so that readers can understand and easily apply them to Java-based applications they would develop in the future.

Although this book is intended as a textbook for undergraduate- and postgraduate-level courses on Advanced Java, it can also be used as a supplementary textbook for undergraduate/postgraduate courses on network programming, server-side programming, Enterprise Java, and GUI programming. The book is also a useful resource for researchers to learn to write different kinds of distributed applications effectively and efficiently using various Java concepts. In addition, it will provide useful background and reference information for professionals working in the area of Java-based web applications.

CONTENT AND STRUCTURE

The book is organized into twenty eight chapters, each covering a unique topic in detail. The chapters have been grouped into three parts:

- Part I—Inside Java
- Part II—Network Programming
- Part III—Enterprise Java

In Part I (Chapters 1–11), important Java concepts such as Exception Handling, Multi-threading, Garbage Collection, Collection Framework, Generic Programming, Reflection, JNI, AWT and Swing, and Java and XML, among others, have been discussed. Part II (Chapters 12–18) includes networking concepts such as Socket programming, RMI, The JavaMail API, and Java XML-RPC. Part III (Chapters 19–28) covers concepts of Java Enterprise Edition such as Servlet, JSP, JDBC, Hibernate, JNDI, JMS, CORBA, and JSF.

Chapter 1 gives a quick summary of six important Java tools (`jhat`, `jdb`, `javap`, `javadoc`, and `jcmd`) out of many powerful tools that come with JDK to help Java developers in better programming. Other tools have been discussed in the remaining chapters.

Chapter 2 covers Java exception handling. It helps programmers to understand what exceptions are and how they are handled. It also gives a brief description of exception classes and their hierarchy.

In *Chapter 3*, we discuss multi-threaded processes in Java. A multi-threaded process has two or more parts which can run concurrently and each part can do a designated task at the same time. Multi-threading enables us to write programs in a way where multiple activities can proceed concurrently in the same program.

Chapter 4 first describes the basics of the working of Garbage Collection inside HotSpot. It then gives an overview of the available garbage collectors with their functions and performance metrics. It also demonstrates how to select and configure a collector and set sizes for the memory areas on which the collector operates. Finally, it lists some of the most commonly used options that affect garbage collector behaviour.

Chapter 5 explains a powerful unified architecture, known as collection framework, provided by Java. Java provides high-quality implementation of collection interfaces resulting in unquestionable performance and quality of programs. Java not only provides the different implementations of an interface, but also allows us to interchange these implementations seamlessly.

In *Chapter 6*, we talk about Java generics, which was one of the extensions added to Java 1.5. Generics allows us to write parameterized classes, interfaces, and methods where parameters are type names. This also helps us to detect more bugs at compile time and fix them then and there.

Chapter 7 throws light on the concept of Java reflection APIs. The reflection API in Java enables us to examine and/or modify the properties, behaviour, or other elements of an object at run-time. An understanding of reflection will help us in comprehending the tools (NetBeans, Eclipse, Spring) that use this API.

Chapter 8 covers the Java Native Interface (JNI) which is an API that allows Java code to interoperate with applications and libraries written in other programming languages such as C and C++. It is a two-way interface that allows Java applications to invoke the native method, and native methods to interact with the Java code.

Chapter 9 gives us a detailed understanding of Java AWT concepts, background philosophy, and practical concerns with an introduction to *Swing* which is an extension to AWT.

Chapter 10 expounds on the Java APIs for XML (eXtensible Markup Language), which is a key technology for structured data representation and transfer. It is used virtually everywhere, from small- to large-scale legacy applications. Java also promotes portability and is an obvious choice to work with XML documents. Java APIs for XML make it easier to use XML from the Java programming language. It also provides sample applications that you can run.

Chapter 11 outlines how applications process some input and generate some output. Java provides a rich set of classes and interfaces as a separate package `java.io` for such Input and Output (I/O). Java also provides another package `java.nio` containing Non-blocking I/O (NIO) API, which, in some situations, can give a big performance boost over blocking IO. In this chapter, we have also given an overview of how all these classes are grouped with their purposes.

Chapter 12 demonstrates how one can use Java network APIs to write basic network programs easily and quickly. Java has some distinct advantages over other programming languages as far as network applications are concerned. In addition, Java can handle network security issues extremely well. Features such as platform independence and garbage collection allows us to develop efficient and elegant network applications without worrying about system crashes, spread of viruses, or stealing of sensitive data.

In *Chapter 13*, we lay emphasis on Java implementation of socket API. Sockets can be used as lower-level tools for IPC in local processes as well as processes running on different computers. Sockets are particularly useful when we want to write client–server applications.

In *Chapter 14*, we explore how Java's object-oriented version of RPC (known as Remote Method Invocation) can be easily used to develop sophisticated networking applications. This technology elevates network programming to a higher plane.

Chapter 15 deals with the primary protocols for delivery and accessing of emails such as Simple Mail Transfer Protocol (SMTP), Post Office Protocol (POP), and Internet Message Access Protocol (IMAP).

In *Chapter 16*, we cover the structure of applets, their execution philosophy, and other applet-specific issues. Applets are Java programs that usually run within web browsers and give more power to the browsers.

Chapter 17 outlines XML-RPC, the XML-based Remote Procedure Call (RPC) protocol. In this protocol, eXtensible Markup Language (XML) is used to describe a Remote Procedure Call. It is a very simple and portable way to call remote procedures over HTTP.

Chapter 18 illustrates the Simple Object Access Protocol (SOAP), which is an extension to XML-RPC. SOAP can be used in a wide variety of systems ranging from messaging systems to RPC.

Chapter 19 brings to the fore almost all the aspects of Java security mechanism from secure language features to the security APIs, tools, and built-in provider services, highlighting key packages and classes.

Chapter 20 elucidates the powerful Java server-side technology called Servlets. They usually run inside a Java-enabled web server and extend its capabilities. Since servlets are written in Java and Java is an extremely powerful language, even a simple web server bundled with servlets becomes unquestionably powerful.

Chapter 21 describes the Java Server pages which is an extension to Servlets. It is one of the many server-side technologies used to build dynamic web applications that has caught the attention of web developers due to several reasons.

In *Chapter 22*, we discuss an important technique called Java DataBase Connectivity (JDBC), which allows us to access databases through Java programs. It provides Java classes and interfaces to fire SQL and PL/SQL statements, process results (if any), and perform other operations common to databases.

Chapter 23 presents Hibernate, an open source Object Relational Mapping (ORM) tool. It allows us to persist Plain Old Java Objects (POJO) to the database.

Chapter 24 examines the Java Naming and Directory Service. It allows us to associate (called binding) names with objects and to find (called lookup) those objects later by their names.

Chapter 25 reviews another Java technology used to write distributed applications that can communicate in a loosely coupled way. Messaging is often used to coordinate programs in dissimilar systems or written in different programming languages.

In *Chapter 26*, we study some other J2EE technologies, especially, JavaBean and EJB. Since JavaBean is the fundamental component technology and is a basic building block of EJB, we have primarily focused on this technology in this chapter.

Chapter 27 simplifies the generic concept of CORBA (Common Object Request Broker Architecture), which is a specification that describes how heterogeneous objects can interoperate. CORBA objects can be created/accessed using virtually any programming language (such as Java, C, C++, Smalltalk, and Ada) and can exist on any platform (such as Windows, Unix, Linux, and Solaris).

In *Chapter 28*, we look into the primary concepts of **J**ava **S**erver **F**aces (JSF), which is a Java-based framework for creating web-based user interfaces. It combines the power of Struts and Swing and follows Model–View–Controller (MVC) architecture. Many examples, starting with a simple example JSF application, have been provided.

ACKNOWLEDGEMENTS

Bringing together important advanced Java concepts under a common roof is no easy task. The exercise was even more difficult due to the large volume of the manuscript. I, therefore, had a very tough time. However, the support from colleagues and many other key people led to successful completion of this project. I thank all of them.

I am extremely grateful to the reviewers, as their feedback helped me in improving the technical accuracy and presentation of the chapters.

It is said that "behind every successful man, there is a woman". People will decide if I am successful. However, the woman in front, not behind me, is none other than my beloved wife Banhishikha Roy. No words can describe her contribution towards this work. I acknowledge her patience from the bottom of my heart. She always took some time out to help me develop the manuscript. This book would not have been successfully completed without her understanding and cooperation.

The other "woman" is my six-year-old little girl, Rimisha. While working on the more demanding topics of the manuscript, my little daughter's presence, even late at night, would calm me and bring a smile to my face. I love her dearly

I have taken utmost care to eliminate any technical or typographical errors in the book and urge readers to send in their comments, constructive criticism, and suggestions, preferably through email (u_roy@it.jusl.ac.in and royuttam@gmail.com). I appreciate your feedback and hope you enjoy reading this book.

Uttam K. Roy

BRIEF CONTENTS

DETAILED CONTENTS

PART II: NETWORK PROGRAMMING 271

PART ONE
INSIDE JAVA

CHAPTER – 1

JAVA TOOLS

KEY OBJECTIVES

After completing this chapter readers will be able to—

- write doc comments and use javadoc to generate HTML documentation files
- understand how to use the Java debugger jdb
- get an idea about packaging of a set of files into a single one and vice versa
- understand how to fire diagnostic commands to JVM using jcmd
- learn how to analyze JVM heap dump file used jhat tool
- learn how to quickly find the method signatures of a class using javap

1.1 INTRODUCTION

Java beginners often use `javac` and `java` to compile and run Java programs. However, JDK comes with a lot of other powerful tools such as `jar, jhat, jdb, javap, javadoc, jcmd, javah, keytool, jconsole, jps, jstatd, jstat, jinfo, jmap, jstack` and many more to enable Java developers to program better. This chapter gives a quick reference of the first six (not in order) tools available default with the Java JDK. Other tools have been discussed in various other chapters. For example, `jstat` has been discussed in detail in Chapter 4 and `javah` has been discussed in Chapter 8.

1.2 JAVADOC

Documentation is an important part of program code. It not only helps others to understand the program, but helps the author to remind how his/her own older programs also work. Since external documentation may easily become outdated as the program changes, Java encourages us to write documentation directly in the source code. It requires less efforts to update documentation as and when program code changes.

Java standardizes the syntax and semantics of writing documentation. It also provides a tool `javadoc` to generate HTML files to view the documentation from a web browser in a convenient way.

Note that Java also uses this tool to generate Java API specification from the source code. In fact, if we have the source code, we ourselves can generate this. We can also generate HTML documentation similar to the Java API reference pages using `javadoc`. This section discusses how to write documentation and how to generate HTML files using `javadoc` command.

Since documentation comments (or simply doc comments) go directly in the source code, we must hide it from Java compiler. So, documentation is written as special comments between the character sequence `/**` and `*/` that begin and end the comment respectively. Note that the starting delimiter must be `/**` (not `/*`), otherwise, `javadoc` tool will not process the comments. Here is an example of single line comment:

```
/** This is a single line java doc comment. */
```

Comments can spread multiple lines:

```
/**
 This is an example of comments
 that spans multiple lines.
*/
```

The `javadoc` preserves all white spaces between /** and */. However, if leading asterisks on each line are used, white spaces (blanks and tabs) preceding the initial asterisk (*) characters are discarded. Here is an example:

```
/**
  * This is also an example of comments
  * that spans multiple lines.
  */
```

A doc comment may be attached with only class, interface, constructor, method, or field declarations by writing the comment immediate before them. The following is a comment attached with a class `X`.

```
/** Represents the class of two-dimensional geometrical points. */
public class Point {}
```

Similarly, the following attaches a comment with a method.

```
public class Point {
  private int x, y;
  /** Returns x coordinate of the point */
  public int getX() { return x; }
}
```

The first sentence of each doc comment should be a summary sentence, containing a concise but complete description of the declared entity. The `javadoc` tool ignores any doc comment placed in the body of a method.

```
public class Point {
  private int x, y;
  public int getY() {
    /** This comment will not be processed by javadoc */
    return y;
  }
}
```

So far, we have seen how to write a simple doc comment. Let us now generate the HTML files, using `javadoc` command. It parses the declarations and documentation comments in the specified file(s) and produces a set of HTML pages describing, by default, the public and protected classes, interfaces, constructors, methods, and fields. We can pass either a series of Java package names or source files to `javadoc` as argument(s). Here is an example:

```
javadoc Point.java
```

This generates a set of files. The output of this command is show below:

```
Creating destination directory: "point\"
Loading source file Point.java...
Constructing Javadoc information...
Standard Doclet version 1.7.0_07
Building tree for all the packages and classes...
Generating point\Point.html...
Generating point\package-frame.html...
Generating point\package-summary.html...
Generating point\package-tree.html...
Generating point\constant-values.html...
Building index for all the packages and classes...
Generating point\overview-tree.html...
Generating point\index-all.html...
Generating point\deprecated-list.html...
Building index for all classes...
Generating point\allclasses-frame.html...
Generating point\allclasses-noframe.html...
Generating point\index.html...
Generating point\help-doc.html...
```

As we can see, a set of files is generated in the current directory. The `index.html` file is the front page with frames. If we open this file using a browser, it looks like this:

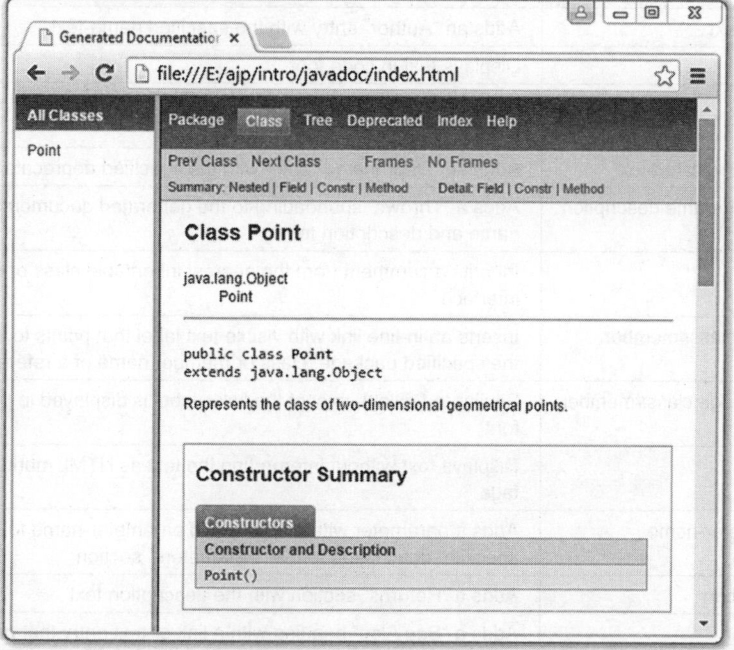

We can place HTML tags inside the description part as usual. For example, the below example makes use of `<b>` tag to impose more importance:

```
The <b>javc</b> is an import tool.
```

In addition to main description, doc comment may have an optional tag section. The main description starts after the starting delimiter /** and must end before the tag section. The tag section contains special tags, which are used to generate well-formatted API about the code being documented.

The tags take the form `@tagname`. For example, in comments for methods we can use `@param` and `@return` tags (if applicable) to describe the method's parameters and return value, respectively. The `@param` tag should be followed by the parameter's name, and then a description of that parameter. Here is an example:

```
/**
  @param x        the X coordinate of the point
*/
public void setX(int x) { this.x = x; }
```

Similarly, the `@return` tag is followed simply by a description of the return value.

```
/**
  @return      the X coordinate of the point
*/
public int getX() { return x; }
```

The argument to a tag includes any text following the tag up to, but not including, either the next tag, or the end of the doc comment.

The summary of frequently used tags is shown in Table 1.1:

Table 1.1: Build doc comments tags

Tag with syntax	Description
@author name-text	Adds an "Author" entry with the specified name-text
{@code text}	Displays text in code font
{@docRoot}	Represents the relative path to the generated document's (destination) root directory from any generated page.
@deprecated deprecated-text	Adds an "Deprecated" entry with the specified deprecated-text
@exception class-name description	Adds a "Throws" subheading to the generated documentation, with the class-name and description text
{@inheritDoc}	Inherits a comment from the nearest inheritable class or implementable interface
{@link package.class#member label}	Inserts an in-line link with visible text label that points to the documentation for the specified package, class or member name of a referenced class
{@linkplain package.class#member label}	Similar to {@link}, except the link's label is displayed in plain text than code font
{@literal text}	Displays text without interpreting the text as HTML markup or nested javadoc tags
@param parameter-name description	Adds a parameter with the specified parameter-name followed by the specified description to the "Parameters" section
@return description	Adds a "Returns" section with the description text
@see reference	Adds a "See Also" heading with a link or text entry that points to reference
@serial field-description | include | exclude	Used in the doc comment for a default serializable field
@serialData data-description	Documents the data written by the writeObject( ) or writeExternal( ) methods
@serialField field-name field-type field-description	Documents an ObjectStreamField component
@since since-text	Adds a "Since" heading with the specified since-text to the generated documentation

(Contd)

Table 1.1: (*Contd*)

@throws class-name description	Similar to @exception tag
{@value package.class#field}	When {@value} is used in the doc comment of a static field, it displays the value of that constant
@version version-text	Adds a "Version" subheading with the specified version-text to the generated docs when the -version option is used

Some types of tags can be repeated while others cannot. For example, `@return` tag should appear only once whereas `@see` tag may appear any number of times. This implies that the tag section may contain any number of tags. Tag names are case-sensitive.

There are two kinds of tags: *block tags*, and *in-line tags*. The block tags (also called standalone tags) take the form `@tagname` and in-line tags appear within curly braces, as `{@tagname}`. A block tag must start at the beginning of a line or after any leading spaces and an optional asterisk. Otherwise `javadoc` will ignore them. An in-line tag can appear anywhere in the comment. Here is an example:

```
/**
  See this infinite loop {@code while(true);}
*/
```

We can also use one argument custom tags in the form `@tagname`. Here is an example:

```
@task   Re-visit the documentation
```

To enable this tag, use `-tag` option to the `javadoc` int in the following form:

```
-tag  tagname:Xaoptcmf:"caption"
```

Here `tagname` is the tag to be processed and `caption` is the heading to be used for this tag. The `Xaoptcmf` part of the argument determines where in the source code the tag is allowed to be placed, and whether the tag can be disabled (using X). Here is an example:

```
javadoc -tag task:a:"Remainder" Point.java
```

It tells that the tag `@task` is allowed to be placed in all places, and the heading for this tag will be `Remainder`.

1.3 JAVAP

This command line tool displays information in brief about the methods, constructors and fields present in the specified class(es). The syntax of using `javap` is:

```
javap <options> <classes>
```

The name of the class(es) must be a fully qualified class name (i.e., including package name). Here is an example:

```
javap java.lang.Object
```

This displays the information of the class `Object` (the root class of Java class hierarchy) in the package `java.lang`. Here is the sample output:

```
Compiled from "Object.java"
public class java.lang.Object {
  public java.lang.Object();
  public final native java.lang.Class<?> getClass();
  public native int hashCode();
  public boolean equals(java.lang.Object);
  protected native java.lang.Object clone()throws
java.lang.CloneNotSupportedException;
  public java.lang.String toString();
```

```
    public final native void notify();
    public final native void notifyAll();
    public final native void wait(long) throws java.lang.InterruptedException;
    public final void wait(long, int) throws java.lang.InterruptedException;
    public final void wait() throws java.lang.InterruptedException;
    protected void finalize() throws java.lang.Throwable;
    static {};
}
```

Note that `javap` does not show the code of the methods/constructors. It shows only the prototypes of methods/constructors. It is useful especially to those who want to quickly find the method signatures of a class. For example, if you do not have any IDE and want to quickly know the methods available on `java.lang.String` class, use the following simple command:

```
javap java.lang.String
```

The javap command displays its output to stdout. If you want to store the output in a file, use the following command instead:

```
javap java.lang.String > out.txt
```

If no option is specified, `javap` tool prints the package, protected, and public fields and methods of the specified classes. In fact the output of the command can be customized using options. The set of options themselves can be viewed using `–help` or `--help` or `-?` options or without using any options as follows:

```
javap
```

It displays the available options with a brief description as follows:

```
Usage: javap <options> <classes>
where possible options include:
  -help  --help  -?        Print this usage message
  -version                 Version information
  -v  -verbose             Print additional information
  -l                       Print line number and local variable tables
  -public                  Show only public classes and members
  -protected               Show protected/public classes and members
  -package                 Show package/protected/public classes
                           and members (default)
  -p  -private             Show all classes and members
  -c                       Disassemble the code
  -s                       Print internal type signatures
  -sysinfo                 Show system info (path, size, date, MD5 hash)
                           of class being processed
  -constants               Show static final constants
  -classpath <path>        Specify where to find user class files
  -bootclasspath <path>    Override location of bootstrap class files
```

The options are self-explanatory. For example `-p` option is used to show all including the private members of the class. This tool can also be used to disassemble the byte code in a readable format using `-c` option. Note a Java class file contains the so called byte code, which is translatable to op-codes/mnemonics. Consider the following simple Java class:

```
public class HelloWorld {
  public static void main(String[] args) {
    System.out.print("Hello World!");
  }
}
```

Compile this program and use the following command to see the contents of the `HelloWorld` class file in op-code format:

```
javap -c HelloWorld
```

A part of the output is shown here:

```
Compiled from "HelloWorld.java"
public class HelloWorld {
  public HelloWorld();
    Code:
       0: aload_0
       1: invokespecial #1  // Method java/lang/Object."<init>":()V
       4: return  public static void main(java.lang.String[]);
    Code:
       0: getstatic     #2 // Field java/lang/System.out:Ljava/io/PrintStream;
       3: ldc           #3 // String Hello World!
       5: invokevirtual #4 // Method java/io/PrintStream.print:(Ljava/lang/String;)V
       8: return
}
```

It is easy to see the relation between the source code and the byte code To print more information, use the following command:

```
javap -c -s -verbose HelloWorld
```

1.4 JCMD

This tool is used to send diagnostic commands to a specified JVM. To demonstrate how to work with `jcmd`, we shall first write a simple Java program as follows:

```
public class LoopForEver {
  public static void main(String[] args) {
    while(true);
  }
}
```

The code is really simple having only an infinite loop. The loop is inserted deliberately so that it makes a JVM up all the time and we can inspect the JVM properties in the meanwhile. Compile the program and run it in a terminal using the following command:

```
java LoopForEver
```

This makes a JVM running indefinitely. The `jcmd` expects lvmid of the target JVM. A lvmid, is typically, but not necessarily, the operating system's process identifier for the JVM process. To find lvmid of the JVM, we can use the command without any arguments:

```
jcmd
```

It displays all JVMs running on the local machine listed by lvmid followed by main class as follows:

```
432 LoopForEver
3724 sun.tools.jcmd.JCmd
```

To know the commands that we can give to a JVM, specify the lvmid along with help to the command as follows:

```
jcmd 432 help
```

This displays a list of commands that we can give to the JVM identified by the lvmid 432. Here is a sample output of the command:

```
432:
The following commands are available:
VM.commercial_features
ManagementAgent.stop
ManagementAgent.start_local
ManagementAgent.start
Thread.print
GC.class_histogram
GC.heap_dump
GC.run_finalization
GC.run
VM.uptime
VM.flags
VM.system_properties
VM.command_line
VM.version
help
```

We can then apply any of the listed commands. To get help about a specific command specify the command after help. For example, to see how to use `GC.heap_dump` command, use the following command:

```
jcmd 4680 help GC.heap_dump
```

This generates a help content as follows:

```
4680:
GC.heap_dump
Generate a HPROF format dump of the Java heap.

Impact: High: Depends on Java heap size and content. Request a full GC unless
the '-all' option is specified.

Syntax : GC.heap_dump [options] <filename>

Arguments:
        filename :  Name of the dump file (STRING, no default value)

Options: (options must be specified using the <key> or <key>=<value> syntax)
        -all : [optional] Dump all objects, including unreachable objects
(BOOLEAN, false)
```

So, to store the snapshot of the JVM heap in a file `myHeap`, we can use the following command:

```
jcmd 432 GC.heap_dump myHeap
```

This dump file can be analyzed using a tool like `jhat` (**j**ava **h**eap **a**nalysis **t**ool) discussed later in this chapter. Here is another command that gives the JVM version:

```
jcmd 432 VM.version
432:
Java HotSpot(TM) Client VM version 23.3-b01
JDK 7.0_07
```

The following command shows the flags (including default flags) used to start the JVM:

```
jcmd 432 VM.flags
432:
-XX:InitialHeapSize=16777216 -XX:MaxHeapSize=268435456 -XX:-
UseLargePagesIndividualAllocation
```

There is also a command `PerfCounters.print` that displays all the performance-related counters of the specified JVM.

```
jcmd 432 PerfCounter.print
```

A small portion of the output is shown here:

```
432:
java.ci.totalTime=1690
java.cls.loadedClasses=353
java.cls.sharedLoadedClasses=0
java.cls.sharedUnloadedClasses=0
java.cls.unloadedClasses=0
java.property.java.class.path="."
java.property.java.endorsed.dirs="D:\Java\jdk1.7.0_07\jre\lib\endorsed"
java.property.java.ext.dirs="D:\Java\jdk1.7.0_07\jre\lib\ext;C:\Windows\Sun\Jav
a\lib\ext"
java.property.java.home="D:\Java\jdk1.7.0_07\jre"
java.property.java.library.path="D:\Java\jdk1.7.0_07\bin;C:\Windows\Sun\Java\bi
n;C:\Windows\system32;C:\Windows;D:\Java\
jdk1.7.0_07\bin;C:\Windows\system32;C:\Windows;C:\Windows\System32\Wbem;C:\Wind
ows\System32\WindowsPowerShell\v1.0\;D:\M
ySQL\MySQL Server 5.0\bin;C:\Program Files (x86)\SSH Communications
Security\SSH Secure Shell;."
java.property.java.version="1.7.0_07"
java.property.java.vm.info="mixed mode"
java.property.java.vm.name="Java HotSpot(TM) Client VM"
java.property.java.vm.specification.name="Java Virtual Machine Specification"
java.property.java.vm.specification.vendor="Oracle Corporation"
java.property.java.vm.specification.version="1.7"
java.property.java.vm.vendor="Oracle Corporation"
java.property.java.vm.version="23.3-b01"
java.rt.vmArgs=""
...
```

Another powerful feature of jcmd is that it allows us to control Java Flight Recordings (JFR) from command line. To do this JFR must be enabled by starting the application using the flags `-XX:+UnlockCommercialFeatures -XX:+FlightRecorder` to JVM as follows:

```
java -XX:+UnlockCommercialFeatures -XX:+FlightRecorder LoopForEver
```

We can see that JFR commands have been enabled by using `jcmd`. The commands relevant to Java Flight Recorder are: `JFR.start`, `JFR.stop`, `JFR.check` and `JFR.dump`. The JFR.start command is used to control how and when actual recording should happen. For example, to start a recording after 2 seconds with duration 30 seconds on the JVM with the identifier 432 and save it to the file "r30s.jfr" in the current directory, use the following:

```
jcmd 432 JFR.start name=test delay=2s duration=30s filename=r30s.jfr
```

This recording is identified by the name "test", which is used by other JFR commands. A flight recording can be fired by specifying options to the JVM directly. For example, the following does the same thing as above:

```
java -XX:+UnlockCommercialFeatures -XX:+FlightRecorder -
XX:StartFlightRecording=delay=20s,duration=30s,name=test,filename=r30s.jfr
LoopForEver
```

The `JFR.check` displays the status of all recording command. For example:

```
jcmd 432 JFR.check
```

To stop a recording, use `JFR.stop` command specifying the name of the recording to be stopped as follows:

```
jcmd 432 JFR.stop name=test
```

Finally, to dump the recordings to a file, we can use The `JFR.dump` command as follows:

```
jcmd 432 JFR.dump name=test file_name=r30s.jfr
```

Note that `jcmd` must be used on the same machine where the JVM is running, and have the same effective user and group identifiers that were used to launch the JVM.

1.5 JHAT

The `jhat` (**j**ava **h**eap **a**nalysis **t**ool) is a useful tool to retrieve information from a heap dump file created using a tool like `jmap`.

It is a valuable tool for debugging and understanding programs. It allows us to navigate object structures to learn how objects are interconnected in a program at runtime. It also allows us to trace the references to a given object from the root set, which is particularly useful for tracking down unnecessary object retention known as "memory leaks". It takes the following form:

```
jhat [ options ] <heap-dump-file>
```

It parses the specified dump file and starts a web server. A web browser may then be used to get desired data. The web server supports a few pre-designed queries as well as custom queries written in OQL (**O**bject **Q**uery **L**anguage), which is a language similar to SQL to query heap dumps.

We shall use the same LoopForEver.java program to demonstrate this tool. To use `jhat`, we have to dump heap information in a file. There are several ways to generate a java heap dump:

- Use jmap with -dump option to obtain a heap dump at runtime;
- Use jconsole option to obtain a heap dump via HotSpotDiagnosticMXBean at runtime;
- Use java by specifying -XX:+HeapDumpOnOutOfMemoryError VM option; Heap dump will be generated when OutOfMemoryError is thrown;
- Use jcmd;
- Use hprof.

The standard tool `jmap` may be used for this purpose. However, `jmap` expects a local VM identifier (lvmid), which is typically, but not necessarily, the operating system's process identifier for the JVM process. We can use Java tools such as `jcmd` or `jps` to find such lvmid. We used `jcmd` as follows:

```
jcmd
```

A sample output of this command is shown below:

```
5000 LoopForEver
3468 sun.tools.jcmd.JCmd
```

We can easily see that the lvmid of the process is 5000. This ID can be used to create a dump file using `jmap` command as follows:

```
jmap -dump:file=myHeap 5000
```

Here `myHeap` is the name of the file where we want to dump and 5000 is the lvmid of the JVM running the application. If everything is fine, you will see the following message:

```
Dumping heap to E:\ajp\intro\myHeap ...
Heap dump file created
```

The file `myHeap` contains a snapshot of all the live objects and classes at the moment it was created. Diagnosed process may be terminated after dumping heap with `jmap`. There is also a straightforward way to generate the dump file using `java` command as follows:

```
java -Xrunhprof:file=myHeap,format=b LoopForEver
```

When this program terminates (terminate using `Ctrl C` as this program loops forever), a dump file is generated. This is useful if your program does not take sufficient time to run to create the dump file using `jmap` command. The `jcmd` command can also be used to create the dump file as follows:

```
jcmd 5000 GC.heap_dump myHeap
```

The dump file is now ready to be used by `jhat`. Use the following command to start `jhat`:

```
jhat myHeap
```

If everything goes right, the following message appears:

```
Reading from myHeap...
Dump file created Tue Jan 27 12:03:28 IST 2015
Snapshot read, resolving...
Resolving 5941 objects...
Chasing references, expect 1 dots.
Eliminating duplicate references.
Snapshot resolved.
Started HTTP server on port 7000
Server is ready.
```

The `jhat` can obviously be started on a separate computer having the dump file. Usually analyzers choose to zip the dump and move it to machine more accessible to them and with enough resource. The `jhat` parses the heap dump and make the data available on a web server that it runs by default on port 7000. Use `-port` option to start the web server on a different port. To check the data provided by `jhat`, use the following URL in a web browser while `jhat` is still running.

```
http://172.16.5.82:7000/
```

For local computers, instead of IP address, we can use `localhost` or any loopback address such as `127.0.0.1`. The page looks like this:

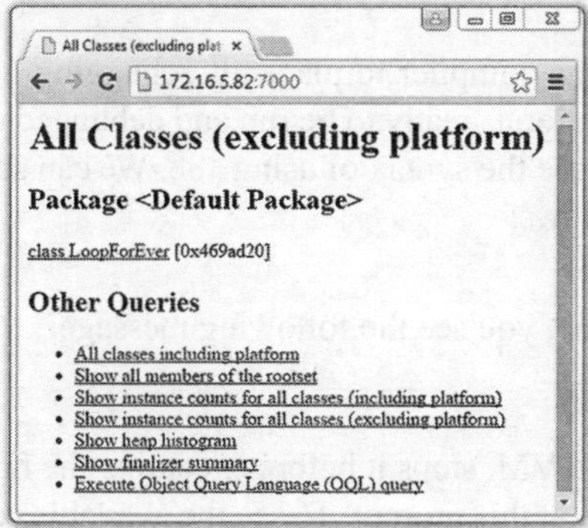

As we can see, this page contains some readymade queries.

They let us surf along all the classes and objects. We shall be able to check how many instances of each class were alive in the moment the heap was created. By clicking on a query link, we can reach other pages containing other queries. The last link is interesting as it allows us to write custom queries using OQL. The jhat also provides a useful page to get help on OQL. The URL of this page with the default port is:

```
http://172.16.5.82:7000/oqlhelp/
```

1.6 JDB

A good programmer should have good skills to debug programs. This skill enables the programmer to find any subtle bugs or defects which are not visible during code review or comes when a particular situation occurs and removes them. The old method of debugging that uses print statements here and there in the program makes the program simply ugly. Although, they can be removed before delivering the program finally, they make a simple program almost unreadable.

This section introduces you to the command line, interactive, Java runtime debugger known as `jdb` which is a very useful tool to debug Java code. The `jdb` tool allows us to query to a JVM and displays information. The JVM may be started by the `jdb` itself or may be an existing one.

We shall first use `jdb` to start a JVM and to debug an application. To demonstrate how `jdb` works, we shall use the following Java program:

```
public class Test {
  int v = 4;
  public static void main(String[] args) {
    int x = 2, y = 3;
    int z = add(x, y);
    Test t = new Test();
    t.set(6);
    System.out.println(x+"+"+y+"="+z);
  }
  public static int add(int a, int b) {
    int c =  a + b;
    return c;
  }
  public void set(int x)  {   v = x;  }
}
```

Although, it is a very simple and correct program that does not do any useful task, it keeps the program logic simple and helps us concentrate on only debugging the program. Compile this program with the `-g` option as follows:

```
javac -g Test.java
```

The `-g` option tells the compiler to place all debugging information in the generated class file `Test.class`. The application is ready to be run and debugged using `jdb`. Like other commands, you can use `-help` option to see the syntax of using `jdb`. We can start a debugging session for our `Test.class` application as follows:

```
jdb Test
```

If everything goes fine, you see the following message:

```
Initializing jdb ...
>
```

This starts a new Java VM, stops it before executing the first statement of the class. We can now apply various commands at this prompt. To see the available commands we can use `help` command.

We need to give `run` command at the prompt to start the application. However, if we run the application, it will exit immediately as the main method does not have anything that will make the application waiting. All we see is the output of the main method. But that is just not what we want to see. To see program state at different time of its execution, we set a breakpoint before applying the `run` command, so that when the program is run, the execution stops at that breakpoint. We can set breakpoints in two ways: using `stop in` or `stop at` commands. The former sets a breakpoint in a specified method and the latter sets a breakpoint at a given line number and their respective syntax are:

```
stop in <class id>.<method>[(argument_type,...)]
stop at <class id>:<line>
```

Let's set a breakpoint at the beginning of the main() method as follows:

```
> stop in Test.main(java.lang.String[])
Deferring breakpoint Test.main(java.lang.String[]).
It will be set after the class is loaded.
>
```

We must specify class name. However, specifying the parameter is mandatory if there are overloaded methods. So the following command will also work:

```
stop in Test.main
```

Since the application has not yet started, the class `Test` has not yet been loaded in the JVM, the breakpoint is not immediately set. Instead it postpones setting the breakpoint till class is actually loaded. We can now give the `run` command.

```
> run
run Test
Set uncaught java.lang.Throwable
Set deferred uncaught java.lang.Throwable
>
VM Started: Set deferred breakpoint Test.main

Breakpoint hit: "thread=main", Test.main(), line=3 bci=0
4         int x = 2, y = 3;

main[1]
```

The `jdb` loads the class Test (that was specified when we started `jdb`) and sets the breakpoint that we configured earlier and tries to execute main method and allows JVM to proceed. The JVM reaches the first breakpoint and stops. It is also possible to run any class by specifying it as an argument to the run command. Anyway, we can see the line about to be executed using list command.

```
main[1] list
1     public class Test {
2       int v = 4;
3       public static void main(String[] args)
4 =>      int x = 2, y = 3;
5         int z = add(x, y);
6         Test t = new Test();
7         t.set(6);
8         System.out.println(x+"+"+y+"="+z);
9       }
10      public static int add(int a, int b) {
```

The line to be executed is shown by =>. To execute current line `next` command is used:

```
main[1] next
>
Step completed: "thread=main", Test.main(), line=4 bci=2
4         int y = 3;
```

It executes the current line and shows the next line to be executed. Let us apply another `next` command:

```
main[1] next
>
Step completed: "thread=main", Test.main(), line=5 bci=4
5         int z = add(x, y);
```

If a line contains a method call, the next command completes that too. To step over the function call, we use `step` command:

```
main[1] step
>
Step completed: "thread=main", Test.add(), line=11 bci=0
11         int c =  a + b;
```

As we can see, the control has now gone inside the `add()` method. This way we can issue as many `next` and `step` commands as we want to execute instructions. To finish the execution of the current function `add()` and to go back to the caller `main()`, we can use `step up` command:

```
main[1] step up
>
Step completed: "thread=main", Test.main(), line=5 bci=9
5         int z = add(x, y);
```

Let us apply the `next` command twice. Then to see the values of all local variables including the arguments passed in a method, we can use `locals` command:

```
main[1] locals
Method arguments:
args = instance of java.lang.String[0] (id=372)
```

```
Local variables:
x = 2
y = 3
z = 5
t = instance of Test(id=373)
```

To print the value of a specific variable, use `print` command:

```
main[1] print x
  x = 2
```

To change the value of a variable x, use `set` command:

```
main[1] set x=10
  x=10 = 10
```

We can verify the assignment using `print` command again:

```
main[1] print x
  x = 10
```

To print the field `v` of the object `t` use `t.v`.

```
main[1] print t.v
  t.v = 4
```

To see detailed information about the object, use `dump` command:

```
main[1] dump t
  t = {
    v: 4
}
```

We can see what all classes are currently loaded in the JVM by using the `classes` command.

```
main[1] classes
```

The following shows a small portion of the output:

```
** classes list **
Test
boolean[]
byte[]
char[]
double[]
float[]
int[]
java.io.BufferedInputStream
java.io.BufferedOutputStream
java.io.BufferedReader
java.io.BufferedWriter
java.io.Closeable
java.io.ExpiringCache
java.io.ExpiringCache$1
java.io.ExpiringCache$Entry
java.io.File
java.io.FileDescriptor
java.io.FileDescriptor$1
java.io.FileInputStream
java.io.FileOutputStream
```

To know the information about a class, we can use `class` command specifying the class as an argument:

```
main[1] class Test
Class: Test
extends: java.lang.Object
```

The class command shows the name of super class, interfaces implemented, nested classes etc. To see which methods are available on a class, use `methods` command:

```
main[1] methods Test
** methods list **
Test <init>()
Test main(java.lang.String[])
Test add(int, int)
Test set(int)
java.lang.Object <init>()
java.lang.Object registerNatives()
java.lang.Object getClass()
java.lang.Object hashCode()
java.lang.Object equals(java.lang.Object)
java.lang.Object clone()
java.lang.Object toString()
java.lang.Object notify()
java.lang.Object notifyAll()
java.lang.Object wait(long)
java.lang.Object wait(long, int)
java.lang.Object wait()
java.lang.Object finalize()
java.lang.Object <clinit>()
```

The `methods` command lists method signatures of the methods written in given class as well as inherited from the super class. Similarly, to see which fields are available on a class, use `fields` command:

```
main[1] fields Test
** fields list **
int v
```

Note that `Test` has only one field v. Watching where in the code, a particular field is being accessed or modified is an important part of debugging. This is done using the watch command. However, to use this command effectively, we first set up another command which gets called when any such watch point is hit. We can do this using the command `monitor`. It takes another command as an argument and executes the latter command when the following scenarios are encountered:

- a field access/modification watch point is reached
- a breakpoint is reached
- next, step, step up, stepi commands are executed
- a method is entered/exited while tracing of methods is ON

Here is an example:

```
main[1] monitor list
```

This way we can set up as many monitors as we want. Each monitor is identified by an integer number which can be used to remove the monitor later. The list of monitors together with their ids can be listed using the same `monitor` command without any argument:

```
main[1] monitor
1: list
```

We can now set up a watch point as follows:

```
main[1] watch Test.v
Set watch modification of Test.v
```

Apply the `next` command to see the behaviour now:

```
main[1] next
>
Field (Test.v) is 0, will be 4: "thread=main", Test.<init>(), line=2 bci=6
2     int v = 4;

1     public class Test {
2 =>    int v = 4;
```

```
    public static void main(String[] args) {
      int x = 2, y = 3;
      int z = add(x, y);
      Test t = new Test();
      t.set(6);
      System.out.println(x+"+"+y+"="+z);
    }
    public static int add(int a, int b) {
```

Use `unwatch` command if you do not watch a field any more

```
main[1] unwatch Test.v
Removed: watch modification of Test.v
```

Use `unmonitor` command to remove the monitor if it is no longer necessary.

```
main[1] unmonitor 1
Unmonitoring 1: list
```

To see all break points at a particular moment use `clear` command:

```
main[1] clear
Breakpoints set:
        breakpoint Test.main
```

To continue the execution continuously (i.e. until a break point is reached) use `cont` command:

```
main[1] cont
> 2+3=5

The application exited
```

And finally, to exit JDB, use `exit` or `quit` command.

Note that `jdb` may be used to connect to an already started JVM using Java Debug Interface (JDI). The JDI is a high-level Java API that defines the mechanisms for communication between debuggers and similar systems and running (usually remote) JVMs. The connection is established with so called *connectors*. The JDK traditionally ships a set of connectors the jdb can use to connect to a JVM such as `SACoreAttachingConnector`, `SADebugServerAttachingConnector`, and `SAPIDAttachingConnector`. You can see the available connectors using the following command:

```
jdb -listconnectors
```

This lists all available connectors with a small description of the arguments they take. The following command instructs `jdb` to use a connector named `sun.jvm.hotspot.jdi.SAPIDAttachingConnector` to connect to a JVM having PID 1234:

```
jdb -connect sun.jvm.hotspot.jdi.SAPIDAttachingConnector:pid=1234
```

Once `jdb` is connected to the JVM, you can fire commands as usual.

1.7 JAR

A Java ARchive (JAR) is a file that bundles multiple files into a single one. A JAR file usually contains the class files and auxiliary resources. Specifically, JAR files bring the following benefits:

- Java programs (including core Java API) are distributed usually as JAR files.
- JAR files use ZIP file format. So, we can compress/decompress files.
- Since, JAR file contains a bundle of files, a set of files can be transferred over the network using single request/response pair that takes less time.
- We can optionally seal packages stored in JAR files to enforce version consistency. Sealing a package within a JAR file ensures the availability of all classes defined in that package.
- This also makes distributing a set of files as a single file easy.

- It is possible to digitally sign a JAR file containing software that requires special privilege. This allows end users to allow/disallow the privilege by checking the signature and the author's digital certificate.
- We can extend the functionality to the Java core platform using JAR files with its packaging for extension features.
- JAR files can contain special file to hold metadata about the actual files. This allows us to configure the application on the fly.

1.7.1 Syntax

Note that JAR files as similar to Unix's/Linux's tar (**t**ape **ar**chive) files and the tool `jar` also has similar command-line options. To check the available options, run the command without any option:

```
jar
Usage: jar {ctxui}[vfmOMe] [jar-file] [manifest-file] [entry-point] [-C dir]
files ...
Options:
    -c  create new archive
    -t  list table of contents for archive
    -x  extract named (or all) files from archive
    -u  update existing archive
    -v  generate verbose output on standard output
    -f  specify archive file name
    -m  include manifest information from specified manifest file
    -e  specify application entry point for stand-alone application
        bundled into an executable jar file
    -0  store only; use no ZIP compression
    -M  do not create a manifest file for the entries
    -i  generate index information for the specified jar files
    -C  change to the specified directory and include the following file
If any file is a directory then it is processed recursively.
The manifest file name, the archive file name and the entry point name are
specified in the same order as the 'm', 'f' and 'e' flags.

Example 1: to archive two class files into an archive called classes.jar:
       jar cvf classes.jar Foo.class Bar.class
Example 2: use an existing manifest file 'mymanifest' and archive all the
           files in the foo/ directory into 'classes.jar':
       jar cvfm classes.jar mymanifest -C foo/ .
```

The output is self explanatory. It not only shows the options available, but some examples as well.

1.7.2 Creating a JAR file

To create a JAR file use `c` option:

```
jar cf jarFile files(s) ...
```

Here `f` specifies the output JAR filename and `files(s)` argument is a space-separated list of one or more files to be bundled in the JAR file. Note that use of - (hyphen) before options is optional for `jar` tool. To see what files are being added, we can optionally use v option. The order of options is not important. Here is an example:

```
jar cvf shapes.jar Point.class Circle.class
```

This packages two files `Point.class` and `Circle.class` in the current directory into a JAR file `shapes.jar` and places it in the current directory. Make sure that the input files exist in the current directory. If everything goes fine, you will see the following output:

```
added manifest
adding: Point.class(in = 255) (out= 192)(deflated 24%)
adding: Circle.class(in = 257) (out= 193)(deflated 24%)
```

Although, files packaged in a JAR are usually Java classes, they can be virtually any kind of files. We can also specify the name of directories whose contents are to be packaged:

```
jar -cvf all.jar shapes/ comp/
```

This packages all files under `shapes` and `comp` directory in a JAR file `all.jar`. If we extract the content, the same directory structure will be created. We can instruct jar to change the directory temporarily during execution using `–C` option.

For example, this command changes to the directory `comp` and adds the `HDD.class` from that directory to `test.jar`:

```
jar cvf test.jar -C comp HDD.class
```

This command changes to the `comp` directory and adds all files to `test.jar` (without creating a `comp` directory in the jar file), then changes back to the original directory and adds `Point.class` to `test.jar`.

```
jar cvf test.jar -C comp . Point.class
```

This command changes to the `comp` directory and adds all files to `test.jar` (without creating a `comp` directory in the jar file), then changes back to the original directory and changes to shapes directory and adds all files to `test.jar` and finally returns to the original directory.

```
jar cvf test.jar -C comp . -C shapes .
```

JAR files use ZIP file format. So, in addition to bundle a set of files into a single one, we can use it for compressing and decompressing files. The following command compresses the file `Circle.class` and puts the resultant data in a file `Circle.jar`:

```
jar cvf Circle.jar Circle.class
```

Note that the size of JAR file need not necessarily be less than the original file. The compression ratio depends on several factors including size of the input file, and the distribution of content and so on. To avoid ZIP compression, we can use `0` option as follows:

```
jar cvf0 Circle.jar Circle.class
```

1.7.3 Viewing Contents of a JAR file

The t option is used to list table of contents of a JAR file as follows:

```
jar tf jar-file
```

Here `jar-file` argument is the path and name of the JAR file whose contents we want to view. For example the following command displays the content of the file `shapes.jar`:

```
jar tf shapes.jar
```

The output is displayed on the screen as follows:

```
META-INF/
META-INF/MANIFEST.MF
Point.class
Circle.class
```

Note that t option merely displays the content of a JAR file; it does not extract the content. The procedure to extract the content of a JAR file is shown in the next section.

1.7.4 Extracting the Content

The general syntax to extract the contents of a JAR file is:

```
jar xf jar-file [archived-file(s)]
```

Here, the `jar-file` argument is the name of the JAR file from which one extracts files and optional `archived-file(s)` argument is the space-separated list of the files to be extracted from the archive. If this `archived-file(s)` argument is not present, the `jar` tool extracts the entire contents. Here is an example:

```
jar xvf shapes.jar
```

This extracts the content of shapes.jar and puts it in the current directory. We've used v option to see the files being extracted. A sample output is shown here:

```
  created: META-INF/
inflated: META-INF/MANIFEST.MF
inflated: Point.class
inflated: Circle.class
```

The jar extracts contents of a JAR file and writes them to the current directory, reproducing the directory structure that the files have in the archive. The original JAR file remains unchanged. The following command extracts only `Point.class` form `shapes.jar`.

```
jar -xvf shapes.jar Point.class
```

This way we can extract as many number of files as we wish.

1.7.5 Updating a JAR file

To add more files or to update the content of some files already in an existing archive, we use `u` option. The following command updates the `Point.class` in `shapes.jar`.

```
jar uvf shapes.jar Point.class
```

This does not change the content of the JAR itself. So the content remains same as follows:

```
META-INF/
META-INF/MANIFEST.MF
Point.class
Circle.class
```

If no files in the archive have the same pathname as the specified file(s), specified file(s) are added to the JAR file. So, the following command adds the file `Rectangle.class` to the `shapes.jar`:

```
jar uvf shapes.jar Rectangle.class
```

The content of the JAR now looks like this:

```
META-INF/
META-INF/MANIFEST.MF
Point.class
Circle.class
Rectangle.class
```

Unfortunately, there is no provision to remove a file from a JAR.

1.7.6 Manifest File

In a JAR file, there exists a special file called *manifest file* that contains "meta" information about the other files that are packaged in the archive and always has the pathname `META-INF/MANIFEST.MF`. This metadata enables the JAR file to support a wide range of functionality, including electronic signing, version control, package sealing, and others.

A manifest's entries take the form of `header: value` pairs. Exactly what file information should be recorded in the manifest depends on how you intend to use the JAR file. If none is specified, `jar` creates a default manifest file with a content as follows:

```
Manifest-Version: 1.0
Created-By: 1.7.0_07 (Oracle Corporation)
```

This tells that the manifest file conforms to version 1.0 of the manifest specification and was created by the JDK version 1.7.0_07. Note that a manifest file typically contains digest information which is not included in the default manifest. A detailed discussion about digests and signing is given in Chapter 19. The generation of default manifest file can be prevented using `M` option.

To add more content to the manifest file, `m` option is used together with the filename containing entries to be added. The general syntax is this:

```
jar cfm jar-file manifest-entry-file input-file(s)
```

Before adding some entries, let us understand the functionality of some entries. Note that the execution of an application starts from a class file containing a special method with the following signature:

```
public static void main(String[] args)
```

A class having this function can act as an entry point of an application. If a class `Start.class` is an entry class (i.e. having a `main()` method), we can specify this using a manifest entry as:

```
Main-Class: Start
```

To add this entry to a JAR file's manifest, create a text file (say myManifest.txt) containing the above line and use the following command:

```
jar -cvfm shapes.jar myManifest.txt Point.class Circle.class Start.class
```

If you extract the JAR file, you will see the content of the manifest file as:

```
Manifest-Version: 1.0
Created-By: 1.7.0_07 (Oracle Corporation)
Main-Class: Start
```

The JAR file has now become runnable and can be run directly using Java command as follows:

```
java -jar shapes.jar
```

The jar tool also has an option e that allows us to specify the main class as follows:

```
jar -cvfe shapes.jar Start Point.class Circle.class Start.class
```

However, to add other entries to the manifest file, `m` option must be used. If a JAR file references other JAR file(s), it can be specified in the manifest file. For example, if a JAR file `shapes.jar` references class of another JAR `start.jar`, it can be specified in the manifest file of `shapes.jar` as follows:

```
Class-Path: start.jar
```

In general any number of JAR files separated by space can be specified. This way, we can add more and more functionality using the manifest file.

KEYWORDS

Block tags—Tags that take the form `@tagname` and must start at the beginning of a line or after any leading spaces and an optional asterisk

Doc comments—Java documentation comments to be processed by javadoc tool

Heap dump—A file that contains data representing the snapshot of a JVM heap

In-line tags—Tags that appear within curly braces, as `{@tagname}` and can appear anywhere in the comment

jar—A Java tool that can bundle multiple files into a single one and vice versa.

javadoc—A Java toll used to generate HTML documentation pages from doc comments

javap—A command line tool that displays information in brief about the methods, constructors and fields present in the specified class(es)

jcmd—A Java tool used to send diagnostic commands to a specified JVM

jdb—A command line, interactive, Java tool used to debug Java code

JDI—A high-level Java API that defines the mechanisms for communication between debuggers and similar systems and running (usually remote) JVMs

jhat—A Java toll used to retrieve information from a heap dump

lvmid—An identifier which typically, but not necessarily, is the operating system's process identifier for the JVM process

OQL—A query language similar to SQL and used to query heap dumps

SUMMARY

Java beginners often use `javac` and `java` to compile and run Java programs. However, JDK comes with a lot of other powerful tools such as `jar`, `jhat`, `jdb`, `javap`, `javadoc`, `javah`, `jcmd`, `keytool`, `jconsole`, `jps`, `jstatd`, `jstat`, `jinfo`, `jmap`, `jstack` and many more to enable Java developers to program better.

Java standardizes the syntax and semantics of writing documentation. It also provides a tool `javadoc` to generate HTML files to view the documentation from a web browser in a convenient way.

The javap command line tool displays information in brief about the methods, constructors and fields present in the specified class(es). It is useful especially to those who want to quickly find the method signatures in a class.

The jcmd tool is used to send diagnostic commands to a specified JVM. Another powerful feature of jcmd is that it allows us to control Java Flight Recordings (JFR) from command line.

The `jhat` (java heap analysis tool) is a useful tool to retrieve information from a heap dump file. It parses the specified dump file and starts a web server. A web browser may then be used to get the desired data. The web server supports a few pre-designed queries as well as custom queries written in OQL (Object Query Language), which is a language similar to SQL to query heap dumps.

Java comes with a command line, interactive, runtime debugger known as `jdb` which is a very useful tool to debug Java code. The `jdb` tool allows us to query to a JVM and displays information.

The jar tool can bundle multiple files into a single one and vice versa. It use ZIP file format. So, in addition to bundling a set of files into a single one, we can use it for compressing and decompressing files.

WEB RESOURCES

`http://docs.oracle.com/javase/7/docs/technotes/tools/solaris/javadoc.html`
javadoc - The Java API Documentation Generator

`http://docs.oracle.com/javase/tutorial/deployment/jar/`
Lesson: Packaging Programs in JAR Files

`http://docs.oracle.com/javase/7/docs/technotes/tools/solaris/jcmd.html`
jcmd

`http://docs.oracle.com/javase/7/docs/technotes/tools/share/jhat.html`
jhat - Java Heap Analysis Tool

`http://docs.oracle.com/javase/7/docs/technotes/tools/windows/jdb.html`
jdb - The Java Debugger

`http://docs.oracle.com/javase/7/docs/technotes/tools/windows/javap.html`
javap - The Java Class File Disassembler

EXERCISES

Objective-type Questions

1. Which of the following is used to compile Java code?
(a) jar (c) javadoc
(b) javac (d) java

2. Which of the following is used to execute Java code?
(a) javap (c) javah
(b) javac (d) java

3. Which of the following is used to create HTML documentation pages?
   (a) javac (c) jdoc
   (b) javadoc (d) jdb

4. Which of the following is used to debug Java programs?
   (a) javac (c) jdoc
   (b) javadoc (d) jdb

5. With javadoc, which of the following denotes a javadoc comment?
   (a) /** (c) /*
   (b) //# (d) //**

6. Which javadoc tag is used to denote a comment for a method parameter?
   (a) @param (c) @parameter
   (b) @method (d) @argument

7. Name the tools that lie in the jdk
   (a) javab, javadoc, javav
   (b) javac, javatxt & javah
   (c) javak, javadoc & javah
   (d) javac, javadoc, javah

8. Java is a ______ programming language
   (a) Second generation
   (b) Third generation
   (c) Fourth generation
   (d) None of these

9. The javac converts program into
   (a) Hexadecimal code
   (b) Octal code
   (c) Byte code
   (d) Object code

10. What is the full form of JDK
   (a) Joint Development Kit
   (b) Java Demonstrate Kit
   (c) Java Development Keyword
   (d) Java Development Kit

11. What is the full form of JVM?
   (a) Joint Virtual Machine
   (b) Java Vital Machine
   (c) Java Virtual Machanic
   (d) Java Virtual Machine

12. Which of the following is the correct form of a Java file name?
   (a) <filename>.java
   (b) Java.<filename>
   (c) <filename>_java
   (d) Java_<filename>

13. Which of the following features is not supported by Java?
   (a) Abstraction (c) Polymorphism
   (b) Pointer (d) Inheritance

14. The jdb is used to
   (a) Create a jar archive
   (b) Debug a Java program
   (c) Create C header file
   (d) Generate Java documentation

15. The jar is used to
   (a) Create a jar archive
   (b) Debug a java program
   (c) Create C header file
   (d) Generate Java documentation

16. What is the meaning of jar?
   (a) Java ARchive
   (b) Java ARray
   (c) Java ARchitecture
   (d) Java Advanced Routine

17. Match the following.
   (i) java 1) is a tool for debugging Java program
   (ii) javah 2) is a tool for creating C-like header files
   (iii) javap 3) runs java bytecode
   (iv) jdb 4) prints Java code representation
   (a) i-3, ii-2,iii-1
   (b) i-3, ii-2, iii-4, iv-1
   (c) i-1, ii-2, iii-3, iv-4
   (d) i-2, ii-1, iii-3, iv-4

18. JVM is a
   (a) Debugger (c) Compiler
   (b) Assembler (d) Interpreter

19. Bytecode is given as input to
   (a) Linker (c) JVM
   (b) Assembler (d) Compiler

20. What is the purpose of debugging?
   (a) Developing software
   (b) Editing software
   (c) Removing errors from code
   (d) All of the above

Subjective-type Questions

1. What does javadoc command do?
2. Explain with examples the syntax of javadoc command.
3. Which delimiters are used to write javadoc comments?
4. Describe briefly the different files generated by javadoc.
5. Describe the structure of javadoc comments.
6. What is difference between block tags and in-line tag?
7. Write the name of a few tags for methods.
8. Write the examples of repeatable and non-repeatable tags.
9. What is the function of javap command?
10. Describe with examples the syntax of javap command.
11. What is the function of jcmd?
12. Describe with examples the syntax of jcmd command.
13. Demonstrate how jcmd can be used as flight recorder command.
14. What is the full form of jhat?
15. What is the function of jhat command?
16. How do you obtain a JVM dump file?
17. What is the function of jdb?
18. Demonstrate how jdm can be used in step by step program debugging.

CHAPTER – 2

EXCEPTION HANDLING

KEY OBJECTIVES

After completing this chapter readers will be able to—

- understand what exceptions are
- get an idea about exception handling mechanism
- learn Java exception class hierarchy
- use keywords try, catch, throw, throws and finally
- learn how to use try-with-resource statement
- write new exception classes

2.1 EXCEPTIONS

Exceptions are exceptional/unusual/abnormal events that occur during the execution of programs. To understand, what exceptions really are, consider the following simple program:

```
class ExceptionTest {
  public static void main(String[] args) {
    int d = 0, result;
    result = 100/d;
    System.out.println(result);
  }
}
```

Since, division by 0 is invalid, we say that an *exception* occurs during the division. Consider the following array declaration.

```
int[] a = new int[4];
a[5] =  6;
```

Since, any index out of the range 0 to 3, is invalid, an *exception* occurs when the second statement is executed. The following array declaration also results in an exception, since the size of any array can never be negative.

```
int b = new int [-3];
```

Consider the following class declarations:

```
class X {}
class Y extends X {}
```

With these declarations, the following type cast results in an exception:

```
X x = new X();
Y y = (Y)x;
```

In the following example, since the string is null, `length()` method will cause an exception.

```
String s = null;
int len = s.length();
```

Since the following string contains characters, `parseInt()` method results in an exception.

```
String s = "abc";
int i = Integer.parseInt(s);
```

With these examples, you might have an idea of what exceptions are now. In practice, there are many exceptional situations that may occur during the execution of a program. A highlight of such exceptions will be discussed in due course.

Anyway, what happens if an exception really occurs? The exception disrupts the normal flow of execution and terminates the program abruptly. Yes, that's the default behaviour of JVM. Consider that a program has the following series of statements:

```
statement 1;
statement 2;
statement 3;
statement 4;
```

If an exception occurs at `statement 2`, rest of the code will not be executed. Indeed, if our first program is executed, JVM terminates the program with the following message:

```
Exception in thread "main" java.lang.ArithmeticException: / by zero
        at ExceptionTest.main(ExceptionTest.java:6)
```

How will you feel if your program, which takes a very long time to run, terminates abnormally just before its completion? Certainly, not good. Fortunately, Java provides a standard and robust framework to cope up with exceptional scenarios, known as *Java Exception Handling*.

2.2 HANDLING EXCEPTIONS

Five keywords are used for exception handling. They are `try`, `catch`, `throw`, `throws` and `finally`. In this mechanism, we place a piece of vulnerable code (i.e., which might cause some exception) in a block called *try block*, which looks like this:

```
try {
   //code to inspect...
}
```

When an exception occurs during the execution of the code in the try block, JVM creates an exception object and declares that something wrong has happened. The exception object contains a lot of useful debugging information such as name of thread, file name, line of code at which exception occurred, name of exception and it's description etc. The process of creating this object and disclosing it is called *throwing* the exception. Throwing an exception disrupts the normal flow of execution. The JVM then tries to find code (called handler) that wants to handle (resolve) the exceptional situation. If found, it passes the newly created object to this handler, which is said to be *catching* the exception. The handler is specified by *catch* block immediately after the try block as follows:

```
try {
  //code to inspect...
}
catch(...) {
  //code to handle the exception
}
```

The catch block declares a parameter that specifies the type of exception it can handle.

2.3 AN EXAMPLE

Let us now apply this mechanism to our division example. Since, the division operation may throw an exception, we guard it using a try block as follows:

```
try {
  result = 100/d;
}
```

If the value of d is zero, an exception occurs during the division operation. The JVM creates an object representing the exception and throws the object which essentially disrupts the normal control of execution and places it just after the try block. The JVM then looks for an appropriate catch block that can hold the object thrown. Note that if JVM does not find any suitable catch block, it forwards the exception to a default handler which prints exception description and stack trace and terminates the program without executing any further instruction. Since, the division operation throws an `ArithmeticException` object, we add a catch block that can receive the exception object as follows:

```
catch(ArithmeticException e) {
  System.out.println("An arithmetic exception occurred.");
  result = 100;
}
```

This causes to receive the thrown object which can be accessed through e. This handler handles the exception by simply printing a message and setting the value of result to 100. The control of execution then comes after the catch block and continues. Here is the complete source code:

```
class ExceptionTest {
  public static void main(String[] args) {
    int d = 0, result;
    try {
      result = 100/d;
    }
    catch(ArithmeticException e) {
      System.out.println("An arithmetic exception occurred.");
      result = 100;
    }
    System.out.println("After catch block");
  }
}
```

If this program is executed, it no longer terminates abruptly. The result of the program is as follows:

```
An arithmetic exception occurred.
After catch block
```

2.4 TYPES OF EXCEPTIONS

Java platform provides a hierarchy of exception classes [Figure 2.1:] that represent various exceptional situations. Let us have a brief overview of these classes.

The hierarchy is created by having one (or more) exception extend another exception. The root of this exception class hierarchy is the `Throwable` class. Conventionally, two subclasses of this class, namely `Exception` and `Error` are provided to indicate exceptional situations.

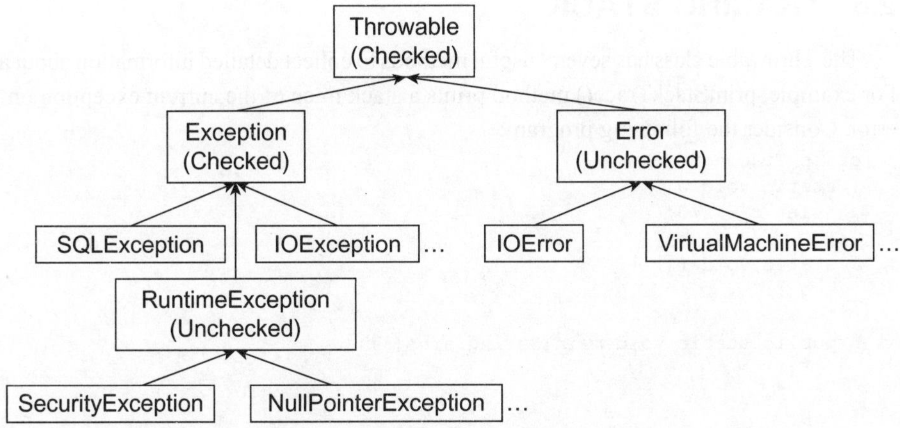

Figure 2.1: Java Exception class hierarchy

The class `Error` represents serious problematic scenarios (we shall call them errors) that applications can neither anticipate nor recover from. Examples of such errors are out of memory error, stack overflow error, class format error, no class definition found error etc.

The class `Exception` represents rest of the exceptional scenarios that applications can catch and handle. Usually, exceptions are categorized into two groups: *checked exceptions* and *unchecked exceptions*.

2.4.1 Checked Exceptions

Checked exceptions are those that must be caught or declared to be thrown. Java considers `Throwable` and any of its subclass that is not also a subclass of either `RuntimeException` or `Error` as checked exceptions. Checked exceptions should be handled in the code to avoid compile time errors.

2.4.2 Unchecked/Runtime Exceptions

Unchecked exceptions (also called runtime exceptions) are those which need not be caught or declared to be thrown explicitly. Note that checked and unchecked exceptions are functionally equivalent. We can do everything with checked exceptions that can also be done with unchecked exceptions, and vice versa.

2.5 CATCHING EXCEPTION

Note that Java exceptions are organized into a hierarchy. The advantage of this hierarchy is that if we write a catch block to catch a certain exception in the hierarchy, then it can also catch all subclasses of that exception too. It means, we can catch all exceptions from that certain exception and down the hierarchy. For example, since `FileNotFoundException` is a subclass of `IOException`, the following catch block can catch `IOException` as well as all other sub classes of `IOException` including `FileNotFoundException`:

```
catch(IOException ioe) {}
```

2.6 TRACING STACK

The Throwable class has several useful methods to collect detailed information about an exception. For example, printStackTrace() method prints a stack trace of the current exception on the standard error. Consider the following program:

```
class TracingStack {
  static void g() {
    int r = 2/0;
  }
  static void f() {
    g();
  }
  public static void main(String args[]) {
    f();
  }
}
```

This results in the following output:

```
Exception in thread "main" java.lang.ArithmeticException: / by zero
        at TracingStack.g(TracingStack.java:3)
        at TracingStack.f(TracingStack.java:6)
        at TracingStack.main(TracingStack.java:9)
```

The first line contains the name and description of the exception whereas rest of the lines locate the source of exception.

2.6.1 Multiple Catch Blocks

A single try block may have multiple catch blocks. This usually happens if try block throws more than one type of exceptions and we want to handle them differently. It takes the following form:

```
try {
  //code that throws exception
}
catch(Exception1 e) {
  //handle this way
}
catch(Exception2 e) {
  //handle that way
}
...
```

When an exception is thrown, the control of execution comes immediately after the enclosing try block. The JVM then searches for a matched catch block and if one is found, it is executed and control goes to the end of the try-catch. This implies that even if multiple catch blocks exist, only matched one (if there is any) is executed. The following example uses two catch blocks:

```
class MultipleCatch {
  public static void main(String args[]) {
    try {
      String a = args[0];
      int b = 2/0;
    }
```

```
        catch(ArrayIndexOutOfBoundsException e) {
          System.out.println(e);
        }
        catch(ArithmeticException e) {
           System.out.println(e);
        }
    }
}
```

The two statements in the try block can throw two exceptions. The former one throws an `ArrayIndexOutOfBoundsException` if no command line argument is passed to this program. If the first statement is passed (i.e., a command line argument is passed), second one throws an `ArithmeticException`. To catch these two exceptions, we have provided two catch blocks. The former one is responsible to catch `ArrayIndexOutOfBoundsException` whereas the later one catches `ArithmeticException`.

Multiple catch blocks may also be used in the case where all the exceptions thrown inside the try-block are the same type or subclasses of that type. The following illustrates that:

```
try{
   //code that throws IOException
}
catch (FileNotFoundException e){ }
catch (IOException e){}
```

Here, all `IOExceptions` are being handled by the second catch block except `FileNotFoundException`. The first catch block handles `FileNotFoundException` differently. Note that only the first catch-block that matches with a thrown exception will only handle an exception.

Catching many exceptions in a try block makes the code ugly. If multiple catch blocks have similar code, in Java SE 7 and later, we can combine multiple catch blocks into a single one using pipe (|) operator as follows:

```
catch(ArrayIndexOutOfBoundsException|ArithmeticException e) {
   System.out.println(e);
}
```

This single catch block can handle `ArrayIndexOutOfBoundsException` as well as `ArithmeticException`. It also reduces code duplication The parameter in a multi-catch block is implicitly final and hence cannot be modified.

Order of catch blocks does matter. Consider the following catch blocks:

```
catch(Exception e) {}
catch(ArrayIndexOutOfBoundsException e) {}
```

Since, `Exception` is the superclass of all the exceptions, all the exceptions (including `ArrayIndexOutOfBoundsException`) will be caught by the first catch block. So, second catch block is unreachable and results in a compilation error. In general, catch blocks must be arranged from most specific to most general. So, the following catch blocks are valid:

```
catch(ArrayIndexOutOfBoundsException e) {}
catch(Exception e) {}
```

Here, the first catch block only catches `ArrayIndexOutOfBoundsException` whereas second one catches everything else.

2.6.2 throw

Java programming language also allows us to explicitly throw an exception using `throw` keyword. The following program unconditionally creates an `Exception` object and throws it:

```
class ThrowTest {
  public static void main(String[] args) {
    try {
      throw new Exception("test");
    }
    catch(Exception e) {
      System.out.println(e);
    }
  }
}
```

Note that in practice, an exception is thrown only if an unusual situation occurs. The above program unconditionally throws an exception only to demonstrate the `throw` clause.

Only objects that are instances of `Throwable` class (or one of its subclasses) may be thrown by the `throw` statement. Similarly, only this class or one of its subclasses can be the argument type in a `catch` clause.

A catch block can take necessary actions after catching an exception. However, if it thinks that it has not been able to handle the exception completely, it can *re-throw* the exception expecting that some code else will handle it completely. Re-throwing an exception is done with the same `throw` keyword except that no new exception object is created. It takes the following form:

```
try {
  //code that throws exception
}
catch(Exception e) {
  //do as much as possible with e
  //then re-throw it
  throw e;
}
```

The following is a concrete example to illustrate this:

```
class ReThrowTest {
  void f() throws Exception {
    try { throw new Exception(); }
    catch(Exception e) {
      System.out.println("Handled paritally in f()");
      throw e;
    }
  }
  void g() {
    try { f(); }
    catch(Exception e) {
      System.out.println("Handled completely in g()");
    }
  }
  public static void main(String[] args) {
    new ReThrowTest().g();
  }
}
```

Here, the catch block in method `f()` catches an exception and prints a message. It thinks that the there is something else to do with this exception and re-throws the exception expecting that the caller will do that. The catch block of caller method `g()` catches the exception and takes further steps. This program results in the following output:

```
Handled partially in f()
Handled completely in g()
```

2.6.3 throws

A method must specify the list of *checked* exceptions that it might (directly/indirectly) raise but does not handle them using `throws` clause as follows:

```
return-type method-name (parameter list) throws list-of-exceptions {
}
```

The `throws` clause goes after the parameter list and before method body. This specification enables callers of the method either to guard themselves by using appropriate try-catch blocks or to re-declare it. Here is an example:

```
void f() throws Exception {
  throw new Exception("throws test");
}
```

This method unconditionally throws an `Exception` object. It specifies, using `throws` clause that it might throw an `Exception` object during its execution. This specification helps the caller to identify the list of exceptions it must deal with. A caller can:

- call the method f() within a try block and provide appropriate catch block to handle the exception.
- declare the exception to be re-thrown using a separate throws clause.
- use both the above together.

The following example uses a try-catch block:

```
void g() {
  try {
    f();
  }
  catch(Exception e) {
    //...
  }
}
```

It is useful if `g()` knows what exactly it should do if `f()` throws an exception. Otherwise, `g()` may re-specify it using a separate `throws` clause as follows:

```
void g() throws Exception {
  f();
}
```

It is also possible to handle the `Exception` using a try-catch block and still declare it to be thrown as follows:

```
void g() throws Exception {
    try {
      f();
    }
    catch(Exception e) {
      //take actions...
      throw e;
    }
  }
```

In this case, `g()` takes necessary steps in the catch block as far as it can and re-throws the caught exception expecting that some code else will handle it completely.

A method can only throw objects of the same class or subclass mentioned in the `throws` clause. In other words, throws clause must include classes (or super classes) whose instances are actually thrown.

```
void f() throws java.io.IOException {
  throw new Exception("throws test");
}
```

The above function is invalid as it throws a super class `Exception` object but declares a `IOException` to be thrown. However, the following is acceptable:

```
void f() throws Exception {
  throw new java.io.IOException("throws test");
}
```

A method that declares a checked exception to be thrown may not actually throw it. For example, the following method declares to throw a checked exception `InterruptedException`, but does not actually throw it:

```
void h() throws InterruptedException { }
```

A throws clause may include a comma-separated list of exceptions:

```
void h() throws InterruptedException, IllegalAccessException,
ClassNotFoundException { }
```

Although, it is not mandatory, we may also specify unchecked exceptions in the `throws` clause.

```
void h() throws NullPointerException { }
```

2.6.4 finally

Sometimes it is very much necessary to execute a piece of statements before a block of code is exited. For example, if a file or a database connection is opened, they should ideally be closed regardless of any problems that may occur. Java exception handling mechanism provides a `try-finally` clause for this purpose. This helps the program to guard (such as recover resources) itself even if an unexpected exception occurs. It takes the following form:

```
try {
  // code with multiple exit points...
}
//zero or more catch blocks
finally {
  //this gets always executed no matter how try block exited
}
```

The `finally` block is similar to `catch` block except that it always gets executed when try block exits no matter how it is exited. As long as finally block does not throw any exception, the control returns to the point from where this finally block was called and try block returns in the appropriate manner.

Let us now inspect when and in which cases a finally block gets executed. In the simplest case, the try block runs to the end with no exception thrown. The finally block will be executed just after the try block.

```
class FinallyTest {
  public static void main(String args[]) {
    try { }
    finally { System.out.println("In finally"); }
  }
}
```

It results in the following output:

```
In finally
```

The try block throws an exception and it is caught by a matching catch block. The finally block will execute right after the catch block executes.

```
class FinallyTest {
  public static void main(String args[]) {
    try { throw new Exception();}
    catch(Exception e) { System.out.println("In catch"); }
    finally { System.out.println("In finally"); }
  }
}
```

It produces the following result:

```
In catch
In finally
```

If catch block throws an exception further, before passing it to the caller, finally block is executed.

```
class FinallyTest {
  public static void main(String args[]) throws Exception {
    try { throw new Exception(); }
    catch(Exception e) {
      System.out.println("In catch");
      throw new Exception();
    }
    finally { System.out.println("In finally"); }
  }
}
```

It also produces the same result. What happens if an exception is thrown but there is no matching catch block? The exception object is thrown to the caller. But, before throwing the exception, the finally block is executed.

```
class FinallyTest {
  public static void main(String args[]) throws Exception {
    try { throw new Exception();}
    finally { System.out.println("In finally "); }
  }
}
```

A return statement is encountered before the try block completes. But, before it returns to caller, the finally block is still executed.

```
class FinallyTest {
  public static void main(String args[]) {
    try { return; }
    finally { System.out.println("In finally "); }
  }
}
```

2.6.4.1 An Example

Since, a finally block is always executed regardless of what happens in the try block, it is a perfect place to write clean up code (such as closing a file or socket/database connection) that may otherwise be bypassed by statements such as `return`, `break`, `continue` etc. Here is an example:

```
FileInputStream fis = new FileInputStream("aFile.txt");
try {
  //file related operations...
}
catch(IOException e) {
  System.out.println(e);
}
finally {
  fis.close();
}
```

If an exception is thrown during file opening, neither try nor finally blocks get executed. Since, the file is not opened, there is no need to close it. Otherwise (i.e., the file is successfully opened), if try block throws an `IOException`, it is caught by the catch block. The finally block will execute right after the catch block executes. This ensures that if the file is opened, it is also closed.

Since, the `finally` block itself may throw an exception, it may be put in an enclosing `try-catch` block as follows:

```
try {
  FileInputStream fis = new FileInputStream("aFile.txt");
  try {
    //file related operations...
  }
  finally {
    fis.close();
  }
}
catch(Exception e) {
  //..
}
```

This can handle all of the checked exceptions. Alternatively, the code of the finally block may be put in another try-catch clause:

```
FileInputStream fis = new FileInputStream("aFile.txt");
try {
  //file related operations...
}
finally {
  try {
    fis.close();
  }
  catch(Exception e} {
    //...
  }
}
```

2.6.4.2 Some Properties

The `finally` block, if used, must be placed after all `catch` blocks. So, the following is illegal as `finally` block does not follow all `catch` blocks:

```
try {
  //...
}
finally { }
catch(Exception e) {}
```

However, probably you have already noticed that a `finally` block may exist without any `catch` block as follows:

```
try {
  //...
}
finally { }
```

Every `try` block may have at most one `finally` block. The following is illegal:

```
try {
  //...
}
finally { }
finally { }
```

2.6.5 try-with-resources Statement

The finally block, no doubt, provides a cleaner way to clean up resources. However, if we forget to close resources, we shall get runtime exceptions which are hard to debug. We might look into the entire program to make sure that all resources will get closed for all possible scenarios. Fortunately, Java 7 and later provides an even better mechanism known as *try with resource statement*. It enables us to create resources in the try statement and use them in the try block. When the try block exits by any means, the Java Runtime Environment automatically close these resources. The try with resource statement look like this:

```
try(Aresource ar = new AResource()) {
  //use it
}
```

The following is an example:

```
try (FileInputStream fis = new FileInputStream("a.txt")) {
  //use this file
}
```

In the try statement, we open a file and use it in the try block. When this try block exits, no matter how it exits, runtime environment will certainly close the file. So, we can freely create resources and use them. The only requirement is that the resource class must directly or indirectly implement `java.lang.AutoCloseable` interface. Hopefully, most of the resources implement this interface, and may be used in try with resource statement.

We can also create our own resource implementing this interface which has a single method `close()` as follows:

```
class MyResource implements AutoCloseable {
  public void close() {
    System.out.println("In MyResource's close()");
  }
}
```

We can then use it in the try statement:

```
class TryWithResourcesTest {
  public static void main(String args[]) throws Exception {
    try (MyResource mr = new MyResource()) {
      //...
    }
  }
}
```

When executed, it prints the following message:

```
MyResource's close()
```

Multiple resource may also be created in the try statement:

```
try (
  FileInputStream fis = new FileInputStream("a.txt");
  FileOutputStream fos = new FileOutputStream("b.txt");
  Socket s = new Socket("localhost",6789);
) {
  //...
}
```

It creates three resources in the try statement separated by semicolon (;). When try exits, the `close()` methods on all these three resources are automatically called in the opposite order of their creation.

Like an ordinary try statement, a try-with-resources statement can have catch and finally blocks. If present, they are executed after the resources created have been closed. Consider the following program:

```
class TryWithResourcesTest {
  public static void main(String args[]) throws Exception {
    try (MyResource mr = new MyResource()) {
      //...
    }
    finally {
      System.out.println("In finally");
    }
  }
}
```

This prints the following message:

```
In MyResource's close()
In finally
```

Note that exceptions may occur when JRE calls `close()` method on resources created in try-with-resource statement. Exception may also occur in the try block. If both occur, earlier exceptions are suppressed and the exception that occurs in the try block is finally thrown. The suppressed exception may be recovered for handling using `getSuppressed()` method of `Throwable` class. The following program illustrates this:

```
class TryWithResourcesTest1 {
   public static void main(String args[]) throws Exception {
     try {
       try (MyResource mr = new MyResource()) {
         System.out.println("Throwing from try block");
         throw new Exception("try block");
       }
     }
     catch(Exception e) {
       System.out.println(e);
       Throwable[] t = e.getSuppressed();
       System.out.println("Suppressed exception...");
       for(int i=0;i<t.length;i++)
        System.out.println(t[i]);
     }
  }
}
class MyResource implements AutoCloseable {
  public void close() throws Exception {
    System.out.println("Throwing from close()");
    throw new Exception("close()");
  }
}
```

In this program, we create resource in the try-with-resource statement and throw an `Exception` from the try block. As expected, before forwarding this exception to the enclosing code, JRE tries to invoke `close()` method on the resource. However, `close()` method itself throws a new `Exception` which gets suppressed and the earlier Exception is finally forwarded to the outer catch block. We have retrieved the suppressed exception using `getSupressed()` method. If we execute the program, the following results:

```
Throwing from try block
Throwing from close()
java.lang.Exception: try block
Suppressed exception...
java.lang.Exception: close()
```

2.6.6 Nested try-catch

It is possible that exception handlers are nested within one another. This means a `try`, `catch` or a `finally` block can in turn contain another set of try-catch-finally blocks. For example, in the following code, a try block contains another try-catch sequence.

```
try {
  statement 1;
  try {
    statement 2;
  }
  catch(Exception e) { }
}
catch(Exception e){ }
```

A catch block can also contain another try-catch sequence as follows:

```
try {
  statement 1;
}
catch(Exception e){
  try {
    statement 2;
  }
  catch(Exception e1) { }
}
```

Or even finally can contain other try-catch blocks:

```
try {
  statement 1;
}
finally {
  try {
    statement 2;
  }
  catch(Exception e) { }
}
```

Consider the following example:

```
FileInputStream fis = null;
try {
  fis = new FileInputStream("aFile.txt");
}
catch(IOException e) {
  fis.close();
}
```

Since, the code in the catch block itself can throw an exception, we can put this code in a separate try-catch as follows:

```
FileInputStream fis = null;
try {
  fis = new FileInputStream("aFile.txt");
}
catch(IOException e) {
  try {
    fis.close();
  }
  catch(Exception e1) { }
}
```

If anything goes wrong in `fis.close()` statement (e.g. fis is null), an exception is thrown, However, inner catch block can catch that exception and handle it.

2.7 CUSTOM EXCEPTION CLASSES

Sometimes it is required to develop meaningful exceptions based on application requirements. Fortunately, Java also allows us to create new exception classes.

Since, only instances of `Throwable` class (or one of its subclasses) may be thrown, user-defined exception classes must inherit (directly or indirectly) this class. The following is a user-defined exception class that extends `Exception` class:

```
class InsufficientAmountException extends Exception {
    long amount;
    InsufficientAmountException(long amount) {
        this.amount = amount;
    }
}
```

To increase readability, it is recommended to append the string "Exception" to the names of all classes that inherit (directly or indirectly) from the `Exception` class. Here is another example:

```
class ExcessiveAmountException extends Exception {
    long amount;
    ExcessiveAmountException(long amount) {
        this.amount = amount;
    }
}
```

We can then use these two exception classes just like ordinary exception classes as follows:

```
class Bank {
    static long MaximumAmount = 15000;
    public void withdraw(long accNo, long amount)
      throws InsufficientAmountException, ExcessiveAmountException {
      long balance = getBalance(accNo);
      if(balance < amount)
         throw new InsufficientAmountException(amount);
      if(amount > MaximumAmount)
         throw new ExcessiveAmountException(amount);
      //else withdraw...
    }
    private long getBalance(long accNo) {
      return 0;
    }
}
```

These exceptions classes can also be used in the catch blocks. The following example illustrates this:

```
class UserException {
  public static void main(String args[]) {
    Bank b = new Bank();
    try {
      b.withdraw(0, 20000);
    }
    catch(ExcessiveAmountException e) {
      System.out.println(e);
    }
    catch(InsufficientAmountException e) {
       System.out.println(e);
    }
  }
}
```

If executed, it results in the following output:

```
InsufficientAmountException
```

KEYWORDS

catch block—Contains code to handle exceptions

Checked Exception—A set of exceptions that must be caught or declared to be thrown

Custom Exception classes—User-defined exception classes that represent meaningful exceptional situations

Error—A subclass of Throwable that represents serious problematic scenarios (we shall call them errors) that applications can neither anticipate nor recover from

Exception—A subclass of Throwable that represents exceptional scenarios that applications can catch and handle

Exception hierarchy—A hierarchy of Java exception classes that represent various exceptional situations

Exceptions—Exceptional or unusual or abnormal events that occur during the execution of programs

finally block—Contains code that always gets executed no matter how try block exited

Nested try-catch— A `try`, `catch` or a `finally` block containing another set of try-catch-finally blocks

Runtime exception—A set of exceptions that need not be caught or declared to be thrown explicitly

throw—A keyword used to throw an exception explicitly

Throwable—The root class of Java exception class hierarchy

throws—A keyword used to specify a set of exceptions a method might throw during its execution

try block—Used to contain a piece of code to be examined

Try-with-resource statement—A construct that allows us to use resources that get closed automatically by the Java Runtime Environment

Unchecked Exceptions—A set of exceptions that need not be caught or declared to be thrown explicitly

SUMMARY

Exceptions are exceptional/unusual/abnormal events that occur during the execution of programs. Five keywords are used for exception handling—`try`, `catch`, `throw`, `throws` and `finally`. A try block contains code to be examined. A try block is followed by one or more catch blocks and/or one finally block. Exceptions are thrown and caught by the respective catch block (if any). The finally block, if present, is always executed irrespective of how try block exits.

In Java, exceptional scenarios are represented by various classes which are organized in a hierarchy. The class Throwable is the root of this class hierarchy. The Throwable class has several useful methods to collect detailed information about an exception. Two subclasses of this class are Exception and Error. The class `Error` represents serious problematic scenarios that applications can neither anticipate nor recover from them. The class `Exception` represents rest of the exceptional scenarios that applications can catch and handle.

Usually, exceptions are categorized into two groups: *checked exceptions* and *unchecked exceptions*. Checked exceptions are those that must be caught or declared to be thrown. Java considers `Throwable` and any of its subclass that is not also a subclass of either `RuntimeException` or `Error` as checked exceptions. Unchecked exceptions (also called runtime exceptions) are those which need not be caught or declared to be thrown explicitly.

It is also possible to explicitly throw an exception using `throw` keyword. A method must specify the list of *checked* exceptions that it might (directly/indirectly) raise but does not handle them using `throws` clause. Java 7 and later provides mechanism known as *try with resource statement* that enables us to create and use resources that get closed automatically by the Java Runtime Environment.

It is possible for exception handlers to be nested within one another. This means a `try`, `catch` or a `finally` block can in turn contain another set of try-catch-finally blocks.

It is also possible to define custom exception classes which must inherit (directly or indirectly) the class Throwable.

WEB RESOURCES

http://docs.oracle.com/javase/tutorial/essential/exceptions/
Lesson: Exceptions

http://www.tutorialspoint.com/java/java_exceptions.htm
Java Exception Handling

http://tutorials.jenkov.com/java-exception-handling/index.html
Java Exception Handling

http://howtodoinjava.com/2013/04/04/java-exception-handling-best-practices/
Java exception handling best practices

http://www.journaldev.com/1696/java-exception-handling-tutorial-with-examples-and-best-practices
Java Exception Handling Tutorial with Examples and Best Practices

http://www.javaworld.com/article/2076700/core-java/exceptions-in-java.html
Exceptions in Java

http://www.javatpoint.com/exception-handling-and-checked-and-unchecked-exception
Exception Handling in Java

http://www.urz.uni-heidelberg.de/Unterstuetzung/Hinweise/Einzel/Java/EckelJavaTutor/TIJ311.htm
Error Handling with Exceptions

EXERCISES

Objective-type Questions

1. The class at the top of exception class hierarchy is ________
   (a) ArithmeticException
   (b) Throwable
   (c) Class
   (d) Exception

2. What will be the output of the program?

```
public class Test {
  public static void main(String[] args) {
    try {
      return;
    }
    finally {
      System.out.println( "Finally" );
    }
  }
}
```

   (a) Finally
   (b) Compilation error.
   (c) The code runs with no output.
   (d) An exception is thrown at runtime.

3. What will be the output of the program?

```
public class Test {
  public static void main(String[] args) {
    try {
      int x = 0;
      int y = 5 / x;
      System.out.println("finished");
    }catch (ArithmeticException ae) {
      System.out.println("Exception");
    }catch (Exception e) {
      System.out.println("Arithmetic
                              Exception");
    }
  }
}
```

   (a) Compilation error.
   (b) finished
   (c) Exception
   (d) Arithmetic Exception

4. An exception thrown from outside try block will
   (a) return the program normally
   (b) be ignored
   (c) terminate the program
   (d) none of the above

5. Which of the following causes an exception
   (a) A run-time error
   (b) A hardware malfunction
   (c) An operating system problem
   (d) A syntax error

6. When does exception occur in Java?
   (a) At compilation time
   (b) At run time
   (c) Any time
   (d) None of the mentioned

7. Which of these keywords is not a part of exception handling?
   (a) try (c) finally
   (b) catch (d) thrown

8. Which of the following keywords is used to examine exceptions?
   (a) try (c) finally
   (b) catch (d) throw

9. Which of the following keywords is used to handle exception?
   (a) try (c) throw
   (b) catch (d) throws

10. Which of the following keywords is used to throw an exception explicitly?
(a) try (c) throw
(b) catch (d) throws

11. The key words used with exception handling are:
(a) try, catch, handle
(b) try, hold, finally
(c) throw, catch, conclude
(d) try, catch, finally

12. Arithmetic Exception is
(a) A checked exception
(b) An unchecked exception
(c) An error
(d) None of the above

13. Which of following exception is thrown by the `int z=2/0;`?
(a) ClassNotFoundException
(b) NullPointerException
(c) ArithmeticException
(d) SecurityException

14. Checked exceptions are processed by
(a) Java compiler
(b) Java interpreter
(c) Both (a) and (b)
(d) None of the above

15. Unchecked exceptions are processed by
(a) Java compiler
(b) Java interpreter
(c) Both (a) and (b)
(d) None of the above

16. Which one of the following statements is correct?
(a) The 'try' block must be followed by a 'catch' block.
(b) The 'try' block must be followed by a 'finally' block.
(c) The 'try' block must be followed by either a 'catch' block or a 'finally' block.
(d) The 'try' block must be followed by at least one 'catch' block and one 'finally' block.

17. Creating an exception object and handling it to the run time system is called
(a) exception handling
(b) catching exception
(c) passing exception
(d) throwing exception

18. Which of the following is an example of runtime exception?
(a) FileNotFoundException
(b) IOException
(c) IllegalClassFormatException
(d) ClassCastException

19. Which of the following is the super class of all exception classes?
(a) Exception (c) RuntimeException
(b) Throwable (d) IOException

20. Which of the following blocks gets executed compulsorily whether exception is caught or not?
(a) finally (c) throws
(b) throw (d) catch

21. Which of the following is true of the object thrown by a throw clause?
(a) It must be an Exception type
(b) It must be a Throwable type
(c) It must be an Error type
(d) It must be a String type

22. Which of the following methods is used to print the description of an exception?
(a) traceException()
(b) printStackTrace()
(c) printDescription()
(d) printStack()

23. Which of the following exceptions is thrown if an array element is accessed beyond the array size?
(a) ArrayIndexOutOfBounds
(b) IndexOutOfBoundsException
(c) IndexOutOfBounds
(d) ArrayIndexOutOfBounds Exception

24. Which of the following is true when we write custom exception classes?
(a) Extend the class Exception
(b) Create our own try and catch block
(c) Use finally block
(d) Use throws keyword

25. Which of the following is true about the Error and Exception classes?
(a) The Error class is final and the Exception class is not.
(b) The Exception class is final and the Error is not.
(c) Both classes extend Throwable.
(d) Both classes implement Throwable.

26. Predict the output of the following Java program.

```
class Test {
    public static void main(String args[]) {
        try {
            throw 2;
        }
        catch(int e) {
            System.out.println
                        ("Exception " + e);
        }
    }
}
```

(a) Exception 2
(b) Exception 0
(c) Compilation Error
(d) None of the above

27. What will be the output of the program?

```
public class Test {
  public static void main(String[] args){
    try {
      int x = 0;
      int y = x / 5;
      System.out.println("finished");
    }catch (ArithmeticException ae) {
      System.out.println("Exception");
    }catch (Exception e) {
     System.out.println("Arithmetic
                       Exception");
    }
  }
}
```

(a) Compilation error
(b) finished
(c) Exception
(d) Arithmetic Exception

28. Which of the following is thrown by the read() method of InputStream class?

(a) Exception
(b) FileNotFoundException
(c) ReadException
(d) IOException

29. What will be the output of the following program?

```
public class Test{
  public static void main(String args[]){
    System.out.print("Before ");
    try {
    }catch(Throwable t){
      System.out.print("Inside ");
    }
    System.out.print("End ");
  }
}
```

(a) Before End
(b) Before Inside
(c) Inside End
(d) Before Inside End

30. What causes an IllegalMonitorStateException?

(a) Two threads call a static synchronized method at the same time.
(b) A thread invokes wait() on an object that is already waiting.
(c) A thread invokes notify() on an object that is not waiting.
(d) A thread calls wait() or notify() before acquiring an object's monitor.

Subjective-type Questions

1. What is the difference between checked and unchecked exceptions?

2. What is the difference between throw and throws keyword?

3. What do you mean by exception propagation?

4. What are the two types of exceptions in Java? What are the differences between them?

5. Why do you use multiple catch blocks?

6. How will you write new exception classes?

7. What is the difference between 'Exception' and 'error' in Java?

8. Describe the principle of 'finally' block.

9. What happens if an exception is not caught?

10. Describe the exception hierarchy in Java

11. What is the difference between ClassNotFoundException and NoClassDefFoundError?

12. What are the advantages of using exception handling?

13. Why are Errors not checked?

14. Why are Runtime Exceptions not checked?

15. What is meant by 're-throwing' an exception? How do you re-throw an exception?

16. Write some important methods of Exception Class?

17. What is the usefulness of multiple catch blocks?

18. What is the use of throws keyword?

19. When do you use a catch block and when do you use a finally block?

20. Write some example scenarios when finally block is not executed.

CHAPTER – 3

MULTI-THREADING

KEY OBJECTIVES

After completing this chapter readers will be able to—

- understand what multi-threaded programs are
- learn how to write multi-threaded programs
- learn how to interrupt, suspend and resume threads
- get an idea about inter-thread communication
- understand what synchronized methods and blocks are
- deal with deadlock

3.1 INTRODUCTION

A thread is a control/flow/path of execution that exists within a process. A process may have one or more threads in it and is referred to as *single-threaded* or *multi-threaded* process respectively. In a single-threaded process, there is only one flow to execution of instructions, whereas a multi-threaded process has multiple sets of instructions that are executed concurrently; it hence has multiple concurrent flows/paths of execution.

So, a multi-threaded process has two or more parts that can run concurrently and each part can do a designated task at the same time. Multi-threading enables us to write programs in a way where multiple activities can proceed concurrently in the same program. However, note that a system having only one execution core executes multiple threads in an interleaved way resulting in no extra benefit in terms of effective execution time.

In this chapter, we shall discuss how to work with multi-threaded processes in Java.

3.2 MAIN THREAD

When we supply a program to the JVM for execution, it creates one thread and associates the program's `main()` method. The thread then executes the statement contained in the `main()` method.

Since, it is the first thread that starts running when a program begins, it is said to be *main/primary* thread. Other threads, if required, may be spawned from this main thread.

Though we do not create the main thread explicitly, we can inspect and control its properties. However, to work with main thread, we must have a reference to the Thread object corresponding to the main thread. This can be accomplished using Thread's static `currentThread()` method that returns a reference to the currently executing thread object. So, a reference to the main Thread object can be obtained using the following statement in the `main()` method:

```
Thread t = Thread.currentThread();
```

We can then access the main thread via this reference. The following program illustrates this:

```
class ThreadInfo {
  public static void main(String args[]) {
    Thread t = Thread.currentThread();

    System.out.println("Current Thread: "+t);
    System.out.println("Name: "+t.getName());
    System.out.println("Id: "+t.getId());
    System.out.println("Priority: "+t.getPriority());
    System.out.println("State: "+t.getState());

    System.out.println("Changing name and priority...");
    t.setName("Primary");
    t.setPriority(8);

    System.out.println("After name and priority change...");
    System.out.println("Current Thread: "+t);
    System.out.println("Name: "+t.getName());
    System.out.println("Priority: "+t.getPriority());
  }
}
```

Every thread has a name for identification purposes. Note that it is just a string. So, multiple threads may have the same name. When a thread is created, a new name is generated for it if none is specified.

The above program first prints some of the thread properties such as its name, id, priority, etc. It then changes the name and priority and displays them again. It results in the following output:

```
Current Thread: Thread[main,5,main]
Name: main
Id: 1
Priority: 5
State: RUNNABLE
Changing name and priority...
After name and priority change...
Current Thread: Thread[Primary,8,main]
Name: Primary
Priority: 8
```

The information between '[' and ']' includes the name of the thread, its priority and the name of thread group where this thread belongs in order. We see indeed that the name of the thread was "main". Later it was changed to "primary".

3.3 USING sleep

A thread should ideally consume minimum CPU cycles. Think about a thread that prints current system time up to second accuracy. Since the second part of time changes only after 1 second, it is better to print the time and wait for one second. This makes processor time available to the other threads of the application or other applications that might be running on a computer system.

A thread can be made suspended using `sleep()` method that has the following overloaded versions:

```
public static void sleep(long millis)
public static void sleep(long millis, int nanos)
```

They cause the currently executing thread to cease execution for the specified duration. The former version takes the duration in milliseconds, whereas the latter one allows us to specify the duration in milliseconds and nanoseconds. Consider the following program:

```
public class SleepDemo {
  public static void main(String args[]) {
    for(;;) {
      System.out.println("Local date and time: "+new java.util.Date());
      try {
        Thread.sleep(1000);
      }catch(InterruptedException ie){}
    }
  }
}
```

In this program, the main thread prints the current date and time and waits for 1 second and repeats this all over again. When it waits, it releases the CPU which can be used by other threads or applications. The following is sample output of this program.

```
Local date and time: Sat Apr 26 11:41:46 IST 2014
Local date and time: Sat Apr 26 11:41:47 IST 2014
Local date and time: Sat Apr 26 11:41:48 IST 2014
Local date and time: Sat Apr 26 11:41:49 IST 2014
Local date and time: Sat Apr 26 11:41:50 IST 2014
Local date and time: Sat Apr 26 11:41:51 IST 2014
Local date and time: Sat Apr 26 11:41:52 IST 2014
Local date and time: Sat Apr 26 11:41:53 IST 2014
...
```

Since this program runs for ever, use `Crtl-C` to terminate the program. Note that duration specified in `sleep()` is not guaranteed to be precise, because it is limited by the facilities provided by the underlying OS. Also, the `sleep()` may throw an `InterruptedException` if the current thread is interrupted. Either case, don't assume that `sleep()` will suspend the thread for precisely the duration specified.

3.4 CREATING THREAD

There are two ways to create threads: by extending the `java.lang.Thread` class and implementing the `java.lang.Runnable` interface.

3.4.1 Extending Thread

One way to create threads is to write a class extending the `Thread` class and overriding its `run()` method as follows:

```
public class SimpleThread extends Thread {
  public void run() {
    for(int i = 0; i < 4; i++)
      System.out.println("In MyThread: "+i);
  }
  //...
}
```

The `run()` method provides the entry point for the thread. It contains codes to be executed concurrently with other threads. Our `run()` method simply prints a message five times. The objects of this class are called threads. The following creates one thread object:

```
SimpleThread st = new SimpleThread();
```

When, this thread starts, the codes in the `run()` method get executed concurrently with other codes. Note that in a uni-processor system, the codes run in interleaved way. Anyway, this thread does not start automatically. It is started using its inherited `start()` method as follows:

```
st.start();
```

When this statement is encountered, JVM creates a new control of execution and associates the `run()` method with it and returns to the caller immediately. The two threads, the current thread and the newly created one are then run concurrently. The current thread executes statements after `start()` method and new thread executes the statements in `run()` method. Here is the complete source code:

```
public class SimpleThread extends Thread {
  public void run() {
    for(int i = 0; i < 4; i++)
      System.out.println("In MyThread: "+i);
  }
  public static void main(String args[]) {
    SimpleThread st = new SimpleThread();
    st.start();
    for(int i = 0; i < 6; i++)
      System.out.println("In main thread: "+i);
  }
}
```

Here, the main thread creates a new thread and calls its `start()` method which spawns a new control of execution and returns to the main thread immediately. The main thread then executes the statements after the `start()` method whereas the new thread executes the `run()` method concurrently. A sample output is shown below:

```
In main thread: 0
In MyThread: 0
In MyThread: 1
In main thread: 1
In main thread: 2
In MyThread: 2
In main thread: 3
In MyThread: 3
In main thread: 4
In main thread: 5
```

Note that the output may vary next time you run the program. This happens because the operating system may use a different interleaving pattern depending on its scheduling policy and other parameters.

3.4.2 Implementing Runnable

Although, we can create threads extending the `Thread` class, it has an inherent problem. Since, Java does not support multiple inheritance for classes, if a class has to extend another class, it cannot extend `Thread`. Fortunately, Java provides an alternative way to create threads where we create a class implementing the `Runnable` interface as follows:

```
public class MyClass implements Runnable {
  public void run() {
    for(int i = 0; i < 4; i++)
      System.out.println("In MyThread: "+i);
  }
  //...
}
```

The class implements the `run()` method of `Runnable` interface. Note that an object of this class is not a thread; it is merely runnable in the sense that its `run()`, method can be executed concurrently with other codes. The thread object is created using any of the following constructors of `Thread` class:

```
public Thread(Runnable target)
public Thread(Runnable target, String name)
```

Both take a runnable object as first argument and create a thread object. So, we use the former one passing a runnable object as follows:

```
Thread t = new Thread(new MyClass());
```

This is an ordinary thread and can be started as usual:

```
t.start();
```

It eventually calls runnable object's `run()` method. Here is the complete source code using `Runnable` interface:

```
public class MyClass implements Runnable {
  public void run() {
    for(int i = 0; i < 4; i++)
      System.out.println("In MyThread: "+i);
  }
  public static void main(String args[]) {
    Thread t = new Thread(new MyClass());
    t.start();
    for(int i = 0; i < 6; i++)
      System.out.println("In main thread: "+i);
  }
}
```

This generates a similar output as shown below:

```
In main thread: 0
In MyThread: 0
In main thread: 1
In MyThread: 1
In main thread: 2
In MyThread: 2
In main thread: 3
In MyThread: 3
In main thread: 4
In main thread: 5
```

Again note that the output may vary every time you run the program.

3.5 INTERRUPTING THREAD

Interrupting a thread means requesting it to stop what it is currently doing and do something else. The request is sent to a thread using its `interrupt()` method that sets the thread's *interrupt flag*. However, how will the thread identify that it has been interrupted?

Note that methods such as `sleep()`, `wait()`, `join()` etc. throw an `InterruptedException` if they find interrupt flag set. So, a thread can use any of these methods in a try block and provide an appropriate catch block which gets executed when it is interrupted. In this way, a thread can determine if it is interrupted or not. The following program demonstrates this:

```
class Timer extends Thread {
  public void run() {
    while(true) {
      System.out.println("Timer running. Date & time: "+new java.util.Date());
      try {
        Thread.sleep(1000);
      }catch(InterruptedException e) {
         System.out.println("Timer was interrupted");
         return;
      }
    }
  }
}
```

```
public class InterruptDemo {
  public static void main(String args[]) throws InterruptedException {
    Timer t = new Timer();
    t.start();
    Thread.sleep(4000);
    t.interrupt();
  }
}
```

Here, main thread creates and starts a child thread that continuously prints current date and time and sleeps for 1 second. The main thread, after 4 seconds, calls child thread's `interrupt()` method that sets child thread's interrupt flag. If the child thread is sleeping at that time, `sleep()` throws an `InterruptedException` when it returns. Otherwise, when `sleep()` method is encountered the next time, it throws an `InterruptedException`. Either case, the catch block is executed and the child thread can respond to this interruption.

It is up to the thread exactly how it will respond to an interrupt. However, it is very common that the thread dies upon interruption. In our example, the child thread prints a message and returns. It is also up to the thread how quickly it will respond. For example, if the thread receives an interrupt in the middle of some heavyweight computation, it can only respond at the end of the computation.

The following is a sample output of the program:

```
Timer running. Date & time: Sun Apr 27 11:45:14 IST 2014
Timer running. Date & time: Sun Apr 27 11:45:15 IST 2014
Timer running. Date & time: Sun Apr 27 11:45:16 IST 2014
Timer running. Date & time: Sun Apr 27 11:45:17 IST 2014
Timer was interrupted
```

Alternatively, a thread may use static `interrupted()` method to check if it was interrupted. The method returns a `true` if the interrupt flag is set; `false` otherwise. So, a thread, on its way to normal work, may devote some time to inspect the method's return value as follows:

```
while(true) {
  //do normal work
  //check it was interrupted
  if(Thread.interrupted()) {
    //it was interrupted, respond
  }
}
```

At any time, if `interrupted()` method returns the value `true`, it understands that an interrupt request was sent to it. The following program illustrates this:

```
class Timer extends Thread {
  public void run() {
    while(true) {
      System.out.println("Timer running. Date & time: "+new java.util.Date());
      if(Thread.interrupted()) {
        System.out.println("Timer was interrupted");
        return;
      }
    }
  }
}
public class InterruptDemo1 {
  public static void main(String args[]) throws InterruptedException {
    Timer t = new Timer();
    t.start();
    Thread.sleep(20);
    t.interrupt();
  }
}
```

The child thread, upon interrupt, responds by printing a message and terminating itself. Here is a sample output of this program:

```
Timer running. Date & time: Sun Apr 27 11:48:23 IST 2014
Timer running. Date & time: Sun Apr 27 11:48:23 IST 2014
Timer running. Date & time: Sun Apr 27 11:48:23 IST 2014
Timer running. Date & time: Sun Apr 27 11:48:23 IST 2014
Timer running. Date & time: Sun Apr 27 11:48:23 IST 2014
Timer running. Date & time: Sun Apr 27 11:48:23 IST 2014
Timer running. Date & time: Sun Apr 27 11:48:23 IST 2014
Timer was interrupted
```

Note that `interrupted()` method clears the interrupt flag of the thread. This means if the method is called twice in succession, the second call would return `false` unless the current thread is interrupted again in the meanwhile.

3.6 SUSPENDING AND RESUMING

A thread may be suspended and resumed using the combination of `wait()` and `notify()` methods. The following program illustrates this:

```
class MyThread extends Thread {
  boolean active = true;
  public void Suspend() { active=false; }
  public synchronized void Resume() {
    active = true;
    notify();
  }
  public synchronized void run() {
    try {
      while(true) {
        if(active) {
          System.out.println("Running...");
          Thread.sleep(500);
        }
        else {
          System.out.println("Suspended...");
          wait();
        }
      }
    }catch(Exception e) {e.printStackTrace();}
  }
}
public class SuspendResume {
  public static void main(String args[]) throws Exception {
    MyThread mt = new MyThread();
    mt.start();
    while(true) {
      Thread.sleep(1000);
      mt.Suspend();
      Thread.sleep(1000);
      mt.Resume();
    }
  }
}
```

The class `MyThread` has a boolean field active that represents the current status of the thread. The methods `Suspend()` and `Resume()` change this flag to suspend and resume a thread respectively. The main thread suspends and resumes after every 1 second. Here is a sample output:

```
Running...
Running...
Running...
```

```
Suspended...
Running...
Running...
Running...
Suspended...
Running...
Running...
Running...
Suspended...
Running...
Running...
Running...
Suspended...
Running...
Running...
Suspended...
```

Since the program runs for ever, press ctrl-C to terminate the program.

3.7 THREAD PRIORITY

In Java, every thread has a priority. Higher priority threads get more preference in terms of CPU, I/O time, etc. than lower priority threads. However, how threads with different priorities should be handled depends absolutely on the underlying platform specifically on its scheduling algorithm. Conceptually, threads of equal priority should get equal chance. Similarly, higher priority threads should ideally receive more importance than lower priority ones.

Priorities are represented by integer numbers from 1 (lowest) to 10 (highest) which are represented by two static final fields `MIN_PRIORITY` and `MAX_PRIORITY` of `Thread` class respectively. A new thread receives its initial priority equal to the priority of its creator thread. The JVM assigns a priority value equal to the final field `NORM_PRIORITY` to the main thread. Java defines these fields as follows:

```
public final static int MIN_PRIORITY = 1;
public final static int NORM_PRIORITY = 5;
public final static int MAX_PRIORITY = 10;
```

The following program prints their values:

```
public class MinMaxPriority {
  public static void main(String args[]) {
    System.out.println("Lowest thread priority: "+Thread.MIN_PRIORITY);
    System.out.println("Normal thread priority: "+Thread.NORM_PRIORITY);
    System.out.println("Highest thread priority: "+Thread.MAX_PRIORITY);
  }
}
```

It generates the following output:

```
Lowest thread priority: 1
Normal thread priority: 5
Highest thread priority: 10
```

The following methods are available to work with priority:

```
public final int getPriority()
public final void setPriority(int newPriority)
```

The former returns the current priority of the thread, whereas the latter assigns the priority specified to the thread. The following program demonstrates their usage:

```
public class PriorityDemo extends Thread {
  public void run() {
    System.out.println("Child's initial priority: "+getPriority());
    setPriority(3);
    System.out.println("After change, child's priority: "+getPriority());
  }
```

```
  public static void main(String args[]) {
    Thread t = Thread.currentThread();
    System.out.println("Main's initial priority: "+t.getPriority());
    t.setPriority(7);
    System.out.println("After change, main's priority: "+t.getPriority());
    new PriorityDemo().start();
  }
}
```

It results in the following output:

```
Main's initial priority: 5
After change, main's priority: 7
Child's initial priority: 7
After change, child's priority: 3
```

Note that a priority merely tells how important a thread should get with respect to others. Programs with multiple threads, specifically with different priorities, may behave differently at different platforms especially on preemptive and non-preemptive ones. The following program demonstrates how two threads with different priorities are handled.

```
class MyThread extends Thread {
  int count = 0;
  public int getCount() { return count; }
  public void run() {
    while(true) count++;
  }
}
public class PriorityTest {
  public static void main(String args[]) throws InterruptedException {
    MyThread t1 = new MyThread();
    MyThread t2 = new MyThread();
    t1.setPriority(Thread.MAX_PRIORITY);
    t2.setPriority(Thread.MIN_PRIORITY);
    t1.start();
    t2.start();
    Thread.sleep(100);
    System.out.println("Thread 1 count: "+t1.getCount());
    System.out.println("Thread 2 count: "+t2.getCount());
  }
}
```

The main thread creates and starts two threads; one having highest priority and the other one having lowest priority. The two threads continuously increment their respective local variable count. The main thread waits for 100 milliseconds and prints the current values of the local count variable of the two threads. A sample output of this program is shown when it was run under Windows 7.

```
Thread 1 count: 43802164
Thread 2 count: 40580567
```

Note that the actual values may vary in different platforms and of course at different times. Since, the two children thread do not finish, terminate the program by pressing Ctrl-C.

3.8 USING join()

Multiple threads run concurrently; one does not wait for the other. However, sometimes it is necessary that a thread should not proceed further until another thread finishes its task. For example, consider a simple program having two threads; one of which sorts an array and the other prints the sorted array. Obviously, the print thread must not start printing until sort thread sorts the array. This type of dependency can be achieved using `join()` method. It makes the caller blocked until the called thread dies.

So, if a thread t2 depends on t1, the code for t2 should look like this:

```
//do independent tasks
t1.join();  //wait for t1 to terminate
//do remaining task
```

The following program illustrates this:

```
class MyThread extends Thread {
  int[] a;
  MyThread(int[] ar) {
    a = ar;
    start();
  }
  public void run() {
    java.util.Arrays.sort(a);
    System.out.println("Child completed sorting.");
  }
}
public class JoinDemo {
  public static void main(String args[]) throws Exception {
    int a[] = {2, 6, 4, 0, 1, 5, 3};
    MyThread t = new MyThread(a);
    t.join();
    System.out.println("Main printing array elements are :");
    for(int i = 0; i < a.length; i++)
      System.out.print(a[i]+" ");
  }
}
```

Here, child thread sorts the array and main thread prints it. The main thread creates a child thread passing an array to be sorted. It then starts the child thread. Since, child thread may take some time to sort the array, main thread must not proceed for printing immediately. That's why it calls child thread's `join()` method that makes the main thread waiting. The join() returns when child terminates after sorting the array. The main thread can then be sure that the array is sorted and can safely print the array. This results in the following output:

```
Child completed sorting.
Main printing array elements are :
0 1 2 3 4 5 6
```

If you omit the `join()` method from the program, it is no longer guaranteed that the elements will be printed in sorted order. Here is a sample incorrect output:

```
Main printing array elements are :
0 1 2 3 4 Child completed sorting.
5 6
```

Here is another example that demonstrates the importance of join() method in a multi-threaded program:

```
class MyThread extends Thread {
  int[] a;
  MyThread(int[] ar) {
    a = ar;
    start();
  }
  public void run() {
    java.util.Arrays.sort(a);
  }
}
public class JoinTest {
  public static void main(String args[]) throws Exception {
    int a[] = {2,3,4,0,1}, b[] = {6,9,8,7,5};
    MyThread t1 = new MyThread(a);
    MyThread t2 = new MyThread(b);
```

```
    t1.join();
    t2.join();
    int result[] = merge(a,b);
    for(int i=0;i<result.length;i++)
      System.out.print(result[i]+" ");
  }
  static int[] merge(int[] a, int[] b) {
    int i=0, j=0, k=0;
    int[] result = new int[a.length+b.length];
    while(i < a.length && j < b.length) {
      if(a[i] < b[j]) result[k++]=a[i++];
      else result[k++] = b[j++];
    }
    while(i<a.length) result[k++] = a[i++];
    while(j<b.length) result[k++] = b[j++];
    return result;
  }
}
```

The main thread has two unsorted arrays `a` and `b`. It wants to sort them and merge them to form a third sorted array. However, main thread itself does not want to sort them; instead it gets them sorted using two new threads. The main thread simply merges them after getting them sorted. So, main thread creates two new threads passing on array to be sorted to each and starts them. The two children threads then concurrently sort their respective array. The task of the main thread is to merge these two sorted arrays to form a third sorted one. However, main thread can start merging if two children threads sort them and terminates. So, it invokes their respective `join()` methods. Here is a sample output:

```
0 1 2 3 4 5 6 7 8 9
```

Omit the two `join()` statements from the program and see the behaviour. You may get a wrong output as follows:

```
0 1 2 3 4 6 9 8 7 5
```

3.9 SYNCHRONIZATION

There are many situations where multiple threads access common objects. When two or more threads access the same object, the state of the object is not guaranteed to be correct all the time if special care is not taken. To understand how it can happen, consider the following simple class:

```
class Counter {
  int val = 0;
  void inc() { val++; }
  void dcr() { val--; }
}
```

The class `Counter` has a single field `val` (initialized to 0) that gets incremented and decremented by two methods `inc()` and `dcr()` respectively. What should be the value of `val` if these two methods on a `Counter` object are invoked same number of times? Obviously, the value should remain 0. However, that may not be the case in a multithreading environment. To illustrate this, see the following program:

```
public class RaceConditionDemo extends Thread {
  Counter c;
  RaceConditionDemo(Counter c) { this.c = c; start(); }
  public void run() {
    for(int i=0;i<10000;i++) c.dcr();
  }
  public static void main(String args[]) throws Exception {
    Counter c = new Counter();
```

```
        RaceConditionDemo rc = new RaceConditionDemo(c);
        for(int i=0;i<10000;i++) c.inc();
        rc.join();
        System.out.println("Final value of c.val: "+c.val);
    }
}
```

Here, the main thread creates a `Counter` object `c` and a child thread with this object. The main thread and the child thread then concurrently invoke `inc()` and `dcr()` methods on `c` 1000 times respectively. At end, main thread prints the final value of `c.val`. When we executed this program 5 times, we got these values: -502, -394, 240, 505 and -664. What is wrong in the above program? Why it is not giving the correct result?

This happens since two non-atomic operations `val++` and `val--` are executed in overlapped way. Note that these are high level instructions. Although, they look simple, JVM translates them into multiple steps. For example, `val++` will probably be translated into the following steps:

A. Get value of `val`
B. Increment this value by 1
C. Put it back to `val`

Similarly, JVM will probably translate `val--` into following:

D. Get value of `val`
E. Decrement this value by 1
F. Put it back to `val`

If these two sets of instructions are executed concurrently, they *may* be interleaved as A B D E C F. If this happens, `val` will have wrong final value -1. If last two instructions are interchanged, the value will again have wrong value 1. Like these two, there are many other such interleaving patterns for which `val` will have incorrect value. This situation is popularly known as *race condition*, and the segment of code where resources are shared by multiple threads is known as *critical section*. For a class like `Counter`, this incorrect result might not be too harmful. However, consider the following class:

```
class Account {
  int balance = 0;
  void inc() { val++; }
  void dcr() { val--; }
}
```

Here, even a small deviation from the correct balance is not acceptable. So, we must have some mechanism to avoid this inconsistency. In general, we can avoid problem, if we can ensure that critical sections are not executed in interleaved fashion.

Fortunately, Java allows us to specify this using the keyword `synchronized`. Two versions exist: *synchronized methods* and *synchronized blocks*. A method is made synchronized by adding a `synchronized` keyword before its declaration:

```
class X{
  synchronized void f() {
    //...
  }
}
```

Let us briefly understand what happens when a method is declared as synchronized. In Java, every object has an internal entity called *internal lock* or *intrinsic lock* or *monitor lock* or simply *lock* or *monitor.* It is like a privilege that only one thread can "own" at any one time. It can also be thought of as a room that one thread can “occupy” at any one time. So, if a thread does own a lock of an object, no other thread can own the lock of the same object until the thread that owns the lock releases it. Addition of a `synchronized` keyword means just requesting to own a lock. When a thread invokes a non-static synchronized method on an object, it makes a request to own the lock of the associated object. If the lock is not yet owned by some thread else, the requesting thread is given the lock. Otherwise, it must wait until the lock is available. However, it must contend with other waiting threads to own the lock. The lock is released when the owner quits the method.

So, a `synchronized` keyword before a method essentially tells the JVM

- not to interleave multiple parallel invocations of the method on the same object.
- to ensure that when one thread is executing a synchronized method on an object, all other threads wait before invoking other synchronized methods on the same object.

With this understanding, we can rewrite our `Counter` class as follows:

```
class Counter {
  int val = 0;
  synchronized void inc() { val++; }
  synchronized void dcr() { val--; }
}
```

Both the methods have been declared with `synchronized` keyword. Let us now understand how two threads access a `Counter` object without interfering. When main thread executes, `inc()` on `c`, it owns `c`'s lock. Before finishing this method, the child thread cannot own the lock of c; therefore cannot execute `dcr()`. Similarly, when child thread executes `dcr()`, it owns the lock of c. During that time main thread waits. So, these methods are executed without any form of interleaving. However, we have no control whatsoever on the order these methods are executed. Needless to say that the program will give the correct result this time.

What would you do if you wanted to synchronize a shorter block of code instead of an entire method? Java has the other option called *synchronized block* that takes the following form:

```
synchronized(o) {
  //code to be synchronized
}
```

Here, o is some object that provides the lock. Our `Counter` class may be written as:

```
class Counter {
  int val = 0;
  Object o = new Object();
  void inc() {
    //other codes
    synchronized(o) {
      val++;
    }
    //other codes
  }
  void dcr() {
    //other codes
    synchronized(o) {
      val--;
    }
    //other codes
  }
}
```

Note that a synchronized method is a specific case of synchronized block where the lock is obtained from the concerned object.

```
synchronized void f() {
  //some code
}
```

The above declaration is equivalent to

```
void f() {
  synchronized(this) {
    //some code
  }
}
```

It is also possible to make a static method synchronized as follows:

```
class X
  synchronized static void g() { /*body*/  }
}
```

However, what happens if it is invoked since a static method is not associated with an object? In this case, the `Class` object associated with the method's class provides the lock. So, it is equivalent to

```
class X {
  static void g() {
    synchronized(X.class) { /*body*/ }
  }
}
```

Since, access to static and non-static methods are handled by different locks and since a static field may be accessed by both non-static and static methods, care should be taken when using both. Consider a slightly modified version of our `Counter` class:

```
class Counter {
  static int val = 0;
  synchronized void inc() { val++; }
  synchronized static void dcr() { val--; }
}
```

Here, the static field is incremented and decremented by a synchronized non-static and a synchronized static method respectively. However, if they are invoked on a `Counter` object `c`, `inc()` uses the `c`'s lock whereas `dcr()` uses lock of `Counter's Class` object. This means that the methods may get interleaved raising an incorrect result again. The following is a potential solution using synchronized block:

```
class Counter {
  static int val = 0;
  void inc() {
    synchronized(Counter.class) {
      val++;
    }
  }
  static void dcr() {
    synchronized(Counter.class) {
      val--;
    }
  }
}
```

Here, both `val++` and `val--` statements are synchronized using the same lock obtained from Counter's Class object.

Synchronized blocks sometimes may make programs more efficient than synchronized methods. Consider the following class declaration:

```
class X {
  int i1, i2;
  void inc1() { i1++; }
  void inc2() { i2++; }
}
```

Suppose that multiple threads access the method `inc1()` and also `inc2()`. So, fields may have incorrect values. Here is a solution using synchronized methods:

```
class X {
  int i1, i2;
  synchronized void inc1() { i1++; }
  synchronized void inc2() { i2++; }
}
```

However, since we have used synchronized methods, execution of `inc1()` unnecessarily blocks `inc2()` and vice versa that reduces amount of concurrency. A more efficient solution using synchronized block may be written as follows:

```
class X {
  int i1, i2;
  Object o1 = new Object(), o2 = new Object();
  void inc1() {
    synchronized(o1) {
      i1++;
    }
  }
  void inc2() {
    synchronized(o2) {
      i2++;
    }
  }
}
```

Here, multiple concurrent execution of `inc1()` and `inc2()` will work properly; at the same time one will not block the other.

3.9.1 Synchronization and Atomicity

Note that the synchronized keyword does not make a method/block atomic.

```
// this block is NOT atomic!
synchronized(o) {
  s1;
  s2;
}
```

It merely tells that if one thread gets a lock on `o`, no other thread can get the lock on the same object `o`. Similarly, the `synchronized` keyword below merely ensures that if one thread gets a lock on `o1`, no other thread can get the lock on the same object `o1`.

```
// this block is NOT atomic!
synchronized(o1) {
  s3;
  s4;
}
```

So, if two threads execute these two blocks, the execution sequence may be s1, s3, s2, s4. This implies that neither of the blocks is atomic. Unfortunately, there is no built-in support for atomic code blocks in Java.

3.10 DEADLOCK

Deadlock is a situation where two or more threads wait for each other indefinitely.

We know that the `synchronized` keyword may cause the executing thread to block while trying to acquire the lock on the specified object. Since, the thread might already hold locks associated with other objects, two or more threads could each be waiting for one another to release a lock. As a result, they will end up waiting forever. Specifically, a deadlock may occur when multiple threads need the same locks but obtain them in different order. The following program illustrates this:

```
class MyThread extends Thread {
  String r1, r2;
  int id;
  MyThread(int i, String s1, String s2) {
    id = i;
    r1 = s1;
    r2 = s2;
    start();
  }
  public void run() {
    synchronized(r1) {
      System.out.println("Thread "+id+" obtained a lock on "+r1);
      try {
        Thread.sleep(1000);
      }catch(Exception e) {}
      System.out.println("Thread "+id+" is waiting to obtain a lock on "+r2);
      synchronized(r2) {
        System.out.println("Thread "+id+" obtained a lock on "+r2);
      }
    }
  }
}
public class DeadlockDemo {
  public static void main(String args[]) throws Exception {
    int a[] = {2, 6, 4, 0, 1, 5, 3};
    String r1 = new String("R1"), r2 = new String("R2");
    MyThread t1 = new MyThread(1, r1, r2);
    MyThread t2 = new MyThread(2, r2, r1);
  }
}
```

Here, main thread creates two string objects r1 and r2 and are passed to the `MyThread's` constructor in opposite order to create two threads `t1` and `t2`. The thread `t1` tries to acquire locks on `r1` and `r2` in this order whereas `t2` wants to acquire locks on the same object but in opposite order. This results in a circular wait and hence deadlock. Here is a sample output:

```
Thread 1 obtained a lock on R1
Thread 2 obtained a lock on R2
Thread 1 is waiting to obtain a lock on R2
Thread 2 is waiting to obtain a lock on R1
```

Note that a deadlock always occurs if the above program is run. In practice, deadlocks may not occur all the time, and instead occur for certain data sets which are often difficult to predict. So, testing for deadlocks is difficult, as deadlocks depend on timing, load, and environment, and thus might happen infrequently or only under certain circumstances. This warns us that extreme care should be taken when writing synchronized multi-threaded programs.

One way to prevent deadlock is to make sure that all locks are always taken in the same order by any thread. For the following two threads, deadlocks cannot occur.

```
MyThread t1 = new MyThread(1, r1, r2);
MyThread t2 = new MyThread(2, r1, r2);
```

Here, both threads obtain locks on r1 and r2 in the same order; hence deadlock can never occur. Lock ordering is a simple but effective way of preventing deadlock. However, it may only be useful if we have complete knowledge of all the locks at compile time. Moreover there may be situations, where lock ordering is not possible.

Another way to prevent deadlock requires threads to acquire all the locks that are needed during execution before proceeding.

```
synchronized(MyThread.class) {
  synchronized(r1) {
    System.out.println("Thread "+id+" obtained a lock on "+r1);
```

```
      try {
        Thread.sleep(1000);
      }catch(Exception e) {}
      System.out.println("Thread "+id+" is waiting to obtain a lock on "+r2);
      synchronized(r2) {
        System.out.println("Thread "+id+" obtained a lock on "+r2);
      }
    }
}
```

This makes use of an additional lock which controls acquisition of two locks in a non-overlapped way. Since, a thread will either acquire all locks or none, there is no circular wait which implies no deadlock. However, since a thread may hold locks, required for short time, during the thread's entire execution period (possibly very long), the effective utilization of the locks may be low. In practice, deadlock prevention or avoidance or detection requires special algorithms, many of which can be found in a standard book on operating system. Unfortunately, there is no best and foolproof algorithm for these purposes. So, a little care of the program design may help us getting out of the deadlock situation. So how will you know that there are chances of deadlock. The following are some conditions where there may be a chance of deadlock:

- The code contains any nested synchronized block
- A synchronized method calls another synchronized method
- The code obtains locks on different objects

3.11 INTER-THREAD COMMUNICATION

We rarely write multi-threaded programs where threads run independently. If threads are really independent, it is probably a good idea to write multiple programs, one for each thread. A useful multithreaded-program is one where multiple threads run concurrently in a cooperating manner to perform a designated task. Consider a simple program having two threads as follows:

The child thread finds (produces) prime numbers and stores them in a variable and main thread prints them. This is a specific example of class producer-consumer problem. Although, this example is not much useful, it helps us in understanding how to write multi-threaded programs where threads communicate with one another.

One simple but elegant solution is to use a variable shared by these two threads. The child thread stores a new prime number here and main thread prints it. The solution must satisfy the following basic requirements:

- Main thread must not print the same prime number more than once i.e. after printing a number, main thread must wait for the child thread to generate a new one.
- Similarly, the child thread must not generate a new prime number before the main thread prints the previous one.

This tells us that a high degree of cooperation is needed between these two threads. A potential solution is shown below:

```
public class ThreadCommSpin extends Thread {
  static int turn = 0;
  int buf[], n = 2;
  public int nextPrime() {
    while(true) {
      boolean prime=true;
      for(int i=2;i<=n/2;i++) if(n%i == 0) {prime = false;break;}
      if(prime) return n++;
      else n++;
    }
  }
```

```
    public ThreadCommSpin(int[] a) {buf = a;start();}
    public void run() {
      while(true) {
        while(turn != 0);
        buf[0]=nextPrime();
        turn = 1;
      }
    }
    public static void main(String args[]) throws Exception {
      int[] a = new int[1];
      ThreadCommSpin st = new ThreadCommSpin(a);
      while(true) {
        while(turn != 1);
        System.out.print(a[0]+" ");
        turn = 0;
      }
    }
  }
```

Both main and child thread use a shared one element array to read and write prime numbers. The coordination is achieved using another shared variable `turn` which determines a thread's turn. It is child's turn if the value of `turn` is 0, else it is main thread's turn. A thread waits by spinning in a while loop until it gets its own turn. This means a thread consumes CPU cycles even if it is not its turn. However, ideally, if a thread finds that it is the other thread's turn, it should wait without consuming any CPU cycles further. So the above solution is inefficient.

Fortunately, to avoid unnecessary polling, Java provides a framework that uses `wait()`, `notify()` and `notifyAll()` methods. These methods are implemented in `java.lang.Object`, hence is available in all Java objects. To write an inter-thread communication solution, let us understand the functionality of these methods:

`wait()`

This method places the invoking thread in the wait set associated with this object. While the thread waits, it relinquishes lock on this object. Since, it relinquishes the lock, it must first acquire the lock. That is why, `wait()` method must be used within a synchronized method/block. The thread becomes disabled until either another thread invokes the `notify()` method or the `notifyAll()` method on the same object, or interrupts the waiting thread.

`notify()`

It wakes up a single thread that is waiting (called `wait()` method) on this object's lock. In case of multiple threads waiting, one of them is arbitrary chosen. The calling thread then relinquishes the lock on the object. The awakened thread then competes in the usual manner with other threads (if any) to get the lock back and proceeds further.

This method must also be called within a synchronized method/block.

`notifyAll()`

This is similar to `notify()` method except that it awakens all waiting threads on the current object.

With this knowledge, we can rewrite our previous program as follows:

```
public class ThreadComm extends Thread {
  static int turn = 0;
  int buf[], n = 2;
  public int nextPrime() {
    while(true) {
      boolean prime=true;
      for(int i=2;i<=n/2;i++) if(n%i == 0) {prime = false;break;}
```

```
      if(prime) return n++;
      else n++;
    }
  }
  public ThreadComm(int[] a) {buf = a;start();}
  public void run() {
    while(true) {
      synchronized(buf) {
        while(turn != 0)
          try {
            buf.wait();
          }catch(Exception e) {e.printStackTrace();}
        buf[0] = nextPrime();
        turn = 1;
        buf.notify();
      }
    }
  }
  public static void main(String args[]) throws Exception {
    int[] a = new int[1];
    ThreadComm st = new ThreadComm(a);
    while(true) {
      synchronized(a) {
        while(turn != 1) a.wait();
        System.out.print(a[0]+" ");
        turn = 0;
        a.notify();
      }
    }
  }
}
```

Here, since the initial value of turn is 0, the main thread waits until child thread generates a prime number and notifies the main thread. Similarly, after generating a prime number, the child thread waits until main threads print it and notifies the child thread. A partial output of this program is shown below:

```
2 3 5 7 11 13 17 19 23 29 31 37 41 43 47 53 59 61 67 71 73 79 83 89 97 101 103
107 109 113 127 131 137 139 149 151 157 163 167 173 179 181 191 193 197 199 211
223 227 229 233 239 241 251 257 263 269 271 277 281 283 293 307 311 313 317 331
337 347 349 353 359 367 373 379 383 389 397 401 409 419 421 431 433 439 443 449
457 461 463 467 479 487 491 499 503 509 521 523 541 547 557 563 569 571 577 587
593 599 601 607 613 617 619 631 641 643 647 653 659 661 673 677 683 691 701 709
...
```

KEYWORDS

Atomic—An indivisible piece of code

Critical section—A segment of code where resources are shared by multiple threads

Deadlock—A situation where two or more threads wait for each other indefinitely

Interrupt—Requesting a thread to stop what it is currently doing and do something else

InterruptedException—An exception which is thrown when a thread is waiting, sleeping, or otherwise occupied, and the thread is interrupted, either before or during the activity

join()—Makes the caller waiting for the called thread to die

Lock—An internal entity used to synchronize code

Main Thread—The first thread that starts running when a program begins

Priority—An integer number from 1 to 10 that represents the importance of a thread

Race condition—A situation where outcome of a program depends on the order of interleaving of threads

Runnable—The interface a thread class implements

sleep()—Causes the currently executing thread to sleep (temporarily cease execution) for the specified number of milliseconds, subject to the precision and accuracy of system timers and schedulers

start()—Causes this thread to begin execution; the Java Virtual Machine calls the run method of this thread.

Synchronized blocks—Blocks of codes created with synchronized keyword

Synchronized methods—Methods declared with the synchronized keyword

Thread—A control or flow or path of execution that exists within a process

SUMMARY

A thread is a control/flow/path of execution that exists within a process. A process may have one or more threads in it and is referred to as *single-threaded* or *multi-threaded* process respectively.

When we supply a program to the JVM for execution, it creates one thread and associates the program's `main()` method. Since, it is the first thread that starts running when a program begins, it is said to be *main/primary* thread. Other threads, if required, may be spawned from this main thread.

There are two ways to create threads; by extending the `java.lang.Thread` class and implementing the `java.lang.Runnable` interface. If a class has to extend another class, it implements the `Runnable` interface to be a thread class. In both the cases, the `run()` method provides the entry point for the thread.

A thread may be suspended temporarily to avoid consuming CPU cycles unnecessarily using sleep() method. A thread may be suspended and resumed using the combination of `wait()` and `notify()` methods.

Interrupting a thread means requesting it to stop what it is currently doing and do something else. The request is sent to a thread using its `interrupt()` method.

In Java, every thread has a priority. Higher priority threads get more preference in terms of CPU, I/O time, etc. than lower priority threads. Priorities are represented by integer numbers from 1 (lowest) to 10 (highest) which are represented by two static final fields `MIN_PRIORITY` and `MAX_PRIORITY` of `Thread` class respectively.

However, sometimes it is necessary that a thread should not proceed further until another thread finishes its task. This type of dependency can be achieved using `join()` method.

Java provides synchronized keyword to deal with race condition. Two versions exist: *synchronized methods* and *synchronized blocks*. A method or a block is made synchronized by adding a `synchronized` keyword before its declaration. The synchronized keyword does not make a method/block atomic. Unfortunately, there is no built-in support for atomic code blocks in Java.

Deadlock is a situation where two or more threads wait for each other indefinitely. Some of the situations where there may be a chance of deadlock are i) The code contains any nested synchronized block ii) A synchronized method calls another synchronized method iii) The code obtains locks on different objects.

A useful multithreaded-program is one where multiple threads run concurrently in a cooperating manner to perform a designated task. Threads communicate using the methods wait(), notify() and notifyAll() methods.

WEB RESOURCES

`http://docs.oracle.com/javase/tutorial/essential/concurrency/`
Lesson: Concurrency

`https://www.ibm.com/developerworks/library/j-thread/`
Writing multithreaded Java applications

`http://www.tutorialspoint.com/java/java_multithreading.htm`
Java - Multithreading

`http://tutorials.jenkov.com/java-concurrency/index.html`
Java Concurrency / Multithreading Tutorial

`http://www.javatpoint.com/multithreading`
Multithreading in Java

`http://www3.ntu.edu.sg/home/ehchua/programming/java/J5e_multithreading.html`
Java Programming Tutorial: Multithreading & Concurrent Programming

`http://www.nakov.com/inetjava/lectures/part-1-sockets/InetJava-1.3-Multithreading.html`
Multithreading and Thread Synchronization

EXERCISES

Objective-type Questions

1. In Java, a thread can be created by
   (a) Extending the Thread class
   (b) Implementing Runnable interface
   (c) Both (a) and (b)
   (d) None of these

2. Which one of the following methods is used to start a thread execution?
   (a) run() (c) resume()
   (b) init() (d) start()

3. When a class extends the Thread class, it should override __________ method
   (a) start() (c) execute()
   (b) init() (d) run()

4. Which two are valid constructors for Thread?
   (i) Thread()
   (ii) Thread(Runnable r, String s)
   (iii) Thread(Runnable r, ThreadGroup g)
   (iv) Thread(String s, ThreadGroup g)
   (v) Thread(int priority)
   (a) (i) and (iii) (c) (i) and (ii)
   (b) (ii) and (iv) (d) (ii) and (v)

5. Which three are methods of the Object class?
   (i) sleep(long ms); (v) interrupt();
   (ii) notify(); (vi) wait(long ms);
   (iii) isInterrupted(); (vii) notifyAll();
   (iv) synchronized();
   (a) (i), (vi), (vii) (c) (i), (ii), (vi)
   (b) (i), (iv), (vi) (d) (ii), (vi), (vii)

6. Consider the following class declaration:
   class X implements Runnable {/*...*/}
   Which of the following code segments is used to start a new thread?
   (a) new Thread(new X()).start();
   (b) new X().start();
   (c) Thread t = new Thread(X); t.start();
   (d) X x = new X(); x.start();

7. Which of the following methods cannot directly cause a thread to stop executing?
   (a) setPriority() (c) notify()
   (b) wait() (d) interrupt()

8. Which of the following methods causes a thread to stop executing?
   (a) wait() (c) terminate()
   (b) stop() (d) pause()

9. Which of the following methods is used to release the CPU voluntarily?
   (a) release() (c) giveUp()
   (b) suspend() (d) yield()

10. Which of the following methods must be implemented in a class that implements Runnable interface?
    (a) start() (c) execute()
    (b) run() (d) call()

11. Which of the following types is used to represent thread priority in Java ?
    (a) float (c) int
    (b) double (d) long

12. What is the output of this program?

```
class Test {
    public static void main(String args[]) {
        Thread t = Thread.currentThread();
        System.out.println(t);
    }
}
```

    (a) Thread[main,5,main]
    (b) Thread[5,main]
    (c) Thread[main,0]
    (d) Thread[main,5]

13. What is the default thread priority used in Java?
    (a) 0 (c) 5
    (b) 1 (d) 10

14. Which of the following constants is used to represent the default priority of a thread?
    (a) DEF_PRIORITY
    (b) DEFAULAT_PRIORITY
    (c) NORM_PRIORITY
    (d) NORMAL_PRIORITY

15. The isAlive() method is used to
    (a) know whether a thread is running or not
    (b) know whether a thread was created or not
    (c) restart a thread after stopping it
    (d) resume a thread after blocking it

16. Which of the following keywords are used to make a method synchronized?
    (a) atomic (c) synchronized
    (b) block (d) unit

17. Which of the following is the priority range in Java?
(a) 1–10 (c) 5–10
(b) 0–9 (d) 1–5

18. Which of the following statements is false?
(a) The sleep() method should be enclosed in try-catch block
(b) The yield() method should be enclosed in try-catch block.
(c) A thread can be temporarily suspended from running by using the wait() method.
(d) A join() causes the caller to wait till the called thread terminates

19. What happens if two threads having same priority are started?
(a) The thread whose name lexicographically precedes the other is executed first.
(b) Both of them will be executed simultaneously.
(c) None of them will be executed.
(d) It is dependent on the operating system.

20. Deadlock is a situation when ________.
(a) two or more threads have circular dependency on an object
(b) two or more threads are trying to access the same object
(c) two or more threads are waiting for a resource
(d) None of these

21. Which of these statements is incorrect?
(a) Two threads in Java can have same priority.
(b) By multithreading CPU's idle time is minimized, and we can take maximum use of it.
(c) By multitasking CPU's idle time is minimized, and we can take maximum use of it.
(d) A thread can exist only in two states, running and blocked.

22. Which of the following interfaces is used to create a thread
(a) Startable (c) Executable
(b) Runnable (d) Thread

23. Which of the following methods contains the body of the thread?
(a) run() (c) stop()
(b) start() (d) main()

24. Which of the following classes or interfaces defines the wait(), notify(),and notifyAll() methods?
(a) Thread (c) Object
(b) Runnable (d) Class

25. Which of the following methods is used to change the priority of a thread?
(a) setPriority() (c) newPriority()
(b) changePriority() (d) updatePriority()

26. How many locks does an object have?
(a) 1 (c) 3
(b) 2 (d) 4

27. A dead thread
(a) is discarded
(b) must wait until all other threads execute before it is restarted
(c) cannot be restarted
(d) is synchronized

28. What is the output of the following program ?

```
public class Test {
   public static void main (String[]
   args) throws Exception {
      Thread.sleep(1000);
      System.out.println("Sleeping");
   }
}
```

(a) Compilation error.
(b) An exception is thrown at runtime.
(c) The code executes normally, but nothing is printed.
(d) The code executes normally and prints "sleeping".

29. Consider the following class

```
public class MyClass implements Runnable
{
   public void run()    {
      // some code here
   }
}
```

Which of the following will create and start this thread?
(a) new Runnable(MyClass).start();
(b) new Thread(MyClass).run();
(c) new Thread(new MyClass()).start();
(d) new MyClass().start();

30. What happens if an unchecked exception is thrown from a try block and there is no matching catch block?
(a) The program ignores the exception.
(b) The program terminates immediately.
(c) The method throws the exception to its caller.
(d) Compilation error.

Subjective-type Questions

1. What are the differences between a process and a thread?
2. What are the benefits of multi-threaded programming?
3. Show the different ways we can create threads in Java with their relative merits and demerits.
4. Explain the life cycle of a thread in Java.
5. Explain with example inter-thread communication techniques.
6. How do you make a method synchronized? How does it differ from a non-synchronized method?
7. Discuss the relative advantages and disadvantages of synchronized methods and synchronized blocks.
8. What is a deadlock? How does it differ from starvation?
9. How will you say that a program may suffer from a deadlock?
10. What is the difference between yield and sleeping?
11. What is race condition? How will you find and solve race condition?
12. How does thread synchronization occur inside a monitor?
13. How can we pause the execution of a Thread for a specific time?
14. What do you understand about Thread Priority?
15. What happens when we make a static method synchronized?
16. What is the function of join( ) method? Write a real world program that uses join() method.
17. Write a Java program to solve the producer-consumer problem in Java?
18. Write a program which will result in deadlock. Now fix the deadlock in your program.
19. Is it possible to create new thread by calling its run() method directly? If not, why?
20. Write some common problems that may arise in multi-threading environment?
21. What is the difference when the synchronized keyword is applied to a static method or to a non-static method?
22. What is difference between notify() and notifyAll()?
23. What happens when start() is called?
24. What is main thread? When is it created?
25. Briefly describe how Java implements synchronization.

CHAPTER – 4

GARBAGE COLLECTION

KEY OBJECTIVES

After completing this chapter readers will be able to—

- understand the importance of garbage collector
- understand how garbage collector works
- get an idea about different garbage collectors
- select and tune parameters of garbage collector
- monitor the performance of garbage collector
- learn a set of useful commands

4.1 INTRODUCTION

Currently Java runs on more than 850 million personal computers worldwide, and on billions of devices worldwide, including mobile and TV devices. One of the key reasons for such legendary success is the ability to tune its performance to realize high performance and massive scalability. This is achieved through the maturing evolution and continuous engineering of its runtime environment and multithreaded garbage collector. Knowing even a little about JVM's garbage collector can greatly help in improving the performance of your Java applications.

HotSpot, originally released as the "Java HotSpot Performance Engine" is JVM maintained and distributed by Oracle. Since, in this book, only Oracle's implementation of Java has been considered, the "JVM" always refers to "HotSpot".

This chapter first describes the basics of how Garbage Collection works inside HotSpot. Then, it gives an overview of available garbage collectors with their functions and performance metrics. It also demonstrates how to select and configure a collector and set sizes for the memory areas on which the collector operates. Finally, it lists some of the most commonly used options that affect garbage collector behaviour.

4.2 EXPLORING JVM

In this section, an overview of the JVM is provided along with an introduction to Garbage Collection and performance.

JVM may be thought of as an abstract computing machine that executes Java programs (in byte codes) in it. A JVM for a specific operating system, along with other tasks, translates the Java byte codes into instructions on the local operating system. The specific part that performs this translation is called Just-In-Time (JIT) compiler. This way, platform independence is achieved. The architecture is shown in Figure 4.1:

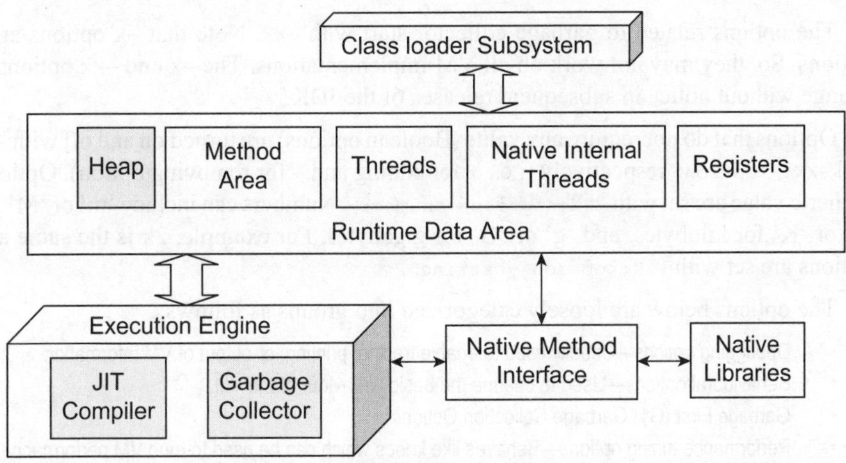

Figure 4.1: JVM architecture

The primary components of JVM architecture are the class loader, the runtime data areas, and the execution engine. The key components related to performance are highlighted in the picture. The section of memory where all objects (local or member) are stored is called *heap*. It is worth noting that class static members are created in method area. The heap is managed by the garbage collector.

4.2.1 Performance

Performance tuning is usually done by choosing the heap size and the most appropriate garbage collector for an application. Performance tuning usually refers to optimizing the following criteria:

- Responsiveness—It refers to how quickly an application or system responds to a request. Tuning responsiveness means minimizing response time.
- Throughput—The percentage of time not utilized in garbage collection.
- Garbage collection overhead—The percentage of total time spent in garbage collection, that is, the inverse of throughput
- Pause time—The duration when application execution is stopped while garbage collection occurs.
- Frequency of collection—How often collection occurs, relative to application execution.
- Promptness—The time between when an object becomes garbage and when the memory becomes available.

4.3 JVM OPTIONS

Several options and environment variables are available that can affect the performance characteristics of the HotSpot JVM. These options start with -X or -XX. The available -X options may be listed using the following command:

```
java -X
```

The partial output of this command is shown below:

```
...
-Xms<size>          set initial Java heap size
-Xmx<size>          set maximum Java heap size
-Xss<size>          set java thread stack size
...
```

The options related to garbage collector start with -XX. Note that -X options are not standard options. So, they may not work on all VM implementations. The -X and -XX options are subject to change without notice in subsequent releases of the JDK.

Options that do not require any value (Boolean options) are turned on and off with `-XX:+<option>` and `-XX:-<option>` respectively (i.e., + for adding and – for removing option). Options that require numeric value are set with `-XX:<option>=<number>`. Numbers can include 'm' or 'M' for megabytes, 'k' or 'K' for kilobytes, and 'g' or 'G' for gigabytes. For example, 2k is the same as 2048. String options are set with `-XX:<option>=<string>`.

The options below are loosely categorized into groups as follows:

- Debugging options—Usually used to enable tracing, printing, or output of VM information.
- Behavioural options—Used to change the basic behaviour of the VM.
- Garbage First (G1) Garbage Collection Options
- Performance tuning options—Behaves like knobs which can be used to tune VM performance.

A detailed list of available options may be found in Appendix.

4.4 GARBAGE COLLECTION

A garbage object (or simply garbage) is one that can no longer be reached through any pointer/reference in the running program. Since, such objects can never be accessed/used, it is worth reclaiming memory occupied by them and allocating to others (if any).

Garbage collection refers to the process of indentifying garbage objects and freeing (called *reclaiming*) heap memory occupied by them. Note that, in a programming language like C/C++, it is solely the programmer's task to track and collect garbage. However, in Java, garbage is collected automatically by a special component (a separate thread), called *garbage collector*. This way, it relieves programmers from memory management and helps them to devote more time on actual logic.

Although Java shields the programmer from garbage collection, it is worth understanding some aspects of this hidden implementation. By knowing some assumptions (represented by parameters) made by garbage collectors, it is possible to tune those parameters to achieve improved performance without knowing actual implementation.

4.5 GENERATIONAL GARBAGE COLLECTOR

The basic function of any garbage collector is to identify garbage objects. One of the possibilities is to start with reachable objects and find other objects reachable from them and so on. The objects left over are garbage objects. The time taken by this approach is proportional to the number of reachable objects. For applications that maintain huge live data, this time (overhead) becomes significant and is not acceptable. Although, there exists other native algorithms, they also essentially examine all reachable objects, thereby not suitable for large applications.

Java intelligently found an efficient algorithm that minimizes the time required to reclaim garbage objects. The algorithm is solely based on some observed facts, most importantly *weak generational hypothesis*, which states that most objects survive for only a short period of time. The property is best described in Figure 4.2:

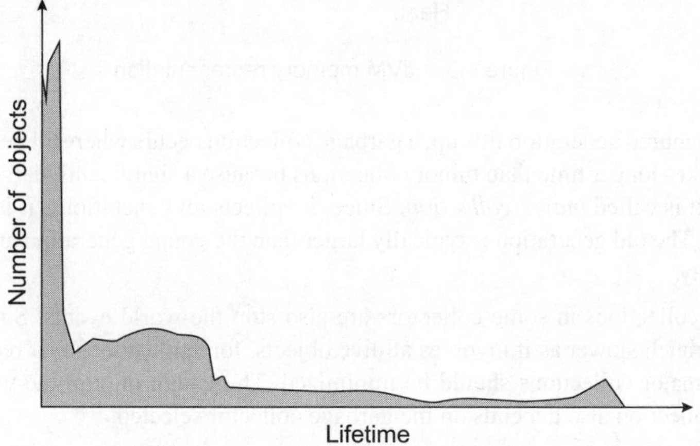

Figure 4.2: Weak generational hypothesis

The x indicates the survival duration of objects and y axis corresponds to the number of objects having that duration. The shaded area shows typical distribution of objects having different lifetimes. The sharp peak at the left indicates that large number of objects have very short lifetime i.e., die immediately after creation and hence candidate for reclaim. However, some objects (for example `Iterator` objects) survives even after a long time so the distribution stretches out to the right. The lump to the right of the initial peak indicates that some objects live for the intermediate duration

Although, not all applications have the same distribution, a surprisingly large number has this behaviour. Java makes use of this property (most objects die young) to devise an efficient garbage collection algorithm.

Keeping the above property in mind, Java divides its heap into two sections that hold objects of different ages. Objects are created in the first section and move to the other section as they become aged. The first section holds short aged objects and is called *young generation*. When it fills up, a garbage collection occurs. Since, according to weak generational hypothesis, most objects in the young generation die soon, very few objects live. So, the collection takes place very quickly as its time is proportional to the number of live objects. That's why this collection is called *minor collection*. During minor collection, no other heap sections are checked for garbage. This generation is typically smaller and its occupancy grows more rapidly.

During any minor collection (for all collectors), all application threads are stopped until the operation completes. This is why minor collections are said to be *stop-the-world* events.

When a young generation object becomes sufficiently aged (i.e., survives a predefined number of minor collections), it is eventually *promoted* or *tenured* to the second section. This section has relatively higher aged objects hence is called *tenured generation* (or old generation) [Figure 4.3:].

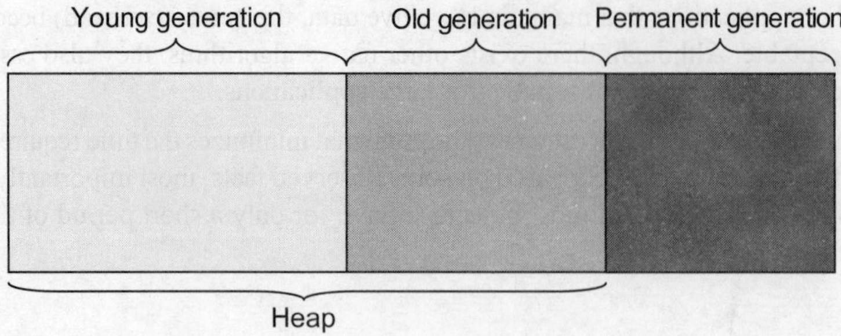

Figure 4.3: JVM memory representation

When tenured generation fills up, a garbage collection occurs where all generations are collected. Since, it takes longer time than minor collections because a significantly larger number of objects is involved, it is called *major collection*. Since, it collects all generations, it is sometimes called *full collection*. The old generation is typically larger than the young generation and its occupancy grows more slowly.

Major collections in some collectors are also stop-the-world events. Since, a major collection is usually much slower as it involves all live objects, for applications that require quick guaranteed response, major collections should be minimized. The length of stop-the-world event for a major garbage collection also depends on the garbage collector selected.

The minor collection algorithm typically puts a premium on speed, since it is frequent. On the other hand, the major collection algorithm is more space efficient, as the old generation takes up most of the heap and works well with low garbage densities.

In addition, beyond heap, JVM stores some objects that are closely related for its own operation. For example objects describing classes and methods and other reflective data are stored here. The permanent generation is populated by the JVM at runtime based on classes in use by the application. In addition, Java SE library classes and methods may be stored here. JVM occasionally loads and unloads objects here and hence these objects are called *permanent generation*.

4.6 HOTSPOT'S GARBAGE COLLECTION

In the previous section, we have described the basic philosophy of generational garbage collection. In this section, let us know how it is implemented in HotSpot.

The organization of generations for all collectors in HotSpot JVM except parallel collector is shown in Figure 4.4:

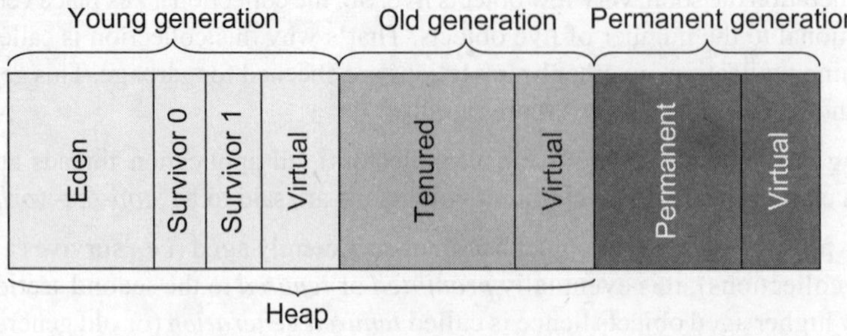

Figure 4.4: JVM memory for non-parallel GC

The same for parallel collector is shown in Figure 4.5: The size of the allocated space to JVM may be specified with the `-Xmx` option. However, it does not use all unless it is needed. The space to be used may be specified using `-Xms` option. If the value of the `-Xms` option is smaller than the value of the `-Xmx` option, some space remains uncommitted and is shown as *virtual* in the figure.

The heap and the permanent generation comprises the entire memory allocated to a JVM. The entire allocated space is divided into the *young*, *tenured* and *permanent* generations.

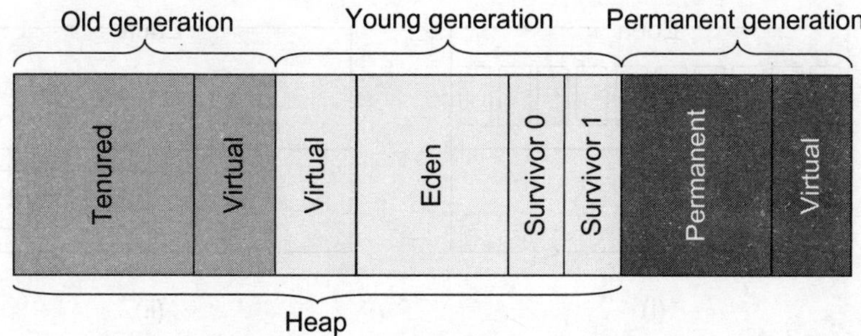

Figure 4.5: JVM memory for parallel GC

The young generation consists of a space called *Eden* and two smaller *survivor spaces* (often referred to as *from* and *to*). We shall refer to these survivor spaces as S0 and S1. When a JVM starts, all these areas are empty [Figure 4.6: (i)]. Most of the objects are initially allocated in Eden [Figure 4.6: (ii)].

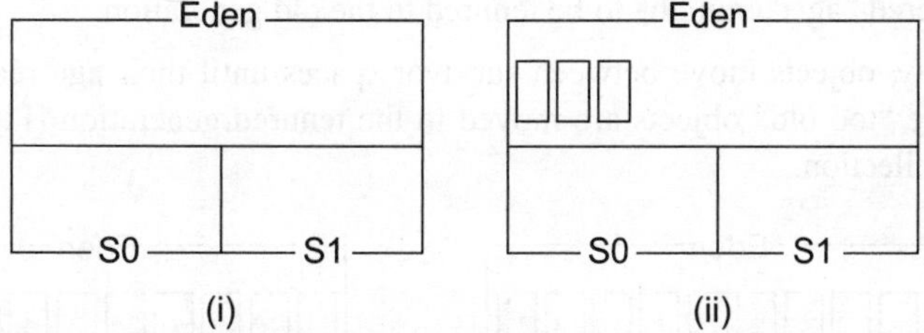

Figure 4.6: Initial young generation (i) Empty Eden (ii) Allocated some objects

When the Eden is full [Figure 4.7: (i)], a minor collection occurs. During this phase, the live objects in Eden are identified. This has been shown in Figure 4.7: (i). The shaded objects are unreachable objects and others are live objects. Live objects are moved to the survivor space S0 and unreferenced objects are deleted [Figure 4.7: (ii)]. Live objects that are too large to fit in S0 are directly copied to the old generation (not shown in figure). The objects in the survivor space are marked with numbers that indicate the number of times the objects survived (1 in our case) during minor collection.

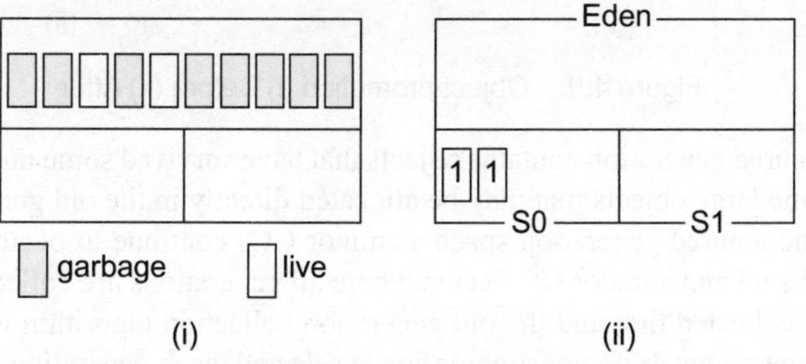

Figure 4.7: 1st Minor collection (i) Before (ii) After

The Eden becomes eventually full again [Figure 4.8: (i)] and as a result second minor collection occurs. During this time not only Eden is checked for garbage, but the survivor space S0 is checked also. The live objects from Eden are moved to the other survivor space i.e., S1. The live objects (if any) from the first survivor space (S0) are also moved to S1 with their age incremented. Now, both Eden and S0 are cleared. If the target survivor space becomes full, the live objects from Eden or other survivor space are tenured, irrespective of their age.

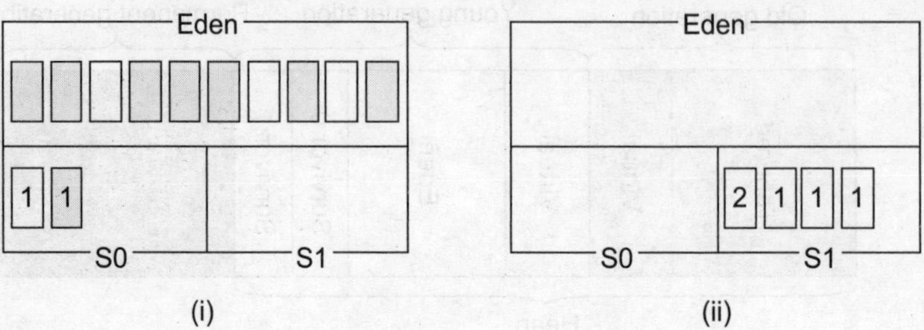

Figure 4.8: 2nd Minor collection (i) Before (ii) After

Note that one survivor space is empty at any time, and serves as the destination of any live objects in Eden and the other survivor space during the next minor collection. Also note that there are differently aged objects in the survivor space. The survivor spaces essentially keep objects that have survived at least one minor collection and have thus been given more chances to die before being considered "aged enough" to be tenured to the old generation.

In this way, objects move between survivor spaces until their age reaches a certain threshold (say 3). These "too old" objects are moved to the tenured generation [Figure 4.9: (ii)] during the next minor collection.

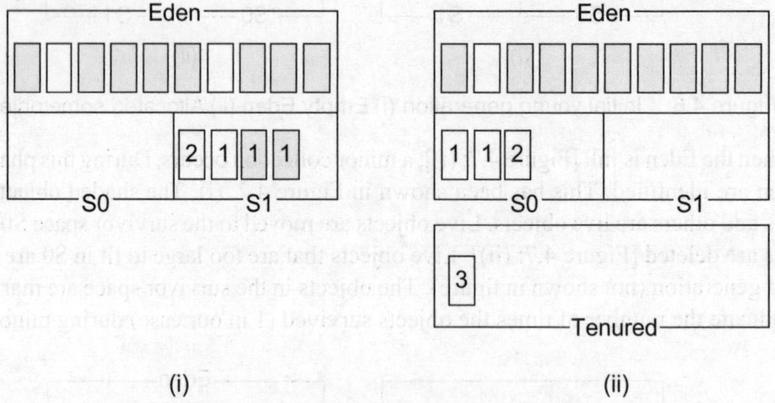

Figure 4.9: Object promotion (i) Before (ii) After

So, the tenured generation contains objects that have survived some number of minor collections as well as some large objects that may be allocated directly in the old generation. Objects continue to move to the tenured generation space as minor GCs continue to occur. Eventually, the tenured generation fills up and a major GC occurs where all generations are collected. Typically, the young generation is collected first and the old generation collection algorithm is run on both the old and permanent generations. If compaction option is selected, each generation is compacted separately.

If the young generation is collected first and the old generation does not have sufficient space to accept objects likely to be promoted, the young generation collection algorithm is not run (except for Concurrent Mark-Sweep collector). Instead, the old generation collection algorithm is run on all generations.

4.7 AVAILABLE COLLECTORS

HotSpot provides multiple garbage collectors to satisfy different requirements for both large and small applications. People who need high performance may select the appropriate garbage collector and configure it to meet their needs best. However, it is not an easy task at all. Java 5.0 and later is intelligent enough to select a garbage collector based on the class of the host where the application runs. Although, this default garbage collector, no doubt, improves the performance to some extent, it is, by no means, always the best choice for every application. To achieve the desired level of performance, it is recommended to select a garbage collector explicitly and tune its parameters.

The HotSpot JVM provides different collectors, each with different performance characteristics: *serial collector*, *parallel collector*, *parallel compact collector* and *concurrent collector*.

4.7.1 Serial Collector

For serial garbage collector, single thread is used to perform all garbage collection responsibilities. That is both young and old generations are collected serially, in a stop-the-world fashion [Figure 4.10:]. The application execution is suspended during the collection.

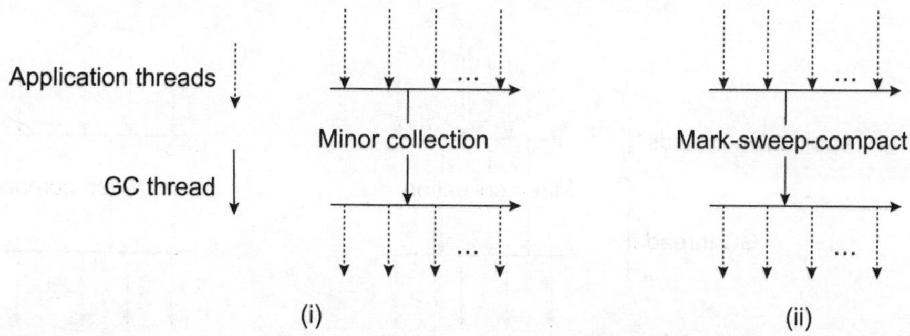

Figure 4.10: Serial collector (i) Young generation collection (ii) Old generation collection

For collecting young generation, the algorithm described in the previous section is used. For old generation, serial collector uses a 3-phase *mark-sweep-compact* collection algorithm, a brief description of which is given below:

This collection algorithm has three phases: *mark, sweep* and *compact*. In mark phase, live objects are identified. In the next phase, the collector sweeps the garbage over the generations. In the compact phase, live objects are slid towards the beginning of the old generation. This leaves free space (if any) as a single contiguous block at the other end.

Since, serial collector always uses single thread, it cannot leverage multi-processor system. That's why, it is recommended to use this collector in a uni-processor system. However, it may be useful on multiprocessors for applications that need heap of up to100 MB.

The strength of this collector however, lies in its single thread as there is no communication overhead between threads. Try avoiding other collectors that cost additional overhead if your application does not need special behaviour.

Use the option -XX:+UseSerialGC to select serial collector. The following command selects a serial collector and prints its details:

```
java -XX:+UseSerialGC -XX:+PrintGCDetails —version
```

A sample output is shown below:

```
java version "1.7.0_07"
Java(TM) SE Runtime Environment (build 1.7.0_07-b11)
Java HotSpot(TM) Client VM (build 23.3-b01, mixed mode, sharing)
Heap
 def new generation   total 4928K, used 369K [0x23f10000, 0x24460000, 0x29460000)
  eden space 4416K,   8% used [0x23f10000, 0x23f6c5f8, 0x24360000)
  from space 512K,   0% used [0x24360000, 0x24360000, 0x243e0000)
  to   space 512K,   0% used [0x243e0000, 0x243e0000, 0x24460000)
 tenured generation   total 10944K, used 0K [0x29460000, 0x29f10000, 0x33f10000)
   the space 10944K,   0% used [0x29460000, 0x29460000, 0x29460200, 0x29f10000)
 compacting perm gen  total 12288K, used 69K [0x33f10000, 0x34b10000, 0x37f10000)
   the space 12288K,   0% used [0x33f10000, 0x33f21408, 0x33f21600, 0x34b10000)
     ro space 10240K,  45% used [0x37f10000, 0x38394650, 0x38394800, 0x38910000)
     rw space 12288K,  54% used [0x38910000, 0x38f97e58, 0x38f98000, 0x39510000)
```

4.7.2 Parallel Collector

The serial garbage collector may not be the best choice for all applications. For example, heavily threaded large applications that run on a multi-processor machine having large memory, expect special behaviour from garbage collector. In such a case, usually parallel collector (also known as the throughput collector) exhibits better performance than the serial one.

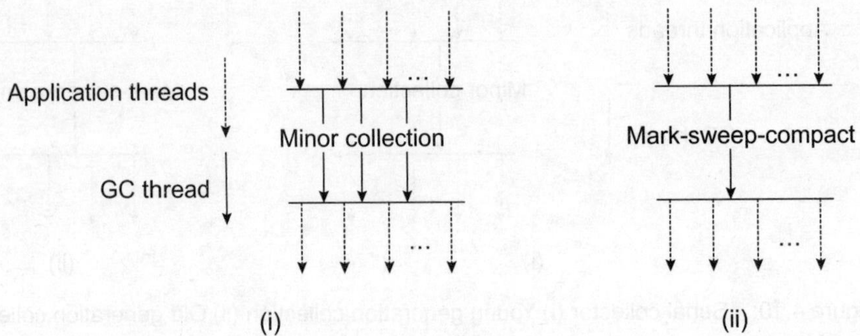

Figure 4.11: Parallel collector (i) Young generation collection (ii) Old generation collection

For parallel garbage collector, as its name implies, multiple threads are used to perform minor collections [Figure 4.11: (i)]. Since, it uses multiple threads leveraging multi-processor system, it can decrease garbage collection overhead significantly and hence increases application throughput. However, it is still a stop-the-world collector. Moreover, it uses the same single-threaded mark-sweep-compact algorithm [Figure 4.11: (ii)] for collecting old generation.

This collector is best suited for applications (having medium to large-sized data sets) that are run on multiprocessor or multi-threaded hardware. Applications having pause time constraints should not use this collector, since infrequent, but potentially long, old generation collections will still occur.

Use the option -XX:+UseParallelGC to select parallel collector. The following command selects a parallel collector and prints its details:

```
java -XX:+UseParallelGC -XX:+PrintGCDetails -version
```

A sample output is shown below:

```
java version "1.7.0_07"
Java(TM) SE Runtime Environment (build 1.7.0_07-b11)
Java HotSpot(TM) Client VM (build 23.3-b01, mixed mode)
Heap
 PSYoungGen      total 4800K, used 416K [0x12e40000, 0x13390000, 0x18390000)
  eden space 4160K, 10% used [0x12e40000,0x12ea8208,0x13250000)
  from space 640K, 0% used [0x132f0000,0x132f0000,0x13390000)
  to   space 640K, 0% used [0x13250000,0x13250000,0x132f0000)
 ParOldGen       total 10944K, used 0K [0x08390000, 0x08e40000, 0x12e40000)
  object space 10944K, 0% used [0x08390000,0x08390000,0x08e40000)
 PSPermGen       total 12288K, used 1363K [0x04390000, 0x04f90000, 0x08390000)
  object space 12288K, 11% used [0x04390000,0x044e4d20,0x04f90000)
```

4.7.3 Parallel Compacting Collector

Note that the parallel collector uses multiple threads for minor collections only. For major collection, still single thread is used which may degrade performance significantly. In Java 5 and later, a concept called *parallel compaction* has been introduced that allows parallel collector to perform even major collections in parallel. The algorithm consists of three phases: *mark*, *summary* and *compact*.

The algorithm divides each generation into fixed-sized *regions*. In the *mark* phase, an initial set of live objects directly reachable from the application code is identified first and is distributed among garbage collection threads. These threads then mark other live objects in parallel [Figure 4.12: (ii)].

The summary phase inspects the density of the live objects in each region. Due to previous compactions, it is expected that regions towards left are denser than regions towards right. The denser regions yield very little space and are not worth the cost of compacting them. So, summary phase starts from the leftmost region and finds a point beyond which compacting is cost-effective. The regions to the left of that point are referred to as the *dense prefix*. Note that the summary phase is currently implemented as a serial phase [Figure 4.12: (ii)]. Parallel summary phase may be implemented but not as important as parallelization of the mark and compact phases.

In the compaction phase, only non-dense regions are compacted.

Use `-XX:+UseParallelOldGC` to enable parallel compaction.

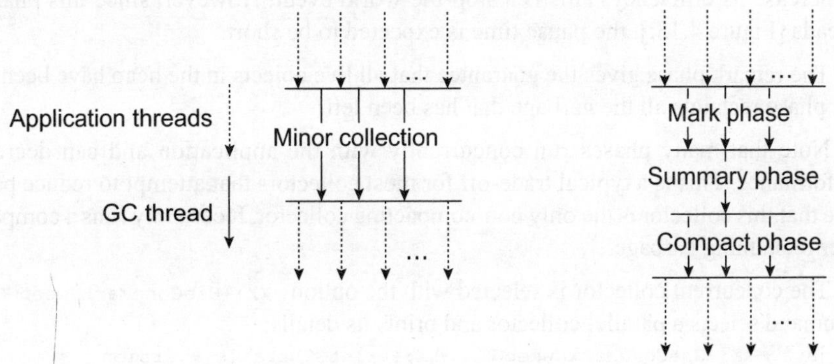

Figure 4.12: Parallel Compact collector (i) Young generation collection (ii) Old generation collection

Applications having pause time constraints may use this collector as it reduces old generation collection time.

4.7.4 Concurrent Collector

Note that all of the serial, parallel and parallel compact collectors are stop-the-world collectors. This means they suspend the application during the garbage collection. This may not be acceptable for application for which response time is much more important.

Fortunately, Java provides a fourth collector called *concurrent collector* (also called *low-latency collector*) that performs most of its work while the application is still running. This makes garbage collection pauses short. Since, old generation collections, though infrequent, result in relatively long pauses, a concurrent mark-sweep algorithm has been introduced for it.

The algorithms have primarily four phases: *initial mark*, *concurrent mark*, *remark* and *concurrent sweep*. In the initial mark phase, only the live objects directly reachable from the application code are identified. This phase is short stop-the-world event and uses a single thread [Figure 4.13:]. In the next phase, the collector concurrently marks all live objects that are transitively reachable from this set. This phase is not the stop-the-world event. So it does not pause the application. However, since the application runs and probably updates reference fields concurrently with this phase, all live objects may not be marked at the end of this phase.

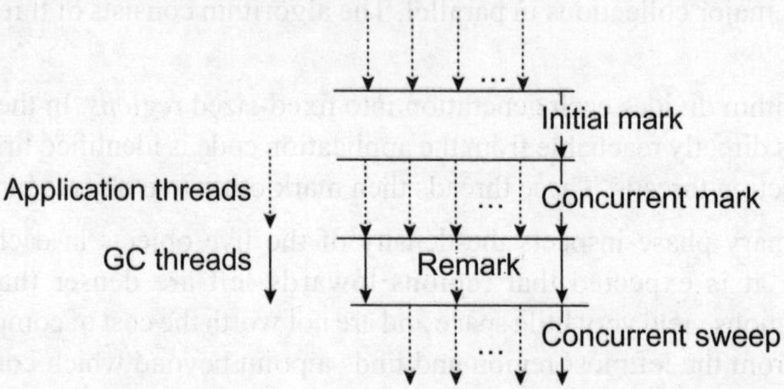

Figure 4.13: Old generation collection in concurrent collector

To cope up with this problem, the collector suspends the application in the remark phase and finalizes marking by revisiting any objects that were modified during the concurrent marking. Since, remark pause is more substantial than the initial mark, multiple threads are run in parallel to increase its efficiency. This is a stop-the-world event. However, since this phase uses multiple threads [Figure 4.13:], the pause time is expected to be short.

The remark phase gives the guarantee that all live objects in the heap have been marked. So, the last phase reclaims all the garbage that has been left.

Note that many phases run concurrently with the application and can decrease application performance. This is a typical trade-off for most collectors that attempt to reduce pause times. Also note that this collector is the only non-compacting collector. It certainly runs a compaction algorithm after reclaiming garbage.

The concurrent collector is selected with the option `-XX:+UseConcMarkSweepGC`. The following command selects a parallel collector and prints its details:

```
java -XX:+UseConcMarkSweepGC  -XX:+PrintGCDetails -version
```

A sample output is shown below:

```
java version "1.7.0_07"
Java(TM) SE Runtime Environment (build 1.7.0_07-b11)
Java HotSpot(TM) Client VM (build 23.3-b01, mixed mode)
Heap
```

```
par new generation    total 4928K, used 369K [0x04390000, 0x048e0000, 0x098e0000)
 eden space 4416K,   8% used [0x04390000, 0x043ec668, 0x047e0000)
 from space 512K,    0% used [0x047e0000, 0x047e0000, 0x04860000)
 to   space 512K,    0% used [0x04860000, 0x04860000, 0x048e0000)
concurrent mark-sweep generation total 10944K, used 0K [0x098e0000, 0x0a390000,
0x14390000)
concurrent-mark-sweep perm gen total 12288K, used 1363K [0x14390000, 0x14f90000,
0x18390000)
```

4.8 SOME COMMANDS

Printing information about current GC used

```
java -XX:+PrintGCDetails -version
```

A sample result for serial collector is shown below:

```
java version "1.7.0_07"
Java(TM) SE Runtime Environment (build 1.7.0_07-b11)
Java HotSpot(TM) Client VM (build 23.3-b01, mixed mode, sharing)
Heap
 def new generation    total 4928K, used 369K [0x23f10000, 0x24460000, 0x29460000)
  eden space 4416K,   8% used [0x23f10000, 0x23f6c668, 0x24360000)
  from space 512K,    0% used [0x24360000, 0x24360000, 0x243e0000)
  to   space 512K,    0% used [0x243e0000, 0x243e0000, 0x24460000)
 tenured generation    total 10944K, used 0K [0x29460000, 0x29f10000, 0x33f10000)
   the space 10944K,   0% used [0x29460000, 0x29460000, 0x29460200, 0x29f10000)
 compacting perm gen  total 12288K, used 69K [0x33f10000, 0x34b10000, 0x37f10000)
   the space 12288K,   0% used [0x33f10000, 0x33f21408, 0x33f21600, 0x34b10000)
    ro space 10240K,  45% used [0x37f10000, 0x38394650, 0x38394800, 0x38910000)
    rw space 12288K,  54% used [0x38910000, 0x38f97e58, 0x38f98000, 0x39510000)
```

Storing GC information in a file gc.txt

```
java -XX:+PrintGCDetails -Xloggc:gc.txt -version
```

Show all VM related settings:

```
java -XshowSettings:vm -version
```

A sample result is shown below:

```
VM settings:
    Max. Heap Size (Estimated): 247.50M
    Ergonomics Machine Class: client
    Using VM: Java HotSpot(TM) Client VM
```

Set maximum Java heap size 120 MB and show VM settings:

```
java -Xmx120m -XshowSettings:vm -version
```

The result is now given below:

```
VM settings:
    Max. Heap Size: 120.00M
    Ergonomics Machine Class: client
    Using VM: Java HotSpot(TM) Client VM
```

Set maximum Java heap size 2 MB and print VM details:

```
java -Xmx2m -XX:+PrintGCDetails -version
```

The result is now given below:

```
Heap
 def new generation    total 960K, used 330K [0x33910000, 0x33a10000, 0x33b10000)
  eden space 896K,   36% used [0x33910000, 0x339629f0, 0x339f0000)
  from space 64K,     0% used [0x339f0000, 0x339f0000, 0x33a00000)
  to   space 64K,     0% used [0x33a00000, 0x33a00000, 0x33a10000)
```

```
tenured generation   total 1024K, used 0K [0x33b10000, 0x33c10000, 0x33f10000)
  the space 1024K,   0% used [0x33b10000, 0x33b10000, 0x33b10200, 0x33c10000)
compacting perm gen  total 12288K, used 96K [0x33f10000, 0x34b10000, 0x37f10000)
  the space 12288K,   0% used [0x33f10000, 0x33f28018, 0x33f28200, 0x34b10000)
   ro space 10240K,  45% used [0x37f10000, 0x38394650, 0x38394800, 0x38910000)
   rw space 12288K,  54% used [0x38910000, 0x38f97e58, 0x38f98000, 0x39510000)
```

4.9 TOOLS

There are tools to monitor GC. The primary monitoring tools in HotSpot JVM are `jstat` and `jmap`. Sometimes, we need other helping tools such as `jps` and `jstatd` to monitor a Java application.

4.9.1 jstatd

It is an RMI server application that monitors for the creation and termination JVMs and allows tools such as `jps`, jstat to monitor these JVMs remotely through it. This requires an RMI registry running on the local host. The `jstatd` tries to find an RMI registry on the default port (1099), or on the port indicated by the -p port option. If no RMI registry is found, it creates one bound to the port indicated by the -p port option or to the default port if -p option is absent.

The `jstatd` can only monitor JVMs for which it has the appropriate access permissions. The following policy file will allow the `jstatd` server to run without any security exceptions.

```
grant codebase "file:D:/Java/jdk1.7.0_07/lib/tools.jar" {
  permission java.security.AllPermission;
};
```

Here, `D:/Java/jdk1.7.0_07` is the Java installation home directory. To use this policy, save it in a file `jstatd.all.policy` and run the `jstatd` server as follows:

```
jstatd -J-Djava.security.policy=jstatd.all.policy
```

The RMI server consults an RMI registry running locally on default port `1099` (starts a new one if no such registry is found). We can now start a JVM and can be monitored remotely by tools such as `jps` and `jstat`.

4.9.2 jps

The jps command lists the local VM identifier, or lvmid, for each instrumented JVM found on the target system. This lvmid is typically, but not necessarily, the operating system's process identifier for the JVM process. This lvmid is required for other tools such as `jmap`, `jstat`. A typical output of jps command is shown below:

```
E:\ajp\gc>jps
3928 Loop
3380 Jps
```

Here, Loop is Java program running under the supervision of a JVM having lvmid 3928. If you want to find the lvmid of JVMs running on a different machine (say `172.16.5.81`), start `jstatd` first as described in the previous section and then use the following command:

```
jps 172.16.5.81
```

4.9.3 jmap

This command prints shared object memory maps or heap memory details of a specified process or executable core file or a remote debug server. The following command prints the heap information for the process having lvmid 3928

```
E:\ajp\gc>jmap -heap 3928
Attaching to process ID 3928, please wait...
Debugger attached successfully.
Client compiler detected.
JVM version is 23.3-b01

using thread-local object allocation.
Mark Sweep Compact GC

Heap Configuration:
   MinHeapFreeRatio = 40
   MaxHeapFreeRatio = 70
   MaxHeapSize      = 268435456 (256.0MB)
   NewSize          = 1048576 (1.0MB)
   MaxNewSize       = 4294901760 (4095.9375MB)
   OldSize          = 4194304 (4.0MB)
   NewRatio         = 2
   SurvivorRatio    = 8
   PermSize         = 12582912 (12.0MB)
   MaxPermSize      = 67108864 (64.0MB)
   G1HeapRegionSize = 0 (0.0MB)

Heap Usage:
New Generation (Eden + 1 Survivor Space):
   capacity = 5046272 (4.8125MB)
   used     = 1690792 (1.6124649047851562MB)
   free     = 3355480 (3.2000350952148438MB)
   33.50576425527598% used
Eden Space:
   capacity = 4521984 (4.3125MB)
   used     = 1549200 (1.4774322509765625MB)
   free     = 2972784 (2.8350677490234375MB)
   34.25929857336956% used
From Space:
   capacity = 524288 (0.5MB)
   used     = 141592 (0.13503265380859375MB)
   free     = 382696 (0.36496734619140625MB)
   27.00653076171875% used
To Space:
   capacity = 524288 (0.5MB)
   used     = 0 (0.0MB)
   free     = 524288 (0.5MB)
   0.0% used
tenured generation:
   capacity = 11206656 (10.6875MB)
   used     = 0 (0.0MB)
   free     = 11206656 (10.6875MB)
   0.0% used
Perm Generation:
   capacity = 12582912 (12.0MB)
   used     = 109832 (0.10474395751953125MB)
   free     = 12473080 (11.895256042480469MB)
   0.8728663126627604% used

10737 interned Strings occupying 806464 bytes.
```

4.9.4 jstat

The jstat tool displays performance statistics for an instrumented HotSpot Java virtual machine (JVM). The target JVM is identified by its virtual machine identifier, or lvmid. The `jstat` command takes options and displays useful information. The following command shows all the options available:

```
jstat –options
```

The function of each option is explained in Table 4.1:

Table 4.1: jstat options

Options	Explanation
class	Statistics on the behaviour of the class loader.
compiler	Statistics of the behaviour of the HotSpot Just-in-Time compiler.
gc	Statistics of the behaviour of the garbage collected heap.
gccause	Summary of garbage collection statistics (same as -gcutil), with the cause of the last and current (if applicable) garbage collection events.
gccapacity	Statistics of the capacities of the generations and their corresponding spaces.
gcnew	Statistics of the behaviour of the new generation.
gcnewcapacity	Statistics of the sizes of the new generations and its corresponding spaces.
gcold	Statistics of the behaviour of the old and permanent generations.
gcoldcapacity	Statistics of the sizes of the old generation.
gcpermcapacity	Statistics of the sizes of the permanent generation.
gcutil	Summary of garbage collection statistics.
printcompilation	HotSpot compilation method statistics.

The following command summarizes the garbage collection statistics for the JVM having lvmid 3928:

```
jstat -gcutil 3928
```

A sample output of the above command is shown below:

```
S0     S1     E      O      P     YGC    YGCT    FGC    FGCT    GCT
0.00  27.01  64.69  0.00   0.87     7   0.011     0   0.000   0.011
```

If you monitor a JVM running on a different host having IP address 172.16.5.81, start `jstatd` in that machine first. Then use the following `jstat` command:

```
jstat -gcutil 3928@172.16.5.81
```

4.10 TUNING MEMORY SIZE

The performance of a collector depends on the size of heap and generations. In this section, we shall discuss which parameters have been defined to control total size of the heap and the sizes of the generations and their impact on the performance.

4.11 TUNING HEAP SIZE

Note that the size of the total allocated space and the space to be used initially may be specified with the -Xmx and -Xms options respectively. If the value of the -Xms option is smaller than the value of the -Xmx option, some space remains uncommitted. The uncommitted space is sometimes called *virtual*. The different generations can grow to the limit of the virtual space as needed.

Note that throughput depends on free space in a generation. Since collections occur when generations fill up, less the free space in a generation, more frequently the generation fills up and collection occurs. This implies throughput proportional to the space available in a generation. To improve throughput, JVM tries to maintain a significant amount of space free in generations. The allowable range of percentage of free space is specified by two boundary values and are set as `-XX:MinHeapFreeRatio=<minimum>` and `-XX:MaxHeapFreeRatio=<maximum>`.

The default values of these two parameters are 40 and 70 respectively. If the percent of free space in a generation falls below this minimum, the generation is grown subject to the maximum size of the generation. Similarly, if the percentage of free space exceeds the maximum the generation is shrunk subject to the minimum size of the generation.

How do these parameters affect the performance? Small `MinHeapFreeRatio` indicates slow startup as generation size is small and is properly sized after many collections. This may slow down the performance of large server applications. Some rules for server applications are:

- Allocate as much memory as possible to the JVM if large pauses are not any problem
- Take –Xms and –Xmx same. This helps us to make sizing decisions. However, if the choice is poor, JVM will fail to make up.
- Since allocation can be parallelized, for more processors, allocate more memory

4.12 TUNING YOUNG GENERATION

The size of the young generation also does matter. The larger the young generation, the less frequently minor collections occur and throughput increases. However, for a given heap size, tenured generation decreases if young generation increases, which increases the frequency of major collections. Since, major collection takes relatively long time, throughput decreases significantly. The size of these two generations is controlled by a parameter called `NewRatio` which is the ratio between young generation size to tenured generation size. This parameter is set as `–XX:NewRatio=<ratio>`. A value 2 of `NewRatio` indicates that the size of tenured generation is double the size of young generation. In addition, the size of young generation is bounded by two parameters `NewSize` and `MaxNewSize`.

4.12.1 Tuning Survivor Space

Although, the size of the survivor space is not an important metric for performance, it may be tuned using the parameter `SurvivorRatio` which is ration between survivor space size to Eden space size and is set as `-XX:SurvivorRatio=<ratio>`. A value 8 of `SurvivorRatio` indicates that the size of Eden space should be 8 times the size of one survivor space.

Smaller survivor space overflows frequently resulting in live objects to be copied directly to the tenured generation. If survivor spaces are too large, most space will remain unused most of the time.

4.13 ACCESSING GC FROM JAVA PROGRAM

Although, not so powerful, we can interact with the garbage collector from within Java programs such as inspecting some parameters, invoking garbage collector. However, parameters can only be set when a JVM starts using command line options.

4.13.1 Inspecting GC Parameters

When a program runs in a JVM, we can also inspect some of its parameters from the program. This is done using the class `java.lang.Runtime` that corresponds to a JVM. This class provides methods to interface with the environment. The following are some methods:

```
public long maxMemory()
public long totalMemory()
public long freeMemory()
```

The `maxMemory()` returns the maximum amount of memory, in bytes, that the virtual machine will attempt to use.

4.13.2 Explicit Garbage Collection

An application can invoke the garbage collector explicitly using static `gc()` method of `System` class.

```
public static void gc()
```

A call to this method causes a major collection.

`System.gc()` is equivalent to the following call:

```
Runtime.getRuntime().gc()
```

Since, `gc()` always causes a major collection to be done even if a minor collection is sufficient, it may greatly impact the performance. Usually, JVM's determination of when it is appropriate is better. So, invoking garbage collector explicitly should be avoided. If there are still problems related to pause time or others, the parameters of the collector may be carefully selected instead. The JVM may be instructed to ignore the explicit call to a collector using `gc()` using `-XX:+DisableExplicitGC` option.

4.13.3 finalize()

Every Java object inherits a method `finalize()` from `Object` class and is called by the garbage collector before it reclaims the object. The intent is for `finalize()` to release system resources such as open files or open sockets before getting collected. So, it gives us the last chance for any object to perform cleanup activity. The following program illustrates this:

```
class FinalizeDemo {
  public void finalize() {
    System.out.println("object is garbage collected");
  }
  public static void main(String args[]) throws Exception {
    new FinalizeDemo();
    System.gc();
  }
}
```

This program creates an unnamed object and calls the garbage collector explicitly using `System.gc()`. Since the object has no reference pointing to it, it is a garbage object and is collected by the garbage collector. The collector calls the `finalize()` method before collecting it. Here is a sample output:

```
object is garbage collected
```

4.14 APPENDIX

Table 4.2: -X options

Option	Purpose
-Xms	Sets the initial heap size for when the JVM starts
-Xmx	Sets the maximum heap size
-Xmn	Sets the size of the Young Generation
-XX:PermSize	Sets the starting size of the Permanent Generation
-XX:MaxPermSize	Sets the maximum size of the Permanent Generation

-XX options

Table 4.3: Debugging Options

Option and Default Value	Description
-XX:-CITime	Displays time spent in JIT Compiler
-XX:ErrorFile=./hs_err_pid<pid>.log	Saves the error data to the specified file if an error occurs
-XX:-ExtendedDTraceProbes	Enables performance-impacting dtrace probes. (Solaris only.)
-XX:HeapDumpPath=./java_pid<pid>.hprof	Path to directory or filename for heap dump
-XX:-HeapDumpOnOutOfMemoryError	Dumps heap to file when java.lang.OutOfMemoryError is thrown.
-XX:OnError="<cmd args>;<cmd args>"	Executes user-defined commands on fatal error
-XX:OnOutOfMemoryError="<cmd args>; <cmd args>"	Executes user-defined commands when an OutOfMemoryError is first thrown.
-XX:-PrintClassHistogram	Displays a histogram of class instances on Ctrl-Break. Equivalent to jmap -histo command
-XX:-PrintConcurrentLocks	Displays java.util.concurrent locks in Ctrl-Break thread dump. Equivalent to jstack -l command
-XX:-PrintCommandLineFlags	Displays flags that appeared on the command line
-XX:-PrintCompilation	Displays message when a method is compiled
-XX:-PrintGC	Displays messages at garbage collection
-XX:-PrintGCDetails	Prints more details at garbage collection
-XX:-PrintGCTimeStamps	Prints timestamps at garbage collection
-XX:-PrintTenuringDistribution	Displays tenuring age information
-XX:-PrintAdaptiveSizePolicy	Enables printing of information about adaptive generation sizing.
-XX:-TraceClassLoading	Traces loading of classes
-XX:-TraceClassLoadingPreorder	Traces all classes loaded in order referenced
-XX:-TraceClassResolution	Traces constant pool resolutions
-XX:-TraceClassUnloading	Traces unloading of classes
-XX:-TraceLoaderConstraints	Traces recording of loader constraints
-XX:+PerfSaveDataToFile	Saves jvmstat binary data on exit
-XX:ParallelGCThreads=n	Sets the number of garbage collection threads in the young and old parallel garbage collectors
-XX:+UseCompressedOops	Enables the use of compressed pointers
-XX:+AlwaysPreTouch	Pre-touch the Java heap during JVM initialization
-XX:AllocatePrefetchDistance=n	Sets the prefetch distance for object allocation
-XX:InlineSmallCode=n	Inline a previously compiled method only if its generated native code size is less than this
-XX:MaxInlineSize=35	Maximum bytecode size of a method to be inlined
-XX:FreqInlineSize=n	Maximum bytecode size of a frequently executed method to be inlined
-XX:LoopUnrollLimit=n	Unroll loop bodies with server compiler intermediate representation node count less than this value

(*Contd*)

Table 4.3: (*Contd*)

-XX:InitialTenuringThreshold=7	Sets the initial tenuring threshold for use in adaptive GC sizing in the parallel young collector
-XX:MaxTenuringThreshold=n	Sets the maximum tenuring threshold for use in adaptive GC sizing
-Xloggc:<filename>	Logs GC verbose output to specified file. The verbose output is controlled by the normal verbose GC flags
-XX:-UseGCLogFileRotation	Enables GC log rotation, requires -Xloggc
-XX:NumberOfGClogFiles=1	Sets the number of files to use when rotating logs, must be >= 1. The rotated log files will use the following naming scheme, <filename>.0, <filename>.1, ..., <filename>.n-1.
-XX:GCLogFileSize=8K	The size of the log file at which point the log will be rotated, must be >= 8K.

Table 4.4: Behavioural Options

Option and Default Value	**Description**
-XX:-AllowUserSignalHandlers	Does not complain if the application installs signal handlers. (Solaris and Linux only.).
-XX:-DisableExplicitGC	Enables calls to System.gc(). Use -XX:+DisableExplicitGC to disable it.
-XX:+FailOverToOldVerifier	Fails over to old verifier when the new type checker fails.
-XX:+HandlePromotionFailure	The youngest generation collection does not require a guarantee of full promotion of all live objects.
-XX:+MaxFDLimit	Bumps the number of file descriptors to max. (Solaris only.)
-XX:PreBlockSpin=10	Spins count variable for use with -XX:+UseSpinning. Controls the maximum spin iterations allowed before entering operating system thread synchronization code.
-XX:-RelaxAccessControlCheck	Relaxes the access control checks in the verifier.
-XX:+ScavengeBeforeFullGC	Does young generation GC prior to a full GC.
-XX:+UseAltSigs	Uses alternate signals instead of SIGUSR1 and SIGUSR2 for VM internal signals.
-XX:+UseBoundThreads	Binds user level threads to kernel threads. (Solaris only.)
-XX:-UseConcMarkSweepGC	Uses concurrent mark-sweep collection for the old generation.
-XX:+UseGCOverheadLimit	Uses a policy that limits the proportion of the VM's time that is spent in GC before an OutOfMemory error is thrown.
-XX:+UseLWPSynchronization	Uses LWP-based instead of thread-based synchronization.
-XX:-UseParallelGC	Uses parallel garbage collection for scavenges.
-XX:-UseParallelOldGC	Uses parallel garbage collection for the full collections. Enabling this option automatically sets -XX:+UseParallelGC.
-XX:-UseSerialGC	Uses serial garbage collection.
-XX:+UseTLAB	Uses thread-local object allocation
-XX:+UseSplitVerifier	Uses the new type checker with StackMapTable attributes.
-XX:+UseThreadPriorities	Uses native thread priorities.
-XX:+UseVMInterruptibleIO	Thread interrupt before or with EINTR for I/O operations results in OS_INTRPT.

Table 4.5: Garbage First (G1) Garbage Collection Options

Option and Default Value	Description
-XX:+UseG1GC	Uses the Garbage First (G1) Collector.
-XX:MaxGCPauseMillis=n	Sets a target for the maximum GC pause time.
-XX:InitiatingHeapOccupancyPercent=n	Percentage of the (entire) heap occupancy to start a concurrent GC cycle.
-XX:NewRatio=n	Ratio of old/new generation sizes. The default value is 2.
-XX:SurvivorRatio=n	Ratio of eden/survivor space size. The default value is 8.
-XX:MaxTenuringThreshold=n	Maximum value for tenuring threshold. The default value is 15.
-XX:ParallelGCThreads=n	Sets the number of threads used during parallel phases of the garbage collectors.
-XX:ConcGCThreads=n	Number of threads concurrent garbage collectors will use.
-XX:G1ReservePercent=n	Sets the amount of heap that is reserved as a false ceiling to reduce the possibility of promotion failure. The default value is 10.
-XX:G1HeapRegionSize=n	With G1 the Java heap is subdivided into uniformly sized regions. This sets the size of the individual sub-divisions.

Table 4.6: Performance Options

Option and Default Value	Description
-XX:+AggressiveOpts	Turns on point performance compiler optimizations that are expected to be default in upcoming releases.
-XX:CompileThreshold=10000	No. of method invocations/branches before compiling [-client: 1,500].
-XX:LargePageSizeInBytes=4m	Sets the large page size used for the Java heap. [amd64: 2m.].
-XX:MaxHeapFreeRatio=70	Maximum percentage of heap free after GC to avoid shrinking.
-XX:MaxNewSize=size	Maximum size of new generation (in bytes).
-XX:MaxPermSize=size	Size of the Permanent Generation.
-XX:MinHeapFreeRatio=ratio	Minimum percentage of heap free after GC to avoid expansion.
-XX:NewRatio=ratio	Ratio of old/new generation sizes.
-XX:NewSize=size	Default size of new generation (in bytes).
-XX:ReservedCodeCacheSize=size	Reserved code cache size (in bytes).
-XX:SurvivorRatio=size	Ratio of eden/survivor space size.
-XX:TargetSurvivorRatio=ratio	Desired percentage of survivor space used after scavenge.
-XX:ThreadStackSize=size	Thread Stack Size (in Kbytes).
-XX:+UseBiasedLocking	Enable biased locking. For more details, see this tuning example.
-XX:+UseFastAccessorMethods	Uses optimized versions of Get<Primitive>Field.
-XX:-UseISM	Uses Intimate Shared Memory.
-XX:+UseLargePages	Uses large page memory.
-XX:+UseMPSS	Uses Multiple Page Size Support w/4mb pages for the heap.
-XX:+UseStringCache	Enables caching of commonly allocated strings.

(*Contd*)

Table 4.6: (*Contd*)

-XX:AllocatePrefetchLines=lines	Number of cache lines to load after the last object allocation using prefetch instructions generated in JIT compiled code.
-XX:AllocatePrefetchStyle=value	Generates code style for prefetch instructions.
-XX:+UseCompressedStrings	Uses a byte[] for Strings which can be represented as pure ASCII.
-XX:+OptimizeStringConcat	Optimizes String concatenation operations where possible.

KEYWORDS

Atop-the-world event—An event when occurs stops all other activities

Concurrent Collector—A type of collector that performs most of its work while the application is still running

finalize()—A method which is called by the garbage collector on an object before it reclaims the object

Garbage Collector—A component of Java that is responsible for indentifying garbage objects and freeing heap memory occupied by them

Generational hypothesis—A hypothesis that states that most objects survive for only a short period of time

Major collection— Process of garbage collection done on all generations

Minor collection—Process of garbage collection done on young generation

Parallel Collector—A type of garbage collector that uses multiple threads perform minor collections

Parallel Concurrent Collector—An extension to parallel collector where major collections are also done in parallel

Permanent generation—The portion of the heap from where objects are occasionally loaded and unloaded

Serial Collector—A type of garbage collector that uses single thread

Tenured generation—The portion of the heap where relatively higher aged objects are kept

Yung generation—The portion of the heap which contains short aged objects

SUMMARY

One of the key reasons of Java's legendary success is its garbage collector which can greatly help in improving performance of your Java applications. Garbage collection refers to the process of indentifying garbage objects and freeing heap memory occupied by them. In Java, garbage is collected automatically by a special component, called *garbage collector*.

The garbage collector uses a hypothesis called *weak generational hypothesis*, which states that most objects survive for only a short period of time. Java divides heap into different segments such as young, old and permanent generations where different aged objects are kept. From time to time garbage collector identifies garbage objects and claims their memory using techniques such as minor and major collections.

JVM provides different collectors, each with different performance characteristics: *serial collector*, *parallel collector*, *parallel compact collector* and *concurrent collector*.

Since, serial collector always uses single thread, it cannot leverage multi-processor system. This collection algorithm has three phases: *mark, sweep* and *compact*. The strength of this collector however, lies in its single thread as there is no communication overhead between threads.

For parallel garbage collector, as its name implies, multiple threads are used to perform minor collections. Parallel collector uses multiple threads for minor collections only. For major collection, still single thread is used which may degrade performance significantly. In Java 5 and later, a concept called parallel compaction has been introduced that allows parallel collector to perform even major collections in parallel.

Java provides a fourth collector called *concurrent collector* (also called *low-latency collector*) that performs most of its work while the application is still running

There are tools to monitor GC. The primary monitoring tools in HotSpot JVM are `jstat` and `jmap`. Sometimes, we need other helping tools such are `jps` and `jstatd` to monitor a Java application.

WEB RESOURCES

http://www.oracle.com/webfolder/technetwork/tutorials/obe/java/gc01/index.html
Java Garbage Collection Basics

http://www.oracle.com/technetwork/java/javase/memorymanagement-whitepaper-150215.pdf
Memory Management in the Java HotSpot™ Virtual Machine

http://www.azulsystems.com/sites/default/files/images/Understanding%20Java%20Garbage%20Collection%20v2%20(1).pdf
Understanding Java Garbage Collection

http://buytaert.net/files/hipeac05-paper.pdf
Garbage Collection Hints

http://mfinocchiaro.files.wordpress.com/2008/07/java-virtual-machine-neutral.pdf
Java Performance Tuning

http://www.academia.edu/1260340/CMS_and_G1_Collector_in_Java_7_Hotspot_Overview_Comparisons_and_Performance_Metrics
Comparisons and Performance Metrics

EXERCISES

Objective-type Questions

1. When is the object B in the following code eligible for garbage collection?

```
void start() {
A a = new A();
B b = new B();
a.s(b);
b = null; /* Line 5 */
a = null; /* Line 6 */
System.out.println("start completed");
/* Line 7 */
}
```

(a) After line 5
(b) After line 6
(c) After line 7
(d) There is no way to be absolutely certain.

2. Where will be the most chance of the garbage collector being invoked?

```
class HappyGarbage01 {
  public static void main(String args[]) {
    HappyGarbage01 h = new HappyGarbage01();
    h.methodA();
  }
 Object methodA() {/* Line 6 */
   Object obj1 = new Object();
   Object [] obj2 = new Object[1];
   obj2[0] = obj1;
   obj1 = null;
   return obj2[0];
  }
}
```

(a) After line 9
(b) After line 10
(c) After line 11
(d) Garbage collector never invoked in methodA()

3. At what point is the Bar object, created on line 6, eligible for garbage collection?

```
class Test {
  String f() {
  String s = new String(); /* Line 3 */
  return s;
 }
 public static void main (String args[]) {
  Test t = new Test(); /* Line 7 */
  String s1 = t.f(); /* Line 8 */
  s1 = new String(); /* Line 9 */
  System.out.println(s1);
  }
}
```

(a) After line 8
(b) After line 9
(c) After line 4, when f() completes
(d) After line 10

4. Which operator is used by Java run time implementations to free the memory of an object when it is no longer needed?

(a) delete (c) new
(b) free (d) None of the mentioned

5. Which function is used to perform some action when the object is to be destroyed?

(a) finalize() (c) main()
(b) delete() (d) None of the mentioned

6. Which of the following statements are incorrect?

(a) Default constructor is called at the time of declaration of the object if a constructor has not been defined.
(b) Constructor can be parameterized.

(c) finalize() method is called when an object goes out of scope and is no longer needed.
(d) finalize() method must be declared protected.

7. How can you force garbage collection of an object?
(a) Garbage collection cannot be forced.
(b) Call System.gc().
(c) Call Runtime.gc().
(d) Set all references to the object to new values(null, for example).

8. When is the Demo object eligible for garbage collection?

```
class Test {
  private Demo d;
  void start() {
    d = new Demo();
    this.takeDemo(d); /* Line 5 */
  } /* Line 6 */
  void takeDemo(Demo demo) {
    demo = null;
    demo = new Demo();
  }
}
```

(a) After line 5
(b) After line 6
(c) After the start() method completes
(d) When the instance running this code is made eligible for garbage collection.

9. After line 8 runs, how many objects are eligible for garbage collection?

```
public class X {
  public static void main(String [] args) {
    X x = new X();
    X x2 = m1(x); /* Line 4 */
    X x4 = new X();
    x2 = x4; /* Line 6 */
    doComplexStuff();
  }
  static X m1(X mx) {
    mx = new X();
    return mx;
  }
}
```

(a) 0 (c) 2
(b) 1 (d) 3

10. Which of the following options is used to set initial heap size?
(a) -Xmx<size> (c) -Xms<size>
(b) -Xss<size> (d) None of the above

11. JVM options start with
(a) -X (c) -JVM
(b) -XX (d) Both a) and b)

12. If garbage collection occurs on young generation, it is called
(a) Major collection
(b) Minor collection
(c) Small collection
(d) Young collection

13. If garbage collection occurs on all generations, it is called
(a) Major collection
(b) Minor collection
(c) Large collection
(d) Young collection

14. The portion of heap where short aged objects are kept is called
(a) New generation
(b) Young generation
(c) Fresh generation
(d) First generation

15. The portion of heap where relatively long aged objects are kept is called
(a) Old generation
(b) Permanent generation
(c) Previous generation
(d) Second generation

16. The garbage collector that uses a single thread is called
(a) Simple collector
(b) One-thread collector
(c) Single collector
(d) Serial collector

17. Which one is not a HotSpot's garbage collector?
(a) Serial collector
(b) Parallel collector
(c) Concurrent collector
(d) Roubust collector

18. Which one of the following is not a HotSpot's monitoring tool?
(a) jstat (c) jps
(b) jmap (d) jvm

19. Which one of the following is not a step in serial collector?
(a) Mark (c) Sweep
(b) Identify (d) Compact

20. Which of the following options is used to select serial collector?
(a) -XX:+UseSerialGC
(b) -XX:+UseParallelOldGC
(c) -XX:+UseConcMarkSweepGC
(d) None of the above

Subjective-type Questions

1. Why are two survior spaces maintained in young generation by HotSpot?
2. How do you identify minor and major garbage collection in Java?
3. What is the structure of Java Heap? What is Perm Gen space in Heap?
4. How do you find GC resulted due to calling System.gc()?
5. What is the difference between Parallel and Paralle compact Garbage collector?
6. When does an Object becomes eligible for Garbage collection in Java?
7. What is finalize method in Java? When does Garbage collector call finalize method in Java?
8. Can we force Garbage collector to run at any time?
9. Does Garbage collection occur in permanent generation space in JVM?
10. How do you monitor garbage collection activities?
11. Which part of the memory is involved in Garbage Collection? Stack or Heap?
12. What is the responsiblity of Garbage Collector?
13. What are the different ways to make an object eligible for Garbage Collection when it is no longer needed?
14. How can the Garbage Collection be requested?
15. What is the purpose of overriding finalize() method?
16. How many times does the garbage collector call the finalize() method for an object?
17. What happens if an uncaught exception is thrown from during the execution of the finalize() method of an object?
18. How do you enable/disable call of finalize() method of exit of the application?

CHAPTER – 5

COLLECTION FRAMEWORK

KEY OBJECTIVES

After completing this chapter readers will be able to—

- understand architecture of collection framework
- familiarize core collection classes and interfaces
- use commonly used collections classes and interfaces
- use commonly used collection algorithms
- evaluate the performance of implementations of interfaces and algorithms

5.1 INTRODUCTION

It is often necessary to store and manipulate a group of objects. Earlier versions (1.2) of Java provided unrelated classes such as `Vector, Hashtable, Stack, Properties, Dictionary` etc. to work with aggregate data. Although, they provided sufficient functionalities, they lacked a common framework. As a result, the way of using these classes varies quite a bit.

In version 1.2, Java provided a unified architecture, known as *collection framework* for representing and manipulating aggregate objects. A *collection* is basically a container that encapsulates multiple objects into a single unit. Examples include a list of employees, a set of numbers, a set of processes, a queue of requests etc.

All collections frameworks primarily contains three parts: *interfaces*, *implementation* and *algorithms.*

Interfaces

These abstract data types define the functionality of collections. These enable collections to be manipulated in a unified way irrespective of their internal implementation. For example, all collection interfaces define a method `add()` that may be used to add an element to the collection. However, the element itself may be added at the end (for queue) or at an arbitrary location (for set) of the collection. Collection interfaces are provided in the package `java.util`.

Implementation

These are classes implementing those interfaces. Although, they use reusable data structures, their behaviour differs for different collection types. We use them to create different types of collections in our program. Implementation classes are provided in `java.util` and `java.util.concurrent` package.

Algorithms

In addition, collection framework defines a set of methods (usually static) for important operations such as searching, sorting, shuffling of objects which implement collection interfaces. These methods behave polymorphically; i.e. work differently on different implementations.

5.2 BENEFITS

Java collection frameworks provide the following benefits:

Less Programming Effort

The framework itself provides interfaces and implementation of commonly used concepts such as sets, lists, queues, maps etc. So, programmers can devote more time on the program logic instead of their implementation.

High Quality and Performance

Java provides high-quality implementation of collection interfaces resulting in unquestionable performance and quality of our programs. Java not only provides different implementations of an interface, but also allows us to interchange these implementations seamlessly. So, a program may suddenly switch a different implementation without minimal effort still maintaining the quality and performance.

Interoperability

Collection framework also facilitates the interoperability among unrelated classes eliminating the need of writing adapter and/or conversion classes. Since, most methods take a `Collection` (top level interface) parameter, different implementations may be passed back and forth.

Quick Learning

Although, Java provided a set of classes for representing group of object prior to version 1.2, these ad hoc classes had a little consistency among them. So programmers had to learn each of them from scratch resulting in high unintentional error. Since, collection interfaces form a hierarchy, understanding relation among them is not difficult. As a result one can become a master in this area in a substantially less time.

Flexible Redesign

Writing a new implementation as a part of this framework is simply a matter of fun. It has become an extremely easy task to write a new implementation and use it in our program without major modification.

5.3 COLLECTION INTERFACES

As mentioned earlier, collection interfaces define behaviour of commonly used concepts and establishes relations among them. The core collection interfaces and their hierarchy is shown in Figure 5.1: For simplicity, the major interfaces are shown here. These interfaces are the foundation of Java collection framework. They create abstract types and enable us to manipulate collections independently of their implementations. All core collection interfaces are generic. However, they may also be used as ordinary interfaces. The detail information about generics may be found in the next chapter.

Note that `Map` doesn't inherit `Collection`. However, it is considered as a part of collections framework.

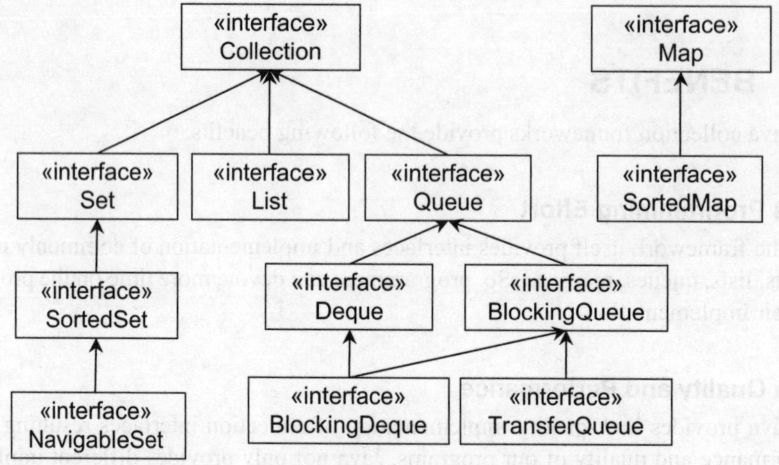

Figure 5.1: Core collection interface hierarchy

The following is a brief description of top level interfaces.

Collection

The root interface in the hierarchy is `Collection` interface. It represents a general group of objects, called *elements*. It defines primitive operations on collections such as adding[`add()`], removing [`remove()`] elements, checking existence of an element [`contains()`], size [`size()`] of collection etc. It also provides methods for bulk operations such as `addAll()`, `removeAll()`, `retainAll()`, `containsAll()`, `clear()` etc. The `toArray()` method acts as bridge between collections and older APIs that expect arrays on input.

Java does not provide a direct implementation of this interface. However, implementations are provided for more specific collection types such as Set, `List`, `Queue` etc.

Set

This interface models the mathematical set that contains an unordered collection of objects without any duplicates. It contains only methods inherited from `Collection`. However, since a set cannot contain duplicate elements, it does add restrictions on those methods. Set also changes the contract of `equals()` and `hashCode()` operations so that `Set` objects can be compared meaningfully irrespective of their implementation. Note that two sets are equal if they contain the same elements.

List

A `List` is an ordered collection and can contain duplicate elements. It is like a dynamic array. It allows us to have precise control over the elements inserted and deleted. We can access elements by their position (integer index). In addition to the operations inherited from `Collection, List` interface provides useful methods to add, remove, replace elements based on specified position and arbitrary range operations on the list.

Queue

This interface models queue where elements are added and removed in a specific order, typically in a first-in-first-out (FIFO) manner. It defines additional operations for insertion, removal and inspection. Although queues typically arrange elements in a FIFO order, other arrangements (such as LIFO) are also possible. Every `Queue` implementation must specify its ordering properties.

Map

It represents key-value pairs. The keys will be unique and each key can map to at most one value. Although, it does not ensure element ordering, some implementations guarantee it. To interoperate with other collection classes/interfaces, it provides three collection views, which allow a map's contents to be viewed as a set of keys, collection of values, or set of key-value mappings.

5.4 COLLECTION IMPLEMENTATION

As noted earlier, Java does not provide any implementation for root interface Collection. Instead it provides implementation of more specific interfaces such as `Set, List, Queue` etc. All collection implementations provide two constructors: one that takes no argument and one that takes a `Collection` argument. The following sections discuss how to work with these collections.

5.4.1 Set

Java provides three general-purpose implementations for `Set` interface: `HashSet`, `LinkedHashSet` and `TreeSet` [Figure 5.2:].

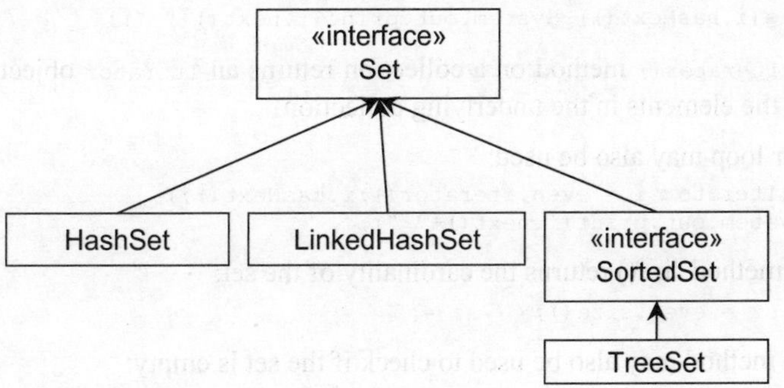

Figure 5.2: Set implementations

Neither of the implementations allows random-access to an element in a set. To retrieve elements from the Set, we can either use `Iterator` or for-each loop.

5.4.1.1 HashSet

Since, `HashSet` implements `Set` interface, it does not guarantee any insertion and iteration orders. However, it may contain `null` element. This class is a hash-based implementation and internally it uses `HashMap` which is one of the `Map` implementations. It offers constant time performance for certain operations such as `add()`, `remove()`, `contains()` and `size()` assuming that the hash function has distributed the elements equitably among the buckets. However, iteration time is proportional to the sum of number of elements and number of buckets. So, number of buckets should not be very high (load factor should not be very small) if iteration time is important.

`HashSet` has multiple constructors that give us the flexibility to create instances in different ways.

```
Set empty = new HashSet();                       //{}
Set even = new HashSet(Arrays.asList(0,2,4)); //{0, 2, 4}
Set copy = new HashSet(even);                  //create from existing Set
Set blank = new HashSet(8);                    //initial capacity 8
Set nullSet = new HashSet(8, 1);              //initial capacity 8, load factor 1
```

Elements in a `HashSet` are added using `add()` method.

```
even.add(6);    //{0, 2, 4, 6}
even.add(8);    //{0, 2, 4, 6, 8}
```

The method `add()` returns `false` if the element already exists else it returns `true`. Elements may be retrieved using the for-each construct as follows:

```
for (Object o:even) System.out.print(o+" ");
```

It prints all the elements of the Set `even`:

```
0 2 4 6 8
```

Alternatively, the iterator may be used to traverse the set. An iterator object iterates over the elements in a collection. Its functionalities are specified by `java.util.Iterator` interface having the following methods:

`hasNext()` – Returns true if there are more elements in the collection; false otherwise

`next()` – Returns the next element

`remove()` – Deletes the last element returned from the collection

Here is an example of how to use iterator:

```
Iterator i = even.iterator();
while(i.hasNext()) System.out.print(i.next()+" ");
```

The `iterator()` method on a collection returns an `Iterator` object which knows how to step through the elements in the underlying collection.

A for loop may also be used:

```
for(Iterator i = even.iterator();i.hasNext();)
  System.out.print(i.next()+" ");
```

The method size() returns the cardinality of the set:

```
int sz = even.size();  //sz = 5
```

This method may also be used to check if the set is empty:

```
if(blank.size() == 0) System.out.println("empty set");
```

Alternatively, `isEmpty()` method may be used:

```
boolean e1 = even.isEmpty();       //e1 = false
boolean e2 = blank.isEmpty();      //e2 = true
if(blank.isEmpty()) System.out.println("empty set");
```

The existence of an element may be checked using contains() method:

```
boolean c1 = even.contains(6);     //c1 = true
boolean c2 = even.contains(10);    //c2 = false
```

To obtain an array containing all of the elements of a set, we use `toArray()` method:

```
Object[] a = even.toArray();
```

The method `remove()` is used to remove the specified element.

```
even.remove(4);//{0, 2, 6, 8}
```

It returns `true` if set contains element or `false` otherwise. To remove all elements, we use the bulk operation `clear()`.

```
even.clear();  //{}
```

Let us now use some of the bulk operations to perform mathematical set operations such as union, intersection, set difference etc. For this purpose, we create two sets as follows:

```
Set s1 = new HashSet(Arrays.asList(1, 2, 3));
Set s2 = new HashSet(Arrays.asList(2, 3, 4, 5));
```

The union of these two sets may then be obtained as follows:

```
Set s3 = new HashSet(s1);  //s3 = {1, 2, 3}
s3.addAll(s2);             //s3 = {1, 2, 3, 4, 5}
```

In the first statement, s3 contains all the elements of s1. In the second statement, all elements of s2 are added to s3 using `addAll()` method.The intersection of s1 and s2 is obtained as follows:

```
s3 = new HashSet(s1);      //s3 = {1, 2, 3}
s3.retainAll(s2);          //s3 = {2, 3}
```

The `retainAll()` method keeps only the elements that are contained in the specified collection. In other words, it removes from this collection all of its elements that are not contained in the specified collection. Similarly, the set difference is obtained as follows:

```
s3 = new HashSet(s1);      //s3 = {1, 2, 3}
s3.removeAll(s2);          //s3 = {1}
```

This implementation is not thread-safe. So, explicit synchronization is needed if multiple threads access a `HashSet` concurrently. Alternatively a synchronized version may be obtained using `Collections.synchronizedSet()` method as follows:

```
Set syncSet = Collections.synchronizedSet(new HashSet());
```

5.4.1.2 LinkedHashSet

Although `Set` interface does not mandate any iteration order, the chaotic ordering provided by `HashSet` may be avoided using `LinkedHashSet` implementation. It is an extension to `HashSet` and uses linked list and hash table internally. It provides the predictable iteration order without incurring the increased cost associated with `TreeSet`. An ordered copy of a specified set may be created using this class as follows:

```
Set aSet = …;
Set orderedSet = new LinkedHashSet(s);
```

This class provides all operations of `Set` interface and has an effect similar to `HashSet` implementation. As it maintains a linked list, it exhibits slightly slower performance than `HashSet`. However, iteration time for a `LinkedHashSet` is proportional to the size of the set, not to its capacity. Note that iteration time for a `HashSet` is proportional to the capacity and is likely to be longer than `LinkedHashSet`.

This implementation is not also thread-safe. Fortunately, Java provides a synchronized version which may be obtained as follows:

```
Set syncSet = Collections.synchronizedSet(new LinkedHashSet());
```

5.4.2 SortedSet

This is an extended interface of `Set` and provides a total ordering on its elements. The elements are arranged according to natural ordering. A Comparator may also be supplied if custom ordering is required. It provides several other methods related to elements ordering.

5.4.2.1 TreeSet

As its name implies, it is a tree-based implementation of `SortedSet` and provides guaranteed log(n) time cost for the basic operations such as `add()`, `remove()` and `contains()`. Like other collection interfaces, it also defines a constructor that takes a `Collection` object.

```
SortedSet ss = new TreeSet(Arrays.asList(2,3,5));   //{2,3,5}
```

This creates an ordered set of three elements with 2 as the first and 5 as the last. These elements can be checked using the following:

```
Object fe = ss.first(); //fe = 2
Object le = ss.last();  //le = 5
```

The `add()` method adds the specified element in tree such that the resultant set remains sorted.

```
ss.add(1);  //ss = {1, 2, 3, 5}
ss.add(4);  //ss = {1, 2, 3, 4, 5}
```

A sorted subset may be obtained using any one of the methods `headSet()`, `tailSet()` and `subSet()`. The `headSet()` returns a view of the portion of this set whose elements are strictly less than the specified element. The `tailSet()` does similar except that it considers the relation 'greater'.

```
SortedSet s1 = ss.headSet(3); //s1 = {1, 2}
SortedSet s2 = ss.tailSet(3); //s2 = {3, 4, 5}
```

The `subSet()` returns a view of the portion of this set whose elements range from the first argument (inclusive), to the second argument (exclusive).

```
SortedSet s3 = ss.subSet(2, 5); //s3 = {2, 3, 4}
```

Note that they do not create any copy. So changes in the original set are reflected in this set, and vice versa.

Note that this implementation is not synchronized. If multiple threads access a tree set concurrently, and at least one of the threads modifies the set, it must be synchronized externally. The easiest way is to use static `synchronizedSortedSet()` method of `Collection` class during creation time:

```
    SortedSet s = Collections.synchronizedSortedSet(new
TreeSet(Arrays.asList(2,3,5)));
```

5.4.3 List

One of the commonly used collection type is `List`. Unlike sets, lists are ordered collection and allow duplicate elements. It defines additional methods for positional (indexed) access to list elements, beyond those specified in the `Collection` interface. List indices start from zero. In addition to normal `Iterator`, `List` interface provides a special iterator, called a `ListIterator`, that allows element insertion and replacement, and bidirectional access. It also provides a method to obtain an iterator that starts at a specified index in the list.

Java provides two implementations of this interface: `ArrayList` and `LinkedList` [Figure 5.3:].

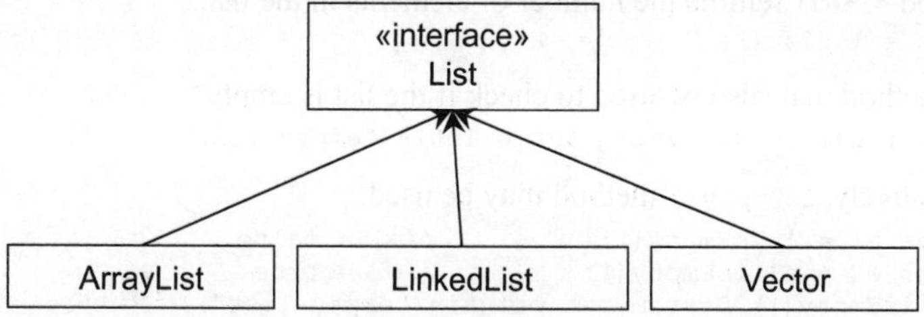

Figure 5.3: List implementations

5.4.3.1 ArrayList

It is a resizable array implementation of `List` interface and is roughly equivalent to `Vector`. Each `ArrayList` instance has a capacity which is always at least as large as the number of elements present. As elements are added and removed, its capacity grows or shrinks automatically. To reduce incremental reallocation, a high capacity may be specified using `ensureCapacity()` adding large number of elements.

Like other collection implementations, `ArrayList` also has multiple constructors that give us the flexibility to create instances in different ways.

```
List el = new ArrayList();                          //empty list
List l = new ArrayList(Arrays.asList(2,3));        //l = 2->3
List l1 = new ArrayList(10);                       //empty, initial capacity 10
```

Since, a `List` is an ordered collection, in addition to the inherited method `add()` that appends the specified element to the end of a list, it provides an overloaded version that inserts the specified element at the specified position.

```
l.add(2);                   //append, l = 2->3->2
l.add(2, 4);                //insert 4 at index 2, l = 2->3->4->2
```

List also allows us to retrieve an element from the specified position. The following retrieves the element from index 1.

```
Object o1 = l.get(1);       //o1 = 3
```

A normal iterator may be used to traverse the entire list. In addition, the `listIterator()` method returns a `ListIterator` that allows bidirectional traversal of the list, inserting/deleting elements during traversal etc. A `ListIterator` has a cursor which is positioned between elements. The elements before and after the cursor are returned by the call of `previous()` and `next()` methods respectively.

```
ListIterator li = l.listIterator();     //sets cursor at the begining
while(li.hasNext()) System.out.print(li.next()+" ");
```

It prints

```
2->3->4->2
```

This time the cursor is set at the end of the list. The following traverses the list in the backward direction:

```
while(li.hasPrevious()) System.out.print(li.previous()+" ");
```

It prints

```
2->4->3->2
```

Like `SortedSet`, `List` also provides a method to view the portion of this list between start index (inclusive) and end index (exclusive).

```
List sl = l.subList(1, 3);    //sl = 3->4
```

Note that any non-structural changes in the returned list are reflected in this list, and vice versa. The method `size()` returns the number of elements in the list:

```
int sz = l.size();    //sz = 4
```

This method may also be used to check if the list is empty:

```
if(el.size() == 0) System.out.println("empty list");
```

Alternatively, `isEmpty()` method may be used:

```
boolean e1 = l.isEmpty();          //e1 = false
boolean e2 = el.isEmpty();         //e2 = true
if(l1.isEmpty()) System.out.println("empty list");
```

Two versions exist to remove elements; one that removes an element from the specified index and one that removes specified element.

```
l.remove(2);                    //remove element from index 2, l = 2->3->2
l.remove(new Integer(3));  //remove the element 2, l = 2->2
```

Also two versions exist to find the position of a given element in the list. They return the index of the first occurrence and last occurrence of the specified element.

```
int first = l.indexOf(2);         //first = 0;
int last = l.lastIndexOf(2);      //last = 1;
```

An element at the specified position in this list may be replaced with the specified element using `set()` method:

```
l.set(0, 4);              //l = 4->2
```

To remove all elements, we use the bulk operation `clear()`.

```
l.clear();                //remove all, l =
```

This implementation is not also thread-safe. The synchronized version may be obtained as follows:

```
List syncList = Collections.synchronizedList(new ArrayList());
```

5.4.3.2 LinkedList

This class implements two collection interfaces, `List` and `Deque` and provides all operations of these two interfaces. Internally uses doubly linked list. So, some operations execute in time proportional to the index value. The usage of LinkedList is similar to ArrayList. The Deque specific operations are described in the following section.

This implementation is not also thread-safe. To get the synchronized version, the following code may be used:

```
List syncList = Collections.synchronizedList(new LinkedList());
```

5.4.4 Queue

It is a collection to hold elements prior to processing. Like `List`, it also represents an ordered collection of elements. Queues implementations can order elements in FIFO (queue), LIFO (stack) and priority basis. These implementations generally do not accept null elements.

Queue provides two forms of methods for inserting, deleting and inspecting elements. One form throws an exception if the operation fails. The other form returns a special value such as null or false, depending on the operation. A summary of basic queue operations is shown in Table 5.1:

Table 5.1: Queue methods

	Methods throwing exception	Methods return special value
Insert	add(e)	offer(e)
Delete	remove()	poll()
Inspect	element()	peek()

Java provides two implementations of this interface: `LinkedList` and `PriorityQueue` [Figure 5.4:].

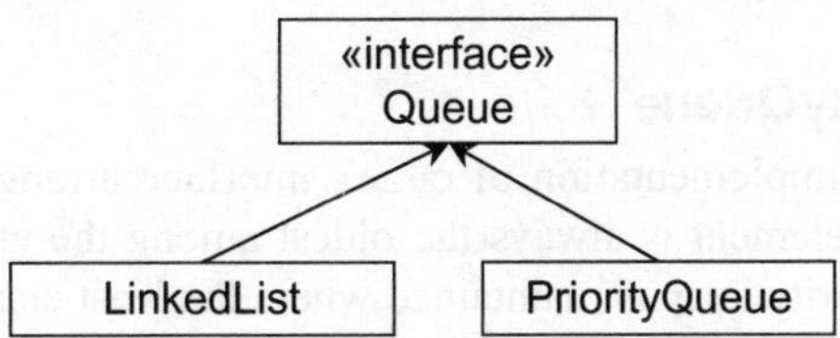

Figure 5.4: Queue implementations

5.4.4.1 LinkedList

Note that `LinkedList` implements two collection interfaces `List` and `Queue`. This section only describes the functionality of `LinkedList` with respect to `Queue`. `LinkedList` has two constructors: zero argument constructor that constructs an empty queue and other constructs a queue containing the elements of the specified collection.

```
Queue empty = new LinkedList();                    //empty queue
Queue q = new LinkedList(Arrays.asList(1,3));      //q = 1->3
```

The queue q has only two elements with 1 at the front and 3 at the rear end. Other elements may be added using either of the two methods, `add()` or `offer()`. The following code adds two elements.

```
q.add(5);          //q = 1->3->5
q.offer(7);        //q = 1->3->5->7
```

Note that elements are added at the rear end of the queue. The `add()` method returns true on success and throws an exception otherwise. The `offer()` method returns true on success and false otherwise. The latter is generally preferable as `add()` behaves differently for success and failure situations. Since, LinkedList is a collection, its elements may be inspected using iterator or for-each loop:

```
for(Object o:q) System.out.print(o+" ");
```

or

```
Iterator i = q.iterator();
while(i.hasNext()) System.out.print(i.next()+" ");
```

Both print all the elements in the queue as follows:

```
1 3 5 7
```

Like adding elements, there are two forms of methods for deleting elements:

```
q.remove();              //q = 3->5->7
q.poll();                //q = 5->7
```

Note that elements are deleted from a queue from the front end. It also provides two methods that return the element at the head of the queue without removing it from the queue.

```
Object e = q.element(); //e = 5
Object e1 = q.peek();   //e1 = 5
```

Although a queue orders elements in FIFO order, a LIFO ordered queue (i.e. stack) may be created as follows:

```
Queue lifo = Collections.asLifoQueue(new LinkedList());
```

Elements are removed in the opposite order they were added in.

```
lifo.add(1);
lifo.add(2);
lifo.add(3);
lifo.add(4);

int m1 = (int)lifo.remove();     //m1 = 4
int m2 = (int)lifo.remove();     //m2 = 3
```

5.4.4.2 PriorityQueue

The `LinkedList` implementation of `Queue` interface arranges elements in FIFO order. This means that the head element is always the oldest among the elements present. In PriorityQueue implementation a priority heap is maintained where the least element always sits at the top (head). Element's class must implement `Comparable` interface which has comparison method `compareTo()`. The elements are compared using `comparedTo()` method and least element sits at the top (head) of the heap. So, head element is always the least among all the elements.

Note that `PriorityQueue` does not specify how other elements are exactly stored in heap. It only ensures that head element is always the least element.

Like other collection implementations, it also provides various constructors:

```
Queue empty = new PriorityQueue(); //empty queue
Queue q = new PriorityQueue(Arrays.asList(7,4,5)); //4 is at head
```

Elements are added using add() or offer() methods. However, it always ensures that least element sits at the head.

```
q.add(3);    //3 is at head
q.add(6);    //3 is still at head
q.offer(2); //2 is at head
```

Note that the iterator returned by the iterator() method does not ensure that elements are traversed in any particular order. So, resultant sequence may not be sorted in natural order.

```
Iterator i = q.iterator();
while(i.hasNext()) System.out.print(i.next()+" ");
```

The above code prints a sample sequence as `2 4 3 7 6 5`. The heap is rearranged after every delete operation:

```
Object o1 = q.remove(); //o1 = 2, 3 is at head now
Object o2 = q.poll();    //o2 = 3, 4 is at head now
```

The head element may be inspected using `element()` or `peek()` methods:

```
Object e = q.element(); //e = 4
Object e1 = q.peek();    //e1 = 4
```

5.4.5 Map

This interface models a set of key-value pairs. The keys are unique and each key corresponds to one value. For example, we may have a collection of login-password pair. The password may be stored/retrieved for a given login. `Map` defines necessary methods such as `put()`, `get()` for this purpose. It also defines other methods such as `remove()`, `containsKey()`, `containsValue()`, `size()`, `isEmpty()` etc.

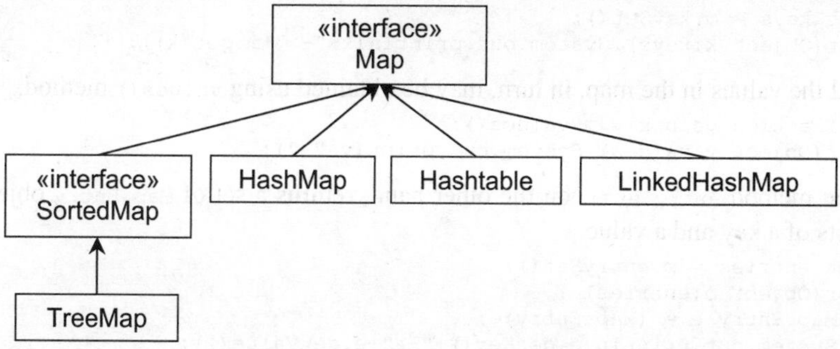

Figure 5.5: Map implementations

The Java provides three general-purpose implementations: `HashMap`, `LinkedHashMap`, and `TreeMap` [Figure 5.5:].

5.4.5.1 HashMap

It implements `Map` interface and provides all map operations. Internally uses hash table and allows null key and value.

The advantage of `HashMap` is that it offers constant time [i.e. O(1)] performance for operations such as `add()`, `remove()`, `contains()` and `size()`. However, iteration time is proportional to the sum of number of key-value pairs present and number of buckets. So, if iteration time is important, number of buckets should not be very high (load factor should not be very small).

Each `HashMap` object is characterized by two parameters: *capacity* and *load factor*. The capacity is the number of buckets in the hash table. The load factor controls when to rebuild the internal data structures.

It provides a number of constructors to create maps:

```
Map m = new HashMap();              //empty map
Map m1 = new HashMap(8);            //initial capacity 8
Map m2 = new HashMap(6, 1);         //initial capacity 6, load factor 1
Map m3 = new HashMap(m);            //m3 = m
```

Key-value pairs are inserted using put() method as follows:

```
m.put("uttam","uttam1");        //key="uttam", value="uttam1"
m.put("bibhas","bibhas1");      //key="bibhas", value="bibhas1"
m.put("parama","parama1");      //key="parama", value="parama"
```

Once the key-value pairs are stored, the value corresponding to a key may be retrieved using the `get()` method specifying the key.

```
String p1 = (String)m.get("uttam"); //p1 = "uttam1"
String p2 = (String)m.get("parama");//p2 = "parama1"
```

There are convenient methods like `containsKey()` and `containsValue()` which may be used to check the existence of any key or value.

```
boolean b1 = m.containsKey("uttam");        //b1 = true
boolean b2 = m.containsKey("banhi");        //b2 = false
boolean b3 = m.containsValue("bibhas1");    //b3 = true
boolean b4 = m.containsValue("samiran");    //b4 = false
```

There are three ways to view the key-value collection in the map: as a set of keys, collection of values and set of key-value entries. The method `keySet()` returns a set of all keys which may be used to retrieve corresponding values.

```
Set keys = m.keySet();
for(Object k:keys) System.out.println(k+"->"+m.get(k));
```

All the values in the map, in turn, may be obtained using `values()` method.

```
Collection values = m.values();
for(Object v:values) System.out.print(v+" ");
```

The method `entrySet()`, on the other hand, returns a set of `Map.Entry` objects each of which consists of a key and a value.

```
Set entries = m.entrySet();
for(Object o:entries) {
  Map.Entry e = (Map.Entry)o;
  System.out.println(e.getKey()+"->"+e.getValue());
}
```

Another common operation is to remove mappings which is done using `remove()` method that removes the entry corresponding to the specified key. Here is an example:

```
m.remove("uttam"); //removes entry for the key "uttam"
```

The method `clear()` removes all the entries from the map.

```
m.clear();
```

The following is an application of `HashMap` that generates a frequency table of the characters found in the specified file pass as a command line argument.

```
import java.io.*;
import java.util.*;
public class CharacterCount {
  public static void main(String[] args) throws Exception {
    Map m = new HashMap();
    FileInputStream fis = new FileInputStream(new File(args[0]));
    while (fis.available() > 0) {
      char a = (char) fis.read();
      Integer freq = (Integer)m.get(a);
      m.put(a, (freq == null) ? 1 : freq + 1);
    }
    Set keys = m.keySet();
    for(Object k:keys) System.out.println(k+"->"+m.get(k));
  }
}
```

Java also provides another hash based Map implementation: `Hashtable`. Although `Hashtable` and `HashMap` are functionally similar, there are subtle differences. For example, `HashMap` is not thread-safe while `Hashtable` is a thread-safe collection. However, `HashMap` exhibits better performance in a single-threaded environment than `Hashtable`. In mult-threaded environment, a synchronized version of map may be obtained as follows:

```
Map syncMap = Collections.synchronizedMap(new HashMap());
```

Alternatively, we may use `java.concurrent.ConcurrentHashMap` which is thread-safe version of `HashMap`. It is more scalable and performs better than synchronized `HashMap` in multi-threaded environment. However, in single-threaded environment HashMap is slightly better.

5.4.5.2 LinkedHashMap

Note that `Map` interface does not mandate any iteration order. The `HashMap` implementation does not also ensure any ordering. This chaotic ordering is not sometimes desirable and may be avoided using `LinkedHashMap` implementation. It extends `HashMap` and uses a doubly linked list and hash table internally. It provides the predictable iteration order. An ordered copy of a specified map may be created using this class as follows:

```
Map aMap = ...
Map orderedMap = new LinkedHashMap(aMap);
```

This class provides all operations of `Map` interface and has an effect similar to `HashMap` implementation. As it maintains a linked list, it exhibits slightly slower performance than `HashMap`. However, iteration time for a `LinkedHashMap` is proportional to the size of the map, not to its capacity. Note that iteration time for a `HashMap` is proportional to the capacity and is likely to be longer than `LinkedHashMap`.

This implementation is not also thread-safe. Fortunately, Java provides a synchronized version which may be obtained as follows:

```
Map syncSet = Collections.synchronizedMap(new LinkedHashMap());
```

5.4.6 SortedMap

This is a sub-interface of `Map` and models sorted maps where entries are ordered with respect to key in natural ordering or using a `Comparator` specified during map creation. It defines some operation meaningful for sorted maps such as `firstKey()`, `lastKey()`, `headMap()`, `tailMap()` etc.

5.4.6.1 TreeMap

It is a red-black tree implementation of `SortedMap` which is a sub interface of `Map`. It takes `log2(n)` time for `get()`, `put()`, `remove()` and `containsKey()` methods. It provides several constructors:

```
SortedMap sm = new TreeMap();         //empty map
SortedMap sm1 = new TreeMap(sm);      //create from existig sorted map
```

A sorted map may also be created from an ordinary unsorted map as follows:

```
Map m = new HashMap();              //unsorted map
m.put("uttam","uttam1");            //add some entries
m.put("bibhas","bibhas1");
m.put("parama","parama1");
m.put("samiran","samiran1");

sm = new TreeMap(m); //get sorted from unsorted one
```

The methods entrySet(), keyset() and values() give the sorted view when iterating over the map.

```
Set keys = sm.keySet();
for(Object k:keys) System.out.println(k+"->"+sm.get(k));
```

This results in the following result:

```
bibhas->bibhas1
parama->parama1
samiran->samiran1
uttam->uttam1
```

The two special keys—the lowest (first) and the highest (last) keys are obtained as follows:

```
String k1 = (String)sm.firstKey(); //k1 = "bibhas"
String k2 = (String)sm.lastKey();  //k2 = "uttam"
```

Analogous to `HashSet`, the head and tail views may be retrieved as:

```
SortedMap hm = sm.headMap("samiran"); //hm = {bibhas=bibhas1, parama=parama1}
SortedMap tm = sm.tailMap("samiran"); //tm = {samiran=samiran1, uttam=uttam1}
```

5.5 ALGORITHMS

Like `Arrays` class which has various methods for manipulating arrays, `Collections` class provides several static methods to perform common collection operations such as sorting, searching etc. Most of these methods operate on `List` objects, except a few which operate on arbitrary `Collection` objects. The following sections briefly describe how to use these methods.

5.5.1 Sorting

Java provides two classes `TreeSet` and `TreeMap` for sorted sets and maps. However, there is no implementation for sorted list. Sorting of a List is done with the `sort()` method.

The `sort()` method arranges the elements of a `List` instance according to an ordering relationship. This method uses a slightly optimized stable merge sort algorithm. Its one form takes a `List` instance and arranges its elements according to natural ordering. The following sorts a list of integers and prints its elements:

```
List l = new ArrayList(Arrays.asList(3, 5, 4, 2, 3, 2, 1, 3));
Collections.sort(l);        //increasing order
System.out.println("Increasing order\n"+l);
```

This program segment merely demonstrates how to use collection algorithms. The element's class must implement `Comparable` interface. This is mandatory since this version of `sort()` uses element's `compareTo()` method to compare them. Otherwise a `ClassCastException` will be thrown. A sample output of the above code segment looks like this:

```
Increasing order
[1, 2, 2, 3, 3, 3, 4, 5]
```

5.5.1.1 Custom Sort

The other form takes a `Comparator` in addition to a `List` and sorts the elements with the `Comparator`. This version is useful if an ordering (e.g. decreasing order) other than natural ordering is required or the element's class does not implement `Comparable` interface. For custom ordering, we first create a class that implements the `Comparator` interface which has single method `compare()`.

```
class IntegerComparator implements Comparator {
  public int compare(Object o1, Object o2) {
    return (Integer)o2 - (Integer)o1;
  }
}
```

The `compare()` method is implemented according to the desired ordering. The above class is capable of comparing two integers in such a way that they may be arranged in decreasing order. We can then sort a given list in decreasing order as:

```
Collections.sort(l, new IntegerComparator());//decreasing order
System.out.println("Decreasing order\n"+l);
```

Alternatively, we can define an unnamed Comparator class and use it as follows:

```
Collections.sort(l, new Comparator() {
      public int compare(Object o1, Object o2) {
        return (Integer)o2 - (Integer)o1;
      }});  //decreasing order
System.out.println("Decreasing order\n"+l);
```

A sample output of the above code segment look like this:

```
Decreasing order
[5, 4, 3, 3, 3, 2, 2, 1]
```

5.5.2 Shuffling

The opposite of sort is shuffle which arranges list elements arbitrarily. Shuffling is sometimes necessary such as generating test cases, data for games etc. using a default or a specified source of randomness. Two versions of `shuffle()` method exist. One operates on a `List` using a default source of randomness.

```
Collections.shuffle(l);
System.out.println("After Shuffling\n"+l);
```

This traverses the list backwards and swaps the current element with a randomly selected element whose position is selected from first to the current position, inclusive. When executed, it produced the following list:

```
After Shuffling
[5, 3, 1, 4, 2, 2, 3, 3]
```

The other form of `shuffle()` requires a `Random` object to be specified explicitly.

```
Collections.shuffle(l, new Random());
```

5.5.3 Manipulation

In addition to sorting and shuffling, `Collections` class also provides a set of methods for manipulating lists in different ways.

5.5.3.1 Reversing

The method `reverse()` reverses the order of the elements in the specified list. The following pair of statements sorts an array in decreasing order:

```
Collections.sort(l);
Collections.reverse(l);
```

The final list will look like this:

```
[5, 4, 3, 3, 3, 2, 2, 1]
```

5.5.3.2 Swapping

The `swap()` method swaps elements of two specified positions of a specified list. The following is equivalent to reversing a list.

```
int sz = l.size();
for(int i=0;i<sz/2;i++)
  Collections.swap(l, i, sz-1-i);
```

5.5.3.3 Copying

The `copy()` method copies all elements of a specified source list to another specified destination list.

```
Collections.copy(l1, l);
```

It copies all elements of l to l1. Note that the size of l1 must be at least equal to the size of l. Other elements, if any, of l1 are not affected.

5.5.3.4 Filling

For re-initialization, `fill()` method may be used. It replaces all of the elements of the specified list with the specified element.

```
Collections.fill(l1,0);
```

This puts a 0 in every position of the list l1.

5.5.3.5 Adding

The `addAll()` method operates on Collection. It adds all of the specified elements to the specified collection. The following adds three integers to the list l1.

```
Collections.addAll(l1, -1, -2, -3);
```

5.5.4 Searching

Searching an element in a collection of elements is common in many programs. The `binarySearch()` method searches the specified list for the specified object. As its name implies, it uses binary search algorithm which requires the list to be sorted prior to use in this algorithm. The behaviour of this algorithm is not defined if it is applied on an unsorted list. It is common to use `sort()` method to sort the List before a call to `binarySearch()`.

It also has two versions: one takes a List and an element to look for and assumes that the List is sorted in ascending order according to the natural ordering. The following are some examples:

```
Collections.sort(l);                          //l=[1, 2, 2, 3, 3, 3, 4, 5]
int in = Collections.binarySearch(l, 4); //in = 6
in = Collections.binarySearch(l, 2);     //in = 1
in = Collections.binarySearch(l, 3);     //in = 3
```

For unsuccessful search, it returns a value (-(insertion point) - 1), where the insertion point is the point at which the value would be inserted into the list.

```
in = Collections.binarySearch(l, 0);     //in = -1
```

So, if the element is not present, it may be inserted using the following:

```
if(in < 0) l.add(-in-1, 0);                //l=[0, 1, 2, 2, 3, 3, 3, 4, 5]

in = Collections.binarySearch(l, 6);   //in = -10
if(in < 0) l.add(-in-1, 6);              //l=[1, 2, 2, 3, 3, 3, 4, 5, 6]
```

5.5.5 Finding Extreme values

The `max()` and `min()` return the maximum and minimum element of the specified list respectively.

```
int min = (int)Collections.min(l);          //min = 0
int max = (int)Collections.max(l);          //max = 6
```

5.5.6 Counting frequency

The `frequency()` method operates on general `Collection`. It returns the number of occurrences of a specified element in the specified collection.

```
int fre = Collections.frequency(l,2);              //fre = 2
fre = Collections.frequency(l,3);                  //fre = 3
```

The following program prints the frequency table of characters of the specified file.

```
import java.util.*;
import java.io.*;
public class FrequencyCount {
  public static void main(String args[]) throws Exception {
    List l = new ArrayList();
    FileInputStream fis = new FileInputStream(new File(args[0]));
    while (fis.available() > 0)
      l.add((char) fis.read());

    for(char c = 'A';c<='z';c++)
    System.out.println(c+" "+Collections.frequency(l,c));
  }
}
```

KEYWORDS

Algorithms—A set of static methods to perform common collection operations such as sorting, searching etc.

ArrayList—A resizable array implementation of `List` interface

Collection—A container that encapsulates multiple objects into a single unit

HashMap—It implements `Map` interface and provides all map operations. Internally uses hash table and allows null key and value

HashSet—This class is a hash-based implementation of Set interface and offers constant time performance for certain operations

LinkedHashMap—It extends `HashMap` and uses a doubly linked list and hash table internally, providing the predictable iteration order

LinkedHashSet—It is an extension to `HashSet` and uses linked list and hash table internally and provides the predictable iteration order without incurring the increased cost associated with `TreeSet`.

LinkedList—A class that implements two collection interfaces, `List` and `Deque` and provides all operations of these two interfaces.

List—An interface that models an ordered collection and can contain duplicate elements.

Map—It represents key-value pairs where keys are unique and each key can map to at most one value

PriorityQueue—The `LinkedList` implementation of `Queue` interface arranges elements in FIFO order.

Queue—This interface models queue where elements are added and removed in a specific order, typically in a first-in-first-out (FIFO) manner.

Set—An interface that models the mathematical set that contains an unordered collection of objects without any duplicates

SortedMap—This is a sub-interface of `Map` and models sorted maps where entries are ordered with respect to key

SortedSet—An extended interface of `Set` and provides a total ordering on its elements

TreeSet—A tree based implementation of `SortedSet` and provides guaranteed log(n) time cost for the basic operations

TreeMap—It is a red-black tree implementation of `SortedMap`.

SUMMARY

In version 1.2, Java provided a unified architecture, known as collection framework for representing and manipulating aggregate objects. All collections frameworks primarily contains three parts: interfaces, implementation and algorithms. The root interface in the hierarchy is Collection that defines primitive operations on collections interface. Other commonly used interfaces are, Set, List, Queue, Map etc.

Java provides three general-purpose implementations for Set interface: HashSet, LinkedHashSet and TreeSet. The HashSet is a hash-based implementation and offers constant time performance for certain operations. LinkedHashSet is an extension to HashSet and uses linked list and hash table internally and avoids the chaotic ordering. The TreeSet is tree based implementation and provides guaranteed log(n) time cost for the basic operations.

One of the commonly used collection type is List. Unlike sets, lists are ordered collection and allow duplicate elements. Java provides two implementations of this interface: ArrayList and LinkedList. It is a resizable array implementation of List interface and is roughly equivalent to Vector. The LinkedList class implements two collection interfaces, List and Deque and provides all operations of these two interfaces. Internally uses doubly linked list.

It is a collection to hold elements prior to processing. Like List, it also represents an ordered collection of elements. Java provides two implementations of this interface: LinkedList and PriorityQueue. The LinkedList implementation of Queue interface arranges elements in FIFO order. This means that the head element is always the oldest among the elements present.

The Map interface models a set of key-value pairs. The keys are unique and each key corresponds to one value. The Java provides three general-purpose implementations: HashMap, LinkedHashMap, and TreeMap.

The HashMap internally uses hash table and allows null key and value. The LinkedHashMap extends HashMap and uses a doubly linked list and hash table internally and avoids chaotic ordering. The TreeMap is a red-black tree implementation of SortedMap which is a sub interface of Map. It takes log2(n) time for get(), put(), remove() and containsKey() methods.

Collections class provides several static methods to perform common collection operations such as sorting, searching etc. Most of these methods operate on List objects, except a few which operate on arbitrary Collection objects.

WEB RESOURCES

http://docs.oracle.com/javase/7/docs/technotes/guides/collections/
The Collections Framework

http://www.digilife.be/quickreferences/PT/Java%20Collections%20Framework.pdf
Java Collections Framework

http://homepage.cs.uiowa.edu/~slonnegr/oosd/22Collections.pdf
Collection Framework

http://www.eecs.yorku.ca/course_archive/2011-12/W/2011/lectures/04%20The%20Java%20Collections%20Framework.pdf
Lecture 4. The Java Collections Framework

http://softeng.polito.it/slides/07-JavaCollections.pdf
Java Collection Framework

http://people.cs.aau.dk/~torp/Teaching/E01/Oop/handouts/collections.pdf
Collections in Java

http://www.tutorialspoint.com/java/java_collections.htm
Java Collections Framework

EXERCISES

Objective-type Questions

1. Which of these packages contains all the collection classes?
   (a) java.lang (c) java.net
   (b) java.util (d) java.awt

2. Which of these classes is not part of Java's collection framework?
   (a) Map (c) Stack
   (b) Array (d) Queue

3. Which of these interfaces is not a part of Java's collection framework?
   (a) List (c) SortedMap
   (b) Set (d) SortedList

4. Which of these methods deletes all the elements from invoking collection?
   (a) clear() (c) delete()
   (b) reset() (d) refresh()

5. What is Collection in Java?
   (a) A group of objects
   (b) A group of classes
   (c) A group of interfaces
   (d) None of the mentioned

6. What is the output of this program?

```
import java.util.*;
class Array {
  public static void main(String args[]) {
    int array[] = new int [5];
    for (int i = 5; i > 0; i--)
        array[5-i] = i;
    Arrays.fill(array, 1, 4, 8);
    for (int i = 0; i < 5 ; i++)
        System.out.print(array[i]);
  }
}
```

   (a) 12885 (c) 58881
   (b) 12845 (d) 54881

7. What is the output of this program?

```
import java.util.*;
class vector {
  public static void main(String args[]) {
    Vector obj = new Vector(4,2);
    obj.addElement(new Integer(3));
    obj.addElement(new Integer(2));
    obj.addElement(new Integer(5));
    obj.removeAll(obj);
    System.out.println(obj
                    .isEmpty());
  }
}
```

   (a) 0 (c) True
   (b) 1 (d) False

8. What is the output of this program?

```
import java.util.*;
class stack {
  public static void main(String args[]){
    Stack obj = new Stack();
    obj.push(new Integer(3));
    obj.push(new Integer(2));
    obj.pop();
    obj.push(new Integer(5));
   System.out.println(obj);
  }
}
```

(a) [3, 5] (c) [3, 2, 5]
(b) [3, 2] (d) [3, 5, 2]

9. What is the output of this program?

```
import java.util.*;
class hashtable {
  public static void main(String args[]) {
    Hashtable obj = new Hashtable();
    obj.put("A", new Integer(3));
    obj.put("B", new Integer(2));
    obj.put("C", new Integer(8));
    obj.remove(new String("A"));
    System.out.print(obj);

  }
}
```

(a) {C=8, B=2} (b) [C=8, B=2]
(c) {A=3, C=8, B=2} (d) [A=3, C=8, B=2]

10. What is the output of this program?

```
import java.util.*;
class Bitset {
  public static void main(String args[]) {
   BitSet obj = new BitSet(5);
   for (int i = 0; i < 5; ++i)
       obj.set(i);
   obj.clear(2);
   System.out.print(obj);
  }
}
```

(a) {0, 1, 3, 4} (c) {0, 1, 2, 3, 4}
(b) {0, 1, 2, 4} (d) {0, 0, 0, 3, 4}

11. Which of these interfaces declares core method that all collections will have?

(a) set (c) Comparator
(b) EventListner (d) Collection

12. Which of these interfaces handles sequences?

(a) Set (c) Comparator
(b) List (d) Collection

13. Which of these interfaces must contain a unique element?

(a) Set (c) Array
(b) List (d) Collection

14. Which of these is Basic interface that all other interfaces inherit?

(a) Set (c) List
(b) Array (d) Collection

15. What is the output of this program?

```
import java.util.*;
class Maps {
  public static void main(String args[]){
    TreeMap obj = new TreeMap();
    obj.put("A", new Integer(1));
    obj.put("B", new Integer(2));
    obj.put("C", new Integer(3));
    System.out.println(obj
                        .entrySet());
  }
}
```

(a) [A, B, C] (c) {A=1, B=2, C=3}
(b) [1, 2, 3] (d) [A=1, B=2, C=3]

16. What is the output of this program?

```
import java.util.*;
class Array {
  public static void main(String args[]){
    int array[] = new int [5];
    for (int i = 5; i > 0; i--)
        array[5 - i] = i;
    Arrays.sort(array);
    for (int i = 0; i < 5; ++i)
      System.out.print(array[i]);;
  }
}
```

(a) 12345 (c) 1234
(b) 54321 (d) 5432

17. Suppose you would like to create an instance of a new Map that has an iteration order that is the same as the iteration order of an existing instance of a Map. Which concrete implementation of the Map interface should be used for the new instance?

(a) TreeMap
(b) HashMap
(c) LinkedHashMap
(d) The answer depends on the implementation of the existing instance.

18. Which class does not override the equals() and hashCode() methods, inheriting them directly from class Object?

(a) String (c) StringBuffer
(b) Double (d) Character

19. Which collection class allows you to grow or shrink its size and provides indexed access to its elements, but whose methods are not synchronized?

(a) HashSet (c) List
(b) LinkedHashSet (d) ArrayList

20. You need to store elements in a collection that guarantees that no duplicates are stored and all elements can be accessed in natural order. Which interface provides that capability?
(a) Map (c) List
(b) Set (d) Collection

21. Which interface does java.util.Hashtable implement?
(a) Map (c) HashTable
(b) List (d) Collection

22. Which interface provides the capability to store objects using a key-value pair?
(a) Map (c) List
(b) Set (d) Collection

23. Which collection class allows you to associate its elements with key values, and allows you to retrieve objects in FIFO (first-in, first-out) sequence?
(a) ArrayList (c) HashMap
(b) LinkedHashMap (d) TreeMap

24. Which collection class allows you to access its elements by associating a key with an element's value, and provides synchronization?
(a) SortedMap (c) TreeSet
(b) TreeMap (d) Hashtable

Subjective-type Questions

1. What is Java Collections Framework? List out some benefits of Collections framework.
2. What are the basic interfaces of Java Collections Framework?
3. What is an Iterator?
4. What is the difference between Enumeration and Iterator interface?
5. What are the different ways to iterate over a list?
6. How does HashMap work in Java?
7. What are the different Collection views provided by Map interface?
8. What is the difference between HashMap and Hashtable?
9. How do you decide between HashMap and TreeMap?
10. What are the similarities and differences between ArrayList and Vector?
11. What is the difference between Array and ArrayList? When will you use Array over ArrayList?
12. What is the difference between ArrayList and LinkedList?
13. Which collection classes provide random access of its elements?
14. Which collection classes are thread-safe?
15. What are concurrent Collection Classes?
16. What is BlockingQueue?
17. What is Queue and Stack? List their differences.
18. What is Comparable and Comparator interface?
19. What is the difference between Comparable and Comparator interface?
20. How can we sort a list of Objects?
21. How can we create a synchronized collection from the given collection?
22. What are the common algorithms implemented in Collections Framework?

CHAPTER – 6

GENERIC PROGRAMMING

KEY OBJECTIVES

After completing this chapter readers will be able to—

- understand the purpose of Java generics
- write generic classes, interfaces and methods
- get an idea about type inference and type erasure
- use generic collections classes and interfaces
- understand bounded type parameter and different wildcards
- know the limitations of Java generics

6.1 INTRODUCTION

Bugs are inevitable in any software. However, careful programming can reduce them. Several extensions were added to JDK 1.5. One of these was Java generics, which helps us to detect more bugs at compile time and fix them then and there. This allows us simply to avoid some runtime errors and handling them prior to coming into play.

Generics allows us to write parameterized classes, interfaces and methods where parameters are type names. If you are already familiar with C++ templates, you'll soon realize that there are both similarities and important differences. If you are not familiar with lookalike constructs from elsewhere, don't worry, all the better; you can start afresh, without unlearning any misconceptions.

Although, the primary usage of generics is to abstract over types when working with collections, it is possible to write custom generic classes, interfaces and methods. The following section describes the basic problems the Java generics solve and how it solves the problem with the help of custom classes.

6.2 MOTIVATION

Since, `java.lang.Object` is top-level class in Java class hierarchy, it is possible to write general-purpose classes and methods that operate on `Object`. To understand this statement, consider the following class:

```
class Wrapper {
  Object o;
  void set(Object o) { this.o = o; }
  Object get() { return o; }
}
```

This class represents a general-purpose wrapper class. Since, internally it maintains a reference of type `Object`, which is the super class of all other types, it can hold arbitrary Java object. So, the following statement is valid:

```
Wrapper w = new Wrapper();
w.set(new String("abc"));
```

It creates a wrapper instance and stores a `String` object in it using its `add()` method. Since, any object may be added, and `get()` method returns it as an `Object` instance, it is necessary to type cast:

```
String s = (String)w.get();
```

Since, the wrapper indeed holds a `String` object, `Object` to `String` casting is correct. Compiler also remains silent as it observes that the statement is syntactically correct. However, the situation may not be as simple as above. A careless programmer (or by mistake), may write a statement as follows:

```
Integer x = (Integer)w.get();
```

Note that type of the object held is `String`. So, casting it to an `Integer` type is illegal. Although, Java can determine this anomaly at runtime and informs us by throwing a `ClassCastException`, there is no provision to determine it at compile time as there is no syntax error in the statement. Since, compiler only cares about syntax, it cannot restrict programmers from such incorrect type casting. Since, the above code still compiles, we wouldn't know anything is wrong until runtime.

It is also possible to keep different type of object at different time.

```
w.set(new String("xyz"));
w.set(new Integer(2));
```

The wrapper object, does not, anyway indicate that it is capable of holding specific type of objects. So, if we want to restrict the contained type to something specific (like `String`), our only option would be to specify the requirement in documentation. If the class had been a generic one, these mistakes could have been caught by the compiler and rectified then and there.

6.3 SOLUTION

Using Java's generics, lets rewrite our `Wrapper` class as follows.

```
class Wrapper <T> {
  T o;
  void set(T o) { this.o = o; }
  T get() { return o; }
}
```

Although, it introduces some new syntax, there is nothing to worry about. It is very much similar to our previous version except that it uses a *formal type parameter* `T`. All occurrences of `Object` have been substituted by `T`. The `<T>` after class name indicates that the class is a generic one. The type parameters can be used throughout the generic declaration in a way almost similar to that of ordinary types.

To refer to this generic type, we supply a concrete type name as argument.

```
Wrapper<String> w;
```

We specify the type argument (`String` in this case) within angular brackets. We might imagine that `Wrapper<String>` stands for a version of `Wrapper` where `T` has been uniformly replaced by `String`. However, it is misleading, because the declaration of a generic is never actually expanded in this way. In fact, during compilation, all generic information will be removed entirely using a process called *type erasure* which we shall discuss in detail later in this chapter.

Like any other variable declaration, the above line does not actually create a new object. It simply declares a reference to a `Wrapper<String>` (pronounced as "Wrapper of String"). To instantiate this class, the new keyword is used, as usual, along with the type name (may be omitted in some cases) within angular brackets between the class name and the parenthesis:

```
w = new Wrapper<String>();
```

We can also do these things in one line, such as:

```
Wrapper<String> w = new Wrapper<String>();
```

To understand the syntax of generic class declaration, you can compare it with method declaration. Remember that during a method declaration, we use formal parameters to hold actual arguments passed during method call. For example,

```
public static int add(int a, int b) {  // int a, int b are formal parameters
    return a + b ;
}
```

During the invocation, the formal parameters are substituted by the actual arguments. For example,

```
// method call: formal parameters substituted by actual arguments
int result = add(2, 3);   // 2 and 3 are actual arguments
```

Type parameters used in the class declaration have the same purpose as the formal parameters used in the method declaration. A class can use formal type parameters to receive type arguments. The type names used during instantiation are called *actual type arguments*. During instance creation, such as `Wrapper<String>`, all occurrences of the formal type parameter `T` are replaced by the actual type argument `String`.

Anyway, with this additional type information, compiler can perform type check during compile-time and ensure that there will be no runtime class cast error. Since, w is a kind of '`Wrapper` of `String`' now, only `String` objects can be stored in it.

```
w.set(new String("abc"));
```

Note that even if w is a generic instance, this syntax is exactly same as the previous one. However, any attempt to store an object other than `String` will result in a compilation error:

```
w.set(new Integer()); //compilation error
```

This wrapper is now targeted at only `String`, meaning only `String` instances can be stored into this wrapper. Accordingly, if we try to keep something else in it, the compiler will complain. The stored element may also be retrieved directly without a type cast as follows:

```
String s = w.get();
```

The compiler knows that this wrapper can only contain `String` instances, so casts are not necessary. An attempt to cast to a different type will also result in a compilation error alerting you to what previously would have been a runtime bug.

```
Integer i = (Integer)w.get();      //compilation error
```

Instead of relying on the programmer to keep track of object types and performing casts, which could lead to failures at runtime difficult to debug and solve, the compiler can help the programmer enforce a greater number of type checks and detect more failures at compile time.

Needless to say wrappers for other types (reference types only) may be created and used using the usual way as and when needed:

```
Wrapper<Integer> wi = new Wrapper<Integer>(); //wrapper of Integer
wi.set(new Integer(4));
Integer i = wi.get();
```

It is possible to make both classes and interfaces generic. A class or an interface is generic if it accepts one or more type parameters. In general, any number of type parameters may be specified. They are specified in angular brackets separated by comma (,) and follow the class (or the interface) name as follows:

```
class Pair <K, V> {/*...*/}
```

These parameters typically appear in the type's methods, either as the type method's parameter list or as the type of its return value.

```
class Pair <K, V> {
  void put(K k, V v);
  V get(K k) {/*...*/}
}
```

Here two type parameters `K` and `V` are introduced after the class name. Then K appears as the argument type of the `get()` and `put()` method and V appears as the return type of `get()` method.

This section simply demonstrates the fundamental concepts of Java generics. We shall discuss several other issues in subsequent sections. However, since Java generics is extensively used in collection framework, let us be quickly familiar with how to use generic collection classes and interfaces.

6.4 COLLECTION FRAMEWORK AND GENERICS

The primary usage of generics is to abstract over types when working with collections. In practice, we hardly write new generic types. However, we should recognize the syntax and learn how to use generics. Before generics, an example usage of collection class looks like this:

```
List l = new ArrayList();
l.add(new Integer(4));
Integer i = (Integer)l.get(0);
```

Look at the cast in the last line. Since, the `get()` method returns an `Object` instance, to assign it to a variable of type `Integer`, the cast is required.

However, the cast is annoying. It not only introduces clutter, but there is also a possibility of `ClassCastException` at run time due to wrong cast being used by mistake. Moreover, if we want to mark a list as being restricted to contain a particular data type, there is no provision before generics.

Most of the collection classes and interfaces including `List` have been upgraded using generics in Java 1.5 version. So, we can rewrite the above program fragment using generics:

```
List<Integer> intList = new ArrayList<Integer>();
intList.add(new Integer(4));
Integer i = intList.get(0);
```

Now, look at the way the variable `intList` has been declared. It is no longer a general list, but a '`List` of `Integer`', written as `List<Integer>`. Indeed the `List` is a generic interface whose declaration looks like:

```
public interface List<E> extends Collection<E> { /*...*/}
```

The type correctness of the program can be checked at compile-time now. When we declare `intList` as `List<Integer>` (i.e '`List` of `Integer`'), this holds true wherever and whenever it is used hereafter, and the compiler guarantees it. Since, `intList` can now contain only `Integer` objects, adding anything else will be a compilation error:

```
intList.add(new String("abc"));    //compilation error
```

Another interesting point is that the cast is no longer necessary. Java also introduces a new for loop to iterate generic lists:

```
for(Integer item : intList)
  System.out.println(item);
```

Similar to generic collection classes, most of the collection classes are also generic. One example of such a generic interface is `Comparable` which is written as:

```
package java.lang;
import java.util.*;
public interface Comparable<T> {
  public int compareTo(T o);
}
```

6.5 TYPE NAMING

Unlike ordinary variables, type variables are named by single uppercase letters. It helps us to differentiate type variables and ordinary class or interface name. The most commonly used type parameter names are:

```
T - Type
S,U,V etc. - 2nd, 3rd, 4th types
V - Value
E - Element (used extensively by the Java Collections Framework)
K - Key
N - Number
```

Table 6.1: summarizes some of the frequently used terms in generics:

Table 6.1: Terminologies in Java generics

Generic Term	Meaning
List<E>	Generic Type, E is called formal parameter
List<Integer>	Parameterized type, Integer is actual argument here
<T extends Comparable>	Upper-bounded type parameter
List<?>	Unbounded wildcard
<? extends T>	Bounded wildcard
<? super T>	Bounded wildcard
List	Raw type
<T extends Comparable<T>>	Recursive bounded type parameter

6.6 GENERIC METHODS AND CONSTRUCTORS

Like classes and interfaces, methods (including constructors) may use type parameters and are called *generic methods*. They are useful if we don't want to make the whole class generic. Generic methods may be a member of generic as well as non-generic classes. The following shows a generic method as part of non-generic class.

```
class X {
  static <T> void print(T t) {
    System.out.println(t.getClass().getName());
  }
}
```

This takes a single type parameter which appears before the return type. It prints the type information of the object passed to it. The type parameter's scope is limited to the method in which it's declared. We call this method like a normal method except that we specify the type parameter before the method name:

```
X.<Integer>print(new Integer(2));
X.<String>print(new String("aa"));
```

The type of object must be same or a subtype of type argument. The value of type parameter may be inferred from method parameter and may be omitted:

```
X.print(new Integer(2));
X.print(new String("aa"));
```

Like generic type, a generic method may take any number of type parameters. Both static and non-static generic methods are allowed. A non-static method may use class's type parameter (if any).

```
class Y <S> {
  <T> void print(S s, T t) {
    System.out.println(s.getClass().getName());
    System.out.println(t.getClass().getName());
  }
}
```

The complete syntax for invoking this method would be:

```
Y<Integer> y = new Y<Integer>();
y.<Integer, String>print(new Integer(2), new String("aa"));
```

However, since the type parameters may be inferred from method parameter, we may omit them:

```
y.print(new Integer(2), new String("aa"));
```

The following section describes more about type inference.

6.7 TYPE INFERENCE

Sometimes it is possible to find some type information automatically from the arguments passed to methods or constructors. This ability is known as *type inference* and may

- Determine the types of the arguments.
- Determine the type that the result is being assigned, or returned (if available).
- Find the most specific type that works with all of the arguments.

The following sections illustrate these.

6.7.1 Generic methods

Type inference sometimes allows us to invoke a generic method like an ordinary method. Consider the following example:

```
class A {
 static <T> void f(T t){};
}
```

The generic method `f()` defines one type parameter named `T`. Java compiler can infer the type argument even if it is not explicitly specified during method call.

```
A.f(2);                              //T is Integer
```

However, we can also specify the type argument explicitly:

```
A.<Integer>f(2);    //Explicit type argument, T is Integer
```

The method argument must be convertible to the explicit type argument. So, the following is correct:

```
A.<Number>f(2);     //OK, T is Number and Integer can be converted to Number
```

However, the following is not correct as `2` cannot be cast to `String`.

```
A.<String>f(2);    //Error, T is String, however Integer can't be cast to String
```

6.7.2 Constructors

Type inference is also possible for constructors. Consider the following class:

```
class X <T> {
  T t;
  <S>X(T t, S s) {}
}
```

The class `X` takes a single type parameter `T`. The constructor for `X` itself takes another type parameter and uses class's type parameter as well. Compiler can infer these type parameters from the constructor call:

```
new X<>("", 3);                              //T is String and S is Integer
```

We can also specify type argument for the class explicitly:

```
new X<String>("", 3);                        //T is String and S is Integer
new X<Object>("", 3);                        //T is Object and S is Integer
```

Both arguments may also be specified explicitly.

```
new <Integer>X<String>("", 3);               //T is String and S is Integer
new <Number>X<String>("", 3);                //T is String and S is Number
new <Integer>X<Object>("", 3);               //T is Object and S is Integer
new <Number>X<Object>("", 3);                //T is Object and S is Number
```

6.7.3 Classes

It is also possible to infer class's type argument even if constructor does not use it. Consider the following class:

```
class X <T> {
  <S>X(S s) {}
}
```

To help compiler to infer class's type argument, we use <> (called diamond) as follows:

```
X<Integer> x = new X<>("");                  //T is Integer, S is String
```

Note that to take advantage of type inference during generic class instantiation, we must use the diamond. Otherwise, the compiler generates an unchecked conversion warning:

```
X<Integer> x1 = new X("");      //warning
```

This happens because the constructor `X()` refers to the `X` raw type.

6.8 BOUNDED TYPE PARAMETERS

The generic classes or methods we have written may take any reference type arguments. For example, the `Wrapper` class can take arbitrary arguments:

```
Wrapper<Integer> wi;
Wrapper<Double> wd;
Wrapper<String> ws;
Wrapper<Exception> we;
Wrapper<Object> wo;
//...
```

However, if we want to restrict that `Wrapper` to only accept certain arguments, we specify it as *bounded type parameter*:

```
class Wrapper <T extends Number> {/*...*/}
```

This tells that the type argument to `Wrapper` can only be either `Number` or anything that extends `Number`. Note that, the keyword `extends` is used in a general sense to mean either `extends` for classes or `implements` for interfaces.

The generic type name is similar to unbounded generic type except that if we try to use any type that is not Number, it results in a compilation error.

```
Wrapper<String> ws;
Wrapper<Exception> we;
Wrapper<Object> wo;
```

The above types are now wrong as neither `String` nor `Exception` nor `Object` is a sub-type of `Number`. However, the following remains still valid:

```
Wrapper<Integer> wi;
Wrapper<Double> wd;
```

Bounded type parameters can be used with interfaces as well as methods.

```
interface MyIntf <T extends Number> {}
static <T extends Number> void printNumber(T t) {}
static <T extends Comparable<T>> int max(T a, T b) {/*...*/}
```

The interface `MyIntf` and the method `printNumber()` only take argument of type `Number` or its sub-type whereas `max()` takes argument of type `Comparable<T>` or its sub-type.

6.8.1 Multiple bounds

A type parameter may have more than one bound and is written as:

```
<T extends C & I1 & I2>
```

It means `T` must be a subtype of `C`, `I1` and `I2`. In general if multiple bounds are specified, the type variable must be a subtype of all listed bound types. If one of the bounds is a class, it must be specified first. Given the following types:

```
class C { /* ... */ }
interface I { /* ... */ }
```

The following bound specification is wrong as the class name is not specified first in the bound list.

```
<T extends I & C>
```

The correct one is:

```
<T extends C & I>
```

We can't have more than one class in multiple bounds. The following are some other examples:

```
<T extends C>                   //T has bound C
<T extends I>                   //T has bound I
<T extends C & I>               //T has bound C and I
<T, S extends C>                //T is unbounded, S has bound C
<T, S extends I>                //T is unbounded, S has bound I
<T, S extends C & I>            //T is unbounded, S has bound C and I
<T extends C, S>                //T has bound C, S is unbounded
<T extends I, S>                //T has bound I, S is unbounded
<T extends C & I, S>            //T has bound C and I, S is unbounded
<T extends C, S extends C>      //Both T and S have bound C
<T extends C, S extends I>      //T has bound C, S has bound I
<T extends I, S extends C>      //T has bound I, S has bound C
<T extends C & I, S extends C & I>      //Both T and S have bound C &
```

Note that Java does not allow us to use `super` keyword when declaring a bounded type parameter. So, the following is wrong:

```
class X <T super Number> {}
```

6.9 GENERICS AND SUB-TYPE

The sub-type and super-type relationships with respect to generics appear to be confusing to beginners. However, understanding them is important and clearly makes you better equipped to work with generics.

In Java, we know that a reference of type `T` may refer to an object of type `S` if `S` is either `T` or `S` is a sub-type of `T`. For example, an `Object` type reference can hold an `Object` or any of its sub-type object such as `Integer`.

```
Object oRef = new Object();              //oRef refers to an Object
String sRef = new String("Java");        //sRef refers to a String
oRef = sRef;                             //oRef now refers to a String
```

Similarly, the following is also valid as `Integer` and `Double` are sub-type of `Number`:

```
Number nRef = new Integer(2);          //nRef refers to an Integer
nRef = new Double(3.2);                //nRef now refers to a Double
```

The same is also true for generics.

```
List<Number> ln = new ArrayList<>();
ln.add(new Integer(2));
ln.add(new Double(3.2));
```

Since, `Integer` and `Double` are sub-type of `Number`, a list of `Number` may hold `Integer` as well as `Double` objects. However, `List<Integer>` is not a subtype of `List<Number>`. Consider the following example:

```
List<Integer> li = new ArrayList<Integer>();
ln = li;
```

Here we have created a `List` of `Integer` and assigned it to a `List` of `Number`. It seems to be obvious as – "a List of Integer is indeed a List of Number". But this is not correct in the generics world! [Figure 6.1:]

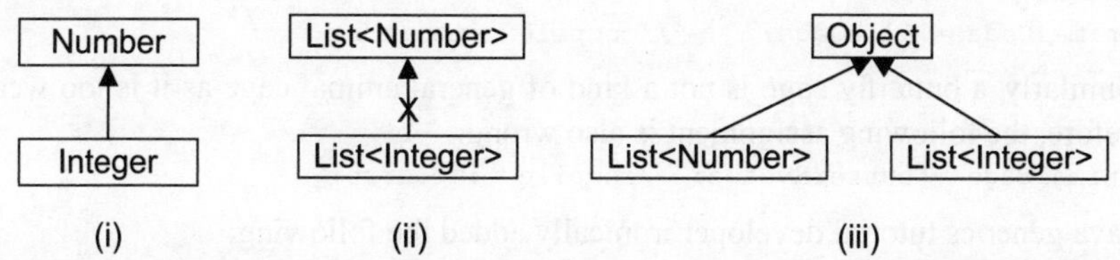

Figure 6.1: Generics and sub-typing (i) Integer is a sub-type of Number (ii) However, List<Integer> is not a sub-type of List<Number> (iii) Their common parent is Object

This piece of code does not compile because if it could have compiled we could add a `Double` object as follows:

```
ln.add(new Double(3.2));
```

This could have resulted in `ClassCastException` at runtime and type safety could not be achieved.

In general, given two concrete types `A` and `B`, `AClass<A>` has no relationship to `AClass<B>`, regardless of whether or not `A` and `B` are related. The common parent of `AClass<A>` and `AClass<B>`

is `Object`. To illustrate this, a beautiful example was given in Java's tutorial. We are also using that example to demonstrate this.

Consider the following type hierarchy:

```
class Animal {/*...*/}
class Lion extends Animal {/*...*/}
class Butterfly extends Animal {/*...*/}
```

Since, `Lion` and `Butterfly` are kind (sub-type) of `Animal`, either may be supplied when an `Animal` is required:

```
Animal a = new Lion();        //a refers to a lion
a = new Butterfly();          //a now refers to a butterfly
```

We know that lions are kept in lion cages (with bars strong enough to prevent the lions from going out):

```
List<Lion> lionCage = new ArrayList<Lion>();
lionCage.add(new Lion());
```

Similarly, butterflies are kept in cages whose bars need not be so strong but should be spaced closely enough to hold in the butterflies:

```
List<Butterfly> butterflyCage = new ArrayList<Butterfly>();
butterflyCage.add(new Butterfly());
```

Now, think about a cage of an animal.

```
List<Animal> animalCage = new ArrayList<Animal>();
```

Since, it is an animal cage, it should ideally be capable of keeping all animals including a lion and a butterfly. So, its bars should not only be strong, but also spaced closely. If such a cage really exists, it is possible to keep a lion as well as a butterfly together there.

```
animalCage.add(new Lion());
animalCage.add(new Butterfly());
```

Now, let us think about this question: "Is a lion cage a kind of animal cage? i.e. is `List<Lion>` a kind of `List<Animal>` or is `List<Butterfly>` a kind of `List<Animal>`". If we think critically, we shall find the answer as "no" in both cases. This is because ideally, if a lion cage could have been a kind of animal cage, we could keep butterflies there since a butterfly is also a kind of animal. However, bars of a lion cage are not close enough to prevent butterflies from escape. Therefore, the following assignment is wrong:

```
animalCage = lionCage;        //compile time error
```

Similarly, a butterfly cage is not a kind of general animal cage as it is too weak to keep lions. Therefore, the following assignment is also wrong:

```
animalCage = butterflyCage; //compile time error
```

Java generics tutorial developer ironically added the following:

Before generics, the animals could be kept in improper kinds of cages. As a result, it would be possible for them to escape.

6.10 WILDCARDS

So, how do you specify a "List of some kind of animal" syntactically? This is represented as:

```
List<? extends Animal> someAnimalCage;
```

and is read as "`List` *of unknown type which is either* `Animal` *or a sub-type of it*". So, for this type of cage, either a lion cage or a butterfly cage may be provided [Figure 6.2:].

```
someAnimalCage = lionCage;
someAnimalCage = butterflyCage;
```

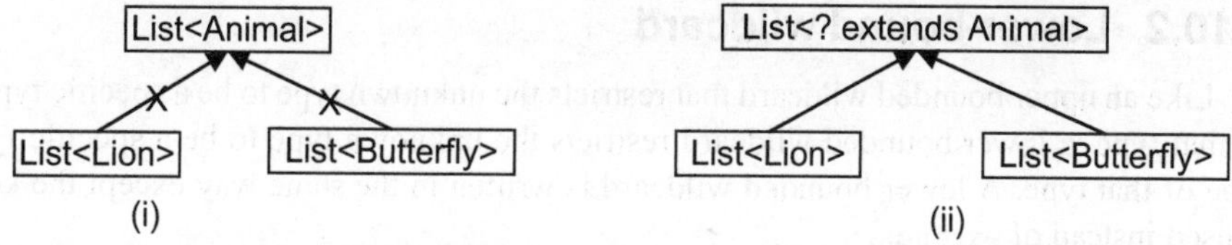

Figure 6.2: Wildcards (i) Without wildcard (ii) With wildcard

In generics, an unknown type is represented by the wildcard character "?". It may be used as the type of a parameter, field, or local variable. Although, it may be used as a return type, being more specific is better. However, the wildcard is never used as a type argument for a generic method invocation, a generic class instance creation, or a super type.

6.10.1 Upper-bound wildcard

Since, `<? extends Animal>` represents any type bounded by the type `Animal`, it is said to be *bounded wildcard* with the *upper bound* `Animal`.

Note that, the keyword `extends` is used in a general sense to mean either `extends` for classes or `implements` for interfaces.

However, we cannot add any lions or butterflies to this kind of cage. This is because, if `someAnimalCage` refers to a lion cage (bars are not so close) and if we put some butterflies there, they will fly away. Similarly, if `someAnimalCage` refers to a butterfly cage (bars are not so strong) and if we put some lions there, they will break the cage and escape. So the following are incorrect:

```
someAnimalCage.add(new Lion());
someAnimalCage.add(new Butterfly());
```

What will the usage of this kind of cage be then? Don't worry. Although, we cannot put anything (except null) there, we can still view its contents.

```
for(Animal an: someAnimalCage)
  an.free();    //assume that the Animal class has a method free()
```

Since, `someAnimalCage` contains `Animal` or any sub-type of `Animal`, it is safe to assign its elements to an `Animal` type variable.

A method may also use such upper-bounded wildcards.

```
static void f(List<? extends Animal> l) {/*...*/}
```

With this declaration, the method `f()` may be invoked supplying both `lionCage` as well as `butterflyCage`:

```
f(lionCage);          //OK
f(butterflyCage);     //OK
```

The method `f()` can access the list elements as type `Animal`:

```
static void f(List<? extends Animal> l) {
  for (Animal elem : l) {
    // ...
  }
}
```

Similarly, if we want to write the method that works on `List<Number>`, `List<Integer>`, `List<Double>`, `List<Float>` etc., we specify it as:

```
static void g(List<? extends Number> l) {/*...*/}
```

In general, for an "in" parameter that serves up data to the function, an upper-bounded wildcard is used.

6.10.2 Lower-bound wildcard

Like an upper bounded wildcard that restricts the unknown type to be a specific type or a subtype of that type, a lower bounded wildcard restricts the unknown type to be a specific type or a super type of that type. A lower bounded wildcard is written in the same way except the keyword `super` is used instead of `extends`.

```
List<? super Integer> list;
```

This represents a '`List` of *unknown type that is either* `Integer` *or any super type of it*'. The list type that this list can hold is `Integer` types. Consider the following lists:

```
List<Number> ln = new ArrayList<Number>();
List<Object> lo = new ArrayList<Object>();
List<Integer> li = new ArrayList<Integer>();
```

With this, the following are correct:

```
list = li;
list = ln;
list = lo;
```

Since, the list can hold an `Integer` type or any of it's super type object, it is always safe to add `Integer` objects to this list.

```
list.add(new Integer(2));
```

However, since we do know what type of list it actually is, list elements can be type cast to `Object` only:

```
for(Object o : list)
  System.out.println(o);
```

It is not possible to specify both upper bound and lower bound for a wildcard simultaneously.

6.10.3 Unbounded wildcard

Java generics also provides another kind of wildcard called *unbounded wildcard* and is represented as '?'. For example, `List<?>` represents a *list of unknown types* and can hold arbitrary types of lists. To appreciate its concept, let us try to write a method that prints the list of any type:

It could look like this:

```
static void printList(List<Object> list) {
  for (Object o : list)
      System.out.print(o + " ");
}
```

Note that even if `String`, `Integer` and `Double` etc. are sub-types of `Object`, `List<String>`, `List<Integer>`, `List<Double>` etc. are not sub-types of `List<Object>`. So, we can only pass `List<Object>` to this method. This means, this method can only print list of `Object` and no other.

To write a generic `printList()` method, we can use `List<?>`:

```
static void printList(List<?> list) {
  for (Object o : list)
      System.out.print(o + " ");
}
```

We can now pass different kinds of lists to this method for printing:

```
List<Integer> li = ...
List<String> ls = ...
List<Double> ld = ...
printList(li);
printList(ls);
printList(ld);
```

Like upper-bounded list, adding elements is not allowed.

```
List<?> list = new ArrayList<String>();
list.add(new Object()); // compile time error
```

When the actual type parameter is `?`, it stands for some unknown type. The `add()` method takes arguments of type `T`, the element type of the list. An argument to `add()` must be a subtype of this unknown type. Since we don't know what type that is, we cannot pass anything in. The sole exception is null, which is a member of every type.

C++ templates do not provide any facility like bounded or unbounded type. This is another point where Java generics differs from C++ templates.

6.10.4 Wildcard and sub-typing

We know that although `Integer` is a subtype of `Number`, there is no relationship between `List<Integer>` and `List<Number>`. Figure 6.3: shows the relationships between several `List` classes declared with both upper and lower bounded and unbounded wildcards.

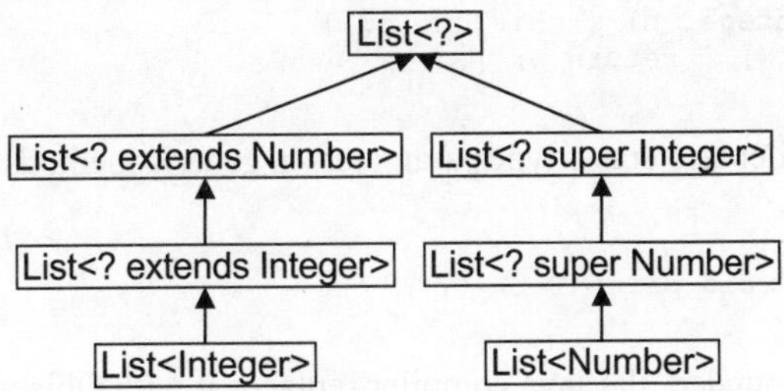

Figure 6.3: A hierarchy of several generic List class declarations

6.11 TYPE ERASURE

Note that generics was introduced for compile time type-checking and has no implication at run time. Accordingly, compiler uses a technique called *type erasure* where it takes the following steps:

- Replace all type parameters with their bounds or Object (for unbounded type parameters). Therefore, the resultant bytecode contains only ordinary classes, interfaces, and methods.
- Insert type casts if necessary to preserve type safety.
- Generate bridge methods to preserve polymorphism in extended generic types.

For example, if we have a generic class like below:

```
class Wrapper <T> {
  T o;
  void set(T o) { this.o = o; }
  T get() { return o; }
}
```

The Java compiler replaces it with Object, since T is unbounded:

```
class Wrapper {
  Object o;
  void set(Object o) { this.o = o; }
  Object get() { return o; }
}
```

This class looks like an ordinary class. The compiler also inserts the required downcast operator in the user codes. For example, consider the following user code:

```
Wrapper<String> w = new Wrapper<String>();
w.set(new String("abc"));
String s = w.get();
```

It will be replaced by

```
Wrapper w = new Wrapper();
w.set(new String("abc"));                //upcast is type-safe
String s = (String)w.get();              // compiler inserts downcast operation
```

Similarly, consider the following class that uses a bounded type parameter:

```
class Wrapper <T extends Integer> {
  T o;
  void set(T o) { this.o = o; }
  T get() { return o; }
}
```

The Java compiler replaces the bounded type parameter T with the bound Integer:

```
class Wrapper <T extends Integer> {
  Integer o;
  void set(Integer o) { this.o = o; }
  Integer get() { return o; }
}
```

The Java compiler also erases type parameters in generic methods. Consider the following generic method:

```
class X {
  static <T> void print(T t)  {/*…*/}
}
```

Since, T is unbounded, the Java compiler replaces it with Object:

```
class X {
  static void print(Object t)  {/*…*/}
}
```

The implication of type erasure is that the type argument is not available at runtime for use in casts or as the argument to the `instanceof` method.

Generics are often compared with templates in C++. However, unlike C++ templates, which creates a new type for each type argument, in Java generics there is just one class file which is used to create instances for all the type arguments.

The full details of erasure are beyond the scope of this book. However, the simple description we just gave isn't far from the truth. It is good to know a bit about this.

6.12 BACKWARD COMPATIBILITY

Note that lots of API classes (such as the Collections classes) were not generic prior to JDK 5.0. So, to get pre-generics behaviour, Java provides *raw types*. A raw type is the name of a generic class or interface without any type arguments. For example, given the generic Wrapper class:

```
class Wrapper <T> {
  T o;
  void set(T o) { this.o = o; }
  T get() { return o; }
}
```

To create a parameterized type, we specify an actual type argument for the formal type parameter T:

```
Wrapper<String> ws = new Wrapper<String>();
```

It is possible to omit the actual type argument which gives rise to a raw type:

```
Wrapper w = new Wrapper();
```

Therefore, `Wrapper` is the raw type of the generic type `Wrapper<T>`. However, a non-generic class or interface type is not a raw type. For backward compatibility, assigning a parameterized type to its raw type is allowed:

```
Wrapper<String> ws = new Wrapper<String>();
Wrapper w = ws;                         // OK
```

However, for reverse assignment, a warning is given:

```
Wrapper w = new Wrapper();              // w is a raw type of Wrapper<T>
Wrapper<String> ws = w;                 // warning: unchecked conversion
```

The warning indicates that the compiler is not responsible for type checks which is postponed till runtime. Since, for raw types, no compilation time type checking is done, we should not use it unless it is unavoidable.

6.13 RESTRICTIONS ON GENERICS

Although, Java generics is an extremely powerful tool, it is not free from drawbacks. The following sections highlight some of its limitations.

6.13.1 Cannot Specify Primitive Type Arguments

Consider the following parameterized type:

```
class X <T> {/*...*/}
```

When instantiating X type objects, it is possible to specify only non-primitive type arguments. So all the following statements give rise to compilation error:

```
X<int> xi;                        //compilation error, int is used
X<double> xd = new X<>();         //compilation error, double is used
X<char> xc = new X<char>();       //compilation error, char is used
```

6.13.2 Cannot Declare Static Fields of Type Parameters

Since, a class's static field is a class-level variable, which is shared by all of the instances of the class, declaring static fields of type parameters are prohibited. So, the following results in a compilation error:

```
class X <T> {
  static T a;  //compilation error
}
```

Consider the following variable declarations:

```
X<Integer> xi = new X<Integer>();
X<Double> xd = new X<Double>();
X<String> xs = new X<String>();
```

If static fields of type parameter would have been allowed, what would be the actual type of a? It cannot be `Integer`, `Double`, and `String` simultaneously. This is why declaring static fields of type parameters is prohibited.

6.13.3 Cannot Create Instances of Type Parameters

It is not possible to create an instance of a type parameter. So, the following class declaration results in a compilation error:

```
class X <T> {
  T t = new T();      //compilation error
}
```

However, using reflection we have a way out:

```
class X <T> {
  T t;
  X(Class<T> c) throws Exception {
    t = c.newInstance();
  }
}
```

6.13.4 Cannot Use instanceof

Since, type erasure removes all type parameters from generic code, it is not possible to ascertain what arguments were passed. Accordingly, verifying which parameterized type for a generic type is being used at runtime is not possible. In fact Java does not allow us to use `instanceof` operator for generic types:

```
List<Integer> l = new ArrayList<Integer>();
if(l instanceof ArrayList<Integer>) {      //compilation error
  /*...*/
}
```

6.13.5 Cannot create Generic arrays

It is not also possible to create arrays of parameterized types. So, the following code results in a compilation error:

```
List<Integer>[] al = new List<Integer>[4]; // compile-time error
```

However, we may cast from `Object[]` to `T[]` with a risk of unchecked cast and warning. That is why it is better to use Collection classes such as `ArrayList` and `HashMap` instead of arrays. Those classes are also implemented on top of array in Java but JDK handles the type-safety using generics carefully.

6.13.6 Limitations on exception

A generic class cannot extend the `Throwable` class directly or indirectly. So, the following classes will result in compile error:

```
//X extends Throwable directly, compilation error
class X<T> extends Throwable { /*... */ }
//Y extends Throwable indirectly, compilation error
class Y<T> extends Exception { /*... */ }
```

A generic type cannot also be used in `throw` clause:

```
try {
throw new ArrayList<Integer>();    //compilation error
}
```

The catch clause cannot also use type parameter:

```
static <T> void f() {
  try { /*... */ }
  catch(T t) {} //compilation error
}
```

However, we can use a type parameter in a `throws` clause:

```
class X<T extends Exception> {
  public void f() throws T { /*... */}    // OK
}
```

6.13.7 Cannot use .class

We cannot use `.class` for parameterized types. So the following are wrong:

```
Class c = List<String>.class;  //illegal
c = List<Integer>.class;  //illegal
c = List<Double>.class;  //illegal
```

This is because unlike C++ templates, in Java generics, a separate class is not generated for each type argument. So, we must use raw type instead of parameterized type:

```
Class c = List.class;
```

KEYWORDS

Bounded type parameter—A type parameter that accepts a restricted set of arguments

Generics—A construct to write parameterized classes, interfaces and methods

Lower-bounded wildcard—The wildcard that represents a set of unknown types restricted by a lower bound

Type argument—An argument passed to generic type or method/constructor call

Type erasure—A technique by which Java compiler translates generic classes/interfaces/methods to their no-generic counterparts

Type inference—Ability to find some type information automatically from the arguments passed to methods or constructors.

Type parameter—A parameter accepted by generic class, interface or method

Upper-bounded wildcard—The wildcard that represents a set of unknown types restricted by an upper bound

Wildcard—The '?' character used to represent an unknown type in generics

Unbounded wildcard—The wildcard that represents any unknown type

SUMMARY

Java generics allows us to write parameterized classes, interfaces and methods where parameters are type names. Although, the primary usage of generics is to abstract over types when working with collections, it is possible to write custom generic classes, interfaces and methods. Instead of relying on the programmer to keep track of object types and performing casts, which could lead to failures at runtime difficult to debug and solve, the compiler can help the programmer enforce a greater number of type checks and detect more failures at compile time.

It is possible to make both classes and interfaces generic. A class or an interface is generic if it accepts one or more type parameters. In general, any number of type parameters may be specified. They are specified in angular brackets separated by comma (,) and follow the class (or the interface) name

Like classes and interfaces, methods (including constructors) may use type parameters and are called generic methods. Sometimes it is possible to find some type information automatically from the arguments passed to methods or constructors. This ability is known as type inference.

It is also possible to restrict the argument that a generic type/method will use using bounded type parameter. It is written as the type parameter followed by the extends keyword followed by the bound. A type parameter may have more than one bound. If one of the bounds is a class, it must be specified first.

The sub-typing differs in generics from traditional sub-typing. In general, given two concrete types A and B, AClass<A> has no relationship to AClass, regardless of whether or not A and B are related. The common parent of AClass<A> and AClass is Object.

To establish sub-typing relationship, wildcard was introduced and is represented by the character '?'. Three versions of wildcard exist. Upper-bounded wildcard represents unknown types which is either a given type or its sub-type. Lower-bounded wildcard represents unknown types which is either a given type or its super-type. Unbounded wildcard represents any unknown types.

Compiler uses a technique called type erasure to convert generic types/methods to their non-generic counterpart. It generates just one class file which is used to create instances for all the type arguments. Although, Java generics is an extremely powerful tool, it is not free from drawbacks. For example, we cannot specify primitive type arguments, cannot declare static fields of type parameters, cannot create instances of type parameters, cannot use instanceof, cannot create generic arrays etc.

WEB RESOURCES

`http://docs.oracle.com/javase/tutorial/java/generics/`
Lesson: Generics

`http://www.eecs.qmul.ac.uk/~mmh/APD/bloch/generics.pdf`
Generics

`http://cs.nyu.edu/courses/spring12/CSCI-GA.3033-014/generics-tutorial.pdf`
Generics in the Java Programming Language

`http://www.agiledeveloper.com/articles/GenericsInJavaPartI.pdf`
Generics in Java – Part I

`http://userpages.umbc.edu/~edelman/341/JavaGenerics.pdf`
Java generics and Collections

EXERCISES

Objective-type Questions

1. Why are generics used?
(a) Generics make code more fast.
(b) Generics make code more optimized and readable.
(c) Generics add stability to your code by making more of your bugs detectable at compile time.
(d) Generics add stability to your code by making more of your bugs detectable at run time.

2. Which of these type parameters is used for a generic class to return and accept any type of object?
(a) K (c) T
(b) N (d) V

3. Which of these type parameters is used for a generic class to return and accept a number?
(a) K (c) T
(b) N (d) V

4. Which of these is a correct way of defining generic class?
(a) class name(T1, T2, ..., Tn) { /* ... */ }
(b) class name <T1, T2, ..., Tn>{ /* ... */ }
(c) class name[T1, T2, ..., Tn] { /* ... */ }
(d) class name{T1, T2, ..., Tn} { /* ... */ }

5. Which of the following is an incorrect statement regarding the use of generics and parameterized types in Java?
(a) Generics provide type safety by shifting more type checking responsibilities to the compiler.
(b) Generics and parameterized types eliminate the need for down casts when using Java Collections.
(c) When designing your own collections class (say, a linked list), generics and parameterized types allow you to achieve type safety with just a single class definition as opposed to defining multiple classes.
(d) All of the mentioned

6. Which of the following characters is used to represent wildcard?
(a) ? (c) #
(b) * (d) @

7. Which of the following is incorrect for class C and interface I1 and I2?
(a) <T extends I1 & C & I2>
(b) <T extends I2 & I1 & C>
(c) <T super C & I1 & I2
(d) <T extends C & I1 & I2>

8. Which of the following variable declarations is incorrect?

(a) List<Integer> li = new ArrayList<Integer>();
(b) List<? extends Number> ld = new LinkedList<Double>();
(c) List<Number> ln = new ArrayList<>();
(d) List<Integer>[] a = new ArrayList <Integer>[10];

9. Which of the following is incorrect?

(a) <T extends Number>
(b) <Tsuper Number>
(c) <? extends Number>
(d) <? super Number>

10. Which of the following reference types cannot be generic?

(a) Anonymous inner class
(b) Interface
(c) Inner class
(d) All of the mentioned

11. Which of the following is incorrect?

(a) List<Interger> is a sub-type of List<Number>
(b) List<? extends Integer> is a sub-type of List<? extends Number>
(c) List<Integer> is a sub-type of List<?>
(d) List<Number> is a sub-type of List <? extends Number>

12. Which of the following represents an unbounded wildcard?

(a) <? extends String>
(b) <? super String>
(c) ?
(d) <? extends Number>

13. What is the output of this program?

```
import java.util.*;
public class genericstack <E> {
  Stack <E> stk = new Stack <E>();
        public void push(E obj) {
    stk.push(obj);
        }
      public E pop() {
    E obj = stk.pop();
        return obj;
      }
}
class Output {
  public static void main(String args[]) {
    genericstack <String> gs = new
                            genericstack<String>();
    gs.push("Hello");
    System.out.println(gs.pop());
  }
}
```

(a) H
(b) Hello
(c) Runtime Error
(d) Compilation Error

14. What is the output of this program?

```
import java.util.*;
public class genericstack <E> {
  Stack <E> stk = new Stack <E>();
  public void push(E obj) {
    stk.push(obj);
    }
      public E pop() {
  E obj = stk.pop();
       return obj;
     }
}
class Output {
  public static void main(String args[]) {
    genericstack <Integer> gs = new
                        genericstack<Integer>();
    gs.push(36);
    System.out.println(gs.pop());
  }
}
```

(a) 0
(b) 36
(c) Runtime Error
(d) Compilation Error

15. What is the output of this program?

```
import java.util.*;
public class genericstack <E> {
  Stack <E> stk = new Stack <E>();
  public void push(E obj) {
    stk.push(obj);
  }
  public E pop() {
    E obj = stk.pop();
    return obj;
  }
}
class Output {
  public static void main(String args[]) {
    genericstack <String> gs = new
                            genericstack<String>();
    gs.push("Hello");
    System.out.print(gs.pop() + " ");
    genericstack <Integer> gs = new
                           genericstack<Integer>();
    gs.push(36);
    System.out.println(gs.pop());
  }
}
```

(a) Error
(b) Hello
(c) 36
(d) Hello 36

16. What is the output of this program?

```
import java.util.*;
public class genericstack <E> {
  Stack <E> stk = new Stack <E>();
  public void push(E obj) {
    stk.push(obj);
  }
  public E pop() {
    E obj = stk.pop();
    return obj;
  }
}
class Output {
  public static void main(String args[]) {
    genericstack <Integer> gs = new
            genericstack<Integer>();
    gs.push(36);
    System.out.println(gs.pop());
  }
}
```

(a) H
(b) Hello
(c) Runtime Error
(d) Compilation Error

17. Which syntax would you use to express a wildcard with a lower-bound of some type?
(a) ?
(b) ? extends type
(c) ? super type
(d) None of the above

18. Which syntax would you use to express a wildcard with an upper-bound of some type?
(a) ?
(b) ? extends type
(c) ? super type
(d) None of the above

19. When was generics first introduced in Java?
(a) JDK 1.4 (c) JDK 1.6
(b) JDK 1.5 (d) JDK 1.7

20. Which of the following character pairs are used to write type parameters?
(a) <> (c) []
(b) {} (d) ()

Subjective-type Questions

1. Briefly explain the concept of Java generics.
2. Write the primary purpose of Java generics.
3. Explain briefly the benefits of using Java generics.
4. What is the benefit of Generics in Collections Framework?
5. Why can't we write code as List<Number> numbers = new ArrayList<Integer>();?
6. Why can't we create generic array, or write code as List<Integer>[] array = new ArrayList<Integer>[10];?
7. Write a generic method to exchange the positions of two different elements in an array.
8. How is a generic type instantiated (to form a parameterized type)?
9. What is the raw type and what are its usefulness?
10. Explain the concept of bounded type parameter.
11. Which specific problem does wildcard solve?
12. Explain with examples the different kinds of wildcards.
13. Identify those types that cannot be used as type arguments.
14. Briefly explain the concept of 'type erasure'?
15. Will the following method compile? If not, why?

```
public static void print(List<?
extends Number> list) {
    for (Number n : list)
        System.out.print(n + " ");
    System.out.println();
}
```

16. Given the following classes:

```
class Shape { /* ... */ }
class Circle extends Shape { /* ... */ }
class Rectangle extends Shape { /* ... */ }
class Node<T> { /* ... */ }
```

Will the following code compile? If not, why?

```
Node<Circle> nc = new Node<>();
Node<Shape>  ns = nc;
```

17. Write the tasks performed by type erasure.
18. What is an "unchecked" warning message?

CHAPTER – 7

REFLECTION

KEY OBJECTIVES

After completing this chapter readers will be able to—

- understand the importance of reflection API
- examine and/or modify the properties or behaviour at run-time
- familiarize with reflection classes and interfaces
- know how to write dynamic proxy
- use annotations to analyze code
- identify some drawbacks of reflection

7.1 INTRODUCTION

One of the reasons why Java language has been so powerful and widely used is due to some of its APIs such as reflection using which one can do a whole lot of unimaginable tasks. The reflection API in Java enables us to examine and/or modify the properties or behaviour or other elements of an object at run-time. For example, given a class name, we can extract all kinds of information about the class such as if it is public or abstract or final, fields and methods contained in that class, their modifiers, its super-class or even interface the class implements. This is possible even if the source code of the class is not available.

Understanding reflection a bit will help us understanding the tools (such as NetBeans, Eclipse, Spring) that use this API.

Most classes and interfaces to implement reflection are provided as a separate package `java.lang.reflect` except one `java.lang.Class` which is considered to be the primary reflection class.

7.1.1 Pros and Cons of Reflection

Reflection is one of the advanced topics in Java. It is a powerful technique and can enable applications to perform operations which would otherwise be impossible. Although, it is hardly used in normal programming, it is the backbone for most of the Java, J2EE frameworks. Some of the examples that use reflection are:

- Reflection is extensively used in hibernate when objects are mapped to database tables.
- IDEs such as NetBeans, Eclipse provide the helpful auto-completion facility using reflection.
- Tomcat also finds servlets from a class name in a web.xml by exercising reflection.
- Spring provides a powerful dependency injection using reflection
- JUnit uses reflection to parse @Test annotation to get the test methods.

So, an understanding on reflection will not only help us to use those frameworks, but will help us to develop such frames on our own.

Although, the power of reflection is unquestionable, it is too dangerous if not used carefully. In addition, it has the following disadvantages:

- Using reflection we can access even private fields and change the value of final fields. This can be a serious pitfall that may cause applications to behave abnormally.
- Since reflection resolves the types dynamically, it is slower than the non-reflective counterpart.
- Since, reflection requires runtime permissions that might not be available in systems running under security manager, it can cause applications to fail at runtime.
- Reflection code is relatively difficult to understand and debug making it less flexible and hard to maintain.

7.2 CLASSES

The foundation of Java reflection API is the class `java.lang.Class`. However, for historical reason, it is placed in `java.lang` package instead of reflection package `java.lang.reflect`. A `Class` object represents a class or an interface in a Java application. These objects are created automatically by the Java Virtual Machine (JVM) as and when classes are loaded. This class provides methods to examine both class level and object level runtime information such as modifiers, fields, methods, constructors etc.

7.2.1 Class

Before doing any inspection on a class, we first obtain a reference to the `Class` object associated with a class/interface. It is the entry point for all of the reflection APIs. There is no public constructor in this class. However, there are several ways to get such an object depending on available information such as an object, name of a class, name of a type etc.

Note that JVM loads certain classes automatically even if they are not used in a Java application. Consequently, a `Class` object for each such loaded class is created by the JVM itself. The methods described below return a reference to that object if it is already created, else loads the class and a new `Class` object is created and returned.

7.2.1.1 Using getClass()

If an object is available, an instance of `Class` representing the object's class may be created using `getClass()` method as follows:

```
String s = new String("Java");
Class c = s.getClass();
```

Here the object `c` represents the class `String`. Note that the method `getClass()` is defined in the `Object` class. Since all classes directly or indirectly extend `Object` class, this method is available on all Java objects.

Note that the class `String` is a built-in Java library class whose source code is even available. So, inspecting such a class at runtime does not make much sense. This means, reflection APIs are not usually used for class whose structure is known in advance. It is useful in a situation where we have little information about a class such as only byte code of a class.

Since, in Java, an enum declaration defines a class (called enum type), its instance may be used in the same way as ordinary Java objects as follows:

```
enum E { yes, no }
E e = E.yes;
Class c = e.getClass();
```

It returns the class for enum type `E`. Since, Java arrays are objects, `getClass()` method may be used on an array instance as follows:

```
int arr[] = new int[10];
Class c = arr.getClass();
```

The returned `Class` object `c` represents the array of int. The non-static `getClass()` method always returns the name of a class, not an interface.

```
interface I {};
class IImpl implements I {}
I i = new IImpl();
Class c = i.getClass()
```

The return `Class` object corresponds to the class `IImpl`, not interface `I`.

7.2.1.2 Using .class

Since, instances of primitive types are not objects, it is not possible to invoke `getClass()` method on those instances. Moreover, since the method `getClass()` is non-static, an object should be available to invoke this method.

Java provides an alternative way to get a `Class` object if only *type name* is known. This type name may be a class name, an interface name, an enum name or even a name of primitive types. So, for built-in primitive type `int`, a `Class` object representing that type is obtained as follows:

```
Class c = int.class;
```

Similarly, the following returns a `Class` object representing the type `int[]`.

```
Class c1 = int[].class;
```

This syntax is valid for class, interface and enum types as well:

```
Class c2 = String.class;
Class c3 = I.class;
Class c4 = E.class;
```

Here, `I` and `E` are interface and enum defined earlier. Since, this .class syntax is valid for all types, it is the most flexible one.

7.2.1.3 Using forName()

There is still another way to get a `Class` object using static `Class.forName()` method. This method takes a fully qualified class/interface name.

```
Class c = Class.forName("java.lang.String");
Class c1 = Class.forName("java.io.Serializable");
```

The `forName()` method also takes mangled array types. Here is an example:

```
Class c = Class.forName("[I");
```

Here, `c` represents an array of primitive type `int`. Here are some other examples:

```
Class c2 = Class.forName("[[I");                    //2-D array of int

Class c3 = Class.forName("[D");                     //array of double

Class c4 = Class.forName("[[D");                    //2-D array of double

Class c5 = Class.forName("[Ljava.lang.String;");    //array of String
```

Note that `forName()` method cannot be used for primitive types.

7.2.1.4 Using TYPE Field

For primitive types, there is another way to obtain `Class` object. We know that for every primitive type and void, there exists a wrapper class. For example, for primitive type `int`, the name of the wrapper class is `java.lang.Integer`. Each wrapper class contains a field named `TYPE` which holds the `Class` for the primitive type being wrapped. This `TYPE` field may also be used to get `Class` for primitive type as follows:

```
Class c = Integer.TYPE;
```

This is essentially equivalent to:

```
Class c = int.class;
```

The following is an example for primitive type `double`:

```
Class c = Double.TYPE;
```

And for `void` type:

```
Class c = Void.TYPE;
```

Note that `Class` objects corresponding to primitive types and array types merely represent an empty public final abstract class. Consequently, inspecting such classes hardly occurs in practice.

7.2.2 Modifier

This class contains 12 static constants; each one represents one of 12 modifiers (public, private, protected etc.) that can be applied on class and its members such as fields, methods and constructors. Each modifier is represented by an integer with a distinct bit position. The values of these constants are summarized in Table 7.1:

Table 7.1: Field summary of Modifier class

Name of fields of Modifier class	Modifier name	Least significant 12 bits of 32-bit int	Value
PUBLIC	public	000000000001	1
PRIVATE	private	000000000010	2
PROTECTED	protected	000000000100	4
STATIC	static	000000001000	8
FINAL	final	000000010000	16
SYNCHRONIZED	synchronized	000000100000	32
VOLATILE	volatile	000001000000	64
TRANSIENT	transient	000010000000	128
NATIVE	native	000100000000	256
INTERFACE	interface	001000000000	512
ABSTRACT	abstract	010000000000	1024
STRICT	strict	100000000000	2048

Since, there is no explicit constant which corresponds to "package" access, it is necessary to check for the absence of all three access modifiers to identify a package modifier. The `Modifier` class also provides static methods to identify set of modifiers that can be applied on class, field, method and constructor. The methods and their return values are summarized in Table 7.2:

Table 7.2: Method summary of Modifier class

Method	Return value	Least significant 12 bits	Set of modifiers
classModifiers()	3103	110000011111	public private protected static final abstract strict
fieldModifiers()	223	000011011111	public private protected static final volatile transient
methodModifiers()	3391	110100111111	public private protected static final synchronized native abstract strict
constructorModifiers()	7	000000000111	public private protected

The following example program illustrates this:

```
import java.lang.reflect.*;
public class FindModifiers {
  public static void main(String args[]) throws Exception {
    System.out.println("Class modifiers:
"+Modifier.toString(Modifier.classModifiers()));
    System.out.println("Field modifiers:
"+Modifier.toString(Modifier.fieldModifiers()));
    System.out.println("Method modifiers:
"+Modifier.toString(Modifier.methodModifiers()));
    System.out.println("Constructor modifiers:
"+Modifier.toString(Modifier.constructorModifiers()));
  }
}
```

Here, `classModifiers()` method returns an int value OR-ing together the modifiers that can be applied to a class. The methods `fieldModifiers()`, `methodModifiers()` and `constructorModifiers()` return similar values corresponding to field, method and constructor respectively. The `toString()` method of `Modifier` class returns a string representation of a given int modifier. Here is a sample output of this program:

```
Class modifiers: public private protected static final abstract strict
Field modifiers: public private protected static final volatile transient
Method modifiers: public private protected static final synchronized native
abstract strict
Constructor modifiers: public private protected
```

7.3 INSPECTING CLASS

The class `Class` provides several methods to get the information about the class, its fields, methods and constructors etc. The following sections describe how one gets information about a class and its members.

7.3.1 Getting Class Information

Before digging into the class, let us gather some information about the class itself such as its simple name, package the class is contained in, if the class is a synthetic class etc. A class is said to be a synthetic class if it is created at runtime. The following program prints some useful information about a specified class:

```
public class GetClassInfo {
  public static void main(String args[]) throws Exception {
    Class c = Class.forName(args[0]);
    System.out.println("Cannonical name: "+c.getCanonicalName());
    System.out.println("Simple name: "+c.getSimpleName());
    Package p = c.getPackage();
    System.out.println("Package name: "+p.getName());
```

```
    System.out.println("Is synthetic class: "+c.isSynthetic());
    System.out.println("Protection domain: "+c.getProtectionDomain());
  }
}
```

This program generated the following result when `java.lang.String` was supplied as an argument.

```
E:\ajp\ref\>java GetClassInfo java.lang.String
Cannonical name: java.lang.String
Simple name: String
Package name: java.lang
Is synthetic class: false
Protection domain: ProtectionDomain  null
 null
 <no principals>
 java.security.Permissions@1f1fba0 (
 ("java.security.AllPermission" "<all permissions>" "<all actions>")
)
```

7.3.2 Getting Class Modifiers

A class/interface/enum may be declared with zero or more of the 7 modifiers `public`, `protected`, `private`, `static`, `final`, `abstract` and `strictfp`. However, not all modifiers are allowed all the time. For example, `final` cannot be applied on interface and an enum cannot be `abstract`. Certain combinations of modifiers are not also possible. For example, `final` and `abstract` cannot be used at the same time.

Anyway, how do you know what modifiers are used for a given class if the source code of the class is not available? For example, what modifiers are used for the Java library class `java.lang.String`? Although, this information is available in Java documentation, documentation for all classes may not always be available.

Fortunately, the `getModifiers()` method returns a set of modifiers for a class/interface encoded as an int. They may be decoded using the methods of class `Modifier`. The following program illustrates this:

```
import java.lang.reflect.*;
public class GetClassModifiers {
  public static void main(String args[]) throws Exception {
    Class c = Class.forName(args[0]);
    System.out.print("Modifiers for "+args[0]+": ");
    System.out.print(Modifier.toString(c.getModifiers()));
  }
}
```

This program accepts a fully qualified name of a class (or interface/enum) and prints set of modifiers used for the class. To find the modifiers for `String`, use the following command:

```
java GetClassModifiers java.lang.String
```

It generates an output as follows:

```
Modifiers for java.lang.String: public final
```

Similarly, for interface `java.lang.Runnable`, it generates the following result:

```
Modifiers for java.lang.Runnable: public abstract interface
```

This program may be supplied a user-defined class as well.

7.3.3 Finding Implemented Interfaces

To get interfaces implemented by a class/interface, we use `getGenericInterfaces()` method of `Class`.

```
public Type[] getGenericInterfaces()
```

It returns an array of `Type`. The `Type` is the common super interface for all types in Java including raw types, parameterized types, array types, type variables and primitive types. The following program accepts a fully qualified class name and prints set of interfaces implemented by the class.

```
import java.lang.reflect.*;
public class GetImplementedInterfaces {
  public static void main(String args[]) throws Exception {
    Class c = Class.forName(args[0]);
    Type[] intfs = c.getGenericInterfaces();
    System.out.println(args[0]+" implements: ");
    for(Type intf : intfs)
      System.out.println(intf);
  }
}
```

To find the list of interfaces implemented by `String`, use the following command:

```
java GetImplementedInterfaces java.lang.String
```

It generates an output as follows:

```
java.lang.String implements:
interface java.io.Serializable
java.lang.Comparable\<java.lang.String\>
interface java.lang.CharSequence
```

7.3.4 Finding Inheritance Hierarchy

To get the super class, we use `getSuperclass()` method.

```
public Class<? super T> getSuperclass()
```

It returns the `Class` representing the superclass of the class. The following program accepts a fully qualified class name and prints the inheritance hierarchy:

```
import java.lang.reflect.*;
public class GetInheritanceHierarchy {
  public static void main(String args[]) throws Exception {
    Class c = Class.forName(args[0]);
    print(c.getSuperclass());
    System.out.print(c);
  }
  static void print(Class<?> c) {
    if(c != null) {
      print(c.getSuperclass());
      System.out.print(c+"<--");
    }
  }
}
```

To find the list of interfaces implemented by `Applet`, use the following command:

```
java GetInheritanceHierarchy java.applet.Applet
```

It generates an output as follows:

```
class java.lang.Object<--class java.awt.Component<--class
                                      java.awt.Container<--class
java.awt.Panel<--class java.applet.Applet
```

7.3.5 Finding Annotations

An annotation is represented by `java.lang.annotation.Annotation` interface. For annotations for class, method, constructor and field, reflection provides the following method in the respective class:

```
public Annotation[] getDeclaredAnnotations()
```

This returns an array of annotations declared for the element type. The following program finds all deprecated constructors and methods of a specified class:

```
import java.lang.reflect.*;
import java.lang.annotation.*;
public class GetAnnotations {
  public static void main(String args[]) throws Exception {
    Class c = Class.forName(args[0]);
    Method[] methods = c.getDeclaredMethods();
    for(Method method : methods) {
      Annotation[] anos = method.getDeclaredAnnotations();
      for(Annotation a : anos)
        if(a.toString().contains("Deprecated")) System.out.println(method);
    }
    Constructor[] cons = c.getConstructors();
    for(Constructor con : cons) {
      Annotation[] anos = con.getDeclaredAnnotations();
      for(Annotation a : anos)
        if(a.toString().contains("Deprecated")) System.out.println(con);
    }
  }
}
```

A sample result for `String` is shown below:

```
public void java.lang.String.getBytes(int,int,byte[],int)
public java.lang.String(byte[],int)
public java.lang.String(byte[],int,int,int)
```

7.4 FINDING CLASS MEMBERS

There are three types of member a class may have: fields, methods and constructors. Java defines an interface `Member` that represents a single member. Each type of member is also represented as a separate class: `Field`, `Method` and `Constructor`. The class `Class` provides numerous methods to obtain those members. These methods may be grouped into two categories: i) methods that return a specific member such as field, method or constructor and ii) methods that return all members. Under each category there are again two sub-categories: i) methods that search only the current class and ii) methods that search for the super-classes and super-interfaces. Methods that only search the current class, return even private members, whereas methods that search super-classes and super-interfaces return only public members. The following sections describe how to use them to get class members.

7.4.1 Getting Fields

A field of a class is represented by the `Field` class that provides information about, and dynamic access to, a single field. The following methods are available to retrieve fields of a class:

```
public Field getDeclaredField(String name)
public Field[] getDeclaredFields()

public Field getField(String name)
public Field[] getFields()
```

The first one returns a single `Field` object corresponding to the specified field name, whereas the second one returns an array of `Field` corresponding to all fields. These two methods search only the fields declared (hence this word appears in the method name) in the class explicitly. The last two are the counterparts of the first two except that they search for super-class and super-interface. The following program accepts a fully qualified class name and prints a description of all declared fields in the class:

```
import java.lang.reflect.*;
public class GetClassFields {
  public static void main(String args[]) throws Exception {
    Class c = Class.forName(args[0]);
    Field[] fields = c.getDeclaredFields();
    System.out.println("No of fields in "+args[0]+": "+fields.length);
    for(Field f : fields)
      System.out.println(f);
  }
}
```

To find all declared fields of `Integer` wrapper class, use the following command:

```
java GetClassFields java.lang.Integer
```

It generates an output as follows:

```
No of fields in java.lang.Integer: 11
public static final int java.lang.Integer.MIN_VALUE
public static final int java.lang.Integer.MAX_VALUE
public static final java.lang.Class java.lang.Integer.TYPE
static final char[] java.lang.Integer.digits
static final char[] java.lang.Integer.DigitTens
static final char[] java.lang.Integer.DigitOnes
static final int[] java.lang.Integer.sizeTable
private final int java.lang.Integer.value
public static final int java.lang.Integer.SIZE
private static final long java.lang.Integer.serialVersionUID
static final boolean java.lang.Integer.$assertionsDisabled
```

If you want to get fields including inherited ones, use `getFields()` method instead. Note that `getFields()` methods only return public inherited methods. Note that there's no built-in method that returns all the fields including the inherited ones. Using reflection, let us now write a program that retrieves all the fields:

```
import java.lang.reflect.*;
public class GetAllClassFields {
  public static void main(String args[]) throws Exception {
    print(Class.forName(args[0]));
  }
  static int v = 0;
  static void print(Class c) {
    if(c != null) {
      print(c.getSuperclass());
      Field[] fields = c.getDeclaredFields();
      indent(v);
      System.out.println("Class: "+c);
      for(Field f : fields) {
        indent(v);
        System.out.println(f);
      }
      v++;
    }
  }
  static void indent(int n) {
    for(int i=0;i<n;i++) System.out.print("  ");
  }
}
```

The method `print()` starts searching from the given class and works its way up the hierarchy recursively until either a field is found, or no super class is available. The `print()` method, on its way, displays all the fields including the private ones. The method `indent()` has been used to indent the output.

7.4.2 Getting Methods

A method of a class is represented by the `Method` class that provides information about, and access to, a single method. The following methods are available to retrieve methods of a class:

```
public Method getDeclaredMethod(String name, Class<?>... parameterTypes)
public Method[] getDeclaredMethods()

public Method getMethod(String name, Class<?>... parameterTypes)
public Method[] getMethods()
```

The functionality of these methods is similar to the methods available for fields except that these return method instead of field. The following program illustrates how to get all declared methods of a specified class:

```
import java.lang.reflect.*;
public class GetClassMethods {
  public static void main(String args[]) throws Exception {
    Class c = Class.forName(args[0]);
    Method[] methods = c.getDeclaredMethods();
    System.out.println("No. of methods in "+args[0]+": "+methods.length);
    for(Method m : methods)
      System.out.println(m);
  }
}
```

Use the following command to find all methods of `Member` interface:

```
java GetClassMethods java.lang.reflect.Member
```

It results in the following output:

```
No. of methods in java.lang.reflect.Member: 4
public abstract java.lang.String java.lang.reflect.Member.getName()
public abstract java.lang.Class java.lang.reflect.Member.getDeclaringClass()
public abstract int java.lang.reflect.Member.getModifiers()
public abstract boolean java.lang.reflect.Member.isSynthetic()
```

Note that this program, retrieves even the private methods of the class. Use the following command to find all methods of `java.lang.Class` class:

```
java GetClassMethods java.lang.Class
```

If you want to get methods including inherited ones, use `getMethods()` method instead. The following finds all methods of a class including inherited and private methods:

```
import java.lang.reflect.*;
public class GetAllClassMethods {
  public static void main(String args[]) throws Exception {
    print(Class.forName(args[0]));
  }
  static int v = 0;
  static void print(Class c) {
    if(c != null) {
      print(c.getSuperclass());
      Method[] methods = c.getDeclaredMethods();
      indent(v);
      System.out.println("Class: "+c);
      for(Method m : methods) {
        indent(v);
        System.out.println(m);
      }
      v++;
    }
  }
  static void indent(int n) {
    for(int i=0;i<n;i++) System.out.print("  ");
  }
}
```

7.4.3 Getting Constructors

Since, constructors are special methods, reflection API provides a separate class `Constructor` that provides information about, and access to, a single constructor. The following methods are available to retrieve constructors of a class:

```
public Constructor<T> getDeclaredConstructor(Class<?>... parameterTypes)
public Constructor<?>[] getDeclaredConstructors()

public Constructor<T> getConstructor(Class<?>... parameterTypes)
public Constructor<?>[] getConstructors()
```

Since, constructors are not inherited, the last two methods return only public constructor(s). The following program retrieves all constructors of a specified class:

```
import java.lang.reflect.*;
public class GetClassConstructors {
  public static void main(String args[]) throws Exception {
    Class c = Class.forName(args[0]);
    Constructor[] cons = c.getDeclaredConstructors();
    System.out.println("No of constructors in "+args[0]+": "+cons.length);
    for(Constructor con : cons)
      System.out.println(con);
  }
}
```

Use the following command to find all methods of `java.lang.Boolean` class:

```
java GetClassConstructors java.lang.Boolean
```

The sample result is shown below:

```
No of constructors in java.lang.Boolean: 2
public java.lang.Boolean(boolean)
public java.lang.Boolean(java.lang.String)
```

7.5 WORKING WITH CLASS MEMBERS

In the previous section, we have retrieved different class members such as fields, methods and constructors. In this section, let us get/set field, call methods, create objects by calling constructors etc.

7.5.1 Field Type

A field may be either any of the eight primitive types (`boolean`, `char`, `byte`, `short`, `int`, `long`, `float`, and `double`) or a reference type (anything which is a direct or indirect subclass of `java.lang.Object`). The class `Field` has two methods to know its type:

```
public Class<?> getType()
public Type getGenericType()
```

They return a `Class` and a `Type` object representing the field respectively. The following simple program shows all field names and their types of given class:

```
import java.lang.reflect.*;
public class GetFieldType {
  public static void main(String args[]) throws Exception {
    Class c = Class.forName(args[0]);
    Field[] fields = c.getDeclaredFields();
    for(Field f : fields)
      System.out.println(f.getType()+" "+f.getName());
  }
}
```

A sample output for `java.lang.String` is shown below:

```
class [C value
int hash
long serialVersionUID
class [Ljava.io.ObjectStreamField; serialPersistentFields
interface java.util.Comparator CASE_INSENSITIVE_ORDER
int HASHING_SEED
int hash32
```

7.5.2 Field Modifiers

We can apply several modifiers (`public`, `private`, `protected`, `transient`, `volatile`, `static` and `final`) to a field. The `getModifiers()` method of Field class returns an encoded integer representing the set of modifiers used to declare the field. The `Modifier` class has a set of methods to identify what modifiers the returned integer represent. The following program lists all static fields of a given class:

```
import java.lang.reflect.*;
public class GetFieldModifier {
  public static void main(String args[]) throws Exception {
    Class c = Class.forName(args[0]);
    Field[] fields = c.getDeclaredFields();
    System.out.println("Static fields of "+args[0]+":");
    for(Field f : fields)
      if(Modifier.isStatic(f.getModifiers()))
        System.out.println(f.getName());
  }
}
```

A sample output for `java.lang.String` is shown below:

```
Static fields of java.lang.String:
serialVersionUID
serialPersistentFields
CASE_INSENSITIVE_ORDER
HASHING_SEED
```

7.5.3 Accessing Fields

The class `Field` has several methods to get and/or set field value. The following program illustrates this:

```
import java.lang.reflect.*;
class X {
  public double pd1 = 1;
  public double pd2 = 2;
}
public class AccessFields {
  public static void main(String args[]) throws Exception {
    X x = new X();
    Class c = x.getClass();
    String fname = args[0];
    Field f = c.getDeclaredField(fname);
    System.out.println("Before, "+fname+": "+f.getDouble(x));
    f.setDouble(x, 4);
    System.out.println("After, "+fname+": "+f.getDouble(x));
  }
}
```

This program, given a field name, first prints the value of the field of an `X` object and changes its value to 4 and finally prints this modified value. The interesting part of this program is that the name of the field is not known at compile time. This shows that reflection API enables us to access any field of a class without knowing the name of the field in advance. The following is a sample output:

```
E:\ajp\ref\>java AccessFields pd2
Before, pd2: 2.0
After, pd2: 4.0
```

The `Field` class also provides a generic `get()` method that returns an `Object` representing the value of the field on the specified `Object`. The value is automatically wrapped in an object if it has a primitive type

7.5.3.1 Accessing Forbidden Fields

Note that get methods throw an exception if the field is inaccessible. Similarly, set methods also throw an exception if the field is inaccessible or final. However, reflection API allows us to make even an inaccessible field accessible or modifying a final field. The `Field` class inherits two methods from `java.lang.reflect.AccessibleObject` which may be used for this purpose:

```
public void setAccessible(boolean flag)
public static void setAccessible(AccessibleObject[] array, boolean flag)
```

The former one sets the `accessible` flag for field to the specified `boolean` value. The value `true` and `false` suppresses and enables Java language access checks respectively. The following program illustrates how to make a private field accessible:

```
import java.lang.reflect.*;
class X {
  private final int pf = 0;
}
public class AccessForbiddenFields {
  public static void main(String args[]) throws Exception {
    X x = new X();
    Class c = x.getClass();
    Field f = c.getDeclaredField("pf");
    f.setAccessible(true);
    System.out.println("pf = "+f.getInt(x));
  }
}
```

The following program prints the value of a private field. Here is a sample output of this program:

```
pf = 0
```

7.5.3.2 Modifying Final Fields

A final field may be made mutable using the same method used in the previous section. Here is an example program that modifies the private final field

```
import java.lang.reflect.*;
class X {
  private final int pf = 0;
}
public class ModifyFinalFields {
  public static void main(String args[]) throws Exception {
    X x = new X();
    Class c = x.getClass();
    Field f = c.getDeclaredField("pf");
    f.setAccessible(true);
    System.out.println("Before: pf = "+f.getInt(x));
    f.setInt(x, 4);
    System.out.println("After : pf = "+f.getInt(x));
  }
}
```

Here is a sample output of this program:

```
Before : pf = 0
After  : pf = 4
```

Note that reflection allows us to access even a private field or modify even a final field. This implies a direct violation of some fundamental concepts such as abstraction etc. So, reflection should only be used if it is unavoidable and if used, utmost discretion must be taken.

7.5.4 Method Modifiers

Like fields, we can apply several modifiers (`public`, `private`, `protected`, `static`, `abstract` `synchronized`, `final`, `native` and `strictfp`) to a method. The `getModifiers()` method of `Method` class returns an encoded integer representing the set of modifiers used to declare the method. The `Modifier` class has a set of methods to identify what modifiers the returned integer represent. The following program lists all public methods of a given class:

```
import java.lang.reflect.*;
public class GetMethodModifier {
  public static void main(String args[]) throws Exception {
    Class c = Class.forName(args[0]);
    Method[] methods = c.getDeclaredMethods();
    System.out.println("Public methods of "+args[0]+":");
    for(Method m : methods)
      if(Modifier.isPublic(m.getModifiers()))
      System.out.println(m.getName());
  }
}
```

Use the following command to get the list of public methods available on `Method` class:

```
java GetMethodModifier java.lang.reflect.Method
```

7.5.5 Method Information

In addition to method modifiers

- a method has a return type,
- may accept some parameters and
- may throw some exceptions.

The return type of a method may be obtained using either of the following methods:

```
public Class\<?\> getReturnType()
public Type getGenericReturnType()
```

The former returns a `Class` and the latter returns a `Type` representing the return type. There are two methods that return a list of parameter a method takes.

```
public Class\<?\>[] getParameterTypes()
public Type[] getGenericParameterTypes()
```

The former returns an array of `Class` whereas the latter returns an array of `Type`. Similarly, the list of exceptions a method throws is obtained using the following methods:

```
public Class\<?\>[] getExceptionTypes()
public Type[] getGenericExceptionTypes()
```

The following program lists information about methods of a specified class:

```
import java.lang.reflect.*;
public class GetMethodInfo {
  public static void main(String args[]) throws Exception {
    Class c = Class.forName(args[0]);
    Method[] methods = c.getDeclaredMethods();
```

```
      System.out.print("Class :"+args[0]);
      for(Method m : methods) {
        System.out.println("\n\nMethod: "+m.getName());
        System.out.println("Return type: "+m.getGenericReturnType());
        System.out.print("Parameters taken:");
        Type[] params = m.getGenericParameterTypes();
        for(Type p : params) System.out.print("  "+p);
        System.out.print("\nExceptions thrown: ");
        Type[] exceptions = m.getExceptionTypes();
        for(Type e : exceptions) System.out.print("  "+e);
      }
    }
  }
```

The output of this program for the input class `java.lang.Object` is shown below:

```
…
Method: wait
Return type: void
Parameters taken:  long
Exceptions thrown:   class java.lang.InterruptedException

Method: wait
Return type: void
Parameters taken:  long  int
Exceptions thrown:   class java.lang.InterruptedException
…
```

7.5.6 Invoking Methods

The reflection API also allows us to invoke a method (both static and non-static) indirectly. This is done using `Method.invoke()` method which looks like this:

```
public Object invoke(Object obj, Object... args)
```

The first argument is the object instance (or null for static method) on which the method is to be invoked and second argument (an array of objects) is the method's parameters (if any). This argument array may be of length 0 or null or absent if the number of formal parameters required by the underlying method is 0.

The following program invokes the method `length()` on a `String` object.

```
import java.lang.reflect.*;
public class InvokingMethods {
  public static void main(String args[]) throws Exception {
    String s = new String("Java");
    Class c = s.getClass();
    Method m = c.getDeclaredMethod("length");
    System.out.println("The length of "+s+" is "+m.invoke(s));
  }
}
```

The output of this program is:

```
The length of Java is 4
```

7.5.6.1 Accessing Forbidden Methods

Like private fields, a private method may be made accessible using `setAccessible()` method. The following simple program demonstrates this:

```
import java.lang.reflect.*;
class X {
  private void f() {
    System.out.println("f() called");
  }
}
```

```
public class AccessForbiddenMethods {
  public static void main(String args[]) throws Exception {
    Method method = X.class.getDeclaredMethod("f");
    method.setAccessible(true);
    method.invoke(new X());
  }
}
```

This program invokes the private method `f()` on a `X` object. Since, the method `f()` is private, before calling it, it has been made accessible using `setAccesssible()` method passing argument `true`.

7.5.7 Debugging with Reflection

This section describes how to use annotations in Java reflection to analyze our code. Suppose, we want to write a program (we shall call it debugger) to test or analyze or debug a given class. The program calls one or more methods (not all) of the given class. Since, the program should work on any arbitrary class which may contain arbitrary methods, it is probably impossible to write such a program traditionally.

One simple but elegant idea is to mark the methods to be called with an annotation. Since annotations provide data about a class that are not part of the programming logic itself, they have no direct impact on the code they annotate. Once this is done, the task of the program will then be finding only marked methods and call them. So, let us first write a maker annotation.

Annotations are just like interfaces except that they are defined using `@interface` before the annotation name. We know that an annotation can be retained till compile time or runtime which is indicated using two constants `RetentionPolicy.SOURCE` and `RetentionPolicy.RUNTIME` respectively. Another built-in annotation `@Target` lets us indicate the kinds of program element to which an annotation type is applicable. With this information, our marker annotation looks like this:

```
import java.lang.annotation.*;
@Target(value = ElementType.METHOD)
@Retention(value = RetentionPolicy.RUNTIME)
public @interface Call {}
```

This is an empty annotation as its purpose is only mark a method. Since, our debugger program inspects this annotation at runtime, the retention policy is indicated as `RetentionPolicy.RUNTIME.` using a separate built-in Java annotation `@Retention`. Moreover, since the marker annotation is written for methods, it is indicated as `ElementType.METHOD` in the `@Target` annotation.

Let us now write a sample class to be tested by our debugger.

```
public class X {
  public void f() { System.out.println("f() called"); }
  @Call
  public void g() { System.out.println("g() called"); }
  @Call
  public void h() { System.out.println("h() called"); }
}
```

Note that two methods `g()` and `h()` have been marked with our annotation `@Call`. This means we want the debugger to call only these two methods. To process this annotation, we write a annotation processor which typically uses Java reflection API for this and looks like this:

```
import java.lang.reflect.*;
public class Debugger {
  public static void main(String args[]) throws Exception {
    X x = new X();
    Method[] methods = x.getClass().getDeclaredMethods();
    for(Method method : methods) {
```

```
            Call c = method.getAnnotation(Call.class);
            if(c != null) {
              try {
                method.invoke(x);
              } catch (Exception e) { e.printStackTrace(); }
            }
          }
        }
      }
```

The `main()` method iterates through h all the methods of the class `X` and calls those methods which have been marked with `@Call` annotation. A sample output of the program is shown below:

```
h() called
g() called
```

If the debugger wants to call a different set of methods, simply annotate them with the `@Call` and recompile the class `X` and start the debugger again.

7.5.8 Getting Constructor Modifiers

Like methods, reflection also provides APIs to find constructors of a class and obtain information such as the its modifiers, parameters, annotations and thrown exceptions etc. Since, the role of constructors is only to instantiate objects, fewer modifiers (only `private`, `protected` and `public`) are meaningful. The following program prints the list of public constructors of the specified class:

```
import java.lang.reflect.*;
public class GetConstrutorModifier {
  public static void main(String args[]) throws Exception {
    Class c = Class.forName(args[0]);
    Constructor[] constructors = c.getDeclaredConstructors();
    System.out.println("Public Construtors of "+args[0]+":");
    for(Constructor con : constructors)
      if(Modifier.isPublic(con.getModifiers()))
      System.out.println(con);
  }
}
```

A sample output for `java.lang.Object` class is shown below:

```
public java.lang.Object()
```

7.5.9 Instantiating Objects

Reflection can do more than just simply list fields, methods and constructors. Through reflection, we can even create instances. The simplest way to instantiate objects is to use `newInstance()` method of `Class`.

```
public T newInstance()
```

This essentially uses zero argument constructor (default constructor) to instantiate objects. The following creates an instance of `String`:

```
String s = String.class.newInstance();
```

What happens if we call `newInstance()` on a class that has no default constructor? Nothing pleasant: an `InstantiationException` will be thrown. Fortunately, Java reflection also allows us to create new instances of a class that require constructor arguments. However, we just have to work a bit more. First we find the required constructor from the class and then call it with the right arguments. The way to find the constructor is to call the `getConstructor()` method with a description of the constructor that we are looking for. We then use `newInstance()` method of `Constructor` that looks like:

```
public T newInstance(Object... initargs)
```

Creating an instance using `newInstance()` is useful when the name of a class is not known in advance. For example, JDBC programmers usually write programs intended to connect to different databases at different times. Since, the name of the driver class is different for different databases, it not possible to create an instance of the driver using "new" syntax which always expects a class name. Using reflection it is simply a matter of trick. The instance creation code will look like this:

```
Class.forName(args[0]).newInstance();
```

Note that the name of the class is passed as a command line argument and the code creates an instance using the default constructor. This code passes the compilation phase successfully and is capable of creating an instance of any class whose name is supplied at runtime. Needless to say that the class with a default constructor must exist.

The following program illustrates how to use `newInstance()` method.

```
import java.lang.reflect.*;
public class InstantiateObjects {
  public static void main(String args[]) throws Exception {
    String s1 = (String)String.class.newInstance();
    Class c = String.class;
    Constructor con = c.getDeclaredConstructor(char[].class);
    char[] chars = {'J', 'a', 'v', 'a'};
    Object[] param = {chars};
    String s2 = (String)con.newInstance(param);
    System.out.println(s2);
  }
}
```

This creates two instances of `String`. The first string `s1` is constructed using `newInstance()` of `Class`. The second string `s2` is constructed with the help of the following constructor:

```
public String(char[] value)
```

Note that the `newInstance()` will throw exceptions if proper arguments are not supplied.

7.5.10 Arrays

In Java, an array is a special object that contains a fixed number of components of the same type. In reflection API, an array is represented by the `Array` class that provides several static methods to dynamically create and access Java arrays.

7.5.10.1 Checking Array types

It is possible to identify if a class corresponds to an array using static `isArray()` method of `Class`. The following program retrieves all array fields of a specified class:

```
import java.lang.reflect.*;
public class GetClassArrayFields {
  public static void main(String args[]) throws Exception {
    Class c = Class.forName(args[0]);
    Field[] fields = c.getDeclaredFields();
    for(Field f : fields)
      if(f.getType().isArray()) System.out.println(f);
  }
}
```

A sample output for `Integer` class is shown below:

```
static final char[] java.lang.Integer.digits
static final char[] java.lang.Integer.DigitTens
static final char[] java.lang.Integer.DigitOnes
static final int[] java.lang.Integer.sizeTable
```

7.5.10.2 Creating New Arrays

The class `Array` provides a static method `newInstance()` to create an array in a reflective way. The following example creates an array of 5 integers and prints its elements:

```
import java.lang.reflect.*;
public class CreateArray {
  public static void main(String args[]) throws Exception {
    int len = 5;
    Object o = Array.newInstance(Integer.class, len);
    for(int i=0;i<len;i++) {
      Array.set(o, i, new Integer(i));
    }
    System.out.println(java.util.Arrays.toString((Object[])o));
  }
}
```

A sample output of this program is shown below:

```
[0, 1, 2, 3, 4]
```

7.6 DYNAMIC PROXY

One of the important facilities of reflection API is the ability to create proxies dynamically. In general, a proxy is a module that sits in the middle of two or more communicating parties and can intercept, inspect or even modify the messages being exchanged. The proxy is a fundamental design pattern that is used quite often in programming. A proxy may be used for various functionalities some of which are mentioned below:

- An access proxy is used to enforce security policies on access to a service or data.
- A remote proxy is used to mask or shield the client from the fact that the underlying object is remote.
- A load balancer proxy is used to distribute incoming requests to set of backend servers.
- A virtual proxy is used to perform lazy or just-in-time instantiation of the real object.
- Accountability
- Logging mechanism

In this section, we shall discuss how to create and install such proxies to intercept method invocation.

7.6.1 Designing Dynamic Proxy

In Java, a proxy is an object that acts as a pass through or a placeholder for object level access. Since, it sits between the caller and the object and can intercept the method call, it can change the real behaviour [Figure 7.1:].

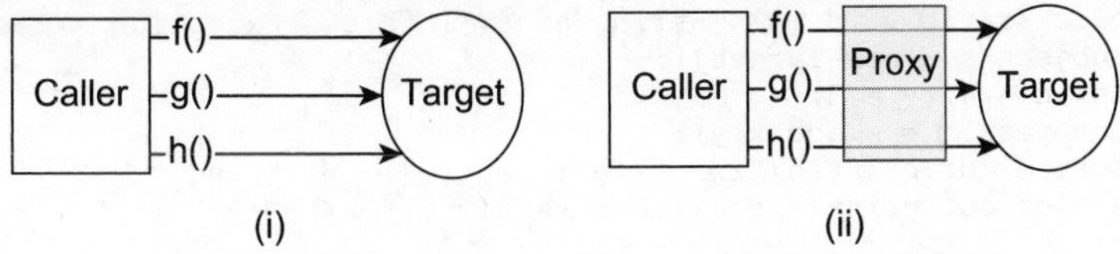

Figure 7.1: Method call (i) Without proxy, (ii) With proxy

One of the fundamental requirements of proxy design is to provide maximum transparency to the client and least coupling between the proxy and the underlying object. This means the method invocation syntax used by the client in a system with a proxy installed should remain same (or slightly different) as it was before the introduction of the proxy [Figure 7.1:]. This usually requires a proxy to either implement an interface or inherit from a known super class [Figure 7.2:].

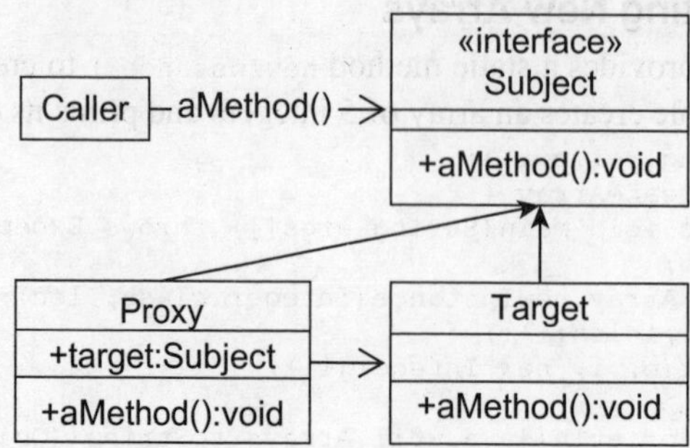

Figure 7.2: Proxy design pattern

Interestingly this implementation class (called proxy class) of an interface may be created at runtime. Since this proxy class is created on the fly, it is known as *dynamic proxy*. Java reflection API provides a class `java.lang.reflect.Proxy` which is used to create such dynamic proxy classes and their instances (called proxy objects).

Before describing how to create and install dynamic proxies, let us first develop a simple application that does not use any proxy. Once we understand this, we shall install a proxy between the caller and the target object.

Since, proxy requires an interface, we shall develop our application using an interface as follows:

```
public interface Subject {
  int add(int a, int b);
}
```

It has a single method `add()` that takes two integers and returns their sum. A sample implementation class will look like this:

```
public class Target implements Subject {
  public int add(int a, int b) {
    System.out.println("In add(): received: " + a + " and " + b);
    int result = a + b;
    System.out.println("In add(): Sent: "+ result);
    return result;
  }
}
```

The method `add()` displays several information to track what happens behind the scene. We can now write a client to use this class as follows:

```
import java.lang.reflect.*;
public class Caller {
  public static void main(String args[]) throws Exception {
    Subject s = new Target();
    int x = 4, y = 3;
    int result = s.add(x,y);
    System.out.println("In caller: sent: " + x +" and "+y);
    System.out.print("In caller: received("+x+"+"+y+"=): " + result);
  }
}
```

This program creates a `Target` object and invokes `add()` method on it. It also prints useful information to track method call and response. The pictorial description and a sample result of this program is shown below:

```
In add(): received: 4 and 3
In add(): Sent: 7
In caller: sent: 4 and 3
In caller: received(4+3=): 7
```

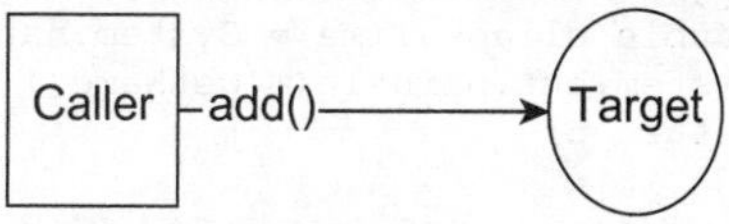

Caller — add() → Target

Let us now install a proxy between the `Caller` and the `Target`. To install a proxy object, we have to create a proxy class first. This proxy class structurally should look like the `Target` which already implements `Subject` interface. So, the proxy class must also implement this interface. The `java.lang.reflect.Proxy` class provides a static method `getProxyClass()` which can be used for this purpose and looks like this:

```
public static Class<?> getProxyClass(ClassLoader loader,
Class<?>... interfaces)
```

Indeed this method takes an array of interfaces and a class loader and returns the `Class` object for a proxy class. The byte code of this proxy class will be generated by the specified class loader and will implement all the supplied interfaces. For our `Subject` interface, we get the proxy class as follows:

```
Class proxyClass = Proxy.getProxyClass(Subject.class.getClassLoader(),new
Class[] { Subject.class });
```

A proxy class created in this fashion will have the following properties:

- Proxy classes are public, final, non-abstract subclasses of java.lang.reflect.Proxy
- The proxy class name begins with the string "$Proxy".
- A proxy class implements exactly the interfaces specified at its creation.
- Each proxy instance has an associated invocation handler object, whose class implements the interface InvocationHandler.
- Each proxy class has one public constructor that takes one argument, an implementation of the interface InvocationHandler, to set the invocation handler for a proxy instance

7.6.2 Invocation Handlers

Proxy itself is not as important as its behaviour which is provided by an implementation of `java.lang.reflect.InvocationHandler`. A method invocation on a proxy instance through one of its proxy interfaces will be dispatched to the `invoke()` method of the instance's invocation handler. The prototype of this method looks like this:

```
Object invoke(Object proxy, Method method, Object[] args)
```

It takes three parameters, processes a method invocation on a proxy instance and returns the result. The first parameter is a reference for the proxy instance that the method was invoked on. The second parameter is the `Method` instance corresponding to the interface method invoked on the proxy instance and the last parameter is an array of objects containing the values of the arguments passed in the method invocation on the proxy instance, or null if interface method takes no arguments. This essentially is the place where we implement the functionality of the proxy.

Before creating a proxy instance, let us write such a handler. Our handler simply keeps track of method invocation time. So, it looks like this:

```
import java.lang.reflect.*;
public class MyLogger implements InvocationHandler {
  Object target;
  public MyLogger(Object t) {target = t;}
```

```
public Object invoke(Object proxy,Method m,Object[] args)throws Throwable
{
    double start = System.nanoTime();
    Object o = m.invoke(target, args);
    double ellapseTime = System.nanoTime() - start;
    System.out.println(m.getName() + "() took "+ellapseTime+" ns");
    return o;
  }
}
```

The `invoke()` intercepts a method call and notes the current system time. It then wants the method call to pass through. For this, it needs a reference to the real object. Since, `invoke()` method does not provide any such reference, it is passed to the constructor which saves the reference in `target`.

Note that the method is called on the target object using reflection. That's why it works generically for all objects and for all methods. We can now call the one argument constructor that takes an invocation handler to create a proxy instance:

```
Target o = new Target();
Subject s = (Subject)proxyClass.getConstructor(new Class[]
{ InvocationHandler.class }).newInstance(new Object[] { new MyLogger(o) });
```

Instead of using the reflection API to access the public constructor, a proxy instance can also be created directly by calling the `newProxyInstance()` method of `Proxy` as follows :

```
Target o = new Target();
Subject s =   (Subject)Proxy.newProxyInstance(o.getClass().getClassLoader(),
o.getClass().getInterfaces(), new MyLogger(o));
```

The `newProxyInstance()` method essentially combines the actions of calling `getProxyClass()` and invoking the constructor with an invocation handler [Figure 7.3:].

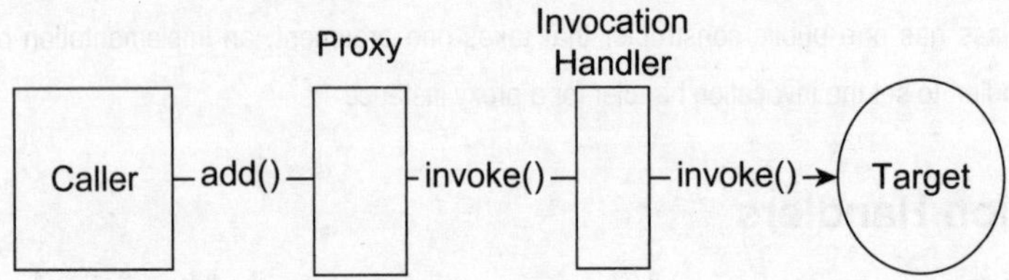

Figure 7.3: Method invocation with proxy installed

The source code of the caller will finally look like this:

```
import java.lang.reflect.*;
public class Caller {
  public static void main(String args[]) throws Exception {
   Target o = new Target();
   Subject s = (Subject)Proxy.newProxyInstance(o.getClass().getClassLoader(),
                                 o.getClass().getInterfaces(), new MyLogger(o));
    int x = 4, y = 3;
    int result = s.add(x,y);
    System.out.println("In caller: sent: " + x +" and "+y);
    System.out.print("In caller: received("+x+"+"+y+"=): " + result);
  }
}
```

A sample output of this program looks like this:

```
In add(): received: 4 and 3
In add(): Sent: 7
add() took 605067.0 ns
In caller: sent: 4 and 3
In caller: received(4+3=): 7
```

7.7 DISADVANTAGE OF REFLECTION

One of the primary drawbacks of reflection is that *reflective code* gets executed more slowly than their non-reflective counterpart. This happens since reflection involves types that are resolved at run-time, but not at compile time. Moreover, since JVM performs a lot of optimization at compile time, codes that use reflection will remain un-optimized and run slower than those codes which did not use reflection API.

Another drawback of reflection is that it allows us to access information that is usually not allowed in non-reflexive code. For example, reflection allows us to access even class's private fields and methods that would otherwise remain inaccessible in non-reflective code. This violates the rule of abstraction and could potentially ruin the code or may make it non-portable.

So, it is suggested that reflective codes not be used unless it is unavoidable.

KEYWORDS

Array—A class that provides several static methods to dynamically create and access Java arrays

Class—A Class object represents a class or an interface in a Java application

Constructor—A class that provides information about, and access to, a single constructor

Field—A class that provides information about, and dynamic access to, a single field

Method—A class that provides information about, and access to, a single method

Modifier—A class contains 12 static constants one each modifiers that can be applied on class and its members such as fields, methods and constructors

Proxy—A module that sits in the middle of two or more communicating parties and can intercept, inspect or even modify the messages being exchanged

Reflection—An API in Java that enables us to examine and/or modify the properties or behaviour or other elements of an object at run-time

Type—A class that represents the type of field

SUMMARY

The reflection API in Java enables us to examine and/or modify the properties or behaviour or other elements of an object at run-time.

The foundation of Java reflection API is the class `java.lang.Class`. A `Class` object represents a class or an interface in a Java application. This class provides methods to examine both class level and object level runtime information such as modifiers, fields, methods, constructors etc.

There are numerous ways to create such an object. There are certain other important classes for introspection. One such class is Modifier that contains 12 static constants one for each modifier. A field of a class is represented by the `Field` class that provides information about, and dynamic access to, a single field. A method of a class is represented by the `Method` class that provides information about, and access to, a single method. Since, constructors are special methods, reflection API provides a separate class `Constructor` that provides information about, and access to, a single constructor.

The reflection API also allows us to invoke a method (both static and non-static) indirectly. This is done using `Method.invoke()` method. Reflection also provides facility to analyze code using annotations.

Like methods, reflection also provides APIs to find constructors of a class and obtain information such as its modifiers, parameters, annotations and thrown exceptions etc. Reflection can do more than just simply list fields, methods and constructors. Through reflection, we can even create instances.

In reflection API, an array is represented by the `Array` class that provides several static methods to dynamically create and access Java arrays.

One of the important facilities of reflection API is the ability to create proxies dynamically.

One of the primary drawbacks of reflection is that *reflective code* gets executed more slowly than their non-reflective counterpart. Another drawback of reflection is that it allows us to access information that is usually not allowed in non-reflexive code.

WEB RESOURCES

http://docs.oracle.com/javase/tutorial/reflect/
Trail: The Reflection API

http://ftp.gwdg.de/pub/languages/java/java.sun.com/jdk1.1/java-reflection.pdf
Java™ Core Reflection API and Specification

http://wwwusers.di.uniroma1.it/~parisi/Risorse/java-reflection-explained-simply-manual-8up.pdf
Java Reflection

http://www.csd.uoc.gr/~hy252/references/JavaReflection.pdf
Java Reflection in Action

http://www.kencooney.com/programming/java/reflection.pdf
Java Reflection

http://www.java2s.com/Tutorial/Java/0125__Reflection/Catalog0125__Reflection.htm
Java Reflection

EXERCISES

Objective-type Questions

1. Which of these packages contains reflection classes and interfaces?
   (a) java.reflection
   (b) java.reflect
   (c) java.lang.reflection
   (d) java.lang.reflect

2. Which of the following is used to get the type of object represented by "obj"?
   (a) Classloader.getInstance(obj);
   (b) obj.getClass().getName();
   (c) obj.toString();
   (d) new Class.getName(obj);

3. What does the following program segment do?

```
import java.lang.reflect.Field;
MyClass myClass = new MyClass();
try {
    Class cl=Class.forName("MyClass");
    Field res=cl.getDeclaredField("count");
    res.set(myClass,"5");
}
catch(Exception e) {}
```

   (a) The first 5 member variables of myClass are copied to "res".
   (b) The value of myClass.count is set to 5.
   (c) 5 copies of the myClass object are created.
   (d) The number of MyClass fields described in "cl" is set to 5.

4. What is primary class in reflection?
   (a) Reflection (c) Class
   (b) Reflect (d) Primary

5. Which of the following methods on an object is used to get a Class object representing the object's type?
   (a) getClass() (c) type()
   (b) getType() (d) class()

6. How do you get a Class object for primitive types?
   (a) [I] (c) 2[I
   (b) I]] (d) [[I

7. Which of the following returns a Class for an array of String?
   (a) Class.forName("[LString;");
   (b) Class.forName("java.lang.String;");
   (c) Class.forName("[Ljava.lang.String;");
   (d) Class.forName("[Ljava.lang.String");

8. The total number of modifiers used for class/interface, fields, methods and constructors is
   (a) 10 (c) 12
   (b) 11 (d) 13

9. What value does classModifiers() return?
   (a) 3103 (c) 3391
   (b) 7 (d) 223

10. What value does fieldModifiers() return?
    (a) 3103 (c) 3391
    (b) 7 (d) 223

11. What value does methodModifiers() return?
    (a) 3103 (c) 3391
    (b) 7 (d) 223

12. What value does constructorModifiers() return?
    (a) 3103 (c) 3391
    (b) 7 (d) 223

13. Which of the following methods is used to call a method using reflection?
    (a) call()
    (b) callMethod()
    (c) invoke()
    (d) invokeMethod()

14. Which of the following methods is used to create an instance of a class?
    (a) newObject()
    (b) createInstance()
    (c) createObject()
    (d) newInstance()

15. Which of the following modifiers cannot be used for a class?
    (a) public
    (b) final
    (c) abstract
    (d) volatile

16. Which of the following methods is used when modifying final fields?
    (a) setField()
    (b) setAccessible()
    (c) makeAccessible()
    (d) makeModifiable()

17. Which of the following methods is used to find the list of interfaces a class implements?
    (a) getGenericInterfaces()
    (b) getInterfaces()
    (c) findGenericInterfaces()
    (d) interfaces()

18. Which of the following classes represents an invocation handler?
    (a) java.reflect.InvocationHandler
    (b) java.InvocationHandler
    (c) java.lang.reflect.InvocationHandler
    (d) java.lang.reflect.Handler

19. Which of the following methods is used to create a dynamic proxy?
    (a) getProxyInstance()
    (b) getProxy()
    (c) createProxyClass()
    (d) getProxyClass()

20. A dynamic proxy is an instance of
    (a) java.lang.reflect.DynamicProxy
    (b) java.reflect.Proxy
    (c) java.lang.reflect.Proxy
    (d) java.Proxy

21. Which of the following is used to create an instance of an array using reflection?
    (a) Array.newInstance()
    (b) Array.instance()
    (c) Array.createArray()
    (d) Array.createInstance()

Subjective-type Questions

1. Write the mangled names that represent a two-dimensional array.
2. Write the names of some popular software where Java reflection is used.
3. How can you construct an object of a given class using reflection?
4. Write the different ways with their relative merits and demerits to get the Class object?
5. What is the primary purpose of Modifier class?
6. Using reflection, how can you tell if a member is public or private?
7. How will you to retrieve modifier's information of a class
8. There is no explicit constant which corresponds to "package" access. So, how will you identify it?
9. Write some of the methods that are used to get information about a class.
10. Write a program that finds and displays inheritance hierarchy of a specified class.
11. What is the difference between getDeclaraedFields() and getFields()?
12. Write a program that shows all public fields of a specified class.
13. Explain how you will modify final fields.
14. Provide a simple example of object reflection in Java.
15. Is Java reflection slow and/or expensive? What are some of the drawbacks of reflection in Java?
16. Write some practical uses of Java reflection?

CHAPTER – 8

JAVA NATIVE INTERFACE

KEY OBJECTIVES

After completing this chapter readers will be able to—

- understand the importance of JNI
- know the basic steps required to develop JNI applications
- get an idea about how Java types are mapped to native types
- understand how native code can talk to Java code
- learn how to pass parameters to native methods and how to access them
- learn how native code can handle exceptions

8.1 INTRODUCTION

Although Java is an extremely powerful language, there are situations where Java alone may not fulfil our requirements. The following are some examples:

- If we want very fast response from a code, C,C++ or assembly code are better options than Java.
- If we want to use an existing library written using a language other than Java
- If our application requires some platform-dependent features

The **J**ava **N**ative **I**nterface (JNI) is an API that allows Java code to interoperate with applications and libraries written in other programming languages such as C, C++. It is a two-way interface that allows Java applications to invoke native method and native methods to interact with Java code. A native method specifically can do the following:

- Access fields and methods of Java objects passed into it
- Access non-static fields and methods of the Java object on which it is invoked
- Access static fields and methods of the class containing it
- Create, delete, modify Java objects
- Catch and throw exceptions
- Load classes, get class information

- Inspect type at runtime
- Create new JVM and run programs in it

Note that your Java program will no longer remain platform-independent if it contains any JNI code. That is why, it is suggested not to use JNI unless it is unavoidable.

8.2 JAVA PROGRAM WITH C/C++

Although it is said that JNI allows Java code to interact with other language codes, JNI currently provides facilities to access C/C++ or assembly code. We shall first use C and then C++ as native language. Let us first write a simple JNI application that calls a C function `print()` that prints a message. The following are basic steps to do this:

- Write a Java class having a native method declaration.
- Compile this class using javac.
- Generate C header file using javah
- Implement the native method in a C program
- Compile C program and create a shared library
- Run the Java program

8.2.1 Writing Java Program

If a Java program wants to invoke a method which is implemented in a different programming language, the method is said to be *native method*. Before invoking such a method, it must be declared first. Declaring a native method looks very similar to that of abstract methods except that the keyword `native` is used instead of `abstract` keyword. So, the declaration of our `print()` method looks like this:

```
public native void print();
```

The native keyword signals that `print()` will be implemented in a native language. Hence, the method body is not provided. Java compiler understands it and does not look for its body. However, before calling this method, JVM must load the library containing the method's native implementation. We use `loadLibrary()` method of `System` class to load a library. Suppose the method is implemented in GCC and the name of the library is `libtest.so`, then the following line is used to load the library:

```
System.loadLibrary("test");
```

Note that the JVM uses standard, but platform-specific, rule to translate the native library name to the actual library name. For example, for JVM in Unix-like system, the native library name `test` is translated in actual library name `libtest.so` while in windows the same is translated in `test.dll`.

Alternatively, we can use the `load()` method that takes the pathname of the library file as follows:

```
System.load("/root/ajp/jni/c/libtest.so");
```

Note that the `load()` method always expects absolute pathname. Since, it is mandatory to load this library before calling the method, it is a good and safe idea to load it in the static block, which gets executed before all other statements. The complete source code (`JNITest.java`) is given below:

```
class JNITest {
  public native void print();
  static {
    System.loadLibrary("test");
```

```
  }
  public static void main(String[] args) {
    new JNITest().print();
  }
}
```

In the main method, we have created an instance of `JNITest` class and invoked the native method `print()`. Note that the syntax to call a native method is exactly same as a regular method call. We shall consistently use the same class name (`JNITest`) throughout the chapter to demonstrate various concepts of JNI. Needless to say that class's content will be different.

8.2.2 Compiling Java Program

Compiling a Java program having native method is not different at all. We use the same syntax used for ordinary Java programs as follows:

```
javac JNITest.java
```

As usual, this generates a class `JNITest.class`.

8.2.3 Create Header File

The Java part of the JNI application is complete. It is time to implement the method `print()` in C. However, since Java and C are two different programming languages, the prototype of this `print()` function in C is not supposed to be same as in Java. So, how do you determine the prototype of `print()` in C? Fortunately, Java comes with a tool `javah` to solve this problem. The tool `javah`, given a Java class containing native method(s) declaration, essentially generates C/C++ header file containing function prototype(s). So, we use it as follows:

```
javah JNITest
```

The name of the header file is the mangled fully-qualified class name with extension `h`. The above command generates a file `JNITest.h` whose content is shown below:

```
/* DO NOT EDIT THIS FILE - it is machine generated */
#include <jni.h>
/* Header for class JNITest */

#ifndef _Included_JNITest
#define _Included_JNITest
#ifdef __cplusplus
extern "C" {
#endif
/*
 * Class:     JNITest
 * Method:    print
 * Signature: ()V
 */
JNIEXPORT void JNICALL Java_JNITest_print(JNIEnv *, jobject);

#ifdef __cplusplus
}
#endif
#endif
```

The generated header file includes a file `jni.h` (`<JAVA_HOME>/include/jni.h`). This header file provides all information the native function needs to interact with Java code. It defines all of the necessary data types and contains macros and typedefs that hide the complexity of mapping Java types to native types. It also includes other platform-specific header files. Since `javah` automatically includes this header file, we usually do not have to explicitly include this file.

As you can see, `javah` generated the prototype of the following C function corresponding to the Java native method `print()`.

```
JNIEXPORT void JNICALL Java_JNITest_print(JNIEnv *, jobject);
```

The name of the function is determined from the following components:

- the prefix Java_
- a mangled fully-qualified class name
- an underscore ("_") separator
- a mangled method name
- for overloaded native methods, two underscores ("__") followed by the mangled argument signature

This set of rules makes a method name unique even if different Java classes have native methods with same name.

The generated C/C++ function will always contain two parameters in addition to the regular parameters originally declared in the native Java method. The first parameter is a pointer to a structure that contains the interface to the JVM. (Note that this `JNIEnv` is not the actual name of the structure. The name of the structure is `JNIEnv_` and `const struct JNINativeInterface_` for C++ and C respectively. We shall discuss more on this later in this chapter). This structure contains all of the functions necessary to interact with the JVM and to work with Java objects. For example, it includes functions for instantiating objects, throwing exceptions, converting native arrays to/from Java arrays, native strings to/from Java strings etc. With this pointer, although it is not that easy, we can virtually do everything that Java code can do.

The second argument differs depending on whether the native method is non-static or static. It is a reference to the object (`jobject`) for a non-static native method and is a reference to its Java class (`jclass`) for static method.

When a native method is called, JVM passes these two arguments to the corresponding C/C++ function from where we can see the JVM back using these two parameters.

The `JNIEXPORT` and `JNICALL` are macros used to specify the calling and linkage convention of both Java native methods and their implementations. In Linux like OS, they are blank macros (defined in `<JAVA_HOME>/include/linux/jni_md.h`) as follows:

```
#define JNIEXPORT
#define JNICALL
```

So, the function prototype essentially looks like an ordinary one as follows:

```
void Java_JNITest_print(JNIEnv *, jobject);
```

Since windows use different calling conventions, their definitions (`<JAVA_HOME>\include\win32\jni_md.h`) are as follows

```
#define JNIEXPORT __declspec(dllexport)
#define JNICALL __stdcall
```

In windows, the function prototype finally looks like this:

```
__declspec(dllexport) void __stdcall Java_JNITest_print(JNIEnv *, jobject);
```

8.2.4 Implement Native Method

In the C implementation file, we include the above generated header file `JNITest.h`.

```
#include "JNITest.h"
```

We then implement the native method as follows:

```
JNIEXPORT void JNICALL Java_JNITest_print(JNIEnv *env, jobject obj){
    printf("In a C function\n");
}
```

The function `Java_JNITest_print()` prints a simple message `"In a C function\n"` so that we can trace the method calls. Here is the complete source code of C implementation file (`JNITestImpl.c`):

```
//JNITestImpl.c
#include "JNITest.h"
#include <stdio.h>
JNIEXPORT void JNICALL Java_JNITest_print(JNIEnv *env, jobject obj){
    printf("In a C function\n");
}
```

8.2.5 Create Shared Library

The implementation of native method is now ready. We shall use GNU C compiler to compile this file and create a shared library. We use the following command to create a library `libtest.so`:

```
cc -shared -I/usr/java/jdk1.7.0_45/include -
I/usr/java/jdk1.7.0_45/include/linux JNITestImpl.c -o libtest.so
```

Note that to compile, we need the system header file `<JAVA_HOME>/include/jni.h`, which in turn includes `<JAVA_HOME>/include/linux/jni_md.h`. So, include these two directories `<JAVA_HOME>/include` and `<JAVA_HOME>/include/linux` during compilation. The symbolic name `<JAVA_HOME>` represents the directory where Java was installed. For our system, Java home directory was `/usr/java/jdk1.7.0_45/`. So, we included two directories `/usr/java/jdk1.7.0_45/include` and `/usr/java/jdk1.7.0_45/include/linux` so that the compiler cc can recognize header files `jni.h` and `jni_md.h`.

8.2.6 Running the Program

Now, we are about to call a native function from a Java program. Use the following command specifying the location of the native library:

```
java -Djava.library.path=. JNITest
```

If everything goes fine, the following message should appear:

```
In a C function
```

The location of the library may also be specified using `LD_LIBRARY_PATH` environment variable as follows:

```
export LD_LIBRARY_PATH=$LD_LIBRARY_PATH:.
```

We can then run the Java program directly as follows:

```
java JNITest
```

For convenience, we write a shell script as follows:

```
#make.sh
javac JNITest.java
javah JNITest
cc -shared -I/usr/java/jdk1.7.0_45/include -
I/usr/java/jdk1.7.0_45/include/linux JNITestImpl.c -o libtest.so
java -Djava.library.path=. JNITest
```

Give the execution permission as follows:

```
chmod +x make.sh
```

We can now perform all JNI tasks by executing this shell script:

```
./make.sh
```

8.3 USING C++

So far we have implemented a native method in C language. JNI also supports methods to be implemented in C++. Implementing the native method in C++ is not very different. Here is a sample implementation (`JNITestImpl.cpp`):

```
//JNITestImpl.cpp
#include "JNITest.h"
#include <iostream>
JNIEXPORT void JNICALL Java_JNITest_print(JNIEnv *env, jobject obj){
  std::cout << "In a C++ function\n";
}
```

Since, we have not used any C++ specific feature, it looks exactly like C implementation except that we used `cout` instead of `printf` and included `iostream` in place of `stdio.h`. Use GNU C++ compiler `g++` to create the library:

```
g++ -shared -I/usr/java/jdk1.7.0_45/include -
I/usr/java/jdk1.7.0_45/include/linux JNITestImpl.cpp -o libtest.so
```

Run the Java program as before. The following message should appear.

```
In a C++ function
```

The shell script will look like this:

```
#make.sh
javac JNITest.java
javah JNITest
g++ -shared -I/usr/java/jdk1.7.0_45/include -
I/usr/java/jdk1.7.0_45/include/linux JNITestImpl.cpp -o libtest.so
java -Djava.library.path=. JNITest
```

8.4 SYNTAX DIFFERENCE IN C/C++

Every native function receives a pointer `JNIEnv` to JNI interface. Accessing functions through `JNIEnv` parameter has different syntax in C and C++. Let us inspect its reason first. See the following typedefs in `jni.h` file:

```
//jni.h
struct JNINativeInterface_;
struct JNIEnv_;

#ifdef __cplusplus
typedef JNIEnv_ JNIEnv;
#else
typedef const struct JNINativeInterface_ *JNIEnv;
#endif
```

So, `JNIEnv` essentially represents `JNIEnv_` and `const struct JNINativeInterface_ *` in C++ and C respectively [see Figure 8.1:]. The declarations of these two structures are shown below:

```
struct JNINativeInterface_ {
...
    jint (JNICALL *GetVersion)(JNIEnv *env);
...
}
```

```
struct JNIEnv_ {
    const struct JNINativeInterface_ *functions;
#ifdef __cplusplus
    jint GetVersion() {
        return functions->GetVersion(this);
    }
    ...
}
```

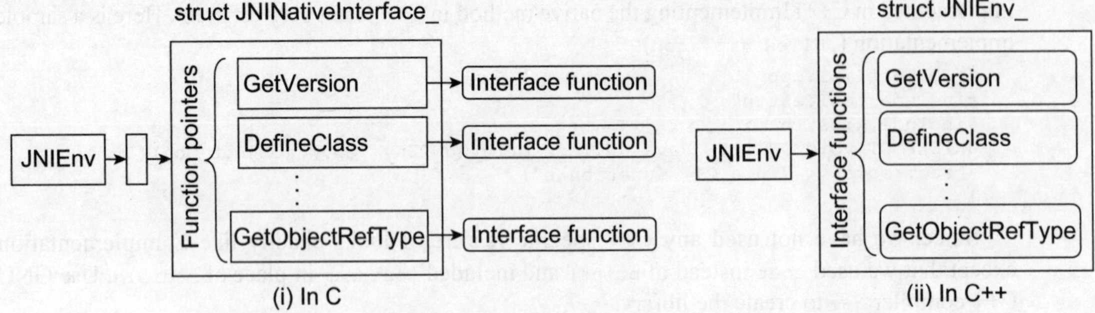

Figure 8.1: JNI interface pointer representation (i) In C (ii) In C++

With this declaration, a function parameter declaration `JNIEnv *env` is translated to `JNIEnv_ *env` and `const struct JNINativeInterface_ **env` in C++ and C respectively. So to invoke a function `GetVersion()`, in C++, we can use either `(*env).GetVersion()` or in short `env->GetVersion()`. The C equivalent syntax is `(*((**env).GetVersion))(env)` or `(*((*env)->GetVersion))(env)` or in short `(*env)->GetVersion()`.

In summary, in C++, we can use `env->`, instead of `(*env)->`. Also, there is no need for the `JNIEnv*` argument in the C++ functions. These imply that invoking a JNI native function in C++ is more convenient than invoking the same in C. Hereafter, we shall use C++ functions unless it is not mentioned explicitly.

8.5 USING JAVA PACKAGE

In this section, we shall discuss how to work with JNI if Java programs belong to a package. We write `JNITest.java` as a part of package `apkg` as follows:

```
package apkg;
class JNITest {
  public native void print();
  static {
    System.loadLibrary("test");
  }
  public static void main(String[] args) {
    new JNITest().print();
  }
}
```

Create a directory `apkg` under your application root directory and place it in `apkg` directory. So, the directory content will look like this:

```
root
 └─apkg
     └─JNITest.java
```

Now, go to the directory `root` and give the following command to compile the Java program:

```
javac apkg/JNITest.java
```

Since, the Java class is kept in a package, we specify fully qualified class name during generation of header file:

```
javah -d include apkg.JNITest
```

You may also put the generated header file in a different directory. We decided to place it in a sub-directory `include`. So, we specified `-d include` option to the `javah` tool. This generates the header file `apkg_JNITest.h` in the `include` sub-directory. So the directory structure looks like this now:

```
root
├──apkg
│     ├──JNITest.java
│     └──JNITest.class
└──include
      └──apkg_JNITest.h
```

Write the implementation file in the `root` directory as follows:

```
//JNITestImpl.cpp
#include "include/apkg_JNITest.h"
#include <iostream>
JNIEXPORT void JNICALL Java_apkg_JNITest_print(JNIEnv *env, jobject obj){
  std::cout << "In a C++ function\n";
}
```

See how the header file is included here. Now compile the C++ program and create library as follows:

```
g++ -shared -I/usr/java/jdk1.7.0_45/include -
I/usr/java/jdk1.7.0_45/include/linux JNITestImpl.cpp -o libtest.so
```

The final directory structure looks like this:

```
root
├───JNITestImpl.cpp
├───libtest.so
├───apkg
│       ├──JNITest.java
│       └──JNITest.class
└───include
        └──apkg_JNITest.h
```

Finally, execute the Java program as follows:

```
java -Djava.library.path=. apkg.JNITest
```

8.5.1 JNI Types and Data Structures

This section discusses how the JNI maps Java types to native C/C++ types. Since, a native language may not support all Java types, a mapping between a Java type to a native type is needed. For example, since C language does not support any `boolean` type, Java `boolean` type is mapped (typedef) to C `unsigned char` which is named as a JNI type `jboolean`. A list of such typedefs can be found in `<JAVA_HOME>/include/jni.h` and `<JAVA_HOME>/include/linux/jni_md.h` (in linux). Some of the declarations are shown below:

```
//jni.h
typedef unsigned char    jboolean;
typedef unsigned short   jchar;
typedef short            jshort;
typedef float            jfloat;
typedef double           jdouble;

typedef jint             jsize;


//jni_md.h
typedef int jint;
#ifdef _LP64 /* 64-bit Solaris */
typedef long jlong;
```

```
#else
typedef long long jlong;
#endif

typedef signed char jbyte;
```

Table 8.1: describes Java primitive types and their machine-dependent native equivalents.

Table 8.1: Type mapping between Java and Linux native code

Java Type	C/C++ type	Native name	Description
boolean	unsigned char	jboolean	unsigned 8 bits
byte	signed char	jbyte	signed 8 bits
char	unsigned short	jchar	unsigned 16 bits
short	short	jshort	signed 16 bits
int	int	jint	signed 32 bits
long	long (for 64-bit) long long (else)	jlong	signed 64 bits
float	float	jfloat	32 bits
double	double	jdouble	64 bits
void	void	void	

The JNI also defines a number of reference types corresponding to different kinds of Java objects. The hierarchy of such JNI reference types is shown in Figure 8.2:

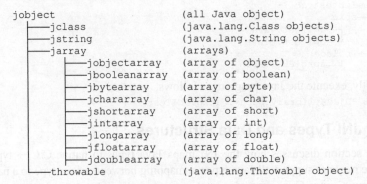

```
jobject                          (all Java object)
    ├──jclass                    (java.lang.Class objects)
    ├──jstring                   (java.lang.String objects)
    ├──jarray                    (arrays)
    │      ├──jobjectarray        (array of object)
    │      ├──jbooleanarray       (array of boolean)
    │      ├──jbytearray          (array of byte)
    │      ├──jchararray          (array of char)
    │      ├──jshortarray         (array of short)
    │      ├──jintarray           (array of int)
    │      ├──jlongarray          (array of long)
    │      ├──jfloatarray         (array of float)
    │      └──jdoublearray        (array of double)
    └──throwable                 (java.lang.Throwable object)
```

Figure 8.2: JNI Reference Types

The JNI uses the Java VM's representation of type signatures. These signatures are used in various JNI functions. Table 8.2: summarizes these type signatures.

Table 8.2: JVM's type signatures

Java Type	Signature	Java Type	Signature	Java Type	Signature
boolean	Z	int	I	void	V
byte	B	long	J	fully-qualified-class	L fully-qualified-class ;
char	C	float	F	type[]	[type
short	S	double	D	method type	(arg-types) ret-type

For clarity and better understanding, some of the declarations and their signatures are shown in Table 8.3:

Table 8.3: JVM's type signatures example

Declaration	Signature	Declaration	Signature
void f()	()V	void f(String)	(Ljava/lang/String;)V
void f(int)	(I)V	void f(int, String)	(ILjava/lang/String;)V
void f(int, int)	(II)V	void f(String, int)	(Ljava/lang/String;I)V
void f(int, double)	(ID)V	void f(int, String[])	(I[Ljava/lang/String;)V
void f(int[])	([I)V	void f(int[], String[])	([I[Ljava/lang/String;)V
void f(int, int[])	(I[I)V	void f(String[],String[])	([Ljava/lang/String;[Ljava/lang/String;)V
void f(int[], double[])	([I[D)V	void f(String[], int[])	([Ljava/lang/String;[I)V
int g()	()I	String g(String)	(Ljava/lang/String;)Ljava/lang/String;
int g(int)	(I)I	String[] g(int, String)	(ILjava/lang/String;)[Ljava/lang/String;
int[] g(int[])	([I)[I	String[] g(String[])	([Ljava/lang/String;)[Ljava/lang/String

8.6 PASSING ARGUMENTS

The native method that we have used so far neither took any argument nor returned any value. Let us now understand how to pass arguments to and use them in native methods.

8.6.1 Passing Primitives

Consider the following Java class having a native method:

```
class JNITest {
 public native byte sqr(byte x);
  static {
    System.loadLibrary("test");
  }
  public static void main(String[] args) {
    byte a = 3;
    System.out.println(a+" * "+a+" = "+new JNITest().sqr(a));
  }
}
```

It declares a native method `sqr()` that receives one `byte` and returns a `byte` which is the square of the value passed. Since, C/C++ does not have a type `byte`, let us see what happens here. The `main()` method invokes `sqr()` with a value 3. Compile this Java program and generate header file as before. The following native function prototype is generated:

```
JNIEXPORT jdouble JNICALL Java_JNITest_sqr(JNIEnv *, jobject, jbyte);
```

Notice that the Java type `byte` is converted to `jbyte` which is actually the typedef of C/C++ `signed char`. The JNI finds that most suitable type in C/C++ corresponding to Java type `byte` is `signed char`. You can find this typedef in `jni_md.h` as follows:

```
typedef signed char jbyte;
```

The implementation of such native method is simple:

```
//JNITestImpl.cpp
#include "JNITest.h"
JNIEXPORT jbyte JNICALL Java_JNITest_sqr(JNIEnv *env, jobject obj, jbyte x) {
  return x * x;
}
```

Compile and generate a library from the above program and run Java programs as before. The following output appears:

```
3 * 3 = 9
```

8.6.2 Passing Strings

To demonstrate how to pass and return Java `String` objects, we have taken the following program:

```
class JNITest {
 public native String greeting(String msg);
  static {
    System.loadLibrary("test");
  }
  public static void main(String[] args) {
    String s = new String("John");
    System.out.println("In Java: Sent-->"+s);
    System.out.println("In Java: received<--"+new JNITest().greeting(s));
  }
}
```

This JNI program declares a native method `greeting()` that receives a Java `String` and also returns a Java `String`. Compile this Java program and generate header file as before. The following native function prototype is generated:

```
JNIEXPORT jstring JNICALL Java_JNITest_greeting(JNIEnv *, jobject, jstring);
```

Here JNI type `jstring` corresponds to Java type `String`. Its declaration looks like this:

```
#ifdef __cplusplus
class _jobject {};
class _jstring : public _jobject {};
typedef _jstring *jstring;
#else
struct _jobject;
typedef struct _jobject *jobject;
typedef jobject jstring;
#endif
```

So, `jstring` is essentially a pointer to an empty struct (in C) or class (in C++) type. Since, a Java `String` is an object, JNI used struct/class to represent them in C/C++. However, JNI couldn't implement the struct/class since a C/C++ string is not an object; it is NULL terminated char array (it is char *). The important question is how to obtain C/C++ char* from Java String then? Fortunately, JNI provides a number of string-related functions that can be accessed through `JNIEnv*`. For example, to get a C++ `char*` from JNI string (`jstring`) `js`, we use the following `GetStringUTFChars()` method as follows:

```
const char *in = env->GetStringUTFChars(js, NULL);
```

We then create a new string from this string preceding a string "Hi ":

```
char out[128];
strcpy(out, "Hi ");
strcat(out, in);
```

The initial string `in` and `js` are destroyed as they are no longer needed.

```
env->ReleaseStringUTFChars(js, in);
```

A list of useful JNI string functions is given in appendix A. Finally, the function returns a JNI string from this out as follows:

```
return env->NewStringUTF(out);
```

The complete source code is given below:

```
//JNITestImpl.cpp
#include "JNITest.h"
#include <string.h>
#include <iostream>
using namespace std;
JNIEXPORT jstring JNICALL Java_JNITest_greeting(JNIEnv *env, jobject obj,
jstring js) {
   // Convert the JNI String (jstring) into C-String (char*)
   const char *in = env->GetStringUTFChars(js, NULL);
   cout << "In C: received<--" << in << '\n';
   // Create a new C-String out
   char out[128];
   strcpy(out, "Hi ");
   strcat(out, in);
   //Release js and in
   env->ReleaseStringUTFChars(js, in);
   cout << "In C: sent->" << out << '\n';
   //Send out
   return env->NewStringUTF(out);
}
```

Compile and generate a library from the above program and run Java programs as before. The following output results:

```
In Java: Sent-->John
In C: received<--John
In C: sent->Hi John
In Java: received<--Hi John
```

8.6.3 Passing Primitive Array

In Java, arrays are reference types. There are 9 types of arrays; one for each of the eight primitive types (`boolean`, `char`, `int`, `byte`, `short`, `long`, `float` and `double`) and one for Java `Object`. For each of these arrays, JNI defines a type, namely `jbooleanArray`, `jcharArray`, `jintArray`, `jbyteArray`, `jshortArray`, `jlongArray`, `jfloatArray`, `jdoubleArray` and `jobjectArray`. In this section, we shall show how to work with JNI primitive arrays. Consider the following Java program:

```
class JNITest {
 public native int[] sort(int[] a);
  static {
    System.loadLibrary("test");
  }
  public static void main(String[] args) {
    int[] a = {5, 4, 6, 3};
    System.out.print("In Java: Sent-->");
    for(int i=0;i<a.length;i++)
      System.out.print(a[i]+" ");
    int[] result = new JNITest().sort(a);
    System.out.print("In Java: Received<--");
    for(int i=0;i<result.length;i++)
      System.out.print(result[i]+" ");
  }
}
```

This JNI program declares a native method `sort()` that receives an `int` array and returns sorted `int` array. The main method passes an unsorted integer array to this native method, which sorts and sends it back to the application. Compile this Java program and generate header file as before. The following native function prototype is generated:

```
JNIEXPORT jintArray JNICALL Java_JNITest_sort(JNIEnv *, jobject, jintArray);
```

In JNI, Java `int` array is represented by the type `jintArray`. Primitive arrays in a native method are also accessed using JNI functions similar to those used for accessing strings. For example, to get C-style array from JNI array `in`, we use `GetIntArrayElements()` function as follows:

```
jint *cArray = env->GetIntArrayElements(in, NULL);
```

The length of the array may be obtained as follows:

```
jsize len = env->GetArrayLength(in);
```

We can now sort the array elements using bubble sort algorithm as follows:

```
for(int i=0;i<len;i++)
  for(int j=0;j<len-i-1;j++)
    if(cArray[j]> cArray[j+1]) {
      int temp = cArray[j];
      cArray[j] = cArray[j+1];
      cArray[j+1] = temp;
    }
```

To demonstrate other array methods, we create a new array, copy elements to this array and destroy the old C-style array as follows:

```
jintArray out = env->NewIntArray(len);
env->SetIntArrayRegion(out, 0 , len, cArray);
env->ReleaseIntArrayElements(in, cArray, NULL);
```

Needless to say, for successful copy, the size of the new array should be same as that of the old array. The complete source code of the C++ implementation is shown below:

```
//JNITestImpl.cpp
#include "JNITest.h"
#include <iostream>
using namespace std;
JNIEXPORT jintArray JNICALL Java_JNITest_sort(JNIEnv *env, jobject obj,
jintArray in) {
  jint *cArray = env->GetIntArrayElements(in, NULL);
  jsize len = env->GetArrayLength(in);
  cout << "\nIn C++: Received<--";
  for(int i=0;i<len;i++)
    cout << cArray[i] << ' ';
  for(int i=0;i<len;i++)
    for(int j=0;j<len-i-1;j++)
      if(cArray[j]> cArray[j+1]) {
        int temp = cArray[j];
        cArray[j] = cArray[j+1];
        cArray[j+1] = temp;
      }
  cout << "\nIn C++: Sent-->";
  for(int i=0;i<len;i++)
    cout << cArray[i] << ' ';
  cout << '\n';
  jintArray out = env->NewIntArray(len);
  env->SetIntArrayRegion(out, 0 , len, cArray);
  env->ReleaseIntArrayElements(in, cArray, NULL);
  return out;
}
```

Compile and generate a library from the above program and run Java programs as before. The following output results:

```
In Java: Sent-->5 4 6 3
In C++: Received<--5 4 6 3
In C++: Sent-->3 4 5 6
In Java: Received<--3 4 5 6
```

A list of useful JNI array functions is given in Appendix A

8.7 ACCESSING JAVA CODE FROM NATIVE PROGRAM

JNI also allows us to access Java code from native code. Suppose, we have invoked a native method `access()` on a Java object `o` as follows:

```
o.access();
```

Then, `access()` can access all members of `o`. In this section, we shall demonstrate how to do this. Consider the following Java program:

```
class JNITest {
  int x = 4;
  void f(){System.out.println("In non-static f()"); }
  static int y = 5;
  static void g() { System.out.println("In static g()"); }
  native void access();
  static {
    System.loadLibrary("test");
  }
  public static void main(String[] args) {
    JNITest o = new JNITest();
    System.out.println("Before: o.x = "+o.x+", o.y = "+o.y);
    o.access();
    System.out.println("After: o.x = "+o.x+", o.y = "+o.y);
  }
}
```

The `JNITest` class has a non-static field `x`, a non-static method `f()`, a static field `y` and a static method `g()` and a native method `access()`. The main method creates a `JNITest` object `o` and calls `access()` method on it. Compile this Java program and generate header file as before. The following native function prototype is generated:

```
JNIEXPORT void JNICALL Java_JNITest_access(JNIEnv *, jobject);
```

The last parameter refers to the Java object on which this method is called. To access a member of `o`, we first get a reference to this object's class via `GetObjectClass()` as follows:

```
jclass cls = env->GetObjectClass(o);
```

To access a field, we must have an ID of the field. There are two JNI functions, one for non-static and one for static, to obtain such field ID:

```
jfieldID fid = env->GetFieldID(cls, "x", "I");
jfieldID fids = env->GetStaticFieldID(cls, "y", "I");
```

These functions take the name of the field and its mangled description of the signature and returns a pointer to an opaque structure. The complete list of signatures may be obtained using `javap` tool with `-s` option as follows:

```
javap -s JNITest
```

See Table 8.3: to understand how to determine the mangled signature description. Once we get the Field ID, we can extract field using appropriate JNI functions as follows:

```
jint x = env->GetIntField(o, fid);
jint y = env->GetStaticIntField(cls, fids);
```

Note that `GetStaticIntField()` function takes a `jclass` argument instead of a `jobject`. These values can also be modified using appropriate Set functions as follows:

```
env->SetIntField(o, fid, 6);
env->SetStaticIntField(cls, fids, 7);
```

To access a method, we obtain a method ID instead of field ID as follows:

```
jmethodID mid = env->GetMethodID(cls, "f", "()V");
jmethodID mids = env->GetStaticMethodID(cls,"g", "()V");
```

The method is then invoked as follows:

```
env->CallVoidMethod(o, mid);
env->CallStaticObjectMethod(cls, mids);
```

The complete source code of C++ implementation of the native function is given below:

```
//JNITestImpl.cpp
#include "JNITest.h"
JNIEXPORT void JNICALL Java_JNITest_access(JNIEnv *env, jobject o) {
  jclass cls = env->GetObjectClass(o);
  jfieldID fid = env->GetFieldID(cls, "x", "I");
  jfieldID fids = env->GetStaticFieldID(cls, "y", "I");
  jint x = env->GetIntField(o, fid);
  jint y = env->GetStaticIntField(cls, fids);
  env->SetIntField(o, fid, 6);
  env->SetStaticIntField(cls, fids, 7);
  jmethodID mid = env->GetMethodID(cls, "f", "()V");
  jmethodID mids = env->GetStaticMethodID(cls,"g", "()V");
  env->CallVoidMethod(o, mid);
  env->CallStaticObjectMethod(cls, mids);
}
```

Compile and generate a library from the above program and run Java programs as before. The following output results:

```
Before: o.x = 4, o.y = 5
In non-static f()
In static g()
After: o.x = 6, o.y = 7
```

A list of useful JNI field and method access functions is given in Appendix A.

8.7.1 Passing Object Array

Note that JNI represents an object array by `jobjectArray` and is handled differently from primitive array. In this section, let us understand how to work with object arrays. Consider the following Java program:

```
class X {
  int id;
  public X(int i) {id = i;}
  public void func() {
    System.out.println("In func, id="+id);
  }
}
class JNITest {
 public native void f(X[] objs);
  static {
    System.loadLibrary("test");
  }
  public static void main(String[] args) {
    X[] objs= {new X(1), new X(2)};
    new JNITest().f(objs);
  }
}
```

This JNI program declares a native method `f()` that receives an array of X objects. The main method creates an array of two such X objects and calls the native method `f()` passing this array. Compile this Java program and generate header file as before. The following native function prototype is generated:

```
JNIEXPORT void JNICALL Java_JNITest_f(JNIEnv *, jobject, jobjectArray);
```

As you can see, the last argument represents an object array. In the native method, we get a method ID corresponding to `func()` method of X class as follows:

```
jclass cls = env->FindClass("X");
jmethodID mid = env->GetMethodID(cls, "func", "()V");
```

The number of elements of this array is obtained as:

```
jsize length = env->GetArrayLength(in);
```

We can then call the method `func()` on each object in this array:

```
for (int i = 0; i < length; i++) {
   jobject jo = env->GetObjectArrayElement(in, i);
   env->CallObjectMethod(jo, mid);
}
```

The complete source of the C++ implementation of the native function is shown below:

```
//JNITestImpl.cpp
#include "JNITest.h"
JNIEXPORT void JNICALL Java_JNITest_f(JNIEnv *env, jobject o, jobjectArray in)
{
  jclass cls = env->FindClass("X");
  jmethodID mid = env->GetMethodID(cls, "func", "()V");
  jsize length = env->GetArrayLength(in);
  for (int i = 0; i < length; i++) {
      jobject jo = env->GetObjectArrayElement(in, i);
     env->CallObjectMethod(jo, mid);
   }
}
```

Compile and generate a library from the above program and run Java programs as before. The following output results:

```
In func, id=1
In func, id=2
```

Passing a string array is similar to passing an object array. Consider the following Java program:

```
class JNITest {
 public native void f(String[] strs);
  static {
    System.loadLibrary("test");
  }
  public static void main(String[] args) {
    String[] strs = {"abc", "xyz"};
    new JNITest().f(strs);
  }
}
```

This JNI program declares a native method `f()` that receives an array of String objects. The main method creates an array of two `String` objects and calls the native method `f()` with this array. Here is a sample C++ implementation of the native method:

```
//JNITestImpl.cpp
#include "JNITest.h"
JNIEXPORT void JNICALL Java_JNITest_f(JNIEnv *env, jobject o, jobjectArray in)
{
  jsize length = env->GetArrayLength(in);
  for (int i = 0; i < length; i++) {
    jstring str = (jstring)env->GetObjectArrayElement(in, i);
    const char *inCStr = env->GetStringUTFChars(str, NULL);
    cout << inCStr1 << '\n';
  }
}
```

Compile and generate a library from the above program and run Java programs as before. The following output results:

```
abc
xyz
```

8.8 CREATING OBJECTS

JNI also allows native code to create new Java objects. Consider the following Java program:

```
class JNITest {
  int a;
  JNITest(int aa) { a = aa; }
  void print() {
    System.out.println("In print(), a = "+a);
  }
 public static native JNITest create();
  static {
    System.loadLibrary("test");
  }
  public static void main(String[] args) {
    JNITest t = create();
    t.print();
  }
}
```

It declares a static native method `create()` that creates and returns a `JNITest` object. The `main()` method creates an instance of `JNITest` using this native method. The `main()` method then calls the object's `print()` method. Compile this Java program and generate header file as before. The following native function prototype is generated:

```
JNIEXPORT jobject JNICALL Java_JNITest_create(JNIEnv *, jclass);
```

In the native method, we first obtain a reference to `JNITest` class:

```
jclass cls = env->FindClass("JNITest");
```

Since, a constructor creates an object, we then get the method ID of the one argument constructor of `JNITest` class:

```
jmethodID midInit = env->GetMethodID(cls, "<init>", "(I)V");
```

Note that for constructors, we pass `<init>` as the method. Since constructors do not return any value explicitly, we specify the return type as V. We can then use methods like `NewObject()` to call the constructor to create a new Java object:

```
jobject newObj = env->NewObject(cls, midInit, 3);
```

The complete source code of the C++ implementation of this native method is given below:

```
//JNITestImpl.cpp
#include "JNITest.h"
JNIEXPORT jobject JNICALL Java_JNITest_create(JNIEnv *env, jclass o) {
  jclass cls = env->FindClass("JNITest");
  jmethodID midInit = env->GetMethodID(cls, "<init>", "(I)V");
  jobject newObj = env->NewObject(cls, midInit, 3);
  return newObj;
}
```

Compile and generate a library from the above program and run Java programs as before. The following output results:

```
In print(), a = 3
```

8.9 EXCEPTION HANDLING IN JNI

This section explains exception handling in JNI. Since JNI handles more than one programming language, exception handling is a little tricky. Although C++ supports a notion of exception handling, it does not completely match with the Java's exception handling mechanism. Actually there is no uniform and general way to throw and catch exceptions in native languages.

The JNI allows native methods to handle outstanding Java exceptions. The unhandled exceptions are propagated back to the VM. The native method may also raise arbitrary Java exceptions. A set of JNI functions is provided for this purpose.

JNI functions use a mechanism to report errors that occur during their execution. They either return an error code or throw a Java exception. JNI functions having a non-void return type (such as `CallIntMethod()`) return error code if an error occurs. This error code is a special value, which does not belong to the set of normal values. Some other functions such as `CallVoidMethod()` or array access functions do not return an error code, but throw an exception.

As mentioned before, since there is no uniform and general way to throw and catch exceptions in native languages, JNI therefore requires to check for possible exceptions after calling JNI functions. There are two ways to determine if an error has occurred or not:

- check the return value (if any) of the last JNI function call or
- call JNI functions, ExceptionOccurred() or ExceptionCheck()

The last mechanism provides a way out even if the JNI function does not even return value. It also provides a more detailed description of the error condition and is usually used to handle errors. Using the last method, a native exception handling code looks like:

```
//a JNI function call
jthrowable ex = env->ExceptionOccurred();
if (ex) {
  //exception occurred handle it
}
```

The method `ExceptionOccurred()` returns an `jthrowable` object that represents the exception occurred. Alternatively, we can use `ExceptionCheck()` method.

```
//a JNI function call
jboolean exceptionOccured = env->ExceptionCheck();
if (exceptionOccured) {
  //exception occurred handle it
}
```

The function of this method is same except that it returns a `jboolean` instead of `jthrowable`. Since, `ExceptionOccured()` returns an object that contains more information about the exception, we usually use it. The description of this exception may be printed using `ExceptionDescribe()` method as follows:

```
env->ExceptionDescribe();
```

This prints the stack trace of this exception and stops the exception propagation. If the propagation of the exception is not stopped, it returns to the Java code that called this native method. To stop this propagation explicitly, we use `ExceptionClear()` method. The native code may also throw an exception using `Throw()` or `ThrowNew()` methods.

```
//throw the caught one
env->Throw(ex)
```

or

```
//throw a new one
jclass newExCls = env->FindClass("java/lang/IllegalArgumentException");
env->ThrowNew(newExCls, "thrown from C++ code");
```

Let us illustrate this using the following Java program:

```
class JNITest {
  private native void catchThrow();
  private void callback(){
    throw new NullPointerException("Thrown by callback");
  }
```

```
  static {
    System.loadLibrary("test");
  }
  public static void main(String[] args) {
    try {
      new JNITest().catchThrow();
    } catch (Exception e) { e.printStackTrace(); }
  }
}
```

This program declares one native method `catchThrow()` which calls the Java method `callback()`. So, here is a sample C++ code to do this:

```
JNIEXPORT void JNICALL Java_JNITest_catchThrow(JNIEnv *env, jobject obj) {
  jclass cls = env->GetObjectClass(obj);
  jmethodID mid = env->GetMethodID(cls, "callback", "()V");
  env->CallVoidMethod(obj, mid);
  …
}
```

Since the method `callback()` unconditionally throws a `NullPointerException`, the native method fetches an exception. We check this exception as follows:

```
jthrowable ex = env->ExceptionOccurred();
if (ex) {
  …
}
```

We then print this exception, clear it and throw a fresh exception as follows:

```
  env->ExceptionDescribe();
  //already cleared by above, we use the following for illustration
  env->ExceptionClear();
  jclass newExCls = env->FindClass("java/lang/IllegalArgumentException");
  env->ThrowNew(newExCls, "Thrown by C++ code");
```

The complete C++ implementation is given below:

```
//JNITestImpl.cpp
#include "JNITest.h"
JNIEXPORT void JNICALL Java_JNITest_catchThrow(JNIEnv *env, jobject obj) {
  jclass cls = env->GetObjectClass(obj);
  jmethodID mid = env->GetMethodID(cls, "callback", "()V");

  env->CallVoidMethod(obj, mid);
  jthrowable ex = env->ExceptionOccurred();
  if (ex) {
    env->ExceptionDescribe();
    env->ExceptionClear();
    jclass newExCls = env->FindClass("java/lang/IllegalArgumentException");
    env->ThrowNew(newExCls, "Thrown by C++ code");
  }
}
```

Compile and generate a library from the above program and run Java programs as before. The following output results:

```
Exception in thread "main" java.lang.NullPointerException: Thrown by callback
        at JNITest.callback(JNITest.java:4)
        at JNITest.catchThrow(Native Method)
        at JNITest.main(JNITest.java:11)
java.lang.IllegalArgumentException: Thrown by C++ code
        at JNITest.catchThrow(Native Method)
        at JNITest.main(JNITest.java:11)
```

Note that Java's type system enforces that a checked exception thrown by a method must be declared in the throws clause of the method. However, it cannot enforce the same exception-checking rules for native methods. This mismatch makes JNI software potentially buggy and often difficult to debug, if an exception is thrown by the native method.

8.10 APPENDIX

JNI Native String Functions

```
jstring NewString(const jchar *unicode, jsize len)
jsize GetStringLength(jstring str)
const jchar *GetStringChars(jstring str, jboolean *isCopy)
void ReleaseStringChars(jstring str, const jchar *chars)
jstring NewStringUTF(const char *utf)
jsize GetStringUTFLength(jstring str)
const char* GetStringUTFChars(jstring str, jboolean *isCopy)
void ReleaseStringUTFChars(jstring str, const char* chars)
void GetStringRegion(jstring str, jsize start, jsize len, jchar *buf)
void GetStringUTFRegion(jstring str, jsize start, jsize len, char *buf)
const jchar * GetStringCritical(jstring string, jboolean *isCopy)
void ReleaseStringCritical(jstring string, const jchar *cstring)
```

JNI Native primitive array Functions

```
jsize GetArrayLength(jarray array)
jobjectArray NewObjectArray(jsize len, jclass clazz, jobject init)
jobject GetObjectArrayElement(jobjectArray array, jsize index)
void SetObjectArrayElement(jobjectArray array, jsize index, jobject val)

j<PrimitiveType>Array New<primitiveType>Array(jsize len)
j<PrimitiveType> * Get<PrimitiveType>ArrayElements(j<primitiveType>Array array,
jboolean *isCopy)
void Release<PrimitiveType>ArrayElements(j<primitiveType>Array array,
j<primitiveType> *elems, jint mode)
void Get<PrimitiveType>ArrayRegion(j<primitiveType>Array array, jsize start,
jsize len, jboolean *buf)
void Set<PrimitiveType>ArrayRegion(j<primitiveType>Array array,
jsize start, jsize len, const jboolean *buf)
void * GetPrimitiveArrayCritical(jarray array, jboolean *isCopy)
void ReleasePrimitiveArrayCritical(jarray array, void *carray, jint mode)
```

JNI Native non-static Field access functions:

```
jfieldID GetFieldID(jclass clazz, const char *name, const char *sig)

jobject GetObjectField(jobject obj, jfieldID fieldID)
jobject SetObjectField(jobject obj, jfieldID fieldID)

jboolean Get<PrimitiveType>Field(jobject obj, jfieldID fieldID)
jboolean Set<PrimitiveType>Field(jobject obj, jfieldID fieldID)
```

JNI Native non-static Method call functions:

```
jmethodID GetMethodID(jclass clazz, const char *name, const char *sig)

jobject CallObjectMethod(jobject obj, jmethodID methodID, ...)
jobject CallObjectMethodV(jobject obj, jmethodID methodID, va_list args)
jobject CallObjectMethodA(jobject obj, jmethodID methodID, const jvalue * args)
```

```
jobject Call<PrimitiveType>Method(jobject obj, jmethodID methodID, ...)
jobject Call<PrimitiveType>MethodV(jobject obj, jmethodID methodID, va_list
args)
jobject Call<PrimitiveType>MethodA(jobject obj, jmethodID methodID, const
jvalue * args)

jobject CallNonvirtualObjectMethod(jobject obj, jclass clazz, jmethodID
methodID, ...)
jobject CallNonvirtualObjectMethodV(jobject obj, jclass clazz, jmethodID
methodID, va_list args)
jobject CallNonvirtualObjectMethodA(jobject obj, jclass clazz, jmethodID
methodID, const jvalue * args)

jobject CallNonvirtual<PrimitiveType>Method(jobject obj, jclass clazz,
jmethodID methodID, ...)
jobject CallNonvirtual<PrimitiveType>MethodV(jobject obj, jclass clazz,
jmethodID methodID, va_list args)
jobject CallNonvirtual<PrimitiveType>MethodA(jobject obj, jclass clazz,
jmethodID methodID, const jvalue * args)
```

JNI Native static Field access functions:

```
jfieldID GetStaticFieldID(jclass clazz, const char *name, const char *sig)

jobject GetStaticObjectField(jclass clazz, jfieldID fieldID)
jobject SetStaticObjectField(jclass clazz, jfieldID fieldID)

jboolean GetStatic<PrimitiveType>Field(jclass clazz, jfieldID fieldID)
jboolean SetStatic<PrimitiveType>Field(jclass clazz, jfieldID fieldID)
```

JNI Native static Method call functions:

```
jmethodID GetStaticMethodID(jclass clazz, const char *name, const char *sig)

jobject CallStaticObjectMethod(jclass clazz, jmethodID methodID, ...)
jobject CallStaticObjectMethodV(jclass clazz, jmethodID methodID, va_list args)
jobject CallStaticObjectMethodA(jclass clazz, jmethodID methodID, const jvalue
* args)

jobject CallStatic<PrimitiveType>Method(jclass clazz, jmethodID methodID, ...)
jobject CallStatic<PrimitiveType>MethodV(jclass clazz, jmethodID methodID,
va_list args)
jobject CallStatic<PrimitiveType>MethodA(jclass clazz, jmethodID methodID,
const jvalue * args)
```

KEYWORDS

javah—A Java tool used to generate artifacts such as function prototype in native languages

JNI—A Java API that allows Java code to interoperate with applications and libraries written in other programming languages such as C, C++

JNICALL—A macro used to specify the calling and linkage convention of both Java native methods and their implementations

JNIEnv—Primary interface to JVM

JNIEXPORT—A macro used to specify the calling and linkage convention of both Java native methods and their implementations

load—Similar to loadLibrary except that it takes absolute pathname of the library

loadLibrary—A method on Java System class to load a native library

Mangled name—A name following some rules to describe something such as method name, its signature etc

native—The keyword used to declare a method as native method

Native method—A method which is implemented in a non-Java programming language, and the method invoked from Java

Native language—Any programming languages other than Java

SUMMARY

The **J**ava **N**ative **I**nterface (JNI) is an API that allows Java code to interoperate with applications and libraries written in other programming languages such as C, C++. It is a two-way interface that allows Java applications to invoke native method and native methods to interact with Java code. The following are basic steps required to develop a JNI-based application:

- Write a Java class having a native method declaration.
- Compile this class using javac.
- Generate C header file using javah
- Implement the native method in a C program
- Compile C program and create a shared library
- Run the Java program

A method is declared as native using the keyword native. The header required to implement a native method in a native language is generated using the tool javah. The file jni.h contains all information the native function needs to interact with Java code.

The shared library is loaded in JVM using either loadLibrary() or load() method. Alternatively, the location of the shared library may be specified using LD_LIBRARY_PATH environment variable.

Each Java type is represented by a corresponding type in native language. JNI also allows us to pass parameters to the native method including primitive arrays, object arrays, strings, objects etc. JNI also allows us to access Java code from native code, such as accessing both static and non-static fields and methods, creating objects etc. Java provides numerous functions for this purpose.

The JNI allows native methods to handle outstanding Java exceptions. The unhandled exceptions are propagated back to the VM. The native method may also raise arbitrary Java exceptions. A set of JNI functions are provided for this purpose.

WEB RESOURCES

`http://docs.oracle.com/javase/1.5.0/docs/guide/jni/spec/jniTOC.html`
Java Native Interface Specification—Contents

`http://www.soi.city.ac.uk/~kloukin/IN2P3/material/jni.pdf`
The Java Native Interface Programmer's Guide and Specification

`http://www3.ntu.edu.sg/home/ehchua/programming/java/JavaNativeInterface.html`
Java Programming Tutorial Java Native Interface (JNI)

`http://homepage.cs.uiowa.edu/~slonnegr/wpj/JNI.pdf`
Java Native Interface

`http://journals.ecs.soton.ac.uk/java/tutorial/native1.1/implementing/`
Java Native Interface Programming

`http://www.javamex.com/tutorials/jni/`
The Java Native Interface (JNI)

`http://www.pacifier.com/~mmead/cs510jip/jni/`
Using the Java Native Interface with C++

EXERCISES

Objective-type Questions

1. Which one of the following methods is called first on a servlet?
   (a) Java Native Implementation
   (b) Java Normalized Interface
   (c) Joint Native Interface
   (d) Java Native Interface

2. Which of the following keywords is used to declare a method as native method?
   (a) primitive
   (c) native
   (b) nativeMethod
   (d) oldMethod

3. Which of the following names will you use in loadLibray method in Linux if the name of a shared library is libtest.so?
   (a) test (c) lib
   (b) libtest (d) libtest.so

4. Which of the following names will you use in loadLibray method in Windows if the name of a shared library is libtest.so?
   (a) lib.dll (c) test.dll
   (b) libtest.dll (d) libtest.so

5. Which of the following languages is used as native language?
   (a) C
   (b) C++
   (c) Both C and C++
   (d) None of the above

6. Which of the following methods is used to load a shared library?
   (a) getLibrary() (c) installLibrary()
   (b) libraryLoad() (d) loadLibrary()

7. Which of the following is a method to load shared library?
   (a) loadLibrary() (c) Both a) and b)
   (b) load() (d) None of the above

8. Which of the following Java tools is used to create native function signature?
   (a) javah (c) javas
   (b) javac (d) javap

9. If the name of the class files is test, what will be the name of the header file generated?
   (a) test.h (c) native_test.h
   (b) java_test.h (d) native.h

10. Which of the following files contains native functions needed to interact with Java code?
   (a) lib.h (c) native.h
   (b) jni.h (d) functions.h

11. A Java Object is represented in native code as
   (a) nativeObject (c) jniObject
   (b) object (d) jobject

12. Which of the following macros is used to specify the calling and linkage convention of both Java native methods and their implementations.
   (a) JNIEXPORT (c) Both a) and b)
   (b) JNICALL (d) None of the above

13. The primary interface to Java language is
   (a) Env (c) JNIEnv
   (b) PrimaryEnv (d) PInterface

14. Which of the following options is used to create a shared library?
   (a) -common (c) -shared
   (b) -s (d) -shareAll

15. What will the mangled signature be if the signature of a function is "void f()"?
   (a) ()V (c) V()
   (b) (I)V (d) ()I

16. Which of the following environment variables specify the location of the library?
   (a) LD_LIBRARY_PATH
   (b) LIBRARY_PATH
   (c) LD_JNI_PATH
   (d) JNI_LIBRARY_PATH

17. How many array types are there in JNI?
   (a) 7 (c) 9
   (b) 8 (d) 10

18. A boolean in Java is converted to C/C++ as
   (a) int (c) signed char
   (b) short (d) unsigned char

19. A char in Java is converted to C/C++ as
   (a) int (c) unsigned short
   (b) short (d) signed char

20. A byte in Java is converted to C/C++ as
   (a) int (c) unsigned short
   (b) short (d) signed char

21. What will the mangled signature be if the signature of a function is "void f(int, int[])"?
   (a) V(I[I) (c) ([II)V
   (b) (II)V (d) (I[I)V

22. A Java type boolean is mangled in JNI as
   (a) Z (c) C
   (b) B (d) S

23. A Java type byte is mangled in JNI as
   (a) Z (c) C
   (b) B (d) S

24. Which of the following is equivalent to delete in C++?
   (a) ReleaseStringUTFChars()
   (b) DeleteStringUTFChars()
   (c) Release()
   (d) FreeStringUTFChars()

25. Which of the following JNI functions is used to create a new string?
    (a) New()
    (b) NewUTF()
    (c) NewStringUTF()
    (d) NewStr()

26. What will the mangled signature be if the signature of a function is "void f(int, double)"?
    (a) (DI)V (c) (ID)V
    (b) V(ID) (d) (IV)D

27. Which of the following JNI methods is used to get array elements?
    (a) GetElements()
    (b) GetIntArrayElements()
    (c) IntArrayElements()
    (d) Elements()

28. Which of the following JNI methods is used to get a reference to an object's class?
    (a) GetObjectClass()
    (b) GetClass()
    (c) Class()
    (d) ObjectClass()

29. Which of the following JNI methods is used to create new Java objects?
    (a) New() (c) NewObject()
    (b) Object() (d) NewJavaObject()

30. Which of the following functions is used to determine if an error has occurred or not?
    (a) ExceptionOccurred()
    (b) ExceptionCheck()
    (c) Both a) and b)
    (d) None of the above

31. Which of the following methods is used to describe an exception?
    (a) ExceptionDescribe()
    (b) Describe()
    (c) Exception()
    (d) JNIExceptionDescribe()

32. Which of the following throws an exception if an error occurs?
    (a) CallIntMethod()
    (b) CallVoidMethod()
    (c) Both a) and b)
    (d) Neither a) nor b)

Subjective-type Questions

1. Explain the advantages and disadvantages of using JNI.
2. Mention some situations when we should use JNI.
3. Write the basic steps required to write a JNI application.
4. How do you load a native shared library in JVM?
5. What is the difference between loadLibrary() and load() method?
6. What is the function of javah tool?
7. Describe the procedure to generate header files using javah.
8. Explain why function call syntax is different in C and C++.
9. How do you determine the name of a JNI function given a native method name?
10. Describe the parameters of a mapped JNI function?
11. Describe the procedure to create a shared library in C/C++.
12. Distinguish between C and C++ pointer representation.
13. Describe the steps required to develop a JNI application that uses package.
14. How are Java types represented in JNI and where are they defined?
15. Show how you pass primitive arrays to a native method.
16. How is a Java string passed to a native method?
17. How do you access Java code from primitive code?
18. What happens when we pass an object array to a native method?
19. Describe the steps required to create Java object from native code.
20. Describe how exceptions are handled in JNI.

CHAPTER – 9

AWT AND SWING

KEY OBJECTIVES

After completing this chapter readers will be able to—

- understand AWT class and interface hierarchy
- identify basic steps needed to write GUI-based programs
- use various AWT components to create GUI
- know about various events and how to handle them
- get an overview of swing API
- use advanced swing components to create GUI

9.1 INTRODUCTION

Working with **G**raphical **U**ser **I**nterface (GUI) is always a fascinating task to the end users as well as interface designers. GUI-based applications provide click and execute environment that make applications more entertaining and interesting. Java provides a rich API, called **A**bstract **W**indow **T**oolkit (AWT), to create various GUI components.

One of the AWT's strongest points is that it has been implemented using each platform's native GUI toolkit, thereby preserving the look and feel of each platform. However, a GUI designed on one platform may look different when displayed on another platform.

It is inherently challenging to design and implement effective GUIs. Moreover, complicated interactions between classes in the AWT sometimes make this task more complex. However, with proper guidance, the creation of GUIs is not only possible, but relatively straightforward. This chapter will give you a detailed understanding of Java AWT concepts, background philosophy and practical concerns with an introduction to *Swing* which is an extension to AWT.

9.2 AWT CLASS HIERARCHY

Java allows programmers to create various graphical components such as window, frame, panel, button, text field, text area, radio button, check box, drop down list, etc. Using these components, we can create an interactive user interface for an application.

There are many (in fact huge) GUI classes in AWT and Swing. In fact, AWT and Swing consists of 12 and 18 packages respectively. Let us start with the AWT classes first to have some basic understanding before moving into Swing. Note that Java programmers usually use swing counterparts of AWT components for their better look and feel.

Fortunately, in AWT, only 2 packages - `java.awt` and `java.awt.event` - are commonly used. Before writing GUI-based applications, let us understand the functionality of some basic components with their relationship [Figure 9.1:].

9.2.1 Component

Components [Figure 9.1:] are graphic elements that can be displayed on the screen and that can interact with the user. For example, buttons, text boxes, checkboxes, radio buttons are all examples of components which are represented by classes `Button`, `TextField`, `Checkbox`, `CheckboxGroup` respectively. All component classes are direct or indirect sub classes of the abstract class `java.awt.Component`. It provides component's basic behaviour, such as adding/removing listeners, getting/setting current coordinates, showing/hiding them etc.

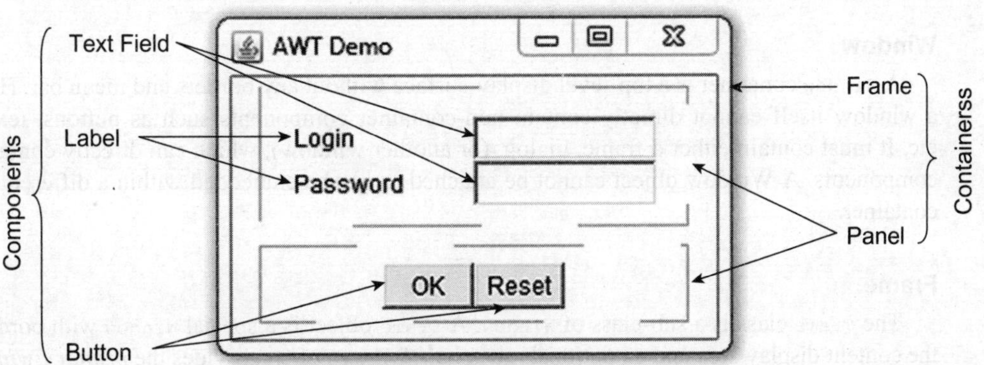

Figure 9.1: Basic GUI elements

9.2.2 Container

Some components (such as buttons, text boxes) cannot stand alone and require some other special components to *contain* them. These special components are called *containers*. Examples of such containers are, window, panel, scroll pane, etc, which are represented by `Window`, `Panel`, and `ScrollPane` classes respectively. The super-class of all these container classes is `Container` class, which defines container's common behaviour such as adding/removing/getting components, choosing a layout, etc. Container keeps track of components added to it using a list.

Note that containers are themselves components, and can thus be placed inside other containers. This nesting of components (including containers) into containers results in a tree of nodes. The root and intermediate nodes are containers and leaves are non-container components such as buttons, text boxes etc. So, each GUI-based application has a top-level container which will hold other components. The commonly used top-level containers are `Window`, `Frame`, and `Dialog`. Figure 9.2: shows the inheritance relationship among AWT component classes.

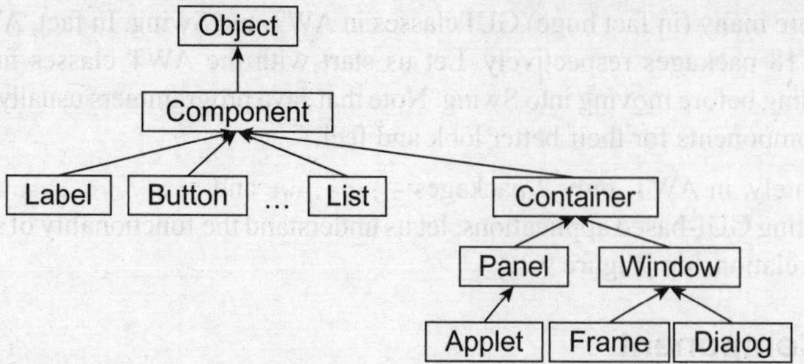

Figure 9.2: AWT components hierarchy

The primary container classes are `Window` and its two subclasses, `Frame` and `Dialog` as well as `Panel`. In addition, a separate container class `Applet`, which is a subclass of `Panel`, is provided specifically to embed Java code in web pages. The detailed description of this `Applet` class can be found in Chapter 16. Here is a brief description of other container classes.

Window

A `Window` container is a top-level display-surface without any borders and menu bar. However, a window itself cannot directly contain non-container components such as buttons, text boxes etc. It must contain either a frame, dialog, (or another window), which can directly contain other components. A Window object cannot be attached to nor be embedded within a different kind of container.

Frame

The `Frame` class is a sub-class of `Window`. A `Frame` object is a special `Window` with border, title, the content display area and an optional menu bar. A `Frame` often provides the *primary window* for a GUI-based application. A GUI-based application typically creates an instance of `Frame` or any of its sub-class created extending it.

Dialog

A Dialog is a top-level window typically used as a *pop-up window* and to take some form of input from the user. It comes with a border, a title-bar (containing an icon, a title and a close button) and a content display area.

Panel

A panel (represented by `Panel` class) is a higher-level container, which is a borderless transparent rectangular box used to organize a set of related components in pattern such as grid or flow. A panel itself is not a visible component. It merely provides some space where we can attach any other components, including other panels.

9.2.3 Controls

The basic AWT non-container component classes (also called controls) are `Label`, `TextField`, `TextArea`, `Button`, `Checkbox`, `CheckboxGroup`, `Choice`, and `List`. New custom component classes may also be created by deriving them from class `Component`. Their visual appearance is shown in Figure 9.3:

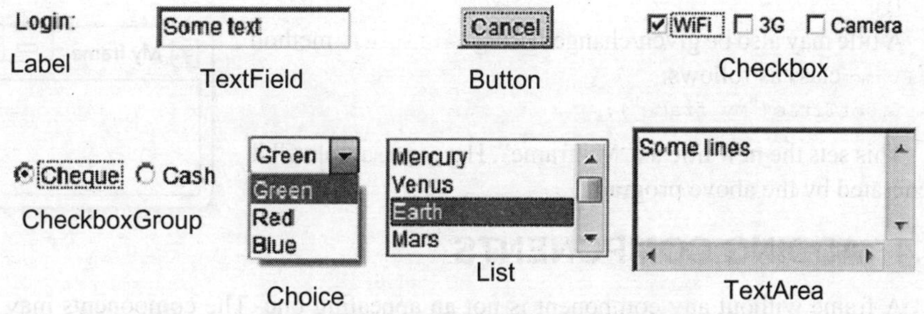

Figure 9.3: Primary GUI components

The following sections describe how to use different AWT components.

9.3 CREATING CONTAINER

Before creating and placing any component, we must create a container. Typically, we create an instance of `Frame` class.

9.3.1 Empty Frame

The following program creates an empty frame.

```
import java.awt.*;
public class FrameDemo {
  public static void main(String args[]) {
    Frame f = new Frame();
    f.setSize(200,100);
    f.setVisible(true);
  }
}
```

The `setSize()` method resizes the frame with specified width and height in pixels. A frame is initially invisible and must be made visible by invoking its `setVisible()` method with the argument `true`. Running this program is as easy as running any other Java application program. Compile and run it using the following pair of commands:

```
javac FrameDemo.java
java FrameDemo
```

A sample GUI is shown here.

9.3.2 Frame with a Title

The frame created in the previous section is too simple and had no title. The title of the frame (say "My frame") may be specified in the constructor.

```
import java.awt.*;
public class TitleDemo {
  public static void main(String args[]) {
    Frame f = new Frame("My frame");
    f.setSize(200,100);
    f.setVisible(true);
  }
}
```

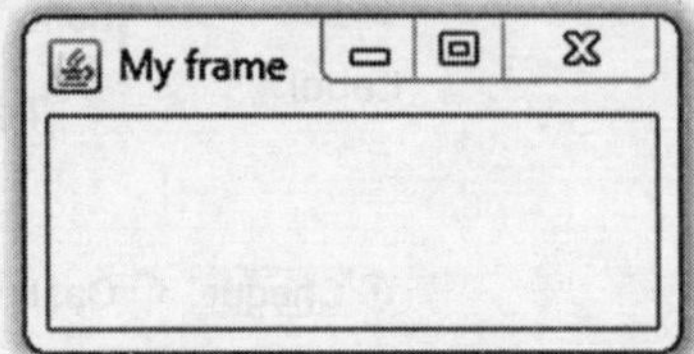

A title may also be given/changed using `setTitle()` method of `Frame` class as follows:

```
f.setTitle("My frame");
```

This sets the new title as "My frame". Here is a sample GUI generated by the above program.

9.4 ADDING COMPONENTS

A frame without any component is not an appealing one. The components may be added to a container using any one of its several overloaded `add()` methods. The following sections describe how to create different components and add them to a container.

9.4.1 Adding a Label

Note that `System.out.println()` cannot display a message on GUI. To place some text on GUI, we create a `Label` object. As its name implies, it is usually used to label other components or to display some textual message. The following program illustrates this:

```
import java.awt.*;
public class LabelDemo {
  public static void main(String args[]) {
    Frame f = new Frame("Label Demo");
    f.setSize(200,100);
    Label l = new Label("Hello World!");
    f.add(l);
    f.setVisible(true);
  }
}
```

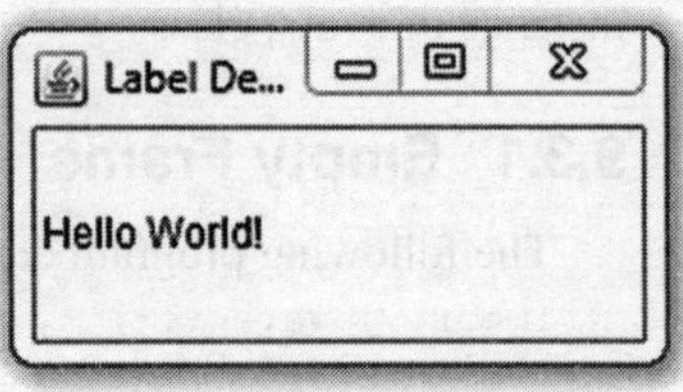

This displays a simple message "Hello World!" Here is a sample output of this program:

9.4.2 Adding a Button

One of the common components found in a GUI is a push button which is represented by `Button` class. When a button is pushed/clicked typically an action is taken. The `Button` class has two constructors.

```
public Button(String label);          // Captioned with specified string
public Button();                      // No caption
```

The first one creates a `Button` object with the given label painted over the button. The second constructor creates a `Button` object with no label. The following program creates a button labelled with "Exit".

```
import java.awt.*;
public class ButtonDemo {
  public static void main(String args[]) {
    Frame f = new Frame("Button Demo");
    f.setSize(200,80);
    f.setLayout(new FlowLayout());
    Button b = new Button("Exit");
    f.add(b);
    f.setVisible(true);
  }
}
```

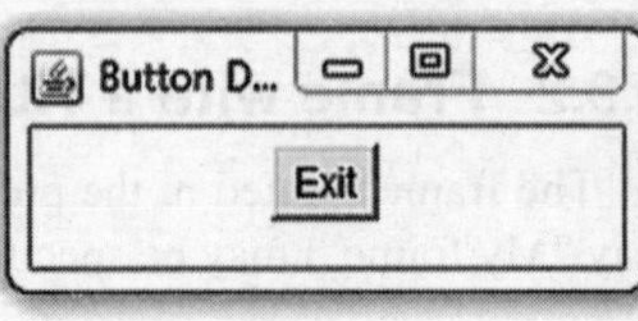

Here is a sample output of this program. One additional thing that we can find in this program is `setLayout()` method whose function is described in the next section.

9.5 LAYOUT

Note that a container may contain multiple components. How are these components arranged? This is controlled by a *layout manager* (represented by `LayoutManager` class) associated with a container. A layout manager is an object that controls the position (layout) and size of components inside a container.

Note that a container can contain another container. For example, a frame can contain panels, which themselves are containers. The layout manager for the frame determines how components (including containers) are sized and positioned inside the frame, and the layout manager for each nested container determines how components are sized and positioned inside that nested container and so on. This simple idea gives us the ability to create complex but beautiful GUI.

The most important layout managers are `FlowLayout`, `GridLayout`, and `BorderLayout`. Each container class has a default layout manager. For example, the default layout manager for the `Frame` and `Dialog` class is the `BorderLayout` whereas `Panel`'s default layout manager is `FlowLayout`. The method `setLayout()` of a container is used to set a layout manager.

9.5.1 FlowLayout

The `FlowLayout` manager arranges the components from left-to-right much like the lines of text in a paragraph. When the space in one row is exhausted, another row is started. The row alignment is determined by the align property. The `FlowLayout` class has the following constructors:

```
public FlowLayout();
public FlowLayout(int align);
public FlowLayout(int align, int hgap, int vgap);
// align: FlowLayout.LEFT or FlowLayout.RIGHT or FlowLayout.CENTER
// Default: hgap=5, vgap=5, align=CENTER
```

The following program illustrates how to use flow layout.

```
import java.awt.*;
public class FlowLayoutDemo {
  public static void main(String args[]) {
    Frame f = new Frame("FlowLayout Demo");
    f.setSize(200,80);
    f.setLayout(new FlowLayout());
    f.add(new Button("OK"));
    f.add(new Button("Cancel"));
    f.setVisible(true);
  }
}
```

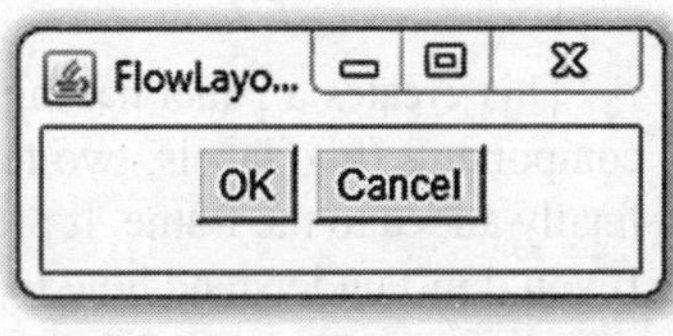

This creates two buttons and places them on a frame in a sequential manner. The actual appearance depends on the width of the display window. The output of this program is shown here.

9.5.2 GridLayout

The `GridLayout` manager arranges a container's components as a grid of rows and columns. The container's display area is divided into *equal-sized* rectangles, and one component is placed in each rectangle. The orientation of components is governed by the container's `ComponentOrientation` property. If the property is `LEFT_TO_RIGHT`, components run left to right and lines flow top to bottom. It the property is `RIGHT_TO_LEFT`, components run right to left and lines flow top to bottom. The `GridLayout` class has the following constructors:

```
GridLayout()                        //Grid layout with 1 row 1 column
GridLayout(int rows, int cols)      //Grid of specified rows and columns.
GridLayout(int rows, int cols, int hgap, int vgap)
//Grid of specified rows, columns, horizontal gap and vertical gap.
```

The following program lays out two buttons into 1 row and two columns:

```
import java.awt.*;
public class GridLayoutDemo {
   public static void main(String args[]) {
      Frame f = new Frame("GridLayout Demo");
      f.setSize(200,100);
      f.setLayout(new GridLayout(1,2));
      f.add(new Button("OK"));
      f.add(new Button("Cancel"));
      f.setVisible(true);
   }
}
```

The output of this program is shown here. A more appealing program that uses grid layout manager is shown below:

```
import java.awt.*;
public class GridLayoutDemo1 {
   public static void main(String args[]) {
      Frame f = new Frame("GridLayout Demo");
      Panel p = new Panel();
      f.setLayout(new FlowLayout());
      p.setLayout(new GridLayout(3,2));
      f.setSize(200,120);
      p.add(new Label("Login"));
      p.add(new TextField());
      p.add(new Label("Password"));
      TextField pass = new TextField();
      pass.setEchoChar('*');
      p.add(pass);

      p.add(new Button("OK"));
      p.add(new Button("Cancel"));
      f.add(p);
      f.setVisible(true);
   }
}
```

This creates a panel having a `GridLayout` manager with three rows and two columns. The six components (two labels, two text fields and two buttons) are then added to this panel. The panel is finally added to the frame. It produces output as shown above. This program also creates text fields. If you don't understand how to do it, don't worry; it is discussed in a separate section.

9.5.3 BorderLayout

A `BorderLayout` manager arranges and resizes a container's components to fit in five regions: north, south, east, west, and center, which are identified by static strings: `NORTH`, `SOUTH`, `EAST`, `WEST`, and `CENTER` defined in `BorderLayout` class. These region names are used in overloaded `add()` method of `Container` having a `BorderLayout` manager.

```
add(Component comp, Object constraints)
```

The second argument is one of these five constants. The method `add()`, without specifying the zone, adds the component to the `CENTER`. Here is an example program that lays five buttons in a frame using the `BorderLayout` layout manager:

```
import java.awt.*;
public class BorderLayoutDemo {
  public static void main(String args[]) {
    Frame f = new Frame("BorderLayout Demo");
    f.setSize(200,120);
    f.setLayout(new BorderLayout());
    f.add(new Button("North"), BorderLayout.NORTH);
    f.add(new Button("South"), BorderLayout.SOUTH);
    f.add(new Button("East"), BorderLayout.EAST);
    f.add(new Button("West"), BorderLayout.WEST);
    f.add(new Button("Center"), BorderLayout.CENTRE);
    f.setVisible(true);
  }
}
```

The sample output is shown here.

9.6 USING PANEL

Panels are often used to organize a set of related components in a pattern such as grid or flow. A panel itself is not a visible component. It merely provides some space where we can attach other components including other panels.

For example, the following program creates a frame with `BoderLayout` manager. It contains a text field at north and a panel at center. The panel, in turn has a `GridLayout` manager and contains 15 buttons.

```
import javax.swing.*;
import java.awt.*;
public class PanelDemo {
  public static void main(String args[]) {
    JFrame f = new JFrame("Calculator");
    f.setSize(150,200);

    // Set up button panel
    Panel p = new Panel();
    p.setLayout(new GridLayout(5,3));
    String[] s = {"0", "+", "-", "*", "/", "="};
    for(int i=1;i<=9;i++)
      p.add(new Button(i+""));
    for(int i=0;i<s.length;i++)
      p.add(new Button(s[i]));

    f.add(new TextField(15), BorderLayout.NORTH);
    f.add(p, BorderLayout.CENTER);
    f.setVisible(true);
  }
}
```

It creates GUI for a simple calculator. A sample output of this program is shown here.

9.7 TEXT FIELD

A text field (represented by `TextField` class) is a basic component where user can type/edit a single line of text. The following program creates a text field with 10 columns:

```
import java.awt.*;
public class TextFieldDemo {
  public static void main(String args[]) {
    Frame f = new Frame("TextField Demo");
    f.setSize(200,80);
    f.setLayout(new FlowLayout());
    f.add(new Label("Name"));
    f.add(new TextField(10));
    f.setVisible(true);
  }
}
```

For multi-line text, we use a text area which is discussed next.

9.8 TEXTAREA

A `TextArea` component has a display area that can show multi-line text. Another advantage of text area over text field is that when the text in the text area becomes larger than the viewable area, scroll bars are enabled automatically, which help users to scroll the text up-down and left-right. Here is a sample program that illustrates how to create text area.

```
import java.awt.*;
public class TextAreaDemo {
  public static void main(String args[]) {
    Frame f = new Frame("Choice Demo");
    f.setSize(200,120);
    f.setLayout(new FlowLayout());
    f.add(new TextArea("Some text", 3, 20));
    f.setVisible(true);
  }
}
```

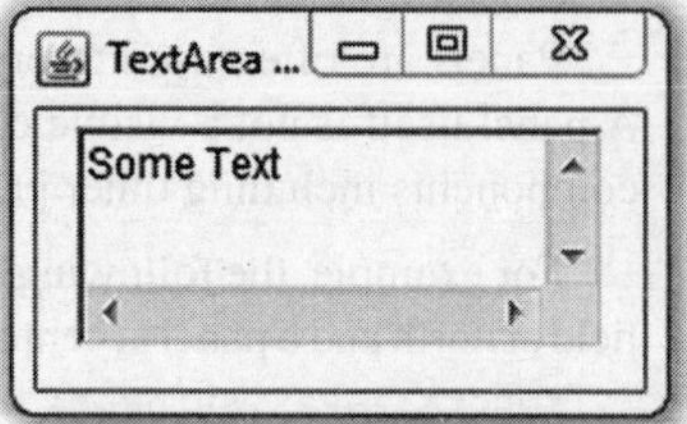

The above program creates a text area with display area 4 lines and 30 characters per line and having initial text "Your text here". A sample output is shown here.

A text area can be made editable or to be read-only using `setEditable()` method.

9.9 LIST

A `List` component, as its name indicates, contains a list of text items that can scroll. The list can be configured so that users can choose either one or multiple items. The following program creates a list with four (4) visible lines.

```
import java.awt.*;
public class ListDemo {
  public static void main(String args[]) {
    String[] colors = {"Red", "Green", "Blue", "Cyan", "Magenta", "Yellow"};
    Frame f = new Frame("List Demo");
    f.setSize(250,120);
    f.setLayout(new FlowLayout());
    List lst = new List(4, false);
    for(int i=0;i<colors.length;i++)
    lst.add(colors[i]);
    f.add(new Label("Colors"));
    f.add(lst);
    f.setVisible(true);
  }
}
```

A sample output is shown here.

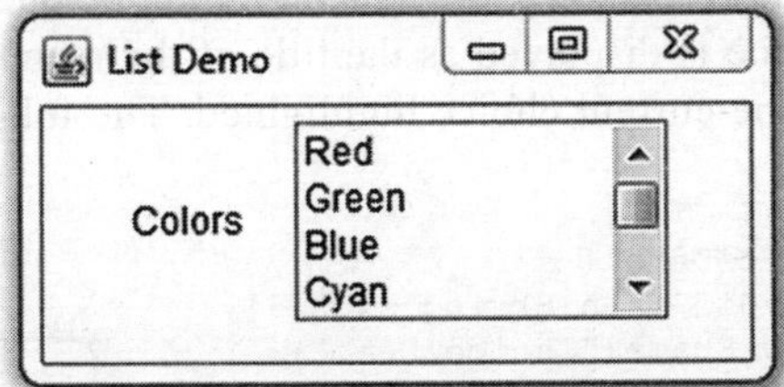

9.10 CHECKBOX

A `Checkbox` object can be in either of the two states: "on" (true) or "off" (false). It has a small rectangular area which remains empty for "off" state and shows a small tick mark (√) for "on" state. Clicking on a check box toggles its state. The following program creates three check boxes in a grid layout:

```
import java.awt.*;
public class CheckBoxDemo {
  public static void main(String args[]) {
    Frame f = new Frame();
    f.setSize(150,100);
    f.setLayout(new GridLayout(3,1));
    f.add(new Checkbox("WiFi", null, true));
    f.add(new Checkbox("3G"));
    f.add(new Checkbox("Camera"));
    f.setVisible(true);
  }
}
```

The screen shot depicts the check boxes and grid layout created by this code example. The check box labelled "WiFi" is in the "on" state, and the other two are in the "off" state.

9.11 CHECK BOX GROUP

Several check boxes can be put in a group using the `CheckboxGroup` class. In a group of check boxes, atmost one can be in the "on" state at any time. Clicking on a check box turns it on and turns all other in the group off. The following program crates a group of three check boxes:

```
import java.awt.*;
public class CheckBoxGroupDemo {
  public static void main(String args[]) {
    Frame f = new Frame();
    f.setSize(150,100);
    f.setLayout(new GridLayout(3,1));
    CheckboxGroup cbg = new CheckboxGroup();
    f.add(new Checkbox("one", cbg, false));
    f.add(new Checkbox("two", cbg, true));
    f.add(new Checkbox("three", cbg, false));
    f.setVisible(true);
  }
}
```

The screen shot depicts the group of check boxes created by this code example. The check box labelled "two" is in the "on" state, and the other two are in the "off" state.

9.12 CHOICE

A `Choice` object represents a pop-up menu of items, one of which may be chosen at any time. The current choice is displayed as the title of the menu. Clicking on the choice causes a menu to appear with the current choice highlighted. The following program creates pop-menu of three items.

```
import java.awt.*;
public class ChoiceDemo {
   public static void main(String args[]) {
      Frame f = new Frame("Choice Demo");
      f.setSize(300,120);
      f.setLayout(new FlowLayout());
      Choice colors = new Choice();
      colors.add("Green");
      colors.add("Red");
      colors.add("Blue");
      f.add(new Label("Choose a color"));
      f.add(colors);
      f.setVisible(true);
   }
}
```

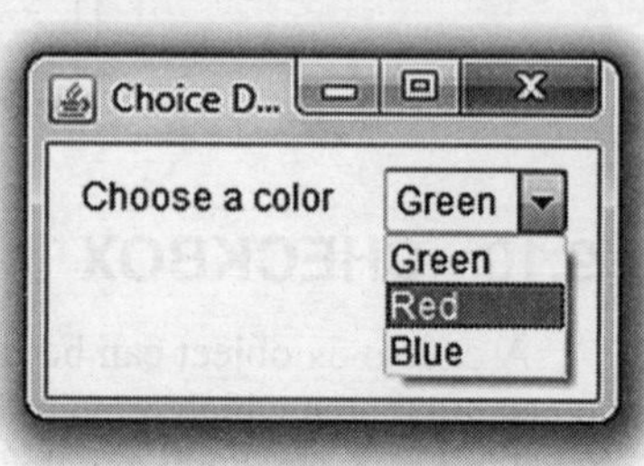

Here is a sample output of this program.

9.13 EVENT HANDLING

The GUI created in the previous sections do nothing except display some components. A useful GUI should respond to user actions. For example, if a user clicks a button captioned "Login", then we should execute a piece of code that takes necessary actions required for login. Similarly, if a user presses a button captioned "Close", codes that close the program should be executed.

However, before taking any action, we must know that the user has taken some actions. The process of determining that an action has been taken is known as listening and the action done by the user is called an *event*. Writing the corresponding code for a user action is called *event handling*. This section describes the Java event handling architecture and how to write event handling codes. Three primary concepts are involved when working with event handling.

- Events: Objects representing different user actions
- Event sources: The components associated with the user actions
- Listeners: Objects interested to listen and handle user actions

9.13.1 Event Sources

AWT components can also respond to different user actions, called *events*, such as clicking a button, typing some text in a text box/ text area, opening/closing a window, etc. Sources of events are various AWT components such as `Button`, `TextField` etc. Events are generated when users interact with the components such as by clicking on a button or writing something in a text field.

9.13.2 Event Classes

When an event is generated, an object (called *event* object) is actually created. There are many event classes corresponding to various kind of events. They have the name of the form `xxxEvent` such as `KeyEvent`, `MouseEvent`, `ActionEvent`, `TextEvent` etc. Table 9.1: shows a summary of primary event classes. The hierarchy of these classes is also shown here.

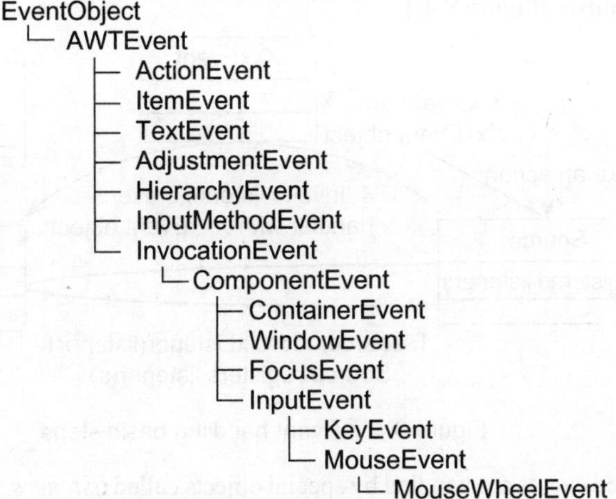

The generated event object is then passed to all the registered listener's appropriate event-handler method(s). So, triggering event eventually invokes method(s) of the listener(s).

Note that a component typically can generate a small set of events, not all. In other words, a specific event is generated by some specific components. For example, `TextEvent` and `AdjustmentEvent` are only generated by text field and scroll bar respectively.

Although, Java AWT defines a wide variety of event classes, not all events are represented by some Java class. This means that not every user action becomes an event. Users can see only those events that Java AWT lets them see.

Table 9.1: Primary event classes

Event Classes	Generated when	Listener Interface
ActionEvent	Button is pressed, menu-item is selected, list-item is double clicked etc.	ActionListener
KeyEvent	Keys are pressed/released, typed etc.	KeyListener
MouseEvent	Mouse is pressed, released, clicked, moved, dragged, entered and exited a component	MouseListener
MouseWheelEvent	Mouse wheel is moved	MouseWheelListener
ItemEvent	Check-box or list item is clicked	ItemListener
TextEvent	Value of textarea or textfield is changed	TextListener
WindowEvent	Window is activated, deactivated, de-iconified, iconified, opened or closed	WindowListener
ComponentEvent	Component is hidden, moved, resized or set visible	ComponentListener
ContainerEvent	Component is added or removed from container	ContainerListener
AdjustmentEvent	Scroll bar is adjusted	AdjustmentListener
FocusEvent	Component gains or loses keyboard focus	FocusListener

9.13.3 Event Listeners

Java follows the well-known subscribe-publish or observer-observable design pattern for its event handling mechanism [Figure 9.4:].

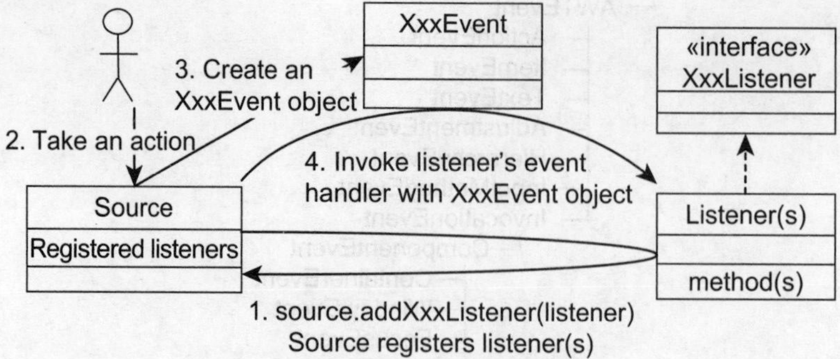

Figure 9.4: Event handling basic steps

The generated events are handled by special objects called *listeners*. The functionality of a listener class is defined by the listener interface. Each event has its own listener interface [see Table 9.1:]. For example, `ActionEvent` has `ActionListener` interface. A listener class interested in processing an action event, must implement the corresponding listener interface `ActionListener`.

To express interest for handling certain component's event, the listener(s) must be registered with the component using its `addXXXListener()` method. When that event occurs, the registered listener's appropriate method is called passing the event object. It means, the listener(s) first *subscribes* to a source's event. The source, upon occurrence of an event, *publishes* the event to all its registered subscribers.

Every method of an event-listener has a single argument of some kind that directly or indirectly inherits `EventObject` class. For example, the argument for methods that handle action events is a type of `ActionEvent`, which is an indirect subclass of `EventObject`. The `EventObject` class defines one very useful method:

```
Object getSource()
```

If a listener is registered with multiple components, it can identify the source object of the event using this method. Note that the `getSource()` method returns an Object. So, a listener, before working with this further, should type caste to desired type. An event class also defines methods to retrieve information about the event. For example, we can query a `KeyEvent` object for information about which key was used, if Alt key was held down etc.

The detailed functionality of each listener is given in Appendix A at the end of this chapter.

9.13.4 Example

Let us first implement the easiest and most common listener, the action listener. An action listener defines what to do when a user performs certain actions such as clicking a button, choosing a menu item, and pressing enter key in a text field.

We first write a handler class that implements `ActionListener` interface as follows:

```
class MyListener implements ActionListener {
  public void actionPerformed(ActionEvent e) {
    //code to be executed for the action...
  }
}
```

The MyListener class implements the single method actionPerformed() defined in ActionLister interface. The handler is ready. However, it is not automatically consulted unless it expresses its interest in receiving action events. The is done by registering an instance of the MyListener class on a component as follows:

```
Button b = new Button("Copy->");
MyListener h = new MyListener();
b.addActionListener(h);
```

Now every time a user performs some action on the button b, the method actionPerformed() of h will be invoked. But what should be written in the actionPerformed() method? For simplicity, let us write a code that simply makes a beep sound. Here is the complete source code of the program:

```
import java.awt.*;
import java.awt.event.*;
public class ActionEventDemo extends Frame {
  ActionEventDemo() {
    setSize(150,80);
    Button b = new Button("ClickMe");
    b.addActionListener(new MyListener());
    add(b);
    setVisible(true);
  }
  public static void main(String args[]) {
    new ActionEventDemo();
  }
}
class MyListener implements ActionListener {
  public void actionPerformed(ActionEvent e) {
    Toolkit.getDefaultToolkit().beep();
  }
}
```

In the above example, the handler class is written as a separate class. It could be an existing class, or an inner class, or even an anonymous inner class. The class ActionEventDemo itself could have implemented the ActionListener interface. The resultant code would then look like:

```
public class ActionEventDemo extends Frame implements ActionListener {
  //...
    b.addActionListener(this);
  //...
  public void actionPerformed(ActionEvent e) {
    Toolkit.getDefaultToolkit().beep();
  }
  //...
}
```

The event handler may be written as an inner class as follows:

```
public class ActionEventDemo extends Frame  {
  //...
    b.addActionListener(new MyListener());
  //...
  class MyListener implements ActionListener {
    public void actionPerformed(ActionEvent e) {
      Toolkit.getDefaultToolkit().beep();
    }
  }
  //...
}
```

An event handler class is often written as an anonymous inner class as follows:

```
public class ActionEventDemo extends Frame {
  //...
    b.addActionListener(new ActionListener() {
      public void actionPerformed(ActionEvent e) {
        Toolkit.getDefaultToolkit().beep();
      }
    });
  //...
}
```

The above handler merely makes a beep sound. Let us develop a more realistic program.

```
import java.awt.*;
import java.awt.event.*;
public class CopyDemo extends Frame {
  TextField t1 = new TextField(), t2 = new TextField();
  CopyDemo() {
    setSize(150,80);
    setLayout(new FlowLayout());
    Button b = new Button("Copy->");
    add(t1);add(b);add(t2);
    b.addActionListener(new ActionListener() {
      public void actionPerformed(ActionEvent e) {
        t2.setText(t1.getText());
      }
    });
    setVisible(true);
  }
  public static void main(String args[]) {
    new CopyDemo();
  }
}
```

This program creates two text fields and a button with caption "Copy->" in between. When the button is clicked, the content of left text field is copied to the right one. Sample screenshots before and after the button click is shown above. Here is another program that illustrates the usage of event handler.

```
import java.awt.*;
import java.awt.event.*;
public class TextEventDemo extends Frame {
  TextField t = new TextField(15);
  TextEventDemo() {
    setSize(180,80);
    setLayout(new FlowLayout());
    add(t);
    t.addKeyListener(new KeyListener() {
      public void keyPressed(KeyEvent e) {}
      public void keyReleased(KeyEvent e) {
        int cp = t.getCaretPosition();
        t.setText(t.getText().toUpperCase());
        t.setCaretPosition(cp);
      }
      public void keyTyped(KeyEvent e) {}
    });
    setVisible(true);
  }
  public static void main(String args[]) {
    new TextEventDemo();
  }
}
```

This program creates a single text field. The content of this text field will always be upper-case characters.

9.13.5 Adapter Classes

A listener class sometimes wants to provide limited functionality. For example, a key listener class may want to provide only `keyReleased()` method, but not all. However, a listener class *must* implement *all* the methods of its listener interface.

It should still not be a problem if the interface has few methods. For example, we may quickly write an empty body for the methods we are not interested in. However, interfaces like `MouseListener` and `WindowListener` have respectively 5 and 7 methods. So, a class implementing these interfaces must at least write the signatures of large number of methods (with an empty body). The resulting collection of empty method bodies can make code harder to read and maintain.

Fortunately, Java provides some ready-made classes called *adapter classes* for each listener interface with more than one method. For example, the `MouseAdapter` class implements the `MouseListener` interface. An adapter class implements empty versions of all its interface's methods.

So, a listener class may be created quickly by extending an adapter class and overriding only the methods of interest, rather than directly implementing all methods of the listener interface. The previous case change program has been written using adapter class.

```
import java.awt.*;
import java.awt.event.*;
public class AdapterDemo extends Frame {
  TextField t = new TextField(15);
  AdapterDemo() {
    setSize(180,80);
    setLayout(new FlowLayout());
    add(t);
    t.addKeyListener(new CaseChanger());
    setVisible(true);
  }
  class CaseChanger extends KeyAdapter {
    public void keyReleased(KeyEvent e) {
      if(e.getSource() instanceof TextField) {
        TextField t = (TextField)e.getSource();
        int cp = t.getCaretPosition();
        t.setText(t.getText().toUpperCase());
        t.setCaretPosition(cp);
      }
    }
  }
  public static void main(String args[]) {
    new AdapterDemo();
  }
}
```

Note that event object contains information about the event such as source of the event. The program above extracts the source of the event using `getSource()` method. The following is another program that uses `MouseMotionAdapter` and displays the x and y coordinates of the mouse pointer.

```
import java.awt.*;
import java.awt.event.*;
public class MouseEventDemo extends Frame {
  Label l = new Label();
  MouseEventDemo() {
    setSize(200,100);
    setLayout(new FlowLayout());
    add(l);
```

```
    this.addMouseMotionListener(new MouseMotionAdapter() {
      public void mouseMoved(MouseEvent e)  {
        l.setText(e.getX()+", "+e.getY());
      }
    });
    setVisible(true);
  }
  public static void main(String args[]) {
    new MouseEventDemo();
  }
}
```

A sample output of the above program is shown here. Note that adapters are classes, not interfaces. So, a class can extend an adapter, provided that it has not already extended another class. Moreover, a class can implement multiple listener interfaces, but cannot extend more than one adapter class as Java does not permit multiple inheritance for classes. However, anonymous inner class may be used to extend an adapter.

```
t.addKeyListener(new KeyAdapter() {
  public void keyReleased(KeyEvent e) {
    //...
  }
});
```

9.14 DIALOG BOXES

Dialog boxes are pop-up sub-windows that appear for a small time, meant to show a message or to take input from the user. Dialog boxes are often used to present error or warning messages. However, they can also present images, directory trees, or just about anything appropriate to the application. The `java.awt.Dialog` control, which represents a top-level window with a title and a border, is used to create dialog boxes.

A dialog box is a child window and must have a parent window. For example, a yes-no dialog box always appears from an existing window. So, all constructors of `Dialog` class take a window as its parent.

A dialog box may be *modal* and *modeless*. A modal dialog box does not allow the user to do any activity without dismissing (closing) it. For example a save as dialog box must be closed before taking any actions on its parent window. Modeless dialog box, on the other hand, allows users to perform activities in parallel without closing it. Example includes a help dialog box. Java supports both styles of dialog boxes.

9.14.1 Simple Dialog

This program creates a simple dialog box having a message and two buttons captioned "Yes" and "No". It appears when the user tries to close the main window. This can be used to verify if the user really wants to close the window.

```
import java.awt.*;
import java.awt.event.*;
public class DialogDemo extends Frame {
  YesNo fd;
  DialogDemo() {
    setSize(200,150);
    addWindowListener(new WindowAdapter() {
      public void windowClosing(WindowEvent e)  {
        fd.setVisible(true);
        if(fd.s == 1) System.exit(0);
      }
    });
```

```
      fd = new YesNo(this);
      setVisible(true);
    }
    public static void main(String args[]) {
      new DialogDemo();
    }
  }
  class YesNo extends Dialog implements ActionListener {
    int s = -1;
    Button y = new Button("Yes"), n = new Button("No");
    YesNo(Frame f) {
      super(f, true);
      setSize(150,100);
      setLayout(new FlowLayout());
      add(new Label("Confirm to close?"));
      add(y);add(n);
      y.addActionListener(this);
      n.addActionListener(this);
    }
    public void actionPerformed(ActionEvent e) {
      setVisible(false);
      s = ((Button)e.getSource()).equals(y)?1:0;
    }
  }
```

Confirm to close?

Yes No

The dialog box is made visible when the user tries to close the main window. This is a modal dialog, which is indicated by passing a value `true` in `super()`. If user presses the button captioned "No", the dialog box disappears and the main window remains open. On the other hand, if user clicks the "Yes" button, the main window as well as the dialog box are closed. A sample output of this program is shown here.

9.14.2 File Dialog

The `FileDialog` class displays a dialog window from which the user can select a file. The following program creates a window containing a button and a text field. When the button is pressed, a file dialog appears where a user can navigate the file system and select file. The selected file is finally shown in the text box.

```
import java.awt.*;
import java.awt.event.*;
public class FileDialogDemo extends Frame {
  FileDialog fd;
  TextField t = new TextField(20);
  FileDialogDemo() {
    setSize(300,150);
    setLayout(new FlowLayout());
    Button b = new Button("Select a file");
    add(b);add(t);
    b.addActionListener(new ActionListener() {
      public void actionPerformed(ActionEvent e) {
        fd.setVisible(true);
        t.setText(fd.getFile());
      }
    });
    setVisible(true);
    fd = new FileDialog(this);
  }
  public static void main(String args[]) {
    new FileDialogDemo();
  }
}
```

9.15 SCROLLBAR

The ScrollBar class represents a very convenient component used to select a value from a range. The component has a movable bar that can go back and forth between a maximum and minimum value. A scrollbar may have either vertical or horizontal orientation, which is represented by two static constants in ScrollBar class: HORIZONTAL and VERTICAL respectively. A commonly used constructor looks as follows:

```
Scrollbar(int orientation, int value, int visible, int minimum, int maximum)
```

where orientation indicates the orientation of the scroll bar, value represents the initial value of the scroll bar, visible is the size of the bubble, minimum and maximum represent lower and upper limit of the range respectively.

This component generates AdjustmentEvent and the corresponding listener interface is AdjustmentListener, which has only one method adjustmentValueChanged(). The following example illustrates use of ScrollBar with AdjustmentEvent.

```
import java.awt.*;
import java.awt.event.*;
public class ScrollBarDemo extends Frame implements AdjustmentListener {
  Label msg   = new Label();
  Scrollbar hs = new Scrollbar(Scrollbar.HORIZONTAL, 0, 60, 0, 300),
            vs = new Scrollbar(Scrollbar.VERTICAL,0, 30, 0, 300);
  public ScrollBarDemo() {
    setSize(200,120);
    hs.addAdjustmentListener(this);
    vs.addAdjustmentListener(this);
    setLayout(new BorderLayout());
    add(hs, BorderLayout.SOUTH);
    add(vs, BorderLayout.EAST);
    add(msg, BorderLayout.CENTER);
    setVisible(true);
  }
  public void adjustmentValueChanged(AdjustmentEvent e) {
    msg.setText("Horozontal: "+hs.getValue() +" ,Vertical: "+ vs.getValue());
  }
  public static void main(String args[]) {
    new ScrollBarDemo();
  }
}
```

It creates two scroll bars, one horizontal and one vertical. Their values are displayed in a label. A sample output is shown here.

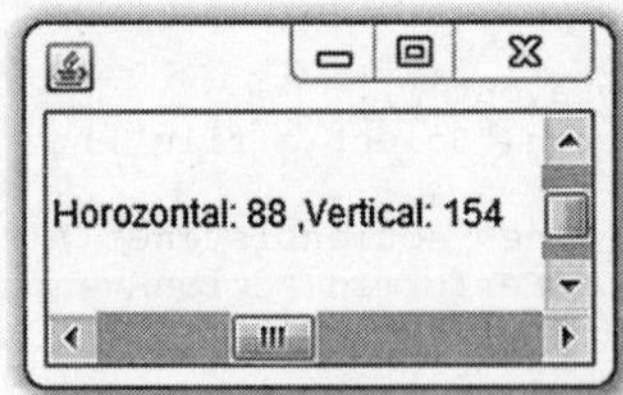

9.16 MENU

Menus are popular GUI components. A menu is a drop-down component displayed from the menu bar attached to a frame. The component hierarchy for menu is shown here. The MenuBar class represents a menu bar which may have one or more menu items represented by MenuComponent class.

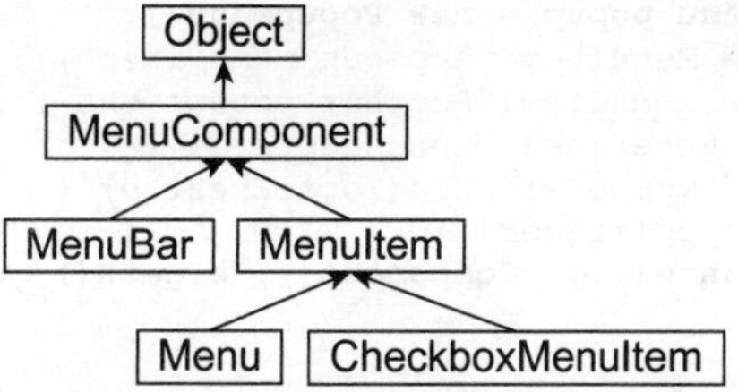

There are two kinds of menu items: simple menu and check box menu. A menu may have sub-menu, which in turn may also have sub-menu and so on. In AWT, creating a sub-menu is easy; we just add one menu to another menu. The following program illustrates this:

```
import java.awt.*;
public class MenuDemo {
  public static void main(String args[]) {
    Frame f = new Frame("Choice Demo");
    f.setSize(200,150);
    f.setLayout(new FlowLayout());
    Menu colors = new Menu("Colors");
    colors.add("Red");
    colors.add("Green");
    Menu shapes = new Menu("Shapes");
    Menu twoD = new Menu("2D shapes");
    Menu threeD = new Menu("3D Shapes");
    twoD.add("Triange");
    twoD.add("Circle");

    threeD.add("Sphere");
    threeD.add("Cube");

    MenuBar lst = new MenuBar();

    shapes.add(twoD);
    shapes.add(threeD);
    lst.add(shapes);
    lst.add(colors);

    f.setMenuBar(lst);
    f.setVisible(true);
  }
}
```

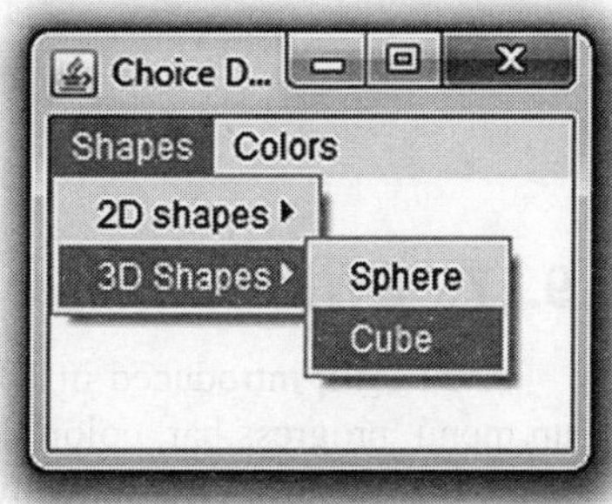

A sample output of this program is shown here.

9.16.1 Popup Menu

A `PopupMenu` component is a small rectangular area, dynamically popped up at a specified position. A popup menu is not tightly bound to a single component. It can appear anywhere across containment hierarchies. It is made visible using the following method:

```
public void show(Component reference, int x, int y)
```

This method will invoke the popup at the x, y coordinate position relative to the component parameter. The following example illustrates this:

```
import java.awt.*;
import java.awt.event.*;
public class PopupMenuDemo {
  public static void main(String args[]) {
    Frame f = new Frame("PopupMenu Demo");
    f.setSize(200,100);
```

```
    final PopupMenu popup = new PopupMenu();
    popup.add(new MenuItem("A popup menu item"));
    popup.add(new MenuItem("Another popup menu item"));
    f.addMouseListener(new MouseAdapter() {
      public void mouseReleased(MouseEvent e) {
        if(e.isPopupTrigger())
          popup.show(e.getComponent(), e.getX(), e.getY());
      }
    });
    f.add(popup);
    f.setVisible(true);
  }
}
```

A sample output is shown here.

9.17 SWING

AWT API, introduced in JDK 1.0, does not support any GUI component for table, tree, pop-up menu, progress bar, color chooser etc. A much more comprehensive set of graphics libraries that enhances the AWT was introduced in JDK 1.1 and was known as *Swing API*. In fact, Swing API includes all AWT components with better look and feel. Specifically, swing has the following features:

More Components—Swing provides a rich set of advanced controls for table, tree, tabbed pane, slider, color chooser etc.

Light Weight—Swing is a lightweight toolkit which does use underlying operating system calls. Instead, swing components are rendered using pure JAVA code.

Pluggable look and feel—The look and feel properties of swing components can be changed at run time.

Highly Customizable—The appearance of swing components is independent of internal representation, and thereby highly customizable.

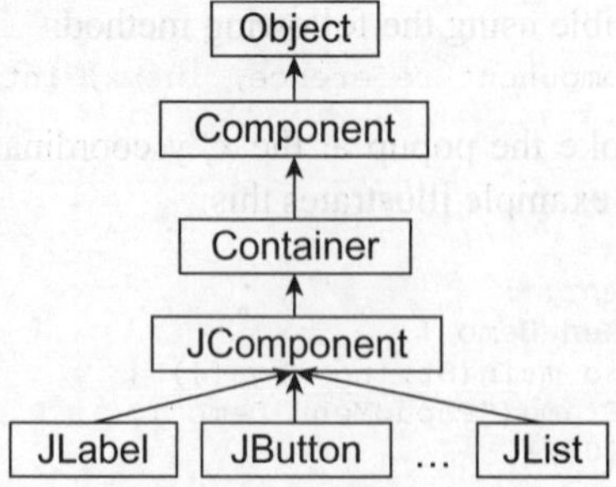

In swing, classes that represent GUI components have names beginning with the letter J. Some examples are `JTextField`, `JButton`, `JLabel` etc. Although, swing includes all AWT components, we shall primarily concentrate on the components that are not available in AWT. Examples of such classes are `JTable`, `JProgressBar`, `JColorChooser` etc. The relationship between AWT and swing components has been shown.

9.17.1 Containment Hierarchy

Each top-level container has a *content pane* where components are added. In addition, the top-level container may have a menu bar by convention positioned outside the content pane. Here is a typical containment hierarchy:

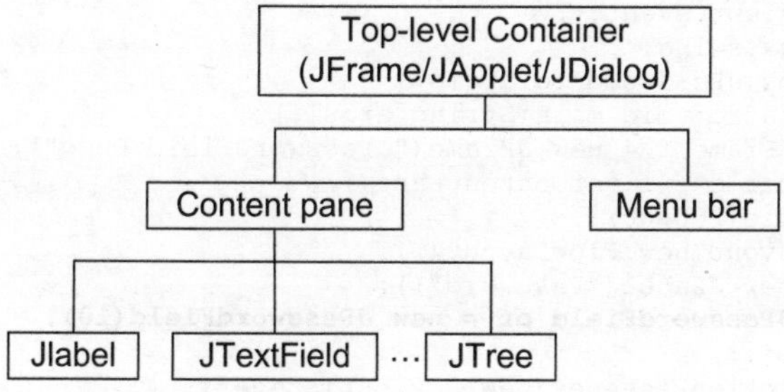

Figure 9.5: Swing containment hierarchy

9.17.2 Adding Components

Swing components are added in a slightly different way from AWT components. Instead of adding them to the container, they are added to the container's *content pane*. Typically, the content pane of a `JFrame` is obtained using its `getContentPane()` method as follows:

```
Container c = f.getContentPane();
```

Once the content pane of a container is obtained, components are added in the usual way. The following sections describe how to add different swing components starting from simple `JTextField`.

9.17.3 JTextField

A text field in swing is represented by `JTextField` and is created in the same way as AWT. However, its look and feel is better than an ordinary AWT text field. The following program displays a basic text field where a user can edit characters.

```
import java.awt.*;
import javax.swing.*;
public class JTextFieldDemo {
  public static void main(String args[]) {
    JFrame f = new JFrame("JTextField Demo");
    Container c = f.getContentPane();
    f.setSize(200,80);
    c.setLayout(new FlowLayout());
    c.add(new JLabel("Name"));
    c.add(new JTextField(10));
    f.setVisible(true);
  }
}
```

A sample output of this program is shown here. The method `setEchoChar()` and `getEchoChar()` are suppressed in `JTextField` to avoid exposing password characters. Instead, a separate class `JPasswordField` that extends `JTextField` is provided for this purpose.

9.17.4 JPasswordField

The `JPasswordField` (a direct subclass of `JTextField`) class represents special text fields (usually used to get passwords) where input characters are suppressed for security reason. Each character entered can be replaced by an echo character. The default echo character is the asterisk (*). The following program displays a password field where a user can enter passwords.

```
import java.awt.*;
import java.awt.event.*;
import javax.swing.*;
public class JPasswordFieldDemo {
  public static void main(String args[]) {
    final JFrame f = new JFrame("JPasswordField Demo");
    Container c = f.getContentPane();
    f.setSize(200,80);
    c.setLayout(new FlowLayout());
    c.add(new JLabel("Password"));
    final JPasswordField pf = new JPasswordField(10);
    c.add(pf);
    pf.addActionListener(new ActionListener() {
        public void actionPerformed(ActionEvent e) {
          String pw = new String(pf.getPassword());
          JOptionPane.showMessageDialog(f,"Password is: " + pw);
        }
    });
    f.setVisible(true);
  }
}
```

A sample output of this program is shown here.

9.17.5 JTable

The `JTable` class lets us create a tabular grid of data. It has many constructors and methods to customize its rendering and editing. Fortunately, it provides defaults for these features so that simple tables can be set up easily. For example, the following program creates a table of 4 rows and 2 columns.

```
import java.awt.*;
import javax.swing.*;
public class JTableDemo {
  public static void main(String args[]) {
    JFrame f = new JFrame("JTable Demo");
    Container c = f.getContentPane();
    f.setSize(200,120);
    f.setLayout(new FlowLayout());
```

```
        int row = 4, col = 2;
        JTable table = new JTable(row, col);
        for(int i=0;i<row;i++) {
          table.setValueAt(i,i,0);
          table.setValueAt(i*i, i,1);
        }
        c.add(table);
        f.setVisible(true);
    }
}
```

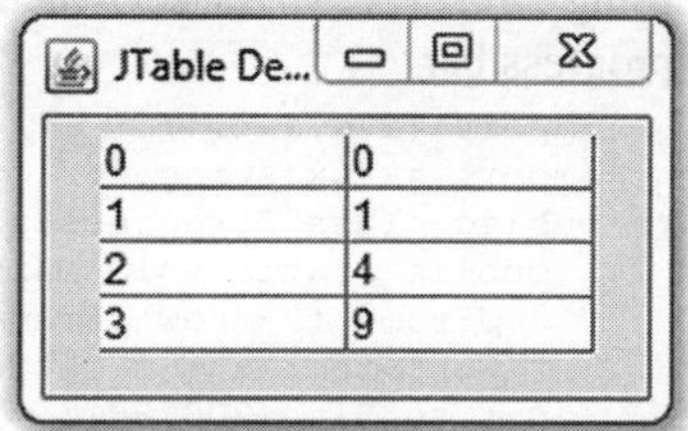

Here is the sample output of the program. The second column holds the square of the number in the first column.

9.17.6 JComboBox

A `JComboBox` object represents a pop-up menu of items, one of which may be chosen at any time. The current choice is displayed as the title of the menu. Clicking on the choice causes a menu to appear with the current choice highlighted. The following program creates pop-menu of three items.

```
import java.awt.*;
import javax.swing.*;
import java.awt.event.*;
public class JComboBoxDemo {
  public static void main(String args[]) {
    JFrame f = new JFrame("JComboBox Demo");
    Container c = f.getContentPane();
    f.setSize(100,150);
    f.setLayout(new FlowLayout());
    final JLabel l = new JLabel();
    String[] colors = { "Red", "Green", "Blue" };
    final JComboBox cl = new JComboBox(colors);
    cl.addActionListener(new ActionListener() {
      public void actionPerformed(ActionEvent e) {
        l.setText("Selected:"+cl.getSelectedItem());
      }
    });
    c.add(l);c.add(cl);
    f.setVisible(true);
  }
}
```

Here is a sample output.

9.17.7 JProgressBar

The `JProgressBar` component is used to visually display the progress of some task. It helps users to have an estimation of how long the task might take to complete or how much work has already been done. A progress bar may be either in *determinate* or *indeterminate* mode.

If it is possible to calculate percentage of work done so far, we use a determinate progress which looks like this:

The percentage is shown by a rectangle which starts out empty and gradually becomes filled in as the task progresses. The textual representation of the percentage, in addition, may be enabled using `setStringPainted()` method. The following program illustrates how to create this kind of progress bar.

```
import java.awt.*;
import javax.swing.*;
public class JProgressBarDemo {
  public static void main(String args[]) throws Exception {
    JFrame f = new JFrame("Choice Demo");
    Container c = f.getContentPane();
    f.setSize(200,80);
    f.setLayout(new FlowLayout());
    JProgressBar pb= new JProgressBar(0, 100);
    pb.setStringPainted(true);
    c.add(pb);
    f.setVisible(true);
    for(int i=0;i<=100;i++) {
      pb.setValue(i);
      Thread.sleep(100);
    }
  }
}
```

A sample output is shown here. However, if we can't immediately determine the length of a long-running task, or a task stuck for a long time, we can show progress bar in indeterminate mode. A progress bar in indeterminate mode, instead of showing any measurable progress, displays an animated bar moving back and forth continuously to indicate that an operation of unknown duration is occurring. In the Java look and feel, indeterminate progress bars look like this:

The modality is set using the method `setIndeterminate()` passing a value `true` (indeterminate mode) or `false` (determinate mode). Note that as soon as it is possible to calculate the remaining time, the progress bar should switch back to its default, determinate mode.

9.17.8 JList

A `JList` component shows a set of items from which one or more may be selected. It provides a very easy way to get user input, especially when you want to give the user a number of specific options. Items can be added easily from an array or vector. This program creates a static list of three items from an array of `String` objects.

```
import java.awt.*;
import javax.swing.*;
import javax.swing.event.*;
public class JListDemo {
  public static void main(String args[]) {
    final JFrame f = new JFrame("JList Demo");
    Container c = f.getContentPane();
    c.setLayout(new FlowLayout());
    String[] languages = {"Java", "C++", "C"};
    JList list = new JList(languages);
    list.addListSelectionListener(new ListSelectionListener() {
      public void valueChanged(ListSelectionEvent e) {
        JList l = (JList) e.getSource();
        Object values[] = l.getSelectedValues();
        for (int i = 0; i< values.length; i++)
```

```
                System.out.println(values[i] + " ");
            }
        });
        c.add(list);
        f.pack();
        f.setVisible(true);
    }
}
```

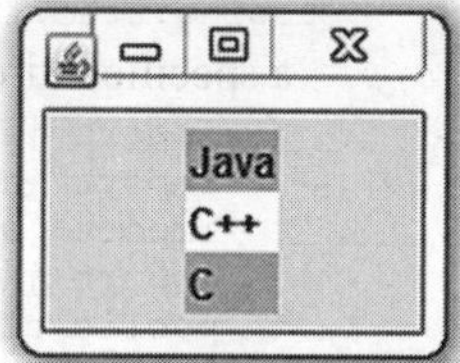

Here is the sample output of the program. To get the selections made, we use `getSelectedValues()` method.

The elements of a `JList` are not editable. A `JList` does not also support scrolling directly. A `JScrollPane` may be associated to have a scrolling list. The event generated by this component is `ListSelectionEvent` and the corresponding listener is `ListSelectionListener`.

9.17.9 JTree

A `JTree` is a sophisticated component that can display data hierarchy using tree. A `JTree` consists of nodes. The top-most node is called 'root'. A node may have children nodes which, in turn, may have further children nodes and so on. Nodes are added using the obvious `add()` method.

The leaf nodes and intermediate nodes are displayed with different icons. Nodes having children may be expanded or collapsed. Expanding a node displays its children and collapsing hides them.

A node in `JTree` is represented by the `TreeNode` interface, which provides methods corresponding to common operations on a node. Fortunately, swing provides an implementation of this interface, the `DefaultMutableTreeNode` class. The following program displays a simple list of components of a computer with their hierarchy using this default node implementation.

```
import java.awt.*;
import javax.swing.*;
import javax.swing.tree.DefaultMutableTreeNode;
public class JTreeDemo {
  public static void main(String args[]) {
    final JFrame f = new JFrame("JTree Demo");
    Container c = f.getContentPane();
    c.setLayout(new FlowLayout());
    DefaultMutableTreeNode root = new DefaultMutableTreeNode("Computer"),
        c1 = new DefaultMutableTreeNode("HDD"),
        c2 = new DefaultMutableTreeNode("CPU"),
        c3 = new DefaultMutableTreeNode("Mouse");
    root.add(c1);root.add(c2);root.add(c3);
    c1.add(new DefaultMutableTreeNode("Seagate"));
    c1.add(new DefaultMutableTreeNode("Samsung"));

    c2.add(new DefaultMutableTreeNode("Intel"));
    c2.add(new DefaultMutableTreeNode("IBM"));

    c3.add(new DefaultMutableTreeNode("Dell"));
    c3.add(new DefaultMutableTreeNode("HP"));

    JTree t = new JTree(root);
    c.add(t);
    f.pack();
    f.setVisible(true);
  }
}
```

A sample expanded output is shown here. Like many other swing components, `JTree` also relies on a model that describes the structure of data. For `JTree`, the model class must implement `javax.`

swing.tree.TreeModel interface. The following program creates a model for file system and displays a specified directory tree.

```
import javax.swing.*;
import javax.swing.event.*;
import javax.swing.tree.*;
import java.io.File;
public class FSTreeDemo {
  public static void main(String[] args) {
    JFrame f = new JFrame("FSTreeDemo");
    f.setSize(300,300);
    FSTreeModel model = new FSTreeModel(args[0]);
    JTree tree = new JTree();
    tree.setModel(model);
    JScrollPane jsp = new JScrollPane(tree);
    f.getContentPane().add(jsp);
    f.setVisible(true);
  }
}
class FSTreeModel implements TreeModel {
  File root;
  public FSTreeModel(String path) { this.root = new File(path); }
  public Object getRoot() { return root; }
  public Object getChild(Object p, int in) {
    String[] c = ((File)p).list();
    return (c == null) || (in >= c.length)?null:new File((File) p, c[in]);
  }
  public int getIndexOfChild(Object p, Object c) {
    String[] l = ((File)p).list();
    if (l == null) return -1;
    String name = ((File)c).getName();
    for(int i = 0; i < l.length; i++)
      if (name.equals(l[i])) return i;
    return -1;
  }
  public int getChildCount(Object p) {
    String[] c = ((File)p).list();
    return c != null? c.length:0;
  }
  public boolean isLeaf(Object node) {  return ((File)node).isFile(); }
  public void addTreeModelListener(TreeModelListener l) {}
  public void removeTreeModelListener(TreeModelListener l) {}
  public void valueForPathChanged(TreePath path, Object newvalue) {}
}
```

A sample output for the drive e:\ (in windows) is shown here. Note that JTree is quite a complex component. Its detailed description is out of the scope of this book.

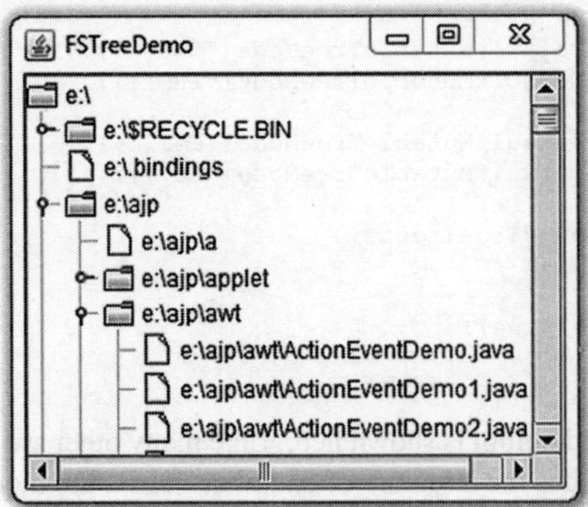

9.17.10 JColorChooser

Another sophisticated but convenient and useful component introduced in swing is `JColorChooser`. It allows users to choose a color from a palette of colors. This component can be placed anywhere within a GUI, including dialog boxes. A `JColorChooser` component has two sections: the tabbed pane of color selection and a preview box. The tabbed pane has three tabs which allows us to select a color from colors models HSV, HSL, RGB and CMYK. The commonly used constructors of `JColorChooser` class are:

```
JColorChooser()
JColorChooser(Color initialColor)
```

The former creates a color chooser with white color initially while the latter creates a color chooser with the specified color initially. The `getColor()` method is used to obtain the color selected. Here is a sample program that uses a color chooser to set the color of some text.

```
import java.awt.*;
import javax.swing.*;
import javax.swing.event.*;
public class JColorChooserDemo {
  public static void main(String args[]) {
    JFrame f = new JFrame("JColorChooser Demo");
    Container c = f.getContentPane();
    f.setSize(650,400);
    f.setLayout(new FlowLayout());
    final JLabel banner = new JLabel("Sample Text",JLabel.CENTER);
    final JColorChooser cc = new JColorChooser(Color.black);
    cc.getSelectionModel().addChangeListener(new ChangeListener() {
      public void stateChanged(ChangeEvent e) {
        Color newColor = cc.getColor();
        banner.setForeground(newColor);
      }
    });
    c.add(banner);
    c.add(cc, BorderLayout.PAGE_END);
    f.setVisible(true);
  }
}
```

The event generated by this component is `ChangeEvent` and the corresponding listener is `ChangeListener`. A sample output of this program is shown below:

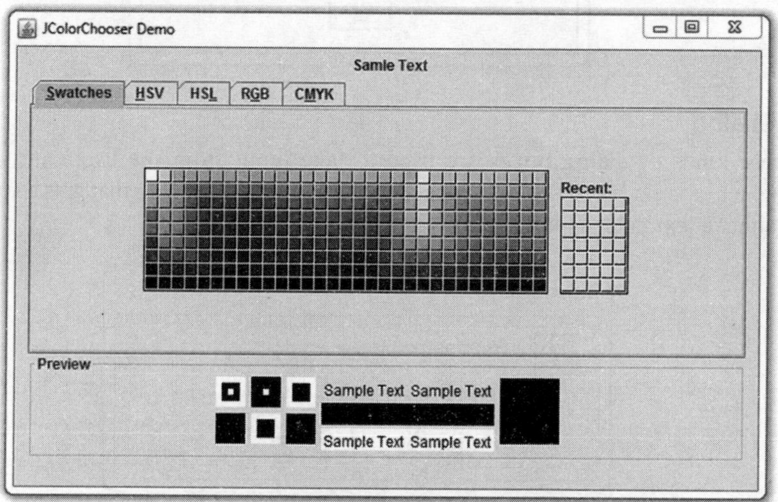

9.17.11 Dialogs

Creating various dialog boxes has become simple in swing. To create simple, standard dialogs, we use the `JOptionPane` class. However, custom dialogs may also be created using the `JDialog` class. We can quickly create and customize several different kinds of dialogs using `JOptionPane`. For example, we can customize layouts, icons to be displayed, title and text, buttons and their captions etc.

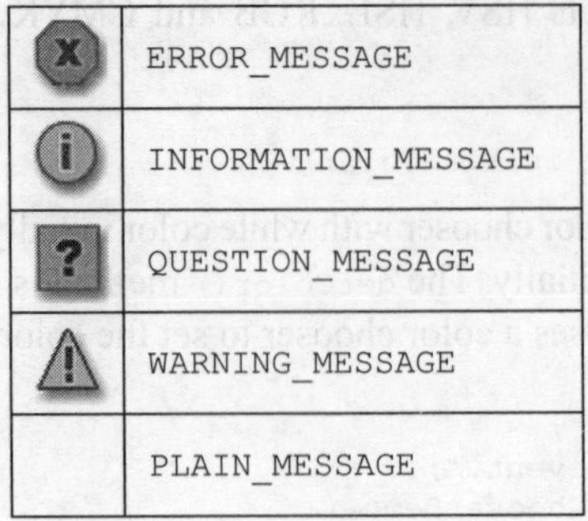

Icon	Constant
X	ERROR_MESSAGE
i	INFORMATION_MESSAGE
?	QUESTION_MESSAGE
!	WARNING_MESSAGE
	PLAIN_MESSAGE

Message Dialog

A message dialog is a modal dialog with one button, labelled "OK". However, the message, icon, and title can be customized. It is created using the following method:

```
void showMessageDialog(Component parent, Object msg, String title, int msgType)
```

Here, `parent` is the parent frame where this dialog is shown, `msg` is the message to be displayed and `title` is the title of the dialog box. The `msgType` represents the icon to be displayed and can have values `ERROR_MESSAGE`, `INFORMATION_MESSAGE`, `WARNING_MESSAGE`, `QUESTION_MESSAGE`, or `PLAIN_MESSAGE` defined in `JOptionPane` class. The icons corresponding to these constants are shown here. The following instantly shows a simple message dialog:

```
JOptionPane.showMessageDialog(f, "How easy to create dialogs!");
```

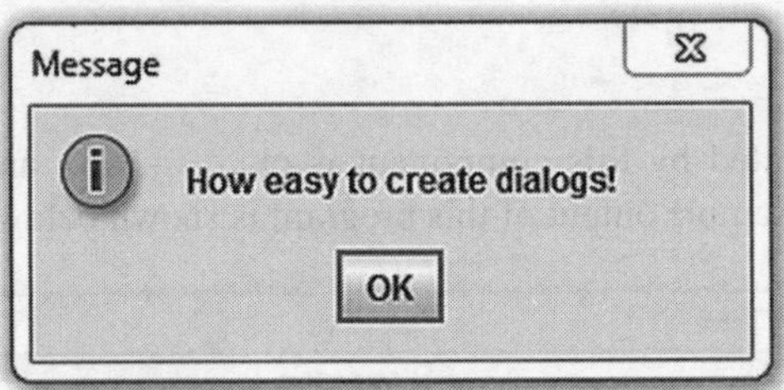

Input Dialog

These kinds of dialog boxes are used to take input from the users and are created using `showInputDialog()` method. It is designed to display a modal dialog that gets a string from the user, using either a text field, an un-editable combo box or a list.

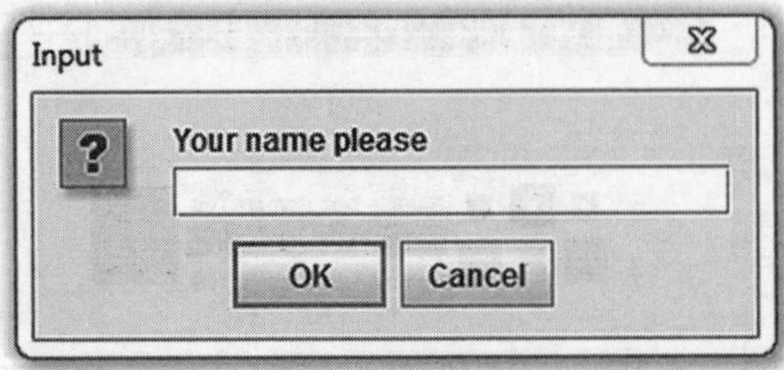

It returns an `Object`, which is generally a `String` reflecting the user's choice. It has several overloaded versions. The simplest one creates a dialog with one text field where users can provide data. Here is an example:

```
String s = (String)JOptionPane.showInputDialog(f, "Your name please");
```

The `showInputDialog()` method can also create a dialog that lets the user to choose one of many options.

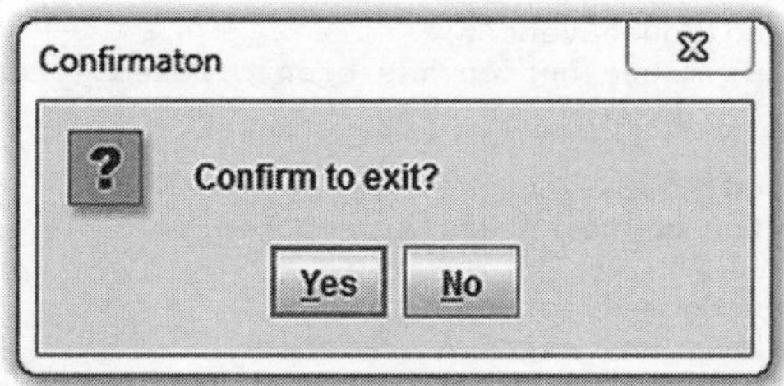

Confirm Dialog

These kinds of dialogs are used to ask the user to confirm something and are created using `showConfirmDialog()` method. The type of buttons to be displayed may be customized using static constants defined in `JOptionPane` class. For example, `YES_NO_OPTION` dialogs have two buttons, and `YES_NO_CANCEL_OPTION` dialogs have three buttons. The following creates a dialog with two buttons.

```
int n = JOptionPane.showConfirmDialog(f,"Confirm to exit?",
"Confirmaton",JOptionPane.YES_NO_OPTION);
```

This method returns an integer indicating the user's action. The possible values are `YES_OPTION`, `NO_OPTION`, `CANCEL_OPTION`, `OK_OPTION`, and `CLOSED_OPTION`. Each option, except for `CLOSED_OPTION`, correspond to the button pressed. The `CLOSED_OPTION` is returned, if dialog window is closed explicitly, rather than pressing a button inside the option pane.

Option Dialog

The option dialog boxes display a variety of buttons with customized button text, and can contain a standard text message or a collection of components. These are created using `showOptionDialog()`. When using `showOptionDialog()` and `showConfirmDialog()` we can either use the standard button text or specify different text. For example, the following creates a dialog with two buttons captioned "Pay now" and "Pay later".

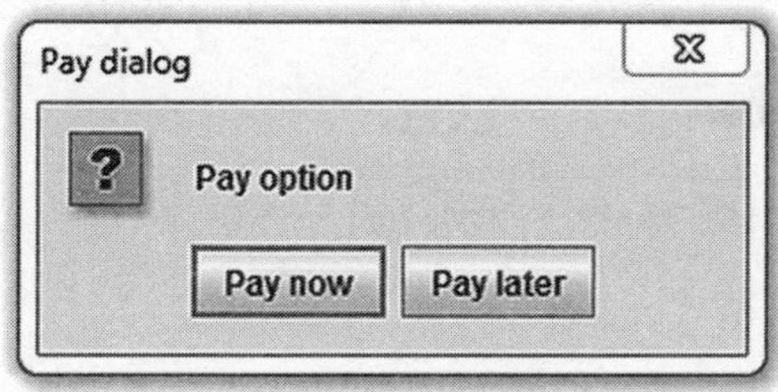


```
String[] options = {"Pay now","Pay later"};
int n = JOptionPane.showOptionDialog(f,"Pay option","Pay
dialog",JOptionPane.YES_NO_OPTION,JOptionPane.QUESTION_MESSAGE, null, options,
options[0]);
```

This method returns an integer similar to `showConfirmDialog()` method.

9.17.12 Appendix A: Methods of Important Event Listener Interfaces

ActionListener

```
void actionPerformed(ActionEvent e)
//Called when an action occurs
```

MouseListener

```
void mouseClicked(MouseEvent e)
//Called when the mouse button has been clicked (pressed and released) on a
component.

void mouseEntered(MouseEvent e)
//Invoked when the mouse enters a component.

void mouseExited(MouseEvent e)
//Called when the mouse exits a component.

void mousePressed(MouseEvent e)
//Invoked when a mouse button has been pressed on a component.

void mouseReleased(MouseEvent e)
//Called when a mouse button has been released on a component.
```

Key//Invoked Listener

```
void keyPressed(KeyEvent e)
//Called when a key has been pressed.

void keyReleased(KeyEvent e)
//Called when a key has been released.

void keyTyped(KeyEvent e)
//Invoked when a key has been typed.
```

ItemListener

```
void itemStateChanged(ItemEvent e)
//Invoked when an item has been selected or deselected by the user.
```

TextListener

```
void textValueChanged(TextEvent e)
//Called when the value of the text has changed.
```

MouseWheelListener

```
void mouseWheelMoved(MouseWheelEvent e)
//Invoked when the mouse wheel is rotated.
```

WindowListener

```
void windowActivated(WindowEvent e)
//Invoked when the Window is set to be the active Window.

void windowClosed(WindowEvent e)
//Called when a window has been closed as the result of calling dispose on the
window.
```

```
void windowClosing(WindowEvent e)
//Called when the user attempts to close the window from the window's system
    menu.

void windowDeactivated(WindowEvent e)
//Invoked when a Window is no longer the active Window.

void windowDeiconified(WindowEvent e)
//Invoked when a window is changed from a minimized to a normal state.

void windowIconified(WindowEvent e)
//Invoked when a window is changed from a normal to a minimized state.

void windowOpened(WindowEvent e)
//Called the first time a window is made visible.
```

ComponentListener

```
void componentHidden(ComponentEvent e)
//Invoked when the component has been made invisible.

void componentMoved(ComponentEvent e)
//Called when the component's position changes.

void componentResized(ComponentEvent e)
//Invoked when the component's size changes.

void componentShown(ComponentEvent e)
//Invoked when the component has been made visible.
```

ContainerListener

```
void componentAdded(ContainerEvent e)
//Invoked when a component has been added to the container.

void componentRemoved(ContainerEvent e)
//Called when a component has been removed from the container.
```

AdjustmentListener

```
void adjustmentValueChanged(AdjustmentEvent e)
//Invoked when the value of the adjustable has changed.
```

FocusListener

```
void focusGained(FocusEvent e)
//Invoked when a component gains the keyboard focus.

void focusLost(FocusEvent e)
//Invoked when a component loses the keyboard focus.
```

KEYWORDS

Abstract Window Toolkit—Java API for building GUI-based applications

Adapter—Class that implements empty versions of all methods of a listener interface

BorderLayout—A layout manager that arranges and resizes a container's components to fit in five regions: north, south, east, west, and center

Components—Graphic elements that can be displayed on the screen and that can interact with the user

Container—Special components that can contain other components

Dialog—A top-level window typically used as a *pop-up window* and to take some form of input from the user

Event—User actions such as clicking a button, typing some text in a text box/text area, opening/closing a window, etc.

Event Listeners—Special objects used to handle generated events

Event sources—Various AWT components that generate events

FlowLayout—A layout manager that arranges the components from left-to-right much like lines of text in a paragraph

Frame—A special `Window` with border, title, the content display area and an optional menu bar

Graphical User Interface—An interface to the users based on graphic components

GridLayout—A layout manager that arranges a container's components as a grid of rows and columns

Layout Manager—An object that controls the position (layout) and size of components inside a container

Panel—A higher-level container, which is a borderless transparent rectangular box, used to organize a set of related components in pattern such as grid or flow

Swing—An extension to AWT providing better look and feel and more GUI components

Window—A top-level display-surface without any borders and menu bar

SUMMARY

GUI-based applications provide click and execute environment that make applications more entertaining and interesting. Java provides a rich API, called **A**bstract **W**indow **T**oolkit (AWT), to create various GUI components.

Java allows programmers to create various graphical components such as window, frame, panel, button, text field, text area, radio button, check box, drop down list, etc. Using these components, we can create an interactive user interface for an application. Components are graphic elements that can be displayed on the screen and that can interact with the user. Some components (such as buttons, text boxes) cannot stand alone and require some other special components to *contain* them. These special components are called *containers*.

Each container is associated with a layout manager that controls the position (layout) and size of components inside a container. The most important layout managers are: `FlowLayout`, `GridLayout`, `BorderLayout`. The `FlowLayout` manager arranges the components from left-to-right much like lines of text in a paragraph. The `GridLayout` manager arranges a container's components as a grid of rows and columns. A `BorderLayout` manager arranges and resizes a container's components to fit in five regions: north, south, east, west, and center.

The basic AWT non-container component classes (also called controls) are `Label`, `TextField`, `TextArea`, `Button`, `Checkbox`, `CheckboxGroup`, `Choice`, `List`. New custom component classes may also be created by deriving them from class `Component`.

Panels are often used to organize a set of related components in a pattern such as grid or flow. A panel itself is not a visible component. It merely provides some space where we can attach other components including other panels.

A useful GUI should respond to user actions such as clicking a button, typing some text in a text box/text area, opening/closing a window etc. The process of determining that an action has been taken is known as listening and the action done by the user is called an event. Writing the corresponding code for a user action is called Event handling.

When an event is generated, an object (called *event* object) is actually created. The generated event object is then passed to all the registered listener's appropriate event-handler method(s).

AWT API, introduced in JDK 1.0, does not support any GUI components for table, tree, pop-up menu, progress bar, color chooser etc. A much more comprehensive set of graphics libraries that enhances the AWT, was introduced in JDK 1.1 and is known as *Swing API*.

WEB RESOURCES

`https://docs.oracle.com/javase/tutorial/uiswing/layout/visual.html`
A Visual Guide to Layout Managers

`http://www.java2s.com/Tutorial/Java/0240__Swing/Catalog0240__Swing.htm`
Swing

`https://docs.oracle.com/javase/tutorial/uiswing/`
Trail: Creating a GUI With JFC/Swing

`http://www.tutorialspoint.com/awt/`
AWT Tutorial

http://www.ntu.edu.sg/home/ehchua/programming/java/j4a_gui.html
Programming Graphical User Interface (GUI)

http://www.javaworld.com/article/2077188/core-java/introduction-to-the-awt.html
Introduction to the AWT

EXERCISES

Objective-type Questions

1. What is the full form of AWT?
   (a) All Windows Tools
   (b) Abstract Window Toolkit
   (c) All Writing Tools
   (d) Absolute Window Toolkit

2. Which of the following methods is used to determine the key pressed?
   (a) getKey() (c) getModifier()
   (b) getActionKey() (d) getSource()

3. Which of these events is generated when a button is pressed?
   (a) MouseEvent (c) PressEvent
   (b) KeyEvent (d) ActionEvent

4. When two or more objects are added as listeners for the same event, which listener is first invoked to handle the event?
   (a) The first object that was added as listener.
   (b) The last object that was added as listener.
   (c) There is no way to determine which listener will be invoked first.
   (d) It is impossible to have more than one listener for a given event.

5. Which of the following components generates action events?
   (a) Buttons (c) Check boxes
   (b) Labels (d) Windows

6. Suppose you want to have an object eh handle the TextEvent of a TextArea object t. How should you add eh as the event handler for t?
   (a) t.addTextListener(eh);
   (b) eh.addTextListener(t);
   (c) addTextListener(eh.t);
   (d) addTextListener(t,eh);

7. What is the preferred way to handle an object's events in Java 2?
   (a) Override the object's handleEvent( ) method.
   (b) Add one or more event listeners to handle the events.
   (c) Have the object override its processEvent( ) methods.
   (d) Have the object override its dispatchEvent( ) methods.

8. Which of these packages contains all the classes and methods required for event handling in Java?
   (a) java.applet (c) java.event
   (b) java.awt (d) java.awt.event

9. What is an event in delegation event model used by Java programming language?
   (a) An event is an object that describes a state change in a source.
   (b) An event is an object that describes a state change in processing.
   (c) An event is an object that describes any change by the user and system.
   (d) An event is a class used for defining object, to create events.

10. Which of these methods are used to register a keyboard event listener?
    (a) KeyListener()
    (b) addKistener()
    (c) addKeyListener()
    (d) eventKeyboardListener()

11. Which of these methods are used to register a mouse motion listener?
    (a) addMouse()
    (b) addMouseListener()
    (c) addMouseMotionListner()
    (d) eventMouseMotionListener()

12. Which of the following classes are derived from the Panel class.
    (a) Applet (c) Frame
    (b) Dialog (d) Button

13. What is a listener in context to event handling?
    (a) A listener is a variable that is notified when an event occurs.
    (b) A listener is an object that is notified when an event occurs.

(c) A listener is a method that is notified when an event occurs.
(d) None of the mentioned

14. Which of these libraries contains top-most Event class?
(a) java.awt.event (c) java.awt
(b) java.lang (d) java.util

15. Which of these methods can be used to determine the type of event?
(a) getID() (c) getEvent()
(b) getSource() (d) getEventObject()

16. Which of these classes is super-class of all the events?
(a) EventObject (c) ActionEvent
(b) EventClass (d) ItemEvent

17. Which of these events will be notified if scroll bar is manipulated?
(a) ActionEvent
(b) ComponentEvent
(c) AdjustmentEvent
(d) WindowEvent

18. What does the following line of code do? Textfield text = new Textfield(10);
(a) Creates text object that can hold 10 rows of text.
(b) Creates the object text and initializes it with the value 10.
(c) Creates text object that can hold 10 columns of text.
(d) The code is illegal.

19. Which of the following methods can be used to change the size of a java.awt.Component object?
(i) dimension()
(ii) setSize()
(iii) area()
(iv) size()
(v) resize()
(a) (ii) & (v) (c) (i), (ii) & (v)
(b) (i), (ii), (iii) & (v) (d) (ii), (iv) & (v)

20. The setBackground() method is part of the following class in java.awt package:
(a) Graphics (d) Container
(b) Applet (e) Object
(c) Component

Subjective-type Questions

1. What is a layout manager and what are the different types of layout managers available?
2. How are the elements of a borderLayout organized?
3. Which containers may have a menu bar?
4. What is the difference between choice and the List?
5. What advantage do Java's layout managers provide over traditional windowing systems?
6. What is the difference between a Window and a Frame?
7. Which is the super-class of all event classes?
8. What method is used to specify a container's layout?
9. What are the advantages of swing over AWT?
10. What interface is extended by AWT event listeners?
11. What is the relationship between an event-listener interface and an event-adapter class?
12. What are events, event sources and event listeners?

CHAPTER – 10

JAVA AND XML

KEY OBJECTIVES

After completing this chapter readers will be able to—

- get an idea about Document Object Model (DOM)
- understand how DOM represents an XML document as a tree structure
- get an idea about DOM objects and interfaces defined by the W3C
- create and navigate a DOM tree for an XML document using Java
- manipulate a DOM tree using Java
- validate an XML document against DTD and schema using Java

10.1 INTRODUCTION

XML (e**X**tensible **M**arkup **L**anguage), is a key technology for structured data representation and transfer. It is used virtually everywhere from small- to large-scale legacy applications. Java also promotes portability and an obvious choice to work with XML documents. Java APIs for XML makes it easier and easier to use XML from the Java programming language.

This chapter gives a detailed description of how to use the Java APIs for XML. It also provides sample applications that you can run.

10.2 XML AND DOM

Document **O**bject **M**odel (DOM) is a language-neutral and platform-independent object model used to represent XML documents. DOM helps scripts and programs to access, add, delete, and edit content, structure, and style of XML documents dynamically.

DOM is standardized by the **W**orld **W**ide **W**eb **C**onsortium (W3C). The primary objective of this standard was to model an HTML document in an object-oriented way so that it could be exposed to scripts, and scripts could access and manipulate HTML documents through this object model dynamically. In this regard, the World Wide Web Consortium (W3C) received several proposals from its member companies. Consequently, the W3C tried to develop an interoperable and language-neutral object model to represent HTML as well as XML documents and the result was DOM. In order to provide a precise specification of the DOM interfaces independent of languages, the W3C chose to use **I**nterface **D**efinition **L**anguage (IDL), defined by **O**bject **M**anagement **G**roup (OMG) in the CORBA 2.2 specification. OMG IDL is widely used to specify interfaces in a language-independent and implementation-neutral way.

The W3C DOM specification is divided into three major parts:

- DOM Core—This portion defines the basic set of interfaces and objects for any structured document.
- XML DOM—This part specifies the standard set of objects and interfaces for XML documents only.
- HTML DOM—This part defines the interfaces and objects for HTML documents only.

In this chapter, we shall highlight only XML DOM. The W3C added some more features to the HTML DOM for better handling.

DOM models a document as a hierarchical structure consisting of different kinds of nodes. Each of these nodes represent a specific portion of the document. This simple idea has made the entire framework elegant. Some kind of nodes may have children of different types. Some nodes cannot have anything below it in the hierarchical structure and are leaf nodes. It also provides standard and specialized set of interfaces and objects to navigate and manipulate (add, modify, delete) DOM tree. DOM is an object-oriented model that encompasses not only the document structure, but the behaviour of the document also. It means, each node of the document tree is not a data structure, but an object which has identity (properties) and activity (methods). The primary objective of DOM is to identify

- interfaces and objects to be used to represent, access, and manipulate documents;
- semantics of these objects and interfaces including both attributes and behaviour;
- collaboration and relationship among these objects and interfaces.

DOM was standardized to be used with any programming language. In this chapter, we shall use Java as the programming language to discuss how to navigate and manipulate the DOM tree. In Chapter 14, we shall show how to do the same using JavaScript.

Let us explain the XML DOM tree with an example. Consider the following simple XML document that contains the specification of a hard disk.

```
<?xml version='1.0'?>
<store>
    <HDD type='SATA'>
        <make>Samsung</make>
        <capacity unit='GB'>80</capacity>
        <speed unit='rpm'>7200</speed>
        <price currency='INR'>1600</price>
    </HDD>
</store>
```

The corresponding XML DOM tree is shown in Figure 10.1:

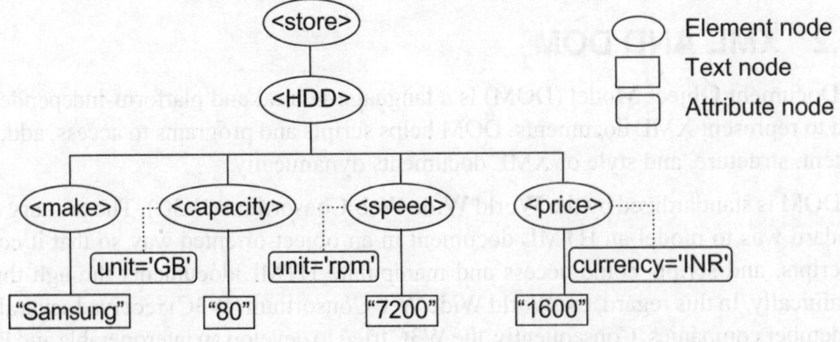

Figure 10.1: XML DOM tree

As mentioned earlier, the DOM tree consists of many types of nodes. Each of these nodes represents a particular component of the XML document. In fact, the hierarchical structure is not a single tree, but a *forest* that consists of many trees. The `Attr`, `Comment`, `CDATASection`, etc. type nodes are not considered as children of any other node. The exact representation of these nodes is implementation-dependent.

Nodes in a DOM tree have structural relationships among them. The topmost node is the *root* node. In Figure 10.2: , `<store>` is the root node. Every DOM tree has exactly one root node. Except the root node, all other nodes have exactly one *parent* node. Nodes except leaf nodes, may have any number of *children*. Nodes having common parent are called *siblings*. For example, the elements `<make>` and `<capacity>`, and `<speed>` and `<price>` are siblings of one another as they have the common parent element `<HDD>`. The elements `<price>` and `<capacity>` are `nextSibling` and `previousSibling`, respectively, of `<speed>`.

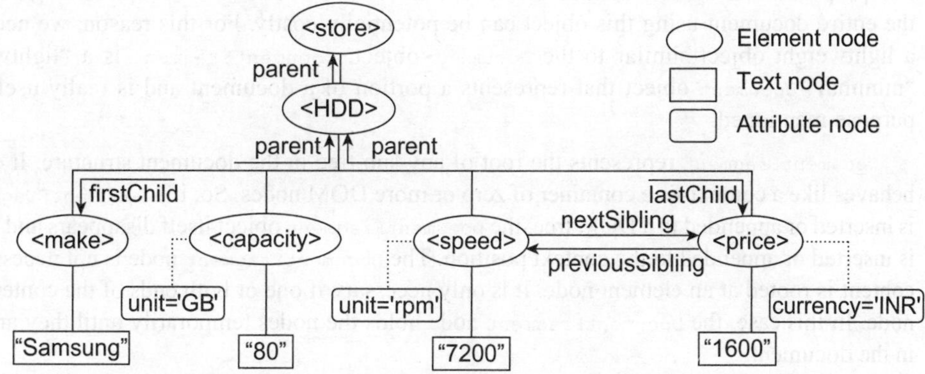

Figure 10.2: Structural relationships among nodes in DOM tree

The fundamental data type in the entire Document Object Model (DOM) is the `Node` interface. All other kinds of nodes implement this interface and hence inherit all the properties and methods of the `Node` interface. However, not all the methods and properties are available on each node type. A specific set of methods and properties are available on each node type. For example, `Text` and `Attr` nodes inherit methods dealing with children from `Node`, but these methods are not valid on `Text` and `Attr` type nodes.

10.3 DOM NODES

All components of an XML document are represented by different kinds of nodes. W3C specified 12 (twelve) types of nodes: `Document`, `DocumentFragment`, `DocumentType`, `EntityReference`, `Element`, `Attr`, `ProcessingInstruction`, `Comment`, `Text`, `CDATASection`, `Entity`, and `Notation`. In this section we shall describe each of these nodes one by one.

`Document`

The W3C `Document` type node represents an entire XML document. Only one `Document` type node exists for each XML document. It is essentially a container of all components of an XML document such as XML declaration (processing instruction), elements, attributes, comments, entities, and so on. Each of these components is represented by a specific type of node.

`Element`

This interface represents an element in the XML document. Elements may have attributes. Those attributes may be obtained from the property `attributes` inherited from the `Node` interface. It also has several useful methods to get an `Attr` node or the value of an attribute by its name.

Attr

An Attr type node represents an attribute of an Element node. An Attr node is associated with an element but is not considered as a child of the element. Therefore, though Attr objects inherit all the properties and methods of the Node interface, some are not valid (i.e., have the value null). For example, the properties parentNode, previousSibling, nextSibling, firstChild, and lastChild are not valid on an Attr object. However, Attr objects have methods to access the name and value of the attributes.

Text

It represents the textual content of an Element type node. The text content of an Element node is represented as a separate Text type node, which is a child node of the element.

DocumentFragment

The implementation of the Document object can be heavyweight as a large number of methods and properties have been defined for it. So, to cut and/or move a document fragment around the entire document using this object can be potentially costly. For this reason, we need to have a lightweight object similar to the Document object. DocumentFragment is a "lightweight" or "minimal" Document object that represents a portion of a document and is really useful for the purpose mentioned.

DocumentFragment represents the root of any sub-tree in the document structure. It essentially behaves like a context-free container of zero or more DOM nodes. So, if a DocumentFragment node is inserted or appended to a DOM tree, the DocumentFragment object itself disappears and its content is inserted or appended to the context position. The DocumentFragment node is not necessary, if the content is rooted at an element node. It is only necessary if one or both ends of the content is a text node. In this case, the DocumentFragment node holds the nodes temporarily until they are dropped in the document.

The W3C provides the createDocumentFragment() method on the Document object to create an empty DocumentFragment container. The DocumentFragment object inherits all the methods and properties of the Node object that may be used to append or insert other nodes to this container.

DocumentType

It provides interfaces to get information about the document, including the list of entities defined for this document. All the properties on this node are read-only.

EntityReference

A node of this type represents an entity reference in the document. However, an XML processor may completely expand references to entities while building the document tree, instead of providing EntityReference nodes. The sub-tree rooted at the node of type EntityReference is an exact copy of the sub-tree rooted at a node of type Entity.

ProcessingInstruction

The ProcessingInstruction interface represents a "processing instruction", which is used in XML to provide specific information about the document to the processor.

Comment

It represents a comment in an XML document. Note that all the characters between the starting '!--' and ending '-->' delimiters are not processed and are called comment.

CDATASection

This type of node represents a CDATA section in the XML document. Note that no lexical check is done on the content of the CDATA section. It is, therefore, useful to include arbitrary text containing characters, which will otherwise be interpreted as XML.

Entity

It represents a known, either unparsed or parsed entity. An XML processor may completely expand entities while building the document tree and in such a case there will be no `EntityReference` nodes in the document tree. An `Entity` node, if present, does not have any parent. W3C DOM Level 3 does not allow the editing of `Entity` nodes. If users want to change the contents of an `Entity` node, the desired changes have to be made to the related `EntityReference` node.

10.4 THE NODE INTERFACE

As mentioned earlier, it is the primary data type for the entire DOM. Every other kind of node inherits all the properties and methods of the `Node` interface. In the next two sections, we shall discuss the frequently used properties and methods available on the `Node` interface.

10.4.1 Node Properties

Some properties of the `Node` interface are read-only. This means that the values of those properties can only be read but they can never be changed. The other properties are read–write. The values of these properties can be read as well as modified. Java provides a read method for each of these properties. For example, the property name is `xxx` on some object `o`, Java provides a method `getXxx()` on `o`. The following important properties are available on the `Node` interface. We shall first discuss the properties, without referring to any language. We shall then discuss how to work with them using Java.

nodeType

This *read-only* property holds a positive integer that indicates the type of the context node. Table 10.1: shows the value of `nodeType` for different kind of nodes as well as constants defined in the W3C DOM specification.

Table 10.1: The values of nodeType property of the Node interface

Node	Value of nodeType	Constant defined
Element	1	ELEMENT_NODE
Attr	2	ATTRIBUTE_NODE
Text	3	TEXT_NODE
CDATASection	4	CDATA_SECTION_NODE
EntityReference	5	ENTITY_REFERENCE_NODE
Entity	6	ENTITY_NODE
ProcessingInstruction	7	PROCESSING_INSTRUCTION_NODE
Comment	8	COMMENT_NODE
Document	9	DOCUMENT_NODE
DocumentType	10	DOCUMENT_TYPE_NODE
DocumentFragment	11	DOCUMENT_FRAGMENT_NODE
Notation	12	NOTATION_NODE

Java provides the `getNodeType()` method on the `Node` object to inspect this property.

This property is typically inspected before obtaining other properties. Note that the only `Element` type node can have children. So, if `nodeType` has the value 1, `childNodes` property (discussed later in this section) on this node is valid. However, if the node is a `Text` node (`nodeType` has the value 3), `childNodes` property is not valid. So, it is always safe to inspect this property before using other node specific properties.

The Java interface `Node` defines the following properties, which help us to determine the type of node we are dealing with.

Table 10.2: lists properties of the `Node` interface.

Table 10.2: The Node interface properties

Property	Meaning
ATTRIBUTE_NODE	It is an Attr type node.
CDATA_SECTION_NODE	It is a CDATASection type node.
COMMENT_NODE	It is a Comment type node.
DOCUMENT_FRAGMENT_NODE	It is a DocumentFragment type node.
DOCUMENT_NODE	It is a Document type node.
DOCUMENT_TYPE_NODE	It is a DocumentType type node.
ELEMENT_NODE	It is an Element type node.
ENTITY_NODE	It is an Entity type node.
ENTITY_REFERENCE_NODE	It is an EntityReference type node.
NOTATION_NODE	It is a Notation type node.
PROCESSING_INSTRUCTION_NODE	It is a ProcessingInstruction type node.
TEXT_NODE	It is a Text node type node.

`nodeName`

This *read-only* property holds the name of a node. The interpretation of this node is different for different types of nodes. Table 10.3: shows the value of this property for different kinds of nodes.

Table 10.3: The values of nodeName property of Node interface

Node	Value of nodeName	Node	Value of nodeName
Element	Name of the element	ProcessingInstruction	Target of the PI
Attr	Name of the attribute	Comment	"#comment"
Text	"#text"	Document	"#document"
CDATASection	"#cdata-section"	DocumentType	Name of DTD
EntityReference	Name of the entity referenced	DocumentFragment	"#document-fragment"
Entity	Name of the entity	Notation	Name of the notation

The Java `Node` interface provides the `getNodeName()` method to inspect this property.

`nodeValue`

This read–write property holds the value of the node. Again, the interpretation of this node is different for different types of nodes. Table 10.4: shows the value of this property for different types of nodes.

Table 10.4: The values of nodeValue property of the Node interface

Node	Value of nodeValue	Node	Value of nodeValue
Element	null	ProcessingInstruction	Content of the PI
Attr	Value of the attribute	Comment	Content of the comment
Text	Content of the text node	Document	Null
CDATASection	Content of the CDATA section	DocumentType	Null
EntityReference	null	DocumentFragment	Null
Entity	null	Notation	Null

The Java `Node` interface provides the `getNodeValue()` method to inspect this property. Consider the following XML document:

```
<?xml version='1.0'?>
<store>
    <HDD type='SATA'>
        <make>Samsung</make>
        <capacity unit='GB'>80</capacity>
        <speed unit='rpm'>7200</speed>
        <price currency='INR'>1600</price>
    </HDD>
</store>
```

For this code segment, suppose `hdd` refers to the `<HDD>` element. This can be done as follows:

```
var hdd = doc.documentElement.firstChild;
```

Then, `hdd.attributes["type"].nodeValue` has the value "`SATA`" and `para.firstChild.nodeValue` has the value "`This is a paragraph`".

childNodes

This property of a node contains all child nodes of the context node. It is valid only on element type nodes. It has a property `length` that indicates number of child nodes. Individual child nodes may be referenced as `childNodes[0]`, `childNodes[1]`, etc. Consider the following code segment:

```
<html>
    <head>
        <title></title>
    </head>
    <body>
        <p>This is a paragraph</p>
    </body>
<html>
```

The `<html>` element is referenced as `document.documentElement` and `document.documentElement.childNodes` is an array of child nodes of the `<html>` element. The `<html>` element has two children: `<head>` and `<body>`. So, `document.documentElement.childNodes[0]` and `document.documentElement.childNodes[1]` refer to `<head>` and `<body>` elements, respectively. Since `<head>` has only one child, the `<title>` element `document.documentElement.childNodes[0].childNodes[0]` refers to the `<title>` element. Similarly, `document.body.childNodes[0]` refers to the `<p>`element.

Accessing elements using `childNodes` may not work correctly in some browsers as they treat blank space between tags as a child text node. This means, for a particular document, `childNodes` property may have different lengths in different browsers. Moreover, if an element changes its location (for example, another element is inserted before it), its index in the `childNodes` property will also change, which may affect some existing JavaScript code that uses `childNodes` and index to access this element. For example, if the `<div>` element is inserted before the `<p>` element, the index of `<p>` in the `childNodes` will be 1, which was 0 before inserting the `<div>` element. The only reliable way to access an element is to use the id of an element. This is described later in this chapter.

firstChild

This property refers to the first child of the context node. Its value is `null` if there is no such node. Note that `document.documentElement` refers to the `<html>` element. So, `document.documentElement.firstChild` refers to the `<head>` element. Similarly, `document.documentElement.firstChild.firstChild` refers to the `<title>` element.

lastChild

This property refers to the last child of the context node. Its value is `null` if no such node exists. The node `document.documentElement.lastChild` refers to the `<body>` element.

nextSibling

It returns the node immediately following this node. If no such node exists, it returns `null`. For example, `document.documentElement.firstChild.nextSibling` refers to the `<body>` element.

previousSibling

It returns the node immediately preceding this node. If no such node exists, it returns `null`. For example, `document.body.previousSibling` refers to the `<head>` element.

attributes

This is an unordered collection containing all attributes specified for the context node or `null` otherwise. Individual attributes may be accessed by name. Consider the following HTML document:

```
<html>
    <head>
        <title>attributes demo</title>
    </head>
    <body bgColor="purple">
    </body>
</html>
```

The following object refers to a list of all the attributes of the `<body>` element.

```
document.body.attributes
```

In JavaScript, it is just an array. JavaScript arrays are associative arrays. So, a specific attribute can be obtained by specifying the name of the attribute as the array index. So, the following object refers to the attribute of the <body> element having the name `bgColor`.

```
document.body.attributes["bgColor"]
```

The value of the `bgColor` attribute of the `<body>` element can then be obtained using the following code:

```
ocument.body.attributes["bgColor"].nodeValue
```

They may also be accessed using a usual ordinal number but DOM does not maintain any specific order for these attribute nodes.

parentNode

Returns the parent node of the context node. Note that `Document`, `DocumentFragment`, `Attr`, `Notation`, and `Entity` nodes do not have a parent and value of this property is `null`. Nodes that have just been created but not added to the tree or nodes that have been deleted, have the value `null` for this property.

10.5 DOCUMENT NODE

It provides several useful properties that can be used to get the information about the XML document.

10.5.1 `Document` Node Properties

`documentElement`

This property of the `Document` node refers to the root node (document element) of the document tree. To navigate the document tree, we generally start from this `documentElement` node.

`docType`

It represents the Document Type Declaration for this document. Its value is `null` if there is no Document Type Declaration.

`documentURI`

It represents the location of the document. Its value is `null` if it is undefined or the document is created dynamically.

`domConfig`

It represents document configuration and maintains a table of recognized parameters. With the help of this property, one can create a new document with the specified configuration. The configuration includes removing the Comment and CDATASection nodes, normalizing the schema, canonicalizing the document, etc.

`inputEncoding`

It returns a string indicating the encoding scheme that was used during the parsing of this document.

`staticErrorChecking`

It indicates whether error checking was enabled or not.

`xmlEncoding`

It is the encoding (specified in the XML declaration) used in the XML document.

`xmlStandalone`

It indicates whether the document can exist independently or requires other resources.

`xmlVersion`

It is the version (specified in the XML declaration) used to write this XML document.

10.5.2 `Document` Node Methods

Since all kinds of nodes can only exist in the context of a document, the `Document` interface provides useful factory methods to create those objects. Each node has the attribute `ownerDocument`, which refers to the context document within which it was created.

`createAttribute`

This method creates and returns the `Attr` type node with the name specified. This attribute can then be set to an element using the `setAttribute` method available on the `Element` type node.

createAttributeNS

This method creates and returns the `Attr` type node with the name and namespace URI specified. This attribute can then be set to an element using the `setAttributeNS` method available on the `Element` type node.

createCDATASection

It creates and returns a `CDATASection` type node with the specified contained string.

createComment

It creates and returns a `Comment` type node with the specified comment string.

createDocumentFragment

It creates and returns an empty `DocumentFragment` node.

createElement

It creates and returns an `Element` type node with the specified element name.

createElementNS

It creates and returns an `Element` type node with the specified element name and namespace URI.

createEntityReference

It creates an `EntityReference` node with the specified node.

createProcessingInstruction

It creates a `ProcessingInstruction` node with the specified name and data string.

createTextNode

It creates and returns a `Text` type node with the specified text content.

getElementById

It returns the `Element` node having the specified id attribute.

getElementsByTagName

It returns a list of `Element` nodes with the specified element name.

getElementsByTagNameNS

It returns a list of `Element` nodes with the specified element name and namespace URI.

importNode

It imports a node from another document to this document. The node of the original document remains unchanged; instead a new copy is created and returned. Some nodes such as `Document`, and `DocumentType`, cannot be imported. It takes a Boolean argument that specifies whether to perform deep copy or shallow copy.

renameNode

It renames an existing `Element` or `Attr` node. It takes three arguments: original name, new namespace URI, and a new qualified name.

10.6 ELEMENT NODE

It provides several useful properties and methods that can be used to get the information about the elements of the XML document.

10.6.1 `Element` Node Properties

`tagName`

It is a read-only property and is valid only for element type nodes. Its value is the tag name of the element. For example, for the `<p>` tag, its value is `P` and for `<body>`, its value is `BODY`

10.6.2 `Element` Node Methods

`getAttribute`

It returns the value of the attribute with the specified attribute name.

`getAttributeNS`

It returns the value of the attribute with the specified attribute name and namespace URI.

`getAttributeNode`

It returns the attribute node with the specified attribute name.

`getAttributeNodeNS`

It returns the attribute node with the specified attribute name and namespace URI.

`getElementsByTagName`

It returns a list of all descendant elements with a specified tag name.

`getElementsByTagNameNS`

It returns a list of all descendant elements with a specified tag name and namespace URI.

`hasAttribute`

It returns a Boolean value that specifies whether the context element has any attribute with the given attribute name.

`hasAttributeNS`

It returns a Boolean value that specifies whether the context element has any attribute with the given attribute name and namespace URI.

`removeAttribute`

It removes the attribute with the specified name.

`removeAttributeNS`

It removes the attribute with the specified name and namespace URI.

`removeAttributeNode`

It removes the specified attribute node.

setAttribute

It adds an attribute with the specified name and value. If the attribute is already present, its value is set by the new value.

setAttributeNS

It adds an attribute with the specified name and value and namespace URI. If the attribute is already present, its value is set by the new value and its prefix is changed to the new prefix.

setAttributeNode

It adds the specified attribute node to the content element. If an attribute with that name is already present, it is replaced by the new one.

setAttributeNodeNS

It adds the specified attribute node to the content element. If an attribute with that name and namespace URI is already present, it is replaced by the new one.

setIdAttribute

It takes two arguments, the name of an attribute and a Boolean value. If the value of the Boolean argument is `true`, this method declares the specified attribute as a user-determined ID attribute. Otherwise, it makes the specified attribute a non-ID attribute.

setIdAttributeNS

It is same as `setIdAttribute`, except that it takes the namespace URI of the attribute as an argument.

setIdAttributeNode

It is same as `setIdAttribute`, except that it takes an attribute node instead of its name.

10.7 TEXT NODE

It provides several useful properties and methods that can be used to get information about the `Text` type nodes in an XML document.

10.7.1 Text Node Properties

isElementContentWhiteSpace

It returns a Boolean value indicating whether the text contains a character that is white space appearing within element content.

wholeText

It returns the text of this node and the text of all other logically-adjacent text nodes concatenated to it in document order.

10.7.2 Text Node Methods

replaceWholeText

It replaces the text of this node and text of all logically-adjacent text nodes with the specified text. Before replacement, it first removes current text node as well as all logically-adjacent text nodes, unless they are recipients of the specified text.

splitText

It splits the node into two nodes. The original node contains text up to a specified offset. The new node contains the rest and is inserted as a next sibling of the original node. The new node is returned.

10.8 ATTR NODE

It provides several useful properties that can be used to get the information about the attributes of an element.

10.8.1 Attr Node Properties

isId

It indicates whether the attribute is an ID attribute.

name

It returns the name of the attribute.

ownerElement

It is the element node to which this attribute is attached.

schemaTypeInfo

It is the type information for this attribute.

specified

It indicates whether a value for this attribute was specified explicitly.

value

It returns the value of the attribute. If value contains any entity references, they are first substituted with their values.

10.9 PARSING XML

In this section, we shall discuss how to access and manipulate an XML DOM tree using Java.

Java implements the W3C DOM specification as a separate package `org.w3c.dom`. Java provides interfaces and objects together with methods and properties according to the DOM specification that can be used to navigate and manipulate the DOM tree. Since Java supports data hiding, properties of an object, as specified by the W3C are not exposed directly. Instead a `get` method for each property is provided. For the property `abc`, the name of the method is `getAbc()`. For example, for the property `firstChild`, it provides the method `getFirstChild()`.

Consider the following XML document `"greeting.xml"`.

```
<?xml version="1.0"?>
<greeting>Hello World!</greeting>
```

The corresponding DOM tree is shown in Figure 10.3:

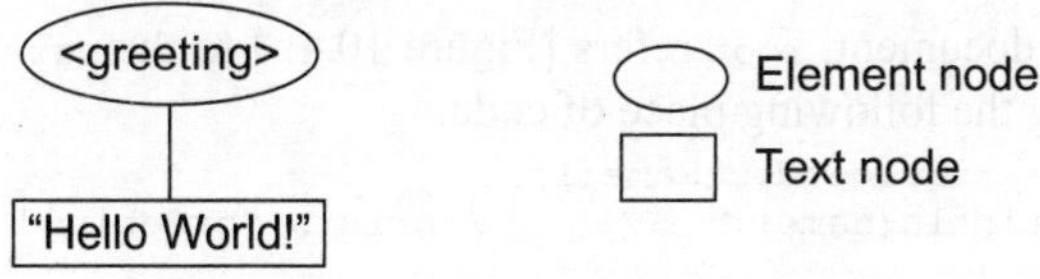

Figure 10.3: DOM tree for "greeting.xml"

10.9.1 Creating Document

To access the DOM tree for this XML document, you have to first create a `Document` object to put your XML into. To do this you have to first create an instance of the parser. The parser parses an XML document, checks well-formedness and creates and returns the `Document` object that represents the entire XML document. The following Java code creates an instance of the parser.

```
DocumentBuilderFactory factory = DocumentBuilderFactory.newInstance();
DocumentBuilder parser = factory.newDocumentBuilder();
```

The following packages must be imported.

```
import javax.xml.parsers.*;
import org.w3c.dom.*;
```

The parser is now ready to parse an XML document. The following overloaded methods are available that can be used to parse an XML document and to create a `Document` object.

```
Document parse(InputStream in)
Document parse(InputStream in, String base)
Document parse(String uri)
Document parse(File xmlFile)
```

The method that is commonly used takes the filename of an XML document. The following line of code parses and creates a `Document` object for the XML file "`greeting.xml`".

```
Document doc = parser.parse("greeting.xml");
```

10.9.2 Navigating DOM Tree

A node in the DOM may be referenced in several ways. Broadly, we can categorize them as follows:

- Start from the `root` node and use structural relationships to reach other nodes.
- Use the `getElementById()` method of the `Document` object to access a particular node directly.
- Use the `getElementsByTagName()` method on the `Document` object to access all element nodes with a common tag name specified.

10.9.2.1 Using Root Node

Remember that W3C defined the property `documentElement` on the `Document` object that refers to the root element of the XML document. Java provides a method `getDocumentElement()` for the same.

```
Element root = doc.getDocumentElement();
```

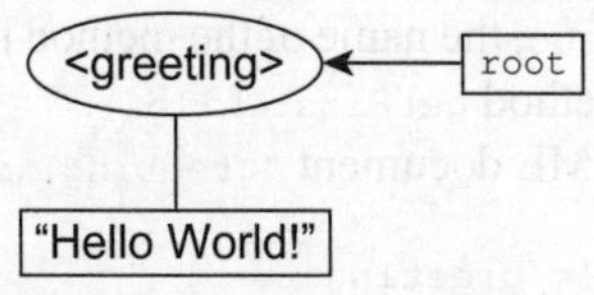

Figure 10.4: Document root

For this XML document, `root` refers [Figure 10.4:] to the `<greeting>` element. You can also verify it by writing the following piece of code:

```
String name = root.getNodeName();
System.out.println(name);              //prints "greeting"
```

Now, suppose we want to get the text content of this element `<greeting>`. The text content of an element is stored in a separate node, which is a child node of this element node. Since, the `root` node has exactly one child, which is the first child of `root`, the `getFirstChild()` method may be used to get a reference to the text node as follows:

```
Node node = root.getFirstChild();
```

Since this node is a Text type node, this line of code could have been written like this:

```
Text node = (Text)root.getFirstChild();
```

The actual text content may be obtained as follows:

```
String txt = node.getNodeValue();
System.out.println(txt);           //prints "Hello World!"
```

10.9.2.2 Getting all Child Nodes

So far we have considered a very simple XML document. Let us now take a more complex XML document `"questions.xml"` as follows:

```
<?xml version="1.0"?>
<question-paper>
  <question id="q1">What is DOM?</question>
  <question id="q2">What are leaves?</question>
</question-paper>
```

This XML document contains some questions. Suppose, we want to extract all questions from this XML file. To do this, get a reference to the root element `<question-paper>` using the procedure described in the previous section.

```
DocumentBuilderFactory factory = DocumentBuilderFactory.newInstance();
DocumentBuilder parser = factory.newDocumentBuilder();
Document doc = parser.parse("questions.xml");
Element root = doc.getDocumentElement();
//root refers to the <question-paper> element
```

The DOM tree corresponding to the XML document is shown in Figure 10.5: .

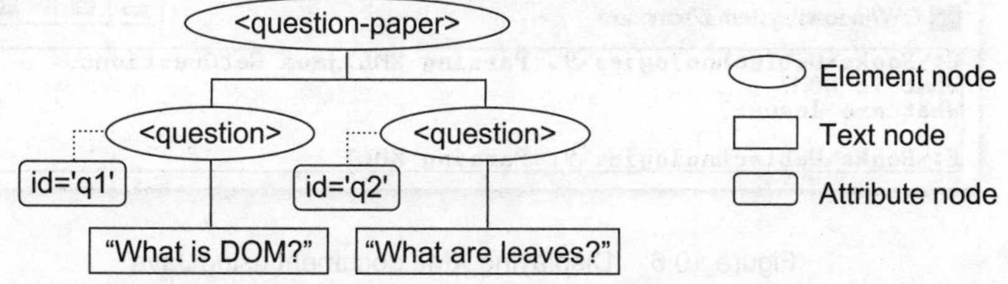

Figure 10.5: DOM tree for "questions.xml"

Let us have a list of all child nodes of this `<question-paper>` element as follows:

```
NodeList children = root.getChildNodes();     //get all child nodes of root
```

The object `children` now contains a list of child nodes of the `root` element, i.e., the `<question-paper>` element. Note that Java represents *new line* character as a `Text` type node also. So, the object `children` contains 3 (three) `Element` nodes one for each `<question>` as well as 4 (four) `Text` nodes, one for each new line character in the `<question-paper>` element. You can verify by printing the length of the `children` list.

```
System.out.println(children.getLength());      //prints 7
```

Individual children can be obtained using the `item()` method on `children` and an index.

```
for(int i = 0; i < children.getLength(); i++) {
   Node node = children.item(i);
   if(node.getNodeType() == Node.ELEMENT_NODE)    //if node is an Element node
      System.out.println(node.getFirstChild().getNodeValue());
}
```

Before applying the `getFirstChild()` method on a node, make sure that the node is an `Element` node and not a `Text` node.

```
if(node.getNodeType() == Node.ELEMENT_NODE)    //if node is an Element node
    System.out.println(node.getFirstChild().getNodeValue());
```

Here is the complete example.

```
import javax.xml.parsers.*;
import org.w3c.dom.*;
class GetQuestions {
    public static void main(String args[]) {
        try {
            DocumentBuilderFactory factory = DocumentBuilderFactory.newInstance();
            DocumentBuilder parser = factory.newDocumentBuilder();
            Document doc = parser.parse("questions.xml");
            Element root = doc.getDocumentElement();
            NodeList children = root.getChildNodes();  //get all children of root
            for(int i = 0; i < children.getLength(); i++) {
                Node node = children.item(i);
                if(node.getNodeType() == Node.ELEMENT_NODE)
                    System.out.println(node.getFirstChild().getNodeValue());
            }
        }catch(Exception e) { e.printStackTrace(); }
    }
}
```

Compile the program using the usual procedure, i.e., using javac compiler as follows:

```
javac GetQuestions.java
```

If everything goes fine, this command generates a class file named `GetQuestions.class`. If you run this program on "`questions.xml`", the output will look as shown in Figure 10.6: .

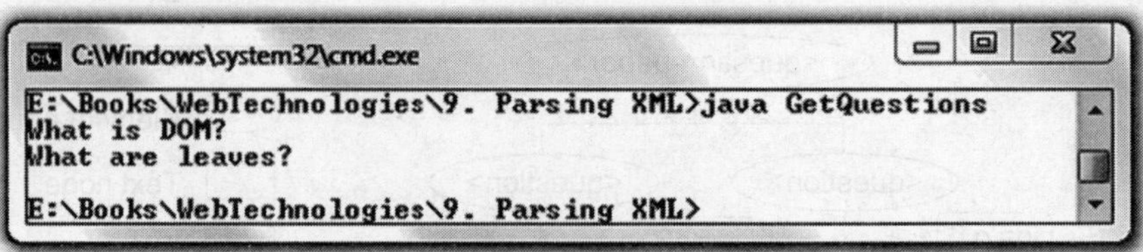

Figure 10.6: Displaying XML document using Java

10.9.2.3 Using getElementsByTagName

A list of elements having a tag name may be obtained using the `getElementsByTagName()` method on the `Document` object. So, a list of `<question>` elements may be obtained in a similar way as follows:

```
NodeList children = doc.getElementsByTagName("question");
```

Since the `<question>` elements are children of the `<question-paper>` element, the `getElementsByTagName()` method may also be invoked on the `root` element as follows:

```
NodeList children = root.getElementsByTagName("question");
```

Questions can now be obtained using a similar procedure.

```
for(int i = 0; i < children.getLength(); i++) {
    Node node = children.item(i);
    System.out.println(node.getFirstChild().getNodeValue());
}
```

However, since the nodes that we have obtained are all element (`<question>`) nodes, there is no need to check whether a node is an `Element` type node or not.

10.9.2.4 Using getElementById

To get a particular element using its unique id attribute, you need to declare a DTD or schema for it. Here is an example.

```
<?xml version="1.0"?>
<!DOCTYPE question-paper [
   <!ELEMENT question-paper (question+)>
   <!ELEMENT question (#PCDATA)>
   <!ATTLIST question id ID #REQUIRED>
]>
<question-paper>
   <question id="q1">What is DOM?</question>
   <question id="q2">What are leaves?</question>
</question-paper>
```

The method `getElementsById()` on the `Document` object is used to get an element with the specified id. So, a particular `<question>` element may be obtained as follows:

```
Element e = doc.getElementById("q1");
```

This line of code retrieves the element having the `id` attribute value "q1". Here is a complete example.

```
import javax.xml.parsers.*;
import org.w3c.dom.*;
class GetElementById {
   public static void main(String args[]) {
      try {
         DocumentBuilderFactory factory = DocumentBuilderFactory.newInstance();
         DocumentBuilder parser = factory.newDocumentBuilder();
         Document doc = parser.parse("questions.xml");
         Element e = doc.getElementById("q1");
         String value = e.getAttribute("id");
         System.out.print(value + ". ");  //print question number
         System.out.println(e.getFirstChild().getNodeValue()); //print question
      }catch(Exception e) { e.printStackTrace(); }
   }
}
```

If you run this program on `"questions.xml"`, the output will look as shown in Figure 10.7: .

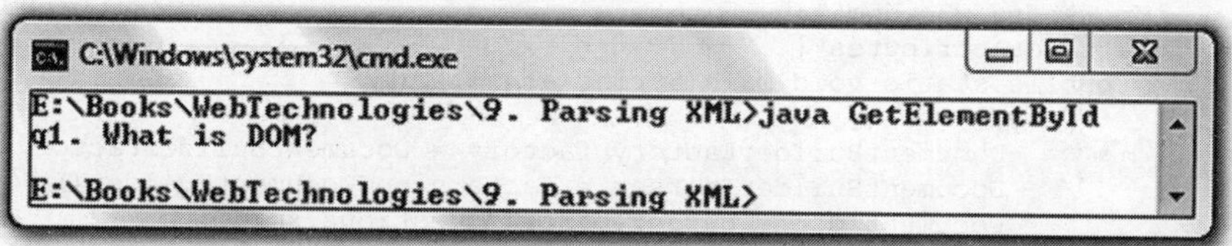

Figure 10.7: Finding an element using the getElementById() method

10.9.2.5 Getting Attributes of an Element

Attributes of an element are obtained using the following method:

```
NamedNodeMap getAttributes()
```

The object returned by the `getAttributes()` method contains all attributes for the context element. Individual attributes may be obtained using the `item()` method and an index. The name and value of an attribute may be obtained using the `getNodeName()` and `getNodeValue()` methods, respectively. The following example prints all attributes (and their values) of an element node.

```
NamedNodeMap attributes = node.getAttributes();    //get all attributes of node
for(int j = 0; j < attributes.getLength(); j++) { //for each attribute
   Node attribute = attributes.item(j);           //get attribute node
   String attName = attribute.getNodeName();      //get attribute name
   String attValue = attribute.getNodeValue();    //get attribute value
   System.out.println(attName + " = " + attValue);//print them
   }
```

Getting a particular attribute using this procedure is not useful as Java does not maintain any specific order of attributes in the list. Moreover, it is not efficient as you need to iterate through the entire list to get the value of a particular attribute. For example, if you want to get the value of the attribute "no", the corresponding code will look like this:

```
NamedNodeMap attributes = node.getAttributes();     //get all attributes of node
String attValue = "";
for(int j = 0; j < attributes.getLength(); j++) { //for each attribute
   Node attribute = attributes.item(j);           //get attribute node
   String attName = attribute.getNodeName();      //get attribute name
   if(attName.equals("no"))
      attValue = attribute.getNodeValue();        //get attribute value
}
System.out.println(attName + " = " + attValue);   //print it
```

Java provides a straightforward solution to achieve this. The value of a specific attribute may be obtained using the following method on the element node.

```
String getAttribute(String attributeName);
```

The following line of code returns the value of the attribute `no` on the element node. Note that the `getAttribute()` method is defined on the `Element` object. So, you need to typecast the `Node` object to the `Element` object first and then apply the `getAttribute()` method. Make sure that the node is really an `Element` type node. Otherwise, a `ClassCastException` will be thrown.

```
String value = ((Element)node).getAttribute("no");
```

If the node is really an `Element` type node, this method can be invoked directly without typecasting.

```
String value = e.getAttribute("no");
```

Here is the complete example.

```
import javax.xml.parsers.*;
import org.w3c.dom.*;
class GetAttributes {
   public static void main(String args[]) {
      try {
         DocumentBuilderFactory factory = DocumentBuilderFactory.newInstance();
         DocumentBuilder parser = factory.newDocumentBuilder();
         Document doc = parser.parse("questions.xml");
         Element root = doc.getDocumentElement();
         NodeList children = root.getElementsByTagName("question");
         for (int i = 0; i < children.getLength(); i++) {
            Node node = children.item(i);
            String value = ((Element)node).getAttribute("no");
            System.out.print(value + ". ");       //print question number
            System.out.println(node.getFirstChild().getNodeValue());
         }
      }catch(Exception e) { e.printStackTrace(); }
   }
}
```

If you run this program on "questions.xml", the output will look as shown in Figure 10.8:

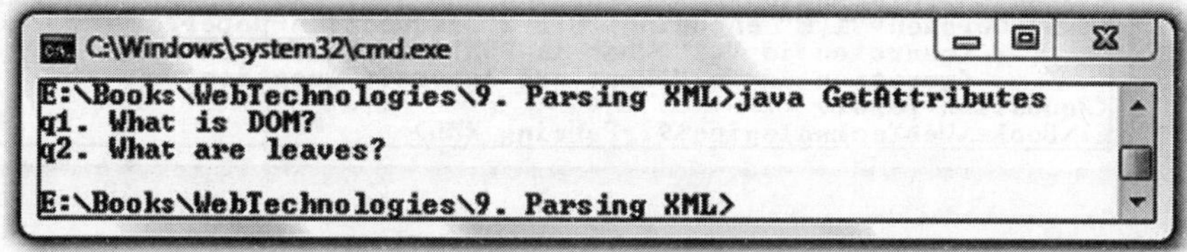

Figure 10.8: Getting attributes of an element

10.9.2.6 Viewing DOM

A DOM tree may be transformed back to an XML document which can then be displayed on the screen or stored in a file. This helps us to visualize and verify the DOM tree after adding or deleting nodes.

```
TransformerFactory tFactory = TransformerFactory.newInstance();
Transformer transformer = tFactory.newTransformer();
DOMSource source = new DOMSource(root);
StreamResult result = new StreamResult(System.out);
transformer.transform(source, result);
```

Here, we first create a `Transformer` object and a `DOMSource` object. The task of the `Transformer` object, as the name implies, is to transform the specified XML document to the specified stream. We want to display the result after transformation to the standard output. So, `System.out` is used to create the result object.

The following packages must be imported.

```
import javax.xml.transform.*;
import javax.xml.transform.dom.DOMSource;
import javax.xml.transform.stream.StreamResult;
```

Here is a program that displays the content of the questions.xml file on the terminal window.

```
import javax.xml.parsers.*;
import org.w3c.dom.*;
import javax.xml.transform.*;
import javax.xml.transform.dom.DOMSource;
import javax.xml.transform.stream.StreamResult;
class View {
   public static void main(String args[]) {
      try {
         DocumentBuilderFactory factory = DocumentBuilderFactory.newInstance();
         DocumentBuilder parser = factory.newDocumentBuilder();
         Document doc = parser.parse("questions.xml");
         Element root = doc.getDocumentElement();
         TransformerFactory tFactory = TransformerFactory.newInstance();
         Transformer transformer = tFactory.newTransformer();
         DOMSource source = new DOMSource(root);
         StreamResult result = new StreamResult(System.out);
         transformer.transform(source, result);
      }catch(Exception e) {e.printStackTrace();}
   }
}
```

It generates the output as shown in Figure 10.9:

```
C:\Windows\system32\cmd.exe
E:\Books\WebTechnologies\9. Parsing XML>java View
<?xml version="1.0" encoding="UTF-8"?><question-paper>
        <question id="q1">What is DOM?</question>
        <question id="q2">What are leaves?</question>
</question-paper>
E:\Books\WebTechnologies\9. Parsing XML>
```

Figure 10.9: Viewing DOM

To write the DOM tree to a file, simply create the `result` object from a file as follows:

```
FileOutputStream out = new FileOutputStream(new File("out.xml"));
StreamResult result = new StreamResult(out);
```

Figure 10.10 shows the transformation from a DOM tree to an XML document.

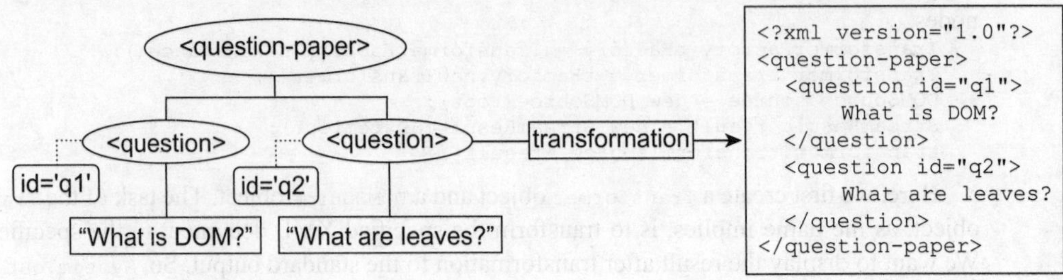

Figure 10.10: DOM tree to XML document transformation

To create a string from a DOM tree, use the following code.

```
StringWriter sw = new StringWriter();
StreamResult result = new StreamResult(sw);
DOMSource source = new DOMSource(root);
transformer.transform(source, result);
String xmlString = sw.toString();
```

The variable `xmlString` now contains the XML document as a string which can be processed further.

10.9.3 Manipulating DOM Tree

So far we have navigated the DOM tree. Let us now discuss how to add, delete, or modify nodes in the DOM tree. We shall use the notation shown in Figure 10.11: to describe the result of different codes that will be used in this section.

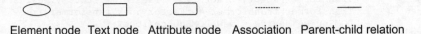

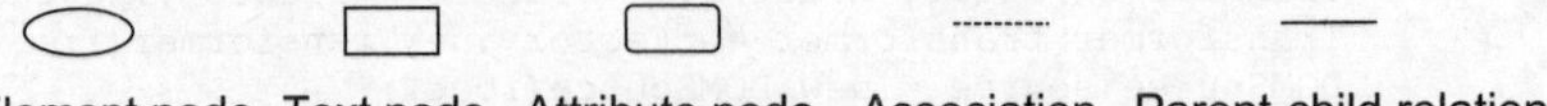

Figure 10.11: Notations used

10.9.3.1 Creating a node

A `Text` type node is created using the `createTextNode()` method on the `Document` node.

```
Text createTextNode(String text)
```

It takes the content of the `Text` node as a string argument. The following line of code creates a `Text` type node with the text “What is DTD?”. Pictorially, the result of this code is shown on the right-hand side.

```
Text txt = doc.createTextNode("What is DTD?");
```

“What is DTD?”

The node `txt` just created does not have any meaning unless it is attached to an `Element` node. Before attaching this `Text` node to an `Element` node, let us create an `Element` node first. An `Element` node is created using the `createElement()` method.

```
Element createElement(String elementName)
```

It takes the name of the element to be created as an argument. The following line of code creates a `<question>` element. The result is shown on the right-hand side pictorially.

```
Element e = doc.createElement("question");
```

<question>

10.9.3.2 Setting an Attribute

An attribute of an element is set using the `setAttribute()` method of the element node.

```
setAttribute(String attributeName, String attributeValue)
```

The following line of code adds the attribute `id` with the value “q3” to the newly created element `e`.

```
e.setAttribute("id", "q3");
```

The result, after attaching an attribute to the nodes, now becomes as shown on the right-hand side.

10.9.3.3 Adding a Node

The `Text` node `txt` can now be attached to the `Element` node `e` using the `appendChild()` method.

```
e.appendChild(txt);
```

Finally, the `Element` node e (together with txt) is attached to the root element at the end.

```
root.appendChild(e);
```

The `appendChild()` method adds a node to the context node at the end of the child list. The element `e` does not have any child so far. So, the node `txt` will become the first child of `e`. The resultant DOM tree is shown in Figure 10.12: .

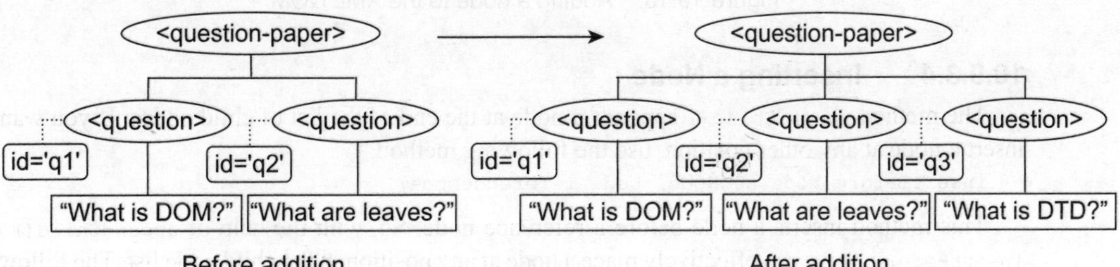

Figure 10.12: DOM tree after adding a <question> element at the end

The complete program is as follows:

```
import javax.xml.parsers.*;
import org.w3c.dom.*;
import javax.xml.transform.*;
import javax.xml.transform.dom.DOMSource;
import javax.xml.transform.stream.StreamResult;
class AppendQuestion {
   public static void main(String args[]) {
      try {
            DocumentBuilderFactory factory = DocumentBuilderFactory.newInstance();
            DocumentBuilder parser = factory.newDocumentBuilder();
            Document doc = parser.parse("questions.xml");
            Element root = doc.getDocumentElement();
            TransformerFactory tFactory = TransformerFactory.newInstance();
            Transformer transformer = tFactory.newTransformer();
            DOMSource source = new DOMSource(root);
            StreamResult result = new StreamResult(System.out);
            System.out.println("Before addition");
            transformer.transform(source, result);
            Text txt = doc.createTextNode("What is DTD?");
            Element e = doc.createElement("question");
            e.appendChild(txt);
            e.setAttribute("id", "q3");
            root.appendChild(e);
            System.out.println("\nAfter addition");
            transformer.transform(source, result);
      }catch(Exception e) {e.printStackTrace();}
   }
}
```

The program first displays the XML document before adding a `<question>` element. It then adds a `<question>` element at the end and displays the modified XML document. If you run this program on "`questions.xml`", the output will look as shown in Figure 10.13:

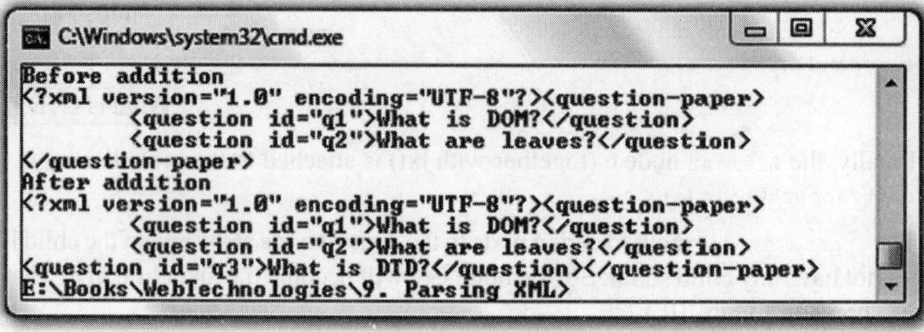

Figure 10.13: Adding a node to the XML DOM

10.9.3.4 Inserting a Node

The method `appendChild()` appends a node at the end of the list of child nodes. If you want to insert a node at any other position, use the following method.

```
insertBefore(Node newNode, Node referenceNode)
```

This method inserts a node before a reference node. So, with the help of `appendChild()` and `insertBefore()`, we can effectively place a node at any position in the child node list. The following code inserts the new <question> node after the first <question>. The resultant DOM tree is shown in Figure 10.14:.

```
NodeList questions = doc.getElementsByTagName("question");    //get all questions
Node firstQuestion = questions.item(0);                       //get first question
root.insertBefore(e, firstQuestion);                          //insert before first question
```

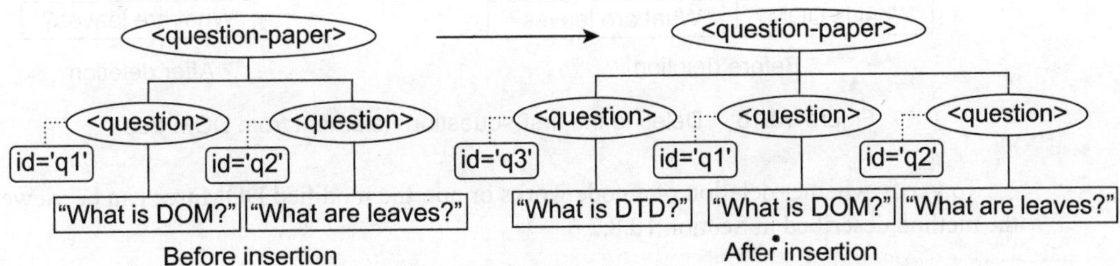

Figure 10.14: DOM tree after inserting a <question> element at the beginning

Let us now insert a <question> element after the first <question> element. Note that inserting after the first <question> element also implies inserting it before the second <question> element. The following piece of code inserts a <question> element after the first question using this concept.

```
NodeList questions = doc.getElementsByTagName("question");  //get all questions
Node firstQuestion = questions.item(0).getNextSibling(); //get first question
Node secondQuestion = firstQuestion.getNextSibling(); //get second question
root.insertBefore(e, secondQuestion);                 //insert before second question
```

The resultant DOM tree is shown in Figure 10.15: .

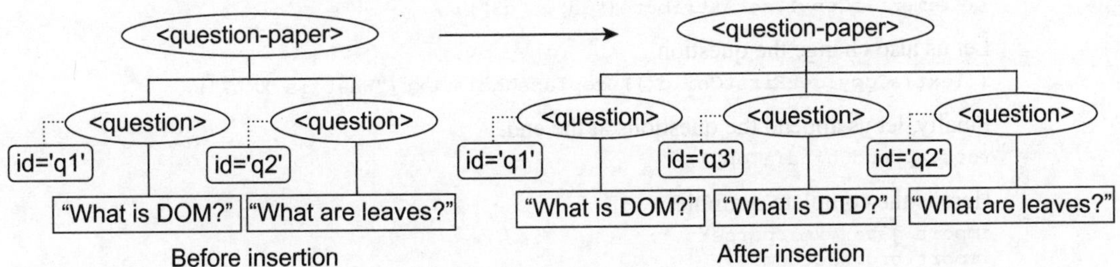

Figure 10.15: DOM tree after inserting a <question> element after first question

10.9.3.5 Deleting a Node

To delete a node from the DOM tree, we use the following method on its parent node.

```
Node removeChild(Node node)
```

If a node is deleted, the entire sub-tree rooted at this node is also deleted. It returns the root of the deleted sub-tree. The following line of code removes the first <question> element from the DOM tree. The effect of deleting the node is shown in Figure 10.16: .

```
NodeList questions = doc.getElementsByTagName("question");  //get all questions
Node firstQuestion = questions.item(0);                     //get first question
root.removeChild(firstQuestion);                            //remove it
```

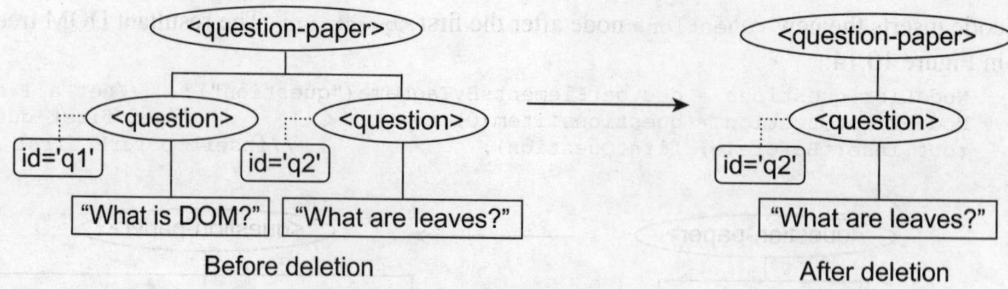

Figure 10.16: Deleting the first <question> element from DOM tree

To verify whether deletion of a node works or not, the modified DOM tree can be viewed using the method described in Section 10.8.2.6.

10.9.3.6 Cloning a Node

An exact copy of a node is created using the `cloneNode()` method on the `Node` interface.

```
cloneNode(boolean deepCopy)
```

It takes a single argument, which indicates whether to perform deep copy or shallow copy. If `true` is specified, the entire sub-tree rooted at the context node is copied recursively. Let us first obtain a reference of the first question.

```
NodeList questions = doc.getElementsByTagName("question");
```

We now clone the node.

```
Node aCopy = questions.item(0).cloneNode(true);
```

The node `aCopy` is now an exact copy of the first question. Since the id attribute must be unique, let us change the id attribute value to "q3" as follows:

```
((Element)aCopy).setAttribute("id", "q3");
```

Let us also change the question.

```
((Text)aCopy.getFirstChild()).replaceWholeText("What is XML?");
```

Finally, let us append the questions at the end.

```
root.appendChild(aCopy);
```

Here is the complete example.

```
import javax.xml.parsers.*;
import org.w3c.dom.*;
import javax.xml.transform.*;
import javax.xml.transform.dom.DOMSource;
import javax.xml.transform.stream.StreamResult;
class CopyQuestion {
  public static void main(String args[]) {
    try {
      DocumentBuilderFactory factory = DocumentBuilderFactory.newInstance();
      DocumentBuilder parser = factory.newDocumentBuilder();
      Document doc = parser.parse("questions.xml");
      Element root = doc.getDocumentElement();

      TransformerFactory tFactory = TransformerFactory.newInstance();
      Transformer transformer = tFactory.newTransformer();
      DOMSource source = new DOMSource(root);
      StreamResult result = new StreamResult(System.out);

      System.out.println("Before addition");
      transformer.transform(source, result);
```

```
        NodeList questions = doc.getElementsByTagName("question");
        Node aCopy = questions.item(0).cloneNode(true);
        ((Element)aCopy).setAttribute("id", "q3");
        ((Text)aCopy.getFirstChild()).replaceWholeText("What is XML?");
        root.appendChild(aCopy);

        System.out.println("\nAfter addition");
        transformer.transform(source, result);
      }catch(Exception e) {e.printStackTrace();}
   }
}
```

The resultant DOM tree is shown in Figure 10.17: .

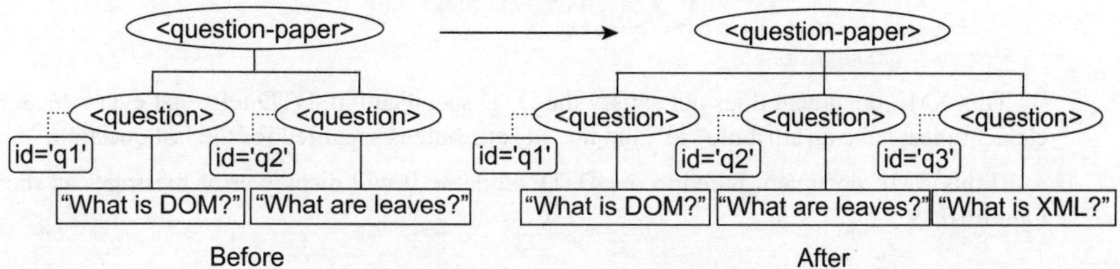

Figure 10.17: Cloning and appending a question

If you run this program on "`questions.xml`", the output will look as shown in Figure 10.18:

```
C:\Windows\system32\cmd.exe
E:\Books\WebTechnologies\9. Parsing XML>java CopyQuestion
Before addition
<?xml version="1.0" encoding="UTF-8"?><question-paper>
        <question id="q1">What is DOM?</question>
        <question id="q2">What are leaves?</question>
</question-paper>
After addition
<?xml version="1.0" encoding="UTF-8"?><question-paper>
        <question id="q1">What is DOM?</question>
        <question id="q2">What are leaves?</question>
<question id="q3">What is XML?</question></question-paper>
E:\Books\WebTechnologies\9. Parsing XML>
```

Figure 10.18: Cloning a node in the DOM tree

10.9.4 Java DTD Validation

Java also provides interfaces to validate an internal DTD. The following program takes an XML file containing DTD as the command line argument and checks whether the document has been written according to the DTD specification. It displays a diagnostic message if an error occurs.

```
import org.w3c.dom.*;
import javax.xml.parsers.*;
public class DTDValidator {
   public static void main(String args[]) {
      try {
   DocumentBuilderFactory factory = DocumentBuilderFactory.newInstance();
        factory.setValidating(true);
        DocumentBuilder parser = factory.newDocumentBuilder();
        Document doc = parser.parse(args[0]);
```

```
        }catch(Exception e) {System.out.println(e);}
    }
}
```

Consider the following xml file "ques.xml":

```
<?xml version="1.0"?>
<!DOCTYPE question-paper [
   <!ELEMENT question-paper (question+)>
   <!ELEMENT question (#PCDATA)>
   <!ATTLIST question id ID #REQUIRED>

]>
<question-paper>
   <question id="q1">What is DOM?</question>
   <question id="q2">What are leaves?</question>
   <question>What is DTD?</question>
</question-paper>
```

This XML document does not satisfy the DTD specification. DTD tells that every <question> element must have an attribute "id", but no "id" attribute is specified for the last question.

If this XML document is fed to our DTD validator, it will display error messages as shown in Figure 10.19:

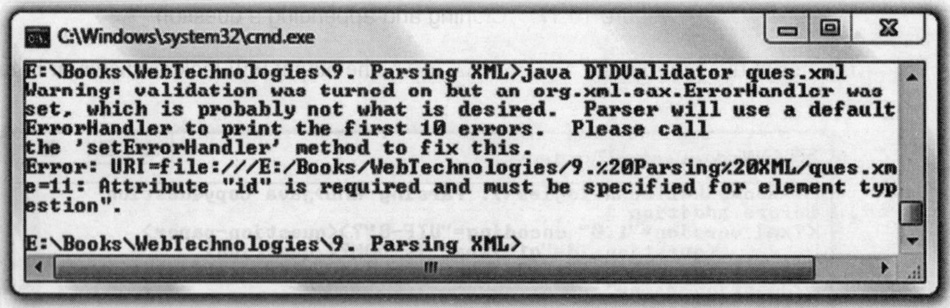

Figure 10.19: XML document validation against DTD

Java also provides interfaces to validate an XML document against an XML schema. The following program takes two arguments: an XML document and an XML schema and performs validation.

```
import java.io.File;
import javax.xml.parsers.*;
import javax.xml.transform.dom.DOMSource;
import javax.xml.validation.Schema;
import javax.xml.validation.SchemaFactory;
import javax.xml.validation.Validator;
import javax.xml.XMLConstants;
import org.w3c.dom.Document;
public class SchemaValidator {
   public static void main(String args[]) {
      try {
         String xmlFile = args[0], schemaFile = args[1];
         // build an XSD-aware SchemaFactory
         SchemaFactory schemaFactory =
SchemaFactory.newInstance( XMLConstants.W3C_XML_SCHEMA_NS_URI );
```

```
            // get the xsd schema specifying the required format for the XML files.
            Schema schemaXSD = schemaFactory.newSchema( new File ( schemaFile ) );

            // Get a Validator that can validate XML files according to the schema.
            Validator validator = schemaXSD.newValidator();

            DocumentBuilderFactory factory = DocumentBuilderFactory.newInstance();
            // Get a parser capable of parsing XML into a DOM tree
            DocumentBuilder parser = factory.newDocumentBuilder();

            // parse the XML purely as XML and get a DOM tree represenation.
            Document document = parser.parse( new File( xmlFile ) );

            // parse the XML DOM tree againts the XSD schema
            validator.validate( new DOMSource( document ) );
        } catch (Exception e) {
            e.printStackTrace();
        }
    }
}
```

KEYWORDS

Attr—Represents an attribute of an `Element` node

CDATASection—Represents a CDATA section in the XML document

Cloning—Creation of an exact copy of an existing node in the DOM tree

Comment—Represents a comment in an XML document

Document—The W3C Document type node represents an entire XML document. Only one Document type node exists for each XML document

DocumentFragment—A "lightweight" or "minimal" `Document` object that represents a portion of a document

DocumentType—Provides interfaces to get the information about the document including the list of entities defined for the document

DOM—A language-neutral and platform-independent object model used to represent XML documents

DOM Core—Defines the basic set of interfaces and objects for any structured documents

DOM tree—DOM models a document as a hierarchical structure consisting of different kinds of nodes, which constitute the DOM tree

Element—Represents an element in the XML document

Entity—Represents a known, either unparsed or parsed entity

HTML DOM—Defines interfaces and objects for HTML documents only

Node—Represents a component of an XML document

Parsing—A procedure for creating a DOM tree from an XML document

Text—Represents the textual content of an `Element` type node

XML DOM—Specifies the standard set of objects and interfaces for XML documents only

XML Validation—A procedure to verify whether an XML document is written according to the constraints specified in a DTD or a schema

SUMMARY

Document Object Model (DOM) is a language-neutral and platform-independent object model used to represent XML documents. DOM is standardized by the World Wide Web Consortium (W3C). The W3C DOM specification is divided into three major parts: DOM Core, XML DOM, and HTML DOM.

DOM models a document as a hierarchical structure consisting of different kinds of nodes. Each of these nodes represents a specific portion of the document.

The primary objective of DOM is to identify

- interfaces and objects to be used to represent, access, and manipulate documents.
- semantics of those objects and interfaces including both attributes and behaviour.
- collaboration and relationship among these objects and interfaces.

Nodes in a DOM tree have structural relationships among them. The topmost node is the root node. DOM tree consists of many types of nodes. The primary node types are `Node`, `Element`, `Document`, `Text`, `Attr`, and `Entity`.

The primary data type for the entire DOM is the Node interface. Every other kind of node inherits all the properties and methods of the Node interface. Some properties of the Node interface are read-only. Others are read–write. Notable properties are `childNodes`, `nodeType`, `nodeName`, `nodeValue`, `firstChild`, `lastChild`, `nextSibling`, `previousSibling`, etc. Java provides a read method for each of these properties.

The `Document` node is another important type node, which represents an entire XML document. It provides several useful properties and methods that can be used to navigate the DOM tree.

The `Element` type represents an element of an XML document. DOM provides a set of useful properties and methods on this type of nodes.

Java implements the W3C DOM specification as a separate package, org.w3c.dom. Java provides interfaces and objects together with methods and properties, according to the DOM specification that can be used to navigate and manipulate the DOM tree.

A node in the DOM may be referenced in several ways. Broadly, we can categorize them as follows:

- Start from the root node and use structural relationships to reach other nodes.
- Use the `getElementById()` method of the Document object to access a particular node directly.
- Use the `getElementsByTagName()` method on the `Document` object to access all element nodes with the common tag name specified.

A DOM tree may be transformed back to an XML document, which can then be displayed on the screen or can be stored in a file. This helps us to visualize and verify the DOM tree after adding or deleting nodes.

Java also provides interfaces to validate an XML document against an internal DTD or an XML schema.

WEB RESOURCES

`http://java.sun.com/j2se/1.4.2/docs/api/org/w3c/dom/package-summary.html`
Package org.w3c.dom

`http://java.sun.com/j2ee/1.4/docs/tutorial/doc/JAXPDOM.html`
Document Object Model

`http://java.sun.com/j2se/1.4.2/docs/guide/plugin/dom/index.html`
Common DOM API

`http://developers.sun.com/sw/building/codesamples/dom/index.html`
Java API for XML Processing API (JAXP) Using DOM

`http://www.ibm.com/developerworks/xml/library/x-domjava/`
Effective XML processing with DOM and XPath in Java

`http://www.java2s.com/Code/Java/XML/DOM-Edit.htm`
`Java and DOM`

EXERCISES

Objective-type Questions

1. What is the full form of DOM?
   (a) Dynamic Object Model
   (b) Distributed Object Model
   (c) Document Object Model
   (d) Dense Object Model

2. How many parts are there in the W3C DOM specification?
   (a) 2 (c) 4
   (b) 3 (d) 5

3. What is the number of parent nodes that a node in the DOM tree can have?
   (a) 1 (c) 3
   (b) 2 (d) 4

4. How many `Document` nodes does a DOM tree have?
   (a) 1 (c) 3
   (b) 2 (d) 4

5. Which of the following is used to inspect the type of a node?
   (a) type
   (b) typeOfNode
   (c) nodeType
   (d) getNodeType

6. What is the value of the `nodeName` attribute for a `Text` node?
   (a) $text (c) #text#
   (b) text# (d) #text

7. What is the value of `nodeType` attribute for a `Text` node?
   (a) 1 (c) 3
   (b) 2 (d) 4

8. Which of the following has a valid `nodeValue` attribute?
   (a) Element (c) Entity
   (b) Attr (d) Document

9. Which of the following has `childNodes` attributes?
   (a) Attr (c) Entity
   (b) Text (d) Element

10. Nodes having a common parent are called
    (a) Child (c) Sibling
    (b) Parent (d) Descendant

11. Which of the following refers to the root element of an XML document?
    (a) `Document`
    (b) `documentElement`
    (c) `Root`
    (d) `rootElement`

12. Which of the following methods is used to create an `Element` type node?
    (a) `newElement()`
    (b) `getElement()`
    (c) `createElement()`
    (d) `element()`

13. Which of the following methods is used to create a `Text` type node?
    (a) `createText()`
    (b) `newTextNode()`
    (c) `newText()`
    (d) `createTextNode()`

14. Which of the following methods is used to create an `Attr` type node?
    (a) `createAttribute()`
    (b) `createAttr()`
    (c) `newAttribute()`
    (d) `newAttr()`

15. Which of the following is used to add an attribute to an `Element` node?
    (a) `setAttr()`
    (b) `setAttribute()`
    (c) `addAttribute()`
    (d) `addAttr()`

16. Which of the following methods is used to get a particular element?
    (a) `getElementsByTagName()`
    (b) `returnElementById()`
    (c) `getElementById()`
    (d) `getElement()`

17. Which of the following attributes returns the name of an element?
    (a) `elementName`
    (b) `name`
    (c) `tagName`
    (d) `getName`

18. Which of the following methods is used to instruct the parser to validate an XML document against a DTD?
    (a) `setValidating()`
    (b) `validate()`
    (c) `doValidate()`
    (d) `getValidating()`

19. Which of the following methods is used to parse an XML document?
    (a) `doParse()` (c) `parseXML()`
    (b) `parse()` (d) `parseXMLDoc()`

20. Which of the following methods is used to clone a node?
    (a) `doClone()`
    (b) `cloneNode()`
    (c) `clone()`
    (d) `doCloneNode()`

Subjective-type Questions

1. How do you add a node at the beginning of a list of child nodes?
2. Discuss how all the attributes of an `element` node are obtained.
3. How do you add a node at the end of a list of child nodes?
4. Describe how a DOM tree is saved in a file.
5. Write a program to display the content of a DOM tree.
6. What is the difference between shallow clone and deep clone?
7. Describe the procedure for validating XML documents against a DTD.
8. Describe the procedure for validating XML documents against a schema.
9. Discuss the difference between the `nextSibling` and `previousSibling` properties with examples.
10. Discuss the difference between the `firstChild` and `lastChild` properties with examples.

CHAPTER – 11

INPUT / OUTPUT

KEY OBJECTIVES

After completing this chapter readers will be able to—

- understand what multi-threaded programs are
- learn how to write multi-threaded programs
- learn how to interrupt, suspend and resume threads
- get an idea about inter-thread communication
- understand what synchronized methods and blocks are

11.1 INTRODUCTION

Often, applications process some input and generate some output. For example, applications may read data from or write to a file, network etc. Java provides a rich set (probably too many) of classes and interfaces as a separate package `java.io` for such Input and Output (I/O). Java also provides another package `java.nio` containing Non-blocking I/O (NIO) API which, in some situations, can give a big performance boost over blocking IO.

The huge number of options may be rather confusing to even expert programmers. In this chapter, we shall give an overview of how all these classes are grouped with their purposes. This grouping helps you in determining the purpose of an I/O class and finding a suitable one for a specific task.

11.2 STREAMS

The I/O operation may pictorially be described as in Figure 11.1: It shows that a program reads data from some resource called *source* and writes data to some resource called *destination*. The source

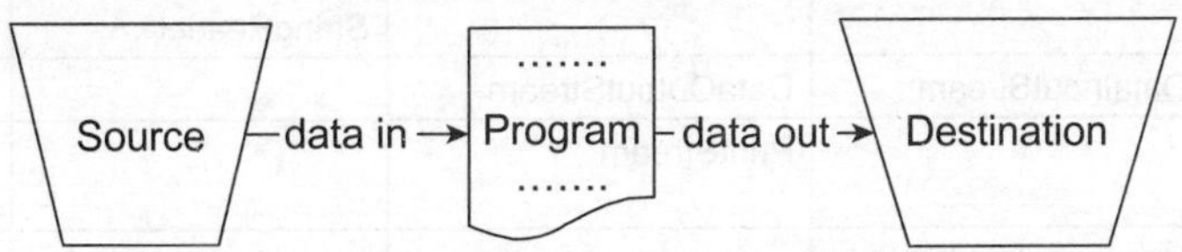

Figure 11.1: Principal of input and output

and destination can be anything that generates, or consumes data. Typical examples of such resources include disk files, peripheral devices, network connections, buffers, pipes etc.

Since properties and behaviours of such resources vary, Java provides a unified way to read from and write to such resources. It introduced the concept of *stream* that flows from one direction to the other and may be used as a carrier of data. Data may be put to or got from the stream. If we put data to the stream, it carries the data along its way. Similarly, we can retrieve data being carried by a stream. Specifically, Java introduced stream classes to simulate this idea and is illustrated in Figure 11.2:

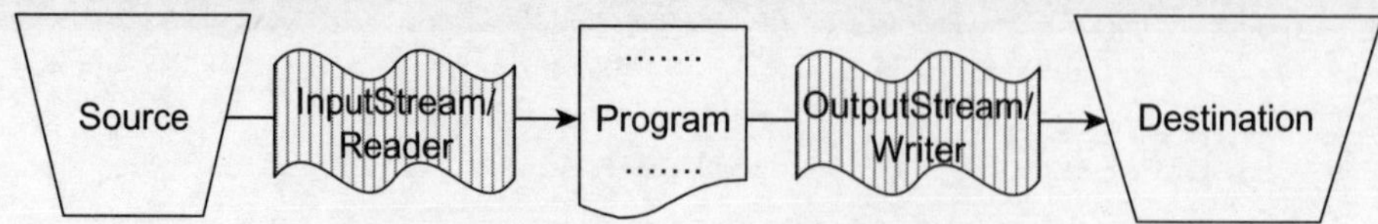

Figure 11.2: Concept of Streams

A program, which wants to read data from some source, uses an `InputStream` or a `Reader` to connect to the source. To get the data from the source, the program simply reads them from the stream. Similarly, if a programs wants to write data to some destination, it uses an `OutputStream` or a `Writer` to connect to the destination. The program simply writes data to the stream and the stream carries them to the destination.

The abstract classes `InputStream` and `OutputStream` represent streams that can carry only sequence of bytes. On the other hand, `Reader` and `Writer` abstract classes can carry sequence of characters. Java IO API also contains a large number of higher level sub-classes that can handle all kinds of data, from primitive values to advanced objects. These classes may be grouped with respect to their purposes such as File Access, Network Access, Array Access, Communication (Pipes), Buffering, Filtering, Parsing, Formatting, String Access. A summary of these classes is shown in Table 11.1:

Table 11.1: Important I/O classes

	Byte stream		**Character stream**	
	Input	**Output**	**Input**	**Output**
Basic	InputStream	OutputStream	Reader InputStreamReader	Writer OutputStreamWriter
Files	FileInputStream RandomAccessFile	FileOutputStream RandomAccessFile	FileReader	FileWriter
Filtering	FilterInputStream	FilterOutputStream	FilterReader	FilterWriter
Buffering	BufferedInputStream	BufferedOutputStream	BufferedReader	BufferedWriter
Parsing	PushbackInputStream StreamTokenizer		PushbackReader LineNumberReader	
Arrays	ByteArrayInputStream	ByteArrayOutputStream	CharArrayReader	CharArrayWriter
Pipes	PipedInputStream	PipedOutputStream	PipedReader	PipedWriter
Objects	ObjectInputStream	ObjectOutputStream		
Strings			StringReader	StringWriter
Data	DataInputStream	DataOutputStream		
Data - Formatted		PrintStream		PrintWriter
Utilities	SequenceInputStream			

11.2.1 Byte Stream

In this section, we shall demonstrate the operation of the most basic kind of streams, byte streams. These are used to input or output 8-bit octets. All byte stream classes are sub-classes of `InputStream` and `OutputStream`. There are many byte stream classes to work with different kinds of resources. Some of the byte input/output stream classes and their hierarchy is shown in Figure 11.3:

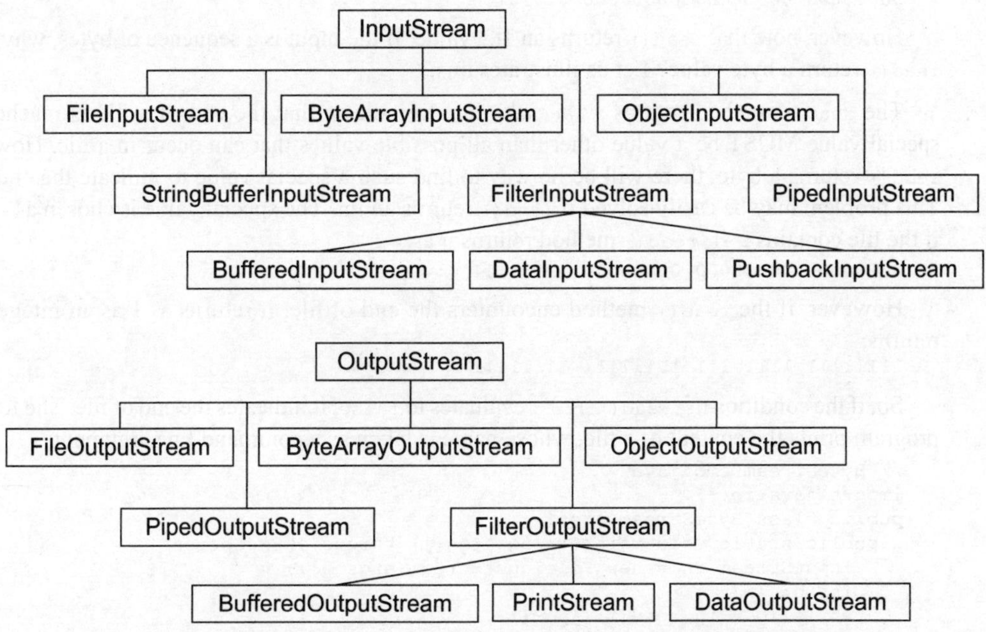

Figure 11.3: Byte-based input/output stream class hierarchy

Files are a common source or destination of data. So let us consider files to illustrate the operation of streams. The byte stream classes for other kind of resources are used in much the same way, except that they are constructed in a different way.

For disk files, the byte stream classes are `FileInputStream` and `FileOutputStream`. These classes act as connectors between a program and a disk file. For data input, we first create an instance of `FileInputStream` using any one of many constructors. The most obvious one takes the name of a file and is used as:

```
InputStream in = new FileInputStream("aFile.txt")
```

Since `FileInputStream` is a sub-class of `InputStream`, it is possible to use an `InputStream` type reference. Pictorially, the situation may be described as follows:

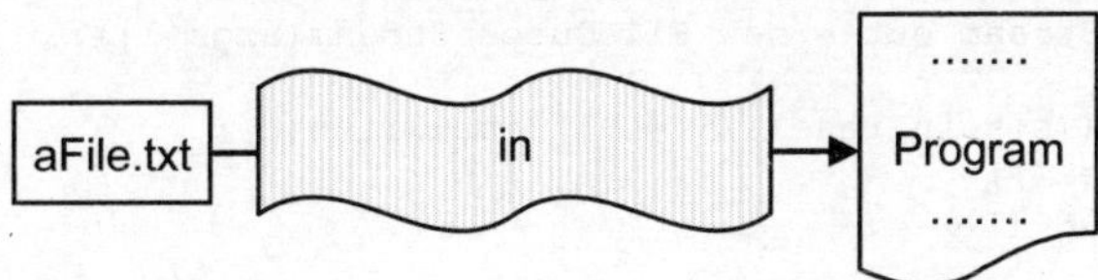

The program can now read data from the file by reading data from `fis` using one of its overloaded `read()` methods.

```
int c = in.read();
```

The `read()` method returns the first 8-bit of the file `aFile.txt`. Consider `aFile.txt` is a simple text file whose content is

```
Test file
```

The `read()` method returns the first byte `01010100` (binary value of character 'T') as an integer. So the least significant byte of a 4-byte integer will contain this value. The remaining bits will be set to zero. So the resultant 32-bit (space is used only for clarity) will look like this:

```
00000000 00000000 00000000 01010100
```

However, note that `read()` returns an `int` value. If the input is a sequence of bytes, why doesn't `read()` return a byte value? Let us illustrates this.

The `read()` method returns a *special value* to indicate that the end of a file is reached. This special value MUST be a value other than all possible values that can occur in a file. However, if `read()` returns a byte, there will be no way to find such a special value to indicate the end of file. This problem may be easily solved if `read()` returns an int. The special value is chosen as -1. Now, if the file contains a -1, `read()` method returns it as:

```
00000000 00000000 00000000 11111111
```

However, if the `read()` method encounters the end of file, it returns a -1 as an integer, i.e. it returns:

```
11111111 11111111 11111111 11111111
```

So, if the condition `fis.read() != -1` evaluates to `false`, it indicates the end of file. The following program prints the content of a file, whose name is taken as a command line argument:

```
// ByteStreamDemo.java
import java.io.*;
public class ByteStreamDemo {
  public static void main(String args[]) throws IOException {
    InputStream in = new FileInputStream(args[0]);
    int b;
    while((b = in.read()) != -1)
      System.out.print((char)b);
    in.close();
  }
}
```

Since, `read()` indeed returns a byte, it is always safe to cast the return value to a char (or even a byte). It is always a good idea to close a file when it is no longer needed using `close()` method that releases any system resources associated with the stream.

The following command prints the source code of the above program:

```
java ByteStreamDemo ByteStreamDemo.java
```

To write byte data to a file, `FileOutputStream` is used in the same way except that `write()` method is used. The following program copies the content of one file to another:

```
import java.io.*;
public class FileCopy {
  public static void main(String args[]) throws IOException {
    InputStream in = new FileInputStream(args[0]);
    OutputStream out = new FileOutputStream(args[1]);
    int b;
    while ((b = in.read()) != -1) out.write(b);
    in.close();
    out.close();
  }
}
```

File names are supplied as command line arguments. The program uses a simple loop that reads the input stream and writes the output stream, one byte at a time as shown:

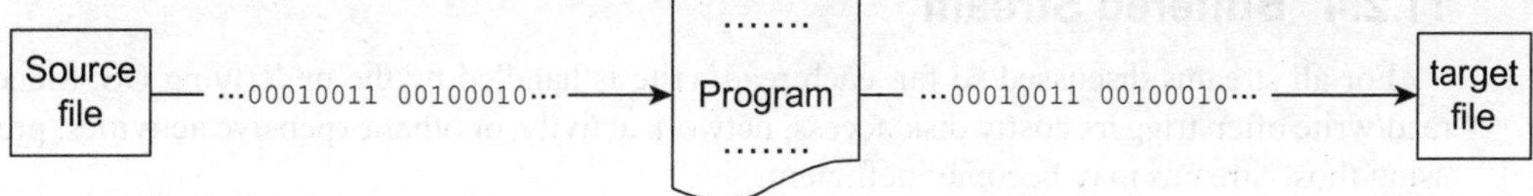

Use the following command to copy the content of a file `src.txt` to `dst.txt`:

```
FileCopy src.txt dst.txt
```

11.2.2 Character Stream

If files contain character data, it is better to use character-oriented streams. These streams automatically translate sequence of bits to 16-bit Unicode characters and vice versa.

All character stream classes are sub-classes of `Reader` and `Writer`. There are also many character stream classes to work with different kind of resources. Like byte streams, there are character stream classes for disk files: `FileReader` and `FileWriter`. The following file copy program uses theses classes:

```
import java.io.*;
public class FileCopy1 {
  public static void main(String args[]) throws IOException {
    Reader in = new FileReader(args[0]);
    Writer out = new FileWriter(args[1]);
    int c;
    while ((c = in.read()) != -1) out.write(c);
    in.close();
    out.close();
  }
}
```

This program is very much similar except that it uses `FileReader` and `FileWriter` for input and output in place of `FileInputStream` and `FileOutputStream`.

Note that character streams internally use byte streams to perform the physical I/O. For example, `FileReader` uses `FileInputStream`, while `FileWriter` uses `FileOutputStream`. However, the translation between characters and bytes is transparent to the users.

11.2.3 Bridging Stream

Sometimes, you may not find a suitable character class for some resource. However, if you have a byte class for that resource, you can convert it to the corresponding character class. Java provides two classes for this purpose: `InputStreamReader` and `OutputStreamWriter`, which act as converters from byte-to-character streams. The constructors of these classes take a byte stream and creates instances of character stream. The following file copy program illustrates the use of these classes:

```
import java.io.*;
public class FileCopy2 {
  public static void main(String args[]) throws IOException {
    Reader in = new InputStreamReader(new FileInputStream(args[0]));
    Writer out = new OutputStreamWriter(new FileOutputStream(args[1]));
    int c;
    while ((c = in.read()) != -1) out.write(c);
    in.close();
    out.close();
  }
}
```

Note that there exists character classes for disk file. This program merely illustrates how to use byte-to-character bridge classes.

11.2.4 Buffered Stream

For all streams discussed so far, each read/write is handled by the underlying OS. Since, each read/write often triggers costly disk access, network activity, or other expensive activities, programs using those streams may become inefficient.

Java provides some special *buffered streams* that can be used to reduce this overhead. Each read/write request on these buffered streams does not always fire a native API. Instead, they use some memory area called *buffer*. A read request on this buffered stream returns data from this buffer as long as data is there. If the buffer is empty before reading, a larger chunk of data is pre-fetched using a single native API call first and placed in the buffer. Similarly, a write request to this buffered stream simply writes data to the buffer. If there is chance that the buffer will overflow, the entire data is written using a single API call first. This way, buffered streams try to reduce the number of native API calls.

Java provides many buffered classes for byte and character-oriented streams. Their constructors typically take an un-buffered stream. So we can create a buffered stream by simply passing an un-buffered stream to the constructor.

11.2.4.1 Buffered Byte Stream

The names of buffered byte stream classes are `BufferedInputStream` and `BufferedOutputStream`. The following is a file copy program that demonstrates the usage of these classes.

```
import java.io.*;
public class FileCopy3 {
  public static void main(String args[]) throws IOException {
    BufferedInputStream in = new BufferedInputStream(new
FileInputStream(args[0]));
    BufferedOutputStream out = new BufferedOutputStream(new
FileOutputStream(args[1]));
    int c;
    while ((c = in.read()) != -1) out.write(c);
    in.close();
    out.close();
  }
}
```

This program is similar to the program `FileCopy.java`. However, it takes significantly less time to copy a large file. For example, when we copied a 1582778 (1.5 MB approx.) byte file using `FileCopy.java` (in Linux), it showed the following output:

```
[root@radix ~]# time java FileCopy audit-1.8-1.src.rpm out.rpm

real    0m7.046s
user    0m1.565s
sys     0m5.442s
```

However, for our `FileCopy3.java`, it took significantly less time and showed the following output:

```
[root@radix ~]# javac FileCopy3.java
[root@radix ~]# time java FileCopy3 audit-1.8-1.src.rpm out.rpm

real    0m0.235s
user    0m0.214s
sys     0m0.017s
```

This suggests us to use buffered streams whenever possible.

11.2.4.2 Buffered Character Stream

The names of buffered byte stream classes are `BufferedReader` and `BufferedWriter`. The following is a file copy program that demonstrates the usage of these classes.

```
import java.io.*;
public class FileCopy4 {
  public static void main(String args[]) throws IOException {
    BufferedReader in = new BufferedReader(new FileReader(args[0]));
    BufferedWriter out = new BufferedWriter(new FileWriter(args[1]));
    String line;
    while ((line = in.readLine()) != null) {
      out.write(line, 0, line.length());
      out.newLine();
    }
    in.close();
    out.close();
  }
}
```

Since a `BufferedReader` is a buffered *stream of characters* (i.e. string), for convenience, it provides a `readLine()` method to read a line of characters (i.e. string).

11.2.5 Reading From Keyboard

Programs often expect data from command line. We can do this in two ways: using standard streams or using the class `Console`. Let us first use standard streams to read data from keyboard.

11.2.5.1 Reading Character

To read characters, we can use standard character stream Reader. The static `System.in` field corresponds to keyboard input. Unfortunately, it is a byte stream. However, we can easily convert it to a character stream using our bridge class `InputStreamReader`. The following program loops to accept characters from the keyboard until the character 'q' is entered.

```
import java.io.*;
public class ReadFromKeyboard {
  public static void main(String args[]) throws IOException {
    Reader cin = new InputStreamReader(System.in);
    System.out.println("Enter characters, 'q' to quit.");
    char c;
    do {
      c = (char) cin.read();
      System.out.print(c);
    } while(c != 'q');
    cin.close();
  }
}
```

11.2.5.2 Reading String

This is a very common requirement in several types of applications where you have to read strings from a keyboard. There are a few ways to do this. The following program uses the buffered character stream `BufferedReader`.

```
import java.io.*;
public class ReadFromKeyboard1 {
  public static void main(String args[]) throws Exception {
    BufferedReader br = new BufferedReader(new InputStreamReader(System.in));
    System.out.println("Enter a line of text");
    String line = br.readLine();
    System.out.println("You entered: "+line);
  }
}
```

This reads an entire line of text and prints the same.

11.2.6 Console

To have more features, especially to read password (the characters should not echo) from command line, the `Console` class may be used. To use this class, we first create an instance of it by invoking static `console()` method of `System` class as follows:

```
Console c = System.console();
```

The password can be read using `readPassword()` method. The following program reads the login name and password from the keyboard and displays them.

```
import java.io.*;
public class ConsoleDemo {
  public static void main (String args[]) throws IOException {
    Console c = System.console();
    String login = c.readLine("Login: ");
    char[] password = c.readPassword("Password: ");
    System.out.println(login+" "+(new String(password)));
  }
}
```

Note that a password is sensitive information and should not be displayed. The program merely shows how to use the `Console` class. Note that the method `readPassword()` does not return a `String`. Since Java String is immutable, it returns a character array, so that password can be overwritten, or removed from the memory as soon as it is no longer needed.

11.3 FORMATTING

Often it is convenient to work with neatly formatted data. Java formatting API assists us to translate data into nicely formatted, human-readable form. These classes are byte stream `PrintStream` and character stream `PrintWriter`. They add functionality to another output stream, specifically the ability to print various data values conveniently. They basically provide three overloaded functions: `print()`, `printf()`, and `format()`. If automatic flushing is enabled, unlike the `PrintStream`, which flushes only when a newline character happens to be output, `PrintWriter` flushes when one of the `println()`, `printf()`, or `format()` methods is invoked.

The `print()` and `println()` methods essentially output a single value after converting the value using the appropriate `toString()` method. The following program illustrates the use of `PrintStream` instance `System.out`.

```
public class PrintStreamDemo {
  public static void main(String args[])  {
    int i = 2, n = i*i;
    System.out.print("The square of ");
    System.out.print(i);
    System.out.println(" is " + n);
  }
}
```

It outputs the following result:

```
The square of 2 is 4
```

The `printf()` and `format()` methods are similar to `printf()` function in C language. They take format string that consists of static text embedded with *format specifiers*. The following program demonstrates it:

```
public class PrintStreamDemo1 {
  public static void main(String args[])  {
    int i = 2, n = i*i;
    System.out.printf("The square of %d is %d%n", i, n);
    System.out.format("%d * %d = %d", 2, 3, 2*3);
  }
}
```

Note that the methods in formatting classes do not throw any exceptions. So, we do not need to include a try/catch block around such method call.

11.4 DATA STREAMS

In addition to byte and character streams, Java provides classes, called *data streams* to handle primitive type values as well as Strings. The following program demonstrates how to write different types of values and read them back.

```
import java.io.*;
public class DataStreamDemo {
  public static void main(String args[]) throws Exception {
    DataOutputStream out = new DataOutputStream(new FileOutputStream("d.dat"));
    out.write(23);                       //byte data
    out.writeInt(32);                    //int data
    out.writeDouble(123.45);             //double data
    out.close();
    DataInputStream in = new DataInputStream(new FileInputStream("d.dat"));
    int    aByte   = in.read();
    int    anInt   = in.readInt();
    double aDouble = in.readDouble();
    System.out.println(aByte+" "+anInt+" "+aDouble);
    in.close();
  }
}
```

Also notice that each specialized write is exactly matched by the corresponding specialized read. It is up to the programmer to make sure that output types and input types are matched in this way.

11.5 OBJECT STREAM

Java provides two powerful classes `ObjectOutputStream` and `ObjectInputStream`, which can be used for object serialization and de-serialization respectively. Object serialization flattens objects into an ordered, or serialized stream of bytes. These bytes can be stored persistently in a file or a database or can even be sent through a network. The ordered stream of bytes can then be read at a later time, or in another environment, to reconstruct the original objects. The last step is known as de-serialization.

Specifically, `writeObject()` method of `ObjectOutputStream` performs the serialization. The serialized data can be stored in a file, in an array, or can be sent through the network. An instance of `ObjectOutputStream` is created accordingly. Similarly, the `readObject()` method of `ObjectInputStream` performs the de-serialization. The data needed for de-serialization may come from a file, an array or a network. An instance of `ObjectInputStream` is created accordingly.

The following program first serializes a `String` object and stores the resultant byte stream in a file "d.dat". It then reconstructs the object from the data stored in file "d.dat".

```
import java.io.*;
public class ObjectStreamDemo {
  public static void main(String args[]) throws Exception {
    ObjectOutputStream out = new ObjectOutputStream(new
FileOutputStream("d.dat"));
    out.writeObject(new String("abc"));              //String object
    out.close();
    ObjectInputStream in = new ObjectInputStream(new FileInputStream("d.dat"));
    String s = (String)in.readObject();
    System.out.println(s);
    in.close();
  }
}
```

Note that a Java object is serializable if its class or any of its super-classes implements either the `java.io.Serializable` interface or its sub-interface, `java.io.Externalizable`. These interfaces do not contain any methods. They merely indicate that instances of classes implanting these interfaces are serializable.

11.6 READING/WRITING ARRAYS VIA STREAMS

Arrays are often used to temporarily store data, as well as source of data. For example, we may load a file into an array, if file data is to be accessed many times. However, if a component expects a stream instead of an array, how do you pass an array there? Don't worry. As mentioned earlier, Java provides I/O classes for virtually every scenario. In this case, it provides `ByteArrayInputStream` or `CharArrayReader` for input and `ByteArrayOutputStream` or `CharArrayWriter` for output.

The following code snippet demonstrates how to use stream-based array classes:

```
byte[] bytes = new byte[1024];
//write data into byte array...
InputStream in = new ByteArrayInputStream(bytes);
//read data from InputStream.

OutputStream out = new ByteArrayOutputStream();
//write data to OutputStream...
byte[] bytes = out.toByteArray();
//read data from byte array...
```

11.7 PIPES

Note that an input stream flows from a source to a program [Figure 11.4: (i)]. Similarly, an output stream flows from a program to a destination [Figure 11.4: (ii)]. If we can join these two streams [Figure 11.4: (iii)], then two programs can communicate.

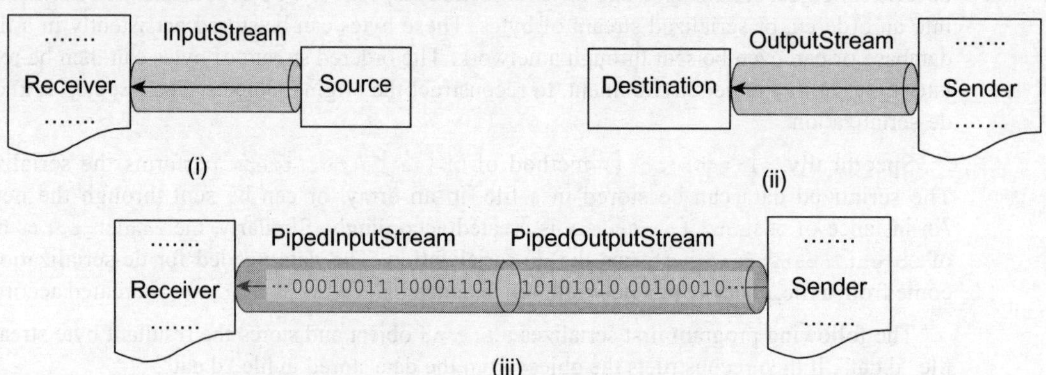

Figure 11.4: Java streams (i) Input stream (ii) Output stream (iii) Pipes

Fortunately, Java provides two classes `PipedInputStream` and `PipedOutputStream` for this purpose. A piped input stream is connected to a piped output stream. The piped input stream then provides whatever data bytes are written to the piped output stream.

Typically, a sender thread first creates a `PipedOutputStream` as follows:

```
PipedOutputStream out = new PipedOutputStream();
```

Pictorially it looks like this:

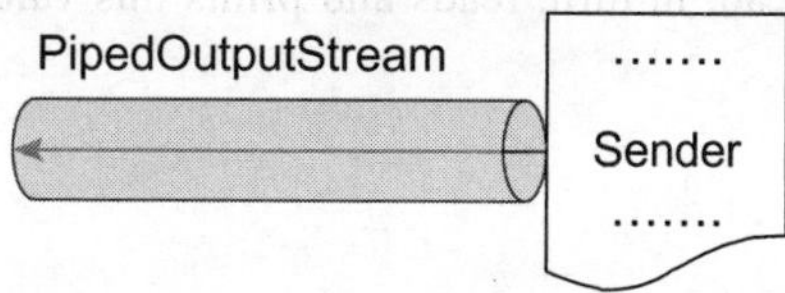

Another receiver thread then creates a `PipedInputStream` and connects to the previously created `PipedOutputStream` as follows:

```
PipedInputStream in = new PipedInputStream(out);
```

The final arrangement is shown in the following:

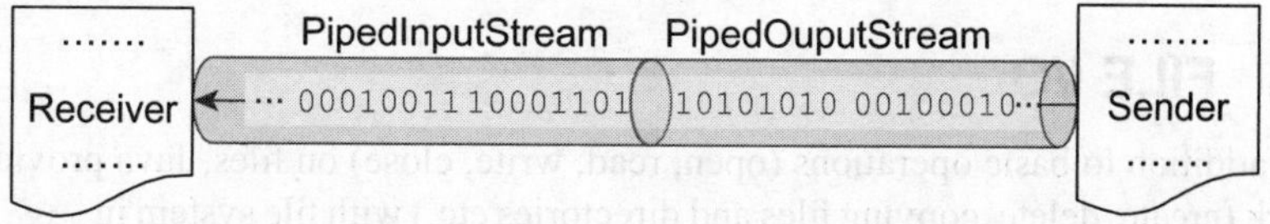

This looks as if two programs are now connected using a single pipe. However, how will the receiver access the `PipedOutputStream`? Typically a third thread (main thread) creates these two streams, joins them and creates two new threads, passing one of these two streams. The following program illustrates this:

```
import java.io.*;
class Sender extends Thread {
  PipedOutputStream output;
  Sender(PipedOutputStream o ) {this.output = o;}
  public void run() {
    try {
      while(true) {
        int v = (int)(Math.random()*100);
        System.out.println("Sent: "+v);
        output.write(v);
        Thread.sleep(1000);
      }
    }catch(Exception e) {}
  }
}
class Receiver extends Thread {
  PipedInputStream input;
  Receiver(PipedInputStream i ) {this.input = i;}
  public void run() {
   try {
      while(true) System.out.println("Received: "+input.read());
   }catch(Exception e) {}
  }
}
public class PipeDemo {
  public static void main(String args[]) throws IOException {

   PipedOutputStream out = new PipedOutputStream();
   PipedInputStream in = new PipedInputStream(out);

   new Receiver(in).start();
   new Sender(out).start();
   }
}
```

The sender thread in the program indefinitely generates a random number and sends its output stream. The received thread, in turn, reads and prints this value. A typical output of this program looks like this:

```
Sent: 38
Received: 38
Sent: 28
Received: 28
Sent: 47
Received: 47
Sent: 49
Received: 49
Sent: 51
Received: 51
…
```

11.8 FILE I/O

In addition to basic operations (open, read, write, close) on files, Java provides a set of classes to work (create, delete, copying files and directories etc.) with file system in `java.nio.file` package and its related package `java.nio.file.attribute`. If you are familiar with a file system, you will find that this API is very intuitive and easy to use.

11.9 PATH

You probably know that a file or a directory in a file system is identified by a sequence of names called *path*. The `Path` interface, as its name implies, is a Java representation of a path in the file system. This is one of the primary interfaces of `java.nio.file` package. This interface provides many methods to perform different operations on paths such as accessing elements of the path, converting the path to other forms, or extracting portions of a path.

11.9.1 Creating a Path

A Path instance may easily be created using one of the overloaded `get()` methods of `Paths` helper class. The `get()` method takes a path string, or a sequence of strings that when joined form a path string. The following are some examples in Windows OS:

```
Path p = Paths.get("E:\\ajp\\io\\sample.txt");
Path p1 = Paths.get("E:/ajp/io/sample.txt");
Path p2 = Paths.get("sample.txt");
Path p3 = Paths.get("E:", "ajp","io", "sample.txt");
Path p4 = Paths.get("E:/ajp/io", "sample.txt");
Path p5 = Paths.get("E:", "ajp/io/sample.txt");
```

Note that the file or directory corresponding to a `Path` might not physically exist. However, we can check the existence of the file/directory, create if it does not exist, open it, delete it, change its permissions, and many more, using methods in the `Files` class.

11.9.2 Retrieving Path Information

A path is a sequence of elements indentified by indices with highest element assigned index 0. The `Path` interface defines numerous methods for retrieving individual elements or a subsequence using these indices.

```
Path p = Paths.get("E:/ajp/io/sample.txt");
System.out.println("toString: "+ p);
System.out.println("getFileName: "+p.getFileName());
```

```
System.out.println("getNameCount: "+p.getNameCount());
System.out.println("getParent: "+p.getParent());
System.out.println("getRoot: "+ p.getRoot());
System.out.println("getName(0): "+p.getName(0));
System.out.println("subpath(0,3): "+p.subpath(0,3));
```

A sample result of this code is:

```
toString: E:\ajp\io\sample.txt
getFileName: sample.txt
getNameCount: 3
getParent: E:\ajp\io
getRoot: E:\
getName(0): ajp
subpath(0,3): ajp\io\sample.txt
```

11.9.3 Path Operations

There are also methods that manipulate a given path. The following sections illustrate some of them.

11.9.3.1 Removing Redundancy

A path may have redundant information. Consider the following paths:

```
E:/ajp/./io/sample.txt
E:/ajp/../ajp/io/sample.txt
E:/Net/../ajp/io/sample.txt
```

For example, the followings paths essentially represent the path `E:/ajp/io/sample.txt`. The `normalize()` method returns a path with redundant name elements eliminated.

```
Path p = Paths.get("E:/Net/../ajp/io/sample.txt");
Path p1 = p.normalize();
```

The path `p1` represents the same path as `p` with name string `E:\ajp\io\sample.txt`.

11.9.3.2 Converting to URI

If it is required to convert the path to a string that can be opened from a browser, we can use `toUri()` method. For example:

```
Path p = Paths.get("E:/ajp/io/sample.txt");
java.net.URI u = p.toUri();;     //u is file:///E:/ajp/io/sample.txt
```

The URI `u` has the name string `file:///E:/ajp/io/sample.txt`.

11.9.3.3 Joining Paths

Two paths can be joined using resolve() method as follows:

```
Path p = Paths.get("E:/ajp");
Path p1 = p.resolve("io/sample.txt");     //p1 is E:\ajp\io\sample.txt
```

The path `p1` refers to the resultant path `E:\ajp\io\sample.txt`. If the path to `resolve()` method itself is an absolute path, the method returns the supplied path itself.

11.9.4 Comparing Paths

The `Path` interface provides a method `equals()` that allows us to check two paths for equality. The `startsWith()` and `endsWith()` methods, on the other hand, may be used to check whether a path begins or ends with a particular string.

```
Path p = Paths.get("E:/ajp/io/sample.txt");
Path p1 = Paths.get("E:/ajp/./io/sample.txt");

if(p.equals(p1.normalize()))
    System.out.println(p +" and "+p1+" are equal");
```

```
if(p.startsWith("e:/"))
  System.out.println("It belongs to drive E");

if(p.endsWith("sample.txt"))
  System.out.println("File name is sample.txt");
```

A sample result of this code snippet is

```
E:\ajp\io\sample.txt and E:\ajp\.\io\sample.txt are equal
It belongs to drive E
File name is sample.txt
```

11.10 FILE

The final class `Files` is another important class in the `java.nio.file` package. It has a rich set of static methods for reading, writing, and manipulating files and directories. These methods typically operate on `Path` objects. The following sections illustrate how to perform different file operations.

11.10.1 Checking Existence

Note that the file or directory corresponding to a `Path` might not physically exist. However, we can check the existence of the file/directory using `exists()` or `notExists()` methods of `Files` class. They respectively return false and true if the file does not exist. Consider that the file `E:/ajp/io/sample.txt` really exists. The following code shows the usage of these two methods:

```
Path p = Paths.get("E:/ajp/io/sample.txt");
boolean b1 = Files.exists(p);                    //b1 is true
boolean b2 = Files.notExists(p);                 //b2 is false
```

11.10.2 Creating File

The `createFile()` method of `Files` class creates a non-existent file. The following code demonstrates this:

```
Path p = Paths.get("E:/ajp/io/blank.txt");
Files.createFile(p);
```

Similarly, the following code creates 9 files with name `f1.jpg, f2.jpg,..., f9.jpg.`

```
for(int i=1;i<10;i++)
Files.createFile(Paths.get("E:/ajp/io/f"+i+".jpg"));
```

Note that `createFile()` throws an `IOException` if the file already exists.

11.10.3 Deleting File

Deleting a file is very easy and may be done using `delete()` method. The following code deletes the 9 .jpg files created in the previous section.

```
for(int i=1;i<10;i++)
Files.delete(Paths.get("E:/ajp/io/f"+i+".jpg"));
```

Note that `delete()` method can even delete directories or links. For directories, the directory must be empty, or the deletion fails. Also, if the file does not exist, a `NoSuchFileException` is thrown.

11.10.4 Copying a File

We can programmatically copy files using overloaded `copy()` methods. The most obvious one takes source and target file paths respectively.

```
Path src = Paths.get("E:/ajp/io/a.txt");
Path dst = Paths.get("E:/ajp/io/copyOfa.txt");
Files.copy(src, dst);
```

However, `copy()` fails if the target file already exists. Java defines some options in enum types `java.nio.file.StandardCopyOption` and `java.nio.file.LinkOption`. The following shows how to replace an existing file if it exists:

```
Files.copy(src, dst, REPLACE_EXISTING);
```

Don't forget to use the following import statement:

```
import static java.nio.file.StandardCopyOption.*;
```

The `copy()` method can also copy directories. However, files inside the directory are not copied. So, the target directory will be empty, even when the original directory contains files. To move files, use `move()` method, which takes similar arguments.

11.10.5 File Attribute

Note that different file systems have different notions of file attributes. So, Java groups related attributes into views. A view specifies file system specific attributes (such as POSIX or DOS), or some common attributes such as file ownership. The basic attributes that are required to be supported by all file system implementations are specified by the view `BasicFileAttributeView`. In addition, Java defines other views such as `DosFileAttributeView`, `PosixFileAttributeView`, `FileOwnerAttributeView`, `AclFileAttributeView`, `UserDefinedFileAttributeView` etc. In this book, we shall discuss only `BasicFileAttributeView`.

The following code illustrates how to obtain basic file attributes:

```
Path p = Paths.get("E:/ajp/io/sample.txt");
BasicFileAttributes attr = Files.readAttributes(p, BasicFileAttributes.class);

System.out.println("isDirectory: " + attr.isDirectory());
System.out.println("isOther: " + attr.isOther());
System.out.println("isRegularFile: " + attr.isRegularFile());
System.out.println("isSymbolicLink: " + attr.isSymbolicLink());
System.out.println("size: " + attr.size());
System.out.println("creationTime: "+ attr.creationTime());
System.out.println("lastAccessTime: " + attr.lastAccessTime());
System.out.println("lastModifiedTime: " + attr.lastModifiedTime());
```

Don't forget to use the following import statement:

```
import java.nio.file.attribute.*;
```

A sample output of this code is shown below:

```
isDirectory: false
isOther: false
isRegularFile: true
isSymbolicLink: false
size: 3110
creationTime: 2014-10-28T06:31:50.740781Z
lastAccessTime: 2014-10-28T06:31:50.740781Z
lastModifiedTime: 2014-10-28T13:04:30.644331Z
```

11.10.6 Reading, Writing, Creating Files

Reading from and writing to files may be done using a pair of methods `readAllBytes()` and `write()`. The following example illustrates this:

```
Path src = Paths.get("E:/ajp/io/sample.txt");
```

```
Path dst = Paths.get("E:/ajp/io/sample1.txt");
byte[] bytes = Files.readAllBytes(src);
Files.write(dst, bytes);
```

This code reads all bytes of the file `sample.txt` and places them in a byte array. It then writes the entire content of the array to the file `sample1.txt`. So, it is basically a file copy program. Java provides a set of open options for different purposes such as truncating, appending, creating a new (if one does not exist) etc. They have been defined in the `java.nio.file.StandardOpenOption` enum type.

If you like to work with streams, `Files` class also provides provisions for them. The following code snippet illustrates this:

```
Path src = Paths.get("E:/ajp/io/sample.txt");
Path dst = Paths.get("E:/ajp/io/sample1.txt");
InputStream in = Files.newInputStream(src);
OutputStream out = Files.newOutputStream(dst);
int b;
while((b = in.read()) != -1) out.write(b);
```

The `Files` class also provides methods to read/write file data using buffered character streams. The following program illustrates this:

```
Charset charset = Charset.forName("US-ASCII");
BufferedReader reader = Files.newBufferedReader(src, charset);
BufferedWriter writer = Files.newBufferedWriter(dst, charset);
String line;
while ((line = reader.readLine()) != null)
    writer.write(line+"\n");
```

Don't forget to use the following import statement:

```
import java.nio.charset.*;
```

11.10.7 Random Access Files

Random access files allows us non-sequential (i.e. random), access to a file's contents and are represented by the `java.nio.channels.FileChannel` class. The only thing that we have to do is to set the cursor at the designated place before reading/writing using its `position()` method. The following program prints the first and last 10 characters of the file sample.text.

```
Path src = Paths.get("E:/ajp/io/sample.txt");
FileChannel fc = FileChannel.open(src, READ, WRITE);
ByteBuffer copy = ByteBuffer.allocate(10);
fc.read(copy);
copy.flip();

while (copy.hasRemaining())  System.out.print((char)copy.get());
copy.flip();
fc.position(fc.size()-10);
System.out.println();
fc.read(copy);
copy.flip();
while (copy.hasRemaining()) System.out.print((char)copy.get());
```

Consider the content of this file is:

```
First line.
Second line.
Last line.
```

Then the above code results in the following output:

```
First line
Last line.
```

11.10.8 Working with Directories

Some methods in Files class do not work properly for directories. For example, although copy() method can copy a directory, it cannot copy its contents. Moreover, there is no method to perform some directory specific operations such as listing directory contents, creating a directory etc. The following sections describe how to work with directories.

11.10.8.1 Listing Directory Contents

To find the contents of a directory, we first get DirectoryStream<Path> object using newDirectoryStream(Path) method. The object basically contains a list of file/directory paths which can be obtained by iterating the object. The following program shows how to print the contents of a directory:

```
import java.nio.file.*;
import java.io.*;
public class ListingDirectory {
  public static void main(String args[]) throws Exception {
    Path dir = Paths.get(args[0]);
    DirectoryStream<Path> stream = Files.newDirectoryStream(dir);
    for (Path file: stream)
      System.out.println(file.getFileName());
  }
}
```

This method takes a directory name as a command line argument and displays the entire contents of a directory: files, links, subdirectories, and hidden files.

11.10.9 Walking Directory Tree

The program in the previous section only prints the content of a given directory. However, it does not look in the sub-directories recursively. The following program recursively traverses a directory tree and prints all the file/directory names on its way:

```
import java.nio.file.*;
import java.io.*;
public class ListingDirectory1 {
  public static void main(String args[]) throws Exception {
    printDir(args[0]);
  }
  public static void printDir(String path) throws Exception {
    Path dir = Paths.get(path);
    DirectoryStream<Path> stream = Files.newDirectoryStream(dir);
    for (Path p: stream) {
      System.out.println(p.toAbsolutePath());
      if(Files.isDirectory(p))
        printDir(path+"/"+p.getFileName());
    }
  }
}
```

The directory to be traversed is specified as a command line argument. To visit all the files in a file tree recursively, we can also use FileVisitor interface, which specifies the required behaviour at key points in the traversal process: when a file is visited, before a directory is accessed, after a directory is accessed, or when a failure occurs. The interface has four methods, visitFile(), preVisitDirectory(), postVisitDirectory(), visitFileFailed(), which correspond to these situations respectively.

To visit the directory tree, we write a class implementing this interface. However, don't worry. You don't have to implement all methods in all the situations. For example, the following programs visit a given directory tree and prints and deletes .class files in its way.

```
import java.nio.file.*;
import java.io.*;
import static java.nio.file.FileVisitResult.*;
import java.nio.file.attribute.*;
class ClassFileRemover extends SimpleFileVisitor<Path> {
  public FileVisitResult visitFile(Path file, BasicFileAttributes attr) throws IOException{
    if(file.toString().endsWith(".class")) {
      Files.delete(file);
    }
    return CONTINUE;
  }
}
public class DirectoryWalkDemo {
  public static void main(String args[]) throws IOException {
    Files.walkFileTree(Paths.get(args[0]), new ClassFileRemover());
  }
}
```

Note that this program deletes files in the given directory. So, choose a directory that does not contain any important file or take a backup before running this program on that directory.

11.10.10 Watching Directory

Java 7 added an extremely powerful feature in NIO package called *Watch Service*, which allows applications to monitor *Watchable* objects (such as directories and files) for various events such as creation, modification and deletion. For example, to recover accidentally deleted files, we may use a watch service to monitor a directory for creating/updating files/directories under it so that we can save a backup copy somewhere else.

The watch service is represented by the `WatchService` class. To get the service, we first create a `WatchService` instance as follows:

```
WatchService watcher = FileSystems.getDefault().newWatchService();
```

A watch service watches objects registered for certain events and notifies the service user if any such events occur on those objects. Any object whose class implements `Watchable` interface may be watched. The `Path` class is perfect for this job. A `Watchable` object is registered with a watch service by invoking its `register()` method. It takes a `WatchService` to register with and one or more events to be monitored on the object. The valid events have been defined in `java.nio.file.StandardWatchEventKinds` class. The following is an example:

```
Path dir = Paths.get("E:/ajp/io/temp");
WatchKey key = dir.register(watcher, StandardWatchEventKinds.ENTRY_MODIFY);
```

The `register()` method returns a `WatchKey` which represents a registration of a `Watchable` object with a `WatchService`. A watch key goes through different states in its lifetime. It is in the *ready* state when created first. On detecting an event (represented by `WatchEvent`), the key goes in the *signaled* state, is queued and can be retrieved by consumers using `poll()` or `take()` methods to retrieve keys.

```
WatchKey key = watcher.take();
```

If a key is in *signaled* state and events are detected further, they are added to the key. However, a *signaled* key is not re-queued for retrieval from the watch service. Events are retrieved (and removed) from key by invoking its `pollEvents()` method and are processed further.

```
for (WatchEvent<?> e : key.pollEvents()) {
  //process event...
}
```

The `WatchEvent` interface defines a set of functions to find necessary information about the event such as its kind, context it occurred on etc. A key goes in the *signaled* state, remains in that state until its `reset()` method is invoked to return the key to the *ready* state. So, to get the key from the watch service, don't forget to reset the key as follows:

```
k.reset();
```

The processing code usually goes in a loop so that processing goes on continuously. The following program installs a watch service for a specified directory, for all kinds of events and prints the kind of event and context.

```
import java.nio.file.*;
import static java.nio.file.StandardCopyOption.*;
public class WatchServiceDemo {
  public static void main(String args[]) throws Exception {
    WatchService watcher = FileSystems.getDefault().newWatchService();
    Path dir = Paths.get(args[0]);
    WatchKey key = dir.register(watcher, StandardWatchEventKinds.ENTRY_MODIFY,
StandardWatchEventKinds.ENTRY_CREATE, StandardWatchEventKinds.ENTRY_DELETE);
    while(true) {
      WatchKey k = watcher.take();
      for (WatchEvent<?> e: key.pollEvents()) {
        System.out.println(e.kind()+" "+e.context());
      }
      k.reset();
    }
  }
}
```

However, the above program does not consider the sub-directories recursively. Let us write a powerful program that installs a watch service for a specified directory and all of its sub-directories and saves a copy as backup to another specified directory whenever events such as file/directory creation of modification occur. This ensures to recover the file from backup directory, even if a file is deleted from the source directory.

```
import java.nio.file.*;
import static java.nio.file.LinkOption.*;
import java.nio.file.attribute.*;
import java.io.*;
import java.util.*;
import static java.nio.file.StandardCopyOption.*;

public class WatchD implements Runnable {
  private final WatchService watcher =
FileSystems.getDefault().newWatchService();
  private final Map<WatchKey,Path> keys = new HashMap<WatchKey,Path>();
  Path src, dst;

  WatchD(Path dir, Path dir1) throws IOException {
    src = dir; dst = dir1;
    register(dir);
  }

  private void register(Path dir) throws IOException {
    Files.walkFileTree(dir, new SimpleFileVisitor<Path>() {
     public FileVisitResult preVisitDirectory(Path dir, BasicFileAttributes
attrs) throws IOException  {
        WatchKey key = dir.register(watcher,
StandardWatchEventKinds.ENTRY_CREATE, StandardWatchEventKinds.ENTRY_MODIFY);
        keys.put(key, dir);
        return FileVisitResult.CONTINUE;
      }
    });
```

```
    new Thread(this).start();
    System.out.println("Ready");
  }
  public void run()  {
    while(true) {
      WatchKey key;
      try {
        key = watcher.take();
        System.out.println(key);
      } catch (InterruptedException x) { return; }

      Path dir = keys.get(key);
      if (dir == null) {
        System.err.println("WatchKey not recognized!!");
        continue;
      }

      for (WatchEvent<?> event: key.pollEvents()) {
        WatchEvent.Kind kind = event.kind();
        if (kind == StandardWatchEventKinds.OVERFLOW) continue;

        WatchEvent<Path> ev = (WatchEvent<Path>)event;
        Path name = ev.context();
        Path child = dir.resolve(name);
        System.out.format("%s: %s\n", event.kind().name(), child);
        Path r = src.relativize(child);
        Path to = Paths.get(dst+"/"+r);//, from = Paths.get(src+"/"+r);
        try {
          Files.copy(child, to, REPLACE_EXISTING);
        }catch(Exception e) {
          Path p1 = Paths.get(src.toString());
          Path p2 = Paths.get(dst.toString());
          for(int i=0;i<r.getNameCount();i++) {
            p1 = p1.resolve(r.getName(i));
            p2 = p2.resolve(r.getName(i));
              try {
      Files.copy(p1, p2, REPLACE_EXISTING);
              }catch(Exception e1) {System.out.println("again"+e);}
          }
        }

        if ((kind == StandardWatchEventKinds.ENTRY_CREATE) &&
Files.isDirectory(child, NOFOLLOW_LINKS)) {
          try {
            register(child);
          } catch (IOException x) {}
        }
      }
      boolean valid = key.reset();
    }
  }
  public static void main(String[] args) throws Exception {
    new WatchD(Paths.get(args[0]), Paths.get(args[1]));
  }
}
```

To use this program, pass source and back directory as follows:

```
java WatchD e:/ajp e:/bkp/ajp
```

Start this program and work on a directory peacefully without worrying about files/directories getting deleted accidentally.

KEYWORDS

Buffered stream—Special streams that internally use buffers and exhibit better performance

BufferedReader—A character-oriented buffered stream used to read data

Console—A Java class used to read data from keyboard

Data Streams—Java stream classes used to handle primitive type values as well as Strings

Files—A Java class that has a rich set of static methods for reading, writing, and manipulating files and directories

InputStream—A byte-oriented stream from which data can be read

ObjectOutputStream—A Java class used for object serialization

ObjectInputStream— A Java class used for object de-serialization

Object Streams—Java stream classes used for object serialization and de-serialization

OutputStream—A byte-oriented stream to which data can be written

Path—A sequence of names used to identify a file or a directory in a file system

PrintStream—A byte stream assists us to translate data into nicely formatted, human-readable form

PrintWriter—A character stream assists us to translate data into nicely formatted, human-readable form

PrintWriter—A character-oriented buffered stream used to write data

Reader—A character-oriented stream from which data can be read

Streams—A logical entity that flows from one direction to the other and may be used as a carrier of data

Watch Service—An I/O service which allows applications to monitor Watchable objects

Watchable objects—The kind of objects a watch service can monitor

Writes—A character-oriented stream to which data can be written

SUMMARY

Java provides a rich set (probably too many) of classes and interfaces as a separate package `java.io` for I/O. It introduced the concept of *stream* that flows from one direction to the other and may be used as a carrier of data. A stream can be byte-oriented or character-oriented. The abstract classes `InputStream` and `OutputStream` represent streams that can carry only sequence of bytes. On the other hand, `Reader` and `Writer` abstract classes can carry sequence of characters. Java IO API also contains a large number of higher level sub-classes that can handle all kinds of data, from primitive values to advanced objects.

All byte stream classes are sub-classes of `InputStream` and `OutputStream`. Similarly, all character stream classes are sub-classes of `Reader` and `Writer`. Java also provides two classes `InputStreamReader` and `OutputStreamWriter`, which act as converters from byte-to-character streams.

Java provides some special *buffered streams* that can be used to reduce overhead. For each read/write request on these buffered streams does not always fire a native API. Instead they use some memory area called *buffer*.

Java formatting API assists us to translate data into nicely formatted, human-readable form. These classes are byte stream `PrintStream` and character stream `PrintWriter`. Java also provides classes, called *data streams* to handle primitive type values as well as Strings. Java provides two powerful classes `ObjectOutputStream` and `ObjectInputStream` and that can be used for object serialization and de-serialization respectively.

The classes `PipedInputStream` and `PipedOutputStream` are used to connect two programs so that they can exchange data.

In addition to basic operations (open, read, write, close) on files, Java provides a set of classes to work (create, delete, copying files and directories etc.) with file system in `java.nio.file` package and its related package `java.nio.file.attribute`. A file or a directory in a file system is identified by a sequence of names called *path*. The `Path` interface, as its name implies, is a Java representation of a path in the file system. The final class `Files` is another important class which has a rich set of static methods for reading, writing, and manipulating files and directories.

Java 7 added an extremely powerful feature in NIO package called *Watch Service*, which allows applications to monitor *Watchable* objects (such as directories and files) for various events such as creation, modification and deletion.

WEB RESOURCES

http://www.tutorialspoint.com/java/java_files_io.htm
Java - Streams, Files and I/O

https://docs.oracle.com/javase/tutorial/essential/io/
Lesson: Basic I/O

http://tutorials.jenkov.com/java-io/index.html
Java IO Tutorial

http://www.mkyong.com/tutorials/java-io-tutorials/
Java I/O Tutorial

EXERCISES

Objective-type Questions

1. Which of these packages contain classes and interfaces used for input and output operations of a program?
   (a) java.util.io (c) java.io
   (b) java.lang.io (d) java.lang

2. Which of these methods of InputStream is used to read integer representation of the next available byte input?
   (a) getInt() (c) readInt()
   (b) read() (d) getInteger()

3. Which of these classes is used for input and output operation when working with bytes?
   (a) Bytes (c) Writer
   (b) Reader (d) InputStream

4. Which of these classes is not a member class of java.io package?
   (a) Integer (c) Writer
   (b) Reader (d) StringReader

5. Which of these classes is used to read bytes from a file?
   (a) FileReader
   (b) FileWriter
   (c) FileInputStream
   (d) InputStreamReader

6. Which of the following data types is returned by every method of OutputStream?
   (a) int
   (b) float
   (c) byte
   (d) None of the mentioned

7. Which of these interfaces is not a member of Java.io package?
   (a) DataInput (c) ObjectFilter
   (b) ObjectInput (d) FileFilter

8. Which of the following is a method of ObjectOutput interface used to finalize the output state so that any buffer is cleared?
   (a) clear() (c) fflush()
   (b) flush() (d) close()

9. Which of these is a method of ObjectOutput interface used to write the object to input or output stream as required?
   (a) write() (c) StreamWrite()
   (b) print() (d) writeObject()

10. Which of the following is a method to clear all the data present in output buffers?
    (a) clear() (c) fflush()
    (b) flush() (d) close()

11. Which of the following classes is used to read characters in a file?
    (a) FileReader (c) FileInputStream
    (b) FileWriter (d) InputStreamReader

12. Which of these methods is used for writing bytes to an outputstream?
    (a) put() (c) printf()
    (b) print() (d) write()

13. Which of the following classes is not related to input and output stream in terms of functioning?
    (a) File (c) InputStream
    (b) Writer (d) Reader

14. Which of the following is specified by a File object?
(a) a file in disk (c) directory in disk
(b) directory path (d) None of the mentioned

15. Which of these methods of FileReader class is used to read characters from a file?
(a) read() (c) get()
(b) scanf() (d) getInteger()

16. Which of these is an interface for control over serialization and deserialization?
(a) Serializable (c) FileFilter
(b) Externalization (d) ObjectInput

17. Which of these classes can be used to implement input stream that uses a character array as the source?
(a) BufferedReader
(b) FileReader
(c) CharArrayReader
(d) FileArrayReader

18. Which of these interfaces extends DataOutput interface?
(a) Serializable (c) ObjectOutput
(b) Externalization (d) ObjectInput

19. Which of these is the method for testing whether the specified element is a file or a directory?
(a) IsFile() (c) Isfile()
(b) isFile() (d) isfile()

20. Which of the following is a process of writing the state of an object to a byte stream?
(a) Serialization (c) File Filtering
(b) Externalization (d) All of the mentioned

21. Which of these is a method to clear all the data present in output buffers?
(a) clear() (c) fflush()
(b) flush() (d) close()

22. Which of the following processes occur automatically by java run time system?
(a) Serialization
(b) Garbage collection
(c) File Filtering
(d) All of the mentioned

23. Which of these classes can return more than one character to be returned to input stream?
(a) BufferedReader
(b) Bufferedwriter
(c) PushbachReader
(d) CharArrayReader

24. DataInput is
(a) an interface that defines methods to read primitive data types.
(b) an abstract class defined in java.io.
(c) a class we can use to read primitive data types.
(d) an interface that defines methods to open files.

25. Which are the valid ways to create DataInputStream streams?
(a) new DataInputStream(new FileInputStream("in.dat");
(b) new DataInputStream("in.dat", "r");
(c) new DataInputStream("in.dat")
(d) new DataInputStream(new File("in.dat"));

26. Given that the file is a File object, which of the following are legal statements to create a new file?
(i) file.create();
(ii) FileOutputStream fos = new FileOutput Stream(file);
(iii) FileWrter out = new FileWriter(file);
(iv) FileInputStream fis = new FileInput Stream(file);
(v) RandomAccessFile raf = new Random AccessFile(file);
(a) (ii), (iii) and (iv)
(b) (ii), (iv) and (v)
(c) (ii) and (iii)
(d) (ii), (iii) and (v)

27. Which exception is thrown by the read() method of InputStream class?
(a) Exception
(b) IOException
(c) FileNotFoundException
(d) ReadException

28. Which of the following statements are true?
(i) Unicode characters are all 16 bits.
(ii) UTF characters are all 24 bits.
(iii) Reader class has methods that can read integers and floats.
(iv) File class may be used to rename a file.
(v) DataOutputStream objects are used to write primitive data to a file.
(a) (i), (iii), (iv) and (v)
(b) (i), (iv) and (v)
(c) (i), (ii) and (iv)
(d) (ii), (iv) and (v)

Subjective-type Questions

1. How would you determine the MIME type of a file?
2. Show the list of all file names from a folder.
3. Write a program to get the list of all files from a folder.
4. How do you read file content using byte array?
5. Write the steps needed to read file content line by line in Java?
6. Write an example that counts the number of times a particular character, such as e, appears in a file. The character can be specified at the command line. You can use xanadu.txt as the input file.
7. Explain the steps required to read property file in static context.
8. How do you read input from console in Java?
9. Write a program to get file list from a folder filtered by extension .java?
10. How do you get file URI reference?
11. When invoking format, what is the best way to indicate a new line?
12. How do you store and read objects from a file?
13. Write a program to create and store property file dynamically?
14. How do you store property file as xml file?
15. How do you get file last modified time?
16. Filter the files by file extensions and show the file names.
17. How do you convert byte array to inputstream?
18. How do you convert inputstream to reader or BufferedReader?
19. The file datafile begins with a single long value that tells you the offset of a single int piece of data within the same file. Write a program that gets the int piece of data. What is the int data?
20. What class and method would you use to read a few pieces of data that are at known positions near the end of a large file? How do you convert byte array to reader or BufferedReader?
21. How do you set file permissions in Java?
22. How do you read a file using BufferedInputStream?
23. What method(s) would you use to determine whether a file is a symbolic link?
24. How do you create temporary file in Java?
25. Write a program to write or store data into temporary file in Java?
26. How do you delete temporary files in Java?
27. How do you write string content to a file in Java?
28. Write a program to write byte content to a file in Java?

PART TWO
NETWORK PROGRAMMING

CHAPTER – 12

BASIC NETWORKING

KEY OBJECTIVES

After completing this chapter readers will be able to—

- get an overview about the Java network classes and interfaces
- Retrieve information about network interfaces
- know how to use URL and URLConnection classes
- access web pages using HTTP and Java network APIs
- know how to encode/decode URL
- use proxies and proxy selectors in Java networking applications

12.1 JAVA AND THE NET

Java has some distinct advantages over other programming languages as far as network applications are concerned. One of the important features of Java is that it supports 16-bit Unicode for International character sets, which is still difficult to implement in other languages. In addition, Java can excellently handle network security issues. These features together with other features such as platform independence and garbage collection allow us to develop efficient and elegant network applications without worrying about the system crashes, spread of viruses, or stealing of sensitive data.

This chapter demonstrates how to use Java network APIs to write basic network programs easily and quickly.

12.2 JAVA NETWORKING CLASSES AND INTERFACES

Java, like other programming languages, provides well-designed classes and interfaces (APIs) to most network features. Table 12.1 shows some of the commonly used network classes and interfaces. The network classes and interfaces are provided basically as three packages `java.net`, `java.rmi`, and `javax.mail`. The first two are parts of the JVM (Java Virtual Machine) and the last one can be downloaded from Oracle's website. With this rich set of interfaces, writing network programs is quite simple. Programmers having experience in network programming in other languages can readily discover how easy it is to develop the same programs in Java. This chapter guides you through some of the basic networking classes and interfaces and provides examples. Advanced network programming concepts may be found in many chapters later.

Table 12.1: Java networking classes and interfaces

NetworkInterface	InetAddress	ServerSocket	Socket
DatagramSocket	DatagramPacket	URL	URLConnection
HttpURLConnection	InetSocketAddress	SocketAddress	Authenticator
PasswordAuthentication	MulticastSocket	URLEncoder	URLDecoder
Remote	Naming	Registry	LocateRegistry
UnicastRemoteObject	RMISecurityManager	RMISocketFactory	RMIClassLoader
RemoteServer	RemoteObject	Session	MimeMessage
Transport	Store	Folder	Message
URLName	Header	ContentType	InternetAddress
MimeBodyPart	MimeMultipart	InternetHeaders	MimeUtility

12.3 GETTING NETWORK INTERFACES

Before developing actual network applications, let us first work with the network interfaces available on a host. A network interface is usually a **N**etwork **I**nterface **C**ard (NIC), that acts as a point of interconnection between a computer and other devices. Each network interface is represented by the Java class `NetworkInterface`.

Systems often run with multiple network interfaces such as wired Ethernet (802.3), WiFi (802.11 a/b/g), Bluetooth (802.15.4) etc. An application can use `NetworkInterface` to specify which NIC to use for a particular network activity.

This class has no public constructor. However, it has many static methods such as `getNetworkInterfaces()`, `getByInetAddress()`, `getByName()`, which can retrieve the interface details from the system. The first one returns the complete list of interfaces on the machine. The last two are used when the IP address or the name of the particular interface is already known. The following example program lists all the network interfaces and their sub-interfaces (if any).

```
//GetNetworkInterfaces.java
import java.net.*;
import java.util.*;
class GetNetworkInterfaces {
  public static void main(String args[]) throws Exception  {
    Enumeration<NetworkInterface> intfs =
NetworkInterface.getNetworkInterfaces();
    while(intfs.hasMoreElements()) {
      NetworkInterface intf = intfs.nextElement();
      System.out.println("\nInterface: "+intf.getName());
      System.out.println("Display name: "+intf.getDisplayName());

      Enumeration<NetworkInterface> subIfs = intf.getSubInterfaces();
      for (NetworkInterface subIf : Collections.list(subIfs)) {
        System.out.printf("\tSub Interface : "+subIf.getName());
        System.out.printf("\tSub Interface Display
name :"+subIf.getDisplayName());
      }
    }
  }
}
```

Network interfaces may have children interfaces, called *sub-interfaces*, which may be obtained using its `getSubInterfaces()` method. Similarly, if a network interface is a sub-interface, `getParent()` returns parent interface. Compile the program using the following command:

```
javac GetNetworkInterfaces.java
```

Now, run the program as follows:

```
java GetNetworkInterfaces
```

A sample output of this program is shown below:

```
Interface: lo
Display name: Software Loopback Interface 1

Interface: eth3
Display name: Realtek PCIe GBE Family Controller

Interface: net4
Display name: Atheros AR9285 802.11b/g/n WiFi Adapter

...
```

We may sometimes like to use a specific interface for data communication. We can query the system for the desired interface by its name as follows:

```
NetworkInterface intf = NetworkInterface.getByName("net4");
```

This interface can then be used subsequently for sending and receiving data (using socket, for example).

Note that network interfaces may not always be physical devices. It may be a logical device implemented by a software. The example includes the loopback interface, which is commonly used in test environments. It is not a physical device but a piece of software simulating a network interface.

12.3.1 Getting Interface Addresses

Each network interface is assigned one or more IP addresses. An IP address is represented by `InetAddress` class. It is sometimes necessary to know the IP address of an interface. This can be done using `getInetAddresses()` method that returns an `Enumeration` of `InetAddress`. The following program shows IP addresses of those interfaces that have at least one IPv4 address assigned.

```
import java.net.*;
import java.util.*;
class GetInterfaceAddresses {
  public static void main(String args[]) throws Exception  {
    System.setProperty("java.net.preferIPv4Stack","true");
    Enumeration<NetworkInterface> intfs =
NetworkInterface.getNetworkInterfaces();
    while(intfs.hasMoreElements()) {
      NetworkInterface intf = intfs.nextElement();
      Enumeration<InetAddress> addresses = intf.getInetAddresses();
      if(addresses.hasMoreElements()) {
        System.out.println("\nName: "+intf.getName());
        System.out.println("Display name: "+intf.getDisplayName());
        while(addresses.hasMoreElements()) {
          InetAddress addr = addresses.nextElement();
          System.out.println("Address: "+addr);
        }
      }
    }
  }
}
```

A sample output of this program is shown below:

```
Name: lo
Display name: Software Loopback Interface 1
Address: /127.0.0.1

Name: net4
Display name: Atheros AR9285 802.11b/g/n WiFi Adapter
Address: /192.168.43.77

Name: eth4
Display name: VMware Virtual Ethernet Adapter for VMnet1
Address: /192.168.226.1

Name: eth5
Display name: VMware Virtual Ethernet Adapter for VMnet8
Address: /192.168.40.1
```

To get IPv6 addresses, comment the line

```
System.setProperty("java.net.preferIPv4Stack","true");
```

The following program prints the hostname and address of the local computer

```
import java.net.*;
class LocalHost {
  public static void main (String args[]) throws UnknownHostException {
     InetAddress ia = InetAddress.getLocalHost();
     System.out.println("Name : "+ia.getHostName());
     System.out.println("Address : "+ia.getHostAddress());
  }
}
```

Here is a sample output:

```
Name : UROY
Address : 192.168.226.1
```

12.3.2 Getting Interface Properties

The `NetworkInterface` has several other useful methods to gather information about a network interface. The following program (`GetInterfaceParameters.java`) displays information about network interfaces whose name is specified as a command line argument.

```
//GetInterfaceParameters.java
import java.net.*;
import java.util.*;
class GetInterfaceParameters {
  public static void main(String args[]) throws Exception  {
    NetworkInterface intf = NetworkInterface.getByName(args[0]);
    System.out.println("\nName : "+intf.getName());
    System.out.println("Display name : "+intf.getDisplayName());
    System.out.println("Up : "+ intf.isUp());
    System.out.println("Loopback : "+ intf.isLoopback());
    System.out.println("PointToPoint : "+intf.isPointToPoint());
    System.out.println("Supports multicast :"+intf.supportsMulticast());
    System.out.println("Virtual : "+intf.isVirtual());

    byte[] mac1 = intf.getHardwareAddress();
    if(mac1 != null) {
      System.out.print("Hardware Address : ");
      for (int k = 0; k < mac1.length; k++)
        System.out.format("%02X%s", mac1[k], (k < mac1.length - 1) ? "-" : "");
      System.out.println();
    }
    System.out.println("MTU :"+intf.getMTU());
  }
}
```

When the program was executed with the argument `eth4`, it generated the following output:

```
Name : net4
Display name : Atheros AR9285 802.11b/g/n WiFi Adapter
Up : true
Loopback : false
PointToPoint : false
Supports multicast :true
Virtual : false
Hardware Address : D0-DF-9A-01-55-E6
MTU :1500
```

12.4 URL

The primary classes to access the Internet are the `java.net.URL` class and the `java.net.HttpURLConnection` class. The class `URL` encapsulates the **U**niform **R**esource **L**ocator (URL), which identifies a resource in the WWW uniquely. A resource can be anything such as a file or a directory, or it can be a reference to a more complicated object, such as a query to a database or to a search engine. The `URL` class provides mechanisms to download web resources to the client computer. It also has methods to retrieve different parts, such as method, hostname, port etc. of a URL.

12.4.1 Creating URL

The class `URL` has several overloaded constructors some of which are mentioned as follows:

```
URL(String url)
URL(String protocol, String host, String file)
URL(String protocol, String host, int port, String file)
```

Any constructor can be used depending upon one's convenience. The most commonly used constructor takes a URL as a string argument and creates a `URL` object. For example, the following code creates a `URL` object for the URL `http://www.yahoo.com`.

```
URL url = new URL("http://www.google.com");
```

The String used in the above example itself represents an absolute URL. We can also create absolute URL objects from a relative URL object and a specification. The general form of this constructor is:

```
URL(URL baseURL, String relativeURL)
```

The following examples show how to use this constructor:

```
URL url = new URL(new URL("https://plus.google.com"), "u/0/?tab=wX");
//Creates the URL https://plus.google.com/u/0/?tab=wX

URL url = new URL(new URL("https://login.yahoo.com/"),
"?.src=ym&.intl=in&.lang=en-IN&.done=http://mail.yahoo.com");
//Creates the URL https://login.yahoo.com/?.src=ym&.intl=in&.lang=en-
IN&.done=http://mail.yahoo.com
```

Each of the URL constructors throws a `MalformedURLException` if the arguments to the constructor refer to a syntactically incorrect URL

12.4.2 Parsing URL

A URL consists of several parts, as follows:

```
protocol://host:[port]/[path[?params][#anchor]]
```

The optional parts are shown in [ ]. Examples of protocols include `HTTP`, `HTTPS`, `FTP`, and `File`. The path is also called filename, and the host is also referred to as the authority. If a URL does not specify a port, a default port for the protocol is used. For example, for HTTP, the default port is 80.

The URL class provides numerous methods to retrieve these parts. For example, we can get the protocol, authority, host name, port number, path, query, filename, and reference from a URL using these methods. The following program (`ParsingURL.java`) prints the different parts of a URL specified as a command line argument.

```
import java.net.*;
public class ParsingURL {
  public static void main(String[] args) throws Exception {
    URL aURL = new URL(args[0]);
    System.out.println("Protocol = " + aURL.getProtocol());
    System.out.println("Authority = " + aURL.getAuthority());
    System.out.println("Host = " + aURL.getHost());
    System.out.println("Port = " + aURL.getPort());
    System.out.println("Default port = " + aURL.getDefaultPort());
    System.out.println("Path = " + aURL.getPath());
    System.out.println("Query = " + aURL.getQuery());
    System.out.println("File = " + aURL.getFile());
    System.out.println("Ref = " + aURL.getRef());
  }
}
```

The program generated the following output when it was supplied the argument

`http://www.uroy.biz:8080/ajp/BasicNetworking/index.html?topic=URL#ParsingURL`

```
Protocol = http
Authority = www.uroy.biz:8080
Host = www.uroy.biz
Port = 8080
Default port = 80
Path = /ajp/BasicNetworking/index.html
Query = topic=URL
File = /ajp/BasicNetworking/index.html?topic=URL
Ref = ParsingURL
```

12.4.3 Web Page Retrieval

Making a connection to a web server in the Internet using socket is sometimes problematic, especially when the client computer is connected to the Internet through a proxy computer that does not support this socket. The Java classes `URL` and `URLConnection` allow client applications to connect to an HTTP server very easily. This mechanism will work even if the clients are behind the firewall and use HTTP proxy. A detailed description of how to specify proxy in a Java program can be found later in this chapter. These classes are special-purpose classes, used for accessing HTTP servers only.

For example, the following code creates a `URL` object for the URL `http://www.google.com.`

```
URL url = new URL("http://www.google.com");
```

You can then call its `openStream()` method to establish an HTTP socket connection with the web server specified by the URL. The method `openStream()` returns an `InputStream` object which can be used to read data from this HTTP socket. The following example displays the content of the URL specified as a command line argument.

```
//URLReadDemo.java
import java.net.*;
public class URLReadDemo {
  public static void main(String args[]) throws Exception {
    int c;
    URL url = new URL(args[0]);
    java.io.InputStream in = url.openStream();
    while (((c = in.read()) != -1))
      System.out.print((char) c);
    in.close();
  }
}
```

Run the program with the argument `http://www.google.com`.

```
java URLReadDemo http://www.google.com
```

A sample output is shown in Figure 12.1:

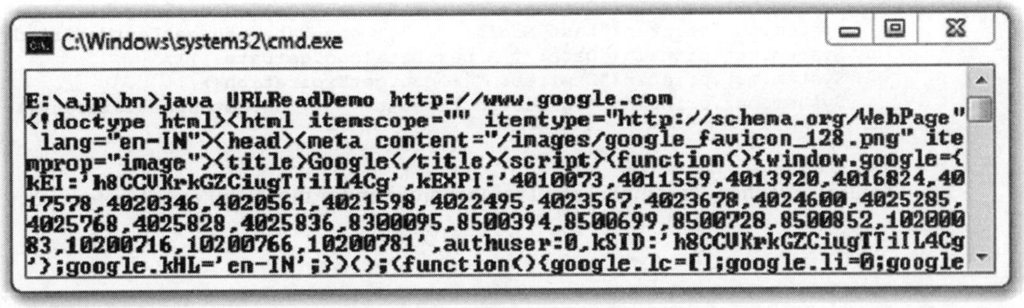

```
C:\Windows\system32\cmd.exe

E:\ajp\bn>java URLReadDemo http://www.google.com
<!doctype html><html itemscope="" itemtype="http://schema.org/WebPage"
 lang="en-IN"><head><meta content="/images/google_favicon_128.png" ite
mprop="image"><title>Google</title><script>(function(){window.google={
kEI:'h8CCVKrkGZCiugTTiIL4Cg',kEXPI:'4010073,4011559,4013920,4016824,40
17578,4020346,4020561,4021598,4022495,4023567,4023678,4024600,4025285,
4025768,4025828,4025836,8300095,8500394,8500699,8500728,8500852,102000
83,10200716,10200766,10200781',authuser:0,kSID:'h8CCVKrkGZCiugTTiIL4Cg
'};google.kHL='en-IN';})();(function(){google.lc=[];google.li=0;google
```

Figure 12.1: Web page retrieval using URL

The class `URL` allows us to only read the content of the URL. It does not allow us to apply other parts of the HTTP protocol, e.g. accessing the header. The class `URLConnection` provides mechanisms to access content as well as to inspect properties of the resource. These properties are HTTP specific and do not make any sense for protocols other than HTTP.

12.5 URLCONNECTION

The class `URLConnection` represents an HTTP connection. The `openConnection()` method on a URL object establishes an HTTP socket connection to the web server and returns a `URLConnection` object that represents the connection. The method `getInputStream()` on this `URLConnection` object returns an `InputStream` object which can be used to read data from this HTTP socket. The following example does the same as the previous example.

```
//URLConnectionDemo.java
import java.net.*;
public class URLConnectionDemo {
  public static void main(String args[]) throws Exception {
    int c;
    URL url = new URL(args[0]);
    URLConnection con = url.openConnection();
    java.io.InputStream in = con.getInputStream();
    while (((c = in.read()) != -1))
      System.out.print((char) c);
    in.close();
  }
}
```

As mentioned in the previous section, `URLConnection` class also provides methods to retrieve information about the resource. Once a connection to a remote server is established, we can inspect the properties of the resource before actually transporting it locally. These attributes are exposed by the HTTP protocol specification and, as such, only make sense for HTTP URLs.

In the following example, we create a URLConnection to examine the document's properties and content:

```
//URLPropertiesDemo.java
import java.util.*;
import java.net.*;
public class URLPropertiesDemo {
```

```
    public static void main(String args[]) throws Exception {
      int c;
      URL url = new URL(args[0]);
      URLConnection con = url.openConnection();
      System.out.println("Content-type: " + con.getContentType());
      System.out.println("Content Encoding: " + con.getContentEncoding());
      System.out.println("Content-length: " + con.getContentLength());
      System.out.println("Last-Modified: " + new Date(con.getLastModified()));
      System.out.println("Date: " + new Date(con.getDate()));
      System.out.println("Expires: " + con.getExpiration());
      System.out.println("Connection Timeout: " + con.getConnectTimeout());
    }
}
```

Figure 12.2: shows a sample output for this program for the URL `http://www.google.com`.

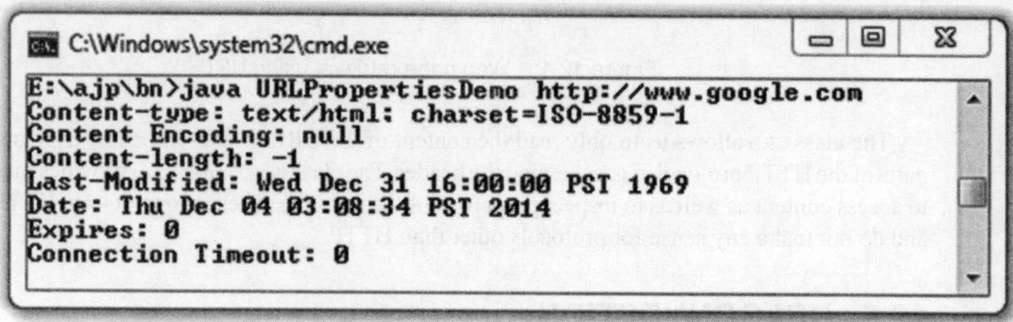

Figure 12.2: www.google.com properties

12.6 HTTPURLCONNECTION

Java also provides HTTP specific sub-class `java.net.HttpURLConnection`, which can be used to set up HTTP parameters and general request properties before making the connection. One of the useful tasks that we can do with this class is automatic redirection.

If the response code of an HTTP response message is 301: Moved Permanently or 302: Temporary Redirect, then a new URL should be contacted. The new redirected URL can be obtained by reading the "Location" header of the HTTP response header. The following example illustrates this:

```
import java.io.*;
import java.net.*;
import static java.net.HttpURLConnection.*;
public class HttpRedirectDemo {
  public static void main(String[] args) throws Exception {
    URL url = new URL(args[0]);
    HttpURLConnection con = (HttpURLConnection) url.openConnection();
    System.out.println("Request URL ... " + url);

    int code = con.getResponseCode();
    if((code != HTTP_OK) && (code == HTTP_MOVED_TEMP || code == HTTP_MOVED_PERM
   || code == HTTP_SEE_OTHER)) {
      System.out.println("Response Code ... " + code);

      // get redirect url from "location" header field
      URL newUrl = new URL(con.getHeaderField("Location"));
```

```
            // open the connection again
            con = (HttpURLConnection) newUrl.openConnection();
            System.out.println("Redirect to URL : " + newUrl);
        }

        BufferedReader in = new BufferedReader(new
    InputStreamReader(con.getInputStream()));
        String line;
        StringBuffer htmlStr = new StringBuffer();
        while ((line = in.readLine()) != null) htmlStr.append(line);
        in.close();
        System.out.println("Content... \n" + htmlStr);
      }
    }
```

A sample output for the URL http://www.yahoo.com is shown below:

```
E:\ajp\bn>java HttpRedirectDemo http://www.yahoo.com
Trying : http://www.yahoo.com
Response code : 301
Redirecting to : https://www.yahoo.com/
Content...
<!DOCTYPE html> <html lang="en-IN" class="dev-desktop uni-purple-border ua-wk
ua-win ua-6.1 ua-wk537
...
```

12.6.1 URLEncoder/URLDecoder

What happens if the URL string has spaces or special characters such as "/", ".", "#" or some other non-ASCII characters such as Bengali, Hindi, Chinese or Japanese characters?

For example, the "#" character has a special meaning when used in an html anchor tag. The space is not allowed on a valid URL format. Also, some characters, such as "~" might not transport properly across the Internet. Such characters must be encoded before using it in a URL. As a rule of thumb, any non-alphanumeric character should be URL encoded. As a result, there will be no harm even if the characters do not have special meanings.

Fortunately, Java has a class `URLEncoder` that can encode these characters so that they can be used in URLs safely. Its `encode()` method takes two parameters, the string to be encoded and the encoding scheme, which is usually supposed to be "UTF-8". Similarly, the class `URLDecoder` is used to get the original string from encoded string. Its `decode()` method takes a string in encoded form and returns a non-encoded version of the string.

Table 12.2: shows some of the often used characters and their URL encodings.

Table 12.2: Some special characters and their URL encodings

;	%3B	#	%23	$	%24	<	%3C
?	%3F	&	%26	,	%2C	>	%3E
/	%2F	=	%3D	<space>	%20 or +	~	%7E
:	%3A	+	%2B	%	%25	%	%25

The number following the % sign is the hexadecimal ASCII code of the character being encoded. Since, the space character is very commonly used, a special code (the "+" sign) has been reserved as its URL encoding. Thus the string "A B" can be URL encoded as either "A%20B" or "A+B". In general, a String is encoded as follows:

- The letters ('a'..'z', 'A'..'Z') and numbers ('0'..'9') remain the same.
- The special characters '.', '-', '*', '_' remain the same.

- Spaces are substituted by '+'
- All other characters are first converted into one or more bytes using the specified encoding scheme. Each byte is then represented by the 3-character string "%xy", where xy is the two-digit hexadecimal representation of the byte.

The following program demonstrates how to encode and decode a string "Hello World!"

```
import java.net.*;
public class URLEncoderDecoder {
  public static void main(String[] args) throws Exception {
    String str = "Hello World!";
    String encodedStr = URLEncoder.encode(str, "UTF-8");
    System.out.println("String : "+str);
    System.out.println("Encoded string : " + encodedStr);
    String decodedStr = URLDecoder.decode(encodedStr, "UTF-8");
    System.out.println("Decoded string : " + decodedStr);
  }
}
```

A sample output of this program is shown here:

```
String : Hello World!
Encoded string : Hello+World%21
Decoded string : Hello World!
```

Similarly, the following string of Bengali characters (The title of a Rabindrasangeet) must be encoded first before using it in a URL.

অকারণে অকালে মোর পড়ল যখন ডাক

The encoded string looks like

```
%E0%A6%85%E0%A6%95%E0%A6%BE%E0%A6%B0%E0%A6%A3%E0%A7%87+%E0%A6%85%E0%A6%95%E0%A6
%BE%E0%A6%B2%E0%A7%87+%E0%A6%AE%E0%A7%8B%E0%A6%B0+%E0%A6%AA%E0%A7%9C%E0%A6%B2+%
E0%A6%AF%E0%A6%96%E0%A6%A8+%E0%A6%A1%E0%A6%BE%E0%A6%95
```

The following encoded URL can then be used to download the notes of the song from the site http://rabindra-rachanabali.nltr.org.

```
http://rabindra-
rachanabali.nltr.org/node/16053?gaan=%E0%A6%85%E0%A6%95%E0%A6%BE%E0%A6%B0%E0%A6
%A3%E0%A7%87+%E0%A6%85%E0%A6%95%E0%A6%BE%E0%A6%B2%E0%A7%87+%E0%A6%AE%E0%A7%8B%E
0%A6%B0+%E0%A6%AA%E0%A7%9C%E0%A6%B2+%E0%A6%AF%E0%A6%96%E0%A6%A8+%E0%A6%A1%E0%A6
%BE%E0%A6%95.xml
```

The following program downloads the file and puts the content in a file অকারণে অকালে মোর পড়ল যখন ডাক.html.

```
import java.io.*;
import java.net.*;
public class URLEncoderDemo {
  public static void main(String args[]) throws Exception {
    int c;
    BufferedReader br = new BufferedReader(new InputStreamReader(new
FileInputStream("in.txt"), "UTF-16"));
    String song = br.readLine();
    String encodedSong = URLEncoder.encode(song, "UTF-8");
    String encodedUrl = "http://rabindra-
rachanabali.nltr.org/node/16053?gaan="+encodedSong+".xml";
    FileOutputStream fos = new FileOutputStream(song+".html");
    URL url = new java.net.URL(encodedUrl);
    InputStream in = url.openStream();
    while (((c = in.read()) != -1)) fos.write((char)c);
    in.close();
    fos.close();
  }
}
```

The name of the song is stored in a file in.txt.

12.7 PROXY

To address security issue, network administrators often install a special component called "proxy server." It is essentially a service that sits between the Internet and the internal network and manages connections between the two worlds. This way, proxies reduce outside security threats while still allowing internal users to access Internet services.

However, Java applications, to be useful, must pass though these proxies. Fortunately, Java provides provisions to work with proxies. The solution lies in activating certain system properties in the Java runtime. Java application needs to specify information about the proxy itself as well as specify user information for authentication purposes. There are many ways we can do it.

12.7.1 Using Command Line Arguments

We can set the required information when starting the JVM for a JAVA application from the command line. For example, if the proxy process runs at port `8080` in the machine having IP address `172.16.15.8`, use the following command to start the application `AnApp`:

```
java -DproxyHost=172.16.15.8 -DproxyPort=8080 AnApp
```

If proxy requires authentication, use two additional arguments

```
java -DproxyHost=172.16.15.8 -DproxyPort=8080 -DproxyUser=user -
DproxyPassword=password AnApp
```

where `user` and `password` are the login and password required by the proxy respectively.

12.7.2 Using System Properties

Alternatively, the same information can be specified in the client programs as follows:

```
System.setProperty("http.proxyHost", "172.16.15.8");
System.setProperty("http.proxyPort", "8080");
```

If proxy requires authentication, use the following two properties.

```
System.setProperty("http.proxyUser", "user");
System.setProperty("http.proxyPassword", "password");
```

12.7.3 Using Proxy Class

In Java 1.5 and later, we can also pass a `java.net.Proxy` instance to the `openConnection()` method of `URL` class. Add this code snippet in your Java network application that wants to use a proxy.

```
URL url = ...
Proxy proxy = new Proxy(Proxy.Type.HTTP, new InetSocketAddress("172.16.15.8",
8080));
URLConnection con = url.openConnection(proxy);
```

12.8 PROXYSELECTOR

This class is used if the information about the proxy is not known or there are many proxies and we are unable to determine a suitable proxy to be used. Specifically, it gives us the flexibility to:

- Decide if a proxy should be used or not for a URL being used.
- Select one (or more) to be used.
- Manage failures when connecting to proxy servers.

Although, `ProxySelector` class is an abstract class, we can use one provided by its `getDefault()` method that returns system-wide proxy selector. However, to use system proxy selector, we must set a system property as follows:

```
System.setProperty("java.net.useSystemProxies", "true");
```

The list of available proxies for a given URL may be obtained as follows:

```
String urlStr = "http://www.google.com";
URL url = new URL(urlStr);

ProxySelector ps = ProxySelector.getDefault();
java.util.List<Proxy> proxies = ps.select(new URI(urlStr));
```

Any one from this list may be used. To use the first one, we write the code

```
Proxy proxy = proxies.get(0);
URLConnection con = url.openConnection(proxy);
```

The entire steps can be summarized by a single statement as follows:

```
Proxy proxy = (Proxy) ProxySelector.getDefault().select(new URI(urlStr)).
iterator().next();
```

KEYWORDS

HttpURLConnection—A Java class that represents an HTTP connection

InetAddress—A Java class that represents an IP address

Interface addresses—The IP address(es) assigned to a network interface

NetworkInterface —A Java class that represents a network interface

Network Interface—Usually a **N**etwork **I**nterface **C**ard (NIC), that acts as a point of interconnection between a computer and other devices.

Proxy—A class that represents a proxy

ProxySelector—A class used to select a proxy from a list of available proxies

Sub-interface—A child interface of an existing interface

URLConnection—A Java class that represents a connection

URLDecoder—A Java class used to decode a URL

URLEncoder—A Java class used to encode a URL

URL—A class that encapsulates the **U**niform **R**esource **L**ocator (URL), which identifies a resource in the WWW uniquely

SUMMARY

Java, like other programming languages, provides well-designed classes and interfaces (APIs) to most network features. The primary network classes and interfaces are provided in the package java.net.

Each network interface is represented by the Java class NetworkInterface. It has many static methods such as getNetworkInterfaces(), getByInetAddress(), getByName(), which can retrieve the interface details from the system. Each network interface is assigned one or more IP addresses which can be obtained using getInetAddresses() method that returns an Enumeration of InetAddress. The NetworkInterface has several other useful methods to gather information about a network interface.

The primary classes to access the Internet are the URL class and the HttpURLConnection class. The class URL encapsulates the Uniform Resource Locator (URL), which identifies a resource in the WWW uniquely. The HttpURLConnection class can be used to inspect the properties of the resource before actually transporting it locally.

Java has classes URLEncoder and URLDecoder that can be used to encode/decode URLs.

Java also provides provisions to work with proxies. A proxy can be specified using command line argument or using system properties or using Proxy instance.

WEB RESOURCES

http://docs.oracle.com/javase/tutorial/networking/
Trail: Custom Networking

https://docs.oracle.com/javase/tutorial/networking/urls/
Lesson: Working with URLs

https://docs.oracle.com/javase/tutorial/networking/nifs/index.html
Lesson: Programmatic Access to Network Parameters

http://computing.dcu.ie/~humphrys/Notes/Networks/java.html
Network programming in Java

http://tutorials.jenkov.com/java-networking/index.html
Java Networking

EXERCISES

Objective-type Questions

1. Which of these packages contains classes and interfaces for networking?
(a) java.util.net (c) java.net
(b) java.util (d) java.network

2. How many bits are present in a single IP address?
(a) 8 (c) 32
(b) 16 (d) 64

3. Which of these classes is used to encapsulate IP address and DNS?
(a) ContentHandler
(b) URL
(c) InetAddress
(d) DatagramPacket

4. What is the full form of URL?
(a) Uniform Reverse Location
(b) Uniform Resource Locator
(c) Universal Resource Locator
(d) Universal Resource Latch

5. Which of these exceptions is thrown by URL class's constructors?
(a) URLNotFoundException
(b) URLSourceNotFound
(c) MalformedURLException
(d) URLNotFound

6. Which of these transfer protocols must be used so that a URL can be accessed by URLConnection class object?
(a) http
(b) https
(c) Any Protocol can be used
(d) None of the mentioned

7. Which of these data members of HttpResponse class is used to store the response from an http server?
(a) status (c) statusResponse
(b) address (d) statusCode

8. Which of these methods is used to know when the last URL was modified?
(a) LastModified()
(b) getLastModified()
(c) GetLastModified()
(d) getlastModified()()

9. Which of these methods is used to know the type of content used in the URL?
(a) ContentType()
(b) contentType()
(c) getContentType()
(d) GetContentType()

10. Which of these classes is used to access actual bits or content information of a URL?
(a) URL (c) URLConnection
(b) URLDecoder (d) All of the mentioned

11. Which of these classes is used to encapsulate IP address and DNS?
(a) DatagramPacket
(b) URL
(c) InetAddress
(d) ContentHandler

12. Which of these methods is used to know the host of a URL?
(a) host() (c) GetHost()
(b) getHost() (d) gethost()

13. Which of these methods is used to know the full URL of a URL object?
(a) fullHost()
(b) getHost()
(c) ExternalForm()
(d) toExternalForm()

14. Which of the following classes is used to represent IPv4 addresses?
(a) InetV4Address
(b) InetAddress4
(c) Inet4Address
(d) IPv4Address

15. Which of the following classes is used to represent IPv6 addresses?
(a) Inet6Address
(b) InetV6Address
(c) InetAddress6
(d) IPv6Address

16. A network interface card is represented by
(a) NetworkHardware
(b) NetworkCard
(c) InterfaceCard
(d) NetworkInterface

17. Which of the following methods is used to get the port of a URL?
(a) port()
(b) getPort()
(c) urlPort()
(d) returnPort()

18. Which of the following methods is used to establish a connection to the server?
(a) connection()
(b) open()
(c) makeConnection()
(d) openConnection()

19. Which of the following classes is used for HTTP?
(a) HttpURLConnection
(b) HttpURL
(c) HttpConnection
(d) HTTP

20. A proxy in Java is represented by
(a) Proxy
(b) JavaProxy
(c) HTTPProxy
(d) GenericProxy

Subjective-type Questions

1. Java API doesn't provide any constructors for InetAddress. How do you create an InetAddress instance?

2. How do you make a connection using URL?

3. When are MalformedURLException and UnknownHostException thrown?

4. How do you get the IP address of a machine from its hostname?

5. What is the difference between URL instance and URLConnection instance?

6. How do you find the hostname corresponding to an IP address?

7. What is the Proxy Server?

8. How do you find the IP address of local machine?

9. How do you specify the timeouts in networking applications? What is a servlet?

CHAPTER – 13

SOCKET PROGRAMMING

KEY OBJECTIVES

After completing this chapter readers will be able to—

- understand the basic idea of Inter-Process Communication
- get an overview of *peer-to-peer* and *client–server* network architecture
- know about the different types of sockets and their functionality
- know what socket address, port and reserved ports are
- use socket-related Java classes
- develop networking applications using TCP and UDP sockets
- understand how to develop iterative and concurrent server applications
- write multicasting application using sockets

13.1 INTRODUCTION

In the previous chapter, we have discussed some of the high level Java mechanisms for **I**nter-**P**rocess **C**ommunication (IPC). In fact, these mechanisms use *sockets* as part of their underlying implementation. In this chapter, we shall discuss sockets as a lower-layer IPC mechanism.

In distributed computing, **I**nter-**P**rocess **C**ommunication (IPC) is the fundamental idea for the exchange of data among multiple processes and/or threads [Figure 13.1:]. It allows processes (probably running on different computers) to communicate by exchanging information to perform a designated task.

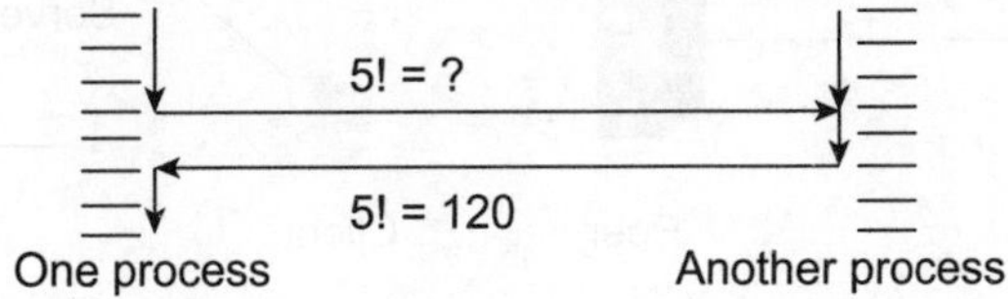

Figure 13.1: Inter-process Communications

For example, consider two processes p1 and p2 running on two different computers connected by a network. The process p1 has the ability to provide the synonym (i.e. words having similar meaning) of a given word. On the other hand, the process p2, who somehow knows the existence of such a useful process p1, at a particular instant of its execution, has obtained a word "buy" whose meaning is not known to p2. In this circumstance, the process p2 may request p1 to provide a synonym of the word "buy". Upon receiving the request, the process p2 responds that the meaning of the word "buy" is basically "purchase". This way, two processes may communicate to get out of the problem.

Most of the operating systems (specially Unix and/or Linux) support tools for IPC such as pipe, FIFO, message queue, shared memory, semaphore etc. All these system-level facilities assume processes can share memory in the user space or system space. Consequently they can only be used if processes reside on the same computer. However, processes running on different computers cannot share memory and therefore memory (and hence those primitive IPC tools) cannot be used as a means for communication.

Socket, on the other hand, can be used as a lower-level tool for IPC for local processes as well as processes running on different computers. Originally, the socket was a low-level programming interface for IPC introduced in Barkley Unix. Accordingly, the concept of socket was made very much similar to Unix I/O that follows *Open-Read-Write-Close* paradigm. The socket follows a similar *Open-Send-Receive-Close* paradigm.

Many programming languages now provide high-level **A**pplication **P**rogramming **I**nterface (API) based on this primitive socket interface. The high-level socket (API) hides the complexities and intricacies of system-level specification and makes programmers devote more time on the application logic. In this chapter, we shall discuss Java implementation of socket API. Sockets are particularly useful when we want to write client–server applications. So, let us have an overview of this mode quickly.

13.2 CLIENT/SERVER PROGRAMS

One of the central ideas of network computing is *client–server* model. Many networking applications including the Internet's primary protocols such as HTTP, SMTP, DNS, etc. use this model. It has some distinct advantages over its counterpart, the *peer-to-peer* model (P2P) where peers are equally privileged, equipotent participants [Figure 13.2:]. Note that sockets may also be used to develop applications for P2P network model.

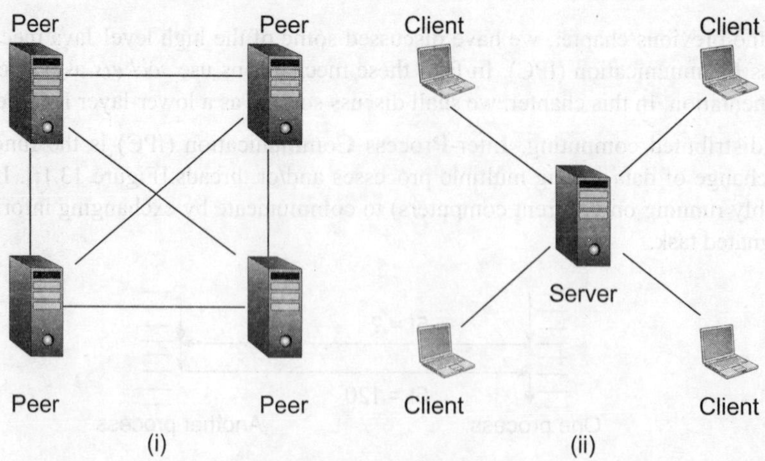

Figure 13.2: Network architecture (i) Peer-to-peer (ii) Client–Server

In client–server programming paradigm, there are two primary components (programs): service providers, known as *server programs* (or simply servers) and service requesters, known as *client programs* (or simply clients). Since, client–server model uses two types of applications, it is sometimes referred to as *two-tier* model. Server programs (which are usually written to provide powerful services) are usually run on high-performance computers and share resources with its clients. Client programs, which usually run on different computers, make use of these resources to perform its designated task.

Each client sends one or more service requests to one or more servers. The servers, in turn, accept these requests, process them and provide the requested service (e.g. sending requested information). This simple but powerful idea can be used in a variety of network applications, though the fundamental concept remains the same.

A server may provide a variety of services such as web service, remote login service, mail service, database service, file service, name service, print service, and many more. One server may provide multiple services. Similarly, one client may get many services from the same or different servers. A program may act as a server or as a client or both (logically). Popular clients include web browsers, chat clients, email clients, etc.

The client process becomes sender of data (if any) at some point of communication and the server process becomes the receiver of that data. At some other instant of communication, the server process becomes the sender of data (if any) and the client process becomes the receiver of that data. Depending on the number of receivers, data communication may be categorized as *uni-cast*, *multi-cast* and *broadcast* [Figure 13.3:].

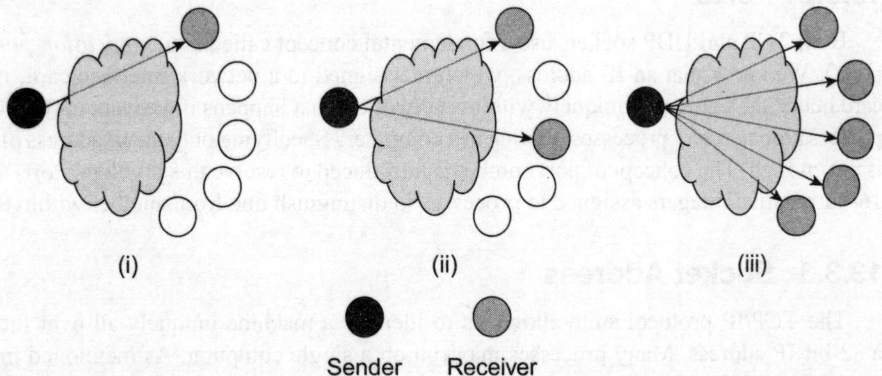

Figure 13.3: Types of communication (i) Uni-cast (ii) Multi-cast (iii) Broadcast communications

When data is sent by one process to another single process, it is known as uni-cast communication. In this case, there is exactly one sender and one receiver. On the other hand, when there exists multiple (but not all) receivers of the data, it is said to be multi-cast. If all are intended receivers, it is said to be broadcast. Note that broadcast is a special case of multicast, when all entities become receivers.

13.3 SOCKETS

A socket, in network terminology, is an end-point for communication between two processes on the network. In Java, sockets are represented by objects for exchanging data. The `java.net` package provides useful classes and interfaces for communication using sockets. Note that a socket is not a connection, it is an endpoint of communication. Sockets objects are also necessary for communication even if there is no connection (e.g. UDP). A connection (usually used for TCP), however, may be represented by the two end points.

13.3.1 Types of Socket

The Java Socket API is built on the top of the underlying transport layer protocol of TCP/IP protocol suit. In TCP/IP there are two transport layer protocols: **T**ransmission **C**ontrol **P**rotocol (TCP) and **U**ser **D**atagram **P**rotocol (UDP). Accordingly, Socket API is categorized into two types. The Socket API that uses TCP as its underlying transport layer protocol is known as TCP Socket (or stream socket) and that which uses UDP is called UDP Socket (or datagram socket). The TCP delivers the data reliably in the same order as they were sent and is known as 'connection-oriented' protocol. On the other hand, UDP does not give any such guarantee on ordering and hence is known as 'connectionless' protocol. Java provides a rich set of classes and interfaces in `java.net` package to support both TCP and UDP sockets. The classes `ServerSocket` and `Socket` (together with other classes) are used to support Transmission Control Protocol (TCP) and provide connection-oriented uni-cast communication. To support User Datagram Protocol (UDP), `DatagramSocket` and `MulticastSocket` classes are used that provide connectionless uni-cast, multi-cast and broadcast communication respectively. So, depending on the application requirement, any one/both of these two types of sockets may be used.

In this chapter, we shall discuss both types of sockets with several programming examples. A side-by-side comparison between these two types of sockets will be done later in this chapter.

13.3.2 Ports

Both TCP and UDP sockets use a fundamental concept called *communication ports* (or simply ports). We know that an IP address, which is assigned to a network interface card, indentifies the card hence the computer uniquely within a network. What happens if we want to refer to a particular process among *many* processes running in a computer? Specifying only the IP address of the computer is not enough. The concept of port number is introduced to resolve this problem. Ports are essentially 16-bit positive integers assigned to processes to distinguish one from another within the computer.

13.3.3 Socket Address

The TCP/IP protocol suite allows us to identify a machine uniquely all over the world using a 32-bit IP address. Many processes may run on a single computer. As mentioned in the previous section, each of these processes is assigned a locally unique positive integer called the port number. Any process can now be identified uniquely all over the world by using this port number together with the IP address of the machine it is running on. This IP address and port number combination can be thought of as an address called the *socket address*. A process willing to send data to another process needs to know only the socket address of the receiver process.

The socket address (i.e. IP address and port number) completes destination address. This means, data first reaches a specific destination IP address (i.e. a computer) and is further routed to the specific process having the destination port number. This way socket address makes the communication between two processes possible. The exact way of communications is illustrated with the help of numerous examples in the following sections.

The same port number may be used for different IP addresses for communication. Since, IP addresses are different, socket addresses are also different and hence processes having those socket addresses are uniquely identifiable.

13.3.4 Socket Address and Java

Usually the notion of socket address is explained with the context of a process. It is said that a process is assigned a locally unique port number. Actually in Java socket programming, port numbers are not assigned to processes; they are assigned to socket objects instead. These socket objects are created in the processes. Three types of socket objects (`ServerSocket`, `DatagramSocket` and `MulticastSocket`) may be created. A process may logically create many socket objects [Figure 13.4:]. Each of these socket objects will have a port number bound to it. Consequently, each socket object has a socket address. This implies that a process does not basically have any socket address; rather socket addresses are assigned to socket objects. Usually, one process creates one socket object. That is why it is sometimes said that a process has a socket address.

Anyway, whatever be the case, it does not disturb Inter-Process Communication (IPC). Actually communication takes place between socket objects and since processes create them, processes can still communicate through these socket objects [Figure 13.4:].

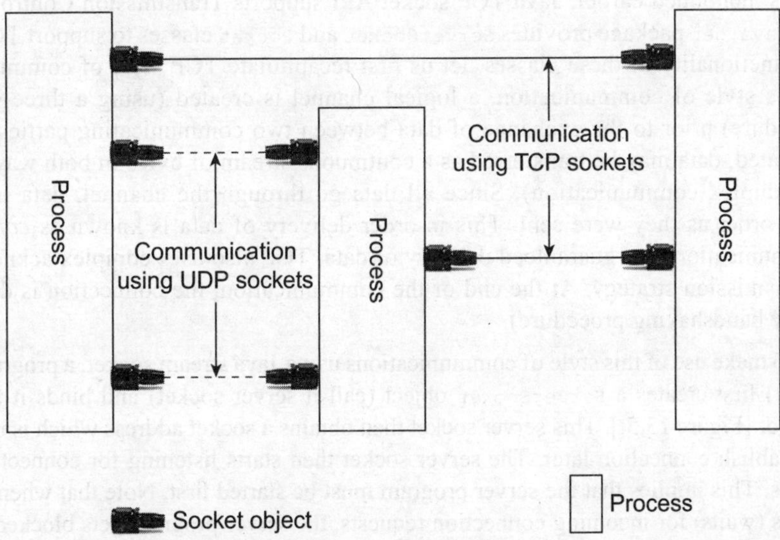

Figure 13.4: Relation between socket objects and processes in Java

13.3.5 Reserved Ports

It was mentioned earlier that each process is assigned a locally unique integer. Ideally, any available (not assigned yet) integer may be used. However, remember that the client must know this port number to make communication possible. If port numbers are assigned arbitrarily, the client processes will not have any idea about them. That is why standard server processes are assigned some fixed port numbers agreed upon at design time. These port numbers are said to be reserved for those well-known processes. According to **I**nternet **A**ssigned **N**umbers **A**uthority (IANA), port numbers from 0 to 1023 are reserved. You should not use these port numbers in your own network programs. However, if you want to implement standard processes (such as HTTP, FTP etc), you should ideally use these reserved ports (80 for HTTP, 20 for FTP) so that others can use them easily. Some reserved port numbers and their corresponding processes are mentioned in Table 13.1:

Table 13.1: Reserved ports

Port	Server	Port	Server	Port	Server	Port	Server
7	Echo	37	Time	110	POP3	434	MobileIP-Agent
18	MSP	43	WhoIs	111	Sun RPC	443	HTTPS
20	FTP Data	80	HTTP	115	SFTP	458	Apple QuickTime
21	FTP Control	53	DNS	118	SQL Services	531	Chat
22	SSH	66	Oracle SQL*NET	161	SNMP	541	rlogin
23	Telnet	69	TFTP	179	BGP	547	DHCP Server
25	SMTP	70	Gopher	197	DLS	563	SNEWS

13.4 TCP SOCKETS

As mentioned earlier, Java TCP socket API supports Transmission Control Protocol (TCP). The `java.net` package provides `ServerSocket` and `Socket` classes to support TCP. To understand the functionality of these classes, let us first recapitulate TCP style of communication quickly. In this style of communication, a logical channel is created (using a three-way handshaking procedure) prior to the exchange of data between two communicating parties. Once a channel is created, data may be transferred as a continuous stream of bytes in both ways simultaneously (full-duplex communication). Since all data go through the channel, data is received in the same order as they were sent. This in-order delivery of data is known as *connection-oriented* communication. For guaranteed delivery of data, TCP also uses complex acknowledgement and retransmission strategy. At the end of the communication, the connection is destroyed (using a 4-way handshaking procedure).

To make use of this style of communications using Java stream socket, a program (usually called server) first creates a `ServerSocket` object (call it server socket) and binds it to an unused port number [Figure 13.5:]. This server socket then obtains a socket address which is used by the clients to establish connection later. The server socket then starts listening for connection requests from clients. This implies that the server program must be started first. Note that when the server socket listens (waits) for incoming connection requests, the server program gets blocked. To accept many connections simultaneously, the server program is usually implemented in a multi-threaded manner and is discussed in Section 13.4.6.

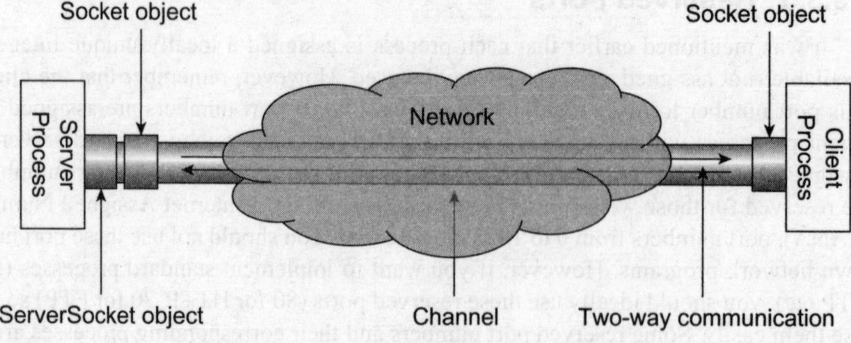

Figure 13.5: Communication using TCP socket

A client is another program started usually on a different computer after the server. The client must somehow know the socket address (IP address/name of the computer where the server program runs and port number of the server socket given by the server program) of the server socket to communicate. It first sends a request for connection establishment to the server socket by creating a `Socket` object and specifying the socket address of the server socket. During the connection establishment, the client should provide its own socket address to the server, so that the server can communicate back (if desired) to the client. The client's port number is usually assigned by the system.

On receiving a request from a client, if everything goes fine, the server establishes a (bidirectional) channel to the client. Once this channel is established, both processes can now communicate in both ways simultaneously [Figure 13.5:].

The heart of the TCP socket API consists of basically two classes: `ServerSocket` and `Socket`. Communication using TCP sockets consists of the following basic steps:

- The server creates a `ServerSocket` object, specifying the port number it listens on.
- The server invokes the `accept()` method on this object. This method makes the server waiting until a request comes from a client.
- The client creates a `Socket` object, specifying the server's name/IP address and port number to connect to.
- The constructor of the `Socket` class attempts to establish a connection to the server socket having specified socket address (i.e. IP address and port number). If the connection is established, it returns a `Socket` object that represents the client end of the logical connection created. The client uses this `Socket` object to communicate with the server.
- The `accept()` method on the `ServerSocket` object also returns a `Socket` object that represents server end of the channel that is connected to the client's socket. The server uses this `Socket` object to communicate with the client.

The temporal flow of control in server and client program is given in Figure 13.6:

Server		Client
1. Creates a `ServerSocket` object, specifying a port number.		
2. Invokes the `accept()` method on this object. This method makes the server waiting for incoming connection request		
		3. Creates a `Socket` object, specifying the name/IP address and port number of the server.
		4. The constructor of the `Socket` class attempts to establish a connection to the specified server and port number.
5. The `accept()` method on the `ServerSocket` object also returns a `Socket` that represents the server side end of the logical connection.	time ↓	5. If the connection is established, it returns a `Socket` object that represents the client side end of the logical connection.
6. Get `InputStream` and an `OutputStream` type objects.		6. Get `InputStream` and an `OutputStream` type object.
		7. Write data using `OutputStream`.
8. Read data using `InputStream`.		
9. Write data using `OutputStream`.		
		10. Read data using `InputStream`.

Figure 13.6: Temporal flow of control in server and client programs using TCP sockets

Each `Socket` object has an `InputStream` and an `OutputStream` associated with it. The client's `InputStream` is connected to the server's `OutputStream`, and the client's `OutputStream` is connected to the server's `InputStream`. Now, both the client and the server can communicate using I/O streams. Let us now understand, how these socket classes are used to develop applications.

13.4.1 The ServerSocket Class

A TCP server socket object is first created using `ServerSocket` class to accept incoming connection requests from clients. The class has four overloaded constructors [See appendix A for details]. The most frequently used one creates a server socket at the specified port.

```
ServerSocket(int port)
```

The port *must* be an unused one otherwise it throws an exception `BindException`. The port must belong to the range from 0 to 65535. The following statement creates a server socket at port 6789.

```
ServerSocket serverSocket = new ServerSocket(6789);
```

Suppose the machine running this server process has one network interface card having IP address `192.168.1.2`. Then the socket address of the process (actually `ServerSocket` object) is `[192.168.1.2, 6789]`. The meaning of this statement is shown in Figure 13.7:

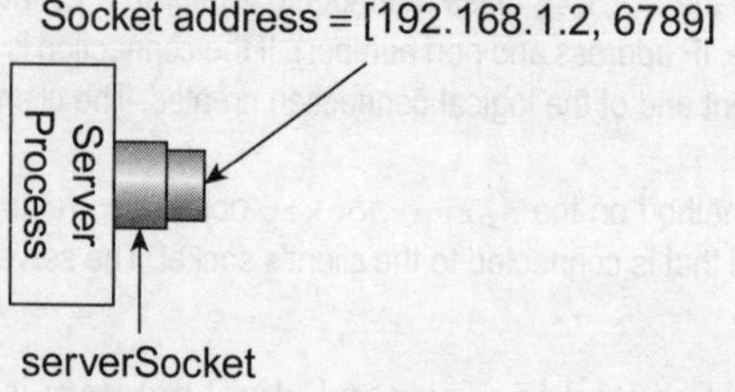

Figure 13.7: Creating a ServerSocket Object

If the machine has multiple network interface cards (hence multiple IP addresses), then the socket created using the above constructor is capable of listening through all these interfaces. So, any one of the IP addresses may be specified in the socket address to connect to this socket object. However, a specific IP address may also be bound to the server socket using a different constructor [See appendix A for details].

Each `ServerSocket` object created has a finite FIFO queue associated with it. This queue stores outstanding connection requests made by the clients. These connection requests are handled by the subsequent call of `accept()` method of the `ServerSocket` object (discussed later in this section). When the queue is full, further connection requests are rejected. The length of this queue may be specified explicitly in the constructor. If nothing is specified (as we have done in our constructor), a queue length of 50 is used.

As mentioned earlier, a process may essentially create many `ServerSocket` objects associated with locally unique port numbers. So, a socket addresses is actually assigned to those `ServerSocket` objects not to the process. Usually, a process creates a single `ServerSocket` object and hence the socket address refers to the `ServerSocket` object as well as the process.

The procedure of assigning a port number to a `ServerSocket` object is sometimes known as *binding* (or association). This binding between a socket and a port may be done by a separate function call `bind()`. Actually, a socket is assigned a port number so that other processes can refer to this socket by this port for further usage.

We have stated that socket address of the `ServerSocket` object can be used by clients to establish connections. However, to accept incoming connections, the server must start listening. This is done by calling the `accept()` method on the server socket as follows [Figure 13.8:]:

```
Socket serverEnd = serverSocket.accept();
```

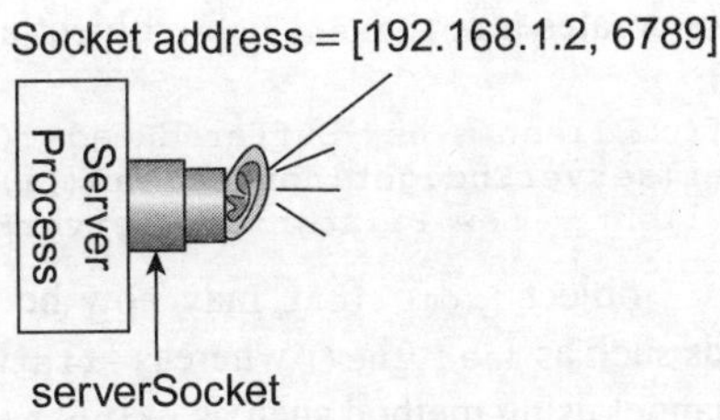

Figure 13.8: Listening for incoming connection requests

This results in the server capable of accepting incoming connections. Note that, connection requests are initially stored in the FIFO queue associated with the server socket object. So, it is possible to send connection requests by clients even if the server has not yet invoked the `accept()` method. If there is already a request (that means it came before a call of `accept()` method), the `accept()` method processes the request. If there is no outstanding connection requests in this queue, the method `accept()` *blocks* the caller (i.e. server process). The process wakes up as soon as a connection request is received. If everything goes well, a *logical channel* between the server process and the client process is created and a `Socket` object is returned which represents the server end of this channel and is used subsequently to communicate with the client.

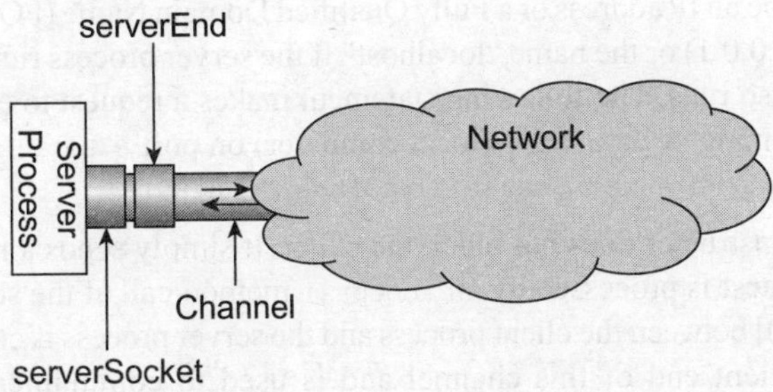

Figure 13.9: Creating a channel

Note that Figure 13.9: merely shows a pictorial view of connection establishment. It appears that server socket becomes used and no channel cannot be attached to it further. However, these sockets are not physical sockets. The pictorial view has been used only for demonstration purpose. Consequently, concepts that exist for physical socket are not applicable here. This implies, programmatically, many logical channels may be attached to our server socket object simultaneously.

Anyway, if further client requests come when the server program is busy serving the current client and no call of `accept()` method is encountered, client requests are initially stored in the FIFO queue associated with this `ServerSocket` object. To establish connections with these clients, the server must process those requests. This is done by calling the `accept()` method on the `ServerSocket` object subsequently. A call of `accept()` method results in processing the request which is at the head of the queue at that instant. Further calls of `accept()` method process client requests (if any) from the queue in First-Come-First-Served (FCFS) basis.

To send data to or receive data from the client, stream objects are created. The `Socket` object provides two useful methods, `getInputStream()` and `getOutputStream()`, which can be used to obtain `InputStream` and `OutputStream` objects, respectively. The `InputStream` object is used to receive data from the socket, whereas the `OutputStream` object is used to send data to the socket. They are usually wrapped by other suitable stream classes to send and receive data conveniently. The following example creates a `BufferedReader` object and a `PrintWriter` object to read from and write to the socket:

```
BufferedReader fromClient = new BufferedReader(new
InputStreamReader(serverEnd.getInputStream()));
PrintWriter  toClient = new PrintWriter(serverEnd.getOutputStream(), true);
```

The `BufferedReader` object `fromClient` may now be used to extract data from the channel using available methods such as `readLine()` whereas `PrintWriter` object `toClient` may be used to push the data to the channel using method such as `println()`. Note that the `readLine()` method of `BufferedReader` object also blocks the caller until an entire line of characters is received.

A summary of constructors and methods of `ServerSocket` class is provided in Appendix A.

13.4.2 The Socket Class

In this section, we shall discuss how to develop a client application. It was mentioned several times that a client process, prior to exchange of data, makes a request to establish a logical connection to the server socket object. This is done using `Socket` class. It has several overloaded constructors which can be used depending upon the requirement. The commonly used one makes a request to establish a socket connection with the specified host and the port.

```
Socket(String host, int port)
```

The host can be an IP address or a Fully Qualified Domain Name (FQDN). It can be any loop-back address (e.g. 127.0.0.1) or the name "localhost" if the server process runs on the computer where the client program also runs. The following statement makes a request to establish a socket connection to the process running at `localhost` (local computer) on port `6789`:

```
Socket clientEnd = new Socket("localhost", 6789);
```

The above constructor does not block the caller. It simply sends a request and returns a `Socket` object. If the request is processed by an `accept()` method call at the server side, a *logical channel* [Figure 13.10: (ii)] between the client process and the server process is created. The object `clientEnd` represents the client end of this channel and is used to communicate with the server process subsequently. In case the server process does not process the request immediately as it is busy in doing some other job, no channel is created at that time [Figure 13.10: (i)]. However, the `Socket` object may be used to get streams for subsequent communications. But, for successful exchange of data, server must process the request and create a channel.

The constructor that we have used basically performs the following tasks:

- Creates a raw socket
- Binds it to an ephemeral port number
- Makes a connection request

If needed, these steps may be done separately. For example, to create a raw (not yet bound) socket, the following code may be used.

```
Socket clientEnd = new Socket();
```

This socket may be bound to some specified port or a port suggested by the system. The following code binds our socket to an ephemeral port.

```
clientEnd.bind(null);
```

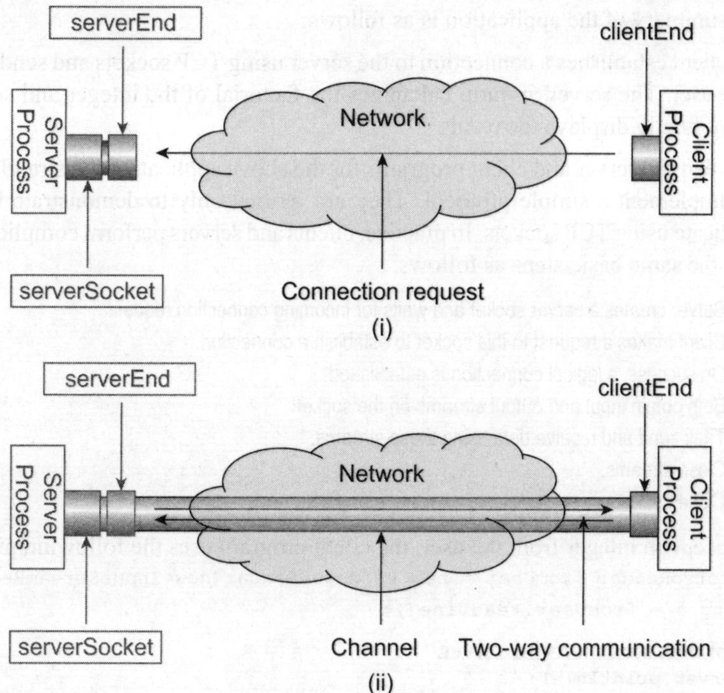

Figure 13.10: Function of socket constructor (i) Connection request sent by client but not processed by the server (ii) Connection request sent by the client and is processed by the server

The argument `null` indicates that the port should be chosen by the system. Finally, a connection request is made as follows:

```
clientEnd.connect(new InetSocketAddress("localhost",6789));
```

The `Socket` has other overloaded constructors also. A summary of constructors and methods of `Socket` class is provided in Appendix B:

Once a `Socket` object is created, the client process, like the server process, obtains `InputStream` and `OutputStream` objects to send data to or receive data from the socket.

```
BufferedReader fromServer = new BufferedReader(new
  InputStreamReader(clientEnd.getInputStream()));
PrintWriter  toServer = new PrintWriter(clientEnd.getOutputStream(), true);
```

The above code creates a `BufferedReader` object and a `PrintWriter` object to read from and write to the socket. At this point both the client and the server are ready to communicate with each other.

13.4.3 An Application

In this section, we shall develop a simple but elegant application using the TCP socket. We shall first write a client program (namely `TCPFactClient.java`) that wants to find the factorial of an integer. We shall also develop a server program (namely `TCPFactServer.java`) that can calculate the factorial of a given integer. We assume that the client has somehow obtained this news that there exists a server program which is capable of calculating the factorial of a specified integer. Consequently, client has decided to make use of this server to have the result. However, to communicate with the server, client needs to know the address and port number of server socket created by the server program. We assume that, client has also collected this information somehow. Let us now see how this client calculates the factorial of a number with the help of server.

The summary of the application is as follows:

The client establishes a connection to the server using TCP sockets and sends an integer obtained from the user. The server, in turn, calculates the factorial of the integer and sends the result back. The client finally displays the result.

Note that the server and client programs for the above application are straightforward and simple as they implement a simple protocol. They are written only to demonstrate how two parties can communicate using TCP sockets. In practice, clients and servers perform complicated tasks. However, they use the same basic steps as follows:

- Server creates a server socket and waits for incoming connection request.
- Client makes a request to this socket to establish a connection.
- On success, a logical connection is established.
- Both obtain input and output streams on the socket.
- They send and receive data using these streams.
- Close streams.
- Close socket.

To accept an integer from the user, the client program uses the following piece of code:

```
BufferedReader fromUser = new BufferedReader(new InputStreamReader(System.in));
String n = fromUser.readLine();
```

Client then sends it to the server.

```
toServer.println(n);
```

The server program retrieves the data using the following piece of code.

```
int n = Integer.parseInt(fromClient.readLine());
```

Since the `readLine()` method of `BufferedReader` class returns a string value, it is necessary to convert the string value to the corresponding integer value. This is accomplished using the `parseInt()` method on the wrapper class `Integer`. Once the number is obtained, the server then calculates the factorial of that number and stores it in a variable `fact` using the following piece of code.

```
int fact= 1;
for(int i=2;i<=n;i++)
   fact*=i;
```

The calculated factorial is then sent back to the client.

```
toClient.println(fact);
```

Finally, the client reads the result from the socket and prints it using the following code:

```
fact = fromServer.readLine();
System.out.println("Received from server: " + fact);
```

13.4.4 Complete Example

Here is the complete source code of the server stored in the file `TCPFactServer.java`.

```
//TCPFactServer.java
import java.io.*;
import java.net.*;
public class TCPFactServer {
  public static void main(String argv[]) throws Exception {
    //create a server socket at port 6789
    ServerSocket serverSocket = new ServerSocket(6789);
    //wait for incoming connection
    System.out.println("Server is listening on port 6789");
    Socket serverEnd = serverSocket.accept();
```

```
        System.out.println("Request accepted");
        //get streams
        BufferedReader fromClient = new BufferedReader(new
    InputStreamReader(serverEnd.getInputStream()));
        PrintWriter toClient = new PrintWriter(serverEnd.getOutputStream(), true);
        //receive data from client
        int n = Integer.parseInt(fromClient.readLine());
        System.out.println("Received from client: " + n);
        int fact = 1;
        for (int i = 2; i <= n; i++)
           fact *= i;
        //send result to the client
        toClient.println(fact);
        System.out.println("Sent to client: " + fact);
      }
    }
```

Here is the complete source code of the client stored in the file `TCPFactClient.java`.

```
    //TCPFactClient.java
    import java.io.*;
    import java.net.*;
    public class TCPFactClient {
      public static void main(String argv[]) throws Exception {
        String fact;
        //create a socket to the server
        Socket clientEnd = new Socket("localhost", 6789);
        System.out.println("Connected to localhost at port 6789");
        //get streams
        PrintWriter toServer = new PrintWriter(clientEnd.getOutputStream(), true);
        BufferedReader fromServer = new BufferedReader(new
    InputStreamReader(clientEnd.getInputStream()));
        BufferedReader fromUser = new BufferedReader
        (new InputStreamReader(System.in));
        //get an integer from user
        System.out.print("Enter an integer: ");
        String n = fromUser.readLine();
        //send it to server
        toServer.println(n);
        System.out.println("Sent to server: " + n);
        //retrieve result
        fact = fromServer.readLine();
        System.out.println("Received from server: "+ fact);
        //close the socket
        clientEnd.close();
      }
    }
```

13.4.5 Running Example Program

We have assumed that both the client and the server programs run on the same computer. If they run on different computers, the client program must specify the address of the computer where the server process is running. For example, if the server program runs on the port 8765 on a computer having IP address `192.168.1.2`, the following line of code should be used by the client to establish a socket connection with the server.

```
Socket clientEnd = new Socket("192.168.1.2", 8765);
```

Now, open a terminal and go to the directory containing the source file `TCPFactServer.java`. To compile the server program use the following command:

```
javac TCPFactServer.java
```

Start the server as follows:

```
java TCPFactServer
```

Now, open another terminal and go to the directory containing the source file `TCPFactClient.java`.

Compile the client program using the following command:

```
javac TCPFactClient.java
```

Now, start the client as follows:

```
java TCPFactClient
```

A sample output is shown in Figure 13.11:

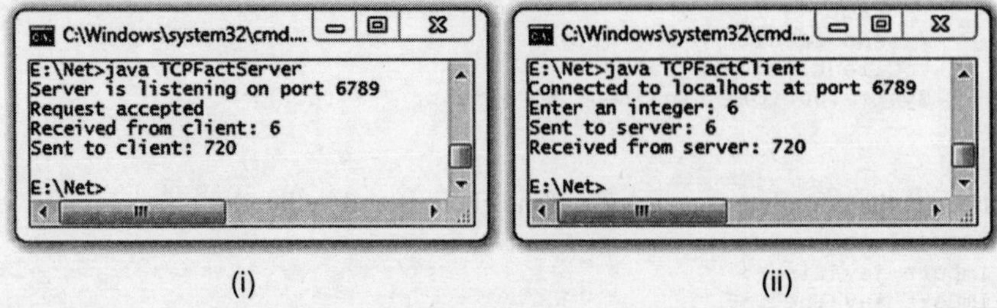

Figure 13.11: Communication using TCP socket (i) TCPFactServer (ii) TCPFactClient

The execution timeline is also shown in Figure 13.12:

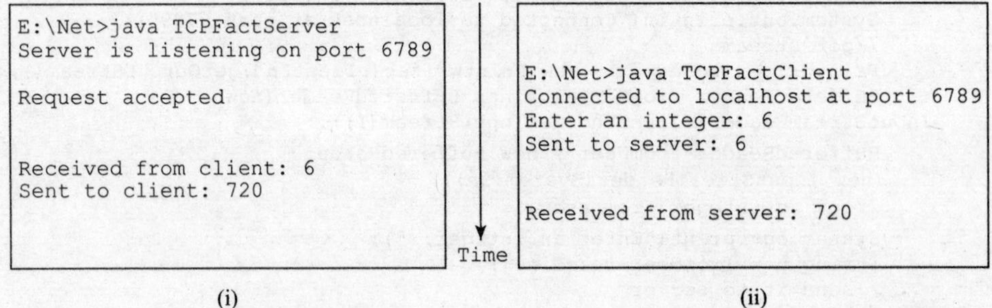

Figure 13.12: Execution timeline of TCP-based application (i) Server (ii) Client program

13.4.6 Handling Multiple Client Requests

Remember that in the server program (`TCPFactServer.java`), call of `accept()` method occurs only once. This means, our server can handle only one request. It quits after serving one client request. Ideally, a server process should be designed in such a way so that it can handle multiple requests (probably coming from many clients). In the following sections, we shall discuss possible implementations of the server to handle multiple requests using i) iterative way and ii) concurrent way.

13.4.6.1 Iterative Solution

One of the possible solutions to handle multiple clients is to implement the server that serves clients one after another. The idea is as follows:

The server program creates a `ServerSocket` object and invokes `accept()` method on it that results in the server program waiting for incoming connections. When a connection request from a client comes, accept method creates a logical connection between the server and the client and returns a `Socket` object that represents the server end of the logical channel. This `Socket` object is then used to handle all the communication with the client. If any more connection requests come during the communication, they initially wait in the First Come First Served (FIFO) queue associated with the server socket object. When the communication with the current client is over, the server again invokes the `accept()` method that takes a request from the head of the queue and repeats the procedure all over again [Figure 13.13:].

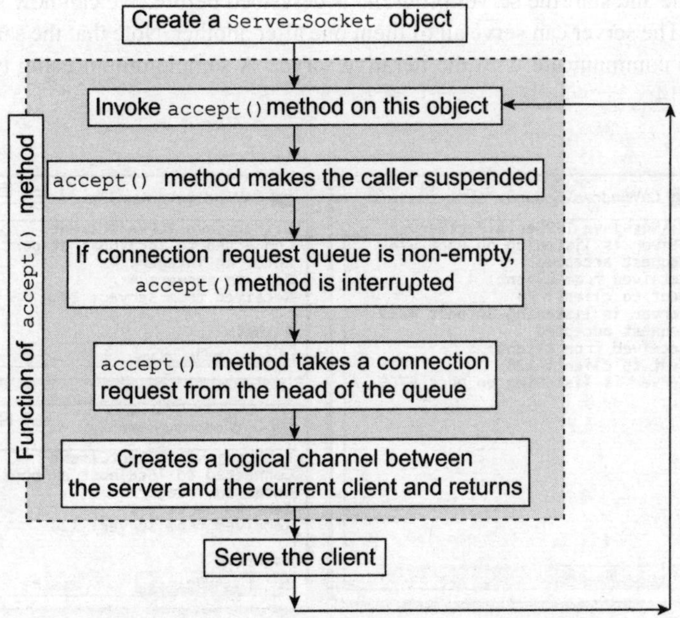

Figure 13.13: Architecture of an iterative server

The following is the source code for our modified server stored in the file `TCPSerialFactServer.java`:

```
//TCPSerialFactServer.java
import java.io.*;
import java.net.*;
public class TCPSerialFactServer {
  public static void main(String argv[]) throws Exception {
    //create a server socket at port 6789
    ServerSocket serverSocket = new ServerSocket(6789);
    while(true) {
      //wait for incoming connection
      System.out.println("Server is listening on port 6789");
      Socket serverEnd = serverSocket.accept();

      System.out.println("Request accepted");
      //get streams
      BufferedReader fromClient = new BufferedReader(new
InputStreamReader(serverEnd.getInputStream()));
      PrintWriter toClient = new PrintWriter(serverEnd.getOutputStream(),
true);
      //receive data from client
      int n = Integer.parseInt(fromClient.readLine());
      System.out.println("Received from client: " + n);
      int fact = 1;
      for (int i = 2; i <= n; i++)
        fact *= i;
```

```
            //send result to the client
            toClient.println(fact);
            System.out.println("Sent to client: " + fact);
         }
      }
   }
```

Compile and start the server program as described before. We can now start as many clients as you wish. The server can serve all of them one after another. Note that the same client program may be used to communicate with the iterative server. A sample output using two clients is shown in Figure 13.14:

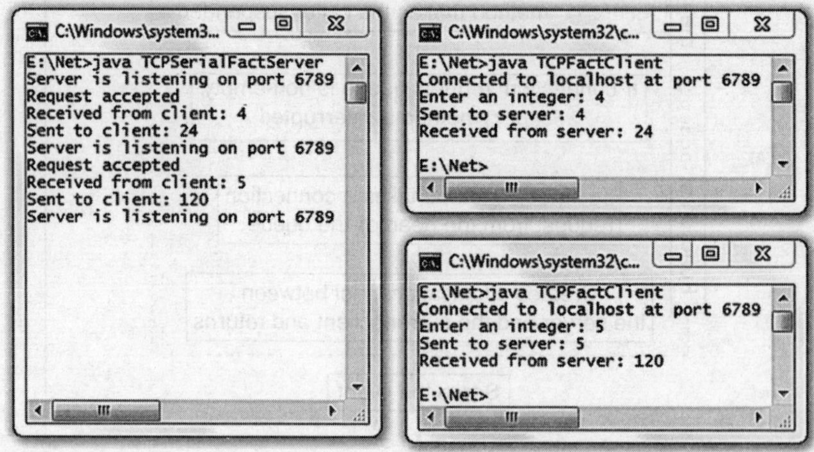

Figure 13.14: TCP Iterative Server and Clients

13.4.7 Concurrently Solution

The iterative server we have designed in the previous section can handle many clients but one at a time. In this design, during communication between the server and a client if a further connection request comes, they wait until the server completes the current communication. These requests are also handled on a First-Come-First-Served basis later. However, this design has some inherent problem. Firstly, a client having longer processing time blocks another client that has relatively smaller processing time and has made a connection request just after the former client. This is because the client that makes a request later has to wait until the server serves the client that made the connection request earlier. Secondly, during a communication session, the server does not usually always use all of its available resources to serve the client. Hence, overall resource utilization at the server end is not optimal. To have a better server-resource utilization and better response time for all the clients, the server may be designed in such a way that it can serve multiple requests concurrently. The following arrangements can be made in the server to implement this:

- Listen for incoming connection.
- Accept a new connection request and create a channel.
- Create a new thread; hand over the channel to this thread
- Go to the listening mode again to accept further connections immediately.
- The thread handles the client request independently using the channel and finally terminates.

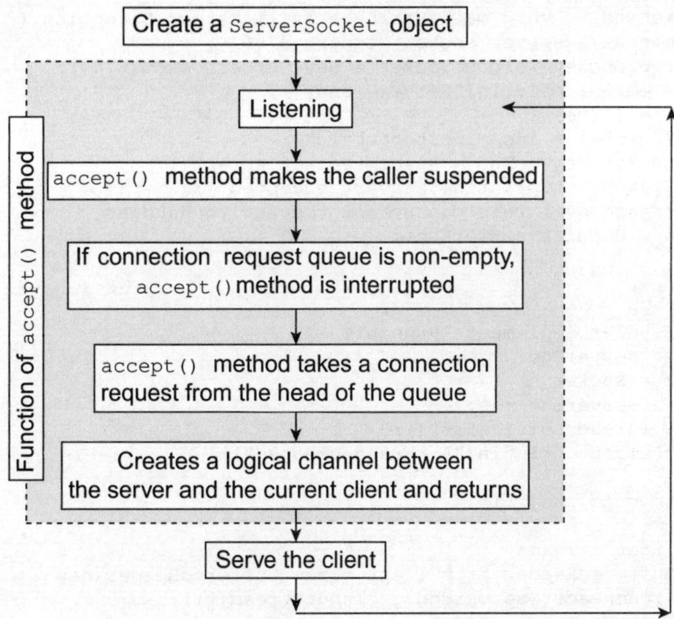

The idea behind the concurrent server is very simple. In this design, the server (main thread) initially listens for incoming client requests. When a request comes, it establishes a socket connection. However, instead of handling the request by itself, it spawns a new thread and handovers this connection to the thread which can handle the client request. The server then immediately goes to the listening mode again so that it can take actions (creating another thread and so on.). The thread runs in parallel and serves the client through the socket connection assigned. So, main thread is solely responsible to accept incoming requests, whereas client requests are explicitly handled by the respective threads. Since, threads run concurrently (OS schedules them), clients are served concurrently. Even if a thread takes a long time to serve a client, other threads (hence other clients) need not wait.

To implement the above idea, we first write a class `Handler` extending `java.lang.Thread` class. So, a `Handler` object represents a thread. The `Handler` objects will be created exclusively to handle client requests. So, a `Handler` object needs something using which it can continue to communicate with a client. Note that, a `Socket` object (that represents one end of the communication channel) may be used to exchange data through the channel. So, we write a constructor in the `Handler` class that takes a `Socket` object as an argument. For our factorial application, this `Socket` object is used to receive an integer from the client and send the factorial of that integer. Since, `Handler` class extends, `java.lang.Thread`, it is necessary to implement the `run()` method. When the thread is started, this method is executed concurrently with other threads. So, we need to write the necessary code in this method to handle a client. The thread is started by the constructor itself so that as soon as the thread object is created, is starts handling the client assigned to it.

The following is the source code for our modified server stored in the file `TCPMTFactServer.java`:

```
//TCPMTFactServer.java
import java.io.*;
import java.net.*;
class TCPMTFactServer {
```

```
    public static void main(String argv[]) throws Exception {
      //create a server socket at port 6789
      ServerSocket welcomeSocket = new ServerSocket(6789);
      System.out.println("Server ready");
      while (true) {
        //wait for incoming connection
        Socket serverEnd = welcomeSocket.accept();
        System.out.println("Request accepted");
        //hand over this connection request to Handler
        new Handler(serverEnd);
      }
    }
  }
  class Handler implements Runnable {
    Socket serverEnd;
    Handler(Socket s) {
      this.serverEnd = s;
      new Thread(this).start();
      System.out.println("A thread created");
    }
    public void run() {
      try {
        //get streams
        BufferedReader fromClient = new BufferedReader(new
  InputStreamReader(serverEnd.getInputStream()));
        PrintWriter toClient = new PrintWriter(serverEnd.getOutputStream(),
          true);
        while (true) {
          //receive data from client
          int n = Integer.parseInt(fromClient.readLine());
          System.out.println("Received " + n);
          if (n == -1) {
            serverEnd.close();
            break;
          }
          int fact = 1;
          for (int i = 2; i <= n; i++)
            fact *= i;
          //send result to the client
          toClient.println(fact);
          System.out.println("Sent: " + fact);
        }
      } catch (IOException e) { }
    }
  }
```

Originally, our server program calculates factorial of one integer given by the client and terminates closing the socket connection. So, each time a client wants to calculate factorial of an integer, it needs to establish a new connection. Note that, establishing a (TCP) connection is done through a 3-way handshaking procedure. Moreover, terminating a connection is even costlier. It uses a 4-way handshaking procedure. Needless to say that this complex procedures of connection establishment and termination impose a significant overhead. To improve the performance in terms of response time, the following idea may be adopted:

After calculating factorial of a given integer, the connection is not closed immediately; rather it is kept open. If the client wants, it may use the same connection to find factorial of more integers. The connection is finally disconnected if both of the communicating parties decide that the connection is no longer needed. This way, the overall response time may be reduced significantly. Keeping this idea in our mind, the `run()` (which actually serves a client) method is modified so that a client can get multiple results though the same connection. Accordingly, we also need to modify out client program slightly so that it can send many integers one by one. To terminate, it sends a −1. The source code for the client stored in `TCPMTFactClient.java` is as follows:

```
//TCPMTFactClient.java
import java.io.*;
import java.net.*;
public class TCPMTFactClient {
  public static void main(String argv[]) throws Exception {
    String fact;
    //create a socket to the server
    Socket clientEnd = new Socket("localhost", 6789);
    System.out.println("connected to localhost at port 6789");
    //get streams
    PrintWriter toServer = new PrintWriter(clientEnd.getOutputStream(), true);
    BufferedReader fromServer = new BufferedReader(new
InputStreamReader(clientEnd.getInputStream()));
    BufferedReader fromUser = new BufferedReader(new
InputStreamReader(System.in));
    while (true) {
      //get an integer from user
      System.out.print("Enter an integer: ");
      String n = fromUser.readLine();
      //send it to server
      toServer.println(n);
      System.out.println("Sent to server: " + n);
      if (n.equals("-1"))
    break;
      //retrieve result
      fact = fromServer.readLine();
      System.out.println("Received from server: " + fact);
    }
    //close the socket
    clientEnd.close();
  }
}
```

Compile and start the server program as described previously. You can now start as many clients as you wish. The server can serve them simultaneously. A sample output using two clients is shown in Figure 13.15:

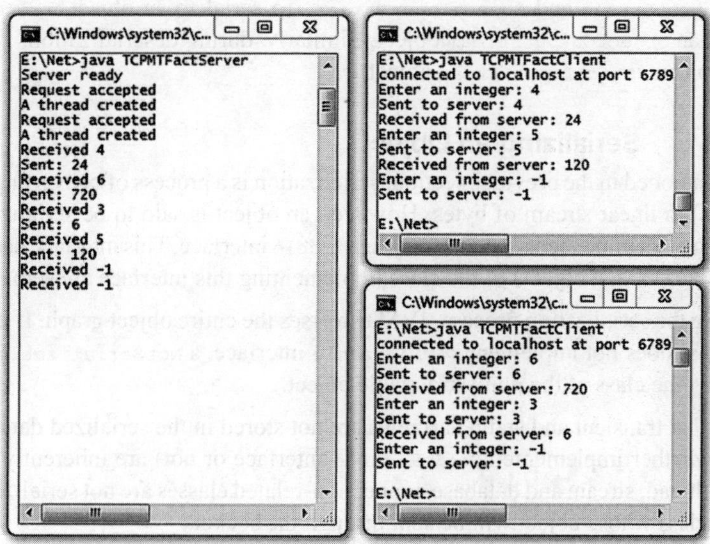

Figure 13.15: TCP Multi-threaded Server and Clients

If the computer where the server program runs is situated in a different network, the client's network must be configured properly. In particular, the IP address of the gateway must be specified. If the client's network is connected to the server's network through a proxy that supports sockets, use the following lines of code:

```
System.setProperty("socksProxyHost", "192.168.1.1");
System.setProperty("socksProxyPort", "1080");
```

Here, 1080 is the port number of the proxy process and 192.168.1.1 is the IP address of the host where the proxy runs. Alternatively, you can pass this information to the Java Runtime Environment during execution as follows:

```
java -DsocksProxyHost=192.168.1.1 -DsocksProxyPort=1080 TCPMTFactClient
```

13.4.8 Sending and Receiving Objects Using TCP

The applications that we have developed so far exchange data as a stream of bytes. It will be more convenient if applications can send and receive objects instead of raw byte stream. Java provides a powerful concept known as *serialization* that can be used to send an object through a socket. The idea behind the object serialization is very simple. The object to be sent is first converted to an equivalent linear stream of bytes. This byte stream is then sent through the socket in the usual way. The object can be restored at the receiving side using *deserialization* process. The serialized data may also be manipulated or even be stored in a persistent storage such as file for further use.

Note that an object to be serialized may have references to other objects, which, in turn, may have references to still more objects. There may be circular references. Objects may also refer to themselves. So, a set of related objects essentially form probably a complex directed graph. Serializing an object, in this case, means serializing all other referenced objects on the graph rooted by the context object also. This is sometimes called deep serialization. Similarly, during the deserialization process, all these objects must be restored (deep deserialization) correctly. However, there is nothing to worry. Java provides the serialization and deserialization facilities implementing all those issues correctly. Programmers need not even know the underlying serialization and deserialization algorithms. These algorithms have been implemented in two high-level stream classes `ObjectOutputStream` and `ObjectInputStream`. To serialize an object, `writeObject()` method is called on an `ObjectOutputStream` object. Similarly, during deserialization, `readObject()` method is called on an `ObjectInputStream` object.

13.4.8.1 Serializing an Object

As mentioned in the previous section, serialization is a process of converting an object (or a graph of objects) to linear stream of bytes. However, an object is said to be serializable provided that its underlying class implements `java.io.Serializable` interface. This interface has no methods or fields. It only indicates that objects of the class implementing this interface are semantically serializable.

During the serialization process, JVM traverses the entire object graph. If it encounters an object whose class does not implement `Serializable` interface, a `NotSerializableException` is thrown identifying the class of the non-serializable object.

Note that transient and static variables are not stored in the serialized data. Also note that some classes (whether implemented `Serializable` interface or not) are inherently non-serializable. For example thread, stream and database connection-related classes are not serializable. Let us now write a simple class whose object will be sent through the socket.

```
class Message implements java.io.Serializable {
  String subject, text;
```

```
   Message(String s, String t) {
      this.subject = s;
      this.text = t;
   }
   String getSubject() {
      return subject;
   }
   String getText() {
      return text;
   }
}
```

This simple class represents a message having a subject and body text. A `Message` object contains only two `String` member variables `subject` and `text` that will contain the subject and body of the message. The class implements `Serializable` interface. The `java.lang.String` class also implements `Serializable` interface. So, `Message` objects are indeed serializable.

Let us now understand the procedure of serializing an object. To serialize an object, we have to create an `ObjectOutputStream` object first. This is a stream that implements serialization part. The actual conversion of our object to the byte array is then done using `writeObject()` method on `ObjectOutputStream` object. This class also defines a set of other useful methods for serializing variables of built-in type. As we have mentioned earlier, the resultant byte array may be used in primarily three ways:

- Store the serialized data in a persistent storage such as file using class `FileOutputStream`
- Store the serialized data in simple byte array using class `ByteArrayOutputStream`
- Send the serialized data through the socket directly without storing them for further usage

The last mechanism is useful to send the data over a TCP socket, whereas the second one may be used to send data as a datagram packet. In this section we shall use the last mechanism. So, an `ObjectOutputStream` object is created using the following way:

```
ObjectOutputStream oos = new ObjectOutputStream(socket.getOutputStream());
```

Since we want to send serialized data over the socket, the `ObjectOutputStream` object is created from socket's `OutputStream`. This `oos` object has now a reference to the socket's `OutputStream`. Let us now create an object to be serialized:

```
Message msg = new Message("Remainder","Return my book on Monday");
```

This is a simple `Message` object that represents a remainder. The `ObjectOutputStream` class contains many methods for serializing various data types. But we are interested in the following method.

```
public final void writeObject(Object x) throws IOException
```

This method serializes the specified object. So, to serialize our Message object, the following code may be used.

```
oos.writeObject(msg);
```

Since, `oos` has a reference to the socket's `OutputStream`, `writeObject()` method serializes `msg` and directly sends the serialized byte array through the socket. At the receiving end, the Message object is restored back from the serialized data using a procedure called deserialization. Here is the complete source code of a program (namely `TCPObjectSender.java`) that sends an object over TCP connection.

```
//TCPObjectSender.java
import java.io.*;
import java.net.*;
public class TCPObjectSender {
   public static void main(String argv[]) throws Exception {
```

```
        String fact;
        //create a socket to the server
        Socket socket = new Socket("172.16.5.81", 6789);
        System.out.println("Connected to localhost at port 6789");
        //Create a Message object to be sent
        Message msg = new Message("Remainder","Return my book on Monday");
        //Create an ObjectOutputStream object
        ObjectOutputStream oos = new
  ObjectOutputStream(socket.getOutputStream());
        //Serialize and send over TCP
        oos.writeObject(msg);
        System.out.println("Sent an object");
        socket.close();
    }
}
```

13.4.8.2 Reconstructing Objects

The counterpart of `ObjectOutputStream` is the `java.io.ObjectInputStream` class that implements deserialization part. Like `ObjectOutputStream`, it also defines a set of useful methods to read the serialized data.

To restore the object back, we first create an `ObjectInputStream` object from an `InputStream` that contains the serialized data. Since serialized data comes through the socket, `InputStream` of the socket is used to create `ObjectInputStream` object as follows:

```
ObjectInputStream in  = new ObjectInputStream(socket.getInputStream());
```

Like, `ObjectOutputStream`, the `ObjectInputStream` class also contains the following method for deserializing an object:

```
public final Object readObject() throws IOException, ClassNotFoundException
```

This method retrieves data for the next `Object` from the input stream. It then deserializes the data to form the object. Since, the return value is `Object` (the top level Java class) we should cast it to the appropriate data type. So, the following code may be used to get out `Message` object back:

```
Message msg = (Message) in.readObject();
```

Here is the complete source code of the program (namely `TCPObjectReceiver.java`) that receives an object over TCP connection.

```
//TCPObjectReceiver.java
import java.io.*;
import java.net.*;
public class TCPObjectReceiver {
   public static void main(String argv[]) throws Exception {
      //create a server socket at port 6789
      ServerSocket serverSocket = new ServerSocket(6789);
      //wait for incoming connection
      System.out.println("Server is listening on port 6789");
      Socket socket = serverSocket.accept();
      System.out.println("Request accepted");
      //Create an ObjectInputStream Object
      ObjectInputStream in  = new ObjectInputStream(socket.getInputStream());
      //Restore the object
      Message msg = (Message) in.readObject();
      //Print the mesaage
      System.out.println("Received a message:");
      System.out.println("subject : " + msg.getSubject()+"\nbody :
 "+msg.getText());
   }
}
```

Compile the sender program `TCPObjectSender.java`, the receiver program `TCPObjectReceiver.java` and `Message.java`. Note that to reconstruct a `Message` object, its class definition is required. So, before starting the receiver program, make sure that the directory contains `Message.class` file. Start the application now. A sample output is shown in Figure 13.16:

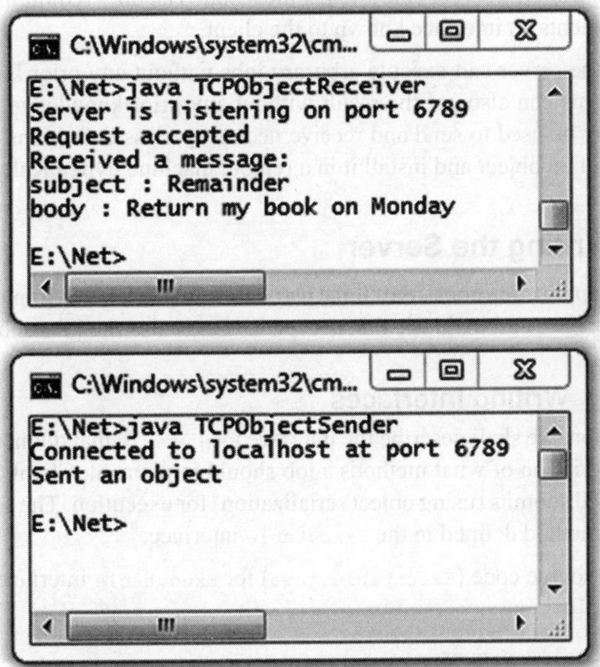

Figure 13.16: Sending and receiving objects through TCP

13.4.9 An Example

In this section, we shall develop a simple but elegant distributed application using TCP socket. In this application [Figure 13.17:], the server accepts jobs from the clients, executes these jobs locally, calculates the execution time, and finally returns the output as well as completion time. This way, clients can execute their jobs remotely on a powerful computer, or a computer having specialized hardware or one that has special permission.

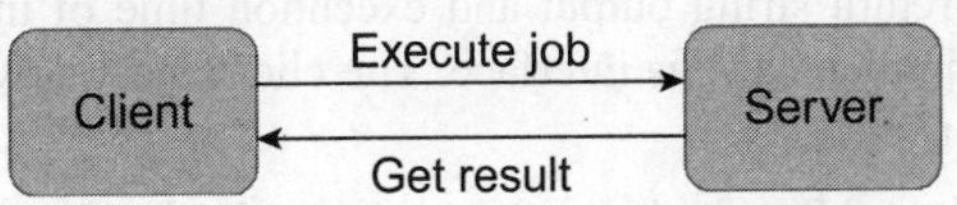

Figure 13.17: Remote job execution scenario

The interesting part of the application is that the server does not have to define the jobs that it executes. Clients can create their custom jobs as and when required and submit them to the server for execution. The only restriction imposed on a job is that its class must implement an interface defined by the server. The class definition of a job is also sent by the client that submits the job through socket. Once the class file is available, the server can execute the job locally using its own resource.

How can a server return the result to the client? If the result's class is a built-in class, the client already has the class definition and can use it easily. However, if the result's class is a server-defined custom class, how can the client get it? Again there is no problem, since the client can download the class definition from the server side and get the result. The only requirement of a result object is that its class implements an interface known to the client.

This way, the server can execute arbitrary jobs without any prior knowledge of the job's class definition. Clients can also get the result without any prior knowledge of result's class definition. The socket may be used to send and receive necessary class definitions. This way, we may change the behaviour of an object and install it in a remote machine dynamically.

13.4.10 Writing the Server

The server application consists of three parts: Result interface, an implementation of that interface, Executable interface and main file that accepts and executes the jobs submitted by the client.

13.4.10.1 Writing Interfaces

In this section, we shall describe the interface `Executable` that defines the client's view of job. It provides a description of what methods a job should implement. Client creates a job implementing this interface and submits (using object serialization) for execution. The server restores the job object and invokes a method defined in the `Executable` interface.

Here is the source code (`Executable.java`) for `Executable` interface.

```
//Executable.java
public interface Executable {
  public String execute();
}
```

The interface has a single method `execute()`. The server will invoke this method on jobs submitted by the clients. This method should return all the output as a single string. The server also calculates the execution time and creates a Result object and sends back to the client.

The `Result` interface describes the structure of the result returned after executing the job. Here is the source code (`Result.java`) for `Result` interface.

```
public interface Result {
    String output();
    double completionTime();
}
```

It defines two methods, `output()` and `completionTime()`. The methods `output()` and `completionTime()` return string output and execution time of the job, respectively. The `Result` object's class must implement this interface. The client must download this `Result` object's class definition to get the result.

Since, Executable and Result objects are exchanged using Java's *object serialization* procedure, classes that implement `Executable` and `Result` must implement the `java.io.Serializable` interface.

13.4.10.2 Implementing Interfaces

The server only defines one class `ResultImpl` which implements `Result` interface. Here is the source code (`ResultImpl.java.`) for `ResultImpl` class.

```
import java.io.Serializable;
public class ResultImpl implements Result, Serializable {
  String output;
  double completionTime;
  public ResultImpl(String o, double c) {
    output = o;
    completionTime = c;
  }
  public String output() { return output; }
  public double completionTime() { return completionTime; }
}
```

An object of this class represents the result of a job in terms of its output and completion time. This result object, generated by a job at the server end, will be transferred to the client side and hence must be serializable. This object is indeed serializable as its class implements the `Serializable` interface. The definition of `ResultImpl` must be downloaded to the client side to reconstruct the result object.

The client only defines one class `Job` which implements `Executable` interface. Here is the source code (`Job.java`.) for `Job` class.

```
//Job.java
import java.io.Serializable;
public class Job implements Executable, Serializable {
  public String execute() {
    int n = 5, prod = 1;
    for(int i = 2; i <= n; i++)
      prod *= i;
    return (new Integer(prod)).toString();
  }
}
```

A `Job` object submitted by the client is transferred to the server side and hence must be serializable. This object is indeed serializable as its class implements the `Serializable` interface. The definition of `Job` must be downloaded to the server side to reconstruct the job object.

13.4.10.3 Implementing Server

```
//TCPServer.java
import java.io.*;
import java.net.*;

public class TCPServer {
  public static void main(String argv[]) throws Exception {

    //create a server socket at port 6789
    ServerSocket serverSocket = new ServerSocket(6789);
    //wait for incoming connection
    System.out.println("Server is listening on port 6789");
    Socket socket = serverSocket.accept();
    System.out.println("Request accepted");

    ObjectInputStream in  = new ObjectInputStream(socket.getInputStream());

    String classFile = (String)in.readObject();

    byte[] b = (byte[])in.readObject();
    FileOutputStream fos = new FileOutputStream(classFile);
    fos.write(b);

    Executable ex = (Executable)in.readObject();
    System.out.print("Starting execution...");
```

```
        double startTime = System.nanoTime();
        String output = ex.execute();
        double endTime = System.nanoTime();
        double completionTime = endTime-startTime;
        System.out.println("[ DONE ]");
        ResultImpl r = new ResultImpl(output, completionTime);

        ObjectOutputStream out  = new ObjectOutputStream(socket.
getOutputStream());
        classFile = "ResultImpl.class";
        out.writeObject(classFile);

        FileInputStream fis = new FileInputStream(classFile);
        byte[] bo = new byte[fis.available()];
        fis.read(bo);
        out.writeObject(bo);

        out.writeObject(r);
        System.out.print("Result sent");
        socket.close();
      }
    }
```

13.4.10.4 Implementing Client

```
//TCPClient.java
import java.io.*;
import java.net.*;
public class TCPClient {
  public static void main(String args[]) throws Exception {
    //create a socket to the server
    Socket socket = new Socket(args[0], 6789);
    System.out.println("Connected to localhost at port 6789");

    ObjectOutputStream out = new ObjectOutputStream(socket.getOutputStream());

    String classFile = "Job.class";
    out.writeObject(classFile);

    FileInputStream fis = new FileInputStream(classFile);
    byte[] b = new byte[fis.available()];
    fis.read(b);
    out.writeObject(b);

    Job aJob = new Job();
    out.writeObject(aJob);

    System.out.println("Submitted a job for execution");
    ObjectInputStream in  = new ObjectInputStream(socket.getInputStream());
    classFile = (String)in.readObject();

    b = (byte[])in.readObject();
    FileOutputStream fos = new FileOutputStream(classFile);
    fos.write(b);

    Result r = (Result)in.readObject();
    System.out.println("result = "+r.output()+", time taken =
"+r.completionTime()+" ns");
    socket.close();
  }
}
```

13.4.10.5 Running the Example

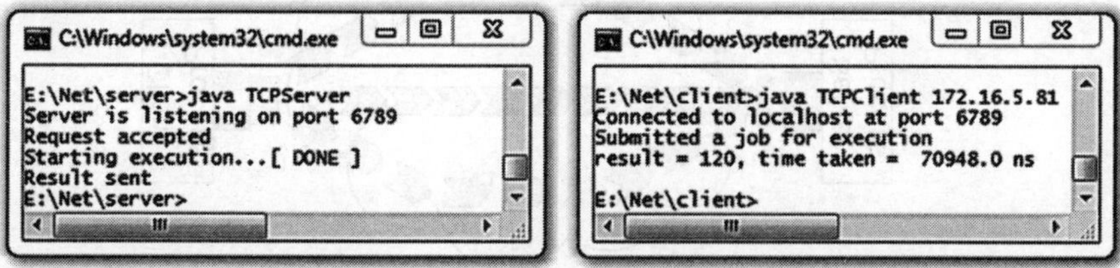

13.5 UDP SOCKETS

In the previous sections, we have discussed how to develop network applications using stream sockets. Communication with a server using stream socket basically consists of two steps. First, create a channel with the server at the desired port. Then, send and receive data through this channel. The stream socket provides reliable communication of ordered stream of bytes, since it uses TCP as the underlying transport layer protocol.

However, TCP provides this reliability and data ordering using complicated algorithms using retransmission (probably many times). Consequently, the performance (in terms of delay) of TCP in case of data loss or network congestion is not satisfactory. Moreover, there exists certain applications (that transmit/receive real time data such as audio, video etc), that expects quick delivery of data instead of ordered and correct delivery. For example, in the case of video transmission, the frames should come continuously, failing of which results in an unpleasant experience to the viewers. However, loss of a few frames in the continuous flow of frames does not degrade the quality of the video so much. For such applications, quick delivery of data is more important than correct and ordered delivery of data. Since, TCP always try to recover an erroneous or lost data frame, it fails to deliver data quickly, in the presence of error and hence is not suitable for real-time applications.

An alternative way to develop such real-time applications is to use datagram sockets that use UDP as the underlying transport layer protocol. In the following sections, we shall discuss how programs exchange data using UDP sockets.

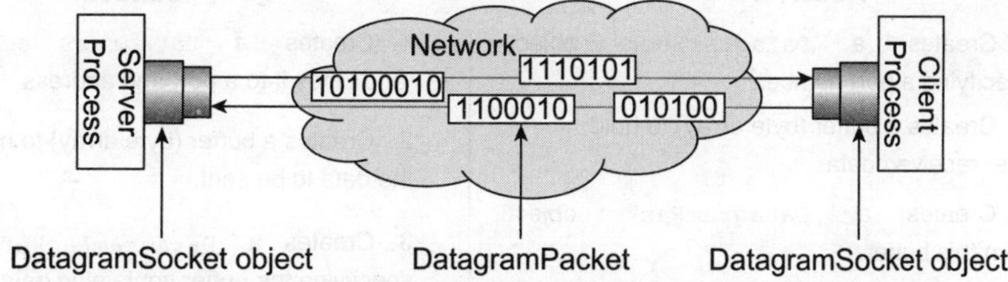

Figure 13.18: Communication using UDP sockets where no explicit communication channel is created

UDP socket allows data communication using a mechanism different from one used in TCP. In the UDP style of communication, no connection with the server socket is established prior to exchange of data [Figure 13.8:]. Instead, two DatagramSocket objects are created and data is sent and received using containers called *datagrams*. The receiver program first creates a datagram socket and waits for the incoming datagrams. A sender program, on the other hand, creates a datagram packet, specifies the IP address and the port number of the server, and puts it on the network. The datagram packet is then forwarded by possibly many intermediate hosts and eventually reaches the server.

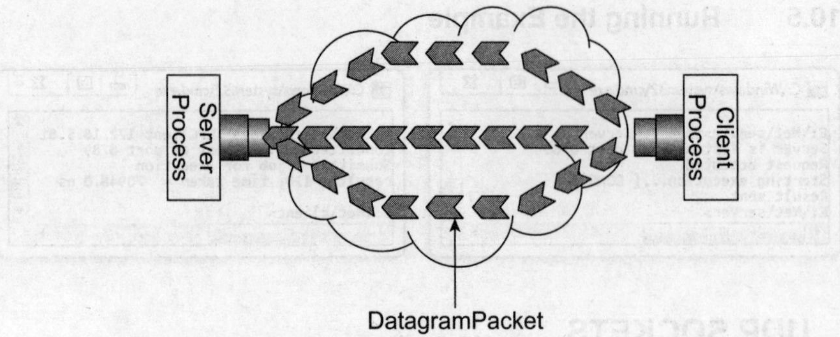

Figure 13.19: Different datagrams may traverse different paths

Note that the packet may be lost on its way or some error may occur in the packet data (payload). Since, recovering the packet may take significant time, UDP does not even try to recover the packet. Instead it concentrates on delivering other packets. It means, UDP does not guarantee that a datagram will arrive at the receiver. It does not also assure that a process will really be there to accept the datagram. Since, datagrams may traverse different paths [Figure 13.19:], there is no guarantee they will reach in the order in which they were sent. Even then, as explained earlier, this style of communication is desired in some situations such as real-time applications.

Let us now understand, how to develop network applications using UDP socket. Java provides two primary classes to develop UDP-based network applications: i) `DatagramSocket` and ii) `DatagramPacket`. A `DatagramPacket` object is a container (called packet) of data to be sent and/or received, whereas `DatagramSocket` is used to send and/or receive those packets. The basic idea [Figure 13.20:] of data communication using UDP socket is as follows:

Both of the communicating parties first create a `DatagramSocket` object. Like TCP socket, this socket is also bound to a port number. Usually, in the receiver program, an unused port number is assigned to the socket by the programmer. In the sender program, the responsibility is usually imposed

Receiver	**Sender**
1. Creates a `DatagramSocket` object, specifying a port number.	1. Creates a `DatagramS ocket` object, and binds it to a port and address.
2. Creates a buffer (byte array) to hold the received data.	2. Creates a buffer (byte array) to hold the data to be sent.
3. Creates a `DatagramPacket` object from this buffer.	3. Creates a `DatagramPacket` object specifying the buffer containing data and socket address of the `DatagramSocket` object created by the receiver.
4. Calls `receive()` method on `DatagramSocket` object passing `DatagramPacket` object as an argument.	4. Calls `send()` method on `DatagramSocket` object passing `DatagramPacket` object as an argument.

time

Figure 13.20: Temporal flow of control in receiver and sender programs using UDP sockets

on the system. A process (call it sender) willing to send data to another process (call it receiver) creates a `DatagramPacket` object specifying the following information:

- A byte array containing the data (payload) to be sent and
- the socket address (IP address and port number) of the `DatagramSocket` object created by the receiver.

The packet is actually sent using `send()` method of `DatagramSocket` object.

On the other hand, the receiver of the packet also creates a `DatagramPacket` object specifying an array where the received data is stored. The packet is received by calling the `receive()` method of `DatagramSocket` object and passing the packet object as an argument. A summary of basic steps to be followed by the sender and receiver is shown in Figure 13.20:

13.5.1 Datagram Packets

Note that data is sent and/or received in terms of packets (also called datagrams). A datagram is represented in Java by a `DatagramPacket` object and can be created using one of the following constructors:

```
DatagramPacket(byte[] data, int size);
DatagramPacket(byte[] data, int size, InetAddress address, int port);
DatagramPacket(byte[] data, int size, int offset);
DatagramPacket(byte[] data, int size, int offset, InetAddress address,
int port);
DatagramPacket(byte[] data, int size, SocketAddress socket);
DatagramPacket(byte[] data, int size, int offset, SocketAddress socket)
```

In our application, to receive data, we shall use the first constructor. It takes two arguments:

- `data`–an array of bytes where the data bytes received are stored and
- `size`–number of bytes to be taken from the packet.

To send data, we shall use the second constructor. It takes four arguments.

- `Data`–an array of bytes containing data to be sent
- `Size`–number of bytes to be sent
- `Address`–IP address assigned to the `DatagramSocket` created by the receiver and
- `Port`–port number assigned to the `DatagramSocket` created by the receiver

There are many other useful methods available on `DatagramPacket` object to get and set the internal properties of the packet. A detailed description of constructors and methods of `DatagramPacket` can be found in Appendix D.

13.5.2 Datagram Server

Let us now develop our factorial application using UDP socket. Note that our server first receives an integer. So, the server first creates a `DatagramSocket` at a port (say 5000) as follows:

```
DatagramSocket socket = new DatagramSocket(5000);
```

The port *must* be an unused one otherwise it throws a `BindException`. The port must belong to the range from 0 to 65535. This port 5000 should be specified by our client in the packet to be sent.

Suppose the machine running this server process has one network interface card having IP address `192.168.1.2`. Then the socket address of the `DatagramSocket` object is `[192.168.1.2, 5000]`. A pictorial description is shown in Figure 13.21:

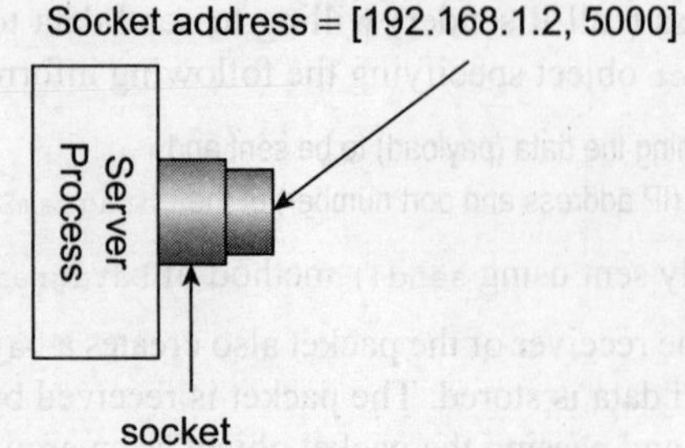

Figure 13.21: Creating a DatagramSocket Object

If the host has multiple network interface cards (hence multiple IP addresses), then this `DatagramSocket` is identifiable by all these interfaces, So, any one of the IP addresses may be specified in the `DatagramPacket` by a sender for delivery of packet. However, if required, a specific IP address may also be bound to the datagram socket using a different constructor [See appendix C for details].

To hold the data sent to this socket, the server program then creates a `DatagramPacket` object where incoming data will be stored.

```
byte[] rbuf = new byte[10];
DatagramPacket rpkt = new DatagramPacket(rbuf, rbuf.length);
```

To receive a `DatagramPacket`, it uses the `receive()` method on the `DatagramSocket` object created.

```
socket.receive(rpkt);
```

The method `receive()` is a blocking one. It means, the `DatagramSocket` waits for a packet to be received. The server comes up when a `DatagramPacket` destined to this socket arrives [Figure 13.22:].

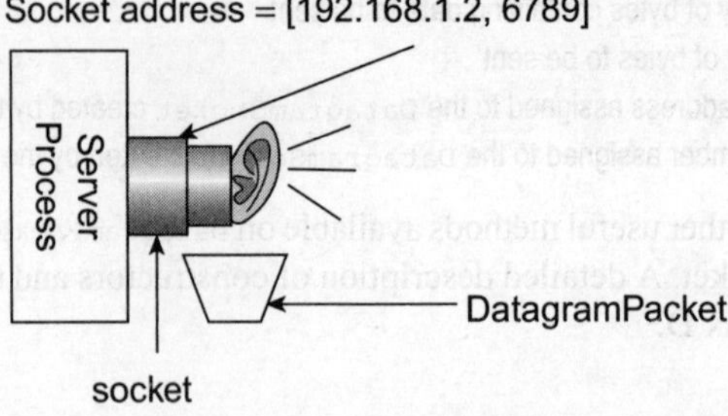

Figure 13.22: DatagramSocket is listening for incoming packets

After receiving a packet destined to it, the server program extracts the data from this packet and puts them on the array specified during creation of the packet. As mentioned earlier, `DatagramPacket` object has many useful methods to explore the packet. The following code creates a string from the data received.

```
String data = new String(rpkt.getData(), 0, rpkt.getLength());
```

Since, in our application, this string is actually an integer, it is converted to an integer using the following piece of code:

```
int n = Integer.parseInt(data);
```

The factorial of this integer is then calculated. To send the result back to the client, the server needs to extract socket information (IP address and port) of `DatagramSocket` object created by the client. This is done using the following piece of code:

```
InetAddress addr = rpkt.getAddress();
int port = rpkt.getPort();
```

The server then creates another `DatagramPacket` object specifying the factorial of the number and the socket information just extracted.

```
String sbuf = String.valueOf(fact).getBytes();
DatagramPacket spkt = new DatagramPacket(sbuf, sbuf.length, addr, port);
```

Finally the packet is forwarded towards the client as follows:

```
socket.send(spkt);
```

Here is the complete source code for our UDP server `UDPFactServer.java`.

```
//UDPFactServer.java
import java.net.*;
import java.io.*;
public class UDPFactServer {
    public static void main(String args[]) throws Exception {
        byte[] rbuf = new byte[10], sbuf = new byte[10];
        //create a server socket at port 5000
        DatagramSocket socket = new DatagramSocket(5000);
        System.out.println("Server ready");
        DatagramPacket rpkt = new DatagramPacket(rbuf, rbuf.length);
        //receive a packet from client
        socket.receive(rpkt);
        //extract data and client information from this packet
        String data = new String(rpkt.getData(), 0, rpkt.getLength());
        InetAddress addr = rpkt.getAddress();
        int port = rpkt.getPort();
        int fact = 1, n = Integer.parseInt(data);
        System.out.println("Received: " + n + " from " + addr + ":" + port);
        for (int i = 2; i <= n; i++)
            fact *= i;
        sbuf = String.valueOf(fact).getBytes();
        DatagramPacket spkt = new DatagramPacket(sbuf, sbuf.length, addr, por
        //send result to the client
        socket.send(spkt);
        System.out.println("Sent: " + fact);

    }
}
```

13.5.3 Datagram Client

Remember that our client first sends an integer to the server to get the factorial of the integer. So, it creates a `DatagramSocket` object.

```
DatagramSocket socket = new DatagramSocket();
```

Note that no port number or IP address of the server is specified here. The above line of code does not create a channel to the server, it simply creates a socket that will be used to send and receive packets. The `DatagramSocket` object is also assigned a locally unique port number by the system. This port number together with the IP address of the client will be encapsulated in the packet sent to the server. The server extracts this information to send the result (if any) back to the client [Figure 13.23:].

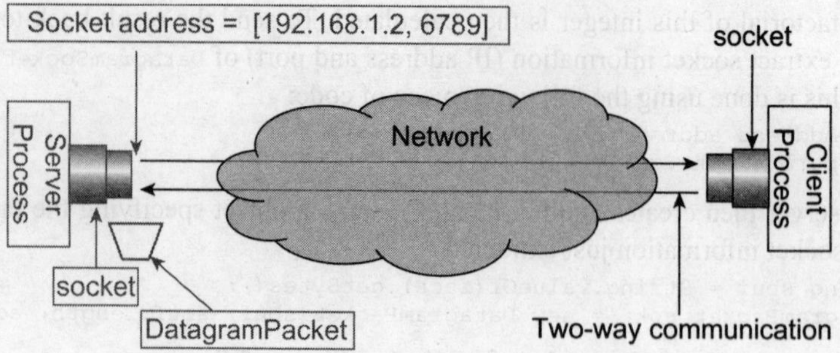

Figure 13.23: Client creates a DatagramSocket

It then accepts an integer from the user and creates a `DatagramPacket` with this data. It also specifies the address and port number of the server in the packet.

```
String data = fromUser.readLine();
sbuf = data.getBytes();
DatagramPacket spkt = new DatagramPacket(sbuf, sbuf.length, addr, 5000);
```

The client then sends the packet using the `send()` method on the `DatagramSocket` object. Whenever a reply comes back, it extracts the data and prints it. Here is the complete source code for UDP client `UDPFactClient.java`.

```
//UDPFactClient.java
import java.net.*;
import java.io.*;
public class UDPFactClient {
   public static void main(String args[]) throws Exception {
      byte[] rbuf = new byte[1024], sbuf = new byte[1024];
      BufferedReader fromUser =
         new BufferedReader(new InputStreamReader(System.in));
      DatagramSocket socket = new DatagramSocket();
      InetAddress addr = InetAddress.getByName(args[0]);
      //get an integer from user
      System.out.print("Enter an integer: ");
      String data = fromUser.readLine();
      sbuf = data.getBytes();
      DatagramPacket spkt = new DatagramPacket(sbuf, sbuf.length, addr, 5000);
      //send it to server
      socket.send(spkt);
      System.out.println("Sent to server: " + data);
      DatagramPacket rpkt = new DatagramPacket(rbuf, rbuf.length);
      //retrieve result
      socket.receive(rpkt);
      data = new String(rpkt.getData(), 0, rpkt.getLength());
      System.out.println("Received from server: " + data);
      //close the socket
      socket.close();
   }
}
```

Compile and run the programs as before. A sample output is shown in Figure 13.24: Note that we started sender and receiver in the same computer to test the correctness of the code. However, if they run on two different computers connected by a network, the sender should specify the socket address (IP and port) of the `DatagramSocket` object created by the receiver program, in the `DatagramPacket`. Also note that the receiver of a datagram should be started first.

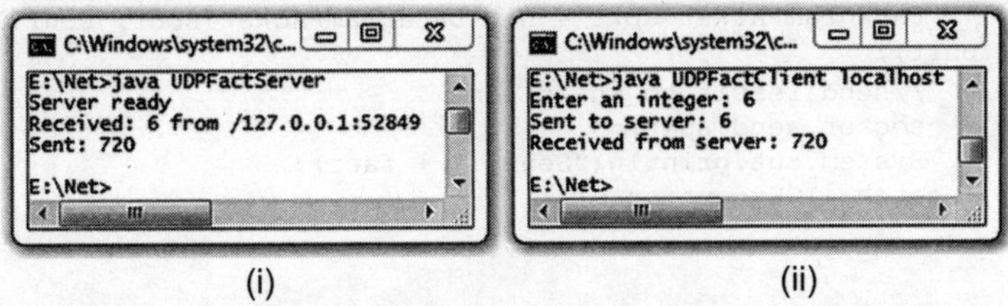

Figure 13.24: Communication using UDP socket (i) UDPFactServer (ii) UDPFactClient

13.5.4 Receiving Multiple Datagrams

We can extend our UDP server so that it can handle multiple requests simultaneously. Here is the complete source code for our multithread UDP server stored in the file `UDPMTFactServer.java`.

```
import java.net.*;
import java.io.*;
public class UDPMTFactServer {
   public static void main(String args[]) throws Exception {
      //create a server socket at port 5000
      DatagramSocket socket = new DatagramSocket(5000);
      System.out.println("Server ready");
      while (true) {
         byte[] rbuf = new byte[10];
         DatagramPacket rpkt = new DatagramPacket(rbuf, rbuf.length);
         //receive a packet from client
         socket.receive(rpkt);
         System.out.println("Receiver a packet");
         //hand over this packet to Handler
         new Handler(rpkt, socket);
      }
   }
}

class Handler implements Runnable {
   DatagramSocket socket;
   DatagramPacket pkt;
   Handler(DatagramPacket pkt, DatagramSocket socket) {
      this.pkt = pkt;
      this.socket = socket;
      new Thread(this).start();
      System.out.println("A thread created");
   }
   public void run() {
      try {
         byte[] sbuf = new byte[10];
         //extract data and client information from this packet
         String data = new String(pkt.getData(), 0, pkt.getLength());
         InetAddress addr = pkt.getAddress();
         int port = pkt.getPort();

         int fact = 1, n = Integer.parseInt(data);
         System.out.println("Received: " + n + " from " + addr + ":" + port);

         for (int i = 2; i <= n; i++)
            fact *= i;
         sbuf = String.valueOf(fact).getBytes();
```

```
            DatagramPacket spkt = new DatagramPacket(sbuf, sbuf.length,
addr, port);
            //send result to the client
            socket.send(spkt);
            System.out.println("Sent: " + fact);
         } catch (IOException e) { }
      }
}
```

To test our multithreaded server, we can write a UDP client as follows:

```
import java.net.*;
import java.io.*;
public class UDPMTFactClient {
   public static void main(String args[]) throws Exception {
      byte[] rbuf = new byte[1024], sbuf = new byte[1024];
      BufferedReader fromUser =
         new BufferedReader(new InputStreamReader(System.in));
      DatagramSocket socket = new DatagramSocket();
      InetAddress addr = InetAddress.getByName(args[0]);
      while(true) {
         //get an integer from user
         System.out.print("Enter an integer: ");
         String data = fromUser.readLine();
         sbuf = data.getBytes();
         DatagramPacket spkt = new DatagramPacket(sbuf, sbuf.length,
addr, 5000);
         //send it to server
         socket.send(spkt);
         System.out.println("Sent to server: " + data);
         if(data.equals("-1")) break;
         DatagramPacket rpkt = new DatagramPacket(rbuf, rbuf.length);
         //retrieve result
         socket.receive(rpkt);
         data = new String(rpkt.getData(), 0, rpkt.getLength());
         System.out.println("Received from server: " + data);
      }
      //close the socket
      socket.close();
      }
}
```

A sample output with two clients is shown in Figure 13.25:

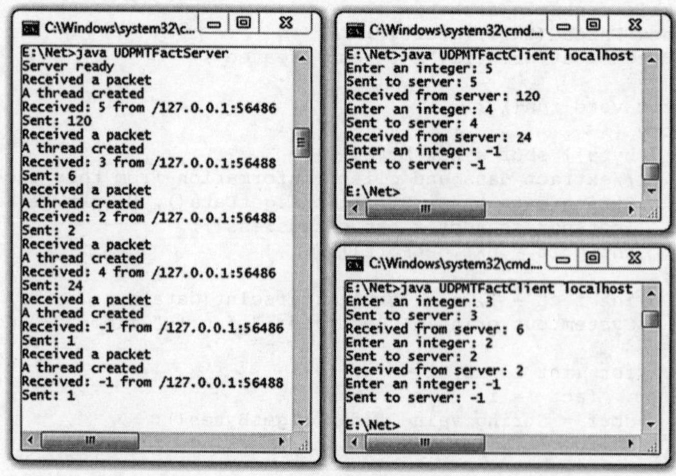

Figure 13.25: UDP Multi-threaded Server and Clients

13.5.5 Sending and Receiving Objects Using UDP

We explained earlier that sending and/or receiving data as objects is more convenient than sending them as a raw stream of bytes. We also developed a simple application where a `Message` object is sent by one program and received by another program using the TCP socket. In this section, we shall discuss how to develop similar applications using UDP sockets.

Note that UDP uses datagram as the container of data to be exchanged. So, whatever data we want to send, is first stored in a byte array which is then encapsulated in a datagram which is finally sent through the network. At the receiver end, the data bytes are extracted from the datagram and converted to the desired format. To send and receive an object, similar steps may be followed.

The object to be sent is first serialized and the resultant data bytes are placed in a byte array. This byte array is used to create a datagram. Finally, this datagram is sent over the network. Upon receiving the datagram, the receiver extracts the byte array from the datagram. These arrays of bytes (which is a linear representation of an object), is used to reconstruct the object using the deserialization procedure. Since we have already discussed how to exchange datagrams using DatagramSocket and DatagramPacket class, the only remaining task that we should know in this case is to create a datagram from a given object and to get the object back from the datagram.

13.5.6 Sending an Object

Let us first discuss the procedure of constructing a datagram containing serialized bytes of an object.

Let us create a Message object to be sent.

```
Message msg = new Message("Remainder","Return my book on Monday");
```

This is the object to be serialized to get the equivalent array of bytes. To serialize this object, we need an ObjectOutputStream object. Since, we want to store the serialized data in a byte array, `ObjectOutputStream` object is created using a `ByteArrayOutputStream` object.

```
ByteArrayOutputStream baos = new ByteArrayOutputStream();
ObjectOutputStream oos = new ObjectOutputStream(baos);
```

When the `ObjectOutputStream` serializes an object, it sends the resultant data to the `ByteArrayOutputStream` object from which the raw byte array may be extracted using `toByteArray()` method. Our `Message` object is serialized as shown in the following:

```
oos.writeObject(msg);
```

Finally, we obtain the array containing serialized data bytes of the `msg` object as follows:

```
byte[] out = baos.toByteArray();
```

So, at last we have an array of bytes. This is used to create a DatagramPacket which is sent over the network using the usual way. Here is the complete source code (stored in the file `UDPObjectSender.java`) of the program that sends a message object:

```
//UDPObjectSender.java
import java.net.*;
import java.io.*;
public class UDPObjectSender {
  public static void main(String[] args) {
    try {
      //Create a DatagramSocket
      DatagramSocket socket = new DatagramSocket();
      //Create a Message object to be sent
      Message msg = new Message("Remainder","Return my book on Monday");
      ByteArrayOutputStream baos = new ByteArrayOutputStream();
      ObjectOutputStream oos = new ObjectOutputStream(baos);
      oos.writeObject(msg);
```

```
            oos.writeObject(msg);
            byte[] out = baos.toByteArray();
            //Muticast group where packet has to sent
            InetAddress group = InetAddress.getByName(args[0]);
            //Port the receiver listens on
            int port = 8379;
            //Create a DatagramPacket with buffer, address and port
            DatagramPacket packet = new DatagramPacket(out, out.length,group, port);
            //Send the packet now
            socket.send(packet);
            System.out.println("Sent an object");
        } catch (Exception e) {
            e.printStackTrace();
        }
    }
}
```

13.5.7 Reconstructing the Object

At the receiver end, the object is reconstructed from the data contained in the datagram. We already know that to receive a datagram, the following piece of code may be used.

```
DatagramSocket socket = new DatagramSocket(8379);
byte[] in = new byte[256];
DatagramPacket packet = new DatagramPacket(in, in.length);
socket.receive(packet);
```

So, the `packet` contains the serialized data (stored in the byte array `in`) of the object. Let us now reconstruct the object using a reverse procedure as follows:

```
ByteArrayInputStream bais = new ByteArrayInputStream(in);
ObjectInputStream ois = new ObjectInputStream(bais);
Message msg = (Message)ois.readObject();
```

So, finally, we have object `msg` which is an exact copy of the object that was sent. Here is the complete source code (stored in the file `UDPObjectReceiver.java`) of the program that reconstructs the message object.

```
//UDPObjectReceiver.java
import java.net.*;
import java.io.*;
public class UDPObjectReceiver {
    public static void main(String[] args) {
        try {
            //Create a MulticastSocket and bind it to port 8379
            DatagramSocket socket = new DatagramSocket(8379);
            //Construct a DatagramPacket to receive packet
            byte[] in = new byte[256];
            DatagramPacket packet = new DatagramPacket(in, in.length);
            System.out.println("Waiting to receive a Message object...");
            //Receive the packet now and display
            socket.receive(packet);
            ByteArrayInputStream bais = new ByteArrayInputStream(in);
            ObjectInputStream ois = new ObjectInputStream(bais);
            Message msg = (Message)ois.readObject();
            System.out.println("Received a message:");
            System.out.println("subject : " + msg.getSubject()+"\nbody :
"+msg.getText());
        } catch (Exception ioe) {
            System.out.println(ioe);
        }
    }
}
```

13.5.8 Running the Application

Compile and run the programs as before. A sample output is shown in Figure 13.26:

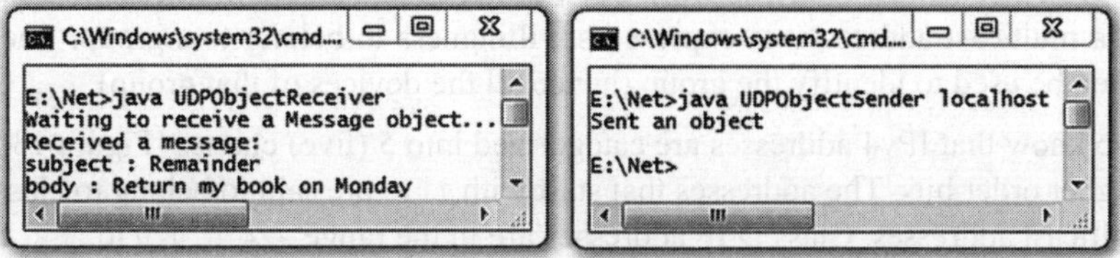

Figure 13.26: Sending and receiving an object using UDP

13.6 MULTICASTING

In all the programs that we have developed so far, the data is destined to only one target. In other words, the number of receivers in all those cases was only one. This type of communication is known as *uni-cast*. Though many applications use this style of communication, there are instances, where a sender application wants to send data to multiple receivers. Multicasting allows sending packets from one host to many other hosts. Packets are sent to a group having an address called *multicast address*. The hosts who are interested to receive the packet must join the group.

Note that one of the possible alternatives of multicasting is to send a packet to each of the intended receivers using UDP or TCP. However, this solution has some inherent problems. For example, the sender should have enough processing power as it sends packets to every receiver. The solution also consumes a significant network bandwidth as packets are duplicated needlessly.

Multicasting handles this problem intelligently. In this method, only one packet is created specifying an address. This address does not represent a specific address. Rather, it essentially represents a group of recipients. To send the packet to multiple intended receivers, the packet is placed on to the network. This packet reaches every host in the network, but only interested hosts accept the packet. Other hosts get the packet but reject it.

13.7 MULTICAST SOCKETS

Java provides `MulticastSocket` class that implements the idea of multicasting and allows an application to send a *single* datagram to a group of recipients in a network (see figure below). The hosts in the group may reside in the same subnet or different subnets connected by multicast-capable routers.

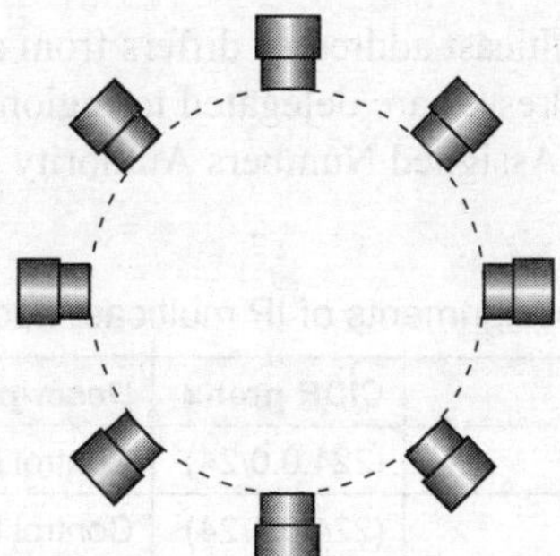

Multicast usually refers to *IP Multicast*, which is a method for efficiently sending packets to multiple receivers at the same time on TCP/IP networks, using multicast addresses.

13.7.1 Multicast Addresses

A *multicast address* is a single IP address that represents multiple network devices forming a group. In other words, many network devices may use a single multicast address. The meaning of using a multicast address is to express its willingness to belong to a group. The multicast address can then be used to identify the group (hence all the devices of that group).

We know that IPv4 addresses are categorized into 5 (five) classes [Figure 13.27:] depending on the higher order bits. The addresses that start with `1110` are said to belong to class D and are known as multicast addresses. Class D IP addresses are in the range `224.0.0.0` to `239.255.255.255`

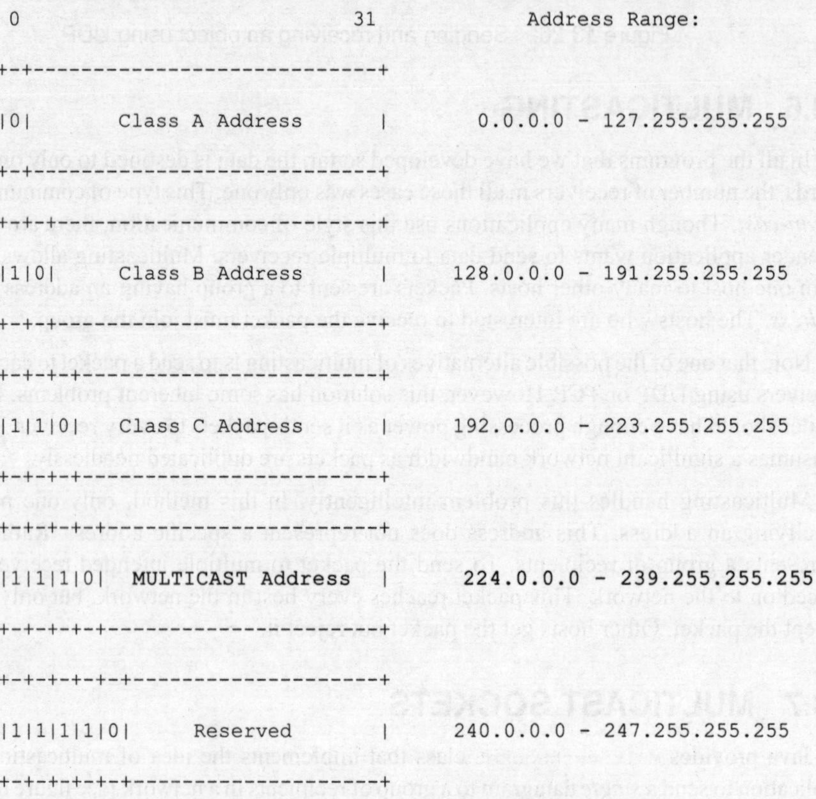

0 31 Address Range:
|0| Class A Address | 0.0.0.0 - 127.255.255.255
|1|0| Class B Address | 128.0.0.0 - 191.255.255.255
|1|1|0| Class C Address | 192.0.0.0 - 223.255.255.255
|1|1|1|0| MULTICAST Address | 224.0.0.0 - 239.255.255.255
|1|1|1|1|0| Reserved | 240.0.0.0 - 247.255.255.255

Figure 13.27: IPv4 address classes

The assignment of IP multicast addresses differs from assignment of unicast IP addresses. Note that IP unicast blocks of addresses are delegated to regional entries. However, multicast addresses are assigned by the Internet Assigned Numbers Authority (IANA) directly. Table 13.2 summarizes the current assignments.

Table 13.2: Current assignments of IP multicast addresses

Range	CIDR prefix	Description
224.0.0.0 - 224.0.0.255	(224.0.0/24)	Control Block for Local Network
224.0.1.0 - 224.0.1.255	(224.0.1/24)	Control Block for Internetwork
224.0.2.0 - 224.0.255.0	-	AD-HOC Block
224.1.0.0 - 224.1.255.255	(224.1/16)	ST Multicast Groups

(*Contd*)

Table 13.2: *(Contd)*

224.2.0.0 - 224.2.255.255	(224.2/16)	SDP/SAP Block
224.252.0.0 - 224.255.255.255	-	DIS Transient Block
225.0.0.0 - 231.255.255.255	-	RESERVED
232.0.0.0 - 232.255.255.255	(232/8)	Block for Source Specific Multicast
233.0.0.0 - 233.255.255.255	(233/8)	GLOP Block
234.0.0.0 - 238.255.255.255		RESERVED
239.0.0.0 - 239.255.255.255	(239/8)	Block for Administratively Scope

13.7.2 MulticastSocket Class

Remember that `DatagramSocket` class itself allows exchanging of packets between exactly two programs. Java provides another class `MulticastSocket` which is a direct subclass of `DatagramSocket` class. Note that this class provides all the functionalities of `DatagramSocket` class. However, it provides a few additional facilities so that a packet can be received by many programs belonging to a common group having an address called multicast address. It also provides methods for joining and leaving a multicast group.

Note that multicasting also allows us to send data across networks. In order to control the scope of multicast (i.e. how far a datagram is allowed to traverse), MulticastSocket allows us to specify a value of Time-To-Live (TTL) field in the IP datagram header. Note that TTL is used to avoid a datagram being looped forever. Routers, upon receiving a packet, decrements the TTL by one and discards the packet if the value becomes 0 (zero).

For multicasting, the TTL field is used to avoid a multicast datagram being traversed forever. and works as follows: A TTL threshold is specified for each interfaces of a router (called multicast capable router). The sender of the packet also specifies a TTL value. The multicast capable router forwards only those multicast datagrams having a TTL value greater than the threshold. A list of TTL threshold with their meaning is shown in Table 15.2:

Table 13.3: TTL threshold list

TTL threshold	Scope
0	Restricted within the same host. Not forwarded multicast packets through any interface.
1	Restricted within the subnet. Not forwarded multicast packets by the router interface.
<32	Restricted within the same department, organization, company etc.
<64	Restricted within the same region
<128	Restricted within the same continent
<255	Unrestricted

In the next few sections, we shall develop a simple multicasting application. Our first application consists of two programs:

- A sender program that sends a single packet containing the message "Hello!" to a group having a multicast address `224.0.0.1`.
- A receiver program that joins the group and listens on port `8379` to receive the hello packet.

Note that the receiver must be started first and must be ready to accept packets. Once the receiver is ready, sender program may be started.

13.7.3 Sending Data

Note that a normal `DatagramSocket` may be used to send any kind of datagram, be it unicast, broadcast or multicast. Since, in our first example, server program will only send packets, a `DatagramSocket` is sufficient to do that. However, a `MulticastSocket` may be created if it is required to send as well as to receive packets. In our first application, we shall use `DatagramSocket`. Later, we shall develop more complex applications where programs will use `MulticastSocket` to send and receive multicast packets.

To send data, let us create a `DatagramSocket` as follows:

```
DatagramSocket socket = new DatagramSocket();
```

An optional port number may be specified if one needs other parties to be able to reach this socket. Since our socket is not intended to receive any packets, port is not specified. This socket is now ready to deliver packets. Let us create a `DatagramPacket` that contains a buffer (byte array) containing a string "Hello!". The following code creates such a buffer:

```
String msg = "Hello!";
byte[] out = msg.getBytes();
```

The `DatagramPacket` may then be created as follows:

```
InetAddress group = InetAddress.getByName("224.0.0.1");
int port = 8379;
DatagramPacket packet = new DatagramPacket(out, out.length, group, port);
```

Note that the multicast address `224.0.0.1` indicates a group consisting of all hosts within the network. We shall use this address so that a receiver program on a remote host within the subnet may also receive packet. We assume that the receiver listens on port `8379`. To send the packet we call `send()` method on the `DatagramSocket` object specifying the packet to be sent.

```
socket.send(packet);
```

13.7.4 Receiving Data

We have mentioned in the previous section that a normal `DatagramSocket` may be used to send any kind of datagram, be it unicast, broadcast or multicast. However, `DatagramSocket` can only receive unicast and broadcast packets. Since our client wants to receive multicast packets (i.e. packets having multicast address in its header), a `MulticastSocket` must be created.

Note that receiving broadcast packets is easier than multicast packets. To receive broadcast packets, processes need not do any extra thing. This is because, broadcast packets are always accepted by the underlying layers and forwarded to the proper applications. However, to receive multicast packets, processes must inform the underlying layer which multicast groups they are interested in. Multicast datagrams are then filtered by underlying MAC or IP (or sometimes both) and datagrams having a previously registered destination group are only accepted and forwarded to the registered processes. When a socket joins a group having an address `addr`, essentially it tells the kernel as follows:

Hey kernel, I know that you reject all multicast datagrams by default. However, I am interested in receiving multicast packets having address `addr`. So, if you get any datagram having destination address `addr`, don't reject them and instead kindly forward them to me (as well as other sockets who are interested in them). Since, a normal `DatagramSocket` does not have any such functionality, we used `MulticastSocket` which provided this additional facility.

The following code creates a `MulticastSocket` that is bound to the port `8379`.

```
MulticastSocket socket = new MulticastSocket(8379);
```

The `joinGroup()` method of a `MulticastSocket` can inform the underlying protocol layers that it is interested in receiving multicast packets having a particular multicast address in the header. To join the group having address `224.0.0.1`, the following code is used.

```
socket.joinGroup(InetAddress.getByName("224.0.0.1"));
```

To join the different groups, this method may be called repeatedly with a different multicast address. The socket will then receive all the packets destined to groups to which it was registered. Similarly, all the sockets of a group will receive copies of multicast packets sent to that group. The only difference between a multicast receiver and a normal receiver is that a multicast receiver joins a group. The remaining part is exactly same as a normal receiver. So, to receive a packet, we create a `DatagramPacket` object as follows:

```
byte[] in = new byte[256];
DatagramPacket packet = new DatagramPacket(in, in.length);
```

Finally the packet is received using `receive()` method.

```
socket.receive(packet);
```

13.7.5 Complete Example

Here is the complete source code of the sender stored in the file `HelloSender.java`.

```
//HelloSender.java
import java.net.*;
public class HelloSender {
  public static void main(String[] args) {
    try {
      //Create a DatagramSocket
      DatagramSocket socket = new DatagramSocket();
      //Fill the buffer with data
      String msg = "Hello!";
      byte[] out = msg.getBytes();
      //Muticast group where packet has to sent
      InetAddress group = InetAddress.getByName("224.0.0.1");
      //Port the receiver listens on
      int port = 8379;
      //Create a DatagramPacket with buffer, address and port
      DatagramPacket packet = new DatagramPacket(out, out.length, group, port);
      //Send to multicast IP address and port
      System.out.println("Sending a packet...");
      //Send the packet now
      socket.send(packet);
      System.out.println("Sent : " + msg);
    } catch (Exception e) {
      e.printStackTrace();
    }
  }
}
```

Here is the complete source code of the receiver stored in the file `HelloReceiver.java`.

```
//HelloReceiver.java
import java.net.*;
public class HelloReceiver {
  public static void main(String[] args) {
    try {
      //Create a MulticastSocket and bind it to port 8379
      MulticastSocket socket = new MulticastSocket(8379);
      //Join to multicast group
      socket.joinGroup(InetAddress.getByName("224.0.0.1"));
      //Construct a DatagramPacket to receive packet
      byte[] in = new byte[256];
      DatagramPacket packet = new DatagramPacket(in, in.length);
```

```
            System.out.println("Waiting to receive a packet...");
            //Receive the packet now and display
            socket.receive(packet);
            String msg = new String(in, 0, packet.getLength());
            System.out.println("Received : " + msg);
         } catch (Exception ioe) {
            System.out.println(ioe);
         }
      }
   }
```

Compile these programs. To run this application, we started three receivers in three separate computers. The sender was then started in one computer. A sample output is shown in Figure 13.28:

Figure 13.28: Sending multicasting packets

13.7.6 Another Multicasting Example

In this application, a program continuously multicasts the score (runs) of a cricket match going on between two teams. The score is generated artificially. Any program that wants to know the current score may join the group and get the score. Since, the sender multicasts the score continuously, the receiver of the score may be started at any time.

Here is the complete source code of the program that multicasts the score stored in the file. ScoreSendor.java.

```
import java.io.*;
import java.net.*;
import java.util.Random;
public class ScoreSender {
  public static void main(String[] args) {
    long score = 0, run;
    Random r = new Random();
    try {
      int port = 8379;
      InetAddress group = InetAddress.getByName(args[0]);
      //Create a DatagramSocket
      DatagramSocket socket = new DatagramSocket();
      while (true) {
        //Fill the buffer with score generated artificially
        do {
          Thread.sleep(1000+r.nextInt(1000));
    }while((run = r.nextInt(7)) == 0);
        score += run;
        String msg = "score: " + score;
        byte[] out = msg.getBytes();
   //Create a DatagramPacket
```

```
            DatagramPacket pkt = new DatagramPacket(out, out.length, group, port);
            //Send the pkt
            socket.send(pkt);
            System.out.println("Sent-->" + msg);
          }
        } catch (Exception e) {
          e.printStackTrace();
        }
      }
    }
```

Here is the complete source code of the program that receives the score stored in the file.

```
ScoreReceiver.java.
    import java.io.*;
    import java.net.*;
    public class ScoreReceiver {
      public static void main(String[] args) {
        byte[] inBuffer = new byte[256];
        try {
          InetAddress address = InetAddress.getByName("224.0.0.1");
          //Create a MulticastSocket
          MulticastSocket socket = new MulticastSocket(8379);
          //Join to the multicast group
          socket.joinGroup(address);
          while (true) {
            DatagramPacket packet = new DatagramPacket(inBuffer, inBuffer.length);
            socket.receive(packet);
            String msg = new String(inBuffer, 0, packet.getLength());
            System.out.println("Received<--" + msg);
          }
        } catch (IOException ioe) {
          System.out.println(ioe);
        }
      }
    }
```

A sample output is shown in Figure 13.29:

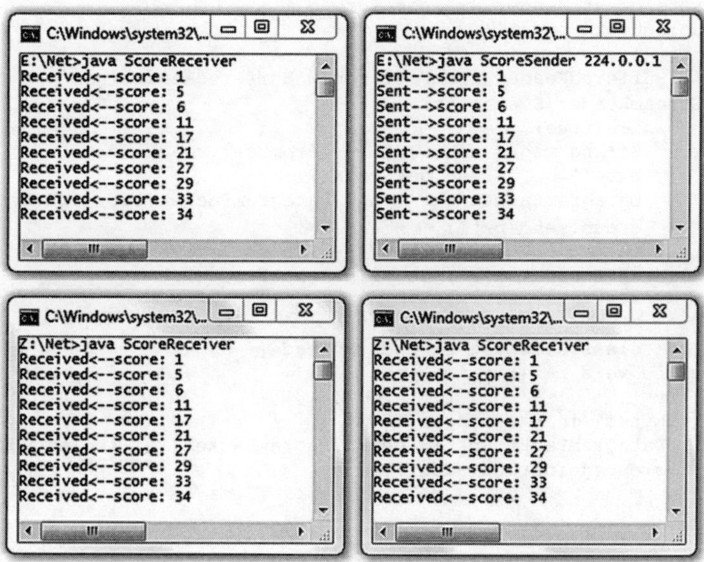

Figure 13.29: Sending and receiving match score

13.7.7 A Text Conference Example

Text mode conferencing and bulletin-board are the oldest models of communication. In these models of communications, text messages are exchanged among two or more people using a terminal. They have some distinct advantages over their counterpart audio/video conferencing.

- They require the least bandwidth as only plain text messages are exchanged.
- Developing applications supporting this model is very easy.

In this section, we shall develop a simple application that supports text conferencing. The application deals with two issues: i) sending text messages supplied by the member to all other participating members of the conference and ii) receiving those text messages. Since a message may arrive, while one is typing a message, we create two child threads from the main thread. One takes the responsibility to send the message being supplied through the keyboard and another one receives the message and displays in the terminal window. Here is the complete source code of the program stored in the file `MulticastSenderReceiver.java`.

```
//MulticastSenderReceiver.java
import java.io.*;
import java.net.*;
public class MulticastSenderReceiver {
  String name;
  InetAddress addr;
  int port = 3456;
  MulticastSocket group;
  public static void main(String[] args){
    new MulticastSenderReceiver(args[0]);
  }
  MulticastSenderReceiver(String name) {
    this.name = name;
    try {
      addr = InetAddress.getByName("224.0.0.1");
      group = new MulticastSocket(port);
      new Receiver().start();
      new Sender().start();
    }catch(Exception e){e.printStackTrace( );}
  }
  private class Sender extends Thread {
    public void run() {
      try {
        BufferedReader fromUser = new BufferedReader(new
InputStreamReader(System.in));
        while(true) {
          String msg = name + ":" + fromUser.readLine();
          byte[] out = msg.getBytes();
          DatagramPacket pkt = new DatagramPacket(out, out.length, addr, port);
          group.send(pkt);
        }
      }catch(Exception e ) {e.printStackTrace();}
    }
  }
  private class Receiver extends Thread {
    public void run() {
      try {
        byte[] in = new byte[256];
        DatagramPacket pkt = new DatagramPacket(in, in.length);
        group.joinGroup(addr);
```

```
      while(true) {
        group.receive(pkt);
        System.out.println(new String(pkt.getData(), 0, pkt.getLength()));
      }
    }catch(Exception e ) {e.printStackTrace();}
  }
 }
}
```

A snapshot of the text conference involving four people is shown in Figure 13.30:

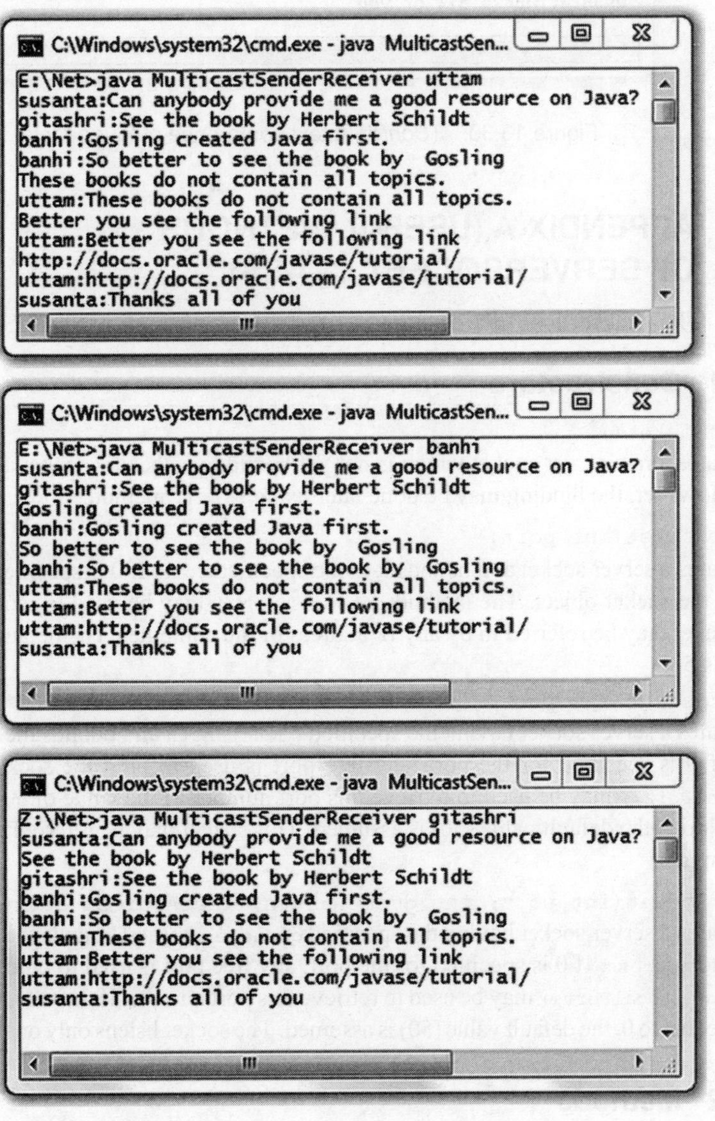

Figure 13.30: A text conference of four people

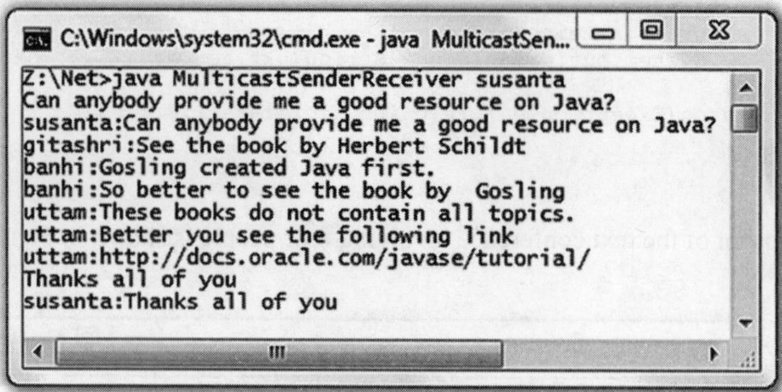

Figure 13.30: (*Contd*) A text conference of four people

13.8 APPENDIX A (USEFUL METHODS OF SERVERSOCKET CLASS)

The following sections give a summary of important methods of ServerSocket class.

13.8.1 Constructors

`ServerSocket()`

Creates a raw server socket which is not yet bound to a specific socket address (IP address and port). However, the binding may be done later using `bind()` method.

`ServerSocket(int port)`

Creates a server socket and bounds it to the specified `port`. If 0 is specified, any free port is used to bind the socket object. The method `getLocalPort()` may be used to retrieve this port number. This socket may be referred to by any IP address of the computer. The default queue length for this socket is 50.

`ServerSocket(int port, int queueLength)`

Creates a server socket having the specified `queueLength` and bounds the socket to the specified `port`. If 0 is specified for the port, any free port is used to bind the socket object. The method `getLocalPort()` may be used to retrieve this port number. If the value of `queueLength` is less than or equal to 0, the default value (50) is assumed. This socket may be referred to by any IP address of the computer.

`ServerSocket(int port, int queueLength, InetAddress address)`

Creates a server socket having the specified `queueLength` and bounds the socket to the specified `port` and `address`. If 0 is specified for the port, any free port is used to bind the socket object. The method `getLocalPort()` may be used to retrieve this port number. If the value of `queueLength` is less than or equal to 0, the default value (50) is assumed. The socket listens only on the specified IP address.

13.8.2 Methods

`Socket accept()`

Processes client requests from the queue associated with the `ServerSocket` object in First-Come-First-Served basis. When there are no requests in the queue, this method waits (blocks the caller) for further incoming connections. Upon receiving a request, it creates a virtual channel between the server and client and returns a `Socket` object that represents the sever-side end of the virtual channel.

`void bind(SocketAddress address)`

Binds the socket to the specified address (IP address and port). This method expects address as `InetSocketAddress` object. The `InetSocketAddress` class extends `SocketAddress` class and implements an IP Socket Address as [IP address, port number] or [hostname, port number] pair. In the latter case, an attempt will be made to resolve the hostname. If resolution fails then the address is said to be unresolved and a `SocketException` is thrown. However, the name can still be used in some circumstances such as connecting through a proxy. If the address is null, `bind()` picks up an ephemeral port and a valid local address to bind the socket. The default queue length for this socket is 50.

`void bind(SocketAddress address, int queueLength)`

Same as previous version except that the length of the queue is set to the specified `queueLength`. If the value of `queueLength` is less than or equal to 0, the default value (50) is assumed.

`InetAddress getInetAddress()`

Returns the address to which the socket is bound or `null` if the socket is not yet bound.

`int getLocalPort()`

Returns the port number this socket is bound or -1 if the socket is not bound yet.

`SocketAddress getLocalSocketAddress ()`

Returns actually an `InetSocketAddress` object that represents the socket address (IP address and port) of the endpoint of this socket or null if the socket is not yet bound.

`boolean isBound()`

Returns `true` if the socket is successfully bound to a socket address, `false` otherwise.

`boolean isClosed()`

Returns `true` if the socket is closed, `false` otherwise.

`int getSoTimeout()`

Returns `SocketOptions.SO_TIMEOUT` value. The value `0` indicates that timeout option is disabled (i.e. infinite timeout).

`void setSoTimeout(int timeout)`

Sets the `SocketOptions.SO_TIMEOUT` value with the specified `timeout` in milliseconds. If a non-zero timeout value is specified and subsequently `accept()` method is called, the `accept()` method waits for only a specified amount of time for the incoming connection request. If no connection request comes within this specified time, a `SocketTimeoutException` is thrown. However, the socket remains valid and a different timeout value may be used (if required) later and `accept()` method may also be called subsequently to have its effect. The timeout value is negative, an `IllegalArgumentException` is raised. A timeout value of 0 (which is also the default timeout) is used for infinite timeout.

`void setReuseAddress(boolean status)`

Sets `SocketOptions.SO_REUSEADDR` value to `true` or `false`. If a `ServerSocket` object is closed using `close()` method, the connection is not closed and the address and port are not freed immediately. It may remain in a timeout state temporarily keeping the connection as it is. This state is known as `TIME_WAIT` state. Note that TCP provides in order delivery of packets. However, since the underlying IP layer does not provide any such guarantee on ordering, IP packets may arrive out of order. The task of TCP layer is to arrange them in the correct order and forward them to the application layer. So, out of order packets may arrive even if the connection is closed. That is why the connection is kept open (temporarily) so that delayed packets may be handled appropriately. So, `TIME_WAIT` state basically means that one side closed the connection but the final confirmation of the close is pending. The connection is finally terminated and all resources are freed. However, it may not be possible for an application to use the same address and port, if there is a connection in the `TIME_WAIT` state involving the address and port. The `setReuseAddress()` method may be used to enable/disable `SO_REUSEADDR` option prior to binding the socket using `bind()` to allow/disallow the socket to be bound even though a previous connection is in a `TIME_WAIT` state.

`boolean getReuseAddress()`

Returns a `true/false` indicating whether or not `SO_REUSEADDR` is enabled/disabled.

`ServerSocketChannel getChannel()`

Returns a `ServerSocketChannel` object (if any) associated with this socket provided that the channel itself was created using static `open()` method of `ServerSocketChannel` class.

`void close()`

Closes the socket. If the socket has an associated channel, the channel is also closed. If a thread is currently blocked on `accept()` method, then the thread throws a `SocketException`.

13.9 APPENDIX B (USEFUL METHODS OF SOCKET CLASS)

The following sections give a summary of important methods of Socket class.

13.9.1 Constructors

`Socket()`

Creates a raw socket which is not yet bound to a specific socket address (IP address and port). However, the binding may be done later using `bind()` method. The connection is not yet established to the server socket. However, the connection may be established later using `connect()` method.

`Socket(InetAddress address, int port)`

Creates a stream socket and connects to the server socket having specified `address` and `port`. The socket is also bound to an ephemeral port and a valid local address.

`Socket(InetAddress host, int port, boolean stream)`

This method is now deprecated. It is used to create stream as well as datagram socket. If the `stream` argument is true, this creates a stream socket. If the `stream` argument is false, it creates a datagram socket. The socket is connected to the server socket having specified `address` and `port`.

`Socket(InetAddress address, int port, InetAddress localAddr, int localPort)`

Creates a socket and connects to the server socket having specified `address` and `port`. The socket is bound to the specified `localAddr` and `localPort`. If a host has more than one IP address, this constructor is used to choose a specific IP address to bind the socket. If 0 (zero) is specified for `port`, system picks up an ephemeral port.

`Socket(Proxy proxy)`

Creates a socket which is not yet connected to a server socket. The connection may be made later using `connect()` method which consults specified proxy host to establish the connection. The proxy mechanism is useful if the client computer is not configured with a gateway and/or DNS host.

`Socket(SocketImpl impl)`

Creates a customized socket. The functionality of the socket is provided by the specified `SocketImpl` object. This `SocketImpl` class provides a plain implementation of the socket. Programmers who want to extend the functionality of a plain socket should create a class that extends `SocketImpl` class and override the methods defined in `SocketImpl` class.

`Socket(String host, int port)`

Creates a stream socket and connects to the specified `port` on the named `host`. The socket is also bound to an ephemeral port and a valid local address.

`Socket(String host, int port, boolean stream)`

This method is now deprecated also. It is used to create stream as well as datagram socket. If the `stream` argument is true, this creates a stream socket. If the `stream` argument is false, it creates a datagram socket. The socket is connected to the specified `port` on the named `host`.

`Socket(String host, int port, InetAddress localAddr, int localPort)`

Creates a socket and connects to the specified `port` on the named `host`. The socket is bound to the specified `localAddr` and `localPort`. If a host has more than one IP address, this constructor is used to choose a specific IP address to bind the socket. If 0 (zero) is specified for `port`, system picks up an ephemeral port.

13.9.2 Methods

`void bind(SocketAddress localEnd)`

Binds the socket to the specified address (IP address and port). This method expects address as `InetSocketAddress` object. The `InetSocketAddress` class extends `SocketAddress` class and implements an IP Socket Address as [IP address, port number] or [hostname, port number] pair. In the latter case, an attempt will be made to resolve the hostname. If resolution fails then the address is said to be unresolved and a `SocketException` is thrown. However, the name can still be used on some circumstances such as connecting through a proxy. If the address is null, `bind()` picks up an ephemeral port and a valid local address to bind the socket.

`void close()`

Terminates the connection. Also closes the socket's `InputStream` and `OutputStream` and hence the socket is not available for further networking. Accordingly, if there is any thread currently working on this socket, the thread throws a `SocketException`. A closed socket can never be rebound or reconnected. If required to, a new socket may be created instead. If the socket has an associated channel, the channel is also closed.

`void connect(SocketAddress address)`

Connects the socket to the specified `address` (IP address and port) of the server socket. This method expects address as `InetSocketAddress` object. The `InetSocketAddress` class extends `SocketAddress` class and implements an IP Socket Address as [IP address, port number] or [hostname, port number] pair. In the latter case, an attempt will be made to resolve the hostname. If resolution fails then the address is said to be unresolved and a `SocketException` is thrown. However, the name can still be used on some circumstances such as connecting through a proxy.

`void connect(SocketAddress address, int timeout)`

Tries to connect this socket to the specified `address` for a specified time in milliseconds. If this method fails to establish a connection within this stipulated time, a `SocketTimeoutException` is thrown. A timeout of 0 (zero) indicates infinite timeout and in this case `connect()` blocks the caller until a connection is established or an error occurs.

`SocketChannel getChannel()`

Returns a `SocketChannel` object (if any) associated with this socket provided that the channel itself was created using static `open()` method of `SocketChannel` class.

`InetAddress getInetAddress()`

Returns the address of the server socket to which this socket is connected. It returns `null` if the socket is not connected.

`InputStream getInputStream()`

Returns an `InputStream` object that may be used to read data bytes from the socket through its `read()` method. The returned object is usually wrapped by other stream classes such as `BufferedReader` to receive data conveniently.

`boolean getKeepAlive()`

Returns a `boolean` indicating whether or not `SocketOptions.SO_KEEPALIVE` is enabled.

`InetAddress getLocalAddress()`

Returns the address to which the socket is bound or `null` if the socket is not yet bound.

`int getLocalPort()`

Returns the port number this socket is bound. A value of –1 is returned if the socket is not yet bound.

`SocketAddress getLocalSocketAddress()`

Returns the socket address (IP address and port number) to which this socket is bound. The returned object is actually an `InetSocketAddress` object representing an IP address and a port number pair. Note that `InetSocketAddress` is a subclass of abstract `SocketAddress` class. The returned object is first converted to the `InetSocketAddress` type. To get the address and port, suitable methods on this resultant object may be used. This method returns a value `null` if the socket is not yet bound.

`OutputStream getOutputStream()`

Returns an `OutputStream` object that may be used to write data bytes to the socket through its `write()` method. The returned object is usually wrapped by other stream classes such as `PrintWriter` to send data conveniently.

`int getPort()`

Returns the port number of the server socket to which this socket is connected. A value of 0 (zero) is returned if this socket is not yet connected.

`int getReceiveBufferSize()`

Returns the value of the `SO_RCVBUF` option for this Socket set by `setReceiveBufferSize()` method. The `SO_RCVBUF` option is the buffer size used by the platform for input on this Socket.

`SocketAddress getRemoteSocketAddress()`

Returns the socket address (IP address and port number) of the server socket to which this socket is connected. The returned object is actually an `InetSocketAddress` object representing an IP address and a port number pair. Note that `InetSocketAddress` is a subclass of abstract `SocketAddress` class. The returned object is first converted to the `InetSocketAddress` type. To get the address and port, suitable methods on this resultant object may be used. This method returns a value `null` if the socket is not yet connected.

`boolean getReuseAddress()`

Returns a `true/false` indicating whether or not `SO_REUSEADDR` is enabled/disabled.

`int getSendBufferSize()`

Returns the value of the `SO_SNDBUF` option for this Socket set by `setSendBufferSize()` method. The `SO_SNDBUF` option is the buffer size used by the platform for output on this Socket.

`int getSoTimeout()`

Returns `SocketOptions.SO_TIMEOUT` value. The value `0` indicates that timeout option is disabled (i.e. infinite timeout).

`boolean getTcpNoDelay()`

Returns `true` if the Nagle's algorithm is enabled, `false` otherwise.

`int getTrafficClass()`

Returns traffic class or Type-of-Service (ToS) that was set by the `setTrafficClass()` method.

`boolean isBound()`

Returns `true` if the socket is successfully bound to a local socket address, `false` otherwise.

`boolean isClosed()`

Returns `true` if the socket is closed, `false` otherwise.

`boolean isConnected()`

Returns `true` if the socket is connected to a server socket successfully, `false` otherwise.

`boolean isInputShutdown()`

Returns `true` if the input stream of the socket is closed, `false` otherwise.

`boolean isOutputShutdown()`

Returns `true` if the output stream of the socket is closed, `false` otherwise.

`void setKeepAlive(boolean on)`

Sets the `SocketOptions.SO_KEEPALIVE` option to `true` or `false`. The purpose of this option is to detect if the peer host crashes or not. Setting this option to `true` instructs the system to check the status of the peer if no data has been exchanged across the socket in either direction for 2 hours (the actual value is implementation dependent). In this case, the TCP sends a keepalive probe to the peer who must respond. A response of ACK indicates that everything is fine and TCP understands the fact and does nothing but repeating the entire procedure after 2 hours of inactivity. If TCP gets a response RST (which indicates that the peer crashed and rebooted) or does not get any response, it closes the socket.

`void setReceiveBufferSize(int size)`

Sets the `SO_RCVBUF` option for this socket to the specified value. The value of `SO_RCVBUF` is used both to set the size of the internal socket receive buffer, and to set the size of the TCP receive window that is advertized to the remote peer.

`void setReuseAddress(boolean on)`

Sets `SocketOptions.SO_REUSEADDR` value to `true` or `false`. If a `Socket` object is closed using `close()` method, the connection is not closed and the address and port associated with the socket are not freed immediately. It may remain in a timeout state temporarily keeping the connection as it is. This state is known as `TIME_WAIT` state. Note that TCP provides in order delivery of packets. However, since the underlying IP layer does not provide any such guarantee on ordering, IP packets may arrive out of order. The task of TCP layer is to arrange them in the correct order and forward them to the application layer. So, out of order packets may arrive even if the connection is closed. That is why the connection is kept open (temporarily) so that delayed packets may be handled appropriately. So, `TIME_WAIT` state basically means that one side closed the connection but the final confirmation of the close is pending. The connection is finally terminated and all resources are freed. However, it may not be possible for an application to use the same address and port, if there is a connection in the `TIME_WAIT` state involving the address and port. The `setReuseAddress()` method may be used to enable/disable `SO_REUSEADDR` option prior to binding the socket using `bind()` to allow/disallow the socket to be bound even though a previous connection is in a `TIME_WAIT` state.

`void setSendBufferSize(int size)`

Sets the `SO_SNDBUF` option for this socket to the specified value. The `SO_SNDBUF` option is a hint for the size the platform's networking code should use to set the underlying network I/O buffers.

`static void setSocketImplFactory(SocketImplFactory fac)`

This method is used to specify the client socket implementation factory for the application. The factory can be specified only once. When a new client socket is created, the `createSocketImpl()` method of socket implementation factory is called to create the actual socket implementation.

`void setSoTimeout(int timeout)`

Sets the `SocketOptions.SO_TIMEOUT` value with the specified `timeout` in milliseconds. If a non-zero timeout value is specified and subsequently `read()` method is called on InputStream associate with this socket, the `read()` method waits for only a specified amount of time for incoming data. If data comes within this specified time, a `SocketTimeoutException` is thrown. However, the socket remains valid and a different timeout value may be used (if required) later and `read()` method may also be called subsequently to have its effect. The timeout value is negative, an `IllegalArgumentException` is raised. A timeout value of 0 (which is also the default timeout) is used for infinite timeout.

`void setTcpNoDelay(boolean on)`

This method is used to enable/disable `TCP_NODELAY` option of the socket. Thet `TCP_NODELAY` option corresponds to the Nagle's algorithm. Note that in this algorithm, written data to the network is not buffered which results in pending acknowledgement of previously written data.

`void setTrafficClass(int tc)`

Sets traffic class or Type-of-Service (ToS) field in the IP header for packets sent from this socket to the specified value. It is just a hint as the underlying network implementation may ignore this value.

`void shutdownInput()`

Sends the input stream for this socket to the *end of stream* state. As a result, any data sent to the input stream side of the socket is acknowledged and then discarded silently. Consequently, if we try to read data from a socket input stream after invoking this method on the socket, the stream will return `EOF`.

`void shutdownOutput()`

Places the output stream for this socket to the *disabled* state. After invoking this method, any previously written data (for a TCP socket) will be sent followed by TCP's normal connection termination sequence. Any attempt to write to a socket output stream after invoking `shutdownOutput()` on the socket, results in an `IOException`.

13.10 APPENDIX C (USEFUL METHODS OF DATAGRAMSOCKET CLASS)

The following sections give a summary of important methods of DatagramSocket class.

13.10.1 Constructors

`DatagramSocket()`

Creates a datagram socket and binds it to any available port on the local host machine. This socket is also bound to all IP addresses. This means that the socket may be referred to by any IP address of the computer.

`protected DatagramSocket(DatagramSocketImpl impl)`

Constructs a datagram socket with the specified `DatagramSocketImpl` object. This socket is not yet bound to any address or port.

`DatagramSocket(int port)`

Creates a datagram socket and binds it to the specified `port` on the local computer. This socket is also bound to all IP addresses. This means that the socket may be referred to by any IP address of the computer.

`DatagramSocket(int port, InetAddress address)`

Creates a datagram socket, bound to the specified `port` and `address`. If the `port` is 0 (zero), an ephemeral port is used. If the `address` is 0.0.0.0, socket is bound to all addresses.

`DatagramSocket(SocketAddress bindAddr)`

Creates a datagram socket and bounds to the specified local socket address.

13.10.2 Methods

`void bind(SocketAddress addr)`

Binds the `DatagramSocket` object to the specified address (IP address and port). This method expects address as `InetSocketAddress` object. The `InetSocketAddress` class extends `SocketAddress` class and implements an IP Socket Address as [IP address, port number] or [hostname, port number] pair. In the latter case, an attempt will be made to resolve the hostname. If resolution fails then the address is said to be unresolved and a SocketException is thrown. However, the name can still be used on some circumstances such as connecting through a proxy. If the address is null, bind() picks up an ephemeral port and a valid local address to bind the socket.

void close()

Closes this datagram socket. If a thread is currently blocked on receive() method, then the thread throws a SocketException.

void connect(InetAddress address, int port)

The functionality of this method is significantly different from the connect() method of Socket class. Connects the socket to a remote socket having specified address and port. Usually, a datagram socket (call it receiver) receives data using receive() method from any other datagram socket (call it sender). If a receiver wants to receive data from a particular sender, it uses connect() method specifying the address and port of the sender socket. Subsequent receive() method calls reject data sent by other sockets. The connect() method may also be used to choose a particular receiver among a group of receivers identified by a multicast address (e.g. 224.0.0.1). All hosts in a multicast group are identified by a single multicast address. If a sender wants to send data to a particular host in this group, the sender may use connect() method specifying the receivers' *own* address and port (which is used in multicast socket address). The sender *must* also use the same address and port in the datagram packet, otherwise an IllegalArgumentException will be thrown.

void connect(SocketAddress addr)

Same as the previous one except the argument is a SocketAddress object that represents the address and port. Actually an InetSocketAddress object that represents IP address and port is passed to this method.

void disconnect()

Disconnects the socket. This method has no effect if the socket is not connected or already closed.

boolean getBroadcast()

Returns true if SO_BROADCAST is enabled, false otherwise.

DatagramChannel getChannel()

Returns the unique DatagramChannel object associated with this datagram socket, if any.

InetAddress getInetAddress()

Returns the address to which this socket is connected. If the socket is not connected it returns null.

InetAddress getLocalAddress()

Returns the local address to which the socket is bound.

int getLocalPort()

Returns the port number on the local host to which this socket is bound.

SocketAddress getLocalSocketAddress()

Returns the socket address (address and port) of the endpoint this socket is bound to.

int getPort()

Returns the port number to which this socket is connected. If the socket is not connected, it returns -1.

int getReceiveBufferSize()

Get value of the SO_RCVBUF option for this DatagramSocket, that is the buffer size used by the platform for input on this DatagramSocket.

SocketAddress getRemoteSocketAddress()

Returns the socket address (address and port) of the endpoint this socket is connected to, or null if the socket is not connected.

boolean getReuseAddress()

Tests if SO_REUSEADDR is enabled.

`int getSendBufferSize()`

Get value of the `SO_SNDBUF` option for this `DatagramSocket`, that is the buffer size used by the platform for output on this DatagramSocket.

`int getSoTimeout()`

Returns `SocketOptions.SO_TIMEOUT` value. The value `0` indicates that timeout option is disabled (i.e. infinite timeout).

`int getTrafficClass()`

Returns traffic class or Type-of-Service (ToS) in the IP datagram header for packets sent from this `DatagramSocket`.

`boolean isBound()`

Returns `true` if the socket is successfully bound to a socket address, `false` otherwise.

`boolean isClosed()`

Returns `true` if the socket is closed, `false` otherwise.

`boolean isConnected()`

Returns `true` if the socket is connected to a remote socket, `false` otherwise.

`void receive(DatagramPacket p)`

Receives a `DatagramPacket` if the packet is intended (i.e. the destination address of the packet matches socket's address) for this socket or the packet is a broadcast one. This method blocks until a datagram is received. When this method returns, the `DatagramPacket`'s buffer is filled with the data received. The packet also contains the IP address and the port number of the sender `DatagramSocket`. The length field of the datagram packet object contains the length of the received message. If the message is longer than the buffer's size, the message is truncated.

`void send(DatagramPacket p)`

Sends a `DatagramPacket` from this socket. The packet contains socket address (IP address and port number) of the intended destination host together with the data (payload). Note that the IP address may be a unicast or multicast or broadcast address. It indicates that a simple DatagramSocket may be used for unicasting, broadcasting and multicasting of packets.

`void setBroadcast(boolean on)`

Sets `SocketOptions.O_BROADCAST` option of the socket to `true/false` that enables/disables the ability of the process to send broadcast messages through datagram sockets. It works only on networks that support the concept of a broadcast message (e.g. Ethernet, token ring, etc.). The default value of this option is `true`.

`static void setDatagramSocketImplFactory(DatagramSocketImplFactory fac)`

Sets the datagram socket implementation factory for the application.

`void setReceiveBufferSize(int size)`

Sets the `SO_RCVBUF` option for this `DatagramSocket` to the specified size. This option is used to give a hint to the size of the underlying network buffer the kernel should use for receiving datagrams. A larger value of this option may allow the network implementation to buffer multiple packets when packets arrive faster than are being received using `receive()` method.

`void setReuseAddress(boolean on)`

Enable/disable the SO_REUSEADDR socket option.

`void setSendBufferSize(int size)`

Sets the `SO_SNDBUF` option for this `DatagramSocket` to the specified size. This option is used to give a hint to the size of the underlying network buffer the kernel should use for sending datagrams. A larger value of this option may allow the network implementation to queue multiple packets when packets are submitted faster than are being sent using `send()` method.

Sets the SO_SNDBUF option to the specified value for this DatagramSocket.

`void setSoTimeout(int timeout)`

Sets the `SocketOptions.SO_TIMEOUT` value with the specified `timeout` in milliseconds. If a non-zero timeout value is specified and subsequently `receive()` method is called on this datagram socket, the `receive()` method waits for only a specified amount of time for incoming data. If data comes within this specified time, a `SocketTimeoutException` is thrown. However, the datagram socket remains valid and a different timeout value may be used (if required) later and `receive()` method may also be called subsequently to have its effect. The timeout value is negative, an `IllegalArgumentException` is raised. A timeout value of 0 (which is also the default timeout) is used for infinite timeout.

`void setTrafficClass(int tc)`

Note that Type-of-Service (TOS) is an 8-bit field in the IP datagram header. This field indicates the abstract parameters of the quality of service desired. The `setTrafficClass()` method is used to set this field with the specified `tc` for datagrams sent from this `DatagramSocket`. However, the underlying network layer may ignore this. The value of `tc` must be in the range 0 to 255, otherwise an `IllegalArgumentException` is thrown. A summary of the TOS field is given below:

```
|<--------------------TOS field------------------->|
  0     1     2     3     4     5     6     7
+-----+-----+-----+-----+-----+-----+-----+-----+
|   PRECEDENCE    |  D  |  T  |  R  |  0  |  0  |
+-----+-----+-----+-----+-----+-----+-----+-----+

     Bits 0-2: Precedence.
     Bit    3: Delay (0 = Normal, 1 = Low Delay).
     Bits   4: Throughput(0 = Normal, 1 = High).
     Bits   5: Reliability(0 = Normal,1 = High).
     Bit  6-7: Reserved for Future Use.

     Precedence
      111 - Network Control
      110 - Internetwork Control
      101 - CRITIC/ECP
      100 - Flash Override
      011 - Flash
      010 - Immediate
      001 - Priority
      000 - Routine
```

13.11 APPENDIX D (USEFUL METHODS OF DATAGRAMPACKET CLASS)

The following sections give a summary of important methods of DatagramPacket class.

13.11.1 Constructors

`DatagramPacket(byte[] buffer, int bytesToRead)`

Creates a `DatagramPacket` to hold received data. The `receive()` method of `DatagramSocket` reads `bytesToRead` bytes of data and stores in `buffer`. The `bytesToRead` must not be greater than `buffer.length` else an `IllegalArgumentException` is thrown.

`DatagramPacket(byte[] buffer,int bytesToSend,InetAddress address,int port)`

Creates a `DatagramPacket` to hold data to be sent to the specified `port` number on the specified `host`. The `send()` method of `DatagramSocket` actually sends first `bytesToSend` bytes of `buffer`. The `bytesToSend` must not be greater than `buffer.length` otherwise an `IllegalArgumentException` is thrown.

`DatagramPacket(byte[] buffer,int offset,int bytesToRead)`

Creates a `DatagramPacket` to hold received data. The `receive()` method of `DatagramSocket` reads `bytesToRead` bytes of data and places in `buffer` starting from specified `offset`. The `bytesToRead` must not be greater than `(buffer.length-offset)` else an `IllegalArgumentException` is thrown.

`DatagramPacket(byte[] buffer,int offset,int bytesToSend,InetAddress address, int port)`

Creates a `DatagramPacket` to hold data to be sent to the specified `port` number on the specified `host`. The `send()` method of `DatagramSocket` actually sends `bytesToSend` bytes of `buffer` starting from the specified `offset`. The `bytesToSend` must not be greater than `(buffer.length-offset)` otherwise an `IllegalArgumentException` is thrown.

`DatagramPacket(byte[] buffer,int offset,int bytesToSend, SocketAddress address)`

Creates a `DatagramPacket` to hold data to be sent to the destination datagram socket having specified socket `addres`. The `send()` method of `DatagramSocket` actually sends `bytesToSend` bytes of `buffer` starting from the specified `offset`. The `bytesToSend` must not be greater than `(buffer.length-offset)` otherwise an `IllegalArgumentException` is thrown.

`DatagramPacket(byte[] buffer,int bytesToSend,SocketAddress address)`

Creates a `DatagramPacket` to hold data to be sent to the destination datagram socket having specified socket `addres`. The `send()` method of `DatagramSocket` actually sends first `bytesToSend` bytes of `buffer`. The `bytesToSend` must not be greater than `buffer.length` otherwise an `IllegalArgumentException` is thrown.

13.11.2 Methods

`InetAddress getAddress()`

Returns the IP address of the host this datagram is destined to or datagram came from.

`byte[] getData()`

Returns the buffer containing the data received or to be sent. The starting position and size (no of bytes) of the data may be obtained using `getOffset()` and `getLength()` methods respectively.

`int getLength()`

Returns the length of the data to be sent or the length of the data received.

`int getOffset()`

Returns the offset of the data to be sent or the offset of the data received in the buffer.

`int getPort()`

Returns the port number on the remote host to which this datagram is being sent or from which the datagram was received.

`SocketAddress getSocketAddress()`

Returns the socket address (IP address and port number) of the remote host that this packet is being sent to or is coming from. The returned object is actually an `InetSocketAddress` object representing an IP address and a port number pair. Note that `InetSocketAddress` is a subclass of abstract `SocketAddress` class. The returned object is first converted to the `InetSocketAddress` type. To get the address and port, suitable methods on this resultant object may be used.

`void setAddress(InetAddress iaddr)`

Sets the IP address of the machine to which this datagram is being sent.

`void setData(byte[] buf)`

Set the data buffer for this datagram packet.

`void setData(byte[] buf, int offset, int length)`

Set the data buffer for this datagram packet. The buffer will contain `length` bytes of data starting from index `offset`.

`void setLength(int length)`

Sets the length of the data in the data buffer for this packet.

`void setPort(int iport)`

Sets the port number on the remote host to which this datagram is being sent.

`void setSocketAddress(SocketAddress address)`

Sets the SocketAddress (usually IP address + port number) of the remote host to which this datagram is being sent.

13.12 APPENDIX E (USEFUL METHODS OF MULTICASTSOCKET CLASS)

The `MulticastSocket` is a direct subclass of `DatagramSocket` class. So, it has all the methods that the `DatagramSocket` class has. In this section only methods specific to `MulticastSocket` class are discussed.

13.12.1 Constructors

`MulticastSocket()`

Creates a multicast socket and binds it to any available port on the local host machine. This socket is also bound to all IP addresses. This means that the socket may be referred to by any IP address of the computer.

`MulticastSocket(int port)`

Creates a multicast socket and binds it to the specified `port` on the local computer. This socket is also bound to all IP addresses. This means that the socket may be referred to by any IP address of the computer.

`MulticastSocket(SocketAddress bindaddr)`

Creates a multicast socket and bounds to the specified local socket address.

13.12.2 Methods

`InetAddress getInterface()`

Returns the address of the network interface used for multicast packets.

`boolean getLoopbackMode()`

Returns the setting for local loopback of multicast packets.

`NetworkInterface getNetworkInterface()`

Returns network interface used for multicasting .

`int getTimeToLive()`

Returns the default time-to-live for multicast packets which are sent out on this socket.

`void joinGroup(InetAddress mcastaddr)`

Adds the socket to the group having specified multicast address.

`void joinGroup(SocketAddress mcastaddr, NetworkInterface netIf)`

Joins to the specified multicast group at the specified interface.

`void leaveGroup(InetAddress mcastaddr)`

Used to leave a multicast group.

`void leaveGroup(SocketAddress mcastaddr, NetworkInterface netIf)`

Leaves a multicast group on a specified local interface.

`void setInterface(InetAddress inf)`

Sets the multicast network interface used by methods whose behaviour would be affected by the value of the network interface.

`void setLoopbackMode(boolean disable)`

Disable/Enable local loopback of multicast packets. The option is used by the platform's networking code as a hint for setting whether multicast data will be looped back to the local socket.

`void setNetworkInterface(NetworkInterface netIf)`

Specify the network interface for outgoing multicast packets sent on this socket.

`void setTimeToLive(int ttl)`

Set the default time-to-live for multicast packets which are sent out on this MulticastSocket to control the scope of the multicasts.

KEYWORDS

Broadcasting—Sending a packet/data to all nodes

Client Socket—Client-side end point of the socket

Datagram Packet—Data container used to send and receive information by UDP

Deserialization—A process of reconstructing the object/data from the byte array obtained during serialization

IP address—A 32-bit address used by the IP layer of the TCP/IP protocol suite to identify a host uniquely

Multicasting—Sending a packet/data to multiple nodes

Multicast Address—An IP address that represents a group of recipients in case of multicasting

Port number—A locally unique positive integer assigned to a process to identify it within the computer uniquely

Reserved ports—Some predefined port numbers allocated to some processes

Serialization—A process of converting an object/data to a linear array of bytes

Server Socket—Server-side end point of the socket

Socket address—A socket address of a process consists of the port number of the process and the computer where it is running. It can be thought of as a channel connecting two entities

TCP socket—A channel established between the client and the server prior to the communication

UDP socket—No dedicated channel established prior to the communication

Unicasting—Sending a packet/data to one node

SUMMARY

Java, like other programming languages, provides well-designed classes and interfaces (APIs) for network programming. The class NetworkInterface is used to retrieve most of the information about the installed network devices.

One of the central ideas of network computing is the client–server model. Many networking applications including Internet's primary protocols such as HTTP, SMTP, DNS, etc. use this model. In this programming paradigm, there are two basic components: service providers, known as servers and service requesters, known as clients. Java allows us to write such client–server programs using TCP as well as UDP sockets.

In the TCP socket, a client establishes a connection to the server socket and sends and receives data through this connection. In the UDP socket data is sent and received in terms of datagrams. Datagrams are containers of data. The client creates a datagram and mentions the socket address of the target host and sends the datagram. The datagram is then forwarded typically by many intermediate routers and eventually reaches its destination host. A UDP socket does not guarantee that the packets will be delivered to the target host, while TCP does. The UDP socket allows us to send packets to the server even if the server is not available at that time but will be up soon.

A server is typically a multithreaded program. For every request that the server process receives, a new thread is created where the new request is handed over while the server goes to the listening state again.

WEB RESOURCES

http://docs.oracle.com/javase/tutorial/networking/sockets/
Lesson: All About Sockets

http://docs.oracle.com/javase/tutorial/networking/datagrams/index.html
Lesson: All About Datagrams

http://www.ibm.com/developerworks/java/tutorials/j-sockets/
Java sockets 101

http://www.java2s.com/Tutorial/Java/0320__Network/javanetSocket.htm
java.net.Socket

http://docs.oracle.com/javase/6/docs/api/java/net/Socket.html
Class Socket

EXERCISES

Objective-type Questions

1. Which of the following statements is used by the server to listen for a connection request from a client?
   (a) Socket s = serverSocket.listen();
   (b) Socket s = serverSocket.wait();
   (c) Socket s = serverSocket.getSocket();
   (d) Socket s = serverSocket.accept();

2. Which of the following is used by a client to establish a socket connection with the server?
   (a) Socket s = serverSocket.getSocket();
   (b) Socket s = serverSocket.accept();
   (c) Socket s = new Socket(ServerName, port);
   (d) Socket s = serverSocket.connect();

3. What happens when a server uses a port to bind an object, but the port is not available?
   (a) The object is bound successfully.
   (b) The server is blocked until the port is available.
   (c) The server encounters a fatal error and must be terminated.
   (d) The exception java.net.BindException occurs.

4. What happens when a client requests connection to a server that has not yet started?
   (a) The exception java.net.ConnectionException occurs.
   (b) The client gets blocked until the server is started.
   (c) The exception java.net.BindException occurs.
   (d) The client encounters a fatal error and must be terminated.

5. Which of the following is used to get an InetAddress object on a socket object skt.
   (a) skt.obtainInetAddress();
   (b) skt.retrieveInetAddress();
   (c) skt.InetAddress();
   (d) skt.getInetAddress();

6. Which of the following can be used for the host name to establish a socket connection with the server running on the same machine with the client?
   (a) "127.0.0.1"
   (b) InetAddress.getLocalHost()

(c) "localhost"
(d) All of the above.

7. To obtain an InputStream on a socket skt, we use ______.
(a) InputStream in = skt.obtainInputStream();
(b) InputStream in = skt.getInputStream();
(c) InputStream in = skt.getStream();
(d) InputStream in = new InputStream(skt);

8. What is the full form of IPC?
(a) Inter-Process Computing
(b) Inter-Process Communication
(c) Internal-Process Communications
(d) Integrated-Process Computing

9. In which layer do socket applications belong?
(a) Application Layer
(b) Transport Layer
(c) Network Layer
(d) None of the above

10. How many bits are there in a socket address
(a) 8 (c) 32
(b) 16 (d) 48

11. Which of the following address pairs is known as socket address?
(a) MAC address, port
(b) IP address, port
(c) IP address, MAC address
(d) Source IP address, destination IP address

12. Which of the following ranges do reserved ports belong to?
(a) 0 to 65535 (c) 0 to 256
(b) -1023 to 1023 (d) 0 to1023

13. Which of the following classes is used to create TCP server socket?
(a) ServerSocket (c) DatagramSocket
(b) Socket (d) MulticastSocket

14. Which of the following methods is used to listen to incoming connections?
(a) accept() (c) receive()
(b) listen() (d) get()

15. Which of the following methods is used to receive a datagram?
(a) accept() (c) receive()
(b) get() (d) store()

16. Which of the following methods is used to assign a socket address to a socket?
(a) assign() (c) bound()
(b) attach() (d) bind()

17. An object is said to be serializable if its class implements
(a) Serializable interface
(b) DoSerialize interface
(c) DoExternalize interface
(d) Convertible interface

18. What is the full form of TCP?
(a) Transmission Control Packet
(b) Transport Control Protocol
(c) Transfer Control Protocol
(d) Transmission Control Protocol

19. What is the full form of UDP?
(a) Useful Datagram Protocol
(b) Useful Datagram Packet
(c) User Datagram Protocol
(d) User Datagram Packet

20. Which of the following IP address classes do multicasting addresses belong to?
(a) Class A (c) Class C
(b) Class B (d) Class D

Subjective-type Questions

1. What is a *socket*?
2. What is meant by *port*? Why is it used?
3. Which are *reserved ports*? Why are they kept reserved?
4. Briefly explain the term *socket address*.
5. Write the names of Java socket classes used to develop TCP socket applications.
6. Write the basic steps to develop TCP socket applications
7. What is meant by *binding* a socket to a socket address. Why is it necessary?
8. How do you develop a server application that can handle multiple client requests concurrently?
9. Compare and contrast TCP and UDP sockets.

10. What is a *ServerSocket* and how is it used?

11. Write the names of Java socket classes used to develop UDP socket applications.

12. Write the basic steps to develop UDP socket applications.

13. What are the differences between *uni-casting* and *multicasting*?

14. How does *multicasting* differ from *broadcasting*?

15. Give some examples where multicasting is used.

16. Mention some advantages and disadvantages of Java Sockets?

17. How do you get the IP address of a machine from its hostname?

18. What are the differences between a TCP socket and a UDP socket? How are they created in Java?

19. Write a Java socket program to get the resource http://www.google.com/index.html using HTTP protocol.

20. What is a serializable object? Give some examples of non-serializable objects in Java.

CHAPTER – 14

REMOTE METHOD INVOCATION

KEY OBJECTIVES

After completing this chapter readers will be able to—

- get an overview about the Remote Procedure Call
- understand the architecture and different components of Java RMI
- know basic steps of writing RMI applications
- write distributed applications using RMI
- know what dynamic object activation is
- get an idea about callback mechanism
- know how dynamic class loading works

14.1 INTRODUCTION

The network programs that we have developed so far use the concept of sockets. Although, socket provides a simple way to write network programs, it is neither very convenient nor the most powerful. This is because everything must be transferred over the network as a stream of bytes. Though, Java provides a rich set of interfaces and classes to accomplish this, writing a complex application using these facilities is undoubtedly not so easy.

Having realized this fact, in the later versions of Java, a new object-oriented version of networking (known as Remote Method Invocation) was incorporated. This technology elevates network programming to a higher plane. In this chapter, we shall explore how this mechanism can be used easily to develop sophisticated networking applications.

14.2 REMOTE METHOD INVOCATION

Java **R**emote **M**ethod **I**nvocation (RMI) is an object-oriented **R**emote **P**rocedure **C**all (RPC) technique. It allows us to invoke methods on an object that exists in a different address space. This address space may exist on the same computer or even on a different computer connected to the source computer by a network. So, it enables objects, distributed in different computers, to communicate with one another. Although it provides a simple but elegant model [Figure 14.1:], it is remarkably powerful and can be used to invoke remote methods easily and in a natural way.

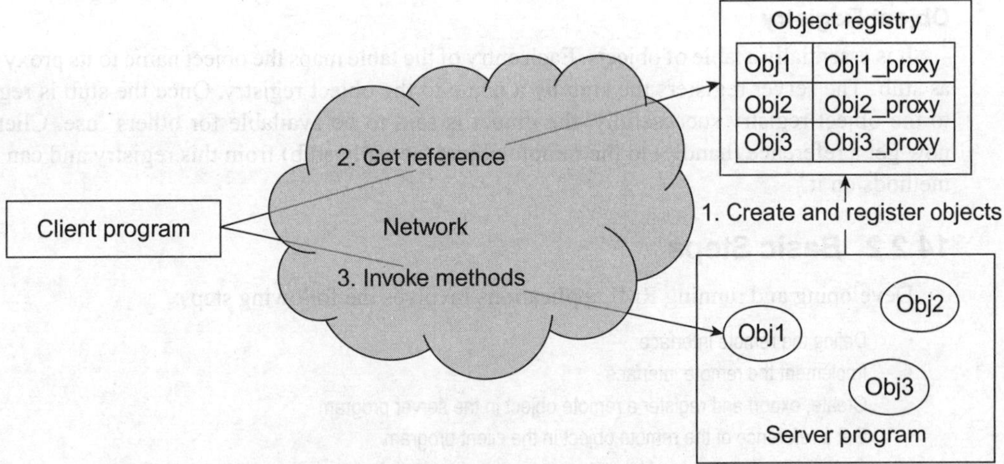

Figure 14.1: RMI programming model

The underlying communication between clients and server in this model takes place seamlessly using sockets. It means that the message from the client is not method invocation in the OO sense. Instead, it is a stream of data that must be interpreted by the server before it can invoke method on the target object. However, RMI application developers need not know this complex socket communication. Originally, in general, RMI architecture was developed taking the following goals into consideration:

- A primary goal of Java RMI technology was to allow programmers to develop distributed Java programs with the same syntax and semantics used for non-distributed programs.
- Another goal was to create a distributed object model that fits the Java programming language and the local object model naturally. RMI architects finally succeeded in creating such a powerful system that extends the safety and robustness of the Java architecture to the distributed computing world.

14.2.1 Application components

Three entities are often involved [Figure 15.1:] in an RMI application: a *server* program, a *client* program and *object registry*.

Server

This is a program that typically creates a *remote* object to be used for method invocation. This object is an ordinary object except that its class implements a Java RMI interface. Upon creation, the object is exported and registered with a separate application called *object registry* (or simply registry).

Client

A client program typically consults the object registry to get a reference (handle) to a remote object with a specified name. It can then invoke methods on the remote object using this reference (handle) as if the object is stored in the client's own address space. The RMI handles the details of communication (using sockets) between the client and the server and passes information back and forth. Note that this complex communication procedure is absolutely hidden to the client and server applications.

Object Registry

It is essentially a table of objects. Each entry of the table maps the object name to its proxy known as stub. The server registers the stub by a name to the object registry. Once the stub is registered to the object registry successfully, the object is said to be available for others' use. Clients can now get a reference (handle) to the remote object (actually stub) from this registry and can invoke methods on it.

14.2.2 Basic Steps

Developing and running RMI applications involves the following steps:

- Define the remote interface
- Implement the remote interface
- Create, export and register a remote object in the server program
- Get a reference of the remote object in the client program
- Compile the Java source files
- Run the application

Define a remote interface

First, we define an interface that contains methods that the server wishes to publish. Since method invocations on remote object occurs in a very different way from local method invocation, an interface for the remote object must be declared as follows:

- The remote interface must be public.
- The remote interface extends (either directly or indirectly) the interface `java.rmi.Remote`. The interface `Remote` is a marker interface and has no methods.

  ```
  public interface java.rmi.Remote {
  }
  ```

  A remote interface implements this `Remote` interface only to indicate that its methods may be invoked remotely.
- Each method in the interface must declare that it throws `java.rmi.RemoteException`. Note that remote objects may fail in a very different way from local objects. Therefore, every method exposes the additional exception `RemoteException` so that programmers can handle this failure appropriately.

Implement the remote interface

We then write a concrete class implementing one or more such remote interfaces. These classes may implement other interfaces or other methods may be added that can only be invoked locally. All classes that are used by these methods as parameters or return type must also be implemented. More than one implementation of the interface may be provided. Caller need not be aware of the underlying implementation.

Implement the server

Implementing a server application that creates an instance of the remote object and registers it to the RMI registry with a name is called *object deployment*. There are many ways to register an object to the RMI registry. We shall describe them separately later in this chapter.

Implement the client

A client application gets a handle to this remote object and invokes methods on it. There are different procedures to get a reference to the remote object. A detailed discussion can be found later in this chapter.

Compile them

Use Java compiler (`javac`) to compile all source files including interfaces and other subsidiary classes. To make the RMI technology work successfully, we should get help from the stub and the skeleton. Note that with Java versions before Java 5.0, programmers had to generate RMI stubs in a separate compilation step using `rmic`. Version 5.0 of Java and beyond no longer require this step. Anyway, the functions of stub and skeleton [see Figure 14.2:] are as follows:

- When a client invokes a remote method, a similar method call occurs on local stub.
- The stub packs (marshals) the necessary information (method name, parameters etc.) and sends to the server-side skeleton. The process of gathering data and transforming it into a standard format before it is transmitted over a network is called marshalling. The stub knows all information (IP address, port) of the skeleton.
- The server-side skeleton, upon receiving the information, unpacks (un-marshals) the information and invokes methods on the actual object. The process of retrieving data from the marshalled data is known as un-marshalling. Finally, it packs the result and sends the result (if any) to the stub.
- The stub unpacks the information and forwards the result to the client.

Start the application

First, start an object registry. In Java, the object registry is started using the application `rmiregistry`. It can also be created dynamically. Then start the server program. Finally, start the client program.

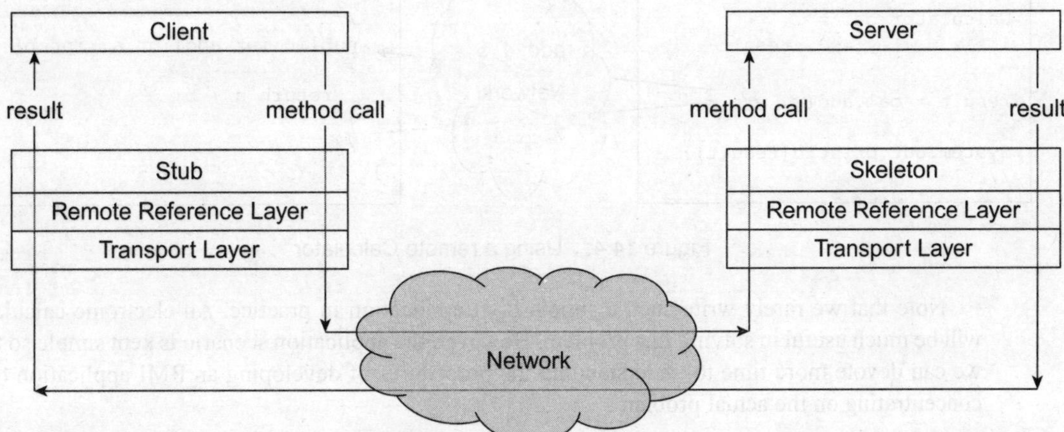

Figure 14.2: RMI architecture

14.3 JAVA RMI INTERFACES AND CLASSES

The Java RMI provides remote method invocation a framework as package `java.rmi`. Application developers use this package to create their programs. Java RMI hides almost all aspects of the distribution and provides a uniform way by which objects (distributed or not) may be accessed. The hierarchy of primary classes and interfaces is shown in Figure 14.3:

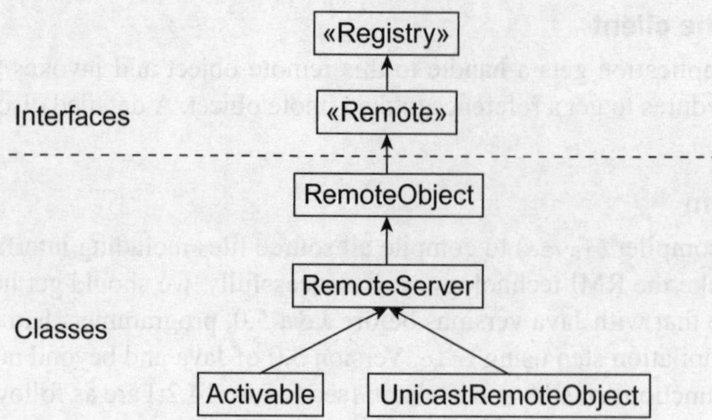

Figure 14.3: RMI class and interface hierarchy

14.4 AN APPLICATION

In this section, we shall develop a simple but elegant distributed application using Java RMI technology. In this application [Figure 14.4:], the server program creates and exports a simple remote object (we call it calculator) which provides one method. The method takes two integers as arguments and returns their sum. A client program gets a reference to the remote object and invokes this method on the remote object to calculate the sum of two integers.

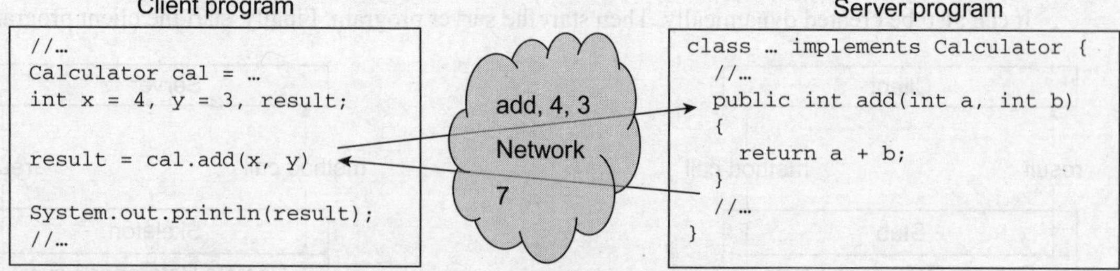

Figure 14.4: Using a remote Calculator

Note that we rarely write such a simple RMI application in practice. An electronic calculator will be much useful in solving this problem. However, the application scenario is kept simple so that we can devote more time to understanding the procedures of developing an RMI application than concentrating on the actual problem.

14.4.1 Writing an interface

At first, communicating programs must agree upon a protocol. This protocol is expressed in an interface and is usually developed by the service provider. An interface is an abstract description of the methods that may be invoked on an object supporting that interface. To support an interface, object's class must provide implementations of those methods.

An interface only provides abstract description (signature) of methods without any implementation. The signature provides necessary information such as name of a method, its return type as well as number, order and type of arguments to be passed to invoke the method. This means the signature provides enough information to determine the method call syntax. A program (call it server program/service provider) creates an object whose class implements this interface (i.e. provides implementations of these methods) and publishes this interface. By publishing an interface, server program conveys the following:

"Hey all of you, I have created an object that is capable of providing a set of important services. If you are interested, you can get these services by calling the corresponding methods on this object. The necessary information (name of the method, argument list and return type) to invoke these methods is given in the interface".

Since method invocations on remote objects occur in a very different way from local method invocation, an interface for the remote object must be declared as follows:

- The remote interface must be public.
- The remote interface extends (either directly or indirectly) the interface `java.rmi.Remote`. The interface `Remote` is a marker interface and has no methods.

```
public interface java.rmi.Remote {
}
```

  A remote interface implements this `Remote` interface only to indicate that its methods may be invoked remotely.
- Each method in the interface must declare that it throws `java.rmi.RemoteException`. Note that remote objects may fail in a very different way from local objects. Therefore, every method exposes the additional exception `RemoteException` so that programmers can handle this failure appropriately.

In our application, remote object wants to provide a single method as follows:

- A method that takes two integers as arguments, adds them up and returns the result

An interface that specifies the above description may then be written as follows:

```
//Calculator.java
import java.rmi.*;
public interface Calculator extends Remote {
   public int add(int a, int b) throws RemoteException;
}
```

The `Calculator` interface defines the client's view of the remote object. The interested programs (call them client programs/service users) make use of this interface to know the details of services (methods) that the object provides. In this way, the `Calculator` interface helps the clients and server to agree upon a protocol.

This interface extends `Remote` interface (provided in `java.rmi` package) and hence becomes a remote interface. Any object, whose class implements this interface, is a remote object whose methods can be invoked from a different JVM.

The interface describes only one method `add()`. This is the method that remote programs will use to find the sum of two integers. Since, this method will be called remotely, it may fail due to problems related to communication or protocol or server. So, using `throws` clause, the method indicates that a `RemoteException` might be thrown by this method during its execution. The exception `RemoteException` (provided in `java.rmi` package) is a checked exception. Consequently, a program that calls this method must prepare it to handle this exception explicitly by either catching or re-throwing the exception

A remote interface must be *public*. Note that a remote interface will most probably be used by classes which do not belong to the same package where the interface is kept. We know that a non-public interface is only accessible from the classes of the same package. Consequently, to make an interface available to every other, it is declared as `public`. Our `Calculator` interface is also declared `public` accordingly.

Note Java's *object serialization* procedure is used by RMI to transfer objects. Consequently, objects/variables that are transferred across different JVMs must be *serializable*. An object is said to be *serializable* if its class implements the `java.io.Serializable` interface. The interface `java.io.Serializable` does not define anything; it just specifies that the object of the class is serializable. In our application, a client passes two integers to invoke the method `add()`. Fortunately, `int` type and all other Java primitive types are serializable. Hence there is nothing to worry about the serialization procedure.

14.4.2 Writing Implementation class

An interface merely helps us in determining method call syntax. It does not provide any method implementation (body). The implementation is provided in another class. In general, an implementation class of a remote object is developed as follows:

- It must declare that it implements at least one remote interface.
- It must provide implementations of all the methods specified in the remote interface.
- Optionally define one or more constructor.

14.4.2.1 Implementing the remote interface

There are two ways to write an implementation class (say `SimpleCalculator` for our application). In the simplest way, an implementation class extends either `java.rmi.server.UnicastRemoteObject` or `javax.rmi.PortableRemoteObject` class [Figure 14.5: (i)]. In this case, the implementation class readily becomes a remote class. The advantage of this scheme is that the objects of this class are exported automatically by the super class's (`UnicastRemoteObject` or `PortableRemoteObject`) constructor when they are created. So, we don't have to export them explicitly. However, the problem of this scheme is that, the implementation class cannot extend any other class further as Java does not support multiple inheritance for classes. So, it is not a good idea to write implementation classes extending `UnicastRemoteObject` or `PortableRemoteObject`.

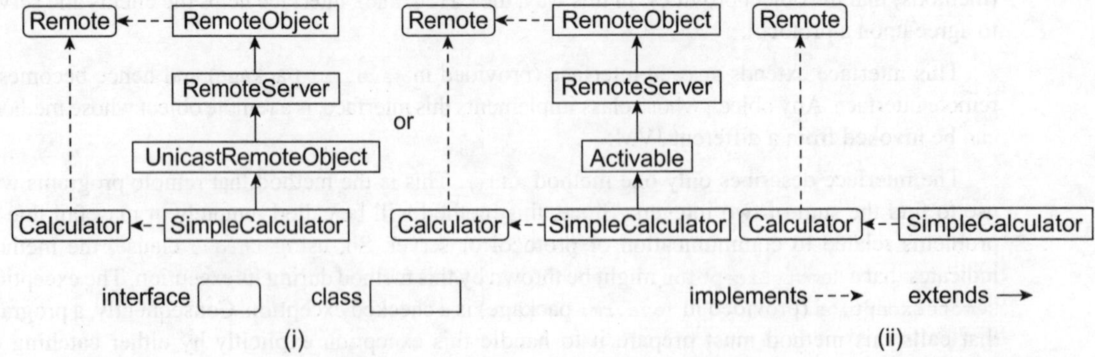

Figure 14.5: Writing implementation class (i) Extending a class (ii) Without extending a class

To avoid the aforesaid problem, there exists another (probably better) scheme. In this scheme implementation class does not extend `UnicastRemoteObject` or `PortableRemoteObject` classes which leave a provision of extending other classes if required later [Figure 15.5: (ii)]. However, instances of this implementation classes have to be exported explicitly, Fortunately, both `UnicastRemoteObject` and `Activatable` classes provide several static overloaded versions of `exportObject()` method for explicit export of remote objects. In this case, though we have to write some extra piece of code, we shall have a provision to extend other classes if really necessary.

In our class implementation, the last described procedure is followed. Accordingly, a sample class is developed whose source code (stored in file `SimpleCalculator.java`) is given below:

```
//SimpleCalculator.java
import java.rmi.*;
public class SimpleCalculator implements Calculator {
  public int add(int a, int b) {
    System.out.println("Received: " + a + "and" + b);
    int result = a + b;
    System.out.println("Sent: " + result);
    return result;
  }
}
```

The implementation class in our example is `SimpleCalculator`. It declares that it implements a remote interface `Calculator` as follows:

```
public class SimpleCalculator implements Calculator {
```

In general, an implementation class may implement any number of remote interfaces. An implementation class may also extend any other implementation class of a remote interface.

14.4.2.2 Providing method implementation

The implementation class must provide definition (body) of all the methods specified in the remote interface(s). For our implementation class `SimpleCalculator`, the only method `add()` is defined as follows:

```
public int add(int a, int b) {
  System.out.println("Received: " + a + "and" + b);
  int result = a + b;
  System.out.println("Sent: " + result);
  return result;
}
```

The implementation of `add()` method is very simple. It returns the sum of two integers passed to this method. The `System.out.println()` methods are used only to print useful messages so that we can track this method invocation.

Note that the method `add()` does not have to indicate that it throws any exception because its body itself does not throw `RemoteException` nor does it throw any other checked exceptions.

When a class declares that it implements an interface, it basically promises to the compiler that it will provide method bodies for all the methods specified in that interface. We know that methods of an interface are implicitly public and abstract. So, if the implementation class doesn't obey its promise (it it does not provide definition of all methods), it becomes an incomplete class, which by definition is called an abstract class. In this case, the compiler will figure this fact out if the class itself does not declare it as abstract class.

In an implementation class, it is possible to define methods not specified in the remote interface. However, those methods can only be invoked locally (i.e. within the virtual machine running the service) and cannot be invoked remotely.

The type of arguments to, or return values from, remote methods may be any valid type in Java, including objects. For objects, the only requirement is that they implement the interface `java.io.Serializable`. It is good to know that almost all classes in `java.lang` and `java.util` packages implement the `Serializable` interface. However, certain types are inherently non-serializable and cannot be passed to or returned from a remote method. Examples of such type include classes related to threads, file descriptors, socket connection, database connection, that makes sense only within a single address space.

The following rules are employed when objects are passed to a remote method.

When a *local* object is passed to a remote method as an argument, the method's formal parameter refers to a *local* temporary object which is an exact copy of the actual object. Consequently, if a method is called in the remote method through the formal parameter, invocation of the method occurs on local object not on the actual object that was passed as an argument. Any changes to this local object's state in the remote method are reflected only in the receiver's local copy, not in the caller's original object. Similarly, any changes to the original object's state by the caller are not reflected in the receiver's copy. Note that, class definition of actual object must exist in the remote method's JVM.

However, if the object passed to a remote method is itself a *remote* object, method's formal parameter refers to a *local* temporary object which is a proxy to the actual object. In this case, a method call through the formal parameter results in a similar method invocation on local proxy object which in turn forwards the method invocation information towards the actual object. A detailed description of this procedure is given later in this chapter.

14.4.2.3 Writing Constructor

Writing the constructor is not mandatory if implementation class does not extend `java.rmi.server.UnicastRemoteObject` or `javax.rmi.PortableRemoteObject` class. However, if the implementation class extends any one of these two classes, a constructor is mandatory for the following reason:

When an implementation class extends `java.rmi.server.UnicastRemoteObject` or `javax.rmi.PortableRemoteObject` class, objects of the implementation class are exported by the super class's constructor automatically upon creation. Since, during this export, super class's constructor could potentially throw a `java.rmi.RemoteException`, we must define a constructor that throws a `RemoteException`, even if the constructor does nothing else. Otherwise, the Java compiler produces an error message.

Since our implementation class does not extend any of those two classes, we have not written any constructor. However, a suitable constructor may always be written if initialization of variables of each newly created instance of the class is needed.

14.4.3 Writing an RMI Server

This is a simple Java application program (call it `CalculatorServer.java`) containing the well-known `main()` method. This program usually performs the following steps:

- Creates an instance of implementation class
- Exports it so that the object can receive method invocation from remote client
- Registers the object to a registry so that remote client can get remote reference to this object

14.4.3.1 Creating a remote object

Creating an instance of the implementation class uses the same syntax used for creating ordinary objects. So, the following piece of code creates an instance of our `SimpleCalculator` class.

```
SimpleCalculator calculator = new SimpleCalculator();
```

14.4.3.2 Exporting the object

The object created above is an ordinary object and is not capable of handling method invocation requests that come from a remote program. To add this capability, it has to be exported. Exporting an object basically means making the object capable of receiving invocations of its methods from remote clients. Note that our implementation class does not extend `UnicastRemoteObject` or `PortableRemoteObject` class. So, we have to export the object explicitly using static `exportObject()` method of the `UnicastRemoteObject` (or `PortableRemoteObject`) class as follows:

```
Calculator stub = (Calculator)UnicastRemoteObject.exportObject(calculator, 0);
```

The first argument of `exportObject()` method is an object to be exported. The second argument is an `int` that specifies the TCP port to be used to listen for incoming remote invocation requests for the object. Usually a `0` (zero) is used for this value which indicates that the port has to be chosen at runtime by RMI or the underlying operating system. However, programmers may specify a specific port to be used for listening. If `exportObject()` method returns successfully, our `SimpleCalculator` object becomes ready to process incoming remote invocations.

Let us now understand the functionality of `exportObject()` method in detail. This is necessary for programmers who want to understand the implementation of Java RMI architecture. A clear understanding of this architecture enables programmers to develop sophisticated network applications without any hassle.

The `exportObject()` method essentially creates and installs a proxy for the `calculator` object at the server end passing the `calculator` object to the proxy. This proxy is known as *skeleton*. This proxy has a reference to the `calculator` object. The task of the skeleton broadly is as follows:

It creates a TCP `ServerSocket` object and listens for the incoming connection requests on the TCP port specified by the second argument. Upon establishing a connection, The `ServerSocket` waits for the incoming remote method call on behalf of our `calculator` object.

Whenever a request for method call (in the packed format) comes to this skeleton, it unpacks the request to obtain the method name and arguments to be used for this method. This unpacking procedure is also called *un-marshalling*. Note that the `calculator` object and its skeleton belong to the same JVM and skeleton has also reference to this local `calculator` object. So, skeleton can invoke the desired method on the actual object and get the result. It then packs (called *marshalling*) the result and sends it back to the caller.

The method `exportObject()` creates and returns another proxy for this object to be uploaded to the object registry. This proxy is called *stub*. The stub knows the port the skeleton listens on as well as the IP address of the computer. This means the stub knows all the information about the skeleton and can communicate with e skeleton as and when necessary. The object registry essentially provides this stub object on request. The type of this stub must be `Calculator`, not the `SimpleCalculator`. This is because stub for a remote object (`SimpleCalculator` in this case) implements the interface (`Calculator`) which is implemented by the exported object.

The communication procedure is shown in Figure 14.6:

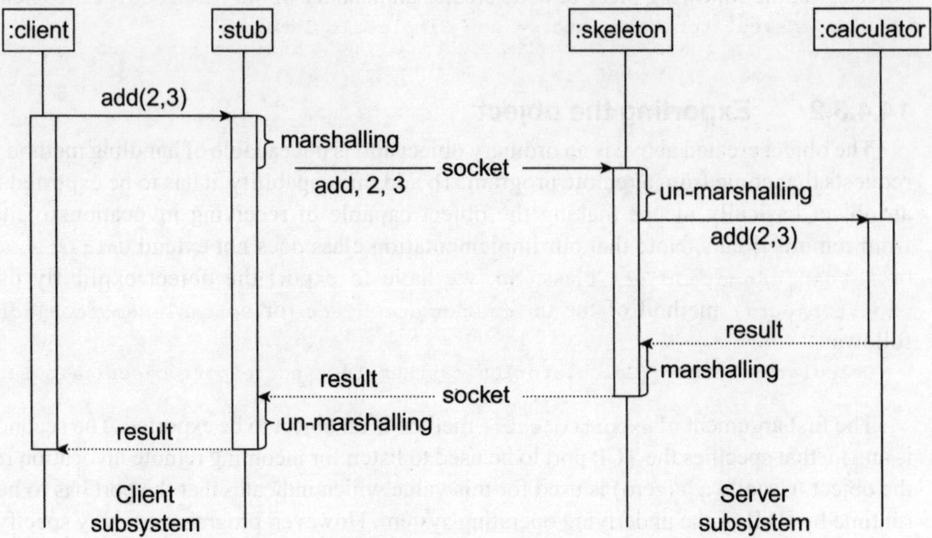

Figure 14.6: Calculator client–server execution pattern

The interesting part of `exportObject()` method is that it creates and loads class files for stub at runtime (if one not found). Consequently, we don't have to generate class files for stub using `rmic` compiler in Java 5.0 and later versions. This method also has another overloaded version as follows:

```
public static RemoteStub exportObject(Remote obj) throws RemoteException
```

This method does not take any port number as arguments and expects existence of pre-generated class files for stub and skeleton. The name of the stub class is determined by concatenating the binary name of the remote object's class with the suffix "_Stub". Indeed, `rmic` compiler generates class files using the aforesaid naming convention. For example, the following command generates a class file `SimpleCalculator_Stub.class` from an implementation class file `SimpleCalculator.class`.

```
rmic SimpleCalculator
```

If the `exportObject()` method does not find an appropriate stub class or is unable to load the stub class, or a problem occurs creating the stub instance, a `StubNotFoundException` is thrown.

To understand the functionality of this stub class, source code may be generated using any suitable Java de-compiler. A sample source generated using DJ Java de-compiler is shown below:

```
import java.lang.reflect.Method;
import java.rmi.RemoteException;
import java.rmi.UnexpectedException;
import java.rmi.server.RemoteObject;
import java.rmi.server.RemoteRef;
import java.rmi.server.RemoteStub;

public final class SimpleCalculator_Stub extends RemoteStub implements
Calculator {
```

```
  private static final long serialVersionUID = 2L;
  private static Method $method_add_0;

  static {
    try    {
      $method_add_0 = Calculator.class.getMethod("add", new Class[] { Integer.TYPE,
Integer.TYPE });
    }
    catch (NoSuchMethodException localNoSuchMethodException)    {
      throw new NoSuchMethodError("stub class initialization failed");
    }
  }

  public SimpleCalculator_Stub(RemoteRef paramRemoteRef)  {
    super(paramRemoteRef);
  }

  public int add(int paramInt1, int paramInt2) throws RemoteException {
    try    {
      Object localObject = this.ref.invoke(this, $method_add_0, new Object[]
{ new Integer(paramInt1), new Integer(paramInt2) }, -7734458262622125146L);
      return ((Integer)localObject).intValue();
    }
    catch (RuntimeException localRuntimeException) {
      throw localRuntimeException;
    }
    catch (RemoteException localRemoteException) {
      throw localRemoteException;
    }
    catch (Exception localException) {
      throw new UnexpectedException("undeclared checked exception",
localException);
    }
  }
}
```

So, if a programmer faces difficulty in generating a stub class (e.g. `rmic` compiler or implementation class is not available etc.), the programmer may use the previous version of `exportObject()` method without any trouble. We also have used this version to avoid generating stub class explicitly. In this case, Java RMI generates a proxy class (having a name like Proxy0) whose functionality is very much similar to the stub class generated by the `rmic`. It then creates and installs a proxy (skeleton) dynamically for the `calculator` object. The method `exportObject()` also creates and returns another proxy (stub) for this object to be uploaded to the object registry. We wrote a Java agent program to find the class data and using a DJ Java de-compiler a source was generated as follows:

```
import java.lang.reflect.*;
import java.rmi.RemoteException;

public final class $Proxy0 extends Proxy implements Calculator {
  public $Proxy0(InvocationHandler invocationhandler){
    super(invocationhandler);
  }
  public final boolean equals(Object obj) {
    try {
      return ((Boolean)super.h.invoke(this, m1, new Object[] { obj
        })).booleanValue();
    }catch(Error _ex) { }
    catch(Throwable throwable) {
      throw new UndeclaredThrowableException(throwable);
    }
  }
```

```
    public final int add(int i, int j) throws RemoteException {
      try {
        return ((Integer)super.h.invoke(this, m3, new Object[] {
          Integer.valueOf(i), Integer.valueOf(j)})).intValue();
      }catch(Error _ex) { }
       catch(Throwable throwable) {
         throw new UndeclaredThrowableException(throwable);
       }
    }
    public final String toString() {
      try {
        return (String)super.h.invoke(this, m2, null);
      }catch(Error _ex) { }
       catch(Throwable throwable) {
         throw new UndeclaredThrowableException(throwable);
       }
    }
    private static Method m1;
    private static Method m0;
    private static Method m3;
    private static Method m2;

    static {
      try {
        m1 = Class.forName("java.lang.Object").getMethod("equals", new Class[] {
                  Class.forName("java.lang.Object") });
        m0 = Class.forName("java.lang.Object").getMethod("hashCode", new
  Class[0]);
        m3 = Class.forName("Calculator").getMethod("add", new Class[] {
                  Integer.TYPE, Integer.TYPE });
        m2 = Class.forName("java.lang.Object").getMethod("toString", new
  Class[0]);
      }catch(NoSuchMethodException nosuchmethodexception) {
         throw new NoSuchMethodError(nosuchmethodexception.getMessage());
       }
       catch(ClassNotFoundException classnotfoundexception) {
         throw new NoClassDefFoundError(classnotfoundexception.getMessage());
       }
    }
  }
```

Java RMI generates this proxy class using the concept of dynamic proxy. It may be noted that the implementation of `add()` method in this class is similar to that of in the stub class generated by `rmic` compiler.

14.4.3.3 Registering the stub

The object's server-side proxy (skeleton) is now ready to accept the incoming method invocation request. The object's stub is also generated. This stub can communicate with the skeleton remotely using socket. So, if we can somehow create an instance of this stub in a remote computer, invoking a method on the remote object through that stub instance will be a matter of time. The stub is obtained from a separate application called registry where the server registers the stub.

To register the stub generated by `exportObject()` method with the object registry, a reference to object registry is needed. A new object registry may be created or an existing one may be used. The class `java.rmi.registry.LocateRegistry` provides many static methods for this purpose. In our example, we shall use an existing object registry which can be started using `rmiregistry` application provided by JVM. The `rmiregistry` application runs as a separate process and allows applications to register remote objects or obtain references to named remote objects. *Java RMI only allows us to run* `rmiregistry` and server in the same computer currently.

The following code is used to get a reference to an existing object registry which is already started on the same computer on default port (1099).

```
Registry registry = LocateRegistry.getRegistry();
```

Specify the port number to the `getRegistry()` method, if object registry runs on a port other than 1099. Instead of using an existing registry, the application itself may explicitly create a registry as follows:

```
Registry registry = LocateRegistry.createRegistry(1099);
```

This creates a registry that listens on port 1099. Note that a registry created using the above piece of code is available provided that the server application is started. Anyway, once we have a reference to the registry, the stub is registered with this object registry as follows:

```
String name = "calculator";
registry.rebind(name, stub);
```

The `rebind()` method essentially binds a specified stub and a name. If there is an existing binding for the specified name, it is overridden. So, the stub for the calculator object is hereafter known as 'calculator'.

When a client requests the object registry to have a reference to the remote object, the stub for the remote object is passed. The client-side application that contacted the object registry creates and installs an instance of this stub in the client's computer and returns a reference to the client. Client basically invokes methods on this local stub object. As mentioned earlier, this stub has complete information about the skeleton, which is object's server-side proxy. The stub creates a socket to the skeleton. It packs the information such as the method name to be invoked, parameters etc. This is called *marshalling*. The stub then sends the packed data to the skeleton through the socket. The skeleton then un-marshals the data and follows the steps as mentioned previously. The entire execution sequence is shown in Figure 14.6: .

The entire piece of code is embedded in a try-catch block.

The source code for server is stored in the file `CalculatorServer.java`. The source code for the `CalculatorServer.java` class is given as follows:

```
//CalculatorServer.java
import java.rmi.*;
import java.rmi.registry.*;
import java.rmi.server.*;
public class CalculatorServer {
  public static void main(String args[]) {
    try {
      SimpleCalculator cal = new SimpleCalculator();
      Calculator stub = (Calculator)UnicastRemoteObject.exportObject(cal,0);
      Registry registry = LocateRegistry.getRegistry();
      String name = "calculator";
      registry.rebind(name, stub);
      System.out.println("Calculator server ready...");
    }catch (Exception e) { e.printStackTrace(); }
  }
}
```

14.4.4 Writing an RMI Client

Clients for `SimpleCalculator` are relatively simple. It is the program that invokes `add()` method on the object created and exported by the server. However, to invoke a method, it has to obtain a reference to the remote object first. A reference to a remote object may be obtained using:

- Registry
- RMI's naming service
- Passing and returning remote objects

In the current application, we shall use the first method. Note that remote references are stored in the object registry. So, client first synthesizes a remote reference to the object registry running on the server host using the `LocateRegistry.getRegistry()` method as follows:

```
Registry registry = LocateRegistry.getRegistry(args[0]);
```

The argument to the `getRegistry()` method is the first command line argument `args[0]` which is the name or IP address of the computer where the registry runs on the default port (1099). If the registry runs on a port other than 1099, you specify the port as the second argument to the `getRegistry()` method. The `getRegistry()` method consults the remote registry (using socket) and essentially returns a local proxy registry (stub for registry which is an instance of `RegistryImpl_Stub` class). Note that this proxy is created and loaded dynamically upon downloading the `RegistryImpl_Stub` class data from the remote object registry. This proxy registry knows all the information of the remote registry (port and IP address) and capable of communicating (using socket) with the remote registry upon request. The information about the registry object (such as class file name) may be verified using the following code:

```
System.out.println(registry);
```

When this statement is executed, it generates an output shown below:

```
RegistryImpl_Stub[UnicastRef [liveRef:[endpoint:[172.16.5.81:1099](remote),objI
D:[0:0:0, 0]]]]
```

Once the client gets a reference to the remote registry, it uses the `lookup()` method on this registry to get a reference to the remote `calculator` object as follows:

```
String name = "calculator";
Calculator cal = (Calculator)registry.lookup(name);
```

Note that the client uses the same name that the server uses to register the object. The lookup method of the proxy registry consults the remote registry, downloads the stub for the `SimpleCalculator` object having the name "calculator" specified as argument. It then creates and installs an instance of the stub (dynamically using the concept of dynamic class loading) and returns a reference to the client. The reference `cal` is actually a local reference to the stub. The information about the cal object (such as class file name) may be verified using the following code:

```
System.out.println(cal);
```

When this statement is executed, it generates an output shown below:

```
Proxy[Calculator,RemoteObjectInvocationHandler[UnicastRef [liveRef:
[endpoint:[172.16.5.81:52704](remote),objID:[-1812e356:1409d599c42:-7fff,
150949126975901178
6]]]]]
```

Note that, `[172.16.5.81:52704]` is the socket address of the skeleton. This stub sits behind the scene and behaves as a proxy of the remote `calculator` object. When client invokes a method using the `cal` reference, a similar method invocation on the stub occurs. The stub then creates a TCP socket connection with the skeleton, marshals the method invocation information and sends the request. When the result comes back from the skeleton, the stub returns the result to the client. The underlying procedure is transparent to the client.

Invoking the `add()` method on the remote object is now as simple as invoking a method on an ordinary local object.

```
int x = 4, y = 3;
int result = cal.add(x,y);
```

Here is the complete source code for the client which is stored in `CalculatorClient.java`.

```
//CalculatorClient.java
import java.rmi.*;
import java.rmi.registry.*;
public class CalculatorClient {
  public static void main(String args[]) {
    try  {
      String name = "calculator";
      Registry registry = LocateRegistry.getRegistry(args[0]);
      //System.out.println(registry);
      //uncomment above line if you want to display the info. about registry
      Calculator cal = (Calculator)registry.lookup(name);
      //System.out.println(cal);
      //uncomment above line if you want to display the info. about cal
      int x = 4, y = 3;
      int result = cal.add(x,y);
      System.out.println("Sent: " + x +" and "+y);
      System.out.print("Received("+x+"+"+y+"=): " + result);
    }catch (Exception e) { e.printStackTrace();  }
  }
}
```

14.5 COMPILING THE PROGRAM

Suppose the server application is developed in the directory `E:\Net\rmi\calculator\server` of a computer having IP address `172.16.5.81`. Hereafter, we shall refer to this directory as `server_home`. Now, put server-side files in `server_home` as shown in Figure 14.7: (i)

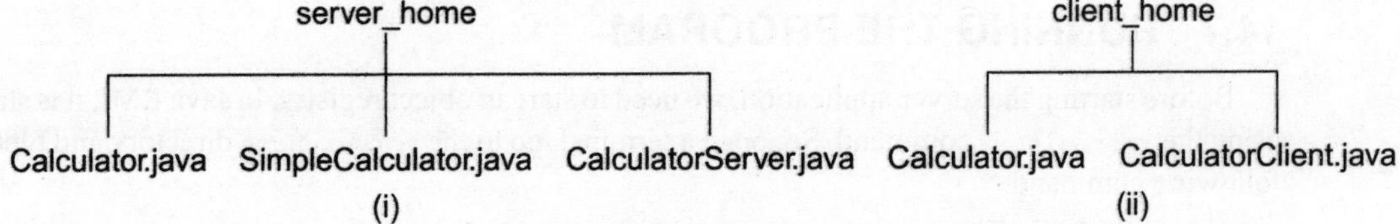

Figure 14.7: Directory content for Calculator (i) Server (ii) Client

Assume that the client application is developed in the directory `E:\Net\rmi\calculator\client` of another computer. We shall refer to this directory as `client_home`. Now, put client-side files in `client_home` as shown in Figure 14.7: (ii).

14.5.1 Compiling Server

Open a terminal and go to the directory `server_home`. This directory contains three files, `Calculator.java`, `SimpleCalculator.java` and `CalculatorServer.java`. Use `javac` command to compile these Java source files as follows:

```
javac *.java
```

This generates the class files `Calculator.class`, `SimpleCalculator.class` and `CalculatorServer.class`

14.5.2 Compiling Client

Go to the directory `client_home`. The `Calculator.class` generated in `server_home` directory is needed by the client to develop its own applications. Get this class file from `server_home` directory and put it in `client_home`. Alternatively, you can put the `Calculator.java` file in `client_home` and generate the class file using the following command

```
javac Calculator.java
```

Now, give the following command to compile client-side source file.

```
javac CalculatorClient.java
```

This generates a class file `CalculatorClient.class`

14.6 GENERATING STUB CLASSES

Java 5.0 and later releases add support for the dynamic generation of stub classes at runtime, obviating the need to use the Java RMI stub compiler, `rmic`, to pregenerate stub classes for remote objects. Note that `rmic` must still be used to pregenerate stub classes for remote objects that need to support clients running on earlier versions.

When remote object is exported (using the constructors or static `exportObject()` methods of the classes `java.rmi.server.UnicastRemoteObject` or `java.rmi.activation.Activatable`) and a pregenerated stub class for the remote object is not found, the remote object's stub will be a `java.lang.reflect.Proxy` instance (whose class is dynamically generated) with a `java.rmi.server.RemoteObjectInvocationHandler` as its invocation handler. A detail about enhancements that have been incorporated in the current version of Java can be found in `http://docs.oracle.com/javase/1.5.0/docs/guide/rmi/relnotes.html`.

However, if a stub class is really needed, use the following command to generate it:

```
rmic SimpleCalculator
```

14.7 RUNNING THE PROGRAM

Before starting the server application, we need to start an object registry. In Java RMI, it is started using the `rmiregistry` command. So, open a terminal, go to the `server_home` directory and type the following command:

```
start rmiregistry
```

The command opens new windows and starts the object registry application on the default port 1099. Note that `rmiregistry` needs `Calculator.class` file when a Calculator object is registered. So, `rmiregistry` should be started from a directory that contains `Calculator.class` file. However, RMI has techniques for loading class dynamically, which will be illustrated in a separate application in detail.

14.7.1 Start Server

Give the following command to start the server:

```
java CalculatorServer
```

It produces a sample output as shown in Figure 14.8:

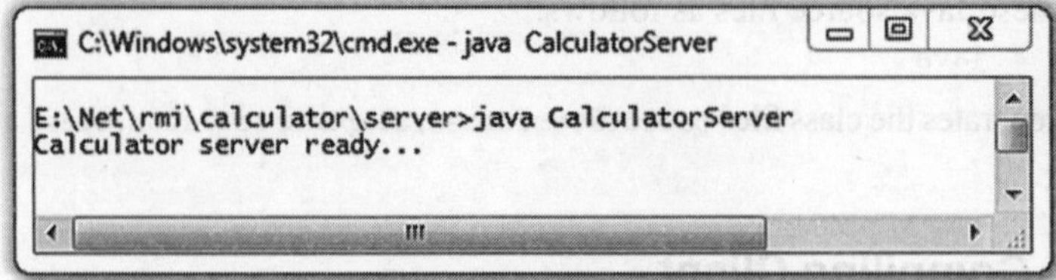

Figure 14.8: Calculator server

14.7.2 Start client

Go to the `client_home` directory and give the following command to start the client:

```
java CalculatorClient 172.16.5.81
```

It produces a sample output as shown in Figure 14.9: (i). The final output of the server application is shown in Figure 14.9: (ii).

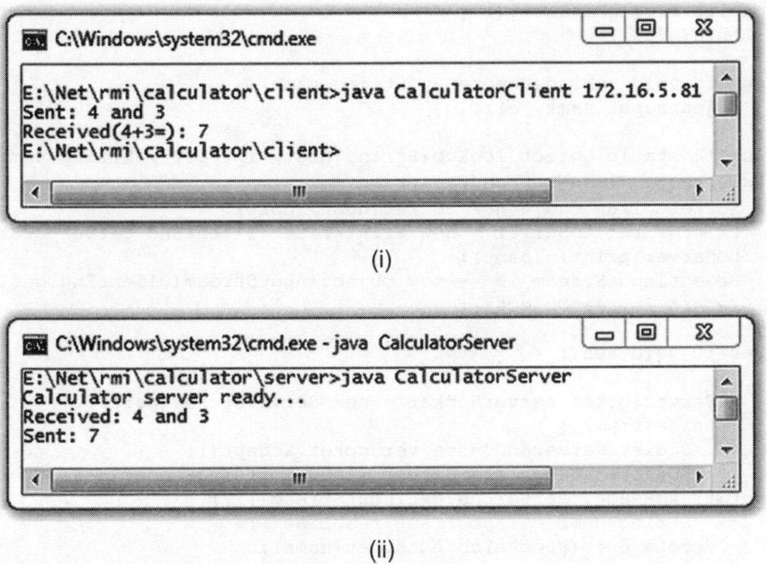

Figure 14.9: Calculator application (i) Client (ii) Server

14.7.3 Understanding object Registry

The registry is essentially an application for the server to register services it offers and a place for clients to query for those services. Let us now understand how this application functions.

When a registry is started using `rmiregistry` command or `Registry.createRegistry()` method, it creates a `ServerSocket` object and listens for incoming connection. If a client program invokes `lookup()` method, it makes a socket connection to the remote registry application and sends the name of the object specified as argument through the connection. The remote registry finds the stub with this name and sends this object over the network back to the client using object serialization. The `lookup()` method, upon receiving the serialized data, reconstructs the object and finally returns it to the caller. The returned object is the client-side proxy of the server object and knows how to communicate with the object through the server-side proxy. So, if we can somehow create an instance of the stub at the client side, invoking a method on the remote object becomes possible readily.

In this section, we shall develop a simple registry that behaves as described above. The following is the complete source code of this registry store in a file `SimpleRegistry.java`.

```
import java.rmi.*;
import java.io.*;
import java.net.*;
import java.util.*;
public class SimpleRegistry implements Runnable {
  int port;
  Hashtable objects = new Hashtable();
  public SimpleRegistry(int prt) {
    this.port = prt;
    new Thread(this).start();
  }
  public SimpleRegistry() {
    this(6789);
  }
  public void rebind(Remote o, String name)    {
    objects.put(name, o);
  }
  public static Object lookup(String host, int port, String name) throws
IOException, ClassNotFoundException {
    Socket clientEnd = new Socket(host, port);
    PrintWriter toServer = new PrintWriter(clientEnd.getOutputStream(), true);
    toServer.println(name);
    ObjectInputStream in  = new ObjectInputStream(clientEnd.getInputStream());
    return in.readObject();
  }
  public void run() {
    try {
      ServerSocket serverSocket = new ServerSocket(port);
      while(true) {
        Socket serverEnd = serverSocket.accept();
        BufferedReader fromClient = new BufferedReader(new
InputStreamReader(serverEnd.getInputStream()));
        String name = fromClient.readLine();
      Remote o = (Remote)objects.get(name);
        ObjectOutputStream oos = new
ObjectOutputStream(serverEnd.getOutputStream());
        oos.writeObject(o);
      }
    }catch(Exception e) {}
  }
}
```

Now modify the calculator server as follows:

```
//Registry registry = LocateRegistry.getRegistry();
//registry.rebind(name, stub);
SimpleRegistry reg = new SimpleRegistry();
reg.rebind(stub, name);
```

The original statements in the server are shown in the comment line. Also modify the calculator client as follows:

```
//Registry registry = LocateRegistry.getRegistry(args[0]);
//Calculator cal = (Calculator)registry.lookup(name);

Calculator cal = (Calculator)SimpleRegistry.lookup(args[0],
Integer.parseInt(args[1]), name);
```

The original statements in the client are shown in the comment line. Compile and run the application as discussed earlier. Note the calculator server creates a `SimpleRegistry`. So, a separate rmiregistry application is not needed. A sample output is shown in Figure 14.10:

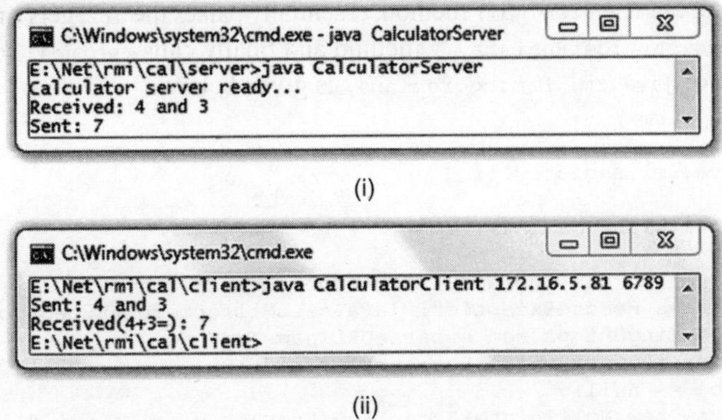

Figure 14.10: Using custom registry (i) Calculator server (ii) Calculator client

14.7.4 Using RMI URL

In our calculator example, server exports and registers a remote object explicitly using a tedious procedure. The client also gets a reference to the remote object using a long method. Java RMI provides a simple addressing mechanism, known as RMI URL, which may be used by the server as well as the client for the same purpose.

The server application creates an object and registers it to the RMI registry using the static `rebind()` method of `java.rmi.Naming` class. The server must specify the port number of RMI registry application and the IP address or name of the computer where it runs. The server must also specify a logical name by which the object will be known to clients. Clients use this name to get a reference to this object.

The entire information may be encapsulated using RMI URL. It is similar to the HTTP URL except that it uses "rmi" as the protocol name. It takes the following form:

```
rmi://host:[port]/objectName
```

The `host` is the IP address or Fully Qualified Domain Name (FQDN) of the computer where the RMI registry runs. The optional `port` is the port number of the RMI registry. The default port number is `1099`. The `objectName` is a logical name of the object. For example, if RMI registry runs in a computer having IP address `172.16.5.81` on port `2000`, and object name is `calculator`, the RMI URL for this object will be as follows:

```
protocol      host        port    name
rmi://172.16.5.81:2000/calculator
```

If RMI registry runs on default port (1099), the above URL reduces to

```
rmi://172.16.5.81/calculator
```

If RMI registry and server run on the same computer, the above URL further reduces to

```
calculator
```

Since, Java RMI only supports to run RMI registry and server on the same computer, the URL of our remote object is simply `calculator`.

Now, create an object and register it using the `Naming.rebind()` method as follows:

```
String url = "calculator";
SimpleCalculator calculator = new SimpleCalculator();
Naming.rebind(url, calculator);
```

The `java.rmi.Naming.rebind()` method, essentially parses the `url`, gets a reference to the registry using `LocateRegistry.getRegistry()` method and finally calls `rebind()` method on this registry. A code snippet of `java.rmi.Naming.rebind()` is given below:

```
package java.rmi;

import java.rmi.registry.*;
//...
public final class Naming {
//...
  public static void rebind(String name, Remote obj)
        throws RemoteException, java.net.MalformedURLException    {
    ParsedNamingURL parsed = parseURL(name);
    Registry registry = getRegistry(parsed);
    if (obj == null)
       throw new NullPointerException("cannot bind to null");
    registry.rebind(parsed.name, obj);
  }
//...
}
```

Since `java.rmi.Naming.rebind()` method expects second argument as `Java.rmi.Remote` type object, the class definition of `SimpleCalculator` needs to be modified slightly in this case as follows:

```
//SimpleCalculator.java
import java.rmi.*;
import java.rmi.server.*;
public class SimpleCalculator extends UnicastRemoteObject implements Calculator
{
  SimpleCalculator()throws RemoteException {}
  public int add(int a, int b) {
    System.out.println("Received: " + a + " and " + b);
    int result = a + b;
    System.out.println("Sent: " + result);
    return result;
  }
}
```

The code that has been added is shown with bold face. Here is the modified source code of `CalculatorServer.Java`.

```
//CalculatorServer.java
import java.rmi.*;
public class CalculatorServer {
  public static void main(String args[]) {
    try {
      String url = "calculator";
      SimpleCalculator calculator = new SimpleCalculator();
      Naming.rebind(url, calculator);
      System.out.println("Calculator server ready...");
    }catch (Exception e)  { e.printStackTrace(); }
  }
}
```

The `Naming.rebind()` method registers the calculator object with the name "calculator" to the registry running on the same machine on the default port. You can now start the rmiregistry and server as before.

The client application can also make use of RMI URL to get a reference. We are assuming that the RMI registry will run on the default port. So, the URL of the remote object for the client looks like this:

```
String url = "rmi://" + args[0] + "/calculator";
```

The name of the object is "calculator". The first command line argument args[0] is the IP address or Fully Qualified Domain Name (FQDN) of the server.

```
Calculator cal = (Calculator)Naming.lookup(url);
```

The code above contacts the RMI registry running in the computer specified by the command line argument and asks for the stub for the object, registered under the name `calculator`. The rest of the client code is the same. Compile the code and start the client application as before.

14.8 CALLBACK

In a typical RMI application, clients invoke methods on remote objects created by the server. Callback mechanism (as the name suggests) allows server to call methods back on remote objects created and passed by the clients. This service is necessary in many cases. Consider the following situations:

When a client invokes a method on a remote object and the method takes a long time to complete, the client has to wait for the method to return. Callback mechanism allows the client to return to whatever it was doing quickly after making a call. The server, having once completed the method execution, sends the response back to the client asynchronously by calling a method on a remote object that was created and passed by the client to the remote object created by the server.

Consider another situation. A client wants to display some data (say score of a game) as soon as it arrives on a server. Since, the client does not have any idea when new data will arrive at the server, it may periodically fetch data from the server. This may result in fetching the same data unnecessarily, probably many times, that leads to consumption of network bandwidth as well as client and server resources. To avoid this problem, instead of getting data by the client from server, the server may send data to the client only when new data arrives.

The implementation of callback mechanism is very simple. As mentioned earlier, Java RMI allows us to pass even a *remote* object (i.e its class implements `Remote` interface) to a remote method. To understand callback mechanism, it is necessary to understand what happens when remote objects are passed in Java RMI.

We know when an object is exported, an instance of its skeleton is created. This skeleton wraps around the object and has similar methods of the remote object. So, when a client creates, exports and passes a remote object to a remote method, the following actions are taken by Java RMI [Figure 14.11:].

- An instance a proxy (stub) of this remote object is created.
- This stub knows everything (port number and IP address) about the arguments object's skeleton.
- This stub is then serialized to have a linear array of bytes.
- This serialized data is sent to the recipient (i.e. remote method) over the network using socket.
- At the recipient, the stub instance is reconstructed and installed.
- Remote methods formal parameter refers to this instance.

Since, remote method's formal parameter now refers to a proxy to the actual object passed by the client, a method call through the formal parameter results in a similar method invocation on local proxy object, which in turn forwards the method invocation information towards the actual object. The server can then asynchronously invoke the remote methods on remote client objects in the same way the client asynchronously invokes methods on remote-server objects.

In the following section, we shall develop a simple application as follows:

A client creates a receiver object and exports it. It then gets a reference to a remote notifier object. The client, to register itself, calls `registerMe()` method of notifier object passing this receiver object. Inside `registerMe()` method, the server calls the `notify()` method back on the receiver object passing a string.

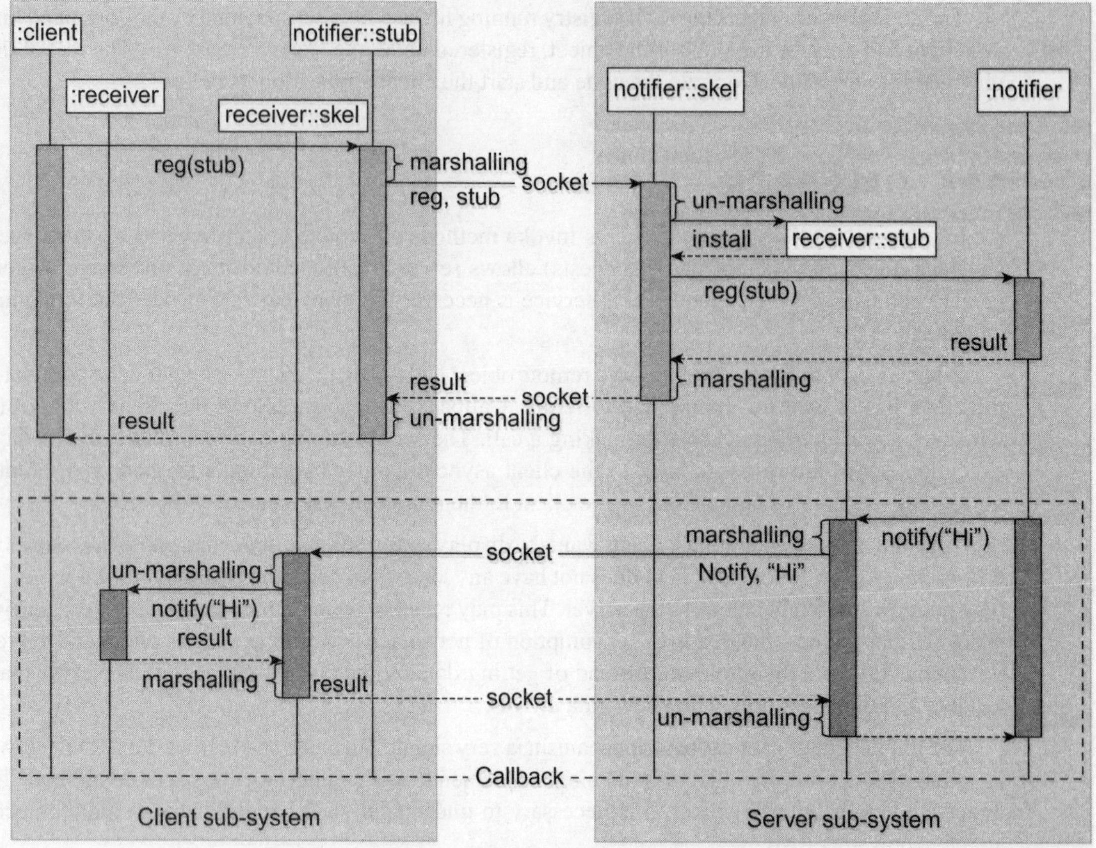

Figure 14.11: RMI callback mechanism

Again note that the application that we are going to develop does not exhibit all the power of callback mechanism. It merely shows us to write an RMI application using call back mechanism.

14.8.1 Creating interfaces

Since, the client and server separately create their remote objects, we need two interfaces:

```
//Receiver.java
import java.rmi.*;
public interface Receiver extends Remote {
   public void notify(String s) throws RemoteException;
}
```

This is the interface for a remote object to be created by client. This declares a single method `notify()` that accepts a String. The interface for server-side object is as follows:

```
//Notifier.java
import java.rmi.*;
public interface Notifier extends Remote {
   public void registerMe(Receiver r) throws RemoteException;
}
```

This interface defines a single method `registerMe()` to register a `Receiver` object.

14.8.2 Implementing interfaces

The following is a simple implementation class for `Notifier`:

```
//SimpleNotifier.java
import java.rmi.*;
public class SimpleNotifier implements Notifier {
  public void registerMe(Receiver r) {
    try {
      System.out.println("registered the receiver : "+r);
      String msg = "A message from SimpleNotifier";
      r.notify(msg);    //callback
      System.out.println("Sent : "+msg);
    }catch(RemoteException e) {}
  }
}
```

The `registerMe()` method simply calls the `notify()` method on specified `Receiver` with a message.

The crucial part for the client to have callback service is to create remote object and export it. A client can do this in two ways:

- Create a class implementing a remote interface and extending `java.rmi.server.UnicastRemoteObject` or `javax.rmi.PortableRemoteObject`. In this case, the object is exported automatically during its instantiation.
- Create a class implementing a remote interface but, the class does not extend `java.rmi.server.UnicastRemoteObject` or `javax.rmi.PortableRemoteObject`. Export the object explicitly using static `exportObject()` method of `java.rmi.server.UnicastRemoteObject` or `javax.rmi.PortableRemoteObject` class.

Since in our previous calculator application, we have used the second method, let us use the first method for this application. The implementation of `Receiver` is as follows:

```
//SimpleReceiver.java
import java.rmi.*;
import java.rmi.server.*;
public class SimpleReceiver extends UnicastRemoteObject implements Receiver,
java.io.Serializable {
  SimpleReceiver() throws RemoteException {}
  public void notify(String msg) {
    try {
      System.out.println("received : " + msg);
    }catch(Exception e) {e.printStackTrace();}
  }
}
```

Note that this implementation class implements `Serializable` interface. This is necessary as Java RMI uses serialization to send and receive objects. It also extends `UnicastRemoteObject`. So, its instance is exported automatically during its creation. The `notify()` method simply displays the string received.

14.8.3 Writing the server

The server application is as simple as our previous Calculator server program. The complete source code for the server (stored in `CallbackServer.java`) is shown below:

```
import java.rmi.*;
import java.rmi.registry.*;
import java.rmi.server.*;
public class CallbackServer {
  public static void main(String args[])    {
    try {
      String name = "notifier";
      SimpleNotifier notifier = new SimpleNotifier();
      Notifier stub = (Notifier)UnicastRemoteObject.exportObject(notifier, 0);
      Registry registry = LocateRegistry.createRegistry(1099);
      registry.rebind(name, stub);
      System.out.println("Notifier ready...");
    }catch (Exception e) { e.printStackTrace(); }
  }
}
```

14.8.4 Writing the client

The complete source code for the client (stored in `CallbackClient.java`) is shown below:

```
import java.rmi.*;
public class CallbackClient {
  public static void main(String args[]) {
    try  {
      String url = "rmi://" + args[0] + "/notifier";
      Notifier notifier = (Notifier)Naming.lookup(url);
      SimpleReceiver recv = new SimpleReceiver();
      notifier.registerMe(recv);
    }
    catch (Exception e) {
      e.printStackTrace();
    }
  }
}
```

Note that the instance `recv` is not exported explicitly. Since, its class (`SimpleReceiver`) extends, `UnicastRemoteObject`, it is exported during its creation by the constructor of `UnicastRemoteObject` class.

14.8.5 Compiling the application

Compile the programs using `javac` command as described earlier.

14.8.6 Running the application

Go to the `server_home` directory and use the following command to start the server.

```
javac CallbackServer
```

Note that, a registry is created on a port 1099 in the server program using static `createRegistry()` method on `LocateRegistry` class. So, starting a registry using `rmic` is no longer needed. We have assumed that the server is started in a computer having IP address `172.16.5.81`.

Now go to the `client_home` directory and use the following command to start the client.

```
javac CallbackClient 172.16.5.81
```

A sample result is shown in Figure 14.12:

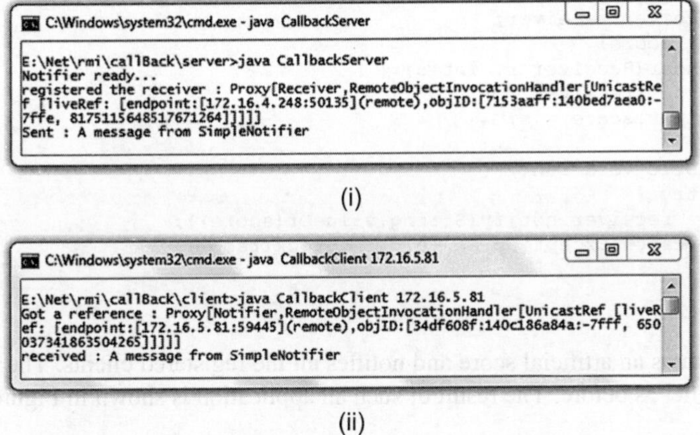

Figure 14.12: RMI callback in action (i) Notifier (ii) Receiver

14.9 ANOTHER CALLBACK APPLICATION

In our previous application, we have shown how to develop a simple callback application. In this section, we shall develop a sophisticated application as follows:

The application consists of a server and one or more clients. The server is capable of notifying the score of a game. The clients register themselves to receive the score from the server. To implement this idea, the same `Notifier` and `Receiver` interfaces are used, The implementation of `Notifier` is as follows:

```
//ScoreNotifier.java
import java.rmi.*;
import java.util.*;
public class ScoreNotifier implements Notifier, Runnable {
  Hashtable receivers = new Hashtable();
  ScoreNotifier() {new Thread(this).start();}
  public void registerMe(Receiver r) {
    try {
      receivers.put(String.valueOf(receivers.size()), r);
      System.out.println("Registered a receiver");
      System.out.println("No of registered receivers: "+receivers.size());
    }catch(Exception e) {e.printStackTrace();}
  }
  public void run() {
      Random rand = new Random();
      int score = 0, run;
      while(true) {
        do {
          try {
            Thread.sleep(1000+rand.nextInt(1000));
          }catch(Exception e) {e.printStackTrace();}
        }while((run = rand.nextInt(7)) == 0);
        score += run;
        int no = receivers.size();
        for(int i = 0;i<no;i++) {
          Receiver r = (Receiver)receivers.get(String.valueOf(i));
     System.out.println("Sending : "+score);
     new Sender(r, score).start();
    }
      }
```

```
   }
   private class Sender extends Thread {
      Receiver receiver;
      int score;
      Sender(Receiver r, int s) {
         this.receiver = r;
         this.score = s;
      }
      public void run() {
         try {
            receiver.notify(String.valueOf(score));
         }catch(Exception e) {e.printStackTrace();}
      }
   }
}
```

It generates an artificial score and notifies all the registered clients. The server program creates such a notifier as before. The result of such an application is shown in Figure 14.13:

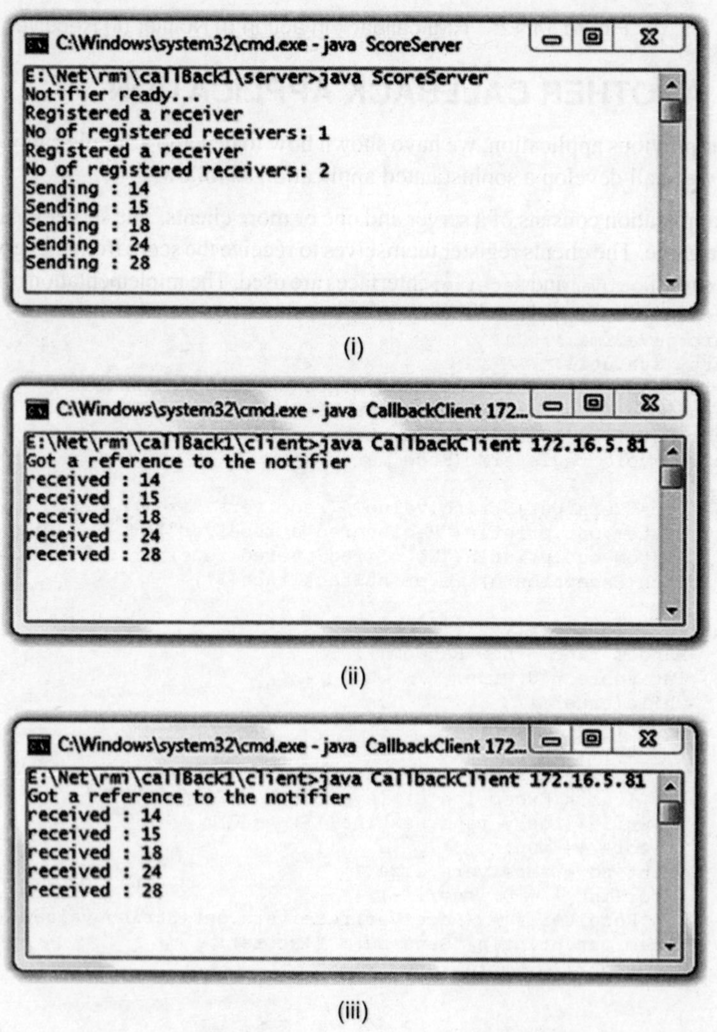

Figure 14.13: Callback (i) Notifier (ii) and (iii) Receiver

14.10 DYNAMIC OBJECT ACTIVATION

In our previous examples, remote objects run all the time even if no method on them is invoked. Java 2 and later releases allow us to register information about *remote object implementations* whose instance should be created and executed *on demand*, instead of running all the time. In fact, the RMI system does not create an instance unless a method invocation request comes. This means, the system acts a *lazy activator*.

14.10.1 Basic idea

In the lazy activation scheme, no instance of a remote object is created by the server program in advance. Instead, information about *remote object implementation* (such as object's class file name, location from which the class can be loaded, data to be used for object bootstrap etc.) is provided to an application called `rmid`. At this moment, the object is said to be in *inactive* (or passive) state. However, a stub of the remote object (which is yet to be created and exported) is obtained from this `rmid` and bound to the registry so that clients can get a remote reference from this registry. When, method invocation request comes, `rmid` checks the existences of the underlying object. If the object does not exist, a new instance is created with the help of information provided during the registration procedure. This newly created object is said to be in *active* state. The process of transforming a passive object into an active object is known as *activation*. This active object is used for a further method invocation request.

14.10.2 Implementation

RMI implements lazy activation using a *faulting remote reference* (also called a fault block). Actually, stub of a remote object contains a faulting remote reference which consists of:

- *an activation identifier* for the remote object
- a *transient* reference referring to the *active* remote object.

The *activation identifier* contains enough information for activating the object. The transient reference is the actual *live* reference to the active remote object. Initially the live reference to a remote object is `null` which indicates that the object is not yet active. When the first method invocation request comes, faulting reference checks the live reference and identifies that the object is in passive state. In this case, it initiates an *activation protocol* (discussed in the next section) to activate the object with the help of activation identifier and sets the live reference to the newly activated remote object. Once the faulting reference obtains the live reference, it forwards method invocations to the underlying remote reference which, in turn, forwards the method invocation to the remote object.

14.10.3 The activation protocol

This is the protocol that specifies how to activate an activatable passive object. The protocol is executed by the components: faulting reference (discussed in the previous section), activator, activation group, and the object to be activated.

Activator

This component itself does not activate the remote object. Instead, it supervises the activation process. The task of an activator is as follows:

- It keeps a database of information (such as object's class file name, location from which the class can be loaded, data to be used for object bootstrap etc.) necessary to activate an object.
- It forwards requests for object activation (along with the necessary information) to the correct activation group inside a remote JVM.
- It manages Java virtual machines, that starts up (when necessary).

Activation group

This is the component that actually activates the object with the specified activation information and returns the activated object back to the activator. The object is then said to belong to this group. The object activation occurs in the following way:

A faulting reference calls the activator (an RMI interface) with an activation identifier to activate the object associated with the identifier. The activator consults the object's activation descriptor consisting of the following information:

- Group identifier of the object that specifies a JVM where it has to be activated
- Remote object's underlying class name
- A URL path from which the class definition of the object can be loaded
- A file name containing initialization data for the object in marshalled (packed) form

The activator forwards the activation request to the group (if it already exists) in which this object should reside. If the activation group is not yet created, the activator creates a new activation group and then forwards the activation request to that group. The activation group reads the activation information from the object's activation descriptor, loads the class for the object and instantiates the object using a special two argument constructor.

After activating the object, the activation group passes a marshalled object reference back to the activator. The activator then records the live reference and activation identifier pair and returns the live (active) reference to the faulting reference. The faulting reference of the stub finally forwards method invocations via the live reference directly to the remote object.

14.10.4 An example

We shall demonstrate RMI object activation procedure by modifying our calculator application. The following are the three steps we shall follow to modify the application:

- Modify the implementation class.
- Modify the Server class.
- Modify the procedure to run the program.

14.10.4.1 Writing implementation class

The heart of RMI object activation is `java.rmi.activation.Activatable` class that provides support for making remote objects activatable. The implementation class of an activatable remote object usually extends this class. So, let us modify our `SimpleCalculator` class as follows:

```
public class SimpleCalculator extends Activatable implements Calculator {
//...
}
```

Also write the following import statement:

```
import java.rmi.activation.*;
```

Now add a two argument constructor as follows:

```
public SimpleCalculator(ActivationID id, MarshalledObject data) throws
RemoteException {
    super(id, 0);
    System.out.println("SimpleCalculator Instantiated.");
}
```

The implementation of `add()` method remains unchanged. Here is the complete source code (written in `SimpleCalculator.java`) of the modified class:

```
//SimpleCalculator.java
import java.rmi.*;
import java.rmi.activation.*;
public class SimpleCalculator extends Activatable implements Calculator {
  public SimpleCalculator(ActivationID id, MarshalledObject data) throws
  RemoteException {
    super(id, 0);
    System.out.println("SimpleCalculator Instantiated.");
  }
  public int add(int a, int b) {
    System.out.println("Received: " + a + " and " + b);
    int result = a + b;
    System.out.println("Sent: " + result);
    return result;
  }
}
```

The modified portion has been shown with bold face font.

14.10.4.2 Writing server class

The server itself does not create an instance of `SimpleCalculator`. Instead, it gathers necessary information to create an activatable remote object. The server then forwards this information to `rmid`, gets a reference to an instance of the activatable class's stub class and finally registers this stub with the rmiregistry. The server then quits silently. The client can consult rmiregistry to get a remote reference.

Each activatable object is said to belong to a group called *activation group*. This activation group is responsible for activating the object on demand. So, we have to get an ID of an activation group. The activation group may be an existing one or a new one (if desired one does not exist). For that reason, we create an *activation group descriptor*. The task of the activation group descriptor is to provide all the information to `rmid` so that it can contact the appropriate existing JVM or spawn a new JVM for the activatable object. It contains the following necessary information:

- The class name of the group to be created
- Location from which the group's class definition may be loaded
- A "marshalled" object that contains group-specific bootstrap data.

An activation group descriptor is created using `ActivationGroupDesc` class. It has two constructors as follows:

```
ActivationGroupDesc(Properties overrides,
ActivationGroupDesc.CommandEnvironment cmd)
```

```
ActivationGroupDesc(String className, String location, MarshalledObject<?> data,
Properties overrides, ActivationGroupDesc.CommandEnvironment cmd)
```

The first constructor (which we shall use in our application) constructs a group descriptor using the default group implementation and code location. Properties are used to override system properties in the group implementation's VM. The command environment controls the command/options used to start a child VM, or can be `null` if `rmid`'s default is accepted. An activation group descriptor is created as follows:

```
Properties props = new Properties();
props.put("java.security.policy", "policy");
ActivationGroupDesc aGroup = new ActivationGroupDesc(props, null);
```

It constructs a group descriptor that uses the system defaults for group implementation, code location and command environment. Since `rmid` runs under a security sandbox, we have specified security policy stored in a file "policy". For simplicity, we use a policy file that gives global permission to anyone from anywhere as follows:

```
grant {
        // Allow everything for now
        permission java.security.AllPermission;
};
```

This group activation descriptor is then forwarded to the `rmid` as follows:

```
ActivationGroupID id = ActivationGroup.getSystem().registerGroup(aGroup);
```

The `getSystem()` method returns a reference to the `ActivationSystem` (rmid), which then registers the specified activation group descriptor. The `rmid` then contacts the appropriate existing JVM or spawn a new JVM for the activatable object and returns an id representing the group. This id is then used to create an activation descriptor of the activatable object as follows:

```
ActivationDesc desc = new ActivationDesc (id, "SimpleCalculator", null, null);
```

The task of an activation descriptor is to provide all the information that `rmid` requires to create a new instance of the implementation class. The second argument is the name of the implementation class (`SimpleCalculator` in our case) for the activatable object. We assume that the location of `SimpleCalculator`'s class is same as `rmid`'s start location. That's why the third argument is specified as `null`. In case the location of the class definition is different, specify it using a URL. We also do not want to pass activatable object's initialization parameter. So, the last argument is also null.

Finally, register the activation descriptor with the `rmid` as follows:

```
Calculator stub = (Calculator)Activatable.register(desc);
```

The static `register()` method of `Activatable` class registers an activation descriptor and returns a reference to the stub of the object to be activated on demand. This stub can then be registered to the rmiregistry as follows:

```
Naming.rebind("calculator", stub );
```

The complete source code for the server (stored in `Server.java`) is given below:

```
import java.util.*;
import java.rmi.*;
import java.rmi.activation.*;
public class Server {
  public static void main( String args[] ) throws Exception    {
    Properties props = new Properties();
    props.put("java.security.policy", "policy");
    ActivationGroupDesc aGroup = new ActivationGroupDesc(props, null);
    System.out.print("Registering activation group descriptor...");
    ActivationGroupID id = ActivationGroup.getSystem().registerGroup(aGroup);
    System.out.println("[ OK ]");
    ActivationDesc desc = new ActivationDesc (id, "SimpleCalculator", null,
null);
    System.out.print("Registering activation descriptor...        ");
    Calculator stub = (Calculator)Activatable.register(desc);
    System.out.println("[ OK ]");
    System.out.println("Obtained stub for the SimpleCalculator");
    Naming.rebind("calculator", stub );
    System.out.println("Stub for SimpleCalculator bound in registry");
  }
}
```

14.10.4.3 Compiling and running the program

Put all the four files `Calculator.java`, `SimpleCalculator.java`, `Server.java` and `policy` in a directory. In our computer, we have put these files in the directory `E:\Net\rmi\activation`. Now, go to the directory and compile these programs as follows:

```
javac *.java
```

To run the application, we have to start the Java's `rmid` application. Go to the directory and use the following command to start `rmid`:

```
start rmid -J-Djava.security.policy=policy
```

Now start the rmiregistry as follows:

```
start rmiregistry
```

Now run the server as follows:

```
java Server
```

A sample result is shown in Figure 14.14:

```
C:\Windows\system32\cmd.exe
E:\Net\rmi\activation>java Server
Registering activation group descriptor...[ OK ]
Registering activation descriptor...      [ OK ]
Obtained stub for the SimpleCalculator
Stub for SimpleCalculator bound in registry
E:\Net\rmi\activation>
```

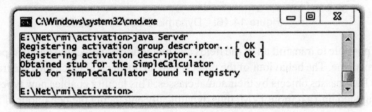

Figure 14.14: Dynamic Object activation server

Assume that rmid and rmiregistry are running in a computer having IP address `172.16.5.81`. Our previous calculator client program can now be started from a remote computer as follows:

```
java CalculatorClient 172.16.5.81
```

A sample result is shown in Figure 14.15: (i). A sample output of `rmid` terminal is shown in Figure 15.14: (ii)

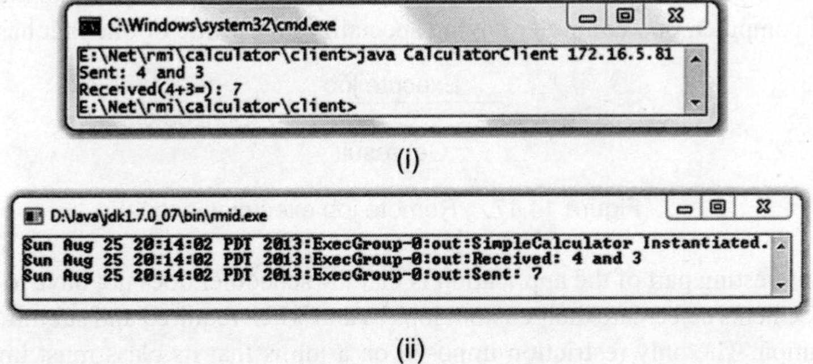

Figure 14.15: Dynamic Object activation (i) Server (ii) Client (iii) rmid

14.11 DYNAMIC CLASS DOWNLOADING

One of the important features of Java RMI is that it allows us to dynamically download the definition of the object's class if the same is not available in the receiver's JVM. Figure 14.16: illustrates how classes are downloaded from a client to a server and from a server to a client using the URL protocol .

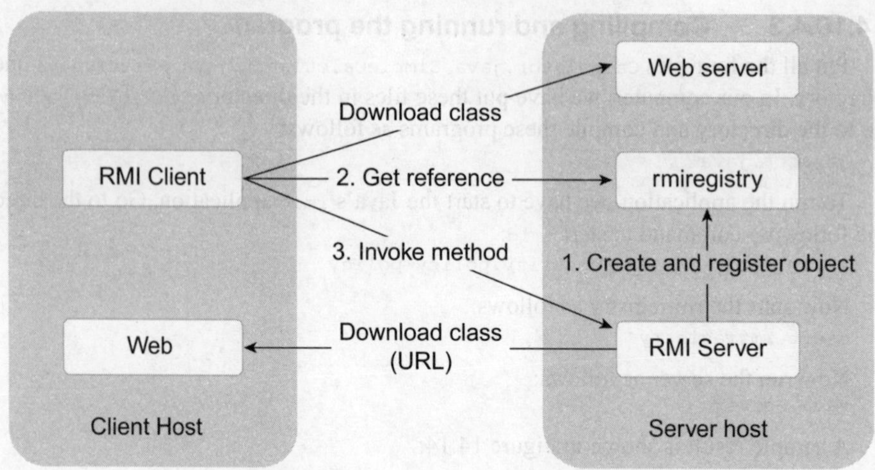

Figure 14.16: Dynamic Class downloading

It is possible to transmit all of the fields and methods of an object to another, possibly remote, Java virtual machine. The behaviour of the objects remain unchanged when they are transmitted to another JVM as RMI passes objects by their actual classes. This facility enables new types and functionalities to be migrated into a remote JVM, thus dynamically enhancing the behaviour of an RMI application.

14.12 AN EXAMPLE

In this section, we shall develop another powerful distributed application using RMI technology that makes use of the power of dynamic class downloading.

In this application [Figure 14.17:], the server creates a remote object called *scheduler*, which accepts jobs from the clients, executes these jobs locally, calculates the execution time, and finally returns the output as well as completion time. This way, clients can execute their jobs remotely on a powerful computer, or a computer having specialized hardware or one that has special permission.

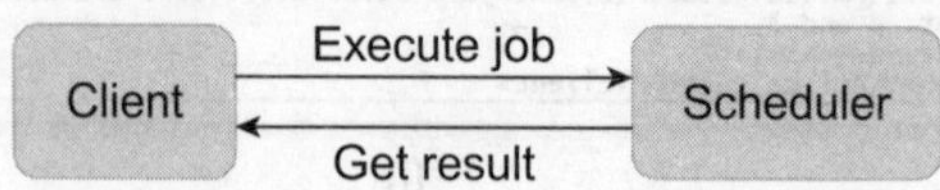

Figure 14.17: Remote job execution scenario

The interesting part of the application is that the scheduler does not have to define the jobs that it executes. Clients can create their custom jobs as and when required and submit them to the scheduler for execution. The only restriction imposed on a job is that its class must implement an interface defined by the scheduler. The class definition of a job can be downloaded at runtime from the client that submits the job using RMI technology. Once the class file is available, the scheduler can execute the job locally using its own resource.

How can a scheduler return the result to the client? If the result's class is a built-in class, the client already has the class definition and can use it easily. However, if the result's class is a scheduler-defined custom class, how can the client get it? Again there is no problem, since the client can download it from the server side and get the result. The only requirement of a result object is that its class implements an interface known to the client.

This way, the scheduler can execute arbitrary jobs without any prior knowledge of the job's class definition. Clients can also get the result without any prior knowledge of the result's class definition. The Java RMI runtime environment will download the necessary class files from the specified location as and when required. This way, Java RMI allows us to change the behaviour of an object and install it in a remote machine dynamically.

14.12.1 Writing an RMI server

The server has three parts: scheduler interface, an implementation of that interface, and code that creates the scheduler object.

14.12.1.1 Write an Interface

In this section, we shall describe the interface `Scheduler` that defines the client's view of the remote object. The `Scheduler` interface makes a connection between the server and the client. Here is the source code (`Scheduler.java`) for `Scheduler` interface.

```
package intf;

import java.rmi.Remote;
import java.rmi.RemoteException;

public interface Scheduler extends Remote {
    Result run(Job aJob) throws RemoteException;
}
```

The interface has a single method `run()` which will be used by clients to submit their jobs. This interface uses two other interfaces `Job` and `Result`. The interface `Job` defines the structure of a job to be submitted by the client. Here is the source code (`Job.java`) for the `Job` interface.

```
package intf;
public interface Job {
   String run();
}
```

The `Job` interface defines a single method `run()` that actually executes the job and returns the result as a `String`. The class of every job submitted by clients must implement this interface and must define the `run()` method. The scheduler must download this class definition to execute the job locally.

The `Result` interface describes the structure of the result returned by the scheduler. Here is the source code (`Result.java`) for `Result` interface.

```
package intf;
public interface Result {
   String output();
   double completionTime();
}
```

It defines two methods, `output()` and `completionTime()`. The methods `output()` and `completionTime()` return output and execution time of the job, respectively. The `Result` object's class must implement this interface. The client must download this `Result` object's class definition to get the result.

Since, Java's *object serialization* procedure is used by RMI to transfer objects, classes that implement `Job` and `Result` must implement the `java.io.Serializable` interface.

14.12.1.2 Implement the interface

The server defines two classes: `SchedulerImpl` and `ResultImpl`, which implements remote interface `Scheduler` and `Result`, respectively. Here is the source code (`ResultImpl.java`.) for `ResultImpl` class.

```
package impl;
import java.io.Serializable;
import intf.Result;
public class ResultImpl implements Result, Serializable {
   String output;
   double completionTime;
   public ResultImpl(String o, double c) {
      output = o;
      completionTime = c;
   }
   public String output() { return output; }
   public double completionTime() {        return completionTime; }
}
```

An object of this class represents the result of a job in terms of its output and completion time. This result object, generated by the scheduler, will be transferred to the client side and hence must be serializable. This object is indeed serializable as its class implements the `Serializable` interface. The definition of `ResultImpl` must be downloaded to the client side to reconstruct the result object.

Here is the source code (`SchedulerImpl.java`.) for `SchedulerImpl` class.

```
package impl;
import java.rmi.RemoteException;
import intf.*;
public class SchedulerImpl implements Scheduler {
   public SchedulerImpl() {
      super();
   }
   public Result run(Job aJob) throws RemoteException {
      double startTime = System.nanoTime();
      String output = aJob.run();
      double endTime = System.nanoTime();
      return new ResultImpl(output, endTime-startTime);
   }
}
```

In the `run()` method of the scheduler object, the job is executed. Note that the class for job object is defined by the client. As a result, the scheduler does not have any idea about the job. So, it simply calls the `run()` method on the job object. The server must download the class definition of the job object from the client side before calling the `run()` method. It calculates the execution time, creates a result object, and returns it.

14.12.1.3 Implement the server

A server first creates an instance of the `SchedulerImpl` class using the usual syntax as follows:

```
SchedulerImpl scheduler = new SchedulerImpl();
```

This object is then exported to the RMI runtime so that it can accept the incoming remote method call using the following piece of code [Figure 14.18]:

```
Scheduler stub = (Scheduler) UnicastRemoteObject.exportObject(scheduler, 0);
```

To register this stub with the object registry, we need to have a reference to object registry.

```
Registry registry = LocateRegistry.getRegistry();
```

The stub is then registered with object registry as follows:

```
String name = "Scheduler";
registry.rebind(name, stub);
```

The entire execution sequence is shown in Figure 14.18. The entire piece of code is embedded in a try-catch block.

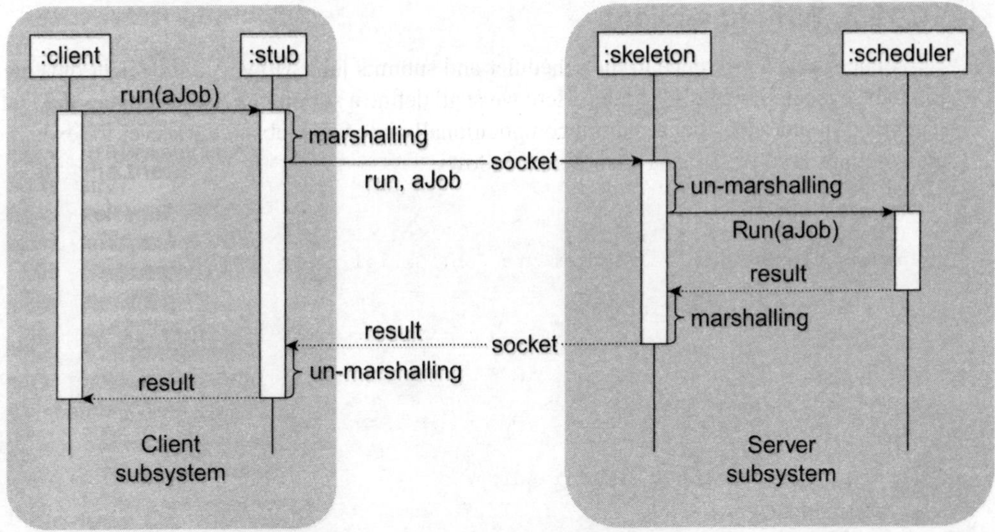

Figure 14.18: Java RMI framework

Since class files of the Job will be downloaded to the Scheduler, it is always safe to install a security manager that will protect access to the system resources by this downloaded code. If the code upon download performs any operation, the security manager will check whether the downloaded code has the privilege to do that operation and takes necessary actions. The following code is used to install a security manager:

```
if (System.getSecurityManager() == null) {
   System.setSecurityManager(new SecurityManager());
}
```

A security policy must be specified which will be used by the security manager. We shall specify the security policy during the execution of the application. The source code for `Server` is stored in the file `Server.java`. The source code for the `Server` class is given as follows:

```
package impl;
import java.rmi.registry.LocateRegistry;
import java.rmi.registry.Registry;
import java.rmi.server.UnicastRemoteObject;
import intf.*;
import impl.*;
public class Server {
   public static void main(String[] args) {
      if (System.getSecurityManager() == null) {
         System.setSecurityManager(new SecurityManager());
      }
      try {
         SchedulerImpl scheduler = new SchedulerImpl();
         Scheduler stub = (Scheduler)
UnicastRemoteObject.exportObject(scheduler, 0);
         Registry registry = LocateRegistry.getRegistry();
         String name = "Scheduler";
         registry.rebind(name, stub);
         System.out.println("SchedulerImpl bound");
      } catch (Exception e) {
         System.err.println("SchedulerImpl exception:");
         e.printStackTrace();
      }
   }
}
```

14.12.2 Writing a client

A client gets a reference to the scheduler and submits jobs. However, the client must define the job to be executed by the scheduler. Here we shall define a simple job that calculates the factorial of a number. In practice, clients submit computationally intensive jobs to the server for execution. The class definition of `Factorial` is shown as follows:

```
package impl;
import intf.*;
import java.io.Serializable;
public class Factorial implements Job, Serializable {
    int n;
    public Factorial(int v) {
        n = v;
    }
    public String run() {
        int result = 1;
        for(int i = 2; i <= n; i++)
            result *= i;
        return String.valueOf(result);
    }
}
```

The `Factorial` class implements the `Job` interface. Its `run()` method calculates and returns the factorial of a specified integer. When a client submits such a `Factorial` job object to the remote scheduler, the object is transferred to the scheduler using Java's serialization procedure. So, `Factorial` job object must be serializable. Since the `Factorial` class implements the `Serializable` interface, objects of the `Factorial` class are indeed serializable.

To reconstruct the `Factorial` job object in the `Scheduler` object's JVM, job object's class definition is needed. The RMI system downloads the class definition of `Factorial` on behalf of the `Scheduler` object. The client must specify the location where the RMI system can find the object's class definition. Now, `Scheduler` object's `run()` method is invoked which, in turn, invokes `Factorial` object's `run()` method where the job is executed.

Clients may also submit other jobs to the remote `Scheduler` object. The `Scheduler` executes these jobs using the same procedure described. It need not know each job's implementation procedure. It only knows that each job it receives implements the `Job` interface and has the method `run()`.

Let us now write the code for the client. The client will first get a reference to the remote registry using the `LocateRegistry.getRegistry()` method as follows:

```
Registry registry = LocateRegistry.getRegistry(args[0]);
```

The argument to the `getRegistry()` method is the first command line argument `args[0]` which is the name or IP address of the computer where the registry runs on the default port (1099). If the registry runs on a port other than 1099, you specify the port as the second argument to the `getRegistry()` method.

The client then uses the `lookup()` method on this registry to get a reference to the remote `Scheduler` object as follows:

```
String name = "Scheduler";
Scheduler scheduler = (Scheduler) registry.lookup(name);
```

To submit a task, the client has to create an instance of the `Factorial` object.

```
Factorial aJob = new Factorial(Integer.parseInt(args[1]));
```

The second command line argument, after converting it to an integer, is passed to the `Factorial` constructor. This argument indicates the integer whose factorial has to be calculated. The client can now submit the job to the remote object for execution.

```
Result r = scheduler.run(aJob);
```

The result of job execution is stored in the `Result` object. Remember that the `Result` interface was implemented by the server. So, the client does not have the definition of `Result` object's class. The RMI system will download the necessary class definition from the location as specified by the server. So, the client can invoke methods on this `Result` object to get the desired result and other information such as completion time.

```
System.out.println("Execution time = " + r.completionTime() + " micro sec(s)");
```

The entire piece of code is embedded in a try-catch block to handle the error that may occur at runtime. A security manager should also be installed to protect the system as `Result` object's class definition is downloaded in the client's JVM.

Here is the complete source code for the client which is stored in `Client.java`.

```
package impl;
import java.rmi.registry.LocateRegistry;
import java.rmi.registry.Registry;
import intf.*;
import impl.*;
public class Client {
   public static void main(String args[]) {
      if (System.getSecurityManager() == null) {
         System.setSecurityManager(new SecurityManager());
      }
      try {
         Registry registry = LocateRegistry.getRegistry(args[0]);
         String name = "Scheduler";
         Scheduler scheduler = (Scheduler) registry.lookup(name);
         Factorial aJob = new Factorial(Integer.parseInt(args[1]));
         Result r = scheduler.run(aJob);
         System.out.println(args[1] + "! = " + r.output());
         System.out.println("Execution time = " + r.completionTime() + " micro
sec(s)");
      } catch (Exception e) {
         e.printStackTrace();
      }
   }
}
```

14.12.3 Compiling the program

In practice, the server should deploy the necessary files for a client program to use. In our case the client must have a `Scheduler`, `Job`, and `Result` interface. The client also needs the `Result` object's class (`ResultImpl` in this case) definition which will be downloaded by the RMI system from the location specified by the server at runtime. So, server must deploy these four classes.

The server will then write the implementation of `Scheduler` and `Result` interface and deploy an object in a computer accessible by the clients. The client programmers can then download the necessary class files and develop their applications which will use the `Scheduler` object.

All the files are packaged as follows:

Server machine

intf: `Scheduler`, `Job`, `Result`

impl: `SchedulerImpl`, `ResultImpl`, `Server`

Client machine

impl: `Factorial`, `Client`

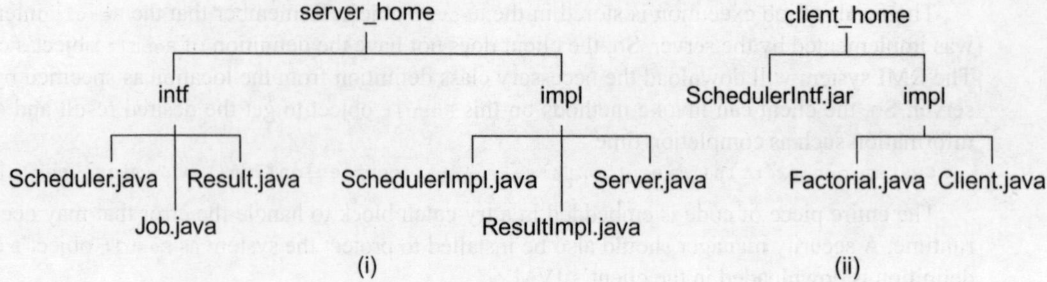

Figure 14.19: Directory configuration for Scheduler (i) Server (ii) Client

Suppose the developer of the server is developing an application in the directory "E:\Net\rmi\scheduler\server" of a computer having IP address `172.16.5.81`. Hereafter, we shall refer to this directory as `server_home`. Create the directory structure and put server-side files as shown in Figure 14.19: (i).

14.12.3.1 Creating Interface classes

Go to the directory `server_home`. Give the following command to compile the interface source files and generate a jar file (`SchedulerIntf.jar`) containing the generated interface class files.

```
javac intf\*.java
jar cvf schedulerIntf.jar intf\*.class
```

Make sure that the directory containing the Java compiler is included in your PATH environment variable. The jar command will generate the following output:

```
added manifest
adding: intf/Job.class(in = 129) (out= 112)(deflated 13%)
adding: intf/Result.class(in = 167) (out= 143)(deflated 14%)
adding: intf/Scheduler.class(in = 222) (out= 169)(deflated 23%)
```

This `SchedulerIntf.jar` file is needed by the client to develop its own application. This file must be put in a network accessible place so that the client can access it. For example, it can be put on a web server accessible by the client.

14.12.3.2 Compiling Server

The impl package contains three source files: `SchedulerImpl.java`, `ResultImpl.java`, and `Server.java`. `SchedulerImpl.java` is the implementation of `Scheduler` interface, `ResultImpl.java` is the implementation of `Result` interface, and `Server.java` creates and exports the Scheduler object. Use the following command to compile these source files.

```
javac impl\*.java
```

The stub and skeleton for `SchedulerImpl` implements the `Scheduler` interface which refers to the `Job` and `Result` interfaces. So, Java's object registry needs the definition for these interfaces. Remember, the class definition of `Result` interface is needed by the client. So, create a jar file containing these four classes and put it in a network accessible place. Give the following command to create the jar file `scheduler.jar`:

```
jar cvf scheduler.jar intf\*.class impl\ResultImpl.class
```

This generates the following sample output:

```
added manifest
adding: intf/Job.class(in = 129) (out= 112)(deflated 13%)
adding: intf/Result.class(in = 167) (out= 143)(deflated 14%)
adding: intf/Scheduler.class(in = 222) (out= 169)(deflated 23%)
adding: impl/ResultImpl.class(in = 688) (out= 417)(deflated 39%)
```

To deploy this jar file, we shall use Apache's tomcat web server running in the server computer (IP address is `172.16.5.81`) on a port `8080`. Put this jar file in the web server's document root. So, the URL of this jar file will be `http://172.16.5.81:8080/scheduler.jar`. We shall specify this URL while running the server application.

14.12.3.3 Compiling Client

Suppose client application is developed in another computer having IP address `172.16.4.248` in directory `E:\Net\rmi\scheduler\client` which we shall refer to as `client_home`. Create the directory structure and put client-side files as shown in Figure 14.19: (ii).

First download the `SchedulerIntf.jar` file from a location specified by the server and put it in the directory `client_home`. In the client computer, there are two files in the impl package `Factorial.java` and `Client.java`. `Factorial.java` is the implementation of the `Job` interface. The `Client.java` gets a reference of the `Scheduler` object and invokes the `run()` method using this reference. Give the following command to compile source files:

```
javac -cp schedulerIntf.jar;. impl/*.java
```

Note that the server needs the implementation of `Job` interface, i.e., `Factorial` class in our case which will be downloaded by the Java RMI system. However, the client must specify the location of this class file. In the client application, we shall again use Apache's tomcat server to deploy the `Factorial` class. Configure the tomcat web server and put the `Factorial.class` in the `impl` subdirectory of document root so that the RMI system can download this file whenever necessary. The base URL of this class file is `http://172.16.4.248:8080/`. We shall specify this URL while running the client application.

14.12.4 Running the application

Remember, we had installed a security manager in the `Server.java` and `Client.java` applications. When we run these applications, we must specify a security policy for them. In this case we shall specify the policy as a file in the form of command line argument. Create a file `server.policy` in the `server_home` directory. The content of the file looks like this:

```
grant codeBase "file:/E:/Net/rmi/scheduler/server" {
    permission java.security.AllPermission;
};
```

Similarly, create another file `client.policy` in the directory `client_home` with the following content:

```
grant codeBase "file:/E:/Net/rmi/scheduler/client" {
    permission java.security.AllPermission;
};
```

Before starting the server application, we need to start an object registry. In Java RMI, it is started using the `rmiregistry` command. So, open a terminal and type the following command:

```
rmiregistry
```

The command does not generate any output; it starts the object registry application on the default port 1099. Give the following command to start the server:

```
java -Djava.rmi.server.codebase=http://172.16.5.81:8080/scheduler.jar
     -Djava.security.policy=server.policy
     impl.Server
```

It produces a sample output as shown in Figure 14.20:

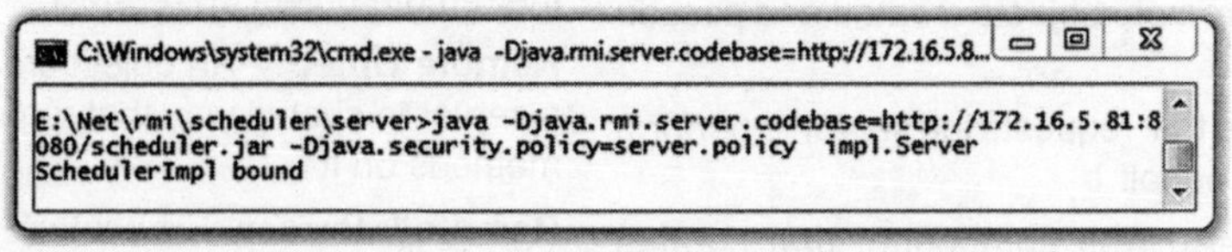

```
C:\Windows\system32\cmd.exe - java -Djava.rmi.server.codebase=http://172.16.5.8...

E:\Net\rmi\scheduler\server>java -Djava.rmi.server.codebase=http://172.16.5.81:8
080/scheduler.jar -Djava.security.policy=server.policy  impl.Server
SchedulerImpl bound
```

Figure 14.20: RMI server

14.12.5 Start client

Give the following command to start the client:

```
java -cp ./schedulerIntf.jar;.
     -Djava.rmi.server.codebase=http://172.16.4.248:8080/
     -Djava.security.policy=client.policy
      impl.Client 172.16.5.81 5
```

It produces a sample output as shown in Figure 14.21:

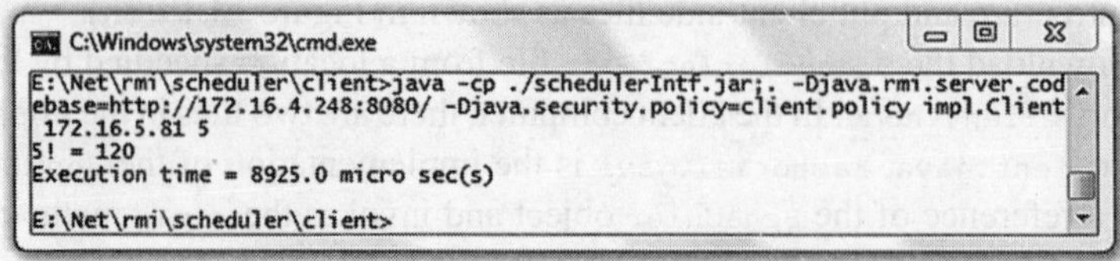
C:\Windows\system32\cmd.exe
E:\Net\rmi\scheduler\client>java -cp ./schedulerIntf.jar;. -Djava.rmi.server.codebase=http://172.16.4.248:8080/ -Djava.security.policy=client.policy impl.Client 172.16.5.81 5
5! = 120
Execution time = 8925.0 micro sec(s)
E:\Net\rmi\scheduler\client>

Figure 14.21: RMI client

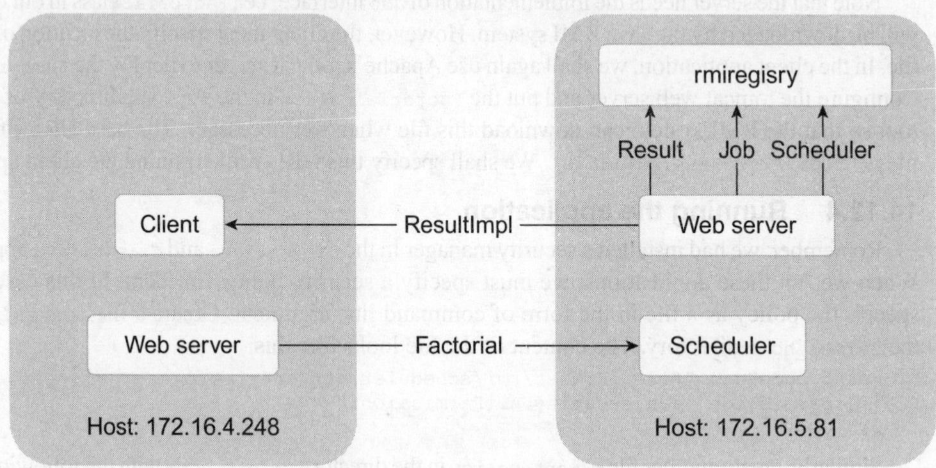
rmiregisry
Result
Job
Scheduler
Client
ResultImpl
Web server
Web server
Factorial
Scheduler
Host: 172.16.4.248
Host: 172.16.5.81

Figure 14.22: Scheduler runtime environment

Figure 14.22: illustrates where Client, rmiregistry, and scheduler find necessary classes at runtime.

KEYWORDS

Activation—The process of transforming a passive object into an active object

Activation protocol—A protocol used to activate an activatable object

Callback—A mechanism that allows server to call methods back on remote objects created and passed by the clients.

Client—A machine that requests the server to perform some tasks on its behalf

Lazy Activator—An RMI component that creates class instances on demand, instead of running all the time

Marshalling—The process of gathering data and transforming it into a standard format before it is transmitted over a network

Object registry—A database that keeps the information about objects and provides a reference to the remote object on request

Remote Object—An object created and exported by a server in such a way that remote clients can invoke methods on it

Remote Interface—The interface of a remote object used to publish the prototypes of methods on a remote object

Remote Method—Methods on a remote object that can be called by remote clients

RMI—A Java mechanism of Remote Procedure Call (RPC) used to invoke methods on a remote object

Stub—An object that resides at the client computer and acts as a proxy of the remote server object

Serialization—The procedure to convert an object to the byte stream used by the Java RMI mechanism

Server—A remote machine which serves us the requested operation

Skeleton—An object that resides at the server computer and acts as a proxy of the remote server object

Un-marshalling—The process of retrieving data from the marshalled data

SUMMARY

Java Remote Method Invocation (RMI) is an object-oriented Remote Procedure Call (RPC) technique. It allows us to invoke methods on a remote object. One of the important features of Java RMI is that it allows us to dynamically download the definition of an object's class if the same is not available in the receiver's JVM. Similarly, it also allows the client to upload an object's implementation to the server dynamically if it is not available on the server.

Primarily four components are involved in a Java RMI application: an interface, its implementation, a server program that creates and exports a remote object, and a client which gets a reference on a remote object and invokes method on it. Java RMI uses a mechanism very much similar to the URL to access remote objects.

A server program typically creates a *remote* object to be used for method invocation. The object is exported and registered with a separate application called *object registry*. A client program typically consults the object registry to get a reference to a remote object with a specified name. It can then invoke methods on the remote object using this reference as if the object is stored in the client's own address space. Object registry is essentially a table of objects. Each entry of the table maps the object name to its proxy known as stub.

The client-side proxy of the remote is known as stub. The function of stub is to communicate with the remote skeleton on behalf of the client's method invocation request. The method invocation information is marshalled and sent to the skeleton. Upon receiving the response, it un-marshals the response, gets the result and sends the result back to the client.

The function of skeleton is to unpack the request to obtain the method name and arguments to be used for this method. This unpacking procedure is also called *un-marshalling*. Skeleton also has reference to a local object and can invoke the desired method on the actual object and get the result. It then packs (called *marshalling*) the result and sends it back to the caller.

The type of arguments to, or return values from, remote methods may be any valid type in Java, including objects. For objects, the only requirement is that they implement the interface `java.io.Serializable`.

Java RMI provides a simple addressing mechanism, known as RMI URL, that may be used to register a remote object and to get a reference to the remote object. One of the powerful features of RMI is callback mechanism which allows server to call methods back on remote objects created and passed by the clients.

Dynamic object activation allows us to register information about *remote object implementations* whose instance should be created and executed *on demand*, instead of running all the time. The RMI system does not create an instance unless a method invocation request comes which makes the system a *lazy activator*. RMI implements lazy activation using a *faulting remote reference*.

WEB RESOURCES

`http://www.oracle.com/technetwork/java/javase/tech/index-jsp-136424.html`
Remote Method Invocation Home

`http://docs.oracle.com/javase/tutorial/rmi/index.html`
Java RMI Tutorial

`http://java.sun.com/javase/technologies/core/basic/rmi/index.jsp`
Remote Method Invocation

`http://docs.oracle.com/javase/7/docs/api/java/rmi/package-summary.html`
Java API Reference for the RMI package

`http://docs.oracle.com/javase/7/docs/platform/rmi/spec/rmi-activation.html`
Remote Object Activation

EXERCISES

Objective-type Questions

1. What is the default port number of RMI?
   (a) 1099 (c) 1090
   (b) 1990 (d) 1909

2. A remote object must be an instance of
   (a) java.rmi.RemoteObject
   (b) java.io.Serializable
   (c) java.lang.Cloneable
   (d) java.rmi.Remote

3. Which of the following is a utility that registers remote objects and provides naming services for locating objects?
   (a) rmiregistry (c) java
   (b) rmic (d) javac

4. Which of the following is an object that resides on the client host and serves as a proxy for the remote server object?
   (a) Stub
   (b) RMI Registry
   (c) Server implementation
   (d) Skeleton

5. __________ is an object that resides on the server host and communicates with the stub and the actual server object.
   (a) Server object interface
   (b) RMI Registry
   (c) Skeleton
   (d) Stub

6. Which of the following command is used in Java RMI to start the object registry on port 1080?
   (a) rmiregistry 1080
   (b) rmiregistry
   (c) objectregistry 1080
   (d) objectregistry

7. Which of the following is used to register a remote object o with a name obj at port 1080 on host it.jusl.ac.in?
   (a) Naming.bind("rmi://it.jusl.ac.in/obj", o);
   (b) Name.rebind("rmi://it.jusl.ac.in:1080/obj", o);
   (c) Naming.rebind("rmi://it.jusl.ac.in:1080/obj", o);
   (d) Name.bind("rmi://it.jusl.ac.in:1080/obj", o);

8. __________ is a sub interface of java.rmi.Remote that defines the methods for the server object.
   (a) Skeleton
   (b) Server object interface
   (c) Server implementation
   (d) RMI Registry

9. To locate a remote object with the name obj at port 1080 on host it.jusl.ac.in, we use
   (a) Remote remoteRef = Name.lookup("rmi://it.jusl.ac.in:1080/obj");
   (b) Remote remoteRef = Name.lookup("//it.jusl.ac.in:1080/obj");
   (c) Remote remoteRef = Name.lookup("http://it.jusl.ac.in:1080/obj");
   (d) Remote remoteRef = Naming.lookup("rmi://it.jusl.ac.in:1080/obj");

10. Which of the following methods is used to export an object?
    (a) exportObject() (c) doExport()
    (b) export() (d) exportIt()

11. What is the full form of RMI?
    (a) Remote Method Interaction
    (b) Registered Method Invocation
    (c) Registered Method Interaction
    (d) Remote Method Invocation

12. Which of the following commands is used to start an object registry?
    (a) startregistry (b) registrystart
    (c) rmiregistry (d) activateregistry

13. Which of the following interfaces must an activatable remote object's class implement?
    (a) DoActivate (b) Activate
    (c) Activable (d) Activatable

14. Which of the following methods in Naming class is used to bind an object?
    (a) doBind() (b) bind()
    (c) register() (d) DoRegister()

15. Which of the following exceptions must be thrown by a remote method?
    (a) NetworkException
    (b) MarshallingException
    (c) CommunicationException
    (d) RemoteException

16. Which of the following methods is used to find an object registry?
(a) findRegistry() (b) getRegistry()
(c) lookupRegistry() (d) searchRegistry()

17. Which of the following methods is used to create a new registry?
(a) createRegistry()
(b) makeRegistry()
(c) newRegistry()
(d) constructRegistry()

18. Which of the following methods on registry is used to get a remote reference?
(a) search() (b) get()
(c) find() (d) lookup()

19. Which of the following interfaces must be implemented by a class for its instances to be serializable?
(a) DoSerialize
(b) MakeSerializable
(c) Serialize
(d) Serializable

20. Which of the following components activates an object?
(a) Activator (b) Activation group
(c) Faulting Reference (d) Stub

Subjective-type Questions

1. What is the difference between RMI and Socket?
2. What is RMI Registry?
3. What are the exceptions thrown by RMI?
4. What is the difference between a stub and a skeleton?
5. Why does RMI require an interface?
6. What is a serializable object? Give some examples of non-serializable objects in Java.
7. Explain the RMI architecture.
8. How do Java RMI clients contact remote Java RMI servers?
9. What is a remote object? Why should we extend UnicastRemoteObject ?
10. What is the difference between RMI and CORBA?
11. What are the services provided by the RMI Object?
12. What are the differences between RMI and a socket?
13. How will you pass parameters in RMI ?
14. What is the difference between using bind() and rebind() methods of Naming Class?
15. Can a class implementing a Remote interface have non-remote methods?
16. What are the layers of RMI Architecture?
17. What is the role of java.rmi.Naming Class?
18. What is the role of Remote Interface in RMI?
19. Why must classes implement Serializable in order to be written to an ObjectOutputStream?
20. Write the format of an RMI URL.

CHAPTER – 15

JAVA MAIL API

KEY OBJECTIVES

After completing this chapter readers will be able to—

- get an idea about SMTP, POP3 and IMAP
- understand how to send emails using JavaMail API
- write Java programs to retrieve emails
- add attachment to an email
- learn how to send html content
- know how to forward and delete emails

15.1 E-MAIL

An electronic mail (or simply email or e-mail), as its name suggests, is a digital version of a message (or letter). This concept was introduced much earlier than evolution of the Internet. Needless to say that the email system was very simple at that time. It was as simple as leaving a message on someone's desk. It allowed a user only to place a message in another user's directory where later one could see the message after logging in.

The current email system is much more powerful. It allows two parties to exchange emails across networks using addresses called *email addresses*. It does not even require the sender and recipient to both be online at the same time. It has, no doubt, become one of the most popular applications of the Internet.

A set of protocols is used for delivery and accessing of such emails. **S**imple **M**ail **T**ransfer **P**rotocol (SMTP) is used to deliver emails, whereas **P**ost **O**ffice **P**rotocol (POP) and **I**nternet **M**essage **A**ccess **P**rotocol (IMAP) are used to access emails.

15.2 JAVAMAIL API

JavaMail is a powerful API that provides a platform-independent framework to send and retrieve electronic-mail (e-mail). Originally, the specification does not mandate support for a specific protocol. However, JavaMail includes support for some well-known protocols such as SMTP, POP and IMAP.

The package `javax.mail` contains classes that encapsulate the different components of the email system. Initially, the detailed layout of these classes and interfaces may wrongly cause you to believe that you are in big trouble. However, once you start working, you will certainly discover that it is a very simple and handy API for incorporating robust mail/messaging functionality in your applications.

The package `com.sun.mail` contains implementation classes for mail protocols such as SMTP, POP and IMAP. Note that JavaMail itself does not implement an email server. It helps us in accessing an existing email server. Since, almost all users have an account in the Gmail server, we shall use it to test the code present in this chapter.

Note that sending email using the Java application has various practical use as follows:

- When a user creates an account, an email, containing critical information to be used by the user later, may be sent automatically at the end of account creation.
- In the middle of an account creation, some web application may send an activation code to the specified email address to verify if the user really owns that email address.
- In case a user forgets the password, an email containing the password may be sent to the user's email address automatically.
- For important updates, emails may be sent automatically to the relevant users.

15.3 INSTALLING JAVAMAIL API

Java 2 Platform, Enterprise Edition (J2EE) 1.3 includes JavaMail API. So, if you have this version installed in your computer, you need not download JavaMail API. However, for other versions of Java, you have to download a jar (**j**ava **ar**chive) file that contains the necessary classes and interfaces. During the development of this manuscript, the version of JavaMail API is 1.5.0. We downloaded the jar file `javax.mail.jar` from `https://java.net/projects/javamail/pages/Home`.

To use this API, include this jar file in you `CLASSPATH` environment variable. If you do not have the right to change this environment variable, specify this jar file (using –cp option) during compilation and execution. If you still can't understand, then follow the instruction given in the 'Running the example' sections.

If you are not using Java SE 6 or newer, you will also need an extension called **J**ava **A**ctivation **F**ramework (JAF). Being a kind of plug-in to Java, it basically helps us to handle multitude data formats such as simple text or extremely complex documents composed of images, audio, video, and even *live* objects. The JAF is provided as a separate package `javax.activation`. The JavaMail API Design Specification (Version 1.5) can be found in the following URL:

`http://javamail.java.net/nonav/docs/JavaMail-1.5.pdf`

15.4 SENDING EMAILS

The **S**imple **M**ail **T**ransfer **P**rotocol (SMTP) is an application layer protocol in the TCP/IP protocol suite which is used to send electronic mails (email). It uses TCP as its underlying transport layer protocol. The SMTP protocol specifies a set of commands and responses to send emails. A sample set of SMTP commands and responses to send an email is shown in Figure 15.1:

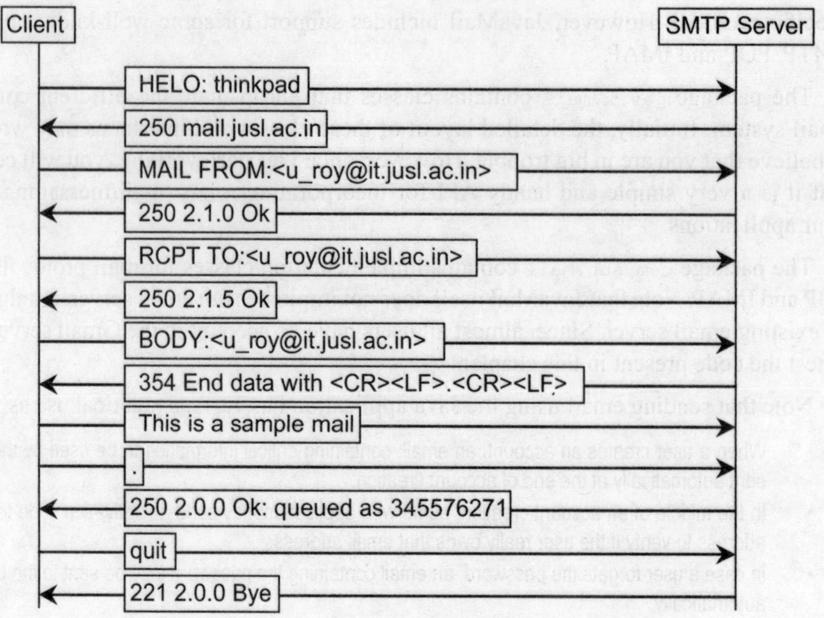

Figure 15.1: A typical SMTP message exchange

In this section, we shall discuss how to send an email containing simple text message. There are three steps to follow to send an email using JavaMail API:

- Create a Session object that stores necessary information such as host name, user name and password to send an email.
- Compose a message.
- Send the message.

15.4.1 Creating a Session Object

The mail handling (i.e. sending and retrieving) task is typically started by obtaining a `javax.mail.Session` object. This final `Session` class represents a mail session. A new `Session` object may be created or an existing one may be used. To get a `Session` object, two static methods `getDefaultInstance()` and `getInstance()` are available on `Session` class.

The former method returns an existing (or a new instance if the method is called for the first time) `Session` object and later creates a fresh one. Since, the default session is potentially available to all code executing in the same Java virtual machine, an application may prefer to create a new instance for its own using `getInstance()` method. It has two overloaded versions:

```
static Session getInstance(Properties props)
static Session getInstance(Properties props, Authenticator authenticator)
```

The `Properties` object is used to configure the session. Configuring a session means specifying email host, port number being used etc. The `Authenticator` object is required if the mail host enforces a user to be authenticated (e.g. providing user name and password).

We know that SMTP itself does not mandate authentication. In practice, there exists some (wrongly configured) mail servers which implements this raw SMTP and hence do not require authentication. However, a good mail server does not open SMTP port (25) directly. Instead, an additional security layer (such as SSL, TSL) is inserted in front of SMTP. Any program that wants to reach the SMTP port, has to pass through this security layer. This security layer takes care of the authentication and finally forwards the request to the SMTP.

Most of the mail servers (such as Gmail, Yahoo) have been configured this way. For these mail servers, we should use the second overloaded version of `getInstance()` that requires an `Authenticator` object. We shall discuss sending mails using mail servers that require authentication in detail later in this chapter.

In our first program, we shall use a mail server (`webmail.jusl.ac.in`) that does not require authentication. So, we shall use the first version of `getInstance()` method. Note that mail servers that do not require authentication are potentially vulnerable for external attack and should always be avoided.

Since, the above mentioned methods take a `Properties` object, let us first create a `Properties` object as follows:

```
Properties props = new Properties();
```

This `Properties` object is used to configure the `Session` object. However, this object does not so far contain any property. So, we must set some necessary properties as follows:

```
String host = "webmail.jusl.ac.in";
props.setProperty("mail.smtp.host", host);
```

This indicates that the mail server `webmail.jusl.ac.in` is to be used for sending mails. You should use IP address or name of the mail server, where you have an account, in place of `webmail.jusl.ac.in`.

Alternatively, an existing `Properties` object may also be used as follows:

```
Properties props = System.getProperties();
```

The `System.getProperties()` method returns the current set of system properties (such as `java.version`, `java.home` etc.) as a `Properties` object. This object is useful if an application wants to use default system properties. However, always make sure that some necessary properties (such as `mail.smtp.host`) are set properly. The set of required properties is determined by the actual procedure used to send the mail.

The `Session` object can be created with this property object as follows:

```
Session session = Session.getInstance(props);
```

Now, this `Session` object has relevant information necessary to `Transport` emails as well as to have access to email `Store`. Let us now compose a message for delivery.

15.4.2 Compose a Message

The abstract class `javax.mail.Message` encapsulates an email message. Since, it is an abstract class, its direct known subclass `javax.mail.internet.MimeMessage` is usually used to create a mail message as follows:

```
MimeMessage msg = new MimeMessage(session);
```

The constructor takes a `Session` object and creates an empty message. When this message is sent, the session object is consulted for information necessary for email delivery. To populate this message, a number of methods are available on `MimeMessage` class. For example, `setSubject()` method sets the subject, and the `setText()` method sets the (plaintext) body content of the message. The following is an example that fills the message:

```
String from = "u_roy@it.jusl.ac.in", to = from;
msg.setFrom(from);
msg.addRecipients(Message.RecipientType.TO, to);
msg.setSubject("A test mail");
msg.setText("Sent a mail without authentication");
```

The addRecipients() method adds an email address to the list of intended receiver's email addresses. The first argument indicates the type of recipients and has possible values Message.RecipientType.TO, Message.RecipientType.CC and Message.RecipientType.BCC. They represent primary (TO), Carbon Copy (CC) and **B**lind Carbon Copy (BCC) recipients respectively.

It has another overloaded version that may be used to specify multiple email addresses:

```
void addRecipients(Message.RecipientType type, Address[] addresses)
```

Here, the second argument is a list of recipient's email addresses.

15.4.3 Sending the Mail

Sending the mail is as simple as follows:

```
Transport.send(msg);
```

The static send() method of Transport class delivers the specified message to all recipient's addresses, which were added to the message using addRecipients() method. If send() method encounters any of the recipient addresses as invalid (e.g. wrong format or non-existing address), during delivery of message, a SendFailedException is thrown.

Note that success does not always imply that the message is really delivered to the ultimate recipient. The failures may occur in later stages of delivery, where usually an undeliverable message is sent back to the user.

Alternatively, we can send mail using a specific instance from the session for SMTP protocol as follows:

```
Transport transport = session.getTransport("smtp");
transport.connect(host, null, null);
transport.sendMessage(msg, msg.getAllRecipients());
transport.close();
```

The connect() method, establishes a connection to the specified host and username and password (null if unnecessary). Finally, the sendMessage() delivers the message. Since, connect() method keeps the connection with the mail server active between messages, this method is useful if sending multiple messages is required. The static send() method makes a separate connection to the server for each method call.

The complete source code (SendEmail.java) is given below:

```
//SendEmail.java
import java.util.*;
import javax.mail.*;
import javax.mail.internet.*;
public class SendEmail {
  public static void main(String [] args){
    String host = "webmail.jusl.ac.in";
    String from = "u_roy@it.jusl.ac.in", to = from;
    Properties props = new Properties();
    props.setProperty("mail.smtp.host", host);
    Session session = Session.getInstance(props);
    try{
      MimeMessage msg = new MimeMessage(session);
      msg.setFrom(from);
      msg.addRecipients(Message.RecipientType.TO, to);
      msg.setSubject("A test mail");
      msg.setText("Sent a mail without authentication");
      Transport.send(msg);
      System.out.println("Sent message successfully....");
    }catch (Exception e) {
      e.printStackTrace();
    }
  }
}
```

15.4.4 Compiling and Running the Program

We assume that all the programs in the chapter are developed in a directory: `E:\Net\mail`. Place the jar file `javax.mail.jar` in this directory. Go to the `E:\Net\mail` directory and use the following command to compile our `SendEmail.java`:

```
javac -cp javax.mail.jar;. SendEmail.java
```

It generates a single class file `SendEmail.class`. To execute the program, use the following command:

```
java -cp javax.mail.jar;. SendEmail
```

To show that the mail has really been sent, a snapshot from the mail server interface is shown in Figure 15.2:

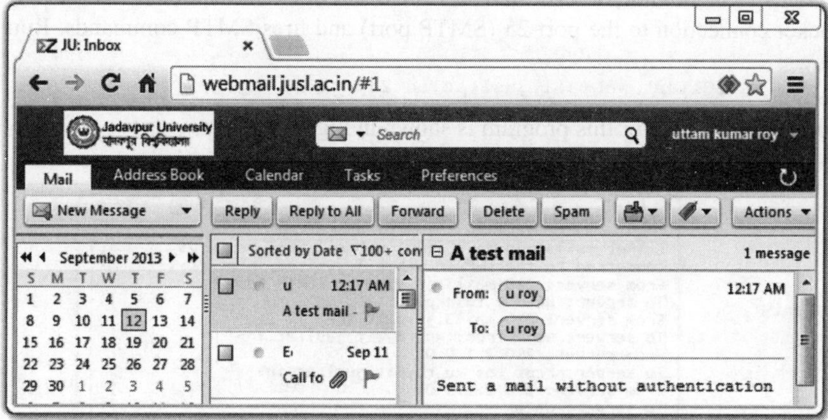

Figure 15.2: Sending email using JavaMail API

15.5 SENDING EMAILS DIRECTLY USING SOCKET

We know that SMTP itself does not mandate any user authorization procedure. This suggests to us to establish a simple TCP socket to the server that implements the basic SMTP and gives commands to send emails. The email server (`webmail.jusl.ac.in`) we have used in our previous program is one such server. The following program sends an email from `u_roy@it.jusl.ac.in` to itself using the basic socket mechanism.

```
import java.io.*;
import java.net.*;
class MailClient {
   public static void main(String argv[]) throws Exception {
      int port = Integer.parseInt(argv[1]);
      BufferedReader inFromUser =
         new BufferedReader(new InputStreamReader(System.in));
      Socket clientSocket = new Socket(argv[0], port);
      if(clientSocket == null) System.out.println("error");
      else {
         System.out.println("connected to the server " + argv[0] + " at port " + port);
       DataOutputStream outToServer =
       new DataOutputStream(clientSocket.getOutputStream());
       BufferedReader inFromServer =
      new BufferedReader(new InputStreamReader(clientSocket.getInputStream()));
       String[] out = { "HELO : thinkpad\n",
                "mail from: <u_roy@it.jusl.ac.in>\n",
                "rcpt to: <u_roy@it.jusl.ac.in>\n",
                "data\n",
                "This is a sample mail\n.\n",
                "quit\n"
                };
```

```
        try {
            System.out.println("From server: " + inFromServer.readLine());
            for(int i = 0; i < out.length; i++) {
                outToServer.writeBytes(out[i]);
                System.out.print("To server: " + out[i]);
                System.out.println("From server: " + inFromServer.readLine());
            }
        }catch(Exception e) {clientSocket.close();}
    }
}
```

Compile the program as follows:

```
javac MailClient.java
```

Note that it does not use JavaMail API and hence does not require `javax.mail.jar` file. It creates a socket connection to the port 25 (SMTP port) and fires SMTP commands. Run the program as follows:

```
java MailClient webmail.jusl.ac.in 25
```

A sample output for this program is shown in Figure 15.3:

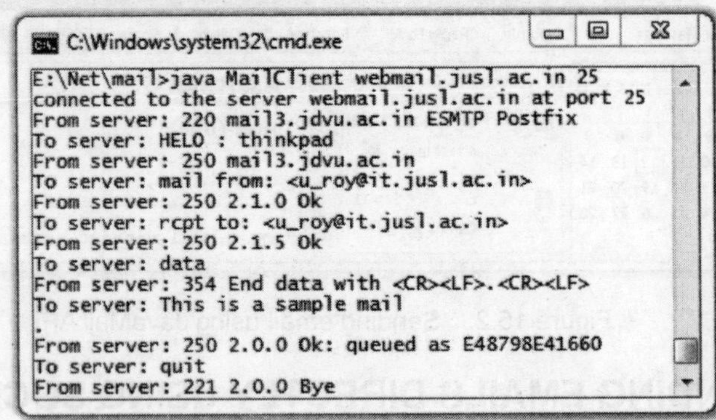

C:\Windows\system32\cmd.exe
E:\Net\mail>java MailClient webmail.jusl.ac.in 25
connected to the server webmail.jusl.ac.in at port 25
From server: 220 mail3.jdvu.ac.in ESMTP Postfix
To server: HELO : thinkpad
From server: 250 mail3.jdvu.ac.in
To server: mail from: <u_roy@it.jusl.ac.in>
From server: 250 2.1.0 Ok
To server: rcpt to: <u_roy@it.jusl.ac.in>
From server: 250 2.1.5 Ok
To server: data
From server: 354 End data with <CR><LF>.<CR><LF>
To server: This is a sample mail
From server: 250 2.0.0 Ok: queued as E48798E41660
To server: quit
From server: 221 2.0.0 Bye

Figure 15.3: Sending email using Java TCP socket

15.6 SECURED SMTP

The first standard for email delivery was **S**imple **M**ail **T**ransfer **P**rotocol (SMTP). As its name implies, it is a very simple protocol and is still in use. However, SMTP is a fairly naive protocol, and provides no facilities to verify the user's identity. This means, any user who has an account in the mail server can send an email to any other user without any password verification.

This basic flaw in the protocol may be exploited by viruses, worms, security frauds and spammers forging identities. This makes the system vulnerable and must be avoided. So, usually an SMTP server runs an authorization protocol (typically **S**ecure **S**ocket **L**ayer (SSL), or **T**ransport **L**ayer **S**ecurity (TLS)) over the SMTP protocol. In this case, usually users are not allowed to connect to the SMTP port directly. A user typically connects to the SSL/TLS first and provides authorization information. The SSL/TLS starts the authorization procedure and if the user passes this authorization procedure, SSL/TLS forwards the request to the actual SMTP server. Some mail servers allow users to connect to the port 25; however, users must go through the authentication procedure first before working with normal SMTP.

SMTP may be made secured using SSL or TLS and the corresponding port number used is shown in Table 15.1:

Table 15.1: Standard ports used by SMTP

Protocol	Port number	Protocol	Port number
SMTP without SSL/TLS	25	SMTP with TLS	587
SMTP with SSL	465		

A detailed description of these two protocols may be found in Chapter 20.

In this section, we shall discuss how to send mails using SSL or TLS and Java mail API. For demonstration purpose, we have created an account in Gmail server having username `usr.some` and password `some.usr`.

First we have to specify that an authentication is required as follows:

```
props.put("mail.smtp.auth", "true");
```

Then, we have to specify which protocol (SSL/TLS) we want to use for authentication.

15.6.1 Using SSL

Most of the mail servers including mail support SSL for user authentication. So, it is a good idea to use SSL to pass through the authentication procedure. The following properties are required for SSL:

```
props.put("mail.smtp.port", "465");
props.put("mail.smtp.socketFactory.class","javax.net.ssl.SSLSocketFactory");
```

The first line indicates that the port number `465` (i.e. SMTP/SSL) is to be used for authentication. If this standard port number is not used for SSL, find it and use it in place of `465`. A list of port numbers used by standard email servers is given later in this chapter. During the mail delivery, the SSL handshake starts immediately when a client connects to this port, and only after the session is encrypted, the SMTP protocol begins.

The second line tells that the client will get help from `javax.net.ssl.SSLSocketFactory` class to talk to SSL server. Indeed, JavaMail API includes this class, which implements SSL. This second line is mandatory if the SMTP server uses SSL (port 465) for authentication, like the Gmail SMTP server does.

15.6.2 Using TLS

If TLS is used as a security layer, the following properties are required:

```
props.put("mail.smtp.starttls.enable", "true");
```

Note that the above piece of code does not use any specialized class to talk to TLS server. This is because TLS uses *plaintext authentication* and hence no specialized authenticator is required. However, to start the authentication procedure, the above line is required.

Note that the previous mechanism uses two ports, `465` (for SSL) and `25` (for SMTP). Port `465` authenticates the user and forwards the request to `25`. For plaintext authentication, only one port may be used instead of two ports. However, one additional command `STARTTLS` is added to SMTP. So, clients connect to regular SMTP port (25) and issue a `STARTTLS` command after which the session is encrypted. Once the session is encrypted regular SMTP starts working.

By setting `mail.smtp.starttls.enable` property to `true`, we tell the client to issue a `STARTTLS` command to start authentication procedure.

However, for smooth transition from SSL to TLS, a separate port (587) for TLS is provided. So, it is possible to connect to this port as follows:

```
props.put("mail.smtp.port", "587");
```

In this case, clients connect to the port `587` where authentication starts and once it is over, regular SMTP starts. However, connecting to this port (`587`) it is not mandatory to use TLS.

15.6.3 Providing Authentication Information

We create two strings, one for username and the other for password:

```
final String user = "usr.some", password = "some.usr";
```

Since, SSL or TLS requires authentication information, we have to pass username and password information. There are many ways we can do this:

- Using `Authenticator` object
- Using `send()` method of `Transport` class.
- Using `connect()` method of `Transport` Class

Using `Authenticator` object

In this case, we create a subclass (usually inner) from abstract `javax.mail.Authenticator` class overriding its `getPasswordAuthentication()` method as follows:

```
class MyAuthenticator extends javax.mail.Authenticator {
    String user, password;
    MyAuthenticator(String user, String password) {
      this.user = user;
      this.password = password;
    }
    protected PasswordAuthentication getPasswordAuthentication() {
      return new PasswordAuthentication(user, password);
    }
}
```

The `getPasswordAuthentication()` method returns a `PasswordAuthentication` instance created from a (username, password) pair. An instance of this class is then registered with the `Session` object during its creation.

```
Authenticator auth = new MyAuthenticator(user, password);
Session session = Session.getInstance(props, auth);
```

When authentication is required, subclass's `getPasswordAuthentication()` method is called. We can also collect username and password using popup dialog as follows:

```
class PopupAuthenticator extends Authenticator {
  protected PasswordAuthentication getPasswordAuthentication() {
    String user = JOptionPane.showInputDialog("Enter username:");
    String password = JOptionPane.showInputDialog("Enter password:");
    return new PasswordAuthentication(user, password);
  }
}
Authenticator auth = new PopupAuthenticator();
Session session = Session.getInstance(props, auth);
```

Alternatively, we can create and use an anonymous inner class as follows:

```
Authenticator auth = new Authenticator () {
  public PasswordAuthentication getPasswordAuthentication(){
    return new PasswordAuthentication(user, password);
  }
};
Session session = Session.getInstance(props, auth);
```

To summarize, we create and use anonymous class during the creation of `Session` object as follows:

```
Session session = Session.getInstance(props,
  new javax.mail.Authenticator() {
    protected PasswordAuthentication getPasswordAuthentication() {
      return new PasswordAuthentication(user, password);
    }
  });
```

Using `send()` method of `Transport` Class

Alternatively, the user name and password may be specified in the `send()` method of transport class directly as follows:

```
Session session = Session.getInstance(props);
Transport.send(msg, user, password);
```

Using `connect()` method of `Transport` Class

We can also send a mail using a specific instance from the session for SMTP protocol as follows:

```
Transport transport = session.getTransport("smtps");
transport.connect(host, user, password);
transport.sendMessage(msg, msg.getAllRecipients());
transport.close();
```

The `connect()` method establishes a connection to the specified host and username and password, whereas `sendMessage()` method delivers the message. Since, `connect()` method keeps the connection (unless the connection is not closed explicitly using `close()` method) open with the mail server, this method is useful if we want to send multiple messages. The static `send()` method makes a separate connection to the server for each method call and closes it once the message is delivered.

The following program (`SendEmail1.java`) sends a mail from the user `usr.some@gmail.com` to itself using SSL.

```
//SendEmail1.java
import java.util.*;
import javax.mail.*;
import javax.mail.internet.*;
public class SendEmail1 {
  public static void main(String [] args) {
    String mailHost = "smtp.gmail.com";
    String from = "usr.some@gmail.com", to = "usr.some@gmail.com";
    final String user = "usr.some", password = "some.usr";

    Properties props = new Properties();
    props.setProperty("mail.smtp.host", mailHost);
    props.put("mail.smtp.auth", "true");

    props.put("mail.smtp.port", "465");
   props.put("mail.smtp.socketFactory.class","javax.net.ssl.SSLSocketFactory");

    //disable two lines above and enable one line below to use TLS

    //props.put("mail.smtp.starttls.enable", "true");

    Session session = Session.getInstance(props,
      new javax.mail.Authenticator() {
        protected PasswordAuthentication getPasswordAuthentication() {
          return new PasswordAuthentication(user, password);
        }
      });
```

```
    session.setDebug(true);
    try{
      MimeMessage msg = new MimeMessage(session);
      msg.setFrom(from);
      msg.addRecipients(Message.RecipientType.TO, to);
      msg.setSubject("A test mail");
      msg.setText("test message");
      Transport.send(msg);
    }catch (Exception e) {
      e.printStackTrace();
    }
  }
}
```

The added portion is shown with bold font. To view the debugging information and to understand how the message is sent, we have used the following line of code:

```
session.setDebug(true);
```

Compile and run the program as described before. A sample output of this program is shown in Figure 15.4:

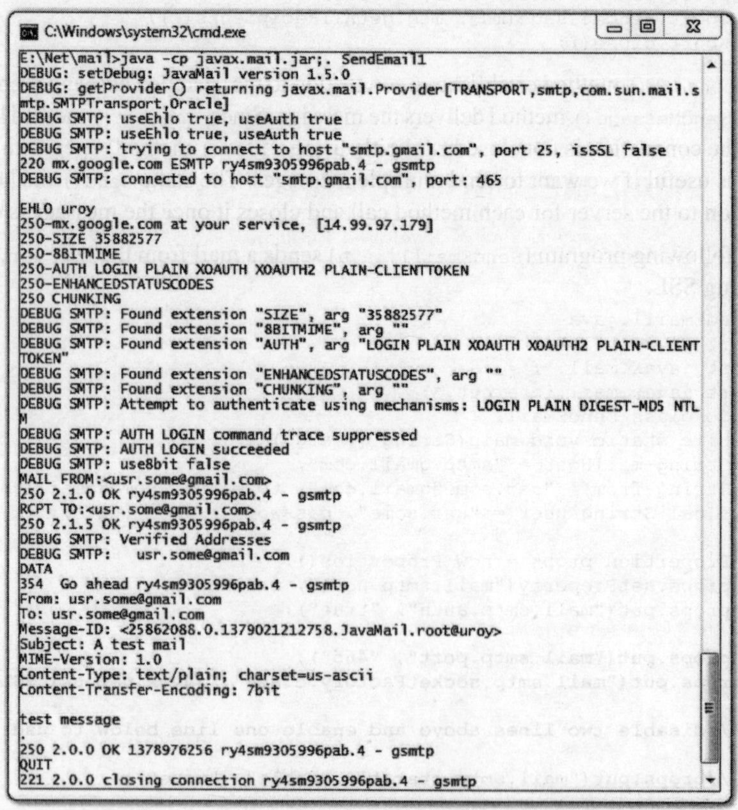

Figure 15.4: Sending email using Java mail API

The following program (`SendEmailTransport.java`) sends a mail from the user `usr.some@gmail.com` to itself using SSL and `Transport` object.

```
//SendEmailTransport.java
import java.util.*;
import javax.mail.*;
import javax.mail.internet.*;
public class SendEmailTransport {
  public static void main(String [] args) {
    String host = "smtp.gmail.com";
    String from = "usr.some@gmail.com", to = "usr.some@gmail.com";
    final String user = "usr.some", password = "some.usr";
    Properties props = new Properties();
    Session session = Session.getInstance(props);
    try{
      MimeMessage msg = new MimeMessage(session);
      msg.setFrom(from);
      msg.addRecipients(Message.RecipientType.TO, to);
      msg.setSubject("A test mail");
      msg.setText("test message");

      Transport transport = session.getTransport("smtps");
      transport.connect(host, user, password);
      transport.sendMessage( msg, msg.getAllRecipients());
      transport.close();
    }catch (Exception e) {
      e.printStackTrace();
    }
  }
}
```

15.7 EMAIL MESSAGE REVISITED

The email messages, we have developed so far, have only text content. In this section, we shall discuss creating messages having text and/or non-text content.

15.7.1 MIME

Note that, SMTP was originally designed to transfer only plain (ASCII) text. The maximum number of characters and lines were also limited. To overcome these limitations, a standard was defined by **I**nternet **E**ngineering **T**ask **F**orce (IETF) in RFC 1521 and 1522 called **M**ultipurpose **I**nternet **M**ail **E**xtension (MIME). MIME is a standard intended for enhancing the capabilities of SMTP. It provides a simple and standard way to represent and encode a wide variety of media types for transmission via SMTP.

MIME especially supports the following:

- Both ASCII and non-ASCII character sets
- Messages having unlimited length
- Multi-font messages
- Multi-media: Image, Audio, and Video messages
- Multi-objects in a single message
- Even raw binary files

Moreover, MIME specification was built to be completely backward compatible and flexible and open to extensions. It enables us describing and organizing new content type by defining additional fields in the email header.

The `javax.mail.internet.MimeMessage` class, which is a subclass of abstract `javax.mail.Message` class, implements MIME messages. A MIME message has basically two parts: *header* and *body*.

The header section contains attributes that specify address(es) and other values necessary to send, route, receive, decode and store the message. Attributes also specify the structure and type of data contained in the message body.

The content of `Message` may consist of a single part or multiple parts. A single part `Message` is one which has only one section of data, whereas multi-part `Message` has a body having multiple sections.

15.7.2 Single-part Message

In this case, the content of a `Message` is represented by a `javax.activation.DataHandler` object, which carries the content and provides useful methods to handle the content. A `DataHandler` object knows how to deal with the content. To add content to a `Message`, the following steps are followed:

- Create some content
- Instantiate a `DataHandler` object
- Place content into that `DataHandler` object
- Place that `DataHandler` object into a `Message` object
- Define attributes for this `DataHandler` object in the `Message` header properly

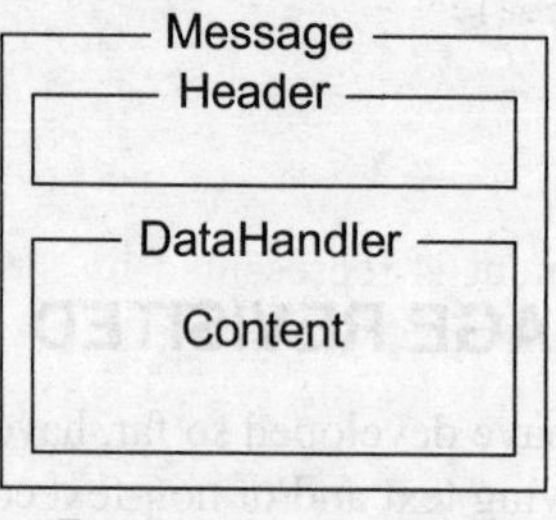

Format of a single part message

The JavaMail API provides two methods `setDataHandler()` and `setContent()` to set the message content:

```
void  setDataHandler(DataHandler dh)
void  setContent(Object obj, String type)
void  setContent(Multipart mp)
```

The first two are used for messages having a single part and the last method is used for multi-part message and is described in the next section.

Using setDataHandler()

In this case, we use `setDataHanlder()` method on `Message` to set a `DataHandler` that encapsulates data. The `DataHandler` class provides a consistent interface to data obtained in different formats and sources. A `DataHandler` object may be created using any of the following constructors:

```
DataHandler(DataSource ds)
DataHandler(Object obj, String mimeType)
DataHandler(URL url)
```

The constructors accept data as either a `DataSource`, which is a stream connected to the data or a Java `Object` or a `URL`. For example, the following example creates a `DataHandler` object from a String:

```
//create a String
String content = "simple string";
//create a DataHandler object with this String
DataHandler dh = new DataHandler(content, "text/plain");
```

The second argument indicates that the content is *plain text* type. Similarly, the following code creates a `DataHandler` object from file data:

```
String filename = "SendEmailTest.java";
DataSource ds = new FileDataSource(filename);
DataHandler dh = new DataHandler(ds);
```

We can now insert the `DataHandler` object `dh` having content into the `Message` object `msg` as follows:

```
//insert content to the message
msg.setDataHandler(dh);
```

Note that the content set by the last `setDataHanlder()` method persists overwriting existing (if any) content.

Using setContent()

In this case, we can set content to a `Message` using its `setContent()` method directly. The following example illustrates this:

```
//create a String
String content = "simple string";
//insert content to the message directly
msg.setContent(content, "text/plain");
```

15.7.3 Multi-part MIME message

In this case, message content is represented by a `Multipart` object. A Multipart object is a container that contains one or more `Bodypart` objects, each of which can in turn contain `DataHandler` objects. For example, if a message has a text content and an attachment, the message is said to have two body parts.

The `javax.mail.internet.MimeMultipart` class, which is a subclass of abstract `javax.mail.Multipart` class, represents a muti-part content. To create a message having multiple parts, the following steps are followed:

- Create a `MimeMultipart` object or create an object of a class that extends `Multipart` class.
- Create one or more `MimeBodyPart` object one for each part of the message content
- Populate these objects using `setContent()` or `setDataHandler()` method as described in the previous section
- Insert the `MimeMultipart` object into the message using `setContent()` method.

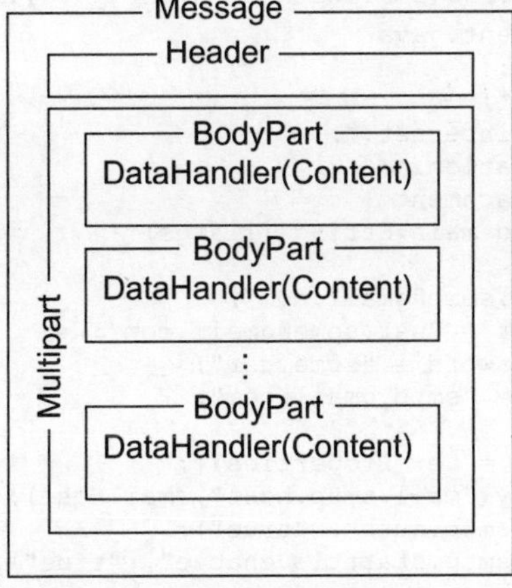

Format of a multi-part message

15.7.4 Composing a Mixed Message

In this section, we shall compose a message which has text content and an attachment (i.e. multiple parts). To create a message having multiple parts, we first create a `MimeMultipart` object:

```
Multipart multipart = new MimeMultipart();
```

Since, there are two body parts (one text and another attachment) in our message, we create two `MimeBodyPart` objects as follows:

```
MimeBodyPart part1 = new MimeBodyPart();
MimeBodyPart part2 = new MimeBodyPart();
```

The first part `part1` holds a text message and the second part `part2` holds an attachment. A piece of text is placed in the first part as follows:

```
part1.setContent("This mail has an attachment.", "text/plain");
```

Since, the content type is plain text, `setText()` may also be used:

```
part1.setText("This mail has an attachment.");
```

The `setText()` method sets the specified String to the `part1` with a MIME type of `text/plain`. Let us now attach a file `EmailWithAttachment.java` with the second part as follows:

```
String filename = "EmailWithAttachment.java";
DataSource source = new FileDataSource(filename);
DataHandler dh = new DataHandler(source);

part2.setDataHandler(dh);
part2.setFileName(filename);
```

Alternatively, to be concise, `attachFile()` method may be used:

```
String filename = "EmailWithAttachment.java";
part2.attachFile(filename);
```

The `attachFile()` uses the given file to provide the data for `part2`. The file name specified is used as the file name for this part and file data is used as the data for this part. The encoding is done appropriately based on file data. These two parts are then added to the `MimeMultipart` object as follows:

```
multipart.addBodyPart(part1);
multipart.addBodyPart(part2);
```

Finally, this `MimeMultipart` object is attached to the actual message and delivered using the following code:

```
msg.setContent(multipart );
Transport.send(msg);
```

The complete source code (`EmailWithAttchment.java`) is given below:

```
// EmailWithAttchment.java
import java.util.*;
import javax.mail.*;
import javax.mail.internet.*;
import javax.activation.*;
class EmailWithAttachment {
 public static void main(String [] args) {

   String to = "usr.some@gmail.com";
   final String user = "usr.some@gmail.com";
   final String password = "some.usr";
   String mailHost = "smtp.gmail.com";

   Properties props = new Properties();
   props.setProperty("mail.smtp.host", mailHost);
   props.put("mail.smtp.auth", "true");
   props.put("mail.smtp.starttls.enable", "true");

   Session session = Session.getInstance(props,
    new javax.mail.Authenticator() {
```

```
    protected PasswordAuthentication getPasswordAuthentication() {
    return new PasswordAuthentication(user,password);
    }
  });
   //session.setDebug(true);
  try{
    MimeMessage msg = new MimeMessage(session);
    msg.addRecipients(Message.RecipientType.TO,to);
    msg.setSubject("Mail with attachment");

    Multipart multipart = new MimeMultipart();

    MimeBodyPart part1 = new MimeBodyPart();
    MimeBodyPart part2 = new MimeBodyPart();

    //part1.setContent("This mail has an attachment.", "text/plain");
    part1.setText("This mail has an attachment.");

    String filename = "EmailWithAttachment.java";
    //DataSource source = new FileDataSource(filename);
    //DataHandler dh = new DataHandler(source);

    //part2.setDataHandler(dh);
    //part2.setFileName(filename);

    part2.attachFile(filename);

    multipart.addBodyPart(part1);
    multipart.addBodyPart(part2);

    msg.setContent(multipart );

    Transport.send(msg);

   System.out.println("msg sent....");
   }catch (Exception e) {e.printStackTrace();}
  }
}
```

15.7.5 Compiling the Program

This program uses `javax.activation` package. If you are using Java SE earlier than 6, then download `javax.activation.jar.zip` file from the following link

`http://www.java2s.com/Code/Jar/j/Downloadjavaxactivationjar.htm`

The, `javax.activation.jar.zip` file contains a single `javax.activation.jar` file. Unzip and put `javax.activation.jar` file in `E:Netmail` directory. Use the following command to compile:

```
javac -cp javax.mail.jar;javax.activation.jar;. EmailWithAttachment.java
```

Note that, Java SE 6 or later already has an activation package included. So, there is no need to download the jar file separately. Use the following command to compile:

```
javac -cp javax.mail.jar;. EmailWithAttachment.java
```

A sample output is shown in Figure 15.5:

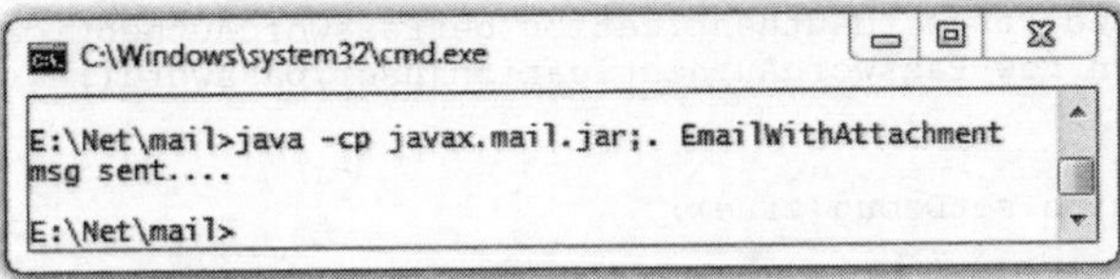

Figure 15.5: Sending an email with attachment

Figure 15.6: shows a snapshot of Gmail interface that indicates that a mail arrived with an attachment.

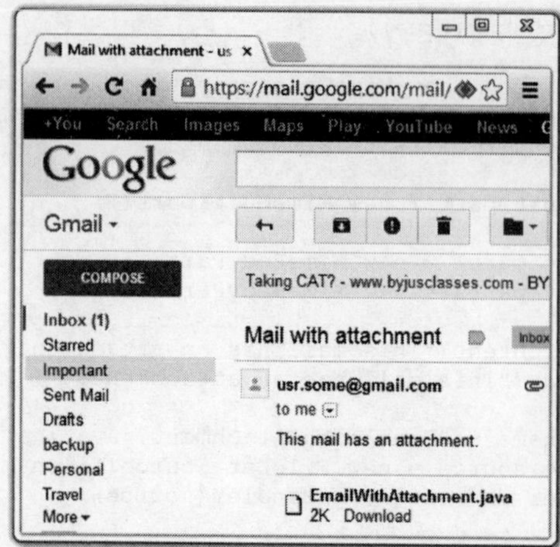

Figure 15.6: Receiving an email with attachment

Google and the Google logo are registered trademarks of Google Inc., used with permission

15.8 EMAIL WITH HTML CONTENT

Sending messages having html content needs a little additional work. All we need to do is to specify content type as `text/html` in `setContent()` method. For example, the following piece of code sets a `<h2>` element to the content:

```
msg.setContent("<h2>Mail with html body.</h2>","text/html");
```

The complete source code of a program (`SendEmail4.java`) that sends a message having html content is shown below:

```
//SendEmail4.java
import java.util.*;
import javax.mail.*;
import javax.mail.internet.*;
public class SendEmail4 {
  public static void main(String [] args) {

    String to = "usr.some@gmail.com";
    String mailHost = "smtp.gmail.com";
    final String user = "usr.some@gmail.com", password = "some.usr";

    Properties props = new Properties();
    props.setProperty("mail.smtp.host", mailHost);
    props.put("mail.smtp.auth", "true");
    props.put("mail.smtp.starttls.enable", "true");

    Session session = Session.getInstance(props,
      new javax.mail.Authenticator() {
   protected PasswordAuthentication getPasswordAuthentication() {
     return new PasswordAuthentication(user,password);
   }
      });
    //session.setDebug(true);
    try{
      MimeMessage msg = new MimeMessage(session);
      msg.setFrom(user);
```

```
      msg.addRecipients(Message.RecipientType.TO, to);
      msg.setSubject("Mail with html body");
      msg.setText("Test message");
      msg.setContent("<h2>Mail with html body.</h2>","text/html");
      Transport.send(msg);
      System.out.println("msg sent....");
    }catch (Exception e) {
      e.printStackTrace();
    }
  }
}
```

Compile and run the program as described previously. A sample output is shown in Figure 15.7:

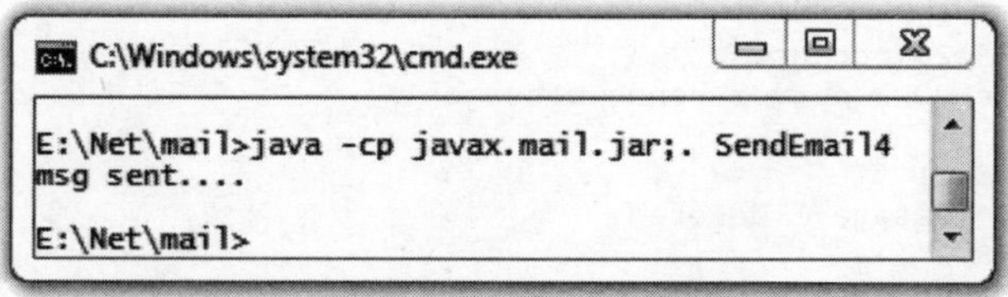

Figure 15.7: Sending mail with html body

15.9 ACCESSING EMAIL

In the previous sections, we have discussed how to send mails. Let us now discuss how to retrieve email messages from a mail server such as Gmail. There exists two primary protocols that describe syntax and semantics to retrieve emails: **P**ost **O**ffice **P**rotocol (POP) and **I**nternet **M**essage **A**ccess **P**rotocol (IMAP) [Figure 15.8:].

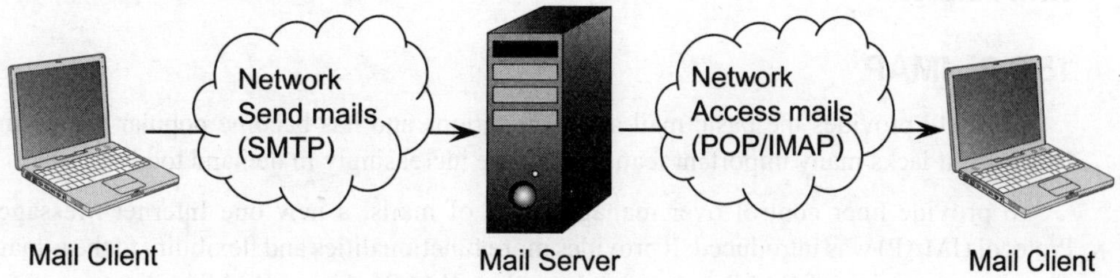

Figure 15.8: Sending and retrieving mails

15.9.1 POP

POP is an acronym for **P**ost **O**ffice **P**rotocol. Its current version is 3.0 and is known as POP3. It is a standard protocol (see RFC 1939 for details) that supports basic functions (download and delete) for electronic mail. Like most Internet protocols, the POP3 is a simple request–response protocol.

A POP3 server listens for connections on standard TCP port 110. Once a connection is established, the communication between the client and server takes places in the form of *commands* and *responses*. The commands are sent by clients while server sends responses.

An example POP3 session is shown below:

```
S: <wait for connection on TCP port 110>
C: <open connection>// e.g. telnet localhost 110
S:    +OK uroy POP3 server (JAMES POP3 Server 2.3.2) ready
C:    user abc
S:    +OK
C:    pass abc
S:    +OK Welcome abc
C:    STAT
S:    +OK 2 320
C:    LIST
S:    +OK 2 messages (320 octets)
S:    1 120
S:    2 200
S:    .
C:    RETR 1
S:    +OK 120 octets
S:    <the POP3 server sends message 1>
S:    .
C:    DELE 1
S:    +OK message 1 deleted
C:    RETR 2
S:    +OK 200 octets
S:    <the POP3 server sends message 2>
S:    .
C:    DELE 2
S:    +OK message 2 deleted
C:    QUIT
S:    +OK Apache James POP3 Server signing off.
C:  <close connection>
S:  <wait for next connection>
```

The telnet application may be used to establish a connection to the pop server. Once the connection has been established, the client application must send username and password information to the email server. If the login credentials are accepted, the user can access the mailbox to download or delete messages.

15.9.2 IMAP

The POP provides the basic mail access functions and has become popular for its simplicity. However, it lacks many important features that are increasingly in demand today.

To provide finer control over manageability of mails, a new one Internet Message Access Protocol (IMAP) was introduced. It provides more functionalities and flexibility to the e-mail clients. The current version of IMAP is 4 and is known as IMAP4. Using IMAP4, clients can manipulate messages stored on a remote server in the same way they manipulate messages stored in the local machine. IMAP has some specific advantages over its competitor POP, some of which are mentioned below:

- In POP, clients get disconnected after downloading messages. However, IMAP4 allows clients stay connected and download messages any time during the session.
- Unlike POP, which allows only one client to be connected to the mailbox at a time, the IMAP allows multiple clients to access a mailbox simultaneously. It also provides facilities to the clients to detect changes made to the mailbox by other connected clients.
- The IMAP4 allows us to retrieve individual parts of the message. This means a client can retrieve the text portion of a message without retrieving attached files.
- In IMAP, clients can detect the message states (such as read, replied, deleted) using flags, which are stored on the server. POP does not specify any such mechanism.

- It is possible to create, rename, and/or delete mailboxes (usually represented as folders) with IMAP4. It enables us in copying and moving messages across mailboxes. It also enables us to create *shared* and *public* folders.
- IMAP4 clients can ask the server to provide messages that meet a search criteria. So, clients need not download all messages to perform this searching.

Although, IMAP overcomes many of the pitfalls of POP, it introduces additional complexity which, in turn, introduces server-side workaround. For example, a malicious client can provide critical search criteria to the server to search messages that can potentially consume significant amount of server resources. Due to tremendous complexity of IMAP fewer e-mail services support IMAP.

15.9.3 Secured Mail Access

Like many other protocols, POP and IMAP, exchange login name, password and data in the clear form. This means that anyone having access to the link between the server and client can listen and probably discover passwords. To overcome this problem, it is strongly recommended to use POP and IMAP that operate only through secure channels.

Usually, to make mail access secured, POP and IMAP are bundled with **T**ransport **L**ayer **S**ecurity (TLS) or **S**ecure **S**ockets **L**ayer (SSL). Most of the mail servers including Gmail use this mechanism. The POP3 protocol, when used with an SSL layer, is called POP3S. Similarly, the IMAP when bundled with SSL is called IMAPS. A list of port numbers used by these protocols is shown in Table 15.2:

Table 15.2: Ports used by POP and IMAP

Protocol	Port number	Protocol	Port number
POP3 with or without TLS	110	POP3/SSL	995
IMAP4 with or without TLS	143	IMAP4/SSL	993

A detailed list of SMTP, POP and IMAP servers may be found in Section 15.14

15.9.4 JavaMail API support

Fortunately, JavaMail API supports both of these protocols. In this section, we shall discuss how JavaMail API allows us to retrieve emails from servers that implement POP and/or IMAP.

To describe message storage, JavaMail API provides two primary classes `Store` and `Folder`. Messages, delivered by a transport protocol or an agent, are placed in `Folder`s. The `Store` class describes a `Folder` hierarchy and an access protocol such as POP, IMAP etc. These access protocols are used to retrieve messages from folders.

15.9.5 Reading Email

To read messages, a `Store` object is first created.

```
Store store = session.getStore("pop3s");
```

This indicates that `store` should use the protocol `pop3s` while retrieving the messages. The protocol `pop3s` is a secured extension to pop3. Alternatively, `imaps` (which is a protocol similar to `pop3s`) may be used:

```
Store store = session.getStore("imaps");
```

Since, both `pop3s` and `imaps` require user name and password to be verified, `connect()` method is used to supply them:

```
String host = "pop.gmail.com", username = "usr.some", password = "some.usr";
store.connect(host, username, password);
```

The `connect()` method takes a host name, user name, and password to authenticate a user. The name of the POP3 server for Gmail is `pop.gmail.com` and is used as host name. There are other overloaded `connect()` methods where missing information is obtained from the `Session` object's properties and `Authenticator` object.

If everything goes fine, we have an access to the message store now. To access messages, we create a `Folder` object that represents a folder containing messages. Folders can contain subfolders as well as messages, thus providing a hierarchical structure.

The following program (`RetrieveEmail.java`) shows how to retrieve all emails of the user `usr.some` from the Gmail POP3 server `pop.gmail.com` using Java mail API and POP3.

```
import java.util.Properties;
import javax.mail.*;
public class RetrieveEmail {
  public static void main(String[] args) throws Exception {
    String host = "pop.gmail.com", protocol = "pop3s";
    String username = "usr.some", password = "some.usr";

    Properties props = new Properties();
    Session session = Session.getInstance(props);
    session.setDebug(true);
    Store store = session.getStore(protocol);
    store.connect(host, username, password);
    Folder inbox = store.getFolder("Inbox");
    if (inbox.exists()) {
      inbox.open(Folder.READ_ONLY);
      Message[] emails = inbox.getMessages();
      for (int i = 0; i < emails.length; i++) {
        System.out.println("Message " + (i + 1));
        emails[i].writeTo(System.out);
      }
      inbox.close(false);
    }
    else
      System.out.println("Inbox not available");
    store.close();
  }
}
```

A sample output of this program is shown in Figure 15.9:

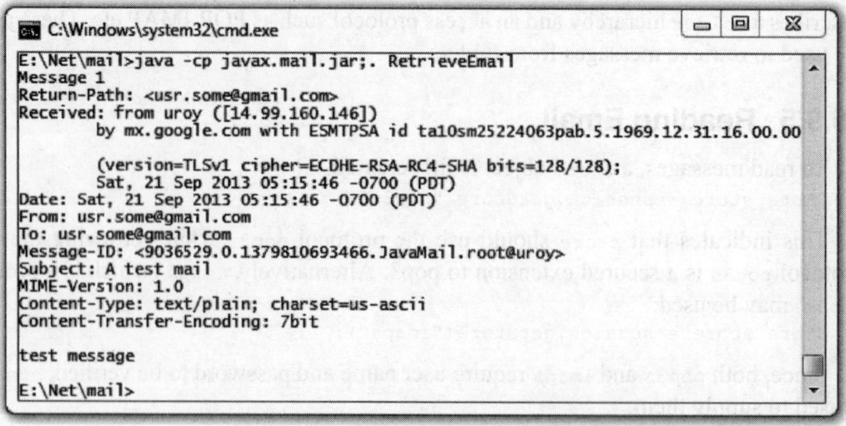

Figure 15.9: Retrieving email using Java mail API and POP3

15.9.6 Using Authenticator

Like sending emails, an `Authenticator` object may also be used to retrieve mails. In this case, instead of passing host, user and password to the `connect()` method of `Store` directly, we configure a `Properties` object to have the host, and create an `Authenticator` object having user and password. These two objects are then supplied to the `Session` object. The following example demonstrates this:

```
String host = "pop.gmail.com", protocol = "pop3s";
String username = "usr.some", password = "some.usr";

Properties props = new Properties();
//provide host
props.put("mail."+protocol+".host", host);
//provide user and password
Authenticator auth = new Authenticator () {
  public PasswordAuthentication getPasswordAuthentication(){
    return new PasswordAuthentication(user, password);
  }
};
Session session = Session.getInstance(props, auth);
Store store = session.getStore(protocol);
store.connect();
```

The protocol `imaps` may be used instead of `pop3s`.

15.10 DELETING MAILS

To delete a message from a folder, the folder must be opened in `READ_WRITE` mode:

```
inbox.open(Folder.READ_WRITE);
```

The message deletion is a two-step process. We first set message's `DELETED` flag to `true`:

```
msg.setFlag(Flags.Flag.DELETED, true);
```

However, setting the `DELETED` flag to `true` on a message does not remove it from the folder. Instead it marks the message as deleted. The message is actually deleted when `expunge()` method on the folder is invoked.

```
inbox.expunge();
```

Alternatively, close the folder using its `close()` method passing the argument `true`.

```
inbox.close(true);
```

The value `true`, tells the `close()` method to call `expunge()` method. Note that POP3 does not support `expunge()` method. So, `close()` method should be called with an argument `true` for POP3.

The following is a program that deletes all the messages from the folder "inbox".

```
import java.util.Properties;
import javax.mail.*;
public class DeleteEmail {
  public static void main(String[] args) throws Exception {
    String host = "pop.gmail.com", protocol = "imaps";
    String username = "usr.some", password = "some.usr";

    Properties props = new Properties();
    Session session = Session.getInstance(props);
    //session.setDebug(true);
    Store store = session.getStore(protocol);
    store.connect(host, username, password);
    Folder inbox = store.getFolder("Inbox");
```

```
      if (inbox.exists()) {
        inbox.open(Folder.READ_WRITE);
        Message[] emails = inbox.getMessages();
        for (int i = 0; i < emails.length; i++) {
          System.out.println("Deleting Message " + (i + 1));
          emails[i].setFlag(Flags.Flag.DELETED,true);
        }
        inbox.close(true);
      }
      else
        System.out.println("Inbox not available");
      store.close();
    }
  }
```

Since, this program is potentially dangerous as it deletes all the messages from a folder, make sure you either have copies of these messages stored elsewhere or the folder does not contain any important messages. A sample output is shown in Figure 15.10:

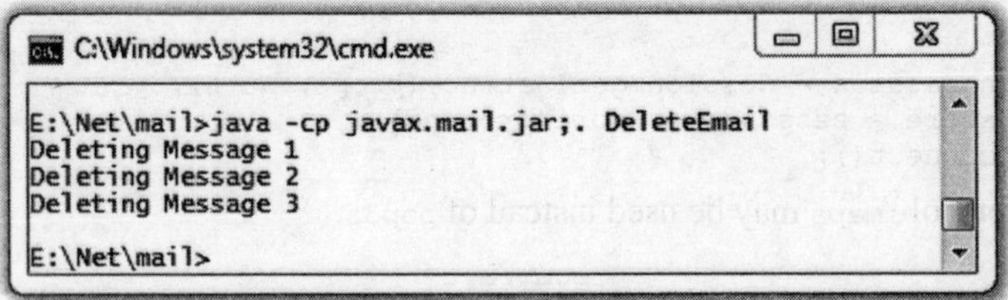

Figure 15.10: Deleting email using Java mail API and IMAP

15.11 REPLYING TO MAILS

To reply to an email received (and retrieved using POP or IMAP), `reply()` method may be used.

```
Message reply(boolean replyToAll)
```

This method returns a new `Message` suitable for reply. This means `reply()` configures headers and attributes of the reply `Message` properly. For example, the sender becomes the recipient, subject is set to the original subject prefixed with "Re: " etc. However, the content of this new Message will be empty. The Boolean parameter indicates whether to reply to only the sender (`false`) or reply to all (`true`). The following example demonstrates how to reply to an email:

```
Message replyMsg = recvMsg.reply(false);
replyMsg.setFrom(new InternetAddress("usr.some@gmail.com"));
replyMsg.setText("Received your mail.");
Transport.send(replyMsg);
```

Make sure that the session properties required to send an email are set properly.

15.12 FORWARDING MAILS

Unlike `reply()`, there is no method to get a message suitable for forwarding. So, forwarding an email is a little complicated. A message to be forwarded has two parts: one that contains the old message and a new part which is added during forwarding. This tells us that a forwarding mail is a multipart message. To create a forwarding email, the following steps are required:

- Create a fresh `Message` which will have two parts
- Set headers and attributes properly

- Create two BodyPart objects
- Fill one BodyPart by new content
- Fill the other BodyPart by old content
- Create a Multipart object
- Add those BodyParts to the Multpart object
- Finally, set this Multipart object as the content of the message

The following creates a fresh message:

```
MimeMessage frdMsg = new MimeMessage(session);
```

Now, set some important headers as follows:

```
frdMsg.setSubject("Fwd: " + message.getSubject());
frdMsg.setFrom(InternetAddress.toString(message.getFrom()));
frdMsg.addRecipients(Message.RecipientType.TO,"usr.some@gmail.com");
```

The message is forwarded to an email address: usr.some@gmail.com. Create a Multipart object that will be set as content to the message:

```
Multipart multipart = new MimeMultipart();
```

Create a BodyPart object and populate it with text content:

```
BodyPart newPart = new MimeBodyPart();
newPart.setText("New Message:\n\n");
```

Now, create another BodyPart object to hold the entire content of the original message:

```
BodyPart oldPart = new MimeBodyPart();
oldPart.setContent(message.getContent(), message.getContentType());
```

Add these two parts to the Multipart object:

```
multipart.addBodyPart(newPart);
multipart.addBodyPart(oldPart);
```

Finally, add this Multipart object to the forwarding message:

```
frdMsg.setContent(multipart);
```

This message is now ready for forwarding and can be sent using the following code:

```
Transport.send(frdMsg);
```

15.13 COPYING EMAILS

Messages are copied from one folder to another using copyMessages() method of Folder class:

```
public void copyMessages(Message[] msgs, Folder dest)
```

This method, if invoked on a folder, copies specified messages to the specified folder. Note that the specified messages must belong to the source folder. For example, to copy all the messages from inbox folder to backup folder, the following code may be used:

```
inbox.open(Folder.READ_ONLY);
Message[] emails = inbox.getMessages();
inbox.copyMessages(emails, backup);
```

Note that the source folder must be opened to get messages from it. However, the destination folder does not have to be opened explicitly. The copyMessages() method invokes the appendMessages() method on the destination folder to append the specified messages.

Also note that the destination folder must exist. If it does not exist, it may be created using the following piece of code:

```
Folder defaultFolder = store.getDefaultFolder();
Folder backup = defaultFolder.getFolder("backup");
backup.create(Folder.HOLDS_MESSAGES);
```

This creates a folder `backup` under the root directory. The following program (`CopyEmail.java`) creates a folder `backup` and copies all the messages from `inbox` to this folder.

```
import java.util.Properties;
import javax.mail.*;
public class CopyEmail {
  public static void main(String[] args) throws Exception {
    String host = "pop.gmail.com", username = "usr.some", password = "some.usr";

    Properties props = new Properties();
    Session session = Session.getInstance(props);
    session.setDebug(true);
    Store store = session.getStore("imaps");

    store.connect(host, username, password);
    Folder inbox = store.getFolder("Inbox");

    Folder defaultFolder = store.getDefaultFolder();
    Folder backup = defaultFolder.getFolder("backup");
    boolean isCreated = backup.create(Folder.HOLDS_MESSAGES);
    System.out.println("created: "+ isCreated);

    inbox.open(Folder.READ_ONLY);
    Message[] emails = inbox.getMessages();
    inbox.copyMessages(emails, backup);
  }
}
```

15.14 LIST OF SMTP, POP3 AND IMAP SERVERS

Default port for SMTP, POP and IMAP:

- SMTP AUTH: Port 25 or 587
- SMTP StartTLS Port 587
- SMTP SSL Port 465
- POP Port 110
- POP SSL Port 995
- IMAP Port 143
- IMAP SSL Port 993
- IMAP StartTLS Port 143

Table 15.3: Standard ports used by SMTP, POP and IMAP

Server	SMTP	POP3	IMAP
AT&T Server	smtp.att.yahoo.com SSL Port: 465	pop.att.yahoo.com SSL Port: 995	-
BT Connect Server	pop3.btconnect.com	mail.btconnect.com	imap4.btconnect.com Port: 143
BT Openworld & BT Internet Server	mail.btopenworld.com mail.btinternet.com	pop.btopenworld.com pop. btinternet.com	imap.btopenworld.com imap.btinternet.com
Comcast Server	smtp.comcast.net Port : 587	pop.comcast.net	imap.comcast.net
Gmail	smtp.gmail.com SSL Port: 465 StartTLS Port: 587	pop.gmail.com SSL Port: 995	imap.gmail.com SSL Port: 993

(Contd)

Table 15.3 (*Contd*)

Server	SMTP	POP3	IMAP
Hotmail Server	smtp.live.com StartTLS Port: 587	pop3.live.com SSL Port: 995	-
NTL @ntlworld.com Server	smtp.ntlworld.com SSL Port: 465	pop.ntlworld.com SSL Port: 995	imap.ntlworld.com SSL Port: 993
O2 Server	smtp.o2.ie smtp.o2.co.uk	pop3.o2.ie pop3.o2.co.uk	imap.o2.ie imap.o2.co.uk
O2 Online Deutschland Server	mail.o2online.de	pop.o2online.de	imap.o2online.de
Orange Server	smtp.orange.net smtp. orange.co.uk	pop.orange.net	imap.orange.net
T-Online Deutschland Server	smtpmaii.t-online.de (AUTH) securesmtp.t-online.de (SSL)	popmail.t-online.de (AUTH) securepop.t-online.de (SSL)	imapmail.t-online.de
Verizon Server hosted on Yahoo Server	outgoing.yahoo.verizon.net	incoming.yahoo.verizon.net	incoming.yahoo.verizon.net
Verizon Server	outgoing.verizon.net SSL Port: 465	incoming.verizon.net SSL Port: 995	incoming.verizon.net
Wanadoo UK Server	smtp.wanadoo.co.uk	pop.wanadoo.co.uk	-
Yahoo	smtp.mail.yahoo.com SSL Port 465	pop.mail.yahoo.com SSL Port: 995	imap.mail.yahoo.com SSL Port: 993
Yahoo Plus	plus.smtp.mail.yahoo.com SSL Port: 465	plus.pop.mail.yahoo.com SSL Port: 995	-
Yahoo UK	smtp.mail.yahoo.co.uk SSL Port: 465	pop.mail.yahoo.co.uk SSL Port: 995	-
Yahoo Deutschland	smtp.mail.yahoo.de SSL Port: 465	pop.mail.yahoo.de SSL Port: 995	
Yahoo AU/NZ	smtp.mail.yahoo.com.au SSL Port: 465	pop.mail.yahoo.com.au SSL Port: 995	
1&1 (1and1) Server	smtp.1and1.com StartTLS Port: 25 or 587	pop.1and1.com SSL Port: 995	imap.1and1.com SSL Port: 993
1&1 Deutschland Server	smtp.1und1.de StartTLS Port: 25 or 587	pop.1und1.de SSL Port: 995	imap.1und1.de SSL Port: 993

KEYWORDS

Authenticator—A class whose objects know how to obtain authentication for a network connection

DataHandler—A Java class that provides a consistent interface to data obtained in different formats and sources

Email—Digital version of a message (or letter)

Email Address—A name that identifies an electronic post office box on a network where e-mail can be sent

Expunge—A method that permanently removes messages marked as DELETED

Folder—An abstract class that represents a folder for mail messages

IMAP4—The Internet Message Access Protocol version 4, used to retrieve emails from a mail server

IMAPS—IMAP bundled with SSL

MIME—An Internet standard that extends the format of email to support ASCII as well as non-ASCII character transmission

Multipart Message—An email message having multiple body parts

PasswordAuthentication—A repository to hold user name and password

POP3—The Post Office Protocol version 3, used to retrieve emails from a mail server

POP3S—The POP3 protocol, when used with an SSL layer

Single-part Message—An email message having a single body part

SMTP—A standard protocol used to send emails from a mail server

SSL—A commonly used protocol for managing the security of a message transmission on the Internet

STARTTLS—A way to take an existing insecure connection, and upgrade it to a secure connection using SSL/TLS

Store—A Java abstract class that models a message store and its access protocol, for storing and retrieving messages

TLS—A successor of SSL that was designed to provide communication security over the Internet

Transport—A Java abstract class that models a message transport

SUMMARY

An electronic mail (or simply email or e-mail), as its name suggests, is a digital version of a message (or letter). **S**imple **M**ail **T**ransfer **P**rotocol (SMTP) is used to deliver emails, whereas **P**ost **O**ffice **P**rotocol (POP) and **I**nternet **M**essage **A**ccess **P**rotocol (IMAP) are used to access emails.

JavaMail is a powerful API that provides a platform-independent framework to send and retrieve electronic mail (e-mail).

There are basically three steps to follow to send an email using JavaMail API: (i) Create a Session object that stores the necessary information such as host name, user name and password to send an email (ii) Compose a message and (iii) Send the message.

This final Session class represents a mail session. The Session class provides access to the protocol providers that implement the Store, Transport, and related classes. To send/retrieve emails, a Session object is created and configured with some necessary properties.

The class MimeMessage represents a MIME style email message. **M**ultipurpose **I**nternet **M**ail **E**xtension (MIME) is a standard intended for enhancing the capabilities of SMTP. It provides a simple and standard way to represent and encode a wide variety of media types for transmission via SMTP.

The message is then sent using Transport class.

A typical SMTP server runs an authorization protocol to make communication secured. There are two protocols available to do this: **S**ecure **S**ocket **L**ayer (SSL) and **T**ransport **L**ayer **S**ecurity (TLS). In this case, a user typically connects to the SSL/TLS first and provides authorization information. The SSL/TLS starts the authorization procedure and if the user passes this authorization procedure, SSL/TLS forwards the request to the actual SMTP server.

There exists two primary protocols that describe syntax and semantics to retrieve emails: **P**ost **O**ffice Protocol (POP) and **I**nternet **M**essage **A**ccess **P**rotocol (IMAP). POP is a standard protocol that supports basic functions (download and delete) for electronic mail. To provide finer control over manageability of mails, IMAP was introduced. IMAP has some specific advantages over its competitor POP.

Usually, to make mail access secured, POP and IMAP are bundled with **T**ransport **L**ayer **S**ecurity (TLS) or **S**ecure **S**ockets **L**ayer (SSL). Most of the mail servers including Gmail use this mechanism. The POP3 protocol, when used with an SSL layer, is called POP3S. Similarly, the IMAP when bundled with SSL is called IMAPS.

WEB RESOURCES

`http://www.ietf.org/rfc/rfc2821.txt`
Simple Mail Transfer Protocol

`http://www.ietf.org/rfc/rfc1939.txt`
Post Office Protocol - Version 3

`http://tools.ietf.org/html/rfc1730`
Internet Message Access Protocol – Version 4

`http://javamail.java.net/nonav/docs/JavaMail-1.5.pdf`
JavaMail API Design Specification, Version 1.5

`https://javamail.java.net/nonav/docs/api/`
JavaMail API documentation

`http://www.oracle.com/webfolder/technetwork/tutorials/obe/java/javamail/javamail.html`
Sending an Email using the JavaMail API

EXERCISES

Objective-type Questions

1. What is the default port number of SMTP?
   (a) 25 (c) 22
   (b) 465 (d) 110

2. What is the full form of SMTP?
   (a) Simple Mail Transportation Protocol
   (b) Simple Mail Transfer Policy
   (c) Simple Message Transfer Protocol
   (d) Simple Mail Transfer Protocol

3. What is the full form of POP?
   (a) Post Office Policy
   (b) Post Object Protocol
   (c) Post Office Protocol
   (d) Permanent Object Protocol

4. What is the full form of IMAP?
   (a) Internet Message Access Protocol
   (b) Internet Mail Access Protocol
   (c) Internet Message Access Policy
   (d) Internet Mail Access Policy

5. What is the full form of MIME?
   (a) Multipurpose Internet Mail Extension
   (b) Multipurpose Internet Message Extension
   (c) Multipurpose Internet Mail Expansion
   (d) Multipurpose Internet Message Expansion

6. Which of the following is used to retrieve emails from a mail server?
   (a) SMTP (c) HTTP
   (b) POP3 (d) FTP

7. Which of the following is used to send emails from a mail server?
   (a) SMTP (c) HTTP
   (b) POP3 (d) IMAP

8. When retrieving mail, which of the following is the proper order of working with classes?
   (a) Store, Folder, Message, Transport
   (b) Session, Store, Folder, Message
   (c) Session, Store, Folder, Transport, Message
   (d) Session, Folder, Message, Transport

9. Which of the following characters is used in an email address?
   (a) @ (c) $
   (b) # (d) %

10. Which of the following packages contains classes and interfaces for sending and retrieving mails?
    (a) javax.email (c) java.email
    (b) java.mail (d) javax.mail

11. Which of the following methods is used to get an instance of Session class?
    (a) getInstance()
    (b) createInstance()
    (c) makeInstance()
    (d) inatance()

12. Which of the following methods of Transport class is used to send an email?
    (a) deliver() (c) send()
    (b) doDeliver() (d) doSent()

13. Which of the following port numbers are used for SMTP with SSL?
    (a) 25 (c) 587
    (b) 465 (d) 22

14. Which of the following properties is used to use TLS?
    (a) mail.smtp.enable
    (b) mail.starttls.enable
    (c) mail.smtp.starttls.enable
    (d) mail.smtp.starttls

15. Which of the following classes is used to create a multi-part message?
    (a) Multipart (c) Manypart
    (b) Multiplepart (d) Multi-part

16. Which of the following methods are used to attach a file to an email message?
    (a) addFile() (c) attachFile()
    (b) appendFile() (d) doAttach()

17. What is the correct content type for html content?
    (a) text/plain (c) html/text
    (b) text/html (d) html/plain

18. Which of the following ports is used for POP3 with SSL?
    (a) 993 (c) 143
    (b) 110 (d) 995

19. Which of the following classes represents message storage?
(a) Storage (c) Folder
(b) Store (d) Message

20. Which of the following methods is used to delete email messages permanently?
(a) expunge() (c) doDelete()
(b) delete() (d) doExpunge()

Subjective-type Questions

1. Mention some limitations of POP.
2. Write some of the advantages of IMAP over POP.
3. Explain the format of an email address.
4. Describe briefly the working principle of SMTP.
5. Write the steps to be followed to send an email using JavaMail API.
6. How does a client authenticate it to the SMTP that uses SSL or TLS?
7. What is meant by secured SMTP and how is that implemented?
8. What do you mean by a mail session?
9. Describe the different procedures to create a Session object.
10. What is the purpose of MIME?
11. Describe briefly the format of a MimeMessage.
12. What are the differences between a single-part message and a multipart message?
13. Describe the procedure of attaching a file to an email.
14. How do you send an email having html content?
15. A message may be sent using static send() method as well as sendMessage() method. Which one will you prefer and why?
16. What do you mean by primary, Carbon Copy and Blind Carbon Copy recipients?
17. Explain briefly the function of SSL in the context of SMTP.
18. Describe briefly the Post Office Protocol.
19. Describe briefly the working principle of IMAP.
20. Explain briefly the function of SSL in the context of POP.
21. Describe the procedure to reply to an email.
22. Write the steps to be followed to forward an email to a given email address.
23. Describe the procedure to copy emails from one folder to another.

CHAPTER – 16

APPLETS

KEY OBJECTIVES

After completing this chapter readers will be able to—

- understand the execution philosophy of applets
- understand the life cycle of an applet
- learn how to embed applets in HTML documents
- get an idea about methods available in the `Applet` class
- write basic applets
- understand the limitations of applets

16.1 CLIENT SIDE JAVA

Applets are Java programs (usually small) that generally run within web browsers [Figure 16.1:]. They are usually incorporated in an HTML page. A web browser downloads the class file of the applet together with the other parts of the web page from the web server. If the browser has a suitable Java Virtual Machine (JVM), it executes the applet in the client computer. Since, applets run within web browsers in the client computer, they are said to be client-side Java technology.

The power of Java is not limited to Java applications only. Applets are also written using Java. Since, these applets can be embedded within web pages, they bring all facilities of Java in the html documents with little restrictions. Accordingly, the importance of Java as a client-side technology in the web is unquestionable.

Usually, applets are downloaded from a remote web server [Figure 16.1:]. Consequently, they should be smaller in size. Larger applets have longer download time giving an unpleasant experience to the visitors.

Note that applets work for the local files also. So, we need not always deploy html files containing applets in a web server. The html documents containing applets may be opened directly in a

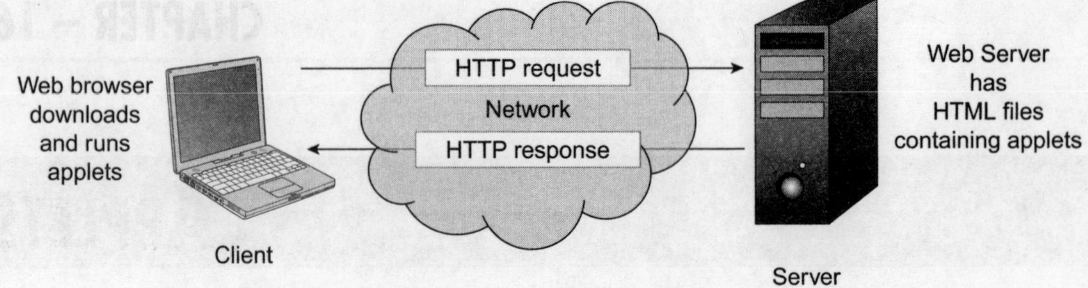

Figure 16.1: Execution of an Applet

Java-enabled browser. They work in the same way as they do upon downloading from a remote server. Java also provides a utility `appletviewer` that may also be used to test applet's functionality as well to run standalone applets.

In this chapter, we shall discuss the structure of applets, their execution philosophy, and other applet-specific issues.

16.2 LIFE CYCLE

Though applets are Java programs, they have certain differences from Java application programs. Applets, unlike Java application programs, do not have any `main()` method. Instead, they have an `init()` method that can be used for a similar purpose. Applets do not have any constructor. The way instances of applets are created and run is completely different from the way objects are created in Java application programs. So, let us understand the philosophy behind an applet.

Development of an applet consists of two basic steps: writing the Java class and incorporating it in an html document. We first concentrate on writing the applet class.

An applet (a Java class) must be created by extending the `java.applet.Applet` class [Figure 16.2:], which provides interfaces between the web browser and the applet. If you want to use swing components, you should create your applets by extending this `javax.swing.JApplet` class instead of `Applet` class. Note that the class, `javax.swing.JApplet` is a subclass of the `Applet` class [Figure 16.2:].

```
java.lang.Object
    java.awt.Component
        java.awt.Container
            java.awt.Panel
                java.applet.Applet
                    javax.swing.JApplet
```

Figure 16.2: The Applet class hierarchy

An applet, from its birth to death, goes through a number of states [Figure 16.3:].

- Instantiated or born
- Running
- Idle or Stopped
- Dead or destroyed

The duration when an applet remains alive is called *life cycle* of the applet. The class `Applet` provides a framework where your applets can run. It has a set of methods to control and supervise the smooth execution of applets [Figure 16.3:]. These methods (also called *life cycle methods*) are called in a specific order during an applet's entire life cycle. An applet usually overrides these methods to do a designated task.

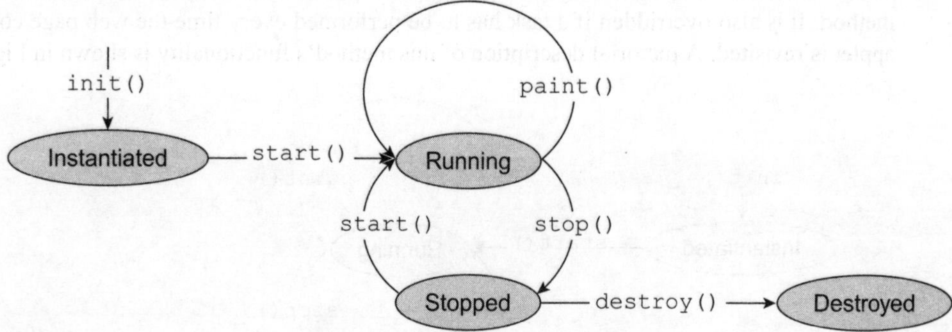

Figure 16.3: Life cycle of an applet

Even though, life cycle methods are called automatically by the browser, we should have sound knowledge about when they are called and what we can do with these methods. The following is a brief description of these life cycle methods.

16.2.1 init()

This is the first method that gets called only once [Figure 16.4:], when an instance of the applet is created and loaded by a web browser. Applets do not have any constructor. Since this method is called before all other methods, it can be used as a constructor. Usually, the piece of code that we write in the constructor goes here. For example, instantiating other objects, initializing variables, setting background and foreground color may be done here. A pictorial description of this method's functionality is shown in Figure 16.4:

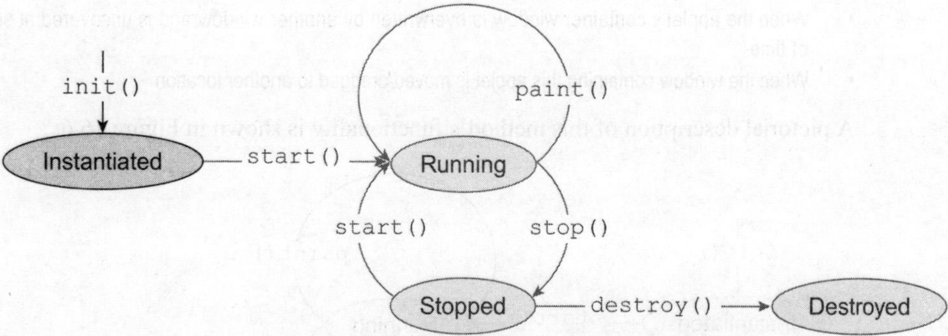

Figure 16.4: Function of init() method

Do not make this method large, resource-consuming, and computationally intensive. Otherwise, your applet will take a long time to load resulting in a bitter experience to the viewers.

16.2.2 start()

This is the second method that gets called in the sequence [Figure 16.5:]. Note that `init()` method merely creates an instance of applet which is not yet active. The `start()` method, as the name implies, *starts* the execution of an applet. It is also called every time an applet is restarted (revisited). Restarting an applet means the applet was running, but stopped for some reason using `stop()` method earlier and needs to be started again. If you want to perform a task after initialization, override this method. It is also overridden if a task has to be performed every time the web page containing the applet is revisited. A pictorial description of this method's functionality is shown in Figure 16.5:

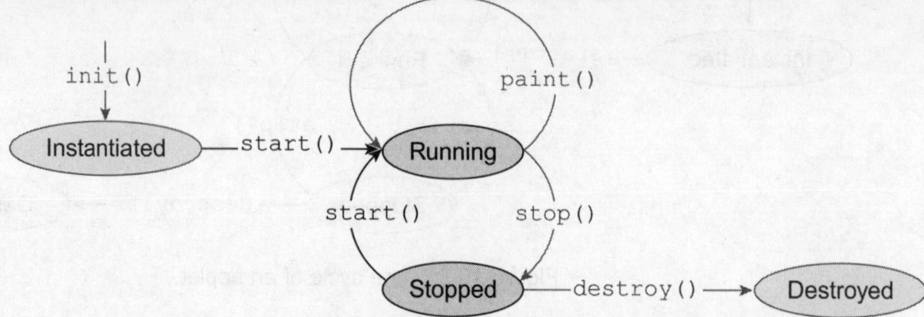

Figure 16.5: Function of start() method

It is also recommended to return from this method quickly. If it is really necessary to do any computationally intensive task in the `start()` method, it is better to create a new thread which will perform the task while `start()` method returns quickly.

16.2.3 paint()

This method is inherited from the `java.awt.Container` class. It is called immediately when the applet starts its execution [Figure 16.6:]. This method is also called when the output of an applet is redrawn. There are several situations when an applet is redrawn.

- When the window containing the applet is minimized and restored
- When the applet's container window is overwritten by another window and is uncovered at some later point of time
- When the window containing this applet is moved/dragged to another location

A pictorial description of this method's functionality is shown in Figure 16.6:

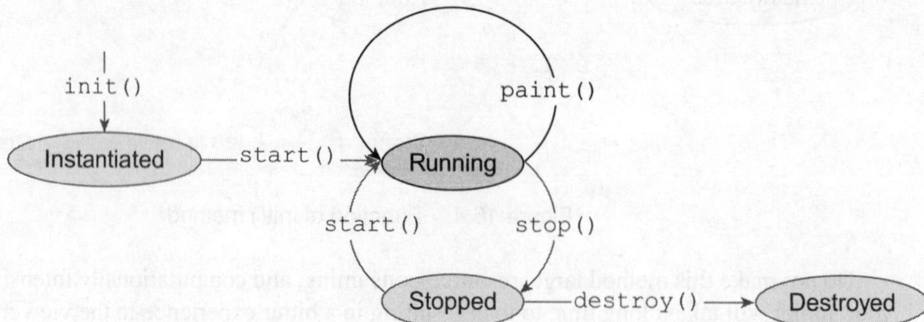

Figure 16.6: Function of paint() method

This method takes a single argument of the type `Graphics`, which encapsulates the graphic window the applet is contained in. It has numerous useful methods that are used to display AWT components such as graphic elements (e.g. lines, ovals, rectangles, etc.), images, strings, etc. on the window. This is the method where we can write our code of what we expect from the applet such as animation etc.

16.2.4 stop()

The method `stop()` makes the applet inactive temporarily. For example, when a visitor switches to another window, leaving the current window containing the applet [Figure 16.7:], this method is called. However, the applet may come back to the running state again using a call of start() method again. This way, an applet can switch between these two states (stopped and running) any number of times in its life cycle.

A pictorial description of this method's functionality is shown in Figure 16.7:

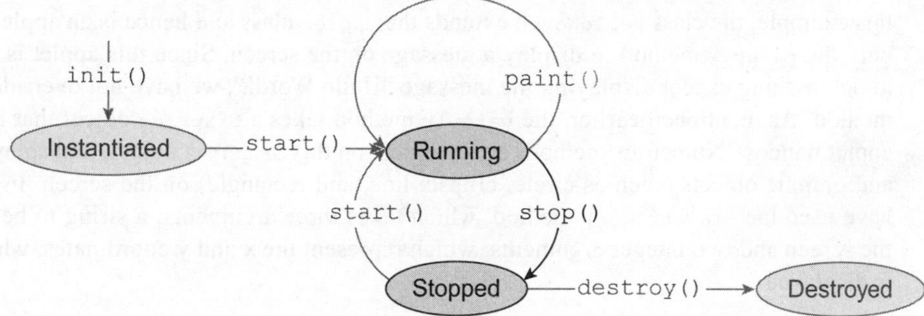

Figure 16.7: Function of stop method

It is the right place to write code to cleanup resources that are not necessary during the inactive period. For example, we should suspend all threads that were started in the `start()` method so that they do not consume system resources. Consequently, if an applet shows some animation, we should suspend it when visitors are not viewing it.

16.2.5 destroy()

This method is called [Figure 16.8:] only once when the browser window containing the applet is closed (exited). This method makes the applet dead (i.e., the applet is not available any more). Typically, you need not override this method. If a browser window containing a running applet is closed, the `stop()` method is called first, which calls `destroy()` method after performing all the necessary tasks to shut down the applet. However, the method is still available to release other resources.

A pictorial description of this method's functionality is shown in Figure 16.8:

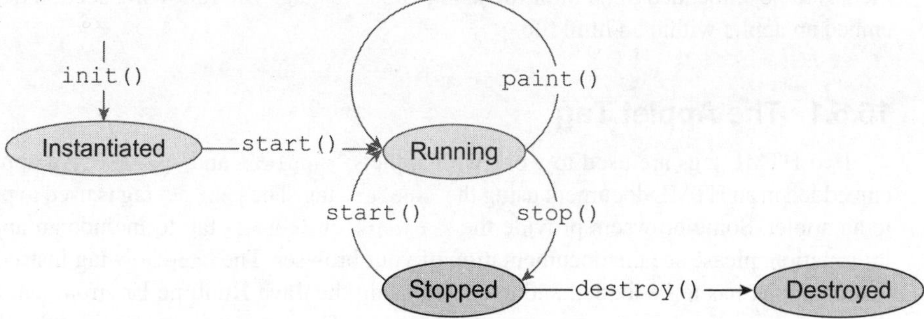

Figure 16.8: Function of destroy method

16.3 WRITING AN APPLET

Let us now write our first applet called `HelloWorld` which will display a simple message "Hello World!" on the screen. The following is the source code of the `HelloWorld` applet stored in the file `HelloWorld.java`.

```
//HelloWorld.java
public class HelloWorld extends java.applet.Applet {
    public void paint(java.awt.Graphics g) {
        g.drawString("Hello World!", 20, 20);
    }
}
```

Your applet must extend either the `java.applet.Applet` or the `javax.swing.JApplet` class. In this example, the class `HelloWorld` extends the `Applet` class and hence is an applet. It overrides only the `paint()` method to display a message on the screen. Since this applet is not supposed to do anything except displaying the message "Hello Word!", we have not overridden any other method. As mentioned earlier, the `paint()` method takes a `Graphics` object that represents the applet window. Numerous methods are available on this `Graphics` object, to display text, images and graphic objects (such as circle, ellipse, line, and rectangle) on the screen. In this case, we have used the `drawString()` method, which takes three arguments: a string to be displayed on the screen and two integer arguments, which represent the x and y coordinates, where the string is displayed .

16.4 GENERATING CLASS FILE

Generating class file for an applet is exactly same as generating class files from application programs. The same `javac` compiler bundled with the **J**ava **D**evelopment **K**it (JDK) is used. To compile our `HelloWorld` applet, go to the directory containing the file `HelloWorld.java` and use the following command:

```
javac HelloWorld.java
```

On successful compilation, it creates a class file named `HelloWorld.class`, which contains the byte code for our `HelloWorld` applet. Make sure that the directory containing the `javac` compiler is included in your `PATH` environment variable.

16.5 RUNNING THE APPLET

Running an applet is different from running a Java application program. To run an applet, its class file has to be embedded in an html file using `<applet>` tag. The following section describes how to embed an applet within an html file.

16.5.1 The Applet Tag

Two HTML tags are used to work with applets: `<applet>` and `<param>`. An applet is typically embedded in an HTML document using the `<applet>` tag. The `<param>` tag is used to pass parameters to an applet. Some browsers provide the `<object>` or `<embed>` tag to include an applet. For more information, please see the documentation of your browser. The `<applet>` tag instructs the browser that an applet has to be loaded and executed using the **J**ava **R**untime **E**nvironment (JRE). It takes three mandatory attributes: `code`, `width`, and `height`. The `code` attribute specifies the class file for this applet to be instantiated. The `width` and `height` attributes indicate the width and height, respectively, of the applet window to be created. For our `HelloWorld` applet, we create a simple HTML file, `HelloWorld.html`, as follows:

```
<!-- HelloWorld.html -->
<html>
   <head><title>Applet Demo</title></head>
   <body>
      <applet code="HelloWorld" height=50 width=150 >
      </applet>
   </body>
</html>
```

Now, open it in a browser. If the browser is Java-enabled, it understands the meaning of the `<applet>` tag. It loads the class file `HelloWorld.class` and executes it and places the result at the place of the `<applet>` tag. Note that the extension `.class` is not used in the `<applet>` tag. Put the `HelloWorld.class` file in the same directory as the `HelloWorld.html` file. The result is shown in Figure 16.9:

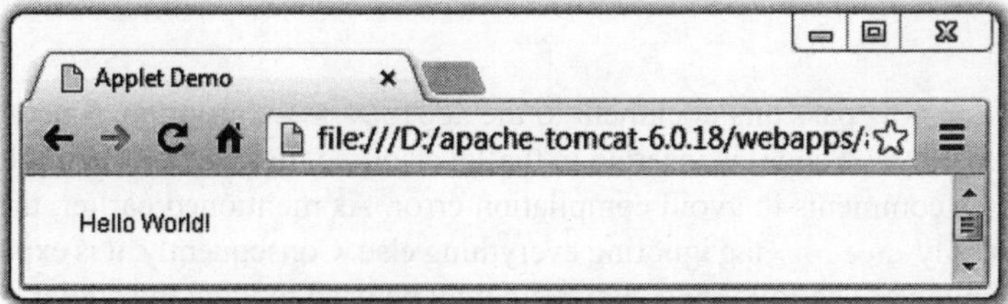

Figure 16.9: Result of HelloWorld applet. The applet was opened in chrome browser directly without deploying it on a web server

If you do not see the applet running, make sure that at least the **J**ava **2** **S**tandard **E**dition (J2SE) platform is installed in your client computer and linked with the browsers. Most often the browsers have their own **J**ava **R**untime **E**nvironment (JRE) to interpret applets. Alternatively, you can use the application `appletviewer`, which comes with JDK, as follows.

```
appletviewer HelloWorld.html
```

The output [Figure 16.10:] now looks exactly the same except that it creates a window with a different appearance.

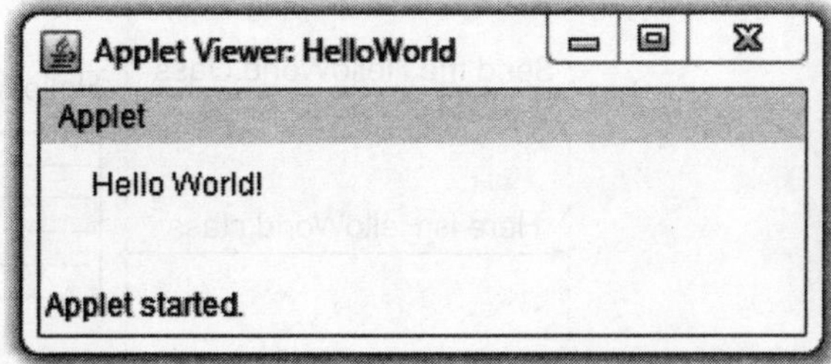

Figure 16.10: Result of HelloWorld applet using appletviewer

The `appletviewer` program comes with JDK and allows us to run applets outside a web browser. It displays applets embedded in the specified document (using `<applet>`, `<object>` or `<embed>` tags)

in its own window. Note that the application `appletviewer` cannot download the class file from the remote web server. It is usually used for testing applets before deploying them to a web server. The `appletviewer` program is usually kept in the `bin` subdirectory of Java's installation directory. To use this program from any directory, make sure that the directory containing the `appletviewer` program is included in your `PATH` environment variable.

Though `appletviewer` functions like a web browser, the way it functions is different. It processes only applet tag (if any) embedded in a document. So, the document containing applets need not always be an html document. Sometimes, for quick development and to avoid creating a separate html file, the applet is embedded in the applet source file (.java file). For example, we can embed our HelloWorld applet in the `HelloWorld.java` file as follows:

```
/*
<applet code="HelloWorld" height=50 width=300>
</applet>
*/
public class HelloWorld extends java.applet.Applet {
    public void paint(java.awt.Graphics g) {
        g.drawString("Hello World!", 20, 20);
    }
}
```

We can now pass this document to the `appletviewer` program. Since, the `<applet>` tag (which is not a valid Java code) is inserted in the Java source file, which is compiled using `javac`, the tag is written as comments to avoid compilation error. As mentioned earlier, the `appletviewer` program looks at only `<applet>` tag ignoring everything else. Consequently, it is expected to display our applet in its windows. The following command may be used to view the applet.

```
appletviewer HelloWorld.java
```

The result is exactly same as shown in Figure 16.10:

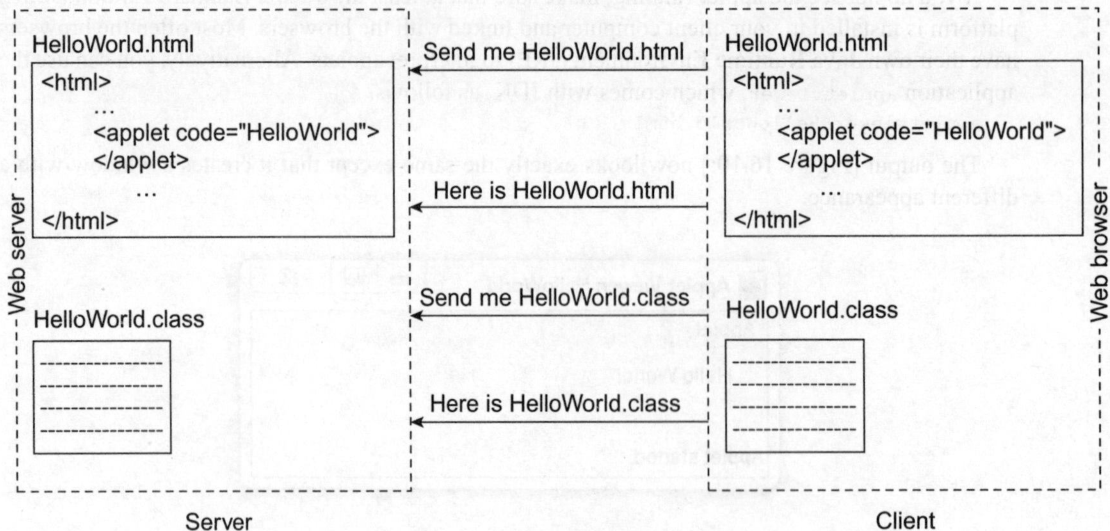

Figure 16.11: The execution of HelloWorld.html deployed in a web server

If you want to deploy the applet on a web server, place these two files in the same folder. The result is shown in Figure 16.12:

Figure 16.12: Result of HelloWorld applet. The applet was deployed on tomcat web server running in a computer having IP address 172.16.5.81

The `<applet>` tag takes several other optional attributes. It takes the following general form:

```
<applet
   code='appletClassFile'
   [codebase='URLOfCodeBase']
   [alt='altervativeText']
   [name='NameOfApplet']
   width='width of Applet window in pixels'
   height='height of Applet window in pixels'
   [align='alignment']
   [vspace='pixels']
   [hspace='pixels']>
```

The optional attributes are shown in square brackets. Let us discuss the functionality of each of these attributes.

`code` — This attribute specifies the name of the class file (without the extension `.class`) that contains the applet's byte code.

`codebase` — It specifies the base URL to be searched for the applet's executable class file. If nothing is mentioned, the directory from where the HTML document containing this applet was downloaded is assumed. In such cases, you must put the applet's class file and the HTML document in the same directory. However, different URLs may also be used with some restrictions.

`alt` — It specifies a message to be displayed if the browser has been able to understand the applet, but has failed to execute it for some reason such as the user turning off the applet.

`name` — This attribute specifies a name for an applet instance. Other applets use this name to find it and communicate with it.

`width` — It is the width of the applet window in pixels.

`height` — It is the height of the applet window in pixels.

`align` — It is used to adjust the position of an applet with respect to the surrounding text and images. It can have the following values:

- `left` — It puts the applet on the left side of the page and causes text to wrap around it.
- `right` — It puts the applet on the right side of the page and causes text to wrap around it.
- `top` — It aligns the top of the applet with the top of the text.
- `bottom` — It aligns the bottom of the applet with the bottom of the text.
- `middle` — This value works differently in different browsers. In some browsers, it aligns the middle of the text with the middle of the applet. In some other browsers, it aligns the bottom of the text with the middle of the applet window.
- `baseline` — It aligns the bottom of the applet with the baseline of the text. The baseline is the bottom line of characters such as a, b, c, d, and e. Some letters such as g, j, and p dangle below this baseline.

`vspace` — It specifies the space to be left above and below the applet window, in pixels.

`hspace` — It specifies the space to be left on the left and right of the applet window, in pixels.

16.6 SECURITY

Java applets were introduced a long time ago to provide animations in web pages. They are not architected for large applications. So, your applets should be small in size and should not perform computationally intensive tasks. Moreover, applets, after being downloaded from the server, are executed on a client machine. Several restrictions are imposed for security reasons. The goal imposing these restrictions is protecting client computer from potentially vulnerable applets. To ensure this goal, applet capabilities are restricted, probably more than necessary. You should be fairly aware of those restrictions if you are going to develop applets. Applets should not be allowed to do the following:

- Reading, writing, creating, destroying, and renaming files on the local file system
- Sending sensitive information to other potentially vulnerable computers over the network
- Creating potentially destructive/malicious processes
- Writing virus programs that destroy your data or perform other malicious events.

Taking these points into consideration, many constraints are imposed, some of which are as follows:

Limitations on Read and Write

Applets cannot access (i.e., read from or write into) the local file system. This restriction is imposed on the applets to prevent searching and sending of valuable information, or even formatting of the hard disk, upon being downloaded onto the client's computer. Applets cannot create any file in the local file system.

Limitations on Connectivity

Applets cannot create any network connection or transfer data to a third party server (i.e., the server which they were downloaded from). If it were allowed, the developer would be able to write malicious applets that send sensitive information from the client's computer to other computers.

Limitations on Native Library Access

Applets are not allowed to access native libraries from other languages such as C++ though Java applications do so. If this was allowed, there would be no way to prevent applets sitting on the client's computer from calling native methods that perform malicious actions.

Limitations on Process Creation

Applets are not allowed to spawn new processes from them. If this was allowed, users could write malicious applets that spawn too many new processes. These processes could make all the resources of the client computer busy. However, applets are allowed to create threads since threads belong to the same address space of the applet and cannot do too many malicious things.

Limitations on Events

Applets cannot detect or handle events that occur outside the applet area.

Limitations on Accessing System Properties

Applets are allowed to read some (not potentially vulnerable) system properties but not all. Table 16.1: shows some of the restricted system properties.

Table 16.1: Restricted System properties

System property	Description
java.class.path	Java classpath
java.home	Directory where the Java was installed
user.dir	Current working directory of the user
user.home	Home directory of the user
user.name	Account name of the user

However, there is a category of applets, called *privileged applets* which may run outside the security boundary and have privilege to access the client computer. Also note that local applets (loaded from local file system) have none of the restrictions that are imposed on the applets loaded over the network. The reason for this is that local applets are considered to be more reliable than unknown applets from the network.

16.7 UTILITY METHODS

The `Applet` class provides a set of useful methods (in addition to the five methods `init()`, `start()`, `paint()`, `stop()`, and `destroy()`) that can be used for different purposes. A brief description of commonly used methods is given here:

`isActive()` — Returns `true` if the applet is active, `false` otherwise. An applet becomes active just before the `start()` method is called and becomes inactive just before the `stop()` method is called.

`resize(int width, int height)` — Sets the size of the applet's window with the specified width and height

`resize(Dimension new)` — Sets the size of the applet with the specified dimension

`showStatus(String message)` — Displays the specified message in the status bar of the browser's window

`getDocumentBase()` — Returns the URL of the document containing this applet

`getCodeBase()` — Returns the URL of the base directory from which this applet was loaded

`getParameter(String param)` — Returns the value of the specified parameter passed to this applet

`getParameterInfo()` — Returns a two-dimensional array of strings that contains information about the parameters that this applet understands.

`getAppletContext()` — Returns a `java.applet.AppletContext` object that represents applet's context, which allows us to query, and affects applet's environment.

`getAppletInfo()` — Returns information about the applet as a string

`getImage(URL url)` — Returns an `Image` object from the specified URL of the image

`getImage(URL base, String name)` — Returns an `Image` object from the specified base URL and relative name of the image

`newAudioClip(URL)` — Creates an `AudioClip` object specified by the URL

`getAudioClip(URL)` — Returns an `AudioClip` object specified by the absolute URL argument

`getAudioClip(URL, String)` — Returns an `AudioClip` object specified by the absolute base URL and relative name arguments

`play(URL)` — Plays an audio clip specified by the absolute URL

`play(URL, String)` — Plays an audio clip specified by the absolute base URL and a relative name

16.8 USING STATUS BAR

You can display a short message on the status bar of the window using the `showStatus()` method. Consider the following applet:

```
//Status.java
public class Status extends java.applet.Applet {
    public void paint(java.awt.Graphics g) {
        setBackground(java.awt.Color.gray);
        g.drawString("This is in the applet window", 20, 30);
        showStatus("This is shown in the status bar");
    }
}
```

Now, create an HTML document containing an `<applet>` tag as follows:

```
<applet code=”Status” width=”300” height=”50”>
</applet>
```

Alternatively, you can embed in the file `Status.java` as explained previously. Now run `appletviewer` specifying the file name containing the applet as an argument. A sample result is shown in Figure 16.13:

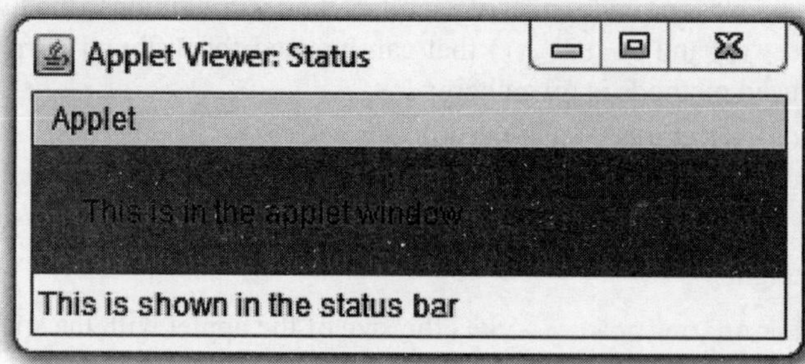

Figure 16.13: Displaying a message on the status bar

16.9 APPLETCONTEXT INTERFACE

The `Applet` API provides an interface, `java.applet.AppletContext`, which can be used to interact with the environment where the applet runs. For example, we can manipulate the content of a web page, load a URL, interact with the JavaScript code embedded in the web page, communicate with other applets running in the same web page, and so on.

An `AppletContext` object is obtained using `getAppletContext()` on the `Applet` object. The prototype declaration of this method is as follows:

```
public java.applet.AppletContext getAppletContext();
```

The following code shows how to obtain an `AppletContext` object.

```
AppletContext ac = getAppletContext();
```

The `AppletContext` interface provides many useful methods, some of which are mentioned as follows:

`AudioClip getAudioC.5lip(URL url);`

Returns an `AudioClip` object from the specified URL

`Image getImage(URL url);`

Returns an `Image` object, which can be painted on the screen, from the specified URL

`Applet getApplet(String appletName)`

Finds and returns an `Applet` object that exist in the same context, with the specified name

`Enumeration getApplets();`

Finds and returns all applets that exist within the same context

`void showDocument(URL url)`

Loads the specified URL in the current window

`void showDocument(URL url, String targetWindow)`

Loads the specified URL in the specified window

`void showStatus(String message)`

Displays a short message on the status bar

`void setStream(String key, InputStream stream)`

Binds the specified stream with the specified key in this applet context

`InputStream getStream(String key);`

Returns the stream associated with the specified key within this applet context

`Iterator getStreamKeys();`

Returns a list of keys of the streams in this applet context

16.10 DOCUMENT BASE AND CODE BASE

The document base is the URL of the HTML file containing this applet. The method `getDocumentBase()` returns this URL.

The code base, on the other hand, is the name of the base directory from where the applet's class file was loaded. The values of the document base and code base are the same, unless the `codebase` attribute of the `<applet>` tag is used to specify a different URL.

Typically, a code base (if specified) refers to a subdirectory of the document base directory where applet's class files may be found. This is because browsers restrict applets from accessing arbitrary directories/URLs. If access permissions are given to the document base, subdirectories have similar permissions. So, specifying a subdirectory as the code base is always safe. Consider the following applet (`Bases.java`), which displays the code base and document base.

```
//Bases.java
public class Bases extends java.applet.Applet {
   public void paint(java.awt.Graphics g) {
      g.drawString("Document base : " + getDocumentBase(), 20, 10);
      g.drawString("Code base : " + getCodeBase(), 20, 30);
   }
}
```

Now, compile this applet and create an HTML page containing the following:

```
<applet code="Bases" codebase="./applets" width="400" height="40">
</applet>
```

The result is shown in Figure 16.14:

Figure 16.14: Document base and code base

16.11 PASSING PARAMETER

Like command line arguments, parameters can be passed to applets. Applets can access those parameters and customize their tasks. This helps applets to function differently in different situations without recompiling the source code.

Parameters are passed to the applet using the `<param>` child tag of the `<applet>` tag. Each `<param>` tag, as its name implies, passes one parameter to the surrounding applet. It has two attributes, `name` and `value`. They indicate the name and value of the parameter to be passed respectively. Consider the following parameter specification:

```
<applet code="ParamDemo" width="200" height="60">
    <param name="fontColor" value="FF0000">
    <param name="bgColor" value="EEEEEE">
</applet>
```

It means that a `ParamDemo` applet is to be instantiated with two parameters `fontColor` and `bgColor`, whose values are `FF0000` and `EEEEEE`, respectively.

16.11.1 Retrieving Parameter

Parameters are retrieved from an applet using the `getParameter()` method. This methods takes the name of the parameter as an argument and returns the value of the parameter as a `String`. The prototype declaration of this method is as follows:

```
public java.lang.String getParameter(java.lang.String);
```

The following code shows how to retrieve the parameters using the `getParameter()` method. The retrieved values are then used to set the background and foreground color of the applet.

```
//ParamDemo.java
import java.awt.*;
import java.applet.*;
public class ParamDemo extends Applet {
    String fontColor, bgColor;
    public void init() {
        fontColor = getParameter("fontColor");
        bgColor = getParameter("bgColor");
    }
    public void paint(Graphics g) {
        setBackground(color(bgColor));
        g.setColor(color(fontColor));
        g.drawString("Font Color :" + fontColor, 20, 20);
        g.drawString("Background color:" + bgColor, 20, 40);
    }
    public Color color(String color) {
        int c = Integer.parseInt(color, 16);
        int red = c / (256 * 256);
        int green = (c / 256) % 256;
        int blue = c % 256;
        return new Color(red, green, blue);
    }
}
```

Note that the method `getParameter()` always returns the value of the specified parameter as a string. It is typically converted to the desired type. For example, in the `ParamDemo` applet, the value of the `fontColor` and `bgColor` parameters is a hexadecimal RGB value. To get the actual color from it, we have first converted it into an integer value using the `Integer.parseInt()` method. Then, we have extracted red, green, and blue components and finally created a color with these components.

The following code results in the output as shown in Figure 16.15:

```
<applet code="ParamDemo" width="200" height="60">
   <param name="fontColor" value="FFFFFF">
   <param name="bgColor" value="AAAAAA">
</applet>
```

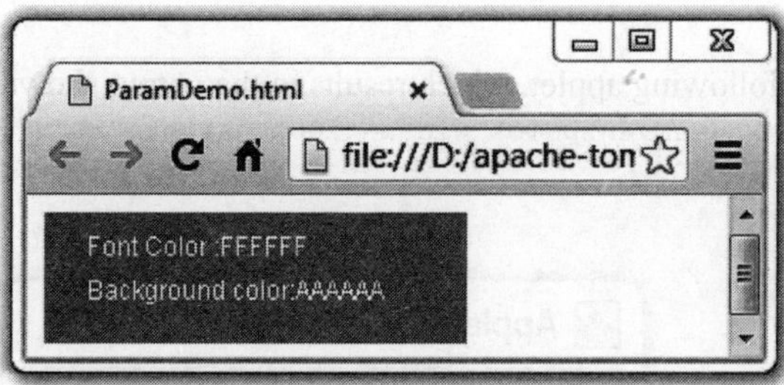

Figure 16.15: Parameter passing in applets

16.12 EVENT HANDLING

The event handling mechanism is the same as the Java Application program. The following applet demonstrates this:

```
//MouseEventDemo.java
import java.awt.*;
import java.applet.*;
import java.awt.event.*;
public class MouseEventDemo extends Applet implements MouseListener {
   String msg = "";
   int x = 0, y = 0;
   public void init() {
      addMouseListener(this);
   }
   public void paint(Graphics g) {
      g.drawString(msg, x, y);
   }
   public void mouseClicked(MouseEvent me) {
      x = me.getX();
      y = me.getY();
      msg = "clicked";
      repaint();
   }
   public void mouseEntered(MouseEvent me) {
      x = y = 10;
      msg = "entered";
      repaint();
   }
   public void mouseExited(MouseEvent me) {
      x = y = 10;
      msg = "exited";
      repaint();
   }
   public void mousePressed(MouseEvent me)
      x = me.getX();
      y = me.getY();
      msg = "pressed";
      repaint();
   }
```

```
    public void mouseReleased(MouseEvent me) {
        x = me.getX();
        y = me.getY();
        msg = "released";
        repaint();
    }
}
```

Now create the following applet, which results in the output shown in Figure 16.16:

```
<applet code="MouseEventDemo" width="200" height="50">
</applet>
```

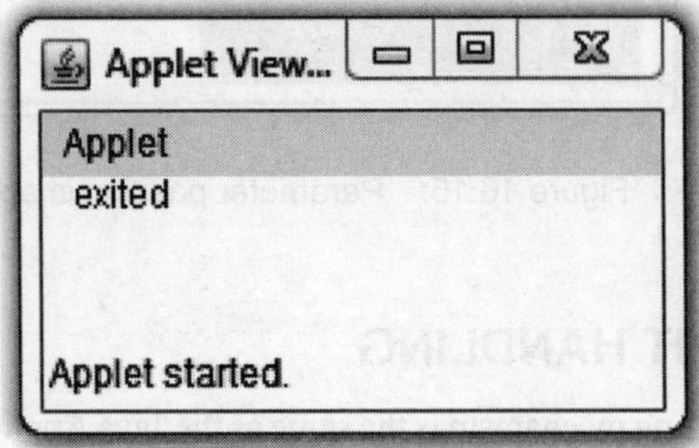

Figure 16.16: Event handling in applets

16.13 COMMUNICATION BETWEEN TWO APPLETS

Sometimes it is necessary for an applet to find other applets and communicate with them to do a complicated task. This happens when several distinct applets are not enough to accomplish a task. In this section, we shall only explain how communication among applets running within the same browser takes place. There is hardly any occasion where applets running in separate browsers want to communicate. If it is really necessary, they can use various technologies, such as sockets, RMI etc., which have already been discussed in the previous chapter.

The important part of applet communications is finding other applets. For this purpose the `AppletContext` interface provides two methods `getApplet()` and `getApplets()`.

16.13.1 Using getApplet() Method

This method is used to find an applet by its name. It has the following form:

```
Applet getApplet(String appletName);
```

The `getApplet()` method returns an `Applet` object with the specified name. The name of an applet is one that is specified by the `name` attribute of the `<applet>` tag.

For example, the name of the following applet is `server`.

```
<applet code="Server" width="200" height="80" name="server">
</applet>
```

Since the `getApplet()` method returns a generic `Applet` object, it is typically converted to your custom applet object. Suppose, the name of your applet class is `Server` and an instance is created with the name "server" (i.e., the value of `name` attribute of `<applet>` tag is "server" as shown above). A reference to this applet can be obtained from another applet `Client` as follows:

```
AppletContext ac = getAppletContext();
Server s = (Server) ac.getApplet("server");
```

Once a reference to an applet is obtained, desired methods can be invoked on it, as and when required.

16.13.2 Using getApplets() Method

This method is useful when one applet want to find another applet which has no name (i.e., no `name` attribute is specified in `<applet>` tag). The `getApplets()` method on the `AppletContext` interface takes the following form:

```
Enumeration getApplets();
```

Essentially, it returns a list of all (including itself) applets available in the same context as this applet. In the following code, `e` is a list of applets.

```
AppletContext ac = getAppletContext();
Enumeration e = ac.getApplets();
```

The finder applet can now iterate through the list to get individual applets. Once the finder, gets references to those applets, it can also invoke methods on them. The following example shows how to find other applets.

```
//GetAppletDemo.java
import java.awt.*;
import java.applet.*;
public class GetAppletsDemo extends Applet {
  String id;
  public void init() {
    id = getParameter("id");
  }
  public void paint(Graphics g) {
    g.drawString("This is applet"+id, 20, 20);
      if(id.equals("1")) {
        setBackground(new Color(238,238,238));
        AppletContext ac = getAppletContext();
        java.util.Enumeration e = ac.getApplets();
        g.drawString("Found following applets:", 20, 40);
        int count=1;
        while(e.hasMoreElements()) {
          GetAppletsDemo a = (GetAppletsDemo)e.nextElement();
            String result = "applet's class name = "+a.getClass().getName()+",
id = "+a.id;
            g.drawString(result, 20, 40+count*20);
            count++;
        }
     g.drawString("Found "+count+"applets", 20, 40+count*40);
      }
      else {
        setBackground(new Color(170,170,170));
      }
   }
}
```

The following applet generates the output shown in Figure 16.17:

```
<applet code="GetAppletsDemo" width="500" height="40">
</applet>
```

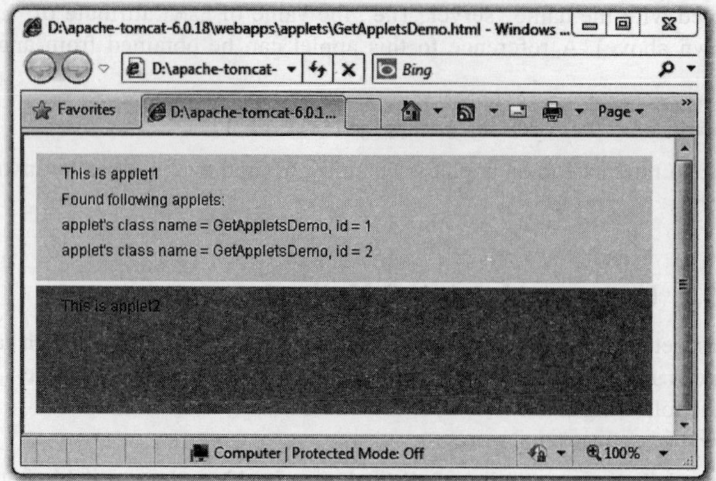

Figure 16.17: Finding all applets

16.13.3 A Sample Application

Now, let us develop a simple but elegant application that demonstrates how two applets communicate with each other. In this application, the applet `Client` sends an integer to another applet `Server`. The `Server` applet simply returns the square of the number. Finally, `Client` displays the result. The source code for the `Server` applet (`Server.java`) is as follows.

```
//Server.java
public class Server extends Applet {
   int val = 1, result = 0;
   public void paint(java.awt.Graphics g) {
      setBackground(java.awt.Color.LIGHT_GRAY);
      g.drawString("Server", 20, 20);
      g.drawString("received :" + String.valueOf(val), 20, 40);
      g.drawString("Sent :" + String.valueOf(result), 20, 60);
   }
   public int sqr(int n) {
      val = n;
      result = n * n;
      repaint();
      return result;
   }
}
```

The `Server` applet has a public method `sqr()`, which takes an integer and returns its square. The `Client` applet will use this method to send an integer and get the result. The source code for the `Client` applet (`Client.java`) is as follows:

```
//Client.java
import java.awt.*;
import java.applet.*;
public class Client extends Applet {
  int n = 2, result;
  Server s;
  public void init() {
    String param = getParameter("calculator");
    AppletContext ac = getAppletContext();
    Server s = (Server)ac.getApplet(param);
    result = s.sqr(n);
  }
```

```
    public void paint(Graphics g) {
        setBackground(Color.LIGHT_GRAY);
        g.drawString("Client", 20,20);
        g.drawString("Sent: \n"+String.valueOf(n), 20,40);
        g.drawString("Recived: "+String.valueOf(result), 20,60);
    }
}
```

Compile these two files and create an HTML file containing the applet declaration as follows:

```
<applet code="Server" width="200" height="80" name="server">
</applet>

<applet code="Client" width="200" height="80" name="client">
<param name="calculator" value="server">
</applet>
```

Create a `Server` applet first, with the name "server". Now, create a `Client` applet and pass the parameter `calculator` with the value "server". The `Client` applet first gets the value of the parameter. It then finds the applet having this name. If you open this HTML document in a browser, it appears as shown in Figure 16.18:

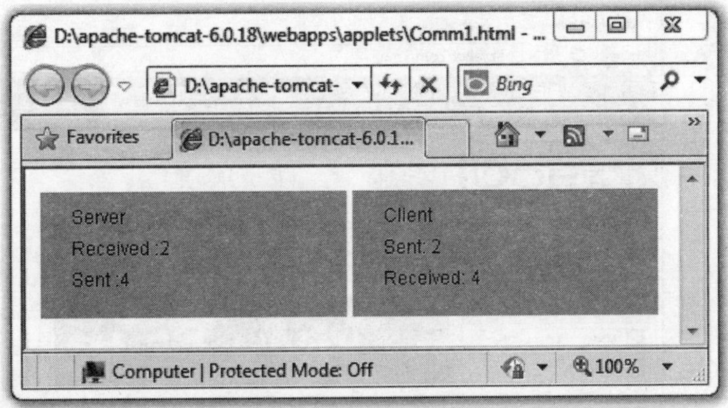

Figure 16.18: Communication between two applets

16.14 LOADING WEB PAGES

You can load a web page in the browser's window using the `showDocument()` method on the `AppletContext` object. It takes the following forms:

```
void showDocument(URL url)
void showDocument(URL url, String targetWindow)
```

The first form takes a URL argument and loads it in the current window. The second form allows us to load the URL in the specified window. The second argument can have the following values:

- `_blank` — Loads the URL in a new unnamed window
- `targetWindow` — Loads the URL in the window having the name `targetWindow`
- `_self` — Loads the URL in the window containing this applet
- `_parent` — Loads the URL of the parent window containing this applet
- `_top` — Loads the URL in the top-level window.

The following applet loads the URL `http://www.yahoo.com` in the applet's window.

```
/LoadDemo.java
import java.awt.*;
import java.applet.*;
import java.net.*;
public class LoadDemo extends Applet {
  AppletContext ac; URL url;
  public void start() {
    ac = getAppletContext();
    url = getCodeBase();
  }
  public void paint(Graphics g) {
    try {
      ac.showDocument(new URL("http://www.yahoo.com"));
    }catch(Exception e) {showStatus("URL not found");}
  }
}
```

The following applet declaration results in the output as shown in Figure 16.19:

```
<applet code="LoadDemo" width="200" height="80">
</applet>
```

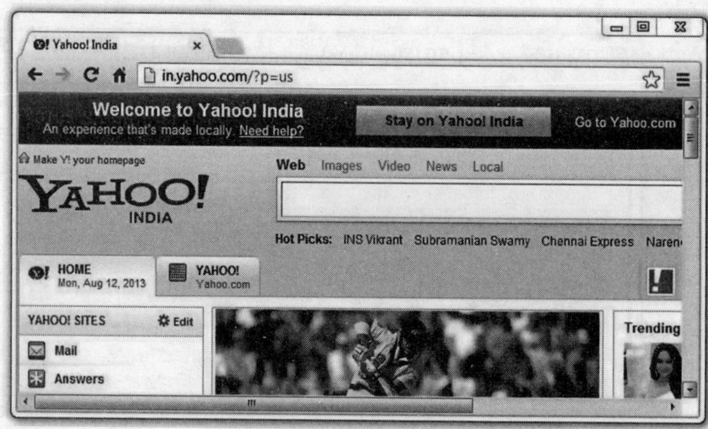

Figure 16.19: Loading a URL using applet

16.15 INTERACTING WITH JAVASCRIPT CODE

Java applets can invoke JavaScript functions that are present in the same html document as the applet. The following applet calls the JavaScrip `doAlert()` function.

```
import java.applet.*;
import java.net.*;

public class AppletToJavaScript extends Applet{
  public void init(){
    String msg = "Hello from Java (using javascript alert)";
    try {
      getAppletContext().showDocument
        (new URL("javascript:doAlert(\"" + msg +"\")"));
      }
    catch (MalformedURLException me) { }
  }
}
```

Now consider the following html file containing a JavaScript `doAlert()` function and an applet.

```
<HTML><HEAD></HEAD><BODY>
<SCRIPT>
function doAlert(s) {
   alert(s);
   }

</SCRIPT>
<APPLET CODE="AppletToJavaScript"
        NAME="myApplet"  MAYSCRIPT
        HEIGHT=10 WIDTH=10>
</APPLET>
</BODY>
</HTML>
```

A sample output is shown in Figure 16.20:

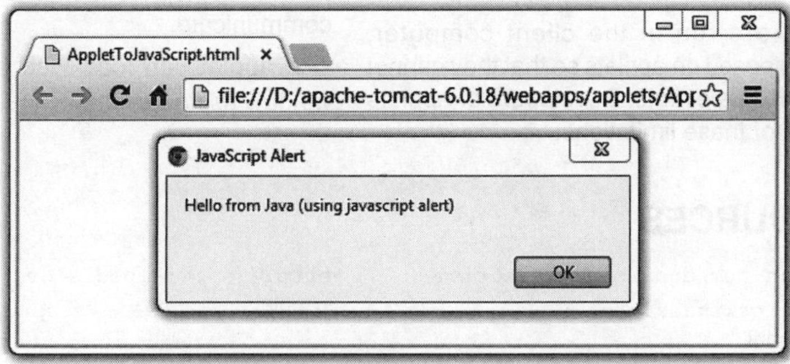

Figure 16.20: Calling a JavaScript function from an applet

KEYWORDS

Active Applets—Applets that are being viewed by the user

Applet class—Base class of all applets

Applet Communication—The process by which applets find other applets and exchange information.

AppletContext—It is the interface that provides methods to query and affect the environment where the applet is running.

Applet tag—An HTML tag used to embed applets in HTML documents

Appletviewer—An application provided by the JDK to view your applets without any browser

Applet—Tiny Java programs that run within the context of a web browser

Codebase—Code base is the name of the base directory from where the applet's class file was loaded.

Document base—The document base is URL of the HTML file that contains an applet

Graphics—An object that represents the canvas of the applet

Inactive Applets—Applets that are stopped possibly because the user selected another window

JApplet—Swing extension of the `Applet` class

Life Cycle— The stages through which an applet passes, from its creation to its destruction.

Param tag—Used to pass parameters to the applets

SUMMARY

We started this chapter with the execution philosophy of applets. Applets are tiny Java programs that run within the context of web browsers. They are embedded in HTML documents. Java-enabled web browsers download the class files for applets and execute them.

Every applet must extend the `java.applet.Applet` class, which provides interfaces to work with the applets. The `Applet` class has five life cycle methods: `init()`, `start()`, `paint()`, `stop()`, and `destroy()`. These methods are executed in that order, from the creation of an applet to its destruction. Our applet class should override these methods as and when necessary. We can also add other methods in the applet class.

Applets are compiled using the same procedure as Java application programs are compiled. HTML provides two tags to work with the applets: `<applet>` and `<param>`. The applets are embedded in an HTML document using the `<applet>` tag. It has several attributes that are used to customize applets.

Since applets are run in the client computer, restrictions are imposed on applets so that they cannot perform any malicious events. Developers of applets should be aware of these limitations.

The `<param>` tag, which is a child tag of the `<applet>` tag, is used to pass parameters to the applets. Applets can retrieve parameters using the `getParameter()` method. We described how to pass and retrieve parameters with extensive examples.

The `Applet` class also provides several other methods that are used to query and affect the properties of applets. Then we described the event handling mechanism in applets. Event handling in applets is exactly the same as in other Java AWT application programs.

Applets can find other applets and communicate with them. We developed a sample application consisting of two applets to demonstrate how applets can communicate.

An applet can load web pages in the browser's window using the `showDocument()` method.

WEB RESOURCES

`http://java.sun.com/docs/books/tutorial/deployment/applet/index.html`
Java Applets Tutorial

`http://java.sun.com/applets/`
Applets: Code samples and Apps.

`http://en.wikipedia.org/wiki/Applet`
Applets

EXERCISES

Objective-type Questions

1. What is an Applet?
   (a) The name of a database
   (b) A kind of fruit
   (c) A Java program that is run through a web browser
   (d) An interactive website

2. What is the difference between a Java Applet and a Java application program?
   (a) All the methods in an applet class are private.
   (b) Applets can create GUI, applications cannot.
   (c) Applets are run in web browsers but applications are not.
   (d) An application is a small program, whereas an applet is large.

3. What is the full form of AWT?
   (a) Adjust Window Table
   (b) Abstract Window Toolkit
   (c) Auto Window Transfer
   (d) Advanced Window Toolkit

4. Which one of the following is a valid declaration of an applet?
   (a) class AnApplet implements Applet {
   (b) public class AnApplet extends applet implements Runnable {
   (c) abstract class AnApplet extends java.applet.Applet {
   (d) public class AnApplet extends java.applet.Applet {

5. Why does an applet have no main() method?
   (a) The browser acts as the main. The applet provides methods for the browser.
   (b) The paint() method is like the main method for an applet.
   (c) Programs that do graphics do not need a main.
   (d) Only simple programs need a main.

6. Which of the following classes must your applet extend?
   (a) Component (c) Applet
   (b) Graphics (d) AWT

7. What is the function of the Graphics object?
   (a) It represents the canvas of the applet and provides drawing methods.
   (b) It represents the status bar.
   (c) It represents the entire screen of the computer monitor.
   (d) It represents the applet background.

8. Which of the following codes is used to display the string "Hello World!" at X=20 Y=50 location? Assume that g holds a Graphics object reference.
   (a) g.println("Hello World!");
   (b) drawString("Hello World!", 20, 50);
   (c) g.drawString(20, 50, "Hello World!");
   (d) g.drawString("Hello World!", 20, 50);

9. Which of the following sets the background color of the applet to white?
   (a) setBackColor(gray);
   (b) setBackGround(gray);
   (c) setBackGround(Color.gray);
   (d) setBackColor(Color.gray);

10. Which of the following packages must be imported to get the class Applet?
    (a) java.applet.Applet
    (b) java.util.*
    (c) java.awt.*
    (d) javax.swing.*

11. Which of the following must be imported to get the graphics components?
    (a) java.util.* (c) java.Graphics
    (b) java.awt.* (d) java.lang.*

12. Which of the following tags is used to pass parameters to applets?
    (a) <parameter> (c) <argc>
    (b) <para> (d) <param>

13. Which of the following tags is used to insert an applet into an HTML document?
    (a) <applet> (c) <insertapplet>
    (b) <body> (d) <embedapplet>

14. Which of the following methods is called by the browser when it wishes to display on the monitor?
    (a) draw() (c) display()
    (b) show() (d) paint()

15. Can the source code for your applet be compiled by the usual javac compiler?
    (a) No, because applets have no main() method.
    (b) Yes, if you are going to run it from the DOS prompt.
    (c) Yes, an applet is just another class as far as the compiler is concerned.
    (d) No, the web browser compiles the code.

16. Which of the following methods is used to draw a rectangle filled in with the current color?
    (a) fillRect() (c) fillOval()
    (b) drawRect() (d) drawOval()

17. If you are using the Graphics object g and wish to change the pen color to blue, what should you do?
    (a) g.setPen(Color.blue)
    (b) setBackground(Color.blue)
    (c) g.setColor(Color.blue)
    (d) g.setBlue( )

18. Which of the following statements is true?
    (a) Applets have main() function.
    (b) Applets cannot use System.out.print() method.
    (c) Applets are JavaScript programs.
    (d) Applets run within a web browser.

19. Which of the following sequences is the correct order of method call?
    (a) start(), init(), paint(), stop(), destroy()
    (b) init(), paint(), start(), stop(), destroy()
    (c) init(), start(), paint(), stop(), destroy()
    (d) start(), init(), paint(), destroy(), stop()

20. Which of the following is not a method of the Applet class?
    (a) move() (c) play()
    (b) resize() (d) isActive()

Subjective-type Questions

1. What are applets?
2. Explain why applets do not have constructors.
3. Explain briefly the applet's life cycle methods.
4. What are the differences between Java applets and Java applications?
5. Write the steps involved in applet development.

6. Write the sequence of applet's life cycle methods in which they are called.
7. Demonstrate with example, how parameters are passed to applets.
8. Describe how parameters are retrieved from an applet.
9. Demonstrate with examples, how applets can communicate with each other.
10. Can applets on different pages communicate with each other?
11. How do you determine the width and height of an applet?
12. Show how URLs are loaded dynamically using applets.
13. Which classes and interfaces does the Applet class contain?
14. Which tags are used in HTML to display an applet?
15. Which methods are available to retrieve information about an applet?
16. Which method is used to display a string on the applet's window? Which function is this method included in?

CHAPTER – 17

JAVA XML-RPC

KEY OBJECTIVES

After completing this chapter readers will be able to—

- understand the operational principle of XML-RPC
- get an idea about Remote Procedure Call
- learn how to use Apache XML-RPC Java library
- write simple XML-RPC clients and servers
- configure Apache XML-RPC servlet to handle XML-RPC requests
- get an idea about introspection mechanism

17.1 INTRODUCTION

XML-RPC, as its name suggests, is an XML-based **R**emote **P**rocedure **C**all (RPC) protocol. In this protocol, e**X**tensible **M**arkup **L**anguage (XML) is used to describe a Remote Procedure Call. Describing an RPC means encoding method invocation information (such as method name, parameter list etc.) and reply from the method. These encoded XML messages are then exchanged between applications using the **H**yper**T**ext **T**ransfer **P**rotocol (HTTP).

It is a very simple and portable way to call remote procedures over HTTP [Figure 17.1:]. The XML-RPC specification promotes a platform-independent framework for describing remote procedure call syntax. So, it can be used with almost all programming languages such as Java, C, C++, Python, PHP, Perl etc. In this chapter, we shall focus on how to use this technology using Java.

XML-RPC was first proposed by Dave Winer in 1998. The primary goal of this technology was to enable heterogeneous application components, running on heterogeneous platforms and operating systems, to interoperate over network connections. The secondary goal was to use a standard protocol to transport RPC messages. Consequently, XML was used to describe messages and the well-known HTTP was used as its transport protocol. The use of HTTP as a transport protocol makes it relatively easier to integrate XML-RPC with the existing web-enabled applications spreading across the computing landscape. Dave Winer described this technology as "RPC over HTTP via XML".

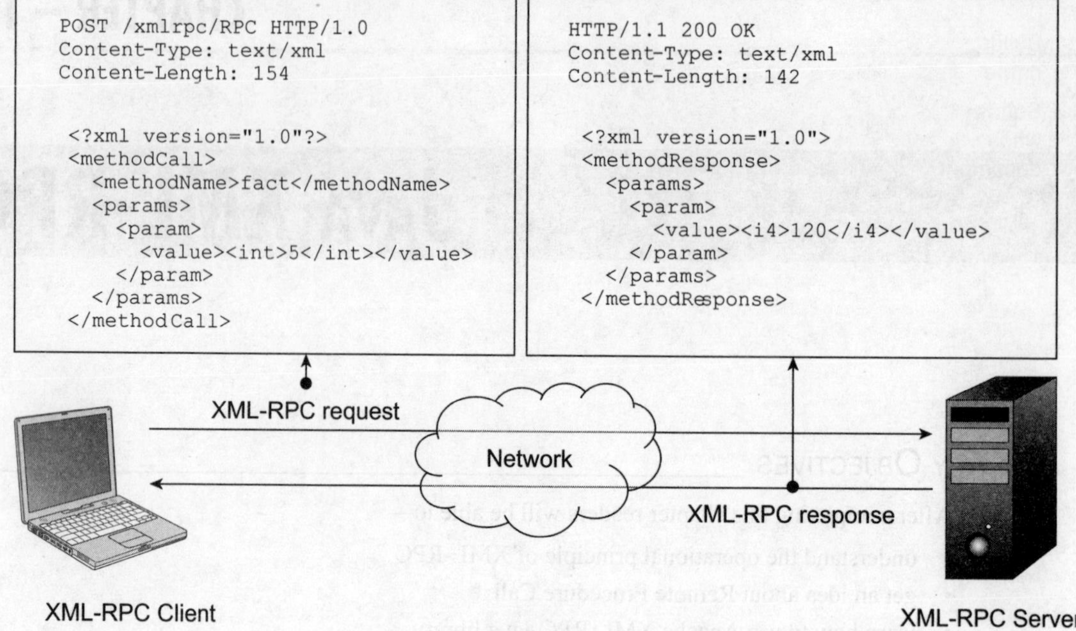

Figure 17.1: XML-RPC Architecture

The extended version has evolved into what is currently known as SOAP (Simple **O**bject Access Protocol).

Like other RPC mechanisms, this protocol also deals with two primary components: a server program and a client program. The server program is one which implements one or more methods, invokes them on request and sends result (if any) back. The client program, on the other hand, makes a request to the server to invoke a method with necessary parameters (if any).

These requests and responses are encoded as a standard XML format known as XML messages [See Figure 17.1:].

17.2 XML-RPC OPERATIONAL PRINCIPLE

The method call and response in XML-RPC happens broadly in the following way [Figure 17.2:]:

- A client encodes the name of a function to be called and its arguments in an XML message as described by XML-RPC specification.
- The client then creates an HTTP post request message with the XML message as body and sends it to the server over the network using HTTP.
- Upon receiving this request message, the server forwards it to an XML-RPC processor.
- The XML-RPC processor parses the message to obtain the name of the function to be called and its argument list.
- The server then calls the function with the specified arguments.
- The return value of the function (if any) is again encoded in an XML message as described by XML-RPC specification.
- The server then creates an HTTP response message with this and the XML message as body and sends it back to the client using HTTP.
- Finally, the client, upon receiving the response message, extracts the information and performs further processing.

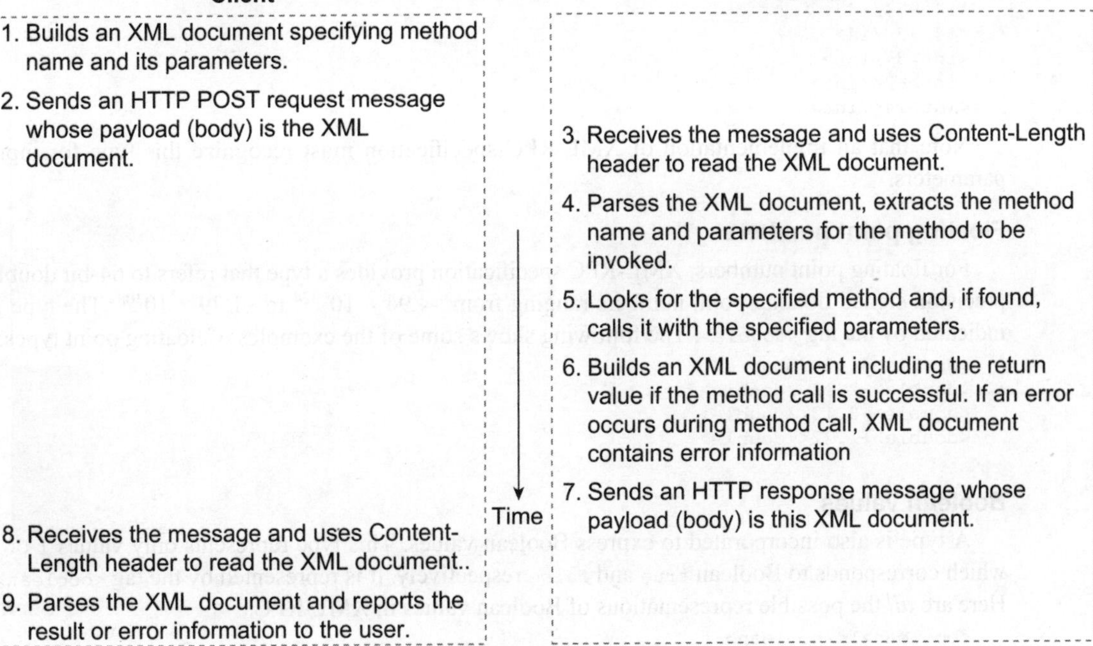

Client
Server
1. Builds an XML document specifying method name and its parameters.
2. Sends an HTTP POST request message whose payload (body) is the XML document.
3. Receives the message and uses Content-Length header to read the XML document.
4. Parses the XML document, extracts the method name and parameters for the method to be invoked.
5. Looks for the specified method and, if found, calls it with the specified parameters.
6. Builds an XML document including the return value if the method call is successful. If an error occurs during method call, XML document contains error information
7. Sends an HTTP response message whose payload (body) is this XML document.
Time
8. Receives the message and uses Content-Length header to read the XML document..
9. Parses the XML document and reports the result or error information to the user.

Figure 17.2: XML-RPC timing diagram

Before developing XML-RPC-based applications, let us now have an overview of supported data types.

17.3 DATA TYPES

A method is usually invoked with some data in the form of parameters. The response from that method may also contain data as a return value. However, unlike method call, which may contain multiple parameters, the response contains at most one return value. A data item in an XML-RPC request or response is embedded within a `<value>...</value>` element. To represent these values, XML-RPC specification defines six *basic data types* and two *compound data types*. Only values of these types may be passed to or returned from the remote method. Note that all the data is written in XML as string values. The specific data type tags are used to indicate how a server/client should interpret the data.

17.3.1 Basic Data Types

XML-RPC specification defines six types for integer, floating point number, Boolean, string, date-time and binary data. These types (except string) are always embedded in `<value>` elements. Only strings may be embedded in a `<value>` element directly omitting the `<string>` element.

Integer

For integers, XML-RPC specification has defined only one type. This type represents a 32-bit (four-byte) signed integer ranging from -2,147,483,648 (-2^{31}) to 2,147,483,647 (2^{31}-1). It is represented by the tag `<int>` or `<i4>`, where `i4` stands for ***4-byte integer***. The following shows some of the examples of integer types:

```
<i4>23</i4>
<i4>-7</i4>
<i4>+3</i4>
<int>3</int>
<int>-2</int>
<int>+4</int>
```

Note that an implementation of XML-RPC specification must recognize this type for input parameters.

Floating point numbers

For floating point numbers, XML-RPC specification provides a type that refers to 64-bit double precision signed floating point numbers ranging from $\sim 4.94 \times 10^{-324}$ to $\sim 1.79 \times 10^{308}$. The type is indicated by the tag `<double>`. The following shows some of the examples of floating point types:

```
<double>3.42</double>
<double>-2.13</double>
<double>-0.13</double>
<double>+1.22</double>
```

Boolean values

A type is also incorporated to express Boolean values. This type represents only values 1 or 0 which corresponds to Boolean `true` and `false` respectively. It is represented by the tag `<boolean>`. Here are *all* the possible representations of Boolean values in XML-RPC:

```
<boolean>1</boolean>
<boolean>0</boolean>
```

Strings

XMP-RPC string type refers to the sequence of ASCII characters. A string value is represented using `<string>` tag. The following is an example representation of a string value in XML-RPC:

```
<string>RPC->Remote Procedure Call</string>
```

However, strings may be embedded in a `<value>` element directly omitting the `<string>` element. Note that `<value>` tag is used as the container of all other types. An XML-RPC implementation must understand both representations. So, the following representation is also valid and is usually used.

```
<value>RPC->Remote Procedure Call</value>
```

XML characters in the form of entity reference are permissible in a string. For example, if we want to use special XML characters, such as '&' and '<', in a string value, we must use the corresponding entity references (e.g., `&` for `&` and `>` for > etc.). The following are some valid string representations that use special characters:

```
<string>XML &amp; RPC</string>
<string>4 &gt; 3</string>
```

The parsers of this XML document should interpret the first string as `XML & RPC` and the second as `4 > 3` as they use the XML entities for the special characters `&` and >.

Date and Time

Dates and times are represented in XML-RPC using a single type and is indicated using `dateTime.iso8601` element. This type conforms to the ISO 8601 standard and hence has this name. It allows us to specify both date and time simultaneously in the `CCYYMMDDTHH:MM:SS` format. Here is one example:

```
<dateTime.iso8601>20130902T06:49:21</dateTime.iso8601>
```

This indicates the date "2nd September, 2013" and time "06:49:21" (using the 24-hour clock format). The following is another example:

```
<dateTime.iso8601>20141015T15:45:00</dateTime.iso8601>
```

The above element represents the date "15th October, 2014" and time "15:45:00" (when this manuscript is being developed).

Binary

We know that control characters (having ASCII code lower than that of space character (32)) are not allowed in XML. So, arbitrary binary data cannot be transported using a sequence of integer values as they may contain these control characters. For this reason, XML-RPC specification introduced a type for raw binary data. This is indicated using `<base64>` tag. A value of this type is a base64 encoded value from binary data. The encoding technique is described in RFC 2045. The following is an example encoding of the string "Hi!":

```
<base64>SGkh</base64>
```

Similarly, the following example shows the encoding of the string "Hello World!"

```
<base64>SGVsbG8gV29ybGQh</base64>
```

17.3.2 Compound Data Types

The basic types represent simple values and are sufficient for simple and less complex applications. However, complex applications may require more complex types to represent compound structure such as array, struct etc. Fortunately, XML-RPC provides two types `array` and `struct` for these compound values.

Array

In XML-RPC, an array is a sequence of data items. However, unlike traditional array where array elements are of same type, XML-RPC allows array elements to be of different types. Also there is no provision for numbering array elements. In general, an array is represented as follows:

```
<array>
  <data>
    <value>An XML-RPC value</value>
    <value>An XML-RPC value</value>
    ...
    <value>An XML-RPC value</value>
  </data>
</array>
```

The sequence of values are written between `<array><data>` and `</data></array>`. Values are specified using `<value>` tag. For example, the following shows an array of 3 integers:

```
<array>
  <data>
    <value><int>2</int></value>
    <value><int>3</int></value>
    <value><int>4</int></value>
  </data>
</array>
```

As mentioned earlier, array elements need not be of the same type. So, the following XML-RPC array is valid.

```
<array>
  <data>
    <value><string>B. S. Roy</string></value>
    <value><int>35</int></value>
    <value><double>48.34</double></value>
  </data>
</array>
```

In the above example, the array elements represent the name, age and weight of a person respectively.

The array elements need not always be basic type. They may be any valid compound types as well. This enables us to create a multidimensional array by embedding arrays within an array. The following shows a two-dimensional array of 2 rows and 3 columns:

```
<array>
  <data>
    <value>
      <array>
        <data>
          <value><int>1</int></value>
          <value><int>2</int></value>
          <value><int>3</int></value>
        </data>
      </array>
    </value>
    <value>
      <array>
        <data>
          <value><int>4</int></value>
          <value><int>5</int></value>
          <value><int>6</int></value>
        </data>
      </array>
    </value>
  </data>
</array>
```

Struct

A struct in XML-RPC is a sequence of name-value pair. Each pair is said to be a member of struct and is represented by `<member>` element. The name of a member is an ASCII string and the value is any valid XML-RPC value including array or struct. A struct has the following general form:

```
<struct>
  <member>
    <name>name1</name>
    <value>value1</value>
  </member>
  <member>
    <name>name2</name>
    <value>value2</value>
  </member>
  …
  <member>
    <name>nameN</name>
    <value>valueN</value>
  </member>
</struct>
```

The following is an example of struct that stores information of a person:

```
<struct>
  <member>
    <name>firstName</name>
    <value><string>Banhishikha</string></value>
  </member>
  <member>
    <name>lastName</name>
    <value><string>Roy</string></value>
  </member>
  <member>
    <name>age</name>
    <value><int>35</int></value>
  </member>
</struct>
```

Similarly, the following example contains information of a method call:

```
<struct>
  <member>
    <name>methodName</name>
    <value><string>sqrt</string></value>
  </member>
  <member>
    <name>y</name>
    <value><int>4</int></value>
  </member>
</struct>
```

This represents a call of a method `sqrt` with parameter `4`. A struct may contain arrays or arrays may also contain struct. This enables XML-RPC programmers to describe even an extremely complex structure in a very easy way. A summary of XML-RPC data types is shown in Table 17.1:

Table 17.1: Basic data types supported by XML-RPC

Type	Range	Examples
int or i4	4-byte integers from 2,147,483,648 (-2^{31}) to 2,147,483,647 (2^{31}-1).	<int>2</int> <i4>3</i4> <int>-4</int>
double	64-bit double precision floating-point numbers from $\sim 4.94 \times 10^{-324}$ to $\sim 1.79 \times 10^{308}$	<double>3.42</double> <double>-2.13</double> <double>-0.13</double>
Boolean	true (1) or false (0)	<boolean>1</boolean> <boolean>0</boolean>
String	sequence of ASCII of characters	<string>XML</string> <string>RPC</string>
dateTime.iso8601	ISO8601 date and time in CCYYMMDDTHH:MM:SS format	<dateTime.iso8601>20130902T06:49:21</dateTime.iso8601>
Base64	Base-64 encoded character sequence as defined in RFC 2045	<base64>SGkh</base64>

17.4 XML-RPC MESSAGES

In XML-RPC, method call and response [Figure 17.1:] are described as HTTP messages having body written in XML. The specification defines three types of messages [Figure 17.3:]: *request message*, *response message* and *fault message*.

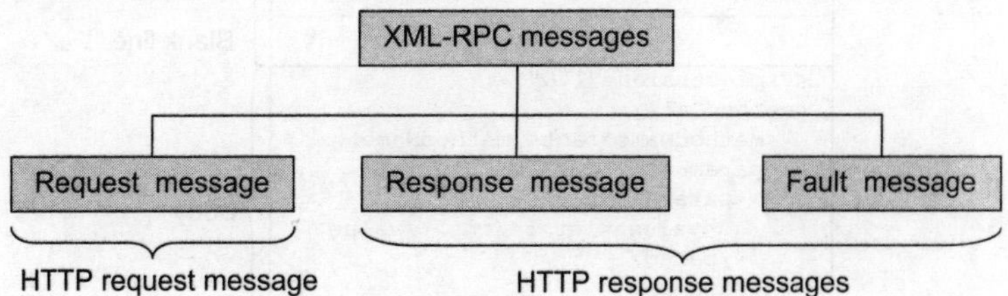

Figure 17.3: XML-RPC messages

XML-RPC request messages are a kind of HTTP request messages, whereas XML-RPC responses and fault messages are HTTP response messages. The following section describes the format of these messages briefly. Understanding message formats helps programmers to write their own implementation of XML-RPC specification as well as to debug and to establish connections between systems in different environments.

17.4.1 Request Message

An XML-RPC request message is basically an HTTP POST request message whose body is an XML document. This XML message body encodes the method call syntax. The message has the root element `<methodCall>` that contains method name and its arguments. The name of the method is represented by the `<methodName>` element and argument list is provided using `<params>` element. The `<params>` element contains a list of `<param>` elements one for each argument. The value of the argument is specified by the `<value>` element. For example, to invoke a method called `fact`, which takes an integer argument, the body of XML-RPC request message looks like this:

```
<?xml version="1.0"?>
<methodCall>
  <methodName>fact</methodName>
  <params>
    <param>
      <value><int>5</int></value>
    </param>
  </params>
</methodCall>
```

And the HTTP request line and header look something like this:

```
POST /xmlrpc/RPC HTTP/1.0
User-Agent: Apache XML-RPC
Host: client.host.name
Content-Type: text/xml
Content-Length: length of XML body in bytes
```

XML-RPC specification does not provide the format of the URL (Uniform Resource Locator) in the request line and can be empty. In the above example, the `/xmlrpc/RPC` is the URL of the processor who will process this request message. The next two lines of the header specify the `User-Agent` and `Host`. The `User-Agent` is the name of the software making the request. The Host is the URL of the client. Note that, these two headers are not mandatory for most of XML-RPC servers.

The last two lines specify mandatory headers `Content-Type` and `Content-Length`. The value of `Content-Type` header is always `text/xml` as the content is an XML document. The value of `Content-Length` is the size of XML message body in number of bytes.

So, the XML-RPC request message (which is an HTTP POST request message) finally looks as shown in Figure 17.4:

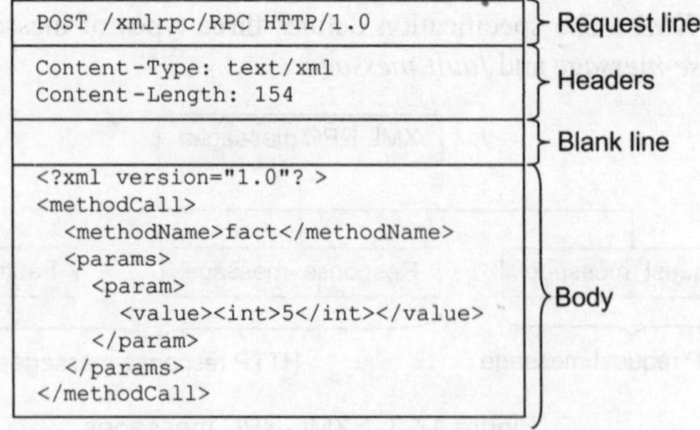
POST /xmlrpc/RPC HTTP/1.0
Request line
Content-Type: text/xml
Content-Length: 154
Headers
Blank line
<?xml version="1.0"? >
<methodCall>
<methodName>fact</methodName>
<params>
<param>
<value><int>5</int></value>
</param>
</params>
</methodCall>
Body

Figure 17.4: A sample XML-RPC Request message

Note that the content of `<methodName>` element is a sequence of alphanumeric characters, underscore, dot, colon, and back slash. The interpretation of this string depends entirely on the server. The string may be the exact name of the method (as shown in the previous example) or method name with object name as a prefix, or may be a name of a file containing a script to be executed etc. The server of the Apache XML-RPC Java library (that we shall use to demonstrate XML-RPC) expects this string as the following format:

```
objectName.methodName
```

Here `objectName` is the name of the object assigned by the server during its creation and `methodName` is the actual name of the method to be invoked.

Note that `<params>` tag may be absent if a method does not take any parameter. So the following is an example of method call without any parameter.

```
<?xml version="1.0"?>
<methodCall>
  <methodName>sayHello</methodName>
</methodCall>
```

The `<value>` tag under `<param>` contains any of the six basic types or two compound types.

17.4.2 Response Message

An XML-RPC response message is basically an HTTP response message whose body is an XML document. This message is sent by the XML-RPC server as a result of method call. In the response line, the server should always return '200 OK' unless an HTTP error occurs. A fault is represented by a separate message and is described in the next section. The header section should contain two headers `Content-Type` and `Content-Length`. The value of `Content-Type` header should be `text/xml` and the value of `Content-Length` is the correct number of bytes in the XML message body.

The body of the message is an XML document whose root element is `<methodResponse>`. This tag contains a single `<params>` tag, which contains a single `<param>` tag. Since a method can only return one value, there exists only one `<param>` tag. An example of a response message body is shown below:

```
<?xml version="1.0">
<methodResponse>
  <params>
    <param>
      <value><i4>120</i4></value>
    </param>
  </params>
</methodResponse>
```

The HTTP response line and header look something like this:

```
HTTP/1.1 200 OK
Content-Type: text/xml
Content-Length: 142
```

So, the XML-RPC response message (which is an HTTP response message) finally looks as shown in Figure 17.5:

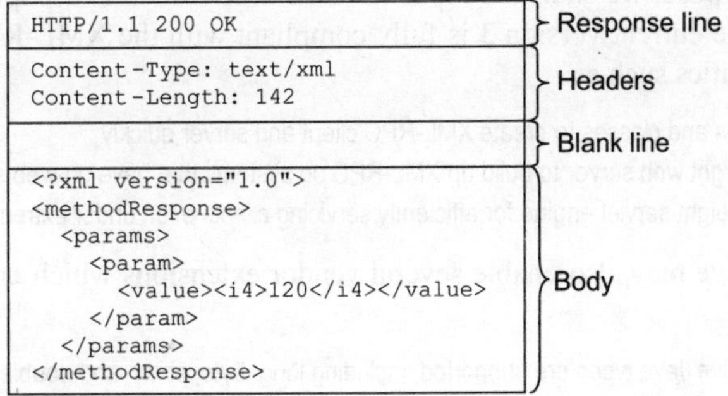

Figure 17.5: A sample XML-RPC Response message

17.4.3 Fault Message

If XML-RPC server faces some problem processing the request, it notifies the client with a special message called *fault message*. Note that a fault message is also a response message except that it has a different format. In this case, the `<methodResponse>` tag contains `<fault>` tag, which designates the message as a fault message. The `<fault>` contains a `<value>`, which is a `<struct>` containing two members. The name of the first member is `faultCode`, whose value is an `<int>`, which indicates the error code. The name of the second member is `faultString`, whose value is a `<string>` which gives an explanation about the error occurred. The following is an example fault message:

```
HTTP/1.1 200 OK
Content-Type: text/xml
Content-Length: 365

<?xml version="1.0"?>
  <methodResponse>
    <fault>
      <value>
        <struct>
          <member>
            <name>faultCode</name>
            <value><int>0</int></value>
          </member>
          <member>
            <name>faultString</name>
            <value>No such handler: fact1</value>
          </member>
        </struct>
      </value>
    </fault>
  </methodResponse>
```

This tells us that a fault occurred as an invalid method 'fact1' was mentioned in the request by the client.

17.5 JAVA XML-RPC

It is well-known that Java is well ahead of its competitors, as far as networking applications are concerned due to its extremely powerful library. So, there is nothing to get surprised if we choose Java as the programming language to develop XML-RPC-based networking applications.

In this section, we shall demonstrate how to build XML-RPC client and server using Java. It describes how to build a variety of different XML-RPC clients, servers and handlers. Some of these use built-in functionality to set up XML-RPC servers and handlers, whereas others prefer handling them directly.

For this purpose, we shall use Apache XML-RPC which is a popular Java implementation of XML-RPC. The current version 3 is fully compliant with the XML-RPC specification. It includes core functionalities such as:

- Interfaces and classes to create XML-RPC client and server quickly
- Light-weight web server to build up XML-RPC on systems that have no web server installed in them
- A light-weight servlet engine for efficiently servicing clients even under extremely high load

Moreover, we may also enable several vendor extensions which enhances the power of XML-RPC greatly.

- All primitive Java types are supported, including long, byte, short, and double.
- Calendar objects are supported. In particular, timezone may be set and time in milliseconds may be sent/received.

- It supports transmitting of DOM nodes, or JAXB objects as well as objects implementing the `java.io.Serializable` interface.
- Instead of default mode, which is based on large internal byte arrays, both server and client can operate in a streaming mode, which preserves resources much better

17.6 INSTALLING THE APACHE XML-RPC JAVA LIBRARY

The web site for Apache XML-RPC Library for Java is `http://ws.apache.org/xmlrpc`. Additional resources (such as documentation) are also available in this site. The examples in this chapter use `org.apache.xmlrpc` package (and other sub packages), which is also available here.

To use Apache XML-RPC Java library, download the necessary `.jar` files from `http://ws.apache.org/xmlrpc/download.html`. This is an open source software, which is another reason for choosing it. We downloaded the zip file `apache-xmlrpc-3.1.3-bin.zip` and unzipped it in E: drive. It creates the following directory structure:

- data (E:)
  - apache-xmlrpc-3.1.3
    - docs
    - lib

The `docs` directory contains documentation and the `lib` directory contains XML-RPC Java library as 5 (five) JAR (**J**ava **AR**chive) files as follows:

```
commons-logging-1.1.jar
ws-commons-util-1.0.2.jar
xmlrpc-client-3.1.3.jar
xmlrpc-common-3.1.3.jar
xmlrpc-server-3.1.3.jar
```

These .jar files are necessary to develop XMP-RPC client–server application. The Java package `org.apache.xmlrpc` contains useful classes for XML-RPC Java clients and server (e.g. `XmlRpcClient`, `XmlRpcServer`, `WebServer`, `XmlRpcServlet` etc.) Include all .jar files in CLASSPATH environment variable. Alternatively, they can be specified during compilation and execution of the application.

17.7 XML-RPC VERSUS JAVA DATA TYPES

Since, we are going to develop XML-RPC application using Java, we must know which XML-RPC types map to which Java types. Apache XML-RPC also provides some extended data types, which may be used if required. However, both client and server must then use Apache XML-RPC. A summary of all these mappings is provided in Table 17.2:

Table 17.2: XML-RPC to Java mapping

Basic data		Apache extension	
XML Tag Name	**Java Type**	**XML Tag Name**	**Java Type**
i4, or int	Integer	ex:nil	None
boolean	Boolean	ex:i1	Byte
string	String	ex:float	Float
double	Double	ex:i8	Long
dateTime.iso8601	java.util.Date	ex:dom	org.w3c.dom.Node

(Contd)

Table 17.2: (*Contd*)

base64	byte[]	ex:i2	Short
struct	java.util.Map	ex:serializable	java.io.Serializable
array	Object[]	ex:bigdecimal	BigDecimal
		ex:biginteger	BigInteger
		ex:dateTime	java.util.Calendar

17.8 EXAMPLE

In this section, we shall develop a simple client–server application using XML-RPC. In this application, the server creates a factorial object on which a single method `fact()` can be invoked. The client invokes this method using the procedure described in XML-RPC specification.

17.8.1 Writing the server

Before setting up the server, let us develop a class for factorial object. The following is the source code of class (stored in `FactImpl.java` file):

```
public class FactImpl {
  public int fact(int n) {
    System.out.println("Received : "+n);
    int prod = 1;
    for(int i = 2; i <= n; i++)
      prod *= i;
    System.out.println("Sent : "+prod);
    return prod;
  }
}
```

This class has only on method `fact()` that takes a single integer (should be non-negative) and returns the factorial of that integer.

Let us now develop a server program that is capable of handling a method invocation request coming from clients over HTTP as XML-RPC request message. The simplest way to do this is to create an instance of `org.apache.xmlrpc.webserver.WebServer` as follows:

```
WebServer webServer = new WebServer(6789);
```

A `WebServer` object is a minimal HTTP server that can handle only XML-RPC messages. It enables us to set up XML-RPC in hosts even if they have no web server installed in them previously. Note that the `WebServer` class does not implement full HTTP and is not capable of serving web pages. The above `webServer` listens for XML-RPC requests on the port `6789`.

This `webServer` itself is not capable of calling a method on an object. This functionality is provided by `org.apache.xmlrpc.server.XmlRpcServer` class. So, internally, it maintains an `XmlRpcServer` object, a reference to which may be obtained as follows:

```
XmlRpcServer rpcServer = webServer.getXmlRpcServer();
```

The `XmlRpcServer` class has a method `execute()`,which can invoke a method for a given `XmlRpcRequest`. This `XmlRpcRequest` class encapsulates an XML-RPC request. The functionality of a `WebServer` object is as follows:

- Upon receiving an XML-RPC request message, it processes its header and XML body.
- It then extracts method name and parameters from the given XML body.
- It creates an `XmlRpcRequest` object with this information.
- It then invokes the `execute()` method on its internal `XmlRpcServer` object passing `XmlRpcRequest` object and records the result

- Finally, it creates an XML body with this result for the XML-RPC response message.
- This XML response body is then embedded in an XML-RPC request message and sent back to the client.

The `rpcServer` object, on the other hand, maintains a list of named objects on which methods may be invoked. However, `rpcServer` does not so far have any such list. To create this list, we instantiate a `org.apache.xmlrpc.server.PropertyHandlerMapping` object as follows:

```
PropertyHandlerMapping mapping = new PropertyHandlerMapping();
```

This object basically maps objects to unique names. In other words, given a name, the underlying object may be obtained. The `addHandler()` method on this object is usually used to create named objects as follows:

```
mapping.addHandler("Factorial", FactImpl.class);
```

The `addHandler()` method takes two parameters. The second parameter is a `Class` (`FactImpl.class` in our case) of the target object and the first parameter is a `String`, which is the name ("Factorial" in our case) of the target object. This name "Factorial" is used by the clients to refer to the object during method invocation.

Note that no object is created at this time. The object is created when the method invocation request comes for the first time. A zero argument constructor is used to create this object. This implies that the object's class must have such a constructor. In our `FactImpl` class, since we have not written any constructor explicitly, a zero argument constructor is present that will be used to create an instance of this class.

Our task is now to inform this mapping to the `rpcServer` as follows:

```
rpcServer.setHandlerMapping(mapping);
```

Finally, we start the web server so that it can listen for HTTP connection.

```
webServer.start();
```

The `start()` method spawns a new thread, which binds this server to the port, it was configured, to accept connections on. The `webServer` is now capable of receiving XML-RPC POST request messages. The complete source of our first server (`Server1.java`) is shown below:

```
//Server1.java
import org.apache.xmlrpc.server.*;
import org.apache.xmlrpc.webserver.*;
public class Server1 {
  public static void main(String args[]) {
    try {
      WebServer webServer = new WebServer(6789);
      XmlRpcServer rpcServer = webServer.getXmlRpcServer();
      PropertyHandlerMapping mapping = new PropertyHandlerMapping();
      mapping.addHandler("Factorial", FactImpl.class);
      rpcServer.setHandlerMapping(mapping);
      webServer.start();
      System.out.println("XML-RPC server ready...");
    }catch(Exception e) {e.printStackTrace();}
  }
}
```

17.8.2 Writing the client

Writing XML-RPC client is relatively simple. The `org.apache.xmlrpc.client` package provides the necessary classes and interface for this. The basic steps are as follows:

- We create an `XmlRpcClient` object and configure it so that it can contact the server.
- We specify the name of the method to be invoked and necessary parameters.
- The method invocation request is done using `execute()` method on this object.
- Finally, we display the result returned by `execute()` method.

First, we create an `XmlRpcClient` object as follows:

```
XmlRpcClient client = new XmlRpcClient();
```

This `client` does not have any information about the XML-RPC server. So, it has to be configured properly. This is done by creating an `XmlRpcClientConfigImpl` object as follows:

```
XmlRpcClientConfigImpl config = new XmlRpcClientConfigImpl();
```

The URL of the XML-RPC server is specified in the `setServerURL()` as follows:

```
config.setServerURL(new URL("http://"+args[0]+":6789/"));
```

We are assuming that during the execution of the client, the IP address of the server is supplied as an argument. Note that the port number `6789`, on which the web server listens, is used here. This configuration information is then passed to the `client`.

```
client.setConfig(config);
```

At this point, the client knows the URL of the server. Now, we have to specify the name method name and its parameters. Since, the `fact()` method takes only one integer as parameter, we create an array of one `Integer` object as follows:

```
int n = 6;
Object[] params = new Object[]{ new Integer(n)};
```

Note that, parameters must always be passed as an array of `Object` elements. So, primitive values may be converted to the `Object` type using their respective wrapper classes. In this case, we have used `Integer` class which is the wrapper class for primitive type `int`. Finally, to invoke the method `fact()` on the server object (known as "Factorial"), the following piece of code is used:

```
Integer result = (Integer)client.execute("Factorial.fact", params);
```

The string `Factorial.fact` refers to the method `fact()` on an object whose name is `Factorial`. Note that, in the server program this name was assigned to the factorial object. The `execute()` method creates XML-RPC request message and forwards it to the server. A sample message is shown below:

```
POST / HTTP/1.1
Content-Type: text/xml
User-Agent: Apache XML RPC 3.1.3 (Sun HTTP Transport)
Cache-Control: no-cache
Pragma: no-cache
Host: 172.16.5.81:6789
Accept: text/html, image/gif, image/jpeg, *; q=.2, */*; q=.2
Connection: keep-alive
Content-Length: 187

<?xml version="1.0" encoding="UTF-8"?>
<methodCall>
  <methodName>Factorial.fact</methodName>
  <params>
    <param>
      <value><i4>6</i4></value>
    </param>
  </params>
</methodCall>
```

Note that the method invocation information is encoded in XML and is included in the body of the request message. The server in turn responds with an XML-RPC message as follows:

```
HTTP/1.1 200 OK
Server: Apache XML-RPC 1.0
Connection: close
Content-Type: text/xml
Content-Length: 155
```

```
<?xml version="1.0" encoding="UTF-8"?>
<methodResponse>
  <params>
    <param>
      <value><i4>720</i4></value>
    </param>
  </params>
</methodResponse>
```

Here, method's return value is also encoded in XML and is included in the body of the response message. The result is then displayed as follows:

```
System.out.println("Received : "+result);
```

The complete source of our first client (`Client1.java`) is shown below:

```
//Client1.java
import org.apache.xmlrpc.client.*;
import java.net.URL;
public class Client1  {
 public static void main (String [] args) {
  try {
    XmlRpcClient client = new XmlRpcClient();
    XmlRpcClientConfigImpl config = new XmlRpcClientConfigImpl();
    config.setServerURL(new URL("http://"+args[0]+":6789/"));
    client.setConfig(config);
    int n = 6;
    Object[] params = new Object[]{ new Integer(n)};
    System.out.println("Sent : "+n);
    Integer result = (Integer)client.execute("Factorial.fact", params);
    System.out.println("Received : "+result);
  } catch (Exception e) {
    e.printStackTrace();
  }
 }
}
```

17.8.3 Running the application

Create the following directory structure in the XML-RPC server computer. Now, place all Apache XML-RPC .jar files in `lib` directory and place `FactImpl.java` and `Server1.java` in `server` directory. Open a terminal and go to the `server` directory. Use the following command to compile Java files.

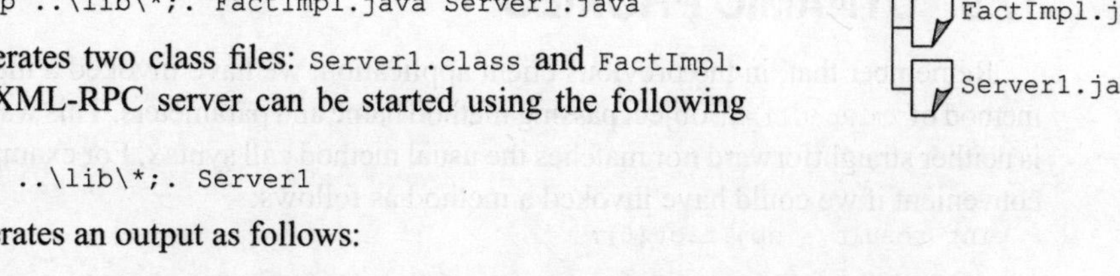


```
javac -cp ..\lib\*;. FactImpl.java Server1.java
```

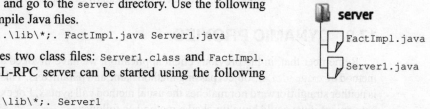

This generates two class files: `Server1.class` and `FactImpl.class`. The XML-RPC server can be started using the following command:

```
java -cp ..\lib\*;. Server1
```

This generates an output as follows:

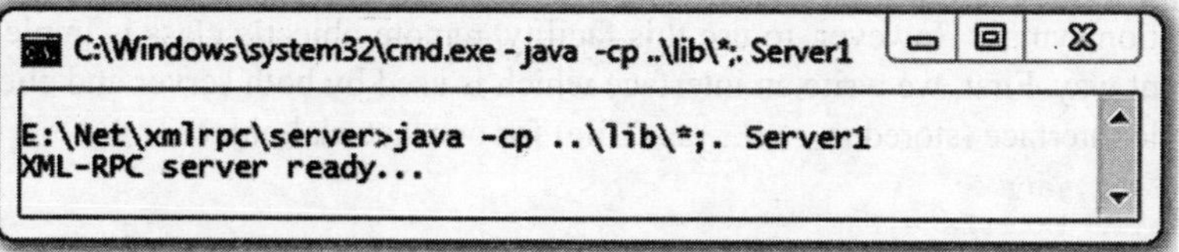

To run our client program, create the following directory structure in another computer. If you do not have another computer, then create this `client` sub-directory under `xmlrpc` directory where you created `lib` and `server` sub-directories previously. Now, place all Apache XML-RPC .jar files in `lib` directory and place `Client1.java` in `client` directory. Open a terminal and go to the `client` directory. Use the following command to compile Java files.

xmlrpc
client
lib
Client1.java

```
javac -cp ..\lib\*;. Client1.java
```

This generates one class files: `Client1.class`. Make sure that the directory containing `javac` compiler is included in the `PATH` environment variable. We assume that the XML-RPC server is running in a computer having IP address `172.16.5.81`. The XML-RPC client can be started using the following command:

```
java -cp ..\lib\*;. Client1 172.16.5.81
```

If the computer running your server has a different IP address, use that address in place of the above mentioned IP address. A sample result for both server and client is shown in Figure 17.6:

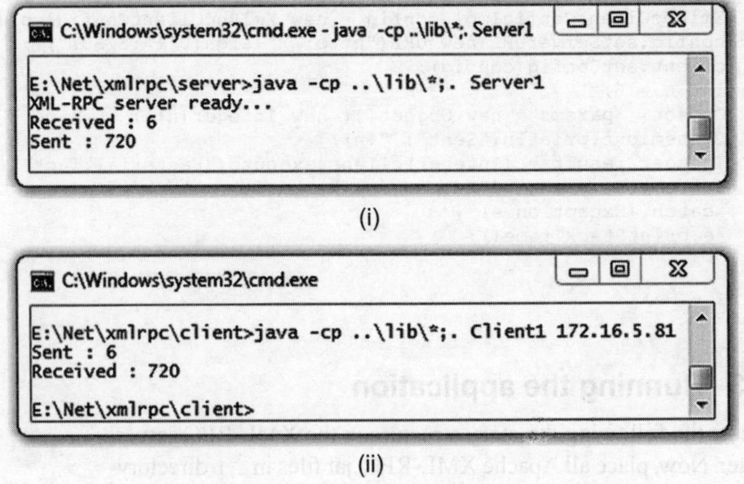
C:\Windows\system32\cmd.exe - java -cp ..\lib*;. Server1
E:\Net\xmlrpc\server>java -cp ..\lib*;. Server1
XML-RPC server ready...
Received : 6
Sent : 720
C:\Windows\system32\cmd.exe
E:\Net\xmlrpc\client>java -cp ..\lib*;. Client1 172.16.5.81
Sent : 6
Received : 720
E:\Net\xmlrpc\client>

(i)

(ii)

Figure 17.6: XML-RPC factorial (i) Server (ii) Client

17.9 DYNAMIC PROXIES

Remember that, in the previous client application, we have invoked a method using `execute()` method of `XmlRpcClient` object passing method name and parameters. This way of method invocation is neither straightforward nor matches the usual method call syntax. For example, it would have been convenient if we could have invoked a method as follows:

```
int result = obj.fact(6);
```

Apache XML-RPC dynamic proxy allows us to invoke remote methods using traditional method invocation syntax. However, to use this facility, remote object's class is implemented in a slightly different way. First, we write an interface which is used by both server and client. The following is a simple interface (stored in `Fact.java` file) for our factorial object.

```
//Fact.java
public interface Fact {
  public int fact(int n);
}
```

The `FactImpl` class should implement this interface. So, modify the `FactImpl.java` file as follows:

```
public class FactImpl implements Fact {
```

The added portion is shown with bold font. Now, use the name of interface during the object mapping as follows:

```
mapping.addHandler(Fact.class.getName(), FactImpl.class);
```

Note that `Fact.class.getName()` method returns the name of the interface (i.e. `Fact`). This is necessary because clients using dynamic proxy always use object's interface name during method invocation. Alternatively, the name may be hardcoded as follows:

```
mapping.addHandler("Fact", FactImpl.class);
```

The modified code is stored in a separate file (`Server2.java`) as follows:

```
//Server2.java
import org.apache.xmlrpc.server.*;
import org.apache.xmlrpc.webserver.*;
public class Server2 {
  public static void main(String args[]) {
    try {
      WebServer webServer = new WebServer(6789);
      XmlRpcServer rpcServer = webServer.getXmlRpcServer();
      PropertyHandlerMapping mapping = new PropertyHandlerMapping();
      mapping.addHandler(Fact.class.getName(), FactImpl.class);
      rpcServer.setHandlerMapping(mapping);
      webServer.start();
      System.out.println("XML-RPC server ready...");
    }catch(Exception e) {e.printStackTrace();}
  }
}
```

The modified portion is shown with bold font. The client, on the other hand, does not use `execute()` method `XmlRpcClient` object to invoke methods. Instead, it creates a `ClientFactory` with a specified `XmlRpcClient` object as follows:

```
XmlRpcClient client = new XmlRpcClient();
//configure this object
ClientFactory factory = new ClientFactory(client);
```

The `newInstance()` method of factory is then used to create a proxy dynamically for a given interface.

```
Fact dProxy = (Fact) factory.newInstance(Fact.class);
```

This `dProxy` can then be used to invoke methods using the usual method invocation syntax.

```
int result = dProxy.fact(n);
```

The dynamic proxy internally calls the server by using the `XmlRpcClient`. The modified code is stored in a separate file (`Client2.java`) as follows:

```
//Client2.java
import org.apache.xmlrpc.client.*;
import java.net.URL;
import org.apache.xmlrpc.client.util.ClientFactory;
public class Client2  {
  public static void main (String [] args) {
   try {
     XmlRpcClient client = new XmlRpcClient();
     XmlRpcClientConfigImpl config = new XmlRpcClientConfigImpl();
     config.setServerURL(new URL("http://"+args[0]+":6789"));
     client.setConfig(config);
     int n = 6;
     //Object[] params = new Object[]{ new Integer(n)};
     System.out.println("Sent : "+n);
     //Integer result = (Integer)client.execute("Factorial.fact", params);
```

```
      ClientFactory factory = new ClientFactory(client);
      Fact dProxy = (Fact) factory.newInstance(Fact.class);
      int result = dProxy.fact(n);
      System.out.println("Received : "+result);
    } catch (Exception e) {
      e.printStackTrace();
    }
  }
}
```

The added portion is shown with bold font and unnecessary code used in `Client1.java` is placed under the comment lines.

Compile and start this application as described previously. Note that the class file for `Fact` interface (i.e. `Fact.class`) in needed by both client and server. A sample result is shown in Figure 17.7:

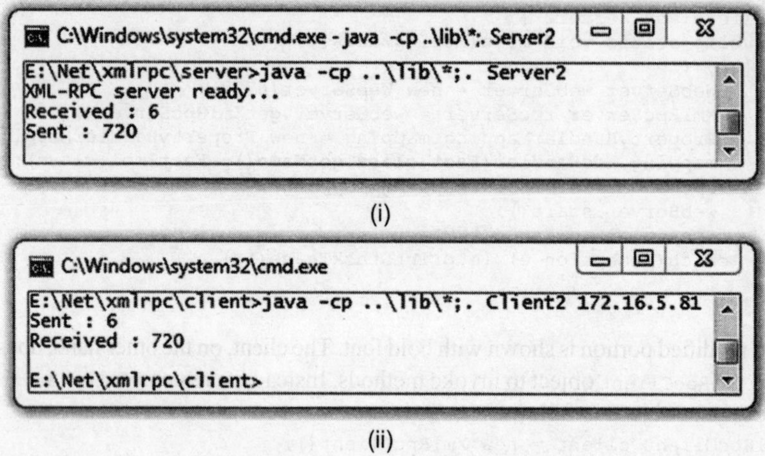
C:\Windows\system32\cmd.exe - java -cp ..\lib*;. Server2
E:\Net\xmlrpc\server>java -cp ..\lib*;. Server2
XML-RPC server ready...
Received : 6
Sent : 720
(i)
C:\Windows\system32\cmd.exe
E:\Net\xmlrpc\client>java -cp ..\lib*;. Client2 172.16.5.81
Sent : 6
Received : 720
E:\Net\xmlrpc\client>
(ii)

Figure 17.7: XML-RPC factorial (i) Server (ii) Client using dynamic proxy

17.10 USING XMLRPCSERVLET

Apache XML-RPC also provides `XmlRpcServlet` class, which has an embedded instance of `XmlRpcServer`. This servlet may be installed to an existing web server (such as tomcat) to serve XML-RPC requests. Note that Apache's tomcat is an extremely versatile web server and full blown servlet engine. Its performance is not questionable even under high load. So, it is a good choice to use this built-in servlet instead of using light-weight `WebServer` class.

In this section, we shall discuss how to make use of this servlet to serve XML-RPC requests. We assume that tomcat is already installed in your computer. The detailed installation procedure may be found in Chapter 20. Consider the home directory of apache tomcat is `D:\apache-tomcat-8.0.0-RC1`. Hereafter, we shall refer to this directory as `tomcat_home`. Create the following directory structure under `webapps` sub directory of `tomcat_home`. Place all XML-RPC `.jar` files (i.e. `commons-logging-1.1.jar, ws-commons-util-1.0.2.jar, xmlrpc-client-3.1.3.jar, xmlrpc-common-3.1.3.jar, xmlrpc-server-3.1.3.jar`) in `WEB-INF\lib` directory. Alternatively, these `.jar` files may be placed in the `lib` subdirectory of `tomcat_home` directory. Inside the `classes` directory, place the file `FactImpl.class`.

Now, create a property file `XmlRpcServlet.properties` under `webserver` directory.

Note that the `XmlRpcServlet` always reads the object mapping information from a file named `XmlRpcServlet.properties`, which must be stored in the directory `org/apache/xmlrpc/server/webserver/`, relative to a directory recognized by tomcat. Alternatively, this property file may be added to any of the .jar files in lib directory. Enter the following line in this file.

```
Factorial=FactImpl
```

```
xmlrpc
  lib
  server
    org
      apache
        xmlrpc
          webserver
            XmlRpcServlet.properties
```

The `XmlRpcServlet` reads this property file and binds objects with names as specified in the file. The left-hand side of '=' sign is the name of the object whose class name is written to the right side of '='. In our case, the name of object is `Factorial` and its value is the fully qualified name of the `FactImpl` class. This name is used by the client during method invocation. Now, append the following entries to `<web-app>… </web-app>` element in the war file `WEB-INF\web.xml` file.

```
<servlet>
  <servlet-name>XmlRpcServlet</servlet-name>
  <servlet-class>org.apache.xmlrpc.webserver.XmlRpcServlet</servlet-class>
</servlet>

<servlet-mapping>
  <servlet-name>XmlRpcServlet</servlet-name>
  <url-pattern>/servlet</url-pattern>
</servlet-mapping>
```

You may take a look at the sample `web.xml` file stored in `tomcat_home\webapps\ROOT\WEB-INF` directory. Start tomcat using executing `startup.bat` in the `tomcat_home\bin` directory. If everything goes fine, our `XmlRpcServlet` is now ready to serve XML-RPC requests. The URL of this servlet is:

```
http://"+args[0]+":8080/xmlrpc/servlet
```

We assume that the IP address of the computer where this tomcat web server runs is given as a command line argument. We also assume that tomcat listens on port 8080 for HTTP requests. Use the above URL to modify either `Client1.java` or `Client2.java` and store it in another file `Client3.java`. The complete source code is given below:

```
//Client3.java
import org.apache.xmlrpc.client.*;
import java.net.URL;
public class Client3  {
 public static void main (String [] args) {
  try {
    XmlRpcClient client = new XmlRpcClient();
    XmlRpcClientConfigImpl config = new XmlRpcClientConfigImpl();
    config.setServerURL(new URL("http://"+args[0]+":8080/xmlrpc/servlet"));
    client.setConfig(config);
    int n = 6;
    Object[] params = new Object[]{ new Integer(n)};
    System.out.println("Sent : "+n);
    Integer result = (Integer)client.execute("Factorial.fact", params);
    System.out.println("Received : "+result);
  } catch (Exception e) {
    e.printStackTrace();
  }
 }
}
```

We can now compile and start this program. A sample result of tomcat terminal and Client3 terminal is shown in Figure 17.8:

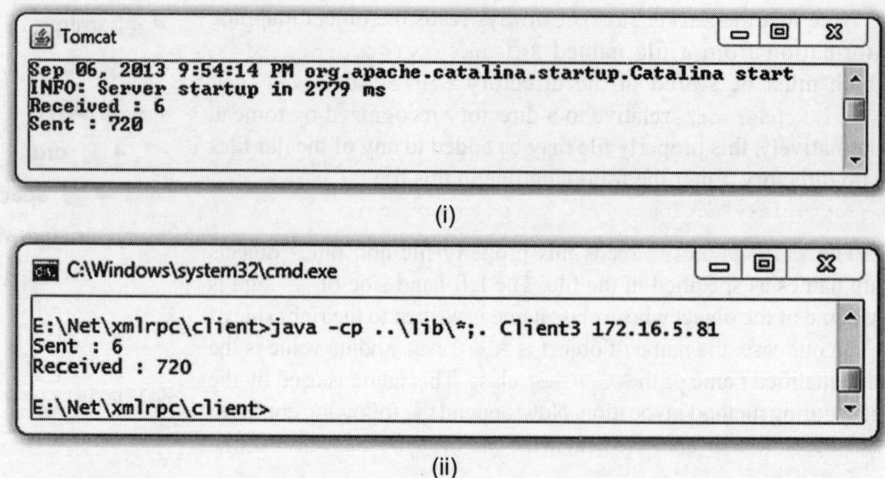
Tomcat
Sep 06, 2013 9:54:14 PM org.apache.catalina.startup.Catalina start
INFO: Server startup in 2779 ms
Received : 6
Sent : 720
(i)
C:\Windows\system32\cmd.exe
E:\Net\xmlrpc\client>java -cp ..\lib*;. Client3 172.16.5.81
Sent : 6
Received : 720
E:\Net\xmlrpc\client>
(ii)

Figure 17.8: Using `XmlRpcServlet` (i) tomcat web server's terminal (ii) Client making XML-RPC request

17.11 USING SERVLETWEBSERVER

The Apache `WebServer` is a minimal HTTP server. Though, it has become very popular amongst Apache XML-RPC programmers, under heavy load, it becomes very slow in comparison to a real servlet engine. This is because, `WebServer` neither handles multiple requests per physical connection nor can it stream requests.

However, if a `WebServer` is really required, Apache recommends to use its enhanced version `org.apache.xmlrpc.webserver.ServletWebServer`. This is a subclass of `WebServer` and provides minimum subset of servlet API. It enables the programmers to bypass complicated tasks involved in setting up a full-blown web server and servlet engine.

The use of the `ServletWebServer` is very simple. We don't have to create and configure even a `XmlRpcServer` object. Instead we create an `XmlRpcServlet` as follows:

```
XmlRpcServlet servlet = new XmlRpcServlet();
```

This servlet is a minimal servlet capable of handling XML-RPC requests. It always reads the object mapping information from a file named `XmlRpcServlet.properties`, which must be stored in the directory `org/apache/xmlrpc/server/webserver/`, relative to the servlet's directory. So, create a directory structure as shown on the right:

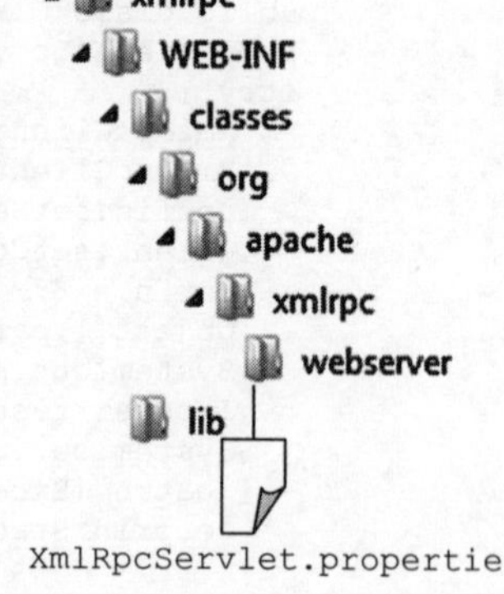
xmlrpc
WEB-INF
classes
org
apache
xmlrpc
webserver
lib
XmlRpcServlet.properties

Make the following entry in this file and put it in the above mentioned directory.

```
Factorial=FactImpl
```

This tells the servlet to create an object from the class `FactImpl` and bound this object to the name "Factorial". This name is used by the client during a method call. Note that this servlet may be an `XmlRpcServlet` or any subclass thereof. However, since servlets are stateless (i.e. multiple threads may use a single servlet concurrently), user defined servlets must not use any unsynchronized instance variables, except those which are read during initialization.

A `ServletWebServer` may then be created with this servlet and a specified port as follows:

```
ServletWebServer webServer = new ServletWebServer(servlet, 6789);
```

The web server is then started as follows:

```
webServer.start();
```

This `ServletWebServer` is now capable of receiving XML-RCP requests and forwarding method invocation information to the specified servlet instance. The complete source code for this server (`ServletServer.java`) is given below:

```
//ServletServer.java
import org.apache.xmlrpc.webserver.*;
public class ServletServer {
  public static void main(String args[]) {
   try {
      XmlRpcServlet servlet = new XmlRpcServlet();
      ServletWebServer webServer = new ServletWebServer(servlet, 6789);
      webServer.start();
      System.out.println("XML-RPC server ready...");
   }catch(Exception e) {e.printStackTrace();}
  }
}
```

To compile and run this program, one additional `.jar` file `servlet-api.jar` for servlet API is needed. This file may be downloaded from the web or may be found in the `tomcat_home\lib` directory if tomcat is already installed. Place this jar file in the `xmcrpc\lib` directory or include it in the CLASSPATH environment variable or specify its location during compilation. We have placed this jar file in `xmcrpc\lib` directory.

To compile the server, go to the `server` directory and use the following command:

```
javac -cp ..\lib\*;. ServletServer.java
```

Now start the server as follows:

```
java -cp ..\lib\*;. ServletServer
```

We can now use our `Client1.java` program to invoke methods as before. A sample result is shown in Figure 17.9:

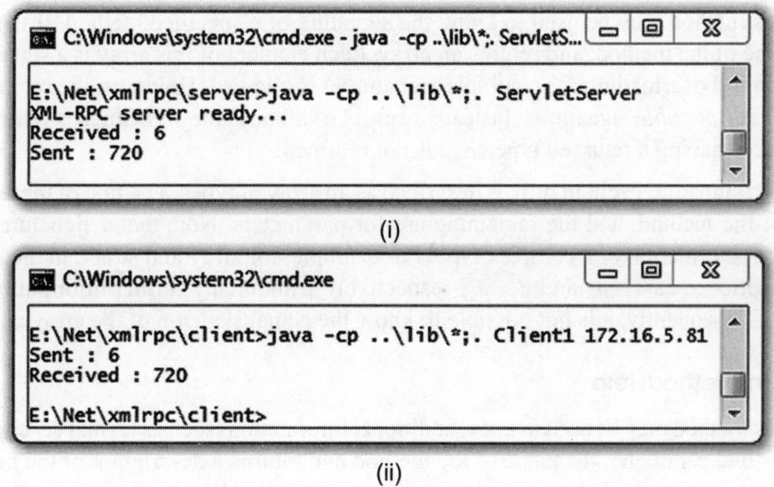
C:\Windows\system32\cmd.exe - java -cp ..\lib*;. ServletS...
E:\Net\xmlrpc\server>java -cp ..\lib*;. ServletServer
XML-RPC server ready...
Received : 6
Sent : 720
(i)
C:\Windows\system32\cmd.exe
E:\Net\xmlrpc\client>java -cp ..\lib*;. Client1 172.16.5.81
Sent : 6
Received : 720
E:\Net\xmlrpc\client>
(ii)

Figure 17.9: Using `ServletWebServer` (i) Server (ii) Client

17.12 INTROSPECTION

Note that, to invoke a remote method, a client must know method's signature (i.e. name of the method and type, number and order of parameters it takes). However, an obvious question is: "How will a client know this information?". Even a more important question is: "How will a client get updated method signature if the signature is changed by the server?".

Most implementations of XML-RPC provide a facility called *introspection* that enables a client to dynamically learn from a server what XML-RPC methods the server implements and what their signatures are.

Note that introspection facility is not a part of the XML-RPC official standard. However, a de facto standard, originally invented around 2001 by Edd Dumbill, has been used by many implementations of XML-RPC including Apache XML-RPC. In this section, we shall illustrate how this facility can be used in Apahe XML-RPC.

Introspection facility basically allows a client to ask three questions to the server as follows:

- What method names do you offer?
- What is the signature of the given method name?
- Can you provide me help on the given method name?

A client may make these queries to the server by invoking special methods `system.listMethods`, `system.methodSignature` and `system.methodHelp` respectively. These special methods always start with the word `system`. An XML-RPC server implementing introspection should be capable of processing these method invocation requests. A short description of these introspection methods is given below:

system.listMethods

This method may be used to find the name of all methods currently implemented by the XML-RPC server. It is a zero argument method that returns names of methods currently supported by the server as an XML-RPC array of strings.

system.methodSignature

This method may be used to know the signature of a specified method. It takes one parameter, the name of the method, and returns an array. Each element of this array is a signature. This implies that method overloading (i.e. multiple signatures) is allowed. However, the returned array may not contain *all possible* signatures. Instead, a subset of all possible signatures is returned. For example, signatures having a returned type `void` is not returned.

Each signature itself, in turn, is described as an array of types. The first of these types is the return type of the method, and the remaining are for parameters. Note that a signature does not provide detailed information of a complex type. For example, for array and struct, in the signature, they are just mentioned as `array` and `struct` respectively without any further information of their internal fields. Consequently, it is not possible to know the actual skeleton of the array and struct at all.

system.methodHelp

This method may be used to know additional information (such as textual description) of a method. It takes one parameter, the name of the method and returns a description of the method in question, for human use. Note that information provided depends solely on the server. The information may be as much or as little a detail including an empty string.

17.12.1 Example

Let us now develop some program that introspects methods implemented by a server.

To provide information about the methods, Apache XML-RPC provides a class `XmlRpcSystemImpl`, which requires a mapping to be provided to it. The static `addSystemHandler()` method is used to provide this mapping as follows:

```
XmlRpcSystemImpl.addSystemHandler(mapping);
```

Let us add this line to our `Server1.java` program and call the resultant program as `IntroServer.java`. The complete source code is provided below:

```
//IntroServer.java
import org.apache.xmlrpc.server.*;
import org.apache.xmlrpc.webserver.*;
import org.apache.xmlrpc.metadata.*;
public class IntroServer {
  public static void main(String args[]) {
    try {
      WebServer webServer = new WebServer(6789);
      XmlRpcServer rpcServer = webServer.getXmlRpcServer();
      PropertyHandlerMapping mapping = new PropertyHandlerMapping();
      mapping.addHandler("Factorial", FactImpl.class);
      rpcServer.setHandlerMapping(mapping);
      XmlRpcSystemImpl.addSystemHandler(mapping);
      webServer.start();
      System.out.println("XML-RPC server ready...");
    }catch(Exception e) {e.printStackTrace();}
  }
}
```

The added piece of code is shown with bold font. To examine the returned information, we have developed a simple client program using socket that sends a simple XML-RPC request message and prints an XML-RPC response message. The following is the source code for this client (`IntroClient.java`):

```
//IntroClient.java
import java.net.*;
import java.io.*;
public class IntroClient {
 public static void main (String[] args) {
  try {
    BufferedReader xmlFile = new BufferedReader(new InputStreamReader(new
FileInputStream(args[1])));
    String xmlBody = "", line, result = "";
    while((line = xmlFile.readLine()) != null)
      xmlBody += line+"\n";

    String reqMsg="POST / HTTP/1.1\n"+
       "Content-Length: "+xmlBody.length() + "\n\n" + xmlBody;
    Socket socket = new Socket(args[0], 6789);
    OutputStream os = socket.getOutputStream();
    os.write(reqMsg.getBytes());
    os.flush();

    InputStream is = socket.getInputStream();
    int ch;
    while( (ch=is.read())!= -1)
      result = result+(char)ch;

    System.out.println("Sent this XML-RPC message-->\n" + reqMsg);
    System.out.print("Received this XML-RPC message-->:\n" + result);
```

```
    } catch (Exception e) {
      e.printStackTrace();
    }
  }
}
```

This program expects the name of a file containing XML body for the XML-RPC request message as an additional command line argument.

17.12.1.1 Listing methods

Compile and start `IntroServer.java` as described before. The client can be started with a different XML file as input. For example, consider the following XML body stored in a file `list.xml`:

```
<?xml version='1.0'?>
<methodCall>
  <methodName>system.listMethods</methodName>
</methodCall>
```

The client can then be started as follows:

```
java -cp ..\lib\*;. IntroClient 172.16.5.81 list.xml
```

A sample result is shown in Figure 17.10:

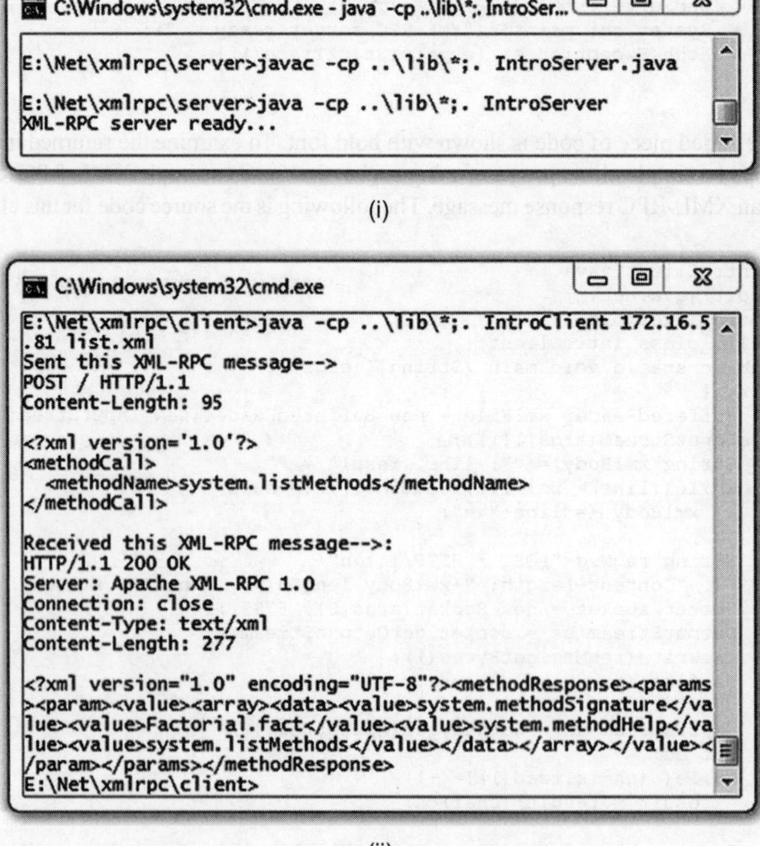

Figure 17.10: Using Apache XML-RPC introspection (i) Server (ii) Client

If we format the XML body of returned message, it looks like this:

```
<?xml version="1.0" encoding="UTF-8"?>
<methodResponse>
  <params>
    <param>
      <value>
        <array>
          <data>
            <value>system.methodSignature</value>
            <value>Factorial.fact</value>
            <value>system.methodHelp</value>
            <value>system.listMethods</value>
          </data>
        </array>
      </value>
    </param>
  </params>
</methodResponse>
```

This indicates that 4 (four) methods (three system methods and one user defined method) are available for invocation.

Alternatively, we can write an XML-RPC client specifying the method name as `system.listMethods`. The following is the source code of such a client:

```
//IntroClient1.java
import org.apache.xmlrpc.client.*;
import java.net.URL;
public class IntroClient1 {
 public static void main (String [] args) {
  try {
    XmlRpcClient client = new XmlRpcClient();
    XmlRpcClientConfigImpl config = new XmlRpcClientConfigImpl();
    config.setServerURL(new URL("http://"+args[0]+":6789"));
    client.setConfig(config);
    Object[] params = null;
    Object[] result = (Object[])client.execute("system.listMethods", params);
    for(int i=0;i<result.length;i++)
      System.out.println(result[i]);
   } catch (Exception e) {
     e.printStackTrace();
   }
  }
}
```

Compile and start this client as follows:

```
java -cp ..\lib\*;. IntroClient1 172.16.5.81
```

A sample result is shown below:

```
system.methodSignature
Factorial.fact
system.methodHelp
system.listMethods
```

17.12.1.2 Finding method signature

To find the signature of a method (say `Factorial.fact`), create the following XML body and store it in a file `signature.xml`.

```
<?xml version='1.0'?>
<methodCall>
  <methodName>system.methodSignature</methodName>
  <params>
```

```
    <param>
      <value><string>Factorial.fact</string></value>
    </param>
  </params>
</methodCall>
```

Start the client using the following command:

```
java -cp ..\lib\*;. IntroClient 172.16.5.81 signature.xml
```

The resultant XML body is shown below:

```
<?xml version="1.0" encoding="UTF-8"?>
<methodResponse>
<params>
  <param>
    <value>
      <array>     <!—array of signatures -->
        <data>
          <value>    <!—one signature found -->
            <array>
              <data>
                <value>int</value> <!—return type -->
                <value>int</value> <!—first argument -->
              </data>
            </array>
          </value>
        </data>
      </array>
    </value>
  </param>
</params>
</methodResponse>
```

It indicates that, for the method `Factorial.fact`, only one signature is available. The signature tells us that the method returns an `int` and takes a single parameter of `int` type.

17.12.1.3 Getting help

To get help for a method (say `Factorial.fact`), create the following XML body and store it in a file `help.xml`.

```
<?xml version='1.0'?>
<methodCall>
  <methodName>system.methodHelp</methodName>
  <params>
    <param>
      <value><string>Factorial.fact</string></value>
    </param>
  </params>
</methodCall>
```

Start the client using the following command:

```
java -cp ..\lib\*;. IntroClient 172.16.5.81 help.xml
```

The resultant XML body is shown below:

```
<?xml version="1.0" encoding="UTF-8"?>
<methodResponse>
<params>
  <param>
    <value>Invokes the method FactImpl.fact(int).</value>
  </param>
</params>
</methodResponse>
```

This tells us that for the method name `Factorial.fact`, server invokes `fact()` method on a `FactImpl` object.

17.13 LIMITATIONS OF XML-RPC

The capabilities of XML-RPC are limited. However, some of these limitations (for example simplicity) are in many ways the advantage of XML-RPC, as they reduce programmer's effort substantially. However, understanding these limitations make it possible to avoid pitfalls or traps when designing complex applications. The following are some of its limitations:

- Choice of data types is limited.
- No facility to represent `NaN` for floating point number.
- Only ASCII characters are allowed in strings.
- There is no provision for passing objects.
- No way to check types of array values.
- No facility to check if a struct has duplicate names.
- Little or no provision for security.
- The XML-RPC specification is now frozen.

KEYWORDS

Basic Type—Types used to represent basic data values such as integers, strings, floating point numbers Booleans etc.

Compound Types— Types used to represent complex data such as arrays and struct etc.

Dynamic Proxy—A mechanism that allows us to invoke methods using traditional method call syntax

Fault String—A string describing an error that occurs during parsing of request message

Handler—An object on which methods may be invoked

Introspection—A protocol that enables a client to dynamically learn from a server what XML-RPC methods the server implements and what their signatures are

Metadata—Information about remote method such as its name and number, type and order of data types it accepts

Property file—A file containing a set of property names and their value

RPC—A mechanism to invoke methods remotely

SOAP—An extended version of XML-RPC

ServletWebServer—An HTTP server provides minimum subset of servlet API

XML-RPC Client—A program that makes method invocation request

XML-RPC fault message—An HTTP message used to send error information back to client

XML-RPC request message—An HTTP message used to encode method invocation request in XML-RPC

XML-RPC response message—An HTTP message used to send result of method invocation back to the client

XML-RPC Server—A program that processes method invocation request, invokes the method and sends the result back

WebServer—A minimal HTTP server provided by Apache XML-RPC to process request messages

SUMMARY

XML-RPC is an XML-based **R**emote **P**rocedure **C**all (RPC) protocol, which uses e**X**tensible **M**arkup **L**anguage (XML) to describe a Remote Procedure Call and **H**yper**T**ext **T**ransfer **P**rotocol (HTTP) to transport encoded messages.

Two primary components are involved in XML-RPC: a server program and a client program. The server program implements one or more methods, invokes them on request and sends result (if any) back. The client program makes a request to the server to invoke a method with necessary parameters (if any).

These requests and responses are exchanged using HTTP messages whose body is an XML document. The XML documents encode method invocation information and reply. These messages are called XML-RPC request and response messages respectively.

To represent values passed to and returned from a remote method, XML-RPC specification defines six *basic data types* for integer, floating point number, Boolean, string, date-time and binary data and two *compound data types* for array and struct.

If XML-RPC server faces some problem processing a request, it notifies the client with a special message called *fault message*, which is a kind of response message having a different format.

Apache XML-RPC is an open source implementation, which is fully compliant to the XML-RPC specification and is used in this chapter. We have demonstrated how to build XML-RPC client and server using Java. It describes how to build a variety of different XML-RPC clients, servers, and handlers. Some of these use built-in functionality to set up XML-RPC servers and handlers, while others prefer handling them directly.

Apache XML-RPC dynamic proxy allows us to invoke remote methods using traditional method invocation syntax.

Apache XML-RPC also provides `XmlRpcServlet` class, which has an automatically embedded instance of `XmlRpcServer`. This servlet may be installed to an existing tomcat web server to serve XML-RPC requests.

XML-RPC specification provides a protocol called *introspection* that enables a client to dynamically learn from a server what XML-RPC methods the server implements and what their signatures are.

WEB RESOURCES

`http://www.tutorialspoint.com/xml-rpc/index.htm`
XML-RPC

`http://ws.apache.org/xmlrpc/`
Apache XML-RPC

`http://www.ibm.com/developerworks/xml/library/j-xmlrpc/index.html`
XML-RPC in Java programming

`http://xmlrpc.scripting.com/default.html`
XML-RPC Specification

`http://xmlrpc-c.sourceforge.net/introspection.html`
XML-RPC Introspection

`http://scripts.incutio.com/xmlrpc/introspection.html`
Introspection

EXERCISES

Objective-type Questions

1. What is the full form of RPC?
(a) Redundant Procedure Call
(b) Remote Proxy Call
(c) Remote Procedure Call
(d) Remote Patient Care

2. What is the full form of XML?
(a) eXtra Markup Language
(b) X-Markup Language
(c) eXpandable Markup Language
(d) eXtensible Markup Language

3. Which of the following protocols is used as transport protocol in XML-RPC?
(a) HTTPS (c) FTP
(b) SMTP (d) HTTP

4. Which one of the following types is a valid XML-RPC data type?
(a) <int> (c) <double>
(b) <float> (d) <char>

5. Which one of the following types is compound data type in XML-RPC?
(a) <linked-list> (c) <queue>
(b) <struct> (d) <stack>

6. Which of the following is a correct date format in XML-RPC?
(a) CCYYDDMM (c) DDMMCCYY
(b) MMDDCCYY (d) CCYYMMDD

7. Which of the following tags is used in a request message?
(a) `<methodCall>`
(b) `<methodRequest>`
(c) `<methodInvocation>`
(d) `<callMethod>`

8. Which of the following tags is used to specify name of the method?
(a) `<methodName>` (c) `<method_Name>`
(b) `<method-Name>` (d) `<method>`

9. An XML-RPC request message is an HTTP
(a) PUT message
(b) GET message
(c) HEAD message
(d) POST message

10. Which of the following tags is used in a response message?
(a) `<methodResponse>`
(b) `<response>`
(c) `<methodResult>`
(d) `<methodReturn>`

11. Which of the following tags is used in a fault message?
(a) `<error>` (c) `<methodError>`
(b) `<fault>` (d) `<methodFault>`

12. Which of the following classes is used to create a minimal web server?
(a) HTTPServer
(b) XmlRpcWebServer
(c) XmlRpcHTTPServer
(d) WebServer

13. Which of the following classes is capable of invoking methods on remote objects?
(a) `XmlRpcRequest`
(b) `XmlRpcResponse`
(c) `XmlRpcClient`
(d) `XmlRpcServer`

14. Which of the following methods is used to add a handler?
(a) putHandler() (c) handlerAdd()
(b) addHandler() (d) appendHandler()

15. Which of the following methods is used to configure an XML-RPC client?
(a) configClient() (c) configAdd()
(b) addConfig() (d) setConfig()

16. Which of the following servlet classes can handle XML-RPC requests?
(a) `XmlRpcServlet`
(b) `ApacheServlet`
(c) `RpcServletRequest`
(d) `XmlRpcServletRequest`

17. Introspection is an ability to
(a) Declare a method as public
(b) To write method documentation
(c) To discover servers
(d) Find information about remote methods

18. Which of the following is an introspection method?
(a) system.getMethods
(b) system.sendMethods
(c) system.retrieveMethods
(d) system.listMethods

19. Which of the following system methods is used to know method signature?
(a) system.listSignature
(b) system.getHelp
(c) system.methodSignature
(d) system.getSignature

20. Which of the following is an extension to XML-RPC?
(a) SOAP (c) FTP
(b) HTTPS (d) Servlet

21. An XML-RPC message is an HTTP ________ message
(a) HEAD (c) GET
(b) POST (d) DELETE

22. Whcih of the following types does not require a <value> element?
(a) int
(b) boolean
(c) date and time
(d) string

23. Which of the following is used to represent integers?
(a) int4 (c) B4
(b) i4 (d) b32

24. How many bits are used to represent integers?
(a) 8 (c) 32
(b) 16 (d) 64

25. How many bits are used to represent floating point numbers?
(a) 8 (c) 32
(b) 16 (d) 64

26. Which of the following is a valid date and time?
(a) D20141015T15:45:00
(b) T15:45:00D20141015
(c) 20141015T15:45:00
(d) 15:45:00D20141015

27. Which of the following elements is used to represent elements of a struct?
(a) <element> (c) <field>
(b) <member> (d) <part>

28. A fault message is represented as
(a) struct (c) boolean
(b) array (d) string

29. Which of the following methods is used to call a remote method?
(a) call() (c) execute()
(b) invoke() (d) refer()

30. What is the default name of the file XmlRpcServlet always
(a) XmlRpcServlet.properties
(b) XmlRpcServlet.xml
(c) XmlRpc.properties
(d) Servlet.properties

31. Which of the following methods is used to start a web server?
(a) run() (c) listen()
(b) init() (d) start()

32. The facility to dynamically get information about the server methods is called
(a) introspection (c) search
(b) reflection (d) digging

Subjective-type Questions

1. Explain XML-RPC architecture.
2. Briefly write the operational principle of XML-RPC.
3. In XML-RPC, which data types are supported?
4. Describe with example how arrays are represented in XML-RPC.
5. How does struct differ from array?
6. For each of the XML-RPC types, write the corresponding Java types.
7. Write with examples the format of XML-RPC request and response messages.
8. What is a fault message? Why is it used?
9. Write briefly the functionality of WebServer class?
10. What are the limitations of WebServer class?
11. Write the relative merits and demerits of WebServer and ServletWebServer
12. What is meant by dynamic proxy with respect to Apache XML-RPC?
13. Explain the usefulness of introspection.
14. Write some of the advantages of XML-RPC.
15. Write some of the limitations of XML-RPC.
16. What happens if a client specifies a nonexistent method name?
17. What are the different ways in which an XML-RPC server can be created?
18. What is the difference between array and struct?
19. How do you represent multi-dimensional arrays?
20. How do you represent raw binary bit-stream?

CHAPTER – 18

JAVA AND SOAP

KEY OBJECTIVES

After completing this chapter readers will be able to—

- understand SOAP architecture
- know the working principle of web service
- learn the format of a SOAP message
- develop, deploy and invoke simple web services
- know how to deploy web services on tomcat
- what asynchronous clients are and how to write them

18.1 INTRODUCTION

Simple **O**bject **A**ccess **P**rotocol (SOAP), as its name implies, is a simple and lightweight mechanism to exchange information between peers. It specifies a modular packaging model to encode information to be changed. Specifically, it uses XML documents, called *SOAP messages*, to represent information.

However, it does not specify any application semantics such as a programming model or implementation specific semantics. As a result SOAP can be used in a wide variety of systems ranging from messaging systems to RPC.

18.2 DIFFERENCES WITH XML-RPC

XML-RPC was designed to be as simple as possible, while allowing complex data structures to be transmitted, processed and returned. In fact, the specification itself is seven pages long, including examples and an FAQ, and is fairly easy to understand. An ordinary programmer, after reading its specification, should not find any difficulty whatsoever in implementing XML-RPC in his/her software.

Simplicity is also XML-RPC's greatest limitation. Though almost all of our RPC needs can be achieved using it, there are certain things that we just can't do such as passing an object to a function, or specifying which portion of a receiving application the message is intended for etc.

SOAP tried to pick up where XML-RPC left off by implementing user defined data types, the ability to specify the recipient, message specific processing control, and other features. Consequently, the SOAP specification became 40 pages long and is complex.

Literally it is not "lightweight" and it threw out the most important feature of XML-RPC, its simplicity. SOAP extensively uses namespaces and attributes specification tags in almost every element of a message. As a result, it incurs significantly more overhead. However, it adds much more information about what is being sent.

18.3 SOAP ARCHITECTURE

SOAP was designed as an object-access protocol by Dave Winer et al. in 1998. Its specification is currently maintained by the XML Protocol Working Group of the World Wide Web Consortium. SOAP architecture consists of three parts:

- The SOAP envelope construct that defines an overall framework to express message content, the message exchangers.
- The SOAP encoding rules that define a mechanism that can be used successfully to exchange application-specific type values.
- The SOAP RPC representation defines a protocol that can be used for remote procedure calls and responses.

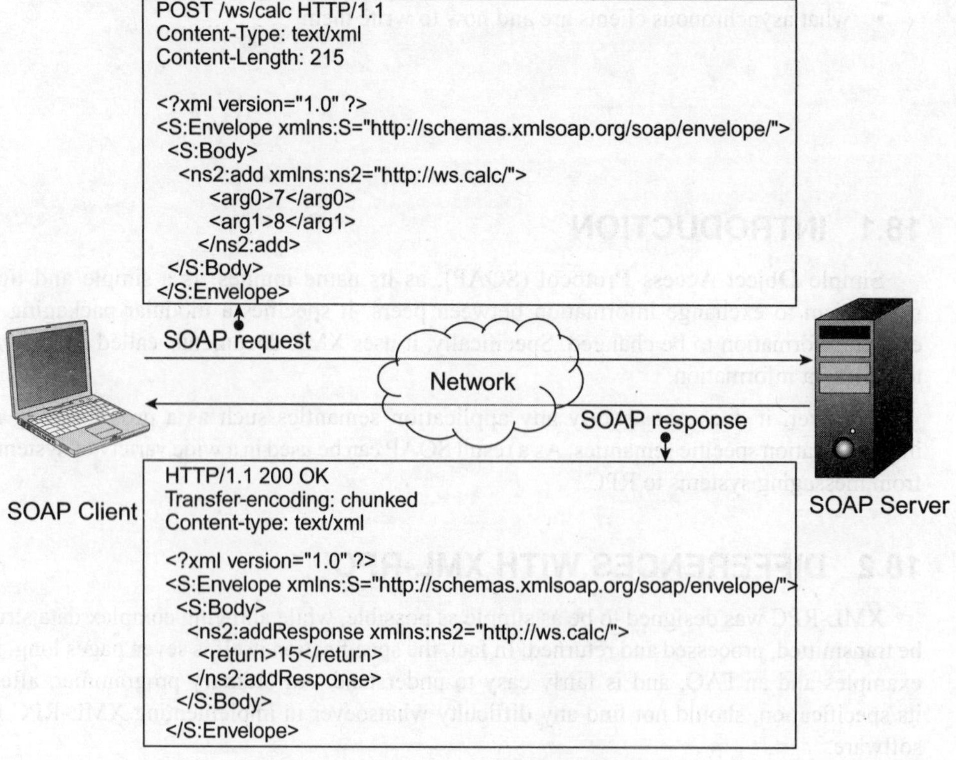
POST /ws/calc HTTP/1.1
Content-Type: text/xml
Content-Length: 215
<?xml version="1.0" ?>
<S:Envelope xmlns:S="http://schemas.xmlsoap.org/soap/envelope/">
<S:Body>
<ns2:add xmlns:ns2="http://ws.calc/">
<arg0>7</arg0>
<arg1>8</arg1>
</ns2:add>
</S:Body>
</S:Envelope>
SOAP request
Network
SOAP response
HTTP/1.1 200 OK
Transfer-encoding: chunked
Content-type: text/xml
<?xml version="1.0" ?>
<S:Envelope xmlns:S="http://schemas.xmlsoap.org/soap/envelope/">
<S:Body>
<ns2:addResponse xmlns:ns2="http://ws.calc/">
<return>15</return>
</ns2:addResponse>
</S:Body>
</S:Envelope>
SOAP Client
SOAP Server

Figure 18.1: RPC using SOAP

This simple idea can potentially be used in combination with a variety of communication protocols, However, the only bindings defined in the specifications so far describe how to use SOAP in combination with HTTP and HTTP Extension Framework.

The RPC part specification describes a standard, XML-based way to encode requests and responses, such as

- Requests to invoke a method including parameters
- Responses from a method including out parameters
- Errors

Figure 18.1: shows how a remote method can be invoked using HTTP POST messages according to SOAP specification.

18.4 SOAP FLAVORS

There are two versions of SOAP specification 1.1 and 1.2. Since these versions are referred to frequently while working with SOAP, it is important to understand the relations between these two. This section outlines the changes and benefits brought by SOAP Version 1.2.

Both SOAP Version 1.1 and 1.2 are standardized by World Wide Web Consortium (W3C). Intuitively, version 1.2 extends the specification version 1.1. Some changes are significant, while other changes are minor. In a single sentence, SOAP Version 1.2 is cleaner, better for web integration, more versatile and faster. The following is a summary of significant changes made in Version 1.2.

- SOAP Version 1.2 provides clear processing model.
- SOAP 1.2's testing and implementation requirements lead to better interoperability.
- SOAP 1.1 is based on XML 1.0. SOAP 1.2 is based on XML Information Set (XML Infoset).
- SOAP 1.2 provides the ability to define transport protocols other than HTTP.
- SOAP 1.2 includes HTTP binding for better integration to the World Wide Web.
- Introduced SOAP with Attachments API for Java (SAAJ) in Version 1.2.
- SOAP Version 1.2 delivers a very well-defined extensibility model.

A detailed list of changes can be found in http://www.w3.org/TR/2001/WD-soap12-20010709/#changes and http://www.w3.org/2003/06/soap11-soap12.html

18.5 SOAP MESSAGES

The primary part of the SOAP is the messaging framework. It specifies a set of XML elements for "packaging" information for exchange between peers. The schema for SOAP messages can be downloaded from `http://schemas.xmlsoap.org/soap/envelope/`.

Any SOAP message is an XML document having the following minimal specification.

- The mandatory root element `<Envelop>`.
- The `<Envelop>` element contains an optional `<Header>` element followed by a mandatory `<Body>` element.

Here is a sample template that shows the structure of a SOAP message:

```
<soap:Envelope xmlns:soap="http://schemas.xmlsoap.org/soap/envelope/">
  <soap:Header> <!-- optional -->
    <!–control information goes here... -->
  </soap:Header>
  <soap:Body>  <!-- mandatory -->
    <!-- payload or Fault element goes here... -->
  </soap:Body>
</soap:Envelope>
```

The elements must always belong to the namespace `http://schemas.xmlsoap.org/soap/envelope/`. The root element `<Envelop>` and namespace together make an XML document a SOAP message. Parsers can simply look at the root element to identify a SOAP message. The `<Envelop>` contains an optional `<Header>` element and one mandatory `<Body>` element that contains payload. Here is a simple SOAP message:

```
<?xml version="1.0" ?>
<soap:Envelope xmlns:soap="http://schemas.xmlsoap.org/soap/envelope/">
  <soap:Body>
    <c:add xmlns:c="http://ws.calc/">
      <arg0>7</arg0>
      <arg1>8</arg1>
    </c:add>
  </soap:Body>
</soap:Envelope>
```

This message represents a call of a method `add()` with two argument values `7` and `8`. The `<Body>` element can have any number of attributes or children elements from any namespace. This is ultimately where the data, which we want to send, goes in.

The receiver of the above message may send the result using another message as follows:

```
<?xml version="1.0" ?>
<soap:Envelope xmlns:soap="http://schemas.xmlsoap.org/soap/envelope/">
  <soap:Body>
    <c:addResponse xmlns:c="http://ws.calc/">
      <return>15</return>
    </c:addResponse>
  </soap:Body>
</soap:Envelope>
```

A SOAP messages can be validated against the underlying schema which can be downloaded from `http://schemas.xmlsoap.org/soap/envelope/`. We downloaded it and put it in a file SOAP.xsd. There are various XML document validators available on the web. We downloaded one such free command line validator from `https://dl.dropbox.com/u/10564628/xsd11-validator.jar`. Suppose the name of the file containing the above SOAP message is `soap.xml`. Then we can check if this XML document is a SOAP message using the following command:

```
java -jar xsd11-validator.jar -sf SOAP.xsd -if soap.xml
```

Like most existing protocols, SOAP also distinguishes controls information and payload. The `<Header>` contains application specific control information. Like `<Body>`, the `<Header>` element can also have any number of attributes or children elements and must be qualified by any namespace (except the SOAP namespace). However, SOAP itself does not specify any built-in headers. These elements influence processing of payload. Here is an example of SOAP message that uses `<Header>` element.

```
<?xml version="1.0" ?>
<soap:Envelope xmlns:soap="http://schemas.xmlsoap.org/soap/envelope/">
  <soap:Header>
    <s:mode xmlns:s="sample">cheque</s:mode>
  </soap:Header>
  <soap:Body>
    <pay>10000</pay>
    <to>B. S. Roy</to>
  </soap:Body>
</soap:Envelope>
```

The body contains an instruction to pay an amount 10000. The header tells that the payment should be made by cheque.

If the receiver of a SOAP message finds anything wrong, it can inform the sender about it by sending a special response message, called *fault message*, back to the sender. The `<Fault>` element is used for this purpose. It is an optional element and if it appears, must be the child of `<Body>` element. This provides a standard error representation that makes possible for a generic architecture to differentiate between success and error. Here is an example of fault message:

```
<?xml version="1.0" ?>
<soap:Envelope xmlns:soap="http://schemas.xmlsoap.org/soap/envelope/">
  <soap:Body>
    <soap:Fault xmlns:ns4="http://www.w3.org/2003/05/soap-envelope">
      <faultcode>soap:Client</faultcode>
      <faultstring>Cannot find dispatch method for
{http://ws.calc/}add1</faultstring>
    </soap:Fault>
  </soap:Body>
</soap:Envelope>
```

This says that an error occurred due to `Client` as it couldn't dispatch method for `add1`. The `<Fault>` element has two mandatory children `<faultcode>` and `<faultstring>`. The former one holds a code for identifying fault and the latter gives a human readable explanation of the fault.

18.6 SOAP BINDING

One of the important features of SOAP is that it enables exchange of messages using various underlying protocols. Since it is not bound to a specific protocol, a communicating peer can choose any suitable protocol for SOAP message transport without affecting the message itself.

However, the only bindings defined in the specifications so far describe how to use SOAP in combination with HTTP and HTTP Extension Framework. HTTP binding maps SOAP request/response message to HTTP request/response message. In the next section, we shall describe how to send SOAP messages over HTTP.

18.7 RPC USING SOAP

Although SOAP was originally intended for exchanging any type of messages, it is primarily used for Remote Procedure Call (RPC). So, it still defines a convention for encapsulating and exchanging RPC calls and responses. Here is a sample HTTP SOAP request message.

```
POST /ws/calc HTTP/1.1
Accept: text/xml, multipart/related
Content-Type: text/xml; charset=utf-8
SOAPAction: "http://ws.calc/Calculator/addRequest"
User-Agent: JAX-WS RI 2.2.4-b01
Host: 172.16.5.81:9999
Connection: keep-alive
Content-Length: 215

<?xml version="1.0" ?>
<S:Envelope xmlns:S="http://schemas.xmlsoap.org/soap/envelope/">
  <S:Body>
    <ns2:add xmlns:ns2="http://ws.calc/">
      <arg0>4</arg0>
      <arg1>3</arg1>
    </ns2:add>
  </S:Body>
</S:Envelope>
```

A SOAP request message is an HTTP POST request message with two mandatory headers `Content-Type` and `Content-Length`. The body of the HTTP request message is a SOAP message which represents the call of a method add with two arguments 4 and 3. The corresponding response method may look like this:

```
HTTP/1.1 200 OK
Transfer-encoding: chunked
Content-type: text/xml; charset=utf-8
Date: Sun, 30 Mar 2014 07:53:06 GMT

<?xml version="1.0" ?>
<S:Envelope xmlns:S="http://schemas.xmlsoap.org/soap/envelope/">
  <S:Body>
    <ns2:addResponse xmlns:ns2="http://ws.calc/">
      <return>7</return>
    </ns2:addResponse>
  </S:Body>
</S:Envelope>
```

Here, the body of the HTTP request message is also a SOAP message which represents the return value 7 from the server.

18.8 WEB SERVICE

A *web service*, as its name suggests, is an application component that provides a service which is available over the web. An application that uses this service is called service consumer/client. The communication (request and response) between a service provider and a consumer takes place through XML messages. Since, XML is used as a communication language, web service is independent of any programming language, operating system.

Usually, web services are built on the top of HTTP and SOAP messages are used for communication. The description (operations offered, message formats, bindings, location etc.) of a web service is provided as an XML document which is written in a language called **W**eb **S**ervice **D**escription **L**anguage (WSDL). In the following section, we shall discuss how to develop, deploy and use a simple web service using Java.

18.9 JAX-WS

Java **A**PI for **X**ML **W**eb **S**ervices (JAX-WS) is an Application Programming Interface (API) for developing web services and clients. It is one of the Java XML programming APIs. JAX-WS web services and clients use SOAP messages for communication and HTTP for message transport.

The web service developer specifies the operations by defining methods in a Java interface and also provides implementation of those methods. A client creates a proxy (a local object representing the service) and then simply calls methods on the proxy. JAX-WS runtime system converts the calls and responses to and from SOAP messages. The developer need not generate or parse SOAP messages. The JAX-WS runtime hides the internal complexity from the application developer.

Though, JAX-WS is a part of the Java EE, it can also be used in Java SE version 6 and onwards. The reason of including JAX-WS in Java SE is that it does not require any servlet of EJB container. This also makes HTTP a competitor of RMI as a distributed computing technology. We shall start with some examples to demonstrate how to develop, deploy and use simple web services using the Java SE 7.0 environment. We shall then show how to use tomcat to work with web service. An overview of the JAX-WS packages can be found in Table 18.1:

Table 18.1: Primary JAX-WS package with short description

Package	Description
javax.jws	APIs for Java to WSDL mapping annotations
javax.jws.soap	APIs for mapping the Web Service to SOAP

(*Contd*)

Table 18.1: (*Contd*)

javax.xml.ws	The Core JAX-WS APIs
javax.xml.ws.http	APIs for XML/HTTP Binding
javax.xml.ws.handler	APIs for message handlers
javax.xml.ws.soap	APIs for SOAP/HTTP Binding
javax.xml.ws.spi	SPIs for JAX-WS
javax.xml.ws.spi.http	HTTP SPI used for portable deployment of JAX-WS in containers
javax.xml.ws.wsaddressing	APIs for WS-Addressing

Note that JAX-WS programming model extends the foundation provided by the Java API for XML-based RPC (JAX-RPC) programming model. It was introduced to simplify developing web services and clients and provides greater platform independence for Java applications by the use of dynamic proxies and Java annotations. The tools included in this model support JAX-WS 2.0, 2.1, and 2.2.

The JAX-WS strategically aligns itself with the current industry trend. It extensively uses a document-centric messaging model which essentially replaces the remote procedure call programming model as specified by JAX-RPC. However, it still supports the JAX-RPC programming model and applications. It introduced some new features that were absent in JAX-RPC some of which are mentioned below:

- Better platform independence for Java applications
- Annotations
- Invoking Web services asynchronously
- Data binding with JAXB 2.2
- Dynamic and static clients
- Message Transmission Optimization Mechanism (MTOM)
- Multiple payload structures
- SOAP 1.2 support
- Support for method parameters and return types

18.9.1 Developing Web Service

We shall develop a web service for our calculator application. In this web service, we shall not explore the sophisticated features of JAX-WS. Instead, we shall concentrate on how to write and invoke a web service. The discussion about the extended features may be found later in this chapter.

Our web service will have a single operation `add()`. We first write an interface `Calculator` as follows:

```
package calc.ws;
import javax.jws.WebMethod;
import javax.jws.WebService;
import javax.jws.soap.SOAPBinding;
import javax.jws.soap.SOAPBinding.Style;

//Service Endpoint Interface
@WebService
@SOAPBinding(style = Style.RPC)
public interface Calculator {
  @WebMethod public int add(int a, int b);
}
```

Writing an endpoint interface is not always required. However, it makes testing and using the web service from other Java clients far easier. This is an ordinary Java interface except that it uses some annotations. JAX-WS uses annotations extensively, to simplify the development and deployment of web service.

An interface, to be a web service interface, must be annotated by `@WebService`. The `@SOAPBinding` annotation maps this web service to SOAP. The element `style` instructs to use RPC encoding style for messages sent to and from the web service. Note that SOAP supports two kinds of encoding: *RPC style* and *document style*. The default is document.

The `@WebMethod` tells that the method `add()` has to be exposed as a web service operation. Although the specification says that the annotation is mandatory, often the code runs without it. The exposed method must be public. The interface is ready and acts as a contract between the web service and the client. The next step is to write an implementation of this interface.

```
package calc.ws;
import javax.jws.WebService;
//Service Implementation
@WebService(endpointInterface = "calc.ws.Calculator")
public class SimpleCalculator implements Calculator {
  @Override
  public int add(int a, int b) {
    System.out.println("Received: " + a + " and " + b);
    int result = a + b;
    System.out.println("Sent: " + result);
    return result;
  }
}
```

This class defines the method `add()` declared in `Calculator` interface. When a class implements an endpoint interface, it is mandatory to use a `@WebService` annotation with a `endpointInteface` element specifying the fully qualified name of the interface. In the above implementation class, `endpointInterface` element tells that the name of the service endpoint interface defining the service's contract is `calc.ws.Calculator`.

18.9.2 Deploying Web Service

JAX-WS includes a class `javax.xml.ws.Endpoint` to easily publish and configure a web service. We do not need a container to deploy a web service. Instead, we can end up with a bootstrap class that calls one of the `publish()` method of `Endpoint` class. This bootstrap class may be the same service implementation or a different class. We shall use a separate class for publishing web service. Here is the essential line of code in the bootstrap class:

```
Endpoint.publish("http://172.16.5.81:6789/ws/calc", new SimpleCalculator());
```

This essentially publishes an endpoint for `SimpleCalculator` object with the URL `http://172.16.5.81:6789/ws/calc`. The necessary server infrastructure is created by the JAX-WS implementation and configured using some default configuration. For custom configuration, we can use other overloaded methods of `Endpoint` class. We assume that the IP address of the machine publishing this web service is 172.16.5.81. If you have a different address, change it.

The following is a complete source code (`CalculatorPublisher.java`) of the web service publisher:

```
import calc.ws.*;
import javax.xml.ws.Endpoint;
public class CalculatorPublisher {
  public static void main(String[] args) {
```

```
   Endpoint.publish("http://172.16.5.81:6789/ws/calc", new
SimpleCalculator());
   }
}
```

To compile and run the programs, create the following directory structure.

```
pub
 ├─CalculatorPublisher.java
 ├─calc
 └──ws
        Calculator.java
        SimpleCalculator.java
```

Go to the directory `pub` and use the following command to compile all classes:

```
javac calc\ws\*.java *.java
```

To publish the web service, run the publisher using the following command

```
java CalculatorPublisher
```

You can check if the web service is published successfully or not by typing the following URL in a web browser:

```
http://172.16.5.81:6789/ws/calc
```

If everything goes well, the browser's screen looks as shown in Figure. 18.2:

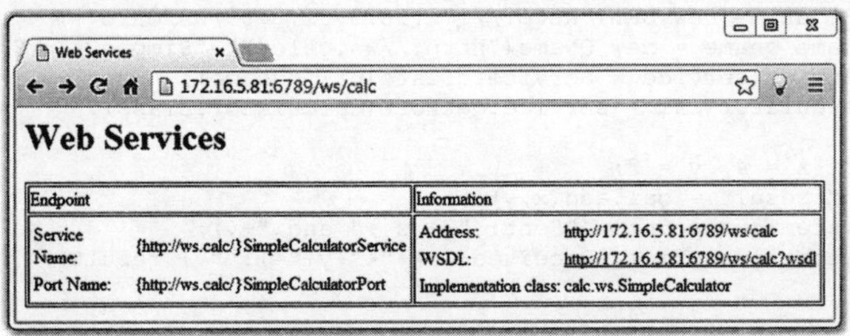

Figure 18.2: Web services screen

Note that in practice, we hardly use `Endpoint` class to publish a web service; instead application server is used for publishing the web services based on your web service SEI and other classes. We shall see how to publish a web service using Apache's tomcat servlet container later in this chapter.

18.9.3 Invoking Web Service

To invoke a web service, a client first creates a `Service` object that encapsulates a web service, which is a set of related ports. A port, in turn, includes a port type, bound to a particular protocol, and a particular endpoint address. A `Service` object is usually created from WSDL contract which is available via WSDL URL.

In this section, we shall create the `Service` object manually using its static `create()` method and the next section describes how to create it from WSDL using `wsimport` command. The `create()` method has many overloaded versions. The commonly used one takes a URL and a QName as follows:

```
URL url = new URL("http://172.16.5.81:6789/ws/calc");
QName qname = new QName("http://ws.calc/", "SimpleCalculatorService");

Service service = Service.create(url, qname);
```

The first argument specifies the location of the web service's WSDL file and the second gives the qualified name of the web service. Since this Service is created from a WSDL file, the port(s)

binding ID, QName, and endpoint address are known to the Service. Anyway, this `Service` object is then used to create a local proxy to the web service:

```
Calculator cal = service.getPort(Calculator.class);
```

The parameter specifies the service endpoint interface that is supported by the returned proxy. Since, endpoint interface for the `SimpleCalculator` web service is `Calculator`, we have specified it. Note that JAX-WS runtime system selects protocol binding (and a port) and configures the proxy accordingly. The returned proxy should not be reconfigured by the client further. Note that to run the client, service endpoint interface `Calculator` is needed. However, it is not difficult to obtain/create this endpoint interface. There are also ways to write a client program without using the endpoint interface. We shall discuss this method in the next section.

Invoking an operation on the web service is now as simple as invoking a method on a local object:

```
int x = 4, y = 3;
int result = cal.add(x,y);
```

The complete source code of the client (`CalculatorClient.java`) is shown below:

```
import java.net.URL;
import javax.xml.namespace.QName;
import javax.xml.ws.Service;
import calc.ws.*;
public class CalculatorClient {
  public static void main(String[] args) throws Exception {
    URL url = new URL("http://172.16.5.81:6789/ws/calc");
    QName qname = new QName("http://ws.calc/", "SimpleCalculatorService");
    Service service = Service.create(url, qname);
    Calculator cal = service.getPort(Calculator.class);

    int x = 4, y = 3;
    int result = cal.add(x,y);
    System.out.println("Sent: " + x +" and "+y);
    System.out.print("Received("+x+"+"+y+"=): " + result);
  }
}
```

Create the following directory structure in a machine for the web service client.

```
client
  │ CalculatorClient.java
  └──calc
       └─ws
              Calculator.java
```

Note that the service endpoint interface Calculator.java is needed by this client. Had there been a provision, you may download it or may write one such interface manually. Open a terminal, go to the `client` directory and use thje following command to compile client files:

```
javac calc\ws\*.java *.java
```

Now, execute the client to invoke the web service as follows:

```
java CalculatorClient
```

A sample result is shown in Figure 18.3:

Figure 18.3: Web service (i) Publisher (ii) Consumer

18.9.4 Tracking SOAP messages

If you want to see the underlying SOAP messages at the publisher side, insert the following line of code in `CalculatorPublisher.java`:

```
System.setProperty("com.sun.xml.internal.ws.transport.http.HttpAdapter.dump",
"true");
```

Similarly, insert the following line of code to see SOAP messages at the client side:

```
System.setProperty("com.sun.xml.internal.ws.transport.http.client.HttpTransport
Pipe.dump", "true");
```

You will see that the client sends a SOAP message which looks like this:

```
<?xml version="1.0" ?>
<S:Envelope xmlns:S="http://schemas.xmlsoap.org/soap/envelope/">
  <S:Body>
    <ns2:add xmlns:ns2="http://ws.calc/">
      <arg0>4</arg0>
      <arg1>3</arg1><
    /ns2:add>
  </S:Body>
</S:Envelope>
```

The web service responds with the following SOAP message:

```
<?xml version="1.0" ?>
<S:Envelope xmlns:S="http://schemas.xmlsoap.org/soap/envelope/">
  <S:Body>
    <ns2:addResponse xmlns:ns2="http://ws.calc/">
      <return>7</return>
    </ns2:addResponse>
  </S:Body>
</S:Envelope>
```

To check that the communication really takes place using SOAP messages, we may write a simple Java socket program. The following is a sample socket program that sends a SOAP request message directly to the web service:

```
import java.io.*;
import java.net.*;
class SoapClient {
  public static void main(String args[]) throws Exception {
    int c;
    Socket socket = new Socket("172.16.5.81", 6789);
    InputStream in = socket.getInputStream();
    OutputStream out = socket.getOutputStream();
    InputStream fin = new FileInputStream(args[0]);
    while(((c = fin.read()) != -1)) out.write((char)c);
    while(((c = in.read()) != -1))
      System.out.print((char)c);
    in.close();
  }
}
```

To run this program, create a file (say `request.txt`) containing a HTTP SOAP request message as follows:

```
POST /ws/calc HTTP/1.1
Content-Type: text/xml; charset=utf-8
Content-Length: 215

<?xml version="1.0" ?>
<S:Envelope xmlns:S="http://schemas.xmlsoap.org/soap/envelope/">
  <S:Body>
    <ns2:add xmlns:ns2="http://ws.calc/">
```

```
      <arg0>4</arg0>
      <arg1>3</arg1>
    </ns2:add>
  </S:Body>
</S:Envelope>
```

We can now invoke the web service from this socket program using the following command:

```
java SoapClient request.txt
```

You will see an output similar to as shown below:

```
HTTP/1.1 200 OK
Transfer-encoding: chunked
Content-type: text/xml; charset=utf-8
Date: Sun, 25 May 2014 06:40:35 GMT

c5
<?xml version="1.0" ?>
<S:Envelopexmlns:S="http://schemas.xmlsoap.org/soap/envelope/">
  <S:Body>
    <ns2:addResponse xmlns:ns2="http://ws.calc/">
      <return>7</return>
    </ns2:addResponse>
  </S:Body>
</S:Envelope>
```

Note that we hardly create SOAP messages explicitly in our program. Instead, we use JAX-WS API to invoke web service. JAX-WS runtime system converts the calls and responses to and from SOAP messages. The example given above will help you understanding how the JAX-WS runtime internally works.

18.9.5 Using WSDL

WSDL is used to develop XML files that specify rules for communication between different systems such as:

- How one system can talk to another system
- Which specific data are needed in the request
- What would be the structure of the XML file containing data
- What error messages to display when a certain rule for communication is not observed, to make troubleshooting easier

Web service publisher generates WSDL document for the clients, who can inspect this document to gather knowledge about the syntax of calling the web service. When we published our web service using `publish()` method of `Endpoint` class, a WSDL document was also generated which can be accessed using the URL `http://172.16.5.81:6789/ws/calc?wsdl`. In general, for a web service endpoint URL `U`, the location of the WSDL file will be `U?wsdl`. The WSDL file looks like this:

```
<!--
 Published by JAX-WS RI at http://jax-ws.dev.java.net. RI's version is JAX-WS
 RI 2.2.4-b01.
-->
<!--
 Generated by JAX-WS RI at http://jax-ws.dev.java.net. RI's version is JAX-WS
 RI 2.2.4-b01.
-->
<definitions xmlns:wsu="http://docs.oasis-open.org/wss/2004/01/oasis-200401-
wss-wssecurity-
utility-1.0.xsd" xmlns:wsp="http://www.w3.org/ns/ws-
policy"xmlns:wsp1_2="http://schemas.xmlsoap.org/ws/2004/09/policy" xmlns:
wsam="http://www.w3.o
rg/2007/05/addressing/metadata"xmlns:soap="http://schemas.xmlsoap.org/wsdl
```

```
/soap/" xmlns:tns="h
ttp://ws.calc/" xmlns:xsd="http://www.w3.org/2001/XMLSchema" xmlns="http:
//schemas.xmlsoap.org
/wsdl/"targetNamespace="http://ws.calc/" name="SimpleCalculatorService">
  <types/>
  <message name="add">
    <part name="arg0" type="xsd:int"/>
    <part name="arg1" type="xsd:int"/>
  </message>
  <message name="addResponse">
    <part name="return" type="xsd:int"/>
  </message>
  <portType name="Calculator">
    <operation name="add" parameterOrder="arg0 arg1">
      <input wsam:Action="http://ws.calc/Calculator/addRequest" message="tns:
      add"/>
      <output wsam:Action="http://ws.calc/Calculator/addResponse" message="tns:
      addResponse"/>
    </operation>
  </portType>
  <binding name="SimpleCalculatorPortBinding" type="tns:Calculator">
    <soap:binding transport="http://schemas.xmlsoap.org/soap/http" style="rpc"/>
    <operation name="add">
    <soap:operation soapAction=""/>
    <input>
     <soap:body use="literal" namespace="http://ws.calc/"/>
    </input>
    <output>
     <soap:body use="literal" namespace="http://ws.calc/"/>
    </output>
   </operation>
  </binding>
  <service name="SimpleCalculatorService">
    <port name="SimpleCalculatorPort" binding="tns:SimpleCalculatorPortBinding">
    <soap:address location="http://172.16.5.81:6789/ws/calc"/>
    </port>
  </service>
</definitions>
```

In a nutshell it defines one operation `add()` which takes two int arguments and returns the sum of them. This WSDL file can be used to generate helper classes such as Service Endpoint Interface (SEI), Service and Exception classes etc. using the application `wsimport`. These classes are popularly known as *portable artifacts* (or simply artifacts). The `wsimport` takes URL of WSDL file as a parameter, and generates a set of files, structured in a directory tree. In order to create these artifacts, create a directory (say client1), open a terminal, go to this directory and use the following command to generate JAX-WS artifacts:

```
wsimport -keep http://172.16.5.81:6789/ws/calc?wsdl
```

This will generate the Java artifacts and compile them by importing the `http://172.16.5.81:6789/ws/calc?wsdl`. A sample output of this command is shown below:

```
parsing WSDL...
Generating code...
Compiling code...
```

A sample directory after creating artifacts is shown here:

```
client1
└─calc
  └─ws
        Calculator.class
        Calculator.java
        SimpleCalculatorService.class
        SimpleCalculatorService.java
```

The -keep option tells not to delete (keep) the source artifacts. You may use this option to inspect the generated files. The SEI is Calculator.java and Service class is SimpleCalculatorService.java. The name of the source file representing a service is generally named as <classname>Service.java. The generated service class has many public constructors including a no-argument constructor. This no-argument constructor is used most often which uses WSDL location and service name from the WSDL file.

Developing the client using these artifacts is very easy. We first create a service as follows:

```
SimpleCalculatorService calcService = new SimpleCalculatorService();
```

The service class also has methods each of which returns a local proxy, called *dynamic proxy*, of service implementation. We get a reference to this proxy as follows:

```
Calculator cal = calcService.getSimpleCalculatorPort();
```

The complete source code of the client is shown below:

```
import calc.ws.*;
public class CalculatorClient {
  public static void main(String[] args) {
    SimpleCalculatorService calcService = new SimpleCalculatorService();
    Calculator cal = calcService.getSimpleCalculatorPort();
    int x = 4, y = 3;
    int result = cal.add(x,y);
    System.out.println("Sent: " + x +" and "+y);
    System.out.print("Received("+x+"+"+y+"=): " + result);
  }
}
```

You can now run this client exactly as before.

Since, in the above example, a client generates artifacts from WSDL document, the web service need not implement an interface and may be coded as:

```
package calc.ws;
import javax.jws.*;
import javax.jws.soap.SOAPBinding;
import javax.jws.soap.SOAPBinding.Style;
@WebService
@SOAPBinding(style = Style.RPC)
public class SimpleCalculator {
  @WebMethod public int add(int a, int b) {
    System.out.println("Received: " + a + " and " + b);
    int result = a + b;
    System.out.println("Sent: " + result);
    return result;
  }
}
```

Deploy it using Endpoint class as before. If you now generate the client artifacts in a directory client2, using wsimport, the following files are generated:

```
client2
└─calc
  └─ws
        SimpleCalculator.class
        SimpleCalculator.java
        SimpleCalculatorService.class
        SimpleCalculatorService.java
```

With these artifacts, the client code in the client2 directory will look like this:

```
import calc.ws.*;
public class CalculatorClient {
  public static void main(String[] args) {
    SimpleCalculatorService calcService = new SimpleCalculatorService();
```

```
      SimpleCalculator cal = calcService.getSimpleCalculatorPort();
      int x = 4, y = 3;
      int result = cal.add(x,y);
      System.out.println("Sent: " + x +" and "+y);
      System.out.print("Received("+x+"+"+y+"=): " + result);
    }
  }
```

In the subsequent sections, we shall use the above implementation of our `SimpleCalculator` class.

18.9.6 Document Style

In the previous examples, we used RPC Style for our SOAP Binding. Actually, there are two different ways to encode and construct SOAP messages: *RPC style* and *Document style*. In short, RPC style SOAP messages contain an XML representation of the method's call in their body. This XML representation uses the name of the method and its parameters.

The WSDL document for RPC style merely tells us how to construct a SOAP message. Consider the WSDL document fragment or our previous web service:

```
...
<message name="add">
  <part name="arg0" type="xsd:int"/>
  <part name="arg1" type="xsd:int"/>
</message>
<message name="addResponse">
  <part name="return" type="xsd:int"/>
</message>
...
  <binding name="SimpleCalculatorPortBinding" type="tns:Calculator">
    <soap:binding transport="http://schemas.xmlsoap.org/soap/http" style="rpc"/>
```

It tells us that to call a method add, SOAP body should contain an XML document fragment as follows:

```
<add>
  <arg0>4</arg0>
  <arg1>3</arg1>
</add>
```

However, there is no provision to verify this XML representation.

In Document style, the SOAP body contains an XML document that can be validated against a defined XML schema. Since, this style relies on the pre-defined schema to determine the structure of the SOAP message, it is a more customizable and flexible approach than RPC style. In this section, we shall rewrite our `SimpleCalculator` web service using document style. Using document style web service is very easy. Simply include `@SOAPBinding` annotation as follows:

```
@SOAPBinding(style = Style.DOCUMENT)
```

Actually, `@SOAPBinding` annotation is optional and the default style is document. So, if the annotation is absent, the style is assumed to document.

The WSDL document fragment for this web service looks like this:

```
...
<xsd:schema>
<xsd:import namespace="http://ws.calc/"
schemaLocation="http://172.16.5.81:6789/ws/calc?xsd=1"/>
</xsd:schema>
...
<message name="add">
  <part name="parameters" element="tns:add"/>
</message>
<message name="addResponse">
```

```
  <part name="parameters" element="tns:add"/>
</message>
<message name="addResponse">
  <part name="parameters" element="tns:addResponse"/>
</message>
…
<soap:binding transport="http://schemas.xmlsoap.org/soap/http"
style="document"/>
…
```

It tells that XML document in the SOAP request and response can be validated against the XML schema which can be downloaded from `http://172.16.5.81:6789/ws/calc?xsd=1`. We downloaded it and it looks like:

```
<xs:schema xmlns:tns="http://ws.calc/"
xmlns:xs="http://www.w3.org/2001/XMLSchema" version="1.0"
targetNamespace="http://ws.calc/">
  <xs:element name="add" type="tns:add"/>
  <xs:element name="addResponse" type="tns:addResponse"/>
  <xs:complexType name="add">
    <xs:sequence>
      <xs:element name="arg0" type="xs:int"/>
      <xs:element name="arg1" type="xs:int"/>
    </xs:sequence>
  </xs:complexType>
  <xs:complexType name="addResponse">
    <xs:sequence>
      <xs:element name="return" type="xs:int"/>
    </xs:sequence>
  </xs:complexType>
</xs:schema>
```

This schema helps us to create XML document in the SOAP message on the fly. You can also generate WSDL and schema from implementation class using the following command:

```
wsgen -keep -wsdl -cp . calc.ws.SimpleCalculator
```

It generates `SimpleCalculatorService.wsdl` (WSDL file) and `SimpleCalculatorService_schema1.xsd` (schema) files.

18.9.7 Using tomcat to deploy web service

Usually, a web service runs under the supervision of a servlet container such as Tomcat, JBoss etc. We need to perform the following steps, at a minimum:

- Create the web application deployment descriptor (web.xml) and a proprietary web service deployment descriptor (for example, sun-jaxws.xml).
- Package generated artifacts, service implementation class and those descriptors into a web archive (.war file).
- Deploy the .war archive into the servlet container.

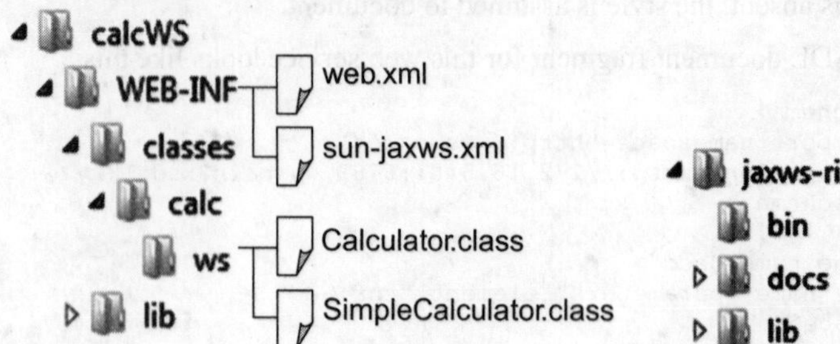

To deploy a JAX-WS Web Service using tomcat, we need JAX-WS API that can be downloaded from `https://jax-ws.java.net/`. We downloaded `jaxws-ri-2.2.8.zip` and when unzipped, the following directory structure was created. The API jars can be found in `jaxws-ri/lib`. Create a web application directory (say `calcWS`) in tomcat's `webapps` directory. The API jars may be copied in the application's lib (i.e. `calcWS/WEB-INF/lib`) directory. In that case, the jars will be only available to the including web application. If you want them available from all applications, place those jar files in tomcat's `lib` directory. We placed them in the application's `lib` directory.

Now we create a standard web deployment descriptor `web.xml` for the deployment. It specifies `WSServletContextListener` as listener class and `WSServlet` as servlet class. A sample `web.xml` is shown below:

```
<?xml version="1.0" encoding="ISO-8859-1"?>
<web-app xmlns="http://xmlns.jcp.org/xml/ns/javaee"
  xmlns:xsi="http://www.w3.org/2001/XMLSchema-instance"
  xsi:schemaLocation="http://xmlns.jcp.org/xml/ns/javaee
                      http://xmlns.jcp.org/xml/ns/javaee/web-app_3_1.xsd"
  version="3.1"
  metadata-complete="true">
  <listener>
    <listener-class>
      com.sun.xml.ws.transport.http.servlet.WSServletContextListener
    </listener-class>
  </listener>
  <servlet>
    <servlet-name>ws</servlet-name>
    <servlet-class>
      com.sun.xml.ws.transport.http.servlet.WSServlet
    </servlet-class>
  </servlet>
    <servlet-mapping>
      <servlet-name>ws</servlet-name>
      <url-pattern>/ws</url-pattern>
    </servlet-mapping>
</web-app>
```

Note that in the current tomcat version 8.0, the use of web deployment descriptor `web.xml` is not mandatory. It works fine without `web.xml` file. Since, older versions needs this file, we have used it for illustration.

We then create a web service deployment descriptor. The name of this file for JAX-WS is `sun-jaxws.xml`. A sample file is shown below:

```
<?xml version="1.0" encoding="UTF-8"?>
<endpoints xmlns="http://java.sun.com/xml/ns/jax-ws/ri/runtime" version="2.0">
  <endpoint name="Calculator" implementation="calc.ws.SimpleCalculator"
    url-pattern="/ws/calc"/>
</endpoints>
```

This essentially tells that for URL pattern `ws/calc`, the corresponding implementation class is `calc.ws.SimpleCalculator`.

Now, start the tomcat . If everything goes fine, our web service will be deployed successfully and the following message appears:

```
...
INFO: Deploying web application directory D:\apache-tomcat-8.0.0-
RC1\webapps\calcWS
Apr 08, 2014 10:10:7 AM com.sun.xml.ws.transport.http.servlet.WSServletDelegate
<init>
INFO: WSSERVLET14: JAX-WS servlet initializing
Apr 08, 2014 10:10:7 AM
```

```
com.sun.xml.ws.transport.http.servlet.WSServletContextListener
contextInitialized
INFO: WSSERVLET12: JAX-WS context listener initializing
Apr 08, 2014 10:10:7 AM
com.sun.xml.ws.transport.http.servlet.WSServletContextListener
contextInitialized
INFO: WSSERVLET12: JAX-WS context listener initializing
…
```

This can be verified by typing the following URL at the address bar of a web browser:

```
http://172.16.5.81:9090/calcWS/ws/calc
```

You can now create a consumer of this web service as discussed earlier.

18.9.8 Using Ant to build war file

If you want to build a web archive (WAR) file, create the following directory structure. Place all JAR files from `jaxws-ri/lib` in `calcWS/WebContent/WEB-INF/lib` directory.

```
calcWS
   build.xml
 ├─src
 │  └─calc
 │     └─ws
 │          Calculator.java
 │          SimpleCalculator.java
 └── WebContent
     └─WEB-INF
        │    sun-jaxws.xml
        │    web.xml
        └─lib
```

There are various tools to build a web archive. We shall use the well-known Apache ant which needs a build file (`build.xml`). The following is a sample ant `build.xml` file:

```
<project name="calcWS" default="war" basedir=".">
  <description>Web Services build file</description>
  <!-- set global properties for this build -->
  <property name="src" location="src"/>
  <property name="build" location="build"/>
  <property name="dist"  location="dist"/>
  <property name="webcontent"  location="WebContent"/>

  <target name="compile" description="compile the source " >
   <mkdir dir="${build}"/>
   <!-- Compile the java code from ${src} into ${build} -->
   <javac srcdir="${src}" destdir="${build}"/>
  </target>

  <target name="war" depends="compile" description="generate war" >
    <!-- Create the war distribution directory -->
    <mkdir dir="${dist}/war"/>
    <!-- Follow standard WAR structure -->
    <copy todir="${dist}/war/build/"><fileset dir="${webcontent}"/></copy>
    <copy todir="${dist}/war/build/WEB-INF/classes/"><fileset
dir="${build}"/></copy>

    <jar jarfile="${dist}/war/calcWS.war" basedir="${dist}/war/build/"/>
  </target>

</project>
```

Open a terminal, go the directory `calcWS` and use the following command to build the WAR file:

```
ant
```

Make sure that the `ant` application is in our PATH environment variable. If everything goes fine, the following message appears:

```
Buildfile: E:\ajp\soap\calcWS\build.xml

compile:
    [mkdir] Created dir: E:\ajp\soap\calcWS\build
    [javac] Compiling 2 source files to E:\ajp\soap\calcWS\build

war:
    [mkdir] Created dir: E:\ajp\soap\calcWS\dist\war
     [copy] Copying 31 files to E:\ajp\soap\calcWS\dist\war\build
     [copy] Copying 2 files to E:\ajp\soap\calcWS\dist\war\build\WEB-
INF\classes

      [jar] Building jar: E:\ajp\soap\calcWS\dist\war\calcWS.war

BUILD SUCCESSFUL
Total time: 2 seconds
```

The war file `calcWS.war` is stored in `calcWS/dist/war/` directory. Place this file in tomcat's `webapps` directory and restart the server. The SimpleCalculator web service will be deployed.

18.9.9 Asynchronous Client

The clients that we have written so far are called *synchronous* clients as they wait for the response to return. If processing of request takes a very long time, a synchronous client cannot continue its work. Fortunately, JAX-WS provides a feature called *asynchronous* request–response that allows a client application to continue its work and handle the response later on. This section describes how to create a client that asynchronously invokes an `add()` operation in a calculator web service.

When using asynchronous request-response, a client, instead of invoking the operation directly, invokes an asynchronous flavor of the same operation. The SEI, we generated so far, does not have asynchronous methods included in the interface. We use JAX-WS bindings to add the asynchronous callback or polling methods on the interface. To generate a service endpoint interface having such asynchronous methods, we use `enableAsyncMapping` binding declaration. There are two ways to specify binding declarations. In the first approach, all binding declarations are written in a separate document, called an *external binding file*. In the second approach, the binding declarations are embedded directly inside a WSDL document.

Using external binding file

A sample external binding file (`bind.xml`) at minimum, is shown below:

```
<!--bind.xml-->
<bindings xmlns="http://java.sun.com/xml/ns/jaxws">
  <enableAsyncMapping>true</enableAsyncMapping>
</bindings>
```

The `<bindings>` element is used as a container for JAX-WS binding declaration. The elements must belong to the `http://java.sun.com/xml/ns/jaxws` namespace. The only child element `<enableAsyncMapping>` indicates that asynchronous methods should be generated. We then use the following command to create artifacts:

```
wsimport -b bind.xml -keep http://172.16.5.81:6789/ws/calc?wsdl
```

The file containing JAX-WS binding information is specified using `-b` option of `wsimport` tool.

Using embedded binding

The binding declaration may be written inside the WSDL file directly on any of the following nodes.

- <definitions>—Applies to all operations of all portType attributes.
- <portType>—Applies to all operations in the portType.
- <operation>—Applies to the operation only.

Download the WSDL file from `http://172.16.5.81:6789/ws/calc?wsdl` and save it in a file `calc.xml` (say). Now, modify this file as follows:

```
<portType name="SimpleCalculator">
  <bindings xmlns="http://java.sun.com/xml/ns/jaxws">
    <enableAsyncMapping>true</enableAsyncMapping>
  </bindings>
...
</portType>
```

The inserted code is shown using bold face. Use the following command to generate the artifacts:

```
wsimport -keep calc.xml
```

Either case, it generates the following asynchronous methods along with the normal synchronous methods in the resultant service endpoint interface `SimpleCalculator`.

```
public int add(int arg0, int arg1);
public Response<Integer> addAsync(int arg0, int arg1);
public Future<?> addAsync(int arg0, int arg1, AsyncHandler<Integer>
asyncHandler);
```

For clarity the annotations have been removed from the actual declaration. JAX-WS supports two models to invoke methods asynchronously: *polling* and *callback*. The first is for ordinary synchronous method and the last two are asynchronous polling and callback methods respectively. We have omitted the annotations for better clarity. Asynchronous invocations require special consideration. For example, instead of invoking the method `add()` directly, we invoke `addAsync()` method.

18.9.9.1 Polling

Consider the second method generated by `wsimport` application:

```
public Response<Integer> addAsync(int arg0, int arg1);
```

In the polling method, a client typically invokes this asynchronous method as follows.

```
SimpleCalculator cal = ...
int x = 4, y = 3;
Response<Integer> response = cal.addAsync(x,y);
```

This method `addAsync()` does not block the client and lets client to continue its own work. The client periodically checks for a response by polling the returned `Response` object. The response is available when `isDone()` method of this object returns `true`. The following code segment illustrates this:

```
while (!response.isDone()) {
  // do something here
}
```

When this loop exits (i.e. response is available), the client gets the result using `get()` method of `Response` as follows:

```
int result = response.get();
```

The complete source code of the client that used polling is shown below:

```
import javax.xml.ws.*;
import async.client.*;
public class CalculatorClientPoll {
  public static void main(String[] args) {
    SimpleCalculatorService calcService = new SimpleCalculatorService();
    SimpleCalculator cal = calcService.getSimpleCalculatorPort();
    int x = 4, y = 3;
    Response<Integer>  response = cal.addAsync(x,y);
    System.out.println("Sent: " + x +" and "+y);
```

```
    try {
      while (!response.isDone()) {
        Thread.sleep(10);
        System.out.println("Printing a message");
      }
      int result = response.get();
      System.out.print("Received("+x+"+"+y+"=): " + result);
    }catch(Exception e) {e.printStackTrace();}
  }
}
```

The `sleep()` method is merely used to avoid printing too many messages on the screen. When executed, this client produced the following result:

```
Sent: 4 and 3
Printing a message
Printing a message
Printing a message
Received(4+3=): 7
```

This implies that the client was printing a message after requesting the service. After some time, the client receives the result from the service, prints and exits.

18.9.9.2 Callback

In this model of method invocation, the client does not continuously poll for response; it instead sets up a handler and continues its normal work. The handler gets notified when the response is available. The asynchronous operation takes an additional parameter, an `AsyncHandler` object that refers to the handler.

```
public Future<?> addAsync(int arg0, int arg1, AsyncHandler<Integer>
asyncHandler);
```

The client provides an `AsynchHandler` instance as a callback handler to accept and process the inbound response object. This handler implements `javax.xml.ws.AsynchHandler` interface which has single method `handleResponse()`. The handler defines this method which gets called when an asynchronous response is received from the server. The response is delivered to the callback handler in the form of a `javax.xml.ws.Response` object. Here is a sample callback handler:

```
class MyHandler implements AsyncHandler<Integer> {
  private int result;
  public void handleResponse(Response<Integer> response) {
    try {
      result = response.get();
    } catch (Exception e) { e.printStackTrace(); }
  }
  int get(){ return result; }
}
```

This handler, upon receiving a response, extracts the result from `Response` object and stores it in a variable result, which can be retrieved later using `get()` method. The client code looks similar to polling method except that it passes a AsyncHandler object as follows:

```
SimpleCalculator cal = …
int x = 4, y = 3;
MyHandler mh = new MyHandler();
Future<?> response = cal.addAsync(x,y, mh);
while (!response.isDone()) {
  // do something here
}
```

When this loop exits (i.e. response is available), the client gets the result using `get()` method of `MyHandler` as follows:

```
int result = mh.get();
```

The complete source code of callback asynchronous client is shown below:

```
import javax.xml.ws.*;
import async.client.*;
import java.util.concurrent.Future;
public class CalculatorClientCallBack {
  public static void main(String[] args) {
    SimpleCalculatorService calcService = new SimpleCalculatorService();
    SimpleCalculator cal = calcService.getSimpleCalculatorPort();
    int x = 4, y = 3;
    MyHandler mh = new MyHandler();
    Future<?> response = cal.addAsync(x,y, mh);
    System.out.println("Sent: " + x +" and "+y);
    try {
      while (!response.isDone()) {
        Thread.sleep(10);
        System.out.println("Printing a message");
      }
      int result = mh.get();
      System.out.print("Received("+x+"+"+y+"=): " + result);
    }catch(Exception e) {e.printStackTrace();}
  }
}
```

When executed, this client produced the following result:

```
Sent: 4 and 3
Printing a message
Printing a message
Printing a message
Printing a message
Received(4+3=): 7
```

KEYWORDS

Ant—A tool from Apache used to build web and applications

Asynchronous client—A web service client that does not wait for the response to return and continues its own work

Body—A child element of <Envelope> containing payload

Envelope —The root element of a SOAP message

Header—Optional child element of <Envelop> containing control information

JAX-WS—Java API for XML Web Services (JAX-WS) is an Application Programming Interface (API) for developing web services and clients

Polling—Checking for something continuously

Simple Object Access Protocol—A minimal set of conventions for invoking code using XML over HTTP defined by World Wide Web Consortium

SOAP messages—HTTP POST messages with an XML document as body used to exchange information between SOAP server and client

SOAP Fault Message—A SOAP message sent by a SOAP server to a SOAP client to indicate an error

SOAP Request Message—A SOAP message sent by a SOAP client to a SOAP server

SOAP Response Message—A SOAP message sent by a SOAP server to a SOAP client

Synchronous client—A web service client that waits for the response to return

Web Service—An application component that provides a service which is available over the web

@WebService—An annotation used to declare an interface as a web service

Web Service Cient—An application that consumes a web service

@WebMethod—An annotation used to expose a method as a web service operation

@SOAPBinding—An annotation used to indicate the SOAP encoding to be in use

WSDL—A language used to describe a web service

wsgen—A Java tool to generate schema, WSDL document etc.

wsimport—A Java tool to generate SOAP artifacts

SUMMARY

Simple **O**bject **A**ccess **P**rotocol (SOAP), as its name implies, is a simple and lightweight mechanism to exchange information between peers. SOAP tried to pick up where XML-RPC left off by implementing user defined data types, the ability to specify the recipient, message specific processing control, and other features. SOAP can be used in a wide variety of systems ranging from messaging systems to RPC.

SOAP was designed as an object-access protocol by Dave Winer et al. in 1998. Its specification is currently maintained by the XML Protocol Working Group of the World Wide Web Consortium.

The primary part of the SOAP is the messaging framework. Any SOAP message is an XML document having the following minimal specification:

- The mandatory root element `<Envelop>`.
- The `<Envelop>` element contains an optional `<Header>` element followed by a mandatory `<Body>` element.

A SOAP message may be a Request message or a Response Message. In addition, it defines another message to indicate erroneous situations.

Although SOAP was originally intended for exchanging any type of messages, it is primarily used for Remote Procedure Call (RPC). It still defines a convention for encapsulating and exchanging RPC calls and responses.

Java **API** for **XML** **W**eb **S**ervices (JAX-WS) is an Application Programming Interface (API) for developing web services and clients. JAX-WS programming model extends the foundation provided by the Java API for XML-based RPC (JAX-RPC) programming model. JAX-WS uses annotations extensively, to simplify the development and deployment of web service.

WSDL is used to develop XML files that specify web services. Web service publisher generates WSDL document for the clients, who can inspect this document to gather knowledge about the syntax of calling the web service. JAX-WS provides several useful tools such as wsimport, wsgen to work with web service. JAX-WS also provides libraries to deploy a web service through an existing web server such as tomcat. JAX also supports synchronous as well as asynchronous clients.

WEB RESOURCES

`http://docs.oracle.com/javaee/5/tutorial/doc/bnayn.html`
The Java EE 5 Tutorial

`http://www.tutorialspoint.com/listtutorial/Java-Web-Service-Tutorial-(With-SOAP-UI)--Part-03/4455`
Java Web Service Tutorial (With SOAP UI)- Part 03

`http://www.informit.com/library/content.aspx?b=STY_XML_21days&seqNum=228`
A SOAP Example in Java

`http://www.mkyong.com/webservices/jax-ws/jax-ws-hello-world-example-document-style/`
JAX-WS Hello World Example – Document Style

`http://examples.javacodegeeks.com/enterprise-java/jws/jax-ws-soap-handler-example/`
JAX-WS SOAP Handler Example

EXERCISES

Objective-type Questions

1. SOAP stands for
   (a) Simultaneous Object Access Protocol
   (b) Simple Object Access Policy
   (c) Simple Object Access Protocol
   (d) Standard Object Access Protocol

2. Which of the following is NOT the purpose of the binding section of a WSDL document?
   (a) To indicate the transport protocol of a portType operation.
   (b) To indicate how the body of a SOAP message is constructed.
   (c) To indicate how the header of a SOAP message is constructed.
   (d) To indicate the message transmission sequence of a portType operation.

3. Which of the following is the root element of every SOAP message?
   (a) <Root> (c) <Container>
   (b) <Envelop> (d) <Header>

4. Which of the following is a mandatory element in a SOAP message?
   (a) <Header> (c) <faultcode>
   (b) <Envelop> (d) <return>

5. WSDL stands for
   (a) Web Service Designing Language
   (b) Web Service Definition Language
   (c) Web Site Description Language
   (d) Web Service Description Language

6. JAX-WS stands for
   (a) Java API for XML Web Site
   (b) Java API for XHTML Web Service
   (c) Java API for XML Wide Service
   (d) Java API for XML Web Service

7. Which of the following does SOAP extend?
   (a) HTTP (c) WSDL
   (b) XML (d) XML-RPC

8. Which of the following annotations is used for declaration of a web service?
   (a) @SOAPBinding (c) @WebService
   (b) @WebMethod (d) @Style

9. What is the default encoding style?
   (a) Document (c) XML
   (b) RPC (d) None of the above

10. Which of the following statements is correct if a SOAP message contains the following statement?
    <SOAP-ENV:Envelope xmlns:SOAP-ENV="http://schemas.xmlsoap.org/soap/envelope/">
    (a) The SOAP processor will go to http://schemas.xmlsoap.org/soap/envelope/ to find out the meaning of Envelope.
    (b) SOAP-ENV is a name in namespace xmlns.
    (c) The tag <Envelope> mentioned above is not the same as the tag <Envelope> of the namespace http://www.w3.org/2001/09/soap-envelope
    (d) SOAP 1.2 standard is used when constructing this SOAP message.

11. In WSDL, a <portType> refers to
    (a) TCP/IP or UDP port on the server
    (b) the operations that can be performed, and the messages that are involved
    (c) the actual protocol used in the Web Service
    (d) only the operations that can be performed

12. Which of the following classes is used to publish a web service?
    (a) Publisher (c) WebService
    (b) Endpoint (d) WSPublisher

13. Which of the following methods is used to publish a web service?
    (a) export() (c) disclose()
    (b) upload() (d) publish()

14. The soap:binding element has two attributes. They are
    (a) style attribute and transport attribute
    (b) actor and name
    (c) encoding and soapAction
    (d) message and parts

15. In WSDL a <port> refers to
    (a) TCP/IP or UDP port on the server
    (b) Represents the actual service used
    (c) Exposes a <service> using a specific protocol binding
    (d) Defines the operation

16. Which of the following statements is correct for the SOAP message given below?
    <SOAP-ENV:Body>
    <ns1:getPriceResponse xmlns:ns1="urn:examples:priceservice" SOAP-ENV:encodingStyle= "http://www.w3.org/2001/09/soap-encoding">
    <return xsi:type="xsd:double">54.99<return>
    </ns1:getPriceResponse/>
    </SOAP-ENV:Body/>
    (a) The SOAP processor will follow SOAP 1.1 standard to encode the number 54.99.
    (b) The service tries to return a double number of value 54.99 as a result.
    (c) The namespace of double is urn:examples:priceservice
    (d) This message is most probably generated by Apache Soap or related engine

17. Which of the following is correct about SOAP and XML-RPC?
    (a) SOAP can do RPC while XML-RPC cannot.
    (b) SOAP is platform and language independent while XML-RPC is not.
    (c) SOAP specification has a part that particularly defines data types while XML-RPC has not.
    (d) SOAP follows XML Schema when defining data types while XML-RPC does not

18. What does SOAP define?
    (a) The overall structure of the XML message
    (b) The conventions representing the remote procedure call in the XML message
    (c) A binding to HTTP
    (d) The conventions to wrap and send an error back to the sender
    e) All of the above

19. Which of the following is true about Simple Object Access Protocol (SOAP) ?
    (a) SOAP is a protocol used in conjunction with web services technology.
    (b) SOAP outlines and defines the specifications used to describe a web service to its requester.
    (c) A SOAP message is formatted in HTML.
    (d) SOAP is platform dependent.

20. Which of the following tools is used to compile WSDL file?
    (a) wsgen (c) wscompile
    (b) wsimport (d) wsc

21. Which of the following classes represents a web service?
    (a) Service (c) WS
    (b) WebService (d) WebServiceClass

22. Which of the following is used for document style encoding?
    (a) @SOAPBinding(style = Style.RPC)
    (b) @SOAPBinding(style = Style.DOCUMENT)
    (c) @Binding(style = Style.DOCUMENT)
    (d) @SOAPBinding(style = Style.DOC)

23. The SOAP elements must always belong to the namespace
    (a) http://jax-ws.dev.java.net
    (b) http://schemas.xmlsoap.org/ws/2004/09/policy
    (c) http://schemas.xmlsoap.org/soap/envelope
    (d) http://schemas.xmlsoap.org/wsdl/soap

24. The name of the tomcat web service servlet is
    (a) WebServiceServlet
    (b) TomcatWSServlet
    (c) TomcatServlet
    (d) WSServlet

25. Which of the following tags is used to enable asynchronous method generation?
    (a) addAsync (c) addAsynchronous
    (b) addAsyn (d) AsyncAdd

26. Which of the following interfaces must an asynchronous callback handler implement?
    (a) AsynchronouscHandler
    (b) Handler
    (c) AsynHandler
    (d) AsyncHandler

27. What is the return type of asynchronous methods?
    (a) Future (c) void
    (b) Response (d) Either a) or b)

28. If the URL of a web service is http://172.16.5.81:6789/ws/calc, what will the URL of the WSDL file be?
    (a) http://172.16.5.81:6789/ws/wsdl
    (b) http://172.16.5.81:6789/ws/calc?wsdl
    (c) http://172.16.5.81:6789/ws/calc?wsdldoc
    (d) http://172.16.5.81:6789/ws/calc?wsdlfile

29. The JAX-WS <bindings> element may be written in
    (a) <definitions> (c) <operation>
    (b) <portType> (d) all of the above

30. What is the default name of sun's web service deployment descriptor?
    (a) sun-jaxws.xml
    (b) sun-jaxws.properties
    (c) jaxws.xml
    (d) jaxws.properties

31. Which of the following is used to generate schema and WSDL from web service implementation file?
    (a) wsimport (c) Both a) and b)
    (b) wsgen (d) None of the above

32. SEI stands for
    (a) Service Endpoint Implementation
    (b) Simple Endpoint Interface
    (c) Service Endpoint Interface
    (d) Sample Endpoint Interface

Subjective-type Questions

1. What is SOAP and how does it relate to XML?
2. Write the purpose of Header element in SOAP document.
3. Describe the structure of SOAP messages. Also write the rules associated with the SOAP message structure.

4. How are SOAP messages embedded in POST method of HTTP protocol?
5. Write the use of SoapMethod attribute in HTTP header.
6. Discuss the various Fault elements associated with SOAP fault.
7. Write the SOAP request message to call a method "getPhoneNumber" with parameter "name" taking value "John". Use SOAP encoding. Also write the SOAP response message for the same. Write about the fault elements.
8. Compare Web Services with CORBA
9. Identify the purpose of envelope and encoding namespace.
10. Explain the role of XML in SOAP.
11. Describe the basic steps to develop a web service client.
12. What is the difference between SOAP and other remote access techniques?
13. What are the elements that should be contained in SOAP message?
14. What is the function of a SOAP body element?
15. What do you mean by SOAP encoding?
16. Give examples where SOAP is used.
17. What are Transport methods in SOAP?
18. What is the difference between a synchronous and asynchronous client?
19. What is the difference between an asynchronous polling and asynchronous callback?
20. Describe the basic steps to develop an asynchronous client.
21. Explain how to develop an asynchronous callback client?
22. Define Web Services.
23. What is the function of WSDL?
24. Describe the process of communication between Client and Web Service.

PART THREE
ENTERPRISE JAVA

CHAPTER – 19

SECURITY

KEY OBJECTIVES

After completing this chapter readers will be able to—

- get an overview about the Java security classes and interfaces
- write secured Java socket programs
- use keytool utility to work with keys, certificates and stores
- know how to make RMI applications secured
- know the importance of signed, sealed and guarded objects
- use jarsigner tool to sign and verify JAR files
- understand how to work with security manager

19.1 INTRODUCTION

Often, security is not considered as a fundamental design element in a programming language. Consequently, software developers incorporate security mechanisms at the end of a project despite recent high-profile attacks. However, Java uses a completely different philosophy where security is considered as a crucial design element. It is aware of many security policies and permissions even before the first class is loaded.

Note that, only attackers do not insert malicious code; poorly written applications may inadvertently compromise system-level resources or affect the performance of other applications. Java applications are hardly victimized by viruses due to the language's insistence on a firm policy and permission design.

Unfortunately, this topic has become one of the most confusing topics. This is mostly because many example codes circumvent security features by granting all permissions to all codes. Needless to say that these sample policies shouldn't be applied in real-world applications; they remain otherwise dangerous.

This chapter explores almost all the aspects of Java security mechanism including developing custom permission classes.

19.2 JAVA SECURITY ARCHITECTURE

Java programming language, with its core features and security extensions, enables us in writing powerful secure applications. Security includes language safety, cryptography, **P**ublic **K**ey **I**nfrastructure (PKI), authentication, secure communication, and access control. In this chapter, we shall discuss the basics of security and its implementation in Java, with numerous examples to illustrate the concepts.

This section gives an overview of Java security, from secure language features to the security APIs, tools, and built-in provider services, highlighting key packages and classes where applicable.

19.2.1 Language Security

The Java language itself provides secure class loading and verification mechanism to ensure that only legitimate Java code is executed. Java programs are compiled into machine-independent representation called *bytecode*. When these bytecodes are executed, they are verified by a special component of Java Runtime Environment, called *bytecode verifier*. The verifier thoroughly checks if the bytecodes strictly conform to the language specification and violate language rules or namespace regulations. The verifier also checks for illegal typecasts, stack overflows or underflows and memory management violations. This ensures that only legitimate bytecodes are executed in the Java runtime.

In addition, Java itself is type-safe and provides automatic memory management, garbage collection, and range-checking on arrays etc. enhancing the robustness of application code.

The Java language also enables developers to restrict access to their classes, methods, and fields using different access modifiers such as `private`, `protected`, `public` and package. The unrestricted access specifier is `public`. The most restrictive specifier is `private`. The `protected` specifier allows access to any subclass, or to other classes within the same package. Package-level access only allows access to classes within the same package.

19.2.2 Basic Security

Java security technology spans a wide range of areas, including cryptography, public key infrastructure, secure communication, authentication, access control and language safety. It contains a rich set of APIs, tools, and implementations of commonly used security algorithms, mechanisms, and protocols. These together provide the programmers a comprehensive security framework for developing and managing applications.

Three principles were adopted while designing security APIs: *Implementation independence*, *Implementation interoperability* and *Algorithm extensibility*.

The first principle says that the applications themselves need not implement security; instead they can make use of the security services from Java. These services are implemented as providers which are represented by the class `java.security.Provider`. Oracle's implementation of Java includes a number of built-in pre-configured providers that implement a basic set of security services. Applications may rely on these providers, which are plugged into the Java platform via a standard interface.

The second principle says that providers are functionally similar and interoperable. This means applications using different providers may seamlessly interoperate.

The last principle says that athough applications usually rely on built-in providers, they are free to use proprietary services or emerging standards that have not yet been implemented. The Java platform is helpful enough to install such custom providers implementing those services.

The following sections give an overview of various security areas such as cryptography, authentication, etc.

19.2.3 Java Cryptography Architecture (JCA)

The Java Cryptography Architecture (JCA) is a framework for accessing and developing cryptographic functionality. The JCA is a major part of Java Security Architecture and contains services such as

- Symmetric stream encryption
- Symmetric bulk encryption
- Asymmetric encryption
- Password-based encryption (PBE)
- Elliptic Curve Cryptography (ECC)
- Message digest algorithms
- Digital signature algorithms
- Key agreement algorithms
- Key generators
- Message Authentication Codes (MACs)
- (Pseudo-)random number generators

The cryptography APIs are organized into two distinct packages. The `java.security` package and `javax.crypto` package.

The former package contains the classes and interfaces for the security framework. This includes access control related classes and supports generation and storage of cryptographic public key pairs, a number of cryptographic operations such as message digest and signature generation. This package also includes classes that support signed/guarded objects and secure random number generation.

The `javax.crypto` packages the classes and interfaces for cryptographic operations (such as encryption, key generation and key agreement, and Message Authentication Code generation) and supports secure streams and sealed objects. The encryption includes symmetric, asymmetric, block, and stream ciphers.

The Java platform includes built-in providers for many of the most commonly used cryptographic algorithms, including the RSA, DSA, and ECDSA signature algorithms, the DES, AES, and ARCFOUR encryption algorithms, the MD5, SHA-1, and SHA-256 message digest algorithms, and the Diffie-Hellman and ECDH key agreement algorithms. These default providers implement cryptographic algorithms in Java code.

The Java comes with security providers that implement commonly used cryptographic algorithms, including the RSA, DSA, and ECDSA signature algorithms, the DES, AES, and ARCFOUR encryption algorithms, the MD5, SHA-1, and SHA-256 message digest algorithms, and the Diffie-Hellman and ECDH key agreement algorithms. Java also includes a built-in provider, named SunPKCS11, that acts as a bridge to a native PKCS#11 (v2.x) token.

The cryptography is often divided as two categories: *secret key cryptography* and *public key cryptography*. Let us have a brief overview of these two:

19.2.3.1 Secret-key Cryptography

In this category of cryptography, both the sender and receiver share the key only known to the communicating parties. Since, often the same key is used for encryption and dycryption, the key is also referred to as *symmetric key*. One of its important advantages is that it can encrypt data with arbitrary size. Though there are many powerful key generation algorithms, the main challenge is exchanging the secret key in a safe way. Moreover if the secret key is somehow disclosed, the entire purpose is lost.

19.2.3.2 Public-key Cryptography

In this both communicating peers maintain a pair of two keys. One of the two keys is only known to that party and is known as *private key*. The other one may be known to everybody and is known as *public key* and hence its name. These two keys are related in such a way that one can be used to decrypt data entrypted by the other. The advantage of this method lies in the use of public key. Intruders can even know this key but cannot proceed too much further.

However, public key encryption algorithms do not support encryption of arbitrary size. For example, RSA can encrypt maximum data as follows:

```
Maximum data size (in bytes) = RSA key size (in bytes) - header
```

For RSA PKCS#1 v1.5 padding, the header size is 11 bytes. So, for a key size of 256 bytes (i.e. 2048 bits), the maximum size of data that RSA can encrypt is 245 (=256 – 11) bytes. Although, a larger key may be chosen, it takes too much time for encryption/decryption unrealistic for real-time applications. That is why, public key encryption algorithms are not meant for general data encryption. Instead, they are usually used to encrypt secret keys, authentication codes etc. For encryption of arbitrary data, the following strategy may be employed (and is also recommended):

1. Generate a symmetric (secret) key with preferred size.
2. Get the public key certificate from the intended receiver.
3. Encrypt the symmetric key with RSA using receiver's public key obtained from the certificate and send the encrypted key.
4. Decrypt the symmetric key (secret) with the RSA using receiver's private key.
5. Encrypt the data with the symmetric key and send it to the receiver.
6. Decrypt the data with the symmetric key.

Steps 1–4 are done only once, whereas steps 5–6 are repeated until the data exchange is over.

19.2.4 Public Key Infrastructure (PKI)

This is a framework that deals with the exchange of information based on public key cryptography. The fundamental idea of public key cryptography is digitally signed *public key certificates*. Java provides APIs to work with these certificates such as creating, building, and validating certificates. The API supports X.509/PKIX compliant digital certificates. The API consists of two packages `java.security` and `java.security.cert`.

19.2.4.1 Public Key Certificates

In public key cryptography, a certificate (also known as a digital certificate) is an electronic document that contains a digital signature and a public key. This signature and key together identify entities such as a person or an organization etc. The certificate is typically used to verify that a public key belongs to an individual.

19.2.4.2 Certificate Format

The format of pubic key certificate was specified as a part of the well-known standard X.509. The structure of an X.509 digital certificate is summarized as follows:

- Certificate
  - Version
  - Serial Number
  - Algorithm ID
  - Issuer

- Validity
  - Not Before
  - Not After
- Subject
- Subject Public Key Info
  - Public Key Algorithm
  - Subject Public Key
- Issuer Unique Identifier (optional)
- Subject Unique Identifier (optional)
- Extensions (optional)
  - ...
- Certificate Signature Algorithm
- Certificate Signature

Java security API provides classes and interfaces to represent such certificates and working with them. We shall write several programs in Java to do various certificate-related operations.

19.2.4.3 Digital Signature

A digital signature is a scheme for ensuring the authenticity of a message or document. The signatory of a digital signature has a pair of keys one of which is called *public key* (assumed to be known to anybody), and the other is called *private key* (assumed to be known only to the signatory). Given a piece of target data (usually another key), its summary, called a *digest* is created using a hash function. The digest data summary is used in conjunction with the DSA algorithm to create the digital signature that is sent with the message. Signature verification involves the use of the same hash function.

The digest is then encrypted using DSA algorithm in conjunction with the signatory's private key. This encrypted version of the data's digest is known as signature of the data. The target data and its signature are then sent (as a single entity or separately) to another application, which in turn, verifies the signature of the data using DSA and the signatory's public key. If the signature is correct, the data is said to reach as an integral part (i.e. without any modification).

19.2.4.4 Key and Certificate Store

Java platform allows us to store keys and certificates in persistent store via `java.security.KeyStore` and `java.security.cert.CertStore` respectively. In addition to standard PKCS11 and PKCS12 key store types, Java also provides a built-in store in a format known as JKS (Java Key Store) format. This JKS key store can be manipulated using a Java tool called `keytool`. A detailed usage of this tool is demonstrated later in this chapter.

19.2.5 PKI Tools

Java comes with tools to work with keys and certificates and keystores. The tool `keytool` can be used to do the following:

- Create private/public key pairs using various key generation allgorithms
- Create self-signed certificates
- Display, import, and export X.509 certificates stored in files
- Issue certificate (PKCS#10) requests to be sent to CAs
- Create certificates based on certificate requests
- Import certificate replies (obtained from the CAs sent certificate requests)
- Designate public key certificates as trusted

The `jarsigner` tool is used to sign JAR (Java ARchive) files and/or to verify signatures on signed JAR files. A detailed discussion about these tools can be found later in this chapter.

19.3 SECURE COMMUNICATION

The Java platform also provides API support and provides implementations for a number of standard secure communication protocols. The primary protocols used for secure communication are SSL and TLS. Although, SSL and TLS are not the only protocols currently in use for security, they are very common for applications that could involve sensitive data (i.e. passwords etc.). A little knowledge about these protocols will greatly help us in understanding how a secure link between a client and a server is really established. Since, the term *privacy* (or simply securiy) comes first whenever we talk about general security, we shall also start writing programs for secure communication.

19.4 SSL

Secure Socket Layer (SSL) is a protocol used to make communication secured and is a primary choice of the Internet community. The purpose of SSL is capable of securing any transmission over TCP, such as HTTP, SMTP, FTP etc. The location of SSL in TCP/IP protocol suit is shown in Table 19.1:

Table 19.1: TCP/IP with SSL

TCP/IP Layers	**Protocols**
Application Layer	HTTP, SMTP, POP, IMAP, NNTP, LDAP, FTP
Secure Socket Layer	SSL/TLS
Transport Layer	TCP/UDP
Internet Layer	IP

SSL was first conceived by Netscape in 1994 and is now under the control of Internet Engineering Task Force (IETF). In 1999, IETF renamed SSL to Transport Layer Security (TLS), and released the first specification, version TLS 1.0. Although TLS 1.0 is a modest upgrade to the most recent version of SSL, version 3.0, the differences between SSL 3.0 and TLS 1.0 are minor. Other upgraded versions of TLS (1.1 and 1.2) are also available. However, they are not as widely supported as TLS 1.0 and SSL 3.0.

19.4.1 What does SSL do?

We must take care of the following issues before transferring critical information (such as password, credit card number etc) over a public network:

- Anyone, who has access to the network, may intercept and view the information. This unauthorized third party is sometimes known as an attacker.
- The attacker may also change the data, on its way to the receiver.
- The attacker may also relay some previously received data to the receiver.
- It is necessary to be sure that the party whom you are communicating with is really who you think it is.

SSL addresses all of these issues and provides solutions to the above mentioned problems using several different cryptographic concepts. For example, it uses public-key cryptography with digital signatures to provide authentication, and secret-key cryptography to provide for privacy and data integrity.

19.4.2 How does it do?

The following is a brief description of SSL handshake messages.

1. The client sends a message containing SSL version, the cipher suites supported by the client, a random byte string that is used in subsequent computations, etc.
2. The server responds with a message containing the cipher suite chosen, the session ID and another random byte string and its digital certificate. If the server requires client authentication, it requests the client's certificate.

3. The client tries to verify the server's digital certificate. If the server is successfully authenticated, client goes to the next step, else warns the user about the problem.
4. The client creates a pre-master secret key, encrypts it using server's public key obtained from the server's certificate in step 2 and sends the encrypted to the server.
5. If the server requested client authentication, client generates a data unique to this handshake, encrypts with the client's private key and sends it along with the client's digital certificate to the server.
6. If the server has requested client authentication, the server attempts to authenticate the client. If the client is authenticated successfully, the server uses its private key to decrypt the pre-master secret, then performs a series of steps (which the client also performs, starting from the same pre-master secret) to generate the master secret.
7. Both the client and the server use the master secret to generate the session keys, which are symmetric keys used to encrypt and decrypt information exchanged during the SSL session and to verify its integrity.
8. The client sends a message to the server informing it that future messages from the client are encrypted with the session key. It also sends a separate encrypted message indicating that the client portion of the handshake is complete.
9. The server sends a message to the client informing it that future messages from the server are encrypted with the session key. It also sends a separate encrypted message indicating that the server portion of the handshake is complete.
10. The entire SSL handshake is now complete, and the SSL session starts.

19.4.3 An Example

In this section, we shall develop a simple but elegant client–server socket application using SSL. In this application, the client sends a string to the server. The server prints the string and sends it back to the client. The client finally prints it. Although this application is very simple, it demonstrates basic steps required to develop almost all SSL-based secure applications.

19.4.3.1 Writing the Server

In a traditional (non-SSL) socket application, the server program first creates a `java.net.ServerSocket` object. In an SSL-enabled socket application, the equivalent object is `javax.net.ssl.SSLServerSocket` object and is created in a slightly different way. All constructors of `SSLServerSocket` class are protected. Consequently, those constructors cannot be used to instantiate `SSLServerSocket` objects. The instances are created using `SSLServerSocketFactory` class. An instance of this factory is usually created as follows:

```
SSLServerSocketFactory factory = (SSLServerSocketFactory)
SSLServerSocketFactory.getDefault();
```

The `SSLServerSocket` object is then created using `createServerSocket()` method on this factory:

```
SSLServerSocket sss = (SSLServerSocket) factory.createServerSocket(6789);
```

This creates an `SSLServerSocket` object that listens on port `6789`. The server then starts listening when an `accept()` method is invoked as follows:

```
SSLSocket ss = (SSLSocket) sss.accept();
```

The server is then ready to accept incoming connections. The complete source code (`SSLServer.java`) is given below:

```
import javax.net.ssl.*;
import java.io.*;
public class SSLServer {
  public static void main(String[] args) {
    try {
      SSLServerSocketFactory factory = (SSLServerSocketFactory)
           SSLServerSocketFactory.getDefault();
      SSLServerSocket sss = (SSLServerSocket) factory.createServerSocket(6789);
      SSLSocket ss = (SSLSocket) sss.accept();
```

```
        BufferedReader in = new BufferedReader(new
             InputStreamReader(ss.getInputStream()));
        PrintWriter out = new PrintWriter(ss.getOutputStream(), true);

        String line = null;
        while ((line = in.readLine()) != null) {
           System.out.println("received<-- "+line);
           out.println(line);
           System.out.println("sent      --> "+line);
        }
      } catch (Exception e) { e.printStackTrace(); }
    }
}
```

This program simply sends strings, obtained from the client, back to the client.

19.4.3.2 Writing the Client

The client first creates a `SSLSocketFactory` as follows:

```
SSLSocketFactory factory = (SSLSocketFactory) SSLSocketFactory.getDefault();
```

The counterpart of `Socket` in SSL is `SSLSocket` which is created as follows:

```
SSLSocket ss = (SSLSocket) factory.createSocket(args[0], 6789);
```

The complete source code (`SSLClient.java`) is given below:

```
import javax.net.ssl.*;
import java.io.*;
public class SSLClient {
  public static void main(String[] args) {
    try {
      SSLSocketFactory factory = (SSLSocketFactory)
           SSLSocketFactory.getDefault();
      SSLSocket ss = (SSLSocket) factory.createSocket(args[0], 6789);

      BufferedReader br = new BufferedReader(new InputStreamReader(System.in));
      BufferedReader in = new BufferedReader(new
           InputStreamReader(ss.getInputStream()));
      PrintWriter out = new PrintWriter(ss.getOutputStream(), true);

      String line = null;
      while ((line = br.readLine()) != null) {
        out.println(line);
        System.out.println("sent      --> "+line);
        System.out.println("received<-- "+in.readLine());
      }
    } catch (Exception e) { e.printStackTrace(); }
  }
}
```

19.4.3.3 Compiling and Running the Application

Compile the server program using the following command:

```
javac SSLServer.java
```

Similarly, compile the client program using the following command:

```
javac SSLClient.java
```

Since, SSL uses certificates, we create a private/public keypair and a self signed certificate for the server and store them in a JKS key store file `server.ks` using Java's `keytool` utility as follows:

```
keytool -genkey -keystore server.ks
```

The keytool asks for information necessary to generate a certificate. Provide the necessary information when asked. A sample output is shown in Figure 19.1:

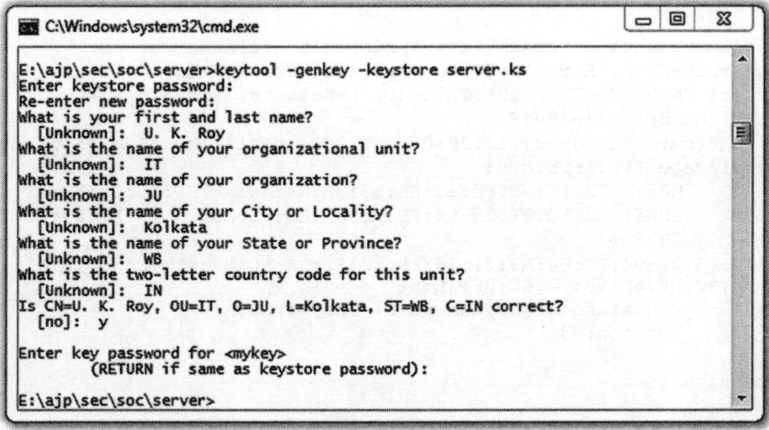

Figure 19.1: Generating a key store using keytool

The entire information may also be passed as command line arguments as follows:

```
keytool -genkey -alias mykey -keyalg RSA -keystore server.ks -storepass 123456
-keypass 123456 -dname "CN=U. K. Roy, OU=IT, O=JU, L=Kolkata, ST=WB, C=IN"
```

The list of keystore entries may be displayed using the following command

```
keytool -list -storepass 123456 -keystore server.ks
```

It generates a samle output as follows:

```
Keystore type: JKS
Keystore provider: SUN

Your keystore contains 1 entry

mykey, May 27, 2014, PrivateKeyEntry,
Certificate fingerprint (SHA1):
32:1D:8F:05:04:CB:03:62:C8:09:29:C5:F9:B3:D7:9D:F4:BC:AC:F0
```

We then extract (called export) the server's certificate and store it in a separate file `server.cer`.

```
keytool -export -alias mykey -keystore server.ks -storepass 123456 -file server.cer
```

During export, keytool asks for the password of the key store. Use the same password used to create the key store. A sample output is shown in Figure 19.2:

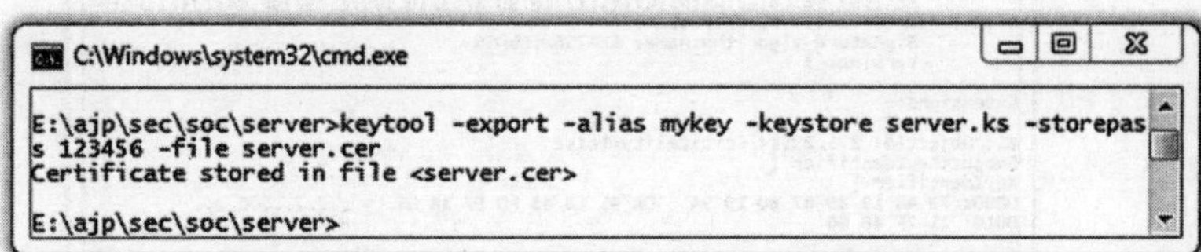

Figure 19.2: Generating a certificate using keytool

The content of this certificate file may be displayed using the following command:

```
keytool -printcert -file server.cer
```

This generates a sample output as follows:

```
Certificate fingerprint (SHA1):
32:1D:8F:05:04:CB:03:62:C8:09:29:C5:F9:B3:D7:9D:
F4:BC:AC:F0

E:\ajp\sec\soc\server>keytool -printcert -file server.cer
Owner: CN=U. K. Roy, OU=IT, O=JU, L=Kolkata, ST=WB, C=IN
Issuer: CN=U. K. Roy, OU=IT, O=JU, L=Kolkata, ST=WB, C=IN
Serial number: 47e38e48
Valid from: Tue May 27 13:20:08 IST 2014 until: Mon Aug 25 13:20:08 IST 2014
Certificate fingerprints:
         MD5:  72:1F:9D:F8:35:EB:B3:3B:AA:A4:A4:F6:DD:ED:7C:F1
         SHA1: 32:1D:8F:05:04:CB:03:62:C8:09:29:C5:F9:B3:D7:9D:F4:BC:AC:F0
         SHA256:
4B:CD:03:2B:94:FE:04:A3:21:74:E5:52:8D:2A:F0:83:9E:7E:20:1D:91:
F5:99:90:DF:86:9B:7D:EB:BB:3B:62
         Signature algorithm name: SHA1withDSA
         Version: 3

Extensions:

#1: ObjectId: 2.5.29.14 Criticality=false
SubjectKeyIdentifier [
KeyIdentifier [
0000: DE 14 6A 59 9D 48 45 57   2B 36 C3 B6 FC E8 C1 65  ..jY.HEW+6.....e
0010: 3D A4 C1 3B                                        =..;
]
]
```

The usage of keytoll to work with keys, certificates and stores is discussed in detail later in this chapter.

This certificate will be sent by the server to the client in step 2 of SSL handshake. A client maintains a list of certificates it relies (trusts) on in a separate store called *trust store*. Note that the trust store only contains public certificates, whereas a key store can store private/pub key pair as well as certificates. Copy this certificate file in the client's home directory which hereafter will be referred to as `client_home`. Go to the `client_home` directory and use the following command to generate a trust store for the client:

```
keytool -import -v -keystore client.ts -storepass 123456 -file server.cer
```

Information about the certificate is displayed and a prompt appears asking if you want to trust the certificate. Type yes (or y), then press Enter. A sample output is shown in Figure 19.3:

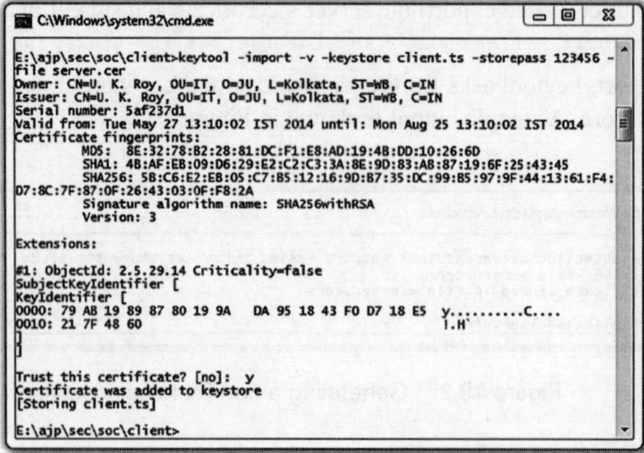

Figure 19.3: Generating a trust store using keytool

At this moment, both client and server are ready to communicate securedly after successful SLL handshake. Start the SSL server first using the following command:

```
java -Djavax.net.ssl.keyStore=server.ks -Djavax.net.ssl.keyStorePassword=123456
SSLServer
```

Note that the key store file and its password are passed to Java interpreter using command line arguments. Start the client using the following command

```
java -Djavax.net.ssl.trustStore=client.ts -
Djavax.net.ssl.trustStorePassword=123456 SSLClient localhost
```

Here, we provide the trust store file and its password. A sample output of the application is shown in Figure 19.4:

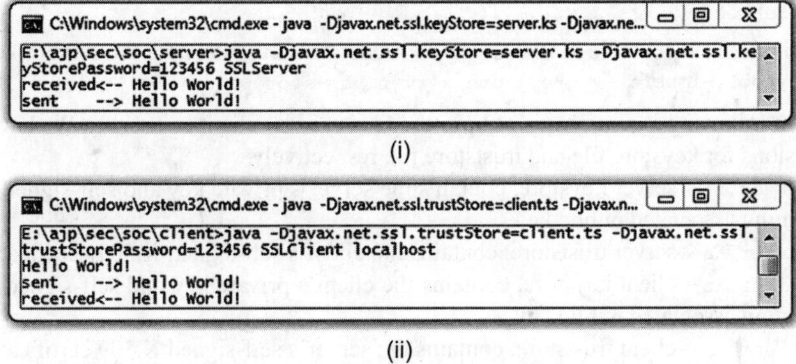

Figure 19.4: Socket communication over SSL (i) Server (ii) Client

The key store and trust store files and their password may also be specified using some Java properties. Add the following lines in `SimpleSSLServer.java`:

```
System.setProperty("javax.net.ssl.keyStore", "server.ks");
System.setProperty("javax.net.ssl.keyStorePassword", "123456");
```

Also add the following lines in `SimpleSSLClient.java`:

```
System.setProperty("javax.net.ssl.trustStore", "client.ts");
System.setProperty("javax.net.ssl.trustStorePassword", "123456");
```

After recompilation, we can then run the server and client directly whose output is shown in Figure 19.5:

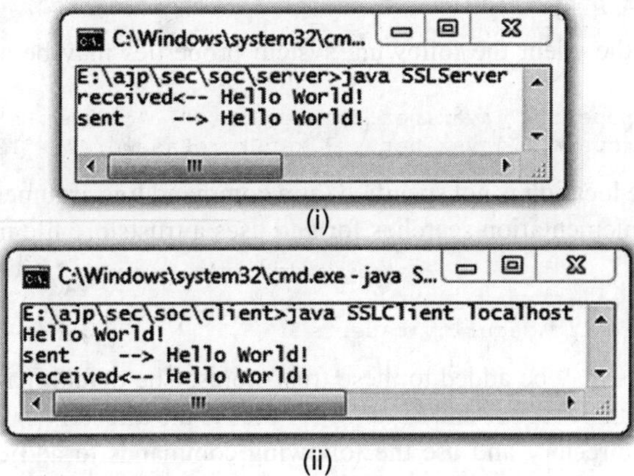

Figure 19.5: Communication over SSL Socket (i) Server (ii) Client

19.4.4 Using Client Authentication

SSL allows server to authenticate a client if the server wants to do so. Add the following entry in `SimpleSSLServer.java`:

```
ss.setNeedClientAuth(true);
```

This configures the socket (in the server mode) that requires client authentication. Client must send its certificate now, otherwise the server stops the negotiations and terminates the connection. So, we create a keystore at the `client_home` directory and export its certificate:

```
keytool -genkey -alias mykey -keyalg RSA -keystore client.ks -storepass 123456
-keypass 123456 -dname "CN=B. C. Dhara, OU=IT, O=JU, L=Kolkata, ST=WB, C=IN"

keytool -export -alias mykey -keystore client.ks -storepass 123456 -file
client.cer
```

Copy `client.cer` file in `server_home`. Generate a trust store for the server:

```
keytool -import -v -keystore server.ts -storepass 123456 -file client.cer
```

The following is a summary of keystore files used by client and server. We have used .ks and .ts extensions for keystore file and truststore file respectively.

`server.ks`—server keystore, contains the server's private key and self-signed X.509 certificate containing associated public key.

`server.ts`—server truststore, contains the client's self-signed X.509 certificate.

`client.ks`—client keystore, contains the client's private key and self-signed X.509 certificate containing associated public key.

`client.ts`—client truststore, contains the server's self-signed X.509 certificate.

If keystore and truststore are not specified using `System.setProperty()` method, then start the server using the following command:

```
java -Djavax.net.ssl.keyStore=server.ks -Djavax.net.ssl.keyStorePassword=123456
-Djavax.net.ssl.trustStore=server.ts -Djavax.net.ssl.trustStorePassword=123456
SSLServer
```

And start the client using the following command:

```
java -Djavax.net.ssl.keyStore=client.ks -Djavax.net.ssl.keyStorePassword=123456
-Djavax.net.ssl.trustStore=client.ts -Djavax.net.ssl.trustStorePassword=123456
SSLClient localhost
```

Instead of passing trust store information to the server at command line, the following system properties may be set:

```
System.setProperty("javax.net.ssl.trustStore", "server.ts");
System.setProperty("javax.net.ssl.trustStorePassword", "123456");
```

Similarly, in the client the following system properties may be specified to provide keystore information:

```
System.setProperty("javax.net.ssl.keyStore", "client.ks");
System.setProperty("javax.net.ssl.keyStorePassword", "123456");
```

If a trust store location is not specified (as a command line argument or using system property), the SunJSSE implementation searches for and uses a truststore file in the following locations (in order):

```
JAVA_HOME\jre\lib\security\jssecacerts
JAVA_HOME\jre\lib\security\cacerts
```

So, certificates may be added to these trust stores. The default password for Java trust store is "changeit". Copy `server.cer` and `client.cer` files to the directory `JAVA_HOME\jre\lib\security`. Now, go to this directory and use the following commands to add `client.cer` and `server.cer` certificate files to the system trust store file `cacerts`.

```
keytool -import -v -alias server -keystore cacerts -storepass changeit -file
client.cer
keytool -import -v -alias client -keystore cacerts -storepass changeit -file
server.cer
```

Check if the certificates are really added using the following command:

```
keytool -list -storepass changeit -keystore cacerts
```

The relevant portion will look like this:

```
...
client, May 29, 2014, trustedCertEntry,
Certificate fingerprint (SHA1):
32:1D:8F:05:04:CB:03:62:C8:09:29:C5:F9:B3:D7:9D:F4:BC:AC:F0
server, May 29, 2014, trustedCertEntry,
Certificate fingerprint (SHA1):
8A:09:40:D4:16:0F:9C:FE:9C:AC:29:F8:4F:6F:0B:A5:C8:28:4A:5E
...
```

Now, both server and client can be started without specifying the trust store. When these certificates are no longer needed, remove them from `cacerts` using the following commands:

```
keytool -delete -alias client -keystore cacerts -storepass changeit
keytool -delete -alias server -keystore cacerts -storepass changeit
```

19.4.5 Using KeyStore

Java platform also provides a class `java.security.KeyStore` for a storage facility for cryptographic keys and certificates. The following server program (`SSLServer1.java`) loads key store and trust store information from files `server.ks` and `server.ts` respectively.

```
import javax.net.ssl.*;
import java.io.*;
import java.security.*;
public class SSLServer1 {
  public static void main(String[] args) {
    try {
        char[] password = "123456".toCharArray();
        KeyStore ks = KeyStore.getInstance("JKS");
        ks.load(new FileInputStream("server.ks"), password);

        KeyStore ts = KeyStore.getInstance("JKS");
        ts.load(new FileInputStream("server.ts"), password);

        KeyManagerFactory kmf = KeyManagerFactory.getInstance("SunX509");
        kmf.init(ks, password);

        TrustManagerFactory tmf = TrustManagerFactory.getInstance("SunX509");
        tmf.init(ts);

        SSLContext sslContext = SSLContext.getInstance("TLS");
        sslContext.init(kmf.getKeyManagers(), tmf.getTrustManagers(), null);

        SSLServerSocketFactory factory =
(SSLServerSocketFactory)sslContext.getServerSocketFactory();

//        SSLServerSocketFactory factory = (SSLServerSocketFactory)
SSLServerSocketFactory.getDefault();
        SSLServerSocket sss = (SSLServerSocket) factory.createServerSocket(6789);
        SSLSocket ss = (SSLSocket) sss.accept();

        ss.setNeedClientAuth(true);

        BufferedReader in = new BufferedReader(new
```

```
InputStreamReader(ss.getInputStream()));
        PrintWriter out = new PrintWriter(ss.getOutputStream(), true);

        String line = null;
        while ((line = in.readLine()) != null) {
          System.out.println("received<-- "+line);
          out.println(line);
          System.out.println("sent    --> "+line);
        }
      } catch (Exception e) {
        e.printStackTrace();
      }
    }
}
```

Similarly, the following client program loads key store and trust store information from files `client.ks` and `client.ts` respectively.

```
import javax.net.ssl.*;
import java.io.*;
import java.security.*;

public class SSLClient1 {
  public static void main(String[] args) {
    try {
      char[] password = "123456".toCharArray();
      KeyStore ks = KeyStore.getInstance("JKS");
      ks.load(new FileInputStream("client.ks"), password);

      KeyStore ts = KeyStore.getInstance("JKS");
      ts.load(new FileInputStream("client.ts"), password);

      KeyManagerFactory kmf = KeyManagerFactory.getInstance("SunX509");
      kmf.init(ks, password);

      TrustManagerFactory tmf = TrustManagerFactory.getInstance("SunX509");
      tmf.init(ts);

      SSLContext sslContext = SSLContext.getInstance("TLS");
      sslContext.init(kmf.getKeyManagers(), tmf.getTrustManagers(), null);

      SSLSocketFactory factory =
(SSLSocketFactory)sslContext.getSocketFactory();
     // SSLSocketFactory factory = (SSLSocketFactory)
SSLSocketFactory.getDefault();
      SSLSocket ss = (SSLSocket) factory.createSocket(args[0], 6789);

      BufferedReader br = new BufferedReader(new InputStreamReader(System.in));
      BufferedReader in = new BufferedReader(new
InputStreamReader(ss.getInputStream()));
      PrintWriter out = new PrintWriter(ss.getOutputStream(), true);

      String line = null;
      while ((line = br.readLine()) != null) {
        out.println(line);
        System.out.println("sent    --> "+line);
        System.out.println("received<-- "+in.readLine());
      }
    } catch (Exception e) {
       e.printStackTrace();
    }
  }
}
```

This application can be run without specifying key store and trust store information at runtime.

19.4.6 Ignoring Server Certificates

A client may not always require server authentication. The following client program demonstrates how to turn off server authentication:

```
import javax.net.ssl.*;
import java.io.*;
import java.security.*;
import java.security.cert.*;

public class SSLClientIgnore {
  public static void main(String[] args) {
    try {
      TrustManager[] trustAllCerts =    {
      new X509TrustManager() {
        public X509Certificate[] getAcceptedIssuers() {return null;}
        public void checkClientTrusted(X509Certificate[] certs,
String authType) {}
        public void checkServerTrusted(X509Certificate[] certs,
String authType) {}
      }
    };

    SSLContext sc = SSLContext.getInstance("SSL");
    sc.init(null, trustAllCerts, new SecureRandom());
    SSLSocketFactory factory =  (SSLSocketFactory)sc.getSocketFactory();

//        SSLSocketFactory factory = (SSLSocketFactory)
SSLSocketFactory.getDefault();
      SSLSocket ss = (SSLSocket) factory.createSocket(args[0], 6789);

      BufferedReader br = new BufferedReader(new InputStreamReader(System.in));
      BufferedReader in = new BufferedReader(new
InputStreamReader(ss.getInputStream()));
      PrintWriter out = new PrintWriter(ss.getOutputStream(), true);

      String line = null;
      while ((line = br.readLine()) != null) {
        out.println(line);
        System.out.println("sent    --> "+line);
        System.out.println("received<-- "+in.readLine());
      }
   } catch (Exception e) {
       e.printStackTrace();
    }
  }
}
```

In this program, we override the default trust manager with one that trusts all certificates. This client works even if server does not provide any certificate.

If you are using a URL connection then the following will also disable server authentication:

```
HttpsURLConnection.setDefaultSSLSocketFactory( sc.getSocketFactory() );
```

Note that a client that does not authenticate a server is vulnerable to several attacks and it is suggested to avoid it as far as possible.

19.4.7 Working with HTTPS

This section describes how to configure tomcat web server to support HTTP over SSL. To create a key store file `tomcat.ks` for tomcat, go to the `tomcat_home` directory and use the following command:

```
keytool -genkey -alias tomcat -keyalg RSA -keystore tomcat.ks -storepass 123456
-keypass 123456 -dname "CN=U. K. Roy, OU=IT, O=JU, L=Kolkata, ST=WB, C=IN"
```

Modify the `tomcat_home\conf\server.xml` files as follows:

```
<Connector port="8443" protocol="HTTP/1.1" SSLEnabled="true"
           maxThreads="150" scheme="https" secure="true"
           keystoreFile="tomcat.ks" keystorePass="123456"
           clientAuth="false" sslProtocol="TLS" />
```

Restart the tomcat server. The tomcat is now ready to work with HTTP over SSL on port 8443. To talk to this tomcat server we have written a HTTPS client whose complete source code (`HTTPSClient.java`) is shown below:

```
// HTTPSClient.java
import javax.net.ssl.*;
import java.io.*;
import java.net.*;
import javax.net.*;
import java.security.*;
import java.security.cert.X509Certificate;

public class HTTPSClient {
  public static void main(String args[]) throws Exception {
    String urlString = "https://127.0.0.1:8443/index.jsp";
    URL url = new URL(urlString);
    TrustManager[] trustAllCerts =   {
      new X509TrustManager() {
        public X509Certificate[] getAcceptedIssuers() {return null;}
        public void checkClientTrusted(X509Certificate[] certs, String
authType) {}
        public void checkServerTrusted(X509Certificate[] certs, String
authType) {}
      }
    };
    SSLContext sc = SSLContext.getInstance("SSL");
    sc.init(null, trustAllCerts, new SecureRandom());
    SocketFactory factory =  sc.getSocketFactory();
    Socket socket = factory.createSocket(url.getHost(), url.getPort());
    PrintWriter out = new PrintWriter(new
OutputStreamWriter(socket.getOutputStream()), true);
    BufferedReader in = new BufferedReader(new
InputStreamReader(socket.getInputStream()));
    out.println("GET " + urlString + " HTTP/1.1\n");
    String line;
    while ((line = in.readLine()) != null)
      System.out.println(line);
  }
}
```

Run the client as follows:

```
java HTTPSClient
```

Note that this client does not need any trust store. The trust manager used in this program overrides `checkServerTrusted()` method. Since, the body of this method is empty, it accepts server response without authenticating the server.

Alternatively, the tomcat's certificate may be added to the system trust store file (i.e. `JAVA_HOME\jre\lib\security\cacerts`). To do this, go to the `tomcat_home` directory and export the public certificate for tomcat to a file `tomcat.cer` using the following command:

```
keytool -export -alias tomcat -keystore tomcat.ks -storepass 123456 -file tomcat.cer
```

Now, copy `tomcat.cer` file, generated in `tomcat_home` directory to the directory `JAVA_HOME\jre\lib\security`. Now, go to this directory and use the following command to add `tomcat.cer` certificate file to the system trust store file `cacerts`.

```
keytool -import -v -keystore cacerts -storepass changeit -file tomcat.cer
```

The https client can now use the default socket factory without using a custom trust manager as follows:

```
SocketFactory factory = SSLSocketFactory.getDefault();
```

The server's certificate is then verified with the entries in the `cacerts` file which indeed contains a certificate for tomcat.

19.5 KEYTOOL REVISITED

Java provides a utility `keytool` (stored in `java_home/bin` directory) used to administer keystores containing cryptographic keys, X.509 certificate chains, and trusted certificates. Programmers use this tool to administer their own private/public key pairs and associated digital certificates for use of self-authentication or data integrity. It also allows users to manage secret keys used in symmetric encryption/decryption (e.g. DES). For a list of options, use the following command:

```
keytool -h
```

Before using this tool, let us quickly understand the different related concepts such as key store, trust store, etc

19.5.1 KeyStore

A keystore, as the name implies, is a repository of keys and certificates and can be a file or a h/w device. There are different standards for keystore file formats. PKCS #12 is a portable industry standard for storage and/or transport of private keys, certificates, miscellaneous secrets, and other items. It is one of the PKCS (**P**ublic-**K**ey **C**ryptography **S**tandards) family of standards published by RSA Laboratories. Files conforming to PKCS #12 usually have extensions `.p12` or `.pfx`.

In addition to supporting PKCS #12 standard, Java has its own proprietary standards (hence not portable) JKS (**J**ava **K**ey **S**tore) provided by "SUN" and its extension JCEKS (**J**ava **C**ryptography **E**xtension **K**ey **S**tore) provided by "SunJCE" that support almost the same functionalities of PKCS #12. The JCEKS keystore gives much stronger protection (see Table 19.2:) for stored private keys by using Triple DES encryption. Moreover, only JCEKS keystores can store secret keys. JKS and JCEKS files usually have extensions `.jks` and `.jceks` respectively.

Table 19.2 Keystore file format

Name of standard	Provider	Public/private keys and certificates	Secret keys
PKCS #12	RSA Laboratories	Can store	Can't store
JKS	SUN	Can store	Can't store
JCEKS	SunJCE	Can store	Can store

A keystore is protected by a store password, which is specified at the time of its creation. This password is required for any access to the keystore further. Furthermore, each secret or private key inside a keystore can be protected by an individual password. Since, there is no need to keep public key certificates secret, they do not have passwords.

Java introduced the `keytool` application for manipulating such keystores. It can also be used to generate *self-signed certificates* for test purposes. Before using `keytool` utility, let us understand the format of a keystore.

19.5.2 Keystore Entries

In a JKS type keystore, each entry may be either of the following two types:

Key Entries

This type of entry may contain either a secret key (called secret key entry) or a private key together with a certificate chain for the corresponding public key (called private key entry). Note that each of these key entries contains very sensitive cryptographic key information, which is optionally stored in a protected format to prevent unauthorized access.

Trusted Certificate Entries

Each of these types of entries contains a single trusted public key certificate of some party. The certificate is said to be *trusted* since the owner of the keystore trusts party having this certificate whose issuer vouches this by signing the certificate. These types of entries are used to authenticate other parties.

19.5.2.1 Truststore

A keystore having only trusted certificate entries is also called *truststore*. So, a truststore is a specific kind of keystore having only certificate entries.

19.5.3 Keystore Aliases

All keys and trusted certificates stored in the keystore are accessed through aliases. An alias is a unique name associated with a certificate entry that keytool uses to uniquely identify each certificate under its control. Aliases are case-insensitive. An alias is specifically used to add, delete, modify, import or export an entry to the keystore using `keytool` command with different options.

The following is a list of useful commands for managing keys. When passwords for key store and key are prompted, supply a suitable password (at least six characters long). We used the password "123456" for all examples in this chapter.

The `keytool` assumes a default keystore file `.keystore` which is located in your home directory or profile directory (for example `C:\Users\root` for Windows 7 and `$HOME` in Unix/Linux). To use another keystore, the option `-keystore` is used with `keytool` command.

19.5.4 Public Key Generation

Generate a private/public key pair with its associated self signed certificate:

```
keytool -genkey -keystore test.ks -dname "CN=Test, OU=IT, O=JU, L=Kolkata,
ST=WB, C=IN"
```

The defaults for various option values are given below:

```
-alias "mykey"
-keyalg
     "DSA" (for option -genkeypair or -genkey)
     "DES" (for option -genseckey)
-keysize
     1024 (for option -genkeypair or -genkey)
     56   (for option -genseckey and -keyalg is "DES")
     168  (for option -genseckey and -keyalg is "DESede")
-validity 90 (in days)
```

The signature algorithm (`-sigalg` option) for a certificate is determined from the private key generation algorithm. For `DSA` and `RSA` key generation algorithms, the `-sigalg` option defaults to `SHA1withDSA` and `MD5withRSA` respectively.

To refer to a particular entry in the keystore, `-alias` option is used. The following adds an entry named `test` to the key store `test.ks`.

```
keytool -genkey -alias test -keystore test.ks -dname "CN=Test, OU=IT, O=JU, L=Kolkata, ST=WB, C=IN"
```

The following adds an entry named `test` to the key store `test.ks` using RSA.

```
keytool -genkey -alias test -keyalg RSA -keystore test.ks -dname "CN=Test, OU=IT, O=JU, L=Kolkata, ST=WB, C=IN"
```

If an application references a key store file without specifying the type, the type as specified (usually `jks`) by the `keystore.type` property in the Java security properties file `<JAVA_HOME>\lib\security\java.security` is assumed. Consequently, by default, `keytool` uses JKS as the format of the keystore and truststore. Use `-storetype` option set to `pkcs12` or `jks` to work with PKCS12 or JKS keystores and truststores respectively.

19.5.5 Changing Password

```
keytool -storepasswd -keystore test.jks
```

Asks for the old and new password for the key store `test.jks`.

19.5.6 Generating a Certificate Chain

The following commands creates four key pairs named ca1, ca1, ca2, and ca4:

```
keytool -alias ca1 -dname CN=ca1 -genkeypair -keystore test.jks -storepass 123456 -keypass 123456
keytool -alias ca2 -dname CN=ca2 -genkeypair -keystore test.jks -storepass 123456 -keypass 123456
keytool -alias ca3 -dname CN=ca3 -genkeypair -keystore test.jks -storepass 123456 -keypass 123456
keytool -alias ca4 -dname CN=ca4 -genkeypair -keystore test.jks -storepass 123456 -keypass 123456
```

The following command extracts ca1's self signed certificate and stores in a file ca1.pem:

```
keytool -export -rfc -alias ca1 -keystore test.jks -storepass 123456 -file ca1.pem
```

The following command creates a certificate sign request for ca2's certificate and stores in file `ca2.csr` in PEM format.

```
keytool -alias ca2 -certreq -keystore test.jks -storepass 123456 -file ca2.csr
```

The following command creates a certificate for ca2 signed by ca1 and stores in a file `ca2.pem`:

```
keytool -alias ca1 -gencert -infile ca2.csr -keystore test.jks -storepass 123456 -rfc -outfile ca2.pem
```

The following creates a chain of certificates; ca2's certificate signed by ca1 followed by ca1's self signed certificate:

```
type ca1.pem >> ca2.pem
```

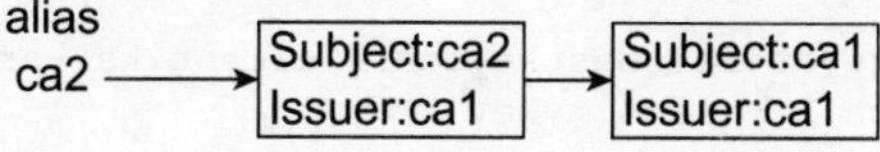

This certificate chain is then imported to the keystore having alias ca2:

```
keytool -alias ca2 -importcert -file ca2.pem -keystore test.jks -storepass 123456
```

Similarly, the following series of commands creates a chain of three certificates:

```
keytool -alias ca3 -certreq -keystore test.jks -storepass 123456 -file ca3.csr
keytool -alias ca2 -gencert -infile ca3.csr -keystore test.jks -storepass 123456 -rfc -outfile ca3.pem
type ca1.pem >> ca3.pem
keytool -alias ca3 -importcert -file ca3.pem -keystore test.jks -storepass 123456
```

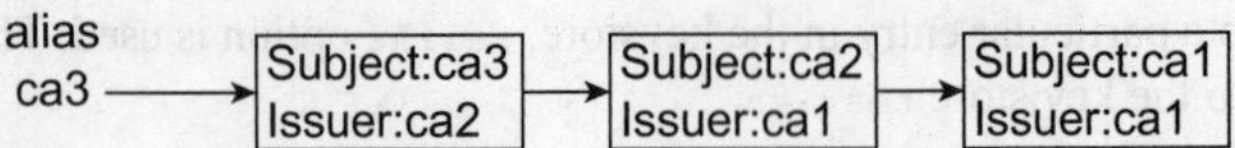

Similarly, the following series of commands creates a chain of four certificates:

```
keytool -alias ca4 -certreq -keystore test.jks -storepass 123456 -file ca4.csr
keytool -alias ca3 -gencert -infile ca4.csr -keystore test.jks -storepass
123456 -rfc -outfile ca4.pem
type ca1.pem >> ca4.pem
keytool -alias ca4 -importcert -file ca4.pem -keystore test.jks -storepass
123456
```

alias
ca4
Subject:ca4
Issuer:ca3
Subject:ca3
Issuer:ca2
Subject:ca2
Issuer:ca1
Subject:ca1
Issuer:ca1

19.5.7 Generating a Certificate Using Openssl

In the area of cryptographic functionality, OpenSSL is a well-know powerful opensource library that includes a command line utility that can be used to perform a variety of cryptographic functions. This section introduces some of the powerful openSSL commands. To work with openSSl, download a suitable version from `http://www.openssl.org/`. We downloaded a file `openssl-0.9.8h-1-bin.zip` and unzipped in a directory `E:\ajp\sec\openssl`. Include the directory `E:\Net\ss\openssl\bin` in your PATH environment variable. Additionally, on windows, the environment variables used by openssl have to be set as follows:

```
set RANDFILE=E:\ajp\sec\openssl\rnd
set OPENSSL_CONF=E:\ajp\sec\openssl\share\openssl.cnf
```

Now, OpenSSL is ready to use. The following are some useful commands to work with cryptography.

Creating Self-signed Certificate

```
openssl genrsa -des3 -out CA.key 1024
openssl req -new -key CA.key -out CA.csr
openssl x509 -req -days 365 -in CA.csr -signkey CA.key -out CA.crt
```

Creating Certificate Signed by the Server

```
openssl genrsa -des3 -out client.key 1024
openssl req -new -key client.key -out client.csr
openssl x509 -req -CA CA.crt -CAkey CA.key -in client.csr -out client.crt -days
365 -Cacreateserial
```

Creating Java Key Store (JKS) from a Private Key and Certificate

With a private key and public certificate, creating a JKS key store can be done in two steps: create a PKCS12 key store using openssl first, then convert it into a JKS using keytool.

```
openssl pkcs12 -export -name mykey -in client.crt -inkey client.key -out
keystore.p12
keytool -importkeystore -destkeystore client.ks -srckeystore keystore.p12 -
srcstoretype pkcs12 -alias mykey
```

Converting Der Key File to Pem Key File

```
openssl rsa -inform der -in p.der -out p.pem
```

Creating a JKS Key store from a Chain of Certificates

Use the following command to create a PEM certificate file containing a chain of certificates.

```
copy client.crt com.crt
type CA.crt >> com.crt
```

In this case, the PEM certificate file `com.crt` contains two certificates, `client.crt` and `CA.crt`. Now, create a PKCS12 key store from this combined certificate.

```
openssl pkcs12 -export -name mykey -in com.crt -inkey client.key -out com.p12
```

This PKCS12 file com.p12 contains an entry named "mykey" containing client's private key and a chain of two certificates. Now, import (convert) this PKCS12 file in a JKS file com.ks.

```
keytool -importkeystore -destkeystore com.ks -srckeystore com.p12 -srcstoretype pkcs12 -alias mykey
```

Secret Key Generation

Generate a secrete (sysmmetric) key using DES:

```
keytool -genseckey -keyalg DES -storetype jceks -keystore sec.ks
```

Note that only JCEKS keystores can store secret keys. So, `-storetype` is mentioned as `jceks`. Generate a 128-bit secret (sysmmetric) key using AES:

```
keytool -genseckey -keyalg AES -keysize 128 -storetype jceks -keystore sec.ks
```

Currently supported secret key generation algorithms are DES, AES, ARCFOUR, Blowfish, DESede, HmacSHA1, HmacSHA256, HmacSHA384, HmacSHA512 and RC2.

Viewing Key Store Entries

To view the contents of a keystore, `-list` option is used. View the content of the entry `mykey` of the key store `test.jks`.

```
keytool -list -alias mykey -keystore test.jks
```

If no alias is specified, it displays all entries of key store `test.jks`:

```
keytool -list -keystore test.jks
```

The `-list` option does not, by default, display certificate information. Use –v to see the certificate information:

```
keytool -v -list -keystore test.jks
```

To see certificate in PEM format, use `-rfc` option:

```
keytool -rfc -list -keystore test.jks
```

Deleting Key Store Entries

Delete an entry identified by alias `mykey` from the key store `test.jks`.

```
keytool -delete -alias mykey -keystore test.jks
```

Exporting Certificate

Export the certificate corresponding to alias `mykey` in the keystore `test.jks` in a file `test.cer`.

```
keytool -export -alias mykey -keystore test.jks -file test.cer
```

This command exports the certificate at the bottom of the certificate chain in that keystore entry identified by alias mykey. If, instead, mykey is the alias for a trusted certificate entry, then that trusted certificate is exported. The specified alias must correspond to a private/public key entry. Note that for secret key entry, no certificate is stored, hence exporting certificate will not work. To export the certificate in PEM format, use `-rfc` option:

```
keytool -export -alias mykey -keystore test.jks -jfc -file test.pem
```

Viewing Certificate

View the content of a certificate file `test.cer`.

```
keytool -printcert -file test.cer
```

The `keytool` utility understands both DER as well as PEM certificate encodings.

Converting Keystore Format

Convert from JKS to PKCS12 format:

```
keytool -importkeystore -srckeystore test.jks -srcstoretype jks -destkeystore
test.pfx -deststoretype pkcs12
```

Convert from JKS to JCEKS format:

```
keytool -importkeystore -srckeystore test.jks -srcstoretype jks -destkeystore
test.jceks -deststoretype jceks
```

Convert from PKCS12 to JKS format:

```
keytool -importkeystore -srckeystore test.pfx -srcstoretype pkcs12 -destkeystore
test.jks -deststoretype jks
```

Convert from PKCS12 to JCEKS format:

```
keytool -importkeystore -srckeystore test.pfx -srcstoretype pkcs12 -destkeystore
test.jceks -deststoretype jceks
```

Convert from PKCS12 to PEM format:

```
openssl pkcs12 -in test.pfx -out test.pem
```

Generating Certificate Signing Request

Certificates generated by `keytool` can be exported in a form suitable for submission to a Certificate Authority such as VeriSign. The following is an example:

```
keytool -keystore test.ks -certreq -alias mykey -keyalg dsa -file out.csr
```

This stores the signing request data in a file `out.csr`.

19.6 GENERATING KEYS

Though Java's `keytool` utility is a powerful tool for key generation and manipulation, Java provides some useful classes and interfaces to work with both public and secret keys.

19.6.1 Public Key Generation

A public key is generated using `java.security.KeyGenerator` class as follows:

```
String alg = "RSA";
KeyPairGenerator keyPairGenerator = KeyPairGenerator.getInstance(alg);
KeyPair keyPair = keyPairGenerator.genKeyPair();
PrivateKey pri = keyPair.getPrivate();
PublicKey pub = keyPair.getPublic();
```

This generates a private and public key pair using RSA algorithm with default parameters. The overloaded `initialize()` methods of `KeyPairGenerator` class may be used to specify algorithm-specific parameters such as key length, randomness etc. Currently, the supported public key generation algorithms are RSA, DSA, EC and DiffieHellman (or simply DH).

19.6.2 Private Key Generation

The class `javax.crypto.KeyGenerator` is used to generate secret (symmetric) keys which are used in secret key cryptography. The following generates a key using DES algorithm:

```
KeyGenerator generator = KeyGenerator.getInstance("DES");
SecretKey secretKey = generator.generateKey();
```

The overloaded `init()` methods of `KeyGenerator` class may be used to specify algorithm specific parameters such as key length, randomness etc. Currently, the supported secret key generation algorithms are DES, AES, ARCFOUR, Blowfish, DESede, HmacSHA1, HmacSHA256, HmacSHA384, HmacSHA512 and RC2.

19.7 WORKING WITH KEYSTORE

A keystore, in Java, is represented by a `java.security.KeyStore` instance, which is created using its static `getInstance()` method specifying keystore type and optionally a provider:

```
KeyStore ks = KeyStore.getInstance(KeyStore.getDefaultType());
```

This creates a `KeyStore` object of type as specified in the Java security properties file. The following creates a KeyStore object of specified type "jks".

```
KeyStore ks = KeyStore.getInstance("jks");
```

Specify keystore type "jceks" or "pkcs12" (case-insensitive) in `getInstance()` method for JCEKS and PKCS12 type keystores respectively.

19.7.1 Reading Keystore

The following program reads a JKS-type keystore file and prints information about all the entires:

```
import java.io.*;
import java.util.*;
import java.security.*;
import java.security.cert.Certificate;
public class ReadJKS {
  public static void main(String[] args) throws Exception {
    char[] password = args[1].toCharArray();
    KeyStore ks = KeyStore.getInstance("JKS");
    ks.load(new FileInputStream(args[0]), password);
    Enumeration e = ks.aliases();
    while(e.hasMoreElements()) {
      String alias = (String)e.nextElement();
      KeyStore.ProtectionParameter protParam = new
KeyStore.PasswordProtection(password);
      KeyStore.PrivateKeyEntry pkEntry =
(KeyStore.PrivateKeyEntry)ks.getEntry(alias, protParam);

      PrivateKey pri = pkEntry.getPrivateKey();
      System.out.println(pri);
      java.security.cert.Certificate[] certs = pkEntry.getCertificateChain();
      for(java.security.cert.Certificate cert:certs)
        System.out.println(cert);
    }
  }
}
```

19.7.2 Extracting Private Keys from Keystore

The `keytool` command does not allow us to extract the private key from a key store. A simple Java program may be written to do this. The following program gets the key and the corresponding certificate and saves them in files `key.der` and `cert.der` in DER format:

```
import java.io.*;
import java.security.*;
public class ReadKeyStore {
  public static void main(String[] args) throws Exception {
    char[] password = "123456".toCharArray();
    KeyStore ks = KeyStore.getInstance("JKS");
    ks.load(new FileInputStream(args[0]), password);

    String alias ="mykey";
    FileOutputStream kos = new FileOutputStream("key.der");
    Key pri = ks.getKey(alias, password);
    kos.write(pri.getEncoded());
```

```
        FileOutputStream cos = new FileOutputStream("cert.der");
        java.security.cert.Certificate cert = ks.getCertificate(alias);
        cos.write(cert.getEncoded());
    }
}
```

Use the following command to create a keystore `test.jks`:

```
keytool -genkey -keystore test.jks -dname "CN=Test, OU=IT, O=JU, L=Kolkata, ST=WB, C=IN"
```

Run the above Java program as follows:

```
java ReadKeyStore test.jks
```

These private keys and certificates may be used in other applications.

19.7.3 Storing Private Key and Certificate in Keystore

The following program creates an entry in the key store file aStore.jks from a given key and a certificate file. These key and certificates may be generated using the previous program.

```
import java.security.*;
import java.io.*;
import java.security.spec.*;
import java.security.cert.Certificate;
import java.security.cert.CertificateFactory;
import java.util.*;
public class WriteKeyStore  {
  public static void main ( String args[]) throws Exception {
    char[] password = "123456".toCharArray();
    String alias = "aKey", name = "aStore.jks";
    KeyStore ks = KeyStore.getInstance("JKS", "SUN");
    ks.load( null , password);

    FileInputStream fis = new FileInputStream(args[0]);
    byte[] kdata = new byte[fis.available()];
    fis.read(kdata);

    PKCS8EncodedKeySpec kp = new PKCS8EncodedKeySpec (kdata);
    KeyFactory kf = KeyFactory.getInstance("DSA");
    PrivateKey pri = kf.generatePrivate (kp);

    CertificateFactory cf = CertificateFactory.getInstance("X.509");

    Collection c = cf.generateCertificates(new FileInputStream(args[1])) ;
    Certificate[] certs = new Certificate[c.size()];

    int in = 0;
    for(Iterator i = c.iterator(); i.hasNext();)
      certs[in++] = (Certificate)i.next();
    ks.setKeyEntry(alias, pri, password, certs );
    ks.store(new FileOutputStream ( name ),password);
    System.out.println ("Key and certificate stored.");
  }
}
```

Run the above Java program as follows:

```
java WriteKeyStore key.der cert.der
```

These stores may be used in other applications.

19.8 WORKING WITH CERTIFICATES

A public key certificate (or simply certificate) is a document to bind a party to a public key which is vouched by usually another party using its private key. In Java, such a certificate is represented by `java.security.Certificate` class that abstracts the common functionality of different certificate formats such as X.509 and PGP. An X.509 certificate is encapsulated by, `java.security.cert.X509Certificate` class which is a subclass of `Certificate`. To work with certificates, an instance of `java.security.cert.CertificateFactory` class is created first using its static `getInstance()` method specifying the certificate format as string.

```
CertificateFactory cf = CertificateFactory.getInstance("X.509");
```

This creates a certificate factory for X.509 certificates. Once this factory is created, we can work with X.509 certificates.

19.8.1 Reading Certificate Information

The `generateCertificate()` method of `CertificateFactory` returns a `Certificate` object and populates it with the data obtained from specified `InputStream`. The following is a sample program to demonstrate this:

```
import java.io.*;
import java.security.cert.*;
public class ReadCertificate {
  public static void main(String args[]) throws Exception {
    CertificateFactory cf = CertificateFactory.getInstance("X.509");
    Certificate c = cf.generateCertificate(new FileInputStream(args[0]));
    System.out.println(c);
  }
}
```

To view the content of a certificate file `test.cer`, use the following command:

```
java ReadCertificate test.cer
```

Note that `generateCertificate()` method can understand DER (**D**istinguished **E**ncoding **R**ules), PEM (**P**rivacy-enhanced **E**lectronic **M**ail) and PKCS#7 certificate file format. If a file contains multiple certificates (possibly unrelated), use `generateCertificates()` method which returns a `Collection` of certificates. Here is an example:

```
Collection c = cf.generateCertificates(new FileInputStream(args[0]));
for(Iterator i = c.iterator();i.hasNext();) {
  Certificate cert = (Certificate)i.next();
  System.out.println(cert);
}
```

19.8.2 Creating Certificate

The following program (`GenerateCertificate.java`) creates a certificate (`c.cer`) using `RSA` key generation and `SHA1` signature algorithm. This program also creates a key store (`c.jks`) file and a trust store (`c.ts`) for this certificate.

```
//GenerateCertificate.java
import sun.security.x509.*;
import java.security.cert.*;
import java.security.*;
import java.math.BigInteger;
import java.util.Date;
import java.io.*;

public class GenerateCertificate {
  public static void main(String args[]) {
    try {
      String enAlg = "RSA", sigAlg = "SHA1with"+enAlg;
      KeyPairGenerator kpg = KeyPairGenerator.getInstance(enAlg);
      KeyPair kp = kpg.generateKeyPair();
      PrivateKey priv = kp.getPrivate();
```

```
            X509CertInfo ci= new X509CertInfo();
            //populate certificate info
            ci.set(X509CertInfo.VERSION, new
      CertificateVersion(CertificateVersion.V3));
            BigInteger sn = new BigInteger(64, new SecureRandom());
            ci.set(X509CertInfo.SERIAL_NUMBER, new CertificateSerialNumber(sn));
            String dn = "CN=myName, OU=myOU, O=myO, L=MyL, S=myS, C=myC";
            X500Name issuer = new X500Name(dn);
            ci.set(X509CertInfo.ISSUER, new CertificateIssuerName(issuer));
            Date from = new Date();
            Date to = new Date(from.getTime() + 365*24*60*60*1000l);
            CertificateValidity duration = new CertificateValidity(from, to);
            ci.set(X509CertInfo.VALIDITY, duration);
            ci.set(X509CertInfo.SUBJECT, new CertificateSubjectName(issuer));
            ci.set(X509CertInfo.KEY, new CertificateX509Key(kp.getPublic()));
            AlgorithmId aid = new AlgorithmId(AlgorithmId.sha1WithRSAEncryption_oid);
            ci.set(X509CertInfo.ALGORITHM_ID, new CertificateAlgorithmId(aid));

            X509CertImpl cert = new X509CertImpl(ci);
            //self sign
            cert.sign(priv, sigAlg);

            FileOutputStream os = new FileOutputStream("c.cer");
            os.write(cert.getEncoded());
            os.close();

            KeyStore ks = KeyStore.getInstance(KeyStore.getDefaultType());
            char[] password = "123456".toCharArray();
            ks.load(null, password);
            java.security.cert.Certificate[] chain = {cert};
            ks.setKeyEntry("abc", priv, password, chain);
            java.io.FileOutputStream fos = new java.io.FileOutputStream("c.jks");
            ks.store(fos, password);

            KeyStore ts = KeyStore.getInstance(KeyStore.getDefaultType());
            ts.load(null, password);
            ts.setCertificateEntry("abc", cert);
            java.io.FileOutputStream fos1 = new java.io.FileOutputStream("c.ts");
            ts.store(fos1, password);
         }catch(Exception e) {e.printStackTrace();}
      }
   }
```

If you want to use any other key generation algorithm and signature algorithm, specify them in the variables `enAlg` and `sigAlg`.

19.8.3 Converting Certificates

The following program converts one certificate file format to another.

```
// Converter.java
import java.io.*;
import java.security.cert.*;
public class Converter {
  public static void main(String args[]) {
    try {
      InputStream inStream  = new FileInputStream(args[1]);
      CertificateFactory cf = CertificateFactory.getInstance("X.509");
      Certificate cert = (X509Certificate)cf.generateCertificate(inStream);
      byte[] buf = cert.getEncoded();

      if(args[0].equals("fromder")) {
        Writer wr = new OutputStreamWriter(new FileOutputStream(args[2]));
        wr.write("-----BEGIN CERTIFICATE-----".toCharArray());
```

```
        wr.write(new sun.misc.BASE64Encoder().encode(buf));
        wr.write("-----END CERTIFICATE-----".toCharArray());
        wr.flush();
      }
      if(args[0].equals("toder")) {
        FileOutputStream os = new FileOutputStream(args[2]);
        os.write(buf);
        os.close();
      }
    }catch(Exception e) { e.printStackTrace(); }
  }
}
```

From DER to PEM conversion:

```
java Converter fromder c.cer c.pem
```

From DER to PEM conversion:

```
java Converter toder c.pem c.cer
```

Using keytool

Convert a DER file (.crt .cer .der) to PEM

```
keytool -import -keystore temp.jks -storepass 123456 -file c.der
keytool -export -keystore temp.jks -storepass 123456 -rfc -file c.pem
```

Convert a PEM file to DER

```
keytool -import -keystore temp.jks -storepass 123456 -file c.pem
keytool -export -keystore temp.jks -storepass 123456 -file c.der
```

Convert a DER file (.crt .cer .der) to PEM

```
openssl x509 -inform der -in c.cer -out c.pem
```

Convert a PEM file to DER

```
openssl x509 -outform der -in c.pem -out c.cer
```

However, openssl accepts only trusted certificate.

19.8.4 SignedObject

Java `java.security.SignedObject` class ensures the integrity of serializable objects when they are transferred over or stored on untrusted media. The object, before reusing it, can be checked to see if it was modified during its transit. An instance of the `SignedObject` encapsulates the serialized representation of another object along with the signature information necessary to validate the wrapped object's authenticity and integrity. The following constructor is available:

```
SignedObject(Serializable object, PrivateKey key, Signature engine)
```

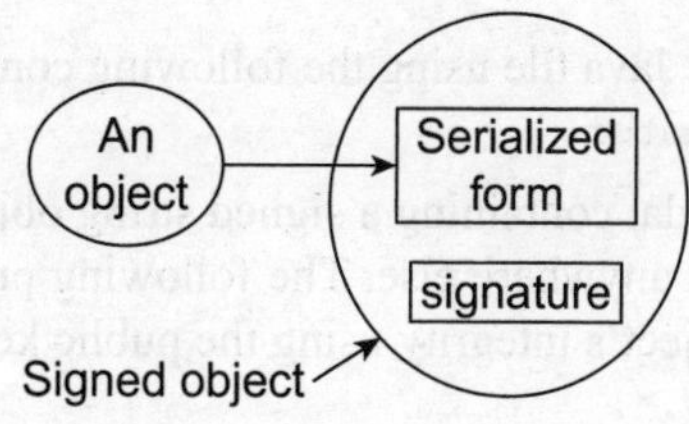

This creates a `SignedObject` from a specified `object`, which is signed with the specified private signing `key` and signature `engine`. The following is a typical example:

```
Serializable obj = ...
PrivateKey key = ...
Signature sig = ...
SignedObject so = new SignedObject(obj, key, sig);
```

Once an instance of `SignedObject` has been created, it can be transferred over or stored on even untrusted media. Upon reconstruction, the integrity of this object can be verified and authenticated using public key associated with the private key that signed the object as follows:

```
SignedObject so = …
PublicKey pub = …
Signature sig = Signature.getInstance(so.getAlgorithm());
if(so.verify(pub, sg)) {
  //the wrapped object remains unchanged, get it and use it
  Object obj = so.getObject();
}
```

A signed object contains the *deep copy* of the original object (in serialized form). Once the original object is wrapped in a signed object, further manipulation of the original object has no side effect on the copy.

Note that to verify the wrapped object's integrity, the public key is needed. This public key may be obtained in the form of public key certificate. The following program creates a `SignedObject` from a `String` and signs it using a private key obtained from a key store `test.ks` and finally stores the `SignedObject` in a file `so.dat`.

```
import java.security.*;
import java.io.*;
public class SignedObjectCreator {
  public static void main(String args[]) throws Exception {
    char[] password = "123456".toCharArray();
    KeyStore ks = KeyStore.getInstance("JKS");
    ks.load(new FileInputStream("test.ks"), password);

    String str = "Hello World!";
    PrivateKey pri = (PrivateKey)ks.getKey("test", password);
    Signature sig = Signature.getInstance("SHA1withRSA");
    SignedObject so = new SignedObject(str, pri, sig);

    ObjectOutputStream oos = new ObjectOutputStream(new
FileOutputStream("so.dat"));
    oos.writeObject(so);
  }
}
```

Create a key store `test.ks` containing one entry having alias `test` using the following command:

```
keytool -genkey -alias test -keyalg RSA -keystore test.ks -storepass 123456
-keypass 123456 -dname "CN=Test, OU=IT, O=JU, L=Kolkata, ST=WB, C=IN"
```

Now, create a public certificate file `test.cer` for this entry using the following command:

```
keytool -export -alias test -keystore test.ks -storepass 123456 -file test.cer
```

Now, execute the above Java file using the following command:

```
Java SignedObjectCreator
```

This generates a file so.dat containing a signed string object. This `so.dat` along with the `test.cer` can now be transferred anywhere else. The following program reconstructs the `SignedObject` and verifies its wrapped object's integrity using the public key obtained from the file `test.cer`.

```
import java.security.*;
import javax.security.cert.X509Certificate;
import java.io.*;
public class SignedObjectVerifier {
  public static void main(String args[]) throws Exception {
    ObjectInputStream ois = new ObjectInputStream(new
FileInputStream("so.dat"));
    SignedObject so = (SignedObject)ois.readObject();
    PublicKey pub = X509Certificate.getInstance(new
```

```
FileInputStream("test.cer")).getPublicKey();
    Signature sg = Signature.getInstance(so.getAlgorithm());
    if (so.verify(pub, sg)) {
      String s = (String)so.getObject();
      System.out.println(s);
    }
  }
}
```

Note that, it is possible to obtain the wrapped object from `SignedObject` without first verifying the sender's authenticity or the message's integrity. This implies that `SignedObject` does not protect the object's content; it merely allows us to verify its integrity. To protect (hide) an object, `SealedObject` may be used.

19.8.5 SealedObject

The `javax.crypto.SealedObject` class, unlike `SignedObject` which deals with integrity, protects an object's confidentiality. A `SealedObject` contains an encrypted version of another object's serialized representation. So, unlike `SignedObject`, wrapped object cannot be retrieved without decryption key. This implies that no one can examine or temper the wrapped object without knowing the decryption key. Moreover, if public key encryption is used, the authenticity of the sender can also be verified. It has the following constructor:

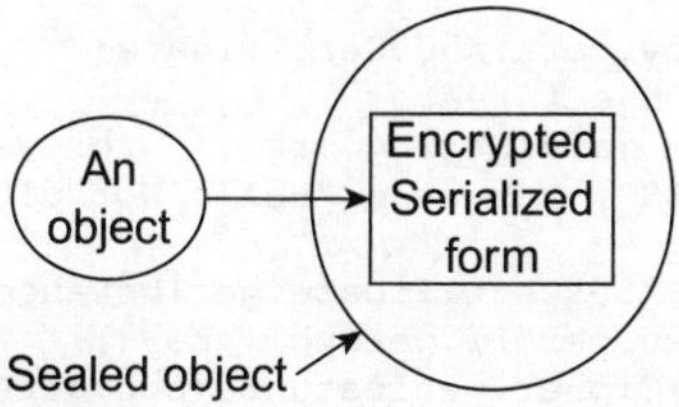


```
SealedObject(Serializable object, Cipher chiper)
```

It creates a `SealedObject` from a specified `Serializable` object and a `Chiper`. The specified `object` is serialized, and this serialized data is sealed (encrypted) using the given `cipher`. The following is a typical example:

```
Serializable object = ...
Cipher cipher = ...
SealedObject so = new SealedObject(serializable, cipher);
```

Once an instance of `SignedObject` has been created, it can be transferred over or stored on even untrusted media. Upon reconstruction, the original object can be retrieved using `getObject()` method. This method decrypts the encrypted content using the corresponding algorithm and correct decryption key, deserializes it and returns the original object. The `getObject()` method has the following overloaded versions:

```
Object getObject(Cipher c)
Object getObject(Key key)
Object getObject(Key key, String provider)
```

So, any one of the following will work:

```
String provider = ...
Chiper chipper = ...
Key decryptionkey = ...

so.getObject(cipher);
so.getObject(decryptionkey);
so.getObject(decryptionkey, provider);
```

Note that to retrieve the original object, the corresponding decryption key is needed. For public key encryption, public key, obtained from the receiver's certificate may be used for encryption. Receiver can then use its private key for decryption. Since, public key cryptography cannot handle data of an arbitrary size, secret key is usually used for encryption. Since, secret key cryptography uses symmetric key, receiver has to obtain the secret decryption key. How will the receiver obtain the secret decryption key without getting it observed or modified? The following strategies may be employed:

1. Generate a symmetric (secret) key with preferred size.
2. Get the public key certificate from the intended receiver.
3. Encrypt the symmetric key with RSA using receiver's public key obtained from the certificate and send the encrypted key.
4. Decrypt the symmetric key (secret) with the RSA using receiver's private key.
5. Encrypt the data with the symmetric key and send it to the receiver.
6. Decrypt the data with the symmetric key.

Steps 1–4 are done only once, whereas steps 5–6 are repeated until the data exchange is over. The following program creates a `SealedObject` from a `String` and signs it using a secret key and finally stores the file `data`. The secret key is encrypted using a public key obtained from (receiver's) certificate file `test.cer`, wrapped in another sealed object which is then stored in a file `key`. Create this `test.cer` file as described in the previous section.

```
import java.security.*;
import java.io.*;
import javax.crypto.*;
import javax.security.cert.X509Certificate;
public class SealedObjectCreator {
  public static void main(String args[]) throws Exception {
    String alg = "DES", target = "Hello World!";

    PublicKey pub = X509Certificate.getInstance(new
FileInputStream("test.cer")).getPublicKey();
    Cipher cipher = Cipher.getInstance(pub.getAlgorithm());
    cipher.init(Cipher.ENCRYPT_MODE, pub);
    KeyGenerator kg = KeyGenerator.getInstance(alg);
    SecretKey sk = kg.generateKey();
    SealedObject so = new SealedObject(sk.getEncoded(), cipher);
    ObjectOutputStream oos = new ObjectOutputStream(new
FileOutputStream("key"));
    oos.writeObject(so);

    cipher = Cipher.getInstance(alg);
    cipher.init(Cipher.ENCRYPT_MODE, sk);
    so = new SealedObject(target, cipher);
    oos = new ObjectOutputStream(new FileOutputStream("data"));
    oos.writeObject(so);
    oos.close();
  }
}
```

This `data` along with the key file `key` can now be transferred anywhere else. The following program first retrieves the secret key using private key obtained from the key store `test.ks`. This secret key is then used further to retrieve wrapped data objects.

```
import java.security.*;
import java.io.*;
import javax.crypto.*;
import javax.crypto.spec.*;
public class SealedObjectDecoder {
  public static void main(String args[]) throws Exception {
    ObjectInputStream ois = new ObjectInputStream(new FileInputStream("key"));
    SealedObject so = (SealedObject)ois.readObject();
```

```
      char[] password = "123456".toCharArray();
      KeyStore ks = KeyStore.getInstance("JKS");
      ks.load(new FileInputStream("test.ks"), password);
      PrivateKey pri = (PrivateKey)ks.getKey("test", password);

      byte[] bytes = (byte[])so.getObject(pri);
      ois = new ObjectInputStream(new FileInputStream("data"));
      so = (SealedObject)ois.readObject();
      SecretKey sk = new SecretKeySpec(bytes, 0, bytes.length,
so.getAlgorithm());
      System.out.println(so.getObject(sk));
    }
  }
```

The following is a pair of sender/receiver socket programs that exchange data using sealed objects. They make use of the basic mechanism used by SSL without using SSL.

```
import java.security.*;
import java.io.*;
import javax.crypto.*;
import javax.security.cert.X509Certificate;
import java.net.*;
public class SealedObjectSender {
  public static void main(String args[]) throws Exception {
    Socket s = new Socket(args[0], 6789);
    ObjectInputStream in = new ObjectInputStream(s.getInputStream());
    ObjectOutputStream out = new ObjectOutputStream(s.getOutputStream());
    java.security.cert.Certificate c =
(java.security.cert.Certificate)in.readObject();
    //authenticate the certificate c here
    PublicKey pub = c.getPublicKey();

    String alg = "DES";
    KeyGenerator kg = KeyGenerator.getInstance(alg);
    SecretKey sk = kg.generateKey();

    Cipher cipher = Cipher.getInstance(pub.getAlgorithm());
    cipher.init(Cipher.ENCRYPT_MODE, pub);
    SealedObject so = new SealedObject(sk.getEncoded(), cipher);
    out.writeObject(so);

    cipher = Cipher.getInstance(alg);
    cipher.init(Cipher.ENCRYPT_MODE, sk);
    BufferedReader fromUser = new BufferedReader(new
InputStreamReader(System.in));
    while(true) {
      so = new SealedObject(fromUser.readLine(), cipher);
      out.writeObject(so);
    }
  }
}
```

```
import java.security.*;
import java.io.*;
import javax.crypto.*;
import javax.crypto.spec.*;
import java.net.*;
public class SealedObjectReceiver {
  public static void main(String args[]) throws Exception {
    ServerSocket ss = new ServerSocket(6789);
    Socket s = ss.accept();
    ObjectOutputStream out = new ObjectOutputStream(s.getOutputStream());
    ObjectInputStream in = new ObjectInputStream(s.getInputStream());
```

```
    char[] password = "123456".toCharArray();
    KeyStore ks = KeyStore.getInstance("JKS");
    ks.load(new FileInputStream("test.ks"), password);
    PrivateKey pri = (PrivateKey)ks.getKey("test", password);

    out.writeObject(ks.getCertificate("test"));

    SealedObject so = (SealedObject)in.readObject();
    byte[] bytes = (byte[])so.getObject(pri);
    so = (SealedObject)in.readObject();
    SecretKey sk = new SecretKeySpec(bytes, 0, bytes.length,
so.getAlgorithm());
    while(true) {
      System.out.println(so.getObject(sk));
      so = (SealedObject)in.readObject();
    }
  }
}
```

To start this application, start the receiver program as follows:

```
java SealedObjectReceiver
```

Now start the sender program as

```
java SealedObjectSender 172.16.5.81
```

Here `172.16.5.81` is the IP address of the receiver computer.

19.8.6 GuardedObject

The operations on a sensitive object should be governed by a permission. This means, each method call on the object should verify if caller thread has proper permission. This tells us to insert security check (probably redundant) in every method including constructor.

Moreover, the user of an object may not always be its creator. This happens especially when an object is transferred across a network using serialization and deserialization. In this case, the security context of an object's caller may be different from that of its creator.

Note that when an object is reconstructed using deserialization, constructor is not used. Therefore, security check code (if any) in the constructor may be bypassed during object reconstruction.

So, if every method requires the permission, it makes sense to require it once, at object level. Java `java.security.GuardedObject` provides object level access control which ensures that permission is checked once. This is done in `getObject()` method, which a caller must use to gain access to the protected object. The basic idea is as follows:

A `Guard` object, which *guards* access to another target object, is first created. Any object can become a Guard provided that the objects class implements the interface `Guard`. It has only one method `checkGuard()` that takes an `Object` argument and performs certain (security) checks. Fortunately, the `java.security.Permission` class (and hence its subclasses) implements the `Guard` interface and can be used as a guard. We create a `PropertyPermission` object as guard as follows:

```
Guard guard = new PropertyPermission("usr.home", "read");
```

This represents a read access to the "usr.home" system property. For simplicity, let us create a String object to be guarded as follows:

```
String pass = new String("123456");
```

The guarded object should be `Serializable` if it is intended to pass across the network. A `GuardedObject` is then created from this `pass` along with its `guard`.

```
GuardedObject go = new GuardedObject(pass, guard);
```

The object `go` embeds the `pass` and `guard` objects. This `GuardedObject` object `go` can be transferred to a different JVM having possibly a different security context. We serialize `go` and put it in a file pass:

```
ObjectOutputStream oos = new ObjectOutputStream(new FileOutputStream("pass"));
oos.writeObject(go);
```

The complete source code is shown below:

```
import java.security.*;
import java.io.*;
import java.util.PropertyPermission;
public class GuardedObjectWrite {
  public static void main(String[] args) throws Exception {
    Guard guard = new PropertyPermission("usr.home", "read");
    String pass = new String("123456");
    GuardedObject go = new GuardedObject(pass, guard);
    ObjectOutputStream oos = new ObjectOutputStream(new
FileOutputStream("pass"));
    oos.writeObject(go);
  }
}
```

We assume that object is reconstructed at the receiver end using a code as follows:

```
ObjectInputStream ois = new ObjectInputStream(new FileInputStream("pass"));
GuardedObject go = (GuardedObject)ois.readObject();
```

To gain access to the guarded object, `getObject()` method is used:

```
String ps = (String) go.getObject();
```

The `getObject()` method in turn invokes the `checkGuard()` method on the guard object that was used to create `GuardedObject`. Our guard object was a `PropertyPermission` object which allows accessing the guarded object to a thread only if the thread has the read access to the `usr.home` system property.

The complete source code is shown below:

```
import java.security.*;
import java.io.*;
public class GuardedObjectRead {
  public static void main(String[] args) throws Exception {
    ObjectInputStream ois = new ObjectInputStream(new FileInputStream("pass"));
    GuardedObject go = (GuardedObject)ois.readObject();
    String pass = (String) go.getObject();
    System.out.println("pass = " + pass);
  }
}
```

19.9 SECURE RMI

The underlying socket communication used by Java's default RMI implementation is not secured. So, how do you develop Java RMI applications that can make remote invocations over secure SSL connections? In this section, we shall modify our calculator RMI application (discussed in the RMI chapter) so that the underlying network communication becomes secured.

In general, Java RMI framework allows us to export a remote object specifying custom socket factories that create sockets of desired type for underlying network communication. These factories may be specified either in the overloaded constructor or `exportObject()` method of `java.rmi.server.UnicastRemoteObject` or `java.rmi.activation.Activatable` class. They take a `java.rmi.server.RMIClientSocketFactory` instance and a `java.rmi.server.RMIServerSocketFactory` instance. The `RMIClientSocketFactory` may be used to control how connections are established and the type of socket to use. On the other hand, the `RMIServerSocketFactory` may be used to control how incoming connections are listened for and accepted as well as the type of sockets to use for incoming connections.

Since, we want our calculator application to work over an SSL connection, our task is now to specify socket factories that create SSL sockets. Fortunately, RMI system provides two classes `SslRMIClientSocketFactory` and `SslRMIServerSocketFactory` (in `javax.rmi.ssl` package) for this purpose which implement `RMIClientSocketFactory` and `RMIServerSocketFactory` over the SSL/TLS protocols respectively.

So, in the calculator server application, let us export our calculator object specifying them as follows:

```
SimpleCalculator cal = new SimpleCalculator();
Calculator stub = (Calculator)UnicastRemoteObject.exportObject(cal,0, new
SslRMIClientSocketFactory(), new SslRMIServerSocketFactory());
```

So, our modified server (`SSLCalculatorServer.java`) looks like this:

```
//SSLCalculatorServer.java
import java.rmi.*;
import java.rmi.registry.*;
import java.rmi.server.*;
import javax.rmi.ssl.*;
public class SSLCalculatorServer {
  public static void main(String args[]) {
    try {
      SimpleCalculator cal = new SimpleCalculator();
      Calculator stub = (Calculator)UnicastRemoteObject.exportObject(cal,0, new
SslRMIClientSocketFactory(), new SslRMIServerSocketFactory());
      Registry registry = LocateRegistry.createRegistry(1099);
      String name = "calculator";
      registry.rebind(name, stub);
      System.out.println("Calculator server ready...");
    }catch (Exception e) { e.printStackTrace(); }
  }
}
```

The modified piece of code has been shown with bold face. The code of the client remains unchanged as it was. To run the application, server creates a keystore `server.ks` using the following command:

```
keytool -genkey -alias mykey -keyalg RSA -keystore server.ks -storepass 123456
-keypass 123456 -dname "CN=U. K. Roy, OU=IT, O=JU, L=Kolkata, ST=WB, C=IN"
```

Now, export this certificate to a certificate file `server.cer` using the following command:

```
keytool -export -alias mykey -keystore server.ks -storepass 123456
-file server.cer
```

Copy this `server.cer` file to client's home directory and import it in the client's trust store `client.ts` using the following command:

```
keytool -import -v -keystore client.ts -storepass 123456 -file server.cer
```

The application is now ready to be started. Start the server as follows:

```
java -Djavax.net.ssl.keyStore=server.ks -Djavax.net.ssl.keyStorePassword=123456
SSLCalculatorServer
```

Start the client as follows:

```
java -Djavax.net.ssl.trustStore=client.ts -Djavax.net.ssl.trustStorePassword=123456
CalculatorClient 172.16.5.81
```

A sample output is shown in Figure 19.6:

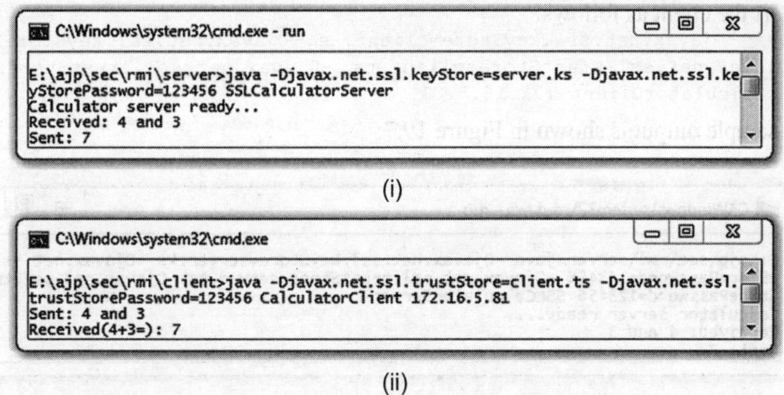

Figure 19.6: RMI over SSL (i) Server (ii) Client

If the server also needs client authentication, the overloaded constructor of `SslRMIServerSocketFactory` may be used when an object is exported as follows:

```
Calculator stub = (Calculator)UnicastRemoteObject.exportObject(cal,0, new
SslRMIClientSocketFactory(), new SslRMIServerSocketFactory(null, null, true));
```

In this case, client creates a certificate and makes an entry in the keystore. Similarly, the server imports this certificate in its truststore.

Note that a remote method invocation takes place in steps:

- A client consults remote registry to get a reference to the stub of the remote object
- The client then invokes methods on the remote object

Our application is so far secured for the second step. The communication with the remote registry still takes place in a non-secure way. To solve this problem, custom socket factories may be specified in the `createRegistry()` and `getRegistry()` methods of `LocateRegistry`. So, modify the calculator server as follows:

```
Registry registry = LocateRegistry.createRegistry(1099, new
SslRMIClientSocketFactory(), new SslRMIServerSocketFactory(null, null, true));
```

Similarly, modify the client (call it `SSLCalculatorClient.java`) as follows:

```
Registry registry = LocateRegistry.getRegistry(args[0], 1099, new
javax.rmi.ssl.SslRMIClientSocketFactory());
```

To run this application, client creates a keystore `client.ks` using the following command:

```
keytool -genkey -alias mykey -keyalg RSA -keystore client.ks -storepass 123456
-keypass 123456 -dname "CN=U. K. Roy, OU=IT, O=JU, L=Kolkata, ST=WB, C=IN"
```

Now, export this certificate to a certificate file `client.cer` using the following command:

```
keytool -export -alias mykey -keystore client.ks -storepass 123456 -file client.cer
```

Copy this `client.cer` file to server's home directory and import it in server's trust store `server.ts` using the following command:

```
keytool -import -v -keystore server.ts -storepass 123456 -file client.cer
```

The application is now ready to be started. Start the server as follows:

```
java -Djavax.net.ssl.keyStore=server.ks -Djavax.net.ssl.keyStorePassword=123456
-Djavax.net.ssl.trustStore=server.ts -Djavax.net.ssl.trustStorePassword=123456
SSLCalculatorServer
```

Start the client as follows:

```
java -Djavax.net.ssl.keyStore=client.ks -Djavax.net.ssl.keyStorePassword=123456
-Djavax.net.ssl.trustStore=client.ts -Djavax.net.ssl.trustStorePassword=123456
SSLCalculatorClient 172.16.5.81
```

A sample output is shown in Figure 19.7:

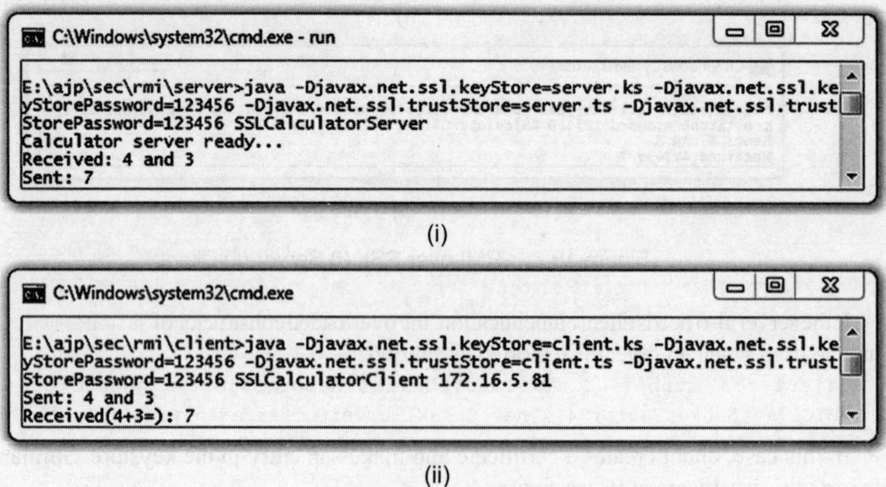

Figure 19.7: RMI over SSL using client authentication (i) Server (ii) Client

19.9.1 Writing Custom Socket Factories

In our previous example, we have used classes provided by the Java RMI framework as custom socket factories. It is also possible to develop our own factories and specify them. To create a custom client socket factory, we implement the `RMIClientSocketFactory` interface which has a single method. Here is a sample implementation (`MySSLClientSocketFactory.java`):

```
//MySSLClientSocketFactory.java
import java.io.*;
import java.net.*;
import java.rmi.server.*;
import javax.net.ssl.*;
public class MySSLClientSocketFactory implements RMIClientSocketFactory,
Serializable {
  public Socket createSocket(String host, int port) throws IOException {
    System.setProperty("javax.net.ssl.keyStore", "client.ks");
    System.setProperty("javax.net.ssl.keyStorePassword", "123456");
    System.setProperty("javax.net.ssl.trustStore", "client.ts");
    System.setProperty("javax.net.ssl.trustStorePassword", "123456");

    SocketFactory factory = SSLSocketFactory.getDefault();
    Socket s = factory.createSocket(host, port);
    return s;
  }
}
```

Here, we have created an `SSLSocket` using default implementation of `SSLSocketFactory` and returned it. We also have set up necessary properties for SSL. Writing a custom server socket factory is similar as follows (`MySSLServerSocketFactory.java`):

```
//MySSLServerSocketFactory.java
import java.io.*;
import java.net.*;
import java.rmi.server.*;
import javax.net.ssl.*;
import javax.net.*;

public class MySSLServerSocketFactory implements RMIServerSocketFactory {
  public ServerSocket createServerSocket(int port) throws IOException {
    System.setProperty("javax.net.ssl.keyStore", "server.ks");
    System.setProperty("javax.net.ssl.keyStorePassword", "123456");
    System.setProperty("javax.net.ssl.trustStore", "server.ts");
    System.setProperty("javax.net.ssl.trustStorePassword", "123456");

    ServerSocketFactory ssf= SSLServerSocketFactory.getDefault();
    ServerSocket ss = ssf.createServerSocket(port);
    ((SSLServerSocket)ss).setNeedClientAuth(true);
    return ss;
  }
}
```

Here, we have created an `SSLServerSocket` using default implementation of `SSLServerSocketFactory` and returned it. We also have set up necessary properties for SSL. The factory also specifies that the server needs client authentication using `setNeedClientAuth()` method.

The server is then modified as follows:

```
Calculator stub = (Calculator)UnicastRemoteObject.exportObject(cal,0, new
MySSLClientSocketFactory(), new MySSLServerSocketFactory());
Registry registry = LocateRegistry.createRegistry(1099, new
MySSLClientSocketFactory(), new MySSLServerSocketFactory());
```

Modify the client as follows:

```
Registry registry = LocateRegistry.getRegistry(args[0], 1099, new
MySSLClientSocketFactory());
```

Start the server as follows:

```
java SSLCalculatorServer
```

Start the client as follows:

```
java SSLCalculatorClient 172.16.5.81
```

19.10 SECURE XML-RPC

An XML-RPC application can be made secure using two ways:

Start the XML-RPC server in an SSL/TLS enabled web server and write an XML-RPC client to communicate with the server or use an SSL enabled XML-RPC framework.

19.10.1 Using XmlRpcServlet

In Chapter 17, we have seen that Apache XML-RPC provides a servlet `XmlRpcServlet`, which has an automatically embedded instance of `XmlRpcServer` and may be installed to an existing tomcat web server to serve XML-RPC requests. To make the communication secured, it is a good idea to configure the tomcat web server so that it runs over SSL. A description is already given in Section 17.6. The procedure of installing `XmlRpcServlet` is also given in Chapter 17. So, configure tomcat to make it SSL-enabled and install `XmlRpcServlet`. Assume that the SSL-enabled tomcat web server runs on a computer having IP address `172.16.5.81` on port `8443`. The URL of the servlet `XmlRpcServlet` will then be `https://172.16.5.81:8443/xmlrpc/servlet`. This URL may be used in the XML-RPC client application. The modified XML-RPC client that uses SSL communication is shown below:

```
//SSLClient.java
import javax.net.ssl.HostnameVerifier;
import javax.net.ssl.HttpsURLConnection;
import javax.net.ssl.SSLSession;

import org.apache.xmlrpc.client.*;
import java.net.URL;
public class SSLClient    {
 public static void main (String [] args) {
  try {
    HttpsURLConnection.setDefaultHostnameVerifier(new HostnameVerifier() {
      public boolean verify(String host, SSLSession ss) { return true; }
    });

    XmlRpcClient client = new XmlRpcClient();
    XmlRpcClientConfigImpl config = new XmlRpcClientConfigImpl();
    config.setServerURL(new URL("https://"+args[0]+":8443/xmlrpc/servlet"));
    client.setConfig(config);

    int n = 6;
    Object[] params = new Object[]{ new Integer(n)};
    System.out.println("Sent : "+n);
    Integer result = (Integer)client.execute("Factorial.fact", params);
    System.out.println("Received : "+result);
   } catch (Exception e) {
     e.printStackTrace();
   }
  }
}
```

The modified code is shown using bold font. To run the application, copy `tomcat.cer` (described in Section 19.4.7) to the client directory and import it in the client's trust store (`client.ts`) using the following command:

```
keytool -import -v -keystore client.ts -storepass 123456 -file tomcat.cer
```

Start the tomcat web server. Now, start the client using the following command:

```
java -cp ..\lib\*;. -Djavax.net.ssl.trustStore=client.ts -
Djavax.net.ssl.trustStorePassword=123456 SSLClient 172.16.5.81
```

19.10.2 Using Secure XML-RPC

Apache XML-RPC version 2.0.1 also provides a framework that works on SSL. The security is provided by two primary class files `SecureWebServer` and `SecureXmlRpcClient` (provided in the package `org.apache.xmlrpc.secure`). The `SecureWebServer` class is used to create a secure XML-RPC server. A sample usage of this class is shown (`SslXmlRpcServer.java`) below:

```
//SslXmlRpcServer.java
import org.apache.xmlrpc.secure.*;
public class SslXmlRpcServer {
   public int fact(int n) {
    System.out.println("Received : "+n);
    int prod = 1;
    for(int i = 2; i <= n; i++)
       prod *= i;
    System.out.println("Sent : "+prod);
    return prod;
   }
```

```
  public static void main(String args[]) {
    SecureWebServer web=new SecureWebServer(6789);
    web.addHandler("Factorial", new SslXmlRpcServer());
    web.start();
    System.out.println("XML-RPC server ready...");
  }
}
```

To create a secure XML-RPC client, we use `SecureXmlRpcClient` class. The source code of this client (`SslXmlRpcClient.java`) is given below:

```
//SslXmlRpcClient.java
import java.util.*;
import javax.net.ssl.*;
import org.apache.xmlrpc.secure.*;
public class SslXmlRpcClient {
  public static void main(String args[]) {
    HttpsURLConnection.setDefaultHostnameVerifier(new HostnameVerifier() {
      public boolean verify(String host, SSLSession ss) { return true; }
    });
    try {
      SecureXmlRpcClient client=new
SecureXmlRpcClient("https://"+args[0]+":6789");
      Vector params= new Vector();
      int n = 5;
      params.add(n);
      System.out.println("Sent : " + n);
      Object result = client.execute("Factorial.fact",params);
      System.out.println("Received : "+result);
    } catch (Exception e) {
      e.printStackTrace();
    }
  }
}
```

To run this application, we have to download a JAR file containing XML-RPC 2.0.1 classes and interfaces. We downloaded `xmlrpc-2.0.1.jar` from `http://www.java2s.com/Code/Jar/x/Downloadxmlrpc201jar.htm`. Since, `SecureWebServer` and `SecureXmlRpcClient` classes use a set of utilities for encoding and decoding text and binary data, we need Apache Commons Codec (TM) software that provides implementations of common encoders and decoders such as Base64, Hex, Phonetic and URLs. These utilities (as `commons-codec-1.9.jar` file) can be downloaded from `http://commons.apache.org/proper/commons-codec/download_codec.cgi`. Now create the following directory structure. Place the JAR files in lib directory. Also place `SslXmlRpcServer.java` and `SslXmlRpcClient.java` in the server and client directory respectively.

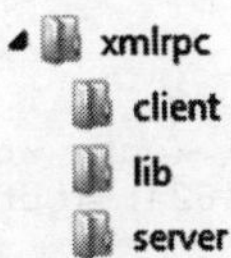

Now go to the server directory and create a key store (server.ks) using the following command:

```
keytool -genkey -alias mykey -keyalg RSA -keystore server.ks -storepass 123456
-keypass 123456 -dname "CN=U. K. Roy, OU=IT, O=JU, L=Kolkata, ST=WB, C=IN"
```

Now, export the certificate to a file server.cer using the following command:

```
keytool -export -alias mykey -keystore server.ks -storepass 123456 -file server.cer
```

Now, copy this server.cer file to the client directory and use the following command to import this certificate in the client's trust store (client.ts):

```
keytool -import -v -keystore client.ts -storepass 123456 -file server.cer
```

The application is now ready to run. Go to the server directory and use the following command to compile the server:

```
javac -cp ..\lib\*;. *.java
```

Now, start the server using the following command:

```
java -cp ..\lib\*;. -Djavax.net.ssl.keyStore=server.ks -
Djavax.net.ssl.keyStorePassword=123456 SslXmlRpcServer
```

Go to the client directory and use the following command to compile the client:

```
javac -cp ..\lib\*;. *.java
```

Now, start the client using the following command:

```
java -cp ..\lib\*;. -Djavax.net.ssl.trustStore=client.ts -
Djavax.net.ssl.trustStorePassword=123456 SslXmlRpcClient 172.16.5.81
```

19.11 SIGNING AND VERIFYING JAR

Java security architecture also provides a facility to digitally sign and verify a **J**ava **AR**chive (JAR) using the tool `jarsigner`. This is a very useful tool that enables parties to exchange data as a single package (created using `jar` utility and consisting of class files, images, sounds and other digital data) ensuring its integrity and authentication. It is used to

- sign JAR files, and
- verify the signatures and integrity of signed JAR files.

19.11.1 Signing JAR

To sign a JAR-bundled file, `jarsigner` needs a private key, which is used to generate digital signatures. We know that a keystore contains private key(s) each of which can be referred to by an *alias*. During signing, the jarsigner tool takes this alias to get the private key. If you already have a keystore use it or create one using the following command:

```
keytool -genkey -alias tom -keyalg RSA -keystore test.jks -storepass 123456 -keypass
123456 -dname "CN=Tom, OU=IT, O=JU, L=Kolkata, ST=WB, C=IN"
```

We also assume that there exists a JAR `test.jar` to be signed. The following is a sample command to create a JAR test.jar:

```
jar cvf test.jar *.class
```

A sample output is shown below:

```
added manifest
adding: First.class(in = 380) (out= 269)(deflated 29%)
adding: GetProps.class(in = 1624) (out= 857)(deflated 47%)
```

We can then use the following command to sign it:

```
jarsigner -keystore test.jks -storepass 123456 test.jar tom
```

The `jarsigner` uses private key from the keystore `test.jks` corresponding to the alias `tom` to generate digital signatures for the JAR file `test.jar`. The signed JAR file also contains a copy of the certificate containing the public key corresponding to the private key used to sign the file. This certificate is used by jarsigner to verify the digital signature of the signed JAR file.

Since no output file is specified, signed JAR file is exactly the same as the input JAR file. The `-signedjar` option may be used to specify the name of the output signed jar file as follows:

```
jarsigner -keystore test.jks -storepass 123456 -signedjar stest.jar test.jar tom
```

When a JAR file is signed, a *digest* is calculated for each file in the JAR. The digest of a file is a hash or encoded representation of the content of the file. The digest changes if and only if the content of the file changes. These digest values are placed in the archive's manifest file (`META-INF/MANIFEST.MF`). Here is a sample manifest file:

```
Manifest-Version: 1.0
Created-By: 1.7.0_07 (Oracle Corporation)

Name: First.class
SHA-256-Digest: W11oZ8EwfXKzq99Gzy1UXi9DnC3o2xWmyJwllmixfD8=

Name: GetProps.class
SHA-256-Digest: DPcVIuZOq6IU2rxGP4jojrWPc4YY141d78WSFwdWuVk=
```

The first two lines say that the manifest conforms to version 1.0 and was created by the 1.7.0_06 version of the JDK. Each pair of rest lines lists

- the file name,
- the name of the digest algorithm used (SHA), and
- an SHA digest value.

In the signed JAR file, two additional files are placed in the META-INF directory:

- a signature file, with extension .SF and
- a signature block file, with extension .DSA, .RSA, or .EC

This can be verified using the following command:

```
jar tvf test.jar
```

This results in a sample output as follows:

```
   237 Sat Jan 18 22:40:26 PST 2014 META-INF/MANIFEST.MF
   399 Sat Jan 18 22:40:26 PST 2014 META-INF/TOM.SF
  1298 Sat Jan 18 22:40:26 PST 2014 META-INF/TOM.RSA
     0 Sat Jan 18 22:40:10 PST 2014 META-INF/
   380 Sun Jan 12 09:53:26 PST 2014 First.class
  1624 Sun Jan 12 08:56:38 PST 2014 GetProps.class
```

This indicates that two additional files `TOM.SF` and `TOM.RSA` have been created and placed under `META-INF` directory. By default the base file name of these files is decided from the alias name. However, it may be specified using `-sigFile` option as follows:

```
-sigFile MYSIG
```

This generates files named `MYSIG.SF` and `MYSIG.RSA`.

19.11.1.1 Signature (.SF) File

The signature file looks similar to the manifest file. However, unlike manifest file where digest values are computed from the file content, the digest values in the signature file are computed from the corresponding entries in the manifest file. Here is a sample signature file:

```
Signature-Version: 1.0
SHA-256-Digest-Manifest-Main-Attributes: 21FX/xw8/ju0AeReBcfmD78H9Mij7
 ZBd84CDIOniLrQ=
SHA-256-Digest-Manifest: hxfdz/3QnAKpMum1COTR06uNLJ+iAqoWvozBZ83NTvQ=
Created-By: 1.7.0_07 (Oracle Corporation)

Name: First.class
SHA-256-Digest: 1M175uZYH+56F+3Kq1Co/ZFagEVmzHBgVXQQvHAx8QI=

Name: GetProps.class
SHA-256-Digest: zRcuvs9fOa4EKXlt/JOPBnLO0+1Ivp/0KdL/obkU8Q8=
```

In addition, the signature file contains a digest for the entire manifest (`SHA-256-Digest-Manifest` header in the previous example) file.

19.11.1.2 Signature Block File

This is the file which actually contains the signature of .SF file which basically summarizes the contents of all source files of the JAR. It has the extension .DSA, .RSA, or .EC depending on the signature algorithm used. The certificate or certificate chain from the keystore containing the public key to be used for authentication (corresponding to the private key used for signing) is also placed in the signature block file. This file is not human-readable.

19.11.2 Verifying JAR

Verifying a JAR file means checking if the signature is valid and if all files remain unchanged as they were when the signature was generated. This involves the following steps:

- Ensure that the .SF file has not been tempered with. This is done by checking if the signature stored in the signature block (.RSA) file was indeed generated using the private key corresponding to the public key whose certificate (or certificate chain) is also stored in the signature block file.
- Ensure that the manifest file has not been tempered with; ensure that no file has not been added/removed from the JAR. This is done by checking the digest listed in each entry in the .SF file with each corresponding section in the manifest.
- Ensure that all source files have not been tempered with. This is done by re-calculating the digest for each file and comparing it with the corresponding digest recorded in the manifest file.

The Java Runtime Environment is responsible for executing those steps. We simply use –verify option do all these steps as follows:

```
jarsigner -verify test.jar
```

If everything goes fine, the following message is generated:

```
jar verified.
```

If verification fails, the appropriate message is shown. For example, if the manifest file is changed, the following message is displayed:

```
jarsigner: java.lang.SecurityException: Invalid signature file digest for Manifest
main attributes
```

To get more information, `-verbose` may be used as follows:

```
jarsigner -verify -verbose test.jar
```

This generates a sample output as follows:

```
             0 Sat Jan 18 23:26:58 PST 2014 META-INF/
          1298 Sat Jan 18 22:40:26 PST 2014 META-INF/TOM.RSA
           399 Sat Jan 18 22:40:26 PST 2014 META-INF/TOM.SF
s          237 Sat Jan 18 23:26:58 PST 2014 META-INF/MANIFEST.MF
sm         380 Sun Jan 12 09:53:26 PST 2014 First.class
sm        1624 Sun Jan 12 08:56:38 PST 2014 GetProps.class

    s = signature was verified
    m = entry is listed in manifest
    k = at least one certificate was found in keystore
    i = at least one certificate was found in identity scope

jar verified.
```

19.12 MULTIPLE SIGNATURES FOR A JAR FILE

Note that signing JAR file does not change the content of constituent files; it merely adds some additional files containing information which may be used for verification. This implies that a JAR may be signed at times as we wish. Every time we sign a JAR, a pair of signature (.SF) and signature block file (.DSA or .RSA or .EC) is created. For example, our resultant `test.jar` can be signed further using a separate keystore alias Jerry as follows:

```
jarsigner -keystore test.jks -storepass 123456 test.jar jerry
```

This adds to additional files `JERRY.SF` (signature file) and `JERRY.RSA` (signature block file) in the directory `META-INF`. This can be verified using the following command:

```
jar tvf test.jar
```

A sample output of the above command is shown below:

```
 237 Sat Jan 18 22:40:26 PST 2014 META-INF/MANIFEST.MF
 399 Sat Jan 18 22:45:32 PST 2014 META-INF/JERRY.SF
1304 Sat Jan 18 22:45:32 PST 2014 META-INF/JERRY.RSA
 399 Sat Jan 18 22:40:26 PST 2014 META-INF/TOM.SF
1298 Sat Jan 18 22:40:26 PST 2014 META-INF/TOM.RSA
   0 Sat Jan 18 22:40:10 PST 2014 META-INF/
 380 Sun Jan 12 09:53:26 PST 2014 First.class
1624 Sun Jan 12 08:56:38 PST 2014 GetProps.class
```

This indeed shows that two more files have been added. Make sure that the keystore file has an alias named `jerry`. If it doesn't exist, create it using the following command:

```
keytool -genkey -alias jerry -keyalg RSA -keystore test.jks -storepass 123456 -
keypass 123456 -dname "CN=Jerry, OU=IT, O=JU, L=Kolkata, ST=WB, C=IN"
```

19.13 ACCESS CONTROL

Although, application developers usually needn't bother about the low-level functions of Java security architecture, an overview of the different components and their interaction is required for smooth understanding.

The heart of the Java security architecture is `SecurityManager` class. Note that not all the actions, taken by various methods of Java libraries, are potentially safe. A small list of these actions is given below:

- Read/write/delete files
- Read/write system properties
- Listen on a local port number
- Accept a socket connection from a specified host and port number
- Open a socket connection to a specified host and port number
- Modify a thread (change its priority, stop it, and so on)
- Create a new class loader
- Create a new process
- Exit from an application
- Load a class from a specified package
- Add a new class to a specified package
- Load a dynamic library containing native methods

Who decided which core actions are unsafe. Obviously, Java security designers made that decision. Anyway, for each of these potentially unsafe actions (see list below), `SecurityManager` class has a method (with name starting with 'check') which determines (by consulting specified policy) if the action is allowed. For example, given a security policy, `checkRead()` and `checkWrite()` method define if a thread is allowed to read from or write to a specified file respectively.

These check methods are invoked by various methods of Java library before performing those sensitive operations. The call of such a check method typically looks like this:

```
SecurityManager security = System.getSecurityManager();
if (security != null) {
   security.checkXXX(argument,  . . . );
}
```

So, the security manager has the opportunity to allow or disallow the operation after consulting a given security policy. This is done by typically creating a `Permission` object (representing access right being sought) and passing it to a special method `checkPermission()`. Current implementation simply passes the Permission object to the static `checkPermission()` method of `AccessController` class, which is the actual workhorse of the security core. This essentially gathers an array of classes representing current calling thread's stack. It then inspects the permissions (in the form of `ProtectionDomains`) associated with each class in this stack. If any class does not have the permission being tested, an `AccessControlException` is thrown. Otherwise the method returns silently.

19.13.1 Installing Built-in Security Manager

By default, the Java interpreter does not provide a security boundary for a Java application. If we want to run a Java application under the supervision of a security manager, we can explicitly inform it in many ways. One way to do this is setting the system property `java.security.manager` using command line argument as follows:

```
java -Djava.security.manager SomeApp
```

This instructs the interpreter to install an instance of the system's default security manager (`java.lang.SecurityManager`). Alternatively, an application can install it using the following piece of code:

```
SecurityManager sm = new SecurityManager();
System.setSecurityManager(sm);
```

The first line creates an instance of the security manager and the second line installs it.

19.13.2 Policy Files

A policy specifies a set of allowable permission(s) to be used by the code from various sources and running as various principals and is represented by a `java.security.Policy` object. A single `Policy` object is installed in the runtime at any given time. Java's default policy implementation expects policy to be specified in files called *policy configuration files*. The policy information contained in these configuration files is loaded in the `Policy` object during its creation. A security manager installed for an application consults this `Policy` object and allows or disallows actions requested by the application. The location of policy files may be specified either in the security property file or at runtime (as command line argument). The security property file `java.security` can be found in in the directory `java.home\lib\security` in Windows and `java.home/lib/security` in Unix like OS where `java.home` refers to the directory that hosts the Java Runtime Environment (JRE). The locations (urls) of policy files are specified in this property file as the values of properties whose names have the form

```
policy.url.n
```

where possible values of `n` are 1, 2, 3,... The policy file locations are specified as values of these properties in the following form:

```
policy.url.n=URL
```

where URL is the location of the policy file. The `java.security` file typically specifies two policy files as follows:

```
policy.url.1=file:${java.home}/lib/security/java.policy
policy.url.2=file:${user.home}/.java.policy
```

The file `java.policy` can indeed be found in the directory `java.home\lib\security` in Windows and `java.home/lib/security` in Unix like OS. This file is called system-wide default policy file as it is consulted first by the Java's built-in security manager. Similarly, a user may place his/her own policy in file `.java.policy` which should be stored in the user's home directory. Other policy files may also be specified subsequently using the value of n as 3, 4, 5,.... A security manager loads the permissions specified in all those policy files in order to take a decision. Make sure that the value of n is continuous.

This has a problem as those steps are required after every reinstallation of Java or after redeployment in a different JVM. However, it may be useful for granting permissions to code that are seldom redeployed.

Additional or a different policy file may also be specified using command line argument `-Djava.security.policy`. Here is an example:

```
java -Djava.security.manager -Djava.security.policy=policyURL SomeApp
```

where `policyURL` is the location of the policy file, which is loaded in addition to all the policy files that are specified in the security property file `java.security`. This `policyURL` may be any regular URL including the name of a policy file in the current directory. Note that in a policy file, we basically *allow* permission. So, once a permission is allowed in a policy file, it cannot be withdrawn in the subsequent policy files. However, newer permissions can always be given in the subsequent policy files.

It is always a good idea to use forward slash(/), instead of backslash (\) as the directory separator as it works both in Windows as well as Linux like OS. Note that, on Windows systems, whenever we specify a file path in a string, we need to include two backslashes for each actual single backslash in the path.

A different policy file is specified in `Djava.security.policy` argument using == (double equals) as follows:

```
java -Djava.security.manager -Djava.security.policy==my.policy SomeApp
```

Here, security manager will ONLY load the policy file `my.policy` ignoring all other policy files specified in the security property file. Note that for `appletviewer`, correct command line argument is `-J-Djava.security.policy`. Also make sure that the value of `policy.allowSystemProperty` in `java.security` file is `true` to work with `Djava.security.policy` command line argument.

An application that uses policy files is described in Section 16.16

19.13.3 Policy File Syntax

In general, a permission merely states that some "thing" can take some "actions" on some "target". For example, in a multi-user OS, a permission means if a user (thing) can read (action) a file (target). Permissions are specified in a policy file using predefined syntax. A policy file contains a list of *entries*. An entry may be of two types: *keystore* entry or *grant* entry. There may be zero or one keystore entry and zero or more grant entries.

19.13.3.1 Keystore Entry

This entry is used to provide the keystore information to retrieve the public keys of the signers specified in the grant entries. If any grant entries specify signer aliases, or principal aliases (see next section), this entry is required and may appear anywhere outside the grant entries in the policy file. It takes the following form:

```
keystore "URL", "type", "provider";
```

where `URL` is the location of the keystore, optional `type` if the keystore type (default is `jks`) and optional `provider` is keystore provider (default is `SUN`). Here is an example of keystore entry:

```
keystore "jerry.jks";
```

The URL of the keystore is relative to the policy file location.

19.13.3.2 Grant Entry

In this entry, actual permissions to be allowed are specified. Each grant entry has zero or more *permission entries*. It may also have `signedBy`, `codeBase` and `principal` entries that collectively specify the code which the permissions have to be applied on. A grant entry takes the following form:

```
grant signedBy "signer_names", codeBase "URL",
        principal principal_class_name "principal_name",
        principal principal_class_name "principal_name",
        ... {

      permission permission_class_name "target_name", "action",
          signedBy "signer_names";
      permission permission_class_name "target_name", "action",
          signedBy "signer_names";
      ...
  };
```

A `signedBy` clause indicates that permissions are applicable only to the code which was signed by the private key corresponding to the public key in the keystore (indicated by keystore entry) entry specified by signedBy value. Consider the following example:

```
keystore "jerry.jks", "jks", "SUN";
grant  signedBy "tom" {
  permission java.io.FilePermission "../data/*", "read";
};
```

This means "any code in a JAR file, which is signed using the private key corresponding to the public key certificate in the keystore whose entry is aliased by tom, has read permission to all files under the sibling data directory".

The value of `signedBy` may be a comma-separated list of aliases to the keystore. For example, `signedBy "tom, jerry"` means, the code must be signed using the private keys corresponding to the public key certificates in the keystore whose entry is aliased by `tom` AND `jerry` to have the designated permission.

The `signedBy` clause is optional and if absent, permissions are applied to all the codes, signed by it or not.

The `codeBase` clause is used to allow permission to that code originated from a location specified by the `codeBase` value. Consider the following example:

```
grant  codeBase "file:/E:/ajp/sec/sm/jerry/*" {
...
};
```

This says that all class files under the specified directory have the listed permissions. Use forward slash(/), not backslash (\), as the directory separator. Moreover, the characters at the end determine the exact meaning of the `codeBase` value.

- A JAR file name matches only the classes in the JAR file.
- A trailing "/" matches all class files (but not JAR files) in the specified directory.
- Trailing "/*" matches all class and JAR files contained in the specified directory.
- A trailing "/-" matches all class and JAR files in the directory and recursively all files in subdirectories contained in that directory.

The `codeBase` clause is optional and if absent, permissions are applied to the code originated from any source.

19.13.3.3 Permission Entry

A permission entry starts with the keyword `permission` followed by the following piece of information

- A permission class name representing a permission type
- The name of a target, permission has to be applied on
- Optional comma separated actions that are allowed to be performed on the target.
- Optional signedBy name/value pair

A permission class is a subclass (directly or indirectly) of abstract java.security permission class and represents access to a system resource. Examples of permission classes include `FilePermission`, `SocketPermission`, `RuntimePermission`, `PropertyPermission` etc. A target is a resource, which the permission is specified for. The "actions" list tells the actions that are permitted for the resource. Here is an example:

```
permission java.io.FilePermission "/tmp/*", "read,write";
```

This grants read/write access to all files in `/tmp` (in Linux). The action is not required for classes such as `java.lang.RuntimePermission`.

The `signedBy` clause for a permission entry is optional. If present, it indicates that the permission class itself must be signed by the specified alias(es) in order to grant the permission.

```
permission aClass "aTarget", "actions", signedBy "tom";
```

This says that for the permission `aClass`, `actions` on `aTarget` are granted if the permission class aClass is placed in a JAR file, which was signed by the private key corresponding to the public key in the certificate specified by the alias `tom`. The `signedBy` clause is ignored for system classes, since they are not subject to policy restrictions.

Examples of Permission Entry

Allows accepting socket connection from 172.16.5.82

```
permission java.net.SocketPermission "172.16.5.82", "accept";
```

Allows connecting to port 6789 on 172.16.4.120.82

```
permission java.net.SocketPermission "172.16.4.120", "connect";
```

Allows accepting connections on, connect to, or listen on any port 999 and above on the local host.

```
permission java.net.SocketPermission "localhost:999-", "accept,connect,listen";
```

19.13.4 Custom Permission Class

New permission classes may be created if built-in permission classes are not adequate. Consider the following scenario:

A department has many students who want to get printouts from a printer. However, only "tom" has the permission to do so. Since, no build-in permission class does not fit well for this situation, we write our own permission class `PrintPermission`. All permission classes must extend either `Permission` or `BasicPermission` (which itself is a subclass of `Permission`). The `Permission` defines more complex permissions that require names and actions, whereas `BasicPermission` defines simpler permissions that only require a name. Our `PrintPermission` also requires only a name and hence can be extended from `BasicPermission` as follows:

```
public class PrintPermission extends java.security.BasicPermission {
  public PrintPermission(String target) {
    super(target);
  }
}
```

We do not override the methods of `BasicPermission` as we don't want extra functions. However, we invoke super class constructor. We also write another minimal class `Student` having a single method `print()` as follows:

```
//Student.java
public class Student {
  String name;
  public Student(String name) { this.name = name;  }
  public void print() {
    SecurityManager sm = System.getSecurityManager();
    if (sm != null) {
      sm.checkPermission(new PrintPermission(name));
    }
    //print document here
  }
}
```

To check if a student really has print permission, this class

- Calls `System.getSecurityManager()` to get the currently installed security manager.
- If there is a security manager (i.e. the result is not null), then
- Create a `PrintPermission` object, and
- Invoke security manager's `checkPermission()` method passing newly created object.

The underlying security framework consults the security policy to see if the student indeed has this permission. A sample application can then be written as:

```
//Dept.java
public class Dept {
  public static void main(String args[]) {
    Student s = new Student("tom");
    s.print();
  }
}
```

Below is a sample policy file that allows print permission for "tom".

```
//sample.policy
grant {
  permission PrintPermission "tom";
};
```

Compile all the source files and start the application using the following command:

```
java -Djava.security.manager -Djava.security.policy=sample.policy
Dept
```

19.14 AN APPLICATION

Here, we shall develop a very simple but elegant application to demonstrate how to make use of all the concepts such as security manager, policy, jar signing and verifying etc. In this application, tom writes a Java program and Jerry wants to have it and run it. Let us now understand the steps they should follow for this purpose.

Suppose, tom has written the following program.

```
//FileSize.java
import java.io.*;
public class FileSize {
  public static void main(String[] args) throws Exception {
    InputStream in = new FileInputStream(args[0]);
    int count = 0;
    while (in.read() != -1) count++;
    System.out.println("Size of "+args[0]+" = "+count+" bytes");
  }
}
```

This application simply prints the size (in bytes) of a file specified as an argument. It is a useful application that anyone else can use, if required, to know the file size. Suppose, Jerry is one such person who wants to get it and run it. So tom generates a class file `FileSize.class` by compiling this program using the following command:

```
javac FileSize.java
```

Tom then creates a JAR file `FileSize.jar` containing the `FileSize.class` file using command:

```
jar cvf FileSize.jar FileSize.class
```

A sample result of this command is shown below:

```
added manifest
adding: FileSize.class(in = 867) (out= 530)(deflated 38%)
```

To sign this JAR file, tom creates a keystore containing private/public key pair as follows:

```
keytool -genkey -alias tom -keyalg RSA -keystore tom.jks -storepass 123456 -
keypass 123456 -dname "CN=Tom, OU=IT, O=JU, L=Kolkata, ST=WB, C=IN"
```

Now you are ready to sign the JAR file. Type the following in your command window

This private key in the keystore entry aliased by `tom` is used to sign the JAR file `FileSize.jar`, to produce result JAR file tom.jar using the following command:

```
jarsigner -keystore tom.jks -storepass 123456 -signedjar tom.jar FileSize.jar tom
```

Tom also exports its certificate in a file `tom.cer` that contains the public key corresponding to the private (that was used to sign the JAR file), which will be required by Jerry to authenticate tom.

```
keytool -export -keystore tom.jks -alias tom -storepass 123456 -file tom.cer
```

Jerry can now download the JAR file `tom.jar` containing the class file `FileSize.class` and use it. However, how can Jerry be sure that the JAR file `tom.jar` has not been tampered or trojaned by an intruder during its transit? Well, this can verified using jarsigner tool as follows:

```
jarsigner -verify tom.jar
```

If everything goes fine, the following message appears:

```
jar verified.
```

If verification fails, an appropriate diagnostic error message is displayed. In that case, Jerry continues to download it again until an unmodified version is obtained. Upon receiving a correct version, Jerry is ready to run the application. Note that the application `FileSize.class` gets the size of a file by reading the content of the entire file. Since it reads a file, it can see sensitive information (if any) present in that file. So, this application is a potentially vulnerable application and should be run within a security sandbox.

Suppose, Jerry wants to know the size of a file `test.txt` situated in the directory other than current directory. For example, suppose `test.txt` is placed in a sibling (having common parent) directory `data`. Jerry can use the following command:

```
java -Djava.security.manager -cp tom.jar FileSize ..\data\test.txt
```

This throws as exception:

```
Exception in thread "main" java.security.AccessControlException: access denied
(
"java.io.FilePermission" "..\data\test.txt" "read")
        at
java.security.AccessControlContext.checkPermission(AccessControlConte
xt.java:366)
        at
java.security.AccessController.checkPermission(AccessController.java:
555)
        at java.lang.SecurityManager.checkPermission(SecurityManager.java:549)
        at java.lang.SecurityManager.checkRead(SecurityManager.java:888)
```

```
        at java.io.FileInputStream.<init>(FileInputStream.java:131)
        at java.io.FileInputStream.<init>(FileInputStream.java:97)
        at FileSize.main(FileSize.java:5)
```

This is because the security manager consults only system and user policy files where no permission to read the file `test.txt` is specified. To allow accessing this file, permission must be given explicitly. This can be specified either in the existing policy files or in a separate policy file and specifying it either in `java.security` file or at runtime. To demonstrate how to work with a policy file, we shall give the permission in a separate policy file. Since, the code is a signed code, Jerry doesn't grant permissions to any file named tom.jar but only to tom.jar archives that tom signed. To do that, Jerry needs to import Tom's certificate in its trust store. So, copy the certificate tom.cer in Jerry's working directory and use the following command:

```
keytool -import -v -keystore jerry.jks -storepass 123456 -alias tom -file tom.cer
```

When you test, make sure that the trust store Jerry does not already contain an entry aliased `tom`. Now, create the following policy file:

```
//jerry.policy
keystore "jerry.jks", "jks";
grant  signedBy "tom" {
  permission java.io.FilePermission "../data/*", "read";
};
```

This tells that any code signed by `tom` has the read access to all files under the sibling directory data of the present working directory. The signature can be verified against the public key which can be found in the certificate in the trust store `jerry.jks` corresponding to the entry `tom`. The verification of the JAR file against Jerry's trust store may also be done explicitly as:

```
jarsigner -verbose -verify -keystore jerry.jks tom.jar
```

If verification is successful, it generates a message as follows:

```
s k      154 Sun Jan 12 13:09:20 PST 2014 META-INF/MANIFEST.MF
         316 Sun Jan 12 13:09:20 PST 2014 META-INF/TOM.SF
        1298 Sun Jan 12 13:09:20 PST 2014 META-INF/TOM.RSA
           0 Sun Jan 12 13:09:16 PST 2014 META-INF/
smk      867 Sun Jan 12 13:09:16 PST 2014 FileSize.class

  s = signature was verified
  m = entry is listed in manifest
  k = at least one certificate was found in keystore
  i = at least one certificate was found in identity scope

jar verified.
```

This policy file can be specified in the command line as follows:

```
java -Djava.security.manager -Djava.security.policy=jerry.policy  -cp tom.jar
FileSize ..\data\test.txt
```

The application reports the number of characters in the specified file without any error. Alternatively, the location of this policy file may be specified as the value of `policy.url.n` in the `java.security` file. For example, if `jerry.policy` is stored in a directory `E:\ajp\sec\sm\jerry`, then add the following line after the line starting with `policy.url.2`:

```
policy.url.3=file:/E:/ajp/sec/sm/jerry/jerry.policy
```

KEYWORDS

Certificate—A digitally signed document from some entity such as person, company, etc. indicating that the public key of some other entity has some particular value

Decryption—A process of getting cleartext back from ciphertext using a cryptographic key

Digital Signature—A string of bits that is computed from some data and the private key of an entity. The signature can be used to verify that the data came from the entity and was not modified in transit

Encryption—A process of converting cleartext to ciphertext using a cryptographic key

jarsigner—A Java tool used to digitally sign and verify a **J**ava **AR**chive (JAR) files

Java Cryptography Architecture—A framework for accessing and developing cryptographic functionality

Key Store—A persistent storage such as files to store keys and certificates

keytool—A Java tool used to manipulate key store and trust store

Message Digest algorithm—A function that takes arbitrary-sized input data (referred to as a message) and generates a fixed-size output, called a digest (or hash)

Permission—Indicates if some entity has the right to access to a system resource

Policy—A set of rules that specifies which permissions are available for code from various sources

Policy File—A file containing policy information

Private Key—A string/number that is supposed to be known only to a particular entity

Provider—Essentially packages that implement various cryptography algorithms

Public Key—A tring/number associated with a particular entity such as an individual or an organization and is intended to be known to everyone who needs to have trusted interactions with that entity

Public Key Infrastructure—A framework that deals with the exchange of information based on public key cryptography

Security Manager—A component that checks the policy currently in effect and perform access control checks for a code being executed

Self-Signed Certificate—A certificate for which the issuer (signer) is the same as the subject

SSL—A protocol used to make communication secured and is a primary choice of the Internet community

SSL Handshake—Set of steps followed in SSL prior to the data exchange

Trust Store—A key store that only stores certificates

SUMMARY

Java programming language, with its core features and security extensions, enables us in writing powerful secure applications. Security includes language safety, cryptography, **P**ublic **K**ey **I**nfrastructure (PKI), authentication, secure communication, and access control.

The cryptography APIs are organized into two distinct packages. The `java.security` package and `javax.crypto` package. The API to support public key infrastructure consists of two packages `java.security` and `java.security.cert`.

Secure **S**ocket **L**ayer (SSL) is a protocol used to make communication secured and is the primary choice of the Internet community. The purpose of SSL is capable of securing any transmission over TCP, such as HTTP, SMTP, FTP etc.

Java provides a utility `keytool` (stored in `java_home/bin` directory) used to administer keystores containing cryptographic keys, X.509 certificate chains, and trusted certificates. Programmers use this tool to administer their own private/public key pairs and associated digital certificates for use of self-authentication or data integrity.

In addition to supporting PKCS #12 standard, Java has its own proprietary standards (hence not portable) JKS (**J**ava **K**ey **S**tore) provided by "SUN" and its extension JCEKS (**J**ava **C**ryptography **E**xtension **K**ey **S**tore) provided by "SunJCE". The JCEKS keystore gives much stronger protection for stored private keys by using Triple DES encryption. Moreover, only JCEKS keystores can store secret keys. Java provides a wide set of classes and interfaces to work with keys, certificates, stores signatures etc.

Java also supports three kinds of objects SignedObject, SealedObject and GuardedObject to ensure object's integrity, confidentially and access control respectively. An instance of the `SignedObject` encapsulates the serialized representation of another object along with the signature information necessary to validate the wrapped object's authenticity and integrity. A `SealedObject` contains an encrypted version of another object's serialized representation. Java `java.security.GuardedObject` provides object level access control which ensures that permission is checked once.

RMI applications can also be made secured by using SSL enabled client and server socket factories used to create socket for underlying communications. It is also possible to make XML-PRC applications secured.

Java security architecture also provides a facility to digitally sign and verify a **J**ava **AR**chive (JAR) using the tool `jarsigner`. This is a very useful tool that enables parties to exchange data as a single package (created using `jar` utility and consisting of class files, images, sounds and other digital data) ensuring its integrity and authentication.

Java allows us to use security manager that allows or disallows the operation after consulting a given security policy. A policy specifies a set of allowable permission(s) to be used by the code from various sources and running as various principals and is represented by a `java.security.Policy` object.

WEB RESOURCES

`http://docs.oracle.com/javase/tutorial/security/`
Trail: Security Features in Java SE

`http://docs.oracle.com/javaee/6/tutorial/doc/gijrp.html`
The Java EE 6 Tutorial

`http://www.oracle.com/technetwork/java/javase/tech/index-jsp-136007.html`
Java SE Security

`http://www.tutorialspoint.com/listtutorials/java/security/1`
JAVA - Security Tutorials

`http://idiotechie.com/java-security-tutorial-step-by-step-guide-to-create-ssl-connection-and-certificates/`
Java Security Tutorial – Step by Step guide to create SSL connection and certificates

EXERCISES

Objective-type Questions

1. A cipher in cryptography is
   (a) An algorithm for performing encryption and decryption
   (b) An encrypted message
   (c) Both (a) and (b)
   (d) None of the above

2. Which one of the following is a cryptographic protocol used to secure HTTP connection?
   (a) Internet Protocol (IP)
   (b) Transmission Control Protocol (SCTP)
   (c) Transport Layer Security (TLS)
   (d) Address Resolution Protocol (ARP)

3. In public key cryptography, the private key is kept by
   (a) sender
   (b) receiver
   (c) both sender and receiver
   (d) None of the above

4. Which one of the following algorithms is not used in asymmetric-key cryptography?
   (a) Electronic code book algorithm
   (b) RSA algorithm
   (c) Diffie-hellman algorithm
   (d) None of the above

5. Which of the following is the most restricted access specifier?
   (a) public (c) protected
   (b) private (d) package

6. JCEKS stands for
   (a) Java Chiper Extension Key Store
   (b) Joint Cryptography Extension Key Store
   (c) Java Cryptography Expansion Key Store
   (d) Java Cryptography Extension Key Store

7. A security provider is represented by
   (a) Security class
   (b) SecurityProvider class
   (c) SecurityImplementer class
   (d) Provider class

8. Which of these packages is used for handling security-related issues in a program?
   (a) java.lang.security (c) javax.security
   (b) java.security (d) javax.sec

9. PKCS stands for
   (a) Private-Key Cryptography Standards
   (b) Public-Key Cryptography Standards
   (c) Public-Key Chiper Standards
   (d) Protected-Key Cryptography Standards

10. Which of the following uses a public key?
   (a) Symmetric key cryptography
   (b) Secret key cryptography
   (c) Private key cryptography
   (d) Public key cryptography

11. Which of the following is not a message digest algorithm?
   (a) DES (c) SHA-1
   (b) MD5 (d) SHA-256

12. What is the full form of PEM?
   (a) Privacy-enhanced Electronic Mail
   (b) Privacy-enhanced Electronic Message
   (c) Private Electronic Mail
   (d) Public Electronic Mail

13. Which of the following is a certificate standard?
   (a) PKCS #12 (c) JCEKS
   (b) JKS (d) X.509

14. Which of the following is not a signature algorithm?
   (a) DSA (c) DES
   (b) RSA (d) ECDSA

15. Which of the following packages is used for certificates?
   (a) javax.security.cert
   (b) java.security.cert
   (c) javax.cert
   (d) java.cert

16. SSL stands for
   (a) Short Socket Layer
   (b) Secure Session Layer
   (c) Secure Socket Layer
   (d) Short Session Layer

17. A key store can contain
   (a) secret key (c) Both a) and b)
   (b) certificate (d) None of the above

18. What is the full form of JKS?
   (a) Java Key Storage
   (b) Java Knowledge Store
   (c) Java Key Store
   (d) Joint Key Store

19. A signature is contained in a
   (a) secret key (c) public key
   (b) certificate (d) None of the above

20. A certificate contains
   (a) Public key (c) Both a) and b)
   (b) Private key (d) None of the above

21. DER stands for
   (a) Double Encoding Rules
   (b) Distributed Encoding Rules
   (c) Distinguished Embedded Rules
   (d) Distinguished Encoding Rules

22. Which of the following is not a standard for key store?
   (a) PKCS #12 (c) JCEKS
   (b) JKS (d) X.509

23. A trust store can contain
   (a) secret key (c) Both a) and b)
   (b) certificate (d) None of the above

24. In Java, which of the following tools is used to manipulate keystores?
   (a) keytool (c) ktool
   (b) javap (d) keychange

25. A public key is represented in Java by
   (a) PublicKey class
   (b) PKey class
   (c) GeneralKey class
   (d) None of the above

26. Which of the following is a certificate format?
   (a) DER (c) PKCS12
   (b) X.509 (d) PKIX

27. The object's integrity is ensured using
   (a) SealedObject (c) GuardedObject
   (b) SignedObject (d) None of the above

28. The object's confidentiality is ensured using
   (a) SealedObject (c) GuardedObject
   (b) SignedObject (d) None of the above

29. The object level access control is provided by
   (a) SealedObject (c) GuardedObject
   (b) SignedObject (d) None of the above

30. Which of the following keys is used to sign an object?
   (a) private key (c) Both a) and b)
   (b) public key (d) None of the above

31. The integrity of a SignedObject is verified using
   (a) private key (c) Both a) and b)
   (b) public key (d) None of the above

32. Which of the following is true about SignedObject?
   (a) All objects can be signed
   (b) Only String objects can be signed
   (c) A SignedObject is a file
   (d) Only Serializable objects can be signed

33. Which of the following methods is used to check the integrity of a signed object?
    (a) check() (c) verify()
    (b) compare() (d) doCheck()

34. Which of the following methods is used to obtain the original object from a signed object?
    (a) getOriginalObject()
    (b) getEmbeddedObject()
    (c) extractObject()
    (d) getObject()

35. Which of the following is true about signed object?
    (a) Private key is required to obtain the embedded object.
    (b) Public key is required to obtain the embedded object.
    (c) No key is required to extract the embedded object.
    (d) The embedded object can never be obtained.

36. Which of the following is true about sealed object?
    (a) Decryption key is required to extract the embedded object.
    (b) Private key is required to obtain the embedded object.
    (c) Public key is required to obtain the embedded object.
    (d) The embedded object can never be obtained.

37. Which of the following options is used with keytool to display the content of a certificate?
    (a) -printcert (c) -showcert
    (b) -displaycert (d) -listcert

38. Which of the following options is used with keytool to display the content of a keystore?
    (a) -print (c) -show
    (b) -display (d) -list

39. Which of the following store type can store secret keys?
    (a) PKCS #12 (c) JCEKS
    (b) JKS (d) None of the above

40. Which of the following options is used with keytool to generate a private/public key pair?
    (a) -getseckey (c) -genkeypair
    (b) -genkey (d) -genbothkey

41. Which of the following is not a secret key generation algorithm?
    (a) DES (c) RC2
    (b) AES (d) DSA

42. Which of the following is not a public key generation algorithm?
    (a) RSA (c) DH
    (b) DSA (d) DES

Subjective-type Questions

1. What is the difference between a SignedObject and SealedObject?
2. Show how objects can be transferred over the network keeping object's confidentiality and intrigrity.
3. What is the purpose of a GuardedObject?
4. What are the advantages of GuardedObject?
5. Explain how an RMI application can be made secured.
6. How will you write and use your own socket factories for RMI applications?
7. Explain how to make an XML-RPC application secured.
8. What does the tool jarsigner do?
9. Show the basic steps required to sign and verify a JAR file using jarsigner tool.
10. What is a message digest?
11. What properties does a message digest satisfy?
12. What do you mean by signing a JAR file multiple times? What is its usefulness?
13. Show the different procedures to install a security manager.
14. What is policy?
15. What are policy files?
16. Briefly describe the syntax of a policy file.
17. What is the purpose of a grant entry in a policy file?
18. What is the purpose of a permission entry in a policy file?
19. How do you write custom permission classes?

CHAPTER – 20

SERVLET

KEY OBJECTIVES

After completing this chapter readers will be able to—

- get an idea about server-side technology
- understand the advantages of Java servlet technology over other similar technologies
- get an idea about the basic execution philosophy of servlets
- understand how to write, deploy, and invoke servlets
- learn how to install and configure Tomcat servlet engine
- learn how to use important concepts such as filters, session tracking, etc.

20.1 SERVER-SIDE JAVA

Like applets (discussed in the previous chapter), servlets are also Java classes. However, unlike applets, which are used to implement client-side of a client–server application, servlets are used at the server-side. They usually run inside a Java-enabled web server and extend its capabilities. This capability is provided by servicing complex requests obtained from the web server, which itself is not capable of handling those requests. Since, servlets are written in Java and Java is an extremely powerful language, even a simple web server bundled with servlets, becomes unquestionably powerful. Consequently, it has become the most popular technology for building interactive web applications.

Note that servlets are not tied to a specific client–server protocol, but are most commonly used with HTTP. That is why, the word *servlet* is often used to mean *HTTP servlet*. Execution of a servlet consists of four basic steps [Figure 20.1:]:

- The client sends a request to the web server.
- The web server interprets it and forwards it to the corresponding servlet.
- The servlet processes the request, generates the output (if any), and sends it back to the web server.
- The web server sends the response back to the client. The browser then displays it on the screen.

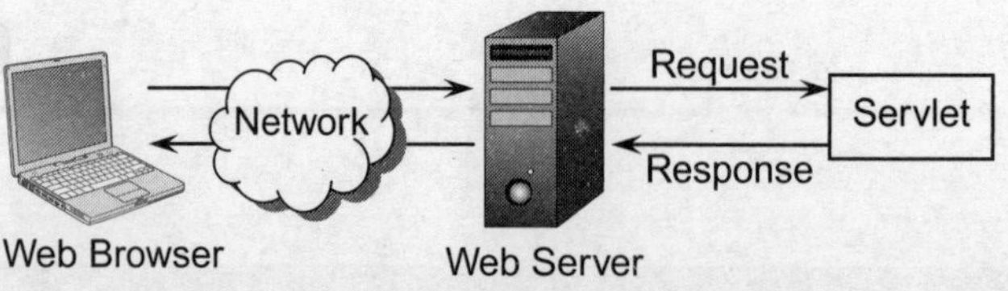

Figure 20.1: Execution of a Java Servlet

It runs entirely within the **J**ava **V**irtual **M**achine (JVM). Since it runs on the server and may be designed to generate simple output, which even older versions of browsers can interpret, there is no browser incompatibility.

20.2 ADVANTAGES OVER APPLETS

Applets, upon download from the server, run in the client's browser. They will function properly, provided a proper **J**ava **R**untime **E**nvironment (JRE) is installed in the client's browser. If the client uses old fashioned browsers and the applets use advanced features, the browsers may fail to execute them.

Servlets, on the other hand, run on the server machine and usually generate simple HTML codes. So, even an older version of the browser can display these HTML pages correctly.

Applets cannot access local resources such as files and databases. Servlets, if configured properly, have full access to system resources. Therefore, servlets are more powerful than applets. However, since applets and servlets are used at the opposite side of a client–server application, making a direct comparison between them should be avoided.

20.3 SERVLET ALTERNATIVES

Numerous parallel technologies to servlets exist. However, each has its own set of problems. Some of the other server-side technologies are discussed briefly here.

20.3.1 Common Gateway Interface (CGI)

CGI is one of the most common server-side solutions. Although widely used, CGI scripting technology has a number of shortcomings, including platform dependence and lack of scalability. A CGI application is an independent program that receives requests from the web server and sends it back to the web server. Some of the common problems of this technology are as follows:

- A new process is created every time the web server receives a CGI request. Since a new process is created and initialized, it may result in considerable increase of response time. Servers may also run out of memory if not configured properly.
- Although, a CGI application can be written in almost every language, most of them are not platform-independent. The common platform-independent language is Perl. Although Perl is a very powerful text processing language, for every request it requires a new interpreter to be started. This increases the overall response time.
- Since a CGI application is a completely separate process, if it terminates abnormally before responding, the web server has no way to identify what happened there. Consequently, it fails to service the request made by the client.

20.3.2 Proprietary APIs

Many proprietary web servers have built-in support for server-side programming. Examples include Netscape's NSAPI, Microsoft's ISAPI, and O'Reilly's WSAPI. However, none of these APIs is free and the newer versions may not be backward compatible. Most of these are developed in C/C++ languages and hence can contain memory leaks and core dumps that can crash the web server.

20.3.3 Active Server Pages (ASP)

Microsoft's **A**ctive **S**erver **P**ages (ASP) is another technology that supports server-side programming. Unfortunately, the only web server that supports this technology is Microsoft's **I**nternet **I**nformation **S**erver (IIS), which is not free. Although some third-party products support ASP, they are not free either.

20.3.4 Server-side JavaScript

Server-side JavaScript is another alternative to servlets. However, the only known servers that support it are Netscape's Enterprise and FastTrack servers. This ties you to a particular vendor and hence, if possible, should be avoided.

20.4 SERVLET STRENGTHS

Java servlet technology has some distinct advantages over other competent technologies. Truly speaking, except JSP (which is, in fact, an extension to servlet), no technology can compete with servlet technology. The following are some advantages of Java servlet technology.

20.4.1 Efficient

When a servlet gets loaded in the server, it remains in the server's memory as a single object instance. Each new request is then served by a lightweight Java thread spawned from the servlet. This is a much more efficient technique than creating a new process for every request, as done in CGI. Servlets also have more alternatives for optimizations, such as caching the previous computation and keeping database/socket connections open etc.

20.4.2 Persistent

Servlets can maintain the session by using the session tracking/cookies, a mechanism that helps them track information from request to request. Critical information can also be saved to a persistent storage and can be retrieved from it when the servlet is loaded the next time.

20.4.3 Portable

Servlets are written in Java and so they are portable across operating systems and server implementations. This allows servlets to be moved across new operating systems seamlessly. We can develop a servlet on a Windows machine running the Tomcat or any other server and later we can deploy that servlet effortlessly on any other operating system such as a Unix server running an iPlanet/Netscape application server. So, servlets are truly **W**rite **O**nce **R**un **A**nywhere (WORA) programs.

20.4.4 Robust

Since servlets can use the entire rich Java library, they can provide extremely robust solutions. Java has a very powerful exception handling mechanism and provides a garbage collector to handle memory leaks. It also has a very large and rich class library with network and file support, database access, distributed object components, DOM support, security, utility packages, etc.

20.4.5 Extensible

Servlets are nothing but Java technology, which is popular for its well-known features such as platform independence, garbage collection, exception handling, and extremely powerful utility packages. Servlets can also make use of Java's object orientation features, especially inheritance.

A sub class inherits all the features of its super class. Additional features and methods can be added and hence it is easily extendable.

20.4.6 Secure

Servlets run in a Java-enabled web server. So, they can use security mechanisms from both the web server and the Java Security Manager.

20.4.7 Cost-effective

There are a number of free web servers available [Table 20.1:] for personal and commercial use. Java Development Kit (JDK) is also free and can be downloaded from `http://java.com`. So, applications can be developed practically without any cost.

Table 20.1: Standalone web server

Product	Source	Product	Source
Apache Web Server	Apache	Web Server	ZEUS
WebSphere Application Server	IBM	iPlanet	Netscape
Weblogic Application Server	BEA	J Application Server	GenStone
Resin	Caucho	Netscape Enterprise Server	Netscape
JRUN	Adobe	LiteWebServer	Gefion
Orion Application Server	Orion	Java Web Server	Sun
Oracle Application Server	Oracle	CtO-JStar	JavaOne
Dynamo Application Server	ATG	iServer	ServerTec
J2EE Server	Pramati	Domino Go WebServer	Lotus
AppServer	Borland	Java Servlet Server 2.0	Paperclips
Jetty	Eclipse Foundation	KonaSoft Enterprise Server	KonaSoft
Jigsaw Server	W3C	Enhydra	ObjectWeb

Table 20.2: also shows some other add-on software that support Java servlet technology.

Table 20.2: Add-on Servlet engine

Product	Source	Product	Source
Tomcat	Jakarta Project	JRun web server	Allaire
JServ	Java-Apache Project	ServletExec	New Atlanta

20.5 SERVLET ARCHITECTURE

Servlet architecture consists of two packages: `javax.servlet` and `javax.servlet.http`. The first package contains top-level interfaces and classes that are used and extended by all other servlets either directly or indirectly. The second package is provided for servlets that can handle HTTP requests. Figure 20.2: shows the Servlet architecture.

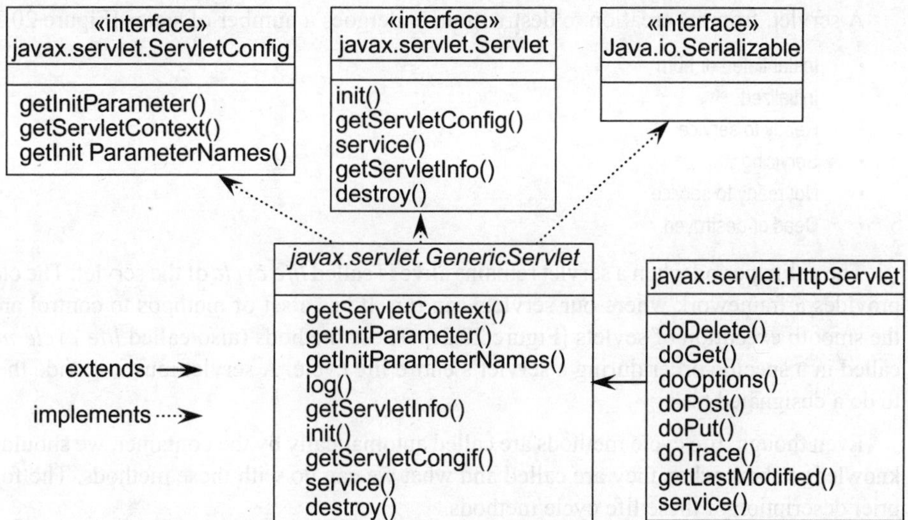

Figure 20.2: Servlet architecture

The top-level interface of the servlet architecture is `javax.servlet.Servlet`. It provides the basic functionalities of all the servlets that are created by implementing this interface directly or indirectly. For example, the `init()` method initializes the servlet, the `service()` method serves the client request, and the `destroy()` method shuts the servlet down.

20.6 SERVLET LIFE CYCLE

The container in which the servlet has been deployed supervises and controls the life cycle [Figure 20.3:] of a servlet. Typically, this container is nothing but a web server. When the container receives a request from a client and determines that the request should be handled by a servlet, it performs the following steps.

- If an instance of the target servlet does not exist, the container does the following:
  - Finds and loads the servlet class
  - Creates an instance of the servlet class
  - Calls the `init()` method on this servlet instance to initialize it
- The container then invokes the `service()` method on the servlet (newly created or existing servlet), passing a `ServletRequest` type object and a `ServletResponse` type object.
- If the container decides that the servlet is no longer needed, it removes and finalizes the servlet by calling the servlet's `destroy()` method.

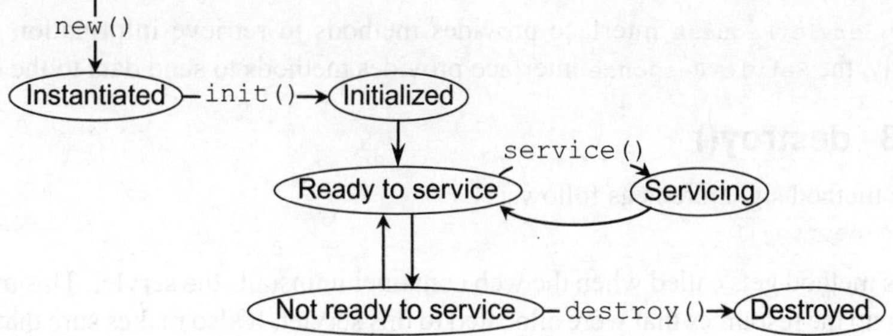

Figure 20.3: Life cycle of a Servlet

A servlet, from its creation to destruction, undergoes a number of states [Figure 20.3:]:

- Instantiated or born
- Initialized
- Ready to service
- Servicing
- Not ready to service
- Dead or destroyed

The entire period when a servlet remains alive is called *life cycle* of the servlet. The class `Servlet` provides a framework where our servlets can run. It has a set of methods to control and supervise the smooth execution of sevlets [Figure 20.2:]. These methods (also called *life cycle methods*) are called in a specific order during a servlet's entire life cycle. A servlet must override these methods to do a designated task.

Even though, life cycle methods are called automatically by the container, we should have sound knowledge about when they are called and what we can do with these methods. The following is a brief description of these life cycle methods.

20.6.1 init()

A servlet's life begins here. This method is called *only once* by the web container, just after it instantiates and loads the servlet. So, it is a good idea to read the persistent configuration data, initialize resources that will be used during the rest of the time, and perform any other one-time activity by overriding the `init()` method. Once the servlet is initialized, it becomes ready to handle the client's request. The prototype of the `init()` method is as follows:

```
void init(ServletConfig)
```

The web container passes a `ServletConfig` object, which contains the startup configuration for this servlet such as initialization parameters. To serve requests, this init() method must complete and return successfully.

20.6.2 service()

This is the most important method, whose signature is as follows:

```
void service(ServletRequest request, ServletResponse response)
```

This method gets called each time the web container receives a request intended for this servlet. The web container calls the `service()` method on a servlet with two objects: a `ServletRequest` type object `request` and a `ServletResponse` type object `response`. The `request` object encapsulates the communication from the client to the server, while the `response` object encapsulates the communication from the servlet back to the client.

The `ServletRequest` interface provides methods to retrieve information sent by the clients. Similarly, the `ServletResponse` interface provides methods to send data to the clients.

20.6.3 destroy()

The method signature is as follows:

```
void destroy();
```

This method gets called when the web container uninstalls the servlet. This method is overridden to clean up the resources that were allocated to this servlet. It also makes sure that any persistent state is synchronized with the servlet's current in-memory state.

20.6.4 Other Methods

The `javax.servlet.Servlet` interface also provides the following methods to inspect the properties of a servlet at runtime.

```
ServletConfig getServletConfig();
```

Returns a `ServletConfig` object, which contains the initialization parameters and startup configuration used for this servlet. The returned object is the object that was passed to the `init()` method during the servlets instantiation.

```
String getServletInfo();
```

Returns a `String` object containing information about the servlet, such as its version, author, copyright, etc.

20.7 GENERICSERVLET

The class `javax.servlet.GenericServlet` implements the `javax.servlet.Servlet` interface and, for convenience, the `javax.servlet.ServletConfig` interface. A servlet class is usually created by extending either the `GenericServlet` class or its descendant `javax.servlet.http.HttpServlet` class unless the servlet needs another class as a parent. If a servlet does need to be a subclass of another class, it must implement the `Servlet` interface directly. This would be necessary when, for example, RMI or CORBA objects act as servlets. In such a case, the servlet class must implement all the methods of the `Servlet` interface.

The `GenericServlet` class defines (as its name suggests) a generic protocol-independent servlet, in the sense that it can be extended to provide implementation of any protocol, such as HTTP, FTP, and SMTP.

The `GenericServlet` class was created to make writing servlets easier. It provides implementations of the life cycle methods `init()` and `destroy()`, as well as methods in the `ServletConfig` interface. The servlet writer has to implement only the `service()` method. This is required because it is the method that is called every time a client requests for the servlet. The prototype of this method is shown as follows.

```
public void service(javax.servlet.ServletRequest request,
        javax.servlet.ServletResponse response)
        throws javax.servlet.ServletException, java.io.IOException;
```

This method expects two arguments. The `ServletRequest` type object `request` encapsulates the client request and is used to extract information from the client's request. On the other hand, `ServletResponse` type object `response` contains information to be sent back to the client.

20.8 HTTPSERVLET

The `HttpServlet` class extends `GenericServlet` and provides a framework for handling HTTP requests. Servlets that want to handle only HTTP requests are usually created by extending this class. It provides an implementation for the `service()` method. So, you do not have to implement the `service()` method if you extend the `HttpServlet` class. The `service()` method in the `HttpServlet` class reads the method type stored in the HTTP request message and invokes a specific method based on this value. Specifically, if the method type is GET, it calls `doGet()`; if the method type is POST, it calls `doPost()`; and so on. These are the methods that we need to override. Default implementations of these methods are also provided. The list of all such methods is given in Figure 20.4:.

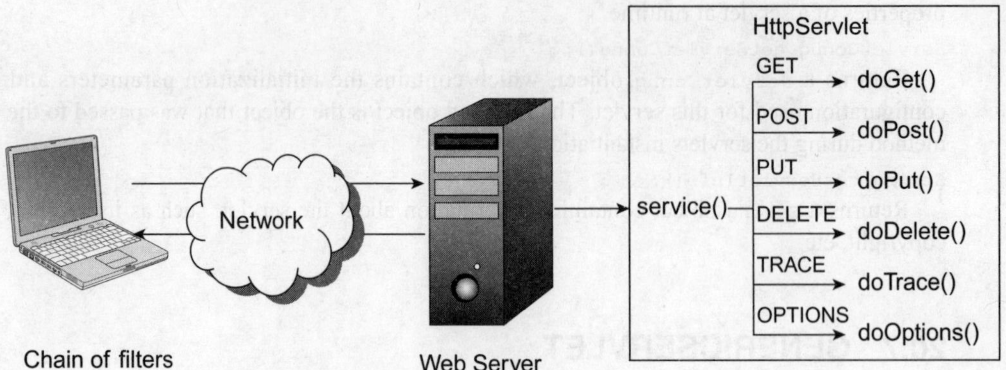

Figure 20.4: Http Servlet in action

Each of these methods takes two arguments: an `HttpServletRequest` type object and an `HttpServletResponse` type object. The following is the prototype of the `doGet()` method:

```
void doGet(HttpServletRequest request, HttpServletResponse response)
```

The `HttpServletRequest` interface extends the `ServletRequest` interface and provides all the functionalities of the `ServletRequest` interface. Additionally, it provides methods to retrieve HTTP-specific information such as headers, method, URL, cookies sent, etc.

The `HttpServletResponse` interface extends the `ServletResponse` interface and provides all the functionalities of the `ServletResponse` interface. Additionally, it provides methods to send HTTP-specific information back to the client.

Servlets created by extending the `HttpServlet` class can handle multiple simultaneous requests. For each request, a thread is created, which runs its `service()` method. If you want to create a single-threaded servlet, your servlet must also implement the `SingleThreadModel` interface as follows:

```
public class SimpleServlet extends HttpServlet implements SingleThreadModel { }
```

The interface `SingleThreadModel` does not define any method. It is used to merely declare that the servlet should use a single thread.

20.9 FIRST SERVLET

Our first servlet is a simple servlet designed to handle the HTTP GET method. Create the following servlet `HelloWorldServlet.java` using any text editor.

```
import java.io.*;
import javax.servlet.*;
import javax.servlet.http.*;
public class HelloWorldServlet extends HttpServlet {
  public void doGet(HttpServletRequest request, HttpServletResponse response)
    throws IOException, ServletException {
      response.setContentType("text/html");
      PrintWriter out = response.getWriter();
      out.println("<html><head><title>Hello World Servlet</title></head>");
```

```
            out.println("<body>");
            out.println("<h1>Hello World!</h1>");
            out.println("</body></html>");
            out.close();
        }
    }
```

The class `HelloWorldServlet` extends the `HttpServlet` class. So, it can handle HTTP requests. It is written to handle only the GET method. Therefore, only the `doGet()` method is overridden. The output of this servlet is a text document containing html tags. This is mentioned using the `setContentType()` method. To send the data back to the client, a `PrintWriter` object is obtained by calling the `getWriter()` method on the `response` object. Finally, it sends the following HTML document.

```
<html><head><title>Hello World Servlet</title></head>
<body>
<h1>Hello World!</h1>
</body></html>
```

At the end, we close the `PrintWriter` object. It is not mandatory as the web container closes the `PrintWriter` or `ServletOutputStream` automatically, when the `service()` method returns. An explicit call to `close()` is useful when you want to perform some processing after responding to the client's request. This also tells the web container that the response is completed and the connection to the client may be closed as well.

20.9.1 Installing Apache Tomcat web server

To install these servlets, we need a web server. Any web server that supports servlets may be used. A list of web servers supporting servlets may be found in Table 20.1 and Table 20.2. Note that the procedure for installing servlets varies from web server to web server. Please refer to the documentation of your web server for definitive instructions. All the servlets are tested in this book using Tomcat web server provided by Apache software foundation. Tomcat is a lightweight, easily configurable free web server and is widely used by users who are new to servlets.

Let us now discuss how to install and configure the Tomcat web server.

Before installing Tomcat, make sure that you have installed either Java 6 Standard Edition (JDK 1.7) or Java 5 Standard Edition (JDK 1.6) in your computer. Download and install Java from `http://java.com/en/download/index.jsp`. Once you have installed, include the Java "bin" directory in the PATH environment variable. For example, if you have installed Java in `D:\Java\jdk1.7.0_07`, include `D:\Java\jdk1.7.0_07\bin` subdirectory in the PATH environment variable. Additionally, create an environment variable JAVA_HOME and set it by the Java installation directory (`D:\Java\jdk1.7.0_07` in our case).

Download the necessary files from `http://tomcat.apache.org/`. When I was writing this book, the latest version was `Tomcat 8.0`. It is recommended to download a `.zip` or `.zip.tar` file for the beginners. If you have downloaded an installer file, install it. If it is a `.zip` file or `.zip.tar` file, simply unzip it in a folder. We shall assume that you have installed Tomcat in the `D:\apache-tomcat-8.0.0-RC1` directory.

Tomcat has a predefined directory structure. A typical directory structure is shown in Figure 20.5:

Figure 20.5: Tomcat directory structure

Suppose `$TOMCAT_HOME` represents the root of the Tomcat installation directory. According to Figure 20.5:, it represents the `D:\apache-tomcat-8.0.0-RC1` directory. The following are some key Tomcat directories under `$TOMCAT_HOME`:

- `\bin` — Startup, shutdown, and other scripts. The `*.bat` (for Windows) files and Unix/Linux counterparts `*.sh` files.
- `\conf` — Configuration XML files. The primary configuration file is `server.xml`, which describes how the server starts, behaves and finds other information. All the information in the configuration files is loaded whenever the web server starts up. So, any change to the files needs a restart of the web server.
- `\lib` — Binary jar files are needed for the server to function. You should put your custom jar files in this directory. Tomcat can find them at runtime.
- `\webapps` — It contains web applications. The directory `ROOT` under it contains the default web application, which can be accessed using the URL `http://172.16.5.81:8080`, where `172.16.5.81` is the IP address of the computer where this web server is running. You should create your own directory under it. We shall create a directory `net` (short for network programming) to put our servlet files. So, the document root of our website will be `http://172.16.5.81:8080/net`.

20.9.2 Building and Installing Servlet

To compile our `HelloWorldServlet.java` file, servlet class files are required. Tomcat comes with a .jar file that contains necessary class files. For Tomcat 8.0, the name of this .jar file is `servlet-api.jar`. You can find this jar file usually in the `$TOMCAT_HOME\lib` directory.

Compile the `HelloWorldServlet.java` using the following command:

```
javac -cp d:\apache-tomcat-8.0.0-RC1\lib\servlet-api.jar HelloWorldServlet.java
```

This generates the file `HelloWorldServlet.class` that contains the byte code for our servlet. Create the following directory structure under the `webapps` subdirectory.

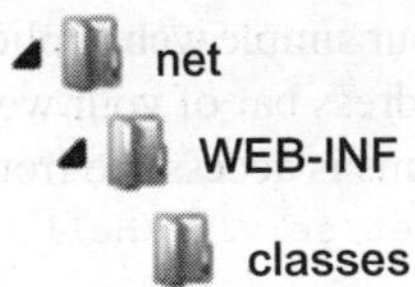

Put this `HelloWorldServlet.class` file in the `$TOMCAT_HOME\webapps\net\WEB-INF\classes` directory.

The servlet class file is now ready to use. However, we have to inform the web server about the existence of this servlet and the URL that will be used to refer to this servlet. This is specified in the `$TOMCAT_HOME\net\WEB-INF\web.xml` file, which is the configuration XML file for this website. If the file does not exist, create this file first.

Now, insert the following lines in this file. Some IDE provides interfaces to generate the same information. However, it is recommended to beginners to do it manually. When you have sufficient knowledge about how to install servlets and how they work, you may use IDEs.

```
<servlet>
   <servlet-name>HelloWorld</servlet-name>
   <servlet-class>HelloWorldServlet</servlet-class>
</servlet>
```

This code maps the servlet class (`HelloWorldServlet.class`) file to a servlet name (`HelloWorld`). The `<servlet>` tag tells the Tomcat that an instance of the servlet has to be created. The name of the class file (without the extension `class`) for this servlet is specified by the `<servlets-class>` tag. Once this instance is created, it can be referred to by a name specified by the `<servlet-name>` tag. You then need to map this servlet name to a URL to be used to invoke this servlet. This is a URL relative to the document root for this website.

```
<servlet-mapping>
    <servlet-name>HelloWorld</servlet-name>
    <url-pattern>/servlet/HelloWorld</url-pattern>
</servlet-mapping>
```

The above `<servlet-mapping>` tag indicates that the servlet having the name `HelloWorld` can be invoked using the URL pattern `/servlet/HelloWorld` relative to the document root. In our case, the document root is `http://172.16.5.81:8080/net`. So, the complete URL of this servlet will be `http://172.16.5.81:8080/net/servlet/HelloWorld`.

20.9.3 Invoking Servlet

Invoking this servlet is very easy. Start the Tomcat web server. If everything goes correct, your web application will be deployed successfully. A sample output containing Tomcat startup message is shown in Figure 20.6:

```
Select Tomcat
INFO: Deploying web application directory D:\apache-tomcat-8.0.0-RC1\webapps\man
ager
Aug 10, 2013 11:45:00 PM org.apache.catalina.startup.HostConfig deployDirectory
INFO: Deploying web application directory D:\apache-tomcat-8.0.0-RC1\webapps\net

Aug 10, 2013 11:45:00 PM org.apache.catalina.startup.HostConfig deployDirectory
INFO: Deploying web application directory D:\apache-tomcat-8.0.0-RC1\webapps\ROO
T
Aug 10, 2013 11:45:00 PM org.apache.coyote.AbstractProtocol start
INFO: Starting ProtocolHandler ["http-nio-8080"]
Aug 10, 2013 11:45:00 PM org.apache.coyote.AbstractProtocol start
INFO: Starting ProtocolHandler ["ajp-nio-8009"]
Aug 10, 2013 11:45:00 PM org.apache.catalina.startup.Catalina start
INFO: Server startup in 1348 ms
```

Figure 20.6: Tomcat startup screen (in windows)

The deployment message for our simple web application is highlighted in the output screen. Now, type the following URL in the address bar of your web browser and press enter. Make sure that the computer where the web server runs is accessible from your computer.

```
http://172.16.5.81:8080/net/servlet/HelloWorld
```

It generates the result as shown in Figure 20.7:

Figure 20.7: The result of HelloWorld servlet

20.10 PASSING PARAMETERS TO SERVLETS

Like command line arguments, parameters can be passed to servlets. Servlets can access those parameters and customize their tasks. This helps servlets to function differently in different situations without recompiling the source code.

There are two ways in which you can pass parameters to a servlet: using URL and using HTML form.

20.10.1 Passing Parameters Directly to a Servlet

Parameters can be passed to servlets directly using URL. In this case parameters and their values are attached directly to the URL when you use the URL to call the servlet. The URL and parameters are separated by '?' character. The character ? says "here are the parameters". Each parameter takes the form `name=value`. Multiple parameters are separated by the '&' character Consider the following URL.

```
http://172.16.5.81:8080/net/servlet/check?login=abc&password=xyz
```

In this example, two parameters are passed `login` and `password` whose values are `abc` and `xyz`, respectively.

Certain special characters such as space and quote (") are not allowed directly in the URL. These characters are encoded in the `%hh` format where `hh` is the hex code of the character. For example, `%20`, `%22`, and `%7E` represent the space, quote, and tilde (~) characters, respectively.

20.10.2 Passing Parameters Directly to a Servlet

One of the disadvantages of passing parameters using URLs is that users can view the parameter names with their values passed. So, it is not safe to send sensitive information using this method. Moreover, the number of parameters that we can pass is also limited. HTML forms can be used to pass parameters in a convenient way. The following HTML code can be used to pass the same information as the previous example.

```
<form method='post' action='http://172.16.5.81:8080/net/servlet/check'>
   Login:<input type='text' name='login'><br />
   Password:<input type='password' name='password'><br/>
   <input type='submit' value='Login'>
</form>
```

The POST method is used here. In this case, the values of all form fields are embedded in the body of the HTTP request message and hence cannot be viewed directly. However, servlets can retrieve them using the usual way.

The servlet URL used in `action` attribute is an absolute URL. A relative URL may also be used as follows:

```
action='servlet/check'
```

The URL `servlet/check` is a URL relative to the current URL (i.e. the URL of the page from which this servlet is invoked). The actual URL may be found by appending this path to the current URL. For example, if `http://172.16.5.81:8080/net/login.htm` calls this servlet, the absolute URL of the servlet is `http://172.16.5.81:8080/net/servlet/check`

20.11 RETRIEVING PARAMETERS

The three methods of the `ServletRequest` interface may be used to retrieve parameters. Their signatures are as follows:

```
public abstract java.lang.String getParameter(java.lang.String);
public abstract java.lang.String[] getParameterValues(java.lang.String);
public abstract java.util.Enumeration getParameterNames();
```

The `getParameter()` method returns the value of the specified parameter. Make sure that the parameter has exactly one value. If there are multiple parameters with the same name, use the `getParameterValues()` method, which returns an array of string values of the specified parameter.

The `getParameterNames()` method returns all the parameters as an enumeration. The values of the individual parameters can be obtained by iterating through the enumeration and using the `getParameter()` method for each of these parameters. The following example shows how to retrieve values of two parameters, `login` and `password`, and return back to the client.

```
// GetParameterServlet.java
import java.io.*;
import javax.servlet.*;
import javax.servlet.http.*;
public class GetParameterServlet extends HttpServlet {
   public void doPost(HttpServletRequest request, HttpServletResponse response)
     throws IOException, ServletException {
      response.setContentType("text/html");
      PrintWriter out = response.getWriter();
      out.println("<html><head><title>Hello World Servlet</title></head>");
      out.println("<body>");
      String login = request.getParameter("login");
      String password = request.getParameter("password");
      out.println("<h2> login:" + login + "<br>password:" + password +
"</h2>");
      out.println("</body></html>");
   }
}
```

Compile the servlet, and put the generated `GetParameterServlet.class` file in the `$TOMCAT_HOME\webapps\net\WEB-INF\classes` directory. Make the following entry in the `web.xml` file, and restart the web server.

```
<servlet>
   <servlet-name>GetParameter</servlet-name>
   <servlet-class>GetParameterServlet</servlet-class>
</servlet>
<servlet-mapping>
   <servlet-name>GetParameter</servlet-name>
   <url-pattern>/servlet/check</url-pattern>
</servlet-mapping>
```

Now an html file (call it login.html) is as follows:

```
<!--login.html-->
<html>
  <body>
    <form method='post' action='servlet/check'>
      Login:<input type='text' name='login'><br />
      Password:<input type='password' name='password'><br/>
      <input type='submit' value='Login'>
    </form>
  </body>
</html>
```

Put this html file in the following directory:

```
$TOMCAT_HOME\webapps\net
```

a

We can now call the above servlet using this html file or using the following URL:

```
http://172.16.5.81:8080/net/servlet/check?login=abc&password=xyz
```

The form output is shown in Figure 20.8 (i), while a sample response from the servlet is shown in Figure 20.8 (ii).

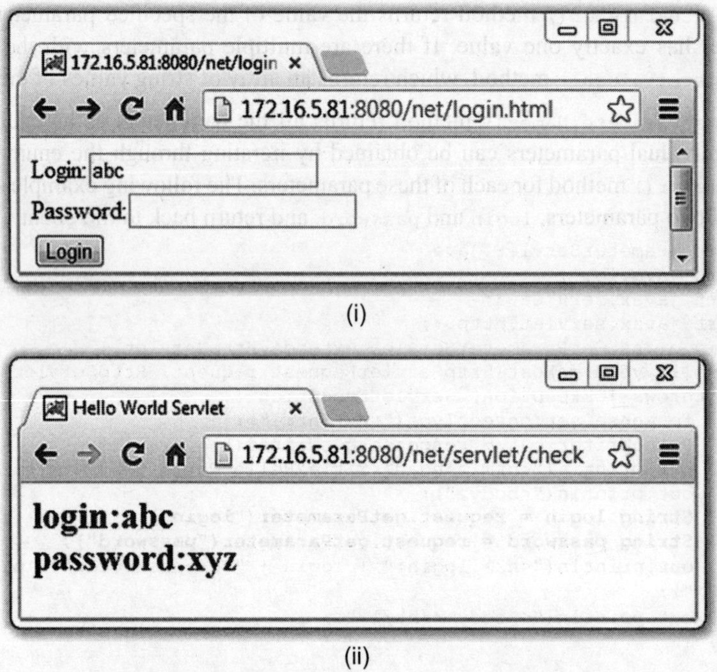

Figure 20.8: Passing and retrieving parameters in servlet (i) Passing parameter (ii) Retrieving parameter

In practice, servlets hardly return the parameter with their values back to the client. Typically, they consult the database for further processing. In our case, the servlet will possibly verify the login name and password information against the information stored in the database and depending upon the result, either allow or disallow the user to login.

20.12 SERVER-SIDE INCLUDE

Server-Side Include (SSI) allows us to embed (include) servlets within HTML pages. The HTML files containing servlets typically have the extension `.shtml`. The web server understands this extension and forwards it to an internal servlet. This internal servlet parses the HTML document and executes the referenced servlets and sends the result back to the web server after merging it with the original HTML document. This lets us include dynamically generated content in an existing HTML file, without having to serve the entire page via a CGI program or other dynamic technologies.

Tomcat uses `org.apache.catalina.ssi.SSIServlet` as its internal servlet. To enable SSI support, remove the XML comments from around the SSI servlet and servlet-mapping configuration in `$TOMCAT_HOME/conf/web.xml`. Also modify the `<context>` tag in `$TOMCAT_HOME/conf/context.xml` as follows:

```
<Context privileged="true">
  …
  <WatchedResource>WEB-INF/web.xml</WatchedResource>
  …
</Context>
```

The syntax for including servlets in HTML documents varies widely from web server to web server. Tomcat SSI directives have the following syntax:

```
<!--#directive attribute="value" attribute="value" ... -->
```

Tomcat SSI directives are formatted like an HTML comment. So, if SSI is not correctly configured, the browser will ignore it. Otherwise, the directive will be replaced by its results before sending the page to the client. A brief description of the directives is given below:

echo

It just inserts the value of a variable. For example, the following directive inserts the value of the local date.

```
<!--#echo var="DATE_LOCAL" -->
```

This generates the following result:

```
Sunday, 11-Aug-2013 04:10:02 PDT
```

There are a number of standard variables including all the environment variables that are available to servlets. Additionally, you can define your own variables with the `set` directive. A list of SSI servlet variables is given in Appendix A at the end of this chapter.

printenv

It returns the list of all defined variables.

```
<!--#printenv -->
```

It results in the following:

```
HTTP_USER_AGENT=Mozilla/5.0 (Windows NT 6.1; WOW64) AppleWebKit/537.36 (KHTML,
like Gecko) Chrome/28.0.1500.95 Safari/537.36 HTTP_ACCEPT_LANGUAGE=en-
US,en;q=0.8
HTTP_ACCEPT=text/html,application/xhtml+xml,application/xml;q=0.9,*/*;q=0.8
LAST_MODIFIED=08/11/13 DOCUMENT_URI=/net/SSI.shtml
HTTP_ACCEPT_ENCODING=gzip,deflate,sdch REMOTE_PORT=56237 SERVER_SOFTWARE=Apache
Tomcat/8.0.0-RC1 Java HotSpot(TM) Client VM/23.3-b01 Windows 7
SERVER_NAME=172.16.5.81 SCRIPT_FILENAME=D:\apache-tomcat-8.0.0-
RC1\webapps\net\SSI.shtml DATE_LOCAL=08/11/13 SERVER_ADDR=172.16.5.81
SERVER_PROTOCOL=HTTP/1.1 REQUEST_METHOD=GET DOCUMENT_NAME=SSI.shtml
SERVER_PORT=8080 SCRIPT_NAME=/SSI.shtml REMOTE_ADDR=172.16.5.81
DATE_GMT=08/11/13 REMOTE_HOST=172.16.5.81 HTTP_HOST=172.16.5.81:8080
HTTP_CONNECTION=keep-alive UNIQUE_ID=BEBC7FB2030AF4392C5871ED88FBCFB1
QUERY_STRING= GATEWAY_INTERFACE=CGI/1.1 org.apache.catalina.ssi.SSIServlet=true
REQUEST_URI=/net/SSI.shtml
```

config

We can use the `config` directive, with a `timefmt` attribute, to modify the formatting of the date and time as follows:

```
<!--#config timefmt="%A %B %d, %Y" -->
<!--#echo var="DATE_LOCAL" -->
```

This generates the following result:

```
Sunday August 11, 2013
```

fsize

This directive returns the size of the file specified by the `file` attribute.

```
<!--#fsize file="SSI.shtml" -->
```

This directive returns the size of the file `SSI.shtml` in kilobytes.

flastmod

The last modification time of a file is inserted using `flastmod` directive whose `file` attribute specifies the file name. The following code inserts the last modification time of the file named `SSI.shtml`.

```
<!--#flastmod file="SSI.shtml" -->
```

You need to replace the `SSI.shtml` with the actual file name you want to refer to. Note that this piece of code does not give the last modification time of an arbitrary file. It is better to use the `echo` directive to print the value of the `LAST_MODIFIED` environment variable, which specifies the last modification time of the file where this directive is included.

```
<!--#echo var="LAST_MODIFIED" -->
```

include

The most common use of SSI is to include the result of a server-side program such as servlet or CGI. The following directive includes the result of our `HelloWorld` servlet in the place of the directive.

```
<!--#include virtual="servlet/HelloWorld" -->
```

The attribute `virtual` specifies the server-side script to be used. Note that the servlet URL used here is relative to the `.shtml` file containing this directive.

So, create a file `SSI.shtml` containing a single line as follows and put in the `$TOMCAT_HOME\webapps\net` directory.

```
<!--#include virtual="servlet/HelloWorld" -->
```

It generates the same output as our `HelloWorld` servlet, as shown in Figure 20.9.

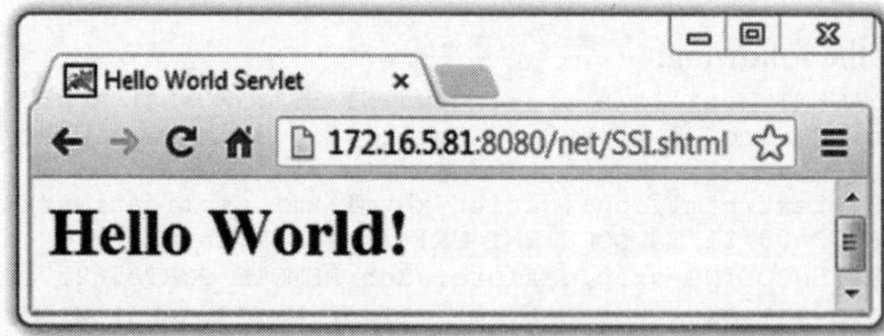

Figure 20.9: Using include directive of SSI

The `include` directive is useful if you want to insert the result of the same servlet in different pages. Use the following to insert a header in every page.

```
<!--#include virtual="header.html" -->
```

Note that the `include` directive can insert the result of any type of file. The following example includes two html files `header.html` and `footer.html`.

```
<!--#include virtual="header.html" -->
SSI allows us to include other documents within HTML pages.
<!--#include virtual="footer.html" -->
```

It first inserts the content of `header.html` whose content is shown below:

```
<!--header.html-->
<h1>SSI: Server Side Include</h1>
```

Then a single line of text is inserted. Finally, it inserts the content of another file `footer.html` whose content is shown below:

```
<!--header.html-->
<h4>Note:syntax of SSI varies widely from web server to web server. </h4>
```

A sample output is shown in Figure 20.10:

Figure 20.10: Including multiple documents

set

It is used for creating variables and setting their values for later use. The following directive creates a variable `SSI` with the value `"Server Side Include"`.

```
<!--#set var="SSI" value="Server Side Include" -->
```

Similarly, the following code creates a variable `sum` with the value `"0"`.

```
<!--#set var="sum" value="0" -->
```

set

It is used for creating variables and setting their values for later use. The following directive creates a variable `SSI` with the value `"Server Side Include"`.

```
<!--#set var="SSI" value="Server Side Include" -->
```


if elif endif else

This directive is used to write conditional sections. For example:

```
<!--#config timefmt="%A" -->
<!--#if expr="$DATE_LOCAL = /Sunday/" -->
<p>Today is Sunday</p>
<!--#elif expr="$DATE_LOCAL = /Saturday/" -->
<p>Today is Saturday</p>
<!--#else -->
<p>Week day</p>
<!--#endif -->
```

20.13 COOKIES

HTTP is stateless. This means that every HTTP request is different from others. Sometimes, it is necessary to keep track of a sequence of related requests sent by a client to perform some designated task. This is called *session tracking*.

Cookies are one of the solutions to session tracking. A *cookie* is [key, value] pair created by the server and is installed in the client's browser when the client makes a request for the first time. Browsers also maintain a list of cookies installed in them and send them to the server as a part of subsequent HTTP requests. The server can then easily identify that this request is a part of a sequence of related requests. This way, cookies provide an elegant solution to session tracking.

The servlet API supports cookies. A cookie is represented using the `javax.servlet.http.Cookie` class and is created using the following constructor:

```
Cookie(String key, String value)
```

A cookie is added by the `addCookie()` method of the `HttpServletResponse` class. Similarly, the server can get all cookies sent by the web browser using the `getCookies()` method of the `HttpServletRequest` class.

```
import java.io.*;
import javax.servlet.*;
import javax.servlet.http.*;
public class CookieDemo extends HttpServlet {
  public void doGet(HttpServletRequest request, HttpServletResponse response)
    throws IOException, ServletException {
    PrintWriter out = response.getWriter();
    Cookie[] cookies = request.getCookies();
    boolean found = false;
    if(cookies != null)
      for(int i=0;i<cookies.length;i++)
        if(cookies[i].getName().equals("session_started")) {
          found = true;
          out.println("You started this session on : " );
          out.println(cookies[i].getValue());
        }
        if(!found) {
          String dt = (new java.util.Date()).toString();
          response.addCookie(new Cookie("session_started", dt));
          out.println("Welcome to out site...");
        }
  }
}
```

When a client makes the call for the first time, the web browser does not send any cookie. The servlet looks for the cookie with the name "`session_started`". Naturally, it cannot find the cookie. It creates, installs, and sends a cookie with the name "`session_started`" using the following code.

```
response.addCookie(new Cookie("session_started", dt));
```

For subsequent calls, web browsers send this cookie with a request. Our servlet finds it, and retrieves the start time of this session and finally sends this value. So, when you access this servlet for the first time, you will see an output as shown in Figure 20.11: (i). Any subsequent request generates the output shown in Figure 20.11: (ii).

(i)

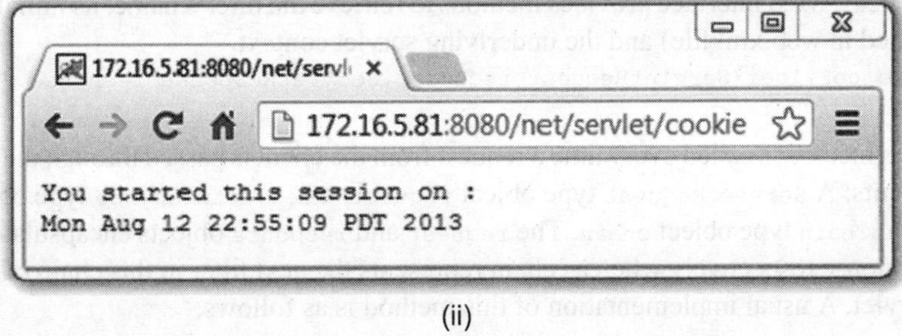

(ii)

Figure 20.11: Working with cookies (i) First access (ii) Subsequent access

20.13.1 Limitations of Cookies

Cookies work correctly, provided that the web browsers have enabled cookie support. In addition to the security concerns, there are some technical limitations:

- . Cookies can carry small pieces of information and are not a standard way of communication.
- Some web browsers limit the number of cookies (typically 20 per web server) that can be installed. To avoid this problem, more than one block of information may be sent per cookie.
- The value of a cookie should never exceed 4 KB. If the value of a cookie is larger than 4 KB, it should be trimmed to fit.
- Cookies cannot identify a particular user. A user can be identified by a combination of user account, browser, and computer. So, users who have multiple accounts and use multiple computers/browsers have multiple sets of cookies. Consequently, cookies cannot differentiate between multiple browsers running in a single computer.
- Intruders can snoop, steal cookies, and attack sessions. This is called *session hijacking*.

20.14 FILTERS

Filters are objects that are installed [Figure 20.12:] between the client and the server to inspect requests and responses. They can transform the request or modify the response or both. Note that filters are not servlets and hence cannot create actual responses. Filters process requests before they reach a servlet and/or process responses after leaving a servlet. In general, a filter can do the following:

- Intercept and inspect requests before dispatching them to the servlets
- Modify requests' headers and data and discard or filter requests
- Intercept and inspect responses before dispatching them to the clients
- Modify requests' headers and data and discard or filter responses

A filter can work on behalf of a single servlet or a group of servlets. Similarly, zero or more filters can be installed for a servlet. Filters are typically used in the following areas:

- Authentication
- Logging and auditing
- Image compression
- Data compression
- Encryption
- Tokenization
- XML transformation

A filter class must implement the `javax.servlet.Filter` interface, which provides a framework for the filtering mechanism. It defines the following methods to be implemented by each filter class:

```
void init(FilterConfig config)
```

The web container, after instantiating a filter, calls this method once to install it and to set its configuration object. The method completes successfully; the filter can then start servicing. This method takes a `FilterConfig` object that contains information that may be used to configure the filter.

The `FilterConfig` interface provides methods to retrieve the filter's name, its initialization parameters (specified in web.xml file) and the underlying servlet context.

```
void doFilter(ServletRequest request, ServletResponse response, FilterChain
chain)
```

This method is called every time a request from the client is passed through the filter. It takes three arguments: A `ServletRequest` type object `request`, a `ServletResponse` type object `response` and a `FilterChain` type object `chain`. The `request` and `response` objects encapsulate the client request and response respectively whereas chain represents the next filter in this chain of filters installed for the servlet. A usual implementation of this method is as follows:

Upon receiving the client request, it processes the request and takes necessary actions (e.g. changing/formatting the content or header etc.) as much as it can do. The filter should then hand over the control to the next filter in this chain by calling `doFilter()` method on `chain`. The next filter takes further actions and forwards the request to the next filter in the chain. This way the client request propagates towards the servlet. If there is no further filter in the chain, the `doFilter()` on `chain` forwards the request to the servlet.

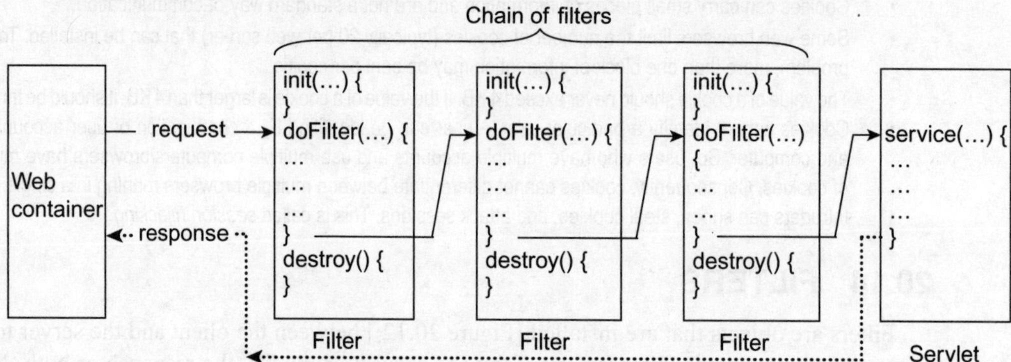

Figure 20.12: Function of filters

However, if a filter in the chain decides, it may not forward the request to the next filter; in this case, the request will not reach the servlet at all. In this way, filters can drop malicious requests intended for the servlet.

```
void destroy()
```

The method is called by the web container to uninstall the filter. Once this method is called on a filter, the `doFilter()` method is not called further, hence it stops functioning.

Let us now develop a simple filter that forwards only those requests that come from the host having the IP address "172.16.4.248". Requests from all other hosts are discarded.

```
import java.io.*;
import javax.servlet.*;
public class Firewall implements Filter {
   private FilterConfig config = null;
   public void init(FilterConfig config) throws ServletException {
      this.config = config;
   }
   public void doFilter(ServletRequest request, ServletResponse response,
      FilterChain chain) throws IOException, ServletException {
      if (request.getRemoteAddr().equals("172.16.4.248"))
         chain.doFilter(request, response);
   }
```

```
    public void destroy() {
        config = null;
    }
}
```

Compile this file using the following command.

```
javac -cp d:\apache-tomcat-8.0.0-RC1\lib\servlet-api.jar Firewall.java
```

Note that the file `servlet-api.jar` is necessary to compile the above filter class. Put the `Firewall.class` file in the `$TOMCAT_HOME\webapps\net\WEB-INF\classes` directory.

20.14.1 Deploying Filter

To use this filter, you must specify it in the `web.xml` file using the `<filter>` tag.

```
<filter>
    <filter-name>myFirewall</filter-name>
    <filter-class>Firewall</filter-class>
</filter>
```

This notifies the server that a filter named `myFirewall` is implemented in the `Firewall` class. So, the web server creates an instance of this filter and installs it during start up. Now, add the following lines in the `web.xml` file.

```
<filter-mapping>
    <filter-name>myFirewall</filter-name>
    <url-pattern>/servlet/HelloWorld</url-pattern>
</filter-mapping>
```

This code states that a filter should function for the URL pattern `/servlet/HelloWorld` that corresponds to our `HelloWorld` servlet. Now, try accessing the `HelloWorld` servlet from a host having IP address 172.16.4.248. A response will be received as before. But, if the servlet is accessed from any machine other than 172.16.4.248, no response will be received.

20.15 PROBLEMS WITH SERVLET

Servlets are not useful for generating presentation content such as HTML. Consider the following piece of code.

```
out.println("<html>");
out.println("  <head>");
out.println("    <title>Hello World Servlet</title>");
out.println("  </head>");
out.println("  <body>");
out.println("      <h1>Hello World!</h1>");
out.println("  </body>");
out.println("</html>");
```

The purpose of the code is to generate the following HTML code.

```
<html>
    <head>
        <title>Hello World Servlet</title>
    </head>
    <body>
        <h1>Hello World!</h1>
    </body>
</html>
```

This is acceptable if you want to generate smaller HTML files. However, if the size of the HTML document is large, it is a tedious process to generate it.

Another drawback of the servlet over **J**ava **S**erver **P**ages (JSP) is that you have to recompile the source yourself after any modification is done. Moreover, the web server has to be restarted to get the effect of modified code. However, JSP can perform these tasks automatically on our behalf.

Servlets often contain presentation logic as well as processing logic, which makes the code difficult to read, understand and extend. If the presentation logic changes, the servlet code has to be modified, recompiled, and redeployed.

20.16 SECURITY ISSUES

Different authors write servlets that are run using the resources of the server computer under the supervision of a web server. So, before installing servlets in the web server, make sure that they come from trusted sources. Certain access constraints should be imposed on the servlets depending on their sources.

The concept of *sandbox* may be incorporated. A *sandbox* is a container of servlets where restrictions are imposed. The administrator of the web server decides which servlets are given which permissions, so that they cannot compromise with the system's security.

In addition to these security issues, the author of the servlet should consider the following points:

- Take sufficient care while writing the file upload code. If not implanted carefully, users may fill the hard disk of the server by uploading large files.
- Review the code that accesses files/database based on the user input. For example, do not allow users to execute arbitrary SQL commands. If allowed, users may fire some harmful SQL commands that can delete database tables.
- Make sure that the request comes from an authorized user. Do not rely on the existence of a session variable.
- Make sure that you have not used the `System.exit()` method anywhere in your program. This will terminate the web server.
- Do not display sensitive parameter values in the web page.

20.17 APPENDIX A: LIST OF SSI SERVLET VARIABLES

Variable Name	Description
AUTH_TYPE	Authentication type (BASIC, FORM, etc.) used for this user
CONTENT_LENGTH	The length of the data passed to this servlet
CONTENT_TYPE	Type of data sent (e.g. text/html etc.)
DATE_GMT	Current date and time in GMT
DATE_LOCAL	Current date and time in the local time zone
DOCUMENT_NAME	The current filename
DOCUMENT_URI	Virtual path to the file
GATEWAY_INTERFACE	The revision of the CGI (if enabled: "CGI/1.1") that the server uses
HTTP_ACCEPT	A list of the MIME types acceptable to the client.
HTTP_ACCEPT_ENCODING	A list of the compression types acceptable to the client.
HTTP_ACCEPT_LANGUAGE	A list of the languages that the client can accept.
HTTP_CONNECTION	Connection type (persistent or non-persistent) sought:
HTTP_HOST	The web site that the client requested
HTTP_REFERER	The URL of the document that the client linked from

Variable Name	Description
HTTP_USER_AGENT	The browser the client is using to issue the request
LAST_MODIFIED	Last modification date and time of the current document
PATH_INFO	Extra path information passed to this servlet
PATH_TRANSLATED	The translated version of the path given by the variable PATH_INFO
QUERY_STRING	The query string passed to this servlet
QUERY_STRING_UNESCAPED	Query string with all shell meta-characters escaped with "\"
REMOTE_ADDR	The IP address of the remote host making the request
REMOTE_HOST	The name of the remote host making the request
REMOTE_PORT	The port number at remote IP address of the host making the request
REMOTE_USER	The authenticated name of the user
REQUEST_METHOD	The HTTP method (GET, POST etc.) used
REQUEST_URI	The web page originally requested by the client
SCRIPT_FILENAME	The location of the current web page on the server
SCRIPT_NAME	The name of the web page
SERVER_ADDR	The server's IP address
SERVER_NAME	The server's hostname or IP address
SERVER_PORT	The port on which the server received the request
SERVER_PROTOCOL	The protocol used by the server. E.g. "HTTP/1.1"
SERVER_SOFTWARE	The name and version of the server software that is answering the client request
UNIQUE_ID	A token used to identify the current session if one has been established

KEYWORDS

Cookie—A key–value pair used for session tracking

Filters—Objects that are installed between the client and the server to inspect requests and responses

GenericServlet—The class `GenericServlet` implements the Servlet and ServletConfig interfaces and defines a generic protocol-independent servlet

HttpServlet—The `HttpServlet` class extends `GenericServlet` and provides a framework for handling HTTP requests

HttpServletRequest—An interface that represents an HTTP request from the client

HttpServletResponse—An interface that represents an HTTP response from the servlet

Life Cycle methods—The methods such as `init()`, `service()`, `destroy()` that run during the life cycle of a servlet

Multi-threaded servlet—A servlet that can handle multiple simultaneous requests

Single-threaded servlet—A servlet that can service one request at a time

Server Side Include—Server-Side Include (SSI) allows us to embed (include) servlets within HTML pages, using SSI directives

Servlet life cycle—The set of states that a servlet goes through, from creation to destruction

Servlet interface—Top-level interface of the servlet architecture, which provides the basic functionalities of all servlets that are created by implementing this interface directly or indirectly

ServletConfig interface—Represents the configuration of a servlet

ServletRequest—An interface that represents a request from the client

ServletResponse—An interface that represents a response from the servlet

Web container—The environment/engine where servlets or other server-side programs run

SUMMARY

Servlet is a Java technology for server-side programming. A servlet is a Java module that runs inside a Java-enabled web server and services requests obtained from a web server.

Java servlet technology has some distinct advantages over other competent technologies in terms of efficiency, persistency, portability, robustness, extensibility, etc. Servlets run in the server machine and usually generate simple HTML codes. So, even a very old browser can display generated HTML pages correctly.

The basic servlet architecture consists of two packages: `javax.servlet` and `javax.servlet.http`. The first package contains top-level interfaces and classes that are used and extended by all other servlets. The second package is provided to use for servlets that can handle HTTP requests.

The container in which the servlet is deployed, supervises and controls the life cycle of a servlet. During its lifetime, methods such as `init()`, `service()`, and `destroy()` are called in some specific order.

The `GenericServlet` class defines a generic protocol-independent servlet in the sense that it can be extended to provide implementation of any protocol such as HTTP, FTP, and SMTP. On the other hand, `HttpServlet` class extends GenericServlet and provides a framework for handling HTTP requests.

There are two ways in which you can pass parameters to a servlet: using URL and using HTML form. One of the disadvantages of passing parameters using URLs is that users can view the parameter names with their values passed. So, it is not safe to send sensitive information using this method. Moreover, the number of parameters that we can pass is also limited. HTML forms can be used to pass parameters in a convenient way. The methods of the `ServletRequest` interface are used to retrieve parameters.

Server-Side Include (SSI) allows us to embed (include) servlets within HTML pages, using SSI directives. This lets us include dynamically generated content in an existing HTML file, without having to serve the entire page via a CGI program or other dynamic technologies.

Sometimes, it is necessary to keep track of a sequence of related requests sent by a client to perform some designated task. This is called session tracking. Cookies are one of the solutions to session tracking.

Filters are objects that are installed between clients and servers to inspect requests and responses. They can transform requests or modify responses.

WEB RESOURCES

`http://docs.oracle.com/javaee/6/tutorial/doc/bnafd.html`
Java Servlet Technology

`http://www.tutorialspoint.com/servlets/`
Servlets Tutorial

`http://www.javatpoint.com/servlet-tutorial`
Servlets Tutorial

`http://www.java2s.com/Tutorial/Java/0400__Servlet/Catalog0400__Servlet.htm`
Servlet

`http://www.ibm.com/developerworks/java/tutorials/j-intserv/`
Introduction to Java Servlet technology

EXERCISES

Objective-type Questions

1. Which one of the following methods is called first on a servlet?
   (a) start() (b) initialize() (c) init() (d) doInit()

2. Which of the following is the name of a web server?
   (a) Netscape (b) Borland (c) W3C (d) Tomcat

3. Which is the top-level class/interface in the servlet class hierarchy?
   (a) javax.servlet.Servlet
   (b) javax.servlet.HttpServlet
   (c) javax.servlet.GenericServlet
   (d) javax.servlet.TopServlet

4. Which of the following statements is false regarding servlets?
   (a) The init() function is called only once during the instantiation of the servlet.
   (b) The HttpServlet class implements the Servlet interface.
   (c) The HttpServlet can handle HTTP requests.
   (d) The GenericServlet class implements the Servlet interface.

5. A servlet is instantiated when
   (a) a client makes a request for the first time
   (b) the web server starts up
   (c) the client makes a request
   (d) the source code is compiled

6. Which of the following interfaces must a single threaded servlet implement?
   (a) NoMultiThread
   (b) SingleThread
   (c) OneThreadModel
   (d) SingleThreadModel

7. How many arguments does the service() method take?
   (a) 1 (c) 3
   (b) 2 (d) 4

8. Which of the following methods is used to retrieve the value of a specified parameter?
   (a) getParameter()
   (b) retrieveParameter()
   (c) parameter()
   (d) getParam()

9. Which of the following tags is used to make a named servlet?
   (a) <servlet-name>
   (b) <servlet-class>
   (c) <servlet>
   (d) <servlet-mapping>

10. Which of the following tags maps a named servlet to a URL pattern?
    (a) <servlet>
    (b) <servlet-name>
    (c) <servlet-class>
    (d) <servlet-mapping>

11. Which of the following SSI directives displays the value of a variable?
    (a) display (c) echo
    (b) print (d) show

12. What is the full form of SSI?
    (a) Server Side Include
    (b) Server Side Integration
    (c) Same Side Include
    (d) Same Side Integration

13. Which of the following SSI directives is used to insert the content of a server-side program?
    (a) insert (c) paste
    (b) include (d) import

14. Which of the following methods is used to add a cookie to the response?
    (a) addCookie() (c) installCookie()
    (b) sendCookie() (d) insertCookie()

15. What is the name of the servlet configuration file?
    (a) servlet.xml (c) web.xml
    (b) config.xml (d) server.xml

16. Which of the following packages contains Servlet interface?
    (a) javax.server.servlet
    (b) javax.servlet
    (c) java.server.servlet
    (d) java.servlet

17. The servlet initialization parameters are specified in the __________ deployment descriptor file as part of a servlet element.
    (a) web.xml (c) web.txt
    (b) web.doc (d) web.ini

18. Which of the following identifies the correct method a servlet developer should use to retrieve data provided by the client?
    (a) getParameter() against the HttpServletRequest object
    (b) getInputStream() against the HttpServletRequest object
    (c) getBytes() against the HttpServletRequest object
    (d) getQueryString() against the HttpServletRequest object

19. Which package provides interfaces and classes for writing servlets?
    (a) javax.servlet
    (b) javax.java.servlet
    (c) javax.awt.servlet
    (d) javax.swing.servlet

20. The Web server that executes the servlet creates an __________ object and passes this to the servlet's service method (which, in turn, passes it to doGet or doPost).
    (a) HttpRequest
    (b) HttpResponse
    (c) Request
    (d) HttpServletResponce

21. Which method can be used to access the ServletConfig object ?
    (a) getServletInfo()
    (b) getServletConfig()
    (c) getInitParameters()
    (d) getConfig()

Subjective-type Questions

1. What is a servlet?
2. What are the advantages of servlets over CGI?
3. What is the task of the `javax.servlet.Servlet` interface?
4. What are the two objects that a servlet receives when it accepts a call from a client?
5. What information does `ServletRequest` allow access to?
6. What type of constraints can `ServletResponse` interface set on the client?
7. Describe the life cycle of a servlet.
8. Describe how an HTTP Servlet handles its client requests.
9. Differentiate between the single-threaded and multi-threaded servlet model.
10. What are the differences between servlets and applets?
11. Mention some uses of Servlets.
12. How can you invoke other web resources such as servlets /JSPs?
13. How can you include other Resources in the Response?
14. What information does the `ServletResponse` interface give to the servlet methods for replying to the client?
15. What do you understand by servlet mapping?
16. What are the advantages of Cookies over URL rewriting?
17. What is session hijacking?

CHAPTER – 21

JAVA SERVER PAGES

KEY OBJECTIVES

After completing this chapter readers will be able to—

- understand the advantages of JSP technology over other competitive technologies
- learn the architecture of JSP pages and their execution philosophy
- get an idea about the different components of JSP pages
- get an overview about the methods used to track sessions
- create and use JavaBean components
- create and use custom tags

21.1 INTRODUCTION AND MARKETPLACE

Java Server Pages (JSP) is a server-side technology that enables web programmers to generate web pages dynamically in response to client requests. Among many server-side technologies used to build dynamic web applications, JSP is the one that has pulled the attention of web developers due to several reasons.

JSP is basically a high-level extension to the Java servlet technology. It enables us to insert pure Java code in an HTML document directly. These pages are executed under the supervision of an environment called *web container*. The web container first compiles the page on the server and generates a servlet, which is loaded in the **J**ava **R**untime **E**nvironment (JRE) automatically. The interesting part is that the web container only generates the servlet from the page if its last modification time is newer than the time when the servlet was generated last. The servlet serves the client requests in the usual way. This makes the development of web applications convenient, simple, and fast. Maintenance also becomes very easy.

JSP technology provides excellent server-side programming for web applications that need database access. JSP not only provides cross-web-server and cross-platform support, but also integrates the WYSIWYG (**W**hat **Y**ou **S**ee **I**s **W**hat **Y**ou **G**et) features of static HTML pages with the extreme power of Java technology.

JSP also allows us to separate the dynamic content of our web pages from the static HTML content. We can write regular HTML files in the usual way. We can then insert Java code for the dynamic parts using special tags, which usually start with `<%` and end with `%>`.

Usually, JSP files have the extension `jsp`. They are also installed in a place where we can place our normal web pages. Many web servers let us define aliases for JSP pages or servlets. So, a URL that appears to reference an HTML file may actually point to a JSP page or servlet.

21.2 JSP AND HTTP

Java Server Pages specification extends the idea of Java servlet API, to provide a robust framework to developers of web applications for creating dynamic web content. Currently, JSP or servlet technology supports only HTTP. However, a developer may extend the idea of servlet or JSP to implement other protocols such as FTP or SMTP. Since, JSP uses HTML, XML, and Java code, the applications are secure, fast, and independent of server platforms. It allows us to embed pure Java code in an HTML document. It is important to note that JSP specification has been defined on top of the Java servlet API. Consequently, it follows all servlet semantics and has all powers that a servlet has.

The life cycle and many of the capabilities, especially the dynamic aspects of JSP pages, are exactly the same as Java servlet technology. So, much of the discussion in this chapter refers to Chapter 20.

21.3 JSP ENGINES

To process JSP pages, a web container that can understand JSP (sometimes referred to as JSP engine) code is needed. It is interesting to note that what we know as the *JSP engine* is nothing but a specialized servlet, which runs under the supervision of the servlet engine. This JSP engine is typically connected with a web server or can be integrated inside a web server or an application server. Many such servers are freely available and can be downloaded for evaluation and/or development of web applications. Some of them are Tomcat, Java Web Server, WebLogic, and WebSphere.

Once you have downloaded and installed a JSP-capable web server or application server in your machine, you need to know where to place the JSP files, what their URLs will be and how to access them from the web browser or another application using those URLs. Since, Tomcat from Apache is an open source, free and easily configurable JSP engine, we shall use it to test all our JSP pages in this chapter.

21.3.1 Tomcat

Tomcat implements servlet 2.2 and JSP 1.1 specifications. It is very easy to install and can be used as a small stand-alone server for developing and testing servlets and JSP pages. For large applications, it is usually integrated into the more powerful Apache Web server.

Since, we shall use Tomcat JSP engine to test our JSP pages in this chapter, let us know how to install Tomcat in our machine first.

- Download the appropriate version of Tomcat from the Apache site `http://tomcat.apache.org\`
- Uncompress the file in a directory. If it is an installer file in Windows, install it in a directory by double clicking on the installer file.
- Set the environment variable `JAVA_HOME` to point to the root directory of your JDK hierarchy. For example, if the root directory of your JDK is `D:\Java\jdk1.7.0_07`, the JAVA_HOME environment variable should point to this directory. Also make sure that the directory (usually bin) containing the Java compiler (`javac`) and interpreter is in your `PATH` environment variable.

- Go to the `bin` directory under the tomcat installation directory and start Tomcat using the command-line command `startup.bat` (in Windows) or `startup.sh` (in Unix/Linux). If everything goes well, you will see an output in Windows as shown in Figure 21.1:

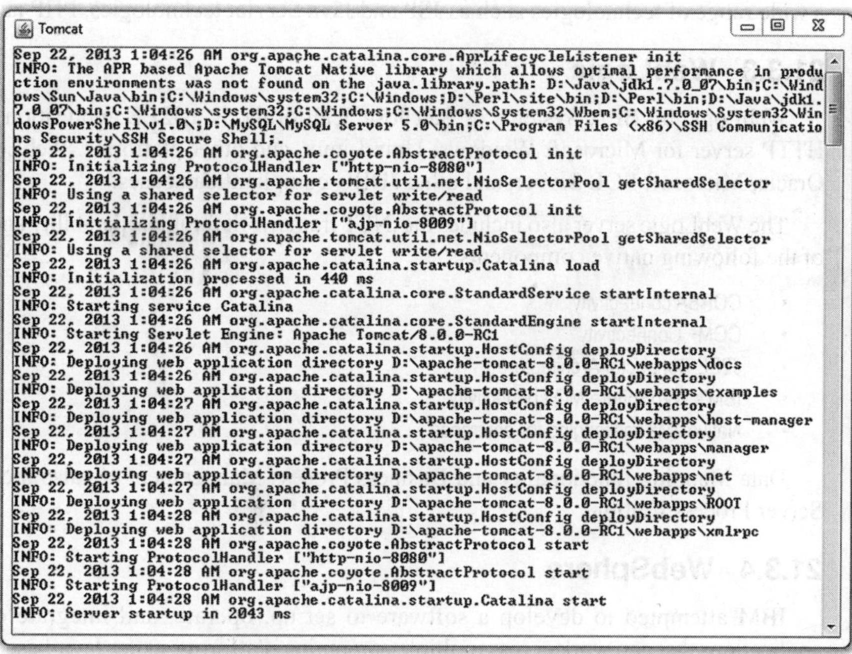

Tomcat
Sep 22, 2013 1:04:26 AM org.apache.catalina.core.AprLifecycleListener init
INFO: The APR based Apache Tomcat Native library which allows optimal performance in produ
ction environments was not found on the java.library.path: D:\Java\jdk1.7.0_07\bin;C:\Wind
ows\Sun\Java\bin;C:\Windows\system32;C:\Windows;D:\Perl\site\bin;D:\Perl\bin;D:\Java\jdk1.
7.0_07\bin;C:\Windows\system32;C:\Windows;C:\Windows\System32\Wbem;C:\Windows\System32\Win
dowsPowerShell\v1.0\;D:\MySQL\MySQL Server 5.0\bin;C:\Program Files (x86)\SSH Communicatio
ns Security\SSH Secure Shell;.
Sep 22, 2013 1:04:26 AM org.apache.coyote.AbstractProtocol init
INFO: Initializing ProtocolHandler ["http-nio-8080"]
Sep 22, 2013 1:04:26 AM org.apache.tomcat.util.net.NioSelectorPool getSharedSelector
INFO: Using a shared selector for servlet write/read
Sep 22, 2013 1:04:26 AM org.apache.coyote.AbstractProtocol init
INFO: Initializing ProtocolHandler ["ajp-nio-8009"]
Sep 22, 2013 1:04:26 AM org.apache.tomcat.util.net.NioSelectorPool getSharedSelector
INFO: Using a shared selector for servlet write/read
Sep 22, 2013 1:04:26 AM org.apache.catalina.startup.Catalina load
INFO: Initialization processed in 440 ms
Sep 22, 2013 1:04:26 AM org.apache.catalina.core.StandardService startInternal
INFO: Starting service Catalina
Sep 22, 2013 1:04:26 AM org.apache.catalina.core.StandardEngine startInternal
INFO: Starting Servlet Engine: Apache Tomcat/8.0.0-RC1
Sep 22, 2013 1:04:26 AM org.apache.catalina.startup.HostConfig deployDirectory
INFO: Deploying web application directory D:\apache-tomcat-8.0.0-RC1\webapps\docs
Sep 22, 2013 1:04:26 AM org.apache.catalina.startup.HostConfig deployDirectory
INFO: Deploying web application directory D:\apache-tomcat-8.0.0-RC1\webapps\examples
Sep 22, 2013 1:04:27 AM org.apache.catalina.startup.HostConfig deployDirectory
INFO: Deploying web application directory D:\apache-tomcat-8.0.0-RC1\webapps\host-manager
Sep 22, 2013 1:04:27 AM org.apache.catalina.startup.HostConfig deployDirectory
INFO: Deploying web application directory D:\apache-tomcat-8.0.0-RC1\webapps\manager
Sep 22, 2013 1:04:27 AM org.apache.catalina.startup.HostConfig deployDirectory
INFO: Deploying web application directory D:\apache-tomcat-8.0.0-RC1\webapps\net
Sep 22, 2013 1:04:27 AM org.apache.catalina.startup.HostConfig deployDirectory
INFO: Deploying web application directory D:\apache-tomcat-8.0.0-RC1\webapps\ROOT
Sep 22, 2013 1:04:28 AM org.apache.catalina.startup.HostConfig deployDirectory
INFO: Deploying web application directory D:\apache-tomcat-8.0.0-RC1\webapps\xmlrpc
Sep 22, 2013 1:04:28 AM org.apache.coyote.AbstractProtocol start
INFO: Starting ProtocolHandler ["http-nio-8080"]
Sep 22, 2013 1:04:28 AM org.apache.coyote.AbstractProtocol start
INFO: Starting ProtocolHandler ["ajp-nio-8009"]
Sep 22, 2013 1:04:28 AM org.apache.catalina.startup.Catalina start
INFO: Server startup in 2043 ms

Figure 21.1: Starting tomcat server

- Tomcat is now running on port 8080 by default. You can test it by using the URL `http://127.0.0.1:8080\`. The page shown in Figure 21.2: appears.

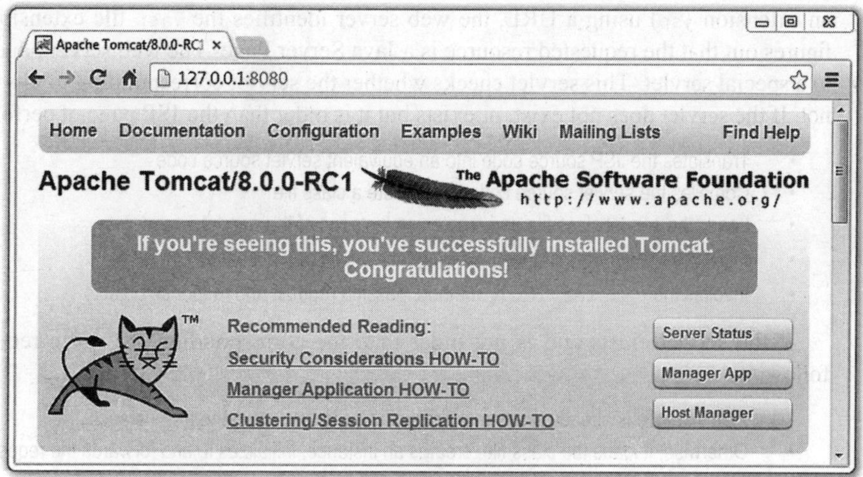

Figure 21.2: Tomcat home page

21.3.2 Java Web Server

The Java System Web Server by Sun is a leading web server that delivers secure infrastructure for medium and large business technologies and applications. Sun claims that it delivers 8x better performance than Apache 2.0 with Tomcat. It is available on all major operating systems and supports a wide range of technologies such as JSP and Java Servlet technologies, PHP and CGI.

21.3.3 WebLogic

WebLogic by BEA Systems of San Jose, California, is a J2EE application server and also an HTTP server for Microsoft Windows, Unix/Linux, and other platforms. WebLogic supports DB2, Oracle, Microsoft SQL Server, and other JDBC-compliant databases.

The WebLogic server also includes the .NET framework for interoperability and allows integration of the following native components:

- CORBA connectivity
- COM+ Connectivity
- J2EE Connector Architecture
- IBM's WebSphere MQ connectivity
- Native JMS messaging for enterprise

Data Mapping functionality and Business Process Management are also included in WebLogic Server Process Edition.

21.3.4 WebSphere

IBM attempted to develop a software to set up, operate, and integrate electronic business applications that can work across multiple computing platforms, using Java-based web technologies. The result is WebSphere Application Server (WAS). It includes both the run-time components and the tools that can be used to develop robust and versatile applications that will run on WAS.

21.4 HOW JSP WORKS

When a client such as a web browser sends a request to a web server for a JSP file (usually having an extension `jsp`) using a URL, the web server identifies the `.jsp` file extension in the URL and figures out that the requested resource is a Java Server Page. The web server hands over the request to a special servlet. This servlet checks whether the servlet corresponding to this JSP page exists or not. If the servlet does not exist, or exists but it is older than the JSP page, it performs the following:

- Translates the JSP source code into an equivalent servlet source code
- Compiles the servlet source code to generate a class file
- Loads the servlet class file and creates an instance of this servlet
- Initializes the servlet instance by calling the `jspInit()` method
- Invokes the `_jspService()` method, passing request and response objects

If the servlet exists and is not older than the corresponding JSP page requested, it does the following:

- If an instance is already running, it simply forwards the request to this instance.
- Otherwise, it loads the class file, creates an instance, initializes it, and forwards the request to this instance.

During development, one of the advantages of JSP pages over servlets is that the build process is automatically performed by the JSP engine. When a JSP file is requested for the first time, or if it is changed, the translation and compilation phase occurs. The subsequent requests for the JSP page directly go to the servlet byte code, which is already in the memory.

21.5 JSP AND SERVLET

Java servlet technology is an extremely powerful technology. However, when it is used to generate large, complex HTML code, it becomes a bit cumbersome.

In most servlets, a small piece of code is written to handle application logic and a large code is written using several `out.println()` statements that handle output formatting (see Chapter 20). Since the codes for application logic and formatting are closely tied, it is difficult to separate and reuse portions of the code when a different logic or output format is required.

JSP separates the static presentation templates from the logic, to generate the dynamic content, by encapsulating it within external JavaBean components. These components are then instantiated and used in a JSP page using special tags and scriptlets. When the presentation template is changed by the web designer, the JSP engine recompiles the JSP page and reloads it in the **J**ava **R**untime **E**nvironment (JRE).

Another problem of servlets is that each time the servlet code is modified, it needs to be recompiled and the web server also needs to be restarted. The JSP engine takes care of all these issues automatically. Whenever a JSP code is modified, the JSP engine identifies it and translates it into a new servlet. The servlet code is then compiled, loaded, and instantiated automatically. The servlet remains in the memory and serves requests subsequently without any delay.

JSP uses technologies based on reusable component engineering such as JavaBean component architecture and **E**nterprise **J**ava**B**ean (EJB) technology. So, JSP does not require significant developer expertise, like Java servlets. Consequently, in the application development life cycle, page designers can now play a major role. JSP pages can be moved easily across web servers and platforms, without any significant changes or effort.

For these reasons, web application developers turn towards JSP technology as an alternative to servlet technology.

21.5.1 Translation and Compilation

Every JSP page gets converted to a normal servlet behind the scene by the web container automatically. Figure 21.3: shows one such translation.

date.jsp (a JSP file)

```
<html>
    <head><title></title></head>
    <body>
        <%= new java.util.Date() %>
    </body>
</html>
```

Translation

```
...
public final class date_jsp extends
org.apache.jasper.runtime .HttpJspBase
    implements org.apache.jasper.runtime.JspSourceDependent {
...
```

date_jsp.java (a servlet)

Figure 21.3: JSP to servlet translation

Each type of data in a JSP page is processed differently during the translation phase. The translation and compilation phases may result in errors. These errors (if any) are generated when a user requests the page for the first time.

The JSP engine returns a `ParseException`, if an error occurs during the translation phase. In such a case, the servlet source file will be empty or incomplete. The last incomplete line describes the cause of error in the JSP page. If an error occurs during the compilation phase, the JSP engine returns a `JasperException` and a message that describes the name of the JSP page's servlet and the line that caused the error.

Now, let us take a specific example to understand this translation procedure. Consider the following JSP page. You may not understand the syntax used in this file. We shall discuss it in the rest of this chapter.

```
<html>
<head><title>Square table</title></head>
<body>
    <table border="1">
        <caption>Temperature Conversion chart</caption>
        <tr><th>Celsius</th><th>Fahrenheit</th></tr>
    <%
        for(int c = 0; c <= 100; c+=20) {
            double f = (c*9)/5.0 + 32;
            out.println("<tr><td>" + c + "</td><td>" + f + "</td></tr>");
        }
    %>
    </table>
  </body>
</html>
```

This is a simple JSP page that prints temperature conversion (from Celsius to Fahrenheit) chart. If you open this page in Google chrome, it looks as shown in Figure 21.4:

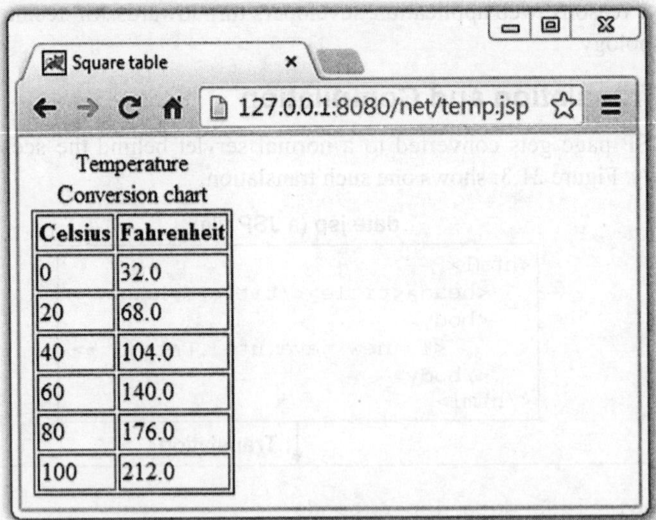

Figure 21.4: Temperature Conversion Chart

When you request this page for the first time, the JSP engine translates the JSP page into the following servlet source code (`temp_jsp.java` created in `tomcat_home\work\Catalina\localhost\net\org\apache\jsp` directory).

```
package org.apache.jsp;

import javax.servlet.*;
import javax.servlet.http.*;
import javax.servlet.jsp.*;

public final class temp_jsp extends org.apache.jasper.runtime.HttpJspBase
    implements org.apache.jasper.runtime.JspSourceDependent {

  private static final javax.servlet.jsp.JspFactory _jspxFactory =
          javax.servlet.jsp.JspFactory.getDefaultFactory();

  private static java.util.Map<java.lang.String,java.lang.Long> _jspx_dependants;

  private javax.el.ExpressionFactory _el_expressionfactory;
  private org.apache.tomcat.InstanceManager _jsp_instancemanager;

  public java.util.Map<java.lang.String,java.lang.Long> getDependants() {
    return _jspx_dependants;
  }

  public void _jspInit() {
    _el_expressionfactory =
_jspxFactory.getJspApplicationContext(getServletConfig().getServletContext()).g
etExpressionFactory();
    _jsp_instancemanager =
org.apache.jasper.runtime.InstanceManagerFactory.getInstanceManager(getServletC
onfig());
  }
  public void _jspDestroy() {
  }
  public void _jspService(final javax.servlet.http.HttpServletRequest request, final
javax.servlet.http.HttpServletResponse response)
        throws java.io.IOException, javax.servlet.ServletException {

    final javax.servlet.jsp.PageContext pageContext;
    javax.servlet.http.HttpSession session = null;
    final javax.servlet.ServletContext application;
    final javax.servlet.ServletConfig config;
    javax.servlet.jsp.JspWriter out = null;
    final java.lang.Object page = this;
    javax.servlet.jsp.JspWriter _jspx_out = null;
    javax.servlet.jsp.PageContext _jspx_page_context = null;


    try {
      response.setContentType("text/html");
      pageContext = _jspxFactory.getPageContext(this, request, response,
                null, true, 8192, true);
      _jspx_page_context = pageContext;
      application = pageContext.getServletContext();
      config = pageContext.getServletConfig();
      session = pageContext.getSession();
      out = pageContext.getOut();
      _jspx_out = out;

      out.write("<html>\r\n");
      out.write("\t<head><title>Square table</title></head>\r\n");
      out.write("\t<body>\r\n");
      out.write("\t\t<table border=\"1\">\r\n");
      out.write("\t\t\t<caption>Temperature Conversion chart</caption>\r\n");
      out.write("\t\t\t<tr><th>Celsius</th><th>Fahrenheit</th></tr>\r\n");
      out.write("\t\t");
```

```
            for(int c = 0; c <= 100; c+=20) {
               double f = (c*9)/5.0 + 32;
               out.println("<tr><td>" + c + "</td><td>" + f + "</td></tr>");
            }

         out.write("\r\n");
         out.write("\t\t</table>\r\n");
         out.write("\t</body>\r\n");
         out.write("</html>\r\n");
       } catch (java.lang.Throwable t) {
         if (!(t instanceof javax.servlet.jsp.SkipPageException)){
           out = _jspx_out;
           if (out != null && out.getBufferSize() != 0)
             try { out.clearBuffer(); } catch (java.io.IOException e) {}
           if (_jspx_page_context != null)
    _jspx_page_context.handlePageException(t);
           else throw new ServletException(t);
         }
       } finally {
         _jspxFactory.releasePageContext(_jspx_page_context);
       }
     }

}
```

The JSP page's servlet class extends `HttpJspBase`, which in turn implements the `Servlet` interface. In the generated servlet class, the methods `_jspInit()`, `_jspService()`, and `_jspDestroy()` correspond to the servlet life cycle methods `init()`, `service()`, and `destroy()`, respectively which were discussed in Chapter 20. The `_jspService()` method is responsible for serving client's requests. JSP specification prohibits the overriding of the `_jspService()` method. However, the developers are allowed to override the `_jspInit()` and `_jspDestroy()` methods within their JSP pages, to initialize and shut down servlets, respectively.

By default, the servlet container dispatches the `_jspService()` method using a separate thread to process concurrent client requests, as shown in Figure 21.5:

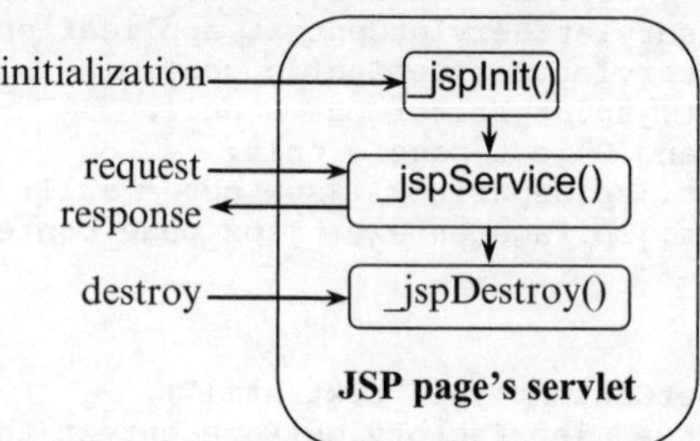

Figure 21.5: Life cycle of JSP's servlet

The static HTML part is simply printed to the output stream associated with the servlet's `service()` method. The code in `<%` and `%>` is copied in the `_jspService()` method.

21.6 ANATOMY OF A JSP PAGE

A JSP page basically consists of two parts: HTML/XML markups and JSP constructs. A large percent of your JSP page, in many cases, just consists of static HTML/XML components, known as *template text*. Consequently, we can create and maintain JSP pages using traditional HTML/XML tools.

We use three primary types of JSP constructs in a typical JSP page: *scripting elements*, *directives*, and *actions*.

Java code that will become an integral part of the resultant servlet is inserted using *scripting elements*. *Directives* let us control the overall structure and behaviour of the generated servlet. *Actions* allow us to use existing components, and otherwise control the behaviour of the JSP engine.

There are three kinds of scripting elements: *scriptlets*, *declarations*, and *expressions*. *Scriptlets* allow us to insert any Java-server-relevant API in the HTML or XML page provided that the syntax is correct. *Declarations* allow us to declare variable and methods. *Expressions* are used to print the value of Java expressions.

21.7 JSP SYNTAX

The syntax of JSP is almost similar to that of XML. ALL JSP tags must conform to the following general rules:

- Tags must have their matching end tags.
- Attributes must appear in the start tag.
- Attribute values in the tag must be quoted.

White spaces within the body text of a JSP page are preserved during the translation phase. To use special characters such as '%', add a '\' character before it. To use the '\' character, add another '\' character before it.

21.8 JSP COMPONENTS

A JSP page consists of the following components:

- Directives
- Scripting Elements
    - Declarations
    - Expressions
    - Scriptlets
- Actions

Table 21.1 lists some JSP tags and their meanings.

Table 21.1: JSP tags

JSP tag	Meaning
<%@...%>	Used for JSP directives such as page and include
<%!...%>	Used for variables, methods, and inner class declarations
<%=...%>	Used for JSP expressions
<%...%>	Used for JSP scriptlets that can contain arbitrary Java statements

21.8.1 Directives

A JSP page may contain instructions to be used by the JSP container to indicate how this page is interpreted and executed. Those instructions are called *directives*. Directives do not generate any output directly, but tell the JSP engine how to handle the JSP page. They are enclosed within the `<%@` and `%>` tags. The commonly used directives are `page`, `include`, and `taglib`.

21.8.1.1 page directive

The following is the syntax of the page directive:

```
<%@ page
      [ language="java" ]
      [ extends="package.class" ]
      [ import="{package.class | package.*}, ..." ]
      [ session="true | false" ]
      [ buffer="none | 8kb | sizekb" ]
      [ autoFlush="true | false" ]
      [ isThreadSafe="true | false" ]
      [ info="text" ]
      [ errorPage="relativeURL" ]
      [ contentType="MIMEType [ ;charset=characterSet ]"    |    "text/html ;
charset=ISO-8859-1"]
         [ isErrorPage="true | false" ]
%>
```

The page directive has many attributes, which can be specified in any order. Multiple page directives may also be used, but in this case, except for the import attribute, no attribute should appear more than once. The code in boldface indicates the default values. Let us discuss the function of some attributes.

import

The value of this attribute is a list of fully qualified names of classes separated by commas (,), to be imported by the JSP file. To import all the classes of a package, use ".*" at the end of the package name. The following directive imports all the classes in the java.io and java.reflect packages and the class Vector that belongs to the java.util package.

```
<%@ page import="java.io.*, java.reflect.*, java.util.Vector" %>
```

The classes can then be referred from declarations, expressions, and scriptlets within the JSP document, without using the package prefix. You must import a class before using it. You can use import as many times as you wish in a JSP file. For example, the line of code we have just discussed can be written as three directives, as follows:

```
<%@ page import="java.io.*" %>
<%@ page import="java.reflect.*" %>
<%@ page import="java.util.Vector" %>
```

Those directives are converted to the corresponding import statement in the generated servlet file. You need not import the classes of the packages java.lang, javax.servlet, javax.servlet.http, and javax.servlet.jsp, as they are imported implicitly.

session

This attribute indicates whether the JSP file requires an HTTP session. The following syntax is used:

session="**true** | false"

If true is specified (this is the default value), the JSP file has a session object that refers to the current or new session. If the value is false, no session object is created. If your JSP file does not require a session, the value should be set to false for performance consideration.

buffer

Syntax:

```
buffer="none | sizekb"
```

The buffer attribute indicates the size in kilobytes (default is 8kb) of the output buffer to be used by the JSP file. The value none indicates a buffer with zero size. In such a case, the output is written directly to the output stream of the response object of the servlet.

autoFlush

Syntax:

```
autoFlush="true | false"
```

The autoFlush attribute specifies whether the buffer should be flushed automatically (true) when it is full. If set to false, a buffer overflow exception is thrown when the buffer becomes full. The default value is true. The value of autoFlush can never be set to false when the buffer is set to none.

isThreadSafe

Syntax:

```
isThreadSafe="true | false"
```

This attribute indicates whether the JSP page can handle multiple threads simultaneously. If true (default value) is specified, the JSP container is allowed to send multiple concurrent client requests to this JSP page. In this case, we must ensure that the access to shared resources by multiple concurrent threads is effectively synchronized. If false is specified, the JSP container sends clients requests one by one using a single thread. This attribute basically provides information to the underlying servlet on whether it should implement the SingleThreadModel interface or not. Tomcat generates the following servlet class declaration if false is specified.

```
public final class ThreadDemo_jsp extends org.apache.jasper.runtime.HttpJspBase
    implements org.apache.jasper.runtime.JspSourceDependent,
                 javax.servlet.SingleThreadModel {
```

In this case, the JSP container loads multiple instances of the servlet in the memory. It then distributes concurrent client requests evenly among these servlet instances for processing in a round-robin fashion.

If true is specified, the following code is generated:

```
public final class ThreadDemo_jsp extends org.apache.jasper.runtime.HttpJspBase
    implements org.apache.jasper.runtime.JspSourceDependent {
```

info

Syntax:

```
info="text"
```

It allows us to specify a descriptive information about the JSP page. This information can be retrieved using the Servlet.getServletInfo() method.

contentType

Syntax:

```
contentType="MIMEType [ ;charset=characterSet ]"
```

It specifies the MIME type and encoding used in the generated response to be sent to the client. MIME types and encoding supported by the JSP container can only be specified. The default MIME type and character encoding are text/html and ISO-8859-1, respectively.

errorPage and isErrorPage

Syntax:

```
errorPage="relativeURL"
isErrorPage="true | false"
```

When an uncaught exception occurs in a JSP page, the JSP container sends information explaining the exception, which is undesirable for some cases such as commercial sites. The errorPage attribute specifies the relative path name of another JSP page to be displayed, in case an error occurs in the current page. In the error page, the `isErrorPage` attribute must be set to `true`. The error page can access the implicit `exception` variable that represents the exception that has occurred as well as other implicit variables. It can then send some message understandable by the clients, by consulting those objects.

21.8.1.2 include directive

This directive inserts the content of a file in a JSP page, during the translation phase when the JSP page is compiled.

Syntax:

```
<%@ include file="relativeURL" %>
```

If the file to be included is an HTML or text file, its content is directly included in the place of the `include` directive. The following example includes an HTML file `header.html` in a JSP page.

```
<%@ include file="header.html" %>
```

If the included file is a JSP file, it is first translated and then included in the JSP page.

```
<%@ include file="login.jsp" %>
```

Make sure that the tags in the included file do not conflict with the tags used in including the JSP page. For example, if the including JSP page contains tags such as `<html>` and `<body>`, the included file must not contain those tags.

The include process is said to be static as the file is included at compilation time. JSP 1.1 specifies that once the JSP file is compiled any changes in the included file will not be reflected. However, some JSP containers, such as tomcat, recompile the JSP page if the included file changes.

21.8.2 Comments

Comments are used to document the JSP pages and can be inserted anywhere in the JSP page. The general syntax is as follows:

```
<%-- JSP comment --%>
```

Anything between `<%--` and `--%>` is ignored by the JSP engine and is not even added to the servlet's source code. Here is an example:

```
<%-- Prints current date and time --%>
<%= new java.util.Date(); %>
```

The Java-like comments may also be used in scriptlets and declarations. They are added to the servlet, but not interpreted and hence are not sent to the client.

```
<%
   //get all cookies
   Cookie[] cookies = request.getCookies();
   /*
   Following code checks whether the request contains
   a cookie having name "user"
   */
   String user = null;
   for(int i = 0; i < cookies.length; i++)
      if(cookies[i].getName().equals("user"))
         user = (String)cookies[i].getValue();
   if(user != null) {
      //proceed
   }
%>
```

The HTML comments are enclosed in `<!--` and `-->` and added to the servlet source code as well as to the response, but browsers do not display them on the screen. Consider the following code:

```
<!-- This page was generated at server on
<%= (new java.util.Date()) %>
-->
```

This generates the following HTML comment. This is sent to the client, but not displayed on the screen.

```
<!-- This page was generated at server on
Sun Sep 22 04:14:07 PDT 2013
-->
```

21.8.3 Expressions

JSP 2.0 specification includes a new feature, *Expression*. It is used to insert usually a small piece of data in a JSP page, without using the `out.print()` or `out.write()` statements. It is a faster, easier, and clearer way to display the values of variables/parameters/expressions in a JSP page. The general syntax of JSP expressions is as follows:

```
<%= expressions %>
```

The expression is embedded within the tag pair `<%=` and `%>`. Note that no semicolon is used at the end of the expression. The expression is evaluated, converted to a `String` and inserted in the place of the expression using an `out.print()` statement. For example, if we want to add 3 and 4 and display the result, we write the JSP expression as follows:

```
3 + 4 = <%= 3+4 %>
```

The expression is translated into the following Java statements in servlet source code.

```
out.write("3 + 4 = ");
out.print( 3+4 );
```

If everything works fine, you should see the following output:

```
3 + 4 = 7
```

The expression can be anything, as long as it can be converted to a string. For example, the following expression uses a `java.util.Date` object.

```
Date and time is : <%= new java.util.Date() %>
```

JSP expressions can be used as attribute values as well as tag names of JSP elements. Consider the following JSP code.

```
<%
   java.util.Date dt = new java.util.Date();
   String dateStr = dt.toString();
   String time = "currentTime";
%>
<<%= time %> value="<%= dateStr %>" />
```

This generates the following tag:

```
<currentTime value="Sun Sep 22 04:12:50 PDT 2013" />
```

JSP also has an equivalent tag for expression as follows:

```
<jsp:expression>
   expressions
</jsp:expression>
```

21.8.4 Scriptlets

You can insert an arbitrary piece of Java code using the JSP *scriptlets* construct in a JSP page. This code will be inserted in the servlet's `_jspService()` method. Scriptlets are useful if you want to insert complex code which would otherwise be difficult using expressions. A scriptlet can contain any number of variables, class declarations, expressions, or other language statements. Scriptlets have the following form:

```
<% scriptlets %>
```

For example, the following scriptlet inserts the current date and time in the JSP page.

```
<%
   java.util.Date d = new java.util.Date();
   out.println("Date and time is : " + d);
%>
```

The resultant servlet code looks like this:

```
…
public final class scriptlet_jsp extends org.apache.jasper.runtime.HttpJspBase
    implements org.apache.jasper.runtime.JspSourceDependent {
…
  public void _jspService(final javax.servlet.http.HttpServletRequest request,
final javax.servlet.http.HttpServletResponse response)
        throws java.io.IOException, javax.servlet.ServletException {
…

   java.util.Date d = new java.util.Date();
   out.println("Date and time is : " + d);
…
```

This results in the following:

```
Date and time is : Sun Sep 22 04:15:50 PDT 2013
```

JSP also has the following XML equivalent for scriptlet:

```
<jsp:scriptlet>
  scriptlets
</jsp:scriptlet>
```

21.8.4.1 Conditional Processing

Several scriptlets and templates can be merged, to do some designated task. The following example illustrates this:

```
<%
int no = (int)(Math.random()*10);
if(no % 2 == 0) {
%>
Even
<% } else { %>
Odd
<% } %>
```

This code gets converted into something like

```
int no = (int)(Math.random()*10);
if(no % 2 == 0) {

      out.write("\r\n");
      out.write("Even\r\n");
  } else {
      out.write("\r\n");
      out.write("Odd\r\n");
  }
```

21.8.5 Declarations

JSP *declarations* are used to declare one or more variables, methods, or inner classes, which can be used later in the JSP page. The syntax is as follows:

```
<%! declarations %>
```

Examples are

```
<%! int sum = 0; %>
<%! int x, y , z; %>
<%! java.util.Hashtable table = new java.util.Hashtable(); %>
```

These variable declarations are inserted into the body of the servlet class, i.e., outside the _jspService() method that processes the client requests. So, variables declared in this way become instance variables of the underlying servlet.

```
<%! int sum = 0; %>
```

This is translated in the servlet as follows:

```
...
public final class scriptlet_jsp extends org.apache.jasper.runtime.HttpJspBase
    implements org.apache.jasper.runtime.JspSourceDependent {
  int sum = 0;
  public void _jspService(final javax.servlet.http.HttpServletRequest request,
final javax.servlet.http.HttpServletResponse response)
        throws java.io.IOException, javax.servlet.ServletException {
  ...
```

Note that variables created using *scriptlets* are local to the _jspService() method. Instance variables are created and initialized once the servlet is instantiated. This is sometimes useful, but sometimes not desirable. The following declarations create an instance variable, lastLoaded.

```
<%! java.util.Date lastLoaded = new java.util.Date();%>
The servlet was last loaded on <b><%=lastLoaded%></b>
```

This generates the following result:

The servlet was last loaded on **Sun Sep 22 04:19:12 PDT 2013**

Similarly, the following piece of code displays the number of times the JSP page is referred after the page is loaded.

```
<%! int count = 0;%>
This page is referred <%= ++count %> times after last modification
```

Variables generated using declarations are available in scriptlets. A declaration has the scope of entire translation unit. It is valid in the JSP file as well as in all the files included statically. Declarations are not valid in dynamically included files.

JSP also has the following XML equivalent for declaration:

```
<jsp:declaration>
  declarations
</jsp:declaration>
```

21.8.6 Scope of JSP Objects

In a JSP page, objects may be created using directives, actions, or scriptlets. Every object created in a JSP page has a scope. The scope of a JSP object is defined as the availability of that object for use from a particular place of the web application. There are four object scope: *page*, *request*, *session*, and *application*.

page

Objects having *page* scope can be accessed only from within the same page where they were created. JSP implicit objects out, exception, response, pageContext, config, and page have *page* scope. We have discussed implicit objects in the next section. JSP objects created using the <jsp:useBean> tag also have *page* scope.

request

A request can be served by more than one page. Objects having *request* scope can be accessed from any page that serves that request. The implicit object request has the *request* scope.

session

Objects having *session* scope are accessible from pages that belong to the same session from where they were created. The `session` implicit object has the *session* scope.

application

JSP objects that have *application* scope can be accessed from any page that belong to the same application. An example is `application` implicit object.

21.8.7 Implicit Objects

Web container allows us to directly access many useful objects defined in the `_jspService()` method of the JSP page's underlying servlet. These objects are called *implicit objects* as they are instantiated automatically. The *implicit objects* contain information about request, response, session, configuration, etc. Some implicit objects are described in Table 21.2:

Table 21.2: JSP Implicit Objects

Variable	Class	Description
out	javax.servlet.jsp.JspWriter	Output stream of the JSP page's servlet.
request	Subtype of javax.servlet.ServletRequest	Current client request being handled by the JSP page
response	Subtype of javax.servlet.ServletResponse	Response generated by the JSP page to be returned to the client
config	javax.servlet.ServletConfig	Initialization information of the JSP page's servlet
session	javax.servlet.http.HttpSession	Session object for the client
application	javax.servlet.ServletContext	Context of the JSP page's servlet and other web components contained in the same application.
exception	java.lang.Throwable	Represents error. Accessible only from an error page
page	java.lang.Object	Refers to JSP page's servlet processing the current request
pageContext	javax.servlet.jsp.PageContext	The context of the JSP page that provides APIs to manage the various scoped attributes. It is extensively used by the tag handlers.

request

This object refers to the `javax.servlet.http.HttpServletRequest` type object that is passed to the `_jspService()` method of the generated servlet. It represents the HTTP request made by a client to this JSP page. It is used to retrieve information sent by the client such as parameters (using the `getParameter()` method), HTTP request type (`GET`, `POST`, `HEAD`, etc), and HTTP request headers (cookies, referrer, etc). This implicit object has request scope.

```
<%
  String name = request.getParameter("name");
  out.println("Hello " + name);
%>
```

For the URL `http://127.0.0.1:8080/net/getParameterDemo.jsp?name=Monali`, it displays the following:

```
Hello Monali
```

A JSP page can retrieve parameters sent through an HTML form. Consider the following form:

```
<form method='post' action='jsp/add.jsp'>
<input type='text' name='a' size='4'>+
<input type='text' name='b' size='4'>
<input type='submit' value='Add'>
</form>
```

Here is the code for the `add.jsp` file.

```
<%
    int a = Integer.parseInt(request.getParameter("a"));
    int b = Integer.parseInt(request.getParameter("b"));
    out.println(a + " + " + b + " = " + (a + b));
%>
```

The result is shown in Figure 21.6:

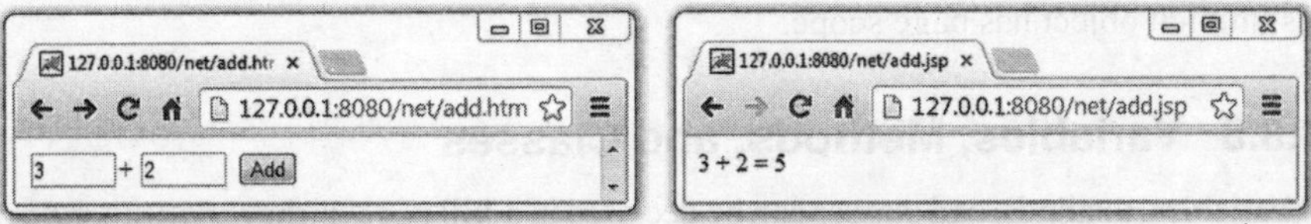

Figure 21.6: Retrieving form data from JSP page

response

This object refers to the `javax.servlet.http.HttpServletResponse` type object that is passed to the `_jspService()` method of the generated servlet. It represents the HTTP response to the client. This object is used to send information such as HTTP response header and cookies. This implicit object has page scope.

pageContext

This `javax.servlet.jsp.PageContext` type object refers to the current JSP page context. It is used to access information related to this page such as request, response, session, application, and underlying servlet configuration. This implicit object has page scope.

session

This `javax.servlet.http.HttpSession` type object refers to the session (if any) used by the JSP page. Note that no `session` object is created if the `session` attribute of the `page` directive is turned off and any attempt to refer to this object causes an error. It is used to access session-related information such as creation time and ID associated to this session. This implicit object has session scope.

application

This `javax.servlet.ServletContext` object refers to the underlying application and is used to share data among all pages under this application. This implicit object has application scope.

out

It denotes the character output stream that is used to send data back to the client. It is a buffered version of `java.io.PrintWriter` called `javax.servlet.jsp.JspWriter` type object. The object `out` is used only in scriptlets. This implicit object has page scope.

```
<% out.println("Hello World!"); %>
```

JSP expressions are placed in the output stream automatically and hence we do not use this `out` object there explicitly.

config

This `javax.servlet.ServletConfig` type object refers to the configuration of the underlying servlet. It is used to retrieve initial parameters, servlet name, etc. This implicit object has page scope.

page

This object refers to the JSP page itself. It can be used to call any instance of the JSP page's servlet. This implicit object has page scope.

exception

This represents an uncaught exception, which causes an error page to be called. This object is available in the JSP page for which the `isErrorPage` attribute of the `page` directive is set to `true`. This implicit object has page scope.

21.8.8 Variables, Methods, and Classes

Variables, methods, and classes can be declared in a JSP page. If they are declared in the declaration section, they become part of the underlying servlet class. For example, variables declared in the declaration section become instance variables and are accessible from any method of the JSP page's servlet class.

Consider the following variable declaration:

```
<%! double PI = 22/7.0; %>
```

The resultant servlet code will look like this:

```
...
public final class method_jsp extends org.apache.jasper.runtime.HttpJspBase
    implements org.apache.jasper.runtime.JspSourceDependent {
double PI = 22/7.0;
...
```

These variables are also shared among multiple threads. Classes and methods can be declared in a similar way as follows:

```
<%!
int add(int a, int b) {
   return a + b;
}
class AnInnerClass {
}
%>
```

The resultant servlet source code will look like this:

```
...
public final class method_jsp extends org.apache.jasper.runtime.HttpJspBase
    implements org.apache.jasper.runtime.JspSourceDependent {
int add(int a, int b) {
   return a + b;
}
class AnInnerClass {
}
...
```

Variables, methods, and classes declared in the declaration section are available in scriptlets. So, the following scriptlet is valid for this declaration.

```
<%out.println(add(2, 3));%>
```

It displays the following:

```
5
```

JSP allows us to declare variables and classes, but not methods, in the scriptlet section. Variables declared in the scriptlet section are local to the `_jspService()` method. They are created each time the client makes a request and destroyed after the request is over. Similarly, classes declared in the scriptlet section become inner classes of the `_jspService()` method. Consider the following code:

```
<%
double temp = 0;
class TempClass {
}
%>
```

The resultant servlet code looks like this:

```
...
public final class method_jsp extends org.apache.jasper.runtime.HttpJspBase
    implements org.apache.jasper.runtime.JspSourceDependent {
...
  public void _jspService(final javax.servlet.http.HttpServletRequest request,
final javax.servlet.http.HttpServletResponse response)
        throws java.io.IOException, javax.servlet.ServletException {
...
double temp = 0;
class TempClass {
}
```

21.8.8.1 Synchronization

Note that variables declared in the declaration section become instance variables. Instance variables become shared automatically among all request handling threads. You must handle synchronization issue to access these variables. Consider the following piece of code:

```
<%!int n = 1;%>
<%
for (int i = 0; i < 5; i++) {
   out.println("Next integer: " + n++ + "<br>");
   Thread.sleep(500);
}
%>
```

The code is intended to print five consecutive integers. Each time this JSP page is invoked, it increments the instance variable `n` five times and displays the value. The code segment works fine if only one request is dispatched to this JSP page at a time. However, if two or more requests are sent to this JSP page, the result is not displayed correctly. To demonstrate this and to allow collision, a delay is given between two consecutive `out.println()`. A sample output is shown in Figure 21.7: , if two requests are sent simultaneously.

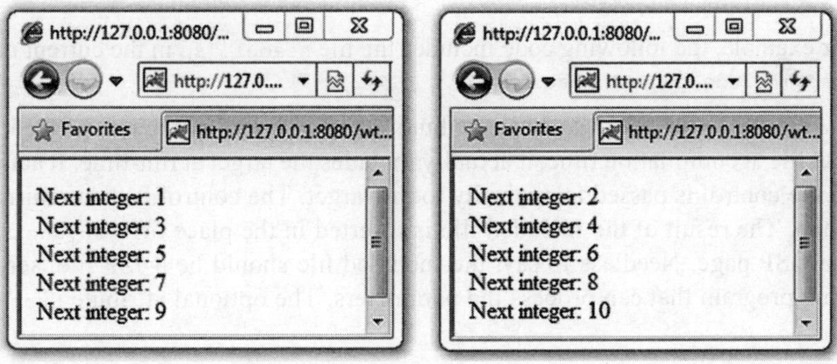

Figure 21.7: Accessing JSP page without synchronization

One of the solutions of this problem is to make the `for` loop atomic so that only one request can access it at a time.

```
<%!
   int n = 1;
   Object o = new Object();
%>
<%
synchronized(o) {
   for (int i = 0; i < 5; i++) {
      out.println("Next integer: " + n++ + "<br>");
      Thread.sleep(500);
   }
}
%>
```

Another way to solve this problem is to inform the JSP container that this page is not thread-safe, so that the container dispatches requests one by one.

```
<%@ page isThreadSafe="false" %>
<%!int n = 1; %>
<%
for (int i = 0; i < 5; i++) {
   out.println("Next integer: " + n++ + "<br>");
   Thread.sleep(500);
}
%>
```

In either case, the result will be correct.

21.8.9 Standard Actions

The JSP engine provides many built-in sophisticated functions to the programmers for easy development of the web applications. These functions include instantiating objects in a JSP page, communicating with other JSP pages and servlets, etc. JSP *actions* are nothing but XML tags that can be used in a JSP page to use these functions.

Note that the same thing can be achieved by writing Java code within scriptlets. However, JSP action tags are convenient ways to use those functions. They also promote component framework as well as application maintainability. The following section describes the commonly used JSP action tags.

include

This action tag provides an alternative way to include a file in a JSP page. The general syntax of the `include` action tag is

```
<jsp:include page="relativeURL | <%=expression%>" flush="true" />
```

For example, the following code includes the file `header.jsp` in the current page:

```
<jsp:include page="header.jsp" />
```

It is similar to the `include` directive but instead of inserting the text of the included file in the original file at compilation time, it actually includes the target at run-time. It acts like a subroutine where the control is passed temporarily to the target. The control is then returned to the original JSP page. The result of the included file is inserted in the place of `<jsp:include>` action in the original JSP page. Needless to say, the included file should be a JSP file, servlet, or any other dynamic program that can process the parameters. The optional attribute `flush` can only take the value `true`.

Let us illustrate with an example. Suppose the content of `date.jsp` is as follows:

```
Date and time: <%= new java.util.Date() %>
```

Now, consider the file `include.jsp`, which has included the `date.jsp` file using the `<jsp:include>` action tag as follows:

```
Before<br>
<jsp:include page="date.jsp" />
<br>After
```

This generates the following result:

```
Before
Date and time: Wed Dec 02 19:56:54 IST 2009
After
```

In `jspService()` method, the following code is inserted:

```
public void _jspService(final javax.servlet.http.HttpServletRequest request,
final javax.servlet.http.HttpServletResponse response)
        throws java.io.IOException, javax.servlet.ServletException {
...
  out.write("Before<br>\r\n");
  org.apache.jasper.runtime.JspRuntimeLibrary.include(request, response,
"date.jsp", out, false);
  out.write("\r\n");
  out.write("<br>After");
...
```

The value of the `page` attribute may be a dynamically generated file name. The following example illustrates this:

```
<%
String fileName = "sortByName.jsp";
String criteria = request.getParameter("sortCriteria");
if(criteria != null) fileName = criteria + ".jsp";
%>
<jsp:include page="<%=fileName%>" />
```

So, if the `include.jsp` page is invoked using the URL `http://127.0.0.1:8080/net/include.jsp?sortCriteria=sortByRoll`, the include action effectively becomes:

```
<jsp:include page="sortByRoll.jsp" />
```

Note that the file `sortByRoll.jsp` must exist. Otherwise, an exception will be thrown. If the `include.jsp` page is invoked using the URL `http://127.0.0.1:8080/net/include.jsp`, the include action effectively becomes

```
<jsp:include page="sortByName.jsp" />
```

param

The JSP `<jsp:param>` action allows us to append additional parameters to the current request. The general syntax is as follows:

```
<jsp:param name="parameterName" value="parameterValue | <%=expression%>" />
```

The `name` and `value` attributes of the `<jsp:param>` tag specify the case sensitive name and value of the parameter, respectively.

It is typically used with the `<jsp:include>` and `<jsp:forward>` action tags. For example, the following code passes the control to the JSP page `process.jsp` temporarily, with two additional parameters, `user` and `sessionId`.

```
<jsp:include page="process.jsp">
   <jsp:param name="user" value="monali" />
   <jsp:param name="sessionId" value="12D43F3Q436N43" />
</jsp:include>
```

The value of the `value` attribute may be a dynamic value, but the value of the `name` attribute must be static. The following example illustrates this:

```
<% String user = request.getParameter("user"); %>
<jsp:include page="process.jsp">
   <jsp:param name="user" value="<%=user%>" />
   <jsp:param name="sessionId" value="<%=System.currentTimeMillis()%>" />
</jsp:include>
```

forward

This action tag hands over the current request to the specified page internally at the server side. If the current page has already generated any output, it is suppressed. The output will only be caused by the page that has handled the request last in the forward chain. The control is never returned to the original page. The general syntax of the JSP forward action tag is

```
<jsp:forward page="relativeURL | <%=expression%>" />
```

Consider the `forward.jsp` file, which forwards the current request to the `date.jsp` file using the `<jsp:forward>` action as follows:

```
Before<br>
<jsp:forward page="date.jsp" />
<br>After
```

This transfers the control to the `date.jsp` page. The result the file `forward.jsp` has generated so far (`Before<br>` in our case) is cleared. The output is due to the page `date.jsp` only, as follows.

```
Date and time: Sun Sep 22 09:31:15 PDT 2013
```

Like the `<jsp:include>` action tag, the value of the `page` attribute of `<jsp:forward>` may be a dynamic file name. The following example illustrates this:

```
<% String mailbox = request.getParameter("mailbox") + ".jsp";%>
<jsp:forward page="<%=fileName%>" />
```

Additional parameters may be specified using the `<jsp:param>` action as follows:

```
<%
   String mailbox = request.getParameter("mailbox") + ".jsp";
   String user = request.getParameter("user");
%>
<jsp:forward page="<%=fileName%>" >
   <jsp:param name="user" value="<%=user%>" />
<jsp:forward>
```

plugin

The `<jsp:plugin>` action is used to generate an HTML file that can download the Java plug-in on demand and execute applets or JavaBeans. It is an alternative way to deploy applets through Java plug-in. Since JSP pages are dynamic in nature, the developers of web applications can make use of Java plug-in to generate browser-specific tags to insert applets on the fly in a much easier and flexible way.

The `<jsp:plugin>` action generates the `embed` or `object` tag for the applet to be executed, depending upon the browser used. When the JSP is translated, the `<jsp:plugin>` action element is substituted by either an `<embed>` or an `<object>` HTML tag. The following code specifies an applet.

```
<jsp:plugin type="applet" code="Message" >
<jsp:params>
    <jsp:param name="message" value="Hello World!"/>
</jsp:params>
<jsp:fallback>
       <p> Unable to start Plug-in. </p>
</jsp:fallback>
</jsp:plugin>
```

The `type` attribute of the `<jsp:plugin>` tag specifies the type (`bean` or `applet`) of plug-in to be used and the `code` attribute specifies the name of the file (without extension) containing the byte code for this plug-in. In the above example, the `<jsp:plugin>` action inserts an applet whose code can be found in the class file `Message.class`.

The `<jsp:plugin>` action tag has a similar set of attributes as the `<applet>` tag. The `<jsp:params>` and `<jsp:param>` actions are used to pass parameters to the plug-in. The `<jsp:fallback>` tag specifies the message to be displayed if the Java plug-in fails to start due to some unavoidable reason.

Here is the source code for the `Message` applet (`Message.java`).

```
public class Message extends java.applet.Applet {
    String msg;
    public void init() {
        msg = getParameter("message");
    }
    public void paint(java.awt.Graphics g) {
        g.drawString(msg, 20, 20);
    }
}
```

This applet takes a single parameter `message` and displays its value at location (20, 20) on the browser's screen, relative to the applet window.

As mentioned earlier, the web server generates either an `<embed>` or an `<object>` tag, depending upon the browser that requested the JSP page. For example, the following code is generated if Tomcat 8.0 is used as the web server and Internet Explorer 8.0 makes the request.

```
<object classid="clsid:8AD9C840-044E-11D1-B3E9-00805F499D93"
codebase="http://java.sun.com/products/plugin/1.2.2/jinstall-1_2_2-
win.cab#Version=1,2,2,0">
<param name="java_code" value="Message">
<param name="type" value="application/x-java-applet">
<param name="message" value="Hello World!">
<comment>
<EMBED type="application/x-java-applet"
pluginspage="http://java.sun.com/products/plugin/"java_code="Message"
message="Hello World!"/>
<noembed>

        <p> Unable to start Plug-in. </p>

</noembed>
</comment>
</object>
```

Though JSP specification includes the `<jsp:plugin>` action tag, different vendors may implement it differently. For detailed information, read the documentation of the web server.

useBean

It is used to instantiate a JavaBean object for later use. We shall discuss this action in Section 23.9.1 in detail.

setProperty

It is used to set a specified property of a JavaBean object. A detailed description of this action may be found in Section 23.9.2.

getProperty

It is used to get a specified property from a JavaBean object. This action has been discussed in Section 23.9.3 in detail.

21.8.10 Tag Extensions

One significant feature added in the JSP 1.1 specification is *tag extension*. It allows us to define and use custom tags in a JSP page exactly like other HTML/XML tags, using Java code. The JSP engine interprets them and invokes their functionality. So, Java programmers can provide application functionality in terms of custom tags, while web designers can use them as building blocks without any knowledge of Java programming. This way, JSP tag extensions provide a higher-level application-specific approach to the authors of HTML pages.

Though a similar functionality can be achieved using JavaBean technology, it lacks many features such as nesting, iteration, and cooperative actions. JSP tag extension allows us to express complex functionalities in a simple and convenient way.

21.8.10.1 Tag Type

JSP specification defines the following tags, which we can create and use in a JSP file.

Simple Tags

Tags with no body or no attribute. Example:

```
<ukr:copyright>
```

Tags with Attributes

Tags that have attributes but no body. Example:

```
<ukr:hello name="Monali" />
```

Tags with Body

Tags that can contain other tags, scripting elements, and text between the start and end tags. Example:

```
<ukr:hello>
    <%= name%>
</ukr:hello>
```

Tags Defining Scripting Variables

Tags that can define scripting variables, which can be used in the scripts within the page. Example:

```
<ukr:animation id="logo" />
<% logo.start(); %>
```

Cooperating Tags

Tags that cooperate with each other by means of named shared objects. Example:

```
<ukr:tag1 id="obj1" />
<ukr:tag2 name="obj1" />
```

In this example, `tag1` creates a named object called `obj1`, which is later used by `tag2`.

21.8.10.2 Writing Tags

In this section, we shall discuss how to define and use simple tags. The design and use of a custom tag has the following basic steps:

- Tag Definition
- Provide Tag Handler
- Deploy the tag
- Use the tag in the JSP file

Tag Definition

Before writing the functionality of a tag, you need to consider the following points:

- Tag Name—The name (and prefix) that will be used for the tag we are going to write
- Attributes—Whether the tag has any attribute and whether it is mandatory
- Nesting—Whether the tag contains any other child tag. A tag directly enclosing another tag is called the *parent* of the tag it encloses
- Body Content—Whether the tag contains anything (such as text) other than child tags

Provide Tag Handler

The functionality of a tag is implemented using a Java class called *tag handler*. Every tag handler must be created by directly or indirectly implementing the `javax.servlet.jsp.tagext.Tag` interface, which provides the framework of the JSP tag extension. In this section, we shall develop a simple tag named `<ukr:hello>`, which has a single optional attribute, `name`. The `<ukr:hello>` tag prints "Hello <name>" or "Hello World!" depending upon whether the attribute `name` is specified or not.

Note that the tag `<ukr:hello>` does not do much. It helps us understand the basic steps that we must follow to write a custom tag. In practice, custom tags will do complex tasks, but the procedure for developing such tags is exactly the same as the `<ukr:hello>` tag. After creating the `<ukr:hello>` tag, it is used in either of the following ways:

```
<ukr:hello name="Monali" />
```

This prints "Hello Monali".

```
<ukr:hello />
```

This prints "Hello World!". Here is the complete source code for the hello tag handler (`HelloTag.java`).

```
package tag;
import javax.servlet.jsp.tagext.SimpleTagSupport;
import javax.servlet.jsp.JspException;
import javax.servlet.jsp.JspWriter;
import java.io.IOException;
public class HelloTag extends SimpleTagSupport {
   String name = "World!" ;
   public void doTag() throws JspException, IOException {
      JspWriter out = getJspContext().getOut();
      out.println("Hello " + name);
   }
   public void setName(String name) {
      this.name = name;
   }
}
```

Though each tag handler must implement the `javax.servlet.jsp.tagext.Tag` interface, it is convenient to use one of the default implementations, the `TagSupport` or `SimpleTagSuport` class. Our tag is one without any body and hence we have used the `SimpleTagSupport` class. Each tag handler must define some predefined methods [Table 21.3:] that are called by the JSP engine. For example, the JSP engine calls the `doStartTag()` and `doEndTag()` methods when the start tag and the end tag, respectively, are encountered. The class `SimpleTagSupport` implements most of the work of a tag handler. The implementation of our class is simple, as it extends the `SimpleTagSupport` class. We have only implemented the `doTag()` method, which is called when the JSP engine encounters the start tag.

Table 21.3: Tag Handler Methods

Tag Handler Type	Methods
Simple	doStartTag, doEndTag, release
Attributes	doStartTag, doEndTag, set/getAttribute1...N
Body, No Interaction	doStartTag, doEndTag, release
Body, Interaction	doStartTag, doEndTag, release, doInitBody, doAfterBody

The hello tag has one attribute, `name`, whose value the handler must access. The JSP engine sets the value of an attribute `xxx` using the method `setXxx()` of the handler. This `setXxx()` method is invoked after the start tag, but before the body of the tag. So, we have inserted one method `setName()`, which will be used by the JSP engine to pass the value of the attribute `name`. Inside the handler, we have stored this value in a variable `name`. If a tag has multiple attributes, the corresponding tag handler must have separate set functions, one for each of these attributes.

Finally, we write the string "Hello" appended with the value of the `name` attribute to the servlet output stream. A reference to this output stream is obtained using the `getOut()` method on `javax.servlet.jsp.JspContext`, which is returned by the `getJspContext()` method.

Deploy the Tag

Save this code in file `HelloTag.java` and put it in the application's `/WEB-INF/classes/tag` directory. To compile this file, we need the necessary tag classes that are provided as the jar file `jsp-api.jar`. This jar file can be found in the `lib` directory of Tomcat's installation directory. Make sure that this jar file is in your classpath during compilation. You can use the following command in the `/WEB-INF/classes/tag` directory to compile the `HelloTag.java` file.

```
javac -classpath ../../../../../lib/jsp-api.jar HelloTag.java
```

This will generate the `HelloTag.class` file in the `/WEB-INF/classes/tag` directory. If everything goes fine, restart the web server. The tag class is now ready to use.

Now, we have to map the tag `hello` with this tag handler class, `HelloTag`. This is done in an XML file called **T**ag **L**ibrary **D**escriptor (TLD). A TLD contains information about a tag library as well as each tag contained in the library. The JSP engine uses TLDs to validate tags used in the JSP pages. The Tag Library Descriptor is an XML document conforming to a DTD specified by Sun Microsystems.

We shall name our tag library file as `tags.tld` and put it in the application's `/taglib` directory. For example, if the application's root directory is `net`, put the `tags.tld` file in the `/net/taglib` directory. Make the following entry in the `tags.tld` file.

```
<?xml version="1.0"?>
<taglib>
   <tlib-version>1.0</tlib-version>
   <jsp-version>1.2</jsp-version>
   <short-name>Simple tag library</short-name>
   <tag>
      <description>Prints Hello 'name'</description>
      <name>hello</name>
      <tag-class>tag.HelloTag</tag-class>
      <body-content>empty</body-content>
      <attribute>
         <name>name</name>
         <required>false</required>
         <rtexprvalue>true</rtexprvalue>
      </attribute>
   </tag>
</taglib>
```

Each <tag> element in the TLD file describes a tag. The <name> element specifies the name of the tag that will be used in the JSP file. The <tag-class> element associates the handler class with this tag name. In this case, the `tag.HelloTag` class is the handler of the tag `hello`. Each <attribute> element specifies the attribute that can be used for this tag. Our tag can have only one attribute, `name`. The <required> element specifies whether the attribute is mandatory (`true`) or optional (`false`). A tag without a body must specify that its `body-content` is empty.

Use the Tag in the JSP File

The tag `hello` is now ready to use. Use the following entry in the JSP page `tag.jsp` and put it in the applications root directory, i.e., `/net` in our case.

```
<%@ taglib prefix="ukr" uri="/taglib/tags.tld" %>
<ukr:hello name="Monali"/>
```

The `taglib` directive includes a tag library whose tags will be used by the JSP page. It must appear before using any custom tags it refers to. The `uri` attribute specifies a URI that uniquely identifies the TLD. The `prefix` attribute specifies the prefix to be used for every tag defined in this TLD. The prefix distinguishes tags in one library from those in others, if they contain tags with the same name. Now, write the following URL in the address bar of your web browser and press enter.

```
http://127.0.0.1:8080/net/tag.jsp
```

It displays

```
Hello Monali
```

For the following code

```
<%@ taglib prefix="ukr" uri="/taglib/tags.tld" %>
<ukr:hello />
```

The code

```
Hello World!
```

```
<%@ taglib prefix="ukr" uri="/taglib/tags.tld" %>
<%!String name="Kutu"; %>
<ukr:hello name="<%=name%>"/>
```

displays

```
Hello Kutu
```

21.8.11 Iterating a Tag Body

Sometimes, it is necessary to iterate a specific code several times. For example, suppose we want to generate a table containing integers and their factorial value. We can write scripts to do this, as follows:

```
<%
for(int i = 2; i <= 6; i++) {
%>
<%=i%>!=<ukr:fact no="<%=i%>" /><br>
<%
}
%>
```

We have assumed that there exists a tag handler for <ukr:fact> as follows:

```
package tag;
import javax.servlet.jsp.tagext.SimpleTagSupport;
import javax.servlet.jsp.JspException;
import java.io.IOException;
import javax.servlet.jsp.JspWriter;
```

```
public class FactTag extends SimpleTagSupport {
   int no;
   public void doTag() throws JspException, IOException  {
      int prod = 1;
      for(int j = 1;j <= no; j++)
         prod *= j;
      JspWriter out = getJspContext().getOut();
      out.println(prod);
   }
   public void setNo(int no) {
      this.no = no;
   }
}
```

It would be better, if the same table uses the following code:

```
<ukr:FactTable start="2" end="6">
   ${count}! = ${fact}<br>
</ukr:FactTable>
```

We can reduce the amount of code in the scripting element by moving the flow of control to the tag handlers. The basic idea is to write a tag called iteration tags that iterates its body.

The iteration tag retrieves two parameters start and end. It calculates the factorial of each number between these two numbers (both inclusive) and assigns them to a scripting variable. The body of the tag retrieves the numbers and their factorials from scripting variables. Here is the handler for the iteration tag.

```
package tag;
import javax.servlet.jsp.tagext.SimpleTagSupport;
import javax.servlet.jsp.JspException;
import java.io.IOException;
public class FactorialTag extends SimpleTagSupport {
   int start, end;
   public void doTag() throws JspException, IOException  {
      for(int i = start; i <= end; i++) {
         int prod = 1;
         for(int j = 1; j <= i; j++)
            prod *= j;
         getJspContext().setAttribute("count", String.valueOf(i) );
         getJspContext().setAttribute("fact", String.valueOf(prod) );
         getJspBody().invoke(null);
      }
   }
   public void setStart(int start) {
      this.start = start;
   }
   public void setEnd(int end) {
      this.end = end;
   }
}
```

This handler, in each iteration, stores the value of the integer and its factorial in the `count` and `fact` variable, respectively, using the following code.

```
getJspContext().setAttribute("count", String.valueOf(i) );
getJspContext().setAttribute("fact", String.valueOf(prod) );
```

The body of the tag is iterated as follows:

```
getJspBody().invoke(null);
```

Now, make the following entry in the `tags.tld` file.

```
<?xml version="1.0"?>
<taglib>
   <tlib-version>1.0</tlib-version>
   <jsp-version>1.2</jsp-version>
   <short-name>Simple tag library</short-name>
   <tag>
      <description>Calculates factorial from 'start' to 'end'</description>
      <name>FactTable</name>
      <tag-class>tag.FactorialTag</tag-class>
            <body-content>scriptless</body-content>
      <attribute>
         <name>start</name>
         <required>true</required>
         <rtexprvalue>true</rtexprvalue>
      </attribute>
      <attribute>
         <name>end</name>
         <required>true</required>
         <rtexprvalue>true</rtexprvalue>
      </attribute>
   </tag>
</taglib>
```

Obtaining the factorial tables is now very simple. Consider the following code.

```
<%@ taglib prefix="ukr" uri="/taglib/tags.tld" %>
Factorial table<br>
<ukr:FactTable start="2" end="6">
   ${count}! = ${fact}<br>
</ukr:FactTable>
```

In the body of the tag, the values of the count and fact variables are retrieved using expression language. Note that the JSP page does not contain a single piece of script. It is displayed as follows:

```
Factorial table
2! = 2
3! = 6
4! = 24
5! = 120
6! = 720
```

21.8.12 Sharing Data Between JSP Pages

All JSP pages participate in an HTTP session unless the `session` attribute of the `page` directive is set to `false`. An HTTP session is represented by the implicit object `session`. This `session` object has session scope and is thus shared among all the pages within the session.

This session object can be used as a shared repository of information such as beans and objects among JSP pages of the same session. For example, `login.jsp` page may store the user name in the session, while subsequent pages such as `home.jsp` can use it. Consider the code segment in `login.jsp`:

```
login.jsp:

String user = request.getParameter("user");
session.setAttribute("user", user);
```

Now, see the code segment in `home.jsp`.

```
String user = (String)session.getAttribute("user");
```

21.9 BEANS

JavaBeans are reusable Java components that allow us to separate business logic from presentation logic. Technically, a JavaBean class is a Java class that meets the following requirements:

- It has a public, no argument constructor.
- It implements the `java.io.Serializable` or `java.io.Externalizable` interface.
- Its properties are accessible using methods that are written following a standard naming convention.

With this simple definition, properly designed beans can be used virtually in all Java environments such as JSP, servlet, applet, or even in Java applications. Note that most of the existing classes are either already bean classes or they can be converted to bean classes very easily.

The methods of a bean must follow a naming convention. If the name of a bean property is `xxx`, the associate reader and writer method must have the name `getXxx()` and `setXxx()`, respectively. The following is a sample class declaration for JavaBean `Factorial`:

```
package bean;
public class Factorial implements java.io.Serializable {
    int n;
    public int getValue() {
        int prod = 1;
        for(int i = 2; i <= n; i++)
            prod *= i;
        return prod;
    }
    public void setValue(int v) {
        n = v;
    }
}
```

Since no constructor is defined explicitly in this class, a zero argument constructor is inserted in the `Factorial` class. The `Factorial` bean class has one property, `value`. So, the name of the reader method is `getValue()`. Similarly, the name of the writer method is `setValue()`. The name of the member variable need not be `value`; it is the property that we want to manipulate on a `Factorial` bean.

Save this code in the file `Factorial.java` and store it in the application's `/WEB-INF/classes/bean` directory. Compile the class exactly like other Java classes. Use the following command in the `/WEB-INF/classes/bean` directory.

```
javac Factorial.java
```

This generates a class file, `Factorial.class`. If everything goes fine, restart the tomcat web server. Tomcat loads all the class files under `/classes` directory and adds its subdirectories to the CLASSPATH of the Java Runtime Environment (JRE). Those class files can now be used exactly like other Java classes.

There are three action elements that are used to work with beans.

21.9.1 useBean

A JSP action element `<jsp:useBean>` instantiates a JavaBean object into the JSP page. The syntax is

```
<jsp:useBean id="object_name" class="class_name" scope="page | request |
session |application"/>
```

Here, the `id` attribute refers to the name of the object to be created and the attribute `class` specifies the name of the JavaBean class from which the object will be instantiated. The attribute `scope` specifies the area of visibility of the loaded bean. The effect of the `<jsp:useBean>` element is equivalent to instantiating an object as follows:

```
<% class_name object_name = new class_name(); %>
```

For example, to instantiate a Factorial bean in a JSP page, the following action is used:

```
<jsp:useBean id="fact" scope="page" class="bean.Factorial" />
```

This is equivalent to the following scriptlet:

```
<% bean.Factorial fact = new bean.Factorial(); %>
```

Once a bean object is loaded into a JSP page, we can use two other action elements to manipulate it.

21.9.2 setProperty

The `<jsp:setProperty>` action tag assigns a new value to the specified property of the specified bean object. It takes the following form:

```
<jsp:setProperty name="obj_name" property="prop_name" value="prop_value"/>
```

The object name, property name, and its value are specified by the `name`, `property`, and `value` attributes, respectively. This is equivalent to calling the `setProp_name()` method on the specified object `obj_name` as follows:

```
<% obj_name.setProp_name(prop_value); %>
```

To set a property of our bean object `fact`, we use the following:

```
<jsp:setProperty name="fact" property="value" value="5" />
```

The equivalent scriptlet is as follows:

```
<% fact.setValue(5); %>
```

21.9.3 getProperty

The `<jsp:getProperty>` action element retrieves the value of the specified property of the specified bean object. The value is converted to a string. It takes the following form:

```
<jsp:getProperty name="obj_name" property="prop_name"/>
```

The object name and its property name are specified by the `name` and `property` attributes, respectively. This is equivalent to calling the `getProp_name()` method on the specified object `obj_name` as follows:

```
<%= obj_name.getProp_name() %>
```

To get the value of the property `value` of our `fact` bean object, we use the following:

```
<jsp:getProperty name="fact" property="value" />
```

The equivalent scriptlet is as follows:

```
<%= fact.getValue() %>
```

21.9.4 Complete Example

The following is a complete JSP page:

```
<table border="1">
    <caption>Factorial table</caption>
    <tr><th width="50">n</th><th width="100">n!</th></tr>
    <jsp:useBean id="fact" scope="page" class="bean.Factorial" />
    <%
    for(int i = 2; i < 6; i++) {
    %>
    <jsp:setProperty name="fact" property="value" value="<%=i%>" />
    <tr><td><%=i%></td><td><jsp:getProperty name="fact" property="value" />
    </td></tr>
    <%
    }
    %>
</table>
```

It generates the output shown in Figure 21.8:

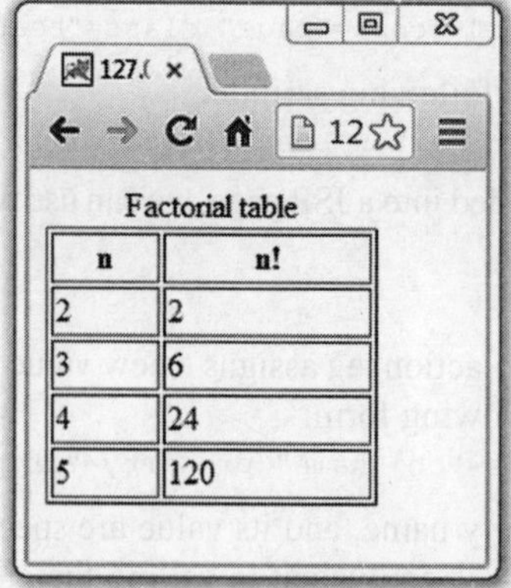

Figure 21.8: Using Beans in JSP

21.9.5 Other Usage

Once a bean object is loaded into the page, it can be used exactly like other objects in scripting elements in the same JSP page. Consider the following code:

```
<jsp:useBean id="fact" scope="page" class="bean.Factorial" />
```

This is equivalent to the following instantiation:

```
<% bean.Factorial fact = new bean.Factorial(); %>
```

Now, the bean object can be accessed using its name, as follows:

```
<%fact.setValue(6);%>
<%=fact.getValue()%>
```

This displays the following output:

```
720
```

21.10 SESSION TRACKING

Since HTTP is a stateless protocol, the web server cannot remember previous requests. Consequently, the web server cannot relate the current request with the previous one. This creates a problem for some applications that require a sequence of related request–response cycles. Examples include online examination systems, email checking systems, and banking applications. How does the server know how many questions you have answered so far or when you started the examination?

We shall use a simple application to demonstrate session tracking using different methods. In this application, the server initially dynamically generates an HTML file to display the integer 0, with two buttons captioned “prev” and “next”. If the user clicks on the *next* button, the server sends the integer next to the one displayed. Similarly, when *prev* button is clicked, the server sends the integer previous to the one displayed.

Note that each time the server receives a request, it has to remember the number it sent in the previous step. Let us now discuss the different methods used for session tracking.

21.10.1 Hidden fields

An HTML hidden field is created using the `<input>` tag, with the `type` attribute `hidden`. For example, the following creates a hidden field.

```
<input type="hidden" name="user" value="monali" >
```

The interesting part about hidden fields is that web browsers do not display them, but send the name–value pair of each hidden field exactly like other input elements when the enclosing form is submitted. So, hidden fields may be used to send information back and forth between server and client to track sessions, without affecting the display. Hidden fields are ideal for applications that do not require a great deal of information.

Let us now implement the application mentioned, using hidden fields.

```
<%@page import="java.util.*"%>
<html>
   <head><title>Hidden field demo</title></head>
   <body>
      <%
         int current = 0;
         String last = request.getParameter("int");
         String button = request.getParameter("button");
         if(button != null) {
            if(button.equals("next"))
               current = Integer.parseInt(last) + 1;
            else
               current = Integer.parseInt(last) - 1;
         }
         out.println(current);
      %>
      <br>
      <form name="myForm" method="post">
         <input type="hidden" name="int" value="<%=current%>">
         <input type="submit" name="button" value="prev">
         <input type="submit" name="button" value="next">
      </form>
   </body>
</html>
```

In this method, the JSP page uses a single hidden field in the generated HTML file named “int”. The value of this hidden field is the integer being sent currently. The hidden field, together with the two submit buttons captioned “prev” and “next”, are put in a form. So, the web browser receives an HTML file like this:

```
<html>
   <head><title>Hidden field demo</title></head>
    <body>

        0

        <br>
        <form name="myForm" method="post">
           <input type="hidden" name="int" value="0">
           <input type="submit" name="button" value="prev">
           <input type="submit" name="button" value="next">
        </form>
    </body>
</html>
```

The HTTP POST method is used in the form and no `action` attribute is specified. When the user clicks any of the two submit buttons, the value of this hidden field (which is the integer currently displayed) is sent to the same JSP page behind the scene. The JSP page extracts this value and understands that this value was sent in response to the previous request. This way, the hidden field helps the JSP page to remember information sent earlier. It also determines the button whose click event generates this request. The JSP page can then easily calculate the value to be sent next, depending on the button clicked.

The advantage of this method is that it does not require any special support from the client's side. Hidden fields are supported by all browsers and the underlying information propagation is absolutely transparent to the user.

Note that users can view the source code of the HTML page and consequently see the value of the hidden field. So, the JSP page should not pass sensitive information such as passwords in the hidden field.

21.10.2 URL Rewriting

This is another simple but elegant method to track sessions and is widely used. It does not require any special support from the web browser. Remember that HTTP allows us to pass information using HTTP URL. This method makes use of that concept. The session information is appended to the URL. Here is the solution using URL rewriting.

```
<%@page import="java.util.*"%>
<html>
   <head><title>URL rewriting demo</title></head>
   <body>
      <%
         int last = 0;
         String param = request.getParameter("int");
         if(param != null) last = Integer.parseInt(param);
            out.println(last);
      %>
      <br>
      <a href="intUrl.jsp?int=<%=last-1%>">prev</a>
      <a href="intUrl.jsp?int=<%=last+1%>">next</a>
   </body>
</html>
```

In this case, the JSP page generates and sets the URL to be called for the hyperlinks "prev" and "next". For example, the web gets this HTML page for the first time:

```
<html>
   <head><title>URL rewriting demo</title></head>
   <body>

0

<br>
<a href="intUrl.jsp?int=-1">prev</a>
<a href="intUrl.jsp?int=1">next</a>
   </body>
</html>
```

When a user clicks on the "prev" hyperlink, the integer that should be sent by the JSP page for this request is appended to the URL. The JSP page simply extracts this information and sends it back with the new URLs for those two hyperlinks. A similar sequence of events happen when a user clicks on the "next" button.

21.10.3 Cookies

This method requires support from the web browsers. In this method, session information is represented by a named token called *cookie*. The JSP page sends this cookie to the web browser. The browser must be configured properly to accept it. Upon receiving a cookie, the web browser installs it. This cookie is then sent back to the server with the subsequent requests. The JSP page can then extract session information from this cookie. This way, the server can identify a session.

By default, most browsers support cookies. However, due to security reasons, very often cookie support is disabled and in that case session management will not work correctly. The following is the JSP page for the application we discussed earlier.

```
<html>
    <head><title>Cookie demo</title></head>
    <body>
        <%
            int current = 0;
            Cookie cookie = null;
            Cookie[]  cookies = request.getCookies();
            if(cookies != null)
                for(int i = 0; i < cookies.length; i++)
                    if(cookies[i].getName().equals("last"))
                        cookie = cookies[i];
            if(cookie != null) {
                String button = request.getParameter("button");
                if(button != null) {
                    if(button.equals("next"))
                        current = Integer.parseInt(cookie.getValue()) + 1;
                    else
                        current = Integer.parseInt(cookie.getValue()) - 1;
                }
            }
            response.addCookie(new Cookie("last", String.valueOf(current)));
            out.println(current);
        %>
        <br>
        <form name="myForm" method="post">
            <input type="submit" name="button" value="prev">
            <input type="submit" name="button" value="next">
        </form>
    </body>
</html>
```

The JSP page first looks for a cookie named "last". If it finds the cookie, the value of the cookie is obtained using the `getValue()` method. Depending on the button clicked, the integer to be sent next is calculated and stored in the variable `current`. This integer, together with a new cookie with the name "last" having the current value set is sent to the web browser. However, if the JSP page does not find any cookie with the name "last", which happens during the first time, it sends a new cookie having the value 0, which is the initial value of the variable `current`.

21.10.4 Session API

JSP technology (and its underlying servlet technology) provides a higher level approach for session tracking. The basic building block of this session API is the `javax.servlet.http.HttpSession` interface. The `HttpSession` objects are automatically associated with the client by the cookie mechanism. An `HttpSession` object is one that persists during a session, until it times out or is shutdown by the JSP page participating in this session.

In a JSP page, an HTTP session is created by default if it is not suppressed by setting the `session` attribute of the `page` directive to `false` as follows.

```
<%@ page session="false" %>
```

This session can be accessed by the implicit object `session`. A JSP page may also create an `HttpSession` object explicitly, using the following method in `HttpServletRequest`.

```
HttpSession getSession(boolean create);
HttpSession getSession();
```

The first version takes a boolean parameter that indicates whether a new session has to be created if one does not exist. If the parameter is `true`, a new session is created if it does not exist. Otherwise, the existing session object is returned. If the parameter is false, it returns the existing session object if it exists, and null otherwise. The second version simply calls the first version with the parameter `true`.

In the `HttpSession` object, we can store and retrieve key–value pair using `setAttribute()`, `getAttribute()`, and `getAttributes()` methods.

```
Object getAttribute(String key);
Enumeration getAttributeNames();
void setAttribute(String key, Object value);
```

The return type of the `getAttribute()` method is `Object`. So you must typecast it to the required type of data that was stored with a key in the session object. If the key specified in the `setAttribute()` method does not already exist in the session, the specified value is stored with this key. Otherwise, the old value is overwritten with the specified value.

The JSP engine uses the cookie mechanism to keep track of sessions. A session object is associated with usually a long alphanumeric ID. This session ID is sent to the client as a cookie with the name `JSESSIONID`, when the client makes a request for the first time using the HTTP response header `Set-Cookie`, as follows:

```
Set-Cookie: JSESSIONID=g52d15acu325dlw532h234
```

For subsequent requests, the client sends this cookie back to the server using the HTTP request header `Cookie` as follows:

```
Cookie: JSESSIONID=g52d15acu325dlw532h234
```

The server can then identify that this request has come from the same client. However, if the client does not accept cookies, this mechanism fails. In that case, programmers may use the URL rewriting mechanism, where each URL must have the session ID appended. The JSP engine, on behalf of programmers, provides a straightforward mechanism to implement URL rewriting. The `HttpServletResponse` object provides methods to append this session ID automatically. These methods identify whether the client is configured to accept cookies. They append the session ID only if the client does not accept cookies.

```
java.lang.String encodeURL(java.lang.String);
java.lang.String encodeRedirectURL(java.lang.String);
```

The `encodeRedirectURL()` method is used for the `sendRedirect()` and `encodeURL()` method is used for the rest to create such URLs.

Here is the solution of our application using `HttpSession` API:

```
<%@page import="java.util.*"%>
<html>
   <head><title>Hidden field demo</title></head>
   <body>
      <%
         int current = 0;
         String last = (String)session.getAttribute("last");
         if(last != null) {
            String button = request.getParameter("button");
               if(button != null) {
                  if(button.equals("next"))
                     current = Integer.parseInt(last) + 1;
                  else
                     current = Integer.parseInt(last) - 1;
               }
         }
         session.setAttribute("last", String.valueOf(current));
         out.println(current);
      %>
```

```
        <br>
        <form name="myForm" method="post">
            <input type="submit" name="button" value="prev">
            <input type="submit" name="button" value="next">
        </form>
    </body>
</html>
```

21.11 USERS PASSING CONTROL AND DATA BETWEEN PAGES

Sometimes, we need to hand over the control to another page, with the necessary data passed to it. In this section, we shall discuss how to pass control across pages with data passed to them.

21.11.1 Passing Control

Sometimes, a JSP page wants to pass the control to another server-side program for further processing. For example, in an e-mail application, the `login.jsp` page on user verification may want to forward the request to the `home.jsp` page. This is done using the `<jsp:forward>` action in the `login.jsp` page as follows:

```
String user = request.getParameter("user");
String password = request.getParameter("password");
//verify the user here
<jsp:forward page="home.jsp" />
```

Once the JSP engine encounters the `<jsp:forward>` action, it stops the processing of the current page and starts the processing of the page (called target page) specified by the `page` attribute. The rest of the original page is never processed further.

The `HttpServletRequest` and `HttpServletResponse` objects are passed to the target page. So, the target page can access all information passed to the original page. You can pass additional parameters to the target page using the `<jsp:param>` action as follows.

```
String user = request.getParameter("user");
String password = request.getParameter("password");
//verify the user here
double startTime = System.currentTimeMillis();
<jsp:forward page="home.jsp">
   <jsp:param name="startTime" value="<%=startTime%>" />
</jsp:forward>
```

The target page can access these parameters in the same way as the original parameters, using the `getParameter()` and/or `getParameterNames()` methods.

21.11.2 Passing Data

The scope of an object indicates from where the object is visible. JSP specification defines four types of scopes: `page`, `request`, `session`, and `application`. The objects having `page` scope are only available within the page. So, objects that are created with `page` scope in a page are not available in another page where the control is transferred using the `<jsp:forward>` action. If you make an object visible across multiple pages across the same request, create the object with `request` scope. The following example illustrates this.

```
<!--original.jsp-->
<jsp:useBean id="fact" scope="request" class="bean.Factorial" />
<%fact.setValue(5);%>
<jsp:forward page="new.jsp" />
```

This page creates a bean object with the `request` scope and sets the value property with 5. It then passes the control to the `new.jsp` page, which looks like this.

```
<!--new.jsp-->
<jsp:useBean id="fact" scope="request" class="bean.Factorial" />
<%=fact.getValue()%>
```

Since the bean was saved as the `request` scope in the `original.jsp` page, the `<jsp:useBean>` action in the `new.jsp` page finds and uses it.

For the URL `http://127.0.0.1:8080/net/original.jsp`, the following is displayed:

```
120
```

Depending upon your requirement, you may create an object having any one of the four scopes.

21.12 SHARING SESSION AND APPLICATION DATA

The objects having `request` scope are available in all pages across a single request. However, sometimes objects should be shared among multiple requests.

Think about an online examination system. JSP pages requested from the same browser must share the same user name that was provided during the login procedure. This is required because different users have different sets of data such as expiry time, number of questions answered so far, number of correct answers, and so on. This type of information can be shared through `session` scope.

The objects having `session` scope are available to all pages requested by the same browser. The implicit object `session` is one such object. This session object can be used to store and retrieve other objects. So, objects may be shared across pages in the same session using this `session` object. The following is a code fragment used in `login.jsp`.

```
<!—login.jsp-->
<%
String user = request.getParameter("user");
String password = request.getParameter("password");
//verify the user here
double startTime = System.currentTimeMillis();
session.setAttribute(user, String.valueOf(startTime));

<jsp:forward page="exam.jsp" />
%>
```

It stores the time when the user starts its session in the session object and forwards the request to `exam.jsp`. The `exam.jsp` will be called many times by the user. The `exam.jsp` retrieves the start time for this user, checks whether the user has exhausted its time limit, and takes necessary actions.

```
String user1 = (String)session.getAttribute("user");

double startTime = Double.parseDouble((String)session.getAttribute("user"));
double currentTime = System.currentTimeMillis();
if(currentTime - startTime > 600000) { //duration is 10 minutes
   //the time is over, forward the request to the page logout.jsp
%>
<jsp:forward page="logout.jsp" />
<%
}
%>
```

Now, think about the same online examination system where different users are giving the examination using different browser windows, but using the same database. For efficiency purposes, information should be shared among pages even if the pages are requested by different users. This type of information can be shared through application scope.

The objects that have application scope are shared by all pages requested by any browser. One such implicit object is `application`. Consider the following code fragment in the `login.jsp` page:

```
Object obj = application.getAttribute("config");
if(obj == null) {
   ExamConfig conf = new ExamConfig();
   application.setAttribute("config", conf);
}
```

It looks for an object having the name "config" in the `application` object. If no such object exists, it creates an `ExamConfig` object and stores one such object in the `application` object. When the `ExamConfig` object is created, connection to the database is established. This database connection can now be shared by all other pages related to this application.

Here is the code fragment used in the `exam.jsp` page.

```
ExamConfig conf = (ExamConfig)application.getAttribute("config");
Statement stmt = conf.getConnection().createStatement();
//use stmt to fire SQL query
```

All requests that use the `exam.jsp` file can simply use the same object stored in the application object to get the `Statement` object and fire the SQL query using JDBC technology.

KEYWORDS

Actions—XML tags that can be used in a JSP page to use functions provided by the JSP engine

Bean—Reusable Java components, which allow us to separate business logic from presentation logic

Cookie—A name–value pair

Declarations—Used to declare one or more variables, methods, or inner classes that can be used later in the JSP page

Directives—Instructions used in the JSP page to inform the JSP engine how this page is interpreted and executed

Expression—A faster, easier, and clearer way to display values of variables/parameters/expressions in a JSP page

Implicit Objects—A web container allows us to directly access many useful objects defined in the `_jspService()` method of the JSP page's underlying servlet. These objects are called implicit objects.

JSP Engine—A specialized servlet that supervises and controls the execution of JSP pages

Plug-in—The `<jsp:plugin>` action is used to generate an HTML file that can download a Java plug-in on demand and execute applets or JavaBeans.

Scope—The scope of a JSP object is defined as the availability of that object for use from a particular place of the web application.

Scriptlets—Sections in a JSP page where we can insert an arbitrary piece of Java code

Session tracking—A procedure using which JSP pages can relate a sequence of requests

Tag extension—Allows us to define and use custom tags in a JSP page exactly like other HTML/XML tags, using Java code

Template text—The static HTML/XML components in a JSP page

Translation—The procedure for converting a JSP page to its servlet source code

Web container— JSP pages run under the web server called web container.

SUMMARY

JSP allows us to directly embed Java code in the HTML pages. To process JSP pages, a JSP engine is needed. It is interesting to note that what we know as the "JSP engine" is nothing but a specialized servlet that runs under the supervision of the servlet engine. Commonly used JSP engines include Apache's Tomcat, Java Web Server, IBM's WebSphere, etc.

JSP technology was developed on top of servlet technology. The JSP pages are finally converted to servlets automatically.

A JSP page basically consists of static HTML/XML components called template text as well as JSP constructs. JSP constructs consist of directives, declarations, expressions, scriptlets, and actions.

A JSP page may contain instructions to be used by the JSP container to indicate how this page is interpreted and executed. Those instructions are called directives.

Expressions are used to insert usually small pieces of data in a JSP page without using `out.print()` or `out.write()` statements.

You can insert an arbitrary piece of Java code using JSP scriptlets construct in a JSP page.

JSP declarations are used to declare one or more variables, methods, or inner classes that can be used later in the JSP page.

JSP actions are XML tags that can be used in a JSP page to use functions provided by the JSP engine.

In a JSP page, objects may be created using directives, actions, or scriptlets. Every object created in a JSP page has a scope. The scope of a JSP object is defined as the availability of that object for use from a particular place of the web application. There are four object scopes: page, request, session, and application.

A web container allows us to directly access many useful objects defined in the `_jspService()` method of the JSP page's underlying servlet. These objects are called implicit objects as they are instantiated automatically. The implicit objects contain information about request, response, session, configuration, etc.

Variables, methods, and classes can be declared in a JSP page. If they are declared in the declaration section, they become part of the class.

JSP tag extension allows us to define and use custom tags in a JSP page exactly like other HTML/XML tags, using Java code.

JavaBeans are reusable Java components called beans which allow us to separate business logic from presentation logic. There are three action elements that are used to work with beans. A JSP action element `<jsp:useBean>` instantiates a JavaBean object into the JSP page. The `<jsp:setProperty>` action tag assigns a new value to the specified property of the specified bean object. The `<jsp:getProperty>` action element retrieves the value of the specified property of the specified bean object.

There are many ways to track sessions in JSP. Hidden fields may be used to send information back and forth between server and client to track sessions, without affecting the display. This is another simple but elegant method to track sessions and is widely used. Cookies are also used to track sessions. JSP technology (and its underlying servlet technology) provides a higher level approach for session tracking.

WEB RESOURCES

http://www.oracle.com/technetwork/java/javaee/jsp/index.html
JavaServer Pages Technology

http://www.oracle.com/technetwork/java/syntaxref12-149806.pdf
Java Server Pages (JSP) v2.0 Syntax Reference

http://docs.oracle.com/javaee/5/tutorial/doc/bnalj.html
Custom Tags in JSP Pages

http://en.wikipedia.org/wiki/JavaServer_Pages
JavaServer Pages

http://www.visualbuilder.com/jsp/tutorial\
JSP Tutorial Home

http://download.oracle.com/otn-pub/jcp/7322-jsp-1.0-fr-spec-oth-JSpec/jsp1_0-spec.pdf?AuthParam=1379914991_d1f98c766f1707c0ca2dc883ea1246a2
JavaServer Pages Specification 1.0

http://tomcat.apache.org/tomcat-8.0-doc\
Apache Tomcat 8.0, Documentation Index

http://tomcat.apache.org/tomcat-8.0-doc/jasper-howto.html
Apache Tomcat 8.0, Jasper 2 JSP Engine How To

http://tomcat.apache.org/tomcat-8.0-doc/config/context.html
Apache Tomcat 8, The Context Container

EXERCISES

Objective-type Questions

1. What is the full form of JSP ?
   (a) Java Servlet Pages
   (b) Java Server Pages
   (c) Java Small Pages
   (d) Java Special Pages

2. Which of the following statements is true?
   (a) JSP and servlets are completely different technologies.
   (b) Servlets are built on JSP technology and all servlets are ultimately converted to JSP pages.

(c) Servlet is a client-side technology, whereas JSP is a server-side technology.
(d) JSPs are built on servlet technology and all JSPs are ultimately translated to servlets.

3. What is the advantage of using RequestDispatcher over sendRedirect() to forward a request to another resource?
   (a) The RequestDispatcher does not use the reflection API.
   (b) sendRedirect() is no longer available in the current servlet API.
   (c) The RequestDispatcher does not require a round trip to the client, and thus is more efficient and allows the server to maintain request state.
   (d) sendRedirect() is not a cross-web server mechanism.

4. In which one of the following cases is the scriptlet better suited?
   (a) Code that handles cookies
   (b) Code that deals with logic that relates to database access
   (c) Code that deals with session management
   (d) Code that deals with logic that is common across requests

5. Which of the following handles a request first in a page-centric approach?
   (a) A JSP page
   (b) A session manager
   (c) A servlet
   (d) A JavaBean

6. Which of the following can be included using the JSP include action?
   (a) Servlet (c) Plain text file
   (b) Another JSP (d) All of the above

7. Which of the following is used to read parameters from a JSP page?
   (a) <jsp:getParam/> action
   (b) <jsp:param> action
   (c) request.getParameter() method
   (d) <jsp:readParam/> action

8. Which of the following is not a method of JSP's servlet ?
   (a) _jspService() (c) jspService()
   (b) _jspDestroy() (d) _jspInit()

9. Which of the following JSP actions is used to include a file in another file?
   (a) <jsp:import> (c) <jsp:read>
   (b) <jsp:include> (d) <jsp:get>

10. What is a JSP page translated into?
    (a) CGI (c) Applet
    (b) Servlet (d) JavaBean

11. Which of the following is not true regarding cookies?
    (a) Cookie class has a two-argument constructor.
    (b) The response object is used to add a cookie.
    (c) The request object is used to get the cookie.
    (d) The request object is used for creating cookies.

12. Which of the following scopes does the implicit object exception have?
    (a) page (c) session
    (b) request (d) application

13. Which of the following tags is used to override the JSP file's initialization method?
    (a) <%= %> (c) <% %>
    (b) <%@ %> (d) <%! %>

14. Which of the following scopes is not valid with respect to JavaBean in JSP?
    (a) request (c) session
    (b) response (d) application

15. Which of the following statements is true regarding HttpServletResponse.sendRedirect()?
    (a) Server itself redirects the current request.
    (b) sendRedirect() executes on the client.
    (c) Server sends a redirection instruction to the client.
    (d) Server drops the current request.

16. Which of the following tags is used for scriptlets?
    (a) <%= %> (c) <% %>
    (b) <%@ %> (d) <%! %>

17. Which of the following attributes of the page directive is used to indicate that the current page is an error page?
    (a) errorPage (c) anErrorPage
    (b) isErrorPage (d) pageError

18. Which of the following tags is used for expressions?
    (a) <%= %> (c) <% %>
    (b) <%@ %> (d) <%! %>

19. Which of the following is not a JSP engine?
    (a) Tomcat
    (b) Java Web Server
    (c) WebLogic
    (d) Apache James

20. Which of the following is not a JSP implicit object?
    (a) request (c) in
    (b) response (d) out

Subjective-type Questions

1. Write some advantages of JSP over servlet.
2. What is the key difference between HttpServletResponse.sendRedirect() and <jsp:forward>?
3. What is the benefit of using JavaBeans to separate business logic from presentation markup within the JSP environment?
4. What is the function of a JSP engine?
5. Compare and contrast between JSP and servlet.
6. Briefly describe the structure of a JSP page.
7. Explain with examples the page directive.
8. What is the purpose of include directive in a JSP page?
9. What is the difference between a declaration and a scriptlet?
10. What do you mean by the scope of JSP objects?
11. Explain with examples the different types of scopes.
12. What do request and response implicit object represent?
13. Write the usage of session and application implicit objects.
14. What do JSP action tags do? Write the names of some JSP action tags.
15. Describe briefly how to create custom tags in JSP.
16. What are the different types of custom tags? Explain with examples.
17. Write the necessary properties that Java Bean components must have.
18. What are the different session tracking technologies available in JSP?
19. Describe how hidden fields can be used to track sessions. What are the problems of using hidden fields?
20. Write the method of passing data between two JSP pages.

CHAPTER – 22

JAVA DATABASE CONNECTIVITY (JDBC)

KEY OBJECTIVES

After completing this chapter readers will be able to—

- get an idea about different types of JDBC drivers
- learn how to use JDBC technology in Java Server Pages
- know how to load JDBC drivers
- retrieve database metadata
- call stored procedures
- understand scrollable and updatable result set

22.1 INTRODUCTION

Many Java applications need access to databases. **J**ava **D**ata**B**ase **C**onnectivity (JDBC) allows us to access databases through Java programs. It provides Java classes and interfaces to fire SQL and PL/SQL statements, process results (if any), and perform other operations common to databases. Since Java Server Pages can contain Java code embedded in them, it is also possible to access databases from Java Server Pages. The classes and interfaces for database connectivity are provided as a separate package, `java.sql`.

22.2 JDBC DRIVERS

A Java application can access almost all types of databases such as relational, object, and object-relational. The access to a specific database is accomplished using a set of Java interfaces, each of which is implemented by different vendors differently. A Java class that provides interfaces to a specific database is called JDBC driver. Each database has its own set of JDBC drivers. Users need not bother about the implementation of those Java classes. They can concentrate on developing database applications. Those drivers are provided (generally freely) by database vendors. This way,

JDBC hides the underlying database architecture. JDBC drivers provided by database vendors convert database access requests to database-specific APIs.

JDBC drivers are classified into four categories depending upon the way they work.

22.2.1 JDBC-ODBC Bridge (Type 1)

This is the *Type 1* driver. This type of driver cannot talk to the database directly. It needs an intermediate ODBC (**O**pen **D**ata**B**ase **C**onnectivity) driver, with which it forms a kind of bridge. The driver translates JDBC function calls to ODBC method calls. ODBC makes use of native libraries of the operating system and is hence platform-dependent. For this mechanism to function correctly, the ODBC driver must be available in the client machine and must also be configured correctly, which is generally a long and tedious process. For this reason, the Type 1 driver is used for experimental purposes or when no other JDBC driver is available. Sun provides a Type 1 JDBC driver with JDK 1.1 or later.

22.2.2 Native-API, Partly Java (Type 2)

This is very similar to the Type 1 driver. However, it does not forward the JDBC call to the ODBC driver. Instead, it translates JDBC calls to database-specific native API calls. This driver is not a pure Java driver, as it interfaces with non-Java APIs that communicate with the database. This approach is a little bit faster than the earlier one, as it interfaces directly with the database through the native APIs. However, it has limitations similar to the previous one. This means that the client must have vendor-specific native APIs installed and configured in it.

22.2.3 Middleware, Pure Java (Type 3)

In this case, the JDBC driver forwards the JDBC calls to some middleware server [Figure 22.1: (ii)] using a database-independent network protocol. The middleware server acts as a *gateway* for multiple (possibly different) database servers and can use different database-specific protocols to connect to different database servers. This intermediate server sends each client request to a specific database. The results are then sent back to the intermediate server, which in turn sends the result back to the client. This approach hides the details of connections to the database servers and makes it possible to change the database servers without affecting the client.

22.2.4 Pure Java Driver (Type 4)

These types of drivers communicate with the database directly by making socket connections. It has distinct advantages over other mechanisms, in terms of performance and development time. Since, it talks with the database server directly, no other subsidiary driver is needed. In this book, we shall use only the Type 4 driver.

22.3 JDBC ARCHITECTURE

The JDBC architecture is sometimes classified as: two-tier and three-tier. Type 2 and 4 drivers use two-tier and Type 1 and 3 use three-tier architecture. Figure 22.1: (i) and (ii) show the JDBC two-tier and three-tier architectures.

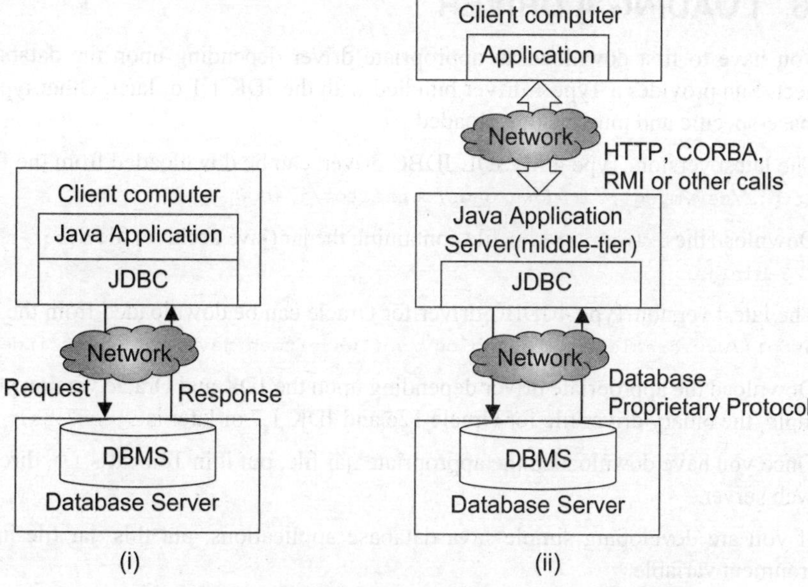

Figure 22.1: JDBC architecture (i) Two-tier (ii) Three-tier

22.4 JDBC CLASSES AND INTERFACES

Java provides an API for accessing and processing data stored in a data source (usually a relational database). A summary of JDBC classes and interfaces with a brief description is shown in Table 22.1:

Table 22.1: Java JDBC classes and interfaces

Class/Interface	Description
DriverManager	The basic service for managing a set of JDBC drivers
Connection	A connection (session) with a specific database
Statement	The object used for executing a static SQL statement and returning the results it produces
ResultSet	A table of data representing a database result set, which is usually generated by executing a statement that queries the database
PreparedStatement	An object that represents a precompiled SQL statement
CallableStatement	The interface used to execute SQL stored procedures
DatabaseMetaData	Comprehensive information about the database as a whole
ResultSetMetaData	An object that can be used to get information about the types and properties of the columns in a ResultSet object.

In this chapter, we shall demonstrate how to use JDBC with respect to JSP.

22.5 BASIC STEPS

The following basic steps are followed to work with JDBC:

- Loading a Driver
- Making a connection
- Executing an SQL statement

22.6 LOADING A DRIVER

You have to first download an appropriate driver depending upon the database you want to connect. Sun provides a Type 1 driver bundled with the JDK 1.1 or later. Other types of drivers are database-specific and must be downloaded.

The latest version, Type 4 MySQL JDBC driver, can be downloaded from the following site:

```
http://dev.mysql.com/downloads/connector/j/#downloads
```

Download the `.zip` or `.tar.gz` file containing the jar (**j**ava **ar**chive) file `mysql-connector-java-5.1.26-bin.jar`.

The latest version Type 4 JDBC driver for Oracle can be downloaded from the following site:

```
http://www.oracle.com/technology/software/tech/java/sqlj_jdbc/index.html
```

Download the appropriate driver depending upon the JDK and Oracle version you are using. For example, the binary driver file for Oracle 12c and JDK 1.7 or later is `ojdbc7.jar`.

Once you have downloaded the appropriate .jar file, put it in Tomcat's `lib` directory and restart the web server.

If you are developing simple Java database applications, put this .jar file in the `CLASSPATH` environment variable.

So far, we have downloaded and installed the JDBC driver. For it to start functioning, an instance of the driver has to be created and registered with the `DriverManager` class so that it can translate the JDBC call to the appropriate database call. The JDBC class `DriverManager` is an important class in the `java.sql` package. It interfaces between the Java application and the JDBC driver. This class manages the set of JDBC drivers installed on the system. It has many other useful methods, some of which will be discussed in Section 26.17.

One way to register a driver with the driver manager is to use the static with a driver class name as an argument. For example, the Type 1 driver provided by Sun can be instantiated and registered with the driver manager as follows:

```
Class.forName("sun.jdbc.odbc.JdbcOdbcDriver");
```

The method `forName()` creates an instance of the class whose name is specified as an argument using its default constructor. The instance created in this fashion must register itself with the `DriverManager` class. The .jar file for MySQL contains two driver class files with the name `Driver.class`, one in the `com.mysql.jdbc` package and the other in the `org.gjt.mm.mysql` package. So, you may use any one of the following:

```
Class.forName("com.mysql.jdbc.Driver");
Class.forName("org.gjt.mm.mysql.Driver");
```

One can perform this registration procedure by explicitly creating an instance and passing it to the static `registerDriver()` method of the `DriverManager` class. The method `registerDriver()` in turn registers the driver with the driver manager. Some JDBC vendors such as Oracle recommend the latter mechanism.

```
DriverManager.registerDriver(new oracle.jdbc.driver.OracleDriver());
```

A similar procedure can be followed for other drivers as well. The implementation of the MySQL driver file `com.mysql.jdbc.Driver` looks like this.

```
public class Driver extends NonRegisteringDriver implements java.sql.Driver {
   static {
      try {
```

```
            java.sql.DriverManager.registerDriver(new Driver());
        } catch (SQLException E) {
            throw new RuntimeException("Can't register driver!");
        }
    }
    public Driver() throws SQLException {}
}
```

Since the static block registers the driver with the driver manager automatically, only creating an instance is sufficient. So, one might use the following code as well:

```
new com.mysql.jdbc.Driver();
```

Now, the driver is ready to translate the JDBC call.

22.7 MAKING A CONNECTION

Once a driver is instantiated and registered with the driver manager, the connection to the database can be established using methods provided by the `DriverManager` class. For each connection created, `DriverManager` makes use of the appropriate driver registered to it. The following methods are available on the `DriverManager` class to establish a connection. All methods return a `Connection` object on successful creation of the connection.

```
public static Connection getConnection(String url, String login, String passwd)
public static Connection getConnection(String url)
public static Connection getConnection(String url, Properties)
```

The `Connection` object encapsulates the session/connection to a specific database. It is used to fire SQL statements as well as commit or roll back database transactions. It also allows us to collect useful information about the database dynamically and to write custom applications. Many connections can be established to a single database server or different database servers.

The primary argument that the `getConnection()` method takes is a database URL. This argument identifies a database uniquely. `DriverManager` uses this URL to find a suitable JDBC driver installed earlier, which recognizes the URL and uses this driver to connect to the corresponding database.

The URL always starts with `jdbc:`. The format of the rest of the JDBC URL varies widely for different databases. Some are mentioned in Table 22.2: The format of the MySQL JDBC URL is as follows:

```
jdbc:mysql://[host]:[port]/[database]
```

Here, `host` is the name (or IP address) of the machine running the database at the port number `port` and `database` is a name of a database. Suppose a MySQL database, `test`, is running in a machine, `uroy`, at port `3306`, the corresponding URL will be

```
jdbc:mysql://uroy:3306/test
```

A database connection can be established using this URL as follows:

```
Connection con = DriverManager.getConnection("jdbc:mysql://uroy:3306/test",
"root", "nbuser");
```

Similarly, the following code segment creates a database connection to the Oracle database `mirora` running in the machine `miroracle` at port `1521`.

```
Connection  con =
DriverManager.getConnection("jdbc:oracle:thin:@miroracle:1521:mirora", "scott",
"tiger");
```

Table 22.2 shows the JDBC URL formats.

Table 22.2: JDBC URL format

<table>
<tr><th colspan="3">MySQL</th></tr>
<tr><td>Jar file</td><td colspan="2">mysql-connector-java-nn-bin.jar</td></tr>
<tr><td>Download URL</td><td colspan="2">http://dev.mysql.com/downloads/connector/j/5.1.html</td></tr>
<tr><td>Driver</td><td colspan="2">com.mysql.jdbc.Driver</td></tr>
<tr><td>URL format</td><td colspan="2">jdbc:mysql://[host]:[port]/[database]</td></tr>
<tr><td>Sample URL</td><td colspan="2">jdbc:mysql://uroy:3306/test
jdbc:mysql://localhost:3306/sample</td></tr>
<tr><th colspan="3">Oracle</th></tr>
<tr><td>Jar file</td><td colspan="2">ojdbc6.jar (Java 1.6)
ojdbc7.jar (Java 1.7)</td></tr>
<tr><td>Download URL</td><td colspan="2">http://www.oracle.com/technology/software/tech/java/sqlj_jdbc/index.html</td></tr>
<tr><td>Driver</td><td colspan="2">oracle.jdbc.driver.OracleDriver</td></tr>
<tr><td>URL format</td><td colspan="2">jdbc:oracle:[type]:@[host]:[port]:[service]
jdbc:oracle:[type]:[host]:[port]:[SID]
jdbc:oracle:[type]:[TNSName]</td></tr>
<tr><td rowspan="2">Sample URL</td><td>thin</td><td>jdbc:oracle:thin:@miroracle:1521: ORCL_SVC
jdbc:oracle:thin:@172.16.4.243:1521: ORCL_SID
jdbc:oracle:thin:@(description=(address=(host=localhost)(protocol=tcp)(port=1521))(connect_data=(sid=ORCL)))
jdbc:oracle:thin:@TNS-NAME</td></tr>
<tr><td>Oci</td><td>jdbc:oracle:oci:@miroracle:1521: ORCL_SVC
jdbc:oracle:oci:@172.16.4.243:1521: ORCL_SID
jdbc:oracle:oci:@(description=(address=(host=localhost)(protocol=tcp)(port=1521))(connect_data=(sid=ORCL)))
jdbc:oracle:oci:@TNS-NAME</td></tr>
<tr><th colspan="3">Sun JDBC-ODBC Bridge</th></tr>
<tr><td>Jar file</td><td colspan="2">Bundled with JDK</td></tr>
<tr><td>Driver</td><td colspan="2">Sun.jdbc.odbc.JdbcOdbcDriver</td></tr>
<tr><td>URL format</td><td colspan="2">JDBC:ODBC:[data source name]</td></tr>
<tr><td>Sample URL</td><td colspan="2">JDBC:ODBC:test</td></tr>
<tr><th colspan="3">DB2</th></tr>
<tr><td>Jar file</td><td colspan="2">db2jcc.jar</td></tr>
<tr><td>Download URL</td><td colspan="2">http://www-01.ibm.com/software/data/db2/ad/java.html</td></tr>
<tr><td>Driver</td><td colspan="2">Com.ibm.db2.jdbc.net.DB2Driver</td></tr>
<tr><td>URL format</td><td colspan="2">Jdbc:db2://[host]:[port]/[database]</td></tr>
<tr><td>Sample URL</td><td colspan="2">jdbc:db2://172.16.4.243:50000/test</td></tr>
<tr><th colspan="3">Pervasive</th></tr>
<tr><td>Jar file</td><td colspan="2">pvjdbc2.jar</td></tr>
<tr><td>Driver</td><td colspan="2">com.pervasive.jdbc.v2.Driver</td></tr>
<tr><td>Download URL</td><td colspan="2">http://www.pervasive.com/developerzone/access_methods/jdbc.asp</td></tr>
<tr><td>URL format</td><td colspan="2">jdbc:pervasive://[host]:[port]/[database]</td></tr>
<tr><td>Sample URL</td><td colspan="2">jdbc:pervasive://uroy:1583/sample</td></tr>
</table>

(Contd)

Table 22.2: (*Contd*)

PostgreSQL	
Jar file	postgresql-nn.jdbc3.jar
Download URL	http://jdbc.postgresql.org/download.html
Driver	org.postgresql.Driver
URL format	jdbc:postgresql://[host]:[port]/[database]
Sample URL	jdbc:postgresql://[localhost]:[5432]/[test]
JavaDB/Derby	
Jar file	derbyclient.jar
Download URL	http://db.apache.org/derby/derby_downloads.html
Driver	org.apache.derby.jdbc.ClientDriver
URL format	jdbc:derby:net://[host]:[port]/[database]
Sample URL	jdbc:derby:net://[172.16.4.243]:[1527]/[sample]

The second overloaded version of the `getConnection()` method takes only a string argument. This argument must contain URL information, together with other parameters such as user name and password. The parameters are passed as a name–value pair separated by "&" using the same syntax as the HTTP URL. The general syntax of such a URL is as follows:

```
basicURL?param1=value1&param2=value2…
```

The following is an example of such a string argument for the MySQL database.

```
jdbc:mysql://uroy:3306/test?user=root&password=nbuser
```

Alternatively, parameters can be put in a `java.util.Properties` object and the object can be passed to the `getConnection()` method. The following is an example using Properties.

```
String url = "jdbc:mysql://uroy:3306/test";
java.util.Properties p = new java.util.Properties();
p.setProperty("user", "root");
p.setProperty("password", "nbuser");
Connection con = DriverManager.getConnection(url, p);
```

22.8 EXECUTE SQL STATEMENT

Once a connection to the database is established, we can interact with the database. The `Connection` interface provides methods for obtaining different statement objects that are used to fire SQL statements via the established connection. The `Connection` object can be used for other purposes such as gathering database information, and committing or rolling back a transaction. The following section describes the different types of statement objects and their functionality.

22.9 SQL STATEMENTS

The `Connection` interface defines the following methods to obtain statement objects.

```
Statement createStatement()
Statement createStatement(int resultSetType,
                          int resultSetConcurrency)
Statement createStatement(int resultSetType,
                          int resultSetConcurrency,
                          int resultSetHoldability)

PreparedStatement prepareStatement(java.lang.String)
```

```
PreparedStatement prepareStatement(String sql,
                                   int resultSetType,
                                   int resultSetConcurrency)
PreparedStatement prepareStatement(String sql,
                                   int resultSetType,
                                   int resultSetConcurrency,
                                   int resultSetHoldability)

CallableStatement prepareCall(java.lang.String)
CallableStatement prepareCall(String sql,
                              int resultSetType,
                              int resultSetConcurrency)
CallableStatement prepareCall(String sql,
                              int resultSetType,
                              int resultSetConcurrency,
                              int resultSetHoldability)
```

The JDBC `Statement`, `CallableStatement`, and `PreparedStatement` interfaces define the methods and properties that enable you to send SQL or PL/SQL commands and receive data from your database.

22.9.1 Simple Statement

The `Statement` interface is used to execute static SQL statements A `Statement` object is instantiated using the `createStatement()` method on the `Connection` object as follows:

```
Statement stmt = con.createStatement();
```

This `Statement` object defines the following methods to fire different types of SQL commands on the database.

executeUpdate()

This method is used to execute DDL (CREATE, ALTER, and DROP), DML (INSERT, DELETE, UPDATE, etc.) and DCL statements. In general, if an SQL command changes the database, the `executeUpdate()` method is used. The return value of this method is the number of rows affected.

Assume that `stmt` is a `Statement` object. The following code segment first creates a table named `accounts`.

```
String create =   "CREATE TABLE accounts (          "+
                  "  accNum        integer primary key,  "+
                  "  holderName    varchar(20),          "+
                  "  balance       integer               "+
                  ")";
stmt.executeUpdate(create);
```

Once the table is created, data can be inserted into it using the following code segment.

```
String insert = "INSERT INTO accounts VALUES(1,'Uttam K. Roy', 10000)";
stmt.executeUpdate(insert);
insert = "INSERT INTO accounts VALUES(2,'Bibhas Ch. Dhara', 20000)";
stmt.executeUpdate(insert);
```

The following JSP page (`DDL.jsp`) creates a table accounts and insert two rows in the table. Make sure that the MySQL JDBC driver is in the `/lib` directory under the Tomcat installation directory.

```
<!--DDL.jsp-->
<%@page import="java.sql.*"%>
<%
  try {
    new com.mysql.jdbc.Driver();
    String url = "jdbc:mysql://uroy:3306/test?user=root&password=nbuser";
    Connection conn = DriverManager.getConnection(url);
    Statement stmt = conn.createStatement();
```

```
      String create = "CREATE TABLE accounts (            " +
            "  accNum      integer     primary key,  " +
            "  holderName varchar(20),              " +
            "  balance     integer                " +
            ")";
      stmt.executeUpdate(create);

      String insert = "INSERT INTO accounts VALUES(1,'Uttam K. Roy', 10000)";
      stmt.executeUpdate(insert);
      insert = "INSERT INTO accounts VALUES(2,'Bibhas Ch. Dhara', 20000)";
      stmt.executeUpdate(insert);
      stmt.close();
      conn.close();
      out.println("Created table accounts");
    } catch (Exception e) {
      out.println(e);
    }
%>
```

executeQuery()

This is used for DQL statements such as SELECT. Remember, DQL statements only read data from database tables; it cannot change database tables. So, the return value of this method is a set of rows that is represented as a `ResultSet` object.

The result of the `executeQuery` method is stored in an object of type `ResultSet`. This result set object looks very much similar to a table and hence has a number of rows. A particular row is selected by setting a cursor associated with this result set. A cursor is something like a pointer to the rows. Once the cursor is set to a particular row, individual columns are retrieved using the methods provided by the `ResultSet` interface. The cursor is placed before the first row of result set when it is created first. JDBC 1.0 allows us to move the cursor only in the forward direction using the method `next()`. JDBC 2.0 allows us to move the cursor both forward and backward as well as to move to a specified row relative to the current row. These types of result sets are called scrollable result sets, which will be discussed in Section 22.12.

Since the cursor does not point to any row (it points to a position before the first row), users have the responsibility to set the cursor to a valid row to retrieve data from it. To retrieve data from a column, methods of the form `getX()` are used, where `X` is the data type of the column. The following is an example that retrieves information from the `accounts` table created earlier.

```
String query = "SELECT * FROM accounts";
ResultSet rs = stmt.executeQuery(query);
while(rs.next()) {
   out.println(rs.getString("accNum"));
   out.println(rs.getString("holderName"));
   out.println(rs.getString("balance"));
}
```

execute()

Sometimes, users want to execute SQL statements whose type (DDL, DML, DCL, or DQL) is not known in advance. This may happen particularly when statements are obtained from another program. In that case, users cannot decide which method they should use. In such cases, the `execute()` method is used. It can be used to execute any SQL commands. Since it allows us to execute any SQL commands, the result can either be a `ResultSet` object or an integer. However, how does a user know it? Fortunately, this method returns a Boolean value, which indicates the return type. The return value `true` indicates that the result is a `ResultSet` object, which can be obtained by calling its `getResultSet()` method. On the other hand, if the return value is `false`, the result is an update count, which can be obtained by calling the `getUpdateCount()` method.

The following JSP page (`execute.jsp`) takes an arbitrary SQL statement as a parameter and fires this SQL statement on the database.

```
<!--execute.jsp-->
<%@page import="java.sql.*"%>
<%
   response.setHeader("Pragma", "no-cache");
   response.setHeader("Cache-Control", "no-cache");
   response.setDateHeader("Expires", -1);
   try {
      String query = request.getParameter("sql");
      if (query != null) {
         new com.mysql.jdbc.Driver();
         String url = "jdbc:mysql://uroy:3306/test";
         Connection con = DriverManager.getConnection(url, "root", "nbuser");
         Statement stmt = con.createStatement();
         if (stmt.execute(query) == false) {
            out.println(stmt.getUpdateCount() + " rows affected");
         }
         else {
            ResultSet rs = stmt.getResultSet();
            ResultSetMetaData md = rs.getMetaData();
            out.println("<table border=\"1\"><tr>");
            for (int i = 1; i <= md.getColumnCount(); i++) {
               out.print("<th>" + md.getColumnName(i) + "</th>");
            }
            out.println("</tr>");
            while (rs.next()) {
               out.println("<tr>");
               for (int i = 1; i <= md.getColumnCount(); i++) {
                  out.print("<td>"+ rs.getString(i) + "</td>");
               }
               out.println("</tr>");
            }
            out.println("</table>");
            rs.close();
         }
         stmt.close();
         con.close();
      }
   }
   catch (Exception e) {
      out.println(e);
   }
%>
<form name="sqlForm" method="post">
   SQL statement:<br><input type="text" name="sql" size="50"><br />
   <input type="reset"><input type="submit" value="Execute">
</form>
```

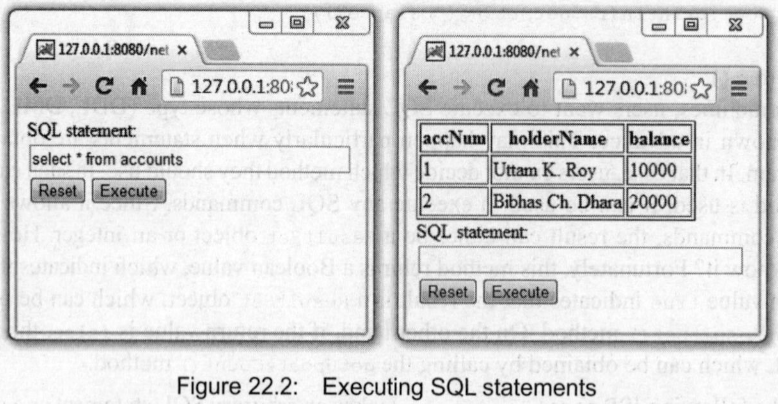

Figure 22.2: Executing SQL statements

Note that this JSP page allows you to fire any valid SQL query, including DML. So, the JSP page must perform user verification before providing this interface.

22.9.2 Atomic Transaction

The database transaction made by the `executeUpdate()` method is committed automatically. This may lead to data inconsistency if a series of related statements are executed. Consider the following simple table for a banking application.

```
accounts(accNum, holderName, balance)
```

The bank manager wants to write a Java program to transfer some amount of money `amount` from the source account `src` to the destination account `dst`. The basic task of this program will be to subtract `amount` from the source account balance and add `amount` to the destination account balance. A sample JSP page looks like this:

```
<!--manager.jsp-->
<%@page import="java.sql.*"%>
<%!
   Connection con;
   Statement stmt;
   String query;
   public void jspInit() {
      try {
         new com.mysql.jdbc.Driver();
         String url = "jdbc:mysql://uroy:3306/test";
         con = DriverManager.getConnection(url, "root", "nbuser");
         stmt = con.createStatement();
      }catch(Exception e) {}
   }
   public boolean transfer(int src, int dst, int amount) {
      try {
         query = "SELECT balance FROM accounts WHERE accNum=" + src;
         ResultSet rs = stmt.executeQuery(query);
         rs.next();
         int srcBal = rs.getInt("balance") - amount;
         query = "SELECT balance FROM accounts WHERE accNum=" + dst;
         rs = stmt.executeQuery(query);
         rs.next();
         int dstBal = rs.getInt("balance") + amount;
         return doTransfer(src, dst, srcBal, dstBal);
      } catch (SQLException e) {
         return false;
      }
   }
   public boolean doTransfer(int src, int dst, int srcBal, int dstBal) {
   try {
      query = "UPDATE accounts SET balance=" + srcBal + " WHERE accNum=" + src;
      stmt.executeUpdate(query);
      query = "UPDATE accounts SET balance=" + dstBal + " WHERE accNum=" + dst;
      //If anything goes wrong here, destination account will contain wrong
      //result.
      stmt.executeUpdate(query);
      return true;
   } catch (SQLException e) {
      return false;
   }
   }
%>
<%
try {
   int src = Integer.parseInt(request.getParameter("src"));
   int dst = Integer.parseInt(request.getParameter("dst"));
```

```
    int amount = Integer.parseInt(request.getParameter("amount"));
    transfer(src, dst, amount);
  }catch(Exception e) {out.println(e);}
  %>
```

Note that source and destination accounts must be updated atomically. However, if anything goes wrong after updating the source account and before updating the destination account in the `doTransfer()` method, the destination account will hold an incorrect balance.

This problem can be solved using the `autoCommit()` method available on the `Connection` object. First the `autoCommit` flag of the `Connection` object is set to false. At the end of execution of all related statements, the transaction is committed. If anything goes wrong during the execution of those statements, it can be caught and the transaction gets rolled back accordingly. This way a set of related operations can be performed atomically.

The correct `doTransfer()` method looks like this:

```
public boolean doTransfer(int src, int dst, int srcBal, int dstBal) {
   try {
      con.setAutoCommit(false);
      query = "UPDATE accounts SET balance=" + srcBal + " WHERE accNum=" + src;
      stmt.executeUpdate(query);
      query = "UPDATE accounts SET balance=" + dstBal + " WHERE accNum=" + dst;
      stmt.executeUpdate(query);
      con.commit();
      return true;
   } catch (SQLException e) {
      try {
        con.rollback();
      } catch (SQLException e1) {
      }
      return false;
   }
}
```

`executeBatch()`

This method allows us to execute a set of related commands as a whole. Commands to be fired on the database are added to the `Statement` object one by one using the method `addBatch()`. It is always safe to clear the `Statement` object using the method `clearBatch()` before adding any command to it. Once all commands are added, `executeBatch()` is called to send them as a unit to the database. The DBMS executes the commands in the order in which they were added. Finally, if all commands are successful, it returns an array of update counts. To allow correct error handling, we should always set auto-commit mode to `false` before beginning a batch command.

The following is the method `doTransfer`, rewritten using this mechanism.

```
  public boolean doBatchTransfer(int src, int dst, int srcBal, int dstBal) {
    try {
      String query;
      con.setAutoCommit(false);
      stmt.clearBatch();
      query = "UPDATE accounts SET balance=" + srcBal + " WHERE accNum=" + src;
      stmt.addBatch(query);
      query = "UPDATE accounts SET balance=" + dstBal + " WHERE accNum=" + dst;
      stmt.addBatch(query);
      stmt.executeBatch();
      con.commit();
      return true;
    } catch (SQLException e) {
      try {
        con.rollback();
```

```
      } catch (SQLException e1) {
      }
      return false;
   }
}
```

Since all the commands are sent as a unit to the database for execution, it improves the performance significantly.

22.9.3 Pre-compiled Statement

When an SQL statement is fired to the database for execution using the `Statement` object the following steps get executed:

- DBMS checks the syntax of the statement being submitted.
- If the syntax is correct, it executes the statement.

DBMS compiles every statement unnecessarily, even if users want to execute the *same* SQL statement repeatedly with different data items. This creates significant overhead, which can be avoided using the `PreparedStatement` object.

A `PreparedStatement` object is created using the `prepareStatement()` method of the `Connection` object. An SQL statement with placeholders (?) is supplied to the method `Connection.prepareStatement()` when a `PreparedStatement` object is created. This SQL statement, together with the placeholders is sent to the DBMS. DMBS, in turn, compiles the statement and if everything is correct, a `PreparedStatement` object is created. This means that a `PreparedStatement` object contains an SQL statement whose syntax has already been checked and hence is called pre-compiled statement. This SQL statement is then fired repeatedly, with placeholders substituted by different data items. Note that `PreparedStatement` is useful only if the same SQL statement is executed repeatedly with different parameters. Otherwise, it behaves exactly like `Statement` and no benefit can be obtained.

The following example creates a `PreparedStatement` object:

```
PreparedStatement ps = con.prepareStatement("INSERT INTO user values(?,?)");
```

The SQL statement has two placeholders, whose values will be supplied whenever this statement is sent for execution. Placeholders are substituted using methods of the form `setX()`, where `X` is the data type of the value used to substitute. These methods take two parameters. The first parameter indicates the index of the placeholder to be substituted and the second one indicates the value to be used for substitution. The following example substitutes the first placeholder with "user1".

```
ps.setString(1, "user1");
```

Consider a file, `question.txt`, which contains questions of the form `question_no:question_string` as follows:

```
1:What is the full form of JDBC?
2:How is a PreparedStatement created?
...
```

The following example inserts questions and their numbers stored in this file in the table `questions`.

```
PreparedStatement ps = con.prepareStatement("INSERT INTO questions
values(?,?)");
BufferedReader br = new BufferedReader(new InputStreamReader(new
FileInputStream("question.txt")));
String line = br.readLine();
while (line != null) {
   StringTokenizer st = new StringTokenizer(line, ":");
```

```
        String qno = st.nextToken();
        String question = st.nextToken();
        ps.setString(1, qno);
        ps.setString(2, question);
        ps.executeUpdate();
        line = br.readLine();
    }
```

PreparedStatement has another important role in executing parameterized SQL statements. Consider this solution using the Statement object.

```
Statement stmt = con.createStatement();
BufferedReader br = new BufferedReader(new InputStreamReader(new
FileInputStream(application.getRealPath("/")+"question.txt")));
String line = br.readLine();
while (line != null) {
    StringTokenizer st = new StringTokenizer(line, ":");
    String qno = st.nextToken();
    String question = st.nextToken();
    String query = "INSERT INTO questions values("+qno+",'"+question+"')";
    stmt.executeUpdate(query);
    line = br.readLine();
}
```

This code segment will work fine, provided the question does not contain characters such as "'". For example, if the file question.txt contains a line "3:What's JDBC?", the value of the query will be

```
INSERT INTO questions values(3,'What's JDBC?')
```

This is an invalid query due the "'" character in the word "What's". If you try, you will get an error message like this:

```
com.mysql.jdbc.exceptions.jdbc4.MySQLSyntaxErrorException: You have an error in
your SQL syntax; check the manual that corresponds to your MySQL server version
for the right syntax to use near 's JDBC?')' at line 1
```

PreparedStatement can handle this situation very easily, as it treats the entire parameter as input. So, the example given using the PreparedStatement will work correctly in this case.

22.9.4 SQL Statements to Call Stored Procedures

JDBC also allows the calling of stored procedures that are stored in the database server. This is done using the CallableStatement object. A CallableStatement object is created using the prepareCall() method on a Connection object.

```
CallableStatement prepareCall(String)
```

The method prepareCall() takes a primary string parameter, which represents the procedure to be called, and returns a CallableStatement object, which is used to invoke stored procedures if the underlying database supports them. Here is an example:

```
String proCall = "{call changePassword(?, ?, ?)}";
CallableStatement cstmt = con.prepareCall(proCall);
```

The variable cstmt can now be used to call the stored procedure changePassword, which has three input parameters and no result parameter. The type of ? placeholders (IN, OUT, or INOUT) depends on the definition of the stored procedure changePassword.

JDBC API allows the following syntax to call stored procedures:

```
{call procedure-name [(?, ?, ...)]}
```

For example, to call a stored procedure with no parameter and no return type, the following syntax is used:

```
{call procedure-name}
```

The following syntax is used to call a procedure that takes a single parameter:

```
{call procedure-name(?)}
```

If a procedure returns a value, the following syntax is used:

```
{? = call procedure-name (?, ?)}
```

MySQL procedures are not allowed to return values. So, the last format is not allowed in MySQL. The web developer must know what stored procedures are available in the underlying database. Before using any stored procedure, one can use the `supportsStoredProcedures()` method on the `DatabaseMetaData` object to verify if the underlying database supports the stored procedure. If it supports, the description of the stored procedures can be obtained using `getProcedures()` on the `DatabaseMetaData` object. Consider the following procedure created in MySQL.

```
DELIMITER //
CREATE PROCEDURE changePassword(IN loginName varchar(10), IN oldPassword
varchar(10), IN newPassword varchar(10))
BEGIN
  DECLARE old varchar(10);
  SELECT password INTO @old FROM users WHERE login=loginName;
  IF @old = oldPassword THEN
    UPDATE users SET password=newPassword WHERE login=loginName;
  END IF;
END //
DELIMITER ;
```

This procedure changes the password of a specified user in the table `users`. It takes three parameters: the login id of the user whose password has to be changed, the old password, and a new password.

If you are using MySQL command prompt to create a procedure, you may face a problem. Note that the stored procedures use ";" as the delimiter. The default MySQL statement delimiter is also ";". This would make the SQL in the stored procedure syntactically invalid. The solution is to temporarily change the command-line utility delimiter using the following command;

```
DELIMITER //
```

This command `DELIMITER //` is not related to the stored procedure. The `DELIMITER` statement is used to change the standard delimiter (semicolon) to another. In this case, the delimiter is changed to //, so that you can have multiple SQL statements separated by the semicolon inside stored procedure. After the `END` keyword, we use delimiter // to show the end of the stored procedure. The last command `DELIMITER ;` changes the delimiter back to the standard one (semicolon).

The `IN` parameters are passed to a `CallableStatement` object using methods of the form `setXxx()`. For example, `setFloat()` and `setBoolean()` methods are used to pass `float` and `boolean` values, respectively.

The following code segment illustrates how to call this procedure.

```
<!--CallableStatement.jsp-->
<%@page import="java.sql.*"%>
<%
    try {
      new com.mysql.jdbc.Driver();
      String url = "jdbc:mysql://uroy:3306/test";
      Connection con = DriverManager.getConnection(url, "root", "nbuser");
      String proCall = "{call changePassword(?, ?, ?)}";
      CallableStatement cstmt = con.prepareCall(proCall);
      String login = request.getParameter("login");
      String oldPassword = request.getParameter("oldPassword");
      String newPassword = request.getParameter("newPassword");
      cstmt.setString(1, login);
```

```
        cstmt.setString(2, oldPassword);
        cstmt.setString(3, newPassword);
        if (cstmt.executeUpdate() > 0) {
            out.println("Password changed successfully");
        } else {
            out.println("Couldn't change password");
        }
        cstmt.close();
        conn.close();
    } catch (Exception e) {
        out.println(e);
    }
%>
```

The following URL may be used to change the password for the user from pass1 to newPass1:

```
http://127.0.0.1:8080/net/jdbc/CallableStatement.jsp?login=user1&oldPassword=pa
ss1&newPassword=newPass1
```

Make sure that the table was created and populated with values as shown below:

```
String create = "CREATE TABLE users (                "+
                "   login varchar(20) primary key,   "+
                "   password        varchar(20)      "+
                ")";
stmt.executeUpdate(create);

String insert = "INSERT INTO users VALUES('user1','pass1')";
stmt.executeUpdate(insert);
insert = "INSERT INTO users VALUES('user2','pass2') ";
stmt.executeUpdate(insert);
```

The `CallableStatement` object also allows batch update exactly like `PreparedStatement`. The following is an example:

```
String proCall = "{call changePassword(?, ?, ?)}";
CallableStatement cstmt = con.prepareCall(proCall);

cstmt.setString(1, "user1");
cstmt.setString(2, "pass1");
cstmt.setString(3, "newPass1");
cstmt.addBatch();

cstmt.setString(1, "user2");
cstmt.setString(2, "pass2");
cstmt.setString(3, "newPass2");
cstmt.addBatch();

int [] updateCounts = cstmt.executeBatch();
```

This example illustrates how to use batch update facility to associate two sets of parameters with a `CallableStatement` object.

22.10 RETRIEVING RESULT

A table of data is represented in the JDBC by the `ResultSet` interface. The `ResultSet` objects are usually generated by executing the SQL statements that query the database. A pointer points to a particular row of the `ResultSet` object at a time. This pointer is called *cursor*. The cursor is positioned before the first row when the `ResultSet` object is generated. To retrieve data from a row of `ResultSet`, the cursor must be positioned at the row. The `ResultSet` interface provides methods to move this cursor.

next()

- This method on the `ResultSet` object moves the cursor to the next row of the result set.
- It returns true/false depending upon whether there are more rows in the result set.

Since the `next()` method returns false when there are no more rows in the `ResultSet` object, it can be used in a while loop to iterate through the result set as follows:

```
String query = "SELECT * from users";
ResultSet rs = stmt.executeQuery(query);
while(rs.next()) {
   //process it
}
```

The `ResultSet` interface provides reader methods for retrieving column values from the row pointed to by the cursor. These have the form `getXxx()`, where `Xxx` is the name of the data type of the column. For example, if data types are string and int, the name of the reader methods are `getString()` and `getInt()`, respectively.

Values can be retrieved using either the column index or the name of the column. Using the column index, in general, is more efficient. The column index starts from 1. The following example illustrates how to retrieve data from a `ResultSet` object.

```
String query = "SELECT * from users";
ResultSet rs = stmt.executeQuery(query);
while(rs.next()) {
    String login = rs.getString("login");
    String password = rs.getString("password");
    System.out.println(login+"\t"+password);

}
```

22.11 GETTING DATABASE INFORMATION

Sometimes, it is necessary to know the capabilities of DataBase Management System (DBMS) before dealing with it. This is because different DBMSs often provide different features, implement them differently, and also use different data types. Moreover, the driver may also implement additional features on top of the DBMS. The `DatabaseMetaData` interface provides methods to collect comprehensive information about a DBMS. We can discover features a DBMS supports and develop our application accordingly. For example, before creating a table, one may want to know what data types are supported by this DBMS. The user may also want to know whether the underlying DBMS supports batch update.

A `DatabaseMetaData` object is obtained using the `getMetaData()` method on the `Connection` object as follows:

```
DatabaseMetaData md = con.getMetaData();
```

We can then use various methods on this `DatabaseMetaData` object to collect the required information about the DBMS. The following is a list of commonly used methods:

`getDatabaseMetaData()`

Returns the `DatabaseMetaData` object, which contains detailed information about the underlying database. Some important methods of `DatabaseMetaData` are

`String getSQLKeywords()`

Returns keywords available

`getDatabaseProductName()`

Returns the name of the manufacturer

`getDatabaseProductVersion()`

Returns the current version

`getDriverName()`

Returns driver used

The following JSP page retrieves most of the MySQL database information.

```
<!--DBMetaData.jsp-->
<%@page import="java.sql.*, java.lang.reflect.*"%>
<%
   new com.mysql.jdbc.Driver();
   String url = "jdbc:mysql://uroy:3306/test";
   Connection con = DriverManager.getConnection(url, "root", "nbuser");
   DatabaseMetaData md = con.getMetaData();
   Method[] methods = md.getClass().getMethods();
   Object[] param = new Object[0];
   out.println("<table border=\"1\">");
   for (int i = 0; i < methods.length; i++) {
      if (methods[i].getParameterTypes().length == 0) {
         if (methods[i].getReturnType() == Boolean.TYPE ||
methods[i].getReturnType() == String.class) {
            out.println("<tr>");
            out.println("<td>"+methods[i].getName() + "</td>");
            try {
              out.println("<td>" + methods[i].invoke(md, param)+"</td>");
            }catch(Exception e) {out.println("<td>" + e+"</td>");}
            out.println("</tr>");
         }
      }
   }
   out.println("</table>");
%>
```

The result of this page is shown in Table 22.6.

22.12 SCROLLABLE AND UPDATABLE RESULTSET

The result set returned so far by a query can be navigated in one direction (forward). Moreover the data the result sets contain are read-only. Any change to the result set does not affect the actual database.

Result sets can be *scrollable* in the sense that the cursor can be moved backward and forward. Additionally, a result set can be *updatable*, such that any change to the result set reflects in the database immediately. A result set can be scrollable as well as updatable. *Note that scrollable and updatable result sets incur significant overhead. So, such result sets should be created if the underlying application performs scrolling.*

In addition to *scrollability* and *updatability*, another important concept, called *sensitivity*, is defined. Sensitivity broadly answers the following question:

```
Can a result set see the changes that are made to the underlying database?
```

If a result cannot see any changes, it is said to be insensitive. Otherwise, the sensitivity of a result set is defined with respect to the database operation as well as the operating party. For example, a result set is said to be sensitive to update if it can see any update operation made on the underlying database. The sensitivity rules are shown in Table 22.3:

The `createStatement()` and `prepareStatement()` methods take extra parameters that specify the type of result returned by subsequent execution of SQL statements. The prototype of the `createStatement()` method to generate a scrollable and updatable result set is as follows:

```
Statement createStatement(int resultSetType, int resultSetConcurrency)
```

Here, scrollability and updatability are controlled by the parameters `resultSetType` and `resultSetConcurrency`, respectively.

22.12.1 Scrollability Type

The parameter `resultSetType` can assume the following static integer constants defined in `ResultSet`. Their meaning is as follows:

- `TYPE_FORWARD_ONLY`

  If this constant is used, the cursor starts at the first row and can only move forward.
- `TYPE_SCROLL_INSENSITIVE`

  All cursor positioning methods are enabled; the result set does not reflect changes made by others in the underlying table.
- `TYPE_SCROLL_SENSITIVE`

  All cursor positioning methods are enabled; the result set reflects changes made by others in the underlying table.

The visibility of internal and external changes to scrollable `ResultSet` in Oracle JDBC is shown in Table 22.3:

Table 22.3: Visibility of Internal and External Changes to Scrollable Result Set in Oracle JDBC

Scroll Type		TYPE_FORWARD_ONLY	TYPE_SCROLL_SENSITIVE	TYPE_SCROLL_INSENSITIVE
Internal	DELETE	No	Yes	Yes
	UPDATE	Yes	Yes	Yes
	INSERT	No	No	No
External	DELETE	No	No	No
	UPDATE	No	Yes	No
	INSERT	No	No	No

22.12.2 Concurrency Type

The parameter `resultSetConcurrency` can assume the following static integer constants defined in `ResultSet`. The following is a brief description:

- `CONCUR_READ_ONLY`

  The result set is not updatable.
- `CONCUR_UPDATABLE`

  Rows can be added and deleted; columns can be updated and are visible to others.

22.12.3 Examples

The following example creates a `Statement` object, whose methods will return scrollable, update insensitive, and read-only result sets.

```
Statement stmt = conn.createStatement(ResultSet.TYPE_SCROLL_INSENSITIVE,
ResultSet.CONCUR_READ_ONLY);
ResultSet rs = stmt.executeQuery("SELECT * FROM questions");
```

The `ResultSet` object `rs` is now scrollable, but update insensitive.

Originally, result sets could be navigated only in one direction (forward) and starting at only one position (the first row). In JDBC 2.0, the row pointer can be manipulated as if it were an array index. Some of the important methods available on the scrollable `ResultSet` object are shown in Table 22.4: The following examples demonstrate how to navigate a scrollable result set:

- Move the cursor forward by one row.

```
rs.next();
//or
rs.relative(1);
```

- Move the cursor backward by one row.

```
rs.previous();
//or
rs.relative(-1);
```

- Set the cursor before the first row.

```
rs.beforeFirst();
```

- Set the cursor after the last row.

```
rs.afterLast();
```

- Set the cursor at the first row (row 1).

```
rs.first();
//or
rs.absolute(1);
```

- Set the cursor at the last row.

```
rs.last();
//or
rs.absolute(-1);
```

- Set the cursor at the second row.

```
rs.absolute(2);
```

- Set the cursor at the second last row.

```
rs.absolute(-2);
```

- Move the cursor forward six rows from the current position.

```
rs.relative(6);
//Sets the cursor after the last row, if it goes beyond the last row
```

- Move the cursor backward four rows from the current position.

```
rs.relative(-4);
//Sets the cursor before the first row, if it goes before the first row
```

Table 22.4: Scrollable ResultSet methods

Method	Description
next()	Advances cursor to the next row
previous()	Moves cursor back one row
first()	Sets cursor to the first row
last()	Sets cursor to the last row
beforeFirst()	Sets cursor just before the first row
afterLast()	Sets cursor just after the last row
absolute(int rowNumber)	Sets the cursor to the specified row number. +ve and –ve numbers indicate positions relative to the position before first row and after last row, respectively. For example, 1 and -1 represent first and last row, respectively.
relative(int rows)	Forwards or reverses cursor the specified number of rows relative to the current position. +ve number indicates forwarding and –ve number indicates reversing. For example, relative(1) forwards the cursor one position, which is equivalent to next(). Similarly, relative(-1) moves the cursor one position back and is equivalent to previous(). It throws an SQLException if cursor points before the first row or after the last row.

(Contd)

Table 22.4: *(Contd)*

moveToInsertRow()	Sets the cursor to a special row called "insert row" and remembers the current position before moving the cursor.
moveToCurrentRow()	Sets the cursor to the row from where the cursor was moved to "insert row" using moveToInsertRow().

The following example creates a `Statement` object, whose methods will return scrollable as well as external-update-insensitive and updatable result sets.

```
Statement stmt = conn.createStatement(ResultSet.TYPE_SCROLL_INSENSITIVE,
ResultSet.CONCUR_UPDATABLE);
ResultSet rs = stmt.executeQuery("SELECT * FROM questions");
```

To update a row in a database table, the following steps are used:

- Obtain an updatable result set.
- Move the cursor to the row to be updated using positioning methods available on the `ResultSet` object.
- Update the value of one or more columns in that row using the `updateXxx()` method on the `ResultSet` object, where `Xxx` is the data type of the column.
- Finally, update the database table using the `updateRow()` method.

The following example demonstrates how to update, insert, or delete a row from a database table using an updatable result set.

```
Statement stmt = conn.createStatement(ResultSet.TYPE_SCROLL_SENSITIVE,
ResultSet.CONCUR_UPDATABLE);
ResultSet rs = stmt.executeQuery("SELECT * FROM users");

//Updating existing row
rs.absolute(4);
rs.updateString("password","newPassword");
rs.updateRow();

//inseting new row
rs.moveToInsertRow();
rs.updateString(1, "anik");
rs.updateString(2, "anik123");
rs.insertRow();

//Deleting a row
rs.deleteRow()
```

The following JSP page changes the password of a specified user using the updatable result set.

```
<!--UpdatableResultSetDemo.jsp-->
<%@ page import="java.sql.*" %>
<%
    try {
        String login = request.getParameter("login");
        String oldPassword = request.getParameter("oldPassword");
        String newPassword = request.getParameter("newPassword");

        new com.mysql.jdbc.Driver();
        String url = "jdbc:mysql://uroy:3306/test";
        Connection con = DriverManager.getConnection(url, "root", "nbuser");
        Statement stmt = con.createStatement(ResultSet.TYPE_SCROLL_INSENSITIVE,
ResultSet.CONCUR_UPDATABLE);
        String query = "SELECT * FROM users WHERE login='" + login + "'";
        ResultSet rs = stmt.executeQuery(query);     //rs contains one row
        rs.next();                                   //set cursor at first row
        String password = rs.getString("password");
        if (password.equals(oldPassword)) {
          System.out.println(password);
```

```
            rs.updateString("password", newPassword); //update the password column
            rs.updateRow();                           //update database table
        }
    } catch (Exception e) {out.println(e); }
%>
```

Use the following URL to verify the above JSP page:

```
http://127.0.0.1:8080/net/jdbc/UpdatableResultSetDemo.jsp?login=user2&oldPasswo
rd=pass2&newPassword=newPass2
```

The following example populates the table questions by inserting questions into the updatable result set.

```
<!--UpdatableResultSetDemo1.jsp-->
<%@ page import="java.sql.*, java.io.*, java.util.*" %>
<%
    try {
        new com.mysql.jdbc.Driver();
        String url = "jdbc:mysql://uroy:3306/test";
        Connection con = DriverManager.getConnection(url, "root", "nbuser");
        Statement stmt = con.createStatement(ResultSet.TYPE_SCROLL_INSENSITIVE,
ResultSet.CONCUR_UPDATABLE);
        ResultSet rs = stmt.executeQuery("SELECT * FROM questions");
        BufferedReader br = new BufferedReader(new InputStreamReader(new
FileInputStream(application.getRealPath("/")+"/jdbc/question.txt")));
        String line = br.readLine();
        while (line != null) {
            StringTokenizer st = new StringTokenizer(line, ":");
            String qno = st.nextToken();
            String question = st.nextToken();

            rs.moveToInsertRow();
            rs.updateString(1, qno);
            rs.updateString(2, question);
            rs.insertRow();
            line = br.readLine();
        }
        br.close();
    } catch (Exception e) {out.println(e); }
%>
```

Use the following URL to verify the above JSP page:

```
http://127.0.0.1:8080/net/jdbc/UpdatableResultSetDemo1.jsp
```

Make sure that the table questions exist. Otherwise, create it using the following SQL command:

```
create table questions (
    qno   integer primary key,
    question varchar(100)
);
```

The following example creates a `Statement` object, whose methods will return scrollable as well as external-update-sensitive and updatable result sets.

```
Statement stmt = conn.createStatement(ResultSet.TYPE_SCROLL_SENSITIVE,
ResultSet.CONCUR_UPDATABLE);
ResultSet rs = stmt.executeQuery("SELECT * FROM questions");
```

In this case, if the database table is updated, it is reflected in the result set. Before retrieving data from a row, you should invoke the `refreshRow()` method of the `ResultSet` object so that it contains the updated row. The following JSP page shows how to use an updatable result set.

```
<!--UpdateSensitive.jsp-->
<%@page import="java.sql.*"%>
<%!
    Connection con;
```

```
      Statement stmt;
      ResultSet rs;
      String query;
      public void jspInit() {
         try {
            new com.mysql.jdbc.Driver();
            String url = "jdbc:mysql://uroy:3306/test";
            con = DriverManager.getConnection(url, "root", "nbuser");
            Statement stmt = con.createStatement(ResultSet.TYPE_SCROLL_SENSITIVE,
   ResultSet.CONCUR_UPDATABLE);
            query = "SELECT * FROM users";
            rs = stmt.executeQuery(query);
            System.out.println("loaded");

         }catch(Exception e) {}
      }
   %>
   <table border="1">
   <tr><th>Login name</th><th>Password</th></tr>
   <%
      try {
         response.setHeader("Pragma", "no-cache");
         response.setHeader("Cache-Control", "no-cache");
         response.setDateHeader("Expires", -1);

         rs.beforeFirst();
         while(rs.next()) {
            rs.refreshRow();
            out.println("<tr><td>" + rs.getString("login") + "</td>");
            out.println("<td>" + rs.getString("password")+"</td></tr>");
         }
      }catch(Exception e) {out.println(e);}
   %>
   </table>
```

This JSP page creates the `ResultSet` when this page is requested for the first time. The `ResultSet` is created in the `jspInit()` method. Consequently, it becomes an instance variable. For subsequent requests, it simply uses the `ResultSet` variable.

22.13 RESULT SET METADATA

The `ResultSetMetaData` object is used to retrieve information about the types and properties of the columns and other meta information about a `ResultSet` object. This is sometimes very useful, if you do not know much about the underlying database table. A `ResultSetMetaData` object is obtained using the `getMetaData()` method on the `ResultSet` object as follows:

```
ResultSet rs = stmt.executeQuery("SELECT * FROM questions");
ResultSetMetaData rsmd = rs.getMetaData();
```

It can be used to get some useful information such as number of rows, number of columns, column names, and their type. The following are some commonly used methods on the `ResultSetMetaData` object:

`int getColumnCount()`

Returns the number of columns in the result

`String getColumnName(int)`

Returns the name of a column in a result set. Requires an integer argument indicating the position of the column within the result set

`int getColumnType(int)`

Returns the type of the specified column in the form of `java.sql.Types`

`String getColumnTypeName(int)`

Returns the type of the specified column as a string

`String getColumnClassName(int)`

Returns the fully qualified Java type name of the specified column

`int getPrecision(int)`

Returns the number of decimal positions

`int getScale(int)`

Returns the number of digits after the decimal position

`String getTableName(int)`

Returns the name of the column's underlying table

`int isNullable(int)`

Returns a constant indicating whether the specified column can have a NULL value

The following JSP page shows how to retrieve meta information from a `ResultSet` object.

```
<!--ResultSetMetaData.jsp-->
<%@page import="java.sql.*, java.lang.reflect.*"%>
<%
    try {
        Class.forName("org.gjt.mm.mysql.Driver");
        String url = "jdbc:mysql://uroy:3306/test";
        Connection conn = DriverManager.getConnection(url, "root", "nbuser");
        Statement stmt = conn.createStatement();
        ResultSet rs = stmt.executeQuery("SELECT * FROM questions");
        ResultSetMetaData rsmd = rs.getMetaData();
        Object obj[] = new Object[1];
        Method[] methods = rsmd.getClass().getDeclaredMethods();
        out.println("<table border=\"0\"><tr><td>Method Name</td>");
        for(int j = 0; j < rsmd.getColumnCount(); j++)
           out.println("<td>" + rsmd.getColumnName(j+1) + "</td>");
        out.println("</tr>");
        for (int i = 0; i < methods.length; i++) {
        if(Modifier.isPublic(methods[i].getModifiers()))
               if (methods[i].getParameterTypes().length == 1) {
                   if(!methods[i].getName().equals("isWrapperFor"))
                      if(!methods[i].getName().equals("unwrap")) {
                         out.print("<tr><td>" + methods[i].getName() + "</td>");
                         for(int j=0;j<rsmd.getColumnCount();j++) {
                            obj[0] = new Integer(j+1);
                            out.print("<td>" + methods[i].invoke(rsmd,obj) +
"</td>");
                         }
                         out.println("</tr>");
                      }
               }
        }
        out.println("<table>");
    }catch(Exception e) {e.printStackTrace();}
%>
```

A sample result for MySQL database is shown in Table 22.5:

Table 22.5: Result Set Metadata

Method Name	qno	question
isWritable	true	true
isCaseSensitive	false	false
getPrecision	11	100

(Contd)

Table 22.5: (*Contd*)

isNullable	0	1
getTableName	questions	questions
getScale	0	0
isCurrency	false	false
isSearchable	true	true
isSigned	true	false
getColumnType	4	12
getColumnDisplaySize	11	100
getColumnLabel	qno	question
isAutoIncrement	false	false
getCatalogName	test	test
getColumnClassName	java.lang.Integer	java.lang.String
getColumnTypeName	INT	VARCHAR
getSchemaName		
isDefinitelyWritable	true	true
getColumnCharacterSet	US-ASCII	Cp1252
getColumnCharacterEncoding	null	null
isReadOnly	false	false
getColumnName	qno	question

Table 22.6: Database Metadata

Method Name	**Return value**
autoCommitFailureClosesAllResultSets	false
getDriverName	MySQL Connector Java
allProceduresAreCallable	false
allTablesAreSelectable	false
supportsTransactions	true
getDriverVersion	mysql-connector-java-5.1.26 (Revision: ${bzr.revision-id})
getCatalogSeparator	.
getCatalogTerm	database
getNumericFunctions	ABS,ACOS,ASIN,ATAN,ATAN2,BIT_COUNT,CEILING, COS,COT,DEGREES,EXP,FLOOR,LOG,LOG10,MAX, MIN,MOD,PI,POW,POWER,RADIANS,RAND,ROUND, SIN,SQRT,TAN,TRUNCATE
getProcedureTerm	PROCEDURE
getSQLKeywords	ACCESSIBLE,ALGORITHM,ANALYZE,ASENSITIVE, BEFORE,BIGINT,BINARY,BLOB,CALL,CHANGE, CONDITION,COPY,DATA,DATABASE,DATABASES, DAY_HOUR,DAY_MICROSECOND,DAY_MINUTE, DAY_SECOND,DELAYED,DETERMINISTIC,DIRECTORY, DISCARD,DISTINCTROW,DIV,DUAL,EACH,ELSEIF, ENCLOSED,ESCAPED,EXCHANGE,EXCLUSIVE,EXIT, EXPLAIN,EXPORT,FLOAT4,FLOAT8,FLUSH,FORCE, FULLTEXT,GENERAL,HIGH_PRIORITY,

(*Contd*)

Table 22.6: (*Contd*)

	HOUR_MICROSECOND,HOUR_MINUTE, HOUR_SECOND,IF,IGNORE,IGNORE_SERVER_IDS, IMPORT,INFILE,INOUT,INPLACE,INT1,INT2,INT3,INT4, INT8,ITERATE,KEYS,KILL,LEAVE,LIMIT,LINEAR,LINES, LOAD,LOCALTIME,LOCALTIMESTAMP,LOCK,LONG, LONGBLOB,LONGTEXT,LOOP,LOW_PRIORITY, MASTER_HEARTBEAT_PERIOD,MAXVALUE, MEDIUMBLOB,MEDIUMINT,MEDIUMTEXT,MIDDLEINT, MINUTE_MICROSECOND,MINUTE_SECOND,MOD, MODIFIES,NO_WRITE_TO_BINLOG,OPTIMIZE, OPTIONALLY,OUT,OUTFILE,PARTITION,PURGE, RANGE,READS,READ_ONLY,READ_WRITE,REBUILD, REGEXP,RELEASE,REMOVE,RENAME,REORGANIZE, REPAIR,REPEAT,REPLACE,REQUIRE,RESIGNAL, RETURN,RLIKE,SCHEMAS,SECOND_MICROSECOND, SENSITIVE,SEPARATOR,SHARED,SHOW,SIGNAL, SLOW,SPATIAL,SPECIFIC,SQLEXCEPTION, SQL_BIG_RESULT,SQL_CALC_FOUND_ROWS, SQL_SMALL_RESULT,SSL,STARTING,STRAIGHT_JOIN, TABLES,TABLESPACE,TERMINATED,TINYBLOB, TINYINT,TINYTEXT,TRIGGER,UNDO,UNLOCK, UNSIGNED,USE,UTC_DATE,UTC_TIME, UTC_TIMESTAMP,VARBINARY,VARCHARACTER, WHILE,X509,XOR,YEAR_MONTH,ZEROFILL
getSchemaTerm	
getStringFunctions	ASCII,BIN,BIT_LENGTH,CHAR,CHARACTER_LENGTH, CHAR_LENGTH,CONCAT,CONCAT_WS,CONV,ELT, EXPORT_SET,FIELD,FIND_IN_SET,HEX,INSERT,INSTR, LCASE,LEFT,LENGTH,LOAD_FILE,LOCATE,LOCATE, LOWER,LPAD,LTRIM,MAKE_SET,MATCH,MID,OCT, OCTET_LENGTH,ORD,POSITION,QUOTE,REPEAT, REPLACE,REVERSE,RIGHT,RPAD,RTRIM,SOUNDEX, SPACE,STRCMP,SUBSTRING,SUBSTRING,SUBSTRING, SUBSTRING,SUBSTRING_INDEX,TRIM,UCASE,UPPER
getSystemFunctions	DATABASE,USER,SYSTEM_USER,SESSION_USER, PASSWORD,ENCRYPT,LAST_INSERT_ID,VERSION
getTimeDateFunctions	DAYOFWEEK,WEEKDAY,DAYOFMONTH,DAYOFYEAR, MONTH,DAYNAME,MONTHNAME,QUARTER,WEEK, YEAR,HOUR,MINUTE,SECOND,PERIOD_ADD, PERIOD_DIFF,TO_DAYS,FROM_DAYS,DATE_FORMAT, TIME_FORMAT,CURDATE,CURRENT_DATE,CURTIME, CURRENT_TIME,NOW,SYSDATE,CURRENT_TIMESTAMP, UNIX_TIMESTAMP,FROM_UNIXTIME,SEC_TO_TIME, TIME_TO_SEC
isCatalogAtStart	true
locatorsUpdateCopy	true
nullsAreSortedAtEnd	false
nullsAreSortedHigh	false
nullsAreSortedLow	true
supportsBatchUpdates	true
supportsConvert	false

(*Contd*)

Table 22.6: *(Contd)*

supportsGroupBy	true
supportsOuterJoins	true
supportsSavepoints	true
supportsUnion	true
supportsUnionAll	true
usesLocalFiles	false
getIdentifierQuoteString	`
supportsDataDefinitionAndDataManipulation Transactions	false
dataDefinitionIgnoredInTransactions	false
storesLowerCaseQuotedIdentifiers	true
storesMixedCaseQuotedIdentifiers	false
storesUpperCaseQuotedIdentifiers	true
supportsANSI92IntermediateSQL	false
supportsAlterTableWithAddColumn	true
supportsAlterTableWithDropColumn	true
supportsCatalogsInDataManipulation	true
supportsCatalogsInIndexDefinitions	true
supportsCatalogsInProcedureCalls	true
supportsCatalogsInTableDefinitions	true
supportsIntegrityEnhancementFacility	false
supportsMixedCaseQuotedIdentifiers	false
supportsOpenCursorsAcrossCommit	false
supportsOpenCursorsAcrossRollback	false
supportsOpenStatementsAcrossCommit	false
supportsOpenStatementsAcrossRollback	false
supportsSchemasInDataManipulation	false
supportsSchemasInIndexDefinitions	false
supportsSchemasInProcedureCalls	false
supportsSchemasInTableDefinitions	false
supportsSubqueriesInComparisons	true
supportsSubqueriesInQuantifieds	true
supportsTableCorrelationNames	true
dataDefinitionCausesTransactionCommit	true
supportsCatalogsInPrivilegeDefinitions	true
supportsDataManipulationTransactionsOnly	false
supportsDifferentTableCorrelationNames	true
supportsSchemasInPrivilegeDefinitions	false
supportsStoredFunctionsUsingCallSyntax	true
doesMaxRowSizeIncludeBlobs	true
generatedKeyAlwaysReturned	true
getDatabaseProductName	MySQL

(Contd)

Table 22.6: (*Contd*)

getDatabaseProductVersion	5.0.51b-community-nt
getExtraNameCharacters	#@
getSearchStringEscape	\
nullPlusNonNullIsNull	true
nullsAreSortedAtStart	false
storesLowerCaseIdentifiers	true
storesMixedCaseIdentifiers	false
storesUpperCaseIdentifiers	false
supportsANSI92EntryLevelSQL	true
supportsANSI92FullSQL	false
supportsColumnAliasing	true
supportsCoreSQLGrammar	true
supportsCorrelatedSubqueries	true
supportsExpressionsInOrderBy	true
supportsExtendedSQLGrammar	false
supportsFullOuterJoins	false
supportsGetGeneratedKeys	true
supportsGroupByBeyondSelect	true
supportsGroupByUnrelated	true
supportsLikeEscapeClause	true
supportsLimitedOuterJoins	true
supportsMinimumSQLGrammar	true
supportsMixedCaseIdentifiers	false
supportsMultipleOpenResults	true
supportsMultipleResultSets	true
supportsMultipleTransactions	true
supportsNamedParameters	false
supportsNonNullableColumns	true
supportsOrderByUnrelated	false
supportsPositionedDelete	false
supportsPositionedUpdate	false
supportsSelectForUpdate	true
supportsStatementPooling	false
supportsStoredProcedures	true
supportsSubqueriesInExists	true
supportsSubqueriesInIns	true
usesLocalFilePerTable	false
providesQueryObjectGenerator	false
getURL	jdbc:mysql://uroy:3306/test
isReadOnly	false
getUserName	root@uroy
toString	com.mysql.jdbc.JDBC4DatabaseMetaData@1b6c838

KEYWORDS

Atomic Transaction—A transaction that either does not occur or occurs completely without any interleaving

CallableStatement—Statements that are used to call stored procedures in a database

Connection—A class that encapsulates the session/connection to a specific database

Database Metadata—An object that represents the meta information about a database

DDL Statement—SQL statements typically used to create tables

DCL Statement—SQL statements typically used to control database tables

DML Statement—SQL statements typically used to manipulate tables such as insert and update.

DQL Statement—SQL statements typically used to read values from tables

Driver— A Java class that provides interfaces to a specific database

JDBC—A Java framework that allows us to access databases through Java programs

PreparedStatement—Pre-compiled statements used to fire parameterized queries

ResultSet—The result of a DQL statement

Result Set Metadata—An object that represents the meta information about a result set

Scrollable Result Set—A result set whose pointer (cursor) can be moved back and forth

Statement—An interface is used to execute static SQL statements

Stored Procedure—Subroutine written using SQL

Updatable Result Set—A result set that can be used directly to modify original database tables

SUMMARY

Java DataBase Connectivity (JDBC) allows us to access databases through Java programs. It provides Java classes and interfaces to fire SQL and PL/SQL statements, process results (if any), and perform other operations common to databases.

A Java class that provides interfaces to a specific database is called JDBC driver. JDBC drivers are classified into four categories depending upon the way they work.

The following basic steps are followed to work with JDBC: Loading a Driver, Making a connection and Executing an SQL statement

To work with database, an instance of the driver has to be created and registered with the DriverManager class. Two ways we can do this: using static forName() method of the Java class Class or using static registerDriver() method of the DriverManager class.

Once an instance of the driver is created, we create Connection object using getConnection() method of DriverManager class. The Connection interface provides methods for obtaining different statement objects that are used to fire SQL statements via the established connection. The Connection object can be used for other purposes such as gathering database information, and committing or rolling back a transaction.

A simple Statement object is instantiated using the createStatement() method on the Connection object. This Statement object defines the many methods to fire different types of SQL commands on the database.

Instead of a simple Statement object, a PreparedStatement object is useful if users want to execute the same SQL statement repeatedly with different data items.

JDBC also allows the calling of stored procedures that are stored in the database server. This is done using the CallableStatement object. A CallableStatement object is created using the prepareCall() method on a Connection object.

A table of data is represented in the JDBC by the ResultSet interface. The ResultSet objects are usually generated by executing the SQL statements that query the database. A pointer points to a particular row of the ResultSet object at a time. This pointer is called cursor. The cursor is positioned before the first row when the ResultSet object is generated. To retrieve data from a row of ResultSet, the cursor must be positioned at the row.

The DatabaseMetaData interface provides methods to collect comprehensive information about a DBMS. We can discover features a DBMS supports and develop our application accordingly. For example, before creating a table, one may want to know what data types are supported by this DBMS.

Result sets can be scrollable in the sense that the cursor can be moved backward and forward. Additionally, a result set can be updatable, such that any change to the result set reflects in the database immediately.

The ResultSetMetaData object is used to retrieve information about the types and properties of the columns and other meta information about a ResultSet object. This is sometimes very useful, if you do not know much about the underlying database table. A ResultSetMetaData object is obtained using the getMetaData() method on the ResultSet object.

WEB RESOURCES

http://docs.oracle.com/javase/tutorial/jdbc/basics/
Lesson: JDBC Basics

http://docs.oracle.com/javase/tutorial/jdbc/
JDBC Database Access

http://www.tutorialspoint.com/jdbc/jdbc_tutorial.pdf
JDBC Tutorial

http://www.javatpoint.com/jdbc-tutorial
JDBC Tutorial

http://infolab.stanford.edu/~ullman/fcdb/oracle/or-jdbc.html
Introduction to JDBC

http://tutorials.jenkov.com/jdbc/index.html
Java JDBC

http://www.techmyguru.com/JDBC/
Java Database Connectivity (JDBC) Overview

EXERCISES

Objective-type Questions

1. Which packages contain the JDBC classes?
   (a) java.db.sql and javax.db.sql
   (b) java.jdbc and javax.jdbc
   (c) java.db and javax.db
   (d) java.sql and javax.sql

2. Which of the following drivers converts JDBC calls into network protocol, to communicate with the database management system directly?
   (a) Type 1 driver (c) Type 3 driver
   (b) Type 2 driver (d) Type 4 driver

3. Which of the following types of objects is used to execute parameterized queries?
   (a) ParameterizedStatement
   (b) Statement
   (c) PreparedStatement
   (d) All of the above

4. Which of the following methods on the Statement object is used to execute DML statements?
   (a) executeInsert() (c) executeQuery()
   (b) execute() (d) executeDML()

5. Which type of driver makes a JDBC–ODBC bridge?
   (a) Type 1 driver (c) Type 3 driver
   (b) Type 2 driver (d) Type 4 driver

6. What is the meaning of ResultSet.TYPE_SCROLL_INSENSITIVE
   (a) This means that the ResultSet is insensitive to scrolling.
   (b) This means that the ResultSet is sensitive to scrolling, but insensitive to changes made by others.
   (c) This means that the ResultSet is insensitive to scrolling and insensitive to changes made by others.
   (d) This means that the ResultSet is sensitive to scrolling, but insensitive to updates, i.e. not updateable.

7. Which of the following SQL keywords is used to read data from a database table?
   (a) SELECT (c) READ
   (b) CHOOSE (d) EXTRACT

8. Which of the following statement objects is used to call a stored procedure in JDBC?
   (a) Statement
   (b) PreparedStatement
   (c) CallableStatement
   (d) ProcedureStatement

9. Which of the following objects is used to obtain the DatabaseMetaData object?
   (a) Driver (c) Connection
   (b) DriverManager (d) ResultSet

10. Which of the following methods is used to call a stored procedure in the database?
    (a) execute() (c) call()
    (b) executeProcedure() (d) run()

11. What will be the effect if we call deleteRow() method on a ResultSet object?
   (a) The row pointed to by the cursor is deleted from the ResultSet, but not from the database.
   (b) The row pointed to by the cursor is deleted from the ResultSet and from the database.
   (c) The row pointed to by the cursor is deleted from the database, but not from the ResultSet.
   (d) None of the above

12. If you want to work with a ResultSet, which of these methods will not work on PreparedStatement?
   (a) execute() (c) executeUpdate()
   (b) executeQuery() (d) All of the above

13. Which of the following characters is used as a placeholder in CallableStatement?
   (a) $ (c) ?
   (b) @ (d) #

14. Which one of the following will not get the data from the first column of ResultSet rs, returned from executing the SQL statement: "SELECT login, password FROM USERS"?
   (a) rs.getString(0)
   (b) rs.getString("login")
   (c) rs.getString(1)
   (d) All of the above

15. Which of the following interfaces is used to control transactions?
   (a) Statement (c) ResultSet
   (b) Connection (d) DatabaseMetaData

16. Which one of the following represents the correct order?
   (a) INSERT, INTO, SELECT, FROM, WHERE
   (b) SELECT, FROM, WHERE, INSERT, INTO
   (c) INTO, INSERT, VALUES, FROM, WHERE
   (d) INSERT, INTO, WHERE, AND, VALUES

17. Which of the following is *not* a benefit of using JDBC?
   (a) JDBC programs are tightly integrated with the server operating system.
   (b) Systems built with JDBC are relatively easy to move to different platforms.
   (c) JDBC programs can be written to connect with a wide variety of databases.
   (d) JDBC programs are largely independent of the database to which they are connected.

18. In which of the following layers of the JDBC architecture does the JDBC–ODBC bridge reside?
   (a) database layer
   (b) client program layer
   (c) both client program and database layers
   (d) JDBC layer

19. Which database application model would an enterprise-wide solution most likely adopt?
   (a) The monolithic model
   (b) The two-tier model
   (c) The three-tier model
   (d) The n-tier model

20. Which code segment could execute the stored procedure "calculate()" located in a database server?
   (a) Statement stmt = connection.
       createStatement();
       stmt.execute("calculate()");
   (b) CallableStatement cs = con.
       prepareCall("{call calculate}");
       cs.executeQuery();
   (c) PrepareStatement pstmt = connection.
       prepareStatement("calculate()");
       pstmt.execute();
   (d) Statement stmt = connection.
       createStatement();
       stmt.executeStoredProcedure("calculate()");

Subjective-type Questions

1. Write the differences between Type 2 and Type 3 drivers.
2. How do you get the ResultSet of a stored procedure?
3. What is the purpose of the setAutoCommit( ) method on the Connection object?
4. How do you move the cursor in scrollable resultsets?
5. Describe the procedure we use to retrieve data from the ResultSet.
6. What are the three statements in JDBC and the differences between them?

7. How do you update a ResultSet programmatically?
8. Why do we use PreparedStatement instead of Statement?
9. What is stored procedure? How do you create a stored procedure?
10. How do you insert and delete a row programmatically?
11. What are batch updates? How are they useful?
12. What are the four types of JDBC drivers?
13. How can you use PreparedStatement ?
14. Explain the different types of JDBC drivers with their working principle.
15. What are two-tier and three-tier JDBC architecture?
16. Write the basic steps to be followed to work with JDBC.
17. Write the different types of SQL statements that can be created in JDBC with their functionality.
18. What does execute() method do? When should we use it?
19. Briefly describe how you would make a set of transactions atomic.
20. What are the advantages of pre-compiled statements over simple statements?
21. Describe briefly how do you call stored procedures in JDBC.
22. What do you mean by database metadata? How do you get them?
23. What are scrollable and updatable result sets?
24. What do you mean by result set metadata? How do you get them?

CHAPTER – 23

HIBERNATE

KEY OBJECTIVES

After completing this chapter readers will be able to—

- understand the advantage of hibernate framework over JDBC
- learn how to install and work with hibernate framework
- write and run hibernate applications
- understand the life cycle of hibernate objects
- get an idea about Hibernate Query Language
- get an overview of hibernate tools

23.1 INTRODUCTION

Hibernate is an open source Object Relational Mapping (ORM) tool. It allows us to persist Plain Old Java Objects (POJO) to the database. The POJO refers to normal Java objects that do not do any special function nor implement any special interfaces of any of the Java frameworks such as EJB, JDBC, DAO, JDO, etc. Although hibernate internally uses JDBC API to interact with the database, it simplifies the development of Java application to interact with the database. The following are some of the advantages of using hibernate:

- It is an open source framework under the LGPL licence and hence may be freely downloaded.
- Hibernate allows us to use database independent queries written in Hibernate Query Language (HQL). So, changing the underlying database is simply a matter of modifying very few lines of code.
- Hibernate internally uses several levels of caching. Hence, the performance of hibernate framework is unquestionable.
- This framework also provides the facilities to create database tables automatically. So, programmers need not know SQL syntax.
- It also supports caching queries and provides statistics about query and database status.

23.2 INSTALLING HIBERNATE

We assume that the latest version of Java is already installed on your computer. Download .zip (for windows) or .tgz (for Unix) from `http://hibernate.org/orm/downloads`. We downloaded the file `hibernate-release-4.3.1.Final.zip` and when unzipped, a set of files was generated. A sample screen shot is shown in Figure 23.1:

Name	Date modified	Type	Size
documentation	1/22/2014 12:07 PM	File folder	
lib	1/22/2014 12:07 PM	File folder	
project	1/22/2014 12:07 PM	File folder	
changelog.txt	1/22/2014 11:59 AM	Text Document	332 KB
hibernate_logo.gif	4/17/2013 12:37 PM	GIF image	2 KB
lgpl.txt	4/17/2013 12:37 PM	Text Document	26 KB

Figure 23.1: Content of `hibernate-release-4.3.1.Final.zip` file

The `lib` directory contains a set of folders containing Hibernate library. The primary JAR files to use hibernate API are stored in `lib/required` folder. Modify your `CLASSPATH` environment variable to point these JAR files or specify them using –cp option of Java and javac command. If you are using an IDE such as Eclipse, place them in your project library directory.

23.3 BASIC STEPS

A typical hibernate application is developed using the following steps:

- Writing a POGO class
- Creating a database table
- Creating configuration and mapping files
- Write code to save, retrieve, update, delete objects

23.4 WRITING POJO CLASS

The first step is to create a Java POJO class. We consider a simple class `Book` as follows:

```
//Book.java
public class Book {
   private int b_id;
   private int b_price;
   private String b_title;
   public Book(){}
   public Book(String t, int p) {
     this.b_title = t;
     this.b_price = p;
   }
   public int getId() { return b_id; }
   public void setId(int id ) { this.b_id = id; }
   public String getTitle() { return b_title; }
   public void setTitle(String t ) { this.b_title = t; }
   public int getPrice() { return b_price; }
   public void setPrice(int p ) { this.b_price = p; }
}
```

This contains three private fields `b_id`, `b_price` and `b_title` and get and set methods for these fields. The `b_id` field works like an index, whereas `b_title` and `b_price` fields store the title and price of a book respectively. It is a good idea to write a class in hibernate as JavaBeans compliant class.

23.5 CREATING A TABLE

The next step is to create a database table. Since, MySQL is one of the most popular open-source database systems available today, we shall use it to demonstrate hibernate. We assume that a MySQL instance is running in the host having IP address 172.16.5.81 and the user name and password to access this database are `root` and `nbuser` respectively. We also assume that a database `test` is already created and configured. If it does not exist, create it using the following command at the MySQL command prompt:

```
mysql> create database test;
Query OK, 1 row affected (0.00 sec)
```

Now, connect to `test` database using the following SQL command:

```
mysql> connect test;
Connection id:    88
Current database: test
```

Our database is now ready. We can create tables in it. For each class, there should exist a database table which will hold object's state (attribute values). Since, a `Book` object will have three fields (`b_id`, `b_title` and `b_price`), let us create a table `tbl_book` having three columns using the following SQL command:

```
create table tbl_book (
  no  int auto_increment,
  name varchar(80),
  pr int,
  primary key (no)
);
```

Here `no`, `name` and `pr` columns correspond to `id`, `title` and `price` fields of the `Book` class respectively.

23.6 WRITING A HIBERNATE APPLICATION

We then write a simple Java hibernate application. This first application simply stores a single `Book` object in the table book.

In this application, we first import necessary classes to work with hibernate. Two primary hibernate API packages are `org.hibernate` and `org.hibernate.cfg`. Import classes from these packages:

```
import org.hibernate.*;
import org.hibernate.cfg.*;
```

The first object that we create in a hibernate application is an `org.hibernate.cfg.Configuration` object and is usually created only once as follows:

```
Configuration cfg = new Configuration();
```

Note that hibernate needs to know, in advance, a set of configuration settings related to database and other related parameters. It must also know where to find the mapping information that defines how Java classes relate to the database tables. Hibernate finds necessary information from `Configuration` object that contains the following information:

- Configuration information such as database connection properties and hibernate properties etc. and
- Object to database table mapping information

The configuration information is stored in files called *configuration files*, which may be standard Java properties files or XML files. The object to database table mapping information, on the other hand, may be stored in XML files called *mapping files* or may be specified using annotation. The `Configuration` object loads information from these files/annotations.

The default constructor of `Configuration` class always searches a configuration file named `hibernate.properties` (which is an ordinary Java property file) in the current directory. So, create a file with this name and put configuration information there. For MySQL, it looks like this:

```
#hibernate.properties
hibernate.connection.driver_class com.mysql.jdbc.Driver
hibernate.connection.url jdbc:mysql://172.16.5.81/test
hibernate.connection.username root
hibernate.connection.password nbuser
```

Alternatively, this information may be put in an XML file (say `config.xml`) and passed to the `configure()` method of `Configuration` object as follows:

```
cfg.configure("config.xml");
```

The `config.xml` file looks like this:

```
<?xml version="1.0" encoding="utf-8"?>
<!DOCTYPE hibernate-configuration SYSTEM
"http://www.hibernate.org/dtd/hibernate-configuration-3.0.dtd">
<hibernate-configuration>
  <session-factory>
    <property name="connection.driver_class">com.mysql.jdbc.Driver</property>
    <property name="connection.url">jdbc:mysql://172.16.5.81/test</property>
    <property name="connection.username">root</property>
    <property name="connection.password">nbuser</property>
  </session-factory>
</hibernate-configuration>
```

This file essentially contains same information as `hibernate.properties` file. An XML configuration file must comply with the hibernate 3 configuration DTD, which is available from `http://www.hibernate.org/dtd/hibernate-configuration-3.0.dtd`. We may also use zero argument `configure()` method as follows:

```
cfg.configure();
```

However, this always expects an XML file with name `hibernate.cfg.xml`. Note that XML configuration file, in contrast to property configuration file, is capable of storing more information such as name of mapping files. Moreover, the syntax of XML files may be validated against the above mentioned DTD. That is why it is recommended to use XML files as configuration files instead of flat property files.

The list of supported databases with their dialect are given in Table 23.1:

Table 23.1: Supported database list

RDBMS	Dialect
MySQL5	org.hibernate.dialect.MySQL5Dialect
MySQL5 with InnoDB	org.hibernate.dialect.MySQL5InnoDBDialect
MySQL with MyISAM	org.hibernate.dialect.MySQLMyISAMDialect
Oracle (any version)	org.hibernate.dialect.OracleDialect
Oracle 9i	org.hibernate.dialect.Oracle9iDialect
Oracle 10g	org.hibernate.dialect.Oracle10gDialect

(Contd)

Table 23.1: (*Contd*)

RDBMS	Dialect
Oracle 11g	org.hibernate.dialect.Oracle10gDialect
DB2	org.hibernate.dialect.DB2Dialect
DB2 AS/400	org.hibernate.dialect.DB2400Dialect
DB2 OS390	org.hibernate.dialect.DB2390Dialect
PostgreSQL	org.hibernate.dialect.PostgreSQLDialect
Microsoft SQL Server 2000	org.hibernate.dialect.SQLServerDialect
Microsoft SQL Server 2005	org.hibernate.dialect.SQLServer2005Dialect
Microsoft SQL Server 2008	org.hibernate.dialect.SQLServer2008Dialect
SAP DB	org.hibernate.dialect.SAPDBDialect
Informix	org.hibernate.dialect.InformixDialect
HypersonicSQL	org.hibernate.dialect.HSQLDialect
H2 Database	org.hibernate.dialect.H2Dialect
Ingres	org.hibernate.dialect.IngresDialect
Progress	org.hibernate.dialect.ProgressDialect
Mckoi SQL	org.hibernate.dialect.MckoiDialect
Interbase	org.hibernate.dialect.InterbaseDialect
Pointbase	org.hibernate.dialect.PointbaseDialect
FrontBase	org.hibernate.dialect.FrontbaseDialect
Firebird	org.hibernate.dialect.FirebirdDialect
Sybase	org.hibernate.dialect.SybaseASE15Dialect
Sybase Anywhere	org.hibernate.dialect.SybaseAnywhereDialect

Anyway, so far the `Configuration` object is aware of database connection properties. Now, we have to specify the object to database table mapping information. A mapping document describes persistent fields and associations. The mapping documents are compiled at application startup time and provide necessary information for a class to the Hibernate framework. They are also used to provide support operations such as creating stub Java source files or generating the database schema etc. Mapping may also be specified in two ways:

- Using XML files called mapping files or
- Using annotation

In this section, we shall use XML file to specify mapping. Here is a sample file (`Book.hbm.xml`) that maps `Book` class to `tbl_book` table:

```
<?xml version="1.0" encoding="utf-8"?>
<!DOCTYPE hibernate-mapping PUBLIC
 "-//Hibernate/Hibernate Mapping DTD//EN"
 "http://www.hibernate.org/dtd/hibernate-mapping-3.0.dtd">
<hibernate-mapping>
   <class name="Book" table="tbl_book">
      <id name="id" type="int" column="no"/>
      <property name="title" column="name" type="string"/>
      <property name="price" column="pr" type="int"/>
   </class>
</hibernate-mapping>
```

The name of this mapping file is usually chosen as `[classname].hbm.xml`. A mapping file must have a root element `<hibernate-mapping>..</hibernate-mapping>`. The `<class>` element maps a Java class to a database table specified using name and table attributes respectively. For our example, it says that the Java class `Book` corresponds to the database table `tbl_book`.

The `<id>` element maps a unique property (specified by `name` attribute) in class to the primary key (specified by `column` attribute) of the database table. The above example tells that the unique `id` class property corresponds to primary key `no` in the table. The `<property>` element is used to map a Java class property (specified by `name` attribute) to a column (specified by `column` attribute) in the database table. In the above example, the `title` and `price` Java class properties correspond to `name` and `pr` column of table `tbl_book` respectively.

Note that for each class property `xxx`, hibernate expects get and set methods as `getXxx()` and `setXxx()` respectively. Hibernate uses these methods to get and set member fields. For properties `title` and `price`, Hibernate expects `getTitle()`, `setTitle()` and `getPrice()`, `setPrice()` methods. Needless to say that these methods really exist in our `Book` class. Hibernate uses these methods to get and set corresponding fields. Note that name of the fields need not be same as property name.

The mapping file may contain other elements and attributes, which we shall discuss in due course. Now, tell the `Configuration` object to look for mapping information in the XML file `Book.hbm.xml` as follows:

```
cfg.addResource("Book.hbm.xml");
```

The name of the mapping file may also be specified in the XML configuration file using `resource` attribute of `<mapping>` element as follows:

```
<hibernate-configuration>
  <session-factory>
    <!—Other entries-->
    <!-- List of XML mapping files -->
    <mapping resource="Book.hbm.xml"/>
  </session-factory>
</hibernate-configuration>
```

Our `Configuration` object is now complete. This reads data from configuration and mapping files and finally places them in a high level heavyweight hibernate object, the `SessionFactory` object, an instance of which may be built as follows:

```
SessionFactory factory = cfg.buildSessionFactory();
```

We then create a `Session` object, which is primary runtime interface between a Java application and Hibernate:

```
Session session = factory.openSession();
```

A `Session` object is equivalent to `Connection` object of JDBC. The main function of the `Session` object is to allow creating, reading, updating and deleting instances of mapped entity classes. In our application, we shall simply save a `Book` object. So, we create one such object:

```
Book b = new Book("Advanced Java Programming", 450);
```

For a database write (e.g. insert, update, delete) hibernate needs a logical `Transaction` to be started as follows:

```
Transaction tx = session.beginTransaction();
```

Note that for database read operations, we do not require any logical transaction in hibernate. The `Session` object provides useful methods to save, update, delete objects. We use `save()` to save our `Book` object:

```
session.save(b);
```

Note that Hibernate, by default, does not automatically commit (`autocommit` mode `false`) database transaction. So, the `save()` method merely writes `b` to the database; nothing will persist permanently in the database until the transaction performs a commit explicitly. Hence, we do it using `commit()` method of in `Transaction`:

```
tx.commit();
```

The entire source code (`SaveBook.java`) of our application is shown below:

```
//SaveBook.java
import org.hibernate.*;
import org.hibernate.cfg.*;
public class SaveBook {
  public static void main(String[] args) {
    Configuration cfg = new Configuration();
    cfg.configure("config.xml");
    cfg.addResource("Book.hbm.xml");
    SessionFactory factory = cfg.buildSessionFactory();
    Session session = factory.openSession();
    Book b = new Book("Advanced Java Programming", 450);
    Transaction tx = session.beginTransaction();
    try {
      session.save(b);
      tx.commit();
    }catch (Exception e) {
     if (tx!=null) tx.rollback();
    }
    finally { session.close(); factory.close();}
  }
}
```

23.7 COMPILING AND RUNNING APPLICATION

We created a directory structure under `E:\ajp\hib` (hereafter referred to as `hibernate_home`) shown in Figure 23.2: The directory `book` contains the file `Book.java` and `SaveBook.java` and `hibernate-release-4.3.1.Final` folder contains Hibernate API. The JAR file mysql-connector-java-5.1.26-bin.jar contains MySQL drivers.

Name	Date modified	Type	Size
book	2/21/2014 6:52 PM	File folder	
hibernate-release-4.3.1.Final	2/21/2014 6:52 PM	File folder	
mysql-connector-java-5.1.26-bin.jar	7/24/2013 2:07 AM	Executable Jar File	836 KB

Figure 23.2: Hibernate application home directory structure

Go to the `hibernate_homebook` directory and use the following command to compile `SaveBook.java`:

```
javac -cp ..\hibernate-release-4.3.1.Final\lib\required\*;. SaveBook.java
```

Now, run this application using the following command:

```
java -cp ..\hibernate-release-4.3.1.Final\lib\required\*;..\mysql-connector-java-5.1.26-bin.jar;. SaveBook
```

You may check if the application really added a row in the table book as follows:

```
mysql> select * from tbl_book;
+----+----------------------------+-------+
| id | title                      | price |
+----+----------------------------+-------+
| 32 | Advanced Java Programming  |   450 |
+----+----------------------------+-------+
1 row in set (0.00 sec)
```

23.8 USING ANNOTATION

We mentioned earlier that object to database mapping information may be specified in two ways: (i) using *XML files* (which we have used so far) and (ii) using *annotations*. One minor problem of the former method is that we need to make a separate XML file for this mapping. Annotations avoid this problem by allowing developers to specify mapping directly into the POJO Java source file. Consequently, it also develops to readily understand the object to table correspondence during class file development.

23.9 ENVIRONMENT SETUP FOR HIBERNATE ANNOTATION

The annotations used in hibernate are provided by Oracle (formerly Sun) under `javax.persistence` package and hibernate has provided implementations for annotations given in that package. So, it is necessary to download the distribution package `javax.persistence`. We downloaded the .zip file `javax.persistence.jar.zip` from `http://www.java2s.com/Code/Jar/j/Downloadjavaxpersistencejar.htm` and placed the `javax.persistence.jar` (contained in the .zip file) file in the `hibernate_home\hibernate-release-4.3.1.Final\lib\required` directory. Alternatively, place this Jar file in your CLASSPATH or specify it at compile time and runtime using `-cp` or `-classpath` option. Note that any other JAR file containing `javax.persistence` package may also be used.

23.10 BOOK APPLICATION USING ANNOTATION

Let us use our Book application to understand annotations. Change Book.java as described in the following:

Import annotation interfaces from `javax.persistence` package as follows:

```
import javax.persistence.*;
```

The complete source of the modified annotated `Book.java` is shown below:

```
//Book.java
import javax.persistence.*;
@Entity
@Table(name = "tbl_book")
public class Book {
  private int b_id;
  private int b_price;
  private String b_title;
  public Book(){}
  public Book(String t, int p) {
    this.b_title = t;
    this.b_price = p;
  }

  @Id @GeneratedValue
  @Column(name = "no")
  public int getId() { return b_id; }
  public void setId(int id ) { this.b_id = id; }
```

```
    @Column(name = "name")
    public String getTitle() { return b_title; }
    public void setTitle(String t ) { this.b_title = t; }

    @Column(name = "pr")
    public int getPrice() { return b_price; }
    public void setPrice(int p ) { this.b_price = p; }
}
```

The XML mapping file `Book.hbm.xml` is no longer needed. So, delete the following line from `SaveBook.java`:

```
cfg.addResource("Book.hbm.xml");
```

Add annotation class to the hibernate Configuration object:

```
cfg.addAnnotatedClass(Book.class);
```

The position of `@Id` annotation determines how Hibernate should access properties on objects. If it is placed on any field, Hibernate accesses object properties directly through fields. In this case, if a field name is different from a column name, `@Column` annotation must be present for that field and must provide association.

On the other hand, if `@Id` annotation is placed on any method, object properties are accessed through get and set methods. So, get and set methods must be present. In that case if property name corresponding to a get method is different from column name, `@Column` annotation must be present for that get method and must provide association.

In our previous example, `@Id` annotation is placed on the `getId()` method. Hence, Hibernate uses get and set methods to access object properties. The following annotation instructs Hibernate to access fields of Book object directly:

```
//Book.java
import javax.persistence.*;
@Entity
@Table(name = "tbl_book")
public class Book {
  @Id @GeneratedValue
  @Column(name = "no")
  private int b_id;

  @Column(name = "pr")
  private int b_price;

  @Column(name = "name")
  private String b_title;
  public Book(){}
  public Book(String t, int p) {
    this.b_title = t;
    this.b_price = p;
  }
}
```

Since, Hibernate accesses fields directly, get and set methods are not necessary for Hibernate. However, if an application wants to access those private fields, suitable methods are necessary.

23.11 FUNCTION OF DIFFERENT ANNOTATIONS

@Entity

It is used to declare a class as an Entity bean. The class should have at least a package scoped no-argument constructor.

@Table

This optional annotation is used to specify the table to store persistent objects. The value of `name` attribute refers to the table name. If none are used, Hibernate uses the class name as the table name.

@Id

It is used to specify the identifier property of the entity bean.

@GeneratedValue

This optional annotation is used to specify the primary key generation strategy to use. If none are used, default AUTO will be used.

@Column

This optional annotation is used to map a field or a property to a table column. If none are specified, by default, the property name will be used as the column name.

23.12 OBJECT LIFE CYCLE

Objects in Hibernate go through any of the three states: *transient*, *persistent* and *detached.*

Transient State

When an object is just instantiated, it is said to be in transient state. A transient object does not yet correspond to any row in the database table. Consequently, any modification on a transient object has no effect on the underlying table. Consider the following example:

```
Book aBook = new Book("Hibernate", 450);
```

Here, `aBook` is a transient object. Hibernate is not aware of `aBook` so far.

Persistent State

When an object is associated with a hibernate session in some way, it is said to be in persistent state. The following are some ways to associate an object with a session:

- Load an already existing object from database
- Store/Update an object to database

The Session interface provides a number of persistence methods to associate an object with the session such as `save()`, `update()`, `saveOrUpdate()`, `merge()`, `load()`, `get()`, `persist()`, etc.

A persistent object corresponds to a row of the database table. Persistent objects are stored in the session's cache. When a session is flushed (using `commit()` or `rollback()`), all persistent objects in session's cache are saved to the database. So, it is not mandatory to explicitly save or update persistent objects, upon modification, to the database, if they are part of an active transaction. They are saved when the transaction is committed.

Detached State

A detached object is one which was in a session's cache earlier, but no longer remains there. This may happen if

- cache is completely cleared (using `clear()` method), or
- object is removed from cache (using `evict()` method) or

- session is closed (using `close()` method),
- transaction is committed.

Unlike a transient object, a detached object did correspond to a table row. However, it does not currently correspond to any table row. A detached object, however, may be attached to a session later which makes it persistent again.

23.13 HIBERNATE QUERY LANGUAGE

Hibernate Query Language (HQL) is a query language similar to SQL but operates on persistent objects instead of tables. Hibernate translates HQL queries into SQL queries which in turn perform action on database. The advantage of HQL over SQL is that, we can avoid database portability issues and take benefits of Hibernate's SQL generation and caching strategies.

An HQL query is represented as a `Query` object which is created using `createQuery()` method of Session passing the query string to the method. Here is an example:

```
String str = "from Book";
Query query = session.createQuery(str);
```

Here "FROM Book" is an HQL query and `query` is a Query object that represents the query. The Query interface has a list of useful methods that are used to work with queries such as executing them, specifying parameters etc. Here is an example that prints the information of all persistent objects:

```
List<Book> books = query.list();
for (Book b : books)
  System.out.println(b.getId() +" "+b.getTitle()+" "+ b.getPrice());
```

The following sections describe how to use different HQL clauses.

23.13.1 From

This clause is used to obtain entire persistent objects.

```
Query query = session.createQuery("from Book");
List<Book> books = query.list();
for (Book b : books)
  System.out.println(b.getId() +" "+b.getTitle()+" "+ b.getPrice());
```

This prints the information of all persistent `Book` objects. The method `list()` executes the query and returns all of `Book` objects as a list.

23.13.2 Select

Unlike from clause which always returns entire objects, select clause can be used to obtain individual properties of the objects.

```
Query query = session.createQuery("select title, price from Book");
List<Object[]> list = (ArrayList)query.list();
```

The query only selects `title` and `price` properties of Book objects. The list() methods returns a list of Object arrays each of which has two elements—one for title and the other for the price. It can be extracted as follows:

```
for(Object[] item : list) {
  String title = (String)item[0];
  int price = ((Integer)item[1]).intValue();
  System.out.println(title+" "+price);
}
```

23.13.3 Where

It is used to filter result and can be used with `from` or `select` clause.

```
Query query = session.createQuery("from Book where price < 400");
List<Book> books = query.list();
```

The following uses `where` with `select`:

```
Query query = session.createQuery("select * from Book where price < 400");
List<Object[]> list = (ArrayList)query.list();
```

23.13.4 Filtering

It enables us to filter data obtained from the database using some query according to a custom condition. Filters have a unique name for identification and can accept parameters and can also be used with XML mapping and annotation. There are two steps to work with filters: define a filter and attach it to a mapping element. A filter in mapping file is defined using `<filter-def>` tag as follows:

```
<filter-def name="priceFilter">
    <filter-param name="price" type="java.lang.Integer" />
</filter-def>
```

This filter `priceFilter` is then attached to a class or collection:

```
<class>
  …
  <filter name="priceFilter" condition="pr &lt; :price"/>
</class>
```

Using the filter is as simple as follows:

```
Filter filter = session.enableFilter("priceFilter");
filter.setParameter("price", 400);
Query query = session.createQuery("from Book");
List<Book> books = query.list();
```

This list contains only those books whose price is less than 400.

23.13.5 Order by

This clause is used to sort the result of an HQL query either in ascending (asc) or descending (desc) order. The following query sorts the result with respect to id in ascending order:

```
Query query = session.createQuery("from Book order by id");
```

The following query sorts the result with respect to price in descending order:

```
Query query = session.createQuery("from Book order by price desc");
```

23.13.6 Group by

This is similar to SQL group by clause. Here is a simple example:

```
Query query = session.createQuery("select count(price), price from Book group
by price");
List<Object[]> list = (ArrayList)query.list();
```

This finds number of books for each price category.

23.13.7 Parameter Binding

A parameter may be passed to an HQL query by concatenating it as follows:

```
String val = "What is Hibernate?";
Query query = session.createQuery("FROM Book where title='"+val+"'");
List<Book> books = query.list();
```

This works fine as long as name does not contain any special character such as "'". For example if the name is `What's Hibernate?`, the resultant query `FROM Book where title='What is Hibernate?` becomes invalid due to the character "'" in the word `What's`. This situation can be handled in two ways: using named parameters or positional parameters.

Named Parameter

It first defines a named parameter using a colon followed by a parameter name. For example, the following defines a named parameter `:title`.

```
Query query = session.createQuery("FROM Book where title=:title");
```

The value of this named parameter may be set using `setParameter()` method as follows:

```
query.setParameter("title", val);
```

The rest of the code now works fine. Alternatively, `setString()` method may be used:

```
query.setString("title", val);
```

The Query interface has many set methods, one for each data type. The `setProperties()` method may also be used in general:

```
Book bk = new Book();
bk.setTitle(val);
query.setProperties(bk);
```

Positional Parameters

This is similar to prepared statements in SQL. In this case a parameter is defined using question mark (?).

```
Query query = session.createQuery("FROM Book where title=?");
```

We specify their values using `setParameter()` or `setString()` method. Since, parameters defined in this fashion are unnamed, we specify their positions (hence its name) instead of their names:

```
query.setParameter(0, val);
```
or
```
query.setString(0, val);
```

The basic disadvantage of this method is that if positions of parameters change, we must also change their indexes in set method.

23.13.8 Update

This is used to update one or more properties of one or more objects. The following is a simple example:

```
Query query = session.createQuery("update Book set price=400 where id=1");
int result = query.executeUpdate();
System.out.println("Rows affected: " + result);
```

23.13.9 Delete

This clause deletes one or more persistent objects. The following query when executed, deletes all Book objects having price property greater than 400.

```
Query query = session.createQuery("delete from Book where price > 400");
```

23.13.10 Insert

HQL currently supports record insertion from one object to another. Here is a simple example:

```
Query query = session.createQuery("insert into Book(title, price) select title,
price from Book where id=1");
```

23.13.11 Aggregate Methods

HQL supports a set of aggregate methods, similar to SQL and works the same way. Here is a simple example:

```
Query query = session.createQuery("select count(*) from Book");
```

23.14 USING NATIVE SQL QUERY

Since, every HQL query will finally be translated into SQL query, applications using HQL queries takes more time to run. Fortunately, Hibernate allows us to use SQL queries in our applications as well. It is sometimes useful to use database-specific features such as query hints or the CONNECT keyword in Oracle. Hibernate also allows us to query, store procedures etc. in SQL. An SQL query is created using `createSQLQuery()` method as follows:

```
SQLQuery query = session.createSQLQuery("select no, name, pr from tbl_book");
```

Note that the result of this query is an Object array. The types of array elements are determined from ResultSetMetadata. It is the responsibility of the programmer to convert array elements in proper type.

```
List<Object[]> list = (ArrayList)query.list();
for(Object[] item : list) {
  Integer id = (Integer)item[0];
  String title = (String)item[1];
  Integer price = (Integer)item[2];
  System.out.println(id+" "+title+" "+price);
}
```

However, we can (and should) explicitly indicate the data type of fields being retrieved. Below is a description of how this can be achieved.

```
query.addScalar("no", org.hibernate.type.IntegerType.INSTANCE);
query.addScalar("name", org.hibernate.type.StringType.INSTANCE);
query.addScalar("pr", org.hibernate.type.IntegerType.INSTANCE);
```

However, it requires us to manually parse the results. This can be avoided by indicating what data type is being retrieved using `addEntity()` method:

```
query.addEntity(Book.class);
```

The rest of the code works as before:

```
List<Book> books = query.list();
for (Book b : books)
  System.out.println(b.getId() +" "+b.getTitle()+" "+ b.getPrice());
```

23.15 NAMED QUERIES

Using too many queries makes Java code ugly. Fortunately, Hibernate provides a technique called *named queries* that lets us separate queries from the coding section of the application. Developers place queries in mapping xml file (.hbm files) or annotated class and assign unique names to them. A Java application can refer to those queries by their name. The following are some advantages of named queries:

- Since, queries are no longer scattered in Java code, it greatly helps in code cleanup.
- It is possible to use the same query multiple times without writing the same query multiple times.
- Their syntax is checked when the session factory is created, making the application fail safe in case of an error.
- If queries are placed in the mapping file, no recompilation is required in case of query modification. However, since most of the cases queries are cached, reloading of session factory is required which may result in server restart up.

However, named queries sometimes make debugging difficult as we have to locate the actual query definition being executed and understand that as well. In terms of performance, named queries do not make much difference nor put any extra cost. Hibernate supports both HQL as well as native SQL named queries.

23.15.1 Defining Named Queries

The named queries may be defined in the mapping file or in an annotated class.

Using Mapping File

We define an HQL named query using <query> tag in the mapping file as follows:

```
<hibernate-mapping default-access="property">
  ...
  <query name="find_All_Books_HQL">
      from Book
  </query>
  ...
</hibernate-mapping>
```

If there is a <class> element, put it before <query> element. The <query> tag has a mandatory attribute name which specifies the name assigned to the query and referred by the application. The query itself is written within the <query> tag. Since a query may contain some special characters (such as <, > etc), it is usually placed within CDATA section as follows:

```
<query name="find_Books_price_less_than_300_HQL">
  <![CDATA[from Book where price < 300]]>
</query>
```

An SQL named query is defined using <sql-query> tag as follows:

```
<sql-query name="find_All_Books_SQL">
  <return class="Book"/>
  select * from tbl_book
</sql-query>
```

The <return> tag specifies entity object to be returned by the SQL query. The CDATA section is usually used to embed query as it may contain special characters such as <, > etc. as follows:

```
<sql-query name="find_Books_price_less_than_300_SQL">
  <return class="Book"/>
  <![CDATA[select * from tbl_book where pr < 300]]>
</sql-query>
```

Using Annotation

Named HQL queries may be defined in an annotated class using @NamedQueries annotation as follows:

```
@NamedQueries({
  @NamedQuery(name="find_All_Books_HQL", query="from Book")
})
```

The @NamedQueries annotation contains a comma-separated list of queries, each of which is specified by @NamedQuery annotation. @NamedQuery annotation has two important attributes: name and query. The name specifies the name of the query by which it will be referred and the query specifies the actual HQL query string to be executed in database. Multiple queries are defined as follows:

```
@NamedQueries({
  @NamedQuery(name="find_All_Books_HQL", query="from Book"),
  @NamedQuery(name="find_Books_price_less_than_300_HQL",
    query="from Book where price < 300")
})
```

SQL named queries are defined using `@NamedNativeQueries` and `@NamedNativeQuery` annotations.

```
@NamedNativeQueries({
  @NamedNativeQuery(name="find_All_Books_SQL", query = "select * from tbl_book",
    resultClass=Book.class
  ),
})
```

The `resultClass` attribute specifies entity to be returned by the SQL query. Multiple queries are defined as follows:

```
@NamedNativeQueries({
  @NamedNativeQuery(name="find_All_Books_SQL", query = "select * from tbl_book",
    resultClass=Book.class),
  @NamedNativeQuery(name="find_Books_price_less_than_300_SQL",
    query = "select * from tbl_book where pr < 300", resultClass=Book.class)
})
```

The names of queries must be unique in XML mapping files or annotations. In practice, it's always a good idea to place all named queries in a separate file and include it in the Java code or in the configuration file. Here is an example of named query file (`NQ.hbm.xml`):

```
<?xml version="1.0" encoding="utf-8"?>
<!DOCTYPE hibernate-mapping SYSTEM
 "http://www.hibernate.org/dtd/hibernate-mapping-3.0.dtd">
<hibernate-mapping>
  <query name="find_All_Books_HQL"><![CDATA[from Book]]></query>
  <sql-query name="find_All_Books_SQL">
    <return class="Book"/>
    <![CDATA[select * from tbl_book]]
  </sql-query>
</hibernate-mapping>
```

To include this file in Java code, use `addResource()` of `Configuration` object as follows:

```
Configuration cfg = new Configuration();
//add configuration file
cfg.addResource("NQ.hbm.xml");
```

Alternatively, include the mapping resource in the configuration file (say `config.xml`) using `<mapping resource="NQ.hbm.xml"/>` and add the configuration file as follows:

```
cfg.configure("config.xml");
```

23.15.2 Calling Named Queries

Once a query is defined, it's name may be used in `getNamedQuery()` method to create a `Query` object as follows:

```
Query query = session.getNamedQuery("find_All_Books_HQL");
```

Execute the query calling its list() method:

```
List<Book> books = query.list();
```

This list can then be iterated to obtain information about all Book objects as follows:

```
for (Book b : books)
  System.out.println(b.getId() +" "+b.getTitle()+" "+ b.getPrice());
```

Here is the complete source code (`NamedQueryTest.java`) of Java program that uses named query stored in `NQ.hbm.xml` file:

```
//NamedQueryTest.java
import org.hibernate.*;
import org.hibernate.cfg.*;
import java.util.*;
public class NamedQueryTest {
```

```
public static void main(String[] args) {
  Configuration cfg = new Configuration();
  cfg.configure("config.xml");
  cfg.addResource("Book.hbm.xml");
  cfg.addResource("NQ.hbm.xml");

  SessionFactory factory = cfg.buildSessionFactory();
  Session session = factory.openSession();
  Transaction tx=session.beginTransaction();

  try {
    Query query = session.getNamedQuery("find_All_Books_HQL");
    List<Book> books = query.list();
    for (Book b : books)
      System.out.println(b.getId() +" "+b.getTitle()+" "+ b.getPrice());

    tx.commit();
  }catch (Exception e) {
   e.printStackTrace();
   if (tx!=null) tx.rollback();
  }
  finally { session.close();factory.close();}
 }
}
```

23.16 GENERATING DDL

Hibernate also provides useful classes to generate DDL. The generated schema may be printed to the console, stored in a file for later use or even exported to a database. The `org.hibernate.tool.hbm2ddl.SchemaExport` class can be used for these purposes. The SchemaExport object is created from a given Configuration object as follows:

```
SchemaExport schemaExport = new SchemaExport(cfg);
```

The schema is then created using its `create()` method:

```
boolean print = true, export = true;
schemaExport.create(print, true);
```

This runs the schema creation script. The drop() method is automatically executed before running the creation script. The variables `print` and `export` indicate that the schema has to be printed to the console and exported to the database. The following is the complete source code of the program:

```
//GenerateDDL.java
import org.hibernate.cfg.*;
import org.hibernate.tool.hbm2ddl.*;
public class GenerateDDL {
  public static void main(String[] args) {
    Configuration cfg = new Configuration();
    cfg.configure("config.xml");
    cfg.addResource("Book.hbm.xml");
    SchemaExport schemaExport = new SchemaExport(cfg);
    schemaExport.setDelimiter(";");
    schemaExport.setOutputFile("out.sql");
    boolean print = true, export = true;
    schemaExport.create(print, true);
  }
}
```

The program also stores the schema in a file out.sql containing the following SQL statements:

```
drop table if exists tbl_book;
create table tbl_book (
```

```
        no integer not null auto_increment,
        name varchar(255),
        pr integer,
        primary key (no)
    );
```

If you check the database, you will find that the table `tbl_book` is created by the above program.

```
mysql> desc tbl_book;
+-------+--------------+------+-----+---------+----------------+
| Field | Type         | Null | Key | Default | Extra          |
+-------+--------------+------+-----+---------+----------------+
| no    | int(11)      | NO   | PRI | NULL    | auto_increment |
| name  | varchar(255) | YES  |     | NULL    |                |
| pr    | int(11)      | YES  |     | NULL    |                |
+-------+--------------+------+-----+---------+----------------+
3 rows in set (0.01 sec)
```

23.17 SYNTAX OF O/R MAPPING FILE

The root element of an XML mapping document is `<hibernate-mapping>`, which has many optional attributes. The list of possible attributes with their possible values is shown below:

```
<hibernate-mapping package="package.name" auto-import="true|false"
   schema="schemaName" catalog="catalogName" default-cascade="cascade_style"
   default-access="field|property|ClassName" default-lazy="true|false"/>
```

A short description of each of these attributes is given below:

`package`: Specifies a package prefix to be used for unqualified class names

`auto-import` (default is `true`): Specifies whether we can use unqualified class names in the query language

`schema`: The name of a database schema

`catalog`: The name of a database catalog

`default-cascade` (default is none): The default cascade style

`default-access` (default is `property`): Specifies the strategy Hibernate should use to access all properties. It may be a custom implementation of PropertyAccessor. When `default-access` is property, Hibernate identifies property names corresponding to table columns from mapping files. It then uses corresponding get and set methods to access the values of the object fields.

`default-lazy` (default is `true`): Specifies the policy for unspecified lazy attributes of class and collection mappings

The <class> element

This element maps the domain object with the corresponding entity in the database. The <hibernate-mapping> element allows us to nest several persistent <class> mappings. However, it recommended to map only a single persistent class in one mapping file and name it after the persistent superclass, e.g. Book.hbm.xml, Employee.hbm.xml. The list of possible attributes with their possible values is shown below:

```
<class
name="ClassName"
table="tableName"
discriminator-value="discriminator_value"
mutable="true|false"
schema="owner"
catalog="catalog"
proxy="ProxyInterface"
```

```
    dynamic-update="true|false"
    dynamic-insert="true|false"
    select-before-update="true|false"
    polymorphism="implicit|explicit"
    where="arbitrary sql where condition"
    persister="PersisterClass"
    batch-size="N"
    optimistic-lock="none|version|dirty|all"
    lazy="true|false"
    entity-name="EntityName"
    catalog="catalog"
    check="arbitrary sql check condition"
    rowid="rowid"
    subselect="SQL expression"
    abstract="true|false"
    />
```

The following is a brief description of each of the possible attributes:

`name (optional):`

The fully qualified Java class name of the persistent class/interface. If this attribute is absent, it is considered that the mapping is for a non-POJO entity.

`table (optional - defaults to the unqualified class name):`

The name of table in database

`discriminator-value (optional - defaults to the class name):`

A value that distinguishes individual subclasses, used for polymorphic behaviour

`mutable (optional, defaults to true):`

Specifies if the instances of the class are mutable

`schema (optional):`

Override the schema name specified by the root `<hibernate-mapping>` element

`catalog (optional):`

Override the catalog name specified by the root `<hibernate-mapping>` element

`proxy (optional):`

Specifies an interface to use for lazy initializing proxies

`dynamic-update (optional, defaults to false):`

Specifies that update SQL statement should be generated at runtime and contain only those columns whose values have changed

`dynamic-insert (optional, defaults to false):`

Specifies that insert SQL statements should be generated at runtime and contain only the columns whose values are not null

`select-before-update (optional, defaults to false):`

Specifies that Hibernate should never perform an SQL update unless it is certain that an object is actually modified

`polymorphism (optional, defaults to implicit):`

Determines whether implicit or explicit query polymorphism is used

`where (optional):`

Specifies an arbitrary SQL WHERE condition to be used when retrieving objects of this class

`persister (optional):`

Specifies a custom ClassPersister

`batch-size (optional, defaults to 1):`

Specifies the batch size for fetching instances of this class by identifier

`optimistic-lock (optional, defaults to version):`

Determines the optimistic locking strategy

`lazy (optional):`

Lazy fetching may be completely disabled by setting lazy="false"

`entity-name (optional):`

Hibernate version 3 allows a class to be mapped multiple times and also allows entity mappings that are represented by Maps or XML at the Java level. In these cases, we provide an arbitrary name for the entity explicitly.

`catalog (optional):`

The name of a database catalog used for this class and its table

`check (optional):`

An SQL expression used to generate a multi-row check constraint for automatic schema generation

`rowid (optional):`

Hibernate can use the rowid extra column (for databases such as Oracle) for fast updates if this option is set to rowid

`subselect (optional):`

Maps an immutable and read-only entity to a database subselect. Useful if you want to have a view instead of a base table, but don't

`abstract (optional):`

Used to mark abstract super classes in `<union-subclass>` hierarchies

23.18 GENERATOR CLASS

The `<generator>` sub-element of `<id>` specifies how to generate the unique identifier for the persistent objects. Hibernate defines many generator classes which implement `org.hibernate.id.IdentifierGenerator` interface. It is also possible to write a generator class implementing this interface. The type of generator is indicated in the `<generator>` element using class attribute as follows:

```
<generator class="generator type"></generator>
```

Some of the built-in generator classes with their functions are discussed in Table 23.2:

Table 23.2: Built-in generator classes with their functions

Generator type	Description
assigned	Default strategy. Application must assign the id.
increment	It generates the unique id. The first generated identifier is usually 1 and is incremented by 1.
identity	Similar to increment, but database dependent.
sequence	It uses the sequence of the database. Creates a sequence HIBERNATE_SEQUENCE automatically if there is none. Database specific.
hilo	It uses high and low (hence the hilo) algorithm to generate the id.

(Contd)

Table 23.2: (*Contd*)

Generator type	Description
native	It tries to use identity, sequence or hilo depending on the availability in the database.
seqhilo	It uses high and low algorithm on the specified sequence name.
uuid	It uses 128-bit UUID algorithm to generate the String id which is unique within a network as IP is used. It is represented by 32 hexadecimal digits.
guid	It uses GUID generated by database of type string.
select	It uses the primary key returned by the database trigger.
foreign	It uses the id of another associated object, mostly used with <one-to-one/> association.
sequence-identiy	It uses a special sequence generation strategy. It is supported in Oracle 10g drivers only.

23.19 HIBERNATE TOOLS

Hibernate tools is a set of utilities used to automatically generate various resources such as

- Java source files, database schemas and DAO classes from mapping file
- Mapping file from database schema etc.

It only works either as an Eclipse plug-in or in JBoss Developer Studio or with Apache Ant. When used with Eclipse, it provides an editor to edit mapping files and a console. The editor also supports auto-completion and syntax highlighting and semantic auto-completion for class names, property/field names, table names and column names. The console allows us to configure database connections, provides visualization of classes and their relationships with tables and allows us to execute HQL queries interactively against database and view the query results.

In this section, we shall discuss how to use Hibernate Tools with Ant. If you are new to Ant, you can read its manual from `http://ant.apache.org/manual/index.html`. We shall create a stand-alone ant build file with the minimum number of required libraries.

23.19.1 Using Hibernate Tools with Ant

This section describes how to install and configure Hibernate Tools to work with Apache Ant. If it is not already installed in your machine, download it from `https://ant.apache.org/bindownload.cgi`. We downloaded `apache-ant-1.9.3-bin.zip` and when unzipped in `D:` drive (in windows), the following directory structure was created. The primary utility `ant.bat` may be found in `bin` directory. To use this utility, either place this directory in your PATH environment variable or use fully qualified path name of this utility.

```
apache-ant-1.9.3
    bin
    etc
    lib
    manual
```

A set of JAR files is needed to work with Hibernate tools. We downloaded the following JAR files from `www.java2s.com`: and placed in a directory `antlib`.

```
dom4j-1.6.1.jar
freemarker-2.3.19.jar
hibernate3.jar
hibernate-tools.jar
javax.persistence.jar
jtidy-r872-jdk15.jar
log4j-1.2.15.jar
mysql-connector-java-5.1.13.jar
org.apache.commons-logging-1.0.4.jar
slf4j-api-1.5.8.jar
```

The primary JAR file for Hibernate tools is `hibernate-tools.jar`. The JAR `hibernate-3.2.2.jar` contains core Hibernate and annotation library. The rest of the files are required by Ant build utility. The Hibernate Tools is now ready to work with Ant.

23.19.2 Ant Task

The ant runs on a specified XML file containing build information. If none is supplied, ant assumes a file `build.xml`. A typical structure of this file is shown below:

```
<project>
  …
</project>
```

Create an ant task for our Hibernate Tool in the `<project>` element as follows:

```
<project>
  …
  <path id="libpath">
    <fileset dir="antlib" includes="*.jar"/>
  </path>

  <taskdef name="MyTask" classname="org.hibernate.tool.ant.HibernateToolTask"
        classpathref="libpath" />
  …
</project>
```

This makes a task called `MyTask` and the class `org.hibernate.tool.ant.HibernateToolTask` implements the task. This task can now be used anywhere in the Ant build.xml file:

```
<project>
  <path id="libpath">
    <fileset dir="antlib" includes="*.jar"/>
  </path>

  <taskdef name="MyTask" classname="org.hibernate.tool.ant.HibernateToolTask"
        classpathref="libpath" />
  <MyTask destdir="./target">
    …
  </MyTask>
…
</project>
```

The required attribute `destDir` specifies that directory to be used to place generated files by exporters.

23.19.3 Configuring Task

The task, to do its function, reads metadata from some files which are specified as follows:

```
<configuration configurationfile="config.xml">
   <fileset dir="." includes="Book.hbm.xml"/>
</configuration>
```

This tells the task to read configuration and mapping data from files `config.xml` and `Book.hbm.xml` respectively. These are the files we used earlier to develop hibernate application. Only use the following DOCTYPE for correct operation:

```
http://hibernate.sourceforge.net/hibernate-mapping-3.0.dtd
```

Since it gathers metamodel information from standard files, it is called *standard configuration*. Given a configuration file and XML mapping files this configuration is usually used to generate database schema and Java POJO and DAO source files, documentation files etc. In general, a standard configuration takes the following form:

```
<configuration
  configurationfile="hibernate.cfg.xml"
  propertyfile="hibernate.properties"
  entityresolver="EntityResolver classname"
  namingstrategy="NamingStrategy classname"
>
    <fileset...>
  </configuration>
```

In addition to standard configuration, Hibernate tools also support annotation and JDBC-based configurations. An annotation-based configuration is used to read the meta model from annotated class and is created using `<annotationconfiguration>` tag as follows:

```
<annotationconfiguration configurationfile="config.xml" />
```

The annotated class is specified in the config.xml as follows:

```
<mapping class="Book"/>
```

Given an annotated class this can be used to create database schema, mapping file and DAO class, documentation files etc.

A JDBC-based configuration is used to perform reverse engineering of a database from a JDBC connection using `<jdbcconfiguration>` tag. Here is an example JDBC configuration:

```
<jdbcconfiguration configurationfile="config.xml" />
```

It reads the connection properties from an XML configuration file and may be used to generate Java POJO and DAO source files, mapping files, documentation etc. A JDBC configuration takes all attributes of `<configuration>` tag together with the following additional attributes:

```
<jdbcconfiguration
  ...
  packagename="package.name"
  revengfile="hibernate.reveng.xml"
  reversestrategy="ReverseEngineeringStrategy classname"
  detectmanytomany="true|false"
  detectoptmisticlock="true|false"
>
  ...
  </jdbcconfiguration>
```

23.19.4 Exporters

These are the tags which actually convert the Hibernate metamodel into various artifacts. The following section describes various exporters available in the Hibernate Tool distribution.

Schema Exporter

For standard or annotation configuration and given a metamodel, this exporter (`<hbm2ddl>`) generates SQL DDL statements, which can be stored in a file and/or exported to the database directly.

```
<MyTask destdir="./dest">
  <configuration configurationfile="config.xml">
    <fileset dir="." includes="Book.hbm.xml"/>
  </configuration>
   <hbm2ddl export="true" outputfilename="out.sql"/>
</MyTask>
```

It is used with standard configuration and generates the following SQL DDL query and stores it in a file `out.sql`:

```
create table tbl_book (
    no integer not null auto_increment,
    name varchar(255),
    pr integer,
    primary key (no)
);
```

The notation `export="true"` instructs the exporter to fire this query to the database also. The result may be checked using the following SQL statements:

```
mysql> desc tbl_book;
+-------+--------------+------+-----+---------+----------------+
| Field | Type         | Null | Key | Default | Extra          |
+-------+--------------+------+-----+---------+----------------+
| no    | int(11)      | NO   | PRI | NULL    | auto_increment |
| name  | varchar(255) | YES  |     | NULL    |                |
| pr    | int(11)      | YES  |     | NULL    |                |
+-------+--------------+------+-----+---------+----------------+
3 rows in set (0.01 sec)
```

Annotation configuration may also be used to generate the same as follows:

```
<MyTask destdir="./dest">
    <classpath><path location="." /></classpath>
  <annotationconfiguration configurationfile="config.xml" />
  <hbm2ddl export="true" outputfilename="out.sql"/>
</MyTask>
```

An additional <classpath> tag is necessary in this situation. In general <hbm2ddl> takes the following form:

```
<hbm2ddl drop="true|false" create="true|false" export="true|false"
 update="true|false" outputfilename="filename.ddl" delimiter=";"
 format="true|false" >
```

POJO Class Exporter

This exporter (<hbm2java/>) generates Java POJO source files from any type of configuration. It takes the following form:

```
<hbm2java jdk5="true|false" ejb3="true|false" />
```

The jdk5 attribute controls if the code is JDK 5 compatible and ejb3 controls if the code should contain annotations. Here is an example:

```
<MyTask destdir="./dest">
   <configuration configurationfile="config.xml">
    <fileset dir="." includes="Book.hbm.xml"/>
   </configuration>
   <hbm2java/>
</MyTask>
```

When used, it generated a POJO class `Book.java` in the `dest` directory as follows:

```
// default package
// Generated Mar 1, 2014 5:19:24 AM by Hibernate Tools 3.2.1.GA
/**
 * Book generated by hbm2java
 */
public class Book  implements java.io.Serializable {
  private int id;
  private String title;
  private int price;
  public Book() { }
  public Book(String title, int price) {
       this.title = title;
```

```
        this.price = price;
    }
    public int getId() {  return this.id; }
    public void setId(int id) { this.id = id; }
    public String getTitle() { return this.title; }
    public void setTitle(String title) { this.title = title; }
    public int getPrice() { return this.price; }
    public void setPrice(int price) { this.price = price; }
}
```

The following example generates an annotated Java source file.

```
<hbm2java ejb3="true" />
```

DAO Exporter

Hibernate tools also allows us to create DAO via `<hbm2dao>` exporter as follows:

```
<MyTask destdir="./dest">
   <configuration configurationfile="config.xml">
    <fileset dir="." includes="Book.hbm.xml"/>
   </configuration>
   <hbm2dao/>
</MyTask>
```

When used, it generated a DAO class file `BookHome.java` for Book in the `dest` directory as follows:

```
// default package
// Generated Mar 1, 2014 5:19:24 AM by Hibernate Tools 3.2.1.GA

import java.util.List;
import javax.naming.InitialContext;
import org.apache.commons.logging.Log;
import org.apache.commons.logging.LogFactory;
import org.hibernate.LockMode;
import org.hibernate.SessionFactory;
import org.hibernate.criterion.Example;

/**
 * Home object for domain model class Book.
 * @see Book
 * @author Hibernate Tools
 */
public class BookHome {
  private static final Log log = LogFactory.getLog(BookHome.class);
  private final SessionFactory sessionFactory = getSessionFactory();
  protected SessionFactory getSessionFactory() {
    try {
      return (SessionFactory) new InitialContext().lookup("SessionFactory");
    } catch (Exception e) {
      log.error("Could not locate SessionFactory in JNDI", e);
    throw new IllegalStateException("Could not locate SessionFactory in JNDI");
    }
  }
  public void persist(Book transientInstance) {
    log.debug("persisting Book instance");
    try {
      sessionFactory.getCurrentSession().persist(transientInstance);
      log.debug("persist successful");
    } catch (RuntimeException re) {
      log.error("persist failed", re);
      throw re;
    }
  }
  ...
}
```

This DAO class can then be used to load, store `Book` objects to the database. However, this generated class `BookHome.java` does not use persistence methods such as `persist()` within a transaction boundary, which is required for correct function of these methods. Usually, a layer above the DAO is used to control the Transaction boundaries. This might be Container Managed Transaction (CMT) or a manually managed transaction boundary. We use the latter method and insert a constructor as follows:

```
public BookHome(SessionFactory sf) {this.sessionFactory = sf;}
```

We also change the declaration of `sessionFactory` as follows:

```
private final SessionFactory sessionFactory;
```

To test this DAO, we write a test class DAOTest.java as follows:

```
//DAOTest.java
import org.hibernate.*;
import org.hibernate.cfg.*;
public class DAOTest {
  public static void main(String[] args) {
    Configuration cfg = new Configuration();
    cfg.configure("config.xml");
    cfg.addResource("Book.hbm.xml");
    SessionFactory factory = cfg.buildSessionFactory();
    BookHome dao = new BookHome(factory);
    Transaction tx=factory.getCurrentSession().beginTransaction();
    Book b = new Book("Introduction to Hibernate", 400);
    dao.persist(b);
    tx.commit();
    factory.getCurrentSession().close();
    factory.close();
  }
}
```

Don't forget to add the following property in `config.xml` file:

```
<property name="hibernate.current_session_context_class">thread</property>
```

The `BookHome.java` needs a package `org.apache.commons.logging` which can be found in `org.apache.commons-logging-1.0.4.jar` file. Put all the necessary JAR files in a directory `required` under the current directory. Use the following command to compile source files:

```
javac -cp .\required\*;. Book.java BookHome.java DAOTest.java
```

Run the application as follows:

```
java -cp .\required\*;. DAOTest
```

Check the database as follows:

```
mysql> select * from tbl_book;
+----+---------------------------+------+
| no | name                      | pr   |
+----+---------------------------+------+
|  1 | Introduction to Hibernate |  400 |
+----+---------------------------+------+
1 row in set (0.00 sec)
```

Mapping File Exporter

This exporter is used to generate hibernate mapping files and is usually intended to use with `<annotationconfiguration>` or `<jdbcconfiguration>`. Here is an example:

```
<jdbcconfiguration configurationfile="config.xml" />
<hbm2hbmxml/>
```

It generates a set of mapping files one for each table in the database specified by config.xml file.

```
<annotationconfiguration configurationfile="config.xml" />
<hbm2hbmxml/>
```

This generates mapping files one for each <mapping class=".."/> entry in config.xml file.

Configuration File Exporter

The <hbm2cfgxml> exporter generates XML configuration file with name hibernate.cfg.xml.

```
<jdbcconfiguration configurationfile="config.xml" />
<hbm2cfgxml ejb3="false"/>
```

The resultant configuration file hibernate.cfg.xml contains properties used in config.xml and adds a few more and adds mapping entries for each mapped class. Depending on the value of optional (default is false) attribute ejb3, the mapping entries take the form <mapping resource="..."/> (false) or <mapping class=".."/> (true).

Documentation Exporter

The <hbm2doc> generates HTML documentation for Java Source files and database schema. It takes the following form:

```
<hbm2doc>
```

HBM Query Exporter

The <query> exporter is used to execute HQL statements and optionally storing the result in a file. It takes the following form:

```
<query destfile="filename">HQL statement</query>
```

The following JAR file is needed to work with query exporter:

```
antlr_2.7.6.jar
commons.collections-3.2.1.jar
javassist-3.10.0.GA.jar
javax.transaction.jar
```

The following example stores the title of the books having price less than 300 in a file out.txt.

```
<query destfile="out.txt">select title from Book where price &lt; 300</query>
```

Multiple statement can be executed using nested <hql> elements as

```
<query destfile="filename">
  <hql>HQL statement1</hql>
  <hql>HQL statement2</hql>
  ...
</query>
```

Here is an example:

```
<query destfile="out.txt">
   <hql>select title from Book where price &lt; 300</hql>
   <hql>select count(*) from Book where price &lt; 300</hql>
</query>
```

This first stores the titles of the books having price less than 300 and finally appends the number of such books. Note that currently <query> exporter only supports DDL statements.

23.19.5 Controlling Reverse Engineering

A JDBC configured Ant task reads database metadata and creates a Hibernate metamodel. During this reverse engineering, a default strategy is used to map SQL types to Java types, to determine class names etc. For example, an SQL type `VARCHAR` is converted to Java `String` etc. However, this strategy may be customized by the user. This is done by providing the strategy as an XML file (usually `hibernate.reveng.xml`) and specifying it as a value `revengfile` attribute of `<jdbcconfiguration>` tag as follows:

```
<jdbcconfiguration configurationfile="config.xml"
revengfile="hibernate.reveng.xml"/>
```

The following additional JAR files are needed to work with custom reverse engineering:

```
cglib-2.1_3.jar
asm-1.5.3.jar
```

A sample reverse engineering strategy file takes the following form:

```
<?xml version="1.0" encoding="UTF-8"?>
<!DOCTYPE hibernate-reverse-engineering SYSTEM
"http://hibernate.sourceforge.net/hibernate-reverse-engineering-3.0.dtd" >
<hibernate-reverse-engineering>
  …
</hibernate-reverse-engineering>
```

To control the reverse engineering process `<hibernate-reverse-engineering>` tag contains various tags which must match (schema-selection*, type-mapping?, table-filter*, table*).

Schema Selection

By default the reverse engineering reads all tables from all schemas. This is sometimes unnecessary and may slow down the process. The `<schema-selection>` tag is used to select only necessary schemas which in turn can speed-up the process significantly. It takes the following form:

```
<schema-selection match-schema="schema"  match-catalog="catalog"
  match-table="table" />
```

The following example instructs reverse engineer to process all tables from the schema `test`.

```
<schema-selection match-schema="test" />
```

The following results in processing only table `tbl_book` from schema `test`:

```
<schema-selection match-schema="test" match-table="tbl_book"/>
```

Type Mappings

The `<type-mapping>` tag specifies how the database types should be mapped to Hibernate types. It takes the following form:

```
<type-mapping>
 <sql-type
  jdbc-type="a java.sql.Types"
  length="a numeric value"
  precision="a numeric value"
  scale="a numeric value"
  not-null="true|false"
  hibernate-type="a hibernate type name"
 />
</type-mapping>
```

Here is an example:

```
<type-mapping>
 <sql-type jdbc-type="VARCHAR" length='1' hibernate-type='char' />
</type-mapping>
```

This specifies that a JDBC type `VARCHAR` with length 1 should be mapped to Hibernate type `char` instead of default type `string`. The following maps `VARCHAR` with length 10 as `char[]`.

```
<sql-type jdbc-type="VARCHAR" length='10' hibernate-type='char[]' />
```

Table Filters

The <table-filter> tag is used to include or exclude specific tables based on the schema. It takes the following form:

```
<table-filter
   match-catalog="catalog_matching_rule"
   match-schema="schema_matching_rule"
   match-name="table_matching_rule"
   exclude="true|false"
   package="package.name"
/>
```

The following results in processing of only table tbl_book.

```
<table-filter match-name="tbl_book" />
```

Table Configuration

The <table> tag enables us to explicitly specify how to reverse engineer a particular table. For example, we can specify class and property names corresponding to table and table columns, which identifier generator should be used for the primary key etc. It takes the following form:

```
<table catalog="a catalog" schema="a schema" name="a table" class="a class" >
  <primary-key.../>
  <column.../>
  <foreign-key.../>
</table>
```

Here is an example:

```
<table schema="test" name="tbl_book" class="Book" >
  <column name="no" property="id"/>
  <column name="name" property="title"/>
  <column name="pr" property="price"/>
</table>
```

This tells that the name of the resultant class corresponding to table tbl_book should be Book and names of the properties corresponding to table columns no, name and pr should be id, title and price respectively.

23.19.6 Controlling POJO Code Generation

Hibernate tools also support controlling certain aspects of custom POJO code generation using <meta> tag to be used in mapping file. The <meta> tag has different attributes that tells what information has to be placed in the resultant POJO code. Here is an example:

```
<hibernate-mapping default-access="property">
  <class name="Book" table="tbl_book">
    <meta attribute="class-description">
      Javadoc for the Book class
      @author UKR
    </meta>
    <meta attribute="implements">Resource</meta>
    <id name="id" type="int" column="no">
      <meta attribute="field-description">Unique id</meta>
      <generator class="native"/>
    </id>
    <property name="title" column="name" type="string"/>
    <property name="price" column="pr" type="int">
      <meta attribute="field-description">The price of the book</meta>
      <meta attribute="scope-field">protected</meta>
    </property>
  </class>
</hibernate-mapping>
```

When used, this generated the following class:

```
// default package
// Generated Mar 3, 2014 7:19:01 PM by Hibernate Tools 3.4.0.CR1
/**
 *        Javadoc for the Book class
 *        @author UKR
 *
 */
public class Book  implements Resource,java.io.Serializable {
    /**
     * Unique id
    */
    private int id;
    private String title;
    /**
     * The price of the book
    */
    protected int price;
   public Book() { }
   public Book(String title, int price) {
      this.title = title;
      this.price = price;
   }
   /**
    *      * Unique id
    */
   public int getId() { return this.id; }
   public void setId(int id) { this.id = id; }
   public String getTitle() { return this.title; }
   public void setTitle(String title) { this.title = title; }
   /**
    *      * The price of the book
    */
   public int getPrice() { return this.price; }
   public void setPrice(int price) { this.price = price;}
}
```

The result of `<meta>` tag has been shown with bold face. A short description of list of attributes of `<meta>` tag is shown in Table 23.3:

Table 23.3: Meta tag attributes

Meta Attribute	Description
class-code	Extra code to be inserted at the end of the class
class-description	Javadoc description of classes
default-value	Default initial value for a field
extends	Class that the current class should extend
extra-import	Extra import to be inserted at the end of all other imports
field-description	Javadoc description of fields and properties
generated-class	Override the name of the actual class generated
gen-property	If property should be generated
implements	Interface the class should implement
interface	Generates an interface instead of class

(Contd)

Table 23.3: (*Contd*)

Meta Attribute	Description
property-type	Overrides the default type of property
scope-class	Scope of the class
scope-field	Scope of the field
scope-get	scope of the get method
scope-set	Scope of the set method
use-in-equals	Include this property in the equals() and hashCode() methods
use-in-tostring	Include this property in the toString() method

KEYWORDS

Column annotation—A hibernate annotation used to map a field or a property to a table column

Configuration—A class whose instance allows the application to specify properties and mapping documents to be used

Configuration files—Standard Java properties files or XML files containing hibernate configuration information

Detached—A detached object is one which was in a session's cache earlier, but no longer remains there

Entity annotation—A hibernate annotation used to declare a class as an Entity bean

Exporters—Tags which actually convert the Hibernate metamodel into various artifacts such as schema, POJO class, DAO etc.

GeneratedValue annotation—A hibernate annotation used to specify the primary key generation strategy to use

Generator class—Specifies how to generate primary key in the database table

Hibernate Tools—A set of utilities used to automatically generate various resources

HQL—A query language similar to SQL but operates on persistent objects instead of tables

Id annotation—A hibernate annotation used to specify the identifier property of the entity bean

Mapping files—XML files containing object to database table mapping information

Named Queries—HQL queries that can be identified by their names

Object Life Cycle—The period objects in Hibernate go through different states

Persistent—When an object is associated with a hibernate session in some way, it is said to be in persistent state

POJO—Java objects that do not do any special function nor implement any special interfaces of any of the Java frameworks

Reverse Engineering—Creating hibernate metamodel from database metadata

Session—The main runtime interface between a Java application and Hibernate that abstracts the notion of a persistence service

Table annotation—A hibernate annotation used to specify the table to store persistent objects

Transaction—An interface that defines the contract for abstracting applications from the configured underlying means of transaction management

Transient—When an object is just instantiated, it is said to be in transient state

SUMMARY

Hibernate allows us to persist Plain Old Java Objects (POJO) to the database. Hibernate supports virtually all databases.

A typical hibernate application is developed using the following steps

- Writing a POGO class
- Creating a database table
- Creating configuration and mapping files
- Write code to save, retrieve, update, delete objects

A hibernate application starts with a Configuration object that contains information such as database connection properties and hibernate properties etc. and object to database table mapping information. These are specified using configuration files and mapping files and or/annotations.

This information is actually place in a SessionFactory object. The interface between Java application and hibernate is the Session object which is created from SessionFactory object. A `Session` object is equivalent to `Connection` object of JDBC. The main function of the `Session` object is to allow creating, reading, updating and deleting instances of mapped entity classes. For a database write (e.g. insert, update, delete) hibernate needs a logical transaction which is represented by a `Transaction` object.

Objects in Hibernate go through any of the three states: *transient*, *persistent* and *detached*. When an object is just instantiated, it is said to be in transient state. When an object is associated with a hibernate session in some way, it is said to in persistent state. A detached object is one which was in a session's cache earlier, but no longer remains there.

Hibernate **Q**uery **L**anguage (HQL) is a query language similar to SQL but operates on persistent objects instead of tables. Hibernate translates HQL queries into SQL queries which in turn perform action on database. The advantage of HQL over SQL is that, we can avoid database portability issues and take benefits of Hibernate's SQL generation and caching strategies.

Hibernate provides a technique called *named queries* that lets us separate queries from the coding section of the application. Hibernate also provides useful classes to generate DDL.

Hibernate tools is a set of utilities used to automatically generate various resources such as

- Java source files, database schemas and DAO classes from mapping file
- Mapping file from database schema, etc.

It only works either as an Eclipse plug-in or in JBoss Developer Studio or with Apache Ant. We discussed how to use Hibernate Tools with Ant. Exporters are tags which actually convert the Hibernate metamodel into various artifacts. Some of the useful exporters are POJO class exporter, DAO exporter, Mapping file exporter, configuration file exporter, HBM query exporter etc. With the help of reverse engineering, it is also possible to create hibernate metamodel from database metadata.

WEB RESOURCES

`http://docs.jboss.org/hibernate/core/3.3/reference/en/html/tutorial.html`
Hibernate Tutorial

`http://www.tutorialspoint.com/hibernate`
Hibernate Tutorial

`http://www.roseindia.net/hibernate/`
Complete Hibernate 3.0 and Hibernate 4 Tutorial

`http://www.dzone.com/tutorials/java/hibernate/hibernate-tutorial/hibernate-tutorial.html`
Hibernate Tutorials

`http://www.javaworld.com/article/2072999/data-storage/get-started-with-hibernate.html`
Get started with Hibernate

`http://www.mkyong.com/tutorials/hibernate-tutorials/`
Hibernate Tutorial

`http://www.javatpoint.com/hibernate-tutorial`
Hibernate Tutorial

EXERCISES

Objective-type Questions

1. Which of the following is true about hibernate?
 (a) Hibernate is a framework.
 (b) Hibernate is an Object-Relational Mapping (ORM) library for the Java language.
 (c) Hibernate provides a mapping for object-oriented domain model to a traditional relational database.
 (d) All of the above

2. What is the root level element in a hibernate mapping file?
 (a) <hibernate-mapping>
 (b) <session-mapping>
 (c) <sessionfactory-mapping>
 (d) None of the above

3. How does bhm.xml file include other hbm.xml files?
   (a) <mapping resource="activity.hbm.xml"/>
   (b) <include resource="activity.hbm.xml"/>
   (c) <add resource="activity.hbm.xml"/>
   (d) None of the above

4. What is dirty checking in Hibernate?
   (a) Object state changes in order to synchronize the updated state with the database
   (b) Remove the dirty data from database
   (c) Check the data when inserted into database
   (d) None of the above

5. What does "<generator class="native" />" means?
   (a) Generate primary key
   (b) Generate tables based on configuration
   (c) Generate sql statement on configuration
   (d) None of the above

6. Is it possible to declare mappings for multiple classes in one mapping file?
   (a) True (c) Can't say
   (b) False (d) None of the above

7. What does session.evict() method do?
   (a) Remove the object and its collections from the second level cache
   (b) Remove the object and its collections from the first level cache
   (c) Remove the object and its collections from the data base
   (d) None of the above

8. Which of the following statements is correct?
   (a) Only the Session that you obtained with sf.getCurrentSession() is flushed and closed automatically.
   (b) Only the Session that you obtained with sf.openSession() is flushed and closed automatically.
   (c) Only the Session that you obtained with sf.getNewSession() is flushed and closed automatically.
   (d) None of the above

9. What does hibernate.hbm2ddl.auto create mean?
   (a) Create session object automatically
   (b) Create Sessio Factory object automatically
   (c) Create tables automatically
   (d) None of the above

10. Is Hibernate Session threadsafe?
   (a) No (c) No relation with thread
   (b) Yes (d) None of the above

11. How can you make a property be read from the database but not modified in anyway?
   (a) By using the isinsert="false" and isupdate="false" attributes.
   (b) By using the isinsert="no" and isupdate="no" attributes.
   (c) By using the insert="false" and update="false" attributes.
   (d) None of the above

12. Which statement is correct?
   (a) session.contains() method to determine if an instance belongs to the database.
   (b) session.contains() method to determine if an instance belongs to the session cache.
   (c) Both are correct
   (d) None of the above

13. How can you get a session object?
   (a) SessionFactory.getSession();
   (b) SessionFactory.openSession();
   (c) SessionFactory.get();
   (d) (session)SessionFactory.getObject();

14. Which of the following is FALSE about Session in hibernate?
   (a) Session is a non-threadsafe object.
   (b) You can share the session between threads.
   (c) Session represents a single unit-of-work with the database.
   (d) Session is the primary interface for the persistence service.

15. What is the name of the default configuration file?
   (a) config.xml
   (b) hibernate.config.xml
   (c) cfg.hibernate.xml
   (d) hibernate.cfg.xml

16. Which of the following is not a function of the Session interface?
   (a) Acts as Factory for Transaction
   (b) Wraps a JDBC connection
   (c) Holds a mandatory first-level cache of persistent objects, used when navigating the object graph or looking up objects by identifier
   (d) Created during application initialization

17. Which of the following is not a method on Session interface?
   (a) save() (c) saveorupdate()
   (b) remove() (d) load()

18. Which of the following is the default generator type?
    (a) increment (c) assigned
    (b) identity (d) sequence

19. What is the full form of POJO?
    (a) Plain Ordinary Java Object
    (b) Plain Old Java Object
    (c) Primitive Old Java Object
    (d) Primary Old Java Object

20. Where can you specify object to database mapping information?
    (a) Mapping files
    (b) Classes
    (c) Both a) and b)
    (d) None of the above

21. Which of the following does the default constructor of Configuration class search?
    (a) config.properties
    (b) coonfig.xml
    (c) hibernate.properties
    (d) hibernate.cfg.xml

22. What is the root element of a hibernate configuration file?
    (a) <hibernate-configuration>
    (b) <hibernate-mapping>
    (c) <hibernate-config>
    (d) <config-hibernate>

23. Which of the following methods on Session interface is used to obtain a Transaction object?
    (a) startTransaction()
    (b) getTransaction()
    (c) openTransaction()
    (d) beginTransaction()

24. Which of the following packages contains hibernate annotations?
    (a) javax.annotations
    (b) javax.persistence
    (c) javax.hibernate.annotations
    (d) javax.persistence.annotations

25. Which of the following is not a valid object state in hibernate?
    (a) transient (c) detached
    (b) persistent (d) volatile

26. What is the full form of HQL?
    (a) High-level Query Language
    (b) Hibernate Query List
    (c) Hibernate Question Language
    (d) Hibernate Query Language

27. Which of the following is not a valid hibernate annotation?
    (a) Entity (c) Column
    (b) Table (d) Row

28. Which of the following is not HQL keyword?
    (a) choose (c) select
    (b) from (d) where

29. Which of the following methods on Session interface is used to create a Query?
    (a) openQuery() (c) createQuery()
    (b) getQuery() (d) prepareQuery()

30. Which of the following is a hibernate to POJO class exporter?
    (a) <java2hbm> (c) <hbmtojava>
    (b) <hbm2java> (d) <fromhbm2java>

Subjective-type Questions

1. What is Object Relational Mapping (ORM)?
2. Why do you need ORM tools like hibernate?
3. Write the advantages of Hibernate over JDBC?
4. What are POJOs?
5. Discuss the different ways hibernate can be configured.
6. How can you specify hibernate to database mapping information?
7. What happens when both hibernate.properties and hibernate.cfg.xml are in the classpath?
8. Write the sample content of hibernate configuration and mapping files.
9. What are the important tags of hibernate.cfg.xml?
10. What is object/relational mapping metadata?
11. Write the core interfaces and classes with their functionality of hibernate framework.

12. Write the basic steps required to communicate with RDBMS using hibernate.
13. What is the function of Session object in hibernate?
14. What is the function of a SessionFactory object? How will you obtain such an object?
15. What is the difference between getCurrentSession() and openSession() in Hibernate?
16. Describe the life cycle of hibernate objects.
17. What is the difference between transient and detached objects?
18. How do you map Java Objects with Database tables?
19. What are the primary differences between Entity Beans and Hibernate ?
20. What is Hibernate Query Language (HQL)?
21. What is the difference between HQL and SQL?
22. How will you create a primary key using Hibernate?
23. What is the difference between JDBC and JTA transactions in Hibernate?
24. Which interfaces are defined to execute the query in the Hibernate?
25. What is the difference between load() and get()?
26. What is a Named query and why is it used?
27. How will you see Hibernate generated SQL statements on console?
28. What are the benefits of detached objects?
29. How will you reattach detached objects to a session?
30. What can you do with hibernate tools?

CHAPTER – 24

Java Naming and Directory Interface

Key Objectives

After completing this chapter readers will be able to—

- understand what naming and directory services are
- appreciate the importance of JNDI
- get an overview about JNDI classes and interfaces
- write JNDI-based applications
- work with Apache Directory Server
- perform basic naming and directory operations

24.1 NAMING CONCEPTS

Naming is a fundamental concept used in almost every system of the world. Our computing systems are not exceptions. It allows us to associate (called *binding*) names with objects and to find (called *lookup*) those objects later by their names. Names are some people-friendly identifiers. An *object* in the naming system is a nameable/referenceable entity such as an object in a program, an IP address, a file etc. A naming service maps these names to objects. The examples of such naming systems are Domain Name System (DNS), File system, Java's rmiregistry, Java IDL's `tnameserv` and `orbd` etc. The DNS is a naming system since it maps host names to IP addresses.

```
www.google.com→74.124.24.104
```

A file system is also a naming system since it maps a file name to some h/w specific address.

```
D:\progs\test.java→sector, track and cylinder number
```

A naming server typically provides services such as binding, unbinding, and looking up objects by their names. It is also important to note that all name servers do not function in the same way. However, in order to be a naming service, it must at the very least support the facility to bind objects with names and to look up objects by name.

Apart from functional differences, the visible difference is the way each naming service requires names to be specified—its naming convention.

24.1.1 Naming Convention

A name is formed by one or more *name components*. The syntax of names, also called *naming convention*, is specified by the naming system.

For example, in the DNS, a name (e.g. `www.google.com`) is an ordered sequence of name components (`www`, `google` and `com`) separated by dots ('.'). Here, `google` is a subdomain under `com` domain (written as `google.com`) and `www` is a name under `google.com`.

A file name in windows (say `D:\progs\test.java`), on the other hand, starts with a drive name (`D:`) and uses \ (back slash) as the name component separator.

Unix like OS uses `/` (forwards slash) in the file path names.

A name (e.g. `ou=IT,o=JU,c=IN`) in LDAP (Lightweight Directory Access Protocol) compliant server is a comma (,) separated ordered sequence of name components, each of which is a name and value pair separated by equality sign (=). This refers to the organizational unit (ou) IT under organization (o) JU (for Jadavpur University) in the country (c) IN (for India).

24.1.2 Naming Context

A *naming context* [Figure 24.1:] is a collection of zero or more name-to-object bindings. For example, a directory in a file system, that contains a set of (file name, file) bindings, is a context. A *subcontext* is child context of a parent context. For example, a sub directory is a subcontext. A subcontext like its parent can also contain a list of bindings. Contexts and their subcontexts together form a general tree. The root of the context tree is referred to as *initial context* or *root context*.

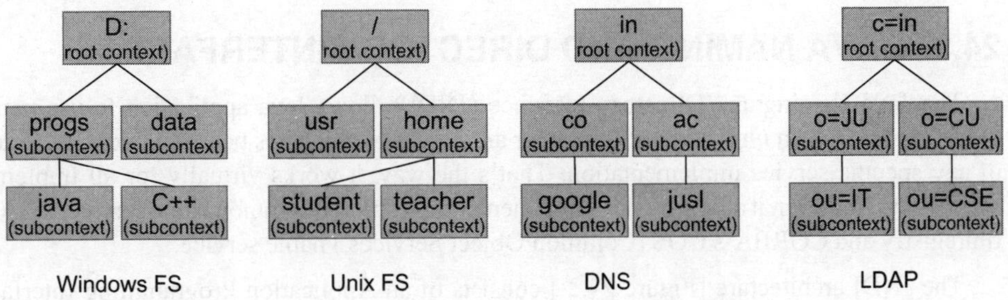

Figure 24.1: Naming Context and Subcontext

Each context is identified by a name unique within its parent context. The fully qualified name of a context starts from the root context and ends with its own name.

Note that not all naming servers allow creating subcontexts. For example, Java's rmiregistry does not permit to create sub contexts.

24.1.3 Binding

The process of associating a name to an object is called *binding*. For example, a DNS name is bound to an IP address; a file name is bound to a file and so on.

Many naming systems don't store objects directly. Instead, they store references to objects. For example, in DNS, the address `207.69.175.36` is a reference to a computer's location on the Internet, not the computer itself.

24.2 DIRECTORY CONCEPTS

A directory service extends the idea of naming service. In addition to associating names with objects, a directory service allows objects to have attributes. Directory service also allows to perform attribute-related operations such as reading, modifying, removing attributes, searching object based-on attributes etc.

For example, an organization will not only have a name, but it will have a (mandatory and optional) set of attributes such as its postal code, street address, telephone number, web link etc. Objects stored in a directory server are called *directory objects*. Virtually, any entity may be represented as a directory object. Attributes describe the entity the directory object represents. An attribute has a name (called identifier) and one or more values. For example, postalCode attribute of an organization has only one value, but telephone number can have many values.

Examples of directory servers include, Novell Directory Service (NDS), Network Information Service (NIS) etc. There are also general directory services that use standard protocols such as X.500 and Lightweight Directory Access Protocol (LDAP).

As mentioned earlier, we can search objects based on their attributes. In that case, we supply query, called *search filter*, consisting of a logical expression in which we specify the attributes that the object or objects must have. This type of searching is known as *content based searching* or *reverse lookup*. For example, we can search all educational institutions situated in Kolkata.

24.2.1 Directory Context

Note that in a name tree, objects can only be bound under a context, not under another object. However, unlike name tree, every node in a directory tree is a context. Consequently, objects can be bound under other objects as well. A directory server, does not distinguish an object and context.

24.3 JAVA NAMING AND DIRECTORY INTERFACE

The Java Naming and Directory Interface (JNDI) allows Java application to use naming and directory. It is not an *implementation*; rather an *interface* which has been defined to be independent of any specific service implementation. That's the way, it works virtually for all implementation seamlessly. However, it also provides implementations for three common name service, LDAP, RMI's rmiregistry and CORBA's COS (Common Object Services) name service.

The JNDI architecture [Figure 24.2:] consists of an Application Programming Interface (API) and a Service Provider Interface (SPI). The SPI helps to plug-in various service providers, whereas API allows applications to use them. The API has two parts: one used to access naming service and the other is used for directory service.

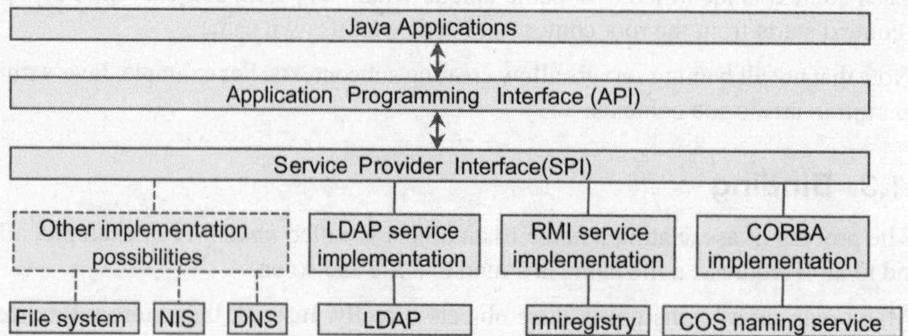

Figure 24.2: JNDI architecture

24.4 AN EXAMPLE

In this section, we shall show how to write a simple Java application using JNDI. We shall rewrite our calculator RMI application that will use JNDI. The `rmiregistry` will be used as the name server. If you have JDK installed, you also have rmiregistry installed. So, you don't have to look for another name server. Since it is an RMI application, the server side includes an interface (`Calculator.java`) and an implementation (`SimpleCalculator.java`) as follows:

```
//Calculator.java
import java.rmi.*;
public interface Calculator extends Remote {
   public int add(int a, int b) throws RemoteException;
}
//SimpleCalculator.java
public class SimpleCalculator implements Calculator {
  public int add(int a, int b) {
    return a + b;
  }
}
```

24.4.1 Writing the Server

To use JNDI interfaces and classes, it imports the naming package:

```
import javax.naming.*;
```

The server, as usual, creates an instance of servant and obtains a stub as follows:

```
SimpleCalculator cal = new SimpleCalculator();
Calculator stub = (Calculator)UnicastRemoteObject.exportObject(cal,0);
```

The next task of the server is to upload this stub to a name server. To work with naming service, we must have a reference to a context in the name tree. The simplest way to create such an object is as follows:

```
Context ctx = new InitialContext();
```

This `ctx` basically refers to a node (context) in the name tree [see Figure 24.1:] maintained by a name server. To work with that name tree, we simply refer to this `ctx` object which, on behalf of us, communicates with the name server. So, this Context object behaves like a proxy. The constructor of the `InitialContext` class does not actually create a Context object; instead it looks for a provider specific factory class that can manufacture such a proxy instance. However, we have not yet provided any information (such as port number, IP address) about the name server; nor have we specified the factory class.

There are different ways to specify the required information. In our example, we shall provide them as command line arguments. Anyway, the server can add a binding using `bind()` method as follows:

```
ctx.bind(args[0], stub);
```

This essentially binds the object `stub` to the context `ctx` with a name specified as the first command line argument. The complete source code (`CalculatorServerJNDI.java`) is shown below:

```
//CalculatorServerJNDI
import java.rmi.server.*;
import javax.naming.*;
public class CalculatorServerJNDI {
  public static void main(String args[]) {
    try {
      SimpleCalculator cal = new SimpleCalculator();
      Calculator stub = (Calculator)UnicastRemoteObject.exportObject(cal,0);
      Context ctx = new InitialContext();
      ctx.bind(args[0], stub);
```

```
            System.out.println("Calculator server ready...");
        }catch (Exception e) { e.printStackTrace(); }
    }
}
```

The relevant modification is shown with bold face.

24.4.2 Writing the Client

A client, like server, also creates a `Context` object as follows:

```
Context ctx = new InitialContext();
```

It then looks up the object supplying the name in the command line using `lookup()` method:

```
Calculator cal = (Calculator)ctx.lookup(args[0]);
```

Since, the type of the object we bound earlier was a `Calculator` type, we can cast the result of `lookup()` to its target class. The complete source code (`CalculatorClientJNDI.java`) is shown below:

```
//CalculatorClientJNDI.java
import javax.naming.*;
public class CalculatorClientJNDI {
  public static void main(String args[]) {
    try {
      Context ctx = new InitialContext();
      Calculator cal = (Calculator)ctx.lookup(args[0]);
      int x = 4, y = 3;
      int result = cal.add(x,y);
      System.out.println("Sent: " + x +" and "+y);
      System.out.print("Received("+x+"+"+y+"=): " + result);
    }catch (Exception e) { e.printStackTrace();  }
  }
}
```

The relevant modification is shown with bold face.

24.4.3 Running Application

Place server related files (`Calculator.java`, `SimpleCalculator.java` and `CalculatorServerJNDI.java`) in a directory, say `E:\ajp\jndi\rmi\server`. Compile all the classes normally. Open a terminal, go to this directory and use the following command to start `rmiregistry` on port `6789`

```
start rmiregistry 6789
```

To start the server, we have to specify the values of two primary properties `java.naming.factory.initial` and `java.naming.provider.url`. The former one specifies the fully qualified name of the factory class, to be used to create a `Context` object, to communicate with the name server. The latter holds location information (port, IP address etc.) of the JNDI provider. The `InitialContext`'s constructor uses this information to create a `Context` object and to connect to the naming server. For `rmiregistry` running on port `6789` in host `172.16.5.81`, the values of these properties are `com.sun.jndi.rmi.registry.RegistryContextFactory` and `rmi://172.16.5.81:6789` respectively. For other name servers, the values of these two properties can be found in Table 24.1: Note that by only changing these two values, we can talk to any name server. Use the following command to start the server:

```
java -
Djava.naming.factory.initial=com.sun.jndi.rmi.registry.RegistryContextFactory -
Djava.naming.provider.url=rmi://172.16.5.81:6789 CalculatorServerJNDI
calculator
```

If everything goes fine, the following message appears:

```
Calculator server ready...
```

Now, place client related files (`Calculator.java`, and `CalculatorClientJNDI.java`) in a directory, say `E:\ajp\jndi\rmi\client`, probably in a different host. Compile all the classes normally. Open a terminal, go to this directory and use the following command to start the client:

```
java -
Djava.naming.factory.initial=com.sun.jndi.rmi.registry.RegistryContextFactory-
Djava.naming.provider.url=rmi://172.16.5.81:6789 CalculatorClientJNDI
calculator
```

If everything goes fine, the following message appears:

```
Sent: 4 and 3
Received(4+3=): 7
```

24.5 SPECIFYING JNDI PROPERTIES

The values of the basic JNDI properties (`java.naming.factory.initial` and `java.naming.provider.url`) may be supplied in different ways. In the previous example, we supplied them as command line arguments. The `InitialContext` class also has an overloaded constructor that takes a `java.util.Hashtable` object. So, we can place JNDI properties in a `Hashtable` object and pass it to the `InitialContext`'s constructor as follows:

```
java.util.Hashtable env = new java.util.Hashtable();
env.put("java.naming.factory.initial","com.sun.jndi.rmi.registry.RegistryContex
tFactory");
env.put("java.naming.provider.url", "rmi://172.16.5.81:6789");
Context ctx = new InitialContext(env);
```

Another way to specify JNDI parameters is to use an application resource file having name `jndi.properties`. It contains a list of key/value pairs in the properties file format. The following is an example of such a property file.

```
#jndi.properties
java.naming.factory.initial=com.sun.jndi.rmi.registry.RegistryContextFactory
java.naming.provider.url=rmi://172.16.5.81:6789
```

The JNDI automatically reads the application resource files from all components in the applications' classpaths and `JRE_HOME/lib/jndi.properties`, where `JRE_HOME` is the file directory that contains Java Runtime Environment (JRE). Note that properties files are text files and should not contain sensitive information, such as passwords.

Table 24.1: shows a list of initial context factory and provider URL for various naming service providers.

Table 24.1: List of initial context factory and provider URL

	java.naming.factory.initial	java.naming.provider.url
rmiregistry	com.sun.jndi.rmi.registry.RegistryContextFactory	rmi://172.16.5.81:1099
file system	com.sun.jndi.fscontext.RefFSContextFactory	file:///D:/
LDAP	com.sun.jndi.ldap.LdapCtxFactory	ldap://172.16.5.81:10389/dc=example,dc=com
orbd, tnameserv	com.sun.jndi.cosnaming.CNCtxFactory	iiop://172.16.5.81:900

24.6 NAME SERVERS

The previous example used rmiregistry name server. In practice, there exists various other name servers such as file system, Java IDL's tnameserv, and orbd. These servers do not support directory service. To illustrate the concepts of directory as well as naming operations, we shall use a simple directory server provided by Apache—known as Apache Directory Server (or simply ApacheDS). The next section describes how to install and use ApacheDS.

24.7 USING APACHEDS

Apache Directory Server (often abbreviated as ApacheDS) is LDAPv3 compatible, open source directory server entirely written in Java. It is a multi-platform application and runs on Mac OS X, Linux and Windows. In this chapter, in addition to file system naming service, Java's rmiregistry and orbd, we shall use ApacheDS to demonstrate the JNDI concepts.

24.7.1 Installing and Starting ApacheDS

To work with ApacheDS, download it from `https://directory.apache.org/apacheds/downloads.html`. Apache provides native installers for several platforms. It also provides a zip and tar.gz archive suitable for any platform. We downloaded `apacheds-2.0.0-M15.zip`. Extract this archive and place the extracted folder (`apacheds-2.0.0-M15`) where you want Apache DS to be installed. We placed the folder in D: drive. Hereafter, we shall refer to this D:\`apacheds-2.0.0-M15` directory as `<ApacheDS_TOP>`).

ApacheDS requires a Java Runtime Environment 6 or later. So, make sure an appropriate version is installed in your machine. Put the directory containing `java` interpreter in your PATH environment variable. Go to `<ApacheDS_TOP>\bin` directory, where you will find two files `apacheds.bat` and `apacheds.sh`, which are startup script for windows and linux respectively. To start ApacheDS in windows, either double click on `apacheds.bat` or open a terminal, go to the `<ApacheDS_TOP>\bin` directory and use the following command:

```
apacheds.bat
```

If everything goes fine, the startup window looks like this:

```
Starting ApacheDS instance 'default'...
[16:02:47] WARN [org.apache.directory.server.core.DefaultDirectoryService] -
You didn't change the admin password of directory service instance 'default'.
Please update the admin password as soon as possible to prevent a possible
security breach.
```

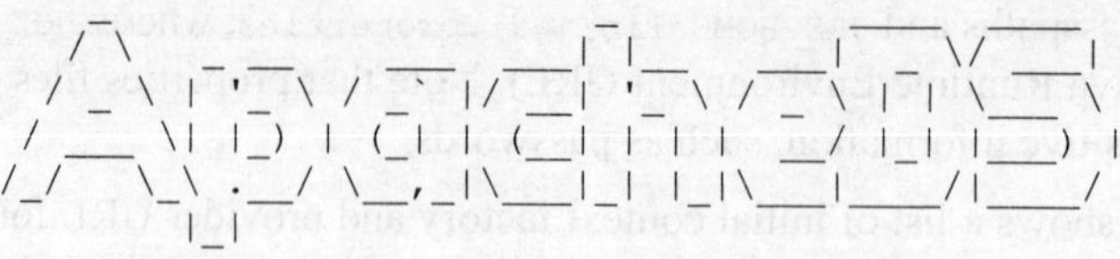

By default the ApacheDS listens on port 10389 (unencrypted or StartTLS) and 10636 (SSL). However, the well-known port for LDAP is 389, which you may choose your ApacheDS to listen on. The server configuration (including port number) is stored in a LDIF file `<ApacheDS_TOP>\instances\default\conf\config.ldif`. The relevant portion for unencrypted LDAL is shown below:

```
...
dn: ads-transportid=ldap,ou=transports,ads-serverId=ldapServer,ou=servers,ads-
directoryServiceId=default,ou=config
ads-systemport: 10389
...
```

And, here is the port specification for SSL-enabled LDAP:

```
dn: ads-transportid=ldaps,ou=transports,ads-serverId=ldapServer,ou=servers,ads-
directoryServiceId=default,ou=config
ads-systemport: 10636
```

Change the port of your choice. Note that a root privilege is required to use a port less than 1024. We stuck on the default ports.

24.7.2 JNDI Properties for ApacheDS

ApacheDS stores entries in distinct areas called *partitions*. Partitions are disconnected from each other, meaning that changes to entries in partition P would never affect entries in partition Q. The entries in a particular partition are stored in naming contexts called the partition suffix. The ApacheDS default instance contains a partition with root suffix `dc=example,dc=com`. Although, a new partition may be created, we shall use this existing partition to demonstrate our JNDI examples.

We shall assume that ApacheDS runs on 10389 in a host 172.16.5.81. The values of these two properties `java.naming.factory.initial` and `java.naming.provider.url` will then be `com.sun.jndi.ldap.LdapCtxFactory` and `ldap://172.16.5.81:10389/dc=example,dc=com` respectively and will be used in all subsequent examples that use ApacheDS as the name server. If you start ApacheDS on a different port, or in a different host, specify them in the value of `java.naming.provider.url` property.

24.8 CALCULATOR RMI APPLICATION USING LDAP

Let us now run our calculator application that will make use of ApacheDS as a naming server instead of rmiregistry. We assume that the ApacheDS is running on 10389 in host 172.16.5.81. To start the server, go the server's home directory and use the following command:

```
java -Djava.naming.factory.initial=com.sun.jndi.ldap.LdapCtxFactory -
Djava.naming.provider.url=ldap://172.16.5.81:10389/dc=example,dc=com
CalculatorServerJNDI cn=calculator
```

Since an LDAP server expects names as pair of values separated by =, we have used name `cn=calculator`. Note that in this case, server and ApacheDS need not necessarily run in the same computer. To start the client, go to the client's home directory and use the following command:

```
java -Djava.naming.factory.initial=com.sun.jndi.ldap.LdapCtxFactory -
Djava.naming.provider.url=ldap://172.16.5.81:10389/dc=example,dc=com
CalculatorClientJNDI cn=calculator
```

24.9 CALCULATOR RMI-IIOP APPLICATION USING JNDI

Let us now redevelop our calculator application using RMI-IIOP and JNDI. We use the same Calculator interface as used in RMI. The implementation of this interface that uses IIOP is shown below:

```
// SimpleCalculator.java
import javax.rmi.PortableRemoteObject;
class SimpleCalculator extends PortableRemoteObject implements Calculator {
  public SimpleCalculator() throws java.rmi.RemoteException {}
  public int add(int a, int b) throws java.rmi.RemoteException {
    return a + b;
  }
  public String[] _ids() {
    String[] id = {"IDL:CalculatorApp/Calculator:1.0"};
    return id;
  }
}
```

24.9.1 Server

The code for the server is shown below:

```
// CalculatorServerJNDI.java
import javax.naming.*;
public class CalculatorServerJNDI {
```

```
    public static void main(String args[]) {
      try {
        SimpleCalculator calc = new SimpleCalculator();
        Context ic = new InitialContext();
        ic.rebind(args[0], calc );
        System.out.println("Calculator Server ready...");
      } catch (Exception e) { e.printStackTrace();}
    }
  }
```

24.9.2 Client

The code for the server is shown below:

```
//CalculatorClientJNDI.java
import javax.naming.*;
public class CalculatorClientJNDI {
  public static void  main( String args[] ) {
    try {
      Context ic = new InitialContext();
      Calculator calc = (Calculator)ic.lookup(args[0]);
      int x =2, y = 3;
      System.out.println("Sent :" + x + " and " + y);
      int result  = calc.add(x, y);
      System.out.println("Received : " + result);
    } catch( Exception e ) {e.printStackTrace();}
  }
}
```

24.9.3 Running the Application

Open a terminal in any machine in the network.

```
start orbd
```

The Java ID naming service now listens on port 900. We assume that the IP address of the machine this service is started on is 172.16.5.81. Compile the server files using the following series of commands:

```
javac SimpleCalculator.java
rmic -iiop SimpleCalculator
javac Calculator.java CalculatorServerJNDI.java
```

Now, start the server:

```
java -Djava.naming.factory.initial=com.sun.jndi.cosnaming.CNCtxFactory -
Djava.naming.provider.url=iiop://172.16.5.81:900 CalculatorServerJNDI
calculator
```

This uploads a reference to the naming service with name "calculator". Compile the client files using the following series of commands:

```
javac Calculator.java
rmic -iiop Calculator
javac CalculatorClientJNDI.java
```

Start the client:

```
java -Djava.naming.factory.initial=com.sun.jndi.cosnaming.CNCtxFactory -
Djava.naming.provider.url=iiop://172.16.5.81:900 CalculatorClientJNDI
calculator
```

24.10 NAMING OPERATIONS

The following sections describe how to perform different name-related operations. We shall use ApacheDS as the name server unless it is specified explicitly.

24.10.1 Adding, Replacing and Removing Binding

A binding is added to a context using its `bind()` method, which takes an object and either a `String` or a `Name`. The following example binds a Java String object with the name `cn=AJavaObject` and associates with the specified initial context.

```
ctx.bind("cn=aJavaObject", new String("JNDI"));
```

The types of objects that are allowed [Table 24.2:] to bind depends on the naming server. For example, LDAP can only bind `Referenceable`, `Serializable` and `DirContext` objects, whereas file system can only bind `Referenciable` or `Reference` objects. Java's `rmiregistry` can only bind `Remote`, `Reference` and `Referenciable` objects and Java IDL's `orbd` and `tnameserv` can only bind CORBA objects. For more information, read the respective server's documentation. So, Java's `String` object (which is only `Serializable`) can be bound to only LDAP naming service.

Table 24.2: Allowable object to be bound with name servers

	Object type					
Name server	Serializable	Referenceable	Reference	Remote	DirContext	CORBA
rmiregistry	X	✓	✓	✓	X	X
file system	X	✓	✓	X	X	X
LDAP	✓	✓	X	X	✓	X
orbd, tnameserv	X	X	X	X	X	✓

The `bind()` method throws a `NameAlreadyBoundException` if the name has already been used to bind some other object. The `rebind()` method works like `bind()`, except that it replaces existing binding (if any) with the specified one.

```
ctx.rebind("cn=aJavaObject", new String("JNDI"));
```

To remove an existing binding, use `unbind()` method specifying the name of the binding:

```
ctx.unbind("cn=aJavaObject");
```

This removes an existing binding having name `aJavaObject` from the current context.

24.10.2 Looking Up

To find an object from the naming tree, we use `lookup()` method specifying name of the object as follows:

```
Object o = ctx.unbind("cn=aJavaObject");
```

Since, the type of the object we bound earlier is a `String`, we can cast the result of `lookup()` to its target class as follows:

```
String s = (String)ctx.lookup(args[0]);
```

24.10.3 Renaming

The name of an object in a context may be renamed using `rename()` method.

```
ctx.rename("old_name", "new_name");
```

This renames the object that was bound to "old_name" to "new_name". The bound object remains unchanged.

24.10.4 Listing

It is sometimes necessary to find all bindings under a certain context. JNDI provides two methods for this: `listBindings()` and `list()`.

24.10.4.1 Using list()

This method returns an enumeration of `NameClassPair`, which consists of the object's name and its class name. The following example illustrates this:

```
//List.java
import javax.naming.*;
public class List {
  public static void main(String args[]) {
    try {
      Context ctx = new InitialContext();
      java.util.Enumeration e = ctx.list(args[0]);
      while(e.hasMoreElements()) {
        NameClassPair ncp = (NameClassPair)e.nextElement();
        System.out.println(ncp.getName()+" <-> "+ncp.getClassName());
      }
    }catch (Exception e) { e.printStackTrace(); }
  }
}
```

This program lists all object's names and their class names. So far, we have used name servers such as rmiregistry and ApacheDS. Let us now use file system naming service. For file system, sun also provides a factory class `com.sun.jndi.fscontext.RefFSContextFactory`. However, this class is not a part of core Java. So, we downloaded the JAR `fscontext.jar` containing this class from `http://www.java2s.com/Code/Jar/f/Downloadfscontextjar.htm` and placed in the class path during runtime. To see the list of file bindings under `D:\apacheds-2.0.0-M15` drive, use the following command:

```
java -cp ..\fscontext.jar;. -
Djava.naming.factory.initial=com.sun.jndi.fscontext.RefFSContextFactory -
Djava.naming.provider.url=file:///D:/ List apacheds-2.0.0-M15
```

A sample result is shown below:

```
bin <-> javax.naming.Context
instances <-> javax.naming.Context
lib <-> javax.naming.Context
LICENSE <-> java.io.File
NOTICE <-> java.io.File
```

24.10.4.2 Using listBindings()

This returns an enumeration of `Binding`, which is a subclass of `NameClassPair`, and additionally contains the object. The following code demonstrates this:

```
//ListBindings.java
import javax.naming.*;
public class ListBindings {
  public static void main(String args[]) {
    try {
      Context ctx = new InitialContext();
      java.util.Enumeration e = ctx.listBindings("");
      while(e.hasMoreElements()) {
        Binding b = (Binding)e.nextElement();
        System.out.println(b.getName()+" <-> "+b.getObject());
      }
    }catch (Exception e) { e.printStackTrace(); }
  }
}
```

To see the list of file bindings under D: drive, use the following command:

```
java -cp ..\fscontext.jar;. -
Djava.naming.factory.initial=com.sun.jndi.fscontext.RefFSContextFactory -
Djava.naming.provider.url=file:///D:/ ListBindings apacheds-2.0.0-M15
```

A sample result is shown below:

```
bin <-> com.sun.jndi.fscontext.RefFSContext@2a15cd
instances <-> com.sun.jndi.fscontext.RefFSContext@fd68b1
lib <-> com.sun.jndi.fscontext.RefFSContext@e45076
LICENSE <-> D:\apacheds-2.0.0-M15\LICENSE
NOTICE <-> D:\apacheds-2.0.0-M15\NOTICE
```

24.11 WORKING WITH SUBCONTEXT

In addition to operations on object bindings, JNDI also allows creating and destroying subcontexts. To create a subcontext, we use `createSubcontext()` providing the name of the subcontext.

```
ctx.createSubcontext("cn=CU");
```

It creates a subcontext `cn=CU` under the current context. To destroy a context, we use `destroySubcontext()` providing the name of the context to be destroyed.

```
ctx.destroySubcontext("cn=CU");
```

This destroys the context `cn=CU` from the context `ctx`.

24.12 WORKING WITH DIRECTORY

To work with directory specific operations, we need the package `javax.naming.directory`. We import all classes under this package, using the following import statement:

```
import javax.naming.directory.*;
```

In a directory, the counterparts of `Context` and `InitialContext` are `DirContext` and `InitialDirContext` respectively. So, obtain a reference to an initial directory context as follows:

```
DirContext dc = new InitialDirContext();
```

The `InitialDirContext` also reads the values of two properties `java.naming.factory.initial` and `java.naming.provider.url`. So, specify them using any one of the procedures described earlier. Let us now discuss how to perform different directory-related operations. We shall use ApacheDS as the name server unless it is specified explicitly. To avoid specifying long JNDI properties repeatedly, we created property file jndi.properties and placed in the directory containing our test programs. The content of this file is shown below:

```
#jndi.properties
java.naming.factory.initial=com.sun.jndi.ldap.LdapCtxFactory
java.naming.provider.url=ldap://172.16.5.81:10389/dc=example,dc=com
```

24.12.1 Reading Attributes

Let us first see how to read all attributes of a directory object. The `getAttributes()` method on `Context` object is used for it. It takes the name of an object and returns an `Attributes` object that holds the unordered collection of attributes the object possesses. The Attributes interface has useful methods to obtain individual attributes or listing all attributes. The following program prints all attributes of the specified directory context:

```
//ReadAttributes.java
import javax.naming.*;
import javax.naming.directory.*;
public class ReadAttributes {
```

```
    public static void main(String args[]) {
      try  {
        DirContext ctx = new InitialDirContext();
        Attributes attrs = ctx.getAttributes(args[0]);
        for (NamingEnumeration ne = attrs.getAll(); ne.hasMore();) {
          Attribute attr = (Attribute)ne.next();
          System.out.println("attribute: " + attr.getID());
          for (NamingEnumeration e = attr.getAll(); e.hasMore();)
          System.out.println("value: " + e.next());
        }
      }catch (Exception e) { e.printStackTrace();  }
    }
  }
```

Use the following command to see all attributes of the ApacheDS partition `dc=example,dc=com`:

```
java ReadAttributes ""
```

A sample result is shown below:

```
attribute: dc
value: example
attribute: objectclass
value: domain
value: top
```

24.12.2 Binding with Attributes

The `DirContext` class is a subclass of Context and provides overloaded methods many of which accept an additional `Attributes` parameter. So, we can use these methods to associate attributes with the object at the time of the binding. Consider the following example:

```
//BindAttr.java
import javax.naming.directory.*;
class BindAttr {
  public static void main(String[] args) {
    try {
      DirContext ctx = new InitialDirContext();
      Attributes attrs = new BasicAttributes(true);
      attrs.put(new BasicAttribute("objectclass", "organization"));
      ctx.bind(args[0], new String("An organization"), attrs);
    } catch (Exception e) { e.printStackTrace(); }
  }
}
```

This associates an attribute `objectclass` having value `organization` with a `String` object and binds it with the name specified as command line argument. The `objectclass` attribute tells that the `String` object is a kind of `organization` object. Run this program using the following command:

```
java BindAttr o=JU
```

Since ApcaheDS specifies that an `organization` object must also have an `o` (o for organization) attribute, the String object must have `o` attributes. We have specified it in its name `o=JU`. We can check this using our previous program as follows:

```
java ReadAttributes o=JU
```

A sample result is shown below:

```
attribute: javaSerializedData
value: [B@70be88
attribute: objectclass
value: organization
value: javaSerializedObject
value: javaObject
value: top
```

```
attribute: javaClassNames
value: java.lang.String
value: java.lang.Object
value: java.io.Serializable
value: java.lang.Comparable
value: java.lang.CharSequence
attribute: javaClassName
value: java.lang.String
attribute: o
value: JU
```

Like replacing a binding in a name service, we can use `unbind()` method to replace a binding in a directory service.

24.12.3 Creating subcontext with Attributes

To create a subcontext having attributes, we use `createSubcontext()` method specifying name of the subcontext and attributes. Here is an example:

```
//AddEntry.java
import javax.naming.directory.*;
public class AddEntry {
  public static void main(String args[]) {
    try  {
      DirContext ctx = new InitialDirContext();
      Attributes attrs=new BasicAttributes(true);
      attrs.put(new BasicAttribute("objectclass", "country"));
      ctx.createSubcontext(args[0], attrs);
    }catch (Exception e) { e.printStackTrace();  }
  }
}
```

This creates a subcontext with an attribute `objectclass` having value `country`. The created subcontext essentially is a `DirContext` object that can contain a set of country bindings. Use the following command to run this:

```
java AddEntry c=India
```

We can check this using our `List.java` program as follows:

```
java List ""
```

A sample result is shown below:

```
o=JU <-> java.lang.String
c=India <-> javax.naming.directory.DirContext
```

24.12.4 Adding Attributes

Attributes may be added, deleted, replaced using `modifyAttributes()` method that takes the following form:

```
void modifyAttributes(Name name, int mod_op, Attributes attrs)
```

The second argument indicates the type of modification and can have any one of the static constants `ADD_ATTRIBUTE, REPLACE_ATTRIBUTE, REMOVE_ATTRIBUTE` of `DirContext` class. The following example adds an attribute `description` to the object having specified name.

```
//AddAttribute.java
import javax.naming.directory.*;
public class AddAttribute {
  public static void main(String args[]) {
    try {
      DirContext ctx = new InitialDirContext();
      Attributes attrs = new BasicAttributes(true);
      attrs.put(new BasicAttribute(args[1],args[2]));
```

```
        ctx.modifyAttributes(args[0], DirContext.ADD_ATTRIBUTE, attrs);
      }catch (Exception e) { e.printStackTrace();   }
    }
}
```

Run this program as follows:

```
java AddAttribute o=JU description A_University
```

This adds an attribute `description` to the object having specified name. We can check this using our `ReadAttributes.java` program as follows:

```
java ReadAttributes o=JU
```

A sample result is shown below:

```
...
attribute: objectclass
value: organization
attribute: description
value: A_University
...
attribute: o
value: JU
```

24.12.5 Modifying Attributes

We use the constant `REPLACE_ATTRIBUTE` for modifying an existing attribute. The following example changes the value of `description` attribute:

```
//ModifyAttribute.java
import javax.naming.directory.*;
public class ModifyAttribute {
  public static void main(String args[]) {
    try {
      DirContext ctx = new InitialDirContext();
      Attributes attrs = new BasicAttributes(true);
      attrs.put(new BasicAttribute(args[1],args[2]));
      ctx.modifyAttributes(args[0], DirContext.REPLACE_ATTRIBUTE, attrs);
    }catch (Exception e) { e.printStackTrace();   }
  }
}
```

Run this program as follows:

```
E:\ajp\jndi\final>java ModifyAttribute o=JU description "One of the top 5
universities in India"
```

We can check this using our `ReadAttributes.java` program as follows:

```
java ReadAttributes o=JU
```

A sample result is shown below:

```
...
attribute: objectclass
value: organization
attribute: description
value: One of the top 5 universities in India
...
attribute: o
value: JU
```

24.12.6 Removing Attributes

We use the constant `REMOVE_ATTRIBUTE` for deleting an existing attribute. The following example deletes the `postalCode` attribute:

```
//RemoveAttribute.java
import javax.naming.directory.*;
```

```
public class RemoveAttribute {
  public static void main(String args[]) {
    try {
      DirContext ctx = new InitialDirContext();
      Attributes attrs = new BasicAttributes(true);
      attrs.put(new BasicAttribute(args[1]));
      ctx.modifyAttributes(args[0], DirContext.REMOVE_ATTRIBUTE, attrs);
    }catch (Exception e) { e.printStackTrace(); }
  }
}
```

Before running this example, make sure that the attribute `postalCode` already exists. You can add it using our AddAttribute.java program as follows:

```
java AddAttribute o=JU postalCode 700032
```

We can now delete this attribute using the following command:

```
java RemoveAttribute o=JU postalCode
```

If you read all attributes of `o=JU`, you will no longer see this attribute.

24.12.7 Batch Operation on Attributes

The `modifyAttributes()` method also has an overloaded version that takes a list of modification requests, each of which is represented by `ModificationItem`. Each `ModificationItem` consists of an Attribute to be used for modification and one of the numeric constants (`ADD_ATTRIBUTE, REPLACE_ATTRIBUTE, REMOVE_ATTRIBUTE`) indicating the type of modification to make. The following example illustrates this:

```
//ModifyAttributes.java
import javax.naming.directory.*;
public class ModifyAttributes {
  public static void main(String args[]) {
    try {
      DirContext ctx = new InitialDirContext();
      ModificationItem[] mi = new ModificationItem[3];
      mi[0] = new ModificationItem(DirContext.ADD_ATTRIBUTE, new
BasicAttribute("description", "Located in Kolkata, India"));
      mi[1] = new ModificationItem(DirContext.REPLACE_ATTRIBUTE, new
BasicAttribute("description", "Located in Kolkata, India"));
      mi[2] = new ModificationItem(DirContext.REMOVE_ATTRIBUTE, new
BasicAttribute("postalCode"));
      ctx.modifyAttributes(args[0], mi);
    }catch (Exception e) { e.printStackTrace(); }
  }
}
```

This adds a `description` attribute, then it changes its value and finally it removes the `postalCode` attribute.

24.12.8 Search

In addition to searching objects by their names, a directory server also allows us to search by attributes. The directory then returns a list of entries satisfying the query. For example, we may want to have all entries having an attribute `o` with value `JU`. The JNDI `DirContext` provides useful methods for various types of searching described in the following sections:

24.12.8.1 Basic Search

In the simplest case, we can search within a given context for entries having specified set of attributes. We first create an `Attributes` object and populate with desired attributes. The following specifies an attribute `o` with value `JU` and `objectclass` with value `organization`.

```
Attributes attrs = new BasicAttributes(true);
attrs.put(new BasicAttribute("o", "JU"));
attrs.put(new BasicAttribute("objectclass", "organization"));
```

We then pass this attribute and context to be searched to the `search()` method as follows:

```
NamingEnumeration result = ctx.search(args[0], attrs);
```

The `search()` method returns `NamingEnumeration` consisting of a list of `SearchResult` object each of which represents an entry satisfying the search. The following program prints details of entries having attributes `o` with value `JU`.

```
import javax.naming.*;
import javax.naming.directory.*;
class BasicSearch {
  public static void main(String[] args) {
    try {
      DirContext ctx = new InitialDirContext();
      Attributes attrs = new BasicAttributes(true);
      attrs.put(new BasicAttribute("o", "JU"));
      attrs.put(new BasicAttribute("objectclass", "organization"));
      NamingEnumeration result = ctx.search(args[0], attrs);
      while (result.hasMore()) {
        SearchResult sr = (SearchResult)result.next();
        System.out.println("name: " + sr.getName());
        for(NamingEnumeration ne = sr.getAttributes().getAll(); ne.hasMore();){
          Attribute attr = (Attribute)ne.next();
          System.out.println("attribute: " + attr.getID());
          for (NamingEnumeration e = attr.getAll(); e.hasMore();)
            System.out.println("value: " + e.next());
        }
      }
    } catch (Exception e) { e.printStackTrace(); }
  }
}
```

Before running this application, add some bindings using the following commands:

```
java BindAttr o=JU
java BindAttr o=CU
java BindAttr o=BU
```

Now, run the program using the following command:

```
java BasicSearch ""
```

A sample output is shown below:

```
name: o=JU
attribute: javaSerializedData
value: [B@28305d
attribute: objectclass
value: organization
value: javaSerializedObject
value: javaObject
value: top
attribute: javaClassNames
value: java.lang.String
value: java.lang.Object
value: java.io.Serializable
value: java.lang.Comparable
value: java.lang.CharSequence
attribute: javaClassName
value: java.lang.String
attribute: o
value: JU
```

The `search()` method returns, by default, all attributes associated with the entries that satisfy the query. However, we can specify a set of attributes the `search()` method should include in the return value. For example, the following specifies that only the `objectclass` attribute should be returned:

```
String[] desiredAttrs = {"objectclass"};
NamingEnumeration result = ctx.search(args[0], attrs, desiredAttrs);
```

This gives the following result:

```
name: o=JU
attribute: objectclass
value: organization
value: javaSerializedObject
value: javaObject
value: top
```

24.12.8.2 Filters

A search may be performed specifying search query, called *search filter*, consisting of logical expressions. For example, the following search filter selects entries that have an attribute `o` with value `JU` and `objectclass` with `organization`.

```
String filter = "(&(o=JU)(objectclass=organization))";
```

The following example essentially does the same thing as our previous example:

```
import javax.naming.*;
import javax.naming.directory.*;
class SearchFilter {
  public static void main(String[] args) {
    try {
      DirContext ctx = new InitialDirContext();
      SearchControls ctls = new SearchControls();
      String filter = "(&(o=JU)(objectclass=organization))";
      NamingEnumeration result = ctx.search(args[0], filter, ctls);
      while (result.hasMore()) {
        SearchResult sr = (SearchResult)result.next();
        System.out.println("name: " + sr.getName());
        for(NamingEnumeration ne = sr.getAttributes().getAll(); ne.hasMore();){
          Attribute attr = (Attribute)ne.next();
          System.out.println("attribute: " + attr.getID());
          for (NamingEnumeration e = attr.getAll(); e.hasMore();)
            System.out.println("value: " + e.next());
        }
      }
    } catch (Exception e) { e.printStackTrace(); }
  }
}
```

Like basic search, we can customize the set of attributes to be returned by the `search()` method as follows:

```
String[] desiredAttrs = {"objectclass"};
ctls.setReturningAttributes(desiredAttrs);
```

KEYWORDS

Address—A specification of a communication endpoint

Atomic name—An indivisible component of a name, as defined by the naming convention of the context in which the name is bound

Attribute—Information associated with a directory object. An attribute consists of an attribute identifier and a set of attribute values.

Binding—The association of an atomic name with an object

Composite name—A name that spans multiple naming systems

Composite namespace—The arrangement of namespaces from autonomous naming systems to form one logical namespace

Composite name resolution—The process of resolving a name that spans multiple naming systems

Compound name—A name in the namespace of a single naming system. It is a sequence of zero or more atomic names composed according to the naming convention of that naming system.

Context—An object whose state is a set of bindings that have distinct atomic names

Context factory—A specialization of an object factory. It accepts information about how to create a context, such as a reference, and returns an instance of the context.

Directory—A connected set of directory objects

Directory entry—Same as directory object

Directory object—An object that is in the directory. Also called a directory entry

Directory service—A service that provides operations for creating, adding, removing, and modifying the attributes associated with objects in a directory

Initial context—The starting point for resolution of names for naming and directory operations

Name—A people-friendly identifier for identifying an object or a reference to an object

Name resolution—The process of resolving a name to the object to which it is bound

Namespace—A set of all names in a naming system

Naming convention—The set of syntactic rules that govern how a name is generated. These rules determine whether a name is valid or invalid in the context in which the name is used.

Naming service—A service that provides the operations on a naming system

Naming system—A connected set of contexts of the same type (they have the same naming convention)

Schema—A set of rules that specifies the types of objects that a directory may contain and the mandatory and optional attributes that directory objects of different types are to have. It may also specify the structure of the namespace and the relationship between different types of objects.

Search filter—A logical expression specifying the attributes that the directory objects being requested should have. It is used by the directory to locate those objects.

Service provider—An implementation of a context or initial context that can be plugged in dynamically to the JNDI architecture to be used by the JNDI client.

Subcontext—A context that is bound in another context of the same type (it has the same naming convention)

SUMMARY

Naming is a fundamental concept used in almost every system of the world. It allows us to associate (called *binding*) names with objects and to find (called *lookup*) those objects later by their names. The examples of such naming systems are Domain Name System (DNS), File system, Java's rmiregistry, Java IDL's tnameserv and orbd etc.

A name is formed by one or more *name components*. The syntax of names, also called *naming convention*, is specified by the naming system. For example, in the DNS, a name (e.g. `www.google.com`) is an ordered sequence of name components (`www`, `google` and `com`) separated by dots ('.'). A file name in windows (say `D:\progs\test.java`), on the other hand, starts with a drive name (`D:`) and uses `\` (back slash) as the name component separator. A name (e.g. `ou=IT,o=JU,c=IN`) in LDAP (Lightweight Directory Access Protocol) compliant server is a comma (,) separated ordered sequence of name components, each of which is a name and value pair separated by equality sign (=).

A *naming context* is a collection of zero or more name-to-object bindings. A *subcontext* is child context of a parent context. Contexts and their subcontexts together form a general tree. The root of the context tree is referred to as *initial context* or *root context*. The process of associating a name to an object is called *binding*. For example, a DNS name is bound to an IP address; a file name is bound to a file and so on.

A directory service extends the idea of naming service. In addition to associating names with objects, a directory service allows objects to have attributes. Directory service also allows to perform attribute related operations such as reading, modifying, removing attributes, searching object based-on attributes etc.

The Java Naming and Directory Interface (JNDI) allows Java application to use naming and directory. This *initial context* is represented by an `InitialContext` object and provides the starting point of name operations. The bind() and lookup() methods are used to bind and find objects respectively. The information about a JNDI server and factory to be used to create initial context is specified by the two properties `java.naming.provider.url` and `java.naming.factory.initial`.

Apache Directory Server (often abbreviated as ApacheDS) is LDAPv3 compatible, open source directory server entirely written in Java. In this chapter, in addition to file system naming service, Java's rmiregistry and orbd, we used ApacheDS to demonstrate the JNDI concepts.

JNDI name related operations are adding, listing, looking up, replacing and removing binding. The directory specific operations are reading attributes, binding with attributes, creating subcontext with attributes, adding, modifying, removing attributes etc.

In addition to searching objects by their names, a directory server also allows us to search by attributes. A search may be performed specifying search query, called *search filter*, consisting of logical expressions.

WEB RESOURCES

`http://docs.oracle.com/javase/jndi/tutorial/`
The JNDI Tutorial

`http://docs.oracle.com/javase/tutorial/jndi/`
Trail: Java Naming and Directory Interface

`http://docs.oracle.com/javase/tutorial/jndi/ldap/jndi.html`
The JNDI Tutorial

`http://directory.apache.org/apacheds/`
ApacheDS

`http://www.javaworld.com/article/2076888/core-java/jndi-overview--part-1--an-introduction-to-naming-services.html`
JNDI overview, Part 1: An introduction to naming services

`http://www.coderpanda.com/jndi-tutorial/`
JNDI Tutorial

EXERCISES

Objective-type Questions

1. What is the full form of JNDI?
(a) Java Network and Directory Interface
(b) Java Naming and Directory Implementation
(c) Java Network and Directory Implementation
(d) Java Naming and Directory Interface

2. What is the full form of LDAP?
(a) Lazy Directory Access Protocol
(b) Lightweight Dynamic Access Protocol
(c) Lightweight Directory Access Protocol
(d) Little Directory Access Protocol

3. Which of the following is not an example of naming service?
(a) DNS (c) file system
(b) rmiregistry (d) HTTP

4. Which of the following is used to obtain the initial context?
(a) InitContext() (c) getInitialContext()
(b) InitialContext() (d) Context()

5. Which of the following is used to bind an object to a name?
(a) assign() (c) bind()
(b) name() (d) map()

6. Which of the following are JNDI properties?
(a) java.naming.factory.initial
(b) java.naming.provider.url
(c) Both a) and b)
(d) None of the above

7. Which of the following methods is used to resolve a name?
(a) lookup() (c) find()
(b) resolve() (d) search()

8. Which of the following is used to rename an existing binding?
(a) change() (c) modify()
(b) renew() (d) rename()

9. Which of the following methods is used to find all bindings?
(a) find() (c) list()
(b) search() (d) enumerate()

10. Which of the following is an example of a directory server?
(a) Apache tomcat (c) Apache
(b) Apache Ant (d) ApacheDS

11. Which of the following characters is used as the separator between name and value in LDAP?
    (a) : (c) .
    (b) = (d) -

12. What is the full form of DNS?
    (a) Directory and Naming Service
    (b) Dynamic Name System
    (c) Dynamic Native System
    (d) Domain Name System

13. A LDAP URL starts with
    (a) jndi (c) iiop
    (b) ds (d) ldap

14. Which of the following Java command line options is used to specify URL of the JNDI provider?
    (a) -Djava.jndi.provider.url
    (b) -Djava.provider
    (c) -Djava.naming.provider.url
    (d) -Djava.naming.url

15. Which of the following Java command line options is used to specify initial context factory?
    (a) -Djava.naming.factory.initial
    (b) -Djava.initial.context
    (c) -Djava.initial.context.factory
    (d) -Djava.factory.initial

16. The association of an object with a name is called
    (a) associating (c) assigning
    (b) binding (d) referencing

17. The procedure of finding an object by its name is known as
    (a) search (c) lookup
    (b) find (d) look for

18. Which of the following is a directory service?
    (a) rmiregistry (c) orbd
    (b) DNS (d) file system

19. A directory context is represented by
    (a) DirectoryContext (c) Dir
    (b) DirContext (d) DContext

20. Which of the following static constants is used to indicate deletion of an attribute?
    (a) DELETE_ATTRIBUTE
    (b) DEL_ATTRIBUTE
    (c) REMOVE_ATTRIBUTE
    (d) THROW_ATTRIBUTE

21. Which of the following static constants is used to indicate deletion of an attribute?
    (a) MODIFY_ATTRIBUTE
    (b) EDIT_ATTRIBUTE
    (c) CHANGE_ATTRIBUTE
    (d) REPLACE_ATTRIBUTE

22. Which of the following types of objects can LDAP bind?
    (a) Serializable (c) Remote
    (b) Reference (d) CORBA

23. Which of the following types of objects can rmiregistry not bind?
    (a) Referenceable (c) Remote
    (b) Reference (d) Serializable

24. Which of the following is used to find initial directory context?
    (a) InitialDirContext()
    (b) InitDirContext()
    (c) InitialContext()
    (d) InitContext()

Subjective-type Questions

1. What is the format of an LDAP URL?
2. What is the relationship between LDAP and JNDI?
3. Explain the importance of JNDI.
4. What is the difference between JDBC, JNDI and Hibernate?
5. What is a naming service?
6. What is a directory service?
7. Distinguish between naming and directory service.
8. Explain the components of JNDI.
9. What is Context and InitialContext?
10. Differentiate among JNDI lookup(), list(), listBindings(), and search() methods.
11. What is an LDAP server? And what is it used for in an enterprise environment ?
12. How will you read all attributes of a directory object?
13. How do you bind an object having attributes to a context?
14. Describe the procedure to add, modify and delete attributes.

15. Discuss how objects can be searched based on their attributes.

16. What are filters? Why are they used?

17. Identify the different components of JNDI and explain their functionality briefly.

18. Describe how to perm a batch of operations on a set of attributes.

19. Explain how to search object by their attributes.

20. Write the syntax of search filter.

CHAPTER – 25

JAVA MESSAGE SERVICE

KEY OBJECTIVES

After completing this chapter readers will be able to—

- get an overview about the Java Message Service and its components
- understand P2P and Pub/Sub model of messaging
- know what synchronous and asynchronous message consumption are
- install and configure Open Message Queue
- write JMS applications
- know how to use JNDI with JMS

25.1 MESSAGING

Messaging is a communication technique between software components or applications. However, unlike *tightly-coupled* communication techniques such as TCP sockets, RMI and CORBA, where both the parties must be available during communication, messaging allows s/w components to exchange messages; they don't have to be available at the same time. This is achieved with the introduction of a third component, called *messaging agent* that provides facilities such as creating, sending, receiving and reading messages. Messaging clients connect to a messaging agent and communicate indirectly. In fact, one need not know anything about the other, thus resulting the communication *loosely-coupled.*

Messaging is often used to coordinate programs in dissimilar systems or written in different programming languages. However, unlike electronic mail, which is a method of communication between people or between software applications and people, it is used for communication between software components or applications.

25.2 JMS API

The Java Message Service (JMS) is a Java API that allows s/w components to create, send, receive and read messages. Formerly developed by Sun, this Message Oriented Middleware (MOM) defines a set of interfaces and associated semantics, which allows Java programs to communicate with other messaging implementations. The mandatory part, which a programmer must know to understand basic messaging concept is very small. However, it supports enough features needed for sophisticated messaging applications.

25.3 JMS COMPONENTS

A JMS application typically has the following components [Figure 25.1:].

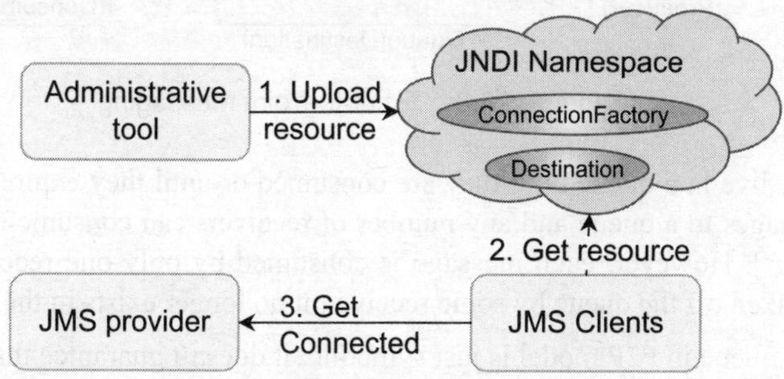

Figure 25.1: JMS Components

JMS Provider

This is a message Oriented Middleware (MOM) that implements JMS specification. It provides requisite API library, a broker that provides message storage/delivery functions. It usually also provides administrative and control features. Some of the well-known providers are Sun's Open Message Queue, Apache's Active MQ and Qpid, JBoss's HornetQ, IBM's Websphere MQ, Progress Software's SonicMQ, ZeroMQ, RabbitMQ etc. In this chapter, we shall use Sun's Open Message Queue, which is also an integral part of J2EE.

JMS Clients

These are Java programs that produce and consume messages.

Administered Objects

There are preconfigured JMS objects created usually by an administrator and are maintained by the broker for client's use. There are two kinds of administered objects: *destinations* and *connection factories*.

A destination is nothing but a message store. It is a target where producers place messages or it is a source consumers retrieve messages or both.

A connection factory object encapsulates a set of configuration properties for a connection. A JMS client uses a connection factory to create a connection to the broker.

Messages

These are objects that JMS clients exchange. In addition to text message, JMS supports messages that contain serialized Java objects and XML documents.

25.4 MESSAGING MODELS

JMS supports two models for exchanging messages between producers and consumers: *Point-to-Point* and *Publish/Subscribe*, which are frequently shortened to p2p (or PTP) and pub/sub respectively. The JMS specification refers to these as *messaging domains*.

25.4.1 Point-to-Point

In this model, the destination, producer and consumer of messages are called *queue, sender* and *receiver* respectively. Senders place messages in queues, and receivers get them [see Figure 25.2:].

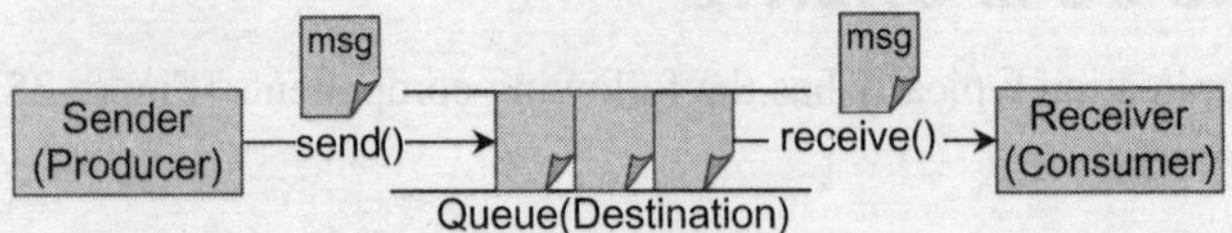

Figure 25.2: Point-to-Point Messaging

Messages live in a queue until they are consumed or until they expire. Any number of senders can put messages to a queue and any number of receivers can consume messages from the queue [Figure 25.3:]. However, each message is consumed by only one receiver. This means once a message is taken off the queue by some receiver, it no longer exists in the queue.

The term queue in P2P model is just symbolic; it doesn't guarantee that messages are delivered in any particular order. Moreover, if more than one potential receiver exists for a queue, receivers are chosen randomly for delivery of messages.

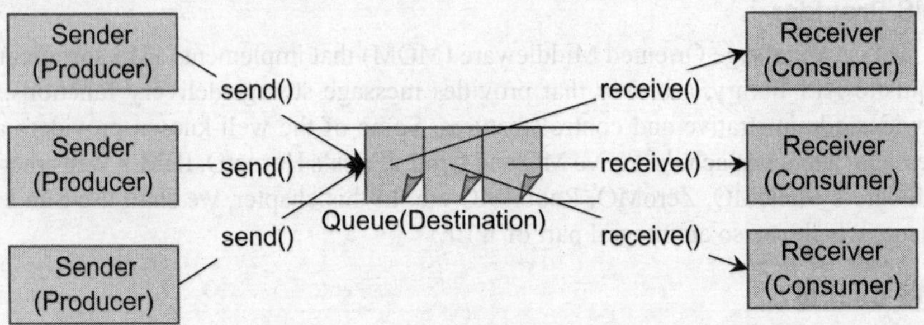

Figure 25.3: Multiple sender, multiple receiver in P2P model

A receiver can get messages by explicitly extracting them from the queue or can register itself to show its interest to get messages. In the former case, a sender and a receiver of a message need not live at the same time. A receiver can still fetch the message later whether or not it was running when the sender produced the message. However, if there is no message in the queue and a receiver tries to extract a message, it gets blocked until a message appears in the queue. This type of message consumption is known as *synchronous consumption.*

However, in P2P model, one receiver (and only one) may also get registered to a queue to get messages and continue the normal flow of execution. The broker can deliver messages as soon as they come in from some sender. This type of message consumption is known as *asynchronous consumption*. What happens if a message appears in a queue and an asynchronous receiver and other synchronous receivers are ready to get messages? Well, wait. We shall discuss more about synchronous and asynchronous consumption of messages later in this chapter.

25.4.2 Publish/Subscribe

In this model, the destination, producer and consumer of messages are called *topic, publisher* and *subscriber* respectively. Subscribers first show their interest in receiving messages on a topic.

Publishers, in turn, produce some messages for the topic. As soon as the messages are produced, they are distributed to *all* current subscribers who showed their willingness earlier [see Figure 25.4:]. So, a client is supposed to get those messages that come after the subscription.

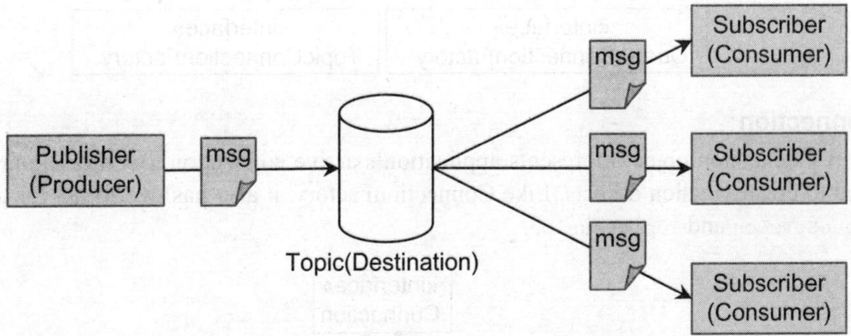

Figure 25.4: Publish-Subscribe Messaging

The primary difference of this model from P2P model is that a message is allowed to be consumed by multiple subscribers. Moreover, messages on a topic remain valid as long as they are being distributed to current subscribers. Messages do not retain the topic even if there is no subscriber for it.

The subscriber, after making a subscription must remain continuously active to receive messages. However, JMS provides a novel facility called *durable subscription*, where the client is allowed to be disconnected for some time. The JMS broker keeps messages published during the disconnection period and delivers them whenever it reconnects.

25.5 MESSAGE CONSUMPTION

JMS allows a message consumer to get messages in two ways: *synchronously* and *asynchronously*.

25.5.1 Synchronous

This style of message consumption happens when a consumer explicitly extracts messages from a destination using `receive()` method. The `receive()` method blocks the caller if no message is available at that time. As a result, the consumer cannot continue its normal mode of execution.

25.5.2 Asynchronous

In this style of message consumption, a consumer simply sets up a listener and continues its normal work. The listener, on behalf of the consumer, listens on thereafter and gets notified by the broker when a message appears in the destination.

25.6 PROGRAMMING MODEL

JMS API defines a set of interfaces [Figure 25.5:] corresponding to different messaging components and provides them as a package `javax.jms`. The primary interfaces are summarized below:

ConnectionFactory

This type of object encapsulates the configuration of a connection and is used to create connection. It has two flavors, one for each messaging models P2P and pub/sub: `QueueConnectionFatory` and `TopicConnectionFactory`.

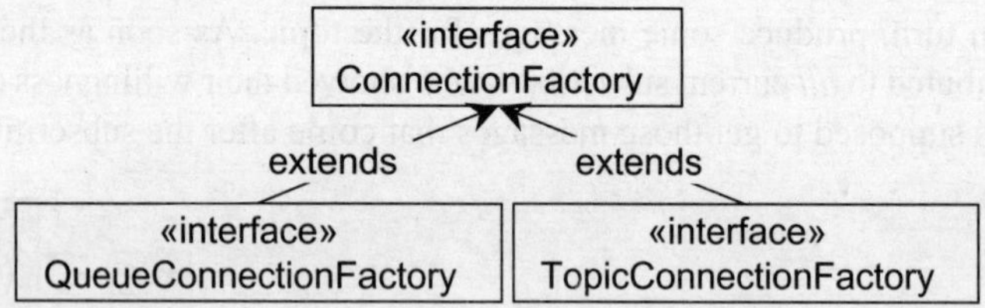

Connection

A Connection object represents application's active connection to a messaging broker. This is used to create Session objects. Like ConnectionFactory, it also has two forms for the two models: `QueueSession` and `TopicSession`.

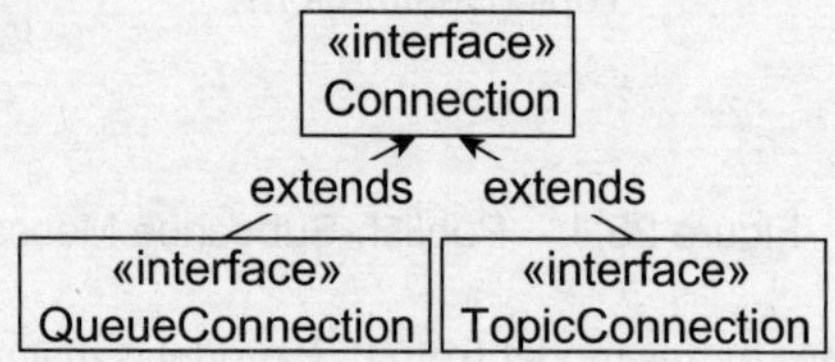

Session

This is a context used to create destinations, producers, consumers, messages etc. It also has two flavors: `QueueSession` and `TopicSession`.

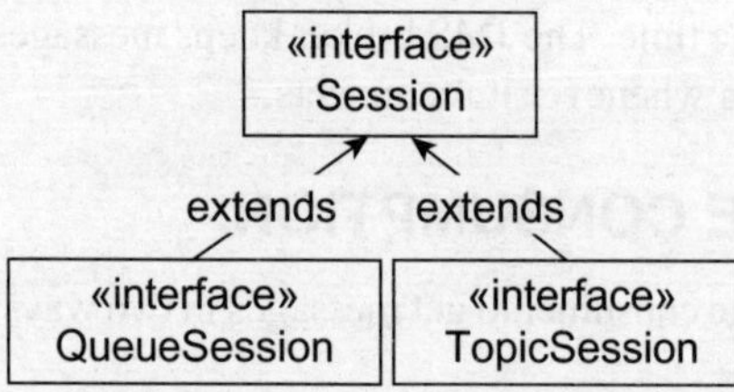

Destination

This is the message store where producers place messages and consumers get messages from. A Destination object may be created from Session or by JNDI lookup. In P2P and pub/sub models, destinations are called queues and topics respectively and are represented by Queue and Topic objects respectively.

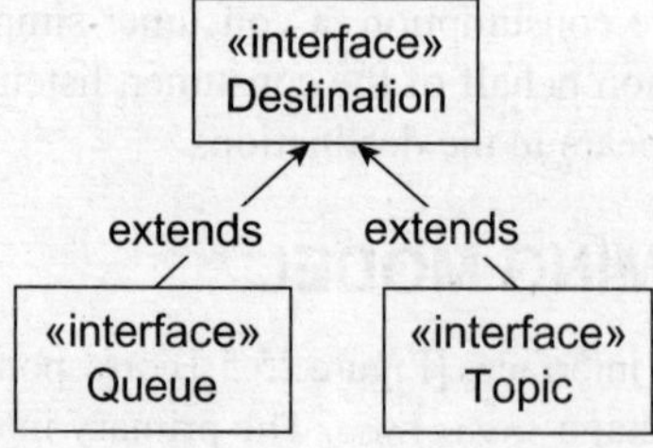

MessageProducer

A `MessageProducer` object is created from `Session` specifying a `Destination` and is used to send messages to the specified destination. It has two forms for two messaging models: `QueueSender` and `TopicPublisher`.

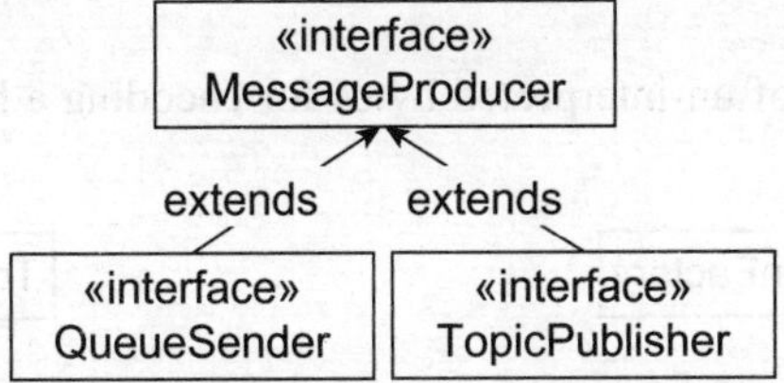

MessageConsumer

A `MessageConsumer` object is created from `Session` specifying a `Destination` and is used to receive messages from the specified destination. It has two forms for two messaging models: `QueueReceiver` and `TopicSubscriber`.

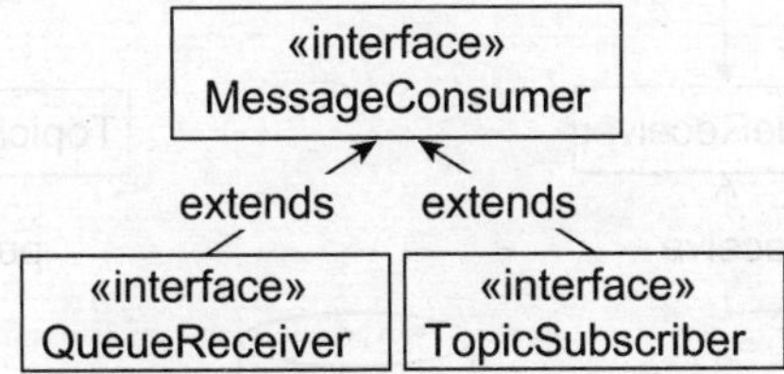

Message

The interface is the root interface of all JMS messages. It defines the message header and the acknowledgement method to be used for all messages. A message usually consists of a header that contains fields used for message routing and identification, application specific property values and a payload that contains the application data being sent. Five types of messages are specified in JMS API [Table 25.1:]:

Table 25.1: JMS generic and model specific interfaces

High-level interface	P2P model	Pub/sub model
ConnectionFactory	QueueConnectionFactory	TopicConnectionFactory
Connection	QueueConnection	TopicConnection
Session	QueueSession	TopicSession
Destination	Queue	Topic
MessageProducer	QueueSender	TopicPublisher
MessageConsumer	QueueReceiver, QueueBrowser	TopicSubscriber

StreamMessage

Contains a stream of Java primitive values.

MapMessage

Contains a set of name-value pairs.

TextMessage

Contains a java.lang.String object. This message type can be used to transport plain-text messages, and XML messages.

ObjectMessage

Contains a Serializable Java object.

BytesMessage

Contains a stream of un-interpreted bytes for encoding a body to match an existing message format.

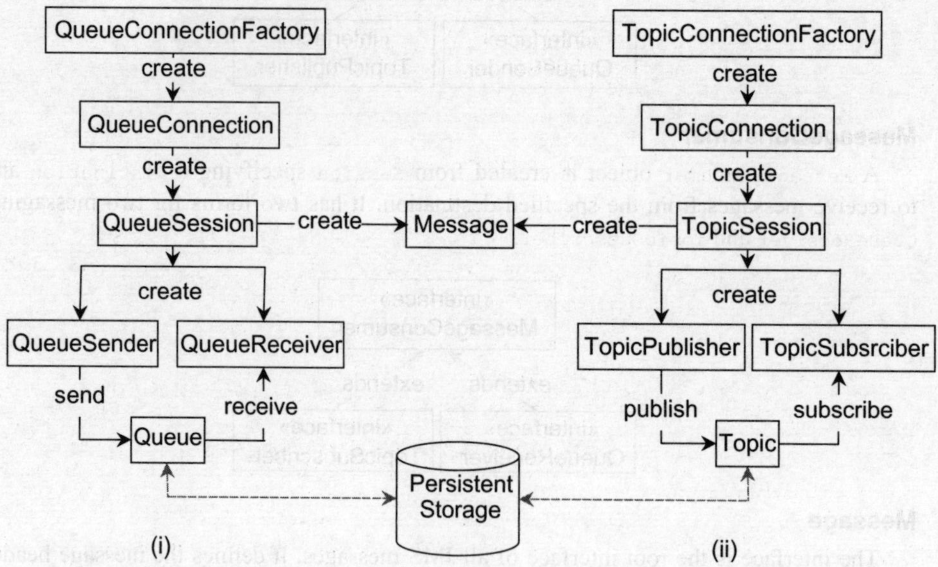

Figure 25.5: JMS programming model (i) P2P model (ii) Pub/Sub model

There are various JMS providers. However, for simplicity, we shall use a full-blown provider such as J2EE server. Instead, we shall use formerly Sun's Open Message Queue, which is lightweight, easy to use and an integral part of J2EE. So, the next section discusses how to get and install Open MQ.

25.7 INSTALLING OPEN MQ

The first step to create a JMS application is to get Open Message Queue. Download the latest release of Open Message Queue from `https://mq.java.net/downloads.html`. We downloaded the zip archive for windows `openmq4_5_2-binary-WINNT.zip`. Unzip the binary (.jar) bundle in a directory, say `D:\openmq4_5_2`. Hereafter, we shall refer to this directory as `<MQ_TOP>`. Edit the file `<MQ_TOP>/etc/mq/imqenv.conf` to set `IMQ_DEFAULT_JAVAHOME` to your JDK home directory. We did this using the following:

```
set IMQ_DEFAULT_JAVAHOME=D:\Java\jdk1.7.0_07
```

Open Message Queue is now ready to function. Go to `<MQ_TOP>/mq/bin` and use the following command to start the broker:

```
imqbrokerd
```

If everything goes fine, the output displayed should be similar to that shown below:

```
D:\openmq4_5_2\mq\bin>imqbrokerd
[08/Mar/2014:05:30:20 PST]
================================================================================
=
Open Message Queue 4.5.2
Oracle
Version:  4.5.2  (Build 2-d)
Compile:  Thu 12/08/2011
```

```
Copyright (c) 2011, Oracle and/or its affiliates.  All rights reserved.
==========================================================================
=
Java Runtime: 1.7.0_07 Oracle Corporation D:\Java\jdk1.7.0_07\jre
[08/Mar/2014:05:30:20 PST]    IMQ_HOME=D:\openmq4_5_2\mq
[08/Mar/2014:05:30:20 PST] IMQ_VARHOME=D:\openmq4_5_2\var\mq
[08/Mar/2014:05:30:20 PST] Windows 7 6.1 x86 uroy (4 cpu) root
[08/Mar/2014:05:30:20 PST] Java Heap Size: max=174784k, current=15744k
[08/Mar/2014:05:30:20 PST] Arguments:
[08/Mar/2014:05:30:20 PST] [B1060]: Loading persistent data...
[08/Mar/2014:05:30:20 PST] Using built-in file-based persistent store:
D:\openmq4_5_2\var\mq\instances\imqbroker\
[08/Mar/2014:05:30:20 PST] [B1270]: Processing messages from transaction log file...
[08/Mar/2014:05:30:21 PST] [B1039]: Broker "imqbroker@uroy:7676" ready.
```

To check the broker startup, use `imqcmd` utility as follows:

```
imqcmd query bkr -u admin
```

Supply the default password of `admin`, when prompted to do so. A sample output is shown below:

```
D:\openmq4_5_2\mq\bin>imqcmd query bkr -u admin
Password:
Querying the broker specified by:

-------------------------
Host        Primary Port
-------------------------
localhost    7676

Version                                              4.5.2
Instance Name                                        imqbroker
Broker ID
Primary Port                                         7676
Broker is Embedded                                   false
Instance Configuration/Data Root Directory           D:\openmq4_5_2\var\mq

Current Number of Messages in System                 0
Current Total Message Bytes in System                0

Current Number of Messages in Dead Message Queue     0
Current Total Message Bytes in Dead Message Queue    0

Log Dead Messages                                    false
Truncate Message Body in Dead Message Queue          false

Max Number of Messages in System                     unlimited (-1)
Max Total Message Bytes in System                    unlimited (-1)
Max Message Size                                     70m

Auto Create Queues                                   true
Auto Create Topics                                   true
Auto Created Queue Max Number of Active Consumers    unlimited (-1)
Auto Created Queue Max Number of Backup Consumers    0

Cluster ID
Cluster is Highly Available                          false
Cluster Broker List (active)                         mq://172.16.5.81:7676/
Cluster Broker List (configured)
Cluster Master Broker
Cluster URL

Log Level                                            INFO
```

```
Log Rollover Interval (seconds)                 604800
Log Rollover Size (bytes)                        268435456

Successfully queried the broker.
```

25.8 WRITING JMS APPLICATION

The following are the basic steps to write a JMS client:

- Create/Look up a ConnectionFactory object.
- Use the ConnectionFactory to create a Connection.
- Use the Connection to create one or more Session objects.
- Create/Look up one or more Destination objects.
- Use a Session and a Destination to create MessageProducer and MessageConsumer objects.
- Send and receive messages.

To write any JMS client, we first need a reference to a `ConnectionFactory` object, which encapsulates the necessary configuration properties for creating connections to the MQ broker. We can easily create such an object by instantiating it explicitly as follows:

```
ConnectionFactory cf = new com.sun.messaging.ConnectionFactory();
```

This object may be obtained by JNDI lookup, which we shall discuss later in this chapter. Since, we have created this object, we have to configure it properly. The minimal configuration requires specifying port number and name or address of the machine where broker is running. We do this as follows:

```
((com.sun.messaging.ConnectionFactory)cf).setProperty(com.sun.messaging.Connect
ionConfiguration.imqAddressList,"172.16.5.81:7676");
```

This ConnectionFactory object is used to create connections with the Sun's Open Message Queue JMS provider. The following is an example:

```
Connection con = cf.createConnection();
```

It represents an open connection (usually a TCP/IP socket) between a JMS client and a broker. It is responsible for authenticating clients, providing connection meta data, creating Session objects etc. and relatively heavyweight object. So, it is recommended to create one Connection object, unless it is unavoidable. This connection initially remains in the *stopped* mode. It means, it does not allow to consume messages from a destination. However, producers may produce their messages, even though there is a stopped connection.

We then create a `Session` object:

```
Session sn = con.createSession(false, Session.AUTO_ACKNOWLEDGE);
```

A `Session` object represents a singled threaded communication session between a JMS client and a JMS broker. It allows us to create producers/consumers, queues/topics, produce/consume messages etc.

This portion is common in all JMS clients. Let us now write code that sends messages to a queue using P2P model.

25.9 WRITING A P2P PRODUCER

A producer in P2P model is called queue sender. Let us write a simple queue sender that produces a simple text message. Since, in P2P model, a message destination is called a queue, let us create a Queue object explicitly as follows:

```
Destination dest = sn.createQueue(args[0]);
```

This creates a `Queue` in the broker with name `AQueue`, if it does not exist already. A `Destination` object is also a JMS administered object and may also be obtained from a JNDI look up, which we shall discuss later in this chapter.

To send messages to a destination, a queue sender uses a `MessageProducer` object, which is created by passing a Destination object to `createProducer()` method of Session:

```
MessageProducer mp = sn.createProducer(dest);
```

It is also possible to create a `MessageProducer` without supplying a destination. The destination is specified later when a message is sent using `send()` method. We then create a text message to be sent as follows:

```
TextMessage tm = sn.createTextMessage();
tm.setText("A test message");
```

A `TextMessage` object is one that contains a `String` object, which has been specified using `setText()` method. Finally, the message is sent to the queue using `send()` method:

```
mp.send(tm);
```

The interesting part is that there is no trace of who will finally read the message. Actually, the producer need not know where or who the consumer is; it just sends messages into queue `AQueue` and what happens from there to the sent messages is not of producer's interest any more.

It is a good idea to close session and connection, so that resources occupied by these objects are released:

```
sn.close();
con.close();
```

The entire source code (`Sender.java`) of the sender is shown below:

```
import javax.jms.*;
public class Sender {
  public static void main(String[] args) {
    try {
      ConnectionFactory cf = new com.sun.messaging.ConnectionFactory();
((com.sun.messaging.ConnectionFactory)cf).setProperty(com.sun.messaging.Connect
ionConfiguration.imqAddressList,"172.16.5.81:7676");
      Connection con = cf.createConnection();
      Session sn = con.createSession(false, Session.AUTO_ACKNOWLEDGE);
      Destination dest = sn.createQueue(args[0]);
      MessageProducer mp = sn.createProducer(dest);
      TextMessage tm = sn.createTextMessage();
      tm.setText("A test message");
      mp.send(tm);
      System.out.println("Message sent:");
      sn.close();
      con.close();
    } catch (Exception e) { e.printStackTrace(); }
  }
}
```

25.9.1 Running Example

To send a message, make sure that the MQ broker is running port 7676 in a machine having IP address 172.16.5.81.

Compile the program as follows:

```
javac -cp jms.jar;imq.jar;. Sender.java
```

The sender can then be executed as follows:

```
java -cp jms.jar;imq.jar;. Sender AQueue
```

If everything goes fine, the following message appears on the screen:

```
Message sent:
```

The content of the queue may also be verified using imqcmd utility as follows:

```
imqcmd query dst -n AQueue -t q -u admin
```

Supply the default password of `admin` when prompted to do so. A sample output is shown below:

```
...
Destination Name                        AQueue
Destination Type                        Queue
Destination State                       RUNNING
Created Administratively                false

Current Number of Messages
    Actual                              1
...
```

25.10 WRITING A P2P SYNCHRONOUS CONSUMER

A consumer in P2P model is called a queue receiver. Let us now see how to write such a receiver to consume the sent message. Like producer, it also creates Session and Destination objects. Then it creates a `MessageConsumer`:

```
MessageConsumer mc = sn.createConsumer(dest);
```

Note that a connection remains in the stopped mode where a consumer is not allowed to consume any message from a destination. So, let's make it running:

```
con.start();
```

Finally, the message is consumed explicitly by invoking `receive()` method. The receiver method just returns a `Message` object and there are no separate methods for receiving just `TextMessage`. So, we type cast it and print text message's content:

```
TextMessage msg = (TextMessage) mc.receive();
System.out.println("Received message: "+msg.getText());
```

Note that the `receive()` method blocks the caller if there is no message in the queue currently. As a result, the consumer cannot continue its normal flow of execution. However, as soon as a message arrives in the queue, it is delivered to the consumer. This way of message consumption is called *synchronous consumption* of message.

The complete source code (SynReceiver.java) is shown below:

```
import javax.jms.*;
public class SynReceiver {
  public static void main(String[] args) {
    try {
      ConnectionFactory cf = new com.sun.messaging.ConnectionFactory();
((com.sun.messaging.ConnectionFactory)cf).setProperty(com.sun.messaging.Connect
ionConfiguration.imqAddressList,"172.16.5.81:7676");
      Connection con = cf.createConnection();
      Session sn = con.createSession(false, Session.AUTO_ACKNOWLEDGE);
      Destination dest = sn.createQueue(args[0]);
      MessageConsumer mc = sn.createConsumer(dest);
      con.start();
      TextMessage msg = (TextMessage) mc.receive();
      System.out.println("Received message: "+msg.getText());
      sn.close();
      con.close();
    } catch (Exception e) { e.printStackTrace(); }
  }
}
```

Compile the program as follows:

```
javac -cp jms.jar;imq.jar;. SynReceiver.java
```

The receiver can then be executed as follows:

```
java -cp jms.jar;imq.jar;. SynReceiver AQueue
```

If everything goes fine, the following message appears on the screen:

```
Received message: A test message
```

The content of the queue may also be verified using `imqcmd` utility as follows:

```
imqcmd query dst -n AQueue -t q -u admin
```

Supply the default password of `admin` when prompted to do so. A sample output is shown below:

```
…
Destination Name                      AQueue
Destination Type                      Queue
Destination State                     RUNNING
Created Administratively              false

Current Number of Messages
    Actual                            0
…
```

It indicates that the message that was produced earlier has been consumed and no longer exists in the queue.

25.11 WRITING A P2P ASYNCHRONOUS CONSUMER

As mentioned in the previous section, the receiver gets blocked and cannot continue its normal execution if it invokes a `receive()` method and the queue is empty. This can be avoided by consuming messages *asynchronously*. In this style of message consumption, consumer simply sets up a listener and continues its normal work. The listener, on behalf of the consumer, listens on thereafter and gets notified by the broker when a message appears in the destination.

A message listener must implement `MessageListener` interface. Here is a sample listener class:

```
public class AListener implements MessageListener {
```

The interface `MessageListener` has a single method `onMessage()`, which takes a single parameter `Message` as follows:

```
void onMessage(Message message)
```

The MQ runtime calls this method to deliver a message. We implement the method as follows:

```
public void onMessage(Message msg) {
  TextMessage tm = (TextMessage) msg;
  try {
    System.out.println("Received: " + tm.getText());
  } catch (Exception e) { e.printStackTrace(); }
}
```

An asynchronous consumer sets up a message listener using its setMessageListener() method:

```
mc.setMessageListener(new AListener());
```

The consumer can then continue its normal work. However, it must be active and therefore must not close the connection and session. Here is the complete source code (AsynReceiver.java.) of asynchronous consumer:

```
import javax.jms.*;
public class AsynReceiver {
  public static void main(String[] args) {
    try {
      ConnectionFactory conFactory = new com.sun.messaging.ConnectionFactory();
((com.sun.messaging.ConnectionFactory)conFactory).setProperty(com.sun.messaging
.ConnectionConfiguration.imqAddressList,"172.16.5.81:7676");
```

```
            Connection con = conFactory.createConnection();
            Session sn = con.createSession(false, Session.AUTO_ACKNOWLEDGE);
            Destination dest = sn.createQueue(args[0]);
            MessageConsumer mc = sn.createConsumer(dest);
            con.start();
            mc.setMessageListener(new AListener());
            System.out.println("Continuing its own work");
        } catch (Exception e) { e.printStackTrace(); }
    }
}
class AListener implements MessageListener {
    public void onMessage(Message msg) {
        TextMessage tm = (TextMessage) msg;
        try {
            System.out.println("Received: " + tm.getText());
        } catch (Exception e) { e.printStackTrace(); }
    }
}
```

Compile and run the program as before. Note that this consumer can continue its work after setting up a listener. The message `Continuing its own work` appears even if there is no message in the queue.

25.12 WRITING A PUB/SUB PRODUCER

A producer in a pub/sub model is called a topic publisher. Let us write a simple topic publisher that produces a simple text message. The code for this topic publisher will look exactly like a queue sender except that it creates a topic instead of a queue as follows:

```
Destination dest = sn.createTopic("ATopic");
```

The complete source code (Publisher.java) is given below:

```
import javax.jms.*;
public class Publisher {
    public static void main(String[] args) {
        try {
            ConnectionFactory cf = new com.sun.messaging.ConnectionFactory();
((com.sun.messaging.ConnectionFactory)cf).setProperty(com.sun.messaging.Connect
ionConfiguration.imqAddressList,"172.16.5.81:7676");
            Connection con = cf.createConnection();
            Session sn = con.createSession(false, Session.AUTO_ACKNOWLEDGE);
            Destination dest = sn.createTopic("ATopic");
            MessageProducer mp = sn.createProducer(dest);
            TextMessage tm = sn.createTextMessage();
            tm.setText("A test message");
            mp.send(tm);
            System.out.println("Message sent:");
            sn.close();
            con.close();
        } catch (Exception e) { e.printStackTrace();}
    }
}
```

25.13 WRITING A PUB/SUB SYNCHRONOUS CONSUMER

A consumer in a pub/sub model is called a topic subscriber. Let us write a simple topic subscriber that consumes a simple text message. The code for this topic publisher will look exactly like a queue sender, except that it creates a topic instead of a queue as follows:

```
Destination dest = sn.createTopic("ATopic");
```

The complete source code (SynSubscriber.java) is given below:

```
import javax.jms.*;
public class SynSubscriber {
```

```
  public static void main(String[] args) {
    try {
      ConnectionFactory conFactory = new com.sun.messaging.ConnectionFactory();
((com.sun.messaging.ConnectionFactory)conFactory).setProperty(com.sun.messaging
.ConnectionConfiguration.imqAddressList,"172.16.5.81:7676");
      Connection con = conFactory.createConnection();
      Session sn = con.createSession(false, Session.AUTO_ACKNOWLEDGE);
      Destination d = sn.createTopic("ATopic");
      MessageConsumer mc = sn.createConsumer(d);
      con.start();
      TextMessage msg = (TextMessage) mc.receive();
      System.out.println("Received message: "+msg.getText());
      sn.close();
      con.close();
    } catch (Exception e) {
      e.printStackTrace();
    }
  }
}
```

This program is exactly same as SynReceiver.java except that it uses `createTopic()` method, instead of `createdQueue()`.

25.14 RUNNING THIS EXAMPLE

In pub/sub model, publishers and subscribers have a timing dependency. A client can consume only messages published after the client has subscribed itself and remains active. Moreover, the JMS system delivers a message to all active subscribers. So, we can start multiple subscribers to receive the same message. Open two terminals and start two subscribers as follows:

```
java -cp imq.jar;jms.jar;. SynSubscriber
```

The subscribers are now ready to receive a single message on topic ATopic. Now start a Publisher that publishes a text message on the same topic.

```
java -cp imq.jar;jms.jar;. Publisher
```

A sample result is shown in Figure 25.6:

Figure 25.6: Publisher/Subscriber example

25.15 WRITING A PUB/SUB ASYNCHRONOUS CONSUMER

An asynchronous topic subscriber looks almost like an asynchronous queue receiver, except that the former creates a topic instead of a queue. The complete source code (AsynSubscriber.java) is shown below:

```
import javax.jms.*;
public class AsynSubscriber {
```

```
  public static void main(String[] args) {
    try {
      ConnectionFactory conFactory = new com.sun.messaging.ConnectionFactory();
((com.sun.messaging.ConnectionFactory)conFactory).setProperty(com.sun.messaging
.ConnectionConfiguration.imqAddressList,"172.16.5.81:7676");
      Connection con = conFactory.createConnection();
      Session sn = con.createSession(false, Session.AUTO_ACKNOWLEDGE);
      Destination dest = sn.createTopic("ATopic");
      MessageConsumer mc = sn.createConsumer(dest);
      con.start();
      mc.setMessageListener(new AListener());
      System.out.println("Continuing its own work");
    } catch (Exception e) { e.printStackTrace(); }
  }
}
class AListener implements MessageListener {
  public void onMessage(Message msg) {
    TextMessage tm = (TextMessage) msg;
    try {
      System.out.println("Received: " + tm.getText());
    } catch (Exception e) { e.printStackTrace(); }
  }
}
```

Note that this program is exactly same as AsynReceiver.java except that it uses `createTopic()` method instead of `createdQueue()`.

We can now start multiple subscribers and publishers as before.

25.16 BROWSING QUEUE

JMS also supports inspecting messages in a queue without receiving them. The following program prints all messages in a queue `AQueue`, else prints a message if the queue is empty.

```
import javax.jms.*;
public class Browser {
  public static void main(String[] args) {
    try {
      ConnectionFactory cf = new com.sun.messaging.ConnectionFactory();
((com.sun.messaging.ConnectionFactory)cf).setProperty(com.sun.messaging.Connect
ionConfiguration.imqAddressList,"172.16.5.81:7676");
      Connection con = cf.createConnection();
      Session sn = con.createSession(false, Session.AUTO_ACKNOWLEDGE);
      Destination dest = sn.createQueue("AQueue");
      QueueBrowser browser = sn.createBrowser((Queue)dest);
      java.util.Enumeration msgs = browser.getEnumeration();
      if ( !msgs.hasMoreElements() )
        System.out.println("No messages in queue");
      else {
        while (msgs.hasMoreElements()) {
          Message tempMsg = (Message)msgs.nextElement();
          System.out.println("Message: " + tempMsg);
        }
      }
      sn.close();
      con.close();
    } catch (Exception e) { e.printStackTrace(); }
  }
}
```

Make sure that a queue with name `AQueue` exists before running the program.

25.17 USING JNDI

JMS has not defined any address syntax by which clients communicate with the broker. Instead, JMS utilizes Java Naming & Directory Interface (JNDI), that provides the following advantages:

- Hides provider-specific details from JMS clients.
- Abstracts JMS configuration information into Java objects that are easily administrated and organized from a common management console.
- Since, there exists JNDI providers for all popular naming services, JMS providers can provide single implementation of administered objects that will run everywhere, thereby eliminating complicated deployment and configuration issues.

Using JNDI, administered objects are created and configured by the MQ administrator and placed on a publicly accessible naming service. These objects can then be used by JMS clients using JNDI interface. This makes client code provider independent and becomes portable from one JMS provider to another. The client can also avoid complicated task for creating and configuring administered objects.

However, for testing purpose or in the early stages of the application, it is more convenient to insert a few lines of code in the client program to connect to the JMS provider directly, instead of using a long procedure needed by JNDI. In the previous sections, we have seen how a client can connect to the JMD provider directly. In this section, we shall discuss the same using JNDI.

So, a client, instead of creating administered object itself, can also look up predefined administered objects such as `ConnectionFactory` and `Destination` using the Java Naming and Directory Interface (JNDI). In this case, the administered objects are created and configured by the MQ administrator and placed in a naming service such as file system, LDAP, rmiregistry etc.

It is expected that JMS providers will provide the tools an administrator needs to create and configure administered objects in a JNDI namespace. Accordingly, MQ provides a utility `imqadmin` for this purpose. A Java program may also be written to create such administered objects. The following is a sample example that uses JNDI:

```
import javax.naming.*;
import javax.jms.*;
//import com.sun.messaging.*;
public class CreateAO {
  public static void main(String[] args) {
    try {
      Context ctx = new InitialContext();
      ConnectionFactory cf = new com.sun.messaging.ConnectionFactory();
((com.sun.messaging.ConnectionFactory)cf).setProperty(com.sun.messaging.
ConnectionConfiguration.imqAddressList,"172.16.4.248:7676");
      ctx.rebind(args[0], cf);
      ctx.rebind(args[1], new com.sun.messaging.Queue());
      ctx.rebind(args[2], new com.sun.messaging.Topic());
      System.out.println("Created and registered three administered objects");
    } catch (Exception e) { e.printStackTrace(); }
  }
}
```

This creates `ConnectionFactory` a `Queue` and a `Topic` objects and binds them to a naming server with names specified as command lines arguments. The `ConnectionFactory` factory object encapsulates the information of a broker running in a host 172.16.4.248 on port 7676 and hence, when used later, is capable of establishing connection with this broker. If your broker runs on a different host, use it in the `setProperty()` method. Note that this program configures administered objects minimally. For other sophisticated configurations such as performance tuning, use `imqadmin` utility that provides a GUI instead. Compile the program as follows:

```
javac -cp imq.jar CreateAO.java
```

Note that the above program is capable of binding administered objects to any naming service, provided that information of the name server is provided as JNDI command line arguments. For example, to register these objects to the (local) file system naming service with base `file:///D:/openmq4_5_2/adminObjects`, use the following command:

```
java -cp imq.jar;fscontext.jar;. -
Djava.naming.factory.initial=com.sun.jndi.fscontext.RefFSContextFactory -
Djava.naming.provider.url=file:///D:/openmq4_5_2/adminObjects CreateAO ACF
AQueue ATopic
```

The names of the connection factory, queue and topic are specified as ACF, AQueue and ATopic Respectively. This essentially creates a file `.bindings` that contains necessary information to establish a connection to the broker running in 172.16.4.248 on port 7676 in the directory `file:///D:/openmq4_5_2/adminObjects`.

Similarly, to register them to the `rmiregistry` on port 6789, use the following command:

```
java -cp imq.jar;. -
Djava.naming.factory.initial=com.sun.jndi.rmi.registry.RegistryContextFactory -
Djava.naming.provider.url=rmi://localhost:6789 CreateAO ACF AQueue ATopic
```

Start rmiregistery as follows:

```
rmiregistry 6789
```

Note that `rmiregistry` must be started in the local machine, as it does not allow us to register objects created in a different machine. This problem may be avoided using an LDAP naming service. We started Apache Directory Server in a machine 172.16.4.248 on port 10389. The administered object can be registered to this LDAP server from any remote computer as follows:

```
java -cp imq.jar;. -
Djava.naming.factory.initial=com.sun.jndi.ldap.LdapCtxFactory -
Djava.naming.provider.url=ldap://172.16.4.248:10389/dc=example,dc=com CreateAO
cn=ACF cn=AQueue cn=ATopic
```

Apache directory sever has two default partitions `dc=example,dc=com` and `ou=system`. We used the former one. A client can then get a reference to `ConnectionFactory` and `Destination` objects, using JNDI as follows:

```
Context ctx = new InitialContext();
ConnectionFactory cf = (ConnectionFactory) ctx.lookup(args[0]);
Destination dest = (Destination)ctx.lookup(args[1]);
```

The complete source code (`ProducerJNDI.java`) of the producer that used JNDI is shown below:

```
import javax.jms.*;
import javax.naming.*;
public class ProducerJNDI {
  public static void main(String[] args) {
    try {
      Context ctx = new InitialContext();
      ConnectionFactory cf = (ConnectionFactory) ctx.lookup(args[0]);
      Destination dest = (Destination)ctx.lookup(args[1]);

      Connection con = cf.createConnection();
      Session sn = con.createSession(false, Session.AUTO_ACKNOWLEDGE);
      MessageProducer mp = sn.createProducer(dest);
      TextMessage tm = sn.createTextMessage();
      tm.setText("A test message");
      mp.send(tm);
```

```
            System.out.println("Message sent:");
            sn.close();
            con.close();
        } catch (Exception e) {
            e.printStackTrace();
        }
    }
}
```

Compile this program using the following:

```
javac -cp jms.jar ProducerJNDI.java
```

Note that this program does not use any provider specific code and hence is capable of working with any JMS provider, provided that JNDI parameters are passed to this program as follows:

```
java -cp jms.jar;imq.jar;fscontext.jar;. -
Djava.naming.factory.initial=com.sun.jndi.fscontext.RefFSContextFactory -
Djava.naming.provider.url=file:///D:/openmq4_5_2/adminObjects ProducerJNDI ACF
AQueue
```

For file system naming service, a JAR file `fscontext.jar` that contains necessary classes for file system JNDI is needed. This file can be found in `<MQ_TOP>/lib` directory. Make also sure that the MQ broker is running on a machine, 172.16.4.248 on port 7676 since the `ConnectionFactory` corresponds to such a broker. For `rmiregistry` naming service running on a computer 172.16.5.1 on port 6789, use the following command:

```
java -cp jms.jar;imq.jar;. -
Djava.naming.factory.initial=com.sun.jndi.rmi.registry.RegistryContextFactory -
Djava.naming.provider.url=rmi://172.16.5.81:6789 ProducerJNDI ACF AQueue
```

For LDAP service, use the following command:

```
java -cp jms.jar;imq.jar;. -
Djava.naming.factory.initial=com.sun.jndi.ldap.LdapCtxFactory -
Djava.naming.provider.url=ldap://172.16.4.248:10389/dc=example,dc=com
ProducerJNDI cn=ACFcn=AQueue
```

The JNDI properties may be specified directly in the program. For file system, it looks like this:

```
java.util.Hashtable env = new java.util.Hashtable();
env.put(Context.INITIAL_CONTEXT_FACTORY,
"com.sun.jndi.fscontext.RefFSContextFactory");
env.put(Context.PROVIDER_URL, "file:///D:/openmq4_5_2/adminObjects");
Context ctx = new InitialContext(env);
```

And run the program simply as follows:

```
java -cp imq.jar;fscontext.jar;. ProducerJNDI ACF AQueue
```

Note that for a file system JNDI, the file system must be local to the JMS client. If it is created by the MQ administrator in a different computer, transfer the `.bindings` file to the JMS client's machine and put it in any directory say `D:/openmq4_5_2/remoteObjects` and specify the directory in the `Djava.naming.provider.url` property as follows:

```
env.put(Context.PROVIDER_URL, "file:///D:/openmq4_5_2/remoteObjects");.
```

Or as a command line argument as

```
-Djava.naming.provider.url=file:///D:/openmq4_5_2/remoteObjects
```

25.18 RELIABILITY MECHANISMS

JMS specification provides many features towards reliable message delivery some of which are discussed briefly in the next few sections.

25.18.1 Acknowledgement

A message is supposed to be consumed successfully if it has been acknowledged. Acknowledgment may be initiated either by the client or by the JMS provider. When and how a message is acknowledged depends on if the session is transacted or not.

For a transacted session, acknowledgments are sent automatically by the provider when a transaction is committed. If a transaction is rolled back, all consumed messages are resent to the destination the messages consumed from.

25.18.2 Message Persistence

By default, messages sent by producers and to be delivered to consumers are stored in stable persistent storage before delivery. The `send()` method does not return successfully until a message is stored. So, if the provider fails later during message delivery due to some reason, or if it is restarted, the messages still sustain. This is known as `PERSISTENT` delivery mode. JMS also provides `NON_PERSISTENT` delivery mode where messages before delivery are not stored in persistent storage. So, messaging may be missing. However, it reduces storage and performance is expected to be better.

A JMS client can instruct the provider to use a specific kind of delivery mode. One way to do this is to use the `setDeliveryMode()` method of the `MessageProducer` interface as follows:

```
mp.setDeliveryMode(DeliveryMode.NON_PERSISTENT);
```

This sets the delivery mode for all messages sent by that producer to `NON_PERSISTENT` mode. We can also use the overloaded `send()` method to set the delivery mode for a specific message as follows:

```
mp.send(message, DeliveryMode.NON_PERSISTENT, 3, 10000);
```

The second argument sets the delivery mode to `NON_PERSISTENT`. The third and fourth arguments set the priority level and expiration time, which are described in the next sections.

25.18.3 Message Priority

JMS specifies ten levels of priority range from 0 (lowest) to 9 (highest) that indicate how urgently messages should be delivered. One way to do this is to use the `setPriority()` method of the `MessageProducer` interface as follows:

```
mp.setPriority(6);
```

This sets the priority level for all messages sent by that producer to 6. We can also use the `send()` method of the `MessageProducer` interface to set the priority for a specific message as follows:

```
mp.send(message, DeliveryMode.NON_PERSISTENT, 6, 10000);
```

The third argument sets the priority level.

25.18.4 Message Expiration

By default, JMS provider retains all the messages in the memory indefinitely. In addition, they are key in persistent storage if `PERSITENT` delivery mode is used. A message may be given an expiry time after which the message is no longer retained in the JMS system. Note that the messages are not deleted as soon as they expire. The JMS provider looks for all expired messages after a certain time interval and deletes such messages from the memory. If an expired message is a persistent one, it is deleted from the persistent message as well.

One way to do this is to use the `setTimeToLive()` method of the `MessageProducer` interface as follows:

```
mp.setTimeToLive(10000);
```

This sets the expiry time for all messages sent by that producer to 10000 milliseconds (10 seconds). We can also use the `send()` method of the `MessageProducer` interface to set the expiry time for a specific message as follows:

```
mp.send(message, DeliveryMode.NON_PERSISTENT, 5, 10000);
```

The fourth argument sets expiry time.

25.18.5 Temporary Destinations

The destinations (queues and topics), we have created so far lasts even after a provider restarts. JMS API also allows to create `TemporaryQueue` and `TemporaryTopic` objects that only last till the connection, in which they are created survives. We create these temporary queues and topic using the `createTemporaryQueue()` and the `createTemporaryTopic()` methods on `Session` interface. The temporary destinations are typically used to implement a simple request/reply mechanism.

25.19 TRANSACTED SESSION

A transaction is the atomic unit of many operations, such as message sends and receives, so that the operations either all succeed or all fail. An application can participate in such transactions by creating a transacted session (or local transaction). The application completely controls the message delivery by either committing or rolling back the session. If all the operations succeed, the transaction is committed. If any one of the operations fails, the transaction is rolled back, and the operations may be attempted again from the beginning.

Think about an application that reliably copies all the messages from a source queue to a destination queue. So, receiving a message from the source and sending it to the destination queue must either occur together or fail both. For this purpose, it can create a transacted session as follows:

```
sn = con.createSession(true, Session.AUTO_ACKNOWLEDGE);
```

The complete source code (Copier.java) is shown below:

```
import javax.jms.*;
public class Copier implements MessageListener {
  Session sn;
  MessageProducer mp;
  public Copier(String args[]) {
    try {
      ConnectionFactory cf = new com.sun.messaging.ConnectionFactory();
((com.sun.messaging.ConnectionFactory)cf).setProperty(com.sun.messaging.Connect
ionConfiguration.imqAddressList,"172.16.5.81:7676");
      Connection con = cf.createConnection();
      sn = con.createSession(true, Session.AUTO_ACKNOWLEDGE);
      Destination from = sn.createQueue(args[0]);
      MessageConsumer mc = sn.createConsumer(from);
      Destination to = sn.createQueue(args[1]);
      mp = sn.createProducer(to);
      con.start();
      mc.setMessageListener(this);
    } catch (Exception e) { e.printStackTrace(); }
  }
  public static void main(String[] args) {
    new Copier(args);
  }

  public void onMessage(Message msg) {
    try {
      mp.send(msg);
      sn.commit();
```

```
        } catch (Exception e) {
          try {
            sn.rollback();
          }catch(Exception e1) {e1.printStackTrace();}
        }

      }
    }
```

KEYWORDS

Administered Objects—Preconfigured JMS objects created usually by an administrator and are maintained by the broker for client's use

Connection—An object that represents application's active connection to a messaging broker and is used to create Session objects

ConnectionFactory—An object that encapsulates the configuration of a connection and is used to create connection

JMS—Java API that allows s/w components to create, send, receive and read messages

JMS Clients—Java programs that produce and consume messages

JMS Provider—A message Oriented Middleware (MOM) that implements JMS specification and provides requisite API library, a broker that provides message storage/delivery functions

Loosely-coupled systems—Systems where both of the communicating parties need not be available during communication

Messages—Objects that JMS clients exchange. In addition to text message, JMS supports messages that contain serialized Java objects and XML documents.

MessageConsumer—An object is created from `Session` specifying a `Destination` and is used to receive messages from the specified destination.

Message Persistence—Message deliver mode that specifies if the message being delivered has to be stored in persistent storage

MessageProducer—An object which is created from `Session` specifying a `Destination` and is used to send messages to the specified destination

Message Priority—An integer ranging from 0 (lowest) to 9 (highest) that indicates how urgently messages should be delivered

Open Message Queue—A JMS provider implemented by Oracle

Point-to-Point messaging—One of the two messaging models of JMS where message are sent by senders, kept in a queue and each message is consumed by exactly one receiver

Pub/Sub messaging—One of the two messaging models of JMS where messages are published by publishers and are distributed to registered subscribers

Session—A context used to create destinations, producers, consumers, messages etc

Temporary destinations—Destinations that only last till the connection, in which they are created survives

Tightly-coupled systems—Systems where both the communicating parties must be available during communication

Transacted Session—Session that support transaction facility

SUMMARY

Messaging is a communication technique between software components or applications. The Java Message Service (JMS) is a Java API that allows s/w components to create, send, receive and read messages.

A JMS application typically has the following components: JMS Provider, JMS Clients, Administered Objects and Messages. JMS supports two models for exchanging messages between producers and consumers: *Point-to-Point* and *Publish/Subscribe.*

In P2P model, the destination, producer and consumer of messages are called *queue, sender* and *receiver* respectively. Senders place messages in queues, receivers get them. Messages live in a queue until they are consumed or until they expire. Any number of senders can put messages to a queue and any number of receivers can consume messages from the queue. However, each message is consumed by only one receiver.

In Pub/Sub model, the destination, producer and consumer of messages are called *topic, publisher* and *subscriber* respectively. Subscribers first show their interest in receiving messages on a topic. Publishers, in turn, produce some messages for the topic. As soon as the messages are produced, they are distributed to *all* current subscribers who showed their willingness earlier.

JMS allows a message consumer to get messages in two ways: *synchronously* and *asynchronously*. This style of message consumption happens when a consumer explicitly extract messages from a destination using `receive()` method. The `receive()` method blocks the caller, if no message is available at that time. As a result, the consumer cannot continue its normal mode of execution. In this style of message consumption, consumer simply sets up a listener and continues its normal work. The listener, on behalf of the consumer, listens on thereafter and gets notified by the broker when a message appears in the destination.

JMS API defines a set of interfaces corresponding to different messaging components and provides them as a package `javax.jms`. The primary interfaces are: ConnectionFactory, Connection, Session, Destination, MessageProducer, MessageConsumer and Message. Five types of messages are specified in JMS API: StreamMessage, MapMessage, TextMessage, ObjectMessage and BytesMessage.

We used formerly Sun's Open Message Queue, which is lightweight, easy to use and an integral part of J2EE. JMS has not defined any address syntax by which clients communicate with the broker. Instead JMS utilizes Java Naming & Directory Interface (JNDI) that provides several advantages.

JMS specification provides many features towards reliable and efficient message delivery such as Acknowledgement, Message Persistence, Message Priority, Message Expirationa, Temporary destinations etc.

WEB RESOURCES

`http://docs.oracle.com/javaee/6/tutorial/doc/bncdq.html`
The Java EE 6 Tutorial

`http://docs.oracle.com/javaee/1.3/jms/tutorial/`
Java Message Service Tutorial

`http://www.novell.com/documentation/extend52/Docs/help/MP/jms/tutorial/`
Java Message Service Tutorial

`http://www.ibm.com/developerworks/java/tutorials/j-jms/j-jms-updated.html`
Java Message Service Tutorial

`http://theopentutorials.com/tutorials/java-ee/ejb3/mdb/java-message-service-jms-api/`
JAVA MESSAGE SERVICE (JMS) API

`http://java.dzone.com/articles/java-messaging-service-jms`
Java Messaging Service (JMS) Point to Point w/ JBoss Tutorial

EXERCISES

Objective-type Questions

1. What is the full form of JMS?
   (a) Java Media Service
   (b) Java Message Service
   (c) Java Message Server
   (d) Java Media Server

2. Which of the following objects does JMS message support?
   (a) dynamic
   (b) nonserialized
   (c) serialized
   (d) All of the above

3. Which of the following packages are JMS APIs contained in?
   (a) java.lang.jms
   (b) java.jms
   (c) java.ext.jms
   (d) javax.jms

4. Which of the following is not a JMS component?
   (a) JMS provider
   (b) JMS client
   (c) JMS administered objects
   (d) JMS cookie

5. Which of the following provided Java Message Service (JMS) specification?
   (a) Sun Microsystems
   (b) Javaloft
   (c) Microsoft
   (d) Apache

6. Which of the following is not a valid JMS message?
   (a) ByteMessage
   (b) ObjectMessage
   (c) CharMessage
   (d) TextMessage

7. Which of the following is FALSE?
   (a) The JMS provider notifies asynchronous consumer when new messages arrive.
   (b) The synchronous consumer collects messages from destination using receive() method.
   (c) An asynchronous consumer client checks the destination periodically for new messages arrival.
   (d) JMS support both synchronous and aynchronous consumption of messages.

8. Which of the following is true about synchronous and asynchronous communications?
   (a) The requester of a service must wait for a response from the service in asynchronous communication.
   (b) In synchronous communication, the requester of a service must wait for a response from the service.
   (c) Both parties must be active in asynchronous communication.
   (d) There is no difference between synchronous and asynchronous communication.

9. Which of the following is not a valid acknowledgement mode?
   (a) AUTO_ACKNOWLEDGE
   (b) CLIENT_ACKNOWLEDGE
   (c) DUPS_OK_ACKNOWLEDGE
   (d) RECEIVER_ACKNOWLEDGE

10. Which JMS component is obtained via JNDI lookups?
   (a) Connection
   (b) ConnectionFactory
   (c) Session
   (d) MessageProducer

11. Which of the following statements is false about synchronous and asynchronous message consumption JMS?
   (a) receive() method is used to consume a message synchronously.
   (b) A message listener is used to consume a message synchronously.
   (c) Messages are consumed asynchronously by using a message listener.
   (d) In asynchronous messaging, the onMessage() method of the listener is invoked when a message arrives.

12. Which of the following is not a role of a JMS Destination component?
   (a) Clients use the destination component as target of messages that it produces.
   (b) Clients use the destination component as source of messages that it consumes.
   (c) Destination component contains location information of a JMS provider.
   (d) Holds JMS messages.

13. Which of the following protocols is an example of an asynchronous protocol?
   (a) Java TCP socket
   (b) Remote Method Invocation (RMI)
   (c) File Transfer Protocol
   (d) Java Messaging Service (JMS)

14. What type of data does a StreamMessage contain?
   (a) Stream of bytes
   (b) Serializable Java object
   (c) Stream of Java primitive types
   (d) Name-value pairs

15. What is TRUE about Message Producers in JMS?
   (a) A message producer is used for sending messages to a destination.
   (b) It uses send() method for pub/sub model.
   (c) It uses publish() method for pub/sub model.
   (d) It uses send() method for P2P model.

16. Which of the following is a preconfigured JMS object?
   a) Message
   b) Destination
   c) Connection
   d) Session

17. Which of the following methods is used to receive messages synchronously in JMS?
(a) receive()
(b) receiveMessage()
(c) receiveNoWait()
(d) syncReceive()

18. Which of the following is true?
(a) RMI supports only loosely-coupled communication.
(b) RMI supports only tightly-coupled communication.
(c) RMI supports both loosely-coupled and tightly-coupled communication.
(d) JMS supports only loosely-coupled communication.

19. What is the priority range in JMS?
(a) 0–9 (c) 0–6
(b) 1–10 (d) 1–7

20. Which of the following requires timing dependencies between the sender(s) and receiver(s)?
(a) P2P Messaging
(b) pub/sub Messaging
(c) Both a) and b)
(d) None of the above

21. The destination in P2P model is called
(a) queue (c) source
(b) topic (d) target

22. The destination in pub/sub model is called
(a) queue (c) source
(b) topic (d) target

23. The message producer in P2P model is called
(a) Publisher (c) Sender
(b) Subscriber (d) Receiver

24. The message consumer in pub/sub model is called
(a) Publisher (c) Sender
(b) Subscriber (d) Receiver

25. Which of the following is not a JMS interface/class?
(a) ConnectionFactory
(b) Connection
(c) Session
(d) Provider

26. Which of the following is not a JMS provider?
(a) Sun's Open Message Queue
(b) Apache's Active MQ
(c) IBM's Websphere MQ
(d) Apache Ant

27. Which of the following is not true in P2P model?
(a) Any number of senders can put messages to a queue.
(b) Any number of receivers can consume messages from the queue.
(c) Each message is consumed by only one receiver.
(d) The message is stored in the queue even after the message is taken off.

28. Which of the following is not true in pub/sub model?
(a) Any number of publishers can put messages to a queue.
(b) Any number of subscribers can consume messages from the queue.
(c) Each message is consumed by only one subscriber.
(d) Messages on a topic remain valid as long as they are being distributed to current subscribers.

29. Which of the following is used to send a message?
(a) MessageProducer
(b) Destination
(c) Session
(d) Connection

30. Which of the methods must a message listener implement?
(a) getMessage() (c) receiverMessage()
(b) onMessage() (d) message()

Subjective-type Questions

1. What is a messaging framework?
2. What is JMS?
3. Are there other Java-based messaging frameworks?
4. What are the benefits of JMS?
5. Identify the different components of JMS.
6. What are administered objects?
7. What is the role of the JMS server?
8. What can a JMS provider do except send and receive messages?

9. What are the differences between P2P and pub/sub messaging models?

10. Give suitable examples where these models may be used.

11. What are the core interfaces and/or classes required for a JMS application?

12. What is the advantage of persistent message delivery compared to non-persistent delivery?

13. What is the difference between the Mailing and Messaging?

14. What are the various message types supported by JMS?

15. What is the role of the JMS Provider?

16. Write the basic steps required to develop a JMS client.

17. What are the differences between loose-coupled and tightly-coupled systems?

18. Discuss the various messaging models supported by JMS. Write some application areas of each of these models.

19. Distinguish between synchronous and asynchronous consumption of messages.

20. Write interfaces and classes specific to P2P and pub/sub model.

21. Discuss the different types of messages supported by JMS.

22. Write the names of some JMS provider.

23. What is the difference between a durable and a non-durable subscriber?

24. What do you mean by browsing a queue?

25. Discuss the different message acknowledgement mechanisms.

26. Distinguish between persistent and non-persistent messages.

27. What is the significance of message priority?

28. Explain the concept of message expiration.

29. What is the usefulness of temporary destinations?

30. Explain the concept of transacted and non-transacted session.

CHAPTER – 26

INTRODUCTION TO J2EE

KEY OBJECTIVES

After completing this chapter readers will be able to—

- have an idea about the technologies used in J2EE
- learn JavaBean technology and its advantages
- understand key JavaBean features such as Introspection, Customization, Persistence, etc
- get an idea about EJB component architecture
- learn Model–View–Controller architecture
- get an idea about struts framework

26.1 OVERVIEW OF J2EE

Today, in the fast-moving and highly demanding world of e-commerce and Information Technology (IT), there is a tremendous need for low-cost, distributed applications (especially transactional applications) for enterprises. These distributed enterprise applications must be designed, implemented, and deployed in less time, with few resources and greater speed.

Fortunately, the Java 2 Enterprise Edition (J2EE) provides a component-based technology for the design, development, assembly, and deployment of low-cost and fast-track enterprise applications. The purpose of J2EE is to simplify the design and implementation of distributed enterprise applications. J2EE offers the following functionalities:

- Multi-tiered distributed application model
- Reusable components
- Flexible transaction control
- Web services support through integrated data interchange on Extensible Markup Language (XML)-based open standards and protocols
- Unified security model

Since J2EE solutions are basically Java-based, they are platform-independent and are not tied to a specific vendor or customer. Customers and vendors are free to select from a wide variety of products and components.

J2EE is not a single technology; it consists of a large set of technologies, some of which are mentioned as follows:

- Enterprise JavaBeans (EJB)
- Java Servlets
- Java Server Pages (JSP)
- Java Message Service (JMS)
- Java Naming and Directory Interface (JNDI)
- Java-XML
- J2EE Connector Architecture
- Java Mail
- Java DataBase Connectivity (JDBC)
- Remote Method Invocation (RMI)
- CORBA
- RMI-IIOP

We have already covered some of these technologies in the previous chapters. In this chapter, we shall discuss some other J2EE technologies, especially, JavaBean and EJB. In Chapter 21, an introduction to JavaBean technology was given. Since JavaBean is the fundamental component technology and is a basic building block of EJB, we must discuss this technology in detail.

26.2 INTRODUCTION TO JAVABEANS

JavaBean technology is a Java-based technology to design and develop reusable and platform-independent software components. These components can then be integrated virtually in all Java-compatible applications. JavaBean components are knows as *beans*. The appearance and features of a bean can be changed or customized using builder tools such as BeanBox and NetBeans.

A bean class is nothing but a usual Java class with the following requirements:

- It must have a public no-argument constructor.
- It has public accessor methods to read and write properties.
- It should implement `Serializable` or `Externalizable` interface.

So, virtually all Java classes are already bean classes or they can be converted to beans with a little effort. For example, the following is an example of a bean class.

```
//Factorial.java
import java.io.*;
public class Factorial implements Serializable {
   protected int n;
   public int getN() {
      return n;
   }
   public void setN(int n) {
      this.n = n;
      long prod = 1;
      for(int i = 2; i <= n; i++)
         prod *= i;
      fact = prod;
   }
   protected long fact;
   public long getFact() {
      return fact;
   }
}
```

Here is another example of a bean class:

```
//State.java
import java.io.Serializable;
public class State implements Serializable {
   protected String state = "off";
   public String getState() {
      return state;
   }
   public void setState(String state) {
      this.state = state;
   }
}
```

Most often, JavaBeans have a GUI representation of themselves. For example, button, calculator, and calendar beans are expected to have a visual representation, so as to be useful. However, some beans do not have any visual representation, and are called *invisible* beans. Invisible beans include a spell checker, random number generator, and temperature monitor.

26.2.1 Properties

A bean typically has one or more *properties* that control appearance and behaviour. Properties are discrete, named attributes of a bean. They constitute the data part of a bean's structure and represent the internal state of a bean. Properties allow us to isolate component state information into discrete pieces that can be easily modified.

In our `Factorial` bean, there are two properties: `n` and `fact`. The property `n` holds an integer value, whose factorial is stored in the property `fact`. Here, `n` is said to be independent property and `fact` is dependent on `n` as the value of `fact` can be calculated from `n`. There need not be such a relationship in all the cases. For example, in the `State` bean, there is only one property `state`. In general, a bean can have any number of properties.

26.2.2 Accessor Methods

The primary way to access bean properties is through accessor methods. An accessor method is a public method of the bean that directly reads or writes the value of a particular bean. For example, the `getN()` method of the `Factorial` bean returns the value of the property `n`. Similarly, `setN()` sets the value of `n`. For the `fact` property, only one method is provided, which returns the value of the property `fact`. In general, a property can have two methods associated with it. The methods that are responsible for reading property values are called *reader* methods. Similarly, methods that are responsible for changing property values are called *writer* methods.

26.3 BEAN BUILDER

Readymade applications are available that provide an environment in which we can build and test beans. Those tools are known as builder tools. Some of the popular bean builder tools are Sun's BeanBox and NetBeans, JBuilder, Borland's Delphi, etc.

A builder tool is able to display several beans simultaneously. It is also able to connect different beans together in a visual manner. So, we can manipulate a bean without writing any piece of code. Most builder tools have a palette of components from which developers can drag and drop components onto a graphical canvas.

The facilities supported by a bean builder vary widely, but there are some common features as follows:

- *Introspection*—ability to analyze a bean to discover properties, methods, and events
- *Properties*—used for customization of the state of a bean

- *Events*—a way used by beans to tell the outside that something is happening, or to react to something that happened outside the bean
- *Customization*—a developer of a bean can customize the behaviour and appearance of the bean within a builder tool
- *Persistence*—a builder tool allows us to customize a bean, and have its state saved away and reloaded later

26.4 ADVANTAGES OF JAVABEANS

Before we discuss the features and facilities supported by JavaBean technology, let us understand what JavaSoft wanted to accomplish by developing this Java-based component technology. In this regard, we can refer to JavaSoft's own JavaBeans mission statement: "Write once, run anywhere, use everywhere". Let us examine each part of this statement to realize what JavaSoft had in mind.

Write Once

A good software component technology should encourage component developers to write code only once. The component should not require rewriting of code to add and/or improve features. Keeping this point in mind, JavaSoft developed JavaBean technology, which allows us to add or improve functionality in the existing code, without re-engineering the original code.

The concept of writing components once also adds sense in terms of version control. This means that developers can make changes to components incrementally, instead of rewriting significant portions from scratch. This results in a steady improvement of functionality, which, in turn, dictates a more consistent software component development through increasing versions.

Run Anywhere

A software technology must be platform independent to have a realistic meaning in today's rapidly varying software environment. This refers to the capability of software components developed using a technology to be executed (run) in any environment. Fortunately, JavaBeans components are ultimately Java components. Consequently, cross-platform support comes automatically.

Good software components should also run across distributed network environments. This can be simply achieved using Java's powerful technology, Remote Method Invocation (RMI), Socket, and RMI-IIOP.

Use Everywhere

This is perhaps the most important part of the JavaSoft's JavaBean mission statement. Well-designed JavaBeans components are capable of being used in a wide range of situations, which include applications, other components, documents, websites, application builder tools, and so on.

In addition to these key features, JavaBean technology has the following built-in features.

JavaBeans are compact components and can be transferred across a low-bandwidth Internet connection that facilitates a reasonable transfer time.

JavaBeans components are so simple that they are not only easy to use, but also easy to develop. Therefore, we can devote more time to embellishing components with interesting features than debugging them.

26.5 BDK INTROSPECTION

A bean builder usually uses Java core reflection API to discover methods of a bean. It then applies the design pattern to discover other bean features (such as properties and events). This procedure is known as *introspection*.

26.5.1 Design Patterns

The JavaBeans framework introduces a lot of rules for names to be used for classes and methods. They are collectively called *design patterns*.

Note that the conventions and design patterns are all optional. However, by following those conventions, we can create really useful beans that can be used within a builder tool as well as in other JavaBean-enabled environments. Builder tools such as BeanBox, NetBeans, and JBuilder use these conventions and design patterns to introspect a bean's properties, methods, and events. Consequently, they can provide an environment where we can customize bean features.

Suppose, a bean has a property called "xxx". JavaBean technology encourages us to use "getXxx" as the name of the reader method and "setXxx" as the name of the writer method. If the property happens to be a Boolean, the reader method could be named "isXxx". For example, our State bean has the property `state`. So, the reader method is "getState" and the writer method is "setState".

A `BeanInfo` class is a class that is used to provide information about a bean explicitly. To do this, a class is created implementing the `BeanInfo` interface. The name of this class should also follow a naming rule. The name of the `BeanInfo` class must be the name of the target bean, followed by the string "BeanInfo". For example, the name of the `BeanInfo` class for the bean `Person` must be "PersonBeanInfo".

Similarly, the name of the `Customizer` class (see Section 26.9) for the bean `MyBean` must be `MyBeanCustomizer`.

JavaBean API provides interfaces and classes that can be used to discover properties and methods of a bean dynamically. The following is a brief description of those interfaces and classes:

`BeanInfo`

The `java.beans.BeanInfo` interface defines a set of methods that allow bean developers to provide information about their beans explicitly. By specifying `BeanInfo` for a bean component, a developer can hide methods, specify an icon for the toolbox, provide descriptive names for properties, define which properties are bound, etc.

`Introspector`

The `java.beans.Introspector` class provides descriptor classes (see Section 26.7) with information about properties, methods, and events of a bean.

The `getBeanInfo()` method of the Introspector class can be used by builder tools and other automated environments to provide detailed information about a bean. The `getBeanInfo()` method relies on the naming conventions for the bean's properties, events, and methods. A call to `getBeanInfo()` results in the introspection process analyzing the bean's classes and super classes. The following example finds the properties and methods of our `Factorial` bean.

```
//IntrospectionDemo.java
import java.beans.*;
public class IntrospectionDemo {
   public static void main( String[] args ) throws IntrospectionException  {
         BeanInfo info = Introspector.getBeanInfo( Factorial.class,
Object.class );
      System.out.println("properties: ");
      for ( PropertyDescriptor pd : info.getPropertyDescriptors() )
         System.out.println(" " + pd.getName());
      System.out.println("methods: ");
      for ( MethodDescriptor pd : info.getMethodDescriptors() )
         System.out.println(" " + pd.getName());
   }
}
```

It generates the output shown in Figure 26.1:

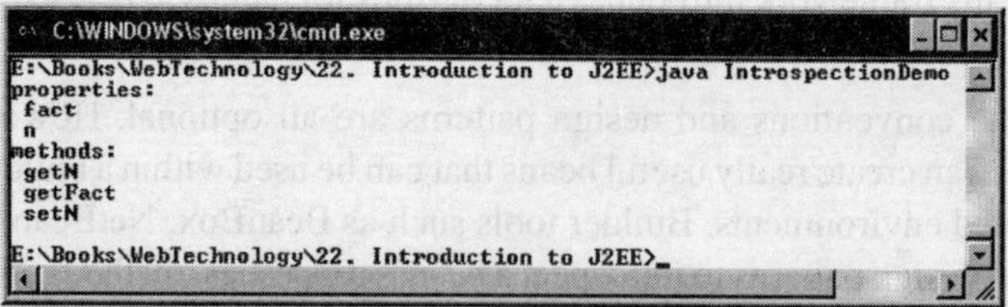

Figure 26.1: Bean Introspection

26.6 PROPERTIES

The properties of a bean represent and control its behaviour and appearance. JavaBean API allows us to create the following primary property types.

26.6.1 Simple Properties

Simple properties of a bean are those that do not depend on other beans or control properties of another bean. Properties are typically declared as `private`. To access them, `get` and `set` methods are used. The names of the `get` and `set` methods follow specific rules, known as *design patterns*. JavaBean-enabled builder/tester tools (such as NetBeans and BeanBox) use these design patterns to do the following:

- Discover the properties of a bean
- Determine the types of the properties
- Display the properties in the property window
- Determine the read/write attribute of the properties
- Find the appropriate property editor for each property type
- Allow us to change the properties

Suppose a bean builder/tester tool encounters the following methods on a bean:

```
public int getValue() { ... }
public void setValue(int v) { ... }
```

The tool infers the following:

- There exists a property name `value`.
- Its type is `int`.
- It is readable and writable.
- It displays the value of this property in the property editor.
- Moreover, it finds the property editor that allows us to change the value of the property.

Creating a Simple Property

The following code is used in the bean to create the property `propertyName`:

```
private PropertyType propertyName = initialValue;
```

Providing a Reader Method

The following code is used to provide a reader method:

```
PropertyType getPropertyName() {
   return propertyName;
}
```

Providing a Writer Method

The following code is used to provide a writer method:

```
void getPropertyName(PropertyType value) {
    propertyName = value;
}
```

The following example shows how to create a simple property:

```
//MyBean.java
public class MyBean {
    private int value = 0;

    /**
     * Get the value of value
     *
     * @return the value of value
     */
    public int getValue() {
        return value;
    }

    /**
     * Set the value of value
     *
     * @param value new value of value
     */
    public void setValue(int value) {
        this.value = value;
    }
}
```

26.6.2 Bound Properties

Sometimes, when a property of a bean changes, you might want to notify another object about this change. This object typically reacts to the change by changing one of its properties. For example, consider two beans `Parent` and `Child`, each having two properties, `firstName` and `familyName`. The `familyName` property of `Child` and `Parent` must have the same value. So, whenever the `familyName` property of `Parent` changes, the `familyName` property of `Child` must also be changed to make them synchronized.

This synchronization can be implemented using the *bound* property. The accessor or modifier methods for a bound property are defined in the same way, except that whenever a bound property changes, a notification is sent to the interested listeners. Whenever a property of a bean changes, a "PropertyChange" event gets fired. The bean generating the event is called *source* bean. We can register one or more "Listener" objects with a source, so that these objects get notified when a bound property of the source bean is updated.

Bean Development Kit (BDK) provides special classes to accomplish coordination between the notifier and listener.

`PropertyChangeListener`

If an object is interested in being notified about the property changes of a source bean, its class must implement the `PropertyChangeListener` interface. This interface defines the following method:

```
void propertyChange(PropertyChangeEvent pce)
```

The listener's class must implement this method. If the listener is registered for a property change event, this method gets called when a bound property of the source bean changes. In this method, the listener object reacts to the property change by modifying one or more of its properties.

PropertyChangeEvent

A `PropertyChangeEvent` object is generated whenever a bound property of a bean changes. This object is then sent from the source bean to all registered `PropertyChangeListener` objects, as an argument of their respective `PropertyChange()` method. This class encapsulates the property change information. It provides several useful methods as follows:

String getPropertyName()

Returns the name of the property that was changed and caused this event firing

Object getOldValue()

Returns the value of the property as an object before it was changed. The bean writer should typecast it to the desired type.

Object getNewValue()

Returns the value of the property as an object after it was changed. The bean writer must typecast it to the desired type.

PropertyChangeSupport

This class is used by the beans having at least one bound property to keep track of registered listeners. It is also used to deliver `PropertyChangeEvent` objects to those registered listeners when a bound property changes. A source bean can instantiate this class as a member field or inherit the functionality of this class by extending it. Figure 26.2 gives the framework for bound property support.

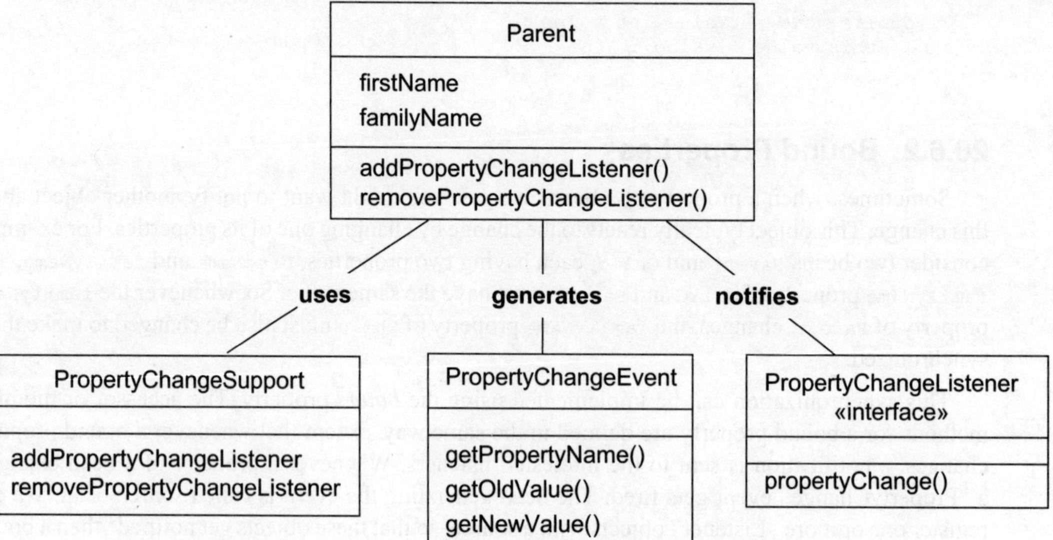

Figure 26.2: Bound Property support framework

Let us now discuss how to write a bound property. The following class acts as a source bean.

```
//Parent.java
import java.beans.*;
public class Parent {
   private String firstName = "Uttam", familyName = "Roy";
   private PropertyChangeSupport pcs;
   public Parent() {
      pcs = new PropertyChangeSupport(this);
   }
   public String getFirstName() {
      return firstName;
   }
```

```
    public void setFirstName(String fname) {
       firstName = fname;
    }
    public String getFamilyName() {
       return familyName;
    }
    public void setFamilyName(String newFamilyName) {
       String oldFamilyName = familyName;
       familyName = newFamilyName;
       pcs.firePropertyChange("familyName", oldFamilyName, newFamilyName);
    }
    public void addPropertyChangeListener(PropertyChangeListener pcl) {
       pcs.addPropertyChangeListener(pcl);
    }
    public void removePropertyChangeListener(PropertyChangeListener pcl) {
       pcs.removePropertyChangeListener(pcl);
    }
}
```

The following bean is a listener that wants to be notified when the `familyName` property of the `Parent` bean changes. So, it implements the `PropertyChangeListener` interface and defines the method `propertyChange()`. In the `propertyChange()` method, it changes its own `familyName` property to the new value of the `familyName` property of the `Parent` bean by using the `getNewValue()` method on the `PropertyChangeEvent` object.

```
//Child.java
import java.beans.*;
public class Child implements PropertyChangeListener {
   private String firstName = "Rimisha", familyName = "Roy";
   public String getFirstName() {
      return firstName;
   }
   public void setFirstName(String fname) {
      firstName = fname;
   }
   public String getFamilyName() {
      return familyName;
   }
   public void setFamilyName(String fname) {
      familyName = fname;
   }
   public void propertyChange(PropertyChangeEvent pce) {
   if(pce.getPropertyName().equals("familyName"))
         setFamilyName((String)pce.getNewValue());

   }
}
```

For demonstration purposes, we have created the following Java application program. Typically, a bean builder (such as BeanBox provided by Sun) may be used.

```
//BoundDemo.java
public class BoundDemo {
   public static void main(String args[]) {
      Parent p = new Parent();
      Child c = new Child();
      p.addPropertyChangeListener(c);
      System.out.println("Before changing family name");
      System.out.println("Parent: " + p.getFirstName() + " " +
p.getFamilyName());
      System.out.println("Child: " + c.getFirstName() + " " +
c.getFamilyName());
```

```
        p.setFamilyName("Biswas");
        System.out.println("After changing family name of parent to 'Biswas'");
        System.out.println("Parent: " + p.getFirstName() + " " +
p.getFamilyName());
        System.out.println("Child: " + c.getFirstName() + " " +
c.getFamilyName());
    }
}
```

This program creates a `Parent` bean and a Child bean. The `Child` bean is then registered with the `Parent` bean. So, whenever the `familyName` property of the `Parent` bean changes, the `Child` bean gets notified and it can change its own `familyName` property. Finally, we have changed the `familyName` property of the `Parent` bean using the `setFamilyName()` method. We have also displayed the details of parent and child before and after changing the property. The output is as shown in Figure 26.3.

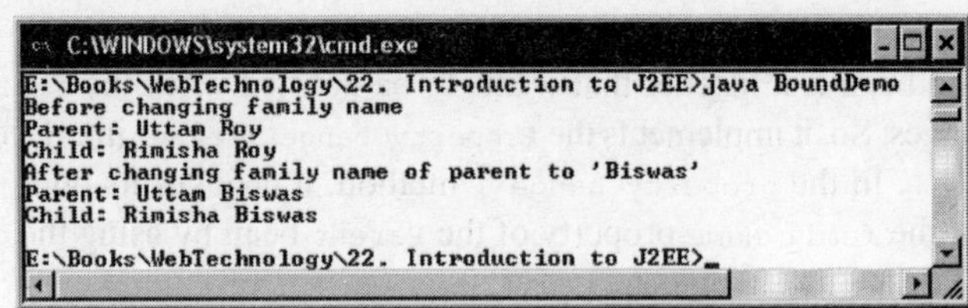

Figure 26.3: Bean bound property demo

26.6.3 Constrained Properties

A *constrained* property of a bean is a special type of property, which can be changed subject to prior permission taken from external object(s). External objects act as *vetoers* and exercise such authority in this case. For example, think about `Broker` and `ShareHolder` beans. The `Broker` can sell the shares at a rate provided `ShareHolder` allows it to do so.

JavaBean API provides a mechanism very similar to the one used for the bound property, which allows other objects to veto the change of the source bean's property. The basic idea for implementing a constrained property is as follows:

- Store the old value of source bean's property if it is to be vetoed.
- Ask listeners (vetoers) of the new proposed value.
- Vetoers are authoritative to process this new value. They disallow by throwing an exception. Note that no exception is thrown if a vetoer gives the permission.
- If no listener vetoes the change, i.e., no exception is thrown, the property is set to the new value; optionally notify "PropertyChange" listeners, if any.

Three objects are involved in this process.

- The *source* bean containing one or more constrained property
- A listener object that accepts or rejects changes proposed by the source bean
- A `PropertyChangeEvent` object encapsulating the property change information

26.6.3.1 Implementing Constrained Property Support

In the source bean, the accessor method for the constrained property is defined in the same way, except that it throws a `PropertyVetoException` as follows:

```
public void setPropertyName(PropertyType pt) throws PropertyVetoException {
    //method body
}
```

A source bean containing one or more constrained properties implements the following functionalities:

- Provides methods to add and remove `VetoableChangeListener` objects to register and unregister them so that they receive notification for property change proposal.
- When a property change is proposed, the source bean sends the `PropertyChangeEvent` object containing the proposed information to interested listeners. This should be done before the actual property change takes place. It allows listeners to accept or refuse a proposal.
- If any one listener vetoes by throwing an exception, continue to notify other listeners (if any) with the old value of the property.

JavaBean API provides a utility class, `VetoableChangeSupport`, similar to `PropertyChangeSupport`. The `VetoableChangeSupport` class provides the methods `addVetoableChangeListener()` and `removeVetoableChangeListener()` to add and remove `VetoableChangeListener` objects, respectively, and keeps track of such listeners. It also provides a method, `fireVetoableChange()`, to send the `PropertyChangeEvent` object to each registered listener when a property change is proposed.

The source bean can instantiate this class as a member field or inherit the functionality of this class by extending it. A `VetoableChangeSupport` object is instantiated as follows:

```
VetoableChangeSupport vcs = new VetoableChangeSupport(this);
```

26.6.3.2 Implementing constrained property listener

If an object's class wants to act as a vetoer, it must implement the `VetoableChangeListener` interface. This interface defines a single method as follows:

```
void vetoableChange(PropertyChangeEvent pce) throws PropertyVetoException;
```

A `VetoableChangeListener` must implement this method. This is the method where the vetoer exercises its power and agrees or disagrees with the proposal. In this method, the listener processes proposed property change and disagrees (vetoes) by throwing a `PropertyVetoException` exception. A typical code looks like this:

```
void vetoableChange(PropertyChangeEvent pce) throws PropertyVetoException {
  if(the_condition_is_not_fulfilled)
    throw new PropertyVetoException("NO", pce);
}
```

Figure 26.4 shows the constrained property support framework.

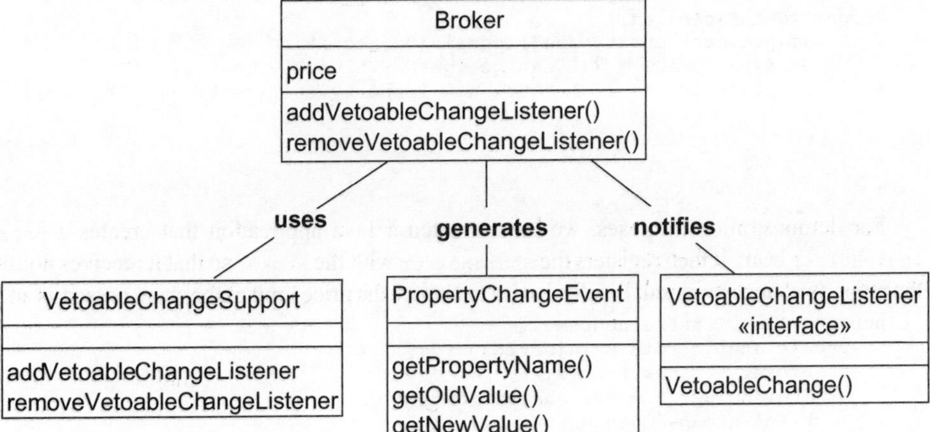

Figure 26.4: Constrained property support framework

26.6.3.3 Example

Let us now demonstrate the constrained property with our `Broker` and `ShareHolder` beans. The `Broker` is the source bean that has a single constrained property, `price`. A `Broker` can sell a share owned by a `ShareHolder`, provided that the `ShareHolder` object allows it. So, `Broker` should take permission before it sells the share. If the permission is given, it actually sells the shares. Otherwise, it does not do anything. The following is the source code of the `Broker` bean.

```
//Broker.java
import java.beans.*;
public class Broker {
   private float price = 10;
   private VetoableChangeSupport vcs;
   public Broker() {
      vcs = new VetoableChangeSupport(this);
   }

   public float getPrice() {
      return price;
   }
   public void setPrice(float newPrice) throws PropertyVetoException {
      float oldPrice = price;
      vcs.fireVetoableChange("price", oldPrice, newPrice);
      System.out.println("Setting new price limit");
      price = newPrice;
   }
   public void  addVetoableChangeListener(VetoableChangeListener pcl) {
      vcs.addVetoableChangeListener(pcl);
   }
   public void removeVetoableChangeListener(VetoableChangeListener pcl) {
      vcs.removeVetoableChangeListener(pcl);
   }
}
```

The `ShareHolder` is the listener bean. It decides whether the `Broker` can sell shares at the specified price. It allows the `Broker` selling shares if the proposed price is greater than or equal to ₹15. Otherwise, it disallows, by throwing the `PropertyVetoException` object. Here is the source code of `ShareHolder`.

```
//ShareHolder.java
import java.beans.*;
public class ShareHolder implements VetoableChangeListener {

   public void vetoableChange(PropertyChangeEvent pce) throws
PropertyVetoException {
      if(pce.getPropertyName().equals("price")) {
         float price = ((Float)pce.getNewValue()).floatValue();
         if(!price >= 15 ) throw new PropertyVetoException("NO", pce);
      }

   }
}
```

For demonstration purposes, we have created a Java application that creates a `Broker` and a `ShareHolder` bean. It then registers the `ShareHolder` with the `Broker` so that it receives notification for the property change proposal. Finally, it tries to change the price limit of the share passed as an argument.

```
public class ConstrainedDemo {
   public static void main(String args[]) {
      Broker b = new Broker();
      ShareHolder s = new ShareHolder();
      b.addVetoableChangeListener(s);
      float price = Float.parseFloat(args[0]);
      try {
```

```
            System.out.println("Old price limit: " + b.getPrice());

            b.setPrice(price);
            System.out.println("New price limit: " + b.getPrice());
         }catch(Exception e) {
            System.out.println("Ah! failed to set price at " + price);
         }
      }
   }
```

Figure 26.5 shows a sample output.

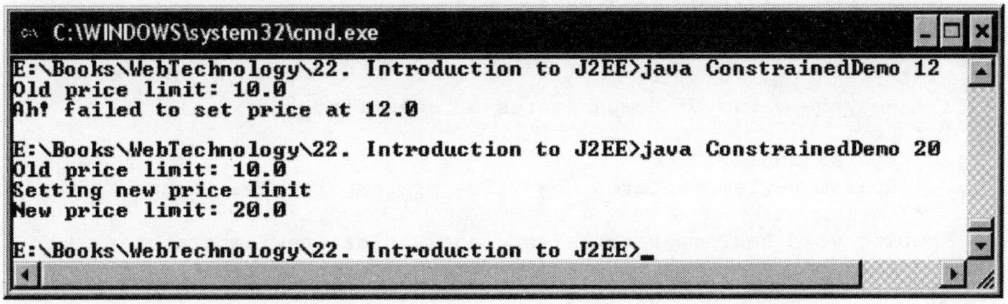

```
C:\WINDOWS\system32\cmd.exe
E:\Books\WebTechnology\22. Introduction to J2EE>java ConstrainedDemo 12
Old price limit: 10.0
Ah! failed to set price at 12.0

E:\Books\WebTechnology\22. Introduction to J2EE>java ConstrainedDemo 20
Old price limit: 10.0
Setting new price limit
New price limit: 20.0

E:\Books\WebTechnology\22. Introduction to J2EE>_
```

Figure 26.5: Bean constrained property demo

26.6.4 Indexed Properties

An index property is an array of properties. It can hold a range of values that can be accessed through accessor functions. To access an individual element, the following methods are specified:

```
public PropertyElementType getPropertyName(int index)
public void setPropertyName(int index, PropertyElementType element)
```

The `get` method takes an array index and returns the element at that index. The `set` method takes two arguments: an index of the property array and its value, and sets the element at the specified index to the specified value. Methods to access the entire array are also specified as follows:

```
public PropertyElementType[] getPropertyName()
public void setPropertyName(PropertyElementType element[])
```

In this case, the `get` method returns the entire property array and the `set` method takes an entire array to be used to set the property array.

The following bean class stores the temperatures of the last seven days.

```
//TemperatureBean.java
public class TemperatureBean {
   private float[] temperatures = new float[7];
   /**
    * Get the value of temperatures
    *
    * @return the value of temperatures
    */
   public float[] getTemperatures() {
      return temperatures;
   }

   /**
    * Set the value of temperatures
    *
    * @param temperatures new value of temperatures
    */
```

```
    public void setTemperatures(float[] temperatures) {
       this.temperatures = temperatures;
    }

    /**
     * Get the value of temperatures at specified index
     *
     * @param index
     * @return the value of temperatures at specified index
     */
    public float getTemperatures(int index) {
       return this.temperatures[index];
    }

    /**
     * Set the value of temperatures at specified index.
     *
     * @param index
     * @param newTemperatures new value of temperatures at specified index
     */
    public void setTemperatures(int index, float newTemperatures) {
       this.temperatures[index] = newTemperatures;
    }
}
```

26.7 BEANINFO INTERFACE

A bean builder typically uses the *introspection* process to discover features (such as properties, methods, and events). In this case, the bean builder exposes all the features to the outside world.

We can also expose the bean's features by using an associated class explicitly. By doing this we obtain the following benefits:

- Hide features we do not want to disclose
- Provide more information about bean features
- Associate an icon with the target bean
- Group bean features into different categories such as normal and advanced groups
- Specify a customizer class
- Expose some bean features explicitly using Java reflection API

The features of a bean are exposed using a separate special class. This class must implement the `BeanInfo` interface. The `BeanInfo` interface defines several methods that can be used to inspect properties, methods, and events of a bean. The following is the declaration of the `BeanInfo` interface:

```
public interface java.beans.BeanInfo{
   public static final int ICON_COLOR_16x16;
   public static final int ICON_COLOR_32x32;
   public static final int ICON_MONO_16x16;
   public static final int ICON_MONO_32x32;
   public abstract java.beans.BeanDescriptor getBeanDescriptor();
   public abstract java.beans.EventSetDescriptor[] getEventSetDescriptors();
   public abstract int getDefaultEventIndex();
   public abstract java.beans.PropertyDescriptor[] getPropertyDescriptors();
   public abstract int getDefaultPropertyIndex();
   public abstract java.beans.MethodDescriptor[] getMethodDescriptors();
   public abstract java.beans.BeanInfo[] getAdditionalBeanInfo();
   public abstract java.awt.Image getIcon(int);
}
```

The BeanInfo interface uses several *descriptor* classes, each of which describes specific features. The following is a list of descriptors:

- `BeanDescriptor`—This descriptor class describes the bean's name, type, and its customizer class, if any.
- `PropertyDescriptor`—This descriptor encapsulates the target bean's properties.
- `MethodDescriptor`—This descriptor encapsulates the target bean's methods.
- `EventSetDescriptor`—This descriptor encapsulates the events that the target bean can fire.

Let us now write a `BeanInfo` class that describes the features of a bean. For this purpose, we shall first write a bean and show how the BeanBox extracts information from this bean. Consider the following bean class:

```
//Person.java
public class Person {
   private String name = "B. S. Roy";
   private String address = "Narayanpur, Kol-136";
   private String PAN = "AGCPR8830P";
   public String getName() {
      return name;
   }
   public void setName(String name) {
      this.name = name;
   }
   public String getAddress() {
      return address;
   }
   public String getPAN() {
      return PAN;
   }
   public void setPAN(String PAN) {
      this.PAN = PAN;
   }
   public void setAddress(String address) {
      this.address = address;
   }
}
```

The bean `Person` has three properties: `name`, `address`, and `PAN`. Each of the three properties has a `get` and a `set` method. Compile this bean using the following command:

```
java Person.java
```

Create a class file, `Person.class`. Create a manifest file, `manifest_person.mf`, as follows:

```
Manifest-Version: 1.0

Name: Person.class
Java-Bean: True
```

Place this file in the same directory as `Person.class`. Now, create a jar file, `person.jar`, using the following command:

```
jar cvfm person.jar manifest_person.mf Person.class
```

It typically generates the following output:

```
added manifest
adding: Person.class(in = 754) (out= 410)(deflated 45%)
```

The bean is now ready to test and use. Load the `person.jar` file in the Bean Box. Create an instance of the `Person` bean and view its properties. It looks as shown in Figure 26.6.

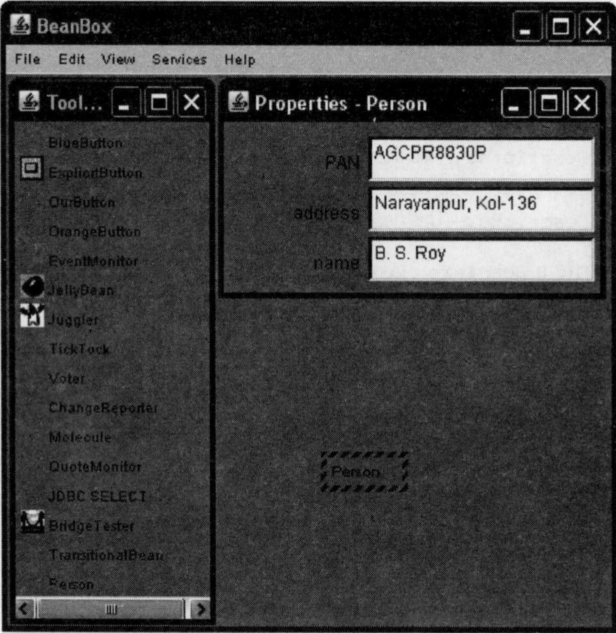

Figure 26.6: Bean introspection

As you can see, BeanBox shows all the properties of the `Person` bean. Suppose we do not disclose the `PAN` property of the `Person` bean, as it is sensitive information. For that purpose, we can write the `BeanInfo` class. The following is the source code of the `BeanInfo` class.

```
//PersonBeanInfo.java
import java.beans.*;
public class PersonBeanInfo extends SimpleBeanInfo {
   private Class personClass = Person.class;
   public PropertyDescriptor[] getPropertyDescriptors() {
      PropertyDescriptor name = null, address = null, PAN = null;
      try {
            name = new PropertyDescriptor("name", personClass);
         name.setDisplayName("Name:");
         name.setPreferred(true);

         address = new PropertyDescriptor("address", personClass);
         address.setDisplayName("Address:");
         address.setPreferred(true);
      } catch (IntrospectionException e) {}
      PropertyDescriptor[] result = {name, address};
      return result;
   }
}
```

To write a `BeanInfo` class, we need to give a name. The name of each `BeanInfo` class follows a naming rule. The name of the `BeanInfo` class of the target bean X must have the name `XBeanInfo`. For example, the name of the `BeanInfo` class of our `Person` bean must be `PersonBeanInfo`. The string "BeanInfo" is appended to the target bean class name.

Since the `BeanInfo` interface implements several methods, we have to implement all of them. Alternatively, a `BeanInfo` class can be created by sub-classing the `SimpleBeanInfo` class. The `SimpleBeanInfo` class is a convenient base class for the `BeanInfo` classes. It implements all the methods, but all are empty. So, the `SimpleBeanInfo` class does not disclose any property of the method at all. We can override a specific method, where we want to return specific information. Since we want to hide the PAN property, we have overridden only the `getPropertyDescriptors()` method. In this method, we have returned an array of only three properties.

Now, modify the manifest file, `manifest_person.mf`, as follows:

```
Manifest-Version: 1.0

Name: Person.class
Java-Bean: True

Name: PersonBeanInfo.class
Java-Bean: False
```

Create the `person.jar` file as shown in Figure 26.7.

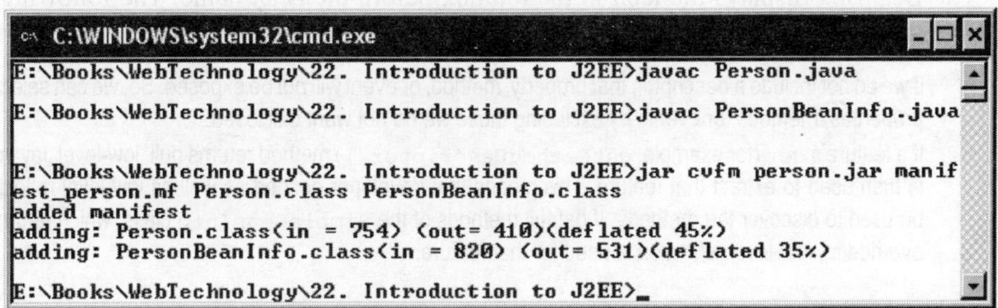

Figure 26.7: Bean introspection

Load the jar file in BeanBox and create a `Person` bean. You can see that only three properties are shown. The result is shown in Figure 26.8.

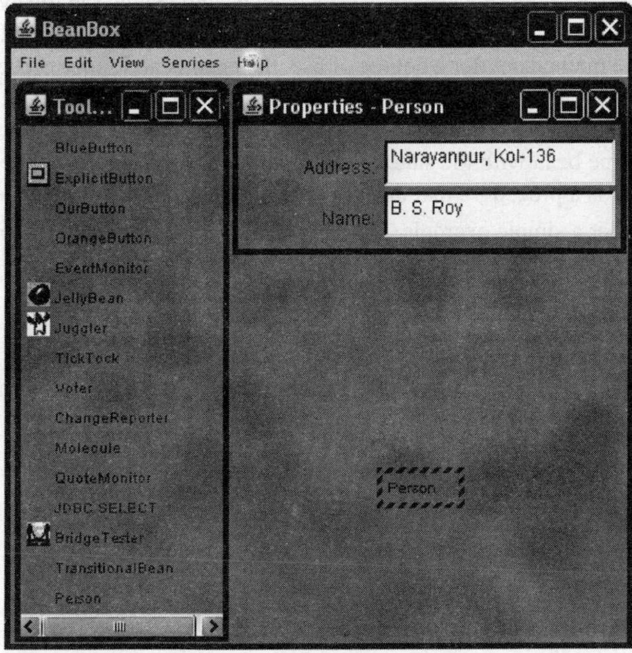

Figure 26.8: Bean introspection

We can also associate an icon with the bean. Override the `getIcon()` method as follows:

```
public java.awt.Image getIcon(int iconKind) {
   if (iconKind == BeanInfo.ICON_MONO_16x16 ||
        iconKind == BeanInfo.ICON_COLOR_16x16 ) {
      java.awt.Image img = loadImage("person16.gif");
      return img;
   }
   if (iconKind == BeanInfo.ICON_MONO_32x32 ||
        iconKind == BeanInfo.ICON_COLOR_32x32 ) {
      java.awt.Image img = loadImage("person32.gif");
      return img;
   }
   return null;
}
```

The BeanBox displays the icon in the toolbox before the bean name. The following important points can be noted:

- If we do not include a descriptor, that property, method, or event will *not* be exposed. So, we can selectively expose properties, methods, or events by excluding those we do not want disclosed.
- If a feature's `get` (for example, `getMethodDescriptor()`) method returns null, low-level Java reflection API is then used to extract that feature. This means that developer-defined as well as low-level reflection can both be used to discover the methods. If default methods of the `SimpleBeanInfo` class, which return null, are not overridden, low-level reflection is used for that feature.

26.8 PERSISTENCE

Sometimes, it is necessary to store the beans for later use. *Persistence* is a procedure to save a bean in non-volatile storage such as a file. The bean can be reconstructed and used later. The important point is that persistence allows bean developers to save the current state of the bean and retrieve the same at some later point of time.

To understand the importance of persistence, let us understand the life cycle of a bean. A bean is first created (possibly using a builder tool). Then its properties are accessed and/or manipulated by calling its public methods. After a degree of use, the bean is no longer needed, and is destroyed and removed from the memory. This is a typical life cycle of a bean. However, think about a situation where you have decided to complete your application temporarily but use of the bean is not yet over. You want the same bean with the state of the bean unchanged whenever the application is restarted later. Persistence is a procedure that does exactly what we have described here.

Let us consider a simple example. Consider the following `Factorial` bean.

```
//Factorial.java
import java.io.*;
public class Factorial implements Serializable {
   protected int n;
   public int getN() {
      return n;
   }
   public void setN(int n) {
      this.n = n;
      long prod = 1;
      for(int i = 2; i <= n; i++)
         prod *= i;
      fact = prod;
   }
   protected long fact;
   public long getFact() {
      return fact;
   }
}
```

This bean has two properties, `n` and `fact`. The property `n` has a `get` method and a `set` method and `fact` has only a `get` method. The `getFact()` method returns the factorial of `n`, which can be specified using the `setN()` method. So, this bean can be used to create a factorial table. Suppose we want to create a table containing factorial of numbers from 2 to 10. So, we can write a code like this:

```
Factorial f = new Factorial();
for(int i = 2; i <= 10; i++) {
   f.setN(i);
   System.out.println(i + "! = " + f.getFact()+ " ");
}
```

However, during the calculation, assume that an external interrupt may occur and in such a case, the application must be terminated. Before terminating, we must save the state of the bean so that we can retrieve the value of the integer up to which we calculated the factorial, so as to find the factorial of the rest of the integers. Java's Serialization procedure may be used to save and retrieve the state of a bean. An object is said to be serializable if its class implements the `Serializable` interface and all members are serializable. The `Serializable` interface does not define any method; it merely indicates that the class implementing it can be serialized. The following code shows how to save the state of a bean.

```
//SaveBean.java
import java.io.*;
public class SaveBean {
   public static void main(String args[]) {
      try {
         Factorial f = new Factorial();
         for(int i = 2; i < 10; i++) {
            f.setN(i);
            System.out.println(i + "! = " + f.getFact()+ " ");
            if(i > Math.random()*10 ) break;
         }
         //save the state of f now
         FileOutputStream fos = new FileOutputStream("out.dat");
         ObjectOutputStream oos = new ObjectOutputStream(fos);
         oos.writeObject(f);
         oos.close();
         System.out.println("Factorial bean saved in file out.dat");
      }catch(Exception e) {e.printStackTrace();}
   }
}
```

The following code demonstrates how to retrieve the bean with its original state.

```
//RetrieveBean.java
import java.io.*;
public class RetriveBean {
   public static void main(String args[]) {
      try {
         FileInputStream fis = new FileInputStream("out.dat");
         ObjectInputStream ois = new ObjectInputStream(fis);
         Factorial f1 = (Factorial)ois.readObject();
         ois.close();
         System.out.println("Factorial bean retrieved from file out.dat");
         for(int i = f1.getN()+1; i <= 10; i++) {
            f1.setN(i);
            System.out.println(i + "! = " + f1.getFact()+ " ");
         }
      }catch(Exception e) {e.printStackTrace();}
   }
}
```

Figure 26.9 shows a sample output that is obtained if you run these two applications.

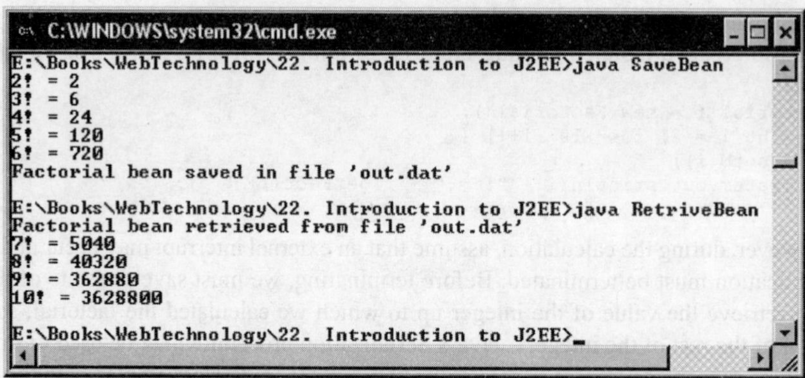

Figure 26.9: Saving and retrieving bean

The JavaBean framework provides a utility class, `XMLEncoder`, which allows us to save a bean in XML format. The following example shows how to save a bean as an XML file:

```
XMLEncoder encoder = new XMLEncoder(
   new BufferedOutputStream(new FileOutputStream("fact.xml")));
encoder.writeObject( f );
encoder.close();
```

It creates the following XML document:

```
<?xml version="1.0" encoding="UTF-8"?>
<java version="1.6.0_10-beta" class="java.beans.XMLDecoder">
 <object class="Factorial">
  <void property="n">
   <int>6</int>
  </void>
 </object>
</java>
```

The bean can later be retrieved from this XML document using the following code:

```
XMLDecoder decoder = new XMLDecoder(
   new BufferedInputStream(new FileInputStream("fact.xml")));
f1 = (Factorial)decoder.readObject();
decoder.close();
```

The object `f1` refers to the original bean now.

26.9 CUSTOMIZER

Bean *customization* allows us to customize the appearance and behaviour of a bean at design time, within a bean-compliant builder tool. There are two ways to customize a bean:

- Using a property editor
- Using Customizers

Property editors are usually supplied by the builder tool, although you can write your own property editor. In this section, we shall discuss how to customize a bean's appearance and behaviour using customizers.

A property editor usually displays all properties that can be manipulated. Sometimes, it is not a good idea to display a large number of properties, most of which are irrelevant. A Customizer class gives us complete control to configure and edit beans. Customizers are used when a specific instruction is needed and property editors are too primitive for this purpose. A Customizer class must do the following:

- A Customizer must be some kind of AWT component that is suitable for display in a dialog box created by the BeanBox. So, it must extend `java.awt.Component` or one of its subclasses. Typically, the Customizer class extends `Panel`.
- It must implement the `Customizer` interface. This interface looks like this:

```
public interface java.beans.Customizer{
    public abstract void setObject(java.lang.Object);
    public abstract void addPropertyChangeListener(java.beans.PropertyCha
ngeListener);
    public abstract void removePropertyChangeListener(java.beans.Property
ChangeListener);
}
```

So, the Customizer class must implement those properties. It must also fire `PropertyChangeEvent` to all registered listeners when a change to the target Bean has occurred.

- Implement a default constructor
- Associate the customizer with its target class via `BeanInfo.getBeanDescriptor`

If a Bean that has an associated Customizer is dropped into the BeanBox, a "Customize..." item is added by the BeanBox in the Edit menu.

26.10 JAVABEANS API

JavaBean API provides a set of related interfaces and classes necessary to design and develop beans in a separate package, `java.beans`. Not all the classes and interfaces are used all the time to develop a bean. For example, the event classes are used by beans that fire property and vetoable change events. However, most of the classes in this package are used by a bean builder/editor. In particular, these classes and interfaces help the bean builder/editor to create user interfaces that the user can use to customize their beans. Tables 26.1, 26.2, and 26.3 respectively show the list of interfaces, classes, and exceptions, which are used to develop beans.

Table 26.1: Javabean interfaces

Interface Name	Description
AppletInitializer	It is designed to work in collusion with java.beans.Beans.instantiate.
BeanInfo	A bean implementor who wants to provide information about their bean explicitly may provide a class that implements this BeanInfo interface.
Customizer	It provides a complete custom GUI for customizing a target JavaBean.
DesignMode	It is intended to be implemented by, or delegated from, instances of BeanContext, in order to propagate to its nested hierarchy of BeanContextChild instances, the current "designTime" property.
ExceptionListener	It is notified of internal exceptions.
PropertyChangeListener	This event gets fired whenever a bean changes a "bound" property.
PropertyEditor	It provides support for GUIs that want to allow users to edit a property value of a given type.
VetoableChangeListener	This event gets fired whenever a bean changes a "constrained" property.
Visibility	A bean may be run on servers where a GUI is not available under some circumstances.

Table 26.2: Javabean classes

Class Name	Description
BeanDescriptor	It provides global information about a bean, including Java class and displayName.
Beans	It provides some general purpose methods to control beans.
DefaultPersistenceDelegate	It is an implementation of the abstract PersistenceDelegate class and is the delegate used by default for classes about which no information is available.
Encoder	A class that is used to create streams or files which encode the state of a JavaBean collection in terms of its public APIs.
EventHandler	It provides support for dynamically generating event listeners, whose methods execute a statement involving an incoming event object and a target object.
EventSetDescriptor	It describes a group of events that a specified Javabean fires.
Expression	It represents a primitive expression where a single method is applied to a target and a set of arguments to return a result.
FeatureDescriptor	It is the common baseclass for PropertyDescriptor, EventSetDescriptor, and MethodDescriptor, etc.
IndexedPropertyChangeEvent	This event gets delivered whenever a component that conforms to the JavaBeans specification (a "bean") changes a bound indexed property.
IndexedPropertyDescriptor	It describes a property that acts as an array and has an indexed read and/or indexed write method to access specific elements of the array.
Introspector	This class provides a standard way for buider tools to learn about the properties, methods, and events that a target JavaBean supports.
MethodDescriptor	It describes a particular method that a JavaBean supports for external access.
ParameterDescriptor	It allows bean implementors to provide additional information for each parameter.
PersistenceDelegate	It takes the responsibility for expressing the state of an instance of a given class in terms of the methods in the class's public API.
PropertyChangeEvent	This event is delivered when a "bound" or "constrained" property is changed.
PropertyChangeListenerProxy	It extends the EventListenerProxy to add a named PropertyChangeListener.
PropertyChangeSupport	It is a utility class that can be used by beans that support bound properties.
PropertyDescriptor	It describes a property that a JavaBean exports through accessor methods.
PropertyEditorManager	It is used to locate a property editor for any given type name.
PropertyEditorSupport	It helps to build property editors.
SimpleBeanInfo	This is a support class to make it easier for people to provide BeanInfo classes.
Statement	A Statement object represents a primitive statement in which a single method is applied to a target and a set of arguments.
VetoableChangeListenerProxy	It extends the EventListenerProxy specifically for associating a VetoableChangeListener with a "constrained" property.
VetoableChangeSupport	It is a utility class that is used by beans that support constrained properties.
XMLDecoder	The XMLDecoder class is used to read XML documents created using the XMLEncoder and is used just like ObjectInputStream.
XMLEncoder	The XMLEncoder class is a complementary alternative to ObjectOutputStream and can be used to generate a textual representation of a JavaBean in the same way that the ObjectOutputStream can be used to create binary representation of Serializable objects.

Table 26.3: Javabean exceptions

Exception Name	Description
IntrospectionException	It is thrown when an exception happens during Introspection.
PropertyVetoException	It is thrown when a proposed change to a property represents an unacceptable value.

26.11 EJB

Enterprise JavaBeans (EJB) is a Java-based comprehensive component architecture for design and development of world-class distributed modular enterprise applications. EJBs are not only platform-independent, but can also run in any application server that implements EJB specifications. The EJB component architecture integrates several enterprise-level requirements such as distribution, transactions, security, messaging, persistence, and Enterprise Resource Planning (ERP) systems.

26.11.1 Benefits of EJB

Unlike other distributed component technologies such as CORBA and Java RMI, the EJB architecture hides most of the underlying system-level semantics such as instance management, object pooling, connection pooling, and thread management. The EJB container performs these tasks on behalf of us.

In the EJB architecture, beans contain the business logic, not the client. Therefore, the client developer can devote more time to the presentation of the client. Since clients do not have to implement business logic, they are thinner. This is very much required if devices running client applications are small and resource-constrained.

EJBs are portable and can run on any EJB compliant server.

It also provides us different types of components for business logic, session, persistence, and enterprise messages.

26.11.2 Usage Scenario

The EJB architecture should be used for those applications that have any of the following requirements:

- The applications must be scalable. The application's components need to be distributed across multiple machines to accommodate a large number of users. EJBs can run on different machines. Moreover, their location will remain transparent to the clients.
- Transactions are required to ensure data integrity. Enterprise beans allow us to perform transactions in a safe way. They also provide mechanisms for accessing shared objects concurrently.
- The application will have a wide variety of clients. Remote clients can easily locate enterprise beans using just a few lines of code. These clients can be thin, various, and numerous.

26.11.3 EJB Architecture

Before discussing the EJB architecture, let us understand the fundamental requirements of the distributed component architecture.

- It must provide mechanisms to instantiate the server-side and client-side proxies. A client-side proxy is created at the client side that represents the actual remote server object and acts as a proxy. A server-server side proxy, on the other hand, is created at the server-side. It must provide the basic mechanism to accept client requests and delegate these requests to the object implementation.

- It must provide a mechanism that allows us to have a reference to the client-side proxy. Using this reference, clients invoke methods. The client-side proxy is responsible for communicating with the server-side proxy.
- It must support a mechanism that can be used to inform the system that a specific component is no longer needed.

To satisfy these requirements, the EJB architecture specifies two types of interfaces: `javax.ejb.EJBHome` and `javax.ejb.EJBObject`. The `javax.ejb.EJBHome` defines the methods that allow a remote client to create, find, and remove EJB objects, as well as home business methods that are not specific to a bean instance. On the other hand, `javax.ejb.EJBObject` defines methods that collectively provide the remote client view of an EJB object.

There are three kinds of beans in the EJB architecture: *Session Beans*, *Entity Beans*, and *Message Driven Beans*.

26.11.4 Session Beans

Session beans perform specific tasks for a client. They are plain remote objects meant for abstracting business logic.

A client invokes methods of the session bean to access an application, which is deployed on the EJB server. The session bean performs business tasks inside the server on behalf of the client, hiding all the complexities from the client.

A session bean, as its name suggests, can be considered as an interactive session. A session bean is not shared. It can handle a single client in the same way that an interactive session may have just one client. A session bean, like an interactive session, is not also persistent. This means that its state is not saved to a database. When the client finishes, its session bean is also terminated. There are two types of session beans: *stateless* and *stateful*.

26.11.4.1 Stateless Session Beans

A stateless session bean does not keep the state between client requests. When a client sends a request for method invocation, the EJB container assigns an instance of a stateless bean. During the method invocation, bean's instance variables may have a state, but that is valid only during the method invocation. When the client makes another request, the same instance may not be assigned to the client, possibly due to the reason that it is already assigned to another client.

Since a stateless bean can be assigned to any client, it supports multiple clients. Therefore, to support the same number of clients, a lesser number of stateless session beans is required than stateful session beans. Session beans are useful for applications that have a large number of clients.

26.11.4.2 Stateful Session Beans

The state of a bean consists of values of its instance variable. Unlike stateless session beans, stateful session beans maintain their states. It means that a client sees the same state of the bean when it interacts with the stateful session bean through multiple method invocation. This is accomplished by assigning the same session bean to the client across multiple requests.

The stateful session bean loses its state when a client terminates. When the client terminates, the state is no longer necessary.

26.11.5 Entity Beans

Entity beans model real world business objects such as customers, orders, and products. They contain business logic that can be saved in a persistent storage for later use. The state of an entity bean persists beyond the lifetime of the application or the EJB server process. In J2EE, the persistency is obtained using a relational database. Usually, each entity bean has an underlying table in a relational database. Each instance of the bean corresponds to a row in that table.

Persistency can be obtained in two ways: *bean-managed* and *container-managed*. In the bean-managed persistency mechanism, the entity bean itself contains the code to save its state in the underlying table. On the other hand, in the container-managed persistence mechanism, the EJB container generates the necessary database access calls automatically.

Container-managed entity beans are not tied to a specific database. Therefore, you can redeploy the same entity bean on different J2EE servers that use different databases without modifying or recompiling the bean's code.

Multiple clients may share entity beans. So, entity beans work within transactions. The EJB container usually supports transaction management. In this case, you only have to specify the transaction attributes in the bean's deployment descriptor. The EJB container will take care of the rest of the procedure.

26.11.6 Message Driven Beans

A Message Driven Bean acts as a listener for the Java Message Service API, processing messages asynchronously. It is similar to an event listener, except that it receives messages instead of events.

The messages may be sent by a wide range of entities such as J2EE components, application clients, other enterprise beans, web components, JMS applications, or even systems that do not use J2EE technology. Message Driven Beans currently process only JMS (Java Message Service) messages, but provisions are left so that they can process other kinds of messages in the future.

The message-driven beans differ from session and entity beans in the sense that clients do not access message-driven beans through interfaces. Message Driven Beans and stateless session beans are similar with respect to the following points:

- They do not maintain state for a client. However, sometimes they can contain state across the handling of client messages such as an open database connection, an object reference to an enterprise bean object, or a JMS API connection.
- All instances are similar. The EJB container can use any instance to process a message. So, it can process multiple messages concurrently.
- One instance of a Message Driven Bean can handle multiple requests.

Note that, session and entity beans allow us to send and receive JMS messages. However, it happens in a synchronous way. We should not use synchronous 'send-receive', which are costly and blocking in a server-side component. Instead, message-driven beans can be used to send and receive messages asynchronously.

26.12 INTRODUCTION TO STRUTS FRAMEWORK

Struts is an application framework for developing Java EE web applications. This is an open-source framework and was originally developed by Craig McClanahan and donated to Apache. Fundamentally, it uses and extends Java servlet API and supports Model–View–Controller (MVC) architecture. It allows us to create flexible, extensible, and maintainable large web applications based on standard technologies, such as Java servlets, JSP, JavaBeans, resource bundles, and XML.

26.12.1 Basic Idea

In a Java EE-based web application, a client usually submits data to the server using the HTML form. These data are then handed over to a servlet or a Java Server Page, which processes them, typically interacts with the database, and finally processes the HTML output that is sent to the client. Since servlet as well as JSP technologies mix application logic with the presentation, they are inadequate for large web projects.

The primary task of struts is to separate application logic that interacts with the database, called *model* from HTML pages that are sent to the client, called *view* and instance that passes information between model and view, called *controller*. For this purpose, struts provide a controller as a servlet, called `ActionServlet`, and allows the writing of templates for the presentation (view), typically in terms of JSP. This special servlet acts as a switchboard to route requests from clients to the appropriate server page. This simple idea makes web applications much easier to design, develop, and maintain. Figure 26.10 describes the struts framework.

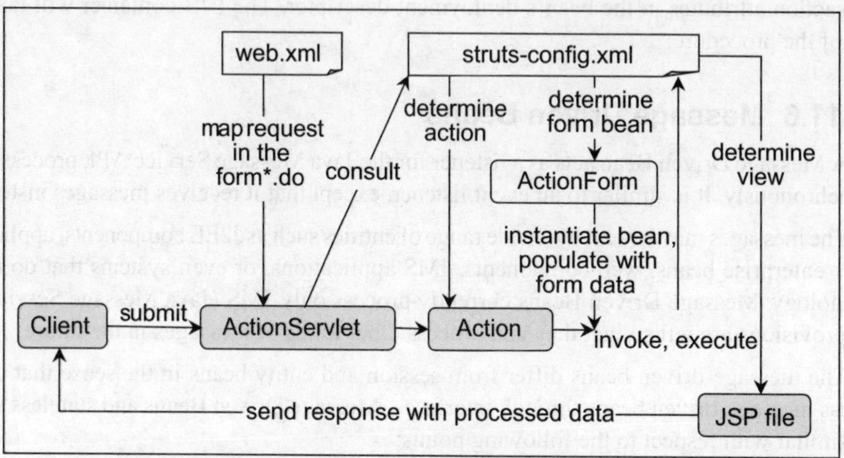

Figure 26.10: Struts framework

That was a high-level description of the struts framework. Let us now discuss the framework technically in more detail.

Every web application has an associated XML file (`WEB-INF/web.xml`) called deployment descriptor. This file must be configured by the web application developer. The deployment descriptor file specifies the configuration of the web application such as servlet mapping, parameter to those servlets, welcome pages, etc. This `web.xml` file is first configured to forward [Figure 26.10:] all requests with a specified pattern (usually `*.do`) to the struts framework's `ActionServlet` using the following entry:

```
<servlet>
    <servlet-name>action</servlet-name>
        <servlet-class>org.apache.struts.action.ActionServlet</servlet-class>
        <init-param>
            <param-name>config</param-name>
            <param-value>/WEB-INF/struts-config.xml</param-value>
        </init-param>
        <init-param>
            <param-name>debug</param-name>
            <param-value>2</param-value>
        </init-param>
        <init-param>
            <param-name>detail</param-name>
            <param-value>2</param-value>
        </init-param>
        <load-on-startup>2</load-on-startup>
</servlet>
```

```
<servlet-mapping>
   <servlet-name>action</servlet-name>
   <url-pattern>*.do</url-pattern>
</servlet-mapping>
```

If you use an IDE such as NetBeans, these entries are automatically inserted. The `web.xml` file also specifies one or more configuration XML file (`struts-config.xml`) that the `ActionServlet` will consult. This `ActionServlet` performs switching functions as mentioned earlier.

Suppose we are developing a web application using `/myapp` as a location relative to the server's document root. In the `struts-config.xml` file, we associate paths with the controller components called Action classes. The following is an example:

```
<action-mappings>
    <action name="LoginForm" path="/login" scope="request"
    type="com.myapp.struts.LoginAction"validate="false">
    </action>
</action-mappings>
```

It specifies that the `ActionServlet` should invoke the controller component `com.myapp.struts.LoginAction` for the URL `http://myhost/myapp/login.do`. We also give a name to this association ("LoginForm" in our case) to refer to it further. Note that the `web.xml` file specified that for the `*.do` pattern URL, `ActionServlet` should be invoked by the web container. So, the `.do` in this URL causes the web container to invoke `ActionServlet` of the struts framework. This `ActionServlet` consults the `struts-config.xml` file and sees the path "login" and invokes `LoginAction`. The form data are temporarily stored in an `ActionForm` type bean. The developer has to write this bean by extending the `ActionForm` class explicitly. `Action` and `ActionForm` are bound using the `name` property of the `<form-bean>` tag. The following is an example:

```
<form-beans>
    <form-bean name="LoginForm" type="com.myapp.struts.LoginForm"/>
</form-beans>
```

This "LoginForm" is the name of the action defined earlier and `com.myapp.struts.LoginForm` is the `ActionForm` bean.

For each `Action`, we can specify the names of the resulting page(s) that has(ve) to be sent to the client as a result of that action. There can be more than one view as the result of an action. Typically, there are at least two: one for "success" and one for "failure". This is accomplished by returning a string from the `execute()` method of `Action` to the `ActionServlet`.

The action form, in turn, can retrieve data sent by the client from `ActionForm` bean. The following example illustrates this:

```
public class LoginAction extends org.apache.struts.action.Action {

    /* forward name="success" path="" */
    private final static String SUCCESS = "success1";
    /* forward name="failure" path="" */
    private final static String FAILURE = "failure";

    /**
     * This is the action called from the Struts framework.
     * @param mapping The ActionMapping used to select this instance.
     * @param form The optional ActionForm bean for this request.
     * @param request The HTTP Request we are processing.
     * @param response The HTTP Response we are processing.
     * @throws java.lang.Exception
     * @return
     */
```

```
public ActionForward execute(ActionMapping mapping, ActionForm  form,
        HttpServletRequest request, HttpServletResponse response)
        throws Exception {
    // extract user data
    LoginForm formBean = (LoginForm) form;
    String name = formBean.getName();
    String email = formBean.getEmail();

    // perform validation
    if ((name == null) || // name parameter does not exist
        email == null || // email parameter does not exist
        name.equals("") || // name parameter is empty
        email.indexOf("@") == -1) {    // email lacks '@'
        formBean.setError();
        return mapping.findForward(FAILURE);
    }
    return mapping.findForward(SUCCESS);
  }
}
```

The parameter `mapping` in the `execute()` method refers to the `ActionServlet` and `form` refers to the associated `ActionForm` bean. The `Action` (the controller component) reports back to the `ActionServlet` using words like "success", "failure", "ready", "OK", "UserError", etc. We specify corresponding view pages in the configuration file as follows:

```
<action name="LoginForm" path="/login" scope="request"
type="com.myapp.struts.LoginAction" validate="false">
  <forward name="success" path="/success.jsp"/>
  <forward name="failure" path="/login.jsp"/>
</action>
```

The `ActionServlet` knows from the configuration file where to forward and what to show as a result. This has the added advantage of reconfiguration of the view layer by simply editing the XML configuration file.

The `ActionForm` beans can be validated ensuring that the user provides valid data in the form. The validation can be carried out on a per-session basis. It allows forms to span multiple pages of the View and Actions in the Controller.

Since the framework works on the server side, the client's view has to be composed at the server before sending it to the client. Typically, some sort of server-side technology such as JSP, Velocity, and XSLT is used for the view layer. Simple HTML files may be used to compose client's view. However, they cannot provide full advantage of all the dynamic features.

KEYWORDS

Accessor methods—Public methods of a bean used to read and write bean properties

Bean builder—A tool that is used to build and/or test beans

BeanInfo interface—Defines several methods that can be used to inspect properties, methods, and events of a bean

Bound property—One which when changed, notifies one or more beans about this change

Constraint property—A constrained property of a bean is a special type of property which can be changed subject to prior permission from external object(s).

Controller—Controls the Model and View components

Customization—Bean customization allows us to customize the appearance and behaviour of a bean at design time, within a bean-compliant builder tool.

Design Patterns—The JavaBeans framework introduces several rules for names to be used for classes and methods. They are collectively called design patterns.

EJB—Enterprise JavaBeans (EJB) is Java-based comprehensive component architecture for design and development of world-class distributed modular enterprise applications.

Entity Beans—Entity beans model real world business objects such as customers, orders, and products. They contain business logic that can be saved in a persistent storage for later use.

Indexed Property—An index property is an array of properties. It can hold a range of values that can be accessed through accessor functions.

Introspection—A procedure to discover properties, methods, and events of a bean dynamically.

Message Driven Beans—A Message Driven Bean acts as a listener for the Java Message Service API, processing messages asynchronously.

Model—Specific code that handles the business logic

Persistence—Persistence is a procedure to save a bean in non-volatile storage such as a file. The bean can be reconstructed and used later.

Session Beans—Session beans perform specific tasks for a client. They are plain remote objects meant for abstracting business logic.

Stateful session beans—Stateful session beans maintain their states across client requests.

Stateless session beans—A stateless session bean does not keep the state between client requests.

View—Takes care of the appearance of web pages

SUMMARY

J2EE is not a single technology; it consists of a large set of technologies.

JavaBean technology is a Java-based technology to design and develop reusable and platform-independent software components. These components can then be integrated virtually in all Java-compatible applications. JavaBean components are knows as beans. The appearance and features of a bean can be changed or customized using builder tools such as BeanBox and NetBeans. A bean class is nothing but a usual Java class with the following requirements:

- It must have a public no-argument constructor.
- It has public accessor methods to read and write properties.
- It should implement `Serializable` or `Externalizable` interface

Properties control the behaviour and appearance of a bean. Usually, beans are developed and tested using tools called bean builder. A bean builder provides several facilities to build a bean.

A bean builder usually uses Java core reflection API to discover the methods of a bean. It then applies design patterns to discover other bean features (such as properties and events). This procedure is known as introspection. The JavaBeans framework introduces a lot of rules for names to be used for classes and methods. They are collectively called design patterns. The different types of bean properties, namely, simple, bound constraint, and indexed properties were explained with extensive examples. JavaBean API provides interfaces and classes to discover properties, methods, and events of a bean. The `BeanInfo` interface defines several methods that can be used to inspect properties, methods, and events of a bean. Sometimes, it is necessary to store the beans for later use. Persistence is a procedure to save a bean in non-volatile storage such as a file. The bean can be reconstructed and used later.

Bean customization allows us to customize the appearance and behaviour of a bean at design time, within a bean-compliant builder tool.

Enterprise JavaBeans (EJB) is a Java-based comprehensive component architecture for design and development of world-class distributed modular enterprise applications. EJBs are not only platform-independent, but also run in any application server that implements EJB specification. The EJB component architecture integrates several enterprise-level requirements such as distribution, transactions, security, messaging, persistence, and Enterprise Resource Planning (ERP) systems. There are three kinds of beans in EJB architecture: Session Beans, Entity Beans, and Message Driven Beans.

Session beans perform specific tasks for a client. They are plain remote objects meant for abstracting business logic. A stateless session bean does not keep the state between client requests. Unlike stateless session beans, stateful session beans maintain their states. Entity beans contain business logic that can be saved in a persistent storage for later use. A Message Driven Bean acts as a listener for the Java Message Service API, processing messages asynchronously.

Struts is an application framework for developing Java EE web applications. It uses and extends Java servlet API and supports Model–View–Controller (MVC) architecture. It allows us to create flexible, extensible, and maintainable large web applications based on standard technologies, such as Java servlets, JSP, JavaBeans, resource bundles, and XML.

WEB RESOURCES

http://java.sun.com/docs/books/tutorial/javabeans/
Trail: JavaBeans

http://java.sun.com/j2ee/1.4/docs/tutorial/doc/
The J2EE 1.4 Tutorial

http://www.ibm.com/developerworks/edu/j-dw-java-gsejb-i.html
Getting started with Enterprise JavaBeans technology

http://java.sun.com/j2ee/tutorial/1_3-fcs/doc/EJBConcepts.html
Enterprise Beans

http://struts.apache.org/
Struts

http://netbeans.org/kb/docs/web/quickstart-webapps-struts.html
Introduction to the Struts Web Framework

http://www.vaannila.com/struts-2/struts-2-tutorial/struts-2-tutorial.html
Struts 2 Tutorial

EXERCISES

Objective-type Questions

1. How do you make an instance variable into a JavaBean property?
   (a) Drop the Bean into the BeanBox property sheet
   (b) Specify get and set methods for the variable
   (c) Declare the instance variable public and static
   (d) Declare the instance variable private and let the BeanBox define get and set methods for the variable

2. JavaBean methods are all
   (a) Properties
   (b) Event listeners
   (c) Identical to methods of other Java classes
   (d) Events

3. Which of the following aspects do properties control?
   (a) How a JavaBean is compiled and dropped into the BeanBox (or other tool)
   (b) The tools you can use to customize a JavaBean
   (c) The communication between JavaBeans
   (d) A JavaBean's appearance and behaviour

4. Which of the following is done using BeanBox's property tool?
   (a) Change the value of a Bean's property
   (b) Add new properties to a Bean
   (c) Delete a Bean's property
   (d) None of the above

5. Bound properties are associated with
   (a) propertyBound event
   (b) valueChanged event
   (c) valueBound event
   (d) propertyChange event

6. A property defined in a JavaBean typically
   (a) is declared as a private type
   (b) has a corresponding get method and set method
   (c) can be saved and retrieved at a later time
   (d) all of the above

7. A bean that receives events generated by a source bean is called
   (a) EventHandler Bean
   (b) Receiver Bean
   (c) Acceptor Bean
   (d) Listener Bean

8. The properties of a Bean
   (a) are defined by the Bean itself
   (b) may be inherited from Bean's super class
   (c) are analogous to instance variables
   (d) All of the above

9. Which of the following mechanisms is used to discover the bean's properties, methods, and events?
   (a) Persistence (c) Customization
   (b) Introspection (d) Event delegation

10. JavaBeans with constrained properties
    (a) instantiate an ActionListener object.
    (b) use methods of the VetoableChangeSupport class.
    (c) instantiate a ConstraintChangeSupport object.
    (d) None of the above

11. Which of the following executes EJB components?
    (a) A web server (c) A web browser
    (b) An EJB container (d) A database server

12. Which of the following interfaces is used to find and remove enterprise beans?
    (a) java.rmi.Home
    (b) javax.ejb.EJBObject
    (c) javax.ejb.EJBHome
    (d) javax.ejb.Object

13. Which of the following is used to create business objects?
    (a) javax.ejb.EntityBean
    (b) javax.ejb.Object
    (c) javax.ejb.SessionBean
    (d) javax.ejb.Business

14. What type of bean is used to embody application processing state information?
    (a) javax.ejb.StateBean
    (b) javax.ejb.Object
    (c) javax.ejb.EntityBean
    (d) javax.ejb.SessionBean

15. Which of the following interfaces must the enterprise bean implement so that an application can invoke its operations?
    (a) javax.ejb.EJBHome
    (b) javax.ejb.EntityBean
    (c) javax.rmi.Remote
    (d) javax.ejb.EJBObject

16. Which of the following is true about a Message-driven bean?
    (a) It has a remote interface.
    (b) It does not feature a component interface.
    (c) It has a local interface.
    (d) It has a client view.

17. What does the EJB architecture specify?
    (a) Distributed object components
    (b) Transactional components
    (c) Server-side components
    (d) All of the above

18. What happens when a reference to a remote method is passed?
    (a) A local copy of the remote object is passed.
    (b) The remote object reference is passed.
    (c) The remote object's stub is passed.
    (d) None of these

19. Each struts action element is uniquely identified by its
    (a) path attribute (c) page attribute
    (b) name attribute (d) input attribute

20. What is the full form of MVC
    (a) Multiple–View–Controller
    (b) Model–View–Cache
    (c) Multiple–View–Cache
    (d) Model–View–Controller

Subjective-type Questions

1. What are JavaBeans?
2. Mention the types of bean properties.
3. How do you create a bound property?
4. Explain with example bean design patterns.
5. How do you create a constrained property?
6. What do you mean by bean customization?
7. What is the purpose of the BeanInfo interface?
8. Explain the importance of bean persistence. How do you make a bean persistent?
9. What is Deployment Descriptor?
10. Mention the advantages of EJB over other component architectures.
11. What is the difference between JavaBean and Enterprise JavaBean?
12. What is a bean managed transaction?
13. What are the differences between stateless and stateful session beans?
14. How does a stateful session bean remember its client state?
15. What is the life cycle of an Entity Bean?

CHAPTER – 27

JAVA AND CORBA

KEY OBJECTIVES

After completing this chapter readers will be able to—

- get an idea about CORBA
- understand the architecture of CORBA and its components
- know basic steps to write CORBA-based client–server applications using Java
- understand the concept of DII and DSI
- learn how to write RMI applications using IIOP
- know how to handle in, out and inout parameters

27.1 INTRODUCTION

CORBA (Common Object Request Broker Architecture) is a specification that describes how heterogeneous objects can interoperate. CORBA objects can be created/accessed using virtually any programming language (such as Java, C, C++, Smalltalk, Ada) and can exist on any platform (such as Windows, Unix, Linux, Solaris). This means that a Java application running under Windows can transparently access C++ objects created on a Unix platform.

Developers need not know what language a CORBA service is written in, or even where it is located physically making CORBA systems extremely versatile. A CORBA object may be shutdown, restarted on a different location and then re-registered with a name server. Clients can simply find the object by looking up the service and then continue to make requests.

The CORBA is specified and controlled by the well-known Object Management Group (OMG), which is a consortium of more than 700 companies that work together to create standards for object computing.

27.2 CORBA ARCHITECTURE

The OMA defines four major parts a CORBA-compliant system should have:

- An Object Request Broker (ORB)—This acts as a software bus for intercommunication of heterogeneous objects.

- CORBAServices—This defines additional system-level services the ORB may provide, such as Security, Naming, and Transactions.
- CORBAFacilities—This part defines application-level services, such as compound documents and other vertical facilities.
- Business Objects—This describes real-world objects and applications, such as a Book or a BankAccount.

27.2.1 IDL

A key feature of CORBA is IDL, a language-neutral Interface Definition Language. Interfaces to CORBA objects are written using IDL. This allows CORBA application developers to describe the service structure of an object without any language specific syntax. IDL interfaces are converted to or obtained from the language specific code using tools provided by the CORBA S/W provider. For example, Java provides a compiler `idlj` for this purpose.

27.2.2 ORB

CORBA objects communicate through a broker called Object Request Broker (ORB). It is a library that enables low-level communication between CORBA compliant applications written in different programming languages. An application, during it life cycle, can ask ORB to do the following:

- Register and look up objects
- Marshal and un-marshal parameters from one programming language to another language
- Publish and retrieve metadata on objects on the local system for another ORB
- Handle security across your machine's local boundary
- Invoke methods statically on a remote object using downloaded stub
- Invoke methods on a remote object using dynamic method invocation
- Automatically activate objects if they are not currently active
- Forward callback methods to appropriate local objects registered with the ORB

However, a developer need not know how those facilities are implemented. They simply use some hooks to use those facilities. This transparency makes CORBA the first choice for writing heterogeneous distributed applications.

27.2.3 IIOP

Communication between ORBs takes place using a TCP/IP-based protocol called Internet Inter-Orb Protocol (IIOP), which defines how CORBA-compliant ORBs pass information back and forth. It is also standardized by OMG.

27.2.4 IOR

CORBA provides several ways to locate CORBA objects. However, the most flexible one is Interoperable Object References (IORs). An IOR contains enough information required for a client ORB to connect to a remote server object or servant. IOR represents a reference to any CORBA object including naming service, transaction service, or customized CORBA servant. It contains the following information:

- IIOP version number
- Host and port number of the server, a request to be forwarded
- Class name and instance data required to create a local proxy (stub)
- A key that uniquely identifies the servant to the ORB exporting the servant
- Other information necessary for method invocations, such as supported ORB services and proprietary protocol support, etc.

A programmer need not know the information contained in an IOR. CORBA provides facilities to convert an IOR to a string (called stringified object reference). This string can then be transferred to other locations. CORBA also provides functions to reconvert the string to remote servant reference (essentially a reference to a local proxy/stub). The process of converting an IOR to a string or a string to a reference is known as *stringification*.

The CORBA standard, for stringification, defines the following two methods on `org.omg.CORBA.ORB`:

```
String object_to_string(org.omg.CORBA.Object o)
org.omg.CORBA.Object string_to_object(String ior)
```

The first one converts the given CORBA object reference to a stringified IOR, whereas the latter converts a stringified IOR produced by the method object_to_string() back to a CORBA object reference.

The representation of IOR is also ORB-implementation independent. So stringified object reference works across different CORBA vendors.

27.3 JAVA IDL

Java SDK provides an API (popularly known as Java-IDL) to support CORBA specification. This means Java-IDL enabled applications can interact with other applications that also support CORBA. The API consists of primarily the following packages: `org.omg.CORBA`, `org.omg.CosNaming`, `org.omg.PortableServer`, `org.omg.PortableInterceptor` and `org.omg.DynamicAny`.

27.4 DEVELOPING CORBA APPLICATIONS

In this section, we shall describe the basic steps needed to develop a distributed application using Java IDL. The following are basic steps used to develop CORBA applications:

- Write an interface using IDL
- Mapping IDL interface to Java
- Implementing the interface
- Writing the server
- Writing the client

We shall consider our Calculator application in this regard. This application was developed earlier using RMI technology. Let us now develop using Java-IDL and understand their relative advantages and disadvantages. This application, in spite of its simplicity, uses all the tasks required to develop almost any CORBA program that uses static invocation.

27.4.1 Write an interface using IDL

Our Calculator object has a single method that takes two integers and returns their sum. The interface for this object in IDL (stored in a file `Calculator.idl`) looks like this:

```
//Calculator.idl
module CalculatorApp {
  interface Calculator {
    long add(in long a, in long b);
  };
};
```

A CORBA module is a container for related interfaces and declarations. It corresponds to a package in Java. The IDL compiler translates a module to a package statement in the Java code. A CORBA interface is similar to Java interface that describes the service of an object. Our calculator object provides a single service (method) that takes two integers and returns their sum.

27.4.2 Mapping IDL interface to Java

To develop an application using Java, this IDL interface is translated to Java code using Java's `idlj` compiler. The `idlj` compiler generates a set of Java files based on option(s) passed to it. We use the following command to generate files required to both client and server:

```
idlj -fall Calculator.idl
```

This generates six files `CalculatorOperations.java`, `Calculator.java`, `CalculatorPOA.java`, `_CalculatorStub.java`, `CalculatorHelper.java` and `CalculatorHolder.java`. The generated files provide standard functionality as follows:

- `CalculatorOperations.java`

  This is a pure Java interface corresponding to CORBA interface and is shared by both the stubs and skeletons. It looks like this:

```
package CalculatorApp;

/**
* CalculatorApp/CalculatorOperations.java .
* Generated by the IDL-to-Java compiler (portable), version "3.2"
* from Calculator.idl
* Wednesday, February 5, 2014 11:58:17 AM PST
*/

public interface CalculatorOperations
{
  int add (int a, int b);
} // interface CalculatorOperations
```

  It is easy to understand how the IDL statements map to the generated Java statements.

- `Calculator.java`

  This is a Java interface that extends `CalculatorOperations` and thus corresponds to CORBA interface. It is derived from `org.omg.CORBA.Object` and ensures the required CORBA functionality. It looks like this:

```
package CalculatorApp;


/**
* CalculatorApp/Calculator.java .
* Generated by the IDL-to-Java compiler (portable), version "3.2"
* from Calculator.idl
* Wednesday, February 5, 2014 11:58:17 AM PST
*/

public interface Calculator extends CalculatorOperations, org.omg.CORBA.Object,
org.omg.CORBA.portable.IDLEntity
{
} // interface Calculator
```

- `CalculatorPOA.java`

  This is the server-side skeleton class. It provides CORBA functionality at the server-side, hence extends `org.omg.PortableServer.Servant`, and implements the `org.omg.CORBA.portable.InvokeHandler` interface and the `CalculatorOperations` interface.

- `_CalculatorStub.java`

  This class is the client-side stub. It provides CORBA functionality for the client, hence extends `org.omg.CORBA.portable.ObjectImpl` and implements the `Calculator` interface.

- `CalculatorHelper.java`

  It provides additional functionality, notably the `narrow()` method which casts a CORBA object reference to its proper type. It is also responsible to read/write data type to CORBA streams, and insert and extract the data type from `Any`s.
- `CalculatorHolder.java`

  This final class, as its name implies, holds a public `Calculator` instance. This is used when the IDL type is an `out` or an `inout` parameter. Since these facilities are not directly available in Java, this holder class provides operations to simulate them by delegating to the methods in the Helper class for reading and writing.

27.4.3 Implementing the interface

To implement the interface, we write a Java class called a *servant*, which inherits from a class called the *servant base*, which is optionally generated by the `idlj` compiler. The servant base class is the CORBA type-specific interface between the ORB and the servant. It unmarshals incoming request, invokes servant methods, marshals results, and instructs the ORB to send the result back to the client ORB.

In our case, we write a servant class `SimpleCalculator` extending `CalculatorPOA` to provide CORBA functionality. Here is our implementation class (`SimpleCalculator.java`):

```
// SimpleCalculator.java
import CalculatorApp.*;
class SimpleCalculator extends CalculatorPOA {
  public int add(int x, int y) {
    System.out.println("Received: " + a + " and " + b);
    int result = a + b;
    System.out.println("Sent: " + result);
    return result;
  }
}
```

A servant class defines methods of the interface it implements. Our `SimpleCalculator` servant defines one, the `add()` method. This adds two integers passed to it and returns the result. It also prints some messages to track method invocation and response.

27.4.4 Writing the server

The trickiest part of any CORBA-based application is to create a servant instance and export it to the ORB so that the other application can invoke methods on the servant. The Object Request Broker (ORB) is represented in Java by `org.omg.CORBA.ORB` class. So, we create an instance of ORB by calling its static `init()` method as follows:

```
ORB orb = ORB.init(args, null);
```

The command line arguments (args) are passed to the `init()` method so that we can set some ORB properties (such as host and port, the naming service running on) at runtime. Now, we need a Portable Object Adapter (POA). We get a reference to the existing POA, the root POA as follows:

```
POA rootpoa = POAHelper.narrow(orb.resolve_initial_references("RootPOA"));
```

We then activate the associated POA manager using the following statement:

```
rootpoa.the_POAManager().activate();
```

The activated POA manager enables the associated POA to start processing requests. We then create an instance of the servant that performs the actual operation as follows:

```
SimpleCalculator cal = new SimpleCalculator();
```

The object is then registered (activated) with the POA and an Interoperable Object Reference (IOR) is obtained. There are many ways to do this. The typical one uses `servant_to_reference()` method as follows:

```
org.omg.CORBA.Object ref = rootpoa.servant_to_reference(cal);
```

This essentially activates the servant and returns an id encapsulating all necessary information required to refer to the servant. This id is used by the clients for method invocation. The invocation request eventually comes to the underlying ORB which consults the associated POA to map the object reference to the servant. These two steps may be explicitly specified as follows:

```
byte[] id = rootpoa.activate_object(cal);
org.omg.CORBA.Object ref = rootpoa.id_to_reference(id);
```

This is also equivalent to:

```
org.omg.CORBA.Object ref = cal._this(orb);
```

To invoke the `add()` method this remote servant, client somehow need this IOR. This IOR may be transferred physically to the client and reconverted to the object type using `narrow()` method of `CalculatorHelper` class. Alternatively, the server may bind this IOR to the naming service from where the client can get the IOR. We use the latter mechanism as it does not require the IOR to be transferred explicitly.

27.4.4.1 Binding IOR to naming service

To get the root context of the name server, we use the following piece of code:

```
org.omg.CORBA.Object objRef = orb.resolve_initial_references("NameService");
```

The `resolve_initial_references()` method returns a generic `org.omg.CORBA.Object`, which is then converted to the naming context (represented by `NamingContextExt` class) type using helper class as follows:

```
NamingContextExt ncRef = NamingContextExtHelper.narrow(objRef);
```

This refers to the root of the naming service and can be used to register IOR by a specified name as an array of `NameComponent`. Let us use a single string "Calculator" as the name of our calculator servant.

```
String name = "Calculator";
NameComponent path[] = ncRef.to_name( name );
```

We register the IOR with this name as follows:

```
ncRef.rebind(path, ref);
```

We finally enable the ORB to wait for invocation requests:

```
orb.run();
```

The following is the complete code for the server (`CalculatorServer.java`):

```
// CalculatorServer.java
import org.omg.CosNaming.*;
import org.omg.CosNaming.NamingContextPackage.*;
import org.omg.CORBA.*;
import org.omg.PortableServer.*;
public class CalculatorServer {
  public static void main(String args[]) {
    try{
      // create and initialize the ORB
      ORB orb = ORB.init(args, null);

      // get a reference to rootpoa
      POA rootpoa =
POAHelper.narrow(orb.resolve_initial_references("RootPOA"));

      // activate the POAManager
      rootpoa.the_POAManager().activate();
```

```
        // create servant
        SimpleCalculator cal = new SimpleCalculator();

        // get IOR corresponding to the servant
        org.omg.CORBA.Object ref = rootpoa.servant_to_reference(cal);

        // get the root naming context
        org.omg.CORBA.Object objRef =
orb.resolve_initial_references("NameService");

        // Convert it to the proper type
        NamingContextExt ncRef = NamingContextExtHelper.narrow(objRef);

        //this the name of the servant
        String name = "Calculator";
        NameComponent path[] = ncRef.to_name( name );

        // register the IOR with the name service
        ncRef.rebind(path, ref);

        System.out.println("CalculatorServer ready and waiting ...");

        // wait for invocations from clients
        orb.run();
      } catch (Exception e) {
        e.printStackTrace();
      }
    }
}
```

27.4.5 Writing the Client

Like server, client also creates and initializes an instance of ORB:

```
ORB orb = ORB.init(args, null);
```

Here, the command line arguments (args) are also passed to the `init()` method so that we can set some ORB properties (such as host and port, the naming service running on) at runtime. Before invoking a method on the remote servant, client first needs to have an IOR to that servant. The IOR may be obtained from the naming service by providing the name of the servant. The root of the naming service is obtained as follows:

```
org.omg.CORBA.Object objRef = orb.resolve_initial_references("NameService");
```

It is then converted to the proper type using helper class as follows:

```
NamingContextExt ncRef = NamingContextExtHelper.narrow(objRef);
```

The client then obtains the IOR of the calculator servant as follows:

```
String name = "Calculator";
org.omg.CORBA.Object ref = ncRef.resolve_str(name);
```

This IOR is then converted to our `Calculator` type using `narrow()` method of `CalculatorHelper` class as follows:

```
Calculator calc = CalculatorHelper.narrow(ref);
```

Method invocation is the easiest part and looks exactly like local invocation. All the complications of marshalling parameters to the wire, routing them to the server-side ORB, unmarshalling, and forwarding to the servant are completely transparent to the client.

```
int x =2, y = 3;
int result = calc.add(x, y);
```

The following is the complete code for the client (`CalculatorClient.java`):

```
import CalculatorApp.*;
import org.omg.CosNaming.*;
import org.omg.CosNaming.NamingContextPackage.*;
import org.omg.CORBA.*;

public class CalculatorClient {
  public static void main(String args[])  {
    try{
      // create and initialize the ORB
      ORB orb = ORB.init(args, null);

      // get the root naming context
      org.omg.CORBA.Object objRef =
orb.resolve_initial_references("NameService");

      // Convert it to the proper type
      NamingContextExt ncRef = NamingContextExtHelper.narrow(objRef);

      // get an IOR from naming service
      String name = "Calculator";
      org.omg.CORBA.Object ref = ncRef.resolve_str(name);

      System.out.println(ref);
      Calculator calc = CalculatorHelper.narrow(ref);

      int x =2, y = 3;
      System.out.println("Sent :" + x + " and " + y);
      int result  = calc.add(x, y);
      System.out.println("Received : " + result);
    } catch (Exception e) {
      e.printStackTrace();
    }
  }
}
```

27.5 COMPILING APPLICATIONS

Create a directory (say server) and place all server-related files, namely `Calculator.idl`, `SimpleCalculator.java` and `CalculatorServer.java`. Use the following command to compile IDL file:

```
idlj -fall Calculator.idl
```

Now, use the following command to compile all the server-related files:

```
javac *.java
```

Now, create a directory (client), probably on a different computer. Place all client-related files, namely `Calculator.idl` and `CalculatorClient.java`. Use the following command to compile the IDL file:

```
idlj -fall Calculator.idl
```

Now, use the following command to compile all the client-related files:

```
javac *.java
```

27.6 RUNNING THE APPLICATION

To run the application, a name service is required.

The server uses this name service to bind reference to the servant implementing Calculator interface. This reference is used by the client for method invocation. Java is shipped with two applications `tnameserv`, a transient naming service, and `orbd`, which is a daemon process containing a Bootstrap Service, a Transient Naming Service, a Persistent Naming Service, and a Server Manager. We shall use `orbd` in our example. The `orbd` runs by default on port 900, though `–ORBInitialPort` option may be used to override the default port. We use the port number 6789.

Open a terminal in any computer (we assume that the IP address of this computer is 172.16.4.248) in the network and use the following command to start `orbd` on port `6789`.

```
orbd -ORBInitialPort 6789
```

Alternatively, the transient name service tnameserv may also be used as follows:

```
tnameserv -ORBInitialPort 6789
```

Note that only persistent binding in the `tnameserv` is the initial naming context. The rest of the namespace is lost if `tnameserv` halts and restarts.

Now, open a terminal in a computer in the network and use the following command to start the server:

```
java CalculatorServer -ORBInitialHost 172.16.4.248 -ORBInitialPort 6789
```

To start the client, open a terminal in another computer in the network and use the following command:

```
java CalculatorClient -ORBInitialHost 172.16.4.248 -ORBInitialPort 6789
```

A sample output is shown in Figure 27.1:

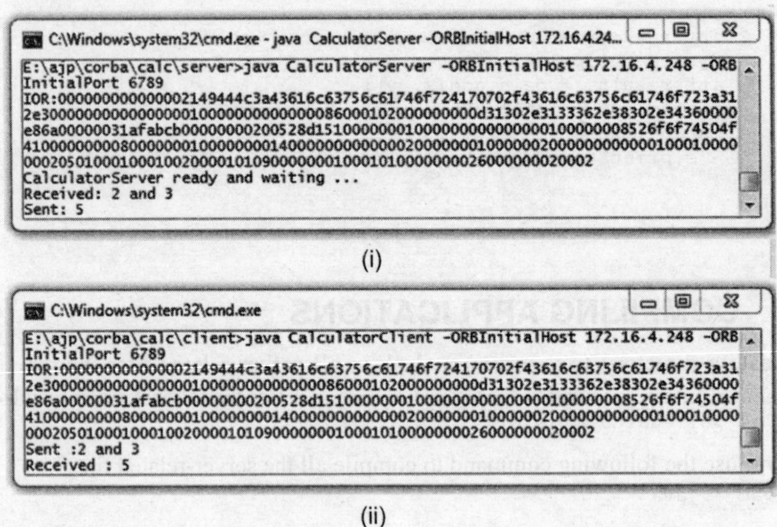

Figure 27.1: Calculator application using Java IDL (i) Server (ii) Client

27.7 USING PROPERTIES

The host and port may be specified in the server as well as client program as follows:

```
Properties props = new Properties();
props.put("org.omg.CORBA.ORBInitialHost","172.16.4.248");
props.put("org.omg.CORBA.ORBInitialPort", "6789");

ORB orb = ORB.init(args, props);
```

In this case, use the following simple commands to start the server and client respectively.

```
java CalculatorServer
java CalculatorClient
```

27.8 STRINGIFIED OBJECT REFERENCE

Note that CORBA uses the concept of stringified object reference to identify CORBA objects. A server program can publish a stringified IOR of a servant and a client can remotely invoke methods on this servant using the IOR. The following program (`CalculatorServerStr.java`) exports a calculator servant and prints its IOR on the screen:

```
// CalculatorServerStr.java
import org.omg.CORBA.*;
import org.omg.PortableServer.*;
public class CalculatorServerStr {
  public static void main(String args[]) {
    try{
      ORB orb = ORB.init(args, null);
      POA rootpoa =
POAHelper.narrow(orb.resolve_initial_references("RootPOA"));
      rootpoa.the_POAManager().activate();
      SimpleCalculator cal = new SimpleCalculator();
      org.omg.CORBA.Object ref = rootpoa.servant_to_reference(cal);
      System.out.println(ref);
      System.out.println("CalculatorServer ready and waiting ..");
      orb.run();
    } catch (Exception e) {
        e.printStackTrace();
      }
  }
}
```

To invoke a method of the calculator servant, the only thing a client needs to know is servant's IOR. The IOR can be transferred to the client machine using different ways such as file transfer and mail attachment. Once the client application has an object reference, it has all the information it needs to connect to the object and make remote invocations on the object's methods. The following client (`CalculatorClientStr.java`) invokes the method add() on the remote object using the given IOR as a command line argument:

```
import CalculatorApp.*;
import org.omg.CORBA.*;
public class CalculatorClientStr {
  public static void main(String args[])  {
    try{
      ORB orb = ORB.init(args, null);
      org.omg.CORBA.Object obj  = orb.string_to_object(args[0]);
      Calculator calc = CalculatorHelper.narrow(obj);
      int x =2, y = 3;
      System.out.println("Sent :" + x + " and " + y);
      int result  = calc.add(x, y);
      System.out.println("Received : " + result);
    } catch (Exception e) {
        e.printStackTrace();
      }
  }
}
```

A sample output is shown in Figure 27.2:

```
C:\Windows\system32\cmd.exe - java CalculatorServerStr
E:\ajp\corba\calc\server>java CalculatorServerStr
IOR:000000000000002149444c3a43616c63756c61746f724170702f43616c63756c61746f723a31
2e3000000000000000010000000000000086000102000000000e31302e38362e3231392e31373300
c46400000031afabcb00000000002022c4226e00000001000000000000000100000008526f6f74504f
4100000000080000000100000000140000000000000200000001000000200000000000010001000
0002050100010001002000001010900000001000101000000000260000000020002
CalculatorServer ready and waiting ...
Received: 2 and 3
Sent: 5
```

(i)

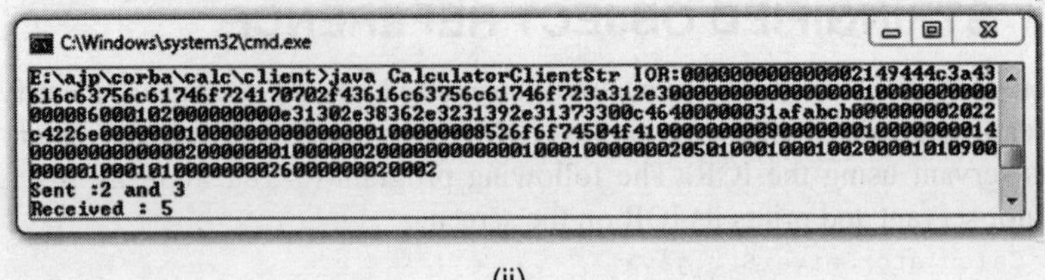

(ii)

Figure 27.2: Calculator application using stringified object reference (i) Server (ii) Client

27.9 USING URL

CORBA defines two URLs `corbaname` and `corbaloc` to provide a human readable/editable way to specify a location where an IOR can be obtained. The following sections describe how to use these two URLS.

27.9.1 Using corbaloc

The `corbaloc` URL is used to specify the location of a CORBA object in a human-readable format with the minimum amount of information necessary. A `corbaloc` URL has the following format:

```
corbcaloc:[iiop]:[Version@]Host[:Port][/ObjectKey]
```

A brief description of different components is given below:

iiop

(Optional) Specifies that the transport protocol should be IIOP. If not present, the protocol defaults to IIOP. So, `corbaloc:iiop:` and `corbaloc::` are equivalent.

Version

(Optional) Specifies the GIOP version supported by the server. The allowed values are 1.0, 1.1 and 1.2; if not present, it defaults 1.0.

Host

Specifies the server's hostname or IP address in dotted decimal format.

Port

(Optional) Specifies the IP port to be used to connect to the server. The default is 900.

ObjectKey

(Optional) A name of the CORBA object on the remote server.

Here is a typical example of a `corbaloc` URL

```
corbaloc:iiop:1.2@172.16.4.248:6789/NameService
```

This refers to the initial naming context of the name service running on a port 6789 in a machine having IP address 172.16.4.248. The following program gets a reference to the initial context of a remote name service using `corbaloc`.

```
import CalculatorApp.*;
import org.omg.CosNaming.*;
import org.omg.CosNaming.NamingContextPackage.*;
import org.omg.CORBA.*;
public class CalculatorClientLoc {
```

```
public static void main(String args[])  {
  try{
    ORB orb = ORB.init(args, null);
    org.omg.CORBA.Object objRef =
orb.string_to_object("corbaloc:iiop:1.2@172.16.4.248:6789/NameService");
    NamingContextExt ncRef = NamingContextExtHelper.narrow(objRef);
    org.omg.CORBA.Object ref = ncRef.resolve_str("Calculator");
    Calculator calc = CalculatorHelper.narrow(ref);
    int x =2, y = 3;
    System.out.println("Sent :" + x + " and " + y);
    int result  = calc.add(x, y);
    System.out.println("Received : " + result);
  } catch (Exception e) {e.printStackTrace();}
 }
}
```

Unlike IOR that contains essentially the complete state of an object reference, the corbaloc URL contains only the object's address. Hence, object references constructed with a corbaloc URL will not have same state as the remote servant; instead they are initialized in a provisional state. The corbaloc URL can be used as a command line argument. The calculator client can be started using the following command:

```
java CalculatorClient -ORBInitRef
NameService=corbaloc:iiop:1.2@172.16.4.248:6789/NameService
```

This tells that the program should contact the name service running on 6789 in a machine having IP address 172.16.4.248.

27.9.2 Using corbaname

The `corbaname` URL provides a mechanism for a client to bootstrap directly. It is typically used to resolve the stringified name from the root naming context.

It is similar to the `corbaloc`, except that it adds the ability to specify an entry within the Naming Service. A `corbaname` URL to an object has two parts. The first part obtains a reference to the naming service and the second part refers to object key within that naming service. These two parts are separated by #. Consider the following example:

```
corbaname:iiop:1.2@172.16.4.248:6789#Calculator
```

Here 172.16.4.248 is the host and 6789 is the port. The part `corbaname:iiop:1.2@172.16.4.248:6789` refers to the root naming context. The part after # refers to the name of the object in question. So, a `corbaname` URL is used to locate a name service and to resolve a name. The following program resolves the calculator servant using `corbaname` URL.

```
import CalculatorApp.*;
import org.omg.CORBA.*;
public class CalculatorClientURL {
  public static void main(String args[])  {
   try{
     ORB orb = ORB.init(args, null);
     org.omg.CORBA.Object ref =
orb.string_to_object("corbaname:iiop:1.2@172.16.4.248:6789#Calculator");
     Calculator calc = CalculatorHelper.narrow(ref);
     int x =2, y = 3;
     System.out.println("Sent :" + x + " and " + y);
     int result  = calc.add(x, y);
     System.out.println("Received : " + result);
   } catch (Exception e) {e.printStackTrace();}
  }
}
```

27.10 USING TIE

In our previous examples, we created servant class extending a class (idlj generated). This type of servant implementation is referred to as *inheritance model*. The problem of this model is that servant cannot extend another class (if it is required) as Java supports only single inheritance for classes. To eliminate this problem, another model (called tie/delegation model) is introduced where servant need not inherit an IDL generated class and hence can extend another class if it is necessary. The drawback of tie model is that it introduces a level of indirection: one extra method call occurs when invoking a method.

In this section, we shall develop server-side of our calculator application using tie model. The servant class is created as follows:

```
class SimpleCalculator implements CalculatorOperations {
  //...
}
```

Not that this class simply implements an interface, the `CalculatorOperations` interface. Since, it does not extend any class, a slot is still there to extend another class. However, this class is an ordinary class and hence an object of this class cannot act as a servant in CORBA environment. The POA cannot bind this object and cannot create an IOR using `servant_to_reference()` method and hence, delete the following line from `CalculatorServer.java`:

```
org.omg.CORBA.Object ref = rootpoa.servant_to_reference(cal);
```

So, how do you publish a `SimpleCalculator` object in CORBA then? The object is tied with POA explicitly using a special class (called tie class). This class may be generated by the `idlj` compiler using `-falltie` option as follows:

```
idlj -falltie Calculator.idl
```

This command, in addition to other files, generates a tie file with name `CalculatorPOATie.java`. To tie our `SimpleCalculator` object with root POA, we create a `CalculatorPOATie` object as follows:

```
CalculatorPOATie tie = new CalculatorPOATie(cal, rootpoa);
```

Now get the IOR as follows:

```
Calculator ref = tie._this(orb);
```

This step also implicitly activates the object. Also add the following import statement:

```
import CalculatorApp.*;
```

The rest of the code is same as before. The server is now ready to work. Compile and start the server as before.

27.11 PERSISTENT OBJECTS

The objects that the server hosted so far are called *transient objects*, as they cannot live beyond the server process. If an object's server process halts, the transient object disappears with it and any object references held by the client becomes invalid. In other words, a transient object has the same lifetime as the execution of the server process that creates it.

However, CORBA specified another type of objects, called *persistent objects* that can live beyond the process that created it. It allows a server process to create an object, register it with the persistent service and exits. The persistence service deals with the object thereafter. If a client has reference to a persistent object and sends an invocation request to the target object, the persistence service creates and activates (if not already done) a server process for the object and then activates (if not already activated) the object itself. The object persists until it is explicitly removed from the persistence service. The entire activation process is transparent to the client.

Note that transient or persistent has nothing to do with the state of the object. An application may create transient objects to access some persistent information maintained in a database. Similarly, some persistent object references may have no state or no persistent state. The persistence merely means duration of existence.

Also note that transiency or persistency is implemented by a specific policy, called `LifeSpanPolicy`, of the underlying POA. This means that any application that wants to provide persistent objects must use POAs with the persistent life span policy. The following section describes how to work with persistent objects.

We first create and initialize an ORB instance:

```
ORB orb = ORB.init(args, null);
```

Then get a reference to the root POA:

```
POA rootpoa = POAHelper.narrow(orb.resolve_initial_references("RootPOA"));
```

The standard life span policy for the `RootPOA` is `TRANSIENT`. So, we create a child POA of `rootPOA` with life span policy set to `PERSISTENT` as follows:

```
Policy[] pPol = new Policy[1];
pPol[0] = rootpoa.create_lifespan_policy(LifespanPolicyValue.PERSISTENT);
POA pPOA = rootpoa.create_POA("childPOA", null, pPol );
```

Activate persistent POA's POAManager, since by default POAManager remains in the 'HOLD' state.

```
pPOA.the_POAManager().activate();
```

Now create a servant and activate the servant with persistent POA:

```
SimpleCalculator cal = new SimpleCalculator();
pPOA.activate_object(cal );
```

Now get a reference and bind it with the naming service as described before. The complete source code of this server (`PersistentCalculatorServer.java`) is shown below:

```
// PersistentCalculatorServer.java
import org.omg.CosNaming.*;
import org.omg.CosNaming.NamingContextPackage.*;
import org.omg.CORBA.*;
import org.omg.PortableServer.*;
public class PersistentCalculatorServer {
  public static void main(String args[]) {
    try{
      ORB orb = ORB.init(args, null);
      POA rootpoa =
POAHelper.narrow(orb.resolve_initial_references("RootPOA"));

      // Create the persistent Policy
      Policy[] pPol= new Policy[1];
      pPol[0] = rootpoa.create_lifespan_policy(LifespanPolicyValue.PERSISTENT);

      // Create a POA specifying this persistent Policy
      POA pPOA = rootpoa.create_POA("childPOA", null, pPol );
      // Activate the PersistentPOA's POAManager
      pPOA.the_POAManager().activate();

      SimpleCalculator cal = new SimpleCalculator();

      // Activate the servant with persistent POA
      pPOA.activate_object(cal );

      org.omg.CORBA.Object ref = pPOA.servant_to_reference(cal);
      org.omg.CORBA.Object objRef =
orb.resolve_initial_references("NameService");
      NamingContextExt ncRef = NamingContextExtHelper.narrow(objRef);
      NameComponent path[] = ncRef.to_name( "Calculator" );
```

```
            ncRef.rebind(path, ref);
            orb.run();
        } catch (Exception e) {
            e.printStackTrace();
        }
    }
}
```

27.11.1 Running Persistent Application

Compile the program as before. Go in the directory containing the class `PersistentCalculatorServer.class` and use the following to start the persistence service, the `orbd` daemon on port 6789:

```
orbd -ORBInitialPort 6789
```

We assume that the daemon is started in a host having IP address 172.16.4.248. Since, a persistent server usually creates a persistent object, registers it and then terminates, the server has to be started in a different way. Fortunately, Java provides a tool `servertool` that allows developer to register, unregister, startup, and shutdown a persistent server. It may be started on any host specifying the port and the host (if different) on which `orbd` is executing as follows:

```
servertool -ORBInitialHost 172.16.4.248 -ORBInitialPort 6789
```

A message and a command prompt appear as follows:

```
Welcome to the Java IDL Server Tool
please enter commands at the prompt

servertool >
```

Use the following command to register an instance of persistence server:

```
servertool > register -server PersistentCalculatorServer -applicationName ps -
classpath .
```

If everything goes fine, the following message appears:

```
server registered (serverid = 260).
```

To see the list of registered server, use `list` command, a sample result of which is shown below:

```
        Server Id        Server Class Name                  Server Application
        ---------        -----------------                  ------------------

           260           PersistentCalculatorServer                ps
```

For more commands, type `help`. Now, start the client in any other computer using the following command:

```
java CalculatorClient -ORBInitialHost 172.16.4.248 -ORBInitialPort 6789
```

27.12 CALLBACK

Sometimes, a client should synchronize itself on a change or update that occurs in a server. For example a client, which displays the score of a game, should always get current score stored in a game server. There are two ways a client can do this:

- Polling: The client can ask the server for the current score periodically.
- Callback: Request server to send score, only when it changes, to the client.

The primary problem of polling method is that the client may have downloaded the same score possibly many times as the client does not have any idea about when the score changes. Alternatively, instead of downloading the score by the client, the responsibility may be imposed on the server. By doing so, the client gets a score only when it changes, thus reducing the number of messages exchanged. This mechanism is called *callback* and has a direct positive impact of network bandwidth.

A callback is an operation invocation made by a server to an object that is implemented by a client. To implement this callback mechanism for score application, we write an IDL as follows:

```
//Callback.idl
module Callback {
  interface Listener {
    void receive(in string s);
  };
  interface Notifier {
    void register(in Listener r);
  };
};
```

In this example, since clients invoke operations on servers and servers invoke operations on clients, IDL defines two interfaces through which each type of application can access the other. Specifically, `Listener` is implemented at the client side and `Notifier` is implemented at the server side. A simple implementation (`ScoreListener.java`) of `Listener` is shown below:

```
// ScoreListener.java
import Callback.*;
class ScoreListener extends ListenerPOA {
  public void receive(String s) {
    System.out.println("received: "+s);
  }
}
```

The `receive()` method gets a string (score) and displays it. A sample `Notifier` implementation (`ScoreNotifier.java`) is shown below:

```
// ScoreNotifier.java
import Callback.*;
import java.util.*;
class ScoreNotifier extends NotifierPOA implements Runnable {
  Hashtable Listeners = new Hashtable();
  public ScoreNotifier() {
    new Thread(this).start();
  }
  public void register(Listener r) {
    System.out.println("Registered a listener: ");
    Listeners.put(r, r);
  }
  public void run() {
    int score = 0, run;Random r = new Random();
    while(true) {
      try {
        do {
          Thread.sleep(1000+r.nextInt(1000));
   }while((run = r.nextInt(7)) == 0);
        score += run;
        Enumeration e = Listeners.elements();
        while(e.hasMoreElements()) {
           Listener rec =  (Listener)e.nextElement();
           System.out.println("Sent: "+score);
           rec.receive(score+"");
        }
      }catch(Exception e) {}
    }
  }
}
```

The `register()` method puts the specified Listener in a `Hashtable`. The listener is created and bound to the ORB by the client. The child thread created from the constructor generates a score artificially and sends it to all the registered Listeners by calling their respective `receive()` method.

The server (`ScoreServer.java`) merely creates a `ScoreNotifier` object and exports it to the naming service:

```
// ScoreServer.java
import org.omg.CosNaming.*;
import org.omg.CosNaming.NamingContextPackage.*;
import org.omg.CORBA.*;
import org.omg.PortableServer.*;
public class ScoreServer {
  public static void main(String args[]) {
    try{
      ORB orb = ORB.init(args, null);
      POA rootpoa =
POAHelper.narrow(orb.resolve_initial_references("RootPOA"));
      rootpoa.the_POAManager().activate();
      ScoreNotifier cal = new ScoreNotifier();
      org.omg.CORBA.Object objRef =
orb.resolve_initial_references("NameService");
      NamingContextExt ncRef = NamingContextExtHelper.narrow(objRef);
      NameComponent path[] = ncRef.to_name( "ScoreNotifier" );
      ncRef.rebind(path, rootpoa.servant_to_reference(cal));
      System.out.println("ScoreServer ready and waiting ...");
      orb.run();
    } catch (Exception e) {
      e.printStackTrace();
    }
  }
}
```

The client, on the other hand, gets a reference to the `ScoreNotifier` object from the name service, creates a `ScoreListener` object, gets it's IOR and passes it to the notifier using in its `register()` method. Remember that the `register()` method stores this IOR in a Hashtable and is used subsequently to send a score created artificially. The source code (ScoreClient.java) is shown below:

```
import Callback.*;
import org.omg.CosNaming.*;
import org.omg.CosNaming.NamingContextPackage.*;
import org.omg.CORBA.*;
import org.omg.PortableServer.*;
public class ScoreClient {
  public static void main(String args[])  {
    try{
      ORB orb = ORB.init(args, null);
      org.omg.CORBA.Object objRef =
orb.resolve_initial_references("NameService");
      NamingContextExt ncRef = NamingContextExtHelper.narrow(objRef);
      Notifier n = NotifierHelper.narrow(ncRef.resolve_str("ScoreNotifier"));
      POA rootpoa =
POAHelper.narrow(orb.resolve_initial_references("RootPOA"));
      rootpoa.the_POAManager().activate();
      ScoreListener sl = new ScoreListener();
      Listener ref = ListenerHelper.narrow(rootpoa.servant_to_reference(sl));
      n.register(ref);
      orb.run();
    } catch (Exception e) {
      e.printStackTrace();
    }
  }
}
```

Compile and run the application as before. A sample result is shown in Figure 27.3:

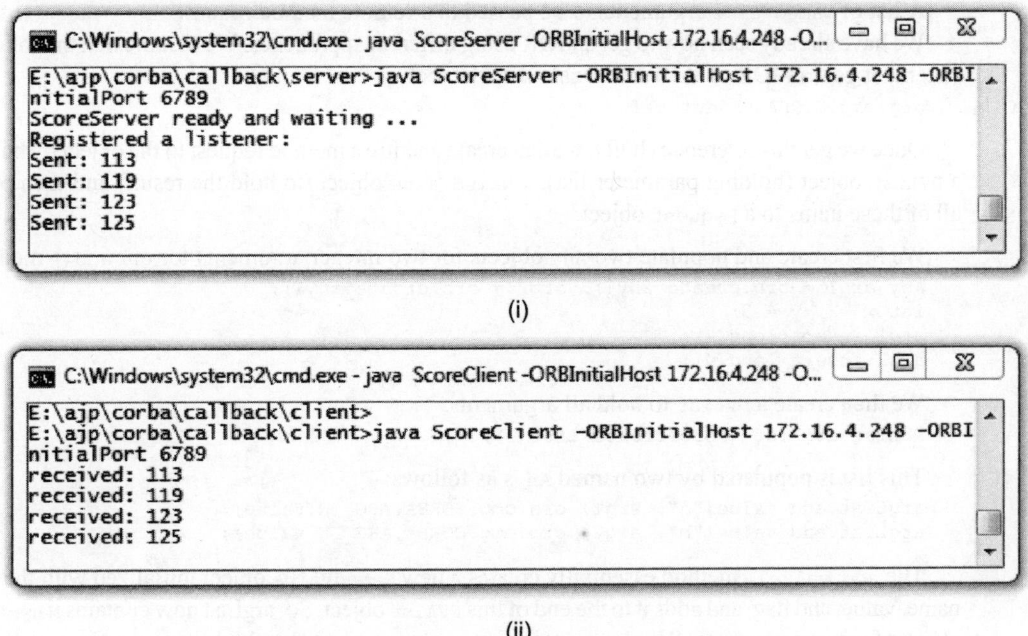

Figure 27.3: CORBA Callback mechanism (i) Server (ii) Client

27.13 USING DYNAMIC INVOCATION INTERFACE (DII)

In our previous examples, for method invocation, client makes use of stub, helper classes, etc., which are generated from the given IDL interface and `idlj` compiler. What happens if the IDL interface is not available? Note that a reference to the remote object may be obtained by querying the naming service. However, how do you invoke a method using this reference if interfaces to the object is not known at compile time? Fortunately, CORBA specification defines an API, called Dynamic Invocation Interface (DII) for this purpose.

To make use of DII, the following steps are required:

- Obtain an IOR to the object
- Create a Request object from this IOR passing method name, parameters and result
- Invoke the request
- Retrieve the result (if any)

The primary classes to work with DII are as follows:

`Request`

This class is the heart of DII, which allows creation and invocation of requests dynamically. A `Request` object basically contains method name (a `String`) together with list of arguments (a `NVList` object) and an optional result from the method (a `NamedValue` object).

`Any`

An `Any` object may contain the Java equivalent of any IDL type and is used to specify an argument.

`NamedValue`

It, as its name implies, is an `Any` value tied with a name and is used to specify a named argument.

`NVList`

A list of NamedValue arguments to be passed to a remote method request.

We have already seen how to get an IOR using different approaches. We assume that the following statement gets an IOR of our remote calculator object:

```
org.omg.CORBA.Object ref = …
```

Once we get this reference (IOR), we can create and fire a method request to the object by building a NVList object (holding parameter list), a NamedValue object (to hold the result) and then putting all of these items to a Request object.

We first create and populate two Any objects for two integer arguments for our add() method:

```
Any arg1 = orb.create_any(), arg2 = orb.create_any();
int x =2, y = 3;
arg1.insert_long(x);
arg2.insert_long(y);
```

We then create a NVList to hold all arguments:

```
NVList argList = orb.create_list(2);
```

This list is populated by two named Anys as follows:

```
argList.add_value("a", arg1, org.omg.CORBA.ARG_IN.value);
argList.add_value("b", arg2, org.omg.CORBA.ARG_IN.value);
```

The add_value() method essentially creates a new NamedValue object initialized with the given name, value, and flag, and adds it to the end of this NVList object. So, argList now contains NamedValue objects for two arguments. We also create a NamedValue object to hold the return value:

```
Any ret = orb.create_any();
ret.type(orb.get_primitive_tc(TCKind.tk_long));
NamedValue resultVal = orb.create_named_value("result", ret,
org.omg.CORBA.ARG_OUT.value);
```

We then create a Request object using _create_request() method of org.omg.CORBA.Object class:

```
Request req = ref._create_request(null, "add", argList, resultVal);
```

The request is fired using invoke() method:

```
req.invoke();
```

Finally the result is extracted as follows:

```
int result = req.return_value().extract_long();
```

The entire piece of code (CalculatorClientDII.java) is given below:

```
//CalculatorClientDII.java
import org.omg.CosNaming.*;
import org.omg.CosNaming.NamingContextPackage.*;
import org.omg.CORBA.*;
public class CalculatorClientDII {
  public static void main(String args[])  {
    try{
      ORB orb = ORB.init(args, null);
      org.omg.CORBA.Object objRef =
orb.resolve_initial_references("NameService");
      NamingContextExt ncRef = NamingContextExtHelper.narrow(objRef);
      org.omg.CORBA.Object ref = ncRef.resolve_str("Calculator");

      Any arg1 = orb.create_any(), arg2 = orb.create_any();
      int x =2, y = 3;
      arg1.insert_long(x);
      arg2.insert_long(y);

      NVList argList = orb.create_list(2);
      argList.add_value("a", arg1, org.omg.CORBA.ARG_IN.value);
      argList.add_value("b", arg2, org.omg.CORBA.ARG_IN.value);
```

```
        Any ret = orb.create_any();
        ret.type(orb.get_primitive_tc(TCKind.tk_long));
        NamedValue resultVal = orb.create_named_value("result", ret,
org.omg.CORBA.ARG_OUT.value);

        Request req = ref._create_request(null, "add", argList, resultVal);
        req.invoke();

        int result = req.return_value().extract_long();

        System.out.println("Sent :" + x + " and " + y);
        System.out.println("Received : " + result);

    } catch (Exception e) {e.printStackTrace();}
  }
}
```

http://docstore.mik.ua/orelly/java-ent/jenut/ch04_05.htm

27.14 USING DYNAMIC SKELETON INTERFACE (DSI)

The Dynamic Skeleton Interface (DSI) is the server-side counterpart of the DII. It allows us to write servants that accept method invocation request even when an IDL interface is not known at compile time and without creating skeleton class. The servant merely defines a method `invoke()` which is called by the ORB providing necessary information (method name, types and values of parameters, result, etc.) encapsulated as a `ServerRequest` object. This `invoke()` method acts as a representative of methods being invoked. This method then performs the task being requested by the client, and constructs and returns the result.

27.14.1 Basic Steps

The following are the basic steps to be followed to write a server that uses DSI concept:

- Write a servant class extending `org.omg.CORBA.DynamicImplementation`
- Implement the `invoke()` method (that takes a `ServerRequest` parameter representing a request from client) as follows:
  - Extract method name using `op_name()`
  - Create an `NVList` to hold method parameters.
  - Populate this list by passing it to `arguments()` method
  - Extract the parameter values from populated `NVList`.
  - Perform the operation, assign new values to `out` and `inout` parameters in the `NVList` as appropriate.
  - Create an `Any` holding result (if any)
  - Pass this `Any` to `set_result()` or `set_except()`, as appropriate.
- Implement the `ids()` method returning an array of repository IDs of the interfaces implemented by this servant.
- Create an instance of the DSI servant and register it with the ORB using `connect()` method of `org.omg.CORBA.ORB`.

27.14.2 An Example

We write a servant for our calculator application that uses DSI extending `org.omg.CORBA.DynamicImplementation` as follows:

```
class SimpleCalculatorDSI extends DynamicImplementation {
//…
  public void invoke(ServerRequest request) {/*…*/}
  public String[] _ids() {/*…*/}
}
```

This class implements two methods `invoke()` and `_ids()`. This invoke method is called by the underlying ORB when a request from a client comes to it. ORB places all method invocation information in a `ServerRequest` object and passes it to the `invoke()` method. Inside this method, we first extract the name of the method specified by the client:

```
String methodName = request.op_name();
```

A DSI servant may want to provide the functionality of many methods. An 'if' statement is inserted for each such method. For our `add()` method of calculator, the following is used:

```
if (methodName.equals("add") == true) {
  //...
}
```

In this if block, we write the functionality of `add()` method. We know that `add()` method takes two parameters and returns the sum of these two parameters. So, the client has certainly specified two arguments which are encapsulated in the `request` object. To hold these two parameters, we create an `NVList` as follows:

```
NVList nvlist = orb.create_list(2);
```

The list is populated with two `Any`s where actually the parameters are stored as follows:

```
Any any1 = orb.create_any(), any2 = orb.create_any();
any1.type(orb.get_primitive_tc(TCKind.tk_long));
any2.type(orb.get_primitive_tc(TCKind.tk_long));
nvlist.add_value("arg1", any1, ARG_IN.value);
nvlist.add_value("arg2", any2, ARG_IN.value);
```

Specifying the type of each Any is necessary so that they can hold parameter value properly. The parameter values encapsulated in `request` object is then transferred to the NVList as follows:

```
request.arguments(nvlist);
```

We then extract those parameter values, add them and put it in `result`.

```
int a = nvlist.item(0).value().extract_long();
int b = nvlist.item(1).value().extract_long();
int result = a + b;
```

The result is placed in another `Any`:

```
Any result_any = orb.create_any();
result_any.insert_long(result);
```

Finally, the result is sent back to the client.

```
request.result(result_any);
```

Inside _ids() method, we simply return the repository ID of our calculator interface:

```
static String[] id = {"IDL:CalculatorApp/Calculator:1.0"};
public String[] _ids() { return id; }
```

The complete source code (`SimpleCalculatorDSI.java`) is shown below:

```
import org.omg.CORBA.*;
class SimpleCalculatorDSI extends DynamicImplementation {
  static String[] id = {"IDL:CalculatorApp/Calculator:1.0"};
  ORB orb;
  SimpleCalculatorDSI(ORB orb) { this.orb = orb; }
  public void invoke(ServerRequest request) {
    try {
      String methodName = request.op_name();
      if (methodName.equals("add") == true) {
        NVList nvlist = orb.create_list(2);
        Any any1 = orb.create_any(), any2 = orb.create_any();
        any1.type(orb.get_primitive_tc(TCKind.tk_long));
        any2.type(orb.get_primitive_tc(TCKind.tk_long));
        nvlist.add_value("arg1", any1, ARG_IN.value);
        nvlist.add_value("arg2", any2, ARG_IN.value);
```

```
            request.arguments(nvlist);
            int a = nvlist.item(0).value().extract_long();
            int b = nvlist.item(1).value().extract_long();
            System.out.println("Received: " + a + " and " + b);
            int result = a + b;
            System.out.println("Sent: " + result);

            Any result_any = orb.create_any();
            result_any.insert_long(result);
            request.result(result_any);
         }
      }
      catch (Exception ex) {ex.printStackTrace();}
   }
   public String[] _ids() { return id; }
}
```

We then create an instance of this dynamic servant:

```
SimpleCalculatorDSI cal = new SimpleCalculatorDSI(orb);
```

It is necessary to register this object to the ORB, so that it can forward (can call its `invoke()` method) client request to it.

```
orb.connect(cal);
```

The IOR of this servant is registered with the naming server using a procedure used earlier. The complete source code of the server is shown below:

```
// CalculatorServerDSI.java
import org.omg.CosNaming.*;
import org.omg.CosNaming.NamingContextPackage.*;
import org.omg.CORBA.*;
public class CalculatorServerDSI {
   public static void main(String args[]) {
      try{
         ORB orb = ORB.init(args, null);
         SimpleCalculatorDSI cal = new SimpleCalculatorDSI(orb);
         orb.connect(cal);
         org.omg.CORBA.Object objRef =
orb.resolve_initial_references("NameService");
         NamingContextExt ncRef = NamingContextExtHelper.narrow(objRef);
         NameComponent path[] = ncRef.to_name( "Calculator" );
         ncRef.rebind(path, cal);
         System.out.println("Calculator Server ready...");
         orb.run();
      } catch (Exception e) {
         e.printStackTrace();
      }
   }
}
```

Compile and run the application as before. This dynamic server works exactly like a normal server. Clients are completely unaware of the fact that a dynamic servant is being used at the server end.

27.15 USING OUT AND INOUT PARAMETER

So far we have used `in` CORBA parameters, which is passed into the operation from the caller. A in CORBA parameter is translated into normal Java parameter. However, a true local copy of the actual argument passed by the caller is created at the receiver's end. So, any modification on the local copy has no effect on the actual argument.

CORBA supports two more types of parameter passing `out` and `inout`. An `out` parameter is one which is passed out of the method to the caller, but no value is passed in. An `inout` parameter, as its name implies, is a combination of `in` and `out`, where the parameter is passed into the operation and returned to the caller.

However, there is no standard mechanism available in Java for these two parameters. So, these concepts are simulated with the help of some classes called *holder classes*. These classes are available for all of the basic IDL datatypes in the `org.omg.CORBA package` and are generated for all named user-defined types, except those defined by typedefs. The holder classes provide a level of indirection and are passed instead of the actual type.

A client creates an instance of the respective holder class for each out and inout parameter. This instance holds some content in its public member value and is passed to the method. The server may then set or modify the content of the holder object. The client gets the modified content and processes further. Since, the encapsulated actual object is modified without affecting the holder object itself, the semantics of `out` and `inout` parameters are supported.

Holder classes for basic IDL types are available in the package `org.omg.CORBA`. The holder class name is of the form `[type]Holder`, where `[type]` is the name of the mapped Java type, with the first letter capitalized. For example, for IDL type long (corresponding Java type is `int`), the name of the Java holder class is `IntHolder`.

Each holder class has a default constructor, a one argument constructor and has a public instance member `value`, which holds the content. The default constructor sets the value field to the default value for the type as defined by the Java language: false for boolean, 0 for numeric and char types, null for strings, null for object references. The source code of `IntHolder` looks like this:

```
package org.omg.CORBA;
/*...*/
public final class IntHolder implements Streamable {
     public int value;
     public IntHolder() { }
     public IntHolder(int initial) { value = initial; }
     /*...*/
}
```

27.15.1 Invoking Operation Using Holder Classes

The following are the basic steps to follow to pass inout and out parameters using holder classes:

- For each IDL out or inout parameter, the client creates an instance of the appropriate holder class
- The contents of the holder instance are set or modified by the receiver, and the client then uses the modified contents after the call returns.
- For the inout parameter, the client must provide a valid content. The method typically uses this content and changes the value if it wishes. The final content is returned to the client at the end of the operation.
- For the out parameter, the client does not initialize the holder with a content. The operation should not use the initial value in the holder and must supply a valid value to be returned to the client.

27.15.2 An Example

Consider the following IDL definition:

```
interface Service {
  void replace(inout string s, in char c, out long times);
};
```

The `replace()` operation replaces all space characters in the string s by the specified character c and returns the number of times the replacement occurred. The first parameter comes in from the caller and the modified string goes out to the caller. Hence it is declared as `inout`. The second one comes from the caller but is not returned back. Accordingly, it is declared as `in`. The last one is only used to send a value back to the caller, hence is declared as `out`. The idlj compiler maps this operation to a Java method as follows:

```
void replace (org.omg.CORBA.StringHolder s, char c, org.omg.CORBA.IntHolder times);
```

A client application can be coded as follows:

```
//Get a reference to the remote CORBA object
Service s = …
StringHolder str = new StringHolder("CORBA parameter passing example");
char c = '_';
IntHolder times = new IntHolder();
System.out.println("Before call: "+str.value+" "+c+" "+times.value);
s.replace(str, c, times);
System.out.println("After call: "+str.value+" "+c+" "+times.value);
```

The implementation of `replace()` method looks like this:

```
  public void replace (org.omg.CORBA.StringHolder s, char c,
org.omg.CORBA.IntHolder times) {
     String temp  = s.value;
     times.value = temp.length() - temp.replace(" ", "").length();
     s.value = s.value.replace(' ', c);
  }
```

A sample output of the client program is shown below:

```
Before call: CORBA parameter passing example _ 0
After call: CORBA_parameter_passing_example _ 3
```

27.16 RMI-IIOP

RMI applications typically use Java Remote Method Protocol (JRMP) for underlying communication. However, they can also use the CORBA's IIOP as the communication protocol. This solution is known as RMI-IIOP, which combines the best features of RMI with the best features of CORBA.

RMI-IIOP utilizes the Java CORBA Object Request Broker (ORB). So, developers can work completely in the Java programming language. So, there is no separate IDL or mapping to learn. The rmic compiler may be used to generate the necessary code for connecting Java applications to others via IIOP. To work with CORBA applications in other languages, IDL may be generated using the `rmic` compiler with the `-idl` option. To generate IIOP stubs and tie classes, we use the `rmic` compiler with the `-iiop` option.

Note that RMI-IIOP provides interoperability with other CORBA objects implemented in different languages, provided that all the remote interfaces are originally defined as Java RMI interfaces.

27.16.1 An Example

In this section, we shall redevelop our calculator application where a client application invokes a method on a remote server object via IIOP.

27.16.1.1 Writing an interface

We use the same Calculator RMI interface used in Chapter 14.

```
import java.rmi.Remote;
public interface Calculator extends java.rmi.Remote  {
  int add (int a, int b) throws java.rmi.RemoteException;
}
```

27.16.1.2 Implementing the interface

Since, object will be accessed via IIOP, its class extends `javax.rmi.PortableRemoteObject`. A sample implementation class (`SimpleCalculator.java`) is shown below:

```
// SimpleCalculator.java
import javax.rmi.PortableRemoteObject;
class SimpleCalculator extends PortableRemoteObject implements Calculator {
  public SimpleCalculator() throws java.rmi.RemoteException {}
  public int add(int a, int b) throws java.rmi.RemoteException {
    System.out.println("Received: " + a + " and " + b);
    int result = a + b;
    System.out.println("Sent: " + result);
    return result;
  }
}
```

Since, super class's constructor might fail to construct the object, defining a constructor that throws a `RemoteException` is necessary, even if it does nothing.

27.16.1.3 Writing the server

In the server, we create an instance of this `SimpleCalculator` and bind it to the CORBA's naming service (`orbd`) via JNDI. The following is the source code of the server (`CalculatorServerJNDI.java`):

```
// CalculatorServerJNDI.java
import javax.naming.*;
public class CalculatorServerJNDI {
  public static void main(String args[]) {
    try {
      SimpleCalculator calc = new SimpleCalculator();
      Context ic = new InitialContext();
      ic.rebind("Calculator", calc );
      System.out.println("Calculator Server ready...");
    } catch (Exception e) { e.printStackTrace();}
  }
}
```

27.16.1.4 Writing the Client

Writing the client is very simple. It gets a reference from the CORBA naming service via JNDI and invokes the add() method. The following is the source code of the client (`CalculatorClientJNDI.java`):

```
//CalculatorClientJNDI.java
import javax.naming.*;
public class CalculatorClientJNDI {
  public static void main( String args[] ) {
  try {
      Context ic = new InitialContext();
      Calculator calc = (Calculator)ic.lookup("Calculator");
      int x =2, y = 3;
      System.out.println("Sent :" + x + " and " + y);
      int result  = calc.add(x, y);
      System.out.println("Received : " + result);
    } catch( Exception e ) {e.printStackTrace();}
  }
}
```

27.16.1.5 Compiling server files

The server side of the application should have the files `Calculator.java`, `SimpleCalculator.java` and `CalculatorServerJNDI.java`. Compile the implementation class first using the following command:

```
javac SimpleCalculator.java
```

To create CORBA-compliant stub and skeleton files, use `rmic` compiler with the `-iiop` option:

```
rmic -iiop SimpleCalculator
```

This generates the client stub `Calculator_Stub.class` and server skeleton `_SimpleCalculator_Tie.class`. Now, compile server source files as follows:

```
javac Calculator.java CalculatorServerJNDI.java
```

27.16.1.6 Compiling Client Files

The client side should have files `Calculator.java`, and `CalculatorClientJNDI.java`. Compile the interface file `Calculator.java` using the following command:

```
javac Calculator.java
```

To create CORBA-compliant stub, use the following file:

```
rmic -iiop Calculator
```

Now, compile the client file:

```
javac CalculatorClientJNDI.java
```

27.16.1.7 Running the Application

Start `orbd` in a host having IP address say `172.16.4.248` on port `6789` as follows:

```
orbd -ORBInitialPort 6789
```

Start the server as follows:

```
java -Djava.naming.factory.initial=com.sun.jndi.cosnaming.CNCtxFactory -
Djava.naming.provider.url=iiop://172.16.4.248:6789 CalculatorServerJNDI
```

Start the client as follows:

```
java -Djava.naming.factory.initial=com.sun.jndi.cosnaming.CNCtxFactory -
Djava.naming.provider.url=iiop://172.16.4.248:6789 CalculatorClientJNDI
```

27.17 IDL TO JAVA LANGUAGE MAPPING

Java 2 SDK 5.0 and onwards includes `idlj` compiler that translates an IDL file to Java interface. A summary of IDL to Java mapping is shown in Table 27.1:

Table 27.1: IDL to Java mapping

IDL Type	Java Type
char, wchar	char
octet	byte
short, unsigned short	short
long, unsigned long	int
long long, unsigned long long	long
float	float
double	double
fixed	java.math.BigDecimal
string, wstring	java.lang.String
boolean	boolean
enum, struct, union	class
sequence, array	array

(*Contd*)

Table 27.1: *(Contd)*

module	package
interface (non-abstract)	signature interface and an operations interface, helper class, holder class
interface (abstract)	signature interface, helper class, holder class
constant (not within an interface)	public interface
constant (within an interface)	fields in the Java signature interface for non-abstract, or the sole Java interface for abstract
exception	class
Any	org.omg.CORBA.Any
type declarations nested within interfaces	"scoped" package
typedef	helper classes
pseudo objects	pseudo interface
readonly attribute	accessor method
readwrite attribute	accessor and modifer methods
operation	method

KEYWORDS

CORBA—A standard defined by the OMG to facilitate the communication of systems that are deployed on diverse platforms

Dynamic Invocation Interface (DII)—An API that allows applications to invoke operations on CORBA objects about which they have no prior information

Dynamic Skeleton Interface (DSI)—An API that enables ORB to deliver method invocation requests to an object implementation when the type of the object implementation is not known at compile time

idlj compiler—A compiler to translate IDL interface definitions to the corresponding Java interfaces, classes, and methods, which can be used to implement client and server code

Initial naming context—A NamingContext object that refers to the root of the COS Naming Service and can be used to create other descendant NamingContext objects

Interface Definition Language (IDL)—A language standardized by OMG for defining the interfaces for all CORBA objects

Internet InterORB Protocol (IIOP)—A TCP/IP based network protocol specified by OMG for inter-ORB communication

Java IDL—A Java API consisting of classes, libraries, and tools that makes CORBA programming possible

Name binding—Assigning a name to an object so that it can be referred to by the name

Naming context—A node in the tree, similar to directory tree, used by COS naming service

Naming service—A CORBA service that enables to name CORBA objects via binding a name to an object reference

Object Management Group (OMG)—A consortium of over 700 members worldwide that establishes industry guidelines and object management specifications in order to provide a common framework for object-oriented application development

Object reference—A CORBA object equivalent to programming language-specific object pointers

Object Request Broker (ORB)—A library to provide CORBA features

Object Request Broker Daemon (ORBD)—A Java tool consisting of a Bootstrap Service, a Transient Naming Service, a Persistent Naming Service, and a Server Manager

Persistent object—An object that can survive beyond the process or thread that created it and until it is explicitly deleted

Portable Object Adapter (POA)—A mechanism that connects a method invocation request using an object reference to the proper servant to serve the request

POA Manager—An object that encapsulates the processing state of its associated one or more POAs

Policy—An object to specify the characteristics of a POA

RMI-IIOP—A Java API that allows to develop RMI applications that communicate via IIOP

Servant—A concrete object or entity that serves method invocation requests

servertool—A Java IDL tool that provides the ease-of-use facilities to programmers to register, unregister, startup, and shutdown a server application

Skeleton—The object-interface-specific ORB component which assists an object adapter in passing requests to particular methods

Static invocation—A mechanism for method invocation on an object when the interface of the object is known at compile time

Stringified object reference—A string obtained from an object reference so that it may be stored on persistent storage or transferred somewhere else

Stub—A local object corresponding to a remote object that forwards method invocation request to the object

tnameserv—A Transient Naming Service provided by Java IDL API

Transient object—An object whose existence is limited by the lifetime of the process or thread that created it

SUMMARY

CORBA (Common Object Request Broker Architecture) is a specification that describes how heterogeneous objects can interoperate. The OMA defines four major parts a CORBA-compliant system should have: An Object Request Broker (ORB), CORBAServices, CORBAFacilities and Business Objects.

A key feature of CORBA is IDL, a language-neutral Interface Definition Language. Interfaces to CORBA objects are written using IDL. This allows CORBA application developers to describe the service structure of an object without any language-specific syntax. IDL interfaces are converted to or obtained from the language specific code using tools provided by the CORBA S/W provider. For example, Java provides a compiler `idlj` for this purpose.

Java SDK provides an API (popularly known as Java-IDL) to support CORBA specification. This means Java-IDL enabled applications can interact with other applications that also support CORBA. The basic steps used to develop CORBA applications are: writing an interface using IDL, mapping IDL interface to Java, implementing the interface, writing the server and writing the client.

Java is shipped with two applications `tnameserv`, a transient naming service, and `orbd`, which is a daemon process containing a Bootstrap Service, a Transient Naming Service, a Persistent Naming Service, and a Server Manager. We used `orbd` in our examples.

CORBA objects can also be identified using URLs. They have two variations known as corbaname and corbaloc. There are two models to implement a servant in CORBA: inheritance model and tie model. Tie model is useful if a servant has to extend a class.

The objects that the server hosted so far are called *transient objects* as they cannot live beyond the server process. CORBA specified another type of objects, called *persistent objects* that can live beyond the process that created it.

CORBA specification defines an API, called Dynamic Invocation Interface (DII) for various purposes such as obtaining an IOR to the object, creating a Request object from this IOR passing method name, parameters and result, invoking the request, retrieving the result (if any). The Dynamic Skeleton Interface (DSI) is the server-side counterpart of the DII. It allows us to write servants that accept method invocation request even when an IDL interface is not known at compile time and without creating skeleton class.

In addition to `in` parameter, CORBA supports two more types of parameter passing `out` and `inout`. Since, there is no standard mechanism available in Java for these two parameters, these concepts are simulated with the help of some classes called *holder classes*.

RMI applications can also use the CORBA's IIOP as the communication protocol. This solution is known as RMI-IIOP, which combines the best features of RMI with the best features of CORBA.

WEB RESOURCES

http://docs.oracle.com/javase/7/docs/technotes/guides/idl/jidlExample.html
Java IDL: The "Hello World" Example

http://docs.oracle.com/javase/7/docs/technotes/guides/idl/GShome.html
Getting Started with Java IDL

http://www.javaworld.com/article/2077037/soa/corba-meets-java.html
CORBA meets Java

http://www.omg.org/
Object Management Group

http://www.javacoffeebreak.com/articles/javaidl/javaidl.html
Java and CORBA - a smooth blend

www.unf.edu/~sahuja/cis6302/corbaexample.doc
CORBA Example

http://paginas.fe.up.pt/~nflores/dokuwiki/lib/exe/fetch.php?media=teaching:0809:java_20tutorial_20and_20guide.pdf
Java IDL tutorial and Guide

EXERCISES

Objective-type Questions

1. What is the full form of CORBA?
   (a) Client Object Request Broker Architecture
   (b) Common Object Request Broker Architecture
   (c) Common Object Response Broker Architecture
   (d) Common Object Request Basic Architecture
2. What is the full form of IDL?
   (a) Interface Dynamic Language
   (b) Intermediate Definition Language
   (c) Interface Declaration Language
   (d) Interface Definition Language
3. What is the full form of IOR?
   (a) International Object Reference
   (b) Inter-operable Open Reference
   (c) Inter-operable Object Reference
   (d) International Open Reference
4. Which of the following is language independent?
   (a) RMI (c) Servlet
   (b) Applet (d) CORBA
5. Which of the following is used in Java programming for objects interacting on different platforms across a network?
   (a) Java IDL
   (b) Java Reflection
   (c) Java Generic programming
   (d) Java ORB
6. OMG stands for
   (a) Open Management Group
   (b) Object Manager Group
   (c) Object Manager General
   (d) Object Management Group
7. ORB stands for
   (a) Open Request Book
   (b) Object Request Broker
   (c) Object Response Broker
   (d) Open Response Book
8. Which of the following is not a part of CORBA core architecture?
   (a) ORB
   (b) CORBAFacilities
   (c) CORBAServices
   (d) GUI
9. The name of IDL compiler in Java is
   (a) idlc (c) jidlc
   (b) idlj (d) jidlj
10. Which of the following is not a task of ORB?
    (a) Register and look up objects
    (b) Marshal and un-marshal parameters from one programming language to another language
    (c) Contact database server
    (d) Publish and retrieve metadata on objects on the local system for another ORB

11. IIOP stands for
    (a) Internet Inter-ORB Policy
    (b) Internet Inter-ORB Protocol
    (c) International Inter-ORB Protocol
    (d) International Inter-ORB Policy

12. Which of the CORBA parameter passing mechanism does Java support?
    (a) in (c) inout
    (b) out (d) All of the above

13. POA stands for
    (a) Pure Object Adapter
    (b) Portable Open Adapter
    (c) Portable Object Adapter
    (d) Portable Object Anomaly

14. Which of the following methods is used to initialize an ORB?
    (a) initialize() (c) getORB()
    (b) init() (d) openORB()

15. Which of the following methods is used to bind an object?
    (a) upload() (c) put()
    (b) register() (d) bind()

16. Which of the following methods is used for typecasting in CORBA?
    (a) typeCast() (c) narrow()
    (b) convert() (d) change()

17. Which of the following is CORBA name server?
    (a) nameserver (c) nameserv
    (b) orbd (d) namingServer

18. Which of the following Java properties is used to specify the IP address of the host where CORBA naming service is running?
    (a) org.omg.CORBA.ORBInitialHost
    (b) org.omg.CORBA.Host
    (c) org.omg.CORBA.InitialHost
    (d) org.omg.CORBA.ORBHost

19. A CORBA URL starts with
    (a) corbaloc (c) Both a) and b)
    (b) corbaname (d) None of the above

20. Which of the following is a servant implementation model?
    (a) tie model
    (b) inheritance model
    (c) Both a) and b)
    (d) None of the above

21. Which of the following types of object does CORBA support?
    (a) Transient objects
    (b) Persistent objects
    (c) Both a) and b)
    (d) None of the above

22. Which of the following classes is used for typecasting?
    (a) Holder class (c) Stub
    (b) Helper class (d) Skeleton

23. What is the default port used by orbd?
    (a) 800 (c) 1099
    (b) 900 (d) 8080

24. DII stands for
    (a) Dynamic Invocation Implementation
    (b) Dynamic Invocation Interface
    (c) Dual Invocation Interface
    (d) Dual Internal Interface

25. DSI stands for
    (a) Dual Skeleton Interface
    (b) Dynamic Server Interface
    (c) Dynamic Server Implementation
    (d) Dynamic Skeleton Interface

26. Which of the following protocols is used between two ORBs?
    (a) HTTP (c) SSL
    (b) JRMP (d) IIOP

27. A module in IDL corresponds to Java
    (a) interface (c) class
    (b) package (d) method

28. Which of the following classes represents an Object Request Broker?
    (a) Broker (c) ObjectRequestBroker
    (b) ORB (d) ObjReqBroker

29. Which of the following methods is used to get a reference to the root POA?
    (a) resolve()
    (b) getReference()
    (c) resolveReference()
    (d) resolve_initial_references()

30. Which of the following methods is used to convert a servant to a CORBA IOR?
    (a) servant2reference()
    (b) servant_to_reference()
    (c) servant_to_IOR()
    (d) servant2CORBA()

Subjective-type Questions

1. What is the purpose of CORBA?
2. Write the functions of different components of CORBA architecture.
3. Illustrate the steps required to develop a simple client–server application using CORBA.
4. What is Dynamic Invocation Interface (DII)?
5. What is Dynamic Skeleton Interface (DSI)?
6. Illustrate the steps required to develop a simple CORBA client using DII.
7. Describe the steps required to develop a simple CORBA server using DSI.
8. What are holder and helper classes? What are their usefulness?
9. What is a servant?
10. Write the functionality of POA.
11. What is initial naming context?
12. What is the function of Object Request Broker (ORB)?
13. What is the purpose of Interface Definition Language (IDL)?
14. What do you mean by activating a POA?
15. What do you mean by Inter-Operable Object Reference?
16. What is the function of an object adapter?
17. What is the difference between transient objects and persistent objects?
18. How will you make an object persistent?
19. What do you mean by callback? How will you implement callback mechanism in CORBA?
20. Write the basic steps required to develop an RMI-IIOP-based application.

CHAPTER – 28

JAVA SERVER FACES

KEY OBJECTIVES

After completing this chapter readers will be able to—

- get an idea about Java Server Faces technology
- understand the advantages of JSF technology over other similar technologies
- get an idea about the basic execution philosophy of JSF life-cycle
- understand how to write, deploy, and invoke JSF pages
- learn how to install and configure JSF with Tomcat
- learn how to use important concepts such as converters, validators, tracking, etc.

28.1 INTRODUCTION

Java Server Faces (JSF) is a Java-based framework for creating web-based user interfaces. It combines the power of Struts and Swing and follows Model-View-Controller (MVC) architecture which is considered to be the best for web frameworks. In an MVC framework, the controller decides which view to show next for a user request. JSF provides a powerful controller servlet for managing the life cycle of web-applications as well as provides a rich component model complete with event handling and component rendering. JSF uses lightweight POJO approach and is hence well-designed and easy-to-use, clean and simple. In a nutshell, using JSF has the following benefits:

- Allows us to create user interfaces using a set of standard, reusable server-side components accessible through tags
- It saves state information of forms components transparently and repopulates forms when they are re-displayed
- Allows us to create custom components
- Encapsulates event handling and component rendering

In this chapter we shall discuss primary concepts with extensive examples starting with a simple example JSF application.

28.2 FIRST APPLICATION

It is good to understand a technology with an application. In our first application, we shall develop a simple JSF application having a page that displays a message "Hello world". In practice, a JSF application typically consists of several pages often backed by Java beans. This application merely helps us in understanding the philosophy of a JSF application.

28.2.1 Installing JSF

We shall set up a basic environment that will facilitate the development, deploy and testing of JSF applications. Professionals often use IDE such as NetBeans, Eclipse, Rational Application Developer etc. However, it is important to know what and how things happen behind the scene to get out of situations if anything goes wrong. Our environment requires

- Java Development Kid (JDK), version 1.5 or higher installed,
- a web server (Tomcat 8) and
- the Mojarra JSF libraries from Oracle.
- A text editor notepad or wordpad
- The command prompt to compile Java programs.
- A web browser to test your JSF applications

Truly speaking, JSF is just a specification. To develop JSF-based web applications, we must obtain and install a reference implementation of this specification. There are many such implementations and any one can be used. The obvious choice is the JSF reference implementation by Oracle. It was developed by the well-known Mojarra project and is freely downloadable from `https://javaserverfaces.java.net/`. This link will guide you to a download page with many download options. The entire library is now included in a single JAR file. Download the most recent version of the JAR file. We downloaded the version `javax.faces-2.2.8-04.jar`. (Release on Dec 09 2014) from `https://maven.java.net/content/repositories/releases/org/glassfish/javax.faces/2.2.8-04/`.

There are many ways to make this library available to web applications running under Tomcat. One way to make it available to a specific application is to place this JAR file into the web application's `WEB-INF\lib` directory. Note that in this case, only this specific web application will have access to that library. If another application needs access to this library, put the JAR file in its own `WEB-INF\lib` directory. Alternatively, we can put the JAR files into a common location so that all web applications can access it. For Tomcat, this location is `<TOMCAT_HOME>\lib`. In this case, all applications running under Tomcat will have access to library. Sometimes, Tomcat requires it to be restarted so that it can load the new JAR files. We put it in our application's directory. `WEB-INF\lib`

JSF applications are simply standard web applications. So, every JSF application has an application root. Create a directory somewhere in your file system. We created a directory `jsf` under `E:\ajp`. So `E:\ajp\jsf` (hereafter referred to as `JSF_HOME`) will act as the root of our JSF application. Every web application root should have a structure. So, we create the following directory structure.

The Java code that gets compiled and distributed with your JSF application will go in a `classes\` directory. Although, we shall not use any Java code in our first example, it's worthwhile creating this folder for further examples.

The `lib\` folder contains resources (such as JAR, xml files) that a web application might need at runtime. Our JSF application needs the JSF library file `javax.faces-2.2.8-04.jar`, which is not a part of Tomcat. So we put it in `lib/` folder.

Every Java-based web application must have a special XML file known as a *deployment descriptor*, whose name is always `web.xml` and resides in the `WEB-INF\` folder. This extremely important file provides information to the servlet engine such as Tomcat about how to configure the environment in which the application will run.

JSF is not a part of servlet and JSP specification, a servlet engine like Tomcat cannot handle JSF requests. So, let us first understand how to make an ordinary servlet engine JSF-compliant. Since, Tomcat itself cannot handle JSF centric requests, it only identifies JSF requests (having a specific pattern) and routes them to a special servlet capable of handling them. So, we must tell the Tomcat which requests are JSF requests and who it should route them to. To distinguish JSF requests from others, a common extension is used rather than having extensions such as .jsp file or. html. JSF 2.0 favors the use of extension `.xhtml` for JSF files and we also use it. The servlet class that understands JSF requests is `javax.faces.webapp.FacesServlet` which is incorporated in `javax.faces-2.2.8-04.jar`.

The entire information is supplied to the Tomcat using application's `web.xml` file by adding the following lines between, `<web-app>` and `</web-app>` tags.

```
<web-app
...
<servlet>
  <servlet-name>Faces Servlet</servlet-name>
  <servlet-class>javax.faces.webapp.FacesServlet</servlet-class>
</servlet>

<servlet-mapping>
  <servlet-name>Faces Servlet</servlet-name>
  <url-pattern>*.xhtml</url-pattern>
</servlet-mapping>

</web-app>
```

Note that value of `<servlet-name>` tag in the `<servlet>` and `<servlet-mapping>` must match. The above codes essentially tell servlet engine that any request that comes in with an extension `.xhtml` should be forwarded to the "Faces Servlet", which is implemented through the Java class named `javax.faces.webapp.FacesServlet`. The class file is included in `javax.faces-2.2.8-04.jar` file placed in application's `lib/` directory.

28.2.2 Writing a JSF Page

The basic configuration is over. It is time to write a simple JSF page. A JSF page, in addition to the html tags, contains namespace qualified special tags, called *JSF tags*. For these tags we need to use the following namespaces of URI in html node.

```
<html xmlns="http://www.w3.org/1999/xhtml"
      xmlns:h="http://java.sun.com/jsf/html" >
```

The following JSF page (`HelloWorld.xhtml`) contains only one JSF tag `<h:outputText>` that renders a text specified in its `value` attribute.

```
<?xml version="1.0" encoding="UTF-8"?>
<!DOCTYPE html PUBLIC "-//W3C//DTD XHTML 1.0 Transitional//EN"
"http://www.w3.org/TR/xhtml1/DTD/xhtml1-transitional.dtd">
<html xmlns="http://www.w3.org/1999/xhtml"
      xmlns:h="http://java.sun.com/jsf/html" >
   <head>
      <title>Simple JSF page</title>
   </head>
   <body>
      <h:outputText value="Hello World!" />
   </body>
</html>
```

This is a very rudimentary JSF page that introduces a few important concepts and helps us to verify that indeed, a basic JSF application is working in our local environment.

Create this file using a standard text editor, such as Microsoft's Notepad, and save the file as `HelloWorld.xhtml` in the application root folder, which for our case is `jsf\`. Note that the extension to this file should be `.xhtml`. The application is now ready to deploy and test.

```
jsf/
 ├HelloWorld.xhtml
 └WEB-INF/
    ├web.xml
    ├lib/
    │ └javax.faces-2.2.8-04.jar
    └classes/
       └ukr/
          └HelloWorld.class
```

28.2.3 Deploying the Application

The final directory structure is shown here. A summary of the entire directory structure is shown in Table 28.1:

Table 28.1: Description of HelloWorld JSF application

Folder or file	Explanation
jsf/	JSF-based web application root directory
HelloWorld.xhtml	The web page to be used by the browser
WEB-INF/	This folder inside the jsf folder holds configuration files such as web.xml, faces-config.xml etc. that are used by web server.
web.xml	This file inside the WEB-INF folder is the Web Application Deployment Descriptor for your application. This is an XML file describing the servlets and other components that make up your application.
lib/	This folder inside the WEB-INF folder holds libraries required by our web application, for example, javax.faces-2.2.8-04.jar file.
javax.faces-2.2.8-04.jar	This file inside the lib folder is the JSF library file.
classes/	This folder inside the WEB-INF folder holds compiled Java classes.

There are many ways to deploy the application. One way to deploy is to place the entire `jsf/` directory in the Tomcat's `webapps` folder. We can also create a WAR (**W**eb **A**pplication a**R**chive) file and place it in the Tomcat's `webapps` directory.

A WAR file has a standard format for distributing and deploying Java EE, web-based applications. The `jar` utility that comes with the JDK can be used to create deployable WAR files.

To create a WAR file, open a terminal, go the `jsf/` directory and use the following command:

```
jar cvf jsf.war *
```

We assume that the Java installation home directory is included in your PATH environment variable. If everything goes fine, an output as shown will be generated:

```
added manifest
adding: HelloWorld.xhtml(in = 385) (out= 257)(deflated 33%)
adding: WEB-INF/(in = 0) (out= 0)(stored 0%)
adding: WEB-INF/classes/(in = 0) (out= 0)(stored 0%)
adding: WEB-INF/lib/(in = 0) (out= 0)(stored 0%)
adding: WEB-INF/lib/javax.faces-2.2.8-04.jar(in = 2572391) (out=
2349858)(deflated 8%)
adding: WEB-INF/web.xml(in = 748) (out= 344)(deflated 54%)
```

The command creates a WAR file `jsf.war` which may be found in `jsf\` directory. This `jsf.war` file contains all the necessary files needed for the HelloWorld JSF application. Put it in the Tomcat's `webapps` directory. Don't forget to restart the Tomcat server. If everything goes fine, a sample screen will appear as follows. The message for our JSF application has been highlighted.

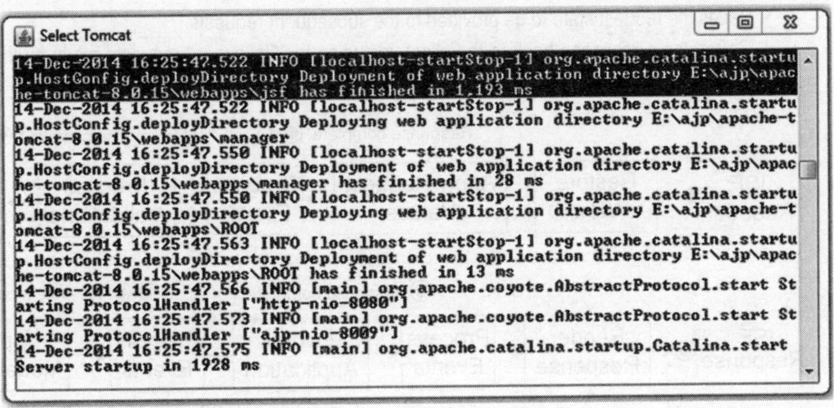

28.2.4 Testing the Application

It is time to open up a web browser and navigate to our JSF application. Use the following URL to open the JSF page:

```
http://127.0.0.1:8080/jsf/HelloWorld.xhtml
```

We are assuming that the Tomcat server is running on port 8080. See the `conf\server.xml` file under Tomcat's installation home directory to find the port it is running on. A sample screen shot is shown below:

28.3 REQUEST PROCESSING LIFE-CYCLE

It is extremely important to JSF programmers to know how JSF requests are processed behind the scenes. Each JSF request, from its submission to completion, known as *life-cycle*, is processed by a series of phases, known as *life-cycle phases* [Figure 28.1:] named as follows:

- Restore View
- Apply Request Values
- Process Validations
- Update Model Values
- Invoke Application
- Render Response

During these phases, a JSF engine performs all necessary jobs such as

- Validates incoming data, converts them to server-side data types and generates error messages when they fail.
- Updates model objects with incoming data.
- Invokes server-side application to perform tasks further.
- Saves the request state to be provided to the subsequent requests.
- Generates a response back to the client, including the "follow-up" requests made by the browser for images, scripts, and style sheets.

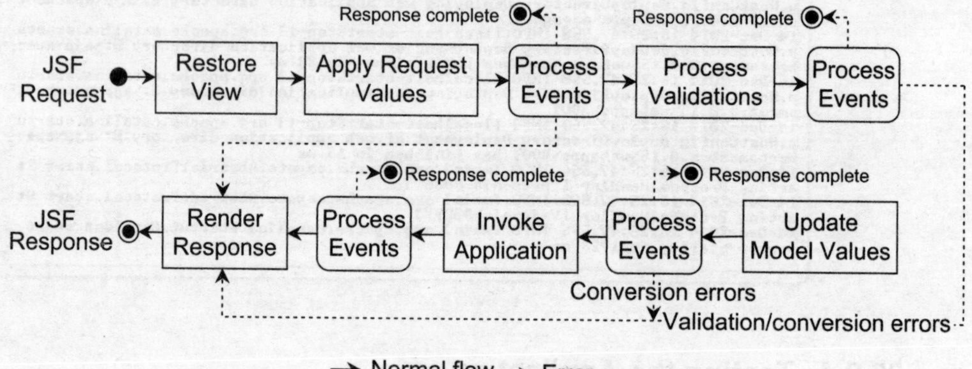

Figure 28.1: JSF request processing life-cycle phases

The following sections give a short description of these phases.

28.3.1 Restore View

When a JSF page is requested, usually by clicking a link or a button component, the request processing life-cycle begins with this phase. Note that for each UI presented in a client, a tree of UI components, called *faces view* is maintained in the server side. In fact the client UI is obtained (rendered) from this view.

The task of this phase is to build a new empty view when a request is made for the first time. The life-cycle then advances to the *Render Response* phase, during which the view is populated with the components corresponding to elements in the page. For subsequent requests, it restores the view (created previously for the first request).

The view also contains validators, converters, event handlers (if any), etc. The tree is saved to be used by other phases in a `FacesContext` type container object which holds all the information required to process current request. All the components, event handlers, converters and validators have the access to this container to extract necessary information.

28.3.2 Apply Request Values

This is the next phase in the request processing life-cycle and is executed only for a *postback* request that refers to some previously requested page. A postback request is usually sent from an already rendered JSF page by submitting a form containing some elements. In this phase, the individual components of restored view tree is updated with the values of form elements. More specifically, the `processDecodes()` method on all the components is called. The process of extracting name-value pair and applying matching incoming value to the UI component is known as *decoding*.

Equivalently, the following happens for each `UIInput` component in the view tree:

```
input.setSubmittedValue(request.getParameter(input.getClientId()));
```

Here `input` is a `UIInput` type component and `request` is `HttpServletRequest`. Note that new values are applied to those components that are capable of holding a value. Components (such as text fields, labels) that implement `javax.faces.component.ValueHolder` interface has an attribute `value` and can hold a value. Components that implement the `EditableValueHolder` interface, can hold values that can be edited by the user. If the `immediate` attribute of these editable components is set to `true`, then converters, validators and value change listeners (if any attached) will also be invoked in this phase. However, failing of any conversions or validations transfers the control directly to the Render Response phase.

Components (such as buttons, links etc.) that implement `ActionSource` interface may generate action events and hence are called *action components*. Action events (if any) associated with these components are queued in this phase. If `immediate` attribute of the action components are set to `true`, then action events are fired in this phase. Otherwise, they are fired in the Invoke Application phase.

Note that not all the phases occur in all the cases in order. A call to `renderResponse()` method at any time, on the current `FacesContext` stops the current processing and skips the control directly to the Render Response phase.

```
FacesContext.getCurrentInstance().renderResponse();
```

Note that this phase does not yet update the business objects that compose the model. It updates only the UI components with the new data.

28.3.3 Process Validations

This phase invokes (if it was not already done in the previous phase) convertors and validators (if any) attached to the components to convert and validate the data captured in the previous phase.

More specifically, the `processValidators()` method is invoked on all the components of view tree. The `processValidators()` method, in turn, calls the associated converters and validators. Any conversion/validation error at this stage causes the control to jump directly to the Render Response phase skipping Update Model Values and Invoke Application phases.

Validators and convertors may be attached to the components in many ways. The following attached a validator to a text component by setting its `required` attribute to `true`.

```
<h:inputText id="login" required="true" />
```

The task of the validator is to check if the value of the text component is empty or not. A detailed discussion on how to attach convertors and validators can be found later in this chapter.

Event listeners for editable components are also called (if not already called in Apply Request Values phase).

28.3.4 Update Model Values

If the process validation phase is passed successfully without any validation error, the model objects are updated with the validated data from the request. However, JSF runtime will update only the bean properties pointed at by an input component's `value` attribute. Also, if the data type of a property is not a String or a Java primitive, data conversion occurs in this phase. If there is any error, similar thing happens as validation errors i.e. the life cycle advances directly to the render response phase so that the page is re-rendered with errors displayed. Any event listener (such as phase listener) registered to this phase is also notified with the event object.

28.3.5 Invoke Application

Event listeners for action components, such as command buttons, links are called (if not already called in Apply Request Values phase i.e. `immediate` attribute was set to `false`).

28.3.6 Render Response

In this phase, the entire component tree is rendered and sent to the client. After the content of the view is rendered, the response state is saved so that subsequent requests can access it and it is available to the restore view phase.

28.4 TRACING PHASES

For better understandability, we can use a phase listener to trace the JSF life-cycle phases and to see what happens in which phase. A phase listener class must implement `PhaseListener` interface which has three methods. Here is a simple phase listener class:

```
package phaseListeners;
import javax.faces.event.*;

public class MyListener implements PhaseListener {
  public void beforePhase(PhaseEvent pe) {
    System.out.println("Start phase : "+pe.getPhaseId());
  }
  public void afterPhase(PhaseEvent pe) {
    System.out.println("End phase : "+pe.getPhaseId());
  }
  public PhaseId getPhaseId() {
    return PhaseId.ANY_PHASE;
  }
}
```

This phase listener is interested in all the phases and hence the `getPhaseId()` method returns the identifier `ANY_PHASE`. The `beforePhase()` and `afterPhase()` methods are called just before and after a phase is started and completed. To active the phase listener to a JSF application, it must be registered in `faces-config.xml` as follows:

```
<lifecycle>
 <phase-listener>phaseListeners.MyListener</phase-listener>
</lifecycle>
```

For an initial request, it produces the following in the system output:

```
Start phase : RESTORE_VIEW 1
End phase : RESTORE_VIEW 1
Start phase : RENDER_RESPONSE 6
End phase : RENDER_RESPONSE 6
```

For a postback request, it produces the following output:

```
Start phase : RESTORE_VIEW 1
End phase : RESTORE_VIEW 1
Start phase : APPLY_REQUEST_VALUES 2
End phase : APPLY_REQUEST_VALUES 2
Start phase : PROCESS_VALIDATIONS 3
End phase : PROCESS_VALIDATIONS 3
Start phase : UPDATE_MODEL_VALUES 4
End phase : UPDATE_MODEL_VALUES 4
Start phase : INVOKE_APPLICATION 5
End phase : INVOKE_APPLICATION 5
Start phase : RENDER_RESPONSE 6
End phase : RENDER_RESPONSE 6
```

28.5 MANAGED BEAN

User Interface (UI) components in a JSF page are often associated with JavaBeans (called *backing beans*) that provide application logic. A JSF page may also use beans for other purposes such as validations, conversions etc. Since these beans are created and managed by a JSF implementation, they are affectionately called *managed beans*. A managed bean is called a backing bean if it is bound with a UI component. Here is an example of a very simple managed bean (`HelloWorld.java`):

```
package ukr;
import javax.faces.bean.ManagedBean;
@ManagedBean
public class HelloWorld {
  public String getMessage() {
    return "Hello World!";
  }
}
```

It has only one method `getMessage()` that returns the string `Hello World!`. The `@ManagedBean` annotation registers the bean to be managed with the FacesServlet implementation. A managed bean is connected to a web page through Expression Language (EL). The `<h:outputText>` component in our previous web page (`HelloWorld.xhtml`) may be connected to this bean as follows:

```
<h:outputText value="#{helloWorld.message}" />
```

The EL `#{helloWorld.message}` retrieves the value of the message property (through `getMessage()` method) of the managed bean `helloWorld`. A detailed syntax of EL expressions is discussed later in this chapter. Note that the name `helloWorld` is used to refer to the managed bean `HelloWorld`. If no name is specified in the `@ManagedBean` annotation, the managed bean's name becomes the class name with the first letter in lowercase.

To compile this file, we need the `javax.faces.bean.ManagedBean` annotation class which is included in the JSF library file `javax.faces-2.2.8-04.jar`. Specify this jar file using `-cp` option of `javac` command. For example, we placed this jar file in the same directory containing `HelloWorld.java` file and used the following command to compile

```
javac -cp javax.faces-2.2.8-03.jar HelloWorld.java
```

It generates the `HelloWorld.class` file. Create a directory `ukr` under `JSF_HOME\WEB-INF\classes` and copy `HelloWorld.class` file there. The final directory content will look exactly as shown in the following page.

The web application is now ready to deploy. One way to do this is to place the entire `jsf/` directory in the Tomcat's `webapps` folder. We can also create a `.war` file and place it in the Tomcat's `webapps` directory. To create a .war file, go to the `jsf/` directory and use the following command:

```
jar cvf jsf.war *
```

```
jsf/
├─HelloWorld.xhtml
└─WEB-INF/
    ├─web.xml
    ├─lib/
    │  └─javax.faces-2.2.8-04.jar
    └─classes
        └─ukr/
            └─HelloWorld.class
```

A sample output of this command is shown below:

```
added manifest
adding: HelloWorld.xhtml(in = 364) (out= 242)(deflated 33%)
adding: WEB-INF/(in = 0) (out= 0)(stored 0%)
adding: WEB-INF/classes/(in = 0) (out= 0)(stored 0%)
adding: WEB-INF/classes/ukr/(in = 0) (out= 0)(stored 0%)
adding: WEB-INF/classes/ukr/HelloWorld.class(in = 366) (out= 270)(deflated 26%)
adding: WEB-INF/lib/(in = 0) (out= 0)(stored 0%)
adding: WEB-INF/lib/javax.faces-2.2.8-04.jar(in = 3127585) (out=
2905152)(deflated 7%)
adding: WEB-INF/web.xml(in = 748) (out= 344)(deflated 54%)
```

This `jsf.war` file contains all the necessary files needed for the HelloWorld JSF application. Put it in the Tomcat's `webapps` directory. Don't forget to restart the Tomcat server. If everything goes fine, a sample screen as follows will appear. The message for our JSF application has been highlighted.

```
Select Tomcat
14-Dec-2014 11:30:47.875 INFO [localhost-startStop-1] org.apache.catalina.startu
p.HostConfig.deployDirectory Deployment of web application directory E:\ajp\apac
he-tomcat-8.0.15\webapps\jsf has finished in 1,210 ms
14-Dec-2014 11:30:47.876 INFO [localhost-startStop-1] org.apache.catalina.startu
p.HostConfig.deployDirectory Deploying web application directory E:\ajp\apache-t
omcat-8.0.15\webapps\manager
14-Dec-2014 11:30:47.900 INFO [localhost-startStop-1] org.apache.catalina.startu
p.HostConfig.deployDirectory Deployment of web application directory E:\ajp\apac
he-tomcat-8.0.15\webapps\manager has finished in 24 ms
14-Dec-2014 11:30:47.900 INFO [localhost-startStop-1] org.apache.catalina.startu
p.HostConfig.deployDirectory Deploying web application directory E:\ajp\apache-t
omcat-8.0.15\webapps\ROOT
14-Dec-2014 11:30:47.978 INFO [localhost-startStop-1] org.apache.catalina.startu
p.HostConfig.deployDirectory Deployment of web application directory E:\ajp\apac
he-tomcat-8.0.15\webapps\ROOT has finished in 78 ms
14-Dec-2014 11:30:47.983 INFO [main] org.apache.coyote.AbstractProtocol.start St
arting ProtocolHandler ["http-nio-8080"]
14-Dec-2014 11:30:47.992 INFO [main] org.apache.coyote.AbstractProtocol.start St
arting ProtocolHandler ["ajp-nio-8009"]
14-Dec-2014 11:30:47.994 INFO [main] org.apache.catalina.startup.Catalina.start
Server startup in 1964 ms
```

In this example, we registered the managed bean using `@ManagedBean` annotation. In general, there are two ways we can register a managed bean with the JSF runtime: using `faces-config.xml` file and using `@ManagedBean` annotation.

28.5.1 Using faces-config.xml File

JSF runtime processes a special file under application's `WEB-INF/` directory. The name of this file is `faces-config.xml` and contains configuration information of the application. We can configure managed bean in this file using `<managed-bean>` tag to enable the JSF framework to instantiate and store them in the appropriate scope as follows:

```
<?xml version="1.0" encoding="UTF-8"?>
<faces-config
...
<managed-bean>
  <managed-bean-name>helloWorld</managed-bean-name>
  <managed-bean-class>ukr.HelloWorld</managed-bean-class>
```

```
    <managed-bean-scope>request</managed-bean-scope>
  </managed-bean>

  </faces-config>
```

This registers the bean exactly the way it was done using @ManagedBean annotation. Note that the file faces-config.xml should contain only application level configuration. So, the above code could have been placed in a separate file (say managed-beans.xml) and tell the web.xml file about its existence as:

```
<context-param>
    <param-name>javax.faces.CONFIG_FILES</param-name>
    <param-value>WEB-INF/managed-beans.xml</param-value>
</context-param>
```

28.5.2 Using @ManagedBean Annotation

In JSF 2.0 and higher, we can use various annotations in the Java classes for different purposes, which make your development easier and faster.

The @ManagedBean annotation in a class automatically registers that class with JSF runtime as a managed bean class. We do not need to configure it in the application configuration resource file using <managed-bean> tag. Here is an example:

```
@ManagedBean
public class HelloWorld {/*...*/}
```

This annotation may have two attributes: name and eager. The value of the name attribute is the name to be used to refer to this bean further. If name attribute is absent, the name of the bean is same as the unqualified class name with the first letter in lower case. For example, the name of the above bean will be helloWorld. The following registers a bean with name now.

```
@ManagedBean(name="now")
class DateBean {/*...*/}
```

If the value of the eager attribute is true, and the scope (discussed in the next section) of the managed bean is "application", the managed bean is instantiated when the application starts. Here is an example:

```
@ManagedBean(name="now", eager="true")
@ApplicationScoped
class DateBean {/*...*/}
```

If the value of eager attribute is unspecified or false, the default "lazy" instantiation of the managed bean occurs.

28.5.3 Scope Annotations

The scope of a managed bean tells JSF runtime when to instantiate the bean and how long the instance should be kept alive. Six kinds of scopes are defined in JSF specification and are represented by scope annotations @NoneScoped, @RequestScoped, @ViewScoped, @SessionScoped, @ApplicationScoped and @CustomScoped annotations. Here is an example:

```
@ManagedBean(name="now")
@SessionScoped
class DateBean {/*...*/}
```

This registers the bean whose instance is created upon the first HTTP request in a session and destroyed when the HTTP session completes. If no scope annotation is used, the @RequestScoped annotation is assumed. The function of other scope annotations is shown in Table 28.2:

Table 28.2: JSF scope annotations

Scope	Description
@RequestScoped	Bean lives during a single HTTP request-response pair. Created upon an HTTP request and destroyed when HTTP response completes.
@SessionScoped	Bean lives during an HTTP session. Created upon the first HTTP request in a session and destroyed when the HTTP session completes.
@ApplicationScoped	Bean lives during the web application entire lifetime. Created upon the first HTTP request (if eager attribute is false) or when the web application starts (if eager attribute is true) and destroyed when the web application stops.
@NoneScoped	Bean lives as a single EL evaluation. Created upon an EL evaluation and destroyed after the EL evaluation.
@ViewScoped	Bean lives during the period a user interacts with the same JSF view in the browser window/tab. Created upon an HTTP request and destroyed when user postbacks a different view.
@CustomScoped	Bean lives during the period the bean's entry in the custom Map which is created for this scope lives.

28.5.4 @ManagedProperty Annotation

This annotation (together with `@ManagedBean`) is used to inject a value into a property. Here is an example:

```
@ManagedBean
public class MyBean {
  @ManagedProperty(value="Hi!")
  private String message;
/*...*/
}
```

This sets the value of `message` field to "Hi". Note that this could have been done by assigning the value "Hi" to the field directly as follows:

```
String message = "Hi";
```

However, the value of `value` attribute may be an EL value expression. This means the `@ManagedProperty` annotation may be used to refer one bean from another. For example, the value of message property of `helloWorld` bean may be injected as follows:

```
@ManagedBean
public class MyBean {
  @ManagedProperty(value="#{helloWorld.message}")
  private String message;
/*...*/
}
```

Note that the scope of referenced bean (`helloWorld` in our case) must not be shorter that the bean making the reference (`myBean` in our case.). The function of `@ManagedProperty` annotation can be implemented using `<managed-property>` tag in `faces-config.xml` file as follows:

```
<managed-bean>
  <managed-bean-name>myBean</managed-bean-name>
  <managed-bean-class>ukr.MyBean</managed-bean-class>
  <managed-bean-scope>request</managed-bean-scope>
  <managed-property>
    <property-name>message</property-name>
    <value>#{helloWorld.message}</value>
  </managed-property>
</managed-bean>
```

This means a bean can be referred to from a configuration resource file. The injected bean may be any bean including the `param` bean that holds the parameters passed with the HTTP request message. So, the value of a bean property may be set dynamically from the HTTP request. Here is an example:

```
@ManagedBean
public class MyBean {
  @ManagedProperty(value="#{param.msg}")
  private String message;
  /*...*/
}
```

This sets the `message` property by the value of `msg` parameter present in the HTTP request. To verify this, use the following tag in a file `ManagedPropertyDemo.xhtml`.

```
<h:outputText value="#{myBean.message}" />
```

Now, use the following URL to access this page:

```
http://127.0.0.1:8080/jsf/ManagedPropertyDemo.xhtml?msg=Hi
```

Since the scope of the `param` bean is *request*, the scope of the `myBean` must also be *request*.

28.6 ACCESSING MANAGED BEAN PROGRAMMATICALLY

We have seen how to access properties of managed bean from both pages and faces configuration files. It is also possible to do the same using Java code from an event listener class or another managed bean. There are many ways to do this. For all cases, we must first have a reference to the current `javax.faces.context.FacesContext` as follows:

```
FacesContext fc = FacesContext.getCurrentInstance();
```

28.6.1 Using javax.faces.context.ExternalContext

If the scope of the bean is known, we can query the containing application environment to have a `Map` object containing registered beans as follows:

```
ExternalContext ec = fc.getExternalContext();
Map m = ec.getApplicationMap();
```

In case of session and request scoped bean, use `getSessionMap()` and `getRequestMap()` methods respectively. A reference to the bean having the name “myBean” can then be obtained as follows:

```
MyBean mb = (MyBean) m.get("myBean");
```

Programmers often love to use the following concise code:

```
MyBean mb=(MyBean)
FacesContext.getCurrentInstance().getExternalContext().getApplicationMap().get(
"myBean");
```

We can now invoke its methods as usual. Note that this method works fine if the scope of the bean is not changed subsequently this code is written. Alternatively, the following methods may be used.

28.6.2 Using javax.el.ELContext

Any EL expression can be evaluated from a Java code with the help of `ELContext` which is obtained as follows:

```
ELContext ec = fc.getELContext();
```

Note that this class in not included in faces JAR file. Download a suitable JAR file containing this class. We downloaded `javax.el-api-2.2.4.jar` from `http://www.java2s.com/Code/Jar/j/Downloadjavaxelapi224jar.htm`. The bean instance can be then obtained as follows:

```
MyBean mb = (MyBean) ec.getELResolver().getValue(ec, null,"myBean");
```

If you want to work with arbitrary EL value expression, we may create a `ValueExpression` object as follows:

```
ExpressionFactory ef = fc.getApplication().getExpressionFactory();
ValueExpression ve = ef.createValueExpression(ec, "#{myBean}", MyBean.class);
```

Note that the expression `#{myBean}` refers to the entire bean instance which can be obtained as shown here:

```
MyBean mb = (MyBean) ve.getValue(ec);
```

The individual properties such as `message` of the bean can also be obtained as follows:

```
ValueExpression ve = ef.createValueExpression(ec, "#{myBean.message}",
String.class);
String msg = (String) ve.getValue(ec);
```

This advantage of this method is that it also allows us to set the value of EL expression as follows:

```
ve.setValue(ec, "abc");
```

Like `ValueExpression`, a `MethodExpression` can be used to invoke a method of a managed bean. For example, the following shows how to invoke the `getMessage()` method of myBean:

```
MethodExpression me =
ef.createMethodExpression(ec,"#{myBean.getMessage}",String.class, new
Class[]{});
String msg = (String)me.invoke(ec, null);
```

28.6.3 Using evaluateExpressionGet() Method

In JSF 2.0, there is a concise way to evaluate an EL expression using `evaluateExpressionGet()` method as follows:

```
Application a = fc.getApplication();
MyBean mb = (MyBean)a.evaluateExpressionGet(fc, "#{myBean}", MyBean.class);
```

However, this method cannot set the value of the EL expression.

28.7 BASIC JSF TAGS

JSF provides various tags to render standard HTML tags. In this section, we shall see which JSF tags are available to generate HTML tags and how to use them. To use these tags, we need to use the following namespaces of URI in html node.

```
<html xmlns:h="http://java.sun.com/jsf/html">
...
</html>
```

<h:outputText>

This tag is used to render a piece of text. Here is an example:

```
<h:outputText value="Hello World!"/>
```

It is rendered in HTML as:

```
Hello World!
```

<h:inputText>

Renders an HTML `<input>` element of type="text". It renders the current value of the component as the value of the "value" attribute. Here is an example:

```
<h:inputText size="10" value="Type your name"/>
```

It is rendered as:

```
<input type="text" name="j_idt4" value="Type your name" size="10" />
```

<h:inputSecret>

Renders an HTML `<input>` element of type="password". The characters entered in this element are not echoed. Here is an example:

```
<h:inputSecret size="10"/>
```

It is rendered as:

```
<input type="password" name="j_idt6" value="" size="10" />
```

<h:inputTextarea>

Renders an HTML `<textarea>` element. The current value of the component is displayed inside the element. Here is an example:

```
<h:inputTextarea value="Hello World!" readonly="true"/>
```

It is rendered as:

```
<textarea name="j_idt8" readonly="readonly">Hello World!</textarea>
```

<h:inputHidden>

Renders an HTML `<input>` element of type="hidden". It renders the current value of the component as the value of the "value" attribute. Here is an example:

```
<h:inputHidden value="next"/>
```

It is rendered as:

```
<input type="hidden" name="j_idt10" value="next" />
```

<h:commandButton>

Renders an HTML `<input>` element of type="submit" button. It renders the current value of the component as the value of the "value" attribute. Here is an example:

```
<h:commandButton value="Logout" onclick="alert('Are to sure to logout?');" />
```

It is rendered as:

```
<input type="submit" name="j_idt12" value="Logout" onclick="alert('Are to sure
to logout?');" />
```

<h:commandLink>

Render an HTML `<a>` anchor element that acts like a form submit button when clicked. Here is an example:

```
<h:commandLink value="Help" action="help" />
```

It is rendered as:

```
<a href="#
"onclick="mojarra.jsfcljs(document.getElementById('j_idt14'),{'j_idt14:j_idt17':
'j_idt14:j_idt17'},'');return false">Help</a>
```

<h:outputLink>

Renders an HTML anchor. The value of the component is rendered as the value of the `href` attribute. Here is an example:

```
<h:outputLink value="help.xhtml" >Help</h:outputLink>
```

It is rendered as:

```
<a href="help.xhtml">Help</a>
```

<h:selectBooleanCheckbox>

Renders a single HTML check box. Here is an example:

```
<h:selectBooleanCheckbox value="Encrypt" id="encrypt"/>
```

It is rendered as:

```
<input id="encrypt" type="checkbox" name="encrypt" />
```

<h:selectManyCheckbox>

Renders a group of HTML check boxes. Here is an example:

```
<h:selectManyCheckbox >
    <f:selectItem itemValue="hdd" itemLabel="HDD" />
    <f:selectItem itemValue="monitor" itemLabel="Monitor" />
</h:selectManyCheckbox>
```

It is rendered as:

```
<table>
    <tr>
<td>
<input name="j_idt24" id="j_idt24:0" value="hdd" type="checkbox" /><label
for="j_idt24:0" class=""> HDD</label></td>
<td>
<input name="j_idt24" id="j_idt24:1" value="monitor" type="checkbox" /><label
for="j_idt24:1" class=""> Monitor</label></td>
    </tr>
</table>
```

<h:selectOneRadio>

Renders a single HTML radio button. Here is an example:

```
<h:selectOneRadio:<h:selectOneRadio >
    <f:selectItem itemValue="cheque" itemLabel="Cheque" />
    <f:selectItem itemValue="cash" itemLabel="Cash" />
</h:selectOneRadio><br/>
```

It is rendered as:

```
<table>
    <tr>
<td>
<input type="radio" name="j_idt28" id="j_idt28:0" value="cheque" /><label
for="j_idt28:0"> Cheque</label></td>
<td>
<input type="radio" name="j_idt28" id="j_idt28:1" value="cash" /><label
for="j_idt28:1"> Cash</label></td>
    </tr>
</table>
```

<h:selectOneListbox>

Renders a single HTML list box. Here is an example:

```
<h:selectOneListbox >
    <f:selectItem itemValue="cheque" itemLabel="Cheque" />
    <f:selectItem itemValue="cash" itemLabel="Cash" />
</h:selectOneListbox>
```

It is rendered as:

```
<select name="j_idt32" size="2"> <option value="cheque">Cheque</option>
    <option value="cash">Cash</option>
</select>
```

<h:selectManyListbox>

Renders multiple HTML list boxes. Here is an example:

```
<h:selectManyListbox >
    <f:selectItem itemValue="hdd" itemLabel="HDD" />
    <f:selectItem itemValue="monitor" itemLabel="Monitor" />
</h:selectManyListbox>
```

It is rendered as:

```
<select name="j_idt36" multiple="multiple" size="2">  <option
value="hdd">HDD</option>
    <option value="monitor">Monitor</option>
</select>
```

<h:selectOneMenu>

Renders an HTML combo box. Here is an example:

```
<h:selectOneMenu >
    <f:selectItem itemValue="cheque" itemLabel="Cheque" />
    <f:selectItem itemValue="cash" itemLabel="Cash" />
</h:selectOneMenu>
```

It is rendered as:

```
<select name="j_idt40" size="1"> <option value="cheque">Cheque</option>
    <option value="cash">Cash</option>
</select>
```

<h:graphicImage>

Renders an image. Here is an example:

```
<h:graphicImage value="back.jpg"/>
```

It is rendered as:

```
<img src="back.jpg" />
```

<h:outputStylesheet>

Includes a CSS style sheet in HTML output. Here is an example:

```
<h:head>
   <h:outputStylesheet library="css" name="myStyles.css"/>
</h:head>
```

It is rendered as:

```
<link type="text/css" rel="stylesheet"
href="/jsf/javax.faces.resource/myStyles.css.xhtml?ln=css" />
```

The `<h:outputStylesheet>` requires a `<h:head>`. Also note that `myStyles.css` file must be put in the directory `webapps/resources/css/`.

<h:outputScript>

Includes a script in HTML output. Here is an example:

```
<h:head>
   <h:outputScript library="js" name="fn.js" />
</h:head>
```

It is rendered as:

```
<script type="text/javascript"
src="/jsf/javax.faces.resource/fn.js.xhtml?ln=js"></script>
```

The `<h:outputScript>` also requires a `<h:head>`. Also note that `fn.js` file must be put in the directory `webapps/resources/js/`.

28.8 EXPRESSION LANGUAGE

The Expression Language (EL) specifies rules to write simple expressions for accessing and manipulating managed beans in an elegant manner. Specifically, EL expressions can set bean properties and can invoke arbitrary static and public methods.

An EL expression is written as `#{...}` or `${...}`. The evaluation of EL expressions may happen at different times and is referred to as *immediate evaluation* and *deferred evaluation*. The former means that the expression is evaluated when the page is rendered and happens for expressions that take the form of `${...}`. Expression in the form of `#{...}`, on the other hand, are evaluated at appropriate time during the page life-cycle and is referred to as deferred evaluation.

EL expression is also categorized as: *value expressions* and *method expressions*. Value expressions can either yield a value or set a value, whereas a method expression invokes a method.

Value expressions can be further categorized into rvalue expression and *lvalue expressions*. Expressions that can only read data, but cannot write it, are called rvalue expressions. Lvalue expressions can both read and write data. Expressions that evaluated immediately (i.e. in the form `${...}`) are always rvalue expressions. Value expressions that use deferred evaluation syntax can act as both rvalue and lvalue expressions as well as method expressions.

Note that ultimately it is upto the framework how it treats `#{...}` or `${...}` expressions. In Facelets, unfortunately, the `${...}` is always treated exactly the same way as `#{...}`. So `${...}` evaluation is also deferred in JSF. So, hereafter we shall only talk about expressions that take the form `#{...}`.

28.8.1 Value Expression

A value expression can be used in static text or in any tag attribute that can accept an expression. Value expressions (both rvalue and lvalue expressions) can refer to JavaBeans, collection objects, implicit object and enumerated types. For example, the following expression references a managed bean named `myBean`:

```
#{myBean}
```

EL expression can contain implicit objects which are listed in Table 28.3:

Table 28.3: JSF implicit objects

Implicit Object	Description
pageContext	The context of the JSP page
initParam	Maps the name of a context initialization parameter to its value
param	Maps a request parameter name to its first value
paramValues	Maps a request parameter name to an array of its values
cookie	Maps a cookie name to a single cookie
header	Maps a request header name to its first value
headerValues	Maps a request header name to an array of its values
pageScope	Maps page-scoped variable names to their values
requestScope	Maps request-scoped variable names to their values
sessionScope	Maps session-scoped variable names to their values
applicationScope	Maps application-scoped variable names to their values

To refer to properties of beans, implicit objects or items of a collection, we use the . or [] notation. For example, to refer to the `message` property, either of the following can be used:

```
#{myBean.message}
#{myBean['message']}
```

We can use . or [] (or combination of them) in a cascaded fashion to refer to a nested property. For example, the following refers to the `first` property of the `message` property of `myBean`.

```
#{myBean.message['first']}
```

If the result of an EL value expression is an array or a List instance, elements of the array or the list can be obtained using [] notation with int indices. Here is an example:

```
#{myBean.colors[0]
```

However, to access Map elements, we use string literal as follows:

```
#{myBean.passwords['user1']
```

EL expressions can contain operators and literals which may be Boolean (true and false), Integer, Floating-point, String (single and back-slashed double quotes) and Null. Here are some examples:

```
#{5.0 gt 3}            //true
#{2 le (3/2)}          //false
#{10 == 11}            //false
#{'a' lt 'b'}          //true
#{'J++' gt 'C++'}      //true
#{17 mod 4}            //1
#{5 div 2}             //2.5
#{1.2 + 1.5}           //2.7
```

It is also possible to write composite expression where more than one expression is written one after another as follows:

```
Text1#{expr1}#{expr2}text2#{expr3}
```

Each expression of the composite expression is converted to a String and then concatenated with any intervening text.

28.8.2 Method Expression

A method expression can be used to invoke arbitrary public methods of a bean, which return a value. A component tag uses method expressions to invoke methods that perform some processing for the component. For example, we can specify a method expression to the `action` attribute of `<h:commandButton>` tag as follows:

```
<h:form>
   <h:commandButton value="Validate" action="#{myBean.validate}"/>
</h:form>
```

Here, when the button is clicked, the method `validate()` on `myBean` is invoked. Like value expressions, we can also use . and the [] operators in method expressions. For example, the above code could have been written as:

```
<h:form>
   <h:commandButton value="Validate" action="#{myBean['validate']}"/>
</h:form>
```

The literal inside the [] is converted to String and is used to find the name of the method that matches it. The above method expressions merely call a method validate that does not take any parameters. However, we can also pass parameters to bean methods. Both the . and [] operators can be used for invoking method calls with parameters, as shown in the following expression syntax:

```
expr1.methodname(parameters)
expr1[expr1](parameters)
```

In the first expression syntax, `expr1` evaluated to represent a bean object, and methodname is a string that represents a method in the bean object. In the second expression, `expr2` is evaluated and cast to a string that represents a method in the bean represented by `expr1`. The parameters in parentheses are the arguments for the method invocation. Parameters can be zero or more values or expressions, separated by commas.

So the following expression invokes a method `validate()` with parameter 'Me'.

```
#{myBean['validate']('Me')}
```

28.8.3 Facelets

There are a set of special tags provided for page layout for web applications. These tags are called *facelets tags*. These tags must be qualified by the following namespace:

```
xmlns:ui="http://java.sun.com/jsf/facelets"
```

28.8.3.1 Templates

Often web pages have common parts such as header and footer. Templates allow us to place common part in a single file and refer to it from pages that need it. So, it allows content to be changed in one place, but used in multiple pages. When working with templates, we use the tags `<ui:insert>`, `<ui:define>`, `<ui:include>` and `<ui:composition>`.

A template is basically a page having some facelets tags that define the layout of the page. Here is an example (myTemplate.xhtml):

```
<html xmlns="http://www.w3.org/1999/xhtml"
   xmlns:ui="http://java.sun.com/jsf/facelets">
 <body>
   <ui:insert name="header" >
      <ui:include src="header.xhtml" />
   </ui:insert> <br/>
   <ui:insert name="content" >
      <ui:include src="contents.xhtml" />
   </ui:insert> <br/>
   <ui:insert name="footer" >
      <ui:include src="footer.xhtml" />
   </ui:insert>
 </body>
</html>
```

The `<ui:insert>` tag, as its name suggests, creates logical named segments. For example, the above template has three sections. The section contents are populated by the `<ui:include>` tag. So the above template is a composition of three documents `header.xhtml`, `contents.xhtml` and `footer.xhtml`, which are ordinary xhtml documents and usually contain `<ui:composition>` tag. This tag is used to group a number of elements which are used inside the template. To illustrate this, the relevant content of `header`.xhtml is given below:

```
<html xmlns:ui="http://java.sun.com/jsf/facelets">
  <body>
    <ui:composition>
      Header
    </ui:composition>
  </body>
</html>
```

The content of the `contents.xhtml` and `footer.xhtml` will look similar. To use this template from another page (say index.html), we can use `<ui:composition>` specifying URL of the template page to its `template` attribute as follows:

```
<ui:composition template="myTemplate.xhtml" />
```

The content of the included template may be re-defined using `<ui:define>` tag as follows:

```
<ui:composition template="myTemplate.xhtml">
   <ui:define name="content">
      New Content
   </ui:define>
</ui:composition>
```

This replaces the content of `content` section by a new line of text. JSF also allows us to pass parameters to template file or an included file using <ui:param>. To hold the parameter in the `header.xhtml`, we write:

```
<ui:composition>
   #{header}
 </ui:composition>
```

To pass a value to the header section, in myTemplate.xhtml, we write

```
<ui:insert name="header" >
  <ui:include src="header.xhtml" >
    <ui:param name="header" value="My Header" />
  </ui:include>
</ui:insert>
```

28.8.3.2 Custom Tags

Open source JSF implementation such as Oracle's JSF offers just a few very standard, reusable UI components for forms, primitive tags for page layout and to display data. Fortunately JSF allows us to enhance their functionality of built-in tags or to create new custom tags. There are two ways to create custom tags: using `<ui:composition>` tag and using Java program.

Using Composition Tag

The following is a list of steps required to implement custom tags:

- Create a source(xhtml) file and define tag contents using <ui:composition> tag.
- Create a tag library descriptor (an XML file) and declare the above custom tag in it.
- Register the tag library descriptor in web.xml.
- Use the above declared tag in an XHTML file.

We shall develop a simple custom tag similar to `<h:inputText>` but has also a label. Here is the content of `labeledInput.xhtml` file.

```
<!--labeledInput.xhtml-->
<html xmlns="http://www.w3.org/1999/xhtml"
  xmlns:h="http://java.sun.com/jsf/html"
  xmlns:ui="http://java.sun.com/jsf/facelets">
  <h:body>
    <ui:composition>
      <h:outputLabel value="#{label}" />
      <h:inputText size="#{size}"/>
    </ui:composition>
  </h:body>
</html>
```

The result of the new tag is a composition of built-in `<h:outputText>` and `<h:inputText>` tags. The new tag will have only two attributes viz. `label` and `size`. This is stored in the directory `jsf/customTags/`. Once the UI of the tag is defined, it is time to give it a name and specify its unique namespace and location of the source file. This is done on an XML file called tag library description. Here is sample tag library descriptor `myTags.xml`.

```
<?xml version="1.0"?>
<!--myTags.xml-->
<facelet-taglib>
  <namespace>http://www.uroy.biz/facelets</namespace>
  <tag>
    <tag-name>labeledInput</tag-name>
    <source>../customTags/labeledInput.xhtml</source>
  </tag>
</facelet-taglib>
```

This defines a custom tag `labeledInput` in namespace `http://www.uroy.biz/facelets`. The file is saved in `WEB-INF/` folder of the web application. Inform the JSF runtime about this tag library in `web.xml` file as follows:

```
</web-app
...
  <context-param>
    <param-name>javax.faces.FACELETS_LIBRARIES</param-name>
    <param-value>/WEB-INF/myTags.xml</param-value>
  </context-param>
</web-app>
```

We can now use newly defined/declared tag in the `test.xhtml` file as follows:

```
<html
  xmlns:ct="http://www.uroy.biz/facelets">
  <body>
    <ct:labeledInput label="First Name:" size="10"/>
    <ct:labeledInput label="Middle Name:" size="5"/>
    <ct:labeledInput label="Last Name:" size="10"/>
  </body>
</html>
```

At the top of the xhtml file, we first define the namespace for our tag. The final directory content is shown here. A sample output of this `test.xhtml` is also shown here:

```
jsf/
 ├─customTags/
 │  ├─labeledInput.xhtml
 │  └─test.xhtml
 └─WEB-INF/
    ├─web.xml
    └─myTags.xml
```

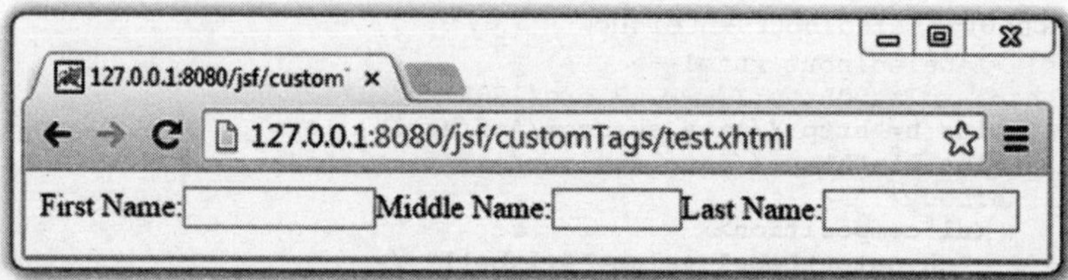

Using Java Program

The previous method merely uses existing tags to compose a new one. To create an absolutely new one, we can write a Java class that defines the behaviour of the tag. All the classes representing the standard components extend `javax.faces.component.UIComponentBase` class that defines the default behaviour of a component class. Here is an example:

```
package tags;
import javax.faces.component.*;
import javax.faces.context.*;
@FacesComponent(value = "tags.toUpper")
public class ToUpper extends UIComponentBase {
  public String getFamily() {
    return "toUpper";
  }
  public void encodeBegin(FacesContext context) throws java.io.IOException {
    String value = (String) getAttributes().get("value");
    if (value != null)
      context.getResponseWriter().write(value.toUpperCase());
  }
}
```

This class corresponds to a simple tag which will have a `value` attribute. The class translates the string in the `value` attribute to upper-case characters. The class is then registered in a tag library `myTags.xml` as follows:

Tag library: myTags.xml

```
<facelet-taglib>
  <namespace>http://www.uroy.biz/facelets</namespace>
  <tag>
    <tag-name>toUpper</tag-name>
    <component>
      <component-type>tags.toUpper</component-type>
    </component>
  </tag>
</facelet-taglib>
```

Inform the JSF runtime about this tag library in `web.xml` file as before. We can now place this tag in the `test.xhtml` file as follows:

```
<html
  xmlns:ct="http://www.uroy.biz/facelets">
  <body>
    <ct:toUpper value="Java Server Faces"/>
  </body>
</html>
```

The final directory content is shown here:

```
jsf/
 ├─customTags/
 │  └─test.xhtml
 └─WEB-INF/
    ├─web.xml
    ├─myTags.xml
    └─classes/
       └─ToUpper.class
```

28.8.3.3 Composite Components

JSF 2.0 addressed all the concerns to create a custom tag by introducing composite components which can be created using the following steps:

- Create a folder resources/ under the web application root.
- Create another folder under resource/ and create an xhtml file in this directory.
- Define the content of the composite component in the xhtml file using <c:interface>, <c:attribute> and <c:implementation> tags.
- Use the component from another xhtml file using namespace http://java.sun.com/jsf/<folder-name> where folder-name is folder in resources directory containing the custom component.

Here is a file (labeledInput.xhtml) that defines a composite tag for a labelled input text.

```
<?xml version="1.0" encoding="UTF-8"?>
<!DOCTYPE html PUBLIC "-//W3C//DTD XHTML 1.0 Transitional//EN"
"http://www.w3.org/TR/xhtml1/DTD/xhtml1-transitional.dtd">
<html xmlns="http://www.w3.org/1999/xhtml"
   xmlns:h="http://java.sun.com/jsf/html"
   xmlns:c="http://java.sun.com/jsf/composite">
   <c:interface>
     <c:attribute name="label" />
     <c:attribute name="size" />
   </c:interface>
```

```
    <c:implementation>
      <h:outputLabel value="#{cc.attrs.label}" />
      <h:inputText size="#{cc.attrs.size}" />
    </c:implementation>
</html>
```

When defining composite component, the `#{cc.attrs.attribute-name}` expression is used to access the attributes defined for the composite component's interface. So `#{cc.attrs.label}` and `#{cc.attrs.size}` expressions refer to the values of the attribute label and size attribute of composite component tag.

Now store the file `labeledInput.xhtml` in a folder named `resources/test/`, under the web application web directory. This directory `resources/` is considered to hold JSF components. To use this component, we can use the test.xhtml file as follows:

```
<html
  xmlns:ct="http://java.sun.com/jsf/composite/test">
  <body>
    <ct:labeledInput label="First Name:" size="10"/>
    <ct:labeledInput label="Middle Name:" size="5"/>
    <ct:labeledInput label="Last Name:" size="10"/>
  </body>
</html>
```

Note that the component library is accessed using the name space `http://java.sun.com/jsf/composite/test`. In general, if the components are stored in a directory `sample`, they can be accessed using the namespace `http://java.sun.com/jsf/composite/sample`. In our case the component itself is accessed through the `<ct:labeledInput>` tag.

28.8.3.4 Remove

Although, JSF engine does not process contents commented by `<!--` and `-->`, they do present in the rendered HTML page in the commented form and hence can be viewed by the clients. For example, the following JSF code

```
<!-- <h:outputText value="Hello World!" />-->
```

will appear at the client side as

```
<!-- &lt;h:outputText value="Hello World!" /&gt;-->
```

Moreover, JSF processes the value expression even commented by `<!--` and `-->` and outputs the result to the generated HTML page. For example, if #{myBean.message} returns a sting "Hi", the following JSF code

```
<!--<h:outputText value="#{myBean.message}" /&gt;-->
```

will appear at the client as

```
<!--&lt;h:outputText value="Hi" /&gt;-->
```

This way some sensitive server-side code may get disclosed at the client side. JSF `<ui:remove>` may be used to prevent the JSF specific code to be rendered on client side. For example, the above JSF code may be hidden as:

```
<ui:remove><h:outputText value="#{myBean.message}" /></ui:remove>
```

It does not output anything as desired.

28.8.4 Converter Tags

The value provided to a component is a string. Conversion from strings to Java objects and vice versa is necessary in many cases. For example, consider a text field where a user supplies his/her Date of Birth (DoB) in a pattern `dd-MM-yyyy` corresponding to a `java.util.Date` property of the backing bean.

The string must be converted properly to store the converted data in the property. Similarly, when the user response comes back, the text field must hold the `Date` value converted in `dd-MM-yyyy` pattern. Moreover, if the user doesn't fill Dob field in the correct format, a message indicating the conversion failure should be displayed.

Oracle's JSF provides many built-in convertor classes (Implementing the `javax.faces.convert.Converter` interface) to perform standard conversions between strings and simple data types in the package `javax.faces.convert`. Table 28.4: shows the list.

Table 28.4: JSF built-in converter classes

Class	Name	Conversion between
BooleanConverter	javax.faces.Boolean	String and java.lang.Boolean (and boolean primitive) values
CharacterConverter	javax.faces.Character	String and java.lang.Character (and char primitive) values
ByteConverter	javax.faces.Byte	String and java.lang.Number values
ShortConverter	javax.faces.Short	String and java.lang.Short (and short primitive) values
IntegerConverter	javax.faces.Integer	String and java.lang.Integer (and int primitive) values
BigIntegerConverter	javax.faces.BigInteger	String and java.math.BigInteger values
LongConverter	javax.faces.Long	String and java.lang.Long (and long primitive) values
FloatConverter	javax.faces.Float	String and java.lang.Float (and float primitive) values
BigDecimalConverter	javax.faces.BigDecimal	String and java.math.BigDecimal values
DoubleConverter	javax.faces.Double	String and java.lang.Double (and double primitive) values
DateTimeConverter	javax.faces.DateTime	String and java.util.Date values
NumberConverter	javax.faces.Number	String and java.lang.Number values

These classes are registered in JSF under a symbolic name shown in the middle column. Out of these 12 classes, last two classes `DateTimeConverter` and `NumberConverter` also have their own tags `<f:convertDateTime>` and `<f:convertNumber>` respectively. We can specify the format and type of the component data by configuring these tag attributes. Here is an example:

```
<!--date.xhtml-->
<html xmlns="http://www.w3.org/1999/xhtml"
   xmlns:h="http://java.sun.com/jsf/html"
   xmlns:f="http://java.sun.com/jsf/core">
   <body>
      <h:form>
         <h:inputText value="#{dateBean.date}" >
            <f:convertDateTime pattern="dd-MM-yyyy" />
         </h:inputText>
         <h:commandButton value="submit" /><br/>
      </h:form>
      <h:messages style="color:red" />
   </body>
</html>
```

The `<f:convertDateTime>` tag in the above code can convert a string in `dd-MM-yyyy` format to a `Date` type object and vice versa. Please note that the pattern is `dd-MM-yyyy` and not `dd-mm-yyyy`. The backing bean to hold the date is this:

```
package converter;
import java.util.Date;
import javax.faces.bean.*;
@ManagedBean
@SessionScoped
```

```
public class DateBean {
  private Date date = new Date();
  public Date getDate() {
    return date;
  }
  public void setDate(Date date) {
    this.date = date;
  }
}
```

The `date.xhtml` produces the following output:

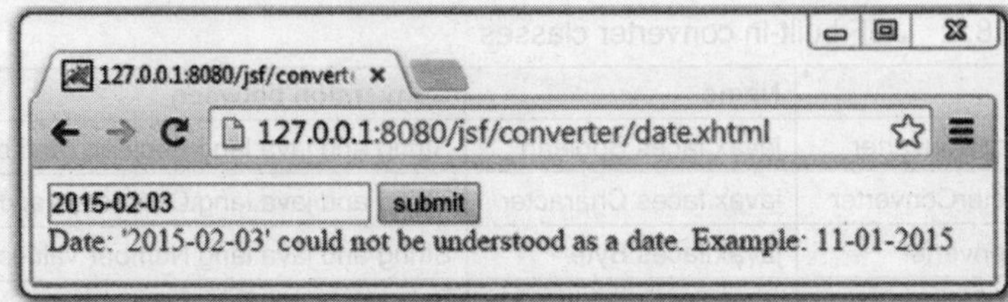

The converter classes (specifically which do not have tags) can also be used in the following ways:

- Add the converter attribute to a component using name of the converter as the value.
- Nest the f:converter tag within a component. Use this tag's converterID attribute to reference the converter's name.

For example, the text box in the above could have been written as:

```
<h:inputText value="#{dateBean.date}" converter="javax.faces.DateTime" />
```

However, the default date format will be "dd MMM, yyyy". Equivalently, The `<f:converter>` may be used as follows:

```
<h:inputtext value="#{datebean.Date}" >
  <f:converter converterid="javax.Faces.Datetime" />
</h:inputtext>
```

Other classes which do not have tags may be used using either of the above two ways. If JSF's built-in converter classes do not fulfil our requirement, we can also write a custom converter of our own. Here are the basic steps to write a custom convertor:

- Create a class implementing javax.faces.convert.Converter interface.
- Implement getAsObject() and getAsString() methods of above interface.
- Assign a unique id to the custom convertor using either @FacesConvertor annotation or faces-config.xml file.

Here is an example:

```
package converter;
import javax.faces.convert.*;
import javax.faces.context.FacesContext;
import javax.faces.component.UIComponent;
import javax.faces.application.FacesMessage;
@FacesConverter("converter.URLConverter")
public class URLConverter implements Converter {
    @Override
    public Object getAsObject(FacesContext fc, UIComponent c, String val)  {
      try {
        return new java.net.URL(val);
      }catch(java.net.MalformedURLException e) {
        FacesMessage msg = new FacesMessage(e.toString());
        msg.setSeverity(FacesMessage.SEVERITY_ERROR);
        throw new ConverterException(msg);
      }
    }

    @Override
```

```
    public String getAsString(FacesContext fc, UIComponent c, Object val) {
        return val.toString();
    }
}
```

Here, the method `getAsObject()` converts the given string value into a URL object and `getAsString()` method converts the given object into a string representation. The `@FacesConverter` annotation registers this converter class with name "converter.URLConverter" for further reference. It could have been registered in the `faces-cinfig.xml` file as follows:

```
<converter>
  <converter-id>converter.URLConverter</converter-id>
  <converter-class>converter.URLConverter</converter-class>
</converter>
```

We can then refer to this converter by its name using either `converter` attribute of a component as follows:

```
<h:inputText value="#{converterBean.url}" converter="converter.URLConverter" />
```

or using `<f:converter>` tag as follows:

```
<f:converter converterId="converter.URLConverter" />
```

The corresponding backing bean is shown below:

```
package converter;
import javax.faces.bean.*;
import java.net.URL;
@ManagedBean(name="converterBean")
@SessionScoped
public class Bean {
    private URL url;
    public URL getUrl() { return url; }
    public void setUrl(URL url) {  this.url = url; }
}
```

A converter may also be registered by the `@ManagedBean` annotation. Consider the following is used for our `URLConverter` class:

```
@ManagedBean
@SessionScoped
public class URLConverter implements Converter {
/*...*/
}
```

This converter can be referred to as

```
<h:inputText value="#{converterBean.url}" converter="#{uRLConverter}" />
```

28.8.5 Displaying Messages

Oracle's JSF implementation provides two tags `<h:messages>` and `<h:message>` to display messages in the client UI. The former is used to display all messages at once. By default, component-specific messages are shown. Set its `globleOnly` attribute to `true` to display only global messages as follows:

```
<h:messages globalOnly="true" />
```

This tag can be placed anywhere in a JSF page. To display messages for a specific component, `<h:message>` tag is used. Its `for` attribute refers to the `id` attribute of the component whose messages are to be displayed:

```
<h:inputText id="login" required="true" />
<h:message for="login"/>
```

A message may be a summary or a detailed description or both. The `<h:message>` and `<h:messages>` tags, by default, show the detail and summary message respectively. However, they can be controlled using the Boolean `showSummary` and `showDetail` attributes.

```
<h:message for="login" />                    <!--detailed -->
<h:message for="login" showSummary="true"/>  <!--both detailed and summary-->
<h:message for="login" showDetail="false"/>  <!--none -->

<h:messages />                               <!--summary -->
<h:messages showDetail="true"/>              <!--both summary and detail-->
<h:messages showSummary="fa   lse"/>         <!--none-->
```

28.8.6 Validations

Often code that processes data expect clean, correct and useful data. So it is a good idea to validate data prior to forwarding them to processing code. Like other frameworks, JSF also provides facilities to validate data of editable components in the Process Validations phase of request processing life-cycle.

The most commonly used validation happens when a form field cannot be left empty (i.e. user must provide some information) and is implemented in JSF as an attribute `required`. All tags that implement `EditableValueHolder` interface has this attribute. Here is an example:

```
<h:inputText required="true" />
```

Oracle's JSF provides some useful tags that can be leveraged to implement validation of any user input. These tags must be qualified by the namespace URI `http://java.sun.com/jsf/core`. Here is an example:

```
<h:inputText value="#{validateBean.temperature}">
  <f:validateLongRange minimum="-273" />
</h:inputText>
```

The above text box corresponds to the `validateBean`'s `temperature` property that holds the temperature in Celsius. Since the lowest possible temperature is –273° C, it is restricted using `minimum` attribute of `<f:validateLongRange>` tag. A list of built-in validation tags with brief description is shown in Table 28.5:

Table 28.5: Oracle's JSF validator tags

Validator class	Tag	Description
LengthValidator	validateLength	Checks if the length of a component's local String value is within a particular range.
DoubleRangeValidator	validateDoubleRange	Checks if a component's local value is within a range of floating-point values.
LongRangeValidator	validateLongRange	Checks if a component's local value is within a range of long values.
RegexValidator	validateRegEx	Checks if a component's local value matches against a regular expression.
RequiredValidator	validateRequired	Checks if a component's local value is empty or not.
BeanValidator	validateBean	Registers a bean validator for the component.

To validate a value against a pattern, the powerful `<f:validateRegex>` tag may be used specifying the regular expression to its `pattern` attribute. Here is an example:

```
<h:form >
   <h:inputText >
     <f:validateRegex pattern="^\w{4,8}$" />
   </h:inputText>
   <h:commandButton value="Click" />
</h:form>
```

This tells that the value of the text box must only contain 4 to 8 alphanumeric characters. Note that server-side data validation requires a client–server round trip. Data may be validated, if possible, at the client side using JavaScript code as follows:

```
<h:form id="myForm">
   <h:inputText id="txt" />
   <h:commandButton value="Click"
      onclick="var v = document.getElementById('myForm:txt').value;
               if(v.match(/^\w{4,8}$/)) return true;
               else return false;"  />
</h:form>
```

Note that JSF renderer may not retain the tag attributes values. For example, for the id attribute value "txt" will be substituted by the "myform:txt" which we have used in our `getElementById()` method. If the JSF implementation follows a different convention, or a different JSF implementation is used, the above code may not work properly.

Data validation may be done using a method of a backing bean. The declaration of the method will look like this:

```
public void <METHOD_NAME> (FacesContext context, UIComponent component, Object
value) { .. }
```

JSF framework automatically calls this method at an appropriate time in the life-cycle. Here is a method added to our `ValidateBean` class:

```
package validate;

/*...*/
public class ValidateBean {
   /*...*/
   public void checkValue (FacesContext context, UIComponent component, Object
value) throws ValidatorException {
      if(Integer.parseInt((String)value) < -273) {
         String summary = "temp can't be less than -273", detail= summary;
         throw new ValidatorException(new
FacesMessage(FacesMessage.SEVERITY_ERROR, summary, detail ));
      }
   }
}
```

If the value is found to be less than −273, this exits by throwing a `ValidatorException()` passing an instance of `javax.faces.application.FacesMessage` else the code exits normally. The message is queued in the messages list and displayed to the user. This method is now ready to be bound with a component using `validator` attribute:

```
<h:inputText validator="#{validateBean.checkValue}" />
```

JSF also allows us to write a custom validator class that implements `javax.faces.validator.Validator` interface and provides the `validate()` method. Here is a sample example that validates temperature:

```
package validate;
import javax.faces.component.*;
import javax.faces.context.*;
import javax.faces.validator.*;
import javax.faces.application.*;

@FacesValidator
public class TemperatureValidator implements Validator {
   @Override
   public void validate (FacesContext context, UIComponent component, Object
value) throws ValidatorException {
     if(Integer.parseInt((String)value) < -273) {
       String summary = "temp can't be less than -273", detail= summary;
```

```
            throw new ValidatorException(new
    FacesMessage(FacesMessage.SEVERITY_ERROR, summary, detail ));
        }
      }

    }
```

The `@FacesValidator` annotation registers the class with the runtime as a validator. Since no value is specified for the `@FacesValidator` annotation, the name of validator will be the name of the class with the first letter in lower case i.e. `temperatureValidator`. The registration can be in the faces-config.xml file as follows:

```
<validator>
  <validator-id>temperatureValidator</validator-id>
  <validator-class>validate.TemperatureValidator</validator-class>
</validator>.
```

This validator is then referred to in the `validatorId` attribute of `<f:validator>` tag:

```
<h:inputText>
  <f:validator validatorId="temperatureValidator" />
</h:inputText>
```

28.9 AJAX

Since, AJAX is an extremely powerful technology, JSF provides the tag `<f:ajax>` to support AJAX capabilities in a standard way. Note that Ajax allows web pages to communicate with the web server asynchronously and can refresh a part of the web page. This is implemented with its `execute` and `render` attributes. The `execute` attribute holds space-separated ids of the components whose values have to be sent to the server. The result of the AJAX request is placed in a component whose id is specified in the `render` attribute. Here is an example(`AjaxTest.xhtml`):

```
<html xmlns="http://www.w3.org/1999/xhtml"
  xmlns:h="http://java.sun.com/jsf/html"
  xmlns:f="http://java.sun.com/jsf/core">
  <body>
    <h:form>
      <h:inputText  id="in" value="#{expander.shortName}"/>=
      <h:outputText id="out" value="#{expander.longName}"/><br/>
      <h:commandButton value="Get full form">
        <f:ajax execute="in" render="out"/>
      </h:commandButton>
    </h:form>
  </body>
</html>
```

This page contains three components: a text box, a label and a button. Users type an abbreviated form such as JSF, JSP etc in the text box. The `<f:ajax>` tag within opening and closing `<h:commandButton>` tags makes the button Ajaxable. This means, when the button is clicked, an AJAX request is sent to the server instead of submitting the whole form. The value of the text box having id attribute value `in` is sent to the server. Upon response, the result (expanded form) is placed in the component having the id `out`. The managed bean that performs the expansion is shown below:

```
package ajax;
import javax.faces.bean.*;
@ManagedBean(name="expander", eager=true)
@ApplicationScoped
public class Expander {
  java.util.Hashtable db = new java.util.Hashtable();
  String sn="JSP";
  public Expander() {
```

```
        db.put("JSF", "Java Server Faces");
        db.put("JSP", "Java Server Pages");
    }
    public String getShortName() { return sn; }
    public void setShortName(String sn) { this.sn = sn; }
    public String getLongName() {
        Object o =  db.get(sn);
        return o != null? (String)o : "Not found";
    }
}
```

The values of multiple components have to be sent to the server, specify their ids in the `execute` attribute. The result can be placed in multiple components in the same way:

```
<h:form id="f1">
  <h:inputText id="txt1" value="#{aBean.property1}"/>
  <h:outputText id="out1" value="#{aBean.property4}"/>
</h:form>
<h:form>
  <h:inputText  id="txt1" value="#{aBean.property2}"/>
  <h:inputText  id="txt2" value="#{aBean.property3}"/>
  <h:outputText id="out1" value="#{aBean.property4}"/><br/>
  <h:commandButton value="Submit">
    <f:ajax execute="txt1 txt2 f1:txt1" render="out1 f1:out1"/>
  </h:commandButton>
</h:form>
```

To send values of every component in the parent form, use

```
<f:ajax execute="@form" render="out"/>
```

28.10 EVENT HANDLING

In JSF event handling model, an event is represented by an instance of an event class. An event source generates an event which is then delivered to event listener objects registered to receive the event.

JSF supports three kinds of events: *value-change events*, *action events* and *phase change events*. A value-change event occurs when the user changes the value of components (such as `UIInput`, `UISelectOne`, `UISelectMany`, and `UISelectBoolean`), that implements `EditableValueHolder` interface. An action event occurs when the user performs some actions such as clicking on components (such as buttons or links) that implement `ActionSource` interface.

We can specify event listeners using either event attributes or event tags. When attribute is used, we implement a method in a backing bean to handle the event and refer that method in an EL expression from the appropriate attribute of the component. On the other hand, if the listener tag is used, we implement an event listener to handle the event and register the listener on a component by nesting a listener tag inside the UI component tag.

28.10.1 Value Change Listener

A value change listener can be implemented in two ways: Using `valueChangeListener` attribute of the component tag and using `<f:valueChangeListener>` tag

28.10.1.1 Using valueChangeListener Attribute

We first implement a method in a managed bean. The method should look like this:

```
public void methodName(ValueChangeEvent e);
```

Here is an example:

```
@ManagedBean(name = "ehBean")
public class Bean {
  public void valueChanged(ValueChangeEvent e) {
    //take actions
  }
}
```

We can write any code inside the method. This listener method can then be attached with a component using its `valueChangeListener` attribute as follows:

```
<h:form >
<h:inputText valueChangeListener="#{ehBean.valueChanged}" onchange="submit()"/>
</h:form>
```

The `onchange` attribute is used to make a JSF call when a value of the text box is changed. JSF runtime implementation then calls this `valueChanged()` method. Note that for components such as buttons or links, onchange attribute is not necessary. Also note that this method limits us to use only one listener for the component.

28.10.2 Using <f:valueChangeListener> tag

Here, we write a class that implements `ValueChangeListener` interface that has single method public void `processValueChange()`. Here is a sample value change listener class:

```
package eh;
import javax.faces.event.*;
public class MyValueChangeListener implements ValueChangeListener {
  @Override
  public void processValueChange(ValueChangeEvent event) throws
AbortProcessingException {
     //take actions
  }
}
```

We can then attach this listener with a component as follows:

```
<h:form >
  <h:inputText onchange="submit()">
    <f:valueChangeListener type="eh.MyValueChangeListener"/>
  </h:inputText>
</h:form>
```

The type attribute specifies fully-qualified name of the listener class. When the value of the text box changes, the `processValueChange()` method of the listener gets called. This method allows us to attach more than one listener with a component.

28.10.3 Action Listener

An action listener may also be implemented in two ways: Using `actionListener` attribute of the component tag and using `<f:actionListener>` tag.

28.10.3.1 Using actioneListener Attribute

Here, we first implement a method in a managed bean. The method should look like this:

```
public void methodName(ActionEvent e);
```

Here is an example:

```
@ManagedBean(name = "ehBean")
public class Bean {
  public void actionMethod(ActionEvent e) {
    //take actions
  }
}
```

We can write any code inside the method. This listener method can then be attached with a component using its `actionListener` attribute as follows:

```
<h:form >
  <h:commandButton value="Click" actionListener="#{ehBean.actionMethod}"/>
</h:form>
```

When the button is clicked, the form is submitted which makes a JSF call. The JSF runtime implementation then calls this `actionMethod()` method. Note that this method limits us to use only one listener for the component.

28.10.4 Using <f:actionListener> tag

Here, we write a class that implements `ActionListener` interface that has single method public void `processAction()`. Here is a sample value change listener class:

```
package eh;
import javax.faces.event.*;

public class MyActionListener implements ActionListener {
  @Override
  public void processAction(ActionEvent event) throws AbortProcessingException{
    //take actions
  }
}
```

We can then attach this listener with a component as follows:

```
<h:form >
  <h:commandButton value="Click" >
    <f:actionListener type="eh.MyActionListener"/>
  </h:commandButton>
</h:form>
```

The type attribute specifies fully-qualified name of the listener class. When the button is clicked, the `processAction()` method of the listener gets called. This methods allows us to attach more than one listeners with a component.

28.11 AN EVENT HANDLING EXAMPLE

In the previous sections, we have seen how to work with JSF events. Let us now write a simple application that leverages JSF's event model. The application has a simple xhtml file containing two selection boxes. The first one has a list of components (such as HDD, Monitor etc.) present in a computer system. The purpose of the second selection box is to provide a set of options for the component selected. This requires the content of the second selection box to be changed when a user selects a component from the first one. Here is the relevant part of the xhtml file:

```
<h:form>
  Select component:
  <h:selectOneMenu  onchange="submit()" valueChangeListener="#{ehMyBean.set}" >
    <f:selectItems value="#{ehMyBean.items}" />
  </h:selectOneMenu>
  Size:
  <h:selectOneMenu >
     <f:selectItems value="#{ehMyBean.spec}" />
  </h:selectOneMenu>
</h:form>
```

The backing bean is shown here:

```
package eh;
import java.util.*;
import javax.faces.bean.*;
import javax.faces.event.*;
```

```
@ManagedBean(name = "ehMyBean", eager = true)
@SessionScoped
public class MyBean {
   Map<String, String[]> maps = new LinkedHashMap<String,String[]>();;
   String[]  spec;
   public MyBean(){
      maps.put("HDD", new String[] {"200 GB", "500 GB"});
      maps.put("Monitor", new String[] {"20'", "21'"});
      spec = maps.get("HDD");
   }
   public void set(ValueChangeEvent e){
      spec = maps.get(e.getNewValue());
   }
   public String[] getSpec() { return spec; }
   public Object[] getItems(){return maps.keySet().toArray();}
}
```

A sample screen shot of this application is shown here:

28.12 PAGE NAVIGATION

A web site typically contains a number of pages. A page can navigate another page using

- Implicit navigation.
- Navigation rules (including conditional rules) defined in managed beans.
- Navigation rules defined in JSF configuration file named faces-config.xml.

28.12.1 Auto Navigation

The simplest way to refer to a page from another is to use `action` attribute of `<h:commandButton>` or `<h:commandLink>` tag.

```
<h:form>
   <h:commandButton action="check" value="Login" />
</h:form>
```

When this button captioned "Login" is clicked, the request is forwarded to a page `check.xhtml` which is expected to exist in the same directory of the current page. The `<h:commandLink>` tag may be used in the same way as follows:

```
<h:form>
  <h:commandLink action="help" value="Help" />
</h:form>
```

Here, when the link captioned "Help" is clicked, the request is forwarded to a page `help.xhtml`.

JSF by default forwards requests to navigated page and the URL of the application does not change. To redirect the request to the navigated page, we can pass the value of the `faces-redirect` parameter as `true` as follows:

```
<h:commandButton action="check?faces-redirect=true" value="Login" />
```

28.12.2 Using Managed bean

The value of `action` attribute may be view name returned by a managed bean method as follows:

```
<h:form>
  <h:commandButton action="#{loginBean.redirect}" value="Login" />
</h:form>
```

Here the view name is obtained by calling the `redirect()` method of `loginBean` which looks like this:

```
package navigation;
import javax.faces.bean.*;
@ManagedBean
public class LoginBean {
  public String redirect() {
    return "check";
  }
}
```

The method returns the view name "check". So when the button is clicked, JSF forwards the request to the page `check.xhtml`. The bean method may take a parameter:

```
public String redirect(String str) { return str; }
```

This is referred to as:

```
<h:commandButton action="#{loginBean.redirect('check')}" value="Login" />
```

Ability to pass a parameter to bean method gives us more control on page navigation. For example, the bean method may return different view names based on the parameter passed as follows:

```
public String redirect(String str) { return "page"+str; }
```

We can now use the same method to navigate different pages as follows:

```
<h:commandButton action="#{loginBean.redirect('1')}" value="Page1" />
<h:commandButton action="#{loginBean.redirect('2')}" value="Page2" />
```

allows us to navigate a page conditionally.

28.12.3 Using Navigation Rule in Faces-config.xml

Navigation rules may be specified explicitly in faces-config.xml as follows:

```
<navigation-rule>
  <from-view-id>index.xhtml</from-view-id>
  <navigation-case>
    <from-action>#{controller.method1}</from-action>
    <from-outcome>page</from-outcome>
    <to-view-id>p1.xhtml</to-view-id>
  </navigation-case>
  <navigation-case>
    <from-action>#{controller.method2}</from-action>
    <from-outcome>page</from-outcome>
    <to-view-id>p2.xhtml</to-view-id>
  </navigation-case>
</navigation-rule>
```

This specifies a set of rules to be used to find pages from the page `index.xhtml`. This first rule says that for form action `#{controller.method1}` that outcomes `page`, the page `p1.xhtml` is to be used. Similarly, for form action `#{controller.method2}` that outcomes `page`, the page `p2.xhtml` is to be used. Note that the target view is determined from the form action as well as outcome. This means even if the outcome of two different form actions is same, different target views may be specified.

KEYWORDS

Apply Request Values—The second phase of JSF request processing life-cycle where submitted values are stored in the component tree

Converter tags—JSF tags that can convert String data to other Java type and vice versa

Deferred evaluation—Evaluation of EL expressions that takes place at different phases of JSF request processing life-cycle

Expression Language—A language that specifies rules to write simple expressions for accessing and manipulating managed beans in an elegant manner

Facelets tags—JSF tags used for page layout for web applications

Invoke Application—The fifth phase of JSF request processing life-cycle where event listeners are invoked (if not already invoked)

Immediate evaluation—Evaluation of EL expressions that takes place when the page is rendered

Java Server Faces— A Java-based framework for creating web-based user interfaces

Life-cycle phases—Steps of JSF request processing life-cycle

Lvalue expressions—Expressions that can read and write data

Managed Bean— A bean created and managed by a JSF implementation

Method Expression—An EL expression that can invoke a method

Process Validations—The third phase of JSF request processing life-cycle where converters and validators are invoked

Rvalue expressions—Expressions that can only read data, but cannot write

Render Response—The last phase of JSF request processing life-cycle where the client interface is generated

Request Processing Life-Cycle—Duration between a JSF request to JSF response

Restore View—The first phase of JSF request processing life-cycle where the component tree is either created or restored

Update Model Values—The fourth phase of JSF request processing life-cycle where model objects are updated

Value Expression—An EL Expression that can either yield a value or set a value

SUMMARY

Java **S**erver **F**aces (JSF) is a Java-based framework for creating web-based user interfaces. Each JSF request, from its submission to completion, known as *life-cycle*, is processed by a series of phases, known as *life-cycle phases:* Restore View, Apply Request Values, Process Validations, Update Model Values, Invoke Application and Render Response.

User Interface (UI) components in a JSF page are often associated with JavaBeans. Since these beans are created and managed by a JSF implementation, they are affectionately called *managed beans*. The `@ManagedBean` annotation registers the bean to be managed with the FacesServlet implementation. We can also configure managed bean in faces configuration file faces-config.xml using `<managed-bean>`.

The scope of a managed bean tells JSF runtime when to instantiate the bean and how long the instance should be kept alive. Six kind of scopes are defined in JSF specification and are represented by scope annotations `@NoneScoped`, `@RequestScoped`, `@ViewScoped`, `@SessionScoped`, `@ApplicationScoped` and `@CustomScoped` annotations. This annotation `@ManagedProperty` is used to inject a value into a property.

The properties of managed bean can be accessed from pages, faces configuration files as well as Java code.

The Expression Language (EL) specifies rules to write simple expressions for accessing and manipulating managed beans in an elegant manner. Specifically, EL expressions can set bean properties and can invoke arbitrary static and public methods. The evaluation of EL expressions may happen at different times and is referred to as *immediate evaluation* and *deferred evaluation*. EL expressions are also categorized as: *value expressions* and *method expressions*.

Value expressions can either yield a value or set a value, whereas a method expression invokes a method.

Templates allow us to place common part in a single file and refer to it from pages that need it. JSF also allows us to enhance the functionality of built-in tags or to create new custom tags.

Data conversion and validation are important concepts of JSF. Oracle's JSF provides many built-in convertor classes to perform standard conversions between strings and simple data types in the package `javax.faces.convert`. JSF also provides facilities to validate data of editable components in the Process Validations phase of request processing life-cycle.

JSF provides the tag `<f:ajax>` to support AJAX capabilities in a standard way. Event handling in JSF is done in a standard way.

WEB RESOURCES

`http://docs.oracle.com/javaee/6/tutorial/doc/bnaph.html`
JavaServer Faces Technology

`https://netbeans.org/kb/docs/web/jsf20-intro.html`
Introduction to JavaServer Faces 2.x

`http://www.tutorialspoint.com/jsf/`
JavaServer Faces (JSF) Tutorial

`http://www.exadel.com/tutorial/jsf/jsftutorial-kickstart.html`
JSF KickStart: A Simple JavaServer Faces Application

`http://www.vogella.com/tutorials/JavaServerFaces/article.html`
JSF (JavaServer Faces) - Tutorial

`http://www.java-samples.com/jsf/`
JSF (JavaServer Faces) - Tutorial

`http://www.javabeat.net/jsf-2/`
JSF 2 Tutorials and Examples

EXERCISES

Objective-type Questions

1. What is the use of the <h:column> tag?
(a) Tag provides a row into dataTable
(b) Tag provides a column into dataTable.
(c) Tag provides a cell into dataTable.
(d) None of the above

2. What is the full form of JSF?
(a) Java Server Finding
(b) Java Service Facility
(c) Java Server Faces
(d) Java Simple Facility

3. The name of servlet capable of processing JSF requests is
(a) JSFServlet
(b) JSFServiceServlet
(c) JavaServerFacesServlet
(d) FacesServlet

4. What is the name of the default faces configuration file?
(a) faces-config.xml
(b) config.xml
(c) config-faces.xml
(d) jsf-config.xml

5. What is namespace for JSF tags to render HTML tags?
(a) http://www.w3.org/1999/xhtml
(b) http://java.sun.com/jsf/html
(c) http://java.sun.com/jsf/facelets
(d) http://java.sun.com/jsf/composite

6. Which of the following is not a phase in JSF request processing life-cycle?
(a) Restore View
(b) Apply Request Values
(c) Process Validations
(d) Prepare Response

7. What is namespace for JSF tags to facelet tags?
(a) http://www.w3.org/1999/xhtml
(b) http://java.sun.com/jsf/html
(c) http://java.sun.com/jsf/facelets
(d) http://java.sun.com/jsf/composite

8. How many phases are there in JSF request processing life-cycle?
(a) 5 (c) 7
(b) 6 (d) 8

9. Which of the following phases is responsible to update model objects?
   (a) Restore View
   (b) Apply Request Values
   (c) Process Validations
   (d) None of the above

10. Which of the following phases is invoked for the first request?
   (a) Process Validations
   (b) Render Response
   (c) Invoke Application
   (d) Update Model Values

11. Which of these listeners can be registered for any phase?
   (a) phase listener
   (b) action listener
   (c) value change listener
   (d) None of the above

12. What is the first phase called in JSF request processing life-cycle?
   (a) Render Response
   (b) Invoke Application
   (c) Update Model Values
   (d) Restore View

13. Which of the following annotations used to register a bean as managed bean?
   (a) @CreateManagedBean
   (b) @RegisterManagedBean
   (c) @ManagedBean
   (d) @RegisterAsManagedBean

14. Which of the following tags is used in the faces configuration file to register a bean as managed bean?
   (a) <managed-bean>
   (b) <create-managed-bean>
   (c) <register-managed-bean>
   (d) <register-bean>

15. Which of the following scope annotations is assumed if none is specified?
   (a) @NoneScoped
   (b) @RequestScoped
   (c) @SessionScoped
   (d) @ApplicationScoped

16. Which of the following annotations is used for property injection?
   (a) @InjectProperty
   (b) @InjectManagedProperty
   (c) @UpdateProperty
   (d) @ManagedProperty

17. What is the full form of EL?
   (a) Expression Literal
   (b) Example Language
   (c) Expression Language
   (d) Efficient Language

18. Which of the following tags is used to render HTML anchor tag?
   (a) <h:commandButton>
   (b) <h:commandLink>
   (c) <h:outputLink>
   (d) All of the above

19. Which of the following characters is used to indicate immediate evaluation of EL expression?
   (a) $ (c) &
   (b) # (d) *

20. Which of the following characters is used to indicate deferred evaluation of EL expression?
   (a) $ (c) &
   (b) # (d) *

Subjective-type Questions

1. What are the advantages of JSF?
2. How do you configure the configuration file? Is it possible to have more than one Faces Configuration file?
3. Explain briefly the life-cycle phases of JSF.
4. How are the components of JSF rendered?
5. How do you declare the page navigation (navigation rules) in faces-config.xml file?
6. What are the differences between a Backing Bean and Managed Bean?
7. How do you pass a parameter to the JSF application using the URL string?

8. Describe briefly JavaServer Faces event and listener model.

9. What is the use of immediate attribute?

10. How do you print out html markup with h:outputText?

11. What is the differences between action and actionlistener in JSF components ?

12. Briefly describe the concept of Validators and Converters in JSF.

13. How do you show confirmation dialog when a user clicks a button?

14. How do you access web.xml init parameters from Java code?

15. How do you pass parameters to methods using El expressions?

Answers to Objective-type Questions

Chapter-1: Java Tools

Q. No	Answer	Q. No	Answer	Q. No	Answer	Q. No	Answer
1.	b	2.	d	3.	b	4.	d
5.	a	6.	a	7.	d	8.	b
9.	c	10.	d	11.	d	12.	a
13.	b	14.	b	15.	a	16.	a
17.	b	18.	d	19.	c	20.	c

Chapter-2: Exception Handling

Q. No	Answer	Q. No	Answer	Q. No	Answer	Q. No	Answer
1.	d	2.	a	3.	c	4.	c
5.	a	6.	b	7.	d	8.	a
9.	b	10.	c	11.	d	12.	a
13.	c	14.	a	15.	b	16.	c
17.	d	18.	d	19.	b	20.	a
21.	b	22.	b	23.	d	24.	a
25.	c	26.	c	27.	b	28.	d
29.	a	30.	d				

Chapter-3: Multi-threading

Q. No	Answer	Q. No	Answer	Q. No	Answer	Q. No	Answer
1.	c	2.	d	3.	d	4.	c
5.	d	6.	a	7.	c	8.	a
9.	d	10.	b	11.	c	12.	a
13.	c	14.	c	15.	a	16.	c
17.	a	18.	b	19.	d	20.	A
21.	d	22.	b	23.	a	24.	c
25.	a	26.	a	27.	c	28.	d
29.	c	30.	b				

Chapter-4: Garbage Collection

Q. No	Answer	Q. No	Answer	Q. No	Answer	Q. No	Answer
1.	d	2.	d	3.	b	4.	d
5.	a	6.	c	7.	a	8.	d
9.	d	10.	c	11.	d	12.	b
13.	a	14.	b	15.	a	16.	d
17.	d	18.	d	19.	b	20.	a

Chapter-5: Collection Framework

Q. No	Answer	Q. No	Answer	Q. No	Answer	Q. No	Answer
1.	b	2.	d	3.	d	4.	a
5.	a	6.	c	7.	c	8.	a
9.	b	10.	a	11.	d	12.	b
13.	a	14.	d	15.	d	16.	b
17.	c	18.	c	19.	d	20.	b
21.	a	22.	a	23.	b	24.	d

Chapter-6: Generic Programming

Q. No	Answer	Q. No	Answer	Q. No	Answer	Q. No	Answer
1.	c	2.	c	3.	b	4.	b
5.	c	6.	a	7.	d	8.	d
9.	b	10.	a	11.	a	12.	c
13.	b	14.	b	15.	d	16.	d
17.	c	18.	b	19.	b	20.	a

Chapter-7: Reflection

Q. No	Answer	Q. No	Answer	Q. No	Answer	Q. No	Answer
1.	d	2.	b	3.	b	4.	c
5.	a	6.	d	7.	b	8.	c
9.	a	10.	d	11.	c	12.	b
13.	c	14.	d	15.	d	16.	b
17.	a	18.	c	19.	d	20.	c
21.	a						

Chapter-8: Java Native Interface

Q. No	Answer	Q. No	Answer	Q. No	Answer	Q. No	Answer
1.	d	2.	c	3.	a	4.	c
5.	c	6.	d	7.	c	8.	a

9.	a	10.	b	11.	d	12.	c
13.	c	14.	c	15.	a	16.	a
17.	c	18.	d	19.	c	20.	d
21.	d	22.	a	23.	b	24.	a
25.	c	26.	c	27.	b	28.	a
29.	c	30.	c	31.	a	32.	b

Chapter-9: AWT and Swing

Q. No	Answer	Q. No	Answer	Q. No	Answer	Q. No	Answer
1.	b	2.	c	3.	d	4.	b
5.	a	6.	a	7.	b	8.	d
9.	a	10.	c	11.	c	12.	a
13.	b	14.	d	15.	a	16.	a
17.	c	18.	c	19.	a	20.	b

Chapter-10: Java and XML

Q. No	Answer	Q. No	Answer	Q. No	Answer	Q. No	Answer
1.	c	2.	b	3.	a	4.	a
5.	c	6.	d	7.	c	8.	b
9.	d	10.	c	11.	b	12.	c
13.	d	14.	a	15.	b	16.	c
17.	c	18.	a	19.	b	20.	b

Chapter-11: Input/Output

Q. No	Answer	Q. No	Answer	Q. No	Answer	Q. No	Answer
1.	c	2.	b	3.	d	4.	a
5.	c	6.	d	7.	c	8.	b
9.	d	10.	b	11.	a	12.	b
13.	a	14.	c	15.	a	16.	b
17.	c	18.	c	19.	b	20.	a
21.	b	22.	a	23.	c	24.	a
25.	a	26.	d	27.	b	28.	b

Chapter-12: Basic Networking

Q. No	Answer	Q. No	Answer	Q. No	Answer	Q. No	Answer
1.	c	2.	c	3.	c	4.	a
5.	c	6.	a	7.	d	8.	b
9.	c	10.	d	11.	c	12.	b

13.	d	14.	c	15.	a	16.	d
17.	b	18.	d	19.	a	20.	a

Chapter-13: Socket Programming

Q. No	Answer	Q. No	Answer	Q. No	Answer	Q. No	Answer
1.	d	2.	c	3.	d	4.	a
5.	d	6.	d	7.	b	8.	b
9.	a	10.	d	11.	b	12.	a
13.	a	14.	a	15.	c	16.	d
17.	a	18.	d	19.	c	20.	d

Chapter-14: Remote Method Invocation

Q. No	Answer	Q. No	Answer	Q. No	Answer	Q. No	Answer
1.	a	2.	d	3.	a	4.	a
5.	c	6.	a	7.	c	8.	b
9.	d	10.	a	11.	d	12.	c
13.	d	14.	b	15.	d	16.	b
17.	a	18.	d	19.	d	20.	b

Chapter-15: Java Mail API

Q. No	Answer	Q. No	Answer	Q. No	Answer	Q. No	Answer
1.	a	2.	d	3.	c	4.	a
5.	a	6.	b	7.	a	8.	b
9.	a	10.	d	11.	a	12.	c
13.	b	14.	c	15.	a	16.	c
17.	b	18.	d	19.	c	20.	a

Chapter-16: Applets

Q. No	Answer	Q. No	Answer	Q. No	Answer	Q. No	Answer
1.	c	2.	c	3.	b	4.	d
5.	a	6.	c	7.	a	8.	d
9.	c	10.	a	11.	b	12.	d
13.	a	14.	d	15.	c	16.	a
17.	c	18.	d	19.	c	20.	a

Chapter-17: Java XML-RPC

Q. No	Answer	Q. No	Answer	Q. No	Answer	Q. No	Answer
1.	c	2.	d	3.	d	4.	a
5.	b	6.	d	7.	a	8.	a
9.	d	10.	a	11.	b	12.	d
13.	c	14.	b	15.	d	16.	a
17.	d	18.	d	19.	c	20.	A
21.	b	22.	d	23.	b	24.	c
25.	d	26.	c	27.	b	28.	a
29.	c	30.	a	31.	d	32.	a

Chapter-18: Java and SOAP

Q. No	Answer	Q. No	Answer	Q. No	Answer	Q. No	Answer
1.	c	2.	c	3.	b	4.	b
5.	d	6.	d	7.	d	8.	c
9.	a	10.	c	11.	b	12.	b
13.	d	14.	a	15.	c	16.	b
17.	d	18.	d	19.	a	20.	b
21.	a	22.	b	23.	c	24.	d
25.	a	26.	d	27.	d	28.	b
29.	d	30.	a	31.	b	32.	c

Chapter-19: Security

Q. No	Answer	Q. No	Answer	Q. No	Answer	Q. No	Answer
1.	b	2.	c	3.	b	4.	a
5.	b	6.	d	7.	d	8.	b
9.	b	10.	d	11.	a	12.	a
13.	d	14.	c	15.	b	16.	c
17.	c	18.	a	19.	b	20.	a
21.	d	22.	d	23.	b	24.	a
25.	a	26.	a	27.	b	28.	a
29.	c	30.	a	31.	b	32.	d
33.	c	34.	d	35.	c	36.	a
37.	a	38.	d	39.	c	40.	c
41.	d	42.	d				

Chapter-20: Servlet

Q. No	Answer	Q. No	Answer	Q. No	Answer	Q. No	Answer
1.	c	2.	d	3.	a	4.	b
5.	b	6.	d	7.	b	8.	a
9.	c	10.	d	11.	c	12.	a
13.	b	14.	a	15.	c	16.	b
17.	a	18.	b	19.	a	20.	d
21.	b						

Chapter-21: Java Server Pages

Q. No	Answer	Q. No	Answer	Q. No	Answer	Q. No	Answer
1.	b	2.	d	3.	c	4.	d
5.	a	6.	d	7.	c	8.	c
9.	b	10.	b	11.	d	12.	a
13.	d	14.	b	15.	c	16.	c
17.	b	18.	a	19.	d	20.	c

Chapter-22: Java Database Connectivity (JDBC)

Q. No	Answer	Q. No	Answer	Q. No	Answer	Q. No	Answer
1.	d	2.	d	3.	c	4.	b
5.	a	6.	b	7.	a	8.	c
9.	c	10.	a	11.	b	12.	b
13.	c	14.	a	15.	b	16.	a
17.	a	18.	d	19.	d	20.	b

Chapter-23: Hibernate

Q. No	Answer	Q. No	Answer	Q. No	Answer	Q. No	Answer
1.	d	2.	a	3.	a	4.	a
5.	a	6.	a	7.	b	8.	a
9.	c	10.	b	11.	c	12.	b
13.	b	14.	a	15.	d	16.	b
17.	b	18.	c	19.	b	20.	c
21.	c	22.	a	23.	d	24.	b
25.	d	26.	d	27.	d	28.	a
29.	c	30.	b				

Chapter-24: Java Naming and Directory Interface

Q. No	Answer	Q. No	Answer	Q. No	Answer	Q. No	Answer
1.	d	2.	c	3.	d	4.	b
5.	c	6.	c	7.	a	8.	d
9.	c	10.	d	11.	b	12.	d
13.	d	14.	c	15.	a	16.	b
17.	a	18.	d	19.	b	20.	c
21.	d	22.	a	23.	d	24.	a

Chapter-25: Java Message Service

Q. No	Answer	Q. No	Answer	Q. No	Answer	Q. No	Answer
1.	b	2.	c	3.	d	4.	d
5.	a	6.	c	7.	c	8.	b
9.	d	10.	b	11.	b	12.	c
13.	d	14.	c	15.	d	16.	b
17.	a	18.	b	19.	a	20.	a
21.	a	22.	b	23.	c	24.	b
25.	d	26.	d	27.	d	28.	c
29.	a	30.	b				

Chapter-26: Introduction to J2EE

Q. No	Answer	Q. No	Answer	Q. No	Answer	Q. No	Answer
1.	b	2.	c	3.	d	4.	a
5.	d	6.	d	7.	d	8.	d
9.	b	10.	b	11.	b	12.	c
13.	a	14.	d	15.	d	16.	b
17.	d	18.	c	19.	a	20.	d

Chapter-27: Java and CORBA

Q. No	Answer	Q. No	Answer	Q. No	Answer	Q. No	Answer
1.	c	2.	d	3.	c	4.	d
5.	a	6.	d	7.	b	8.	d
9.	b	10.	c	11.	b	12.	s
13.	c	14.	b	15.	a	16.	c
17.	c	18.	a	19.	c	20.	c
21.	c	22.	a	23.	b	24.	b

25.	d	26.	d	27.	b	28.	b
29.	d	30.	b				

Chapter-28: Java Server Faces

Q. No	Answer	Q. No	Answer	Q. No	Answer	Q. No	Answer
1.	b	2.	c	3.	d	4.	a
5.	b	6.	d	7.	c	8.	b
9.	d	10.	b	11.	a	12.	d
13.	c	14.	a	15.	b	16.	d
17.	c	18.	d	19.	a	20.	b

INDEX